Sports
Collectors
Digest

Complete Guide to

BASEBALL
MEMORABILIA

Mark K. Larson

Published by

**krause
publications**

700 E. State Street • Iola, WI 54990-0001
Telephone: 715/445-2214

Please call or write for our free catalog of sports publications.
Our toll-free number to place an order or obtain a free catalog is 800-258-0929 or please use our
regular business telephone 715-445-2214 for editorial comment and further information.

Library of Congress Catalog Number: 92-71451
ISBN: 0-87341-455-1
Printed in the United States of America

Contents

Preface

One of these years, when I'm rich and famous for being a children's book author, instead of the self-proclaimed "celebrity" author of a baseball memorabilia book, I'll make an appearance at the annual "Field of Dreams" party. I'll be there as a fan, not as a memorabilia expert.

But I'm going to pass again this year on my sister Lynn's and brother-in-law Bruce's annual baseball bash. It's the 7th annual, complete with the usual ballpark food (popcorn, peanuts, hot dogs, bratwurst and beer). Since many of our memories of playing baseball go back to Little League, the Bad News Bears will be shown on the giant big-screen TV downstairs, just to take us back to that simpler time when all you really wanted was a chance to play. The traditional encore presentation of Field of Dreams will follow, on all three screens.

(Bruce is a basketball coach, so he can justify having a big-screen TV, right? The better to watch the Chicago Bulls with. I do, however, have a hunch it was purchased in the spirit of their Field of Dreams party. After all, he's the one who, with his buddies, thought about heading to the Baseball Hall of Fame in Cooperstown from Michael Jordan territory late one Saturday night, but instead opted for the much closer Field of Dreams in Dyersville, Iowa, a magical place they'd been to before. Thus, they were able to minimize the trouble with their understanding wives when they called home that Sunday morning.)

If you haven't played hooky to experience the Field of Dreams (and you've purchased this book because of the memories, not the prices, it includes), the field is probably calling you to come visit. Take your glove and a kid or two, too. I was there one beautiful Saturday morning with my buddy Dean "Duke" Tuomi, on our way to taking a few youngsters to Mickey Owen's Baseball Camp in Missouri. The only thing which could have made it better would have been to wake up there to a crowing rooster...

I didn't bring my glove, but I did have my camera. And, as a print journalist who learned everything not to do with a camera while I was taking my mandatory photography class, I did get a pretty decent photo of the scene. It's sitting on my stereo at home...

When I look at it, there are fleeting nostalgic moments, as I remember back to the days of radio broadcasters Merle Harmon and Bob Uecker bringing me the sights and sounds of Milwaukee Brewers games from good old Milwaukee County Stadium. I remember all the Pittsburgh Pirates vs. Milwaukee Brewers wiffle ball games I had with my neighbor Bob Bonadurer, and still have the notebook filled with all our head-to-head stats. I remember those trips to the stadium, where the novelty of emerging from the tunnel to an expansive field of green grass still hasn't worn off. I remember watching #19, Robin Yount, on his way to the Hall of Fame...

As I write this, things don't look good in Milwaukee. There's a political mess going on involving the funding of a new stadium, and although some of the signs in the seats have said "This Bud's For Us," Brewer owner Bud Selig might be forced to sell, or move, his team if a new stadium isn't built...

There are lots of memories from that old building...ones which I could never sell. So I, like diehard baseball fans in general, are a bit disheartened with the way things are in Milwaukee right now. And getting my annual "Field of Dreams" invitation this time around was perhaps a bit melancholic.

Sure, there will be plenty of American Legion games to fill the void if the Brewers leave town. Legion games are quite a refreshing brand of baseball, and a change of pace from what we know today as the business of Major League Baseball. But it just wouldn't be the same...

So I guess maybe I'll have to do what Bruce did. Pack up the car and head to Dyersville. Or, maybe buy a new wiffle ball and teach my nephew the pitch I could throw which hit off the basketball backboard above Bob's head. Or dig out my baseball cards and stuff...

Or maybe head over to Duke's house again, for supper, and a few hours of his stories as we uncover more of his baseball memorabilia treasures...

Introduction

This third-edition book is meant to serve collectors who want checklists and fair, accurate prices for baseball collectibles, other than baseball cards, from the 1900s to 1990s. It's a compilation of material taken from the Krause Publications archives - which includes back issues of Sports Collectors Digest, Baseball Card News and Baseball Cards/Sports Cards magazine - and is an outgrowth of the company's line of baseball card price guides. These prices reflect those which were current advertised market prices since late 1995 until May 1996, taken in general from those advertisers who have specialized in the particular areas. At least two comparable sources have been used to determine the prices and ranges of the items, some of which are being cataloged for the first time ever. The condition of the items being priced is, unless noted, Excellent or Mint. Remember, the buyer and seller ultimately determine an item's price.

Each chapter has been repriced (although games in Chapter 18 and player model gloves in Chapter 3 have remained constant) and reedited; typos and errors in the second edition have been corrected (even my favorite one, which turned up in 1992 Kenner statues - "Malt" Williams, who plays for the San Francisco Giants). The author's desk copy of #2, which has a front cover which is curling back on itself, is dog-eared and has chicken scratches throughout it, indicating where mistakes were made, and what new values should be. Although the number of pages has increased by 16, this third edition has fewer photos; there's more room for expanded and/or additional checklists which were omitted from the previous editions.

Dave Miedema's information on uniforms remains condensed in Chapter 2, maintaining room for Dave Bushing's overviews on bat and glove collecting in Chapter 3. Chapter 4 has been expanded and includes values for collectible plates. Chapter 8, which provides checklists of who has been featured on all the major sport magazines' covers, has been increased to include Baseball Magazine covers. Chapter 9, which lists the top 25 books which every collector should have in his sports library, has been expanded to include quite a few more historical overviews and biographies/autobiographies. Chapter 10, commemoratives, has been expanded in the cachets section and adds several pages devoted to team-issued commemoratives. Chapter 12 includes several team-related postcard sets, along with the Perez-Steele postcards. Chapter 16 has more examples of team-related pennants. Chapter 17 offers the most thorough coverage and prices realized from some of the biggest sports memorabilia auctions from 1992-96, plus a few unique photos. Chapter 18 lists a variety of items, which, if you can't find them in the rest of the book, may very well be mentioned in this section. Several items which have appeared in Krause Publications' Standard Catalog of Baseball Cards have also been included in this chapter.

With its third edition of The Complete Guide to Baseball Memorabilia, Krause Publications has maintained the standard for a major comprehensive memorabilia book. Competitors have published books since the first edition of this book was released in 1992, but that added competition has been beneficial; KP has made each successive edition of this book bigger and better than the last one, and a few notches above the competitions' efforts.

The author and publisher would be interested in your thoughts regarding this book - what's good, what you disliked, what needs to be added or deleted, or explained in more detail or made less confusing. Also, there are items which invariably will turn up in someone's attic which haven't been mentioned in this book. So, send descriptions, pictures and checklists along, too. Thanks.

Autographs

Hall of Famer Harmon Killebrew has been a popular signer on the show circuit.

The most common memorabilia which is autographed includes baseballs, index cards, photographs and postcards, Hall of Fame plaques and postcards, Perez-Steele postcards, equipment (shoes, bats, hats, jerseys), programs and books, letters and documents, bank checks, and cut signatures, which have been taken from another piece of writing, such as a manuscript, letter or check.

Autographs can be obtained by several ways. The most personable, and perhaps memorable, experience would be acquiring the autograph from the player at the ballpark. This is the best place to catch a player, and the best time to get his signature. But get there early, before practice; once a player is into his game routine he doesn't want to be distracted. Give yourself an edge over fans who are rude and obnoxious with their requests by being polite and courteous. Having a pen ready and keeping your request simple and fast also helps.

Another alternative is at a baseball card show. Show promoters often impose time/or quota limitations, so if you know a player is going to be signing at a show it's wise to get tickets in advance and get there early.

Dealers and card show promoters also often hold private signings with the players, during which the player fills the mail-order requests sent to the dealer. Non-flat items which are signed sometimes require an extra fee. These private signings are usually advertised in hobby publications. Authenticity is generally guaranteed, and most dealers also have a return policy.

Direct requests can be sent to the player via the mail in care of his team's address, which is the best way, or his home, but the results can be unpredictable, due to the amount of mail the players receive. Some players also believe mail sent to their homes is an invasion of their privacy, so your request might go unheeded.

When dealing through the mail, send less valuable items; you don't want the post office to lose or damage them. Always include a self-addressed, stamped envelope or package with the required postage for its return. A courteous, creative, brief request, which distinguishes and sets off your letter from the others, will yield better results.

Specify if the item is to be personalized or dated, and don't ask the player to sign more than two items. Perhaps you can include an extra for the player to keep, but players are becoming wary of those who request several autographs, perhaps to be sold at a later date. Thus, sometimes the player, in return for his autograph, might ask for a donation to his favorite charity.

Auctions are another source for autographed material. These events, whether by telephone or live, often offer quality material. Items may also turn up at antique shops and flea markets, but questions regarding authenticity, value, condition and scarcity may occur if the seller has limited knowledge of the item.

Trading is always another easy means in acquiring material. A trading network can be established if you take out a classified advertisement in a hobby publication such as Sports Collectors Digest.

Prices for autographed materials are set by the principles of supply and demand, based on regional interest, scarcity, condition (not faded, dirty, shellacked, smudged, scuffed, ripped), player popularity, and significance of the event commemorated. Factors for autographed baseballs also include the signature form (style, placement, nickname), type of ball and writing medium used.

Individually-signed baseballs usually have the autograph on the sweet spot, the shortest distance between two seams. Team balls, those which should include the signatures of all the key players, starters and bench players, generally reserve the sweet spot for the manager's signature.

The more complete the ball is with key players, the more valuable it is. It's also easier to pinpoint the year being represented. But having other signatures, such as those of umpires and broadcasters, detracts from the value.

Some baseballs have just select players who have signed it. These group-signed balls commemorate a particular accomplishment or event, such as the Shot Heard 'Round the World (Bobby Thomson and Ralph Branca), or the living members of the 500 Home Run Club.

When examining an item for authenticity, consider the writing medium used. Was the player alive when the ink, such as in a felt-tip pen or ball-point pens, was available? Quilled pens were prominent in the mid-1800s until fountain pens were developed in 1884. Ball-points became prominent in the 1940s, felt tips in the 1960s and Sharpies in the 1970s. However, whatever medium is used, don't retrace the signature.

Another subtle hint in detecting a faked signature is to check the manufacturer of the ball and the president's signature on it. This may help distinguish deceased players who could not possibly have signed the ball.

Official manufacturers have been - 1) American League baseballs: Reach (1901 to 1974), Spalding (1975-1976), and Rawlings (1977 to present); 2) National League baseballs: Spalding (1876 to 1977), Rawlings (1978 to present); 3) American Association baseballs: Mahn (1882), Reach (1833 to 1891) and 4) Federal League: Victor. Rawlings has produced commemorative balls for use in World Series and All-Star games.

Young and old seek out Hall of Famer Ted Williams for his signature.

American League presidents whose signatures should be on baseballs used during their tenures have been: Byron B. Johnson (1901 to 1927), Ernest S. Barnard (1927 to 1931), William Harridge (1931 to 1959), Joseph E. Cronin (1959 to 1973), Leland S. MacPhail Jr. (1974 to 1983) and Robert W. Brown (1984 to present). National League presidents have been: John A. Heydler (1918 to 1934), Ford C. Frick (1934 to 1951), Warren C. Giles (1951 to 1969), Charles S. Feeny (1970 to 1986), A. Bartlett Giamatti (1986 to 1989), and William D. White (1989 to present).

Realize, however, that signatures can vary, based on the writing tool, item being signed, person's age, popularity, health and mood, time spent during a signing session, and circumstances when it was signed. Learn the player's signature evolution. Slant, size, characters, flamboyancy, legibility and capitalization may all change during a player's career and after.

Forgeries can sometimes be detected by uncommon breaks, peculiarities in pressure and movement in strokes, and changes in thickness in the letters. Facsimile signatures also exist; they are exact reproductions which are printed or screened on the item, often through computer-based technology. Rubber stamps and ghost writers have also been used by players to sign their mail.

When collecting autographed material, become familiar with collector terminology in your area of interest. Utilize the knowledge of skilled, reputable, experienced dealers and maintain good rapport with them. They can be future sources in helping you build a collection.

Also, the Baseball Autograph Handbook, second edition, and Team Baseballs, both by Mark Allen Baker, or hobby publications, such as Sports Collectors Digest, are also good sources. But in the end, before buying, use your own best judgment. Don't buy an item if it's questionable.

Collections can be stored in a file cabinet or display case, with background information on the event and purchase also included. The best conditions for display cases are when effective, indirect lighting is used, so as to not damage or fade the item. The ideal temperature and humidity conditions are 65 to 70 degrees and 50 percent humidity. More valuable items can be kept in safe-deposit boxes.

It's wise to periodically check your collection for signs of deterioration, but avoid excessive handling. Restoration is best left to a professional conservator who's done that type of work before.

Hall of Fame autograph gallery

Hank Aaron (1934-) 1982

Availability: Plentiful
Demand: Average

Cut signature	$7-$10
Single-signature ball	$30-$40
3x5 index card	$20-$25
Photograph/baseball card	$25-$30
HOF plaque postcard	$20-$30
Perez-Steele postcards	$22-$30

Grover Cleveland Alexander (1887-1950) 1938

Availability: Limited
Demand: Average

Cut signature	$225-$300
Single-signature baseball	$2,500-$5,000
3x5 index card	$450-$700
Photograph/baseball card	$700-$900
HOF plaque postcard	$1,000
Perez-Steele postcards	Impossible

Walt Alston (1911-1984) 1983

Availability: Above average
Demand: Average

Cut signature	$12-$15
Single-signature baseball	$650-$700
3x5 index card	$40-$50
Photograph/baseball card	$700
HOF plaque postcard	$85-$150
Perez-Steele postcards	$750-$800

Cap Anson (1852-1922) 1939

Availability: Limited
Demand: Strong

Cut signature	$1,000-$1,150
Single-signature baseball	$12,500-$17,000
3x5 index card	$1,000-$1,500
Photograph/baseball card	$3,500
HOF plaque postcard	Impossible
Perez-Steele postcards	Impossible

Luis Aparicio (1934-) 1984

Availability: Plentiful
Demand: Little

Cut signature	$3-$5
Single-signature baseball	$25

3x5 index card	$5-$8
Photograph/baseball card	$15
HOF plaque postcard	$12-$15
Perez-Steele postcards	$10-$20

Luke Appling (1907-1991) 1964

Availability: Plentiful
Demand: Little

Cut signature	$5
Single-signature baseball	$75
3x5 index card	$8-$10
Photograph/baseball card	$25-$35
HOF plaque postcard	$10-$15
Perez-Steele postcards	$40

Richie Ashburn (1927-)1995

Availability: Plentiful
Demand: Average

Cut signature	$4-$5
Single-signature baseball	$25-$30
3x5 index card	$10
Photograph/baseball card	$15-$20
HOF plaque postcard	$12
Perez-Steele postcards	Impossible

Earl Averill (1902-1983) 1975

Availability: Plentiful
Demand: Little

Cut signature	$5-$7
Single-signature baseball	$450-$500
3x5 index card	$15
Photograph/baseball card	$70-$85
HOF plaque postcard	$25
Perez-Steele postcards	$450-$550

Frank Baker (1886-1963) 1955

Availability: Average
Demand: Average

Cut signature	$65-$100
Single-signature baseball	$1,250-$3,500
3x5 index card	$200-$250
Photograph/baseball card	$800
HOF plaque postcard	$700
Perez-Steele postcards	Impossible

Dave Bancroft (1891-1972) 1971

Availability: Average
Denmand: Average

Cut signature	$30-$50
Single-signature baseball	$2,500-$2,800
3x5 index card	$100
Photograph/baseball card	$250
HOF plaque postcard	$600
Perez-Steele postcards	Impossible

Ernie Banks (1931-) 1977

Availability: Plentiful
Demand: Little

Cut signature	$3-$5
Single-signature baseball	$35
3x5 index card	$10-$13
Photograph/baseball card	$20-$25
HOF plaque postcard	$15-$25
Perez-Steele postcards	$20-$35

Al Barlick (1915-) 1989

Availability: Plentiful
Demand: Little

Cut signature	$4-$5
Single-signature baseball	$20-$25
3x5 index card	$3-$8
Photograph/baseball card	$10-$15
HOF plaque postcard	$8-$10
Perez-Steele postcards	$15

Edward Barrow (1868-1953) 1953

Availability: Average
Demand: Average

Cut signature	$60
Single-signature baseball	$3,300
3x5 index card	$150
Photograph/baseball card	$400
HOF plaque postcard	Impossible
Perez-Steele postcards	Impossible

Jake Beckley (1867-1918) 1971

Availability: Scarce
Demand: Strong

Cut signature	$1,200-$1,300
Single-signature baseball	$4,800-$5,500
3x5 index card	$1,700
Photograph/baseball card	$3,500
HOF plaque postcard	Impossible
Perez-Steele postcards	Impossible

Cool Papa Bell (1903-1991)1974

Availability: Above Average
Demand: Average

Cut signature	$5
Single-signature baseball	$160-$175
3x5 index card	$10
Photograph/baseball card	$50-$60
HOF plaque postcard	$25-$30
Perez-Steele postcards	$35-$80

Johnny Bench (1947-) 1989

Availability: Plentiful
Demand: Average

Cut signature	$5
Single-signature baseball	$35-$40
3x5 index card	$8
Photograph/baseball card	$25-$30
HOF plaque postcard	$22-$30
Perez-Steele postcards	$15-$30

Chief Bender (1883-1954) 1953

Availability: Average
Demand: Average

Cut signature	$100
Single-signature baseball	$2,000-$3,500
3x5 index card	$250
Photograph/baseball card	$450-$500
HOF plaque postcard	$1,200
Perez-Steele postcards	Impossible

Yogi Berra (1925-) 1971

Availability: Plentiful
Demand: Little

Cut signature	$5
Single-signature baseball	$30-$35
3x5 index card	$8
Photograph/baseball card	$20-$25
HOF plaque postcard	$15-$20
Perez-Steele postcards	$15-$25

Jim Bottomley (1900-1959) 1974

Availability: Limited
Demand: Average

Cut signature	$100-$150
Single-signature baseball	$1,700-$2,700
3x5 index card	$300
Photograph/baseball card	$400
HOF plaque postcard	Impossible
Perez-Steele postcards	Impossible

Lou Boudreau (1917-) 1970

Availability: Plentiful
Demand: Little

Cut signature	$3-$5
Single-signature baseball	$25-$30
3x5 index card	$7
Photograph/baseball card	$10-$12
HOF plaque postcard	$6-$10
Perez-Steele postcards	$10-$25

Roger Bresnahan (1879-1944) 1945

Availability: Average
Demand: Average

Cut signature	$350-$500
Single-signature baseball	$3,000-$6,000
3x5 index card	$600-$650
Photograph/baseball card	$1,200
HOF plaque postcard	Impossible
Perez-Steele postcards	Impossible

Lou Brock (1939-) 1985

Availability: Plentiful
Demand: Little

Cut signature	$3-$5
Single-signature baseball	$28-$35
3x5 index card	$8-$10
Photograph/baseball card	$20
HOF plaque postcard	$10
Perez-Steele postcards	$20

Dan Brouthers (1858-1932) 1945

Availability: Scarce
Demand: Strong

Cut signature	$600-$1,250
Single-signature baseball	$7,500-$8,000
3x5 index card	$1,700
Photograph/baseball card	$5,000
HOF plaque postcard	Impossible
Perez-Steele postcards	Impossible

Mordecai Brown (1876-1948) 1949

Availability: Limited
Demand: Average

Cut signature	$250-$300
Single-signature baseball	$3,000-$5,500
3x5 index card	$350-$500
Photograph/baseball card	$900
HOF plaque postcard	Impossible
Perez-Steele postcards	Impossible

Morgan Bulkeley (1837-1922)1937

Availability: Average
Demand: Average

Cut signature	$800-$1,450
Single-signature baseball	$6,000
3x5 index card	$1,200
Photograph/baseball card	$4,000
HOF plaque postcard	Impossible
Perez-Steele postcards	Impossible

Jim Bunning (1931-)1996

Availability: Average
Demand: Average

Cut signature	$3
Single-signature baseball	$35
3x5 index card	$10
Photograph/baseball card	$15
HOF plaque postcard	Impossible
Perez-Steele postcards	Impossible

Jesse Burkett (1868-1953) 1946

Availability: Average
Demand: Average

Cut signature	$375-$450
Single-signature baseball	$4,300-$5,500
3x5 index card	$700
Photograph/baseball card	$1,000
HOF plaque postcard	$1,500
Perez-Steele postcards	Impossible

Roy Campanella (1921-1993) 1969

Availability: Limited
Demand: Strong

Cut signature	$100-$275
Single-signature baseball	$400-$3,500
3x5 index card	$150-$400
Photograph/baseball card	$250-$700
HOF plaque postcard	$250-$325
Perez-Steele postcards	$175-$200

Rod Carew (1945-) 1991

Availability: Plentiful
Demand: Little

Cut signature	$3-$5
Single-signature baseball	$30-$40
3x5 index card	$7-$9
Photograph/baseball card	$20
HOF plaque postcard	$20
Perez-Steele postcards	$25

Max Carey (1890-1976) 1961

Availability: Plentiful
Demand: Average

Cut signature	$7
Single-signature baseball	$750
3x5 index card	$15
Photograph/baseball card	$75-$125
HOF plaque postcard	$60-$75
Perez-Steele postcards	Impossible

Steve Carlton (1944-) 1994

Availability: Average
Demand: Above Average

Cut signature	$3-$5
Single-signature baseball	$25-$30
3x5 index card	$8
Photograph/baseball card	$20-$25
HOF plaque postcard	$25
Perez-Steele postcards	$30

Alexander Cartwright (1820-1892) 1938

Availability: Limited
Demand: Strong

Cut signature	$600-$700
Single-signature baseball	Unknown
3x5 index card	$750
Photograph/baseball card	$3,000
HOF plaque postcard	Impossible
Perez-Steele postcards	Impossible

Henry Chadwick (1824-1908) 1938

Availability: Scarce
Demand: Strong

Cut signature	$1,000-$1,500
Single-signature baseball	Unknown
3x5 index card	$1,200
Photograph/baseball card	$3,200
HOF plaque postcard	Impossible
Perez-Steele postcards	Impossible

Frank Chance (1877-1924) 1946

Availability: Average
Demand: Average

Cut signature	$600-$750
Single-signature baseball	$5,500-$7,000
3x5 index card	$750
Photograph/baseball card	$2,000
HOF plaque postcard	Impossible
Perez-Steele postcards	Impossible

Happy Chandler (1898-1991) 1982

Availability: Plentiful
Demand: Little

Cut signature	$4-$5
Single-signature baseball	$100
3x5 index card	$12
Photograph/baseball card	$30-$35
HOF plaque postcard	$15-$20
Perez-Steele postcards	$25-$35

Oscar Charleston (1896-1954) 1976

Availability: Scarce
Demand: Above average

Cut signature	$600
Single-signature baseball	$7,000
3x5 index card	$1,000-$1,750
Photograph/baseball card	$3,000
HOF plaque postcard	Impossible
Perez-Steele postcards	Impossible

Jack Chesbro (1874-1931) 1946

Availability: Limited
Demand: Above average

Cut signature	$600-$1,150
Single-signature baseball	$6,500-$10,000
3x5 index card	$750
Photograph/baseball card	$2,000-$2,750
HOF plaque postcard	Impossible
Perez-Steele postcards	Impossible

Fred Clarke (1872-1960) 1945

Availability: Average
Demand: Average

Cut signature	$100
Single-signature baseball	$1,500-$3,000
3x5 index card	$200
Photograph/baseball card	$400
HOF plaque postcard	$400-$500
Perez-Steele postcards	Impossible

John Clarkson (1861-1909) 1963

Availability: Scarce
Demand: Strong

Cut signature	$1,200-$1,845
Single-signature baseball	Unknown
3x5 index card	$2,000
Photograph/baseball card	$2,500
HOF plaque postcard	Impossible
Perez-Steele postcards	Impossible

Roberto Clemente (1934-1972) 1973

Availability: Average
Demand: Strong

Cut signature	$100-$150
Single-signature baseball	$2,000-$4,000
3x5 index card	$200
Photograph/baseball card	$350-$600
HOF plaque postcard	Impossible
Perez-Steele postcards	Impossible

Ty Cobb (1886-1961) 1936

Availability: Average
Demand: Strong

Cut signature	$175-$250
Single-signature baseball	$2,500-$2,750
3x5 index card	$325
Photograph/baseball card	$1,200
HOF plaque postcard	$875-$1,000
Perez-Steele postcards	Impossible

Mickey Cochrane (1903-1962) 1947

Availability: Average
Demand: Average

Cut signature	$60-$75
Single-signature baseball	$750-$2,000
3x5 index card	$125-$150
Photograph/baseball card	$350
HOF plaque postcard	$500
Perez-Steele postcards	Impossible

Eddie Collins (1887-1951) 1939

Availability: Average
Demand: Above average

Cut signature	$85-$100
Single-signature baseball	$2,250-$5,000
3x5 index card	$175-$225
Photograph/baseball card	$400
HOF plaque postcard	$550
Perez-Steele postcards	Impossible

Jimmy Collins (1870-1943) 1945

Availability: Scarce
Demand: Strong

Cut signature	$500-$750
Single-signature baseball	$6,000
3x5 index card	$700-$950
Photograph/baseball card	$1,500
HOF plaque postcard	Impossible
Perez-Steele postcards	Impossible

Earle Combs (1899-1976) 1970

Availability: Plentiful
Demand: Average

Cut signature	$15-$17
Single-signature baseball	$500-$2,000
3x5 index card	$40
Photograph/baseball card	$350
HOF plaque postcard	$100
Perez-Steele postcards	Impossible

Charles Comiskey (1859-1931) 1939

Availability: Average
Demand: Average

Cut signature	$350-$375
Single-signature baseball	$4,500-$8,000
3x5 index card	$450-$500
Photograph/baseball card	$1,200
HOF plaque postcard	Impossible
Perez-Steele postcards	Impossible

Jocko Conlan (1899-1989) 1974

Availability: Plentiful
Demand: Little

Cut signature	$5
Single-signature baseball	$100-$125
3x5 index card	$8-$10
Photograph/baseball card	$35
HOF plaque postcard	$15-$20
Perez-Steele postcards	$60-$500

Thomas Connolly (1870-1963) 1953

Availability: Average
Demand: Average

Cut signature	$200-$275
Single-signature baseball	$2,345-$7,000
3x5 index card	$250-$350
Photograph/baseball card	$900
HOF plaque postcard	$1,000-$1,200
Perez-Steele postcards	Impossible

Roger Connor (1857-1931) 1976

Availability: Limited
Demand: Above average

Cut signature	$1,000-$1,185
Single-signature baseball	$5,600-$8,000
3x5 index card	$1,700
Photograph/baseball card	$2,500
HOF plaque postcard	Impossible
Perez-Steele postcards	Impossible

Stan Coveleski (1889-1984) 1969

Availability: Plentiful
Demand: Little

Cut signature	$5
Single-signature baseball	$450
3x5 index card	$8-$12
Photograph/baseball card	$80
HOF plaque postcard	$20-$30
Perez-Steele postcards	$325-$400

Sam Crawford (1880-1968) 1957

Availability: Average
Demand: Average

Cut signature	$35-$65
Single-signature baseball	$1,900-$2,500
3x5 index card	$75-$125
Photograph/baseball card	$250
HOF plaque postcard	$250-$400
Perez-Steele postcards	Impossible

Joe Cronin (1906-1984) 1956

Availability: Above average
Demand: Little

Cut signature	$8-$10
Single-signature baseball	$225-$500
3x5 index card	$25
Photograph/baseball card	$100
HOF plaque postcard	$35-$50
Perez-Steele postcards	$700-$750

Candy Cummings (1848-1924) 1939

Availability: Scarce
Demand: Strong

Cut signature	$1,500-$1,750
Single-signature baseball	Unknown
3x5 index card	$1,700
Photograph/baseball card	$4,500
HOF plaque postcard	Impossible
Perez-Steele postcards	Impossible

Ki Ki Cuyler (1899-1950) 1968

Availability: Average
Demand: Average

Cut signature	$100-$150
Single-signature baseball	$1,500-$3,500
3x5 index card	$175
Photograph/baseball card	$400-$425
HOF plaque postcard	Impossible
Perez-Steele postcards	Impossible

Ray Dandridge (1913-) 1987

Availability: Plentiful
Demand: Little

Cut signature	$4-$5
Single-signature baseball	$35-$50
3x5 index card	$7
Photograph/baseball card	$20-$25
HOF plaque postcard	$12-$20
Perez-Steele postcards	$15-$20

Leon Day (1916-1995) 1995

Availability: Average
Demand: Average

Cut signature	$10
Single-signature baseball	$75-$100
3x5 index card	$15
Photograph/baseball card	$30-$40
HOF plaque postcard	Impossible
Perez-Steele postcards	Impossible

Dizzy Dean (1911-1974) 1953

Availability: Average
Demand: Average

Cut signature	$25-$50
Single-signature baseball	$675-$800
3x5 index card	$75
Photograph/baseball card	$250-$350
HOF plaque postcard	$125-$150
Perez-Steele postcards	Impossible

Ed Delahanty (1867-1903) 1945

Availability: Scarce
Demand: Strong

Cut signature	$1,500
Single-signature baseball	Unknown
3x5 index card	$2,000
Photograph/baseball card	$4,000
HOF plaque postcard	Impossible
Perez-Steele postcards	Impossible

Bill Dickey (1907-1993) 1954

Availability: Plentiful
Demand: Little

Cut signature	$6-$8
Single-signature baseball	$150-$200
3x5 index card	$12
Photograph/baseball card	$50
HOF plaque postcard	$35-$45
Perez-Steele postcards	$45-$80

Martin DiHigo (1905-1971) 1977

Availability: Limited
Demand: Strong

Cut signature	$650-$675
Single-signature baseball	$4,000
3x5 index card	$800-$1,000
Photograph/baseball card	$1,500-$2,000
HOF plaque postcard	Impossible
Perez-Steele postcards	Impossible

Joe DiMaggio (1914-) 1955

Availability: Plentiful
Demand: Strong

Cut signature	$20-$25
Single-signature baseball	$200-$250
3x5 index card	$60
Photograph/baseball card	$100-$150
HOF plaque postcard	$90-$135
Perez-Steele postcards	$250-$300

Bobby Doerr (1918-) 1986

Availability: Plentiful
Demand: Little

Cut signature	$5
Single-signature baseball	$20-$25
3x5 index card	$3-$7
Photograph/baseball card	$10-$13
HOF plaque postcard	$6-$10
Perez-Steele postcards	$15-$20

Don Drysdale (1936-1993) 1984

Availability: Plentiful
Demand: Little

Cut signature	$5-$8
Single-signature baseball	$75-$125
3x5 index card	$10
Photograph/baseball card	$30-$45
HOF plaque postcard	$25
Perez-Steele postcards	$30-$35

Hugh Duffy (1866-1954) 1945

Availability: Average
Demand: Average

Cut signature	$250-$300
Single-signature baseball	$2,200-$3,500
3x5 index card	$350-$450
Photograph/baseball card	$600-$750
HOF plaque postcard	$900
Perez-Steele postcards	Impossible

Leo Durocher (1905-1991) 1994

Availability: Above average
Demand: Above average

Cut signature	$6
Single-signature baseball	$65-$90
3x5 index card	$10
Photograph/baseball card	$40
HOF plaque postcard	Impossible
Perez-Steele postcards	Impossible

Billy Evans (1864-1956) 1973

Availability: Limited
Demand: Above average

Cut signature	$125-$225
Single-signature baseball	$2,000-$4,000
3x5 index card	$300-$350
Photograph/baseball card	$500-$525
HOF plaque postcard	Impossible
Perez-Steele postcards	Impossible

Johnny Evers (1881-1947) 1946

Availability: Limited
Demand: Average

Cut signature	$225-$300
Single-signature baseball	$3,500-$6,000
3x5 index card	$400
Photograph/baseball card	$1,000-$1,200
HOF plaque postcard	$1,100
Perez-Steele postcards	Impossible

Buck Ewing (1859-1906) 1939

Availability: Scarce
Demand: Strong

Cut signature	$1,000
Single-signature baseball	$3,000
3x5 index card	$2,400
Photograph/baseball card	$2,500-$4,000
HOF plaque postcard	Impossible
Perez-Steele postcards	Impossible

Red Faber (1888-1976) 1964

Availability: Above average
Demand: Average

Cut signature	$10-$15
Single-signature baseball	$450-$1,800
3x5 index card	$35-$45
Photograph/baseball card	$75-$100
HOF plaque postcard	$85
Perez-Steele postcards	Impossible

Bob Feller (1918-) 1962

Availability: Plentiful
Demand: Little

Cut signature	$2-$5
Single-signature baseball	$20-$25
3x5 index card	$5-$7
Photograph/baseball card	$10-$12
HOF plaque postcard	$7-$12
Perez-Steele postcards	$15-$35

Rick Ferrell (1905-1995) 1984

Availability: Plentiful
Demand: Little

Cut signature	$4-$5
Single-signature baseball	$40-$60
3x5 index card	$7-$9
Photograph/baseball card	$20
HOF plaque postcard	$8
Perez-Steele postcards	$15-$30

Rollie Fingers (1946-) 1992

Availability: Average
Demand: Average

Cut signature	$3-$5
Single-signature baseball	$22-$30
3x5 index card	$7-$10
Photograph/baseball card	$20
HOF plaque postcard	$8
Perez-Steele postcards	$20

Elmer Flick (1876-1971) 1963

Availability: Above average
Demand: Average

Cut signature	$15-$20
Single-signature baseball	$2,200-$2,500
3x5 index card	$40-$60
Photograph baseball card	$175-$250
HOF plaque postcard	$300-$450
Perez-Steele postcards	Impossible

Whitey Ford (1926-) 1974

Availability: Plentiful
Demand: Little

Cut signature	$4-$5
Single-signature baseball	$30
3x5 index card	$8
Photograph/baseball card	$20
HOF plaque postcard	$12-$20
Perez-Steele postcards	$20-$30

Bill Foster 1995

Availability: Average
Demand: Little

Cut signature	$10
Single-signature baseball	$75
3x5 index card	$15
Photograph/baseball card	$40
HOF plaque postcard	Impossible
Perez-Steele postcards	Impossible

Rube Foster (1878-1930) 1981

Availability: Limited
Demand: Above average

Cut signature	$2,000
Single-signature baseball	$13,000
3x5 index card	$3,800
Photograph/baseball card	$3,150-$5,500
HOF plaque postcard	Impossible
Perez-Steele postcards	Impossible

Jimmie Foxx (1907-1967) 1951

Availability: Average
Demand: Average

Cut signature	$70-$200
Single-signature baseball	$2,800-$3,000
3x5 index card	$250-$350
Photograph/baseball card	$500-$900
HOF plaque postcard	$525
Perez-Steele postcards	Impossible

Ford Frick (1894-1978) 1970

Availability: Average
Demand: Average

Cut signature	$15-$20
Single-signature baseball	$300-$800
3x5 index card	$40-$50
Photograph/baseball card	$75-$100
HOF plaque postcard	$125
Perez-Steele postcards	Impossible

Frankie Frisch (1898-1973) 1947

Availability: Above average
Demand: Average

Cut signature	$15-$18
Single-signature baseball	$1,700-$1,800
3x5 index card	$40-$75
Photograph/baseball card	$100-$150
HOF plaque postcard	$100-$150
Perez-Steele postcards	Impossible

Pud Galvin (1855-1902) 1965

Availability: Scarce
Demand: Strong

Cut signature	$1,000-$1,300
Single-signature baseball	$10,000-$12,000
3x5 index card	$2,500
Photograph/baseball card	$3,000
HOF plaque postcard	Impossible
Perez-Steele postcards	Impossible

Lou Gehrig (1903-1941) 1939

Availability: Average
Demand: Strong

Cut signature	$600-$650
Single-signature baseball	$5,000-$7,000
3x5 index card	$800
Photograph/baseball card	$2,000-$4,000
HOF plaque postcard	Unknown
Perez-Steele postcards	Impossible

Charlie Gehringer (1903-1993) 1949

Availability: Plentiful
Demand: Little

Cut signature	$5
Single-signature baseball	$100-$150
3x5 index card	$10-$15
Photograph/baseball card	$40-$85
HOF plaque postcard	$25-$40
Perez-Steele postcards	$25-$65

Bob Gibson (1935-) 1972

Availability: Plentiful
Demand: Little

Cut signature	$4-$5
Single-signature baseball	$25-$32
3x5 index card	$8
Photograph/baseball card	$18-$21
HOF plaque postcard	$12-$15
Perez-Steele postcards	$20

Josh Gibson (1911-1947) 1972

Availability: Limited
Demand: Strong

Cut signature	$700-$950
Single-signature baseball	$4,500-$6,500
3x5 index card	$800
Photograph/baseball card	$1,200-$1,700
HOF plaque postcard	Impossible
Perez-Steele postcards	Impossible

Warren Giles (1896-1979) 1979

Availability: Above average
Demand: Average

Cut signature	$15-$20
Single-signature baseball	$250-$1,000
3x5 index card	$35-$45
Photograph/baseball card	$75-$125
HOF plaque postcard	Impossible
Perez-Steele postcards	Impossible

Lefty Gomez (1908-1989) 1972

Availability: Plentiful
Demand: Little

Cut signature	$7-$8
Single-signature baseball	$100-$150
3x5 index card	$15-$20
Photograph/baseball card	$35-$45
HOF plaque postcard	$20-$25
Perez-Steele postcards	$40-$65

Goose Goslin (1900-1971) 1968

Availability: Average
Demand: Average

Cut signature	$40-$50
Single-signature baseball	$800-$2,700
3x5 index card	$75-$100
Photograph/baseball card	$300
HOF plaque postcard	$700-$3,000
Perez-Steele postcards	Impossible

Hank Greenberg (1911-1986) 1956

Availability: Above average
Demand: Average

Cut signature	$10-$20
Single-signature baseball	$500-$700
3x5 index card	$35-$75
Photograph/baseball card	$75-$100
HOF plaque postcard	$50-$75
Perez-Steele postcards	$300-$325

Clark Griffith (1869-1955) 1946

Availability: Average
Demand: Average

Cut signature	$100-$135
Single-signature baseball	$1,000-$2,200
3x5 index card	$150-$175
Photograph/baseball card	$350
HOF plaque postcard	$600
Perez-Steele postcards	Impossible

Burleigh Grimes (1893-1985) 1964

Availability: Plentiful
Demand: Little

Cut signature	$6-$8
Single-signature baseball	$80-$225
3x5 index card	$12-$20
Photograph/baseball card	$45-$60
HOF plaque postcard	$20-$30
Perez-Steele postcards	$150-$200

Lefty Grove (1900-1975) 1947

Availability: Above average
Demand: Average

Cut signature	$17-$25
Single-signature baseball	$1,200-$1,300
3x5 index card	$40
Photograph/baseball card	$200
HOF plaque postcard	$100-$125
Perez-Steele postcards	Impossible

Chick Hafey (1903-1973) 1971

Availability: Above average
Demand: Average

Cut signature	$18-$35
Single-signature baseball	$425-$1,500
3x5 index card	$50
Photograph/baseball card	$75-$175
HOF plaque postcard	$600
Perez-Steele postcards	Impossible

Jesse Haines (1893-1978) 1970

Availability: Above average
Demand: Average

Cut signature	$12-$35
Single-signature baseball	$300-$950
3x5 index card	$20-$40
Photograph/baseball card	$75-$125
HOF plaque postcard	$75
Perez-Steele postcards	Impossible

Billy Hamilton (1866-1940) 1961

Availability: Limited
Demand: Strong

Cut signature	$500-$1,500
Single-signature baseball	$4,250-$5,500
3x5 index card	$750
Photograph/baseball card	$2,150-$2,500
HOF plaque postcard	Impossible
Perez-Steele postcards	Impossible

Ned Hanlon (1857-1937) 1996

Availability: Limited
Demand: Little

Cut signature	Unknown
Single-signature baseball	Unknown
3x5 index card	Unknown
Photograph/baseball card	Unknown
HOF plaque postcard	Impossible
Perez-Steele postcards	Impossible

Will Harridge (1883-1971) 1972

Availability: Above average
Demand: Average

Cut signature	$40-$85
Single-signature baseball	$875-$2,500
3x5 index card	$125
Photograph/baseball card	$225-$300
HOF plaque postcard	Impossible
Perez-Steele postcards	Impossible

Bucky Harris (1896-1977) 1975

Availability: Above average
Demand: Average

Cut signature	$20-$25
Single-signature baseball	$450-$1,200
3x5 index card	$40
Photograph/baseball card	$200
HOF plaque postcard	$150-$200
Perez-Steele postcards	Impossible

Gabby Hartnett (1900-1972) 1955

Availability: Above average
Demand: Average

Cut signature	$30-$35
Single-signature baseball	$1,000-$2,000
3x5 index card	$60-$75
Photograph/baseball card	$200-$250
HOF plaque postcard	$200-$325
Perez-Steele postcards	Impossible

Harry Heilmann (1894-1951) 1952

Availability: Average
Demand: Above average

Cut signature	$175-$250
Single-signature baseball	$2,000-$2,500
3x5 index card	$300-$350
Photograph/baseball card	$475-$500
HOF plaque postcard	Impossible
Perez-Steele postcards	Impossible

Billy Herman (1909-1992) 1975

Availability: Plentiful
Demand: Little

Cut signature	$4-$5
Single-signature baseball	$50-$60
3x5 index card	$7
Photograph/baseball card	$25-$30
HOF plaque postcard	$8-$12
Perez-Steele postcards	$15-$25

Harry Hooper (1887-1974) 1971

Availability: Above average
Demand: Average

Cut signature	$12-$15
Single-signature baseball	$450-$1,200
3x5 index card	$20
Photograph/baseball card	$80-$150
HOF plaque postcard	$115
Perez-Steele postcards	Impossible

Rogers Hornsby (1896-1963) 1942

Availability: Average
Demand: Above average

Cut signature	$75-$150
Single-signature baseball	$2,500
3x5 index card	$200
Photograph/baseball card	$500-$700
HOF plaque postcard	$650
Perez-Steele postcards	Impossible

Waite Hoyt (1899-1984) 1969

Availability: Plentiful
Demand: Little

Cut signature	$6-$10
Single-signature baseball	$175-$450
3x5 index card	$15
Photograph/baseball card	$50-$80
HOF plaque postcard	$30-$35
Perez-Steele postcards	$450-$550

Cal Hubbard (1900-1977) 1976

Availability: Above average
Demand: Average

Cut signature	$22-$30
Single-signature baseball	$500-$1,000
3x5 index card	$60
Photograph/baseball card	$175-$250
HOF plaque postcard	$500
Perez-Steele postcards	Impossible

Carl Hubbell (1903-1988) 1947

Availability: Plentiful
Demand: Little

Cut signature	$5-$7
Single-signature baseball	$160-$175
3x5 index card	$10
Photograph/baseball card	$25-$30
HOF plaque postcard	$20-$35
Perez-Steele postcards	$60-$80

Miller Huggins (1879-1929) 1964

Availability: Limited
Demand: Above average

Cut signature	$700-$750
Single-signature baseball	$4,500-$6,000
3x5 index card	$1,000
Photograph/baseball card	$1,500
HOF plaque postcard	Impossible
Perez-Steele postcards	Impossible

William Hulbert (1832-1882) 1995

Availability: Limited
Demand: Little

Cut signature	Unknown
Single-signature baseball	Unknown
3x5 index card	Unkown
Photograph/baseball card	Unkown
HOF plaque postcard	Impossible
Perez-Steele postcards	Impossible

Catfish Hunter (1946-) 1987

Availability: Plentiful
Demand: Little

Cut signature	$3-$5
Single-signature baseball	$22-$28
3x5 index card	$6-$7
Photograph/baseball card	$12-$14
HOF plaque postcard	$8-$12
Perez-Steele postcards	$10-$20

Monte Irvin (1911-) 1973

Availability: Plentiful
Demand: Little

Cut signature	$3-$5
Single-signature baseball	$20-$25
3x5 index card	$7
Photograph/baseball card	$10-$12
HOF plaque postcard	$7-$12
Perez-Steele postcards	$10-$20

Reggie Jackson (1946-) 1993

Availability: Above average
Demand: Above average

Cut signature	$4-$7
Single-signature baseball	$55-$60
3x5 index card	$12
Photograph/baseball card	$30-$35
HOF plaque postcard	$25-$65
Perez-Steele postcards	$45-$60

Travis Jackson (1903-1987) 1982

Availability: Plentiful
Demand: Little

Cut signature	$7
Single-signature baseball	$140-$350
3x5 index card	$15-$25
Photograph/baseball card	$40-$80
HOF plaque postcard	$35
Perez-Steele postcards	$75-$80

Fergie Jenkins (1943-) 1991

Availability: Plentiful
Demand: Little

Cut signature	$3-$5
Single-signature baseball	$22-$28
3x5 index card	$7
Photograph/baseball card	$12-$15
HOF plaque postcard	$10-$15
Perez-Steele postcards	$10-$15

Hugh Jennings (1869-1928) 1945

Availability: Limited
Demand: Strong

Cut signature	$500-$825
Single-signature baseball	$4,750-$6,000
3x5 index card	$900
Photograph/baseball card	$1,000-$1,500
HOF plaque postcard	Impossible
Perez-Steele postcards	Impossible

Ban Johnson (1864-1931) 1937

Availability: Average
Demand: Average

Cut signature	$175-$200
Single-signature baseball	$2,700-$3,500
3x5 index card	$250
Photograph/baseball card	$500-$550
HOF plaque postcard	Impossible
Perez-Steele postcards	Impossible

Judy Johnson (1900-1989) 1975

Availability: Plentiful
Demand: Little

Cut signature	$5-$7
Single-signature baseball	$75-$200
3x5 index card	$10
Photograph/baseball card	$30-$60
HOF plaque postcard	$25
Perez-Steele postcards	$80-$90

Walter Johnson (1887-1946) 1946

Availability: Limited
Demand: Strong

Cut signature	$260-$450
Single-signature baseball	$2,950-$3,500
3x5 index card	$500
Photograph/baseball card	$1,000-$1,300
HOF plaque postcard	Unknown
Perez-Steele postcards	Impossible

Addie Joss (1880-1911) 1978

Availability: Scarce
Demand: Strong

Cut signature	$1,500
Single-signature baseball	$7,500-$10,000
3x5 index card	$2,500
Photograph/baseball card	$3,900-$4,000
HOF plaque postcard	Impossible
Perez-Steele postcards	Impossible

Al Kaline (1934-) 1980

Availability: Plentiful
Demand: Little

Cut signature	$4-$5
Single-signature baseball	$25-$30
3x5 index card	$7
Photograph/baseball card	$15
HOF plaque postcard	$12-$15
Perez-Steele postcards	$20-$25

Tim Keefe (1857-1933) 1964

Availability: Scarce
Demand: Strong

Cut signature	$600-$1,500
Single-signature baseball	$7,000
3x5 index card	$800
Photograph/baseball card	$2,000
HOF plaque postcard	Impossible
Perez-Steele postcards	Impossible

Wee Willie Keeler (1872-1923) 1939

Availability: Limited
Demand: Strong

Cut signature	$1,000-$1,400
Single-signature baseball	$8,000
3x5 index card	$2,000
Photograph/baseball card	$3,000-$3,250
HOF plaque postcard	Impossible
Perez-Steele postcards	Impossible

George Kell (1922-) 1883

Availability: Plentiful
Demand: Little

Cut signature	$3-$5
Single-signature baseball	$20-$24
3x5 index card	$7
Photograph/baseball card	$10-$12
HOF plaque postcard	$6-$10
Perez-Steele postcards	$10-$15

Joe Kelley (1871-1943) 1971

Availability: Limited
Demand: Strong

Cut signature	$800-$1,100
Single-signature baseball	$7,300-$8,000
3x5 index card	$1,000
Photograph/baseball card	$1,500-$2,250
HOF plaque postcard	Impossible
Perez-Steele postcards	Impossible

George Kelly (1895-1984) 1973

Availability: Plentiful
Demand: Little

Cut signature	$7-$8
Single-signature baseball	$100-$350
3x5 index card	$15
Photograph/baseball card	$50-$75
HOF plaque postcard	$30
Perez-Steele postcards	$300-$325

Mike Kelly (1857-1894) 1945

Availability: Scarce
Demand: Strong

Cut signature	$1,800-$2,000
Single-signature baseball	$7,000
3x5 index card	$3,500
Photograph/baseball card	$5,000
HOF plaque postcard	Impossible
Perez-Steele postcards	Impossible

Harmon Killebrew (1936-) 1984

Availability: Plentiful
Demand: Little

Cut signature	$3-$5
Single-signature baseball	$25-$32
3x5 index card	$8
Photograph/baseball card	$20
HOF plaque postcard	$12-$15
Perez-Steele postcards	$10-$25

Ralph Kiner (1922-) 1975

Availability: Plentiful
Demand: Little

Cut signature	$3-$5
Single-signature baseball	$25
3x5 index card	$7-$10
Photograph/baseball card	$15
HOF plaque postcard	$10-$15
Perez-Steele postcards	$10-$25

Chuck Klein (1904-1958) 1980

Availability: Average
Demand: Average

Cut signature	$95-$200
Single-signature baseball	$1,500-$3,000
3x5 index card	$300
Photograph/baseball card	$400-$500
HOF plaque postcard	Impossible
Perez-Steele postcards	Impossible

Bill Klem (1874-1951) 1953

Availability: Average
Demand: Average

Cut signature	$230-$400
Single-signature baseball	$2,750-$3,500
3x5 index card	$600
Photograph/baseball card	$900-$1,200
HOF plaque postcard	Impossible
Perez-Steele postcards	Impossible

Sandy Koufax (1935-) 1971

Availability: Plentiful
Demand: Little

Cut signature	$5-$10
Single-signature baseball	$65-$70
3x5 index card	$15
Photograph/baseball card	$45-$50
HOF plaque postcard	$30
Perez-Steele postcards	$35-$70

Nap Lajoie (1875-1959) 1937

Availability: Average
Demand: Strong

Cut signature	$125-$250
Single-signature baseball	$4,500-$4,950
3x5 index card	$350
Photograph/baseball card	$900-$1,000
HOF plaque postcard	$750
Perez-Steele postcards	Impossible

Kenesaw Landis (1866-1944) 1944

Availability: Above average
Demand: Average

Cut signature	$140-$225
Single-signature baseball	$2,000-$3,500
3x5 index card	$300
Photograph/baseball card	$525-$650
HOF plaque postcard	Impossible
Perez-Steele postcards	Impossible

Tony Lazzeri (1903-1946) 1991

Availability: Average
Demand: Above average

Cut signature	$100-$275
Single-signature baseball	$1,300-$4,000
3x5 index card	$450
Photograph/baseball card	$500-$700
HOF plaque postcard	Impossible
Perez-Steele postcards	Impossible

Bob Lemon (1920-) 1976

Availability: Plentiful
Demand: Little

Cut signature	$3-$5
Single-signature baseball	$20-$30
3x5 index card	$3-$7
Photograph/baseball card	$12-$15
HOF plaque postcard	$6-$10
Perez-Steele postcards	$10-$20

Buck Leonard (1907-) 1972

Availability: Plentiful
Demand: Little

Cut signature	$5
Single-signature baseball	$40-$50
3x5 index card	$7-$10
Photograph/baseball card	$25-$35
HOF plaque postcard	$10
Perez-Steele postcards	$15-$30

Freddie Lindstrom (1905-1981) 1976

Availability: Plentiful
Demand: Average

Cut signature	$12-$15
Single-signature baseball	$200-$700
3x5 index card	$20
Photograph/baseball card	$75-$100
HOF plaque postcard	$40
Perez-Steele postcards	Impossible

John Lloyd (1884-1964) 1977

Availability: Limited
Demand: Above average

Cut signature	$700
Single-signature baseball	$5,600-$7,000
3x5 index card	$750
Photograph/baseball card	$1,200-$2,500
HOF plaque postcard	Impossible
Perez-Steele postcards	Impossible

Ernie Lombardi (1908-1977) 1986

Availability: Above average
Demand: Average

Cut signature	$25-$30
Single-signature baseball	$525-$1,200
3x5 index card	$50
Photograph/baseball card	$225-$300
HOF plaque postcard	Impossible
Perez-Steele postcards	Impossible

Al Lopez (1908-) 1977

Availability: Plentiful
Demand: Little

Cut signature	$5-$7
Single-signature baseball	$75-$85
3x5 index card	$10
Photograph/baseball card	$28-$35
HOF Plaque postcard	$30
Perez-Steele postcards	$45-$75

Ted Lyons (1900-1986) 1955

Availability: Plentiful
Demand: Little

Cut signature	$7-$8
Single-signature baseball	$125-$225
3x5 index card	$10
Photograph/baseball card	$45-$75
HOF plaque postcard	$30-$35
Perez-Steele postcards	$200-$250

Connie Mack (1862-1956) 1937

Availability: Average
Demand: Average

Cut signature	$65-$100
Single-signature baseball	$1,000
3x5 index card	$150-$200
Photograph/baseball card	$350-$400
HOF plaque postcard	$600
Perez-Steele postcards	Impossible

Larry MacPhail (1890-1975) 1978

Availability: Above average
Demand: Average

Cut signature	$60
Single-signature baseball	$785-$1,700
3x5 index card	$175
Photograph/baseball card	$300-$400
HOF plaque postcard	Impossible
Perez-Steele postcards	Impossible

Mickey Mantle (1931-1995) 1974

Availability: Plentiful
Demand: Average

Cut signature	$15-$50
Single-signature baseball	$175-$250
3x5 index card	$75
Photograph/baseball card	$125
HOF plaque postcard	$75
Perez-Steele postcards	$125-$350

Heinie Manush (1901-1971) 1964

Availability: Average
Demand: Average

Cut signature	$18-$30
Single-signature baseball	$1,500-$2,200
3x5 index card	$60
Photograph/baseball card	$200-$300
HOF plaque postcard	$250-$300
Perez-Steele postcards	Impossible

Rabbit Maranville (1891-1954) 1954

Availability: Average
Demand: Average

Cut signature	$120-$150
Single-signature baseball	$1,600-$2,000
3x5 index card	$250
Photograph/baseball card	$350-$425
HOF plaque postcard	Impossible
Perez-Steele postcards	Impossible

Juan Marichal (1938-) 1983

Availability: Plentiful
Demand: Little

Cut signature	$4-$5
Single-signature baseball	$25
3x5 index card	$8
Photograph/baseball card	$15-$18
HOF plaque postcard	$12
Perez-Steele postcards	$10-$20

Rube Marquard (1889-1980) 1971

Availability: Plentiful
Demand: Little

Cut signature	$8-$10
Single-signature baseball	$450-$700
3x5 index card	$15
Photograph/baseball card	$100-$150
HOF plaque postcard	$45
Perez-Steele postcards	Impossible

Eddie Mathews (1931-) 1978

Availability: Plentiful
Demand: Little

Cut signature	$4-$5
Single-signature baseball	$25-$38
3x5 index card	$7
Photograph/baseball card	$15-$25
HOF plaque postcard	$10
Perez-Steele postcards	$10-$20

Christy Mathewson (1880-1925) 1936

Availability: Limited
Demand: Strong

Cut signature	$700-$1,000
Single-signature baseball	$11,500-$13,000
3x5 index card	$1,400
Photograph/baseball card	$2,900-$3,000
HOF plaque postcard	Impossible
Perez-Steele postcards	Impossible

Willie Mays (1931-) 1979

Availability: Plentiful
Demand: Little

Cut signature	$7-$10
Single-signature baseball	$45-$50
3x5 index card	$15
Photograph/baseball card	$25-$35
HOF plaque postcard	$25
Perez-Steele postcards	$30-$60

Joe McCarthy (1887-1978) 1957

Availability: Average
Demand: Average

Cut signature	$15
Single-signature baseball	$650-$1,000
3x5 index card	$25
Photograph/baseball card	$100-$150
HOF plaque postcard	$50-$80
Perez-Steele postcards	Impossible

Tom McCarthy (1864-1922) 1946

Availability: Limited
Demand: Above average

Cut signature	$1,500-$1,675
Single-signature baseball	$4,000-$4,250
3x5 index card	$2,000
Photograph/baseball card	$4,000-$4,250
HOF plaque postcard	Impossible
Perez-Steele postcards	Impossible

Willie McCovey (1938-) 1986

Availability: Plentiful
Demand: Little

Cut signature	$4-$5
Single-signature baseball	$30
3x5 index card	$8
Photograph/baseball card	$20-$25
HOF plaque postcard	$12
Perez-Steele postcards	$10-$25

Joe McGinnity (1871-1929) 1946

Availability: Scarce
Demand: Above average

Cut signature	$800-$1,250
Single-signature baseball	$5,000-$9,000
3x5 index card	$1,500
Photograph/baseball card	$4,000-$5,000
HOF plaque postcard	Impossible
Perez-Steele postcards	Impossible

Bill McGowan (1871-1954) 1992

Availability: Average
Demand: Little

Cut signature	$300
Single-signature baseball	$5,000
3x5 index card	$400
Photograph/baseball card	$2,000
HOF plaque postcard	Impossible
Perez-Steele postcards	Impossible

John McGraw (1873-1934) 1937

Availability: Limited
Demand: Strong

Cut signature	$425-$500
Single-signature baseball	$3,500-$6,000
3x5 index card	$750
Photograph/baseball card	$1,250-$1,500
HOF plaque postcard	Impossible
Perez-Steele postcards	Impossible

Bill McKechnie (1886-1965) 1962

Availability: Above average
Demand: Average

Cut signature	$60-$75
Single-signature baseball	$1,500-$2,000
3x5 index card	$150
Photograph/baseball card	$300-$350
HOF plaque postcard	$300
Perez-Steele postcards	Impossible

Ducky Medwick (1911-1975) 1968

Availability: Above average
Demand: Average

Cut signature	$20-$25
Single-signature baseball	$500-$1,700
3x5 index card	$45
Photograph/baseball card	$150-$200
HOF plaque postcard	$125
Perez-Steele postcards	Impossible

Johnny Mize (1913-1993) 1981

Availability: Plentiful
Demand: Little

Cut signature	$5
Single-signature baseball	$35-$60
3x5 index card	$7-$8
Photograph/baseball card	$30-$35
HOF plaque postcard	$12-$15
Perez-Steele postcards	$20-$35

Joe Morgan (1943-) 1990

Availability: Plentiful
Demand: Little

Cut signature	$3-$5
Single-signature baseball	$25-$30
3x5 index card	$7
Photograph/baseball card	$15-$25
HOF plaque postcard	$12-$18
Perez-Steele postcards	$15-$20

Stan Musial (1920-) 1969

Availability: Plentiful
Demand: Little

Cut signature	$4-$10
Single-signature baseball	$50
3x5 index card	$15
Photograph/baseball card	$30-$35
HOF plaque postcard	$25
Perez-Steele postcards	$30-$80

Hal Newhouser (1921-) 1992

Availability: Average
Demand: Average

Cut signature	$3-$5
Single-signature baseball	$22-$27
3x5 index card	$7
Photograph/baseball card	$12
HOF plaque postcard	$8
Perez-Steele postcards	$15-$20

Kid Nichols (1869-1953) 1949

Availability: Average
Demand: Above average

Cut signature	$125-$200
Single-signature baseball	$3,200-$4,000
3x5 index card	$300
Photograph/baseball card	$475-$500
HOF plaque postcard	$1,000
Perez-Steele postcards	Impossible

James O'Rourke (1852-1919) 1945

Availability: Scarce
Demand: Strong

Cut signature	$1,500-$1,750
Single-signature baseball	$5,200-$10,000
3x5 index card	$2,500
Photograph/baseball card	$3,500-$3,700
HOF plaque postcard	Impossible
Perez-Steele postcards	Impossible

Mel Ott (1909-1958) 1951

Availability: Average
Demand: Above average

Cut signature	$100-$200
Single-signature baseball	$2,500-$3,500
3x5 index card	$275
Photograph/baseball card	$500-$725
HOF plaque postcard	$650
Perez-Steele postcards	Impossible

Satchel Paige (1906-1982) 1971

Availability: Above average
Demand: Above average

Cut signature	$25-$40
Single-signature baseball	$900-$990
3x5 index card	$80-$125
Photograph/baseball card	$200-$235
HOF plaque postcard	$140
Perez-Steele postcards	$3,500

Jim Palmer (1945-) 1990

Availability: Plentiful
Demand: Little

Cut signature	$4-$5
Single-signature baseball	$25
3x5 index card	$7
Photograph/baseball card	$15-$20
HOF plaque postcard	$10-$15
Perez-Steele postcards	$15-$25

Herb Pennock (1894-1948) 1948

Availability: Average
Demand: Average

Cut signature	$175
Single-signature baseball	$1,625-$2,500
3x5 index card	$200
Photograph/baseball card	$350
HOF plaque postcard	Impossible
Perez-Steele postcards	Impossible

Gaylord Perry (1938-) 1991

Availability: Plentiful
Demand: Little

Cut signature	$3-$5
Single-signature baseball	$20-$25
3x5 index card	$7
Photograph/baseball card	$12-$15
HOF plaque postcard	$10
Perez-Steele postcards	$15

Ed Plank (1875-1926) 1946

Availability: Limited
Demand: Strong

Cut signature	$1,500-$1,775
Single-signature baseball	$8,000
3x5 index card	$2,200
Photograph/baseball card	$3,200-$3,500
HOF plaque postcard	Impossible
Perez-Steele postcards	Impossible

Charles Radbourne (1854-1897) 1948

Availability: Scarce
Demand: Strong

Cut signature	$1,425-$2,000
Single-signature baseball	$7,500
3x5 index card	$2,500
Photograph/baseball card	$3,200-$3,500
HOF plaque postcard	Impossible
Perez-Steele postcards	Impossible

Pee Wee Reese (1918-) 1984

Availability: Plentiful
Demand: Little

Cut signature	$4-$7
Single-signature baseball	$50-$60
3x5 index card	$10
Photograph/baseball card	$30-$40
HOF plaque postcard	$20-$30
Perez-Steele postcards	$15-$35

Sam Rice (1890-1974) 1963

Availability: Above average
Demand: Average

Cut signature	$16-$20
Single-signature baseball	$625-$1,500
3x5 index card	$40
Photograph/baseball card	$125-$150
HOF plaque postcard	$100-$135
Perez-Steele postcards	Impossible

Branch Rickey (1881-1965) 1967

Availability: Average
Demand: Average

Cut signature	$75-$175
Single-signature baseball	$1,100-$2,500
3x5 index card	$200
Photograph/baseball card	$525-$750
HOF plaque postcard	Impossible
Perez-Steele postcards	Impossible

Eppa Rixey (1891-1963) 1963

Availability: Average
Demand: Average

Cut signature	$60-$65
Single-signature baseball	$800-$3,500
3x5 index card	$100
Photograph/baseball card	$250-$350
HOF plaque postcard	Impossible
Perez-Steele postcards	Impossible

Phil Rizzuto (1918-) 1994

Availability: Above average
Demand: Average

Cut signature	$4-$5
Single-signature baseball	$25
3x5 index card	$7
Photograph/baseball card	$12-$18
HOF plaque postcard	$12
Perez-Steele postcards	$35

Robin Roberts (1926-) 1976

Availability: Plentiful
Demand: Little

Cut signature	$4-$5
Single-signature baseball	$25
3x5 index card	$7
Photograph/baseball card	$12
HOF plaque postcard	$8
Perez-Steele postcards	$12-$20

Brooks Robinson (1937-) 1983

Availability: Plentiful
Demand: Little

Cut signature	$4-$5
Single-signature baseball	$25-$30
3x5 index card	$7
Photograph/baseball card	$15-$18
HOF plaque postcard	$8
Perez-Steele postcards	$10-$20

Frank Robinson (1935-) 1982

Availability: Plentiful
Demand: Little

Cut signature	$4-$5
Single-signature baseball	$30
3x5 index card	$8
Photograph/baseball card	$20
HOF plaque postcard	$12-$20
Perez-Steele postcards	$25

Jackie Robinson (1919-1972) 1962

Availability: Above average
Demand: Above average

Cut signature	$120-$175
Single-signature baseball	$2,200-$2,500
3x5 index card	$300
Photograph/baseball card	$575-$700
HOF plaque postcard	$600-$700
Perez-Steele postcards	Impossible

Wilbert Robinson (1863-1934) 1945

Availability: Limited
Demand: Above average

Cut signature	$700-$750
Single-signature baseball	$4,225-$6,000
3x5 index card	$750
Photograph/baseball card	$2,000
HOF plaque postcard	Impossible
Perez-Steele postcards	Impossible

Edd Roush (1893-1988) 1962

Availability: Plentiful
Demand: Little

Cut signature	$8-$9
Single-signature baseball	$80-$160
3x5 index card	$10
Photograph/baseball card	$45-$75
HOF plaque postcard	$30-$80
Perez-Steele postcards	$65-$80

Red Ruffing (1904-1986) 1967

Availability: Plentiful
Demand: Little

Cut signature	$20
Single-signature baseball	$195-$500
3x5 index card	$35
Photograph/baseball card	$70-$125
HOF plaque postcard	$100
Perez-Steele postcards	$350-$400

Amos Rusie (1871-1942) 1977

Availability: Limited
Demand: Above average

Cut signature	$700-$1,100
Single-signature baseball	$5,000-$6,500
3x5 index card	$750
Photograph/baseball card	$2,000-$2,300
HOF plaque postcard	Impossible
Perez-Steele postcards	Impossible

Babe Ruth (1895-1948) 1936

Availability: Average
Demand: Strong

Cut signature	$495-$700
Single-signature baseball	$4,000-$4,200
3x5 index card	$1,000
Photograph/baseball card	$2,225-$2,500
HOF plaque postcard	$4,500
Perez-Steele postcards	Impossible

Ray Schalk (1892-1970) 1955

Availability: Above average
Demand: Average

Cut signature	$35-$45
Single-signature baseball	$600-$1,700
3x5 index card	$75-$85
Photograph/baseball card	$225-$350
HOF plaque postcard	$300-$450
Perez-Steele postcards	Impossible

Mike Schmidt (1949-) 1995

Availability: Average
Demand: Strong

Cut signature	$5-$10
Single-signature baseball	$40-$60
3x5 index card	$15
Photograph/baseball card	$35-$55
HOF plaque postcard	$40
Perez-Steele postcards	Impossible

Red Schoendienst (1923-) 1989

Availability: Plentiful
Demand: Little

Cut signature	$4-$5
Single-signature baseball	$25
3x5 index card	$7-$10
Photograph/baseball card	$12-$15
HOF plaque postcard	$10
Perez-Steele postcards	$10-$20

Tom Seaver (1944-) 1992

Availability: Above average
Demand: Above average

Cut signature	$5-$7
Single-signature baseball	$40-$45
3x5 index card	$10
Photograph/baseball card	$30
HOF plaque postcard	$25
Perez-Steele postcards	$35-$40

Joe Sewell (1898-1990) 1977

Availability: Plentiful
Demand: Little

Cut signature	$4-$5
Single-signature baseball	$80-$125
3x5 index card	$8
Photograph/baseball card	$25-$30
HOF plaque postcard	$15
Perez-Steele postcards	$25-$60

Al Simmons (1902-1956) 1953

Availability: Average
Demand: Average

Cut signature	$70-$175
Single-signature baseball	$925-$2,800
3x5 index card	$225-$325
Photograph/baseball card	$500
HOF plaque postcard	$800
Perez-Steele postcards	Impossible

George Sisler (1893-1973) 1939

Availability: Above average
Demand: Average

Cut signature	$25
Single-signature baseball	$550-$1,200
3x5 index card	$50
Photograph/baseball card	$135-$175
HOF plaque postcard	$125
Perez-Steele postcards	Impossible

Enos Slaughter (1916-) 1985

Availability: Plentiful
Demand: Little

Cut signature	$3-$5
Single-signature baseball	$20-$25
3x5 index card	$7
Photograph/baseball card	$10-$15
HOF plaque postcard	$6-$10
Perez-Steele postcards	$10-$20

Duke Snider (1926-) 1980

Availability: Plentiful
Demand: Little

Cut signature	$4-$5
Single-signature baseball	$25-$30
3x5 index card	$7
Photograph/baseball card	$15-$20
HOF plaque postcard	$10-$15
Perez-Steele postcards	$10-$25

Warren Spahn (1921-) 1973

Availability: Plentiful
Demand: Little

Cut signature	$3-$5
Single-signature baseball	$20-$25
3x5 index card	$7
Photograph/baseball card	$12-$15
HOF plaque postcard	$8
Perez-Steele postcards	$20-$30

Al Spalding (1850-1915) 1939

Availability: Limited
Demand: Strong

Cut signature	$750-$1,250
Single-signature baseball	$6,000-$12,000
3x5 index card	$1,750
Photograph/baseball card	$1,800-$2,200
HOF plaque postcard	Impossible
Perez-Steele postcards	Impossible

Tris Speaker (1888-1958) 1937

Availability: Average
Demand: Above average

Cut signature	$100-$200
Single-signature baseball	$2,900-$3,000
3x5 index card	$225-$275
Photograph/baseball card	$500-$700
HOF plaque postcard	$600
Perez-Steele postcards	Impossible

Willie Stargell (1940-) 1988

Availability: Plentiful
Demand: Little

Cut signature	$3-$5
Single-signature baseball	$22-$30
3x5 index card	$7
Photograph/baseball card	$10-$15
HOF plaque postcard	$8
Perez-Steele postcards	$10-$15

Casey Stengel (1890-1975) 1966

Availability: Average
Demand: Above average

Cut signature	$10-$40
Single-signature baseball	$480-$1,000
3x5 index card	$80-$100
Photograph/baseball card	$125-$150
HOF plaque postcard	$100
Perez-Steele postcards	Impossible

Bill Terry (1898-1989) 1954

Availability: Plentiful
Demand: Little

Cut signature	$7
Single-signature baseball	$160
3x5 index card	$10
Photograph/baseball card	$45-$50
HOF plaque postcard	$25-$30
Perez-Steele postcards	$65-$80

Sam Thompson (1860-1922) 1974

Availability: Scarce
Demand: Strong

Cut signature	$1,200-$2,125
Single-signature baseball	$8,000-$10,000
3x5 index card	$3,250
Photograph/baseball card	$6,000
HOF plaque postcard	Impossible
Perez-Steele postcards	Impossible

Joe Tinker (1880-1948) 1946

Availability: Average
Demand: Average

Cut signature	$300
Single-signature baseball	$6,000
3x5 index card	$375-$400
Photograph/baseball card	$900-$1,200
HOF plaque postcard	$1,000
Perez-Steele postcards	Impossible

Pie Traynor (1899-1972) 1948

Availability: Above average
Demand: Average

Cut signature	$40-$100
Single-signature baseball	$1,175-$1,200
3x5 index card	$125-$175
Photograph/baseball card	$300
HOF plaque postcard	$450
Perez-Steele postcards	Impossible

Dazzy Vance (1891-1961) 1955

Availability: Average
Demand: Average

Cut signature	$70-$200
Single-signature baseball	$1,500-$3,200
3x5 index card	$250-$300
Photograph/baseball card	$650-$750
HOF plaque postcard	$600
Perez-Steele postcards	Impossible

Arky Vaughan (1912-1952) 1985

Availability: Average
Demand: Above average

Cut signature	$150-$175
Single-signature baseball	$1,525-$3,500
3x5 index card	$250
Photograph/baseball card	$500-$650
HOF plaque postcard	Impossible
Perez-Steele postcards	Impossible

William Veeck (1914-1986) 1991

Availability: Above average
Demand: Average

Cut signature	$10-$40
Single-signature baseball	$550-$2,000
3x5 index card	$75
Photograph/baseball card	$250-$325
HOF plaque postcard	Impossible
Perez-Steele postcards	Impossible

Rube Waddell (1876-1914) 1946

Availability: Scarce
Demand: Strong

Cut signature	$1,000-$1,400
Single-signature baseball	$7,000-$12,500
3x5 index card	$1,500
Photograph/baseball card	$4,500
HOF plaque postcard	Impossible
Perez-Steele postcards	Impossible

Honus Wagner (1874-1955) 1936

Availability: Average
Demand: Strong

Cut signature	$175-$275
Single-signature baseball	$4,000
3x5 index card	$350
Photograph/baseball card	$725-$800
HOF plaque postcard	$1,200
Perez-Steele postcards	Impossible

Bobby Wallace (1873-1960) 1953

Availability: Average
Demand: Average

Cut signature	$175-$225
Single-signature baseball	$3,000-$4,500
3x5 index card	$300
Photograph/baseball card	$625-$700
HOF plaque postcard	$800
Perez-Steele postcards	Impossible

Ed Walsh (1881-1959) 1946

Availability: Average
Demand: Average

Cut signature	$100-$150
Single-signature baseball	$2,725-$3,600
3x5 index card	$200
Photograph/baseball card	$350-$400
HOF plaque postcard	$350
Perez-Steele postcards	Impossible

Lloyd Waner (1906-1982) 1967

Availability: Plentiful
Demand: Little

Cut signature	$12-$15
Single-signature baseball	$500
3x5 index card	$15-$20
Photograph/baseball card	$150
HOF plaque postcard	$30
Perez-Steele postcards	$3,500

Paul Waner (1903-1965) 1952

Availability: Average
Demand: Above average

Cut signature	$50-$100
Single-signature baseball	$2,300-$2,500
3x5 index card	$125
Photograph/baseball card	$200-$300
HOF plaque postcard	$350
Perez-Steele postcards	Impossible

Monte Ward (1860-1925) 1964

Availability: Limited
Demand: Strong

Cut signature	$1,000-$1,450
Single-signature baseball	$8,350-$12,000
3x5 index card	$1,500
Photograph/baseball card	$3,000-$3,250
HOF plaque postcard	Impossible
Perez-Steele postcards	Impossible

Earl Weaver (1930-) 1996

Availability: Average
Demand: Average

Cut signature	$5
Single-signature baseball	$25
3x5 index card	$7
Photograph/baseball card	$15
HOF plaque/baseball card	Impossible
Perez-Steele postcards	Impossible

George Weiss (1895-1972) 1971

Availability: Above average
Demand: Average

Cut signature	$40-$45
Single-signature baseball	$675-$3,500
3x5 index card	$75-$100
Photograph/baseball card	$250-$300
HOF plaque postcard	Unknown
Perez-Steele postcards	Impossible

Mickey Welch (1859-1941) 1973

Availability: Limited
Demand: Strong

Cut signature	$1,700-$2,000
Single-signature baseball	$5,800-$8,500
3x5 index card	$2,750
Photograph/baseball card	$4,000
HOF plaque postcard	Impossible
Perez-Steele postcards	Impossible

Zack Wheat (1888-1972) 1959

Availability: Above average
Demand: Average

Cut signature	$20-$50
Single-signature baseball	$975-$1,600
3x5 index card	$80
Photograph/baseball card	$175-$200
HOF plaque postcard	$200-$350
Perez-Steele postcards	Impossible

Hoyt Wilhelm (1923-) 1985

Availability: Plentiful
Demand: Little

Cut signature	$3
Single-signature baseball	$20
3x5 index card	$5
Photograph/baseball card	$10-$14
HOF plaque postcard	$8-$15
Perez-Steele postcards	$15

Billy Williams (1938-) 1987

Availability: Plentiful
Demand: Little

Cut signature	$4-$5
Single-signature baseball	$20-$25
3x5 index card	$7
Photograph/baseball card	$10-$15
HOF plaque postcard	$8
Perez-Steele postcards	$10-$15

Ted Williams (1918-) 1966

Availability: Plentiful
Demand: Average

Cut signature	$10-$30
Single-signature baseball	$160
3x5 index card	$50
Photograph/baseball card	$75-$90
HOF plaque postcard	$60
Perez-Steele postcards	$80-$325

Vic Willis (1876-1947) 1995

Availability: Limited
Demand: Little

Cut signature	$250
Single-signature baseball	Unknown
3x5 index card	$425
Photograph/baseball card	$750
HOF plaque postcard	Impossible
Perez-Steele postcards	Impossible

Hack Wilson (1900-1948) 1979

Availability: Limited
Demand: Above average

Cut signature	$235-$300
Single-signature baseball	$2,400-$3,000
3x5 index card	$450
Photograph/baseball card	$675-$800
HOF plaque postcard	Impossible
Perez-Steele postcards	Impossible

George Wright (1847-1937) 1937

Availability: Limited
Demand: Strong

Cut signature	$800-$900
Single-signature baseball	$5,725-$8,500
3x5 index card	$1,200
Photograph/baseball card	$2,750
HOF plaque postcard	Impossible
Perez-Steele postcards	Impossible

Harry Wright (1835-1895) 1953

Availability: Scarce
Demand: Strong

Cut signature	$1,200-$1,600
Single-signature baseball	$5,000
3x5 index card	$2,000
Photograph/baseball card	$3,500
HOF plaque postcard	Impossible
Perez-Steele postcards	Impossible

Early Wynn (1920-) 1972

Availability: Plentiful
Demand: Little

Cut signature	$4-$5
Single-signature baseball	$20-$25
3x5 index card	$7
Photograph/baseball card	$15-$20
HOF plaque postcard	$10
Perez-Steele postcards	$20-$25

Carl Yastrzemski (1939-) 1989

Availability: Plentiful
Demand: Little

Cut signature	$5-$8
Single-signature baseball	$35-$45
3x5 index card	$12
Photograph/baseball card	$25-$30
HOF plaque postcard	$20
Perez-Steele postcards	$15-$30

Tom Yawkey (1903-1976) 1980

Availability: Average
Demand: Average

Cut signature	$70-$100
Single-signature baseball	$1,050-$2,000
3x5 index card	$125-$175
Photograph/baseball card	$325-$400
HOF plaque postcard	Impossible
Perez-Steele postcards	Impossible

Cy Young (1867-1955) 1937

Availability: Average
Demand: Strong

Cut signature	$175-$300
Single-signature baseball	$3,400-$3,500
3x5 index card	$350
Photograph/baseball card	$700-$825
HOF plaque postcard	$1,000
Perez-Steele postcards	Impossible

Ross Youngs (1897-1927) 1972

Availability: Scarce
Demand: Strong

Cut signature	$1,000-$1,150
Single-signature baseball	$7,000
3x5 index card	$1,500
Photograph/baseball card	$2,500
HOF plaque postcard	Impossible
Perez-Steele postcards	Impossible

Gallery of Superstars

Roberto Alomar

Cut signature	$4
Single-signature baseball	$19
3x5 index card	$7
Photograph/baseball card	$12

Sparky Anderson

Cut signature	$3
Single-signature baseball	$30-$35
3x5 index card	$5
Photograph/baseball card	$13-$15

Albert Belle

Cut signature	$6
Single-signature baseball	$40
3x5 index card	$10
Photograph/baseball card	$25

Vida Blue

Cut signature	$3
Single-signature baseball	$25
3x5 index card	$4
Photograph/baseball card	$15

Bert Blyleven

Cut signature	$4
Single-signature baseball	$22
3x5 index card	$7
Photograph/baseball card	$12

Wade Boggs

Cut signature	$4
Single-signature baseball	$35
3x5 index card	$8
Photograph/baseball card	$20

Barry Bonds

Cut signature	$8
Single-signature baseball	$60
3x5 index card	$12
Photograph/baseball card	$35

George Brett

Cut signature	$4
Single-signature baseball	$40

3x5 index card	$10
Photograph/baseball card	$30

Jose Canseco

Cut signature	$5
Single-signature	$40
3x5 index card	$17
Photograph/baseball card	$35

Orlando Cepeda

Cut signature	$3
Single-signature baseball	$25
3x5 index card	$5
Photograph/baseball card	$14

Will Clark

Cut signature	$4
Single-signature baseball	$40
3x5 index card	$8
Photograph/baseball card	$20

Roger Clemens

Cut signature	$4
Single-signature baseball	$50
3x5 index card	$8
Photograph/baseball card	$20-$25

Andre Dawson

Cut signature	$5
Single-signature baseball	$30
3x5 index card	$6
Photograph/baseball card	$18

Dwight Evans

Cut signature	$2
Single-signature baseball	$25
3x5 index card	$5
Photograph/baseball card	$12

Carlton Fisk

Cut signature	$3
Single-signature baseball	$40
3x5 index card	$8
Photograph/baseball card	$20

Nellie Fox

Cut signature	$20
Single-signature baseball	$900
3x5 index card	$50
Photograph/baseball card	$250

Steve Garvey

Cut signature	$2
Single-signature baseball	$25
3x5 index card	$6
Photograph/baseball card	$12

Mark Grace

Cut signature	$2
Single-signature baseball	$25
3x5 index card	$7
Photograph/baseball card	$13

Ken Griffey Jr.

Cut signature	$5
Single-signature baseball	$45
3x5 index card	$10
Photograph/baseball card	$30

Rickey Henderson

Cut signature	$5
Single-signature baseball	$35
3x5 index card	$8
Photograph/baseball card	$25

Gil Hodges

Cut signature	$30
Single-signature baseball	$1,450
3x5 index card	$50
Photograph/baseball card	$295

Bo Jackson

Cut signature	$7
Single-signature baseball	$32
3x5 index card	$15
Photograph/baseball card	$21

Joe Jackson

Cut signature	$1,500
Single-signature baseball	$20,000
3x5 index card	$2,000
Photograph/baseball card	$9,000

Tommy John

Cut signature	$3
Single-signature baseball	$19
3x5 index card	$4
Photograph/baseball card	$13

Jim Kaat

Cut signature	$3
Single-signature baseball	$25
3x5 index card	$5
Photograph/baseball card	$15

Jerry Koosman

Cut signature	$2
Single-signature baseball	$22
3x5 index card	$4
Photograph/baseball card	$10

Don Larsen

Cut signature	$2
Single-signature baseball	$25
3x5 index card	$5
Photograph/baseball card	$13

Mickey Lolich

Cut signature	$2
Single-signature baseball	$19
3x5 index card	$4
Photograph/baseball card	$11

Greg Maddux

Cut signature	$6
Single-signature baseball	$60
3x5 index card	$10
Photograph/baseball card	$30

Roger Maris

Cut signature	$25
Single-signature baseball	$615
3x5 index card	$75
Photograph/baseball card	$215

Billy Martin

Cut signature	$15
Single-signature baseball	$180
3x5 index card	$30
Photograph/baseball card	$70

Don Mattingly

Cut signature	$5
Single-signature baseball	$45
3x5 index card	$12
Photograph/baseball card	$24

Bill Mazeroski

Cut signature	$3
Single-signature baseball	$45
3x5 index card	$6
Photograph/baseball card	$24

Mark McGwire

Cut signature	$3
Single-signature baseball	$30
3x5 index card	$8
Photograph/baseball card	$20

Thurman Munson

Cut signature	$20
Single-signature baseball	$925
3x5 index card	$75
Photograph/baseball card	$325

Dale Murphy

Cut signature	$3
Single-signature baseball	$27
3x5 index card	$6
Photograph/baseball card	$16

Eddie Murray

Cut signature	$3
Single-signature baseball	$50
3x5 index card	$9
Photograph/baseball card	$25

Phil Niekro

Cut signature	$3
Single-signature baseball	$25
3x5 index card	$7
Photograph/baseball card	$13

Tony Oliva

Cut signature	$3
Single-signature baseball	$23
3x5 index card	$6
Photograph/baseball card	$11

Al Oliver

Cut signature	$3
Single-signature baseball	$19
3x5 index card	$4
Photograph/baseball card	$12

Dave Parker

Cut signature	$3
Single-signature baseball	$25
3x5 index card	$7
Photograph/baseball card	$11

Tony Perez

Cut signature	$3
Single-signature baseball	$30
3x5 index card	$4
Photograph/baseball card	$15

Kirby Puckett

Cut signature	$6
Single-signature baseball	$60
3x5 index card	$12
Photograph/baseball card	$30

Jim Rice

Cut signature	$2
Single-signature baseball	$20
3x5 index card	$4
Photograph/baseball card	$11

Cal Ripken Jr.

Cut signature	$6
Single-signature baseball	$75
3x5 index card	$12
Photograph/baseball card	$40

Pete Rose

Cut signature	$5
Single-signature baseball	$35
3x5 index card	$10
Photograph/baseball card	$25

Nolan Ryan

Cut signature	$7
Single-signature baseball	$60
3x5 index card	$15
Photograph/baseball card	$40

Mo Vaughn

Ryne Sandberg

Ryne Sandberg

Cut signature	$4
Single-signature baseball	$40
3x5 index card	$10
Photograph/baseball card	$25

Ted Simmons

Cut signature	$2
Single-signature baseball	$23
3x5 index card	$5
Photograph/baseball card	$12

Ozzie Smith

Cut signature	$3
Single-signature baseball	$28
3x5 index card	$10
Photograph/baseball card	$20

Rusty Staub

Cut signature	$2
Single-signature baseball	$23
3x5 index card	$6
Photograph/baseball card	$12

Don Sutton

Cut signature	$2
Single-signature baseball	$25
3x5 index card	$6
Photograph/baseball card	$12

Frank Thomas

Cut signature	$6
Single-signature baseball	$60
3x5 index card	$12
Photograph/baseball card	$40

Luis Tiant

Cut signature	$2
Single-signature baseball	$25
3x5 index card	$4
Photograph/baseball card	$10

Dave Winfield

Cut signature	$3
Single-signature baseball	$45
3x5 index card	$18
Photograph/baseball card	$25

Robin Yount

Cut signature	$5
Single-signature baseball	$45
3x5 index card	$10
Photograph/baseball card	$21

Inactive Players

Players	Baseball	Photo	Players	Baseball	Photo
Carl Abrams	$21	$11	John Candelaria	$18	$10
Joe Adcock	$23	$12	Chico Carrasquel	$22	$10
Tommie Agee	$20	$9	Gary Carter	$30	$15
Willie Aikens	$17	$10	Rico Carty	$22	$12
Danny Ainge	$15	$12	Norm Cash	$200	$30
Dick Allen	$23	$13	Phil Cavarretta	$30	$15
Felipe Alou	$23	$13	Cesar Cedeno	$28	$14
Jesus Alou	$20	$10	Rick Cerone	$15	$8
Matty Alou	$23	$13	Ron Cey	$24	$13
Sandy Amoros	$75	$30	Chris Chambliss	$20	$10
Joaquin Andujar	$18	$10	Jack Clark	$23	$13
Tony Armas	$19	$11	Donn Clendenon	$20	$11
Alan Ashby	$17	$9	Rocky Colavito	$25	$19
Bobby Avila	$20	$15	Dave Concepcion	$25	$15
Bob Bailor	$15	$7	Tony Conigliaro	$100	$50
Dusty Baker	$21	$13	Gene Conley	$18	$10
Sal Bando	$20	$12	Chuck Connors	$150	$23
Floyd Bannister	$14	$7	Cecil Cooper	$20	$13
Jesse Barfield	$19	$10	Roger Craig	$24	$13
Len Barker	$15	$8	Roger Cramer	$150	$20
Kevin Bass	$16	$9	Warren Cromartie	$17	$10
Don Baylor	$24	$14	Jose Cruz	$23	$14
Mark Belanger	$17	$10	Frank Crosetti	$30	$10
Buddy Bell	$20	$12	Babe Dahlgren	$30	$12
George Bell	$18	$10	Kal Daniels	$17	$9
Gus Bell	$40	$19	Alvin Dark	$20	$12
Ewell Blackwell	$20	$10	Alvin Davis	$20	$10
Paul Blair	$20	$12	Glenn Davis	$21	$12
Johnny Blanchard	$20	$10	Tommy Davis	$21	$11
Steve Blass	$15	$8	Willie Davis	$15	$8
Ron Blomberg	$18	$8	Doug DeCinces	$20	$10
Mike Boddicker	$22	$12	Rick Dempsey	$22	$12
Bobby Bonds	$25	$12	John Denny	$22	$12
Bob Boone	$23	$14	Bucky Dent	$24	$14
Ray Boone	$30	$20	Bob Dernier	$15	$8
Jim Bouton	$20	$10	Lou Dials	$30	$18
Larry Bowa	$20	$10	Dom DiMaggio	$45	$35
Clete Boyer	$23	$12	Larry Doby	$30	$20
Ken Boyer	$290	$70	Dave Dravecky	$23	$13
Ralph Branca	$22	$12	Walt Dropo	$20	$10
Rocky Bridges	$25	$10	Leon Durham	$15	$10
Greg Brock	$8	$15	Ryne Duren	$20	$8
Hubie Brooks	$18	$10	Duffy Dyer	$15	$8
Tom Brunansky	$16	$8	Dock Ellis	$20	$11
Bill Buckner	$20	$10	Carl Erskine	$26	$11
Al Bumbry	$18	$10	Nick Esasky	$17	$10
Lou Burdette	$21	$11	Darrell Evans	$22	$12
Jeff Burroughs	$19	$10	Elroy Face	$22	$10
Enos Cabell	$22	$12	Boo Ferriss	$15	$8
Mike Caldwell	$16	$10	Mark Fidrych	$20	$11
Johnny Callison	$15	$8	Ed Figueroa	$15	$8
Bert Campaneris	$20	$12	Mike Flanagan	$22	$12

Players	Baseball	Photo	Players	Baseball	Photo
Curt Flood	$25	$15	Ted Kluszewski	$300	$75
Dan Ford	$24	$13	Ray Knight	$25	$15
George Foster	$20	$10	Tony Kubek	$30	$18
Jim Fregosi	$23	$13	Harvey Kuenn	$200	$35
Bob Friend	$18	$12	Ed Kranepool	$20	$10
Oscar Gamble	$20	$12	Ken Landreaux	$14	$7
Jim Gantner	$15	$9	Tony LaRussa	$24	$13
Phil Garner	$21	$13	Tommy Lasorda	$30	$15
Ralph Garr	$17	$12	Vern Law	$19	$10
Cito Gaston	$25	$13	Bill Lee	$18	$12
Jim Gentile	$20	$8	Ron LeFlore	$23	$12
Cesar Geronimo	$20	$10	Jeffrey Leonard	$18	$10
Kirk Gibson	$24	$14	Johnny Logan	$17	$10
Al Gionfriddo	$15	$10	Vic Lombardi	$20	$8
Dan Gladden	$18	$10	Jim Lonborg	$23	$11
Goose Gossage	$25	$15	Davey Lopes	$22	$12
Mudcat Grant	$20	$10	Greg Luzinski	$20	$10
Bobby Grich	$22	$10	Sparky Lyle	$21	$12
Ken Griffey Sr.	$30	$18	Fred Lynn	$25	$14
Dick Groat	$20	$13	Garry Maddox	$24	$14
Jerry Grote	$23	$12	Bill Madlock	$22	$11
Kelly Gruber	$24	$15	Rick Manning	$17	$8
Pedro Guerrero	$24	$14	Dennis Martinez	$24	$13
Ron Guidry	$28	$15	John Matlack	$17	$8
Don Gullet	$19	$9	Gary Mathews	$22	$12
Harvey Haddix	$55	$22	Lee Mazzilli	$25	$10
Tommy Harper	$20	$11	Gene Mauch	$20	$8
Bud Harrelson	$20	$10	Carlos May	$15	$8
Richie Hebner	$23	$13	Rudy May	$20	$10
Dave Henderson	$20	$10	John Mayberry	$20	$10
George Hendrick	$21	$12	Lee Mazzilli	$15	$8
Ellie Hendricks	$15	$8	Tim McCarver	$29	$15
Tommy Henrich	$22	$10	Mickey McDermott	$15	$10
Keith Hernandez	$30	$15	Oddibe McDowell	$17	$9
Whitey Herzog	$25	$14	Gil McDougald	$17	$8
Ted Higuera	$16	$9	Sam McDowell	$15	$8
Larry Hisle	$19	$10	Tug McGraw	$25	$15
Butch Hobson	$13	$8	Denny McLain	$25	$10
Bob Horner	$20	$10	Dave McNally	$22	$10
Charlie Hough	$20	$10	Hal McRae	$23	$14
Ralph Houk	$24	$13	Kevin McReynolds	$19	$10
Elston Howard	$500	$90	Gene Michael	$15	$8
Frank Howard	$25	$11	Felix Milan	$15	$7
Roy Howell	$14	$8	Minnie Minoso	$28	$20
Al Hrabosky	$25	$18	Wilmer Mizell	$18	$11
Kent Hrbek	$25	$13	Rick Monday	$23	$13
Randy Hundley	$15	$8	Don Money	$21	$13
Joey Jay	$28	$15	Wally Moon	$15	$10
Davey Johnson	$21	$11	Terry Moore	$40	$25
Alex Johnson	$15	$8	Keith Moreland	$15	$10
Jay Johnstone	$25	$12	Omar Moreno	$25	$15
Cleon Jones	$19	$11	Manny Mota	$27	$14
Don Kessinger	$18	$11	Bobby Murcer	$25	$12
Dave Kingman	$25	$10	Craig Nettles	$25	$13

"We Are Family" members Omar Moreno, Bill Madlock and Manny Sanquillen reunite.

Players	Baseball	Photo	Players	Baseball	Photo
Don Newcombe	$25	$12	Bobby Richardson	$19	$10
Joe Niekro	$21	$11	Johnny Riddle	$20	$15
Gary Nolan	$15	$8	Dave Righetti	$20	$10
Joe Nuxhall	$17	$12	Billy Ripken	$15	$8
Blue Moon Odom	$20	$9	Mickey Rivers	$20	$11
Ben Oglivie	$15	$9	Preacher Roe	$25	$15
Sadaharu Oh	$130	$38	Stan Rogers	$20	$10
Claude Osteen	$24	$12	Al Rosen	$25	$15
Amos Otis	$22	$12	Johnny Roseboro	$20	$10
Mickey Owen	$20	$8	Joe Rudi	$24	$14
Andy Pafko	$22	$10	Bill Russell	$21	$12
Alejandro Pena	$21	$11	Deion Sanders	$40	$25
Joe Pepitone	$21	$10	Johnny Sain	$25	$12
Jim Perry	$15	$10	Manny Sanguillen	$30	$18
Johnny Pesky	$21	$11	Ron Santo	$25	$14
Rico Petrocelli	$15	$8	Hank Sauer	$17	$10
Billy Pierce	$20	$12	Steve Sax	$20	$10
Jimmy Piersall	$23	$13	Herb Score	$23	$15
Lou Piniella	$24	$13	George Scott	$23	$11
Vada Pinson	$24	$13	Mike Scott	$18	$10
Johnny Podres	$24	$13	Bobby Shantz	$20	$10
Darrell Porter	$23	$12	Roy Sievers	$15	$8
Boog Powell	$23	$13	Ken Singleton	$20	$10
Willie Randolph	$25	$13	Sibby Sisti	$15	$9
Vic Raschi	$260	$45	Bill Skowron	$20	$12
Dick Radatz	$18	$9	Roy Smalley	$20	$13
Allie Reynolds	$100	$25	Lonnie Smith	$19	$10
J.R. Richard	$23	$14	Reggie Smith	$23	$13

Players	Baseball	Photo	Players	Baseball	Photo
Cory Snyder	$18	$10	Virgil Trucks	$25	$8
Bob Stanley	$15	$8	Bob Uecker	$33	$20
Fred Stanley	$22	$9	Del Unser	$15	$8
Dave Stewart	$24	$13	Johnny VanderMeer	$20	$10
Dave Stieb	$22	$12	Mickey Vernon	$20	$10
Steve Stone	$21	$13	Frank Viola	$24	$12
Mel Stottlemyre	$25	$12	Bill Virdon	$15	$8
Rick Sutcliffe	$22	$12	Pete Vuckovich	$23	$14
Bruce Sutter	$24	$13	Rube Walker	$50	$15
Ron Swoboda	$20	$10	Claudell Washington	$16	$8
Johnny Temple	$17	$10	Bob Watson	$15	$8
Chuck Tanner	$20	$18	Bob Welch	$21	$12
Kent Tekulve	$23	$12	Bill White	$20	$10
Garry Templeton	$24	$12	Roy White	$17	$8
Gene Tenace	$25	$13	Dick Williams	$25	$15
Wayne Terwilliger	$17	$8	Maury Wills	$30	$12
Gorman Thomas	$20	$10	Mookie Wilson	$20	$8
Bobby Thomson	$22	$10	Wilbur Wood	$14	$8
Andre Thornton	$25	$18	Jimmy Wynn	$20	$11
Marv Throneberry	$50	$20	Steve Yeager	$15	$8
Joe Torre	$23	$12	Don Zimmer	$25	$15

Active players

Players	Baseball	Photo	Players	Baseball	Photo
Jim Abbott	$24	$15	Tom Candiotti	$20	$11
Rick Aguilera	$23	$12	Joe Carter	$25	$12
Sandy Alomar Jr.	$19	$12	Vinny Castilla	$21	$12
Moises Alou	$24	$10	Royce Clayton	$24	$12
Wilson Alvarez	$20	$10	David Cone	$25	$15
Brady Anderson	$20	$12	Jeff Conine	$22	$13
Kevin Appier	$22	$13	Wil Cordero	$24	$12
Steve Avery	$30	$15	Chad Curtis	$20	$10
Carlos Baerga	$26	$23	Ron Darling	$20	$10
Jeff Bagwell	$28	$22	Darren Daulton	$23	$11
Harold Baines	$20	$15	Eric Davis	$24	$15
Tim Belcher	$19	$10	Carlos Delgado	$24	$18
Andy Benes	$23	$14	Delino DeShields	$25	$15
Jason Bere	$30	$15	Mike Devereaux	$20	$10
Dante Bichette	$21	$12	Rob Dibble	$17	$10
Craig Biggio	$20	$10	Doug Drabek	$20	$10
Jeff Blauser	$20	$10	Shawon Dunston	$20	$10
Ricky Bones	$17	$10	Len Dykstra	$28	$20
Bobby Bonilla	$30	$17	Dennis Eckersley	$29	$18
Chris Bosio	$19	$10	Jim Edmonds	$24	$12
Rico Brogna	$17	$8	Jim Eisenreich	$18	$10
Kevin Brown	$21	$13	Cal Eldred	$10	$20
Tom Browning	$20	$10	Tony Fernandez	$22	$15
Jay Buhner	$28	$15	Cecil Fielder	$30	$17
John Burkett	$25	$15	Travis Fryman	$25	$16
Ellis Burks	$17	$10	Gary Gaetti	$19	$12
Brett Butler	$24	$13	Andres Galarraga	$24	$16
Ken Caminiti	$18	$9	Ron Gant	$30	$15

Autographs

Players	Baseball	Photo	Players	Baseball	Photo
Kirk Gibson	$20	$10	Otis Nixon	$23	$13
Tom Glavine	$25	$17	Hideo Nomo	$50	$30
Juan Gonzalez	$29	$18	John Olerud	$26	$16
Luis Gonzalez	$24	$12	Paul O'Neill	$25	$13
Tom Gordon	$14	$8	Rafael Palmeiro	$30	$20
Goose Gossage	$25	$15	Tony Pena	$24	$15
Mike Greenwell	$20	$10	Terry Pendleton	$20	$10
Marquis Grissom	$30	$20	Mike Piazza	$30	$20
Tony Gwynn	$35	$21	Tim Raines	$25	$13
Darryl Hamilton	$20	$10	Manny Ramirez	$28	$19
Erik Hanson	$25	$15	Jeff Reardon	$22	$11
Pete Harnisch	$16	$8	Jose Rijo	$25	$15
Charlie Hayes	$24	$12	Ivan Rodriguez	$20	$10
Tom Henke	$22	$12	Bret Saberhagen	$23	$12
Orel Hershiser	$24	$20	Chris Sabo	$24	$12
Ken Hill	$24	$13	Tim Salmon	$28	$20
Dave Hollins	$24	$13	Reggie Sanders	$20	$12
Steve Howe	$22	$12	Benito Santiago	$25	$14
Pete Incaviglia	$19	$10	Steve Sax	$25	$18
Gregg Jefferies	$25	$20	Kevin Seitzer	$20	$10
Howard Johnson	$25	$15	Gary Sheffield	$28	$16
Randy Johnson	$35	$22	Ruben Sierra	$22	$15
Chipper Jones	$40	$20	Don Slaught	$17	$10
Wally Joyner	$18	$10	Heathcliff Slocumb	$22	$13
Dave Justice	$35	$21	John Smiley	$21	$12
Eric Karros	$25	$15	Lee Smith	$24	$15
Jimmy Key	$25	$15	John Smoltz	$30	$15
Chuck Knoblauch	$20	$10	J.T. Snow	$23	$12
John Kruk	$25	$15	Paul Sorrento	$20	$12
Mark Langston	$20	$10	Sammy Sosa	$24	$14
Ray Lankford	$25	$15	Terry Steinbach	$23	$11
Barry Larkin	$21	$12	Kevin Stocker	$20	$10
Mark Lemke	$23	$13	Bill Swift	$21	$12
Pat Listach	$21	$11	Greg Swindell	$13	$6
Kenny Lofton	$30	$20	Danny Tartabull	$19	$11
Javier Lopez	$26	$16	Mickey Tettleton	$24	$12
Mike Macfarlane	$20	$10	Bob Tewksbury	$17	$10
Shane Mack	$21	$11	Jim Thome	$24	$14
Dave Magadan	$19	$10	Alan Trammell	$27	$17
Dennis Martinez	$24	$13	John Valentin	$17	$9
Edgar Martinez	$25	$15	Fernando Valenzuela	$28	$15
Ben McDonald	$25	$12	Todd Van Poppel	$24	$12
Jack McDowell	$28	$15	Andy Van Slyke	$28	$15
Willie McGee	$25	$15	Greg Vaughn	$22	$12
Fred McGriff	$25	$15	Mo Vaughn	$32	$22
Brian McRae	$24	$12	Robin Ventura	$40	$18
Kevin McReynolds	$19	$10	Tim Wakefield	$23	$13
Kent Merker	$21	$11	Walt Weiss	$20	$12
Jose Mesa	$24	$14	Bob Welch	$21	$12
Kevin Mitchell	$30	$17	Lou Whitaker	$25	$15
Paul Molitor	$30	$23	Devon White	$24	$12
Raul Mondesi	$30	$24	Rondell White	$25	$14
Hal Morris	$20	$11	Mark Whiten	$23	$12
Mike Mussina	$25	$17	Matt Williams	$35	$25
Tim Naehring	$17	$9	Mitch Williams	$20	$10
Charles Nagy	$23	$14	Mark Wohlers	$21	$12
David Nied	$20	$10	Todd Zeile	$20	$12

Autographed Team Baseballs

Key signatures follow each team name

1948 New York Yankees

1920 BOSTON (AL) - Barrow, Hendryx, Hooper, Pennock, Hoyt .... $800-$1250
1920 BOSTON (NL) - Maranville, Powell, Mann .... $600-$900
1920 BROOKLYN - Robinson, Konetchy, Myers, Wheat, Grimes,
Marquard.. $1200-$1750
1920 CHICAGO (AL) - Collins, Risberg, Weaver, Leibold, Felsch, Jackson,
Schalk, Faber, Williams, Kerr, Cicotte.. $ uncertain
1920 CHICAGO (NL) - Hollocher, Flack, Robertson, Alexander .... $900-$1400
1920 CINCINNATI - Daubert, Roush .... $450-$700
1920 CLEVELAND - Wambsganss, Chapman, Gardner, Smith, Speaker,
Jamieson, O'Neill, Sewell, Coveleski .... $1300-$2000
1920 DETROIT - Jennings, Heilmann, Cobb, Veach...................................... $1700-$2500
1920 NEW YORK (AL) - Huggins, Pratt, Ruth, Mays, Shawkey.................. $2200-$3400
1920 NEW YORK (NL) - McGraw, Kelly, Bancroft, Frisch, Youngs, Toney,
Nehf, Barnes .... $1700-$2750
1920 PHILADELPHIA (AL) - Mack.. $600-$850
1920 PHILADELPHIA (NL) - Stengel, Williams, Meusel, Wheat, Rixey ...... $800-$1300
1920 PITTSBURGH - Carey, McKechnie, Traynor, Cooper........................... $675-$1000
1920 ST. LOUIS (AL) - Sisler, Tobin, Jacobson, Williams, Shocker .... $425-$675

1920 ST. LOUIS (NL) - Rickey, Fournier, Hornsby, Stock, Doak, Haines .... $1150-$1750

1920 WASHINGTON - Griffith, Judge, Harris, Rice, Milan, Johnson .... $1300-$2000

1921 BOSTON (AL) - Duffy, McInnis, Pratt, Leibold, Menosky, Jones,
Pennock .... $550-$875

1921 BOSTON (NL) - Barbare, Boeckel, Southworth, Powell, Cruise,
Oeschger .... $400-$600

1921 BROOKLYN - Robinson, Schmandt, Johnston, Griffith, Wheat,
Grimes.. $800-$1200

1921 CHICAGO (AL) - Sheely, Collins, Hooper, Strunk, Schalk, Faber .... $725-$1100

1921 CHICAGO (NL) - Evers, Grimes, Flack, Maisel, Barber,
Alexander... $1200-$1800

1921 CINCINNATI - Daubert, Groh, Bressler, Roush, Duncan, Rixey,
Marquard.. $550-$825

1921 CLEVELAND - Speaker, Sewell, Gardner, Jamieson, O'Neill,
Coveleski .... $725-$1200

1921 DETROIT - Cobb, Blue, Heilmann, Veach, Bassler, Jones..................... $800-$1200

1921 NEW YORK (AL) - Huggins, Ward, Baker, Meusel, Ruth, Mays,
Hoyt .... $3000-$6000

1921 NEW YORK (NL) - McGraw, Kelly, Bancroft, Frisch, Youngs, Meusel,
Snyder, Stengel, Nehf.. $2000-$3000

1921 PHILADELPHIA (AL) - Mack, Witt, T. Walker .... $500-$775

1921 PHILADELPHIA (NL) - Konetchy, Williams, Meusel, Bruggy,
Stengel .... $400-$600

1921 PITTSBURGH - Cuthsaw, Maranville, Carey, Bigbee, Traynor,
Cuyler, Cooper... $800-$1200

1921 ST. LOUIS (AL) - Sisler, Tobin, Jacobson, Williams, Severeid, Shocker . $425-$625

1921 ST. LOUIS (NL) - Rickey, Fournier, Hornsby, Stock, Smith, Mann,
McHenry, Clemons, Dillhoefer, Haines, Doak.. $1075-$1600

1921 WASHINGTON - Judge, Harris, Shanks, Rice, Gharrity, Goslin,
Johnson .... $1000-$1500

1922 BOSTON (AL) - Duffy, Burns, Pratt, Harris, Pennock............................. $500-$750

1922 BOSTON (NL) - Marquard .... $400-$575

1922 BROOKLYN - Johnston, Robinson, Myers, Wheat, DeBerry, Ruether,
Vance, Grimes, T. Griffith.. $1000-$1500

1922 CHICAGO (AL) - Sheely, Collins, Hooper, Mostil, Schalk, Evers,
Faber .... $1200-$1750

1922 CHICAGO (NL) - Grimes, Hollocher, Friberg, Miller, O'Farrell,
Hartnett, Alexander.. $800-$1200

1922 CINCINNATI - Daubert, Pinelli, Harper, Duncan, Hargrave, Roush,
Rixey.. $450-$700

1922 CLEVELAND - Speaker, McGinnis, Sewell, Uhle, Jamieson, O'Neill,
Coveleski .... $675-$1000

1922 DETROIT - Cobb, Blue, Rigney, Heilmann, Veach, Bassler.................. $800-$1200

1922 NEW YORK (AL) - Pipp, Meusel, Ruth, Schang, Baker, Bush, Shawkey,
Hoyt, Huggins .... $2000-$3000

1922 NEW YORK (NL) - McGraw, Kelly, Frisch, Bancroft, Youngs, Stengel, Meusel, Snyder, Jackson, Nehf ....$2000-$3000

1922 PHILADELPHIA (AL) - Mack, Hauser, Galloway, Rommel, Miller ....$500-$750

1922 PHILADELPHIA (NL) - Walker, Williams, Lee, Henline .... $325-$500

1922 PITTSBURGH - McKechnie, Tierney, Maranville, Traynor, Russell, Carey, Bigbee, Gooch, Cuyler, Cooper .... $1100-$1600

1922 ST. LOUIS (AL) - Sisler, McManus, Tobin, Jacobson, Williams, Severeid, Shocker .... $400-$650

1922 ST. LOUIS (NL) - Rickey, Hornsby, Toporcer, Stock, Smith, Schultz, Bottomley, Haines .... $1350-$2000

1922 WASHINGTON - Harris, Rice, Goslin, Johnson .... $900-$1400

1923 BOSTON (AL) - Burns, Flagstead, Harris, Ehmke, Chance .... $900-$1400

1923 BOSTON (NL) - McInnis, Southworth, Powell, Marquard .... $375-$550

1923 BROOKLYN - Robinson, Fournier, Johnston, Wheat, Grimes, Vance .... $1100-$1600

1923 CHICAGO (AL) - Collins, Hooper, Falk, Schalk, Faber, Lyons .... $750-$1200

1923 CHICAGO (NL) - Grimes, Friberg, Statz, Miller, O'Farrell, Hartnett, Alexander, Aldridge .... $800-$1000

1923 CINCINNATI - Roush, Duncan, Hargrave, Luque, Rixey .... $400-$600

1923 CLEVELAND - Speaker, Sewell, Summa, Jamieson, Uhle, Coveleski .... $800-$1200

1923 DETROIT - Cobb, Rigney, Heilmann, Manush, Daus .... $900-$1500

1923 NEW YORK (AL) - Huggins, Pipp, Ruth, Witt, Meusel, Gehrig, Pennock, Hoyt.. $2500-$3750

1923 NEW YORK (NL) - McGraw, Kelly, Frisch, Bancroft, Youngs, Jackson, Stengel, Terry, Wilson, Ryan ....$2100-$3150

1923 PHILADELPHIA (AL) - Mack, Hauser .... $475-$700

1923 PHILADELPHIA (NL) - Holke, Tierney, Mokan, Henline........................ $300-$450

1923 PITTSBURGH - McKechnie, Grimm, Maranville, Traynor, Barnhart, Carey, Cuyler, Morrison .... $1000-$1500

1923 ST. LOUIS (AL) - McManus, Tobin, Jacobson, Williams, Severeid, Shocker .... $350-$525

1923 ST. LOUIS (NL) - Rickey, Bottomley, Hornsby, Myers, Smith, Haines .... $1200-$1800

1923 WASHINGTON - Judge, Harris, Rice, Leibold, Goslin, Ruel, Johnson ....$900-$1400

1924 BOSTON (AL) - Harris, Boone, Flagstead, Ruffing.................................... $350-$525

1924 BOSTON (NL) - Stengel, Bancroft, Marquard .... $700-$900

1924 BROOKLYN - Robinson, Fournier, High, Brown, Wheat, Grimes, Vance .... $1000-$1500

1924 CHICAGO (AL) - Evers, Sheely, Collins, Hooper, Mostil, Falk, Schalk, Thurston, Lyons, Faber.. $1300-$1800

1924 CHICAGO (NL) - Grantham, Heathcote, Hartnett, Alexander .... $725-$1200

1924 CINCINNATI - Critz, Pinelli, Walker, Roush, Mays, Rixey .... $400-$600

1924 CLEVELAND - Speaker, Burns, Sewell, Jamieson, Myatt, Shaute, Coveleski .... $800-$1000

1924 DETROIT - Cobb, Blue, Pratt, Heilmann, Manush, Bassler, Gehringer .... $1000-$1550

1924 NEW YORK (AL) - Huggins, Dugan, Ruth, Meusel, Combs, Gehrig, Pennock, Hoyt.. $3000-$4500

1924 NEW YORK (NL) - McGraw, Kelly, Frisch, Jackson, Youngs, Wilson, Snyder, Terry, Lindstrom, Bentley .... $1900-$2900

1924 PHILADELPHIA (AL) - Miller, Simmons, Lamar .... $600-$1000

1924 PHILADELPHIA (NL) - Holke, Wrightstone, Williams......................... $300-$450

1924 PITTSBURGH - McKechnie, Maranville, Traynor, Carey, Cuyler, Cooper... $800-$1225

1924 ST. LOUIS (AL) - Sisler, McManus, Robertson, Jacobson, Williams, Severeid .... $400-$600

1924 ST. LOUIS (NL) - Rickey, Bottomley, Hornsby, Blades, Hafey............ $1300-$1800

1924 WASHINGTON - Harris, Judge, Rice, Goslin, Johnson .... $1000-$1500

1925 BOSTON (AL) - Prothro, Boone, Carlyle, Ruffing .... $300-$500

1925 BOSTON (NL) - Bancroft, Burrus, Welsh, Felix, Stengel, Marquard .... $600-$900

1925 BROOKLYN - Robinson, Fournier, Stock, Cox, Brown, Wheat, Taylor, Vance, Grimes... $900-$1500

1925 CHICAGO (AL) - Collins, Sheely, Hooper, Falk, Schalk, Lyons, Faber, Bender... $900-$1500

1925 CHICAGO (NL) - Maranville, Grimm, Freigau, Jahn, Hartnett, Alexander... $800-$1200

1925 CINCINNATI - Walker, Roush, Hargrave, Rixey....................................... $350-$575

1925 CLEVELAND - Speaker, Burns, Sewell, McNulty, Buckeye .... $550-$925

1925 DETROIT - Cobb, Blue, Heilmann, Wingo, Manush, Gehringer............. $900-$1300

1925 NEW YORK (AL) - Huggins, Gehrig, Ruth, Hoyt, Pennock, Durocher .... $2750-$4175

1925 NEW YORK (NL) - McGraw, Terry, Kelly, Jackson, Lindstrom, Youngs, Meusel, Frisch, Wilson... $1800-$2700

1925 PHILADELPHIA (AL) - Mack, Hale, Miller, Simmons, Lamar, Cochrane, Foxx, Rommel, Grove .... $1400-$2100

1925 PHILADELPHIA (NL) - Hawks, Williams, Harper................................. $300-$475

1925 PITTSBURGH - McKechnie, Grantham, Wright, Traynor, Cuyler, Carey, Barnhart, Smith, Meadows.. $800-$1200

1925 ST. LOUIS (AL) - Sisler, Rice, Jacobson, Williams................................. $375-$600

1925 ST. LOUIS (NL) - Rickey, Bottomley, Hornsby, Hafey, Mueller, Blades, Haines .... $1300-$2000

1925 WASHINGTON - Harris, Judge, Rice, Goslin, Johnson, Coveleski ....$1000-$1500

1926 BOSTON (AL) - Jacobson, Ruffing.. $300-$475

1926 BOSTON (NL) - Bancroft, J. Smith, Brown .... $325-$525

1926 BROOKLYN - Robinson, Herman, Wheat, Maranville, Carey, Grimes, Vance .... $1200-$1800

1926 CHICAGO - McCarthy, Adams, Wilson, Stephenson, Hartnett, Alexander... $900-$1400

1926 CHICAGO (AL) - Collins, Barrett, Mostil, Falk, Schalk, Lyons, Faber .... $600-$900

1926 CINCINNATI - Walker, Roush, Donahue, Rixey .... $325-$575

1926 CLEVELAND - Speaker, Burns, J. Sewell, Summa, Uhle........................ $600-$900

1926 DETROIT - Cobb, Gehringer, Heilmann, Manush, Fothergill .... $800-$1200

1959 New York Yankees

1926 NEW YORK (AL) - Huggins, Gehrig, Lazzeri, Ruth, Combs,
Meusel, Pennock, Hoyt.. $3500-$5000

1926 NEW YORK (NL) - McGraw, Kelly, Frisch, Jackson, Lindstrom,
Youngs, Terry, Ott.. $1800-$2750

1926 PHILADELPHIA (AL) - Mack, French, Simmons, Cochrane,
Foxx .... $1300-$2100

1926 PHILADELPHIA (NL) - Williams, Leach, Mokan, Wilson...................... $250-$400

1926 PITTSBURGH - McKechnie, Grantham, Wright, Traynor, Waner,
Carey, Cuyler, Smith, Cronin, Kremer, Meadows .... $800-$1200

1926 ST. LOUIS (AL) - Sisler, Miller, Rice, Shang.. $350-$500

1926 ST. LOUIS (NL) - Hornsby, Bottomley, Bell, Southworth, Douthit,
Blades, Hafey, Rhem, Haines, Alexander .... $1600-$2300

1926 WASHINGTON - Harris, Myer, Rice, McNeely, Goslin, Johnson,
Coveleski .... $800-$1200

1927 BOSTON (AL) - Tobin, Ruffing .... $300-$450

1927 BOSTON (NL) - Bancroft, High, Richbourg, Brown .... $300-$450

1927 BROOKLYN - Robinson, Carey, Vance.. $800-$1200

1927 CHICAGO (AL) - Schalk, Clancy, Metzler, Falk, Lyons, Faber .... $350-$550

1927 CHICAGO (NL) - McCarthy, Grimm, Webb, Wilson, Stephenson,
Hartnett, Root .... $500-$800

1927 CINCINNATI - Hargrave, Kelly, Rixey... $300-$450

1927 CLEVELAND - Burns, Fonseca, J. Sewell, Jamieson, Miller.................... $300-$450

1927 DETROIT - Gehringer, Heilmann, Manush, Fothergill, Collins .... $375-$625

1927 NEW YORK (AL) - Gehrig, Lazzeri, Ruth, Combs, Meusel, Hoyt, Moore, Pennock .... $8000-$16000

1927 NEW YORK (NL) - McGraw, Terry, Honrsby, Jackson, Lindstrom, Harper, Roush, Grimes .... $1800-$2700

1927 PHILADELPHIA (AL) - Mack, Dykes, Hale, Cobb, Simmons, French, Cochrane, Collins, Wheat, Foxx, Grove .... $2200-$3300

1927 PHILADELPHIA (NL) - Wrightstone, Thompson, Leach .... $275-$400

1927 PITTSBURGH - Harris, Grantham, Traynor, P. Waner, L. Waner, Barnhart, Cuyler, Groh, Cronin, Kremer .... $700-$1000

1927 ST. LOUIS (AL) - Sisler, Miller, Williams, Schang .... $400-$650

1927 ST. LOUIS (NL) - Bottomley, Frisch, Maranville, Haines, Alexander .... $1200-$1750

1927 WASHINGTON - Harris, Judge, Rice, Speaker, Goslin, Ruel, Lisenbee, Hadley, Johnson, Coveleski .... $1200-$1800

1928 BOSTON (AL) - Myer, Williams, Ruffing .... $300-$475

1928 BOSTON (NL) - Hornsby, Sisler, Richbourg .... $800-$1200

1928 BROOKLYN - Robinson, Bissonette, Bancroft, Hendrick, Herman, Carey, Lopez, Vance .... $1000-$1400

1928 CHICAGO (AL) - Schalk, Kamm, Metzler, Lyons, Walsh, Faber .... $500-$775

1928 CHICAGO (NL) - McCarthy, Cuyler, Wilson, Stephenson, Hartnett .... $450-$725

1928 CINCINNATI - Kelly, Allen, Rixey .... $300-$425

1928 CLEVELAND - Fonseca, Sewell, Hodapp, Jamieson .... $300-$425

1928 DETROIT - Gehringer, Heilmann, Rice .... $325-$500

1928 NEW YORK (AL) - Huggins, Gehrig, Lazzeri, Koenig, Ruth, Combs, Dickey, Pipgras, Hoyt, Pennock, Coveleski .... $3500-$5000

1928 NEW YORK (NL) - McGraw, Terry, Jackson, Lindstrom, Ott, Welsh, O'Doul, Hogan, Roush, Benton, Fitzsimmons, Hubbell .... $1300-$1750

1928 PHILADELPHIA (AL) - Mack, Bishop, Hale, Cobb, Miller, Simmons, Cochrane, Foxx, Speaker, Collins, Grove, Quinn .... $2000-$3000

1928 PHILADELPHIA (NL) - Whitney, Klein, Leach .... $300-$500

1928 PITTSBURGH - Grantham, Wright, Traynor, P. Waner, L. Waner, Brickell, Grimes .... $500-$750

1928 ST. LOUIS (AL) - Manush, Crowder .... $300-$450

1928 ST. LOUIS (NL) - McKechnie, Bottomley, Frisch, Maranville, Hafey, Haines, Alexander .... $1200-$1800

1928 WASHINGTON - Harris, Judge, Reeves, Rice, Barnes, Goslin, Cronin, Sisler, Jones .... $500-$750

1929 BOSTON (AL) - Rothrock, Ruffing .... $250-$350

1929 BOSTON (NL) - Sisler, Maranville, Richbourg, Clark, Evers .... $700-$1200

1929 BROOKLYN - Robinson, Bancroft, Gilbert, Herman, Frederick, Bressler, Carey, Vance .... $850-$1300

1929 CHICAGO (AL) - Shires, Reynolds, Lyons, Faber .... $275-$450

1929 CHICAGO (NL) - McCarthy, Hornsby, Cuyler, Wilson, Hartnett, Malone .... $800-$1200

1929 CINCINNATI - Kelly, Dressen, Swanson, Gooch, Rixey .... $275-$425

1929 CLEVELAND - Fonseca, Hodapp, Sewell, Falk, Averill, Sewell, Ferrell .... $300-$500

1929 DETROIT - Harris, Alexander, Gehringer, Heilmann, Rice, Johnson............$300-$500

1929 NEW YORK (AL) - Huggins, Gehrig, Lazzeri, Ruth, Combs, Dickey, Wells, Hoyt, Pennock .... $2800-$4250

1929 NEW YORK (NL) - McGraw, Terry, Jackson, Lindstrom, Ott, Roush, Hubbell .... $1000-$1600

1929 PHILADELPHIA (AL) - Mack, Foxx, Miller, Haas, Simmons, Cochrane, Cronin, Collins, Earnshaw, Grove.................... $800-$1200

1929 PHILADELPHIA (NL) - Hurst, Thompson, Thevenow, Whitney, Klein, Sothern, O'Doul.. $300-$450

1929 PITTSBURGH - Grantham, Bartell, Traynor, P. Waner, L. Waner, Comorosky, Grimes.. $500-$800

1929 ST. LOUIS (AL) - Kress, Schulte, Manush, Ferrell.................... $325-$550

1929 ST. LOUIS (NL) - McKechnie, Bottomley, Frisch, Orsatti, Douthit, Hafey, Wilson, Johnson, Haines, Alexander...................... $900-$1400

1929 WASHINGTON - Johnson, Judge, Myer, Cronin, Rice, Goslin .... $1300-$1850

1930 BOSTON (AL) - Webb, Ruffing................................ $225-$350

1930 BOSTON (NL) - McKechnie, Sisler, Maranville, Grimes .... $450-$750

1930 BROOKLYN - Robinson, Bissonette, Wright, Herman, Frederick, Lopez, Vance.. $650-$1200

1930 CHICAGO (AL) - Watwood, Jolley, Reynolds, Lyons, Appling, Faber .... $250-$400

1930 CHICAGO (NL) - McCarthy, Grimm, Cuyler, Wilson, Hartnett, Hornsby, Kelly.. $900-$1450

1930 CINCINNATI - Durocher, Cuccinello, Heilmann, Walker, Kelly, Rixey.. $900-$1450

1930 CLEVELAND - Morgan, Hodapp, J. Sewell, Porter, Averill, Jamieson, L. Sewell, Ferrell .... $300-$475

1930 DETROIT - Harris, Alexander, Gehringer, McManus, Stone, Hoyt, Greenberg .... $300-$475

1930 NEW YORK (AL) - Gehrig, Lazzeri, Chapman, Ruth, Hoyt, Combs, Ruffing, Gomez, Pennock, Dickey.......................... $2500-$3750

1930 NEW YORK (NL) - McGraw, Terry, Jackson, Lindstrom, Ott, Leach, Hogan, Bancroft, Roush, Hubbell.......................... $1200-$1800

1930 PHILADELPHIA, (AL) - Mack, Foxx, Dykes, Miller, Simmons, Cochrane, Collins, Grove .... $700-$1000

1930 PHILADELPHIA (NL) - Hurst, Whitney, O'Doul, Davis, Alexander, Klein .... $500-$700

1930 PITTSBURGH - Grantham, Bartell, Traynor, P. Waner, L. Waner, Comorosky.. $450-$700

1930 ST. LOUIS (AL) - Kress, Goslin, Ferrell, Manush .... $375-$575

1930 ST. LOUIS (NL) - Street, Bottomley, Frisch, Gelbert, Adams, Watkins, Douthit, Hafey, Wilson, Grimes, Haines, Dean .... $700-$1000

1930 WASHINGTON - Johnson, Judge, Myer, Cronin, Rice, Manush, Goslin, Marberry.. $1500-$2250

1931 BOSTON (AL) - Webb................................ $200-$300

1931 BOSTON (NL) - Maranville, Schulmerich, Berger, McKechnie.............. $300-$500

1931 BROOKLYN - O'Doul, Lopez, Lombardi, Vance, Robinson .... $800-$1200

1931 CHICAGO (AL) - Blue, Appling, Faber, Lyons .... $250-$375
1931 CHICAGO (NL) - Grimm, Hornsby, English, Cuyler, Wilson, Taylor,
Hartnett, Herman .... $750-$1200
1931 CINCINNATI - Hendrick, Cuccinello, Stripp, Roush, Heilmann,
Rixey... $325-$500
1931 CLEVELAND - Morgan, Porter, Averill .... $250-$375
1931 DETROIT - Alexander, Gehringer, Rogell, Stone, Hoyt, Harris............. $300-$500
1931 NEW YORK (AL) - Gehrig, Lazzeri, Sewell, Ruth, Combs, Chapman,
Dickey, Ruffing, Gomez, Pennock, McCarthy.. $3000-$4500
1931 NEW YORK (NL) - Terry, Jackson, Lindstrom, Ott, Leach, Hogan,
Walker, Hubbell, McGraw .... $1000-$1500
1931 PHILADELPHIA (AL) - Mack, Foxx, Simmons, Cochrane, Grove,
Earnshaw, Hoyt.. $700-$1000
1931 PHILADELPHIA (NL) - Hurst, Mallon, Arlett, Klein, Davis.................. $300-$450
1931 PITTSBURGH - Grantham, Traynor, Waner, Waner............................. $425-$700
1931 ST. LOUIS (AL) - Melillo, Kress, Schulte, Goslin, Ferrell .... $300-$450
1931 ST. LOUIS (NL) - Bottomley, Frisch, Hafey, Hallahan, Grimes,
Haines .... $550-$900
1931 WASHINGTON - Cronin, Rice, West, Manush, Crowder, Marberry,
Johnson .... $1200-$1800
1932 BOSTON (AL) - Alexander, Jolley, Morris.................................... $225-$350
1932 BOSTON (NL) - Maranville, Berger, Worthington, McKechnie............... $300-$450
1932 BROOKLYN - Kelly, Wright, Stripp, Wilson, Taylor, O'Doul, Lopez,
Clark, Vance, Hoyt, Carey.. $600-$950
1932 CHICAGO (AL) - Appling, Lyons, Faber...................................... $325-$500
1932 CHICAGO (NL) - Grimm, Herman, Cuyler, Moore, Stephenson,
Hartnett, Hornsby, Warneke, Grimes .... $700-$1000
1932 CINCINNATI - Hendrick, Durocher, Herman, Lombardi, Hafey,
Heilmann, Frey .... $450-$750
1932 CLEVELAND - Cissell, Porter, Averill, Vosmik .... $250-$375
1932 DETROIT - Gehringer, Walker, Harris... $300-$500
1932 NEW YORK (AL) - Gehrig, Lazzeri, Sewell, Ruth, Combs, Dickey,
Ruffing, Gomez, Allen, Pennock, McCarthy .... $1750-$4000
1932 NEW YORK (NL) - Terry, Ott, Lindstrom, McGraw, Hogan, Jackson,
Jo-Jo Moore, Hoyt, Hubbell .... $900-$1325
1932 PHILADELPHIA (AL) - Cramer, Haas, Simmons, Cochrane, Grove,
Mack.. $500-$750
1932 PHILADELPHIA (NL) - Hurst, Bartell, Klein, Davis, Lee, Davis........... $300-$425
1932 PITTSBURGH - Vaughn, Traynor, Waner, Waner............................. $525-$750
1932 ST. LOUIS (AL) - Burns, Scharien, Goslin, Ferrell........................... $300-$450
1932 ST. LOUIS (NL) - Watkins, Martin, Orsatti, Frisch, Bottomley,
Medwick, Dean, Haines... $500-$700
1932 WASHINGTON - Cronin, Reynolds, Manush, Rice, Crowder,
Johnson .... $1200-$1800
1933 BOSTON (AL) - Hodapp, Johnson, Ferrell.................................... $250-$375
1933 BOSTON (NL) - Maranville, Moore, Cantwell, McKechnie.................. $300-$450
1933 BROOKLYN - Wright, Frederick, Wilson, Lopez, Mungo, Carey .... $700-$1000

1964 New York Mets

1933 CHICAGO (AL) - Appling, Swanson, Simmons, Lyons, Faber .... $375-$575
1933 CHICAGO (NL) - Grimm, Stephenson, Hartnett, Cuyler, Bush, Grimes,
Billy Herman .... $400-$600
1933 CINCINNATI - Bottomley, Hafey, Lombardi, Durocher, Rixey .... $400-$600
1933 CLEVELAND - Averill, Johnson .... $800-$1200
1933 DETROIT - Greenberg, Gehringer, Harris .... $375-$600
1933 NEW YORK (AL) - Gehrig, Lazzeri, Sewell, Ruth, Combs, Chapman,
Dickey, Gomez, Allen, Ruffing, Pennock, McCarthy .... $2800-$4200
1933 NEW YORK (NL) - Terry, Ott, Jackson, Hubbell................................... $750-$1000
1933 PHILADELPHIA (AL) - Foxx, Higgins, Cochrane, Grove, Mack............ $400-$600
1933 PHILADELPHIA (NL) - Klein, Fullis, Schulmerich, Davis .... $300-$450
1933 PITTSBURGH - Piet, Vaughan, Traynor, Waner, Lindstrom, Waner,
Hoyt .... $575-$900
1933 ST. LOUIS (AL) - West, Ferrell, Hornsby.. $450-$675
1933 ST. LOUIS (NL) - Collins, Frisch, Durocher, Martin, Medwick,
Hornsby, Haines, Dean, Vance, Grimes... $900-$1500
1933 WASHINGTON - Kuhel, Myer, Cronin, Goslin, Manush, Rice,
Crowder, Whitehill .... $475-$725
1934 BOSTON (AL) - Harris, Reynolds, Johnson, R. Ferrell, W. Ferrell,
Grove, Pennock.. $375-$525
1934 BOSTON (NL) - McKechnie, Jordan, Maranville, Frankhouse................. $325-$450
1934 BROOKLYN - Stengel, Leslie, Stripp, Boyle, Koenecke, Lopez, Mungo
.... $250-$500

1934 CHICAGO (AL) - Appling, Simmons, Conlan .... $400-$575
1934 CHICAGO (NL) - Grimm, Billy Herman, Hack, Cuyler, Klein,
Hartnett .... $325-$600
1934 CINCINNATI - Bottomley, Hafey, Lombardi .... $300-$525
1934 CLEVELAND - Johnson, Trosky, Hale, Knickerbocker, Averill,
Vosmik, Harder .... $775-$1250
1934 DETROIT - Cochrane, Greenberg, Gehringer, Fox, Goslin, Rowe,
Bridges .... $525-$800
1934 NEW YORK (AL) - McCarthy, Gomez, Lazzeri, Dickey, Gehrig,
Ruffing, Grimes, Ruth, Combs .... $2600-$3900
1934 NEW YORK (NL) - Terry, Jackson, Ott, Hubbell .... $400-$575
1934 PHILADELPHIA (AL) - Mack, Foxx, Higgins, Cramer, Johnson .... $300-$500
1934 PHILADELPHIA (NL) - Chiozza, Bartell, J. Moore, Allen, Todd .... $200-$300
1934 PITTSBURGH - Traynor, Vaughan, P. Waner, L. Waner, Lindstrom,
Hoyt, Grimes .... $550-$875
1934 ST. LOUIS (AL) - Hornsby, West, Hemsley .... $400-$675
1934 ST. LOUIS (NL) - Frisch, Collins, Durocher, Martin, Orsatti, Medwick,
Davis, Dean, Haines, Grimes, Vance .... $575-$900
1934 WASHINGTON - Cronin, Manush .... $275-$450
1935 BOSTON (AL) - Cronin, Cooke, R. Johnson, R. Ferrell, W. Ferrell,
Grove .... $300-$500
1935 BOSTON (NL) - McKechnie, Lee, Ruth, Maranville .... $1000-$1500
1935 BROOKLYN - Stengel, Leslie, Stripp, Lopez .... $300-$475
1935 CHICAGO (AL) - Appling, Simmons, Conlan, Lyons, Stratton .... $375-$575
1935 CHICAGO (NL) - Grimm, Herman, Lee, Klein, Demaree, Galan,
Hartnett, Cuyler, Lindstrom, Hack .... $500-$750
1935 CINCINNATI - Bottomley, Herman, Lombardi, Cuyler, Hafey,
Derringer .... $350-$575
1935 CLEVELAND - Johnson, Averill .... $700-$1200
1935 DETROIT - Cochrane, Greenberg, Gehringer, Goslin .... $500-$750
1935 NEW YORK (AL) - McCarthy, Gehrig, Lazzeri, Dickey, Combs,
Ruffing, Gomez .... $1300-$2000
1935 NEW YORK (NL) - Terry, Jackson, Ott, Leiber, Hubbell .... $475-$800
1935 PHILADELPHIA (AL) - Mack, Foxx, Moses, Cramer .... $300-$450
1935 PHILADELPHIA (NL) - Moore, Allen .... $500-$1000
1935 PITTSBURGH - Traynor, Vaughan, P. Waner, L. Waner, Hoyt .... $500-$700
1935 ST. LOUIS (AL) - Hornsby, West, Solters, Andrews .... $450-$675
1935 ST. LOUIS (NL) - Frisch, Collins, Durocher, Martin, Medwick, Haines,
P. Dean, D. Dean .... $350-$575
1935 WASHINGTON - Harris, Myer, Travis, Powell, Manush, Bolton .... $250-$375
1936 BOSTON (AL) - Cronin, Foxx, R. Ferrell, Hanush, Grove .... $400-$600
1936 BOSTON (NL) - McKechnie, Jordan, Cuccinello, Lopez .... $250-$350
1936 BROOKLYN - Stengel, Hassett, Stripp, Bordagaray, Lindstrom .... $275-$425
1936 CHICAGO (AL) - Appling, Lyons, Stratton .... $250-$400
1936 CHICAGO (NL) - Grimm, Herman, Demaree, Hartnett, Klein,
French .... $300-$450
1936 CINCINNATI - Scarsella, Cuyler, Lombardi, Hafey .... $275-$450

1936 CLEVELAND - Trosky, Hale, Weatherly, Averill, Sullivan, Allen........... $200-$325
1936 DETROIT - Cochrane, Gehringer, Simmons, Goslin, Greenberg .... $400-$575
1936 NEW YORK (AL) - McCarthy, Gehrig, Lazzeri, DiMaggio, Dickey, Ruffing, Gomez .... $1150-$1750
1936 NEW YORK (NL) - Terry, Jackson, Ott, Moore, Mancuso, Hubbell .... $450-$700
1936 PHILADELPHIA (AL) - Mack, Finney, Moses .... $250-$375
1936 PHILADELPHIA (NL) - Camilli, Klein, Moore .... $200-$300
1936 PITTSBURGH - Traynor, Suhr, Vaughan, P. Waner, L. Waner, Hoyt..........$425-$700
1936 ST. LOUIS (AL) - Hornsby, Bottomley, Clift, Bell................................ $450-$725
1936 ST. LOUIS (NL) - Frisch, Mize, Durocher, Martin, Alston, Dean, Haines
.... $425-$675
1936 WASHINGTON - Harris, Travis, Chapman, Stone.................................. $200-$350
1937 BOSTON (AL) - Foxx, Cronin, Higgins, Chapman, Cramer, Doerr, Ferrell, Grove.. $450-$550
1937 BOSTON (NL) - Lopez, McKechnie .... $200-$350
1937 BROOKLYN - Hassett, Manush, Phelps, Hoyt, Grimes........................... $350-$500
1937 CHICAGO (AL) - Appling, Stratton, Lyons .... $250-$425
1937 CHICAGO (NL) - Herman, Demaree, Hartnett, Carleton, Grimm .... $275-$400
1937 CINCINNATI - Wallace, Hafey, Cuyler, Lombardi.................................. $350-$500
1937 CLEVELAND - Campbell, Sotters, Pytlak, Feller, Averill .... $225-$375
1937 DETROIT - Greenberg, Gehringer, Goslin, Cochrane .... $400-$700
1937 NEW YORK (AL) - Gehrig, Lazzeri, DiMaggio, Dickey, Gomez, Ruffing, McCarthy.. $1450-$2500
1937 NEW YORK (NL) - Bartell, Ott, Ripple, Moore, Hubbell, Melton, Terry .... $400-$600
1937 PHILADELPHIA (AL) - Moses, Johnson, Mack .... $225-$375
1937 PHILADELPHIA (NL) - Camilli, Whitney, Klein .... $200-$300
1937 PITTSBURGH - Vaughan, Waner, Waner, Todd, Traynor, Hoyt.............. $425-$650
1937 ST. LOUIS (AL) - Clift, Bell, West, Vosmik, Hornsby, Bottomley........... $425-$650
1937 ST. LOUIS (NL) - Mize, Durocher, Padgett, Medwick, Martin, Frisch, Dean, Haines.. $375-$600
1937 WASHINGTON (AL) - Travis, Lewis, Stone, Almada, Simmons, R. Ferrell, Harris.. $300-$425
1938 BOSTON (AL) - Foxx, Doerr, Cronin, Higgins, Chapman, Cramer, Vosmik, Grove.. $550-$900
1938 BOSTON (NL) - Stengel, Lopez, MacFayden .... $350-$575
1938 BROOKLYN - Grimes, Durocher, Phelps, Cuyler, Manush, Hoyt .... $2000-$2750
1938 CHICAGO (AL) - Hayes, Appling, Steinbacher, Walker, Stratton........... $250-$450
1938 CHICAGO (NL) - Herman, Hack, Reynolds, Hartnett, Garbark, Lee, Grimm, Dean, Lazzeri .... $800-$1000
1938 CINCINNATI - McKechnie, McCormick, Berger, Lombardi, Derringer, Vander Meer... $250-$400
1938 CLEVELAND - Trosky, Averill, Heath, Pytlak, Boudreau, Feller............. $250-$400
1938 DETROIT - Cochrane, Greenberg, Gehringer, Walker, Bridges................ $400-$700
1938 NEW YORK (AL) - McCarthy, Gehrig, DiMaggio, Dickey, Ruffing, Gomez... $900-$1200
1938 NEW YORK (NL) - Terry, Ott, Moore, Danning, Hubbell....................... $350-$550

1938 PHILADELPHIA (AL) - Mack, Moses, Johnson .... $400-$600
1938 PHILADELPHIA (NL) - Weintraub .... $250-$325
1938 PITTSBURGH - Traynor, Vaughan, Waner, Waner, Rizzo, Manush,
Brown .... $700-$1000
1938 ST. LOUIS (AL) - McQuinn, Kress, Almada .... $200-$300
1938 ST. LOUIS (NL) - Frisch, Mize, Slaughter, Medwick, Martin .... $400-$650
1938 WASHINGTON - Harris, Myer, Travis, Case, Simmons, Ferrell,
Goslin, Ferrell .... $300-$475
1939 BOSTON (AL) - Cronin, Foxx, Doerr, Williams, Cramer, Grove .... $450-$650
1939 BOSTON (NL) - Stengel, Hassett, Cuccinello, Lopez, Simmons .... $300-$450
1939 BROOKLYN - Durocher, Lazzeri .... $250-$450
1939 CHICAGO (AL) - Kuhel, Appling, McNair, Lyons .... $200-$350
1939 CHICAGO (NL) - Hartnett, Herman, Leiber, Galan, Hartnett, Dean .... $275-$400
1939 CINCINNATI - McKechnie, McCormick, Goodman, Lombardi,
Simmons, Walters, Derringer .... $325-$500
1939 CLEVELAND - Trosky, Hale, Keltner, Boudreau, Feller .... $225-$350
1939 DETROIT - Greenberg, Gehringer, McCosky, Averill, Bridges .... $300-$500
1939 NEW YORK (AL) - McCarthy, Rolfe, Keller, DiMaggio, Selkirk,
Dickey, Ruffing, Gehring, Gomez .... $750-$1400
1939 NEW YORK (NL) - Terry, Bonura, Ott, Demaree, Danning, Lazzeri,
Hubbell .... $325-$550
1939 PHILADELPHIA (AL) - Mack, Moses, Johnson, Collins .... $300-$400
1939 PHILADELPHIA (NL) - Suhr, Arnovich, Davis .... $175-$275
1939 PITTSBURGH - Traynor, Fletcher, Vaughan, P. Waner, L. Waner,
Manush .... $500-$1000
1939 ST. LOUIS (AL) - McQuinn, Laabs .... $200-$300
1939 ST. LOUIS (NL) - Mize, Slaughter, Medwick, P. Martin .... $375-$550
1939 WASHINGTON - Harris, Vernon, Lewis, Case, Wright, Ferrell,
Leonard .... $200-$300
1940 BOSTON (AL) - Cronin, Foxx, Doerr, Williams, Wilson, Grove .... $600-$1000
1940 BOSTON (NL) - Stengel, Rowell, Cooney, Lopez .... $500-$750
1940 BROOKLYN - Durocher, Reese, Medwick .... $450-$800
1940 CHICAGO (AL) - Appling, Wright, Solters, Lyons .... $200-$300
1940 CHICAGO (NL) - Hartnett, Herman, Dean .... $200-$300
1940 CINCINNATI - McKechnie, F. McCormick, Lombardi .... $350-$550
1940 CLEVELAND - Boudreau, Weatherly, Feller, Smith .... $200-$300
1940 DETROIT - York, Gehringer, McCosky, Greenberg, Averill,
Newsom .... $500-$750
1940 NEW YORK (AL) - McCarthy, DiMaggio, Dickey, Ruffing, Gomez .... $450-$700
1940 NEW YORK (NL) - Terry, Ott, Demaree, Danning, Hubbell .... $400-$600
1940 PHILADELPHIA (AL) - Mack, Moses, Hayes, Simmons .... $400-$750
1940 PHILADELPHIA (NL)- .... $250-$400
1940 PITTSBURGH - Frisch, Vaughan, P. Waner, L. Waner, Lopez .... $500-$1000
1940 ST. LOUIS (AL) - Judnich, Radcliff .... $175-$275
1940 ST. LOUIS (NL) - Mize, Slaughter, P. Martin, Medwick .... $325-$475
1940 WASHINGTON - Harris, Lewis, Ferrell, Vernon .... $200-$325
1941 BOSTON (AL) - Cronin, Foxx, Doerr, DiMaggio, Williams, Grove .... $500-$675

1965 New York Mets

1941 BOSTON (NL) - Cooney, Waner, Stengel .... $300-$400

1941 BROOKLYN - Durocher, Camilli, Herman, Reese, Medwick,
Waner .... $750-$1250

1941 CHICAGO (AL) - Appling, Lyons .... $225-$350

1941 CHICAGO (NL) - Hack, Herman, Dean .... $175-$300

1941 CINCINNATI - McKechnie, Lombardi, Waner .... $400-$600

1941 CLEVELAND - Boudreau, Heath, Lemon, Feller .... $200-$400

1941 DETROIT - Gehringer, McCosky, Radcliff, Greenberg, Benton .... $450-$700

1941 NEW YORK (AL) - McCarthy, Rizzuto, DiMaggio, Dickey, Gomez,
Ruffing .... $800-$1200

1941 NEW YORK (NL) - Terry, Bartell, Ott, Hubbell .... $525-$600

1941 PHILADELPHIA (AL) - Mack, Siebert, Moses, Chapman, Collins,
Simmons .... $325-$500

1941 PHILADELPHIA (NL) - Litwhiler, Etten .... $400-$500

1941 PITTSBURGH - Frisch, Vaughan, Lopez, Waner .... $700-$800

1941 ST. LOUIS (AL) - Ferrell .... $200-$325

1941 ST. LOUIS (NL) - Mize, Brown, Slaughter, Hopp, Musial .... $300-$450

1941 WASHINGTON - Harris, Vernon, Travis, Ferrell, Wynn .... $225-$350

1942 BOSTON (AL) - Cronin, Doerr, Williams, Foxx .... $400-$575

1942 BOSTON (NL) - Stengel, Lombardi, Sain, Spahn .... $800-$1000

1942 BROOKLYN - Durocher, Herman, Reese, Vaughan, Reiser,
Medwick, Wyatt, French .... $400-$600

1942 CHICAGO (AL) - Appling, Lyons .... $250-$350

1942 CHICAGO (NL) - Cavarretta, Hack, Novikoff, Foxx .... $250-$400
1942 CINCINNATI - McKechnie, Vander Meer .... $200-$325
1942 CLEVELAND - Boudreau .... $200-$300
1942 DETROIT - Gehringer, Trucks, Newhouser .... $300-$400
1942 NEW YORK (AL) - McCarthy, Gordon, Rizzuto, DiMaggio, Dickey,
Ruffing, Gomez .... $600-$900
1942 NEW YORK (NL) - Ott, Mize, Hubbell .... $500-$800
1942 PHILADELPHIA (AL) - Mack, Collins .... $300-$450
1942 PHILADELPHIA (NL) - Waner .... $500-$750
1942 PITTSBURGH - Frisch, Lopez .... $700-$900
1942 ST. LOUIS (AL) - Ferrell .... $200-$375
1942 ST. LOUIS (NL) - Slaughter, Musial, W. Cooper, M. Cooper,
Beazley .... $750-$1000
1942 WASHINGTON - Harris, Vernon, Wynn .... $200-$300
1943 BOSTON (AL) - Cronin, Doerr .... $300-$550
1943 BOSTON (NL) - Stengel, McCarthy .... $250-$325
1943 BROOKLYN - Durocher, Herman, Vaughan, Bordagaray, Walker,
Olmo, Waner, Hodges, Medwick, Wyatt .... $350-$700
1943 CHICAGO (AL) - Appling, Grove .... $200-$350
1943 CHICAGO (NL) - Cavarretta, Nicholson, Goodman .... $250-$400
1943 CINCINNATI - McKechnie, McCormick, Vander Meer .... $200-$350
1943 CLEVELAND - Boudreau, Smith .... $200-$275
1943 DETROIT - Cramer, Wakefield, Trout, Trucks .... $200-$300
1943 NEW YORK (AL) - McCarthy, Dickey, Chandler .... $1200-$1500
1943 NEW YORK (NL) - Ott, Witek, Medwick, Lombardi, Adams .... $325-$500
1943 PHILADELPHIA (AL) - Mack, Kell .... $200-$350
1943 PHILADELPHIA (NL) - Rowe, Barrett .... $400-$600
1943 PITTSBURGH - Frisch, Elliott, Lopez, Sewell .... $225-$350
1943 ST. LOUIS (AL) - Ferrell, Dean .... $200-$350
1943 ST. LOUIS (NL) - Musial, W. Cooper .... $350-$475
1943 WASHINGTON - Vernon, Wynn, Gomez .... $200-$300
1944 BOSTON (AL) - Cronin, Doerr, Fox, Johnson, Hughson .... $225-$350
1944 BOSTON (NL) - Holmes .... $200-$300
1944 BROOKLYN - Durocher, Walker, Galan, P. Waner, L. Waner,
Vaughan .... $250-$500
1944 CHICAGO (AL) - Schalk .... $200-$325
1944 CHICAGO (NL) - Grimm, Cavarretta, Dallessandro, Foxx ...... $175-$325
1944 CINCINNATI - McKechnie, McCormick, Tiptop, Walters .... $200-$325
1944 CLEVELAND - Boudreau .... $275-$450
1944 DETROIT - Wakefield, Newhouser .... $225-$375
1944 NEW YORK (AL) - McCarthy, Lindell, Martin, Waner .... $250-$425
1944 NEW YORK (NL) - Ott, Weintraub, Medwick, Lombardi, Voiselle .... $400-$600
1944 PHILADELPHIA (AL) - Mack, Simmons .... $250-$400
1944 PHILADELPHIA (NL) .... $300-$500
1944 PITTSBURGH - Russell, Lopez, Sewell, Frisch .... $300-$400
1944 ST. LOUIS (AL) - Kreevich, Potter .... $300-$500
1944 ST. LOUIS (NL) - Marion, Musial, Hopp, W. Cooper, Martin,

M. Cooper .... $400-$500
1944 WASHINGTON - Spence, Ferrell, Wynn.............................. $200-$300
1945 BOSTON (AL) - Cronin.. $200-$300
1945 BOSTON (NL) - Holmes.. $175-$250
1945 BROOKLYN - Durocher, Galan, Walker, Rosen, Olmo .... $200-$350
1945 CHICAGO (AL) - Appling.. $175-$300
1945 CHICAGO (NL) - Grimm, Cavarretta, Johnson, Hack, Wyse .... $350-$500
1945 CINCINNATI - McKechnie.. $225-$325
1945 CLEVELAND - Boudreau, Feller.. $275-$350
1945 DETROIT (AL) - Greenberg, Newhouser .... $325-$450
1945 NEW YORK (AL) - McCarthy, Waner, Ruffing....................... $200-$325
1945 NEW YORK (NL) - Ott, Lombardi, Mungo............................. $300-$650
1945 PHILADELPHIA (AL) - Mack, Kell.. $225-$350
1945 PHILADELPHIA (NL) - Wasdell, Foxx................................. $700-$900
1945 PITTSBURGH - Frisch, Lopez, Waner .... $600-$800
1945 ST. LOUIS (AL) - Muncrief... $600-$800
1945 ST. LOUIS (NL) - Kurowski, Schoendienst, Barrett, Burkhart,
Brecheen .... $200-$350
1945 WASHINGTON - Lewis, Ferrell, Wolff.............................. $200-$300
1946 BOSTON (AL) - Cronin, Doerr, Pesky, DiMaggio, Williams, Ferriss .... $300-$450
1946 BOSTON (NL) - Holmes, Herman, Sain, Spahn............................ $200-$350
1946 BROOKLYN - Durocher, Reese, Medwick, Higbe .... $350-$500
1946 CHICAGO (AL) - Lyons, Appling, Caldwell............................ $250-$350
1946 CHICAGO (NL) - Grimm, Waitkus .... $175-$275
1946 CINCINNATI - McKechnie, Walters .... $200-$300
1946 CLEVELAND - Boudreau, Edwards, Lemon, Feller................ $250-$350
1946 DETROIT - Kell, Newhouser .... $225-$350
1946 NEW YORK (AL) - McCarthy, Rizzuto, DiMaggio, Dickey, Berra,
Ruffing, Chandler .... $550-$1000
1946 NEW YORK (NL) - Ott, Mize, Lombardi .... $500-$650
1946 PHILADELPHIA (AL) - Mack, Valo, McCosky, Kell............... $300-$400
1946 PHILADELPHIA (NL) - Ennis, Rowe .... $200-$300
1946 PITTSBURGH - Frisch, Kiner, Lopez.................................... $800-$950
1946 ST. LOUIS (AL) - Stephens .... $200-$300
1946 ST. LOUIS (NL) - Musial, Schoendienst, Kurowski, Slaughter, Walker,
Garagiola, Pollet... $400-$600
1946 WASHINGTON - Vernon, Grace, Leonard, Wynn................... $200-$300
1947 BOSTON (AL) - Cronin, Doerr, Pesky, Williams, Dobson .... $250-$400
1947 BOSTON (NL) - Elliott, Holmes, Spahn, Sain......................... $200-$325
1947 BROOKLYN - Robinson, Reese, Vaughan, Snider, Hodges, Branca,
Hatten.. $900-$1100
1947 CHICAGO (AL) - Lyons, Appling, Wright............................. $200-$300
1947 CHICAGO (NL) - Grimm, Pafko, Cavarretta......................... $200-$300
1947 CINCINNATI - Galan, Kluszewski, Blackwell........................ $200-$300
1947 CLEVELAND - Boudreau, Mitchell, Feller, Lemon .... $250-$350
1947 DETROIT - Kell.. $250-$350
1947 NEW YORK (AL) - McQuinn, Rizzuto, DiMaggio, Berra, Reynolds,

Shea... $1000-$1250
1947 NEW YORK (NL) - Ott, Mize, Cooper, Jansen .... $350-$600
1947 PHILADELPHIA (AL) - Mack, Valo, Fox, Marchildon .... $225-$350
1947 PHILADELPHIA (NL) - Walker, Leonard, Rowe .... $250-$400
1947 PITTSBURGH - Herman, Greenberg, Kiner..................................... $200-$300
1947 ST. LOUIS (AL) - Dean.. $225-$350
1947 ST. LOUIS (NL) - Musial, Schoendienst, Garagiola, Medwick,
Munger... $275-$400
1947 WASHINGTON - Vernon, Wynn... $200-$300
1948 BOSTON (AL) - McCarthy, Doerr, Pesky, Williams .... $250-$375
1948 BOSTON (NL) - Dark, Sain, Spahn.. $400-$600
1948 BROOKLYN - Durocher, Hodges, Robinson, Reese, Furillo,
Campanella, Roe, Vaughan, Snider, Branca, Erskine .... $600-$900
1948 CHICAGO (AL) - Lyons, Appling.. $200-$300
1948 CHICAGO (NL) - Grimm... $200-$300
1948 CINCINNATI - Kluszewski .... $200-$300
1948 CLEVELAND - Boudreau, Mitchell, Bearden, Lemon, Feller, Paige........ $400-$575
1948 DETROIT - Kell, Cramer, Newhouser, Trucks .... $250-$350
1948 NEW YORK (AL) - Rizzuto, DiMaggio, Berra, Raschi........................ $400-$750
1948 NEW YORK (NL) - Ott, Durocher, Mize.. $400-$600
1948 PHILADELPHIA (AL) - Mack, Fox... $225-$350
1948 PHILADELPHIA (NL) - Sisler, Ashburn, Leonard, Rowe, Roberts......... $300-$450
1948 PITTSBURGH - Kiner... $275-$375
1948 ST. LOUIS (AL) - .... $200-$400
1948 ST. LOUIS (NL) - Schoendienst, Slaughter, Musial, Garagiola,
Medwick .... $275-$400
1948 WASHINGTON - Vernon, Wynn.. $225-$325
1949 BOSTON (AL) - McCarthy, Doerr, Williams, Parnell.......................... $200-$325
1949 BOSTON (NL) - Spahn, Sain.. $275-$350
1949 BROOKLYN - Hodges, Robinson, Reese, Furillo, Roe, Newcombe,
Campanella, Snider, Connors .... $700-$900
1949 CHICAGO (AL) - Appling .... $200-$300
1949 CHICAGO (NL) - Grimm, Frisch, Burgess..................................... $250-$350
1949 CINCINNATI - Kluszewski.. $200-$275
1949 CLEVELAND - Boudreau, Vernon, Mitchell, Lemon, Feller, Wynn .... $225-$300
1949 DETROIT - Kell, Wertz, Evers, Trucks... $200-$300
1949 NEW YORK (AL) - Stengel, Rizzuto, Berra, DiMaggio, Mize, Raschi,
Reynolds .... $1200-$1500
1949 NEW YORK (NL) - Durocher, Mize, Marshall, Thomson, Irvin............... $275-$550
1949 PHILADELPHIA (AL) - Mack, Fox... $225-$325
1949 PHILADELPHIA (NL) - Sisler, Meyer, Roberts............................... $300-$500
1949 PITTSBURGH - Hopp, Kiner.. $300-$500
1949 ST. LOUIS (AL) - Dillinger, Sievers .... $200-$300
1949 ST. LOUIS (NL) - Schoendienst, Musial, Slaughter, Garagiola, Pollet.......... $225-$350
1949 WASHINGTON.. $200-$300
1950 BOSTON (AL) - McCarthy, Dropo, Doerr, Pesky, Williams .... $250-$350
1950 BOSTON (NL) - Jethroe, Spahn, Sain .... $200-$300

1969 Atlanta Braves

1950 BROOKLYN - Hodges, Robinson, Reese, Furillo, Roe, Campanella,
Newcombe, Snider.. $600-$900
1950 CHICAGO (AL) - Fox, Appling.. $200-$300
1950 CHICAGO (NL) - Frisch, Pafko.. $200-$300
1950 CINCINNATI - Kluszewski, Adcock .... $200-$300
1950 CLEVELAND - Boudreau, Rosen, Doby, Mitchell, Lemon, Wynn,
Feller... $250-$350
1950 DETROIT - Kell, Wertz, Groth, Evers .... $300-$400
1950 NEW YORK (AL) - Stengel, Martin, Rizzuto, Bauer, DiMaggio,
Woodling, Berra, Mize, Ford... $675-$1000
1950 NEW YORK (NL) - Dark, Irvin, Jansen, Maglie .... $300-$450
1950 PHILADELPHIA (AL) - Mack, Dillinger, Lehner................................... $300-$400
1950 PHILADELPHIA (NL) - Ennis, Ashburn, Roberts, Simmons,
Konstanty.. $300-$450
1950 PITTSBURGH - Hopp, Kiner.. $200-$300
1950 ST. LOUIS (AL) - .... $200-$275
1950 St. LOUIS (NL) - Musial, Schoendienst, Garagiola.............................. $225-$325
1950 WASHINGTON - Vernon.. $200-$275
1951 BOSTON (AL) - Doerr, Pesky, Boudreau... $200-$300
1951 BOSTON (NL) - Spahn, Sain.. $200-$250
1951 BROOKLYN - Hodges, Robinson, Reese, Snider, Campanella, Roe,
Newcombe .... $575-$675
1951 CHICAGO (AL) - Fox, Minoso.. $200-$300

1951 CHICAGO (NL) - Frisch, Connors, Burgess... $225-$325
1951 CINCINNATI - Kluszewski, Adcock .... $175-$275
1951 CLEVELAND - Lopez, Avila, Feller, Wynn, Lemon.............................. $225-$325
1951 DETROIT - Kell, Trucks.. $250-$400
1951 NEW YORK (AL) - Stengel, Mize, Rizzuto, Brown, DiMaggio,
Mantle, McDougald, Berra, Martin .... $2500-$4500
1951 NEW YORK (NL) - Durocher, Dark, Mays, Irvin, Maglie .... $1000-$1150
1951 PHILADELPHIA (AL) - Fain, Shantz.. $200-$400
1951 PHILADELPHIA (NL) - Ashburn, Roberts.. $175-$275
1951 PITTSBURGH - Kiner, Garagiola.. $275-$375
1951 ST. LOUIS (AL) - Paige, Gaedel... $400-$600
1951 ST. LOUIS (NL) - Schoendienst, Slaughter, Musial, Garagiola................. $225-$325
1951 WASHINGTON - Vernon.. $100-$225
1952 BOSTON (AL) - Boudreau, Goodman, Kell, Williams .... $175-$275
1952 BOSTON (NL) - Grimm, Mathews, Spahn.. $250-$325
1952 BROOKLYN - Hodges, Robinson, Reese, Furillo, Snider, Campanella,
Black, Erskine... $500-$750
1952 CHICAGO (AL) - Fox, Minoso.. $200-$300
1952 CHICAGO (NL) - Fondy, Baumholtz, Sauer, Hacker............................ $175-$275
1952 CINCINNATI - Hornsby, Kluszewski, Adcock .... $275-$400
1952 CLEVELAND - Avila, Rosen, Mitchell, Wynn, Garcia, Lemon,
Feller... $300-$500
1952 DETROIT - Kell, Kuenn .... $200-$300
1952 NEW YORK (AL) - Stengel, Martin, Reynolds, Mantle, Berra,
Raschi, Woodling, Brown, Mize, Rizzuto.. $650-$800
1952 NEW YORK (NL) - Durocher, Dark, Irvin, Maglie, Wilhelm .... $300-$425
1952 PHILADELPHIA (AL) - Fain, Shantz.. $200-$300
1952 PHILADELPHIA (NL) - Ashburn, Roberts.. $200-$300
1952 PITTSBURGH - Groat, Kiner, Garagiola.. $200-$300
1952 ST. LOUIS (AL) - Hornsby, Paige... $350-$500
1952 ST. LOUIS (NL) - Schoendienst, Slaughter, Musial............................. $275-$400
1952 WASHINGTON - Vernon... $175-$250
1953 BOSTON - Boudreau, Goodman, Kell, Williams, Parnell .... $400-$550
1953 BROOKLYN - Hodges, Meyer, Reese, Furillo, Snider, Robinson,
Campanella, Erskine, Gilliam.. $700-$1000
1953 CHICAGO (AL) - Fox, Minoso, Trucks.. $225-$350
1953 CHICAGO (NL) - Fondy, Baumholtz, Kiner, Garagiola, Banks................ $200-$300
1953 CINCINNATI - Hornsby, Kluszewski, Bell .... $275-$400
1953 CLEVELAND - Lopez, Rosen, Westlake, Mitchell, Lemon, Wynn,
Feller... $225-$300
1953 DETROIT - Kuenn, Boone, Kaline... $200-$275
1953 MILWAUKEE - Grimm, Adcock, Mathews, Spahn, Burdette .... $300-$375
1953 NEW YORK (AL) - Stengel, Martin, Rizzuto, Mantle, Berra, Mize,
Ford.. $750-$1200
1953 NEW YORK (NL) - Durocher, Dark, Mueller, Thomson, Irvin................. $275-$450
1953 PHILADELPHIA (AL) - Philley.. $200-$300
1953 PHILADELPHIA (NL) - Ashburn, Roberts.. $175-$275

1953 PITTSBURGH - Kiner, Garagiola.. $200-$300
1953 ST. LOUIS (AL) - .... $175-$250
1953 ST. LOUIS (NL) - Schoendienst, Slaughter, Musial, Haddix, Staley........ $225-$275
1953 WASHINGTON - Vernon, Busby, Porterfield .... $175-$250
1954 BALTIMORE - .... $150-$225
1954 BOSTON - Boudreau, Jensen, Williams .... $400-$500
1954 BROOKLYN - Alston, Hodges, Gilliam, Reese, Furillo, Lasorda,
Robinson, Campanella, Erskine, Newcombe, Snider..................................... $1200-$1400
1954 CHICAGO (AL) - Fox, Kell, Trucks, Minoso...................................... $200-$325
1954 CHICAGO (NL) - Banks, Kiner, Garagiola .... $300-$500
1954 CINCINNATI - Kluszewski, Temple .... $175-$275
1954 CLEVELAND - Lopez, Avila, Lemon, Wynn, Feller.............................. $300-$450
1954 DETROIT - Kuenn, Kaline .... $350-$425
1954 MILWAUKEE - Grimm, Adcock, Mathews, Aaron, Spahn, Burdette .... $275-$400
1954 NEW YORK (AL) - Stengel, Rizzuto, Mantle, Berra, Slaughter, Grim,
Ford .... $500-$900
1954 NEW YORK (NL) - Durocher, Mays, Irvin, Antonelli, Maglie,
Wilhelm .... $1200-$1500
1954 PHILADELPHIA (NL) - Ashburn, Burgess, Roberts............................ $250-$350
1954 PHILADELPHIA (AL) - Finigan.. $175-$250
1954 PITTSBURGH - Gordon... $150-$250
1954 ST. LOUIS - Schoendienst, Musial, Moon... $200-$300
1954 WASHINGTON - Vernon, Killebrew.. $150-$225
1955 BALTIMORE - Robinson.. $225-$325
1955 BOSTON - Goodman, Jensen, Piersall, Williams .... $175-$300
1955 BROOKLYN - Hodges, Gilliam, Reese, Labine, Furillo, Snider,
Campanella, Newcombe, Robinson, Erskine, Koufax .... $2500-$4000
1955 CHICAGO (AL) - Fox, Kell, Donovan, Trucks .... $200-$300
1955 CHICAGO (NL) - Banks .... $175-$250
1955 CINCINNATI - Kluszewski, Burgess... $200-$300
1955 CLEVELAND - Lopez, Smith, Kiner, Colavito, Lemon, Wynn, Score,
Feller.. $375-$525
1955 DETROIT - Kuenn, Kaline, Bunning .... $175-$275
1955 KANSAS CITY - Boudreau, Slaughter.. $200-$275
1955 MILWAUKEE - Mathews, Aaron, Adcock, Spahn, Burdette................... $250-$400
1955 NEW YORK (AL) - Stengel, Mantle, Slaughter, Howard, Martin,
Berra, Rizzuto, Ford, Larsen.. $500-$900
1955 NEW YORK (NL) - Durocher, Mays, Irvin, Antonelli .... $275-$475
1955 PHILADELPHIA - Ashburn, Roberts.. $175-$250
1955 PITTSBURGH - Groat, Clemente, Friend.. $500-$800
1955 ST. LOUIS - Musial, Schoendienst, Boyer, Virdon, Haddix .... $200-$300
1955 WASHINGTON - Vernon, Killebrew.. $150-$225
1956 BALTIMORE - Kell, Gastall, Robinson... $175-$250
1956 BOSTON - Vernon, Jensen, Williams.. $300-$400
1956 BROOKLYN - Hodges, Gilliam, Reese, Furillo, Snider, Campanella,
Koufax, Newcombe, Erskine, Drysdale, Robinson .... $700-$900
1956 CHICAGO (AL) - Fox, Aparicio, Kell.. $200-$300

1956 CHICAGO (NL) - Banks, Irvin .... $200-$275
1956 CINCINNATI - Kluszewski, Robinson .... $225-$325
1956 CLEVELAND - Lopez, Colavito, Lemon, Wynn, Score, Feller .... $300-$400
1956 DETROIT - Kuenn, Kaline, Bunning .... $200-$300
1956 KANSAS CITY - Boudreau, Slaughter, Lasorda .... $200-$300
1956 MILWAUKEE - Grimm, Adcock, Mathews, Aaron, Spahn, Burdette .... $275-$425
1956 NEW YORK (AL) - Stengel, Martin, Mantle, Howard, Rizzuto,
Slaughter, Berra, Bauer, Ford .... $650-$1000
1956 NEW YORK (NL) - White, Schoendienst, Mays, Antonelli .... $275-$475
1956 PHILADELPHIA - Ashburn, Roberts .... $150-$225
1956 PITTSBURGH - Mazeroski, Groat, Clemente, Virdon .... $600-$850
1956 ST. LOUIS - Musial, Boyer, Schoendienst, Peete .... $175-$300
1956 WASHINGTON - Killebrew .... $150-$225
1957 BALTIMORE - Kell, Robinson .... $200-$300
1957 BOSTON - Jensen, Williams, Vernon .... $200-$275
1957 BROOKLYN - Hodges, Gilliam, Reese, Furillo, Snider, Campanella,
Koufax, Drysdale .... $1000-$1300
1957 CHICAGO (AL) - Lopez, Fox, Aparicio .... $200-$300
1957 CHICAGO (NL) - Banks .... $175-$250
1957 CINCINNATI - Robinson, Kluszewski .... $250-$375
1957 CLEVELAND - Colavito, Maris, Wynn, Wilhelm .... $450-$600
1957 DETROIT - Kuenn, Kaline, Bunning .... $180-$270
1957 KANSAS CITY - Martin .... $175-$275
1957 MILWAUKEE - Schoendienst, Mathews, Aaron, Adcock, Spahn .... $1000-$1500
1957 NEW YORK (AL) - Stengel, Slaughter, Berra, Howard, Sturdivant,
Ford .... $700-$900
1957 NEW YORK (NL) - Mays, Schoendienst, McCormick, White .... $250-$350
1957 PHILADELPHIA - Ashburn, Sanford, Roberts .... $275-$375
1957 PITTSBURGH - Mazeroski, Groat, Clemente, Friend .... $900-$1000
1957 ST. LOUIS - Musial, Boyer, Wilhelm .... $200-$300
1957 WASHINGTON - Killebrew .... $150-$225
1958 BALTIMORE - Robinson, Wilhelm .... $150-$225
1958 BOSTON - Runnels, Williams .... $275-$500
1958 CHICAGO (AL) - Fox, Aparicio, Cash, Wynn .... $200-$300
1958 CHICAGO (NL) - Banks .... $175-$250
1958 CINCINNATI - Robinson, Pinson .... $150-$300
1958 CLEVELAND - Vernon, Colavito, Maris, Wilhelm, Lemon .... $200-$300
1958 DETROIT - Martin, Kaline, Kuenn, Bunning .... $200-$300
1958 KANSAS CITY - Maris .... $400-$550
1958 LOS ANGELES - Alston, Hodges, Furillo, Snider, Reese, Drysdale,
Koufax, Howard .... $350-$600
1958 MILWAUKEE - Schoendienst, Mathews, Aaron, Spahn, Burdette .... $525-$800
1958 NEW YORK - Kubek, Mantle, Berra, Howard, Slaughter, Turley,
Ford, Larsen .... $1100-$1350
1958 PHILADELPHIA - Ashburn, Roberts .... $200-$350
1958 PITTSBURGH - Kluszewski, Mazeroski, Groat, Clemente, Friend .... $575-$850
1958 SAN FRANCISCO - Cepeda, Mays, White, McCormick .... $450-$600

1973 Oakland A's

1958 ST. LOUIS - Musial, Boyer .... $175-$250
1958 WASHINGTON - Pearson, Killebrew .... $150-$225
1959 BALTIMORE - Robinson, Wilhelm .... $175-$250
1959 BOSTON - Runnels, Williams .... $150-$250
1959 CHICAGO (AL) - Lopez, Fox, Aparicio, Cash, Kluszewski, Wynn .... $350-$525
1959 CHICAGO (NL) - Banks, Williams .... $175-$250
1959 CINCINNATI - Robinson, Pinson .... $300-$500
1959 CLEVELAND - Martin, Colavito, Perry, Score .... $175-$250
1959 DETROIT - Kuenn, Kaline, Bunning .... $175-$250
1959 KANSAS CITY - Maris .... $200-$400
1959 LOS ANGELES - Alston, Hodges, Gilliam, Snider, Koufax, Furillo,
Drysdale, Howard, Wills .... $800-$1000
1959 MILWAUKEE - Adcock, Mathews, Aaron, Vernon, Slaughter,
Schoendienst, Spahn .... $350-$500
1959 NEW YORK - Stengel, Kubek, Mantle, Berra, Howard, Slaughter, Ford,
Larsen .... $450-$600
1959 PHILADELPHIA - Sparky Anderson, Ashburn, Roberts .... $300-$400
1959 PITTSBURGH - Stuart, Mazeroski, Groat, Clemente, Kluszewski,
Friend .... $600-$800
1959 SAN FRANCISCO - Cepeda, Mays, McCovey, McCormick .... $250-$375
1959 ST. LOUIS - Musial, Boyer, White, McDaniel, Gibson .... $175-$250
1959 WASHINGTON - Killebrew, Allison, Kaat .... $150-$225
1960 BALTIMORE - Hansen, Robinson, Wilhelm .... $175-$250

1960 BOSTON - Runnels, Williams.. $375-$500
1960 CHICAGO (AL) - Lopez, Fox, Aparicio, Kluszewski, Wynn, Score .... $300-$500
1960 CHICAGO (NL) - Grimm, Boudreau, Banks, Santo, Ashburn,
Williams.. $175-$250
1960 CINCINNATI - Robinson, Martin, Pinson .... $250-$350
1960 CLEVELAND - Aspromonte, Kuenn, Piersall, Perry............................. $150-$250
1960 DETROIT - Cash, Colavito, Kaline, Bunning .... $250-$350
1960 KANSAS CITY -.. $150-$225
1960 LOS ANGELES - Alston, Wills, Howard, Davis, Snider, Hodges,
Davis, Koufax, Drysdale, Gilliam .... $425-$500
1960 MILWAUKEE - Adcock, Mathews, Aaron, Schoendienst, Spahn,
Burdette, Torre... $300-$400
1960 NEW YORK - Stengel, Kubek, Maris, Mantle, Howard, Berra, Ford...........$500-$750
1960 PHILADELPHIA - Roberts.. $100-$150
1960 PITTSBURGH - Stuart, Mazeroski, Clemente, Law, Vernon.................. $800-$1200
1960 SAN FRANCISCO - McCovey, Mays, Cepeda, McCormick,
Marichal.. $250-$375
1960 ST. LOUIS - White, Boyer, Musial, McCarver, Gibson .... $250-$350
1960 WASHINGTON - Killebrew, Versalles, Kaat...................................... $175-$275
1961 BALTIMORE - Robinson, Powell, Wilhelm....................................... $150-$225
1961 BOSTON - Jensen, Yastrzemski.. $175-$250
1961 CHICAGO (AL) - Lopez, Fox, Aparicio, Pierce, Wynn .... $175-$250
1961 CHICAGO (NL) - Banks, Santo, Ashburn, Hubbs, Brock, Williams .... $175-$275
1961 CINCINNATI - Robinson, Pinson, Jay.. $325-$500
1961 CLEVELAND - Piersall, McDowell.. $125-$175
1961 DETROIT - Cash, Kaline, Colavito, Bunning, Freehan .... $250-$350
1961 KANSAS CITY -... $75-$250
1961 LOS ANGELES (AL) -... $200-$300
1961 LOS ANGELES (NL) - Alston, Wills, T. Davis, W. Davis, Howard,
Snider, Drysdale, Koufax .... $275-$400
1961 MILWAUKEE - Adcock, Mathews, Aaron, Torre, Spahn, Martin........... $175-$275
1961 MINNESOTA - Lavagetto, Killebrew, Martin, Versalles, Kaat............... $200-$300
1961 NEW YORK - Kubek, Maris, Mantle, Berra, Howard, Tresh, Ford....... $1400-$1800
1961 PHILADELPHIA -... $100-$150
1961 PITTSBURGH - Stuart, Mazeroski, Clemente, Clendenon, Friend .... $550-$850
1961 SAN FRANCISCO - McCovey, Mays, Cepeda, Marichal,
McCormick.. $250-$350
1961 ST. LOUIS - White, Boyer, Musial, Schoendienst, McCarver, Gibson
.... $275-$350
1961 WASHINGTON - Vernon.. $150-$225
1962 BALTIMORE - Robinson, Powell, Roberts, Wilhelm .... $175-$250
1962 BOSTON - Yastrzemski .... $175-$250
1962 CHICAGO (AL) - Lopez, Fox, Wynn, Peters, DeBusschere .... $200-$400
1962 CHICAGO (NL) - Banks, Hubbs, Santo, Brock, Williams .... $172-$275
1962 CINCINNATI - Robinson, Pinson .... $250-$450
1962 CLEVELAND - McDowell.. $125-$200
1962 DETROIT - Cash, Kaline, Colavito, Bunning .... $125-$200

1962 HOUSTON - Aspromonte .... $300-$425
1962 KANSAS CITY .... $100-$175
1962 LOS ANGELES (AL) - Lee Thomas, Fregosi.. $150-$225
1962 LOS ANGELES (NL) - Alston, Gilliam, Wills, Howard, W. Davis,
T. Davis, Snider, Drysdale, Koufax.. $400-$800
1962 MILWAUKEE - Adcock, Mathews, Aaron, Uecker, Spahn .... $300-$400
1962 MINNESOTA - Versalles, Killebrew, Oliva, Kaat................................... $175-$275
1962 NEW YORK (AL) - Tresh, Maris, Mantle, Howard, Berra, Kubek, Terry,
Ford .... $550-$800
1962 NEW YORK (NL) - Stengel, Hodges, Kranepool .... $300-$450
1962 PHILADELPHIA - .... $100-$150
1962 PITTSBURGH - Mazeroski, Groat, Clemente, Clendenon, Stargell......... $500-$750
1962 SAN FRANCISCO - Cepeda, Mays, McCovey, Marichal, McCormick,
Perry.. $400-$600
1962 ST. LOUIS - White, Boyer, Musial, Schoendienst, Gibson .... $275-$350
1962 WASHINGTON - Vernon.. $150-$275
1963 BALTIMORE - Aparicio, Robinson, Powell, Roberts .... $200-$250
1963 BOSTON - Yastrzemski .... $150-$250
1963 CHICAGO (AL) - Lopez, Fox, Peters, Wilhelm, DeBusschere .... $175-$250
1963 CHICAGO (NL) - Banks, Hubbs, Santo, Brock, Williams .... $175-$250
1963 CINCINNATI - Rose, Harper, Pinson, Robinson .... $200-$275
1963 CLEVELAND - Adcock, McDowell, John... $100-$150
1963 DETROIT - Cash, Kaline, Colavito, Lolich, McLain .... $125-$200
1963 HOUSTON - Staub, Aspromonte, Morgan, Umbricht .... $175-$250
1963 KANSAS CITY -... $150-$225
1963 LOS ANGELES (AL) - Fregosi, Chance... $100-$150
1963 LOS ANGELES (NL) - Alston, Gilliam, Wills, Howard, W. Davis,
T. Davis, Koufax, Drysdale .... $450-$650
1963 MILWAUKEE - Mathews, Aaron, Torre, Uecker, Spahn........................ $150-$225
1963 MINNESOTA - Versalles, Killebrew, Oliva, Kaat.................................. $175-$275
1963 NEW YORK (AL) - Maris, Howard, Mantle, Berra, Ford .... $450-$650
1963 NEW YORK (NL) - Stengel, Snider, Kranepool, Hodges........................ $275-$400
1963 PHILADELPHIA - Allen... $100-$150
1963 PITTSBURGH - Clendenon, Mazeroski, Clemente, Stargell, Mota .... $450-$800
1963 SAN FRANCISCO - Cepeda, Mays, McCovey, Marichal, Larsen,
Perry.. $225-$450
1963 ST. LOUIS - Groat, Boyer, McCarver, Musial, Gibson .... $300-$550
1963 WASHINGTON - Vernon, Hodges .... $100-$150
1964 BALTIMORE - Aparicio, Robinson, Powell, Piniella, Roberts .... $200-$275
1964 BOSTON - Herman, Yastrzemski .... $200-$300
1964 CHICAGO (AL) - Lopez, Wilhelm .... $100-$150
1964 CHICAGO (NL) - Banks, Santo, Williams, Brock, Kessinger.................. $150-$225
1964 CINCINNATI - Rose, Robinson, Pinson, Perez .... $175-$250
1964 CLEVELAND - McDowell, Tiant, John.. $100-$150
1964 DETROIT - Cash, Kaline, Freehan, Lolich, McLain .... $150-$200
1964 HOUSTON - Fox, Aspromonte, Staub, Morgan .... $200-$300
1964 KANSAS CITY - Colavito, Campaneris, Odom...................................... $150-$250

1980 Kansas City Royals

1964 LOS ANGELES (AL) - Adcock, Fregosi, Chance .... $75-$100
1964 LOS ANGELES (NL) - Alston, Wills, Howard, W. Davis, T. Davis,
Koufax, Drysdale .... $250-$400
1964 MILWAUKEE - Mathews, Aaron, Carty, Torre, Spahn, Niekro .... $175-$250
1964 MINNESOTA - Versalles, Oliva, Killebrew, Kaat .... $200-$250
1964 NEW YORK (AL) - Berra, Maris, Mantle, Howard, Ford, Stottlemyre
.... $350-$500
1964 NEW YORK (NL) - Stengel, Kranepool .... $350-$500
1964 PHILADELPHIA - Allen, Bunning .... $100-$135
1964 PITTSBURGH - Clendenon, Mazeroski, Clemente, Mota....................... $450-$650
1964 SAN FRANCISCO - Cepeda, Mays, McCovey, Snider, Marichal,
Perry, Larsen... $200-$300
1964 ST. LOUIS - White, Boyer, Brock, McCarver, Uecker, Gibson .... $375-$550
1964 WASHINGTON - Hodges .... $225-$350
1965 BALTIMORE - Powell, Aparicio, Robinson, Blefary, Palmer, Roberts
.... $200-$300
1965 BOSTON - Herman, Yastrzemski .... $200-$275
1965 CALIFORNIA - Fregosi .... $115-$200
1965 CHICAGO (AL) - Lopez, John, Wilhelm.. $125-$175
1965 CHICAGO (NL) - Banks, Santo, Williams .... $100-$150
1965 CINCINNATI - Rose, Robinson, Pinson, Perez .... $200-$400
1965 CLEVELAND - Colavito, McDowell, Tiant.. $125-$325
1965 DETROIT - Cash, Kaline, Freehan, McLain, Lolich................................ $150-$200

1965 HOUSTON - Morgan, Staub, Fox, Roberts.. $150-$225
1965 KANSAS CITY - Campaneris, Hunter, Paige, Odom........................... $200-$400
1965 LOS ANGELES - Alston, Lefebvre, Wills, W. Davis, Koufax,
Drysdale... $350-$550
1965 MILWAUKEE - Mathews, Aaron, Torre, Niekro .... $250-$350
1965 MINNESOTA - Versalles, Oliva, Killebrew, Kaat.................................. $325-$575
1965 NEW YORK (AL) - Mantle, Howard, Maris, Murcer, Stottlemyre,
Ford.. $400-$575
1965 NEW YORK (NL) - Stengel, Kranepool, Swoboda, Berra, Spahn............. $300-$375
1965 PHILADELPHIA - Allen, Bunning, Jenkins .... $150-$250
1965 PITTSBURGH - Mazeroski, Clemente, Stargell .... $1300-$1400
1965 SAN FRANCISCO - McCovey, Mays, Cepeda, Marichal, Perry,
Spahn .... $200-$350
1965 ST. LOUIS - Schoendienst, White, Boyer, Brock, McCarver, Uecker,
Gibson, Carlton.. $300-$350
1965 WASHINGTON - Hodges, Howard, McCormick .... $150-$225
1966 ATLANTA - Mathews, Aaron, Torre, Niekro....................................... $325-$400
1966 BALTIMORE - Aparicio, B. Robinson, F. Robinson, Palmer .... $250-$450
1966 BOSTON - Herman, Yastrzemski, Lonborg... $200-$300
1966 CALIFORNIA - Fregosi .... $80-$120
1966 CHICAGO (AL) - Agee, John, Wilhelm.. $150-$250
1966 CHICAGO (NL) - Banks, Santo, Jenkins, Roberts............................... $125-$200
1966 CINCINNATI - Perez, Rose, Helms, Harper, Pinson .... $125-$175
1966 CLEVELAND - Colavito, Tiant, McDowell... $100-$175
1966 DETROIT - Cash, Kaline, Freehan, McLain, Lolich............................... $125-$200
1966 HOUSTON - Morgan, Staub, Roberts.. $100-$150
1966 KANSAS CITY - Campaneris, Hunter, Odom.. $100-$150
1966 LOS ANGELES - Wills, W. Davis, T. Davis, Koufax, Drysdale,
Sutton.. $175-$400
1966 MINNESOTA - Killebrew, Oliva, Kaat.. $150-$225
1966 NEW YORK (AL) - Maris, Mantle, Howard, Stottlemyre, Ford .... $400-$600
1966 NEW YORK (NL) - Kranepool, Boyer, Swoboda, Ryan .... $175-$250
1966 PHILADELPHIA - White, Allen, Uecker, Bunning, Jenkins .... $100-$150
1966 PITTSBURGH - Clendenon, Mazeroski, Clemente, Stargell, Mota .... $800-$1200
1966 SAN FRANCISCO - McCovey, Mays, Cepeda, Marichal, Perry .... $175-$250
1966 ST. LOUIS - Schoendienst, Cepeda, Brock, McCarver, Gibson,
Carlton .... $250-$400
1966 WASHINGTON - Hodges, Howard .... $125-$200
1967 ATLANTA - Aaron, Carty, Uecker, Niekro... $150-$225
1967 BALTIMORE (AL) - Powell, Aparicio, B. Robinson, F. Robinson,
Palmer.. $200-$300
1967 BOSTON (AL) - Yastrzemski, Howard, Lonborg, Lyle .... $600-$1200
1967 CALIFORNIA (AL) - Fregosi.. $75-$125
1967 CHICAGO (AL) - Colavito, Boyer, John, Wilhelm .... $100-$175
1967 CHICAGO (NL) - Durocher, Banks, Santo, Williams, Jenkins .... $125-$175
1967 CINCINNATI - Pinson, Rose, Bench .... $150-$225
1967 CLEVELAND (AL) - Adcock, McDowell, Tiant................................... $100-$150

1967 DETROIT (AL) - Cash, Kaline, Freehan, Mathews, McLain, Lolich ....$150-$225
1967 HOUSTON - Mathews, Morgan, Staub... $100-$150
1967 KANSAS CITY (AL) - Appling, Jackson, Hunter, Odom......................... $150-$225
1967 LOS ANGELES - Alston, Davis, Drysdale, Sutton.................................. $200-$275
1967 MINNESOTA (AL) - Killebrew, Carew, Oliva, Kaat .... $275-$375
1967 NEW YORK (AL) - Mantle, Howard, Stottlemyre, Ford......................... $350-$450
1967 NEW YORK (NL) - Kranepool, Harrelson, Swoboda, Seaver, Koosman
.... $325-$475
1967 PHILADELPHIA - White, Allen, Uecker, Groat, Bunning...................... $100-$150
1967 PITTSBURGH - Mazeroski, Wills, Clemente, Stargell .... $400-$600
1967 SAN FRANCISCO (NL) - McCovey, Mays, McCormick, Perry, Marichal
.... $175-$250
1967 ST. LOUIS - Schoendienst, Cepeda, Maris, Brock, McCarver, Carlton,
Gibson .... $550-$750
1967 WASHINGTON (AL) - Hodges, Howard .... $175-$250
1968 ATLANTA - Aaron, Torre, Niekro .... $200-$300
1968 BALTIMORE - Weaver, Powell, B. Robinson, F. Robinson.................... $150-$250
1968 BOSTON - Yastrzemski, Howard, Lyle .... $150-$200
1968 CALIFORNIA - Fregosi .... $100-$125
1968 CHICAGO (AL) - Lopez, Aparicio, John.. $100-$150
1968 CHICAGO (NL) - Durocher, Banks, Santo, Williams, Jenkins .... $125-$200
1968 CINCINNATI - Perez, Rose, Pinson, Bench .... $175-$250
1968 CLEVELAND - Tiant, McDowell .... $100-$150
1968 DETROIT - Cash, Freehan, Kaline, McLain, Lolich............................... $375-$600
1968 HOUSTON - Staub, Morgan .... $100-$150
1968 LOS ANGELES - Alston, Davis, Drysdale, Sutton................................ $125-$200
1968 MINNESOTA - Carew, Oliva, Killebrew, Kaat .... $175-$250
1968 NEW YORK (AL) - Mantle, Bahnsen.. $200-$300
1968 NEW YORK (NL) - Hodges, Kranepool, Harrelson, Swoboda, Koosman,
Seaver, Ryan.. $500-$800
1968 OAKLAND - Bando, Jackson, Odom, Hunter, Fingers .... $200-$300
1968 PHILADELPHIA - White, Allen .... $75-$125
1968 PITTSBURGH - Mazeroski, Wills, Clemente, Stargell, Oliver, Bunning
.... $450-$650
1968 SAN FRANCISCO - McCovey, Bonds, Mays, Marichal, Perry,
McCormick... $175-$250
1968 ST. LOUIS - Schoendienst, Cepeda, Maris, Brock, Simmons, Gibson,
Carlton, McCarver.. $450-$600
1968 WASHINGTON - Howard.. $100-$150
1969 ATLANTA - Cepeda, Aaron, Evans, Niekro, Wilhelm........................... $200-$300
1969 BALTIMORE - Weaver, Powell, B. Robinson, F. Robinson, Cueller,
Palmer.. $150-$275
1969 BOSTON - Yastrzemski, Lyle .... $300-$400
1969 CALIFORNIA - Fregosi, Wilhelm .... $75-$125
1969 CHICAGO (AL) - Lopez, Aparicio, John.. $150-$200
1969 CHICAGO (NL) - Durocher, Banks, Santo, Williams, Jenkins .... $125-$200
1969 CINCINNATI - Perez, Rose, Bench .... $175-$250

1986 Los Angeles Dodgers

1969 CLEVELAND - McDowell, Tiant .... $75-$125
1969 DETROIT - Cash, Kaline, Freehan, McLain, Lolich .... $125-$175
1969 HOUSTON - Morgan .... $75-$125
1969 KANSAS CITY - Piniella.. $250-$375
1969 LOS ANGELES - Alston, Sizemore, Wills, Davis, Drysdale, Bunning,
Buckner, Garvey .... $175-$250
1969 MINNESOTA - Carew, Killebrew, Oliva, Nettles, Kaat .... $275-$375
1969 MONTREAL - Staub .... $275-$450
1969 NEW YORK (AL) - Murcer, Munson, Stottlemyre.................................... $200-$275
1969 NEW YORK (NL) - Harrelson, Swoboda, Seaver, Koosman, Ryan .... $750-$2000
1969 OAKLAND - Bando, Jackson, Odom, Hunter, Fingers, Blue..................... $250-$325
1969 PHILADELPHIA - Allen .... $100-$150
1969 PITTSBURGH - Oliver, Mazeroski, Clemente, Stargell, Bunning .... $325-$575
1969 SAN DIEGO - .... $200-$300
1969 SAN FRANCISCO - McCovey, Bonds, Mays, Marichal, Perry .... $125-$250
1969 SEATTLE - Harper .... $400-$600
1969 ST. LOUIS - Pinson, Torre, Simmons, Gibson, Carlton, Schoendienst,
Brock, McCarver .... $125-$225
1969 WASHINGTON - Williams, Howard... $150-$200
1970 ATLANTA - Cepeda, Aaron, Evans, Niekro, Wilhelm............................ $125-$200
1970 BALTIMORE - Weaver, Powell, B. Robinson, F. Robinson, Palmer....... $325-$400
1970 BOSTON - Yastrzemski, Lyle .... $125-$175
1970 CALIFORNIA - Fregosi .... $75-$125

1970 CHICAGO (AL) - Aparicio, John... $150-$200
1970 CHICAGO (NL) - Durocher, Banks, Santo, Williams, Jenkins,
Wilhelm .... $150-$225
1970 CINCINNATI - Anderson, Concepcion, Perez, Rose, Bench................. $225-$300
1970 CLEVELAND - Nettles, Pinson, McDowell... $75-$125
1970 DETROIT - Cash, Kaline, Freehan, Lolich.. $100-$150
1970 HOUSTON - Morgan .... $75-$125
1970 KANSAS CITY - Lemon, Piniella .... $125-$175
1970 LOS ANGELES - Alston, Wills, Garvey, Buckner, Sutton........................ $175-$250
1970 MILWAUKEE - Harper.. $100-$175
1970 MINNESOTA - Killebrew, Oliva, Carew, Perry, Kaat, Tiant .... $200-$400
1970 MONTREAL - Staub, Morton .... $100-$150
1970 NEW YORK (AL) - Murcer, Munson, Stottlemyre.................................... $275-$375
1970 NEW YORK (NL) - Hodges, Koosman, Harrelson, Swoboda, Kranepool,
Seaver, Ryan, Clendenon... $275-$400
1970 OAKLAND - Bando, Jackson, Hunter, Fingers .... $150-$250
1970 PHILADELPHIA - Bowa, McCarver, Bunning, Luzinski.......................... $100-$150
1970 PITTSBURGH - Mazeroski, Clemente, Stargell, Oliver....................... $600-$800
1970 SAN DIEGO -.. $100-$150
1970 SAN FRANCISCO - McCovey, Bonds, Mays, Foster, Perry, Marichal ....$175-$275
1970 ST. LOUIS - Allen, Torre, Brock, Simmons, Gibson, Carlton .... $150-$200
1970 WASHINGTON - Williams, Howard.. $150-$200
1971 ATLANTA - Aaron, Evans, Williams, Cepeda, Niekro, Wilhelm............. $125-$200
1971 BALTIMORE - Weaver, Powell, B. Robinson, F. Robinson, Palmer....... $250-$300
1971 BOSTON - Aparicio, Fisk, Lyle, Tiant.. $125-$175
1971 CALIFORNIA - Fregosi .... $100-$125
1971 CHICAGO (AL) - John.. $100-$125
1971 CHICAGO (NL) - Santo, Williams, Banks, Jenkins .... $100-$150
1971 CINCINNATI - Concepcion, Perez, Rose, Foster, Bench .... $175-$250
1971 CLEVELAND - Chambliss, Nettles, Pinson, McDowell.......................... $100-$125
1971 DETROIT - Martin, Cash, Kaline, Freehan, Lolich.................................. $150-$200
1971 HOUSTON - Morgan .... $75-$125
1971 KANSAS CITY - Lemon, Piniella .... $75-$125
1971 LOS ANGELES - Alston, Wills, Garvey, Buckner, Sutton, Wilhelm........ $175-$250
1971 MILWAUKEE - Harper.. $75-$100
1971 MINNESOTA - Killebrew, Carew, Oliva, Blyleven, Kaat..................... $100-$150
1971 MONTREAL - Staub .... $75-$100
1971 NEW YORK (AL) - Murcer, Munson, Stottlemyre.................................... $250-$450
1971 NEW YORK (NL) - Hodges, Kranepool, Harrelson, Seaver, Ryan,
Koosman .... $250-$375
1971 OAKLAND - Bando, Jackson, Hunter, Blue, Fingers............................... $200-$275
1971 PHILADELPHIA - Bowa, McCarver, Luzinski, Bunning........................ $100-$150
1971 PITTSBURGH - Clemente, Oliver, Stargell, Mazeroski....................... $500-$700
1971 SAN DIEGO -.. $100-$150
1971 SAN FRANCISCO - McCovey, Bonds, Mays, Kingman, Foster,
Marichal, Perry .... $175-$300
1971 ST. LOUIS - Schoendienst, Torre, Brock, Simmons, Carlton, Gibson ....$150-$250

1971 WASHINGTON - Williams, Harrah, Howard, McLain .... $200-$250

1972 ATLANTA - Mathews, Aaron, Evans, Cepeda, Niekro............................ $125-$200

1972 BALTIMORE - Weaver, Powell, Robinson .... $150-$175

1972 BOSTON - Aparicio, Yastrzemski, Fisk, Tiant.. $150-$200

1972 CALIFORNIA - Pinson, Ryan.. $100-$150

1972 CHICAGO (AL) - Allen, Gossage... $50-$125

1972 CHICAGO (NL) - Durocher, Santo, Williams, Jenkins .... $100-$150

1972 CINCINNATI - Anderson, Perez, Morgan, Concepcion, Rose, Bench,
Foster .... $275-$375

1972 CLEVELAND - Nettles, Bell, Perry .... $100-$125

1972 DETROIT - Cash, Northrup, Freehan, Kaline, Lolich............................ $150-$225

1972 HOUSTON - Durocher... $65-$85

1972 KANSAS CITY - Piniella... $85-$110

1972 LOS ANGELES - Alston, Garvey, Robinson, Davis, Sutton, John,
Wilhelm .... $175-$250

1972 MILWAUKEE - Scott.. $75-$110

1972 MINNESOTA - Killebrew, Carew, Oliva, Blyleven, Kaat...................... $125-$175

1972 MONTREAL - Singleton, McCarver.. $100-$150

1972 NEW YORK (AL) - Murcer, Munson, Stottlemyre................................. $200-$275

1972 NEW YORK (NL) - Hodges, Berra, Kranepool, Harrelson, Mays, Staub,
Seaver, Matlack, Koosman .... $200-$300

1972 OAKLAND - Bando, Jackson, Cepeda, Hunter, Fingers, Blue.................. $350-$400

1972 PHILADELPHIA - Bowa, Luzinski, McCarver, Boone, Schmidt,
Carlton .... $125-$175

1972 PITTSBURGH - Stargell, Clemente, Oliver, Mazeroski....................... $500-$725

1972 SAN DIEGO -... $75-$100

1972 SAN FRANCISCO - McCovey, Bonds, Mays, Marichal......................... $200-$300

1972 ST. LOUIS - Schoendienst, Torre, Brock, Simmons, Gibson.................... $150-$200

1972 TEXAS - Williams, Howard, Harrah.. $150-$210

1973 ATLANTA - Mathews, Aaron, P. Niekro, J. Niekro................................. $125-$200

1973 BALTIMORE - Weaver, Powell, Robinson, Bumbry, Palmer.................... $175-$250

1973 BOSTON - Yastrzemski, Aparicio, Fisk, Cepeda, Evans, Tiant .... $100-$175

1973 CALIFORNIA - Pinson, Robinson, Ryan.. $75-$150

1973 CHICAGO (AL) - Kaat, Gossage .... $75-$125

1973 CHICAGO (NL) - Kessinger, Williams, Jenkins.................................... $75-$100

1973 CINCINNATI - Anderson, Perez, Concepcion, Rose, Bench, Foster......... $225-$350

1973 CLEVELAND - Perry .... $85-$125

1973 DETROIT - Martin, Cash, Northrup, Freehan, Kaline, Lolich, Perry .... $150-$180

1973 HOUSTON - Richard .... $75-$100

1973 KANSAS CITY - Piniella, Brett... $175-$300

1973 LOS ANGELES - Alston, Buckner, Cey, Davis, Garvey, Sutton,
John.. $125-$200

1973 MILWAUKEE - Thomas... $80-$120

1973 MINNESOTA - Carew, Oliva, Killebrew, Blyleven, Kaat...................... $100-$150

1973 MONTREAL - Singleton .... $80-$100

1973 NEW YORK (AL) - Nettles, Murcer, Munson, Stottlemyre, McDowell, Lyle .... $200-$235

1973 NEW YORK (NL) - Berra, Harrelson, Staub, Jones, Kranepool, Seaver, Koosman .... $275-$425

1973 OAKLAND - Bando, Jackson, Hunter, Blue, Fingers .... $275-$425

1973 PHILADELPHIA - Bowa, Schmidt, Luzinski, Boone, Carlton .... $125-$175

1973 PITTSBURGH - Oliver, Stargell, Parker .... $125-$175

1973 SAN DIEGO - Winfield .... $100-$125

1973 SAN FRANCISCO - McCovey, Bonds, Matthews, Marichal .... $100-$150

1973 ST. LOUIS - Schoendienst, Torre, Brock, Simmons, McCarver, Gibson .... $100-$150

1973 TEXAS - Martin, Harrah, Burroughs, Madlock .... $65-$125

1974 ATLANTA - Mathews, Evans, Aaron, P. Niekro .... $150-$200

1974 BALTIMORE - Weaver, Powell, Robinson, Palmer .... $200-$300

1974 BOSTON - Yastrzemski, Evans, Fisk, Cooper, Rice, Lynn, McCarver, Marichal .... $150-$225

1974 CALIFORNIA - Robinson, Ryan .... $100-$150

1974 CHICAGO (AL) - Allen, Kaat, Gossage .... $75-$125

1974 CHICAGO (NL) - Kessinger, Madlock .... $75-$100

1974 CINCINNATI - Anderson, Perez, Morgan, Concepcion, Foster, Rose, Bench .... $225-$350

1974 CLEVELAND - G. Perry, J. Perry .... $100-$150

1974 DETROIT - Freehan, Horton, Kaline, Lolich .... $150-$200

1974 HOUSTON - Wilson, Richard .... $75-$100

1974 KANSAS CITY - Brett, Pinson .... $100-$150

1974 LOS ANGELES - Alston, Garvey, Cey, Buckner, Sutton, Marshall, John .... $150-$225

1974 MILWAUKEE - Yount .... $150-$200

1974 MINNESOTA - Carew, Oliva, Killebrew, Blyleven .... $125-$150

1974 MONTREAL - Singleton, Davis, Carter .... $75-$100

1974 NEW YORK (AL) - Nettles, Murcer, Munson, Lyle, McDowell ...... $175-$250

1974 NEW YORK (NL) - Harrelson, Staub, Jones, Kranepool, Koosman, Seaver .... $135-$200

1974 OAKLAND - Bando, Jackson, Hunter, Blue, Fingers .... $250-$375

1974 PHILADELPHIA - Bowa, Schmidt, Luzinski, Boone .... $100-$150

1974 PITTSBURGH - Oliver, Stargell, Parker, Tekulve .... $150-$200

1974 SAN DIEGO - McCovey, Winfield .... $75-$125

1974 SAN FRANCISCO - Kingman, Bonds .... $50-$100

1974 ST LOUIS - Torre, McBride, Brock, Simmons, McCarver, Gibson .... $125-$175

1974 TEXAS - Martin, Hargrove, Harrah, Burroughs, Jenkins .... $100-$145

1975 ATLANTA - Evans, Niekro .... $100-$150

1975 BALTIMORE - Weaver, Robinson, Palmer .... $150-$250

1975 BOSTON - Yastrzemski, Evans, Lynn, Rice, Fisk, Cooper, Conigliaro, McCarver, Tiant .... $375-$550

1975 CALIFORNIA - Ryan .... $200-$275

1975 CHICAGO (AL) - Kaat, Gossage .... $75-$100

1975 CHICAGO (NL) - Madlock .... $75-$125

1983 Detroit Tigers

1975 CINCINNATI - Anderson, Perez, Morgan, Concepcion, Rose, Foster, Bench .... $350-$400
1975 CLEVELAND - Robinson.. $150-$225
1975 DETROIT - Freehan, Horton, Lolich... $75-$115
1975 HOUSTON - Richard .... $65-$95
1975 KANSAS CITY - Brett, Killebrew.. $150-$200
1975 LOS ANGELES - Alston, Garvey, Cey, Buckner, Sutton, John .... $125-$175
1975 MILWAUKEE - Yount, Aaron... $200-$275
1975 MINNESOTA - Carew, Bostock, Oliva, Blyleven .... $200-$300
1975 MONTREAL - Carter .... $75-$125
1975 NEW YORK (AL) - Martin, Nettles, Bonds, Munson, Piniella, Hunter, Lyle, Guidry.. $250-$450
1975 NEW YORK (NL) - Kranepool, Staub, Kingman, Grote, Seaver, Koosman .... $115-$125
1975 OAKLAND - Bando, Jackson, Williams, Blue, Fingers, Odom .... $250-$350
1975 PHILADELPHIA - Allen, Schmidt, Luzinski, Boone, McCarver, Carlton .... $100-$150
1975 PITTSBURGH - Stargell, Parker, Oliver, Candelaria, Tekulve .... $175-$225
1975 SAN DIEGO - McCovey, Winfield.. $85-$125
1975 SAN FRANCISCO - Murcer, Clark.. $45-$100
1975 ST LOUIS - Schoendienst, Brock, Simmons, Hernandez, Gibson............. $100-$150
1975 TEXAS - Martin, Harrah, Jenkins, Perry .... $100-$200
1976 ATLANTA - Murphy, Niekro .... $75-$100

1976 BALTIMORE - Weaver, Jackson, Robinson, Palmer .... $150-$200
1976 BOSTON - Yastrzemski, Evans, Lynn, Rice, Fisk, Cooper, Tiant,
Jenkins .... $175-$300
1976 CALIFORNIA - Ryan.. $125-$175
1976 CHICAGO (AL) - Gossage... $60-$90
1976 CHICAGO (NL) - Madlock .... $60-$90
1976 CINCINNATI - Anderson, Perez, Morgan, Concepcion, Rose, Griffey,
Foster, Bench, Zachry.. $400-$600
1976 CLEVELAND - Robinson, Powell, Bell....................................... $75-$125
1976 DETROIT - Staub, Freehan, Horton, Fidrych............................. $100-$125
1976 HOUSTON - Richard .... $60-$90
1976 KANSAS CITY - Brett.. $125-$200
1976 LOS ANGELES - Alston, Garvey, Cey, Buckner, Sutton, John ... $100-$150
1976 MILWAUKEE - Yount, Aaron, Frisella....................................... $100-$150
1976 MINNESOTA - Carew, Bostock, Oliva, Blyleven .... $75-$125
1976 MONTREAL - Carter, Dawson .... $75-$125
1976 NEW YORK (AL) - Martin, Nettles, Munson, Hunter, Lyle .... $150-$300
1976 NEW YORK (NL) - Kranepool, Harrelson, Kingman, Torre, Koosman,
Seaver, Lolich... $150-$200
1976 OAKLAND - Williams, Blue, Fingers .... $100-$125
1976 PHILADELPHIA - Allen, Bowa, Schmidt, Luzinski, Boone, McCarver,
Carlton, Kaat... $125-$200
1976 PITTSBURGH - Stargell, Parker, Oliver, Candelaria, Tekulve ..... $150-$175
1976 SAN DIEGO - Winfield, McCovey, Jones, Metzger .... $100-$125
1976 SAN FRANCISCO - Evans, Murcer, Clark.................................. $75-$100
1976 ST. LOUIS - Schoendienst, Hernandez, Brock, Simmons .... $125-$200
1976 TEXAS - Harrah, Thompson, Perry, Blyleven .... $75-$100
1977 ATLANTA - Niekro .... $60-$90
1977 BALTIMORE - Weaver, Murray, Robinson, Palmer .... $100-$150
1977 BOSTON - Evans, Lynn, Yastrzemski, Fisk, Rice, Tiant, Jenkins ... $125-$175
1977 CALIFORNIA - Grich, Bonds, Ryan .... $100-$150
1977 CHICAGO (AL) - B. Lemon .... $60-$90
1977 CHICAGO (NL) - Buckner, Trillo, Murcer, R. Reuschel .... $60-$75
1977 CINCINNATI - Anderson, Morgan, Concepcion, Rose, Griffey, Foster,
Bench, Seaver .... $125-$175
1977 CLEVELAND - Robinson, Bell, Eckersley .... $125-$175
1977 DETROIT - Staub, Trammell, Whitaker, Morris.......................... $100-$150
1977 HOUSTON - Richard .... $60-$90
1977 KANSAS CITY - Brett.. $150-$200
1977 LOS ANGELES - Lasorda, Garvey, Cey, Mota, John, Sutton ...... $175-$250
1977 MILWAUKEE - Cooper, Yount... $75-$125
1977 MINNESOTA - Carew, Bostock.. $85-$100
1977 MONTREAL - Perez, Dawson, Carter .... $80-$120
1977 NEW YORK (AL) - Martin, Nettles, Jackson, Munson, Piniella, Guidry,
Lyle, Hunter.. $350-$450
1977 NEW YORK (NL) - Harrelson, Kranepool, Kingman, Grote, Koosman,
Seaver .... $100-$150

1977 OAKLAND - Allen, Armas, Blue .... $60-$90
1977 PHILADELPHIA - Bowa, Schmidt, Luzinski, Boone, McCarver, Carlton,
Kaat .... $125-$175
1977 PITTSBURGH - Stargell, Parker, Oliver, Gossage, Tekulve .... $125-$200
1977 SAN DIEGO - Winfield, Kingman, Fingers.. $100-$150
1977 SAN FRANCISCO - McCovey, Madlock, Clark .... $100-$150
1977 SEATTLE - .... $125-$175
1977 ST. LOUIS - Hernandez, Brock, Simmons .... $80-$120
1977 TEXAS - Perry, Blyleven.. $50-$100
1977 TORONTO.. $150-$200
1978 ATLANTA - Murphy, Horner, Neikro .... $75-$100
1978 BALTIMORE - Weaver, Murray, Palmer .... $125-$175
1978 BOSTON - Evans, Lynn, Yastrzemski, Fisk, Rice, Eckersley .... $100-$150
1978 CALIFORNIA - Bostock, Ryan... $80-$120
1978 CHICAGO (AL) - Bob Lemon .... $60-$90
1978 CHICAGO (NL) - Murcer, Kingman... $60-$90
1978 CINCINNATI - Anderson, Morgan, Concepcion, Rose, Foster, Bench,
Seaver .... $150-$200
1978 CLEVELAND - Bell .... $85-$100
1978 DETROIT - Whitaker, Trammell, Staub, Morris...................................... $100-$150
1978 HOUSTON - Richard .... $60-$90
1978 KANSAS CITY - Brett... $120-$180
1978 LOS ANGELES - Lasorda, Garvey, Cey, Guerrero, John, Sutton .... $150-$225
1978 MILWAUKEE - Molitor, Yount... $80-$120
1978 MINNESOTA - Carew .... $70-$125
1978 MONTREAL - Perez, Dawson, Carter .... $80-$120
1978 NEW YORK (AL) - Martin, Jackson, Lyle, Munson, Guidry, Hunter,
Gossage, Lemon, Piniella .... $275-$400
1978 NEW YORK (NL) - Kranepool, Koosman .... $75-$100
1978 OAKLAND - Armas.. $60-$90
1978 PHILADELPHIA - Schmidt, Luzinski, Boone, Carlton, Kaat.................... $125-$175
1978 PITTSBURGH - Stargell, Parker, Blyleven, Candelaria, Tekulve .... $125-$175
1978 SAN DIEGO - Smith, Winfield, Perry, Fingers .... $125-$175
1978 SAN FRANCISCO - McCovey, Clark, Blue .... $100-$150
1978 SEATTLE -... $60-$90
1978 ST. LOUIS - Boyer, Hernandez, Brock, Simmons................................... $130-$160
1978 TEXAS - Harrah, Oliver, Jenkins .... $75-$100
1978 TORONTO -.. $65-$150
1979 ATLANTA - Murphy, Horner, Niekro .... $75-$125
1979 BALTIMORE - Weaver, Murray, Flanagan, Palmer................................. $175-$250
1979 BOSTON - Lynn, Rice, Fisk, Yastrzemski, Eckersley .... $125-$175
1979 CALIFORNIA - Carew, Lansford, Baylor, Ryan...................................... $125-$175
1979 CHICAGO (AL) - .... $75-$100
1979 CHICAGO (NL) - Buckner, Kingman, Sutter .... $60-$90
1979 CINCINNATI - Morgan, Concepcion, Griffey, Foster, Bench, Seaver
.... $125-$175
1979 CLEVELAND - Harrah.. $60-$90

1979 DETROIT - Anderson, Whitaker, Trammell, Staub, Morris .... $100-$150
1979 HOUSTON - Richard .... $75-$100
1979 KANSAS CITY - Brett, Quisenberry .... $100-$150
1979 LOS ANGELES - Lasorda, Garvey, Cey, Guerrero, Sutcliffe, Sutton .... $100-$150
1979 MILWAUKEE - Molitor, Yount.. $150-$200
1979 MINNESOTA - Castino, Koosman .... $75-$90
1979 MONTREAL - Perez, Dawson, Carter, Staub, Raines .... $100-$150
1979 NEW YORK (AL) - Martin, Nettles, Jackson, Munson, Murcer, John,
Guidry, Tiant, Gossage, Kaat, Hunter .... $175-$250
1979 NEW YORK (NL) - Kranepool .... $85-$100
1979 OAKLAND - Armas, Henderson... $75-$90
1979 PHILADELPHIA - Rose, Trillo, Bowa, Schmidt, Luzinski, Boone,
Carlton, Kaat.. $150-$200
1979 PITTSBURGH - Stargell, Madlock, Parker, Candelaria, Blyleven,
Tekulve .... $275-$375
1979 SAN DIEGO - Smith, Winfield, Perry, Fingers, Lolich............................ $125-$175
1979 SAN FRANCISCO - McCovey, Clark, Madlock, Blue............................. $125-$150
1979 SEATTLE - .... $60-$90
1979 ST. LOUIS - Boyer, Hernandez, Brock, Simmons................................ $125-$175
1979 TEXAS - Bell, Oliver, Jenkins, Lyle .... $65-$95
1979 TORONTO - Griffin, Stieb .... $60-$90
1980 ATLANTA - Horner, Murphy, Niekro .... $90-$125
1980 BALTIMORE - Weaver, Murray, Stone, Palmer .... $150-$225
1980 BOSTON - Perez, Evans, Lynn, Rice, Fisk, Yastrzemski, Eckersley .... $125-$200
1980 CALIFORNIA - Carew, Lansford .... $75-$100
1980 CHICAGO (AL) - Baines .... $60-$90
1980 CHICAGO (NL) - Buckner, Kingman... $60-$90
1980 CINCINNATI - Concepcion, Griffey, Foster, Bench, Seaver .... $75-$100
1980 CLEVELAND - Harrah, Charboneau .... $45-$75
1980 DETROIT - Anderson, Whitaker, Trammell, Gibson, Morris.................... $100-$150
1980 HOUSTON - Morgan, Ryan.. $125-$175
1980 KANSAS CITY - Brett, Quisenberry... $175-$250
1980 LOS ANGELES - Lasorda, Garvey, Guerrero, Welch, Sutton, Howe,
Valenzuela .... $100-$150
1980 MILWAUKEE - Molitor, Yount.. $80-$120
1980 MINNESOTA - Koosman .... $60-$85
1980 MONTREAL - Dawson, Carter, Raines .... $100-$150
1980 NEW YORK (AL) - Nettles, Jackson, Piniella, Murcer, Guidry, Tiant,
Gossage, John, Perry, Kaat... $200-$250
1980 NEW YORK (NL) - Wilson .... $75-$100
1980 OAKLAND - Martin, Henderson .... $140-$210
1980 PHILADELPHIA - Rose, Bowa, Schmidt, Luzinski, Boone, Carlton,
Lyle.. $275-$350
1980 PITTSBURGH - Stargell, Madlock, Parker, Candelaria, Tekulve,
Blyleven.. $150-$175
1980 SAN DIEGO - Smith, Winfield, Fingers... $80-$120
1980 SAN FRANCISCO - Clark, McCovey, Blue .... $75-$120

1988 San Diego Padres

1980 SEATTLE - .... $60-$90
1980 ST. LOUIS - Schoendienst, Hernandez, Simmons, Kaat .... $80-$120
1980 TEXAS - Bell, Oliver, Staub, Jenkins, Perry, Lyle...................................... $75-$100
1980 TORONTO - Stieb .... $60-$90
1981 ATLANTA - Murphy, Butler, Perry, Niekro.. $100-$150
1981 BALTIMORE - Weaver, Murray, Ripken, Palmer...................................... $100-$150
1981 BOSTON - Lansford, Rice, Yastrzemski, Eckersley.................................. $100-$150
1981 CALIFORNIA - Carew, Lynn .... $60-$90
1981 CHICAGO (AL) - Baines, Fisk, Luzinski, Hoyt .... $75-$100
1981 CHICAGO (NL) - Buckner.. $60-$90
1981 CINCINNATI - Concepcion, Griffey, Foster, Bench, Seaver .... $80-$120
1981 CLEVELAND - Harrah, Blyleven .... $60-$90
1981 DETROIT - Anderson, Whitaker, Trammell, Gibson, Morris.................... $100-$125
1981 HOUSTON - Ryan, Sutton .... $100-$125
1981 KANSAS CITY - Brett, Quisenberry .... $75-$100
1981 LOS ANGELES - Garvey, Cey, Guerrero, Sax, Valenzuela, Stewart ....$275-$350
1981 MILWAUKEE - Yount, Molitor, Fingers.. $100-$150
1981 MINNESOTA - .... $60-$90
1981 MONTREAL - Dawson, Raines, Carter .... $150-$175
1981 NEW YORK - Kingman, Staub .... $100-$125
1981 NEW YORK (AL) - Nettles, Jackson, Winfield, Murcer, Piniella, Guidry,
John, Gossage .... $200-$250
1981 OAKLAND - Martin, Henderson .... $125-$200

1981 PHILADELPHIA - Rose, Bowa, Schmidt, Boone, Sandberg, Carlton, Lyle .... $100-$150
1981 PITTSBURGH - Parker, Stargell, Madlock............................... $75-$125
1981 SAN DIEGO - Smith, Kennedy.. $60-$95
1981 SAN FRANCISCO - Morgan, Clark, Blue .... $65-$95
1981 SEATTLE - Henderson .... $50-$85
1981 ST. LOUIS - Hernandez, Kaat... $100-$135
1981 TEXAS - Bell, Oliver, Jenkins... $65-$95
1981 TORONTO - Bell, Barfield, Stieb.. $60-$100
1982 ATLANTA - Murphy, Butler, Niekro .... $90-$150
1982 BALTIMORE - Weaver, Murray, Ripken, Palmer.................... $100-$150
1982 BOSTON - Lansford, Rice, Yastrzemski, Boggs, Perez, Eckersley............ $150-$250
1982 CALIFORNIA - Carew, Jackson, Lynn, Boone, John, Tiant .... $125-$200
1982 CHICAGO (AL) - Baines, Fisk, Luzinski, Hoyt, Lyle .... $75-$125
1982 CHICAGO (NL) - Buckner, Sandberg, Jenkins, Hernandez .... $80-$120
1982 CINCINNATI - Concepcion, Bench, Seaver .... $75-$125
1982 CLEVELAND - Harrah, Blyleven .... $60-$90
1982 DETROIT - Anderson, Whitaker, Trammell, Gibson, Johnson, Morris............$100-$150
1982 HOUSTON - Ryan, Sutton... $75-$125
1982 KANSAS CITY - Brett, Quisenberry... $75-$100
1982 LOS ANGELES - Garvey, Sax, Guerrero, Valenzuela, Stewart .... $100-$150
1982 MILWAUKEE - Yount, Molitor, Vuckovich, Fingers, Sutton.................. $250-$350
1982 MINNESOTA - Hrbek, Brunansky, Viola .... $60-$90
1982 MONTREAL - Oliver, Dawson, Raines, Carter, Reardon......................... $75-$125
1982 NEW YORK (AL) - Lemon, Nettles, Winfield, Piniella, Murcer, Mattingly, John, Guidry, Gossage .... $125-$175
1982 NEW YORK (NL) - Kingman, Foster .... $80-$120
1982 OAKLAND - Martin, Henderson .... $150-$180
1982 PHILADELPHIA - Rose, Schmidt, Carlton, Lyle .... $150-$175
1982 PITTSBURGH - Madlock, Parker, Stargell, Candelaria, Tekulve .... $90-$135
1982 SAN DIEGO - Kennedy, Gwynn .... $80-$120
1982 SAN FRANCISCO - Robinson, Morgan, Clark, Leonard .... $60-$90
1982 SEATTLE - Perry.. $60-$90
1982 ST. LOUIS - Hernandez, Smith, McGee .... $275-$350
1982 TEXAS - Bell.. $60-$90
1982 TORONTO - Barfield, Stieb .... $60-$90
1983 ATLANTA - Murphy, Butler, Niekro .... $60-$90
1983 BALTIMORE - Murray, Ripken, Palmer.................................. $300-$450
1983 BOSTON - Boggs, Rice, Yastrzemski, Eckersley.................... $150-$200
1983 CALIFORNIA - Carew, Lynn, Boone, Jackson, John............... $80-$120
1983 CHICAGO (AL) - Baines, Kittle, Fisk, Hoyt .... $150-$180
1983 CHICAGO (NL) - Buckner, Sandberg, Jenkins, Hernandez .... $100-$150
1983 CINCINNATI - Concepcion, Bench .... $75-$100
1983 CLEVELAND - Franco, Harrah, Blyleven .... $60-$90
1983 DETROIT - Anderson, Whitaker, Trammell, Johnson, Morris .... $125-$150
1983 HOUSTON - Ryan... $100-$150
1983 KANSAS CITY - Brett, Quisenberry, Perry .... $80-$120

1983 LOS ANGELES - Sax, Guerrero, Valenzuela, Welch, Stewart, Hershiser .... $125-$175

1983 MILWAUKEE - Yount, Molitor, Simmons, Fingers .... $100-$200

1983 MINNESOTA - Hrbek, Brunansky, Viola .... $60-$90

1983 MONTREAL - Oliver, Dawson, Raines, Carter .... $75-$100

1983 NEW YORK (AL) - Martin, Nettles, Winfield, Piniella, Murcer, Guidry, Gossage.. $200-$300

1983 NEW YORK (NL) - Strawberry, Foster, Staub, Kingman, Seaver............. $100-$150

1983 OAKLAND - Lansford, Henderson... $75-$85

1983 PHILADELPHIA - Rose, Morgan, Schmidt, Perez, Denny, Hernandez
....$175-$250

1983 PITTSBURGH - Madlock, Parker, Candelaria, Tekulve............................... $60-$90

1983 SAN DIEGO - Garvey, Gwynn .... $100-$150

1983 SAN FRANCISCO - Robinson... $60-$90

1983 SEATTLE - Perry... $60-$90

1983 ST. LOUIS - Smith, McGee, Hernandez .... $100-$125

1983 TEXAS - Bell, Stewart... $60-$90

1983 TORONTO - Bell, Fernandez, Stieb .... $60-$90

1984 ATLANTA - Murphy.. $60-$90

1984 BALTIMORE - Murray, Ripken, Palmer .... $175-$225

1984 BOSTON - Buckner, Boggs, Rice, Clemens .... $85-$110

1984 CALIFORNIA - Carew, Lynn, Boone, Jackson, John................................ $80-$120

1984 CHICAGO (AL) - Baines, Fisk, Seaver.. $75-$90

1984 CHICAGO (NL) - Sandberg, Sutcliffe, Eckersley..................................... $175-$275

1984 CINCINNATI - Rose, Concepcion, Parker, Perez, Davis.......................... $75-$125

1984 CLEVELAND - Franco, Blyleven .... $75-$90

1984 DETROIT - Anderson, Whitaker, Trammell, Johnson, Gibson, Morris, Hernandez.. $350-$500

1984 HOUSTON - Davis, Ryan .... $65-$100

1984 KANSAS CITY - Brett, Saberhagen .... $100-$150

1984 LOS ANGELES - Sax, Guerrero, Valenzuela, Hershiser .... $125-$150

1984 MILWAUKEE - Yount, Sutton .... $100-$125

1984 MINNESOTA - Hrbek, Puckett, Viola .... $85-$150

1984 MONTREAL - Dawson, Raines, Carter, Rose .... $100-$150

1984 NEW YORK (AL) - Berra, Mattingly, Winfield, Piniella, Niekro, Guidry........$125-$175

1984 NEW YORK (NL) - Hernandez, Strawberry, Foster, Gooden .... $125-$150

1984 OAKLAND - Morgan, Lansford, Henderson .... $85-$100

1984 PHILADELPHIA - Schmidt, Carlton.. $100-$150

1984 PITTSBURGH - Madlock, Candelaria, Tekulve .... $65-$90

1984 SAN DIEGO - Garvey, Nettles, Gwynn, Gossage .... $175-$250

1984 SAN FRANCISCO - Oliver, Leonard, Clark... $75-$90

1984 SEATTLE - Davis, Tartabull, Langston.. $60-$90

1984 ST. LOUIS - O. Smith, McGee .... $125-$150

1984 TEXAS - Stewart .... $60-$90

1984 TORONTO - Bell, Fernandez, Stieb .... $100-$125

1985 ATLANTA - Murphy.. $60-$90

1985 BALTIMORE - Weaver, Murray, Ripken, Lynn.. $50-$85

1942 New York Yankees

1941 New York Yankees

1952 St. Louis Browns

1929 Washington Senators

1985 BOSTON - Boggs, Rice, Clemens... $60-$90
1985 CALIFORNIA - Carew, Jackson, Boone, Sutton, John.............................. $80-$120
1985 CHICAGO (AL) - Guillen, Baines, Fisk, Seaver...................................... $75-$100
1985 CHICAGO (NL) - Sandberg, Eckersley .... $60-$90
1985 CINCINNATI - Rose, Concepcion, Parker, Perez, Davis........................... $75-$125
1985 CLEVELAND - Franco, Carter, Blyleven .... $50-$85
1985 DETROIT - Anderson, Whitaker, Trammell, Gibson, Morris...................... $75-$125
1985 HOUSTON - Davis, Ryan .... $75-$100
1985 KANSAS CITY - Brett, Saberhagen .... $300-$400
1985 LOS ANGELES - Sax, Oliver, Hershiser, Valenzuela .... $60-$150
1985 MILWAUKEE - Yount, Fingers.. $60-$90
1985 MINNESOTA - Hrbek, Puckett, Viola, Blyleven .... $75-$100
1985 MONTREAL - Dawson, Raines .... $45-$75
1985 NEW YORK (AL) - Berra, Martin, Mattingly, Winfield, Henderson,
Guidry, Niekro... $125-$175
1985 NEW YORK (NL) - Hernandez, Johnson, Strawberry, Foster, Carter,
Gooden... $200-$300
1985 OAKLAND - Lansford, Kingman, Sutton... $60-$90
1985 PHILADELPHIA - Schmidt, Carlton.. $75-$100
1985 PITTSBURGH - Madlock... $60-$90
1985 SAN DIEGO - Garvey, Nettles, Gwynn, Gossage .... $75-$100

1985 SAN FRANCISCO - Leonard .... $60-$90
1985 SEATTLE - Tartabull, Langston .... $60-$90
1985 ST. LOUIS - Clark, McGee, Coleman .... $175-$250
1985 TEXAS - Harrah .... $70-$95
1985 TORONTO - Fernandez, Bell, Fielder, Stieb .... $100-$150
1986 ATLANTA - Murphy .... $50-$80
1986 BALTIMORE - Weaver, Murray, Ripken, Lynn .... $75-$100
1986 BOSTON - Boggs, Rice, Clemens, Seaver .... $200-$400
1986 CALIFORNIA - Joyner, Boone, Jackson, Sutton .... $60-$90
1986 CHICAGO (AL) - Baines, Fisk, Carlton, Seaver .... $75-$100
1986 CHICAGO (NL) - Sandberg, Palmeiro, Eckersley .... $75-$100
1986 CINCINNATI - Parker, Davis, Concepcion, Perez, Rose .... $60-$90
1986 CLEVELAND - Franco, Carter, Niekro .... $60-$75
1986 DETROIT - Anderson, Whitaker, Trammell, Gibson, Morris .... $100-$125
1986 HOUSTON - Davis, Scott, Ryan .... $75-$100
1986 KANSAS CITY - Howser, Brett, Jackson, Saberhagen .... $60-$90
1986 LOS ANGELES - Guerrero, Valenzuela, Hershiser .... $75-$100
1986 MILWAUKEE - Yount .... $50-$75
1986 MINNESOTA - Hrbek, Puckett, Blyleven, Viola .... $80-$120
1986 MONTREAL - Dawson, Raines .... $50-$75
1986 NEW YORK (AL) - Mattingly, Winfield, Henderson, Guidry, John .... $125-$200
1986 NEW YORK (NL) - Hernandez, Strawberry, Carter, Mitchell, Foster,
Gooden .... $350-$525
1986 OAKLAND - Canseco, McGwire, Stewart .... $100-$125
1986 PHILADELPHIA - Schmidt, Carlton .... $75-$100
1986 PITTSBURGH - Bonds, Bonilla .... $50-$75
1986 SAN DIEGO - Garvey, Gwynn, Gossage .... $60-$75
1986 SAN FRANCISCO - Clark, Carlton .... $50-$75
1986 SEATTLE - Tartabull, Langston .... $60-$75
1986 ST. LOUIS - Smith, McGee .... $75-$100
1986 TEXAS - Sierra .... $60-$75
1986 TORONTO - Fernandez, Bell, Stieb .... $60-$75
1987 ATLANTA - Murphy, Niekro .... $50-$75
1987 BALTIMORE - Murray, Ripken, Lynn .... $60-$85
1987 BOSTON - Boggs, Rice, Clemens .... $75-$100
1987 CALIFORNIA - Joyner, Boone, Buckner, Sutton .... $65-$80
1987 CHICAGO (AL) - Fisk, Baines .... $75-$115
1987 CHICAGO (NL) - Sandberg, Dawson, Palmeiro .... $50-$75
1987 CINCINNATI - Rose, Parker, Davis, Concepcion .... $75-$100
1987 CLEVELAND - Carter, Franco, Niekro, Carlton .... $75-$100
1987 DETROIT - Anderson, Whitaker, Trammell, Gibson, Morris .... $175-$200
1987 HOUSTON - Davis, Ryan .... $100-$165
1987 KANSAS CITY - Brett, Tartabull, Jackson, Saberhagen .... $85-$100
1987 LOS ANGELES - Lasorda, Sax, Guerrero, Hershiser, Valenzuela .... $80-$120
1987 MILWAUKEE - Yount .... $45-$90
1987 MINNESOTA - Hrbek, Puckett, Viola, Blyleven, Carlton .... $300-$400
1987 MONTREAL - Raines .... $75-$100

1987 NEW YORK (AL) - Mattingly, Henderson, Winfield, John, Guidry .... $100-$150
1987 NEW YORK (NL) - Hernandez, Johnson, Strawberry, Carter,
Gooden.. $150-$175
1987 OAKLAND - McGwire, Canseco, Jackson, Stewart, Eckersley .... $100-$150
1987 PHILADELPHIA - Schmidt... $50-$75
1987 PITTSBURGH - Bonilla, Van Slyke, Bonds .... $75-$100
1987 SAN DIEGO - Gwynn, Garvey, Gossage.. $50-$75
1987 SAN FRANCISCO - Clark, Mitchell, Williams .... $100-$150
1987 SEATTLE - Langston.. $50-$75
1987 ST. LOUIS - Smith, McGee .... $175-$225
1987 TEXAS - Sierra.. $60-$90
1987 TORONTO - Fernandez, Bell, McGriff, Stieb, Niekro.............................. $75-$100
1988 ATLANTA - Murphy.. $50-$80
1988 BALTIMORE - Robinson, Murray, Ripken, Lynn...................................... $75-$100
1988 BOSTON - Boggs, Rice, Clemens... $75-$125
1988 CALIFORNIA - Joyner, Boone, Buckner.. $60-$75
1988 CHICAGO (AL) - Fisk, Baines .... $65-$75
1988 CHICAGO (NL) - Grace, Sandberg, Dawson, Palmeiro, Gossage .... $50-$80
1988 CINCINNATI - Sabo .... $75-$100
1988 CLEVELAND - Franco, Carter.. $50-$75
1988 DETROIT - Whitaker, Trammell, Lynn, Morris.. $85-$100
1988 HOUSTON - Davis, Ryan .... $75-$125
1988 KANSAS CITY - Brett, Tartabull, Jackson, Buckner, Saberhagen .... $100-$125
1988 LOS ANGELES - Sax, Gibson, Hershiser, Valenzuela...................... $200-$300
1988 MILWAUKEE - Yount.. $50-$75
1988 MINNESOTA - Hrbek, Puckett, Viola, Blyleven, Carlton .... $60-$85
1988 MONTREAL - Raines.. $50-$75
1988 NEW YORK (AL) - Martin, Mattingly, Winfield, Henderson, John,
Guidry .... $150-$200
1988 NEW YORK (NL) - Hernandez, Johnson, Strawberry, Carter, Gooden ....$75-$150
1988 OAKLAND - McGwire, Lansford, Canseco, Parker, Stewart, Welch,
Eckersley.. $200-$250
1988 PHILADELPHIA - Schmidt... $75-$100
1988 PITTSBURGH - Bonilla, Van Slyke, Bonds, Drabek .... $50-$75
1988 SAN DIEGO - Gwynn .... $60-$80
1988 SAN FRANCISCO - Clark, Mitchell, Williams .... $60-$85
1988 SEATTLE - Langston... $50-$75
1988 ST. LOUIS - Smith, McGee, Guerrero... $45-$70
1988 TEXAS - Sierra .... $50-$75
1988 TORONTO - McGriff, Fernandez, Bell, Stieb.. $60-$85
1989 ATLANTA - Murphy.. $100-$150
1989 BALTIMORE - Robinson, Ripken .... $75-$125
1989 BOSTON - Boggs, Clemens .... $75-$100
1989 CALIFORNIA - Joyner, Blyleven .... $50-$75
1989 CHICAGO (AL) - Fisk, Baines .... $50-$75
1989 CHICAGO (NL) - Grace, Sandberg, Dawson .... $150-$225
1989 CINCINNATI - Davis.. $50-$85

1989 CLEVELAND - Carter .... $50-$75
1989 DETROIT - Anderson, Trammell, Lynn, Morris .... $50-$75
1989 HOUSTON - Davis .... $40-$60
1989 KANSAS CITY - Brett, Jackson, Boone, Tartabull, Saberhagen .... $100-$150
1989 LOS ANGELES - Lasorda, Murray, Randolph, Gibson, Hershiser, Valenzuela .... $125-$175
1989 MILWAUKEE - Yount .... $90-$125
1989 MINNESOTA - Hrbek, Puckett, Viola .... $50-$85
1989 MONTREAL - Raines .... $75-$100
1989 NEW YORK (AL) - Mattingly, Sax, Winfield, Gossage .... $125-$150
1989 NEW YORK (NL) - Johnson, Strawberry, Hernandez, Carter, Gooden .... $75-$145
1989 OAKLAND - LaRussa, McGwire, Canseco, D. Henderson, R. Henderson, Parker, Stewart, Eckersley .... $225-$300
1989 PHILADELPHIA - Dykstra, Schmidt .... $60-$100
1989 PITTSBURGH - Bonilla, Van Slyke, Bonds .... $75-$100
1989 SAN DIEGO - Clark, Gwynn .... $50-$85
1989 SAN FRANCISCO - Clark, Williams, Mitchell, Gossage .... $150-$200
1989 SEATTLE - Griffey Jr. .... $175-$250
1989 ST. LOUIS - Guerrero, Smith, McGee .... $85-$125
1989 TEXAS - Palmeiro, Franco, Sierra, Baines, Ryan .... $75-$100
1989 TORONTO - McGriff, Fernandez, Stieb .... $100-$150
1990 ATLANTA - Justice, Murphy .... $100-$175
1990 BALTIMORE - F. Robinson, C. Ripken Jr. .... $75-$100
1990 BOSTON - Boggs, Clemens .... $100-$150
1990 CALIFORNIA - Joyner, Winfield, Blyleven .... $75-$100
1990 CHICAGO (AL) - Fisk .... $50-$85
1990 CHICAGO (NL) - Dawson, Grace, Sandberg .... $100-$135
1990 CINCINNATI - Larkin, Davis, Piniella .... $225-$300
1990 CLEVELAND - Hernandez .... $40-$60
1990 DETROIT - Anderson, Fielder, Morris, Trammell, Whitaker .... $75-$100
1990 HOUSTON - Davis .... $40-$60
1990 KANSAS CITY - Brett, Tartabull, Jackson, Saberhagen .... $75-$125
1990 LOS ANGELES - Lasorda, Murray, Gibson, Valenzuela .... $85-$125
1990 MILWAUKEE - Yount, Molitor, Parker .... $50-$75
1990 MINNESOTA - Hrbek, Puckett .... $50-$85
1990 MONTREAL - Raines .... $50-$85
1990 NEW YORK (AL) - Mattingly .... $125-$175
1990 NEW YORK (NL) - Strawberry, Johnson, Viola, Gooden .... $100-$125
1990 OAKLAND - McGwire, Randolph, Canseco, R. Henderson, D. Henderson, Baines, McGee, Welch, Stewart, Eckersley .... $150-$200
1990 PHILADELPHIA - Dykstra, Murphy .... $40-$60
1990 PITTSBURGH - Bonds, Bonilla, Van Slyke, Drabek .... $100-$135
1990 SAN DIEGO - Gwynn, Carter, Clark .... $50-$75
1990 SAN FRANCISCO - Clark, Mitchell, Williams .... $75-$100
1990 SEATTLE - Ken Griffey Jr., Ken Griffey Sr. .... $75-$100
1990 ST. LOUIS - Guerrero, Smith, McGee .... $50-$85
1990 TEXAS - Palmeiro, Franco, Sierra, Ryan .... $85-$100

1989 St. Louis Cardinals

1990 TORONTO - McGriff, Stieb, Fernandez .... $60-$85
1991 ATLANTA - Glavine, Pendleton... $150-$200
1991 BALTIMORE - F. Robinson, C. Ripken .... $65-$100
1991 BOSTON - Boggs, Clemens .... $80-$100
1991 CALIFORNIA - Joyner, Winfield .... $45-$65
1991 CHICAGO (AL) - Fisk, Thomas .... $85-$150
1991 CHICAGO (NL) - Sandberg, Dawson .... $75-$100
1991 CINCINNATI - Larkin, Davis, Piniella .... $65-$85
1991 CLEVEIAND - Swindell... $45-$75
1991 DETROIT - Anderson, Whitaker, Trammell, Fielder .... $75-$100
1991 HOUSTON - Bagwell, Harnisch .... $50-$75
1991 KANSAS CITY - Brett, Saberhagen, Tartabull .... $85-$100
1991 LOS ANGELES - Lasorda, Murray, Strawberry .... $65-$90
1991 MILWAUKEE - Yount, Molitor... $85-$100
1991 MINNESOTA - Knoblauch, Morris, Puckett, Hrbek .... $150-$225
1991 MONTREAL - Calderon... $30-$50
1991 NEW YORK (AL) - Mattingly .... $75-$125
1991 NEW YORK (NL) - Johnson, Gooden, Viola... $60-$90
1991 OAKLAND - R. Henderson, Stewart, Eckersley, Canseco .... $80-$120
1991 PHILADELPHIA - Dykstra, Murphy... $50-$85
1991 PITTSBURGH - Bonds, Bonilla... $100-$150
1991 SAN DIEGO - Gwynn, McGriff, Fernandez .... $50-$80
1991 SAN FRANCISCO - Mitchell, Clark... $40-$60

1990 Pittsburgh Pirates

1991 SEATTLE - Griffey Jr., Griffey Sr... $75-$100
1991 ST. LOUIS - O. Smith, L. Smith .... $45-$60
1991 TEXAS - Franco, Ryan, Sierra, Palmeiro .... $60-$85
1991 TORONTO - Carter, Alomar, Stieb .... $80-$125
1992 ATLANTA - Pendleton, Justice, Glavine $325
1992 BALTIMORE - Devereaux, Ripken, Mussina.. $115
1992 BOSTON - Boggs, Clemens $100
1992 CALIFORNIA - Langston $75
1992 CHICAGO (AL) - Thomas, McDowell $85
1992 CHICAGO (NL) - Maddux, Grace, Dawson, Sandberg $125
1992 CINCINNATI - Larkin, Rijo.. $85
1992 CLEVELAND - Baerga, Belle, Nagy $100
1992 DETROIT - Fryman, Whitaker, Trammell, Fielder $85
1992 HOUSTON - Biggio, Bagwell... $40
1992 KANSAS CITY - Brett, Jefferies, Joyner... $85
1992 LOS ANGELES - Karros, Butler $80
1992 MILWAUKEE - Listach, Yount, Eldred, Molitor $60
1992 MINNESOTA - Puckett, Knoblauch... $85
1992 MONTREAL - Grissom, Walker, Martinez... $50
1992 NEW YORK (AL) - Mattingly $90
1992 NEW YORK (NL) - Murray, Bonilla, Cone.. $85
1992 OAKLAND - Eckersley, McGwire, Henderson, Canseco.................................. $150
1992 PHILADELPHIA - Hollins, Dykstra, Kruk, Schilling, Daulton $100

1992 PITTSBURGH - Bonds, Van Slyke, Drabek......................................$125
1992 SAN DIEGO - Gwynn, Sheffield, McGriff.....................................$85
1992 SAN FRANCISCO - Clark, Williams..$110
1992 SEATTLE - Griffey Jr., Martinez..$115
1992 ST. LOUIS - O. Smith, L. Smith, Lankford $60
1992 TEXAS - Sierra, Gonzalez..$125
1992 TORONTO - Alomar, Carter, Winfield, Morris $200
1993 ATLANTA - Maddux, McGriff...$250
1993 BALTIMORE - Ripken, Mussina...$115
1993 BOSTON - Dawson, Clemens, Vaughn..$80
1993 CALIFORNIA - Salmon, Langston...$75
1993 CHICAGO (AL) - Thomas, McDowell $175
1993 CHICAGO (NL) - Sandberg, Grace..$85
1993 CINCINNATI - Larkin, Rijo...$45
1993 CLEVELAND - Baerga, Belle, Nagy $125
1993 COLORADO - Galarraga, Hayes...$150
1993 DETROIT - Whitaker, Trammell, Fielder.......................................$90
1993 FLORIDA - Harvey, Weiss, Destrade...$150
1993 HOUSTON - Swindell, Drabek, Bagwell...$40
1993 KANSAS CITY - Brett, Cone $125
1993 LOS ANGELES - Piazza, Karros..$150
1993 MILWAUKEE - Listach, Hamilton, Vaughn, Yount $50
1993 MINNESOTA - Puckett, Winfield...$100
1993 MONTREAL - D. Martinez, Grissom, Walker.....................................$50
1993 NEW YORK (AL) - Boggs, Mattingly $115
1993 NEW YORK (NL) - Bonilla, Murray, Gooden.....................................$75
1993 OAKLAND - Sierra, McGwire, Eckersley..$75
1993 PHILADELPHIA - Schilling, Dykstra, Kruk, Daulton............................$300
1993 PITTSBURGH - Van Slyke, Bell..$95
1993 SAN DIEGO - Gwynn, Sheffield..$80
1993 SAN FRANCISCO - Bonds, Clark..$150
1993 SEATTLE - Griffey Jr., R. Johnson $85
1993 ST. LOUIS - O. Smith, Lankford $50
1993 TEXAS - Ryan, Gonzalez, Canseco...$125
1993 TORONTO - Alomar, Molitor, Carter, Olerud, Stewart..........................$200
1994 ATLANTA - Maddux, McGriff...$275
1994 BALTIMORE - Ripken, Mussina...$125
1994 BOSTON - Greenwell, Clemens, Vaughn...$125
1994 CALIFORNIA - Salmon, Langston, Edmonds $95
1994 CHICAGO (AL) - Thomas, McDowell, Ventura $125
1994 CHICAGO (NL) - Sandberg, Grace..$95
1994 CINCINNATI - Larkin...$65
1994 CLEVELAND - Baerga, Belle, Lofton, Martinez, Nagy $175
1994 COLORADO - Galarraga, Hayes...$150
1994 DETROIT - Whitaker, Trammell, Fielder, Anderson.............................$95
1994 FLORIDA - Sheffield, Harvey $75
1994 HOUSTON - Drabek, Bagwell...$50

1994 KANSAS CITY - Appier, Cone $95
1994 LOS ANGELES - Piazza, Karros..$150
1994 MILWAUKEE - Eldred, Vaughn $85
1994 MINNESOTA - Puckett, Winfield, Knoblauch..$110
1994 MONTREAL - D. Martinez, Grissom, Walker...$60
1994 NEW YORK (AL) - Boggs, Mattingly, Key, Abbott $125
1994 NEW YORK (NL) - Bonilla..$75
1994 OAKLAND - Sierra, McGwire, Eckersley...$110
1994 PHILADELPHIA - Dykstra, Kruk, Daulton $250
1994 PITTSBURGH - Van Slyke, Bell $85
1994 SAN DIEGO - Gwynn...$80
1994 SAN FRANCISCO - Bonds, Clark..$150
1994 SEATTLE - Griffey Jr., R. Johnson, Piniella..$85
1994 ST. LOUIS - O. Smith, Lankford $65
1994 TEXAS - Ryan, Gonzalez, Canseco...$125
1994 TORONTO - Alomar, Molitor, Carter, Olerud, Stewart...............................$125
1995 ATLANTA - $250
1995 BALTIMORE - $125
1995 BOSTON - $110
1995 CALIFORNIA - $125
1995 CHICAGO (AL) - $110
1995 CHICAGO (NL) - $145
1995 CINCINNATI - $150
1995 CLEVELAND - $250
1995 COLORADO - $135
1995 DETROIT - $100
1995 FLORIDA - $175
1995 HOUSTON - $125
1995 KANSAS CITY - $90
1995 LOS ANGELES - $125
1995 MILWAUKEE -.. $75
1995 MINNESOTA - $90
1995 MONTREAL - $110
1995 NEW YORK (AL) - $125
1995 NEW YORK (NL) - $95
1995 OAKLAND - $75
1995 PHILADELPHIA - $95
1995 PITTSBURGH - $100
1995 SAN DIEGO - $90
1995 SAN FRANCISCO - $140
1995 SEATTLE - $150
1995 ST. LOUIS - $125
1995 TEXAS - $125
1995 TORONTO - $100

Autographed All-Star Baseballs

Key signatures follow each team name

1937 American League All-Stars

1933 American League All-Star Team - Mack, Collins, Gehrig, Ruth.......... $6500-$9750
1933 National League All-Star Team - McGraw, Traynor, Waner, Frisch........... $2500-$3500
1934 American League All-Star Team - Gehrig, Ruth, Foxx .... $5750-$8500
1934 National League All-Star Team - Ott, Traynor, Vaughan, Waner .... $2000-$3000
1935 American League All-Star Team - Foxx, Gehrig, Hornsby .... $4000-$6000
1935 National League All-Star Team - Frisch, Ott, Vaughan........................ $1400-$2100
1936 American League All-Star Team - Foxx, Gehrig, DiMaggio .... $5000-$7500
1936 National League All-Star Team - Ott, Vaughan, Traynor..................... $1200-$1800
1937 American League All-Star Team - Foxx, DiMaggio, Gehrig .... $4500-$6750
1937 National League All-Star Team - Frisch, Ott, Vaughan........................ $1500-$2350
1938 American League All-Star Team - Foxx, DiMaggio, Gehrig .... $4500-$6800
1938 National League All-Star Team - Ott, Vaughan, Frisch........................ $1200-$1800
1939 American League All-Star Team - Foxx, DiMaggio, Gehrig .... $4000-$6000
1939 National League All-Star Team - Ott, Vaughan..................................... $800-$1200
1940 American League All-Star Team - Foxx, Williams, DiMaggio................ $600-$850
1940 National League All-Star Team - Ott, Vaughan..................................... $750-$1200
1941 American League All-Star Team - Foxx, Williams, DiMaggio................ $600-$900
1941 National League All-Star Team - Ott, Vaughan..................................... $650-$1000
1942 American League All-Star Team - Williams, Joe DiMaggio.................... $500-$750

1954 National League All-Stars

1942 National League All-Star Team - McKechnie, Frisch, Ott, Vaughan ....$700-$1200
1943 American League All-Star Team - McCarthy.. $400-$600
1943 National League All-Star Team - Frisch, Ott, Musial .... $500-$750
1944 American League All-Star Team - McCarthy, Cronin............................ $400-$600
1944 National League All-Star Team - Wagner, Ott, Musial .... $500-$750
1945 (There was no All-Star Game)
1946 American League All-Star Team - Williams, DiMaggio......................... $450-$675
1946 National League All-Star Team - Musial .... $500-$750
1947 American League All-Star Team - Williams, DiMaggio .... $500-$725
1947 National League All-Star Team - Ott, Musial .... $525-$800
1948 American League All-Star Team - Williams, DiMaggio......................... $475-$750
1948 National League All-Star Team - Ott, Musial .... $525-$800
1949 American League All-Star Team - Williams, DiMaggio......................... $475-$750
1949 National League All-Star Team - Campanella, Robinson, Musial........... $550-$850
1950 American League All-Star Team - Williams, DiMaggio .... $500-$750
1950 National League All-Star Team - Campanella, Robinson, Musial........... $550-$850
1951 American League All-Star Team - Williams, J. DiMaggio .... $500-$725
1951 National League All-Star Team - Campanella, Robinson, Musial........... $575-$875
1952 American League All-Star Team - Mantle, Paige.................................. $800-$1300
1952 National League All-Star Team - Campanella, Robinson, Musial........... $575-$825
1953 American League All-Star Team - Mantle, Williams, Paige .... $500-$725
1953 National League All-Star Team - Campanella, Robinson, Musial........... $550-$850
1954 American League All-Star Team - Williams, Mantle .... $450-$675
1954 National League All-Star Team - Campanella, Robinson, Musial........... $550-$825
1955 American League All-Star Team - Williams, Mantle .... $400-$600
1955 National League All-Star Team - Musial .... $400-$600
1956 American League All-Star Team - Williams, Mantle, Berra, Martin, Ford .... $450-$675

1971 American League All-Stars

1956 National League All-Star Team - Campanella, Musial .... $500-$750
1957 American League All-Star Team - Williams, Mantle .... $400-$600
1957 National League All-Star Team - Musial .... $400-$600
1958 American League All-Star Team - Williams, Mantle, Martin, Berra,
Ford .... $500-$800
1958 National League All-Star Team - Musial .... $700-$900
1959 American League All-Star Team - Williams, Mantle .... $400-$600
1959 American League 2nd Game All-Stars - Mantle, Maris, Williams .... $475-$725
1959 National League All-Star Team - Musial .... $400-$575
1959 National League 2nd Game All-Stars - Musial .... $400-$575
1960 American League All-Star Team, both teams - Mantle, Maris .... $475-$700
1960 National League All-Star Team, both teams - Clemente .... $425-$650
1961 American League All-Star Team - Mantle, Maris .... $500-$750
1961 American League 2nd Game All-Stars - Mantle, Maris .... $500-$725
1961 National League All-Star Team - Clemente .... $450-$650
1961 National League 2nd Game All-Stars - Clemente .... $450-$650
1962 American League All-Star Team - Mantle, Maris .... $400-$600
1962 American League 2nd Game All-Stars - Mantle, Maris .... $400-$600
1962 National League All-Star Team - Clemente .... $420-$630
1962 National League 2nd Game All-Stars - Clemente .... $425-$625
1963 American League All-Star Team - Fox, Yastrzemski .... $325-$425
1963 National League All-Star Team - Musial, Clemente .... $375-$550
1964 American League All-Star Team - Mantle .... $325-$500
1964 National League All-Star Team - Clemente .... $400-$600
1965 American League All-Star Team - Kaline, Killebrew .... $325-$450
1965 National League All-Star Team - Clemente .... $450-$675
1966 American League All-Star Team - .... $375-$550

1966 National League All-Star Team - Clemente .... $400-$600
1967 American League All-Star Team - Mantle .... $375-$550
1967 National League All-Star Team - Clemente .... $400-$600
1968 American League All-Star Team - Mantle .... $350-$525
1968 National League All-Star Team - .... $350-$525
1969 American League All-Star Team - Williams .... $350-$525
1969 National League All-Star Team - Clemente .... $400-$600
1970 American League All-Star Team - .... $325-$500
1970 National League All-Star Team - Hodges, Clemente .... $400-$600
1971 American League All-Star Team - Munson, Martin .... $375-$550
1971 National League All-Star Team - Clemente .... $400-$600
1972 American League All-Star Team - .... $300-$450
1972 National League All-Star Team - Clemente .... $400-$600
1973 American League All-Star Team - Munson .... $325-$500
1973 National League All-Star Team - .... $300-$450
1974 American League All-Star Team - .... $325-$500
1974 National League All-Star Team - .... $325-$500
1975 American League All-Star Team - Munson, Martin .... $325-$500
1975 National League All-Star Team - .... $300-$425
1976 American League All-Star Team - Munson .... $325-$500
1976 National League All-Star Team - .... $300-$425
1977 American League All-Star Team - Munson, Martin .... $350-$550
1977 National League All-Star Team - .... $275-$425
1978 American League All-Star Team - Martin .... $300-$450
1978 National League All-Star Team - .... $275-$425
1979 American League All-Star Team - .... $300-$450
1979 National League All-Star Team - .... $300-$450
1980 American League All-Star Team - .... $300-$425
1980 National League All-Star Team - .... $250-$375
1981 American League All-Star Team - .... $300-$425
1981 National League All-Star Team - .... $300-$425
1982 American League All-Star Team - .... $300-$450
1982 National League All-Star Team - .... $275-$400
1983 American League All-Star Team - .... $250-$375
1983 National League All-Star Team - .... $250-$375
1984 American League All-Star Team - .... $250-$375
1984 National League All-Star Team - .... $250-$375
1985 American League All-Star Team - .... $250-$375
1985 National League All-Star Team - .... $275-$425
1986 American League All-Star Team - .... $250-$375
1986 National League All-Star Team - .... $250-$375
1987 American League All-Star Team - .... $250-$375
1987 National League All-Star Team - .... $250-$375
1988 American League All-Star Team - .... $225-$350
1988 National League All-Star Team - .... $225-$350
1989 American League All-Star Team - .... $225-$350
1989 National League All-Star Team - .... $225-$350

Collectors can pursue several options for autographed baseballs.

1990 American League All-Star Team - .... $225-$350
1990 National League All-Star Team - .... $225-$350
1991 American League All-Star Team - .... $150-$200
1991 National League All-Star Team - .... $150-$200
1992 American League All-Star Team - .... $150-$225
1992 National League All-Star Team - .... $125-$200
1993 American League All-Star Team - .... $100-$150
1993 National League All-Star Team - .... $100-$150
1994 American League All-Star Team - $250
1994 National League All-Star Team - $250
1995 American League All-Star Team - $300
1995 National League All-Star Team - $275

Uniforms

It's best to try to find a dealer who has a wide variety of jerseys in his inventory.

"Flannels," which often contain other materials such as wool, cotton or a blend of various fibers, are the pot of gold at the end of the uniform rainbow. In today's marketplace, more than 80 percent of the flannels offered for sale or trade were not used before 1960. Flannels were used in major league baseball until 1973, when doubleknits, made primarily of polyester-based fabrics, were introduced over three seasons (1970-1972). Since that time, mesh jerseys, not unlike those used by many teams in the other major sports, have been worn, too, generally as pregame jerseys for batting practice or spring training exhibition contests.

Pregame jerseys are not as sought-after as game-used jerseys, due to the lack of names on backs, the pullover design, and screened-on logos and numbers. Plus, the cheaper quality fabric on many styles, individually or in combinations, leaves the genre relegated to team collectors and budget-minded collectors unable to afford authentic game garb. Lack of year/set/etc. tagging in most teams' offerings hurts the demand as well, although pregame jerseys, due to lack of demand, are far less likely to be forged.

Until the early 1980s, most baseball teams held an elitist mindset - making uniforms available to regular fans was off-base; the average fan was not worthy of owning a hallowed piece of history. Some jerseys made it into circulation through charity auctions or the occasional lucky fan who wrote to a team and actually got one back in the mail. But, unfortunately, much of what made it into circulation in those days was either stolen or obtained through bribes and payoffs to clubhouse people and security personnel. Thus, many authentic shirts were "hot."

Changes in that elitist mindset began to occur in 1978, when the Philadelphia Phillies sold an entire lot of 1977 game-used jerseys to a New Jersey dealer, who then advertised them in hobby papers. This practice of bulk sales to dealers has been continued by many teams in all sports today, allowing the team to sell all of the items at once, at a set price per shirt. This has eliminated the need to have team employees individually price the items. Some teams, however, also filter individually-priced items into the market through their own outlets and shops, publicity caravans, or through charity auctions, which are not as popular with mainstream collectors because oftentimes bidding escalates to ridiculously high levels.

Shirts bought in bulk from the teams generally make their way to buyers at baseball card shows, through mail order catalogs, and in advertisements in hobby publications. Because the initial seller was the team itself, the authenticity of these jerseys is virtually uncontested.

Game-used equipment collectors consider a truly authentic item as having been issued by the team whose logo or name appears on the jersey and must have been worn by the player in question discernibly. It doesn't have to be falling apart, but it shouldn't be fresh off the rack, either, and should show some evidence of laundering.

Two points to consider in establishing authenticity include wear and tagging. A jersey used for an entire season should show some sort of visible wear. The collar and perhaps the armpits should indicate sweat, or laundering out of that perspiration. Letters and numbers on the jersey should feature an even degree of wear; the edges of the characters may be a bit frayed, the letters and numbers may be loose in one or several locations, and the numbers or scripting may be wrinkled or shrunken a wee bit.

Several types of tags exist, and vary in color, design and location. Year tags depicts depict the year of issuance for a jersey. Most often, these embroideries are done on a piece of fabric that is then affixed to the jersey itself. Strip tags are either embroidered or printed (screened) and are shaped in strip fashion, that is, an accentuated rectangular shape with a line of information running horizontally on an even plane. Flag tags are any tags attached to the jersey on only one edge, normally underneath an adjoining, larger tag (such as a manufacturer's label). In some instances, it may be attached underneath a jersey seam or even occasionally be attached to the jersey.

Name tags identify the name of a player who was originally issued the jersey. With only rare exceptions, name tags have only a player's last name. They are generally embroidered, and affixed to a strip-style tag that itself is sewn into the jersey. Name tags come in two varieties, based on their location on the jersey. Tags affixed to the inside back of the shirt collar are classified as "name in collar" tags, usually referred to on sale lists and in inventories as "NIC." Or, the tag may be included in the shirt's tail, with the corresponding notation being "NIT," for "name in tail." Variations of "NIT" include "NOT" (name on tail) and "NIF" or "NOF" (name in/on flap).

Extra length tags, used mainly by Rawlings, were of the flag variety for several years after their late-1970s introduction and are attached on all sides thereafter. They denote extra inches added into a jersey's sizing, done usually for taller players.

Before 1987, several manufacturers supplied major league teams with their game jerseys. Wilson, a Chicago-based firm, was predominant. Notable runnersup included Rawlings, Sand-Knit, Goodman, McAuliffe, and, in the flannel era, MacGregor and Spalding. However, in 1987, Rawlings stepped up as the first designated "official" supplier of Major League Baseball, done at Commissioner Peter Ueberroth's request.

Rawlings, based in the St. Louis area, emerged victorious, and, from 1987-91, made all game attire for 21 of the 26 teams and some for three others. At the end of 1991, Rawlings' agreement with the major leagues ended and Russell, an Atlanta-based firm with experience in football and basketball, but not major league baseball, was awarded the new contract.

Your best bet for obtaining authentic items secondhand (i.e., not from the team directly nor from team outlets) is to visit experienced dealers in the field, whose identities can be learned through reading hobby publications and magazines, or visiting card conventions and through recommendations from card and hobby shops. Dealers who have made bulk purchases of numerous items from one or several teams are a good bet, as are dealers with proven experience and longevity in the field. A dealer with an inventory featuring a varied mix of commons, minor stars and superstars is a better possibility than someone who only carries top-of-the-line players in ample quantities.

Uniform dealers, of course, are still the most frequent and diversely inventoried source for game-used uniform acquisitions. Many such dealers advertise through display or classified advertising in hobby papers and magazines. Most issue mail order catalogs, often available for as little as a self-addressed, stamped envelope. The names you see regularly advertising in hobby periodicals, or set up at shows on the regional or national level, are generally going to be good people with whom to deal.

Most dealers utilize straight sales, although some will auction rare or unusual pieces. Major consignment dealers with multi-page advertisements for phone auctions of all types of memorabilia often include some uniforms and equipment in their ads. These, as well as auction house events, are generally geared towards higher-end material, although some mainstream, affordable equipment may also be included.

If questions arise concerning a jersey's authenticity, seek a second opinion. Most dealers will not object to having another party examine items to ensure authenticity, but the allowed time to gain an outside appraisal should be agreed upon beforehand, and stressed to the third party whose opinions are being sought.

Many forged jerseys, normally knits, are subject to "simulated" wear, such as a uniform forger using sandpaper, a sharp instrument, or other foreign object to abrade and damage portions of the jersey to give it the appearance of moderate to extreme game usage.

Jersey tags may be clandestinely doctored by removing legitimate tags from a lesser-valued authentic jersey and placing them into a phony item capable of being passed off as a high-ticket item. Doctoring is defined as taking an authentic jersey of a common player and changing tagging, numbering, or other factors pertinent to the jersey to upgrade the identity of the advertiser (i.e. doctoring the collar strip tag in a 1964 Andre Rodgers Cubs flannel jersey to a "14" or a "26" to make the jersey appear as if it was worn by Ernie Banks or Billy Williams).

Restoration, however, involves attempting to bring jerseys (especially flannels) back to their original appearance as close as possible. Where restorations differ from doctoring and gain acceptability in the majority of hobby quarters is that, first, no attempt is made to change or upgrade the identity of the major league wearer.

Legitimate restorations never attempt to restructure or refurbish tags, because too much potential for having a restoration slip into the dark side of the realm (doctoring) exists. Tagging is generally what is used to establish just who wore an item in the first place, and how to go about arranging the restoration process - what year and player were involved - so that the proper script or insignia or numbers can be used. A legitimate restoration tries to put things back the way they originally were, not embellish identities or years of usage to make an item more attractive or saleable.

Restorations are generally accepted by hobbyists if four conditions are met: 1) The restoration is true and accurate to the original identity of the jersey's wearer, with no illicit attempts to upgrade that wearer's identity. 2) The restoration should try to match as closely as possible the original appearance of the item being restored. 3) Potential buyers or traders should know in advance about any restorations. 4) Restorations should have a slight markdown in price, depending on how many were done and the degree of quality of them.

Although there are often telltale clues for detecting certain companies' replicated jerseys, some instances of fakery center around styles, teams and years, or specific players. Some of them include: Hank Aaron 1972-74 Atlanta Braves knits; Hank Aaron 1975-76 Milwaukee Brewers; Don Mattingly 1984 New York Yankees jerseys; pre-1987 Detroit Tigers jerseys of Al Kaline, Norm Cash, Mark Fidrych, Alan Trammell and Lance Parrish; mid-1970s Boston Red Sox and Oakland A's jerseys for Fred Lynn, Jim Rice, Carl Yastrzemski, Luis Tiant, Carlton Fisk, Reggie Jackson and Vida Blue; 1970s Houston Astros jerseys for Cesar Cedeno and Bob Watson; and 1970s Cincinnati Reds jerseys for members of the "Big Red Machine" - Pete Rose, Johnny Bench, Joe Morgan and Tony Perez.

Other forgery targets include: Braves (Dale Murphy, Phil Niekro); Reds (Eric Davis); Dodgers (Steve Garvey); Padres (Tony Gwynn, Ozzie Smith, Garry Templeton); Giants (Vida Blue, Will Clark, Dave Kingman, Bill Madlock); Cubs (Ryne Sandberg); Expos (Gary Carter, Andre Dawson); Mets (Gary Carter, Dwight Gooden, Darryl Strawberry, Tom Seaver); Phillies (Steve Carlton, Pete Rose, Mike Schmidt); Pirates (Bill Madlock, Willie Stargell); Cardinals (Keith Hernandez, Ozzie Smith); Orioles (Reggie Jackson, Jim Palmer, Boog Powell, Cal Ripken Jr., Brooks Robinson); Red Sox (Wade Boggs, Roger Clemens, Carl Yastrzemski); Indians (Warren Spahn); Yankees (Reggie Jackson, Thurman Munson, Graig Nettles, Mickey Rivers); Blue Jays (Ron Fairly, Lloyd Moseby); Angels (Frank Robinson, Nolan Ryan); White Sox (Dick Allen, Harold Baines, Carlton Fisk, Ralph Garr, Rich Gossage, Greg Luzinski, Jorge Orta); Royals (George Brett); Twins (Rod Carew, Kent Hrbek, Harmon Killebrew, Kirby Puckett); A's (Jose Canseco, Rickey Henderson, Billy Martin); Mariners (Ken Griffey Jr.).

In most instances, teams issue two of each jersey style to players under their employment. Three sets of attire is not uncommon, but this practice of three homes/three roads is not as common. In rare instances, set 4 and even set 5 shirts have surfaced. Apart from that, extra shirts tend to appear only when replacements are needed for damaged or stolen uniforms, or, in the 1980s especially, some stars have had several jerseys issued to them for several reasons, such as to be used as donations to fundraisers and charity auctions, to be given to friends, or for team employees to perhaps barter with collectors. Thus, some star jerseys from the last several years may exist in more common than twos or threes for a given style, and some may only evidence minor wear.

The jersey market has a wide variety of dollar amounts assigned to its items. Certain common knits of less popular teams and styles can be had for well under $200, while some totally original, authentic flannels have commanded five-figure sums in highly publicized auctions.

Basically speaking, the price range for a "common" knit usually falls in the $100 to $200 range. However, many exceptions exist. Rather than presenting a yearly, team-by-team price guide, this text will examine situations that may cause a jersey price to exceed $200, or perhaps cause a noticeable markup in a jersey from the lower end of the scale.

Scarcity: Supply/demand considerations affect the price guide scale in the equipment market. The highest dollars come with teams whose jerseys are not only scarce, but also sought by a wide range of collectors.

New releases: Higher prices are generally seen for styles that have recently been introduced and whose numbers within the hobby are restricted due to limited time for release, until greater quantities appear.

Sleeve adornments: Although a regularly-issued logo patch will only minimally increase a shirt's price, a commemorative, memoriam, or other specially-issued patch often creates a notable price increase.

High popularity: Some teams' prices, even though their attire is readily available, are driven up due to longstanding fan following or current popularity due to recent on-field success.

Striking styles: Other times, a style, be it rare, common or in-between, hits a chord with collectors and finds a niche as a high-priced item, due to demand for the style itself.

Early 1970s knits: Since the uniform hobby didn't begin hitting full stride until the end of the 1970s, many teams that wore styles for a short time in the 1972-76 time frame may have allowed only a small quantity of styles into the hobby. The focus on preserving jerseys was almost nonexistent in many quarters at that time.

The Phillies were one of the first teams to make jerseys available to fans.

Spring training/old-timers day jerseys: This is an area in which documentation and history of an item is more important than one may assume. Although prices for such items are lower, proving their origins is often more difficult, and sometimes not provable.

Many collectors don't realize that knits, and even newer and better conditioned flannels, can be machine washed for laundering. This can be done safely if a few key points are heeded about the laundering process.

First, never, ever bleach the jerseys. Chlorine bleach will often drastically fade the letters and numbers on a jersey, so a bleached 1977 Dave Concepcion shirt may as well have had him playing for the Cincinnati Pinks! A no-bleach detergent such as Wisk is recommended.

Secondly, hot water cycles are a definite no-no; the heat in the wash cycle will shrink a jersey. If you own a Carlton Fisk jersey, you're built like Carlton Fisk, and you wash the jersey in hot water, pretty soon you'll need to be built like Ozzie Guillen to fit into it. Cold water is recommended, but lukewarm water is also acceptable in many instances.

Finally, don't use a hot dry cycle; it may cause shrinkage. If you must use an automatic dryer, use an air setting, or the lowest setting. If you have the means, and your neighbors aren't into scavenging your back yard, then a closeline and sunshine will do the rest.

Tags bearing an inscription "wash separately by color" are not a concern when repeatedly done. That inscription is to warn parties about the possible fading of the new jersey's coloring onto other items it is washed with.

Simply put, those who follow the laundry tags in a jersey, and don't try to innovate or discard the information those tags offer for caring for jerseys, should have very few problems.

— Dave Miedema

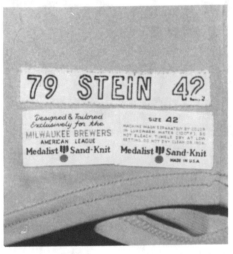

Clockwise, from top left:

1) This 1963 A's gold vest shows a 1959-66 Wilson company label.

2) Harvey Haddix's 1979 Descente Pittsburgh Pirates pinstripe knit jersey shows the label and strip tag - uniform #, size, year.

3) Randy Stein's 1979 Milwaukee Brewers road knit shows a strip tag (year/name/size) and exclusive tag.

4) Rick Reichardt's Washington Senators road flannel has the year tag embroidered directly into the tail.

5) Joe Kerrigan's 1985 Montreal Expos knit shows a Rawlings strip tag (size/year) and flag tag.

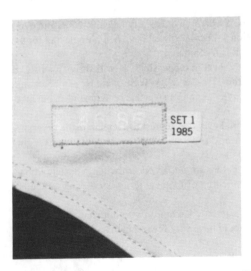

Clockwise, from top left:

1) Rawlings' extra-length tags are attached on the jersey sides.

2) John Henry Johnson's 1987 Milwaukee Brewers road knit shows the occasionally-used 1987 Rawlings company label with flag and strip tags.

3) Sid Monge's 1978 Cleveland Indians road knit shows Rawlings' 1971-88 company label with flag tag.

4) Carlton Fisk's 1991 Chicago White Sox road knit shows a 1988-91 Rawlings company label with flag tag, extra-length tag and tapered tag.

5) Dave Pavlas' 1989 Texas Rangers home spring training knit shows a 1988-89 Rawlings company label with strip tag.

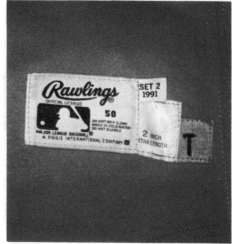

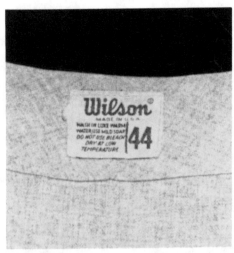

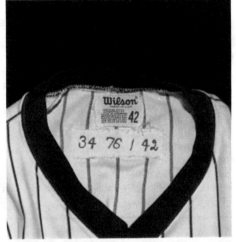

Clockwise, from top left:

1) This jersey is an example of a strip tag showing uniform number, year, set and size.

2) Rick Reichardt's Senators flannel shows a 1967-73 Wilson company label, type 1 small.

3) Ray Burris' 1976 Chicago Cubs home knit shows a 1974-78 Wilson company label (type 2 small) with a strip tag (uniform #/year/set/size).

4) Tom Dettore's 1975 Chicago Cubs road knit shows a 1974-78 Wilson company label with strip tag (uniform #/year/set/size).

5) Bobby Jones' 1984 Texas Rangers blue knit shows a 1979-86 Wilson company label (type 3 small) with year/set tag.

Hank Aaron's Milwaukee Braves jersey is a popular style among collectors.

Game-used jerseys

Hank Aaron: 1967 Atlanta Braves home, game worn..$16,995
Jim Abbott: 1994 New York Yankees home, game worn $695
Rick Aguilera: 1988 Minnesota Twins road, game worn $495
Sparky Anderson: 1974 Cincinnati Reds home, game worn, NOB, signed.............$1,000
Sparky Anderson: 1994 Detroit Tigers road, game worn $850
Cap Anson: 1898 New York Giants road, game worn, NIT $100,000
Luis Aparicio: 1968 Chicago White Sox home, with pants, NOB, signed...............$5,500
Luke Appling: 1971 Chicago White Sox road, game worn, NIC, coaching jersey$3,750
Steve Avery: 1994 Atlanta Braves road, game worn...$695
Harold Baines: 1992 Oakland A's home, game worn $275
Sal Bando: 1968 Oakland A's away, game worn...$700
Don Baylor: 1979 California Angels home, game worn...$995
Don Baylor: 1994 Colorado Rockies road, game worn..$450
George Bell: 1985 Toronto Blue Jays road, game worn..$495
Albert Belle: 1993 All-Star Game jersey, game worn, home, NOB $1,595
Johnny Bench: 1976 Cincinnati Reds road, game worn...$2,495
Johnny Bench: 1981 Cincinnati Reds St. Patrick's Day jersey and cap, game worn, signed
....$1,495
Andy Benes: San Diego Padres road, 1993 All-Star Game, game worn......................$950
Dante Bichette: 1994 Colorado Rockies home, game worn $850
Bert Blyleven: 1987 Minnesota Twins home, game worn $545
Vida Blue: 1986 San Francisco Giants road, game worn, NOB restored.....................$275
Wade Boggs: 1991 Boston Red Sox away, game worn $1,795
Wade Boggs: 1994 New York Yankees home, game worn $1,450

Barry Bonds: 1989 Pittsburgh Pirates road, game worn, NOB $3,000
Barry Bonds: 1994 San Francisco Giants home, game worn $2,195
Bobby Bonds: 1981 Chicago Cubs home, game worn..$400
Bobby Bonilla: 1989 Pittsburgh Pirates road, game worn, NOB $375
Larry Bowa: 1977 Philadelphia Phillies home, game worn $275
Dennis "Oil Can" Boyd: 1987 Boston Red Sox, game worn..............................$195
George Brett: 1984 Kansas City Royals road, game worn, NOB........................$2,700
George Brett: 1991 Kansas City Royals road, game worn $1,995
George Brett: Kansas City Royals blue warm-up jersey $200
Brett Butler: 1986 Cleveland Indians road, game worn, NOB............................$275
Roy Campanella: 1950 Brooklyn Dodgers home, game worn, NIT $16,000
John Candelaria: 1987 California Angels road, game worn................................$225
Jose Canseco: 1991 Oakland A's road, game worn, with pants, NOB $900
Jose Canseco: 1994 Texas Rangers road, game worn..$695
Rod Carew: 1980 California Angels home, game worn $1,095
Steve Carlton: 1969 St. Louis Cardinals road, game worn, signed $1,495
Joe Carter: 1994 Toronto Blue Jays home, game worn, signed $995
Dave Cash: 1978 Montreal Expos home, game worn, NOB................................$175
Ron Cey: 1987 Oakland A's road, game worn, signed $295
Will Clark: 1987 San Francisco Giants home, game worn................................$1,050
Roger Clemens: 1987 Boston Red Sox road, game worn, with pants $1,800
Roberto Clemente: 1957 Pittsburgh Pirates road, restored $15,000
Ty Cobb: 1925 Detroit Tigers home, game worn, NIC....................................$110,000
Cecil Cooper: 1975 Boston Red Sox home, game worn....................................$350
Joey Cora: 1988 San Diego Padres road, game worn $200
Eric Davis: 1985 Cincinnati Reds home, game worn, NOB, signed....................$575
Willie Davis: 1963 Los Angeles Dodgers home, game worn, NIT $1,395
Andre Dawson: 1988 Chicago Cubs home, game worn $695
Rick Dempsey: 1974 New York Yankees road, game worn................................$425
Paul Derringer: 1944 Chicago Cubs home flannel, game worn........................$2,795
Delino DeShields: 1994 Los Angeles Dodgers road, game worn $450
Al Downing: 1974 Los Angeles Dodgers home, game worn $800
Don Drysdale: 1959 Los Angeles Dodgers home, game worn, signed..............$14,500
Shawon Dunston: 1988 Chicago Cubs home, game worn, signed $195
Darrell Evans: 1971 Atlanta Braves home, game worn, NOB $900
Tony Fernandez: 1989 Toronto Blue Jays blue, game worn................................$350
Tony Fernandez: 1991 San Diego Padres road, game worn $225
Cecil Fielder: 1994 Detroit Tigers road, game worn..$895
Carlton Fisk: 1990 Chicago White Sox road, game worn $895
Andres Galarraga: 1994 Colorado Rockies home, game worn $1,150
Ron Gant: 1989 Atlanta Braves home, game worn, signed................................$895
Steve Garvey: 1981 Los Angeles Dodgers home, game worn, NOB, signed............$1,195
Jim Gentile: 1965 Houston Astros home, game worn $1,500
Dan Gladden: 1989 Minnesota Twins home, game worn....................................$295
Fred Gladding: 1965 Detroit Tigers home, game worn....................................$1,250
Tom Glavine: 1994 Atlanta Braves road, game worn..$695
Juan Gonzalez: 1993 Texas Rangers home, game worn, NOB $795
Rich Gossage: 1988 Chicago Cubs road, game worn..$350
Mark Grace: 1988 Chicago Cubs home, game worn $550
Mike Greenwell: 1989 Boston Red Sox road, game worn $475
Ken Griffey Sr.: 1981 Cincinnati Reds road, game worn $425
Ken Griffey Jr.: 1989 Seattle Mariners road, game worn $2,495

Marquis Grissom: 1993 Montreal Expos home, game worn $395
Ron Guidry: 1988 New York Yankees road, game worn...$995
Larry Gura: 1982 Kansas City Royals road, game worn, NOB.................................$175
Tony Gwynn: 1989 San Diego Padres road, game worn $1,050
Moose Haas: 1978 Milwaukee Brewers home, game worn $165
Tommy Harper: Seattle Pilots road jersey, game worn, restored....................$1,200
Charlie Hayes: 1994 Colorado Rockies home, game worn $395
Rickey Henderson: 1991 Oakland A's home, game worn, NOB, signed.................$1,495
George Hendrick: 1976 Cleveland Indians red, game worn $495
Orel Hershiser: 1987 Los Angeles Dodgers road, game worn................................$595
Keith Hernandez: 1988 New York Mets road, NOB, signed....................................$600
Teddy Higuera: 1992 Milwaukee Brewers road, game worn....................................$240
Bob Horner: 1982 Atlanta Braves road, game worn..$350
Kent Hrbek: 1992 Minnesota Twins home, game worn...$695
Catfish Hunter: 1971 Oakland A's road, game worn, NOB $2,250
Bo Jackson: 1987 Kansas City Royals home, game worn $650
Danny Jackson: 1983 Kansas City Royals road, game worn $375
Reggie Jackson: 1968 Oakland A's road vest, game worn...............................$12,995
Reggie Jackson: 1973 Oakland A's home, game worn, NOB $2,995
Reggie Jackson: 1983 California Angels home, game worn, NOB, with pants............$2,795
Gregg Jefferies: 1990 New York Mets home, game worn, NOB $450
Davey Johnson: 1967 Baltimore Orioles home, game worn, NIT............................$1,250
Randy Johnson: 1994 Seattle Mariners home, game worn $795
Chipper Jones: 1993 Atlanta Braves home, game worn.......................................$1,695
Wally Joyner: 1987 California Angels road, game worn, NOB, signed......................$295
Dave Justice: 1992 Atlanta Braves home, game worn, NOB, signed $1,150
Al Kaline: 1974 Detroit Tigers road, game worn $1,695
Eric Karros: 1994 Los Angeles Dodgers road, game worn.....................................$850
Harmon Killebrew: 1961 Minnesota Twins home, game worn, NIC $7,000
Dave Kingman: 1986 Oakland A's gold, game worn, NOB....................................$325
Bruce Kison: 1977 Pittsburgh Pirates black, game worn.......................................$295
Ryan Klesko: 1994 Atlanta Braves home, game worn $595
Ted Kluszewski: 1964 Cincinnati Reds home, game worn....................................$1,800
Chuck Knoblauch: 1993 Minnesota Twins home, game worn $495
Sandy Koufax: 1961 Los Angeles Dodgers home, game worn, NIT......................$19,950
John Kruk: 1994 Philadelphia Phillies road, game worn, NOB, signed $550
Ken Landreaux: 1980s Los Angeles Dodgers road, game worn, NOB $175
Mark Langston: 1993 California Angels home, game worn, signed $225
Carney Lansford: 1988 Oakland A's road, game worn, NOB....................................$750
Barry Larkin: 1993 Cincinnati Reds home, game worn, NOB, signed $695
Tony LaRussa: 1992 Oakland A's home, game worn $375
Ron LeFlore: 1980 Montreal Expos away, game worn, NOB $250
Chet Lemon: 1982 Detroit Tigers home, game worn $325
Kenny Lofton: 1994 Cleveland Indians road, game worn $795
Greg Maddux: 1994 Atlanta Braves road, game worn $1,795
Juan Marichal: 1966 San Francisco Giants home, game worn, NIC, signed............$5,500
Roger Maris: 1960 New York Yankees home, game worn, NIC $25,000
Dennis Martinez: 1988 Montreal Expos road, game worn.......................................$250
Eddie Mathews: 1965 Atlanta Braves road, game worn, signed $12,500
Don Mattingly: 1993 New York Yankees home, game worn....................................$1,495
John Mayberry: 1978 Toronto Blue Jays road mesh pullover $195
Bob McClure: 1987 Montreal Expos road, game worn $100

Willie McCovey: 1972 San Francisco Giants road, game worn, with pants, NIC ....
....$11,500
Jack McDowell: 1995 New York Yankees road, Mantle armband..................................$895
Mark McGwire: 1989 Oakland A's home, game worn..$495
Hal McRae: 1986 Kansas City Royals away, game worn, NOB $275
Andy Messersmith: 1970 California Angels, game worn $550
Kevin Mitchell: 1988 San Francisco Giants, game worn, signed $250
Kevin Mitchell: Seattle Mariners batting practice jersey, grey....................................$195
Paul Molitor: 1988 Milwaukee Brewers road, game worn..$1,095
Bill Monbouquette: 1961 Boston Red Sox road, game worn...$750
Raul Mondesi: 1994 Los Angeles Dodgers home, game worn.....................................$1,250
Joe Morgan: 1968 Houston Astros road, game worn $5,500
Jack Morris: 1983 Detroit Tigers road, game worn, NOB $850
Rance Mulliniks: 1982 Kansas City Royals road, game worn $190
Eddie Murray: 1994 Cleveland Indians road, game worn $795
Eddie Murray: 1995 Cleveland Indians World Series jersey, game worn $2,495
Dale Murphy: 1981 Atlanta Braves road, game worn, signed.......................................$650
Stan Musial: 1960 St. Louis Cardinals road, game worn...$13,500
David Nied: 1993 Colorado Rockies road, game worn, NOB, first year $750
Phil Niekro: 1979 Atlanta Braves road, game worn $895
Hideo Nomo: 1995 Los Angeles Dodgers road, game worn..$6,500
Blue Moon Odom: 1968 Oakland A's green vest, game worn......................................$450
Ron Oester: 1984 Cincinnati Reds home, game worn, signed......................................$145
Sadahara Oh: Taiyo Giants road, game worn, NIC...$2,850
Mel Ott: 1947 New York Giants road, game worn, NIC $45,000
Jim Palmer: 1970 Baltimore Orioles road, game worn, signed....................................$3,500
Rafael Palmeiro: 1990 Texas Rangers road, game worn, NOB, signed......................$650
Dave Parker: 1984 Cincinnati Reds home, game worn..$395
Dave Parker: 1990 Milwaukee Brewers home, game worn $475
Terry Pendleton: 1988 St. Louis Cardinals, game worn, NOB....................................$575
Mike Piazza: 1994 Los Angeles Dodgers road, game worn $1,495
Kirby Puckett: 1985 Minnesota Twins road, game worn, NOB $2,195
Kirby Puckett: 1993 Minnesota Twins home, game worn $995
Jamie Quirk: 1988 Kansas City Royals road, game worn..$175
Tim Raines: 1987 Montreal Expos road, game worn, NOB, signed..............................$595
Manny Ramirez: 1994 Cleveland Indians road, game worn $495
Steve Renko: 1971 Montreal Expos road, game worn $1,000
Jim Rice: 1975 Boston Red Sox road, game worn $1,495
Cal Ripken Jr.: 1994 Baltimore Orioles road, game worn $2,995
Bip Roberts: 1991 San Diego Padres road, game worn $350
Robin Roberts: 1964 Baltimore Orioles home, game worn, signed...........................$4,495
Brooks Robinson: 1957 Baltimore Orioles road, signed $5,000
Frank Robinson: 1973 California Angels home, game worn...$1,695
Ivan Rodriguez: 1995 Texas Rangers home, game worn, All-Star patch $595
Phil Roof: 1966 Kansas City A's home, game worn, signed $600
Pete Rose: 1974 Cincinnati Reds home, game worn, NOB...$2,500
Pete Rose: Cincinnati Reds red warm-up jersey, #14...$250
Pete Rose: Philadelphia Phillies #14 pre-game jersey, signed $895
Pete Rose: 1980 Philadelphia Phillies, game worn...$1,400
Babe Ruth: 1938 Brooklyn Dodgers road, game worn, with pants, NIC...............$110,000
Nolan Ryan: 1987 Houston Astros home, game worn, NOB $4,000
Nolan Ryan: 1990 Texas Rangers road, game worn, with pants $2,750

Bret Saberhagen: 1993 New York Mets road, game worn, signed $600
Tim Salmon: 1992 California Angels road, game worn, NOB $1,395
Ryne Sandberg: 1988 Chicago Cubs home, game worn $1,350
Deion Sanders: 1992 Atlanta Braves road, game worn $695
Mike Schmidt: 1989 Philadelphia Phillies home, game worn $2,495
Mike Scott: 1980 New York Mets road, game worn, NOB $250
Tom Seaver: 1983 New York Mets road, game worn..........................$3,295
Al Simmons: 1943 Boston Red Sox road, game worn, NIC $12,500
John Smiley: 1990 Pittsburgh Pirates home, game worn..........................$175
Ozzie Smith: 1994 St. Louis Cardinals home, game worn..........................$1,350
Duke Snider: 1962 Los Angeles Dodgers road, NIT, signed..........................$11,000
Willie Stargell: 1970 Pittsburgh Pirates home, signed..........................$4,495
Terry Steinbach: 1992 Oakland A's road, game worn, NOB $350
Casey Stengel: 1962 New York Mets road, game worn, with pants $14,750
Rennie Stennett: 1978 Pittsburgh Pirates home, game worn..........................$350
Dave Stewart: 1983 Los Angeles Dodgers home, game worn, NOB $495
Darryl Strawberry: 1988 New York Mets road, game worn, signed $350
Rick Sutcliffe: 1994 St. Louis Cardinals road, game worn, NOB..........................$395
Bruce Sutter: 1985 Atlanta Braves road, game worn $350
Don Sutton: 1974 Los Angeles Dodgers home, NOB, signed $1,495
Don Sutton: 1986 California Angels road, game worn, NOB..........................$925
Danny Tartabull: 1993 New York Yankees home, game worn $695
Frank Thomas: 1994 Chicago White Sox home, game worn $2,500
Alan Trammell: 1994 Detroit Tigers home, game worn $895
Mo Vaughn: 1994 Boston Red Sox home, game worn..........................$795
Robin Ventura: 1994 Chicago White Sox road, game worn $695
Frank Viola: 1988 Minnesota Twins road, game worn, signed $495
Devon White: 1989 California Angels home, game worn, signed $600
Frank White: 1988 Kansas City Royals road, game worn, NOB $350
Hoyt Wilhelm: 1970 Atlanta Braves home, game worn, signed..........................$3,350
Matt Williams: 1988 San Francisco Giants road, game worn $950
Ted Williams: 1960 Boston Red Sox home, game worn $60,000
Dave Winfield: 1993 Minnesota Twins home, game worn..........................$1,200
Mike Witt: 1989 California Angels All-Star Game warm-up jersey, with patch
and tags $250
Carl Yastrzemski: 1978 Boston Red Sox home, signed..........................$1,795
Robin Yount: 1993 Milwaukee Brewers home, game worn..........................$995
Eddie Yuhas: 1953 St. Louis Cardinals home, game worn, NIT..........................$1,500

Replica Jerseys

Hank Aaron: Late 1950s Milwaukee Braves tomahawk, signed..........................$425
Hank Aaron: Late 1960s Atlanta Braves flannel, signed $350
Sparky Anderson: Detroit Tigers home #11, signed..........................$295
Luis Aparicio: Chicago White Sox flannel, signed..........................$275
Ernie Banks: 1969 Chicago Cubs flannel, signed..........................$275
Johnny Bench: 1969 Cincinnati Reds home, signed..........................$250
Yogi Berra: 1952 New York Yankees home flannel, signed $275
Vida Blue: San Francisco Giants home, signed..........................$175
Wade Boggs: New York Yankees home, signed..........................$275

Lou Boudreau: Cleveland Indians flannel, signed..$275
George Brett: Kansas City Royals home, signed..$325
Lou Brock: St. Louis Cardinals flannel, signed $575
Bill Buckner: Chicago Cubs home, signed $185
Roy Campanella: Brooklyn Dodgers, signed $895
Jose Canseco: Oakland A's with elephant patch, signed $275
Jose Canseco: Texas Rangers, signed $225
Rod Carew: California Angels home, signed..$395
Steve Carlton: St. Louis Cardinals flannel, signed $325
Steve Carlton: Philadelphia Phillies home, signed $225
Will Clark: San Francisco Giants home, signed $275
Roger Clemens: Boston Red Sox home, signed..$295
Roberto Clemente: Pittsburgh Pirates home, flannel $195
Ty Cobb: 1920s Detroit Tigers grey flannel..$195
Rocky Colavito: Cleveland Indians grey flannel $195
Eric Davis: Cincinnati Reds home, signed $185
Joe DiMaggio: 1939 New York Yankees pinstripe, signed $2,450
Don Drysdale: Los Angeles Dodgers grey flannel, signed $850
Cecil Fielder: Detroit Tigers road, signed..$250
Rollie Fingers: Oakland A's road flannel, signed..$275
Rollie Fingers: Milwaukee Brewers home, signed $255
Carlton Fisk: Chicago White Sox road, signed $275
Lou Gehrig: 1930s New York Yankees pinstripe flannel..$195
Charlie Gehringer: Detroit Tigers home, signed $575
Bob Gibson: St. Louis Cardinals home, signed..$275
Juan Gonzalez: Texas Rangers home, signed..$275
Dwight Gooden: New York Mets pinstripe, signed $160
Ken Griffey Jr.: Seattle Mariners home, signed $350
Tony Gwynn: San Diego Padres home, signed $250
Rickey Henderson: New York Yankees pinstripe, signed..$250
Keith Hernandez: New York Mets road, signed $150
Orel Hershiser: Los Angeles Dodgers home, signed..$295
Rogers Hornsby: 1920s St. Louis Cardinals grey flannel..$225
Bo Jackson: Chicago White Sox road, signed..$250
Reggie Jackson: 1969 Oakland A's road, flannel, signed..$350
Reggie Jackson: New York Yankees grey, signed..$295
Fergie Jenkins: Chicago Cubs home, signed $250
Al Kaline: Detroit Tigers grey flannel, signed $275
Harmon Killebrew: Minnesota Twins road, signed $250
Barry Larkin: Cincinnati Reds home, signed..$225
Kenny Lofton: Cleveland Indians home, signed..$275
Mickey Lolich: 1968 Detroit Tigers grey, signed $275
Greg Maddux: Atlanat Braves home, signed..$375
Mickey Mantle: 1951 New York Yankees pinstripe, signed $675
Mickey Mantle: 1952 New York Yankees home, signed $675
Mickey Mantle: 1952 New York Yankees away, signed..$600
Juan Marichal: San Francisco Giants road, signed $250
Roger Maris: New York Yankees home..$185
Eddie Mathews: 1957 Milwaukee Braves tomahawk, signed $295
Don Mattingly: New York Yankees road, signed..$275
Willie Mays: San Francisco Giants flannel, signed..$325

Willie McCovey: San Francisco Giants road, signed $250
Mark McGwire: Oakland A's, signed $200
Joe Morgan: 1969 Houston Astros flannel, signed $250
Eddie Murray: Baltimore Orioles or Cleveland Indians, signed $300
Stan Musial: 1942 St. Louis Cardinals flannel, signed $325
Phil Niekro: 1969 Atlanta Braves flannel, signed $275
Jim Palmer: Baltimore Orioles home, signed $275
Tony Perez: Cincinnati Reds home, signed $275
Gaylord Perry: 1962 San Francisco Giants flannel, signed $250
Mike Piazza: Los Angeles Dodgers home, signed $350
Kirby Puckett: Minnesota Twins home, signed $300
Pee Wee Reese: Brooklyn Dodgers away flannel, signed $250
Cal Ripken Jr.: Baltimore Orioles home, signed...$325
Brooks Robinson: Baltimore Orioles grey flannel, signed $225
Frank Robinson: Cincinnati Reds flannel, signed...$250
Pete Rose: 1963 Cincinnati Reds flannel vest, signed...$275
Babe Ruth: 1920s New York Yankees road flannel $200
Nolan Ryan: New York Mets flannel, signed $375
Nolan Ryan: California Angels, signed...$375
Nolan Ryan: Houston Astros, signed $350
Nolan Ryan: Texas Rangers, signed..$350
Ryne Sandberg: Chicago Cubs road, signed...$325
Mike Schmidt: Philadelphia Phillies grey flannel, signed $325
Tom Seaver: 1969 New York Mets home, signed $325
Ozzie Smith: St. Louis Cardinals home, signed $275
Duke Snider: Los Angeles Dodgers flannel, signed $250
Warren Spahn: Milwaukee Braves home, signed $325
Darryl Strawberry: New York Mets road, signed $150
Don Sutton: Los Angeles Dodgers home, signed..$250
Frank Thomas: Chicago White Sox road, signed..$295
Mo Vaughn: Boston Red Sox home, signed $300
Robin Ventura: Chicago White Sox, signed...$200
Frank Viola: Minnesota Twins home, signed $200
Ted Williams: 1939 Boston Red Sox home flannel, signed.....................................$795
Dave Winfield: New York Yankees road, signed $250
Early Wynn: Cleveland Indians flannel, signed $275
Carl Yastrzemski: Boston Red Sox home flannel, signed $595
Robin Yount: Milwaukee Brewers away, signed...$300

Equipment

Lack of information to identify a bat often hinders beginning collectors.

There are basically four categories of bats which collectors pursue. They are:

1) Authentic cracked vs. uncracked, but game-used bat: The player has actually used the bat in a game; it shows wear and tear from use, including scuffs, dents, tape, filing of the handle, uniform #s on the handles, use of pine tar, hollowed ends and cracks. The value of a bat decreases according to the size of the crack.

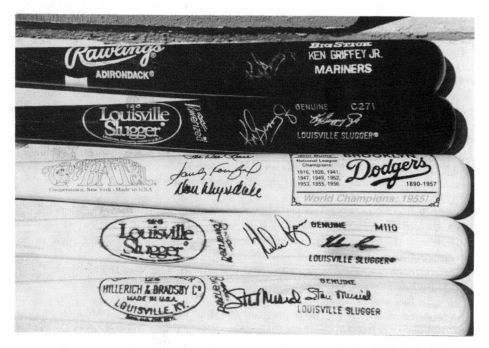

Many collectors have their commemorative bats signed by the players involved.

This bat is made to a player's specifications, with his name and signature on it, or it could be a bat ordered by the team, with the team name branded into it. Pitchers and coaches generally use these bats. Coaches' bats may carry the player's name, but are not necessarily made according to the specifics he used as an active player.

2) Authentic bats, made to the player's specifications, but which have not been used in a game: It's possible the player didn't even own the bat, which could have been ordered by the team for promotions or giveaways, or made for other businesses for resale. These bats are often used for autographing.

3) Retail or store model bats are those which are purchased in sporting goods stores. They are not made according to the player's specifications, but often carry his name as an endorsement. Vintage model bats of stars before the 1950s generally sell well. Naive collectors can end up purchasing these bats for $100 to $200, thinking they are game-used bats when they aren't. Store models can be distinguished from game-used bats because the knobs carry inch markings, a single-digit number, or both initials of the player whose name is on the barrel. Also, if the bat number in the brand oval is followed by any letters, probably player initials, it's likely the bat is a store model.

4) Commemoratives: These bats are made to recognize a particular person, place or event in baseball history, such as a World Series or Hall of Fame induction. These customized bats, generally more desirable than store models, are often created for display purposes and are suitable for autographing, which makes them more valuable. Black Sharpie pens work best.

According to Mark Allen Baker, author of the second edition of the Baseball Autograph Handbook, "lack of accurate information to identify particular bats, along with sources to purchase them from, have been the two greatest obstacles for beginning collectors. Also complicating the hobbyist's acquisition is the lack of the proper terminology to describe a bat. Novice collectors often incorrectly mistake store-bought or retail bats for authentic game-used models. Both collectors and dealers simply do not take enough time to research the background of their acquisitions, often resulting in false advertising of the bat and a worthless acquisition by a novice collector."

The complexities of bat markings will not be delved into, but some general guidelines follow:

Baseball's rules limit the length of bats to 42 inches long and 2 3/4 inches wide. Generally, bats weigh between 30-50 ounces.

These are the most common bat brands used by major leaguers:

1) Hillerich & Bradsby: This company has undergone several name modifications since 1884 until 1979, when its bats became more commonly known as Louisville Sluggers, H&B's most popular style. Since 1945 H&B has labeled bats with player initials and a model number on the knob, which is an identifying number for each individual style. In 1976 those numbers were moved to the barrel of the bat. If the player is contracted with the manufacturer his name is burned into the bat barrel in autograph form. If he isn't, his name is in block letters.

Hillerich & Bradsby adopted the slogan "Powerized" in 1932 and began putting model numbers - which have one letter and at least one number - on the knob in 1944. Those numbers were removed beginning in 1976 and then placed on the barrel. The H&B logo was dropped in 1979, with Louisville Slugger becoming the brand label.

2) A.G. Spalding & Bros. bats, used primarily before the turn of the century.

3) A.J. Reach bats, which were prominent at the beginning of the century.

4) Rawlings, which labels its bats as Adirondacks, and feature a single-colored ring around the neck and a diamond-shaped trademark.

5) Worth, which entered the market in the 1970s and offers its Tennessee Thumper bats.

6) Cooper bats, produced in Canada since 1986.

7) Mizuno bats, made in Japan.

A final caveat, as offered by noted dealer Alan "Mr. Mint" Rosen in his book Mr. Mint's Insider's Guide To Investing in Baseball Cards and Collectibles: "Caveat emptor. It is very difficult to verify a bat actually used by a player in a major-league game. (Was it scuffed at a softball game last week? Did the player himself use it, or did one of his teammates? Was it used only in batting practice? Often, players themselves cannot remember which stick they used.) If you invest in one of these bats, deal only with a dealer who is an expert in the area and insist on written documentation. Reliable dealers usually get these items from unimpeachable sources - the player's attorney or agent, a family member, the clubhouse attendant, or a batboy."

The following are examples of styles and brands of game-used bats and the prices for which they've been listed for sale in Sports Collectors Digest.

Hank Aaron: Hillerich & Bradsby, game used, late 1950s $2,595
Hank Aaron: Adirondack, game used, uncracked, early 1970s $2,295
Joe Adcock: Hillerich & Bradsby, game used, 1965-71 ....$295
Gary Alexander: Adirondack, game used, 1980..$30
Luis Alicea: Louisville Slugger, game used, 1986-89 ....$40
Dick Allen: Hillerich & Bradsby, game used, 1973-75 ....$495
Bobby Allison: Hillerich & Bradsby, game used, 1960s $395
Roberto Alomar: Louisville Slugger, game used, 1990..$425
Roberto Alomar: Cooper, game used, cracked, 1993 ....$250
Sandy Alomar Jr.: Rose, game used, 1994-95..$95
Sandy Alomar Jr.: Adirondack, unused, 1992 All-Star Game $175
Matty Alou: Hillerich & Bradsby, game used, 1965-72...$295
Moises Alou: Adirondack, game used, 1992...$140
Brady Anderson: Louisville Slugger, game used..$85
Luis Aparicio: Hillerich & Bradsby, game used, 1960s...$795
Tony Armas: Louisville Slugger, game used, cracked, 1984-85..$40
Carlos Baerga: Adirondack, game used, 1995, signed...$275
Harold Baines: Adirondack, game used, uncracked, 1991-94, signed.......................................$80
Dusty Baker: Louisville Slugger, game used, 1975-79 ....$100
Steve Balboni: Louisville Slugger, game used, cracked, 1984-85...$40
Sal Bando: Hillerich & Bradsby, game used, 1965-72 ....$175
Don Baylor: Louisville Slugger, game used, 1977-79 ....$150

Hall of Famer Rod Carew signs a bat during a baseball card show appearance.

Albert Belle: Louisville Slugger, game used, 1995 ....$600
Johnny Bench: Adirondack, game used, 1960s, signed $750
Tony Bernazard: Louisville Slugger, game used, two-tone, 1984-85 ....$35
Buddy Biancalana: Worth, game used, cracked, 1988 ....$40
Dante Bichette: Louisville Slugger, game used, 1988...$195
Dante Bichette: Adirondack, game used, cracked, 1995 ....$125
Craig Biggio: Louisville Slugger, game used, 1993-94, signed $195
Jeff Blauser: Louisville Slugger, game used, cracked, 1995...$50
Bruce Bochte: Louisville Slugger, game used, 1975-79..$50
Wade Boggs: Hillerich & Bradsby, game used, 1977-79 (minor leagues) $1,795
Wade Boggs: Louisville Slugger, game used, 1982..$1,295
Wade Boggs: Louisville Slugger, game used, uncracked, 1994 ....$450
Barry Bonds: Louisville Slugger, game used, 1993-95, signed $595
Bobby Bonilla: Louisville Slugger, game used, 1986-89 ....$130
Bob Boone: Louisville Slugger, game used, 1984-85, signed...$265
Bret Boone: Louisville Slugger, game used, 1992-93, signed...$75
Lyman Bostock: Louisville Slugger, game used, 1977-79...$125
Clete Boyer: Hillerich & Bradsby, game used, 1965-72 ....$295
Ken Boyer: Adirondack, game used, 1959 All-Star Game..$1,495
George Brett: Louisville Slugger, game used, uncracked, early 1980s...$1,150
Lou Brock: Hillerich & Bradsby, game used, 1967 All-Star Game, signed...................................$1,595
Lou Brock: Hillerich & Bradsby, game used, 1973-75 ....$495
Jack Brohamer: Louisville Slugger, game used, 1973-75 ....$50
Gates Brown: Hillerich & Bradsby, game used, 1965-72 ....$295
Ollie Brown: Hillerich & Bradsby, game used, 1965-72..$65
Bill Buckner: Louisville Slugger, game used, 1973-75...$150
Jay Buhner: Adirondack, game used, 1994...$150

Ellis Burks: Louisville Slugger, game used, uncracked, 1995 ....$45
Jeff Burroughs: Worth, game used, 1987 ....$70
Brett Butler: Louisville Slugger, game used, 1986-89...$90
Enos Cabell: Louisville Slugger, game used, 1984-85..$20
Ken Caminiti: Adirondack, game used, 1995 ....$80
Jose Canseco: Adirondack, game used, uncracked, 1991, signed $450
Jose Canseco: Cooper, game used, 1995 ....$295
Leo Cardenas: Hillerich & Bradsby, game used, 1973-75, signed $75
Rod Carew: Hillerich & Bradsby, game used, cracked, 1965-72, signed $995
Rod Carew: Louisville Slugger, game used, uncracked, 1979, signed.........................$295
Rod Carew: Adirondack, game used, 1980, signed...$350
Steve Carlton: Louisville Slugger, game used, mid-1980s $750
Gary Carter: Hillerich & Bradsby, game used, 1972-75...$695
Gary Carter: Adirondack, game used, uncracked, mid-1980s..$275
Joe Carter: Louisville Slugger, game used, 1982-83 ....$395
Joe Carter: Louisville, game used, 1995..$195
Rico Carty: Hillerich & Bradsby, game used, 1965-72, signed $225
Cesar Cedeno: Hillerich & Bradsby, game used, 1970-71, signed $140
Ron Cey: Louisville Slugger, game used, 1975-79...$150
Jack Clark: Louisville Slugger, 1984-85...$80
Will Clark: Adirondack, game used, uncracked, 1991, signed $450
Will Clark: Louisville Slugger, game used, uncracked $375
Roberto Clemente: Hillerich & Bradsby, game used, cracked, late 1960s...................$3,295
Rocky Colavito: Hillerich & Bradsby, game used, 1965-72 ....$795
Dave Concepcion: Louisville Slugger, game used, 1984-85, signed $140
Cecil Cooper: Louisville Slugger, game used, 1980...$75
Joey Cora: Rawlings, game used, uncracked, 1993...$45
Al Cowens: Hillerich & Bradsby, game used, 1977-79 ....$40
Vic Davalillo: Louisville Slugger, game used, 1977-79 ....$150
Alvin Davis: Louisville Slugger, game used, 1986-89...$25
Chili Davis: Adirondack, game used, 1995...$100
Eric Davis: Louisville Slugger, game used, 1986-89, signed $90
Tommy Davis: Hillerich & Bradsby, game used, uncracked, 1961-64 ....$350
Willie Davis: Hillerich & Bradsby, game used, 1973-75..$125
Andre Dawson: Louisville Slugger, game used, cracked, early 1980s $275
Doug DeCinces: Adirondack, game used, 1987..$70
Joe DiMaggio: Hillerich & Bradsby, game used, uncracked, 1930s $16,500
Joe DiMaggio: Hillerich & Bradsby, game used, 1945-51...$9,995
Gary DiSarcina: Louisville Slugger, cracked, 1995 ....$50
Bobby Doerr: Hillerich & Bradsby, cracked, repaired, 1949-59....................................$1,200
Dan Driessen: Louisville Slugger, game used, 1984-84...$70
Shawon Dunston: Worth, game used, cracked, 1988-89...$70
Lenny Dykstra: Louisville Slugger, game used, 1986-89..$200
Jim Eisenrich: Louisville Slugger, game used, 1995 ....$45
Mike Epstein: Hillerich & Bradsby, game used, 1973-75...$125
Darrell Evans: Worth, game used, 1988 ....$125
Dwight Evans: Hillerich & Bradsby, 1977-79, signed $395
Dwight Evans: Louisville Slugger, game used, 1984-85...$80
Hoot Evers: Adirondack, game used, 1952-57...$295
Tony Fernandez: Adirondack, game used, 1991..$50
Cecil Fielder: Cooper, game used, cracked, 1994 ....$250
Steve Finley: Cooper, game used, cracked, 1993..$40
Carlton Fisk: Worth, game used, cracked, 1970s, signed $550
Carlton Fisk: Hillerich & Bradsby, game used, 1977-79 ....$1,295
Barry Foote: Adirondack, game used, 1970s $50
George Foster: Louisville Slugger, game used, 1977-79 ....$125

Bill Freehan: Hillerich & Bradsby, game used, 1973-75 .... $495
Jim Fregosi: Hillerich & Bradsby, game used, 1965-71, signed $175
Andres Galarraga: Louisville Slugger, game used, cracked, 1995 .... $175
Ron Gant: Adirondack, game used, 1992 NLCS $350
Jim Gantner: Louisville Slugger, game used, 1991-94 .... $50
Steve Garvey: Adirondack, game used, cracked, late 1970s $325
Steve Garvey: Louisville Slugger, game used, 1985 All-Star Game $595
Cito Gaston: Adirondack, game used, 1970s $110
Lou Gehrig: Hillerich & Bradsby, game used, 1925 .... $13,500
Cesar Geronimo: Hillerich & Bradsby, game used, 1977-79 .... $295
Bob Gibson: Hillerich & Bradsby, game used, 1965-72 .... $995
Dan Gladden: Worth, game used, cracked, 1988 .... $50
Juan Gonzalez: Adirondack, game used, 1995 .... $285
Dwight Gooden: Adirondack, game used, 1984, signed $195
Mark Grace: Adirondack, game used, 1993 .... $295
Mark Grace: Adirondack, game used, cracked, 1995 .... $150
Mike Greenwell: Louisville Slugger, game used, 1995 .... $100
Bobby Grich: Adirondack, game used, cracked, 1981 .... $80
Tom Grieve: Hillerich & Bradsby, game used, 1965-72 .... $110
Ken Griffey Jr.: Louisville Slugger, game used, 1991-95, signed $795
Ken Griffey Sr.: Louisville Slugger, game used, 1973-75 .... $125
Ken Griffey Sr.: Louisville Slugger, game used, 1990 .... $90
Marquis Grissom: Adirondack, game used, 1993 .... $70
Dick Groat: Hillerich & Bradsby, game used, 1965-72 .... $595
Greg Gross: Adirondack, game used, 1970s $70
Pedro Guerrero: Louisville Slugger, game used, 1983-85 .... $85
Ozzie Guillen: Worth, game used, 1995 .... $90
Tony Gwynn: Louisville Slugger, game used, 1981 (minor leagues), signed $1,295
Tony Gwynn: Louisville Slugger, game used, uncracked, 1986-89, signed $395
Tony Gwynn: Adirondack, game used, 1992 All-Star Game $800
Moose Haas: Louisville Slugger, game used, 1980-83 .... $30
Bob Hamelin: Mizuno, game used, 1995 .... $130
Von Hayes: Louisville Slugger, game used, 1986-89 .... $40
Rickey Henderson: Louisville Slugger, game used, 1993 World Series $995
Rickey Henderson: Louisville Slugger, game used, 1995 .... $290
George Hendrick: Louisville Slugger, game used, 1984-85 .... $55
Tommy Henrich: Hillerich & Bradsby, game used, 1940s $1,395
Keith Hernandez: Louisville Slugger, game used, cracked, 1980s $150
Babe Herman: Hillerich & Bradsby, game used, uncracked, 1930s $375
Orel Hershiser: Louisville Slugger, game used, 1984-85 .... $200
Butch Hobson: Hillerich & Bradsby, game used, 1977-79 .... $70
Chris Hoiles: Adirondack, game used, cracked, 1994 .... $70
Elston Howard: Hillerich & Bradsby, game used, pre-1964 .... $1,395
Frank Howard: Hillerich & Bradsby, game used, 1965-72, signed $595
Todd Hundley: Louisville Slugger, game used, cracked, 1995 .... $50
Pete Incaviglia: Cooper, game used, cracked, 1987-90 .... $50
Bo Jackson: Louisville Slugger, game used, 1991-93 .... $295
Joe Jackson: Hillerich & Bradsby, game used, 1921-30 .... $11,000
Reggie Jackson: Louisville Slugger, game used, 1968-72 .... $2,400
Reggie Jackson: Hillerich & Bradsby, game used, 1968-71, signed $1,795
Reggie Jackson: Adirondack, game used, cracked, 1971-79 .... $695
Reggie Jackson: Adirondack, game used, 1985 .... $695
Tommy John: Hillerich & Bradsby, game used, 1977-79 .... $295
Alex Johnson: Hillerich & Bradsby, game used, 1973-75, signed $295
Cliff Johnson: Louisville Slugger, game used, cracked, early 1980s $40
Davey Johnson: Hillerich & Bradsby, cracked 1970s, signed $185

Howard Johnson: Adirondack, game used, 1988 ....$95
Felix Jose: Louisville Slugger, game used, 1986-89..$50
Von Joshua: Hillerich & Bradsby, game used, 1977-79 ....$40
Wally Joyner: Louisville Slugger, game used, 1991-94..$90
Dave Justice: Louisville Slugger, game used, 1995 ....$275
Al Kaline: Hillerich & Bradsby, game used, 1965-72, signed.....................................$795
Al Kaline: Hillerich & Bradsby, game used, chipped, late 1970s................................$450
Ron Karkovice: Louisville Slugger, game used, cracked..$40
Eric Karros: Louisville Slugger, game used, 1992 ....$175
Don Kessinger: Louisville Slugger, game used, 1973-75..$90
Harmon Killebrew: Louisville Slugger, game used, 1965-71, signed.........................$1,595
Harmon Killebrew: Louisville Slugger, game used for 501st home run, 1971 ....$2,000
Dave Kingman: Louisville Slugger, game used, cracked, signed, 1984-85 ....$190
Ted Kluszewski: Hillerich & Bradsby, game used, 1958...$995
Ray Knight: Hillerich & Bradsby, game used, 1977-79..$95
Chuck Knoblauch: Louisville Slugger, game used, 1991-93 ....$175
John Kruk: Louisville Slugger, game used, cracked, 1993..$85
Tony Kubek: Hillerich & Bradsby, game used, 1965-72...$895
Harvey Kuenn: Hillerich & Bradsby, game used, 1965-72 ....$695
Lee Lacy: Adirondack, game used, cracked, 1971-79..$60
Carney Lansford: Hillerich & Bradsby, game used, 1977-79.......................................$65
Barry Larkin: Louisville Slugger, game used, 1986-89 ....$180
Ron LeFlore: Louisville Slugger, game used, 1977-79..$95
Mark Lemke: Louisville Slugger, game used, cracked, 1991-94...................................$80
Chet Lemon: Louisville Slugger, game used, 1990...$45
Nelson Liriano: Louisville Slugger, game used, cracked, 1995 ....$30
Pat Listach: Cooper, game used, cracked, 1993 ....$60
Davey Lopes: Adirondack, game used, 1981..$150
John Lowenstein: Hillerich & Bradsby, game used, 1980s $85
Greg Luzinski: Adirondack, game used, 1971-79...$125
Fred Lynn: Adirondack, game used, 1990 ....$140
Bill Madlock: Louisville Slugger, game used, 1984-85 ....$195
Greg Maddux: Louisville Slugger, 1995, game used, signed $1,295
Mickey Mantle: Louisville Slugger, game used, 1965-68, signed $10,995
Marty Marion: Hillerich & Bradsby, game used, 1940s, signed $850
Roger Maris: Hillerich & Bradsby, game used, cracked, 1960s $2,475
Roger Maris: Hillerich & Bradsby, game used, 1961 ....$4,995
Tino Martinez: Rose, game used, 1995..$110
Eddie Mathews: Hillerich & Bradsby, game used, uncracked, 1968, signed $2,000
Don Mattingly: Worth, game used, 1980s..$495
Don Mattingly: Worth, game used, 1995 ....$350
John Mayberry: Hillerich & Bradsby, game used, cracked, 1973-75 ....$125
Willie Mays: Hillerich & Bradsby, game used, 1965-72...$2,250
Willie Mays: Hillerich & Bradsby, game used, early 1970s......................................$1,895
Bill Mazeroski: Adirondack, game used, 1960 All-Star Game $2,000
Tim McCarver: Hillerich & Bradsby, game used, cracked, 1976................................$285
Willie McCovey: Louisville Slugger, game used, cracked, 1965-71, signed $1,495
Willie McCovey: Louisville Slugger, game used, 1974-75 ....$1,195
Oddibe McDowell: Louisville Slugger, game used, 1986-89.......................................$30
Fred McGriff: Louisville Slugger, game used, 1986-89 ....$195
Mark McGwire: Adirondack, game used, uncracked, 1992 ....$195
Mark McGwire: Adirondack, game used, 1991 All-Star Game, signed........................$595
Hal McRae: Hillerich & Bradsby, game used, 1973-75 ....$60
Hal McRae: Louisville Slugger, game used, 1977-79 ....$95
Kevin McReynolds: Adirondack, game used, 1988 ....$75
Minnie Minoso: Hillerich & Bradsby, game used, 1960 All-Star Game....................$1,495

Kevin Mitchell: Mizuno, game used, cracked, 1994 ....$50
Johnny Mize: Hillerich & Bradsby, game used, 1944-49 ....$995
Paul Molitor: Hillerich & Bradsby, game used, 1977-79.................................$795
Paul Molitor: Cooper, game used, cracked, signed, 1995 ....$250
Rick Monday: Hillerich & Bradsby, game used, uncracked, 1965-71, signed $175
Joe Morgan: Louisville Slugger, game used, 1977-79.......................................$400
Manny Mota: Hillerich & Bradsby, game used, 1965-72 ....$295
Thurman Munson: Hillerich & Bradsby, game used, 1977-79 ....$1,495
Bobby Murcer: Hillerich & Bradsby, game used, 1973-75 ....$175
Eddie Murray: Hillerich & Bradsby, game used, 1977-79, signed....................$1,295
Eddie Murray: Lousville Slugger, game used, cracked, 1988, signed...................$595
Stan Musial: Hillerich & Bradsby, game used, pre-1964................................$4,199
Tim Naehring: Louisville Slugger, game used, 1995...$90
Graig Nettles: Louisville Slugger, game used, 1984-85....................................$195
Phil Niekro: Hillerich & Bradsby, game used, 1977-79...................................$495
Otis Nixon: Cooper, game used, 1995 ....$60
Matt Nokes: Louisville Slugger, game used, 1984-85......................................$80
Ben Oglivie: Louisville Slugger, game used, cracked, 1980-83 ....$60
John Olerud: Adirondack, game used, 1994 ....$125
Tony Oliva: Hillerich & Bradsby, game used, missing knob, early 1970s...........$175
Al Oliver: Louisville Slugger, game used, 1965-72..$100
Jorge Orta: Louisville Slugger, game used, 1977-79..$50
Paul O'Neill: Louisville Slugger, game used, uncracked $180
Rafael Palmeiro: Louisville Slugger, game used, 1986 ....$195
Rafael Palmeiro: Cooper, game used, cracked, 1995..$85
Dave Parker: Louisville Slugger, game used, cracked, 1980-83 ....$125
Lance Parrish: Worth, game used, 1980s $95
Dan Pasqua: Louisville Slugger, game used, cracked, 1994............................$30
Tony Pena: Louisville Slugger, game used, 1986-89 ....$50
Terry Pendleton: Louisville Slugger, game used, 1985 World Series, signed $595
Tony Perez: Adirondack, game used, slight crack, late 1960s $550
Tony Perez: Louisville Slugger, game used, 1986-89, signed...........................$150
Gaylord Perry: Louisville Slugger, game used, early 1980s, signed...................$475
Mike Piazza: Louisville Slugger, game used, 1993...$595
Jim Piersall: Hillerich & Bradsby, game used, 1950s $995
Vada Pinson: Hillerich & Bradsby, game used, 1973-75.................................$250
Kirby Puckett: 1991 Adirondack, ALCS game used $595
Kirby Puckett; 1994 Louisville Slugger, game used..$300
Tim Raines: Louisville Slugger, game used, early 1980s, signed.......................$175
Tim Raines: Louisville Slugger, game used 1982 All-Star Game, signed $495
Manny Ramirez: Louisville Slugger, game used, 1995....................................$325
Willie Randolph: Louisville Slugger, game used, cracked, 1980s......................$95
Jody Reed: Louisville Slugger, game used, 1995 ....$50
Pee Wee Reese: Hillerich & Bradsby, game used, 1949-59 ....$1,595
Rich Reese: Hillerich & Bradsby, game used, 1965-72....................................$85
Ken Reitz: Louisville Slugger, game used, 1975-79...$40
Harold Reynolds: Louisville Slugger, game used, 1984-85..............................$30
Jim Rice: Louisville Slugger, game used, 1984-85..$175
Jose Rijo: Louisville Slugger, game used, 1994 ....$125
Cal Ripken Jr.: Louisville Slugger, game used, 1981......................................$2,250
Brooks Robinson: Hillerich & Bradsby, game used, 1972-75, signed.................$750
Frank Robinson: Hillerich & Bradsby, game used, 1965-71.............................$695
Jackie Robinson: Adirondack, game used, 1952-56 ....$6,995
Pete Rose: Hillerich & Bradsby, game used, 1965-72, signed.........................$1,795
Pete Rose: Hillerich & Bradsby, game used, 1972-75, signed.........................$1,595
Pete Rose: Mizuno, game used, cracked, 1980-83, signed $1,250

Joe Rudi: Hillerich & Bradsby, game used, 1973-75 ....$150
Babe Ruth: Hillerich & Bradsby, game used, uncracked, 1922 ....$8,955
Babe Ruth: Hillerich & Bradsby, game used, 1920s $18,995
Nolan Ryan: Louisville Slugger, game used, 1983-85, signed..$2,495
Tim Salmon: Mizuno, game used, 1995 ....$150
Ryne Sandberg: Adirondack, game used, cracked, 1988 ....$475
Manny Sanguillen: Hillerich & Bradsby, game used, 1965-72, signed.....................................$195
Benito Santiago: Worth, game used, cracked, 1995...$40
Mike Schmidt: Louisville Slugger, game used, 1974-75 ....$1,700
Mike Schmidt: Adirondack, game used, uncracked, 1980s...$750
Red Schoendienst: Adirondack, game used, cracked, 1950s $895
George Scott: Louisville Slugger, game used, 1973-75 ....$50
Tom Seaver: Hillerich & Bradsby, game used, 1972-75, signed...$1,495
Tom Seaver: Hillerich & Bradsby, game used, uncracked, 1977-79.......................................$1,625
Kevin Seitzer: Louisville Slugger, game used, 1986-89...$50
Ruben Sierra: Louisville Slugger, game used, 1991-92, signed $125
Ruben Sierra: Adirondack, game used, 1991 All-Star Game $245
Ted Simmons: Louisville Slugger, game used, 1984-85 ....$150
Moose Skowron: Hillerich & Bradsby, game used, 1950s...$995
Roy Smalley: Louisville Slugger, game used, 1965-72 ....$50
Ozzie Smith: Hillerich & Bradsby, game used, 1977-79, signed $695
Cory Snyder: Louisville Slugger, game used, uncracked, signed $95
Sammy Sosa: Adirondack, game used, 1995 ....$185
Mario Soto: Louisville Slugger, game used, 1984-85 ....$60
Willie Stargell: Hillerich & Bradsby, game used, 1964 All-Star Game, signed $2,495
Willie Stargell: Hillerich & Bradsby, game used, late 1970s...$475
Terry Steinbach: Adirondack, game used, cracked, 1994 ....$70
Rennie Stennett: Louisville Slugger, game used, 1975-79 ....$50
B.J. Surhoff: Adirondack, game used, 1995..$80
Danny Tartabull: Worth, game used, cracked, 1992 ....$80
Mickey Tettleton: Louisville Slugger, game used, cracked, 1984-85, signed $145
Mickey Tettleton: Adirondack, game used, 1995 ....$120
Frank Thomas: Worth, game used, two-toned, 1994, cracked $350
Gorman Thomas: Adirondack, game used, 1981, cracked..$80
Luis Tiant: Hillerich & Bradsby, game used, 1965-72, signed $695
Alan Trammell: Worth, game used, early 1980s, signed $175
Alan Trammell: Louisville Slugger, game used, 1980-83, signed..$395
Andy Van Slyke: Louisville Slugger, game used, 1995 ....$275
Greg Vaughn: Adirondack, game used, 1991 ....$70
Mo Vaughn: Louisville Slugger, game used, 1995...$495
Otto Velez: Hillerich & Bradsby, game used, 1976, cracked $90
Robin Ventura: Louisville Slugger, game used, 1993 ....$175
Pete Vuckovich: Louisville Slugger, game used, 1977-79 ....$75
Bob Watson: Adirondack, game used, 1971-79 ....$95
Walt Weiss: Louisville Slugger, game used, cracked, 1995 ....$45
Walt Weiss: Worth, game used, 1989 ALCS...$235
Bill White: Hillerich & Bradsby, game used, 1950s...$895
Devon White: Louisville Slugger, game used, 1990...$100
Frank White: Adirondack, game used, cracked, 1971-79..$60
Roy White: Hillerich & Bradsby, game used, 1979...$175
Ernie Whitt: Louisville Slugger, game used, 1990 ....$20
Dick Willams: Hillerich & Bradsby, game used, 1950s..$450
Matt Williams: Cooper, game used, slight crack, 1994 ....$295
Dave Winfield: Hillerich & Bradsby, game used, 1973-75, signed..$1,295
Dave Winfield: Cooper, game used, uncracked, 1994..$225
Dave Winfield: Adirondack, game used, 1979 All-Star Game, uncracked $1,850

Jimmy Wynn: Hillerich & Bradsby, game used, cracked, 1976 ....$180
Carl Yastrzemski: Hillerich & Bradsby, game used, 1960-64 ....$1,695
Carl Yastrzemski: Hillerich & Bradsby, game used, 1965-72 ....$995
Carl Yastrzemski: Louisville Slugger, game used, early 1980s $575
Robin Yount: Hillerich & Bradsby, game used, 1973-75 ....$1,995
Robin Yount: Louisville Slugger, game used, 1984-85 ....$295
Richie Zisk: Adirondack, game used, cracked, 1981 ....$60

Unused game bats

Roberto Alomar: Cooper, 1992, C243 ....$150
Carlos Baerga: Louisville Slugger, 1994 ....$250
Carlos Baerga: Adirondack, 1995 World Series $595
Albert Belle: Cooper, B343 ....$150
Barry Bonds: Louisville Slugger H238, 1994 ....$295
Bobby Bonilla: Cooper, S318 ....$75
George Brett: Louisville Slugger, P89, 1983-84, signed $395
Jose Canseco: Cooper, R161 ....$150
Gary Carter: Louisville Slugger, P89, 1984-85 ....$135
Gary Carter: Louisville Slugger, 1982 All-Star Game, signed $450
Joe Carter: Cooper, B343, 1993 World Series $695
Will Cark: Cooper, C271 ....$150
Andre Dawson: Louisville Slugger, 1980-83, C271, signed $195
Tony Fernandez: Cooper, F322, 1993 World Series $175
Cecil Fielder: Cooper, C271 ....$95
Travis Fryman: Adirondack, 1992 All-Star Game $495
Andres Galarraga: Cooper, C243 ....$75
Juan Gonzalez: Cooper, P72 ....$150
Ken Griffey Jr.: Louisville Slugger, C271, 1994, signed $350
Bo Jackson: Louisville Slugger, J93, 1990 ....$125
Reggie Jackson: Louisville Slugger, H174, 1980-83, #44 ....$295
Chipper Jones: Adirondack, 1995 World Series $595
Michael Jordan: Worth, black, signed $275
Eddie Murray: Louisville Slugger, R161, 1983-84, signed $350
Eddie Murray: Adirondack, 1995 World Series, signed $695
John Olerud: Cooper, T141, 1993 World Series $695
Rafael Palmeiro: Cooper, S329 ....$85
Jim Rice: Cooper, R206 ....$85
Jim Rice: Hillerich & Bradsby, M159 ....$295
Ryne Sandberg: Louisville Slugger, B267, 1983-84 ....$295
Mike Schmidt: Adirondack, 1986, 154A $495
Ruben Sierra: Louisville Slugger, 1991-92, T141 ....$125
Ruben Sierra: Louisville Slugger, 1992 All-Star, 484A $350
Matt Williams: Cooper, M110 ....$150
Dave Winfield: Cooper, DW20 ....$150
Robin Yount: Louisville Slugger, 1984-84, P72, signed $350

Team-signed bats

1971 Baltimore Orioles: 1968-72 Reggie Jackson Adirondack model, with 17 signatures, includes Dave McNally, Jim Palmer, Boog Powell, Brooks Robinson and Frank Robinson $1,350

1990 Boston Red Sox: Boston Red Sox bat, with 41 signatures, includes Wade Boggs, Ellis Burks, Roger Clemens, Dwight Evans, Mike Greenwell and Jeff Reardon $325

1995 Boston Red Sox: game-used team bat, with 25 signatures, includes Rick Aguilera, Jose Canseco, Roger Clemens, Mike Greenwell, Mo Vaughn and Tim Wakefield $195

1992 California Angels: Louisville Slugger, game used in spring training, with 25 signatures, includes Jim Abbott, Chuck Finley, Gary Gaetti and Mark Langston...$200

1995 California Angels: Damon Easley's game-used Louisville Slugger, with 25 signatures, includes Jim Abbott, Chili Davis, Chuck Finley, Mark Langston, Tim Salmon,
Lee Smith and J.T. Snow $125

1994 Chicago Cubs: generic Cooper model bat, with 25 signatures, includes Mark Grace, Ryne Sandberg and Sammy Sosa...$150

1959 Chicago White Sox: Billy Martin game used, with 24 signatures, includes Luis Aparicio, Norm Cash, Nellie Fox, Al Lopez and Early Wynn $1,150

1992 Chicago White Sox: Dan Pasqua model bat, with 17 signatures, includes Carlton Fisk, Bo Jackson, Tim Raines, Frank Thomas and Robin Ventura $225

1978 Cincinnati Reds: 1977-79 Pete Rose Hillerich & Bradsby model, with 20 signatures, includes Dave Concepcion, George Foster, Ken Griffey, Pete Rose and Tom Seaver.................$1,150

1995 Colorado Rockies: store model Adirondack, black, with 28 signatures, includes Dante Bichette, Andres Galarraga and Larry Walker...$350

1987 Detroit Tigers: Kirk Gibson model bat, with 29 signatures, includes Sparky Anderson, Darrell Evans, Kirk Gibson, Jack Morris, Alan Trammell and Lou Whitaker $315

1993 Florida Marlins: Jim Corsi game-used bat, with 19 signatures, includes Jeff Conine, Gary Sheffield and Walt Weiss $400

1995 Houston Astros: generic black Adirondack, with 31 signatures, includes Jeff Bagwell, Craig Biggio and Doug Drabek...$295

1982 Kansas City Royals: on a George Brett game-used Louisville Slugger, signed by the entire team..$795

1991 Milwaukee Brewers: on a Paul Molitor Milwaukee Brewers bat, with 24 signatures, includes Paul Molitor, Greg Vaughn and Robin Yount..$150

1995 Montreal Expos: store model Adirondack, with 30 signatures, includes Moises Alou, Will Cordero and Rondell White $175

1969 New York Mets: Gil Hodges pro model Adirondack, with 25 signatures, includes Nolan Ryan and Tom Seaver $450

1956 New York Yankees: Moose Skowron game-used bat, with 22 signatures, includes Mickey Mantle and Casey Stengel $3,250

1990 Oakland A's: generic Adirondack model, with 27 signatures, includes Jose Canseco, Rickey Henderson, Mark McGwire and Dave Stewart...$250

1992 Oakland A's: Oakland A's team bat, with 17 signatures, includes Harold Baines, Jose Canseco, Dennis Eckersley, Rickey Henderson and Mark McGwire..................................$240

1982 St. Louis Cardinals: Steve Braun World Series bat, with 27 signatures, includes Keith Hernandez, Jim Kaat, Willie McGee, Ozzie Smith and Bruce Sutter $495

1991 American League All-Stars: Danny Tartabull bat, with 29 signatures, includes Roberto Alomar, Wade Boggs, Roger Clemens, Cecil Fielder, Carlton Fisk, Ken Griffey Jr., Rickey Henderson, Jack McDowell, Cal Ripken Jr., Ruben Sierra and
Danny Tartabull...$495

Basic tips on bat collecting

Not a week goes by that I don't receive a call regarding the status of a bat in someone's possession. "Is it a game bat or a store bat?" is the usual question, followed immediately by "How much is it worth?"

Then there is the myriad of bat companies, ie. Adirondack, Hillerich & Bradsby, Spalding, Worth, Hanna-Batrite, just to name a few. Which companies made game bats? What length bat did a player use?

So many questions, so little space. But I will try to clarify a few basic tips that may make bat collecting a little less painful, and hopefully, a little more profitable.

First, this article will deal mainly with Hillerich & Bradsby, hereafter H&B bats, since this is what most collectors, especially collectors of older bats, prefer. Adirondack started making bats around 1946 and are now owned by Rawlings. Simple deduction would eliminate Ruth or Cobb Adirondacks from the game bat category. Many players, such as Willie Mays, Gil Hodges and Joe Adcock, started using Adirondack bats during the 1950s.

Hanna Bat Co., of Athens, Ga., also found favor with ballplayers, especially the Yankees of the 1930s. In a legal fight with H&B during that time, Lou Gehrig stated that he occasionally used Hanna Bats. The difficulty lies in knowing which ones are game bats. In regards to Hanna bats of the period, it is almost impossible. You can decipher whether or not the wood is of top quality, whether the dimensions are proper, or if the bat dates from the correct period, but that's about as close as it gets without actual provenance.

Spalding is another popular company that made bats for several players from the late 1870s until World War II. These bats were the preferred tool of men such as Frank Chance, Sam Crawford, Fred Clarke, and a host of others. Again, to tell if you have a game bat or a store model would take an entire article in itself, since there are so many variables.

But on to the subject of H&B bats and why they are probably the easiest of all to decipher, if any of this might be considered easy. I will touch on the quick, generally accepted guidelines for dating and determining possible professional game use. Then, if a bat warrants further examination as to its game possibilities, at least one will know it's worth getting it to an expert for a closer examination.

The place to start looking at any H&B bat, to decide whether the bat has even the remotest possibility of being a game model, is on the knob. The year 1943 is generally considered the first year H&B applied players' model numbers to the bat's knob.

Professional players' bats from 1943 through 1975 will have this number on the knob. These codes will be a letter followed by three or fewer numbers, ie. S2, D29, O1, K55, etc. No professional bat may have more than one letter unless it is an "L," which must come at the end, thus designating a large knob. Joe DiMaggio used a D29 early in his career, then switched to a D29L, which was simply a bat with the same dimensions except for the large knob. H&B bats made during and after 1976 will find the model number moved to the barrel above the player's name.

If your bat has inch marks, a single digit, or two letters followed by a number, they are most likely a store model bat. A single digit, ie. 4, would indicate the length which would be 34". If your Hank Aaron bat has HA3, it is a Hank Aaron store model with a length of 33".

Bats made prior to the 1943 will be void of model designations unless they returned to the factory. If this was the case, the code would be found on both ends of the bat and filled with white paint. If a pre-1943 bat has inch markings, it must be considered a store model bat unless accompanied by a letter from a primary source, ie. ballplayer, family etc., and even then, its value would be a fraction of one without inch marks.

The center label of an H&B bat tells the rest of the story. Let's start with a point that must be made right off. A game model H&B bat made after 1918 must be a model 125. You will find this number in the center of the logo under the slogan "Louisville Slugger."

Prior to 1918, many bats have no model number at all, with only a "dash, dot, dash" where the 125 would normally appear. Other numbers, such as 40, 8, 250, 14, etc., must for general purposes be considered store model designations.

Next, all game model bats made on or after 1931 must have the slogan "Powerized" to the right of the label. This will be found in conjunction with "Bone Rubbed" or "Oil Tempered" which is fine. If you see the slogan "Flame Tempered," again, it must be considered a store model bat.

For dating purposes, I will list the major general center label changes and their respective dates as accurately as I can determine at this time:

1. J.F. Hillerich & Son with a "dash, dot, dash" beneath, 1897-1905.
2. J.F. Hillerich & Son Co., the world "Co." added, 1906-1915.

Top left: barrel marks from a 1921-31 era Paul Waner game bat. Above: the center label of a 1921-31 Waner game-used bat.

Left: The K34 mark, filled in with white paint, is on the knob and also the end of the barrel. The mark was applied to pre-1943 bats when they were returned to the factory for duplication. Above: the center label of a 1921-31 Hillerich & Bradsby Tris Speaker store bat. The T.S. in the label are the player's initials.

At right: the block letter name means the player was not under contract with H&B. Below: the center label of the first model H&B bat. Bradsby's name was added in 1916; the -.- was added around 1917 or 1918.

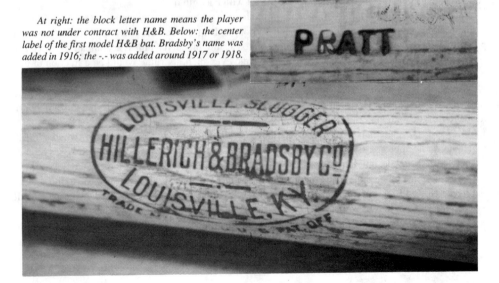

3. Bradsby name incorporated - Hillerich & Bradsby Co., but with the "dash, dot, dash" still below the name in the center, 1916-1921.

4. Same as above but with the words "Made In USA" added under Hillerich & Bradsby, 1922-1979.

5. The number "2" of 125 will be found above the "&" in the center label on bats made after 1960. The "1" will be above 125s made before.

This is called the Malta theory named after bat dating "Columbus," Vince Malta. This theory seems to hold water for all game bats made after 1949 and is used by most collectors and dealers to date labels.

6. A small "r" in a circle after the words "Louisville Slugger" replaced the legend that until then was under the oval. This is assumed to have taken place sometime after the All-Star break in 1964. Any bat with the small "r" is considered a post-1964 bat.

7. Another small "r" found its way above the "d" of Powerized, sometime in 1973.

8. The Hillerich & Bradsby Co. center logo was changed to Louisville Slugger in 1980.

9. "Trade Mark Reg. U.S. Pat. Off." is found under the oval of all H&B bats from 1906 until about 1937, when the "U.S. Pat. Off." was dropped, leaving only the "Trade Mark Reg." This mark continued until sometime around 1943-44 when it was again switched, this time to "Reg. U.S. Pat. Off" which was removed and replaced after 1964 by the small "r".

10. The Liberty Bell Bi-Centennial bats are only from 1976.

Now if that's not enough to confuse anybody who's still awake, consider that the words "Powerized" and it's lightning bolts and assorted accompanying legends changed constantly, and you have real confusion. But that's nothing to what the barrel markings are doing to theories and sanity.

The player's name should appear on the barrel, in script if he had a player's contract with H&B, in block if he did not. What appears above and below this name is enough to drive one mad, but I will list a few supposed "givens."

1. It is assumed that the word "Genuine" appeared above the player's name sometime in 1936, with "Louisville Slugger" appearing below the name sometime in 1937. Prior to that one might find the word "Trade Mark" either above or below with nothing else, "Trade Mark" above with "Reg. U.S. Pat. Off." below, or just the player's name with nothing above or below it, a practice which seems to date from the 1932-36 period.

2. Player model number, ie. S2, moved to barrel above name in 1976.

3. If you see something under the player's name, such as U.C.L.A. or Illinois State, you have a pro-model bat made for a college. They are not considered game-used bats and sell for a slight premium over store models.

And what does all this have to do with anything? If you have a professional model Babe Ruth bat with Genuine above his name and Louisville Slugger below, the bat is 35" in length, a model 125, weighing 40 oz., with no model number on the knob, what do you have?

Ruth retired after the 1935 season, but the word Genuine is not supposed to have been added to bats until 1936. What if that date is wrong and it was actually added at the end of the 1935 season? Is this a game-used bat or a coaches bat? Using the dating technique I've just laid out, it would have to be a coaches bat.

What difference does it make, you may ask? Well, if you were the owner of the above bat, the difference would be about $10,000 that wouldn't end up in your pocket if you went to sell it. So you can see how crucial some of these dating techniques are in relation to certain players and the dates in which they played.

Use the above guidelines to decide whether or not you have a possible game-used H&B bat. If your bat falls into the game category, get it to someone who knows bats. There are lots of ingredients that will help a dealer access the possibility of game use - the proper dating period for a certain player, the correct dimensions (most factory records are incomplete prior to 1930 and sketchy even after that), proper game use, correct model numbers, high quality wood, finish, and on and on and on.

And even after all of this, in most cases, we can only reasonably ascertain that a bat was game used by the player whose name appears on the barrel, and only that the bat was proper for one ordered by him at the time in which he played.

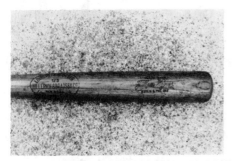

Honus Wagner game bat, 1921-31. The "MADE IN USA" in the center didn't start until 1921; Wagner retired as a player in 1917, so he could only have used the bat as a coach. The difference in value - $15,000.

Store Model Bats

This Jim Bottomley game-used bat from 1921-31 has block letters; the last name only indicates a pre-contract bat.

This 1921-31 Rogers Hornsby game-used bat lacks the "Powerized" stamp, but does have a "MADE IN USA" logo.

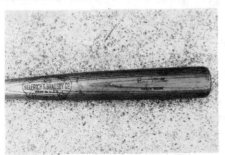

This Bing Miller game-used bat from 1932-36 has the "Powerized" stamp.

This Bill Terry game-used bat from 1937-43 has "TRADE MARK REG." under the label.

Notice that the 2 in 125 is above the & between H&B on this 1960-64 Stan Musial game-used bat. Musial had block letter bats for most of his career.

This is a 1965-72 game-used Luis Aparicio bat. Notice the small trademark symbol after Slugger in the center label, but there is none above the d in "Powerized."

If you venture into the world of collecting game-used bats, get acquainted with a reputable dealer who knows what he is doing and will stand behind his product. Learn as much as you can yourself; an educated collector is good for the hobby. Don't be afraid to ask questions, no matter how trivial they may seem; that's how you learn. Most dealers will share their knowledge because they know that once that confidence is built up, you will become a good customer.

— David Bushing

Store model bats

Hank Aaron: Adirondack $45
Hank Aaron: Wilson $80
Dick Allen: Adirondack...$35
Ernie Banks: Louisville Slugger..$45
Hank Bauer: Adirondack..$45
Johnny Bench: Louisville Slugger $50
Yogi Berra: Hillerich & Bradsby...$65
Bobby Bonds: Louisville Slugger..$45
Johnny Callison: Hillerich & Bradsby $45
Fred Clarke: Gold Medal Spalding, 1908-10..$450
Roberto Clemente: Sears...$85
Roberto Clemente: Hillerich & Bradsby..$75
Mickey Cochrane: Hanna Batrite $60
Rocky Colavito: Spalding...$50
Eddie Collins: Louisville Slugger..$95
Joe DiMaggio: J.C. Higgins...$125
Joe DiMaggio: Revelation..$175
Joe DiMaggio: Louisville Slugger $200
Carlton Fisk: Adirondack $50
Jimmie Foxx: J.C. Higgins...$85
Jimmie Foxx: Hanna Batrite $150
Jimmie Foxx: Louisville Slugger $125
Charlie Gehringer: Louisville Slugger $165
Joe Gordon: Louisville Slugger...$100
Goose Goslin: Diamond Ace...$195
Ken Harrelson: Louisville Slugger $55
Babe Herman: Hillerich & Bradsby...$155
Rogers Hornsby: Louisville Slugger...$275
Cleon Jones: Adirondack $25
George Kell: Spalding..$135
George Kelly: Louisville Slugger $100
Mickey Mantle: Adirondack Big Stick...$75
Mickey Mantle: Hillerich & Bradsby 1960s $195
Mickey Mantle: Louisville Slugger..$100
Roger Maris: Hillerich & Bradsby...$75
Eddie Mathews: Hillerich & Bradsby..$45
Willie Mays: Adirondack..$60
Willie McCovey: Adirondack..$40
Joe Medwick: Hanna Batrite...$35
Felix Milan: Adirondack...$25
Joe Morgan: Hillerich & Bradsby $35
Mel Ott: MacGregor Gold Smith $150
Vada Pinson: Adirondack..$50
Kirby Puckett: Louisville Slugger..$75

Brooks Robinson: Louisville Slugger $65
Frank Robinson: Hillerich & Bradsby..$65
Jackie Robinson: Hillerich & Bradsby...$75
Jackie Robinson: store model, signed $1,995
Pete Rose: Hillerich & Bradsby $60
Babe Ruth: Revelation Bat Co...$95
Babe Ruth: Louisville Slugger $95
Ron Santo: Adirondack...$35
Al Simmons: J.C. Higgins...$125
Tris Speaker: Hanna Batrite $95
Tris Speaker: Hillerich & Bradsby...$295
Willie Stargell: Louisville Slugger $65
Vern Stephens: MacGregor Gold Smith...$100
Joe Torre: Adirondack..$30
Paul Waner: Louisville Slugger $125
Billy Williams: Louisville Slugger $85
Ted Williams: Hillerich & Bradsby..$125
Ted Williams: Hanna Batrite $75
Carl Yastrzemski: Louisville Slugger...$65
Heinie Zimmerman: Spalding, 1916-20 ....$495

Cooperstown Bat Co. Commemorative Bats

Cooperstown Bat Co., Cooperstown, N.Y., has produced several limited-edition bats (500) to commemorate several players, stadiums and teams.

The Cooperstown Bat Co. has a series of bats devoted to "Famous Players."

C.B.C.'s 10 Stadium Series bats include: 1) Fenway Park, 1986; 2) Wrigley Field, 1986; 3) Ebbets Field, 1987; 4) Polo Grounds, 1987; 5) Yankee Stadium, 1987; 6) Forbes Field, 1988; 7) Shibe Park, 1988; 8) Briggs/Tiger Stadium, 1989; 9) Sportsman's Park, 1989; and 10) Comiskey Park, 1990.

C.B.C.'s Famous Players Series includes these players: Pee Wee Reese, 1988; Ted Williams, 1989; Yogi Berra, 1990; Ernie Banks, 1991; Carl Yastrzemski, 1992; Stan Musial, 1993; Duke Snider, 1994; Frank Robinson, 1995; and Mike Schmidt, 1996.

C.B.C. was commissioned by the National Baseball Hall of Fame to produce a limited edition of 500 sets of five bats and a display rack for the inaugural "Class of 1936" - Ty Cobb, Walter Johnson, Christy Mathewson, Babe Ruth and Honus Wagner.

The company also makes bats for autographing. A C.B.C. 1989 Cooperstown Hall of Fame autograph model bat, signed by 18 greats (including Stan Musial, Tom Seaver, Bob Gibson, Steve Carlton, Luis Aparicio, Willie Stargell and Enos Slaughter), was offered in an auction for a minimum bid of $350.

Another C.B.C. Hall of Fame autograph model bat, signed by 24 Hall of Famers (including Stan Musial, Ted Williams, Mike Schmidt, Willie Mays, Hank Aaron, Pete Rose, Johnny Bench, Lefty Gomez, Jocko Conlan, Happy Chandler, Duke Snider, Willie McCovey, Ernie Banks and Lou Brock), was offered in an auction for a minimum bid of $900.

C.B.C.'s Vintage Club Series includes bats for the Brooklyn Dodgers, 1990; Boston Braves, 1991; and Milwaukee Braves, 1992. A Brooklyn Dodgers bat, signed by 34 Dodger greats (including Sandy Koufax, Andy Pafko, Duke Snider, Carl Abrams, Ralph Branca, Don Drysdale, Billy Herman, Mickey Owen and Chuck Connor) was offered in an auction for a minimum bid of $250.

C.B.C. also creates bats for team autograph collectors. The 1992 Major League Team Series had bats for seven teams - California Angels, Chicago White Sox, Cincinnati Reds, Detroit Tigers, Pittsburgh Pirates, San Francisco Giants and Toronto Blue Jays.

The 1991 Major League Team Series features six teams - Chicago Cubs, Kansas City Royals, Los Angeles Dodgers, Oakland Athletics, Philadelphia Phillies and St. Louis Cardinals.

The 1990 Major League Team Series included four teams - Baltimore Orioles, Boston Red Sox, New York Mets and New York Yankees.

C.B.C. has also created three Doubleday Field Bats - in 1983, 1985 and 1989. The 1983 bat is red and brown. Twenty have a plain red band at the throat of the bat; the remaining 124 had a red ring with a brown center stripe. The 1985 version was also red and brown and featured an enlarged drawing of the stadium compared to the first bat. The company has not limited production on these bats, and estimates about 1,900 have been made. About 900 of these were made before 1988 and have the red and brown stripe. Those after 1988 have a red and brown band art reading "Stadium Series."

A limited edition of 1,000 bats were issued 1989 in red and blue to commemorate the 150th anniversary of baseball in America. The text was changed to give the history of the stadium, beginning with the Phinney Lot in 1839 and ending with the 1939 "all-star" game for the dedication of the Hall of Fame. The company did not number the bats in this edition, so there is not an edition number stamped into the knob of the bat.

Bats have also been created to commemorate the Negro League teams; the 1993 and 1994 All-Star Games; the opening of Camden Yards in Baltimore; Cal Ripken's consecutive games played streak; baseball "Immortals" Shoeless Joe Jackson and Ty Cobb; Roberto Clemente; Rusty Staub; Ralph Kiner; Ted Williams' Museum; and the Cincinnati Reds' Big Red Machine.

Louisville Slugger Hall of Fame Induction Bats

Since 1983, Louisville Slugger, in conjunction with the Baseball Hall of Fame, has issued limited-edition bats commemorating the inductions of players, executives, managers and umpires into the Hall of Fame. Their names are engraved into the bat barrels with gold lettering.

Five hundred bats, each numbered, were made per induction ceremony from 1936-87. From 1988 on there have been 1,000 bats made per ceremony. The first 500 are sold through subscription. The Hall of Fame sells the others during the induction ceremonies.

1936 - Ty Cobb, Walter Johnson, Christy Mathewson, Babe Ruth, Honus Wagner .... $495-$575

1937 - Morgan Bulkeley, Ban Johnson, Nap Lajoie, Connie Mack, John McGraw, Tris Speaker, George Wright, Cy Young .... $250-$275

1938 - Grover Alexander, Alexander Cartwright, Henry Chadwick $195

1939 - Cap Anson, Eddie Collins, Charles Comiskey, Candy Cummings, Buck Ewing, Lou Gehrig, Willie Keeler, Charles Radbourn, George Sisler, Al Spalding .... $275-$295

1942 - Rogers Hornsby $195

1944 - Kenesaw Landis $195

1945 - Roger Bresnahan, Dan Brouthers, Fred Clarke, Jimmy Collins, Ed Delahanty, Hugh Duffy, Hugh Jennings, Mike Kelly, James O'Rourke, Wilbert Robinson .... $185-$195

1971 - Dave Bancroft, Chick Hafey, Harry Hooper, Rube Marquard, Satchel Paige, George Weiss $185

1972 - Yogi Berra, Josh Gibson, Lefty Gomez, Will Harridge, Sandy Koufax, Buck Leonard, Ross Youngs, Early Wynn .... $425-$500

1973 - Roberto Clemente, Billy Evans, Monte Irvin, George Kelly, Warren Spahn, Mickey Welch $375

1974 - Cool Papa Bell, Jim Bottomley, Jocko Conlan, Whitey Ford, Mickey Mantle, Sam Thompson .... $350-$500

1975 - Earl Averill, Bucky Harris, Billy Herman, Judy Johnson, Ralph Kiner $225

1976 - Oscar Charleston, Roger Connor, Cal Hubbard, Bob Lemon, Freddie Lindstrom, Robin Roberts $185

1977 - Ernie Banks, Martin DiHigo, John Lloyd, Al Lopez, Amos Rusie, Joe Sewell .... $150-$175

1978 - Addie Joss, Larry MacPhail, Eddie Mathews $185

1979 - Warren Giles, Willie Mays, Hack Wilson $325

1980 - Al Kaline, Chuck Klein, Duke Snider, Tom Yawkey .... $150-$200

1981 - Rube Foster, Bob Gibson, Johnny Mize .... $150-$175

1982 - Hank Aaron, Happy Chandler, Travis Jackson, Frank Robinson $375

1983 - Walter Alston, George Kell, Juan Marichal, Brooks Robinson .... $375-$450

1984 - Luis Aparicio, Don Drysdale, Wes Ferrell, Harmon Killebrew, Pee Wee Reese .... $175-$395

1985 - Lou Brock, Enos Slaughter, Arky Vaughan, Hoyt Wilhelm .... $275-$295

1986 - Bobby Doerr, Willie McCovey, Ernie Lombardi $285

1987 - Ray Dandridge, Jim Hunter, Billy Williams $185

1988 - Willie Stargell $185

1989 - Al Barlick, Johnny Bench, Red Schoendienst, Carl Yastrzemski $195

1990 - Joe Morgan, Jim Palmer $250

1991 - Rod Carew, Fergie Jenkins, Tony Lazzeri, Gaylord Perry, Bill Veeck $225

World Series Black Bats

World Series Black Bats, created by Hillerich and Bradsby, are given to participating players and dignitaries from teams in the Series. They have facsimile signatures of the entire team in gold on a dark black ebony bat.

1934 Detroit Tigers World Series Black Bat .... $2,500-$3,000

1935 Detroit Tigers World Series Black Bat .... $1,500-$2,000

1936 New York Yankees World Series Black Bat .... $2,000-$2,750

1936 New York Giants World Series Black Bat .... $1,200-$1,500

1937 New York Yankees World Series Black Bat .... $1,500-$2,500

1937 New York Giants World Series Black Bat .... $1,000-$1,200

1938 New York Yankees World Series Black Bat .... $1,200-$1,500

1938 Chicago Cubs World Series Black Bat .... $1,200-$1,500

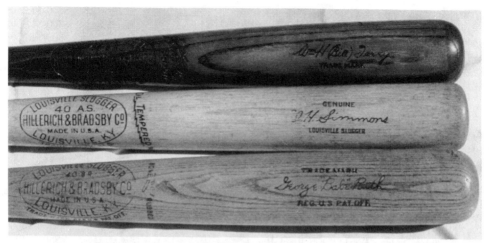

Notice the different labeling on these old-time Hillerich & Bradsby bats.

This 1916-21 era Honus Wagner 40W decal bat is from one of the most beautiful series of store bats ever made.

This is an early JF Hillerich & Son Co. Ty Cobb decal bat, circa 1911-15.

This special bat commemorates the 1971 Baltimore Orioles as American League playoff winners.

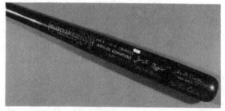

This is a 1941 New York Yankees World Series Black Bat.

Cooperstown Bat Co. has produced several limited-edition commemorative bats.

1939 New York Yankees World Series Black Bat .... $800-$1,250
1939 Cincinnati Reds World Series Black Bat .... $800-$1,000
1940 Cincinnati Reds World Series Black Bat .... $800-$1,250
1940 Detroit Tigers World Series Black Bat .... $800-$1,250
1941 New York Yankees World Series Black Bat .... $800-$1,200
1941 Brooklyn Dodgers World Series Black Bat .... $1,200-$1,500
1942 New York Yankees World Series Black Bat .... $700-$900
1942 St. Louis Cardinals World Series Black Bat .... $600-$800
1943 St. Louis Cardinals World Series Black Bat .... $500-$700
1943 New York Yankees World Series Black Bat .... $500-$700
1944 St. Louis Cardinals World Series Black Bat .... $1,000-$1,200
1944 St. Louis Browns World Series Black Bat .... $1,000-$1,200
1945 Detroit Tigers World Series Black Bat .... $600-$800
1945 Chicago Cubs World Series Black Bat .... $600-$800
1946 St. Louis Cardinals World Series Black Bat .... $500-$700
1946 Boston Red Sox World Series Black Bat .... $1,000-$1,200
1947 New York Yankees World Series Black Bat .... $500-$600
1947 Brooklyn Dodgers World Series Black Bat .... $500-$700
1948 Cleveland Indians World Series Black Bat .... $800-$1,200
1948 Boston Braves World Series Black Bat .... $600-$800
1949 New York Yankees World Series Black Bat .... $450-$650
1949 Brooklyn Dodgers World Series Black Bat .... $500-$700
1950 New York Yankees World Series Black Bat .... $500-$700
1950 Philadelphia Phillies World Series Black Bat .... $600-$800
1951 New York Yankees World Series Black Bat .... $800-$1,200
1951 New York Giants World Series Black Bat .... $700-$900
1952 New York Yankees World Series Black Bat .... $450-$650
1952 Brooklyn Dodgers World Series Black Bat .... $500-$700
1953 New York Yankees World Series Black Bat .... $425-$500
1953 Brooklyn Dodgers World Series Black Bat .... $500-$700
1954 New York Giants World Series Black Bat .... $500-$700
1954 Cleveland Indians World Series Black Bat .... $500-$700
1955 Brooklyn Dodgers World Series Black Bat .... $1,500-$1,900
1955 New York Yankees World Series Black Bat .... $400-$500
1956 New York Yankees World Series Black Bat .... $600-$800
1956 Brooklyn Dodgers World Series Black Bat .... $500-$700
1957 Milwaukee Braves World Series Black Bat .... $500-$700
1957 New York Yankees World Series Black Bat .... $400-$500
1958 Milwaukee Braves World Series Black Bat .... $350-$550
1958 New York Yankees World Series Black Bat .... $300-$400
1959 Los Angeles Dodgers World Series Black Bat .... $500-$700
1959 Chicago White Sox World Series Black Bat .... $800-$1,000
1960 New York Yankees World Series Black Bat .... $300-$400
1960 Pittsburgh Pirates World Series Black Bat .... $500-$700
1961 New York Yankees World Series Black Bat .... $800-$1,000
1961 Cincinnati Reds World Series Black Bat .... $300-$400
1962 New York Yankees World Series Black Bat .... $300-$400
1962 San Francisco Giants World Series Black Bat .... $400-$600
1963 Los Angeles Dodgers World Series Black Bat .... $300-$400
1963 New York Yankees World Series Black Bat .... $300-$400
1964 St. Louis Cardinals World Series Black Bat .... $300-$400
1964 New York Yankees World Series Black Bat .... $300-$400
1965 Los Angeles Dodgers World Series Black Bat .... $350-$450
1965 Minnesota Twins World Series Black Bat .... $350-$500
1966 Baltimore Orioles World Series Black Bat .... $300-$450
1966 Los Angeles Dodgers World Series Black Bat .... $300-$400

1967 Boston Red Sox World Series Black Bat .... $500-$700
1967 St. Louis Cardinals World Series Black Bat .... $350-$450
1968 Detroit Tigers World Series Black Bat .... $500-$700
1968 St. Louis Cardinals World Series Black Bat .... $300-$400
1969 Baltimore Orioles World Series Black Bat .... $250-$350
1969 New York Mets World Series Black Bat .... $800-$1,000
1970 Baltimore Orioles World Series Black Bat .... $200-$300
1970 Cincinnati Reds World Series Black Bat .... $200-$300
1971 Pittsburgh Pirates World Series Black Bat.. $200-$300
1971 Baltimore Orioles World Series Black Bat .... $200-$300
1972 Oakland A's World Series Black Bat... $200-$300
1972 Cincinnati Reds World Series Black Bat .... $200-$300
1973 Oakland A's World Series Black Bat... $200-$300
1973 New York Mets World Series Black Bat .... $300-$400
1974 Oakland A's World Series Black Bat... $200-$300
1974 Los Angeles Dodgers World Series Black Bat .... $200-$300
1975 Cincinnati Reds World Series Black Bat .... $300-$400
1975 Boston Red Sox World Series Black Bat .... $300-$400
1976 Cincinnati Reds World Series Black Bat .... $225-$325
1976 New York Yankees World Series Black Bat .... $200-$300
1977 Los Angeles Dodgers World Series Black Bat .... $225-$325
1977 New York Yankees World Series Black Bat .... $200-$300
1978 Los Angeles Dodgers World Series Black Bat .... $225-$325
1978 New York Yankees World Series Black Bat .... $200-$300
1979 Baltimore Orioles World Series Black Bat .... $200-$300
1979 Pittsburgh Pirates World Series Black Bat.. $250-$350
1980 Kansas City Royals World Series Black Bat .... $200-$300
1980 Philadelphia Phillies World Series Black Bat .... $200-$300
1981 Los Angeles Dodgers World Series Black Bat .... $225-$325
1981 New York Yankees World Series Black Bat .... $200-$300
1982 St. Louis Cardinals World Series Black Bat .... $200-$300
1982 Milwaukee Brewers World Series Black Bat... $150-$250
1983 Baltimore Orioles World Series Black Bat .... $100-$200
1983 Philadelphia Phillies World Series Black Bat .... $250-$350
1984 Detroit Tigers World Series Black Bat .... $350-$450
1984 San Diego Padres World Series Black Bat.. $225-$325
1985 St. Louis Cardinals World Series Black Bat .... $225-$325
1985 Kansas City Royals World Series Black Bat .... $225-$325
1986 New York Mets World Series Black Bat .... $450-$600
1986 Boston Red Sox World Series Black Bat .... $250-$300
1987 Minnesota Twins World Series Black Bat .... $250-$350
1987 St. Louis Cardinals World Series Black Bat .... $200-$300
1988 Los Angeles Dodgers World Series Black Bat .... $150-$250
1988 Oakland A's World Series Black Bat... $100-$200
1989 San Francisco Giants World Series Black Bat .... $100-$200
1989 Oakland A's World Series Black Bat... $100-$200
1990 Oakland A's World Series Black Bat... $100-$200
1990 Cincinnati Reds World Series Black Bat .... $100-$200
1991 Minnesota Twins World Series Black Bat .... $800-$1,000
1991 Atlanta Braves World Series Black Bat .... $500-$700
1992 Toronto Blue Jays World Series Black Bat.. $400-$500
1992 Atlanta Braves World Series Black Bat .... $400-$500
1993 Toronto Blue Jays World Series Black Bat.. $400-$500
1993 Philadelphia Phillies World Series Black Bat .... $400-$500

Pro Insignia Inc.

Pro Insignia produces laser-engraved baseball bats.

Pro Insignia Inc. is a Hudson, Wis.-based company which produces regulation and miniature laser-engraved baseball bats. The bats, which are Rawlings/Adirondack or Worth professional model bats, are produced in limited editions and generally have an issue price of about $50. They are suitable for autographing. Among others, the company has produced commemorative bats for the 1989 (A's, 1,989 bats), 1990 (Reds, 1,990 bats), 1991 (Twins, 1,991 bats) and 1995 (Braves, 1,995 bats) World Series champions; the 1990, 1991 (two bats, 500 each), 1993 (1,993 bats), 1994 (1,994 bats) and 1995 (1,995 bats) All-Star games; the 100th anniversary of the Dodgers (500 bats); the centennial of the St. Louis Cardinals (1,992 bats); the closings of Comiskey Park in Chicago (500 bats), Cleveland Stadium (1,000 bats) and Arlington Stadium (1,000 bats); the 1955 World Champion Brooklyn Dodgers (1,955 bats), 1961 New York Yankees (1,961 bats) and 1966 Baltimore Orioles (1,966 bats); the 1957 World Series between the Milwaukee Braves and New York Yankees (1,957 bats); the 25th anniversaries of the Kansas City Royals, San Diego Padres, Milwaukee Brewers, Philadelphia Phillies and Montreal Expos (500 each); the 40th anniversary of the Baltimore Orioles (1,000 bats); the inaugural seasons for the Colorado Rockies and Florida Marlins (1,000 each); the openings of Jacobs Field in Cleveland (1,994 bats) and Coors Field in Colorado (1,995 bats); and six bats capturing the final standings for each division in the strike-shortened 1994 season (94 each). The company has also created Louisville Sluggers which can be laser-engraved with a collector's name alongside the logo of his favorite team, and team logo bats for the 1995 and 1996 seasons.

Equipment

Cal Ripken Jr. memorabilia became hot when he was on his streak.

While jerseys, bats and autographed baseballs bring the high-end prices for game-used equipment collectibles, there are other avenues for collectors to pursue, although they are not as abundant. These areas include caps, pants, jackets, helmets, shoes, batting gloves, gloves, and miscellaneous items, such as shin guards, equipment bags and wrist bands.

The items in these categories which show the highest prices are usually those which have been obtained in an auction, primarily because of who the player was who used the equipment. Hobby publications such as Sports Collectors Digest offer several ads each issue for equipment. One example offers a 1959 Ted Williams Boston Red Sox game-used team undershirt, grey with navy blue sleeves, and Williams' name in collar, for $2,250.

Caps

Ken Griffey Jr., Cal Ripken Jr. and Nolan Ryan have signed these caps.

Hank Aaron: 1970s Milwaukee Brewers cap, blue/gold with M...$1,250
Johnny Bench: 1970s Cincinnati Reds cap, game used St. Patrick's Day, New Era....................$450
Wade Boggs: 1993-94 New York Yankees cap, game used, New Era..$195

Wade Boggs: 1995 New York Yankees cap, used in the All-Star game, signed $750
Barry Bonds: 1994 San Francisco Giants cap, game used, New Era $225
Bobby Bonilla: 1992-93 New York Mets cap, game used, New Era, signed $95
George Brett: Kansas City Royals cap, game used $550
Lou Brock: 1970s St. Louis Cardinals cap, game used, New Era $350
Ellis Burks: 1994 Colorado Rockies cap, game used, New Era $75
Joe Carter: 1990s Toronto Blue Jays cap, game used, New Era, signed $250
Ron Cey: 1970s Los Angeles Dodgers cap, game used, New Era $125
Will Clark: 1990s San Francisco Giants cap, game used, New Era $195
Will Clark: 1995 Texas Rangers cap, game used, New Era, signed $165
Royce Clayton: 1993 San Francisco Giants cap, game used, New Era, signed $85
Dave Concepcion: 1970s Cincinnati Reds cap, game used St. Patrick's Day, New Era $150
Andre Dawson: 1993 Boston Red Sox, game used, New Era, signed $140
Andre Dawson: 1994 Florida Marlins, game used, signed $125
Bucky Dent: 1970s New York Yankees cap, game used, Wilson $95
Steve Finley: 1990s Houston Astros, game used, New Era, signed $50
Andres Galarraga: 1994 Colorado Rockies, game used, New Era, 125 year pin $150
Juan Gonzalez: 1990s Texas Rangers cap, game used, New Era, signed $145
Mike Greenwell: 1992 Boston Red Sox, game used, New Era, signed $90
Ozzie Guillen: 1990s Chicago White Sox cap, game used, New Era, signed $80
Rickey Henderson: New York Yankees cap, game used, New Era, signed $325
Bruce Hurst: 1993 San Diego Padres cap, game used, New Era $45
Bo Jackson: 1994 California Angles cap, game used, New Era $80
Reggie Jackson: New York Yankees, game used...$550
Tommy John: Chicago White Sox cap, game used $175
Howard Johnson: Detroit Tigers cap, game used $60
Barry Larkin: 1990s Cincinnati Reds cap, game used, New Era, signed $125
Dennis Martinez: 1995 Cleveland Indians, game used, New Era $175
Jack McDowell: 1992 Chicago White Sox cap, game used, New Era, signed $110
Fred McGriff: 1990s San Diego Padres cap, game used, Sports Specialties $125
JoeMorgan: 1978 Cincinnati Reds cap, green, game used on St. Patrick's Day, signed $350
Dale Murphy: Atlanta Braves cap, game used $125
Jim Palmer: 1970s Baltimore Orioles cap, game used, AJD, signed $350
Vada Pinson: 1968 Cincinnati Reds cap, game used, Wilson $150
Kirby Puckett: 1993 Minnesota Twins cap, game used, New Era..$250
Tim Raines: 1980s Montreal Expos cap, game used, New Era, signed..$95
Jim Rice: 1980s Boston Red Sox, game used, Devon, signed $115
Cal Ripken Jr.: Baltimore Orioles cap, game used, signed $450
Brooks Robinson: Baltimore Orioles cap, game used, Tim McAuliffe, 1964 ....$495
Bret Saberhagen: 1993-94 New York Mets cap, game used, New Era $80
Ryne Sandberg: Chicago Cubs cap, game used $175
Gary Sheffield: 1989 Milwaukee Brewers cap, game used, Sports Specialties, signed................$125
Ruben Sierra: 1992 Oakland A's cap, game used, New Era, signed $100
Ruben Sierra: Texas Rangers cap, #21 under bill, game used, signed $250
Darryl Strawberry: Los Angeles Dodger cap, #44 under bill, game used, signed........................$250
Greg Swindell: 1980s Cleveland Indians cap, game used, New Era $75
Mickey Tettleton: 1994 Detroit Tigers cap, game used, New Era, signed $110
Andy Van Slyke: 1980s Pittsburgh Pirates, game used, New Era, signed $125
Larry Walker: 1995 Colorado Rockies cap, game used, New Era, signed $160
Walt Weiss: 1990s Oakland A's cap, game used, New Era, signed $65
Lou Whitaker: Detroit Tigers cap, #1 under bill, game used...$135
Matt Williams: San Francisco Giants cap, game used, 1994 ....$175
Mitch Williams: Chicago Cubs cap, "Thing" under bill, game used $95
Dave Winfield: 1993 Minnesota Twins cap, game used, New Era $150
1995 Cleveland Indians signed cap, includes Carlos Baerga, Albert Belle, Kenny Lofton,
Dennis Martinez, Manny Ramirez, Paul Sorrento, Jim Thome and Dave Winfield......................$150

Pants

Yogi Berra: 1968 New York Mets road pants, signed................................$175
Pat Borders: 1993 Toronto Blue Jays road pants $50
Will Clark: 1991 San Francisco Giants road pants, signed $175
Roger Clemens: 1989 Boston Red Sox road pants.................................$145
Ozzie Guillen: 1986 Chicago White Sox home pants.............................$50
Tom Henke: 1985 Toronto Blue Jays road pants.................................$60
Rick Honeycutt: 1986 Los Angeles Dodgers home pants..........................$50
Jimmy Key: 1984 Toronto Blue Jays road pants $100
Willie Montanez: 1981 Montreal Expos home pants $40
Bill Russell: 1971 Los Angeles Dodgers home pants $75
Mookie Wilson: 1990 Toronto Blue Jays home pants.............................$60

Umpire equipment

Bob Engel: National League umpire's cap, signed $95
Rich Garcia: #19 American League umpire shirt.................................$150
Bill Haller: #1 American League umpire shirt...................................$150
Ted Hendry: American League umpire's cap, signed $75
Mike Reilly: 1970s American League umpire's cap, game used...................$100
Paul Runge: #17 National League umpire shirt..................................$150
Marty Springstead: #4 American League umpire shirt $150
Billy Williams: #24 National League jacket, pants, cap..........................$400
Charlie Williams: National League umpire's cap, signed.........................$95

Jackets

Johnny Bench: 1980s Cincinnati Reds warm-up jacket, Wilson, signed $1,695
George Brett: 1980s Kansas City Royals warm-up jacket, Starter, signed $1,995
Rod Carew: 1970s Minnesota Twins warm-up jacket, Butwin.......................$795
Joe Carter: Cleveland Indians jacket, signed $395
Mark Clear: 1980 All-Star Game jacket, Adidas, with game logo $50
Orel Hershiser: Los Angeles Dodgers warm-up jacket, NOB $475
Kent Hrbek: Minnesota Twins warm-up jacket, 1980s............................$295
Ted Kluszewski: Cincinnati Reds warm-up jacket, Wilson $475
Lou Whitaker: Detroit Tigers Starter heavy jacket, number inside, 1989 ....$495

Game-used batting helmets

Hank Aaron: Milwaukee Brewers batting helmet, mid-1970s.......................$1,500
Roberto Alomar: San Diego Padres batting helmet $695
Roberto Alomar: Toronto Blue Jays batting helmet $795
Carlos Baerga: Cleveland Indians batting helmet $550
Wade Boggs: Boston Red Sox batting helmet $795
Bobby Bonilla: 1992 New York Mets batting helmet $195
George Brett: Kansas City Royals batting helmet, signed $1,275
Mark Brouhard: 1980s Milwaukee Brewers batting helmet.........................$85

Jeff Burroughs: 1988 Toronto Blue Jays batting helmet $125
Jose Canseco: 1980s Oakland A's batting helmet, signed......................................$750
Jose Canseco: Texas Rangers batting helmet, #33, signed...................................$750
Rod Carew: Minnesota Twins batting helmet, signed..$795
Gary Carter: Montreal Expos batting helmet, signed..$795
Will Clark: Texas Rangers batting helmet, 1994, signed.......................................$450
Roberto Clemente: Pittsburgh Pirates batting helmet, 1960s $3,000
Andre Dawson: Boston Red Sox batting helmet, 1994, signed...........................$595
Darrell Evans: Detroit Tigers batting helmet, 1980s..$225
Julio Franco: 1980s Cleveland Indians batting helmet $175
Andres Galarraga: late-1980s Montreal Expos batting helmet............................$150
Juan Gonzalez: Texas Rangers batting helmet, 1993, signed $295
Rickey Henderson: Oakland A's batting helmet, signed $895
Rickey Henderson: Oakland A's batting helmet, worn in 1990 World Series $1,295
Reggie Jackson: California Angels batting helmet, 1984, signed $895
Javy Lopez: Atlanta Braves catcher's helmet, signed $250
Hal McRae: 1980s Kansas City Royals batting helmet..$175
Paul Molitor: Milwaukee Brewers batting helmet, #4, signed...........................$550
Dale Murphy: Atlanta Braves batting helmet, #3, signed $575
Tony Phillips: 1980s Oakland A's batting helmet...$85
Kirby Puckett: 1984-85 Minnesota Twins batting helmet $645
Kirby Puckett: Minnesota Twins batting helmet, #34, signed............................$995
Willie Randolph: 1980s New York Yankees batting helmet $250
Ryne Sandberg: 1991 Chicago Cubs batting helmet...$1,195
Steve Sax: 1980s Los Angeles Dodgers batting helmet.....................................$150
Gary Sheffield: Milwaukee Brewers batting helmet, 1990 ....$175
Ruben Sierra: Texas Rangers batting helmet...$395
Dave Winfield: San Diego Padres batting helmet, mid-1970s $995
Dave Winfield: 1991 California Angeles batting helmet, game used.....................$795
Dave Winfield: New York Yankees batting helmet, game used $1,295
Robin Yount: 1970s Milwaukee Brewers batting helmet, blue with gold M...........$745
Robin Yount: Milwaukee Brewers batting helmet, game used $895
1993 California Angels autographed batting helmet, signed by the entire team
(Mark Langston, J.T. Snow, Chuck Finley, Tim Salmon) $150
1993 Toronto Blue Jays autographed batting helmet, signed by the entire team
(Joe Carter, Roberto Alomar, John Olerud, Devon White, Jack Morris, Dave Stewart).................$195

Replica batting helmets

Dave Justice: Atlanta Braves batting helmet, signed...$110
Mike Schmidt: Philadelphia Phillies batting helmet, signed $160
Tim Salmon: California Angels batting helmet, signed.......................................$100
Ryne Sandberg: Chicago Cubs batting helmet, signed $140
Robin Yount: Milwaukee Brewers batting helmet, signed..................................$150

Game-worn shoes

Johnny Bench: Rawlings spikes, game used, signed...$550
Wade Boggs: Nike spikes, game used..$250
Gary Carter: Brooks cleats, game used, signed $250
Ron Cey: Puma Los Angeles Dodgers, game used, signed.................................$195

Chili Davis: Nike cleats, game used...$50
Cecil Fielder: Pony, black and white, game used $150
Steve Finley: 1995 San Diego Padres cleats, game used, Reebok hightops $75
Juan Gonzalez: Reebok cleats, game used, signed.......................................$195
Ken Griffey Jr.: Nike cleats, used in 1993 All-Star Game, signed $795
Ken Griffey Jr.: Nike cleats, black and teal, 1994, signed..........................$495
Tony Gwynn: Nike turf shoes, name and number on them $295
Darryl Hamilton: Nike cleats, game used..$50
Tom Henke: blue Pony spikes, game used, signed.......................................$100
Reggie Jackson: red Pony, 1986, game used $550
Dave Justice: blue Nike, game used, signed...$250
Eric Karros: 1995 Nike cleats, game used $185
Pat Listach: Reebok high tops, blue and white, game used..........................$95
Ramon Martinez: 1995 Nike cleats, game used $110
Joe Morgan: Mizuno, maroon and white, game used....................................$250
Joe Morgan: 1983 Adidas Philadelphia Phillies cleats, game used...............$350
Hideo Nomo: 1995 Nike cleats, game used $595
Paul O'Neill: Pony cleats, signed..$175
Rafael Palmeiro: Nike turf shoes $100
Tony Perez: Adidas Montreal Expos, game used, signed..............................$195
Jim Rice: Puma cleats, red and blue, signed..$165
Mike Schmidt: Nike spikes, game used, signed $650
Mickey Tettleton: Reebok cleats, signed...$125
Frank Thomas: Reebok high top cleats, "The Big Hurt" stitched in $395
Todd Van Poppel: Reebok cleats, white and green......................................$100
Devon White: Nike cleats, game used $75
Carl Yastrzemski: Spot-Bilt turf shoes, game used $495
Robin Yount: Mizuno cleats, blue and white, game used, signed.................$399

Batting gloves

Wade Boggs: Franklin batting gloves, signed...$125
Barry Bonds: Franklin batting gloves, signed $125
Ellis Burks: Franklin batting gloves $65
Jose Canseco: Mizuno, blue and white, signed..$90
Gary Carter: Mizuno batting glove, blue, signed $75
Joe Carter: Franklin batting gloves, one ripped, signed..............................$110
Will Clark: black Easton batting gloves .... $50 each
Will Clark: Easton batting glove, signed...$65
Will Cordero: Easton batting gloves, signed...$60
Eric Davis: Mizuno batting gloves, scarlet, signed......................................$50
Andre Dawson: Mizuno batting gloves, black, signed .... $60 each
Lenny Dykstra: Franklin batting gloves, red, signed .... $60 each
Cecil Fielder: Franklin batting gloves, black.. $85 each
Julio Franco: Franklin batting gloves..$30
Ken Griffey Jr.: Franklin batting gloves, blue .... $90 each
Ken Griffey Sr.: Franklin batting glove, #30, signed....................................$30
Ozzie Guillen: Saranac batting gloves $65
Tony Gwynn: Franklin batting gloves, signed...$125
Rickey Henderson: Mizuno batting gloves, fluorescent, signed............... $90 each
Chuck Knoblauch: Franklin batting glove, unsigned....................................$35
John Kruk: Easton batting glove, red, signed $60
Barry Larkin: Franklin batting gloves .... $25 each
Don Mattingly: Franklin batting gloves $95

Paul Molitor: Franklin batting gloves..$75
Raul Mondesi: Worth batting gloves, plus wristband, signed.....................$165
Tim Naehring: Nike batting gloves $25
Kirby Puckett: Franklin batting gloves, red.. $75 each
Tim Raines: Franklin batting gloves, blue, signed .... $45 each
Manny Ramirez: Nike batting gloves, signed.. $125
Ivan Rodriguez: Wilson batting gloves...$35
Tim Salmon: Franklin batting gloves $50
Steve Sax: Saranac batting gloves...$65
Mike Schmidt: Franklin batting glove, signed $225
Ozzie Smith: Franklin batting glove, signed...$75
Darryl Strawberry: Easton batting gloves, signed .... $50 each
Mickey Tettleton: Franklin batting gloves $45
Frank Thomas: Worth batting gloves, signed..$195
Alan Trammell: Franklin batting gloves, signed..$85
Robin Ventura: Louisville Slugger batting gloves..$65

Equipment bags

Gary Carter: 1970s Montreal Expos Worth travel bag...............................$250
Frank Robinson: 1970s San Francisco Giants equipment bag $245

Miscellaneous

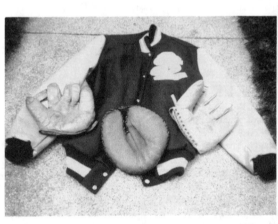

This memorabilia is game-used St. Louis Browns equipment.

1920s baseman's glove..$75
1975 Boston Red Sox catcher's helmet, Carlton Fisk $450
Turn-of-the-century chest protector, very crude, narrow protector $200
Ernie Lombardi 1930s Goldsmith catcher's mitt $100
Gabby Hartnett 1930s Spalding catcher's mitt $100
1930s Wilson catcher's chest protector, all straps intact $95
1930s catcher's chest protector, pro model, game used.......................................$75

1940s Rawlings baseball chest protector, with light trim and patch...$60
1940s McGregor/Goldsmith chest protector...$95
1950s umpire's chest protector...$80
Javy Lopez chest protector, by All-Star, signed..$195
1930s Wilson spitter mask, chest protector and shin guards in traveling train case,
used by a minor leaguer...$375
Turn-of-the-century wire catcher's mask, rectangular eye openings, bird-cage style $200
Turn-of-the-century goggle-eyed mask with straps and pads $200
1880s bird-cage catcher's mask, no welds, all clips and bends $285
1910 Spiderman visor mask with throat protector $375
Circa 1915 wire catcher's mask, "goggle eyes"..$225
1930s-style catcher's mask..$145
1930s catcher's mask, MacGregor, softball, game used..$35
1930s Rawlings shin guards, composition and leather $85
1994 Florida Marlins shin guards, with team logo, game used..$75
Javy Lopez shin guards, by All-Star, signed..$195
Jose Canseco shin guard, by Cosby, signed and numbered $90
Joe Carter Benik knee pad..$40
Butwin 1940s wool St. Louis Cardinals jacket $750
1930s wool baseball hat $30
Kirby Puckett Minnesota Twins game-used wristband...$55
Paul O'Neill Cincinnati Reds wristbands, signed $55
Minnesota Twins 25th anniversary uniform patch, 1985...$30
San Francisco Giants 1984 All-Star Game uniform patch, 1984..$30
Los Angeles Dodgers 25th anniversary uniform patch, 1983 ....$50
Cincinnati Reds 100th anniversary uniform patch, 1994..$50
1933 Washington Senators socks, black and gold, game used $75
1940s Brooklyn Dodgers socks, blue, game used..$95
1960s Houston Astros socks, orange and blue..$50
1978 Boston Red Sox socks, red-white-black, worn by Don Zimmer......................................$60
D&M celluloid umpire indicator, turn-of-the-century, dog logo on the back $80
Turn-of-century reach umpire indicator in original box, celluloid plastic.................................$150
Circa 1880s baseball hand-made ball, thick brown leather...$175
Dusty Baker Los Angeles Dodgers home run #139 baseball, 1979, signed...............................$195
Orlando Cepeda Atlanta Braves home run #314 baseball, 1970, signed...................................$275
Greg Luzinski Philadelphia Phillies home run #33 baseball, 1970, signed...............................$150
Reggie Smith Los Angeles Dodgers home run #255 baseball, 1978, signed..............................$150
Joe Rudi Oakland A's home run #13 baseball, 1970, signed...$150
Baseball used in Dennis Martinez' perfect game on July 28, 1991, vs. Los Angeles,
signed and notated..$695
Baseball used in Fernando Valenzuela's perfect game on June 29, 1990, vs. St. Louis,
signed and notated..$695
Tommy Aaron fungo bat, Louisville Slugger model $250
Whitey Herzog fungo bat, Hillerich & Bradsby, 1972-75, signed...$295
Jim Leyland fungo bat, Louisville Slugger model $150
Bob Rodgers fungo bat, Louisville Slugger model $150
Bobby Valentine fungo bat, Louisville Slugger model..$150
New York Yankees fungo bat, Hillerich & Bradsby model, 1970s..$175
San Diego Padres fungo bat, Louisville Slugger model, early 1970s...$75
Barry Bonds "Tiger Eye" flip-down sunglasses $225
Darryl Strawberry custom-fitted, game-used sunglasses, 1994 with San Francisco $125
Houston Astros Cosby equipment bag, 1970s, orange canvas..$110
Resin bag from Dodger Stadium, circa 1990 ....$15

Game-used gloves

Hank Aaron: 1970s MacGregor, fielder's glove, #44..$7,495
Hank Aaron: 1970s MacGregor glove, first baseman's, #44, signed $4,995
Jim Abbott: Rawlings, signed..$1,195
Richie Allen: Rawlings, fielder's glove, signed...$1,250
Roberto Alomar: Rollin fielder's glove, name stitched in $750
Carlos Baerga: Rollin fielder's glove, name stitched in....................................$650
Johnny Bench: Rawlings catcher's mitt, game used..$2,395
Dante Bichette: Rawlings fielder's glove, name embroidered $695
Dean Chance: Rawlings, game used, 1962-64 ....$1,495
Roger Clemens: Wilson fielder's glove, name sewn in, 1980s $2,000
Darrell Evans: Mizuno, from the 1987 playoffs $695
Ken Griffey Jr.: Rawlings, name embroidered on glove $2,495
Pedro Guerrero: Wilson fielder's glove, name embroidered $295
Tony Gwynn: Rawlings, name embroidered in glove $1,895
Eric Karros: Wilson, game used, 1992-93 ....$1,095
John Kruk: Wilson first baseman's mitt, signed...$750
Willie Mays: MacGregor glove, #24...$10,995
Randy Myers: Mizuno fielder's glove, game used...$595
Jamie Navarro: Wilson fielder's glove, game used $395
Kirby Puckett: Wilson, name embroidered in glove, 1992................................$1,995
Cal Ripken Jr.: Rawlings, name embroidered in glove $2,695
Ryne Sandberg: Rawlings glove, game used $1,995
Ozzie Smith: Rawlings, name stamped in glove..$2,795
Willie Stargell: MacGregor first baseman's mitt, signed $1,650
Billy Swift: Mizuno fielder's glove, game used...$595
Fernando Valenzuela: Rawlings glove, name stamped on it................................$595
Greg Vaughn: Mizuno fielder's glove..$275
Matt Williams: Rawlings fielder's glove, name embroidered.............................$1,195
Dave Winfield: Rawlings first baseman's mitt, game used, 1973 ....$1,195
Robin Yount: Rawlings model, name embroidered on it $1,195

Store-bought gloves

One of the hottest collectibles on the market today seems to be the baseball glove. But what makes a glove collectible? Is it the maker or the style of glove? Is it the player's name who appears embossed on it or is it the condition? The answer is all of the above.

But which of the criteria is most important? Well, in this case, it depends. Baseball gloves, much like baseball cards, derive their value based on several features, which will all be defined.

Let's begin by explaining that this is a treatise on store-bought, over-the-counter gloves, and has little or nothing to do with game-used gloves which may be worth thousands of dollars and must be evaluated individually as to provenance and value. A store-bought glove is just that, an over-the-counter purchase. Those which bear a facsimile autograph of a player will herewith be called an autograph model.

The most important factor in determining the value of a glove is the player's name which appears embossed somewhere on the face of the glove. For example, if you had two identical Draper Maynard G41 gloves in the same condition, one bearing the facsimile autograph of Babe Ruth and the other bearing the facsimile autograph of Babe Young, presuming they are both in used but Excellent condition with all markings easily read, then the Ruth glove would bring in excess of $800, while the identical Young glove would probably sell in the $75 range.

Mickey Mantle player-model gloves are quite rare.

The reason is as obvious as in baseball card collecting. All the 1952 Topps cards are made of the same material and share the same printing process. But the one that illustrates the image of Mickey Mantle is worth thousands of dollars, while the card of Howie Pollet, only one number away from Mantle, would bring less than $100 in any condition. And so it is with glove collecting - the bigger the name, the higher the price, given that all other variants are the same.

The second most important consideration when determining glove value is the condition. Even a relatively common player, if I may borrow the vernacular of the card collecting fraternity, may be worth hundreds of dollars if in Near Mint to Mint condition. This is especially true with older gloves, because it is much harder to find a Near Mint to Mint common player from the 1920s or 1930s than it is to find a similar condition glove from the 1960s or 1970s.

Given this criteria, a Mint condition glove of a relatively obscure player from the 1920s, ie. Bibb Falk, would be worth more than $200, probably much more, while a Mint condition glove of a Hall of Fame member, such as Luis Aparicio, might only bring the same amount or less. It may seem ridiculous, to those who collect more modern era items, that a glove of a Hall of Fame player would bring less than a glove of a player of whom many readers have never heard.

To justify this, one need look no further than any baseball card price guide. Look up the price of any Near Mint E97 Briggs card from 1909-10, then look up the Near Mint price of a 1974 Topps card of Hall of Fame member Reggie Jackson.

That brings us right into the next two very important factors in determining value; supply and demand, or the relative scarcity of some gloves versus the seemingly endless supply of others. Let's take two gloves of players from relatively the same era, Grover C. Alexander and Dave Bancroft.

Both are Hall of Famers and both of their gloves are in great demand amongst serious pre-war glove collectors. Given that both are in Near Mint condition, the Alexander glove, even though he is arguably the more renowned of the two, might bring $500-$700, while a Bancroft would probably bring $800-$1,200. The reason behind the disparity is that Alexander gloves are fairly easy to locate; they appear on the market from time to time. However, there are only a couple of Bancroft models known in private collections.

If a signature model Joe Jackson baseman's mitt exists that was made before his banishment from the major leagues (as a result of the Black Sox scandal in 1919) and it became available on the public market, especially in the auction arena, it would undoubtedly set a new record price paid for a store model glove, regardless of its condition.

While we have already touched on another important factor in determining glove values - age - it deserves its own category. It is impossible to discuss value without the age factor being present. Until recently, very early gloves, because they lacked player endorsements, commanded very little collector attention, which computed to very weak prices as well.

All this is changing now as more and more collectors are beginning to realize how truly scarce the pre-World War I era gloves are in today's marketplace. Two sets of turn-of-the-century fingerless gloves, gloves that were worn either individually or in pairs and had no fingers, traded hands within the last two years for prices in excess of $3,000. Another recent sale of an 1890s baseman's mitt, one which was dated in pen and bore the player's name and college, broke the four digit barrier as well.

Another area in which age plays an important role has to do with the date of manufacture as compared to when the player whose name appears on the glove was active. For example, a Jimmie Foxx baseman's mitt, circa 1930, in Excellent condition, might bring around $500-$600, while a more recently manufactured Jimmie Foxx glove, one made well into the 1960s, sold last year for less than $100. This is an important factor to consider when purchasing a glove - make sure that the date of manufacture corresponds with the time frame in which a player was active.

Rarely, if ever, is a post period glove of any player worth the same amount as one manufactured while the player was still on the diamond. There are dozens of players whose names appeared on gloves long after their playing days ended - Foxx, Ruth, Bill Dickey, Lefty Gomez, Joe DiMaggio, just to name a few. In fact, just like early, or rookie cards, of a player are worth more than later cards of the same player, even while he was still active, so too are earlier model gloves of certain players.

Take Joe DiMaggio, for example. He played in the major leagues from the 1930s until 1951. It is generally accepted that fielders gloves with unlaced fingers are pre-war models or styles, while gloves with the fingers laced are considered post-war models or styles. Various companies produced both laced and unlaced gloves prior to and after World War II, but the terms pre-war and post-war are used to determine the relative era of a fielder's glove using the criteria of whether or not the glove is laced.

If you had two identical Joe DiMaggio gloves, yet one was the laced variation and the other was not, as was the case in 1950 when Spalding manufactured both the earlier style, or unlaced version, as well as the laced model, the earlier would bring a premium, even though both were made the same year, simply because it is the split finger model.

Now, using the same Joe DiMaggio glove as an example, let's discuss two other very important factors in determining glove values. First, does the name Joe DiMaggio appear in cursive, facsimile autograph style, or is it a block style name, each letter independent of the other? Facsimile autograph gloves will always command a higher price than their block style counterparts.

While an excellent condition DiMaggio pre-war style with facsimile autograph may sell somewhere in the $400-$500 range, a like condition and era glove bearing a block stamp might only bring $250-$350. This difference is magnified when the scarcity of a certain player's glove is greater, ie. Lou Gehrig gloves. A signature model Ken-Wel in Excellent condition would sell for $1,500-$2,000; a like conditioned model bearing a block name recently brought $750. All Gehrig gloves are very scarce; less than half a dozen currently reside in private collections. But, as you can see, a signature model glove brings twice the price of its block style counterpart.

Another important value factor has to do with which hand the glove fits on. This is the area that seems to cause the most confusion, even among advanced collectors. The factories, and hence the sporting good stores, used to designate a glove either right hand or left hand by determining which hand the glove actually fit, indicating right hand for a left-handed thrower. As a result, one might find the letters RH somewhere on the box label.

Because of the confusion amongst today's collectors, most now call a glove that fits on the left hand, for a right-handed thrower, a right-handed glove. The best rule of thumb is if you're ordering a glove from a mail order dealer, ask which hand the glove actually fits on. If you see the letters LH in a description of a glove for sale in a mail order ad, it most likely means that the glove is for a left-handed thrower, but always check just to be sure.

And why all this dribble about which hand a glove fits on? The reason is simple economics. Take Mickey Mantle gloves, for example. A recent price paid for a Mickey Mantle MM personal model glove made for right-handed thrower and in Mint condition surpassed the $800 mark. However, a Personal Model Mantle glove in the same Mint condition, but for a left-handed thrower, sold for a mere $175. That's a substantial difference for two almost identical gloves except that one was what collectors call "off-handed."

But what about left-handed gloves of left-handed players, ie. Stan Musial? A Near Mint Heart of the Hide Rawlings Musial baseman's mitt, for a left-handed thrower, sells for $200-250. But the same glove for a right-handed thrower, even though Musial was left handed, would still sell in the same price range, maybe 10 percent less, even though a right-handed Musial would be considered "off-handed."

The reason for this is simple - most collectors are right handed and they want to put the glove on and feel comfortable, so they will buy a nice right-handed model of a left-handed player for nearly the same price, yet they refuse to pay anywhere near the same price for a left-handed glove of a right-handed player.

Does all this make sense, even if left-handed gloves are scarcer? No, but it has to do with supply and demand, and that's what sets the market. What this also means is that if you are left handed, there are some absolute bargains out there on top-of-the-line gloves if you don't mind "off-handed" player's models.

One item we haven't discussed is the quality of the different models. Some players' endorsements may have only been offered on limited versions or models. Still others, like Mantle or Musial, were available on many different models, running the gamut from cheap, dime-store-quality kids gloves to professional, top-of-the-line, leather trimmed, deluxe models. In all instances, the higher the quality, if the player and condition are equal, the higher the price.

We have discussed several factors that determine the actual value and desirability of a collectible glove. There are many more that haven't been discussed, such as how to grade a glove, or how to determine its age, or what's the best marketplace for buying and selling.

Each of these areas might constitute an entire article to completely define, but the above information should help you get a feel for the hobby and how to approach it with some confidence.

— David Bushing

The following information is taken from David Bushing's and Joe Phillips' Vintage Baseball Glove Pocket Price Guide. This comprehensive guide to valuation of vintage gloves estimates there are nearly 1,500 persons involved in the glove collecting hobby. The prices given reflect retail prices based on what dealers or collectors might sell their gloves for and should not be considered as absolute, fixed prices.

Often, gloves were sold in individual boxes and with "hang tags" which were used to price and/or describe the features of the glove. Having them with the glove adds to the overall value of the glove. Pre-war hang tags add $30 with a player photo and can add $50-$150 depending on the player. Post-war tags add $15, and can add $25-$75 depending on the player.

Plain boxes, those without pictures on them, in Good condition (intact, some corners may be split, light scuffing, small surface tears, slight soiling) can add 20-50 percent in value. Post-war plain boxes add 20 percent, 1930-45 add 30 percent, 1920-30 add 40 percent and pre-1920 boxes add 50 percent.

Picture boxes (those with a photo or illustration of the player either posed or in action) in Good condition can add two to six times to the price of the glove. Pre-war boxes of Hall of Famers add four to six times the price, post-war boxes Hall of Famers add two to four times the value, while post-war boxes of non-Hall of Famers adds no more than two times the value.

Other factors involved in value include player popularity and condition of the glove. The guide has established the following grading scale:

Fair/Poor: Gloves in this condition are generally not collectible and often are only good for parts. Irrepairable tears, holes, severe magic marker, dry rot, water damage, and any other major problem.

Good: Glove that has been used considerably. Most of the stamping will be gone or barely visible. Leather very chaffed, thinned in spots, no form left, may still be serviceable but only collectible if an extremely rare model, usually used as a filler until a better similar type is available.

Very Good: Well used but most stamping visible, no form but intact, cloth label gone or worn out, piping frayed and worn.

Excellent: Well used but cared for. Stamping visible. Dark with age but nice patina. Cloth label intact, minor piping wear. Some form left.

Excellent/Mint: The most confusing grade. Much stronger than an Excellent glove but not Near Mint. It is an Excellent glove with certain strong characteristics of a higher grade glove, i.e. super strong, bright signature, perfect cloth label, no oil stains, perfect insides, etc.

Near Mint: A glove that has seen almost no use. Still stiff in form, all stamping strong, most original silver or black ink still within stamping. Perfect insides, perfect cloth patch, has caught but a few balls. Some otherwise Mint gloves may not have been used but have significant enough blemishes such as staining, cracking from dryness, scratches from some handling, to drop it into this category.

Mint: Just that, stone cold new, never played with. This is regardless of age. A Mint glove may show some shelf wear due to years, for example minute piping wear, oxidation around brass grommets, stiff due to no use, slight fading of original color, all of which must be minute and from storage, not from use.

Terms used in the following charts include:

None Known: No glove has been discovered in a manufacturer's catalog or personally.

None Found: These gloves have been found to exist in a manufacturer's catalog, but have not been mentioned as been having been owned or sold by a collector or dealer.

Very Rare: For pre-war gloves, four or less gloves have turned up. For post-war models, eight or less have turned up.

Rare: For pre-war model gloves, five to 10 gloves have turned up. For post-war gloves, 10 to 20 have been found.

Common: For pre-war, this is 11 to 20 gloves. For post-war models this is 21-35.

Very Common: For pre-war gloves, 21 or more have been found. For post-war gloves, 36 or more have been found.

Pre-war gloves (Hall of Famers)

Mint: Add 50 percent to Near Mint values

Joe Jackson is not a Hall of Famer, but his items are highly sought.

+ (increase) or - (decrease) indicates recent trends in the value.

Prices are for USA-made gloves, full size.

* Also have imported models

Player	Very Good	Excellent	Near Mint	Supply
Grover Alexander (+)	$250	$350	$500	Common
Luke Appling (-)	$50	$100	$150	Very Common
Earl Averill	$75	$150	$200	Very Common
Frank Baker (+)	$500	$800	$1,200	None Known
Dave Bancroft	$400	$650	$850	Very Rare
Chief Bender (+)	$500	$800	$1,200	Very Rare
Jim Bottomley (LH) (+)	$250	$350	$500	Rare
Roger Breshnahan (+)	$500	$800	$1,200	Very Rare
Mordecai Brown (+)	$500	$800	$1,200	None Known

Player	Very Good	Excellent	Near Mint	Supply
Max Carey (+)	$250	$350	$500	Rare
Frank Chance (+)	$500	$800	$1,200	None Known
Jack Chesbro (+)	$500	$800	$1,200	None Known
Fred Clarke (+)	$500	$800	$1,200	None Known
Ty Cobb	$750	$1,000	$1,500	Very Rare
Mickey Cochrane (+)	$250	$350	$500	Rare
Eddie Collins (+)	$250	$350	$500	Rare
Jimmy Collins	$400	$650	$850	None Known
Earle Combs (+)	$250	$350	$500	Very Rare
Stan Coveleski	$400	$650	$850	None Known
Sam Crawford (LH) (+)	$500	$800	$1,200	Very Rare
Joe Cronin (-)	$50	$100	$150	Very Common
Kiki Cuyler (-)	$125	$250	$375	Common
Dizzy Dean	$500	$800	$1,200	Very Rare
Bill Dickey (-)	$50	$100	$150	Very Common
Joe DiMaggio (-)	$250	$350	$500	Very Common
Bobby Doerr (-)	$50	$100	$150	Very Common
Johnny Evers (+)	$500	$800	$1,200	None Known
Red Faber	$400	$650	$850	Very Rare
Bob Feller (-)	$50	$100	$150	Very Common
Rick Ferrell (+)	$250	$350	$500	Very Rare
Elmer Flick	$400	$650	$850	None Known
Jimmie Foxx (+)	$250	$350	$500	Common
Frankie Frisch (-)	$125	$250	$375	Common
Lou Gehrig (LH) (+)	$850	$1,000	$1,500	Common
Charlie Gehringer (-)	$125	$250	$375	Very Common
Lefty Gomez (LH) (-)	$125	$250	$375	Rare
Goose Goslin	$75	$150	$200	Very Common
Hank Greenberg (-)	$125	$250	$375	Common
Burleigh Grimes	$400	$650	$850	None Known
Lefty Grove (LH) (-)	$125	$250	$375	Rare
Chick Hafey (+)	$250	$350	$500	Very Rare
Jesse Haines (+)	$250	$350	$500	Very Rare
Bucky Harris	$75	$150	$200	Common
Gabby Hartnett (-)	$125	$250	$375	Common
Harry Heilmann (+)	$250	$350	$500	Common
Billy Herman (-)	$50	$100	$150	Very Common
Harry Hooper (LH) (+)	$500	$800	$1,200	None Known
Rogers Hornsby (-)	$125	$250	$375	Very Common
Waite Hoyt	$400	$650	$850	Very Rare
Carl Hubbell (LH) (+)	$250	$350	$500	Rare
Joe Jackson *	$850	$1,000	$1,500	Very Rare
Travis Jackson (-)	$125	$250	$375	Common
Walter Johnson (+)	$250	$350	$500	Common
George Kelly (+)	$250	$350	$500	Very Rare
Chuck Klein (-)	$125	$250	$375	Common
Nap Lajoie	$850	$1,000	$1,500	None Known
Tony Lazzeri (+)	$250	$350	$500	Very Rare
Freddie Lindstrom (+)	$250	$350	$500	None Found
Ernie Lombardi (-)	$75	$150	$200	Very Common

Player	Very Good	Excellent	Near Mint	Supply
Al Lopez (-)	$50	$100	$150	Very Common
Ted Lyons (-)	$75	$150	$200	Very Common
Heinie Manush (LH)	$75	$150	$200	Very Common
Rube Marquard (LH) (+)	$500	$800	$1,200	None Known
Rabbit Maranville (+)	$250	$350	$500	Rare
Christy Mathewson	$750	$1,000	$1,500	Very Rare
Joe McGinnity	$500	$800	$1,200	None Known
Ducky Medwick (-)	$50	$100	$150	Very Common
Johnny Mize (-)	$50	$100	$150	Very Common
Mel Ott (-)	$75	$150	$200	Very Common
Herb Pennock (LH) (+)	$250	$350	$500	None Found
Eddie Plank (LH) (+)	$500	$800	$1,200	None Known
Pee Wee Reese (-)	$50	$100	$150	Very Common
Sam Rice (+)	$250	$350	$500	Very Rare
Eppa Rixey (LH) (+)	$250	$350	$500	Very Rare
Edd Roush (LH) (-)	$250	$350	$500	Common
Red Ruffing (-)	$125	$250	$375	Common
Babe Ruth (LH) (-)	$500	$800	$1,200	Common
Ray Schalk (-)	$125	$250	$375	Common
Joe Sewell (+)	$250	$350	$500	Very Rare
Al Simmons (-)	$125	$250	$375	Common
George Sisler (LH) (-)	$125	$250	$375	Common
Tris Speaker (LH)	$750	$1,000	$1,500	Very Rare
Bill Terry (LH) (+)	$250	$350	$500	Rare
Joe Tinkers (+)	$500	$800	$1,200	None Known
Pie Traynor (-)	$125	$250	$375	Very Common
Dazzy Vance (-)	$125	$250	$375	Common
Arky Vaughn (+)	$250	$350	$500	None Found
Rube Waddell (LH) (+)	$500	$800	$1,200	None Known
Honus Wagner	$750	$1,000	$1,500	Very Rare
Bobby Wallace (+)	$500	$800	$1,200	None Known
Ed Walsh (+)	$500	$800	$1,200	None Known
Lloyd Waner (-)	$125	$250	$375	Common
Paul Waner (LH) (+)	$250	$350	$500	Very Rare
Zack Wheat (+)	$500	$800	$1,200	Very Rare
Ted Williams (-)	$125	$250	$375	Very Common
Hack Wilson (+)	$250	$350	$500	Very Rare
Cy Young (-)	$250	$350	$500	Very Common
Ross Youngs	$400	$650	$850	None Found

Post-war gloves (Hall of Famers)

Player	Very Good	Excellent	Mint	Supply
Hank Aaron *	$100	$150	$300	Rare
Luis Aparicio (-)	$30	$50	$85	Common
Richie Ashburn (-)	$30	$45	$60	Very Common
Ernie Banks (-)	$50	$85	$125	Common
Johnny Bench * (-)	$30	$50	$85	Very Common

Player	Very Good	Excellent	Near Mint	Supply
Yogi Berra * (-)	$50	$85	$125	Very Common
Lou Boudreau	$30	$50	$85	Very Common
Lou Brock	$65	$125	$175	Very Rare
Roy Campanella (-)	$50	$85	$125	Very Common
Rod Carew	$40	$75	$95	Very Rare
Roberto Clemente (-)	$30	$50	$85	Very Common
Steve Carlton *	$50	$85	$125	Very Rare
Joe DiMaggio * (+)	$150	$250	$375	Common
Don Drysdale *	$40	$75	$95	Common
Bob Feller	$40	$75	$95	Very Common
Rollie Fingers	$40	$75	$95	Very Rare
Whitey Ford (LH) *	$40	$75	$95	Very Common
Bob Gibson	$40	$75	$95	Common
Lefty Gomez	$40	$75	$95	Common
Catfish Hunter *	$40	$75	$95	Common
Monte Irvin	$65	$125	$175	Rare
Joe Jackson	$150	$250	$375	Very Rare
Reggie Jackson	$30	$50	$85	Common
Fergie Jenkins	$40	$75	$95	Rare
Al Kaline * (-)	$30	$50	$85	Very Common
George Kell	$30	$50	$85	Common
Harmon Killebrew (-)	$40	$75	$95	Common
Ralph Kiner	$30	$50	$85	Common
Sandy Koufax (LH) * (+)	$85	$150	$200	Rare
Bob Lemon (-)	$30	$50	$85	Rare
Mickey Mantle * (-)	$225	$350	$500	Rare
Juan Marichal * (-)	$40	$75	$95	Common
Eddie Mathews * (+)	$50	$85	$125	Common
Willie Mays * (-)	$125	$175	$350	Rare
Willie McCovey (-) (LH)	$65	$125	$175	Rare
Joe Morgan *	$40	$75	$95	Very Rare
Stan Musial (LH) *	$100	$150	$300	Common
Hal Newhouser (LH)	$50	$85	$125	Rare
Jim Palmer *	$40	$75	$95	None Known
Gaylord Perry	$40	$75	$95	Rare
Pee Wee Reese	$30	$50	$85	Very Common
Phil Rizzuto	$25	$35	$50	Very Common
Robin Roberts	$30	$50	$85	Very Common
Brooks Robinson * (-)	$30	$50	$85	Common
Frank Robinson * (-)	$40	$75	$95	Common
Red Schoendienst	$30	$50	$85	Very Common
Tom Seaver * (-)	$40	$75	$95	Common
Enos Slaughter	$30	$50	$85	Very Common
Duke Snider (+)	$50	$100	$150	Common
Warren Spahn (LH) (+)	$50	$100	$150	Common
Willie Stargell (LH) *	$40	$75	$95	Rare
Hoyt Wilhelm	$85	$150	$200	Very Rare
Billy Williams *	$40	$75	$95	Rare
Ted Williams *	$100	$150	$300	Rare
Early Wynn	$30	$50	$85	Very Common
Carl Yastrzemski *	$30	$50	$85	Common

Pre-war gloves (star players)

Player	Very Good	Excellent	Near Mint	Availability
Adams, Charles "Babe"	$100	$175	$250	None Known
Archer, Jimmy	$150	$250	$375	None Known
Austin, Jimmy (+)	$150	$250	$375	None Known
Bagby, Jim	$75	$150	$200	None Known
Bartell, Dick (-)	$50	$85	$175	Very Common
Berg, Moe (+)	$500	$800	$1,200	None Known
Berger, Wally (-)	$50	$85	$175	Very Common
Bishop, Max (+)	$100	$175	$250	Very Rare
Blue, Lu (+)	$150	$250	$375	None Known
Bluege, Ossie (+)	$100	$175	$250	Very Rare
Bodie, Ping (+)	$150	$250	$375	None Known
Bonura, Zeke (-)	$75	$150	$200	Rare
Bressler, Rube (+)	$225	$350	$500	None Known
Bridges, Tommy (+)	$100	$175	$250	Very Rare
Brown, Mace (-)	$50	$85	$175	Very Common
Bush, Guy (+)	$75	$150	$200	Rare
Bush, Joe	$150	$250	$375	Very Rare
Camilli, Dolf (-)	$50	$85	$175	Very Common
Carleton, James "Tex"	$75	$150	$200	Rare
Case, George (+)	$150	$250	$375	None Known
Chapman, Ray (+)	$400	$650	$850	None Known
Chase, Hal	$400	$650	$850	None Known
Cicotte, Eddie (+)	$500	$800	$1,200	None Known
Clift, Harlond	$100	$175	$250	Very Rare
Collins, Rip (-)	$35	$65	$125	Very Common
Cooper, Mort	$75	$150	$200	Common
Cooper, Walker	$75	$150	$200	Common
Craft, Harry	$50	$85	$175	Very Common
Cramer, Doc (-)	$75	$150	$200	Common
Cravath, Clifford, "Gravy"	$150	$250	$375	None Known
Crosetti, Frank (-)	$75	$150	$200	Very Common
Crowder, General	$150	$250	$375	None Known
Danning, Harry (-)	$50	$85	$175	Very Common
Daubert, Jake (+)	$225	$350	$500	None Found
Davis, Harry (+)	$225	$350	$500	Very Rare
Dean, Paul (Daffy) (-)	$75	$150	$200	Common
Derringer, Paul	$75	$150	$200	Rare
DiMaggio, Vince (-)	$35	$65	$125	Very Common
Doak, Bill (+15% early models)	$75	$150	$200	Very Common
Doyle, Larry (+)	$225	$350	$500	None Known
Dugan, Joe (+)	$225	$350	$500	None Known
Durocher, Leo (-)	$50	$85	$175	Very Common
Dykes, Jimmy (+)	$150	$250	$375	Very Rare
Earnshaw, George (+)	$100	$175	$250	Very Rare
Falk, Bibb (+)	$150	$250	$375	None Known
Felsch, Hap (+)	$500	$800	$1,200	None Known
Ferrell, Wes (-)	$150	$250	$375	None Found

Player	Very Good	Excellent	Near Mint	Supply
Fitzsimmons, Fred (+)	$150	$250	$375	Very Rare
Flagstead, Ira (+)	$150	$250	$375	Very Rare
Fournier, Jack (+)	$150	$250	$375	None Found
French, Larry (-)	$35	$65	$125	Very Common
Galehouse, Denny (+)	$100	$175	$250	None Found
Gandil, Chick (+)	$500	$800	$1,200	None Known
Gerber, Wally (+)	$150	$250	$375	None Found
Gibson, George (+)	$100	$175	$250	Very Rare
Goodman, Ival (-)	$35	$65	$125	Very Common
Gowdy, Hank (-)	$35	$65	$125	Very Common
Gray, Pete	$225	$350	$500	None Known
Groh, Heinie	$225	$350	$500	Very Rare
Haas, Mule (-)	$50	$85	$175	Very Common
Hack, Stan (-)	$35	$65	$125	Very Common
Hadley, Bump	$100	$175	$250	None Found
Hale, Sammy (+)	$150	$250	$375	None Found
Harder, Mel (+)	$150	$250	$375	None Found
Hargrave, Bubbles (-)	$100	$175	$250	Very Common
Hemsley, Rollie (-)	$35	$65	$125	Very Common
Henrich, Tommy (-)	$50	$85	$175	Rare
Herman, Babe (+)	$100	$175	$250	Very Rare
Higgins, Pinky (-)	$35	$65	$125	Very Common
Johnson "Indian Bob"	$75	$150	$200	None Found
Jones, Sam	$150	$250	$375	None Known
Judge, Joe (+)	$150	$250	$375	Very Rare
Kamm, Willie	$150	$250	$375	None Found
Keller, Charlie (-)	$35	$65	$125	Very Common
Keltner, Ken	$100	$175	$250	Common
Kerr, Dickie (+)	$225	$350	$500	None Known
Koenig, Mark (+)	$225	$350	$500	Very Rare
Kuehl, Joe (+)	$100	$175	$250	Rare
Kurowski, Whitey	$50	$85	$175	Rare
Leach, Tommy	$225	$350	$500	None Known
Leonard, Dutch (+)	$225	$350	$500	None Known
Lewis, Duffy (+)	$225	$350	$500	None Known
Lobert, Hans	$100	$175	$250	None Found
Mancuso, Gus (-)	$50	$85	$175	Very Common
Marberry, Firpo (+)	$225	$350	$500	Very Rare
Martin, Pepper (+)	$150	$250	$375	Very Rare
Mays, Carl	$225	$350	$500	Rare
McInnis, Snuffy J. (+)	$225	$350	$500	None Known
Meyers, Chief (+)	$400	$650	$850	Very Rare
Miller, Bing	$150	$250	$375	Very Rare
Moore, Terry (-)	$35	$65	$125	Very Common
Moses, Wally (-)	$50	$85	$175	Very Common
Mostil, Johnny (-)	$50	$85	$175	Common
Muesel, Bob (+)	$225	$350	$500	Very Rare
Muesel, Irish (+)	$150	$250	$375	Very Rare
Mungo, Van Lingle (+)	$100	$175	$250	Very Rare
Myer, Buddy	$75	$150	$200	Very Rare

Equipment

Player	Very Good	Excellent	Near Mint	Supply
Nickelson, Swish	$50	$85	$175	Common
O'Doul, Lefty (-)	$75	$150	$200	Common
O'Farrell, Bob (-)	$75	$150	$200	Common
Owen, Mickey (-)	$35	$65	$125	Very Common
Pearson, Monte	$35	$65	$125	Very Common
Peckinpaugh, Roger (+)	$225	$350	$500	None Known
Pipp, Wally	$100	$175	$250	Very Rare
Risberg, Swede (+)	$500	$800	$1,200	None Known
Rolfe, Red	$100	$175	$250	Very Common
Rommel, Eddie	$100	$175	$250	Common
Root, Charlie	$75	$150	$200	Common
Rowe, Schoolboy (-)	$50	$85	$175	Common
Ruel, Muddy (+)	$225	$350	$500	Very Rare
Ruether, Dutch (+)	$225	$350	$500	None Known
Schang, Wally (+)	$225	$350	$500	Very Rare
Schocker, Urban (+)	$400	$650	$850	None Known
Schulte, Wildfire (+)	$225	$350	$500	None Known
Schumacher, Hal	$150	$250	$375	None Found
Selkirk, George (-)	$50	$85	$175	Common
Sewell, Luke	$100	$175	$250	Common
Smith, Elmer (+)	$150	$250	$375	None Known
Snodgrass, Fred (+)	$225	$350	$500	None Known
Southworth, Billy (+)	$150	$250	$375	None Found
Stahl, Jake (+)	$225	$350	$500	None Known
Stephenson, Riggs (+)	$150	$250	$375	Rare
Tobin, Jake (+)	$150	$250	$375	None Known
Toporcer, Specs	$150	$250	$375	None Known
Trosky, Hal	$75	$150	$200	Rare
Trout, Dizzy	$75	$150	$200	Rare
Uhle, George (+)	$150	$250	$375	None Known
Vander Meer, Johnny	$75	$150	$200	Rare
Vaughn, Jim (Hippo) (+)	$400	$650	$850	None Known
Veach, Bobby (+)	$150	$250	$375	None Known
Walker, Dixie (-)	$35	$65	$125	Very Common
Waker, Harry (The Hat) (-)	$50	$85	$175	Very Common
Walters, Bucky (-)	$50	$85	$175	Common
Wambsganss, Bill (+)	$400	$650	$850	None Known
Warneke, Lon (-)	$50	$85	$175	Very Common
Weaver, Buck (+)	$500	$800	$1,200	None Known
Whitehill, Earl (+)	$150	$250	$375	Very Rare
Williams, Claude (+)	$500	$800	$1,200	None Known
Williams, Cy (+)	$150	$250	$375	None Known
Williams, Ken	$75	$150	$200	Rare
Willis, Vic (-)	$150	$250	$375	None Known
Wilson, Jimmie (+)	$100	$175	$250	Rare
Wood, Joe (+)	$400	$650	$850	None Known
York, Rudy (-)	$35	$65	$125	Very Common
Zimmerman, Heinie (+)	$225	$350	$500	None Known

Post-war gloves (star players)

Player	Very Good	Excellent	Near Mint	Supply
Abrams, Cal (+)	$45	$65	$95	Common
Adams, Bobby	$30	$45	$60	Rare
Adcock, Joe (+)	$45	$65	$95	Common
Agee, Tommy	$35	$55	$75	None Known
Agganis, Harry	$55	$75	$100	Rare
Allen, Richie	$35	$55	$75	Common
Alley, Gene	$35	$55	$75	None Known
Allison, Bob	$25	$35	$50	Common
Alou, Felipe (+)	$25	$35	$50	Rare U.S.A.
Alou, Matty	$25	$35	$50	Common
Amoros, Sandy	$45	$65	$95	Very Rare
Anderson, Sparky	$45	$65	$95	None Known
Antonelli, Johnny (-)	$30	$45	$60	Common
Avila, Bobby (-)	$35	$55	$75	Common
Bailey, Ed (-)	$35	$55	$75	Very Common
Barber, Steve	$35	$55	$75	None Known
Barney, Rex	$35	$55	$75	None Known
Battey, Earl	$30	$45	$60	Common
Bauer, Hank (+)	$45	$65	$95	Common
Baumhohz, Frank	$35	$55	$75	Very Rare
Beckert, Glenn	$25	$35	$50	Common
Beggs, Joe	$35	$55	$75	Rare
Bell, Gus (-)	$25	$35	$50	Common
Berry, Ken	$35	$55	$75	None Known
Bevins, Floyd	$35	$55	$75	None Known
Bickford, Vern	$35	$55	$75	None Known
Black, Joe (+)	$75	$150	$200	None Known
Blackwell, Ewell	$45	$65	$95	Rare
Blair, Paul	$30	$45	$60	Common
Blasingame, Don	$30	$45	$60	Very Common
Blefary, Curt	$30	$45	$60	Common
Bolling, Frank (+)	$30	$45	$60	None Found
Bolling, Milt	$35	$55	$75	None Found
Boone, Ray	$35	$55	$75	Rare
Boros, Steve	$30	$45	$60	Common
Bouton, Jim	$40	$60	$85	Rare
Boyer, Clete	$35	$55	$75	Rare U.S.A.
Boyer, Ken (+)	$45	$65	$95	Common
Bragan, Bobby	$35	$55	$75	Very Rare
Branca, Ralph	$45	$65	$95	Rare
Brandt, Jackie	$30	$45	$60	Common
Brazle, Al	$35	$55	$75	None Found
Brecheen, Harry	$35	$55	$75	Common
Broglio, Ernie	$25	$35	$50	Rare
Brosnan, Jim (+)	$30	$45	$60	None Found
Brown, Bobby	$35	$55	$75	None Found
Bruton, Bill	$35	$55	$75	Rare

Equipment

Player	Very Good	Excellent	Near Mint	Supply
Buhl, Bob (-)	$30	$45	$60	Common
Bunning, Jim	$35	$55	$75	Common
Burdette, Lew (-)	$35	$55	$75	Common
Burgess, Smoky	$35	$55	$75	Common
Busby, Jim	$30	$45	$60	Common
Byrne, Tommy	$25	$35	$50	None Found
Callison, John	$30	$45	$60	Rare
Campaneris, Bert	$30	$45	$60	Rare
Carey, Andy	$30	$45	$60	Rare
Carlton, Steve	$35	$55	$75	Very Rare USA
Carrasquel, Chico	$30	$45	$60	Very Common
Casey, Hugh	$35	$55	$75	None Known
Cash, Norm	$30	$45	$60	Rare U.S.A.
Cavaretta, Phil	$35	$55	$75	Common
Cepeda, Orlando (-)	$35	$55	$75	Rare U.S.A.
Cerv, Bob	$25	$35	$50	Rare
Cimoli, Gino (+)	$35	$55	$75	Very Rare
Colavito, Rocky	$50	$70	$95	Common
Coleman, Jerry (-)	$35	$55	$75	Common
Collins, Joe	$30	$45	$60	Common
Conigliaro, Tony	$35	$55	$75	Common
Conley, Gene (+)	$55	$75	$100	Very Rare
Connors, Chuck	$100	$175	$300	Very Rare
Consolo, Billy	$35	$55	$75	None Known
Cooper, Walker	$75	$150	$200	Rare
Cottier, Chuck	$35	$55	$75	Very Rare
Courtney, Clint	$30	$45	$60	Common
Covington, Wes (+)	$35	$55	$75	None Found
Cox, Billy	$35	$55	$75	Rare
Craig, Roger	$30	$45	$60	Common
Crandall, Del	$35	$55	$75	Very Common
Crowe, George	$35	$55	$75	None Known
Cuellar, Mike	$35	$55	$75	None Found
Cullenbine, Roy	$35	$55	$75	None Known
Culp, Ray	$35	$55	$75	Rare
Cunningham, Joe	$30	$45	$60	Common
Dark, Al (-)	$30	$45	$60	Very Common
Davalillo, Vic	$35	$55	$75	None Known
Davenport, Jim (-)	$25	$35	$50	Very Common
Davis, Tommy	$30	$45	$60	Rare U.S.A.
Davis, Willie	$30	$45	$60	Rare U.S.A.
DeBusschere, Dave	$35	$55	$75	None Known
Dickson, Murry	$35	$55	$75	None Found
Dierker, Larry	$35	$55	$75	None Known
Dillinger, Bob	$55	$75	$100	Common
DiMaggio, Dom (+)	$55	$75	$100	Very Rare
Doby, Larry (+)	$75	$150	$200	Very Rare
Donovan, Dick	$30	$45	$160	Common
Dropo, Walt	$30	$45	$60	Common
Duren, Ryne	$25	$35	$50	Common

Player	Very Good	Excellent	Near Mint	Supply
Easter, Luke (+)	$55	$75	$100	None Found
Edwards, John	$25	$35	$50	Common
Elliott, Bob	$35	$55	$75	Common
Ellsworth, Dick	$30	$45	$60	Rare
Ennis, Del (-)	$30	$45	$60	Common
Epstein, Mike	$30	$45	$60	Rare U.S.A.
Erskine, Carl	$55	$75	$100	Common
Evers, Hoot	$30	$45	$60	Common
Face, Elroy	$35	$55	$75	Common
Fain, Ferris (-)	$30	$45	$60	Common
Flood, Curt	$40	$60	$85	None Found
Fondy, Dee	$25	$35	$50	Common
Fosse, Ray	$35	$55	$75	Very Rare
Fox, Nelson * Deduct Higgins	$40	$60	$85	Common Wilson
Francona, Tito	$25	$35	$50	Common
Freehan, Bill	$40	$60	$85	Common
Freese, Gene	$35	$55	$75	Rare
Fregosi, Jim	$30	$45	$60	Rare
Friend, Bob	$35	$55	$75	Rare U.S.A.
Furillo, Carl (-)	$40	$60	$85	Very Common
Garagiola, Joe	$55	$75	$100	Common
Garcia, Mike	$45	$65	$95	None Known
Garver, Ned (-)	$30	$45	$60	Very Rare
Gentile, Jim	$30	$45	$60	Rare
Gilliam, Jim (+)	$75	$150	$200	Very Rare
Goodman, Billy	$30	$45	$60	Very Common
Gordon, Joe (-)	$25	$35	$50	Very Common
Gordon, Sid	$35	$55	$75	Rare
Grim, Bob	$45	$45	$60	Common
Groat Dick	$35	$55	$75	Common
Groth, Johnny	$30	$45	$60	Common
Gustine, Frank	$25	$35	$50	Common
Haddix, Harvey	$45	$65	$95	Common
Hansen, Ron	$25	$35	$50	Common
Harrelson, Ken	$35	$55	$75	None Known
Hart, Jim Ray	$35	$55	$75	None Known
Hartung, Clint	$35	$55	$75	None Known
Hegan, Jim (-)	$30	$45	$60	Common
Hemus, Jim (-)	$30	$45	$60	Common
Henrich, Tommy	$40	$60	$85	Common
Herzog, Whitey (+)	$75	$150	$200	Very Rare
Hoak, Don	$35	$55	$75	Common
Hodges, Gil (-)	$40	$60	$85	Very Common
Hoeft Billy	$35	$55	$75	None Known
Holmes, Tommy	$40	$60	$85	Common
Hopp, Johnny	$35	$55	$75	Common
Houk, Ralph	$35	$55	$75	None Known
Howard, Elston (-)	$40	$60	$85	Common
Howard, Frank	$40	$60	$85	Rare
Howell, Dixie	$45	$65	$95	None Found

Equipment

Player	Very Good	Excellent	Near Mint	Supply
Hubbs, Ken	$35	$55	$75	Rare
Hutchinson, Fred	$45	$65	$95	None Known
Jackson, Larry (-)	$25	$35	$50	Very Common
Janowicz, Vic	$35	$55	$75	None Known
Jansen, Larry	$35	$55	$75	Very Rare
Jay, Joey	$25	$35	$50	Rare
Jenson, Jackie (-)	$30	$45	$60	Common
Jethroe, Sam	$40	$60	$85	None Known
Johnson, Dave	$35	$55	$75	Very Rare
Jones, Sam	$35	$55	$75	None Known
Jones, Willie (-)	$40	$60	$85	Common
Kaat, Jim	$40	$60	$85	Rare
Kerr, Buddy	$25	$35	$50	Common
Kessinger, Don	$30	$45	$60	Rare U.S.A.
Kinder, Ellis (+)	$35	$55	$75	None Known
Kline, Ron	$35	$55	$75	None Known
Klipstein, Johnny (+)	$35	$55	$75	None Known
Kluszewski, Ted (-)	$40	$60	$85	Common
Knoop, Bobby	$35	$55	$75	Very Rare
Konstanty, Jim	$35	$55	$75	None Known
Koslo, Dave	$35	$55	$75	None Known
Kubek, Tony	$45	$65	$95	Common
Kucks, Johnny	$25	$35	$50	Rare
Kuenn, Harvey (-)	$30	$45	$60	Very Common
Kurowski, Whitey	$35	$55	$75	Rare
Labine, Clem	$45	$65	$95	Rare
Landis, Jim	$30	$45	$60	Common
Lanier, Max	$45	$65	$95	Rare
Larsen, Don (-)	$40	$60	$85	Common
Lary, Frank	$30	$45	$60	Very Common
Lasorda, Tommy (+)	$75	$150	$200	None Known
Law, Vern	$35	$55	$75	Rare
Lawrence, Brooks	$30	$45	$60	Very Rare
Leja, Frank	$25	$35	$50	Common
Lemon, Jim	$25	$35	$50	Common
Leonard, Dutch	$75	$150	$200	None Known
Lewis, Buddy	$30	$45	$60	Very Rare
Lockman, Whitey	$35	$55	$75	Common
Loes, Billy	$45	$65	$95	Rare
Logan, Johnny (-)	$35	$55	$75	Common
Lolich, Mickey	$35	$55	$75	Rare
Lollar, Sherm (-)	$35	$55	$75	Common
Long, Dale	$35	$55	$75	Common
Lopat, Eddie	$35	$55	$75	None Known
Lopata, Stan	$30	$45	$60	Rare
Lopez, Hector	$35	$55	$75	None Known
Lowrey, Peanuts	$30	$45	$60	Common
Lynch, Jerry	$25	$35	$50	Common
Maglie, Sal	$35	$55	$75	Rare
Maloney, Jim	$35	$55	$75	Rare

Player	Very Good	Excellent	Near Mint	Supply
Malzone, Frank	$35	$55	$75	Rare
Mantilla, Felix	$35	$55	$75	None Known
Marion, Marty (-)	$35	$55	$75	Very Common
Maris, Roger	$55	$75	$100	Common
Marshall, Willard	$25	$35	$50	None Known
Martin, Billy (-)	$35	$55	$75	Very Common
Mauch, Gene	$35	$55	$75	None Known
Maxvill, Dal	$30	$45	$60	Rare
Maxwell, Charlie	$25	$35	$50	Rare
Mazeroski, Bill	$45	$65	$95	Rare U.S.A.
McCarver, Tim	$40	$60	$85	Common
McCormick, Mike F.	$35	$55	$75	Rare
McCormick, Myron (Mike)	$40	$60	$85	Rare
McCosky, Barney	$40	$60	$85	Common
McCullough, Clyde (-)	$25	$35	$50	Very Common
McDaniel, Lindy	$45	$65	$95	None Known
McDermott, Mickey	$45	$65	$95	None Known
McDougald, Gil (-)	$30	$45	$60	Very Common
McDowell, Sam	$35	$55	$75	None Known
McLain, Denny	$45	$65	$95	Rare U.S.A.
McMillan, Ray (-)	$30	$45	$60	Common
McQuinn, George (Claw)	$55	$75	$100	Common
Meyer, Russ (+)	$25	$35	$50	None Known
Miller, Eddie (-)	$30	$45	$60	None Known
Millan, Felix	$35	$55	$75	None Known
Miller, Eddie (-)	$30	$45	$60	Very Common
Miller, Stu	$40	$60	$85	None Known
Milliken, Bob	$45	$65	$95	Common
Minoso, Minnie	$65	$95	$125	Rare
Mitchell, Dale (-)	$45	$65	$95	Common
Mizell, Wilmer	$45	$65	$95	Common
Moon, Wally (-)	$35	$55	$75	Common
Moore, Terry	$40	$60	$85	Common
Moryn, Walt (-)	$30	$45	$60	Common
Mossi, Don (-)	$30	$45	$60	Common
Mueller, Don (-)	$30	$45	$60	Common
Murtaugh, Danny	$35	$55	$75	None Known
Narleski, Ray	$35	$55	$75	None Known
Neal, Charlie	$35	$55	$75	Common
Newcombe, Don	$65	$95	$125	Very Rare
Newsom, Bobo	$45	$65	$95	None Known
Nicholson, Bill	$40	$60	$85	Rare
Niekro, Phil	$45	$65	$95	None Known
Nieman, Bob	$35	$55	$75	Very Rare
Noren, Irv (-)	$30	$45	$60	Common
Nuxall, Joe	$35	$55	$75	Rare
Oliva, Tony	$35	$55	$75	None Known
Osteen, Claude	$35	$55	$75	None Known
Otis, Amos	$30	$45	$60	Common
O'Toole, Jim	$30	$45	$60	Common

Equipment

Player	Very Good	Excellent	Near Mint	Supply
Pafko, Andy (-)	$30	$45	$60	Common
Page, Joe	$45	$65	$95	None Known
Pappas, Milt (+)	$35	$55	$75	None Known
Parker, Wes	$30	$45	$60	Common
Parnell, Mel	$45	$65	$95	Very Rare
Pascual, Camilo	$35	$55	$75	None Known
Pearson, Albie	$30	$45	$60	Rare
Pepitone, Joe	$35	$55	$75	None Known
Perranowsk, Ron	$25	$35	$50	Common
Perez, Tony	$30	$45	$60	Common
Pesky, John (-)	$30	$45	$60	Very Common
Peters, Gary	$35	$55	$75	Rare
Philley, Dave	$30	$45	$60	Rare
Pierce, Billy (-)	$30	$45	$60	Very Common
Piersall, Jimmy	$35	$55	$75	Very Common
Pinson, Vada	$30	$45	$60	Common
Podres, Johnny (-)	$30	$45	$60	Very Common
Pollet, Howie	$40	$60	$85	Rare
Post, Wally	$30	$45	$60	Common
Powell, Boog (+)	$30	$45	$60	Common
Power, Vic (-)	$30	$45	$60	Common
Priddy, Jerry	$30	$45	$60	Rare
Purkey, Bob	$30	$45	$60	Rare
Raffensberger, Ken	$40	$60	$85	None Known
Raschi, Vic	$40	$60	$85	None Known
Reiser, Pete (-)	$30	$45	$60	Very Common
Repulski, Rip (-)	$30	$45	$60	Common
Reynolds, Allie (+)	$75	$150	$200	None Known
Rhodes, Dusty (+)	$40	$60	$85	None Known
Rice, Del (-)	$30	$45	$60	Very Common
Richardson, Bobby	$40	$60	$85	Very Common
Rivera, Jim	$35	$55	$75	Rare
Robinson, Eddie (+)	$40	$60	$85	Very Rare
Roe, Preacher (-)	$40	$60	$85	Very Common
Roebuck, Ed	$35	$55	$75	None Known
Romano, John	$35	$55	$75	Common
Rosar, Buddy	$30	$55	$75	Rare
Rose, Pete	$40	$60	$85	Rare U.S.A.
Roseboro, John	$35	$55	$75	Common
Rosen, Al (-)	$40	$60	$85	Common
Rowe, Schoolboy	$40	$60	$85	Rare
Runnels, Pete (-)	$25	$35	$50	Very Common
Rush, Bob (-)	$30	$45	$60	Very Rare
Rutherford, John	$25	$35	$50	Common
Sain, Johnny (-)	$40	$60	$85	Rare
Sanford, Jack	$35	$55	$75	Very Rare
Santo, Ron	$30	$45	$60	Common
Sauer, Hank (-)	$25	$35	$50	Very Common
Schmitz, Johnny	$25	$35	$50	Rare
Schofield, Dick	$30	$45	$60	None Known

Player	Very Good	Excellent	Near Mint	Supply
Score, Herb	$45	$65	$95	Rare
Scott, George	$25	$35	$50	Common
Seminick, Andy (-)	$25	$35	$50	Very Rare
Shannon, Mike	$25	$35	$50	Common
Shantz, Bobby (-)	$25	$35	$50	V. Common/Non USA
Shea, Frank	$40	$60	$85	None Known
Sherry, Larry	$25	$35	$50	Common
Sherry, Norm	$30	$45	$60	Rare
Shuba, George	$45	$65	$95	Rare
Siebern, Norm	$30	$45	$60	Rare
Sievers, Roy (-)	$25	$35	$50	Very Common
Simmons, Curt (-)	$30	$45	$60	Very Common
Sisler, Dick	$30	$45	$60	Rare
Skinner, Bob	$30	$45	$60	Rare
Skowron, Moose (-)	$30	$45	$60	Very Common
Smalley, Roy	$30	$45	$60	Rare
Smith, Al	$30	$45	$60	Common
Spooner, Karl	$45	$65	$95	Common
Staley, Gerry	$40	$60	$85	None Known
Stanky, Eddie	$35	$55	$75	Common
Stanley, Mickey	$30	$45	$60	Rare
Staub, Rusty	$25	$35	$50	Common
Stephens, Vern (-)	$30	$45	$60	Very Common
Stirnweiss, Snuffy (-)	$30	$45	$60	Very Common
Stuart, Dick (+)	$40	$60	$85	Very Rare
Susce, George	$30	$45	$60	Rare
Sullivan, Haywood	$25	$35	$50	Common
Tanner, Chuck	$35	$55	$75	None Known
Tebbetts, Birdie	$40	$60	$85	Common
Temple, Johnny (-)	$25	$35	$50	Very Common
Terry, Ralph	$30	$45	$60	Common
Terwilliger, Wayne	$35	$55	$75	None Known
Thomas, Frank (-)	$25	$35	$50	Very Common
Thompson, Hank (-)	$25	$35	$50	Very Common
Thomson, Bobby (-)	$30	$45	$60	Common
Tiant, Luis	$35	$55	$75	None Known
Torgeson, Earl (-)	$30	$45	$60	Very Common
Torre, Frank	$30	$45	$60	Very Rare
Torre, Joe	$30	$45	$60	Very Rare USA
Tresh, Tom	$35	$55	$75	Common
Triandos, Gus	$35	$55	$75	Common
Trucks, Virgil	$35	$55	$75	Rare
Turley, Bob	$40	$60	$85	Common
Tuttle, Bill	$25	$35	$50	Very Common
Uecker, Bob	$75	$150	$200	None Known
Valo, Elmer	$30	$45	$60	Very Rare
Verban, Emil	$35	$55	$75	Common
Vernon, Mickey	$35	$55	$75	Common
Versalles, Zoilo	$35	$55	$75	None Known
Virdon, Bill	$30	$45	$60	Rare

Player	Very Good	Excellent	Near Mint	Supply
Waitkus, Eddie	$30	$45	$60	Common
Wakefield, Dick (-)	$30	$45	$60	Common
Walker, Rube (+)	$40	$60	$85	Common
Wertz, Vic (+)	$75	$150	$200	Rare
Westrum Wes	$40	$60	$85	Very Rare
White, Bill (-)	$35	$55	$75	Rare
Williams, Dave	$35	$55	$75	Common
Williams, Dick	$35	$55	$75	Common
Wills, Maury	$35	$55	$75	Rare
Wilson, Earl (+)	$25	$35	$50	None Known
Wooding, Gene	$40	$60	$85	Rare
Yost, Eddie	$35	$55	$75	Rare
Young, Babe	$35	$55	$75	Common
Zarilla, Al (-)	$30	$45	$60	Common
Zernial, Gus (+)	$35	$55	$75	Very Rare
Zimmer, Don (-)	$30	$45	$60	Very Common

Additional player model gloves

Ted Abernathy: 1960s Hollander model, signed..$65
Richie Allen: Spalding model $65
Bobby Allison: 1960s Sonnett model...$125
Luke Appling: Wilson model $85
Richie Ashburn: MacGregor model $45
Ed Bailey: Denkert catcher's mitt $85
Sal Bando: Spalding model..$65
Hank Bauer: 1950s Hurricane model, signed..$85
Gus Bell: 1950s MacGregor model, signed...$75
Buddy Bell: Wilson model...$45
Johnny Bench: 1970s Rawlings catcher's mitt, signed $150
Yogi Berra: 1950s Reach catcher's mitt, signed...$50
Paul Blair: Montgomery Ward model $65
Wade Boggs: Rawlings model $55
Bobby Bonilla: Rawlings model $35
Ken Boyer: Rawlings, three-finger $55
George Brett: 1970s Wilson model, signed...$175
Lou Brock: Franklin model..$75
Roy Campanella: 1950s Wilson catcher's mitt $135
Rod Carew: MacGregor model..$65
Steve Carlton: 1970s Rawlings model, right-handed, signed..$85
Joe Carter: Wilson model...$45
Norm Cash: Wilson first baseman's model $95
Cesar Cedeno: Rawlings model...$45
Ron Cey: MacGregor model $45
Jack Clark: Spalding model $65
Roger Clemens: Wilson model..$65
Roberto Clemente: 1950s Franklin model $150
Roberto Clemente: J.C. Higgins model $145
Tony Conigliaro: 1970s Hurricane model...$110
Alvin Dark: 1950s Spalding model $60
Bill Dickey: 1940s MacGregor Goldsmith catcher's mitt $125

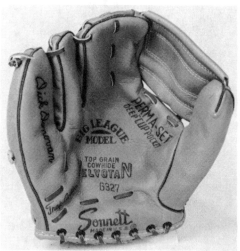

Sonnett, G327 Dick Donovan model.

Sonnett, F4F Bobby Thomson model.

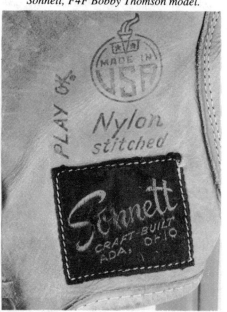

This Hutch cloth label (above) and Sonnett label (right) were attached to gloves produced by the Ohio-based companies.

Sonnett, TW55
Gil Hodges model.

Hutch, 180
Ted Kluszewski model.

Hutch Joe DiMaggio model.

At left is a Bill Dickey glove from the mid-1930s, made for Montgomery Wards stores. At right is a 1920s infielder's glove for a right-handed thrower. Notice the 1-inch web sewed to the thumb and finger.

Left to right: late 1800s baseman's mitt without any webbing; 1910-era fielder's glove with a full web between thumb and finger; a pre-WWII Spalding baseman's mitt with a small cloth patch.

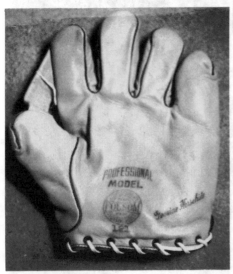

At left is a WWI-era fielder's glove made by Folsum Sporting Goods. Notice the Horsehide mark; horsehide gave way to cowhide during the 1930s. At right is a Rick Ferrell Reach mitt from the 1930s; notice the lack of webbing or break action.

At left, a Rogers Hornsby glove box, circa 1930. Early boxed gloves featuring pictures or illustrations of pre-war Hall of Famers are worth hundreds, even thousands of dollars, with or without the glove.

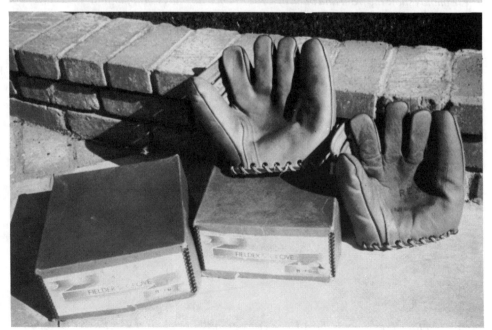

These two Mint pre-war gloves have unlaced fingers and generic boxes.

 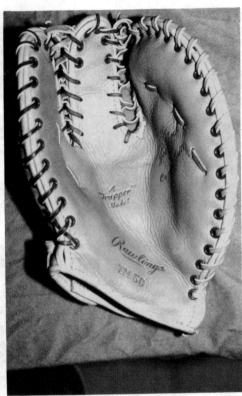

These photos show the front and back of a Joe Adcock Rawlings Trapper mitt, circa 1956-58.

At left is a Rawlings box for the Adcock Trapper mitt; at right is a Wes Parker baseman's mitt, made in Japan, circa 1970.

Joe DiMaggio: 1950s Spalding model, signed...$895
Don Drysdale: 1960s Spalding model, signed...$450
Dwight Evans: 1980s Wilson black model, signed......................................$85
Hoot Evers: Hutch model...$95
Bob Feller: J.C. Higgins model..$50
Ron Fairly: Spalding six-finger model...$85
Carlton Fisk: 1970s Wilson catcher's mitt...$85
Whitey Ford: Spalding model..$70
George Foster: 1970s MacGregor model, signed..$40
Nellie Fox: Wilson model fielder's glove...$140
Steve Garvey: Rawlings first baseman's model..$65
Bob Gibson: 1970s Rawlings model, signed...$100
Kirk Gibson: Wilson model...$65
Pedro Guerrero: Wilson model..$35
Bucky Harris: 1920s Spalding model...$150
Hurricane Hazel: 1950s Rawlings model...$80
Mike Hegan: Spalding first baseman's model...$65
Larry Hisle: Wilson model..$45
Willie Horton: Wilson model..$45
Gil Hodges: Denkert first baseman's mitt..$75
Ken Hunt: Spalding model..$45
Catfish Hunter: 1970s Wilson model...$40
Reggie Jackson: Rawlings model...$45
Tommy John: Wilson model, signed...$65
Harmon Killebrew: 1960s Wilson model..$65
Sandy Koufax: 1950s Denkert model..$350
Harvey Kuenn: 1950s Wilson model...$125
Ron LeFlore: Wilson model..$45
Bob Lemon: 1950s Hurricane model..$50
Johnny Logan: TruPlay model...$35
Ernie Lombardi: Goldsmith catcher's mitt...$125
Greg Luzinski: MacGregor model..$45
Fred Lynn: Wilson model...$75
Billy Martin: 1950s Wilson model...$100
Don Mattingly: Franklin first baseman's mitt...$95
John Mayberry: 1970s MacGregor first baseman's mitt...............................$35
Willie Mays: MacGregor model..$75
Bill Mazeroski: 1950s MacGregor model...$50
Willie McGee: MacGregor model...$45
Johnny Mize: Wilson first baseman's mitt..$95
Rick Monday: Spalding model..$55
Joe Morgan: 1970s MacGregor model, signed..$60
Don Mossi: Nokona model...$45
Stan Musial: 1960s Hawthorne model, signed...$140
Stan Musial: Rawlings model...$85
Graig Nettles: Louisville Slugger model...$40
Amos Otis: Rawlings model...$55
Andy Pafko: J.C. Higgins model..$60
Dave Parker: Rawlings model..$55
Wes Parker: MacGregor model..$30
Joe Pepitone: Trio-Hollander model..$165
Gaylord Perry: 1960s Wilson model, signed...$90
Rico Petrocelli: Spalding model..$55
Jimmy Piersall: 1950s Wilson model...$60
Lou Piniella: Spalding model...$75
Vic Power: Franklin model..$50

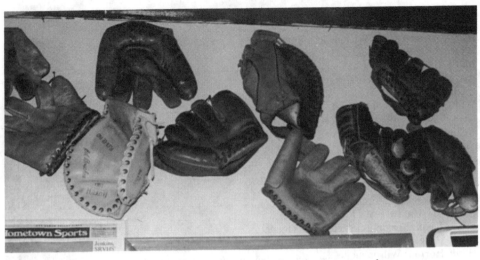

Old store-model gloves can often be found at garage sales.

Willie Randolph: MacGregor model $45
Del Rice: 1960s black Denkert catcher's mitt, 1960s $100
Jim Rice: 1970s Wilson model $40
Cal Ripken Jr.: Rawlings model $65
Phil Rizzuto: Reach model..$145
Brooks Robinson: Rawlings model $45
Frank Robinson: MacGregor model $45
Red Ruffing: 1930s J.C. Higgins model $275
Babe Ruth: 1930s Spalding catcher's mitt...$800
Ryne Sandberg: Rawlings model $65
Ron Santo: 1960s Wilson model, signed $75
Ray Schalk: 1920s Wilson model...$195
Mike Schmidt: Franklin model $45
Tom Seaver: 1970s MacGregor model, signed..$100
Luke Sewell: 1930s Wilson catcher's mitt...$125
Moose Skowron: 1950s Denkert model...$45
Enos Slaughter: 1950s J.C. Higgins model, signed $125
Ozzie Smith: 1970s Rawlings model, signed...$125
Roy Smalley Sr.: Rawlings model...$50
Duke Snider: Rawlings model, unused..$250
Snuffy Sternweiss: Spalding split-finger model $350
Mel Stottlemyre: Spalding model...$30
Bruce Sutter: Wilson model $55
Bill Terry: Ken-Wel fielder's glove..$350
Manny Trillo: Wilson model $55
Johnny Vander Meer: Goldsmith fielder's glove..$295
Bill Virdon: 1950s Denkert model..$65
Frank White: Rawlings model $45
Ted Williams: Sears model..$65
Ted Williams: Hutch model...$200
Dave Winfield: Rawlings model...$45
Carl Yastrzemski: 1970s Spalding, signed twice...$125
Pep Young: 1940s Hutch model...$75
Robin Yount: 1970s Rawlings model...$150
Richie Zisk: Wilson model $55

Statues/Figurines

Hartland Plastics Inc.

Braves and Yankees were well represented in Hartland's intial line of statues.

From 1960-1963, Hartland Plastics Co. in Wisconsin offered a line of molded plastic statues featuring 18 baseball stars.

The approximately 8-inch statues sold well at baseball stadium concession stands and retail stores, for between $2-$4. Up to 150,000 of some players (Babe Ruth, Willie Mays, Mickey Mantle, Yogi Berra, Hank Aaron, Ted Williams and Eddie Mathews) were sold.

There were 5,000 Pittsburgh Pirates Dick Groat statues made. However, although he is considered the most valuable in the set, he wasn't a big seller at the time because he, the 1960 National League MVP, was a one-year wonder. Rocky Colavito's statue, of which about 10,000 were sold, is the second most valuable.

Willie Mays' glove comes in different colors depending on how long it was dyed.

Others in the line were Warren Spahn, Duke Snider, Don Drysdale, Roger Maris, Harmon Killebrew, Luis Aparicio, Nellie Fox, Ernie Banks, and Stan Musial. Twelve statues were hitting poses, two were pitching poses and four were fielding poses. The players, who negotiated contracts with Hartland to use their likenesses, received $500 as royalties, plus 5 percent of gross sales.

Artists created sculptures from countless sketches, then made plastic molds from the sculptures. Details were hand-painted, and intricate paint-spray masks were also used.

Hartland placed its trade stamp on the back belt loop of the player's pants. However, the Ted Williams statue had the stamp printed behind the shoulder and the Rocky Colavito statue had the stamp underneath a shoulder. The Mickey Mantle statue has its stamp on the inside of Mantle's right forearm.

Variations among the statues include:

- Aaron, Mantle, Mathews, Ruth, Spahn and Williams - with or without magnets.
- Willie Mays - his glove and bat come in a variety of colors, depending upon how long they were left in a dye tank.
- Hank Aaron - some early models have his right foot up on the toes, making it difficult for the statue to stand up; later models made his left foot flatter for more support.
- Aparicio, Drysdale, Colavito, Williams - original platforms were dark purple; later models are white.
- Luis Aparicio and Nellie Fox - uniforms have the word "Sox" written in either red (more common) or black.

In addition to baseball players, Hartland, formed in 1950, made western and religious statues, football players and beer signs, which were the company's best sellers. About 25,000 each of a little leaguer and smaller minor leaguer were also created.

In 1963, the firm was sold to Revlon, and production of the statues ceased. After a series of sales of the company to different conglomerates, Hartland closed its plant in 1978. The original molds were taken to the city dump and are buried under a subdivision.

In 1988 William Alley bought the rights to the Hartland name. In 1989-90 the company retooled the original molds and produced a 25th commemorative edition of the 18 stars, 10,000 each, at $25 each. Each figure has a 25th-anniversary label on the back of the belt. The original designer, Frank Fulop, helped in the reproductions as well. A new line of figures began in 1990; there were 10,000 statues each made for each of the original players, plus Roberto Clemente. In 1993 Hartland produced statues for Whitey Ford, Nolan Ryan (home and away), Honus Wagner, Carl Yastrzemski and Cy Young.

In addition to condition (having paint intact, without marks, and including all original parts, including bats), prices for the original Hartland statues are based on the degree of whiteness the statue has maintained - has it stayed white, or faded to cream or yellow?

The Hartland statues were packaged in cardboard boxes. A hang tag was also included on a string. Having these two items also adds to the price of the statue.

These prices are ranges for white (in Excellent to Near Mint) statues; lower-priced off-whites are generally about 50 percent less of the starting range for whites.

Hartland issued reproductions for its 25th anniversary.

- Hank Aaron..........................$200-$250
  Aaron reprint $90
- Luis Aparicio ....$250-$350
  Aparicio reprint $45
- Ernie Banks.........................$300-$350
  Banks reprint $50
- Yogi Berra ....$200-$275
  Berra reprint.................................. $80
- Roberto Clemente reprint $40
- Rocky Colavito ....$500-$750
  Colavito reprint............................. $50
- Don Drysdale......................$300-$400
  Drysdale reprint............................ $50
- Whitey Ford reprint $40
- Nellie Fox ....$100-$250
  Fox reprint $45
- Dick Groat ....$1,000-$1,700
  Groat reprint $60
- Harmon Killebrew ....$450-$500
  Killebrew reprint $75
- Mickey Mantle....................$300-$400
  Mantle reprint.............................. $100
- Roger Maris ....$450-$600

Maris reprint $100
- Eddie Mathews ....$100-$175
  Mathews reprint............................ $60
- Willie Mays.........................$250-$350
  Mays reprint................................. $100
- Stan Musial ....$150-$225
  Musial reprint............................... $50
- Babe Ruth ....$225-$325
  Ruth reprint................................... $65
- Nolan Ryan reprint......................... $50
- Duke Snider ....$350-$450
  Snider reprint $60
- Warren Spahn ....$100-$175
  Spahn reprint................................ $50
- Honus Wagner reprint.................... $40
- Ted Williams......................$200-$250
  Williams reprint........................... $100
- Carl Yastrzemski reprint................ $40
- Cy Young reprint $40
- Little leaguer (bat boy) $150-200
  4" Batter (Minor Leaguer) $125-150
  Complete sets of 18 can be found for
  between $5,000 and $7,000.

Kenner Starting Lineup Statues

Prices, in Mint condition, are for complete sealed packages with the card and statue. The cards themselves are not often collected but are hard to find outside of the original package.

1995 Kenner Starting Lineups

Complete set (58): $675	Cecil Fielder $10	Raul Mondesi $45
Jim Abbott $10	Cliff Floyd $20	Mike Mussina $14
Moises Alou $16	Julio Franco $10	Troy Neel $12
Carlos Baerga $12	Juan Gonzalez........................ $10	Dave Nilsson $13
Jeff Bagwell.......................... $14	Ken Griffey Jr........................ $25	John Olerud $10
Albert Belle $20	Tony Gwynn........................... $16	Paul O'Neill.......................... $12
Geronimo Berroa................... $15	Bob Hamelin.......................... $14	Mike Piazza $20
Dante Bichette $35	Jeffrey Hammonds $14	Kirby Puckett........................ $15
Barry Bonds........................... $13	Randy Johnson $21	Cal Ripken Jr......................... $30
Jay Buhner............................. $18	Jeff King $13	Tim Salmon $12
Jose Canseco......................... $12	Jeff Kent $13	Deion Sanders........................ $16
Chuck Carr $14	Ryan Klesko $35	Reggie Sanders $18
Joe Carter.............................. $10	Chuck Knoblauch $14	Sammy Sosa $16
Andujar Cedeno..................... $14	John Kruk $9	Mickey Tettleton $10
Will Clark.............................. $12	Ray Lankford......................... $9	Frank Thomas........................ $18
Roger Clemens $12	Barry Larkin $13	Andy Van Slyke $10
Jeff Conine $18	Javier Lopez $30	Mo Vaughn............................ $16
Scott Cooper $12	Al Martin $12	Rick Wilkins......................... $14
Darren Daulton $12	Brian McRae.......................... $9	Matt Williams........................ $12
Carlos Delgado...................... $16	Paul Molitor........................... $12	

1995 Kenner Starting Lineup extended

Complete set (9): $290	Tom Pagnozzi......................... $21	Alex Rodriguez...................... $25
Jose Canseco........................... $18	Mike Piazza $30	Mike Schmidt $18
Rusty Greer............................ $19	Manny Ramirez $60	
Kenny Lofton $21	Cal Ripken Jr. $100	

1995 Kenner Cooperstown Collection

Complete set (10): $140	Bob Feller.............................. $14	Eddie Mathews $30
Rod Carew............................. $13	Whitey Ford........................... $13	Satchel Paige $17
Dizzy Dean $14	Bob Gibson $14	Babe Ruth $21
Don Drysdale......................... $13	Harmon Killebrew $30	

1995 Kenner Stadium Stars

Complete set (9): $260	Randy Johnson $50	Frank Thomas......................... $30
Darren Daulton $45	Dave Justice........................... $28	Mo Vaughn............................ $28
Lenny Dykstra $28	Greg Maddux.......................... $45	
Ken Griffey Jr. $32	Mark McGwire $34	

1994 Kenner Starting Lineups

Complete set (65): $585	Andres Galarraga....................$15	Paul Molitor...........................$15
Kevin Appier $11	Juan Gonzalez, ext................$19	Mike Mussina $15
Steve Avery $12	Mark Grace............................$11	John Olerud $18
Carlos Baerga $12	Tommy Greene.......................$11	Rafael Palmiero, ext. $21
Jeff Bagwell...........................$18	Ken Griffey Jr........................$22	Tony Phillips $11
Derek Bell..............................$10	Brian Harper $11	Mike Piazza $55
Jay Bell.................................$10	Bryan Harvey $13	Jose Rijo $12
Albert Belle $19	Charlie Hayes $13	Cal Ripken Jr. $38
Wade Boggs $11	Chris Hoiles $13	Ivan Rodriquez $17
Barry Bonds............................$13	Dave Hollins...........................$12	Tim Salmon $27
John Burkett $10	Gregg Jefferies $12	Ryne Sandberg $19
Steve Carlton, ext. $35	Randy Johnson $25	Curt Schilling $12
Joe Carter $11	Dave Justice...........................$12	Gary Sheffield $12
Will Clark, ext. $18	Eric Karros $11	Gary Sheffield, ext. power $19
Roger Clemens $14	Jimmy Key $15	J.T. Snow $20
David Cone............................$11	Darryl Kile.............................$11	Frank Thomas $19
Chad Curtis............................$12	Chuck Knoblauch $18	Robbie Thompson $11
Darren Daulton $22	Mark Langston $11	Greg Vaughn $11
Delino DeShields....................$10	Kenny Lofton, ext...................$39	Mo Vaughn............................$24
Lenny Dykstra, ext. $20	Don Mattingly $15	Robin Ventura $11
Alex Fernandez.......................$11	Fred McGriff, ext. $20	Matt Williams.........................$13
Cecil Fielder $12	Orlando Merced......................$13	Dave Winfield $13

1994 Kenner Stadium Stars

Complete set (8): $225	Dennis Eckersley $27	Bo Jackson.............................$75
Barry Bonds............................$25	Tom Glavine...........................$26	Kirby Puckett..........................$26
Will Clark $25	Juan Gonzalez.........................$30	Deion Sanders.........................$50

1994 Kenner Cooperstown Collection

Complete set (8): $160	Lou Gehrig $18	Jackie Robinson, 42................$19
set price does not include the	Reggie Jackson $39	Babe Ruth $19
Robinson error	Willie Mays $18	Honus Wagner $39
Ty Cobb $18	Jackie Robinson, 44..............$550	Cy Young $17

1993 Kenner Starting Lineups

Complete set (45): $400	Tom Glavine................$16	Shane Mack $12	Bip Roberts..................$12
Roberto Alomar...........$12	Juan Gonzalez $17	Greg Maddux, ext.......$125	Nolan Ryan...................$37
Carlos Baerga..............$27	Ken Griffey Jr. $29	Jack McDowell............$19	Nolan Ryan, ext., retired
Jeff Bagwell $43	Ken Griffey Jr., with eye	Fred McGriff $16	....................................$190
Barry Bonds, Pitt.........$39	black $25	Mark McGwire............$14	Ryne Sandberg.............$16
Barry Bonds, ext., S.F. .$25	Marquis Grissom $12	Mike Mussina $24	Benito Santiago, ext. $37
Kevin Brown $17	Juan Guzman $12	David Nied, ext. $37	Gary Sheffield $12
Jose Canseco $12	Bo Jackson, ext............$32	Dean Palmer $12	John Smoltz $15
Will Clark....................$12	Eric Karros $21	Terry Pendleton $10	Frank Thomas...............$23
Roger Clemens.............$14	Roberto Kelly $11	Kirby Puckett...............$18	Andy Van Slyke $10
David Cone $13	John Kruk $12	Cal Ripken Jr. $48	Robin Ventura $13
Carlton Fisk, ext. $38	Ray Lankford $12	Cal Ripken Jr., with eye	Larry Walker $16
Travis Fryman $13	Barry Larkin $18	black $48	

1993 Kenner Headline Collection

Complete set (8): $225	Tom Glavine $29	Nolan Ryan $55
Jim Abbott $25	Mark McGwire $22	Deion Sanders $20
Roberto Alomar $29	Cal Ripken Jr. $60	Frank Thomas $35

1993 Kenner Stadium Stars

Complete set (6): $225	Ken Griffey Jr. $35	Frank Thomas $50
Roger Clemens $34	Nolan Ryan $48	
Cecil Fielder $24	Ryne Sandberg $35	

1992 Kenner Starting Lineups

Complete set (46): ... $400

Atlanta Braves
Steve Avery, ext. $28
Tom Glavine $28
Dave Justice $20

Baltimore Orioles
Cal Ripken Jr. $75

Boston Red Sox
Roger Clemens $15

California Angels
Chuck Finley $12

Chicago Cubs
George Bell $12
Ryne Sandberg $21

Chicago White Sox
Bo Jackson spring .. $14
Bo Jackson running $13
Frank Thomas, fielding
.... $67
Frank Thomas, ext.,

batting $58

Cincinnati Reds
Rob Dibble $11
Chris Sabo $10

Cleveland Indians
Albert Belle $40

Detroit Tigers
Cecil Fielder $13

Houston Astros
Craig Biggio $14

Kansas City Royals
Brian McRae $13

Los Angeles Dodgers
Eric Davis, ext. $22
Ramon Martinez $11
Darryl Strawberry .. $10

Milwaukee Brewers

Minnesota Twins
Scott Erickson $9

Kirby Puckett, ext... $29

Montreal Expos
Ivan Calderon $11

New York Mets
Bobby Bonilla, ext. . $24
Howard Johnson $10
Bret Saberhagen, ext.
.... $21

New York Yankees
Kevin Maas $10
Danny Tartabull, ext.
.... $21

Oakland A's
Jose Canseco $12
Dave Henderson $10
Rickey Henderson . $12
Todd Van Poppel, ext.
.... $21

Philadelphia Phillies

Pittsburgh Pirates
Barry Bonds $27

St. Louis Cardinals
Felix Jose $11

San Diego Padres
Tony Gwynn $26
Fred McGriff $19

San Francisco Giants
Will Clark $14
Matt Williams $18

Seattle Mariners
Ken Griffey Jr., regular
.... $25
Ken Griffey Jr., spring
.... $32

Texas Rangers
Juan Gonzalez $27
Nolan Ryan $39
Ruben Sierra $11

Toronto Blue Jays
Roberto Alomar $21
Tom Seaver, ext. $42

1992 Kenner Headline Collection

Complete set (7): $200	Ken Griffey Jr. $35	Nolan Ryan $40
George Brett $50	Rickey Henderson $16	Ryne Sandberg $38
Cecil Fielder $22	Bo Jackson $16	

1991 Kenner Starting Lineups

Complete set (55): $700

Atlanta Braves

Dave Justice, ext. $35

Baltimore Orioles

Glenn Davis, ext. $31
Ben McDonald $13

Boston Red Sox

California Angels

Jim Abbott $15

Chicago Cubs

George Bell, ext. $31
Andre Dawson $18
Shawon Dunston $16
Mark Grace $14
Ryne Sandberg $27

Chicago White Sox

Ozzie Guillen $12
Bo Jackson $11
Tim Raines, ext. $31

Cincinnati Reds

Jack Armstrong $13
Tom Browning $17
Eric Davis $12
Barry Larkin $20
Chris Sabo $12

Cleveland Indians

Sandy Alomar Jr. $15

Detroit Tigers

Cecil Fielder $18
Alan Trammell $17

Houston Astros

Kansas City Royals

Bo Jackson $21

Los Angeles Dodgers

Ramon Martinez $14

Kenner has offered statues of baseball players since 1988.

Darryl Strawberry, ext. $22

Milwaukee Brewers

Minnesota Twins

Kirby Puckett $25

Montreal Expos

Delino DeShields $17

New York Mets

Vince Coleman, ext. $31
John Franco $11
Dwight Gooden $20
Gregg Jefferies $16
Howard Johnson $14
Dave Magadan $13
Darryl Strawberry $10
Frank Viola $12

New York Yankees

Roberto Kelly $11
Kevin Maas $12
Don Mattingly $18
Steve Sax $12

Oakland A's

Jose Canseco $12
Rickey Henderson $12
Mark McGwire $13
Dave Stewart $15

Philadelphia Phillies

Len Dykstra $18

Pittsburgh Pirates

Barry Bonds $42
Bobby Bonilla $16
Doug Drabek $15

St. Louis Cardinals

Todd Zeile $20

San Diego Padres

Benito Santiago $14

San Francisco Giants

Will Clark $16
Kevin Mitchell $12
Matt Williams $50

Seattle Mariners

Ken Griffey Jr. batting $30
Ken Griffey Jr., ext., running . $45
Ken Griffey Sr. ext. $36

Texas Rangers

Nolan Ryan $69

Toronto Blue Jays

Kelly Gruber $17

1991 Kenner Headline Collection

Complete set (7): $250
Jose Canseco........................ $20
Will Clark $28

Ken Griffey Jr. $65
Rickey Henderson $22
Bo Jackson............................. $16

Don Mattingly $42
Nolan Ryan............................. $75

1990 Kenner Starting Lineups

Complete set (92):.......$1,500

Atlanta Braves

Baltimore Orioles

Jeff Ballard $16
Ben McDonald, ext. $28
Cal Ripken Jr. $170
Mickey Tettleton ...$18

Boston Red Sox

Wade Boggs $25
Ellis Burks $15
Roger Clemens $27
Nick Esasky $32
Mike Greenwell $12
Jody Reed $19

California Angels

Jim Abbott, ext. $35

Chicago Cubs

Damon Berryhill $19
Andre Dawson $24
Mark Grace batting $18
Mark Grace power . $22
Greg Maddux $250
Ryne Sandberg $37
Rick Sutcliffe $22
Jerome Walton, ext. $15
Mitch Williams $16

Chicago White Sox

Cincinnati Reds

Todd Benzinger $17
Eric Davis $13
Rob Dibble $17
Barry Larkin $33
Paul O'Neill $25
Chris Sabo $13

Cleveland Indians

Sandy Alomar, ext.. $35

Detroit Tigers

Matt Nokes $12
Gary Pettis $32
Alan Trammell $15
Lou Whitaker $10

Houston Astros

Mike Scott $15

Kansas City Royals

Bo Jackson, ext.......$15

Los Angeles Dodgers

Kirk Gibson $14
Orel Hershiser $21
Eddie Murray $58
Willie Randolph $12

Milwaukee Brewers

Chris Bosio $16
Paul Molitor $29
Gary Sheffield $25
Robin Yount $70

Minnesota Twins

Alan Anderson $14
Wally Backman $32
Gary Gaetti $13
Kent Hrbek $13
Kirby Puckett $33

Montreal Expos

Andres Galarraga ... $26

New York Mets

Ron Darling $18
Dwight Gooden $12
Gregg Jefferies $14
Howard Johnson $14

Kevin McReynolds $13
Juan Samuel $14
Darryl Strawberry bat-
ting $13
Darryl Strawberry field-
ing $13
Frank Viola $13

New York Yankees

Jesse Barfield $12
Roberto Kelly $14
Don Mattingly batting
................................$18
Don Mattingly power
................................$21
Dave Righetti $20
Steve Sax $12
Dave Winfield $36

Oakland A's

Jose Canseco $18
Dennis Eckersley ...$37
Dave Henderson $16
Rickey Henderson . $19
Mark McGwire $16
Dave Stewart $15

Philadelphia Phillies

Len Dykstra $22
Von Hayes $10
Tom Herr $12
Ricky Jordan $12

Pittsburgh Pirates

Barry Bonds $74
Bobby Bonilla $15
John Smiley $12
Andy Van Slyke $15

St. Louis Cardinals

Vince Coleman $13

Pedro Guerrero $12
Joe Magrane $12
Jose Oquendo $18
Ozzie Smith $27

San Diego Padres

Joe Carter, ext........$50

San Francisco Giants

Steve Bedrosian $13
Will Clark power ...$21
Will Clark batting...$21
Kevin Mitchell $12
Rick Reuschel ..:....$18

Seattle Mariners

Ken Griffey Jr. slide
................................$125
Ken Griffey Jr. ext.,
jump......................$120

Texas Rangers

Nolan Ryan $60

Toronto Blue Jays

Fred McGriff $53

**1990 Kenner
Team Lineup
& Award Winners**

Boston Red Sox $50
Chicago Cubs $45
New York Mets $45
New York Yankees $75
Oakland A's...........$125
American League
Lineup....................$50
National League
Lineup....................$50

1989 Kenner Starting Lineups

Complete set (168):.....$3,500

Atlanta Braves

Ron Gant $200
Albert Hall $28
Dion James $19
Dale Murphy $12
Gerald Perry $12
Zane Smith $28
Bruce Sutter $25

Baltimore Orioles

Brady Anderson $50
Cal Ripken Jr. $450
Larry Sheets $22
Pete Stanicek $22

Boston Red Sox

Marty Barrett $15
Wade Boggs $25
Ellis Burks $15
Roger Clemens $27
Mike Greenwell $14
Jim Rice $36
Lee Smith $60

California Angels

Chili Davis $175
Jack Howell $125
Wally Joyner $14
Johnny Ray $150
Dick Schofield $150
Devon White $150
Mike Witt $150

Chicago Cubs

Damon Berryhill $23
Andre Dawson $25
Shawon Dunston $30
Mark Grace $34
Greg Maddux $400
Ryne Sandberg $45
Rick Sutcliffe $20

Chicago White Sox

Harold Baines $15
Ivan Calderon $18
Ozzie Guillen $20
Dan Pasqua $15
Melido Perez $15
Bobby Thigpen $27
Greg Walker $13

Cincinnati Reds

Kal Daniels $15

Eric Davis $12
Bo Diaz $15
John Franco $24
Danny Jackson $13
Barry Larkin $50
Chris Sabo $18
Jeff Treadway $40

Cleveland Indians

Joe Carter $20
Mel Hall $13
Brook Jacoby $13
Doug Jones $14
Cory Snyder $12
Greg Swindell $18

Detroit Tigers

Tom Brookens $35
Mike Henneman $16
Chet Lemon $16
Jack Morris $20
Matt Nokes $12
Luis Salazar $25
Alan Trammell $20
Lou Whitaker $28

Houston Astros

Kevin Bass $13
Glenn Davis $12
Billy Doran $16
Billy Hatcher $13
Mike Scott $10
Dave Smith $12
Gerald Young $15

Kansas City Royals

George Brett $75
Mark Gubicza $13
Bo Jackson $28
Bret Saberhagen $18
Kevin Seitzer $12
Kurt Stillwell $11
Pat Tabler $12
Danny Tartabull $14

Los Angeles Dodgers

Kirk Gibson $16
Orel Hershiser $40
Mike Marshall $20
Mike Scioscia $26
John Shelby $16
Fernando Valenzuela $11

Milwaukee Brewers

Glenn Braggs $15

Rob Deer $12
Ted Higuera $18
Paul Molitor $32
Dan Plesac $14
B.J. Surhoff $20
Robin Yount $75

Minnesota Twins

Gary Gaetti $18
Dan Gladden $16
Kent Hrbek $14
Tim Laudner $15
Kirby Puckett $37
Jeff Reardon $34
Frank Viola $12

Montreal Expos

Tim Raines $13

New York Mets

Gary Carter $25
David Cone $30
Len Dykstra $34
Kevin Elster $20
Dwight Gooden $12
Keith Hernandez $14
Gregg Jefferies $40
Kevin McReynolds ..$18
Randy Myers $30
Darryl Strawberry $12

New York Yankees

Rickey Henderson $20
Al Leiter $17
Don Mattingly $25
Mike Pagliarulo $12
Dave Righetti $22
Don Slaught $22
Dave Winfield $25

Oakland A's

Jose Canseco $18
Dennis Eckersley ...$100
Carney Lansford $20
Mark McGwire $22
Dave Parker $15
Terry Steinbach $25
Dave Stewart $25
Walt Weiss $31
Bob Welch $29

Philadelphia Phillies

Steve Bedrosian $13
Phil Bradley $35
Von Hayes $13
Chris James $13

Juan Samuel $13
Mike Schmidt $75
Milt Thompson $35

Pittsburgh Pirates

Barry Bonds $95
Bobby Bonilla $15
Doug Drabek $22
Mike LaValliere $18
Jose Lind $28
Andy Van Slyke $15
Bob Walk $13

St. Louis Cardinals

Tom Brunansky $17
Vince Coleman $15
Pedro Guerrero $15
Willie McGee $15
Tony Pena $15
Terry Pendleton $23
Ozzie Smith $35
Todd Worrell $25

San Diego Padres

Roberto Alomar $400
Mark Davis $20
Tony Gwynn $130
John Kruk $27
Benito Santiago $21
Marvell Wynne $24

San Francisco Giants

Brett Butler $24
Will Clark $25
Candy Maldonado $13
Kevin Mitchell $15
Robby Thompson $15
Jose Uribe $14

Seattle Mariners

Mickey Brantley $15
Alvin Davis $14
Mark Langston $26
Harold Reynolds $17
Rey Quinones $17

Texas Rangers

Steve Buechele $16
Scott Fletcher $12
Pete Incaviglia $12
Jeff Russell $15
Ruben Sierra $25

Toronto Blue Jays

George Bell $15

1989 Kenner Baseball Greats

Complete set (10): $450	Babe Ruth/Lou Gehrig $50
Willie Mays/Willie McCovey $40	Hank Aaron/Eddie Mathews $50
Johnny Bench/Pete Rose $50	Mickey Mantle/Joe DiMaggio $80
Ernie Banks/Billy Williams $40	Don Drysdale/Reggie Jackson $55
Stan Musial/Bob Gibson $65	Carl Yastrzemski/Hank Aaron $65
Roberto Clemente/Willie Stargell $45	

1989 Kenner One-On-One

Jose Canseco/Alan Trammell $35	Don Mattingly/Wade Boggs $50
Gary Carter/Eric Davis $25	Ryne Sandberg/Vince Coleman $40

1988 Kenner Starting Lineups

Complete set (124): $3,000

Atlanta Braves

Ken Griffey Sr. $30
Dale Musrphy $14
Ken Oberkfell $18
Zane Smith $16
Ozzie Virgil $18

Baltimore Orioles

Mike Boddicker $29
Terry Kennedy $18
Fred Lynn $18
Eddie Murray $65
Cal Ripken Jr. $400

Boston Red Sox

Wade Boggs $22
Ellis Burks $40
Roger Clemens $37
Dwight Evans $18
Jim Rice $20

California Angels

Brian Downing $14
Wally Joyner $10
Donnie Moore $21
Devon White $24
Mike Witt $12

Chicago Cubs

Jody Davis $16
Andre Dawson $25
Shawon Dunston $20
Leon Durham $14
Ryne Sandberg $65
Rick Sutcliffe $19

Chicago White Sox

Harold Baines $15
Carlton Fisk $80
Ozzie Guillen $19
Gary Redus $19
Greg Walker $16

Cincinnati Reds

Buddy Bell $17

Cincinnati Reds

Kal Daniels $14
Eric Davis $10
John Franco $18
Pete Rose $59

Cleveland Indians

Joe Carter $38
Julio Franco $18
Mel Hall $15
Cory Snyder $14
Pat Tabler $16

Detroit Tigers

Willie Hernandez $17
Jack Morris $25
Matt Nokes $28
Alan Trammell $20
Lou Whitaker $25

Houston Astros

Alan Ashby $25
Kevin Bass $15
Glenn Davis $16
Billy Hatcher $16
Nolan Ryan $325
Mike Scott $13

Kansas City Royals

George Brett $80
Dan Quisenberry $20
Bret Saberhagen $16
Kevin Seitzer $16
Danny Tartabull $24

Los Angeles Dodgers

Pedro Guerrero $10
Mike Marshall $25
Steve Sax $14
Franklin Stubbs $25
Fernando Valenzuela ... $18

Milwaukee Brewers

Rob Deer $18
Ted Higuera $18
Paul Molitor $50
B.J. Surhoff $17
Robin Yount $80

Minnesota Twins

Tom Brunansky $28
Gary Gaetti $20
Kent Hrbek $18
Kirby Puckett $55
Jeff Reardon $29
Frank Viola $20

Montreal Expos

Tim Raines $14

New York Mets

Gary Carter $20
Len Dykstra $40
Dwight Gooden $14
Keith Hernandez $17
Howard Johnson $38
Kevin McReynolds $14
Darryl Strawberry $12

New York Yankees

Jack Clark $19
Rickey Henderson $25
Don Mattingly $25
Willie Randolph $18
Dave Righetti $17
Dave Winfield $48

Oakland A's

Jose Canseco $50
Carney Lansford $25
Mark McGwire $35
Dave Parker $28

Philadelphia Phillies

Steve Bedrosian $16
Von Hayes $22

Shane Rawley $16
Juan Samuel $15
Mike Schmidt $60

Pittsburgh Pirates

Barry Bonds $115
Bobby Bonilla $20
Sid Bream $15
Mike Dunne $14
Andy Van Slyke $24

St. Louis Cardinals

Vince Coleman $15
Tommy Herr $17
Willie McGee $17
Ozzie Smith $45
Todd Worrell $36

San Diego Padres

Chris Brown $14
Tony Gwynn $75
John Kruk $37
Benito Santiago $18

San Francisco Giants

Will Clark $37
Jeffrey Leonard $14
Candy Maldonado $20
Rick Reuschel $18

Seattle Mariners

Alvin Davis $17
Mark Langston $29
Ken Phelps $15
Jim Presley $16

Texas Rangers

Charlie Hough $20
Pete Incaviglia $15
Pete O'Brien $15
Larry Parrish $15
Ruben Sierra $28

Toronto Blue Jays

George Bell $14

Salvino Sports Legends

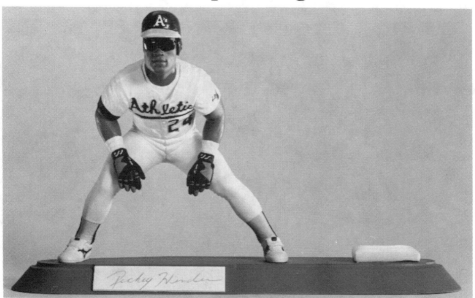

This Salvino statue shows Rickey Henderson stealing his way into the record books.

Many of the sporting world's greatest superstars are honored on hand-signed, limited-edition figurines offered by Salvino Inc. of Corona, Calif.

Original artwork is cast by mold makers to ensure an exact reproduction of the original artwork. Every figurine is individually cast by artisans in cold-cast porcelain and inspected for defects. Every casting is then hand-painted by professionals.

The honored athlete personally autographs signature plaques which are permanently mounted to the figurine base. The authenticity of the autograph is guaranteed and endorsed with a certificate of authenticity numbered to match the figurine. SE means special edition, AP means artist's proof. Values are for Near Mint.

Brooklyn Dodger Collection

Roy Campanella, 2,000	$400
Roy Campanella, 200	$600
Don Drysdale, 2,500	$200
Don Drysdale AP, 300	$225
Sandy Koufax, 2,500	$225
Sandy Koufax SE, 500	$325
Duke Snider home, 1,000	$275
Duke Snider away, 1,000	$275

Heroes of the Diamond

Rickey Henderson home, 600	$275
Rickey Henderson away, 600	$275
Rickey Henderson SE, 550	$375
Reggie Jackson, 1,500	$275
Mickey Mantle fielding, 682	$800
Mickey Mantle batting, 682	$800
Willie Mays N.Y., 750	$400
Willie Mays S.F., 750	$400
Brooks Robinson, 1,000	$275

Dealer specials

Sandy Koufax dealer series, 368	$700
Mickey Mantle batting, 10" #6, 368	$1,100
Mickey Mantle batting, 7" #7, 368	$1,100
Willie Mays home, 368	$700

Others

Harmon Killebrew, 950	$275
Mickey Mantle pinstripe, 365	$900
Mickey Mantle grey, 365	$900
Babe Ruth, 950	$185

Unsigned Yankee Tradition Series

7" hand-painted

Roberto Clemente, 1,750	$75
Mickey Mantle, 2,000	$100
Roger Maris, 2,000	$75
Billy Martin, 2,000	$75

Gartlan Statues

Gartlan USA creates larger-sized and mini statues of each of its players.

Gartlan USA is based in Marlton, N.J., and produces limited-edition ceramic and porcelain sports collectibles, including hand-signed plates and figurines. The larger versions of the statues are about 8 inches tall each; the smaller ones (mini) are about 5 inches tall and generally sell for about $40 each. Plates range in size from 10 1/4" diameter, to 8 1/2" diameter, to 3 1/4" diameter plates. Values are for Near Mint.

Statues

This list of players includes the number made and a current selling price. Artist's proofs are signed by the artist and player.

- Hank Aaron signed figurine, 1,982: $200
- Hank Aaron artist's proof, 300: $350
- Hank Aaron mini, 10,000: $40
- Hank Aaron commemorative, 755: $175
- Hank Aaron Club, club only: $100
- Luis Aparicio signed figurine, 1,984: $100
- Luis Aparicio mini, 10,000: $40
- Luis Aparicio 10 1/4" plate, 1,984: $50
- Luis Aparicio 10 1/4" proof plate, 250: $150
- Luis Aparicio 8 1/2" plate, 10,000: $30
- Luis Aparicio 3 1/4" plate, open: $25
- Al Barlick signed figurine, 1,989: $100
- Al Barlick 3 1/4" plate, open: $20
- Al Barlick Club plate, club only: $50
- "Cool Papa" Bell signed figurine, 1,499: $195
- Johnny Bench signed figurine, 1,989: $225
- Johnny Bench artist's proof, 250: $550
- Johnny Bench mini, 10,000: $50
- Johnny Bench 10 1/4" plate, 1,989:............................$100
- Johnny Bench 3 1/4" plate, open: $20
- Johnny Bench proof plate, 100: $200

- Yogi Berra signed figurine, 2,150: $175
- Yogi Berra artist's proof, 250: $350
- Yogi Berra mini, 10,000: $50
- Yogi Berra 10 1/4" plate, 2,150: $75
- Yogi Berra proof plate, 250: $175
- Yogi Berra 8 1/2" plate, 10,000: $45
- Yogi Berra 3 1/4" plate, open: $15
- George Brett signed figurine, 2,250: $200
- George Brett mini, 10,000: $40
- George Brett Club, club only: $125
- George Brett 10 1/4" plate, 2,000: $100
- George Brett proof plate, 24: $200
- George Brett 3 1/4" plate, open: $15
- George Brett ceramic baseball, open: $20
- George Brett tankard, open:.......................................$30
- Rod Carew signed figurine, 1,991: $150
- Rod Carew mini, 10,000: $40
- Rod Carew induction mini, 125:.................................$150
- Rod Carew 10 1/4" plate, 950: $75
- Rod Carew 8 1/2" plate, 10,000: $40
- Rod Carew 3 1/4" plate, open: $15
- Steve Carlton signed figurine, 3,290: $175
- Steve Carlton artist's proof, 300:................................$450
- Steve Carlton mini, 10,000: $40
- Ray Dandridge signed figurine, 1,987: $175
- Joe DiMaggio signed figurine, 2,214: $900

Hall of Famer Johnny Bench autographs his Gartlan USA statue.

- Joe DiMaggio pinstripe, 325: ....$2,000.
- Joe DiMaggio pinstripe artist's proof, 12:................$7,500
- Carlton Fisk signed figurine, 1,972: $105
- Carlton Fisk artist's proof, 300:................................$350
- Carlton Fisk mini, 10,000:...$40
- Carlton Fisk 10 1/4" plate, 950:................................$100
- Carlton Fisk proof plate, 300:...................................$150
- Carlton Fisk 8 1/2" plate, 10,000: $40
- Carlton Fisk 3 1/4" plate, open: $15
- Carlton Fisk ceramic card, open:.................................$18
- Whitey Ford signed figurine, 2,360: $100
- Whitey Ford artist's proof, 250: $350
- Whitey Ford mini, 10,000:...$50
- Whitey Ford 10 1/4" plate, 2,360: $75
- Whitey Ford proof plate, 250: $150
- Whitey Ford 8 1/2" plate, 10,000: $30
- Whitey Ford 3 1/4" plate, open: $20
- Ken Griffey Jr. signed figurine, 1,989: $200
- Ken Griffey Jr. mini, 10,000: $40
- Ken Griffey Jr. 10 1/4" plate, 1,992: $100
- Ken Griffey Jr. 8 1/2" plate, 10,000: $45
- Ken Griffey Jr. 3 1/4" plate, open: $15
- Ken Griffey Jr. Club plate, club only: $40
- Ken Griffey Jr. ceramic card, open: $12
- Monte Irvin signed figurine, 1,973: $100
- Monte Irvin mini, 10,000:..$40
- Reggie Jackson 3 1/4" plate, open:...............................$15
- Ralph Kiner signed figurine, 1,975: $100
- Ralph Kiner mini, 10,000:...$40
- Buck Leonard signed figurine, 1,972: $195
- Stan Musial signed figurine, 1,969:............................$175
- Stan Musial artist's proof, 300: $300
- Stan Musial mini, 2,269:..$40
- Stan Musial pewter figurine, 500: $850
- Eddie Mathews signed figurine, 1,978: $100
- Eddie Mathews mini figurine, 5,000: $40
- Pete Rose signed figurine, 4,192; $950
- Pete Rose mini, 10,000:..$50
- Pete Rose 10 1/4" platinum plate, 4,192: $300
- Pete Rose 3 1/4" platinum plate, open:..........................$20
- Pete Rose 10 1/4" Diamond plate, 950: $300
- Pete Rose 3 1/4" Diamond plate, open: $16
- Pete Rose Club plate, club only:.................................$100
- Pete Rose 10 1/4" Farewell plate, 50: $500
- Pete Rose tankard, open:...$30
- Mike Schmidt signed figurine, 1,987: $950
- Mike Schmidt artist's proof, 20: $1,500
- Mike Schmidt mini, 10,000:...$50
- Mike Schmidt pinstripe Club, club only:.....................$125
- Mike Schmidt 10 1/4" plate, 1,987: $450
- Mike Schmidt proof plate, 56: $150
- Mike Schmidt 3 1/4" plate, open: $15
- Tom Seaver signed figurine, 1,992:............................$125
- Tom Seaver mini, 10,000:...$40
- Tom Seaver 10 1/4" plate, 1,992: $75
- Tom Seaver 8 1/2" plate, 10,000: $30
- Tom Seaver 3 1/4" plate, open:......................................$15
- Tom Seaver ceramic card, open:....................................$18
- Warren Spahn signed figurine, 1,973: $125
- Warren Spahn mini, 10,000:...$30
- Darryl Strawberry signed figurine, 2,500: $50
- Darryl Strawberry mini, 10,000:...................................$30
- Darryl Strawberry 10 1/4" plate, 1,979: $60
- Darryl Strawberry 8 1/2" plate, 10,000:........................$30
- Darryl Strawberry 3 1/4" plate, open:............................$15
- Frank Thomas signed figurine, 1,994: $200
- Frank Thomas mini, 10,000:...$40
- Frank Thomas Marquee figurine, 10,000: $80
- Frank Thomas 10 1/4" plate, 1,994:.............................$125
- Frank Thomas 8 1/2" plate, 10,000:...............................$30
- Frank Thomas 3 1/4" plate, open:..................................$15
- Frank Thomas ceramic card, open:................................$12
- Ted Williams signed figurine, 2,654: $495
- Ted Williams artist's proof, 250: $500
- Ted Williams mini, 10,000: $50
- Carl Yastrzemski signed figurine, 1,989: $275
- Carl Yastrzemski artist's proof, 250: $500
- Carl Yastrzemski mini, 10,000: $40
- Carl Yastrzemski 10 1/4" plate, 950:...........................$100
- Carl Yastrzemski 8 1/2" plate, 10,000:..........................$30
- Carl Yastrzemski 3 1/4" plate, open:.............................$15
- Carl Yastrzemski ceramic card, open: $18

ProSport Creations

Values are Near Mint

Eddie Mathews	Brooks Robinson	Willie Stargell
edition size: 1,978	*edition size: 1,983*	*edition size: 1,988*
issue price: $175	*issue price: $200*	*issue price: $175*

- Richie Ashburn hand-signed, 1,990 ....$75
  Richie Ashburn mini, 201 ....$40
  Richie Ashburn AP...$100
  Richie Ashburn 9" signed, 50 ....$200
- Rod Carew, 447 ....$100
  Rod Carew AP...$125
- Bill Dickey hand-signed, 947 ....$60
  Bill Dickey mini, 582 ....$40
  Bill Dickey AP..$100
- Whitey Ford hand-signed, 1,876 ....$100
  Whitey Ford mini, 1,499 ....$40
  Whitey Ford AP..$100
- Steve Garvey hand-signed, 232 ....$165
  Steve Garvey AP...$185
- Bob Gibson hand-signed, 1,738 ....$100
  Bob Gibson mini, 1,484 ....$40
  Bob Gibson AP..$125

- Tony Gwynn hand-signed, 672.....................................$125
  Tony Gwynn AP..$150
- Fergie Jenkins hand-signed, 215...................................$125
  Fergie Jenkins AP...$150
- Harmon Killebrew hand-signed, 297 ....$200
  Harmon Killebrew AP...$225
- Eddie Mathews hand-signed, 300 ....$125
  Eddie Mathews AP..$150
- Jim Palmer hand-signed, 1,089.....................................$100
  Jim Palmer AP..$125
  Jim Palmer mini, 576...$40
- Brooks Robinson hand-signed, 800 ....$125
  Brooks Robinson AP $150
- Ozzie Smith hand-signed, 600 ....$225
  Ozzie Smith AP...$250
- Willie Stargell hand-signed, 655...................................$100
  Willie Stargell AP...$140

1995 Micro Stars baseball busts

1. Roberto Alomar...................... $3.25	18. Travis Fryman....................... $3.25	35. Raul Mondesi.......................... $3.75
2. Moises Alou $3.25	19. Andres Galarraga $3.25	36. David Nied............................. $3.25
3. Jeff Bagwell $4.75	20. Juan Gonzalez $3.75	37. Rafael Palmeiro...................... $3.25
4. Jay Bell.................................. $3.25	21. Ken Griffey Jr. $5	38. Mike Piazza............................$5
5. Albert Belle $4.25	22. Tony Gwynn $3.25	39. Kirby Puckett........................ $4.25
6. Dante Bichette........................ $3.25	23. Rickey Henderson................ $3.25	40. Cal Ripken Jr. $7
7. Craig Biggio........................... $3.25	24. Ken Hill................................. $3.25	41. Bret Saberhagen..................... $3.25
8. Wade Boggs $3.25	25. Randy Johnson..................... $3.25	42. Deion Sanders........................ $4.50
9. Barry Bonds $3.75	26. Dave Justice $3.25	43. Gary Sheffield........................ $3.25
10. Jose Canseco $3.25	27. Jimmy Key............................ $3.25	44. Ozzie Smith $3.25
11. Joe Carter $3.25	28. Mark Langston $3.25	45. Sammy Sosa........................... $3.25
12. Will Clark.............................. $3.25	29. Barry Larkin $3.25	46. Frank Thomas $5
13. Roger Clemens...................... $3.25	30. Kenny Lofton $4.75	47. Greg Vaughn.......................... $3.25
14. David Cone $3.25	31. Greg Maddux $5	48. Mo Vaughn............................ $3.25
15. Darren Daulton...................... $3.25	32. Don Mattingly...................... $4.25	49. Robin Ventura........................ $3.25
16. Len Dykstra........................... $3.25	33. Fred McGriff........................ $3.25	50. Matt Williams $4.25
17. Cecil Fielder......................... $3.25	34. Paul Molitor $3.25	

1955 Robert Gould All-Stars statues

One of several issues of miniature plastic player statues from the mid-1950s was the All-Stars series by Robert Gould Inc. of New York. The white plastic statues, which sold for about a quarter, came rubber banded to a baseball card. The cards measure 2 1/2" by 3 1/2" with a white border. A rather crude black-and-white line drawing of the player is set against a green background. There are a few biographical details and 1954 and lifetime stats. An "All Stars" logo is in an upper corner; the card number is in the lower right. The cards are blank-backed. All cards have a pair of notches at the sides and a punch hole to hold the rubber band. Prices shown here are for the cards alone. Cards which retain the statues are valued from two to four times higher. A complete set of cards in Near Mint condition is worth $1,200. Individual cards are worth $40 unless noted.

The players featured are: 1. Willie Mays ($225), 2. Gus Zernial, 3. Al "Red" Schoendienst ($65), 4. Chico Carrasquel, 5. Jim Hegan, 6. Curt Simmons, 7. Bob Porterfield, 8. Jim Busby, 9. Don Mueller, 10. Ted Kluszewski ($60), 11. Ray Boone, 12. Smokey Burgess, 13. Bob Rush, 14. Early Wynn ($60), 15. Bill Bruton, 16. Gus Bell, 17. Jim Finigan, 18. Granny Hamner, 19. Hank Thompson, 20. Joe Coleman, 21. Don Newcombe ($45), 22. Richie Ashburn ($60), 23. Bobby Thomson ($45), 24. Sid Gordon, 25. Gerry Coleman, 26. Ernie Banks ($180), 27. Billy Pierce, 28. Mel Parnell.

1956 Big League Stars Statues

While the plastic statues in this set are virtually identical to the set issued in 1955 by Dairy Queen, the packaging of the Big League Stars statues on a card with all the usual elements of a baseball card makes them more collectible. The DQ Tastee Freeze baseball statues are white, while the Big League versions are bronze colored. The statues measure about 3" tall and were sold in a 4" by 5" cardboard and plastic blister pack for 19 cents. The package features the player's name in a large banner near the top with his team printed below and line drawings of ballplayers in action around the statue. Backs have a player portrait photo and facsimile autograph, position, team, previous year and career stats and a career summary. A perforated tab at the bottom can be pulled out to make a stand for the display. Most packages are found with the hole at the top punched out to allow for hanging on a hook. Values listed here are for complete statue/package combinations. Statues alone sell for $25-$50 for non-Hall of Famers, up to $200 for Mickey Mantle. Packages without the statue should be priced about one-third of the values quoted here. The set is checklisted alphabetically. A complete set is worth $1,925 in Near Mint condition.

The players featured, $55 unless noted, are: John Antonelli, Bobby Avila, Yogi Berra ($180), Roy Campanella ($185), Larry Doby, Del Ennis, Jim Gilliam ($65), Gil Hodges ($115), Harvey Kuenn, Bob Lemon ($80), Mickey Mantle ($375), Eddie Mathews ($135), Minnie Minoso ($65), Stan Musial ($230), Pee Wee Reese ($135), Al Rosen, Duke Snider ($185) and Mickey Vernon.

1968 Topps plaks

1969 Transogram statues/cards

Produced by the Transogram toy company, the 2 1/2" by 3 1/2" cards were printed on the bottom of toy baseball player statue boxes. The cards feature a color photo of the player surrounded by a rounded white border. Below the team photo is the player's name in red and his team and other personal details printed in black. The background is yellow. The cards were designed to be cut off the box, but collectors prefer to find the box intact and, better still, with the statue inside. The first price shown below is for a card in Near Mint, cut from the box; the second is for the statue. A complete set of cards is worth $650 in Near Mint condition.

Among the scarcest of Topps' test issues of the late 1960s, the "All Star Baseball Plaks" were plastic busts of two dozen stars of the era which came packaged like model airplane parts. The busts, which had to be snapped off a sprue, could be inserted into a base which carried the player's name. Packed with the plastic plaks was one of the two checklist cards which featured six color photos per side. The 2 1/8" by 4" checklist cards, popular with superstar collectors, are considerably easier to find today than the actual plaks. A complete set with the two checklist cards ($400 each) is worth $4,500 in Near Mint condition.

1. Max Alvis $40
2. Frank Howard $60
3. Dean Chance $40
4. Catfish Hunter $90
5. Jim Fregosi $40
6. Al Kaline $120
7. Harmon Killebrew $100
8. Gary Peters $40
9. Jim Lonborg $40
10. Frank Robinson $120
11. Mickey Mantle $1,500
12. Carl Yastrzemski $125
13. Hank Aaron $250
14. Roberto Clemente $300
15. Richie Allen $60
16. Tommy Davis $40
17. Orlando Cepeda $60
18. Don Drysdale $120
19. Willie Mays $250
20. Rusty Staub $60
21. Tim McCarver $60
22. Pete Rose $250
23. Ron Santo $60
24. Jim Wynn $40

1. Hank Aaron .... $45/$200
2. Richie Allen .... $6/$50
3. Felipe Alou .... $3/$40
4. Matty Alou .... $2/$50
5. Luis Aparicio .... $15/$75
6. Joe Azcue .... $2/$40
7. Ernie Banks .... $30/$125
8. Lou Brock .... $20/$75
9. John Callison .... $3/$40
10. Jose Cardenal .... $2/$40
11. Danny Cater .... $2/$40
12. Roberto Clemente .... $45/$250
13. Willie Davis .... $2/$40
14. Mike Epstein .... $2/$50
15. Jim Fregosi .... $2/$40
16. Bob Gibson .... $20/$100
17. Tom Haller .... $2/$40
18. Ken Harrelson .... $2/$40
19. Willie Horton .... $2/$40
20. Frank Howard .... $2.50/$40
21. Tommy John .... $6/$75
22. Al Kaline .... $30/$125
23. Harmon Killebrew .... $30/$125
24. Bobby Knoop .... $2/$40
25. Jerry Koosman .... $2.50/$40
26. Jim Lefebvre .... $1/$40
27. Mickey Mantle .... $125/$500
28. Juan Marichal .... $20/$75
29. Lee May .... $2/$40
30. Willie Mays .... $45/$250
31. Bill Mazeroski .... $10/$50
32. Tim McCarver .... $3/$40
33. Willie McCovey .... $30/$125
34. Denny McLain .... $2.50/$40
35. Dave McNally .... $2/$40
36. Rick Monday .... $2/$40
37. Blue Moon Odom .... $2/$40
38. Tony Oliva .... $2/$50
39. Camilo Pascual .... $2/$50
40. Tony Perez .... $6/$60
41. Rico Petrocelli .... $2/$40

42. Rick Reichardt.............................$2/$40
43. Brooks Robinson ....$30/$125
44. Frank Robinson ....$25/$125
45. Cookie Rojas ....$2/$50
46. Pete Rose ....$30/$200
47. Ron Santo ....$2.50/$50
48. Tom Seaver.............................$30/$250
49. Rusty Staub..............................$3/$50
50. Mel Stottlemyre........................$2/$50
51. Ron Swoboda ....$2/$40
52. Luis Tiant ....$2/$40
53. Joe Torre..................................$2/$40
54. Cesar Tovar ....$2/$40
55. Pete Ward ....$2/$40
56. Roy White................................$2/$40
57. Billy Williams ....$20/$75
58. Don Wilson...............................$2/$40
59. Jim Wynn ....$2/$50
60. Carl Yastrzemski ....$30/$150

1970 Transogram

Like the 1969 cards, the 1970 Transogram cards were available on boxes of Transogram baseball statues. The cards are slightly larger at 2 9/16" by 3 1/2". The 30-card set has the same pictures as the 1969 set except for Joe Torre. All players in the 1970 set were included in the 1969 Transogram issue except for Reggie Jackson, Sam McDowell and Boog Powell. Prices are shown for cards in Near Mint condition, cut from the box. A complete set of cards in Near Mint condition is worth $325.

1. Hank Aaron $45
2. Ernie Banks $30
3. Roberto Clemente................................$45
4. Willie Davis...$2
5. Jim Fregosi $2
6. Bob Gibson..$20
7. Frank Howard.....................................$2.50
8. Reggie Jackson $35
9. Cleon Jones..$2
10. Al Kaline $25
11. Harmon Killebrew $25
12. Jerry Koosman....................................$2.50
13. Willie McCovey $25
14. Sam McDowell....................................$3
15. Denny McLain.....................................$6
16. Juan Marichal $20
17. Willie Mays $45
18. Blue Moon Odom $2
19. Tony Oliva $2
20. Rico Petrocelli $2
21. Boog Powell $4
22. Rick Reichardt $2
23. Frank Robinson $20
24. Pete Rose $30
25. Ron Santo $2.50

26. Tom Seaver...$25
27. Mel Stottlemyre $2
28. Joe Torre...$2
29. Jim Wynn $2
30. Carl Yastrzemski $30

1970 Transogram New York Mets

The Transogram Mets set is a second set that the company produced in 1970. The cards are 2 9/16" by 3 1/2" and feature members of the World Champion Mets team. There are 15 cards in the set, which retains the basic color picture with players' names in red and team, position and biographical details in black. As with the other Transogram sets, the cards are most valuable when they are still part of their original box with the statues. Values shown here are for cards in Near Mint condition cut from the box. A complete set of cards is worth $200 in Near Mint condition.

1. Tommie Agee $3
2. Ken Boswell $2
3. Donn Clendenon $3
4. Gary Gentry $2
5. Jerry Grote $3
6. Bud Harrelson.......................................$3
7. Cleon Jones..$3
8. Jerry Koosman......................................$3
9. Ed Kranepool $3
10. Tug McGraw $7
11. Nolan Ryan.......................................$200
12. Art Shamsky $2
13. Tom Seaver..$60
14. Ron Swoboda $2
15. Al Weiss $2

Sports Impressions

Sports Impressions offers a wide variety of players who have been featured on plates and as figurines. Mini 5-inch figurines generally have a price range of $35 to $45. Regular figurines (7") range from $90 to $100. Mini plates generally sell for $20. Regular-size (10 1/4") plates generally range from $75 to $150, while a Mickey Mantle gold plate sells for up to $200.

Sports Impressions statues and plates

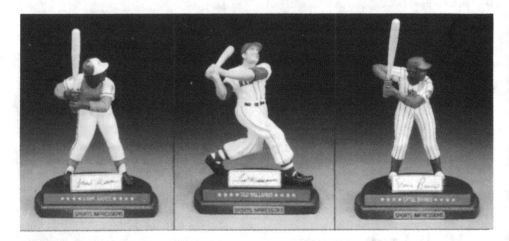

- Hank Aaron 7" Braves figurine, 5,755 ....$75-150
- Hank Aaron 5" Braves figurine $50
- Hank Aaron, 975, signed, 1995 issue $150
- Roberto Alomar, 7" Blue Jays figurine, 975 .....$100
- Ernie Banks 7" Cubs figurine, 5,512 ....$75-$150
- Ernie Banks 5" Cubs figurine $50
- Johnny Bench 7" Reds figurine, 975 ....$150
- Johnny Bench 6" Reds figurine, 2,950 ....$50
- Wade Boggs 7" Red Sox figurine, 2,500....$75-$125
- Wade Boggs 10 1/4" Red Sox plate, 2,000...........$50
- Wade Boggs 10 1/4" Red Sox gold plate, 1,000 ....$125
- Wade Boggs mini Red Sox plate $20
- Barry Bonds 8" Giants figurine, 975 ....$100
- Ralph Branca 7" Giants figurine, 1,951 ....$75
- Jose Canseco 10" A's figurine, 1,988.......$100-$150
- Jose Canseco 7" A's figurine, 2,500 ....$100-$150
- Jose Canseco 5" A's figurine $50
- Jose Canseco 10 1/4" A's plate, 10,000...............$50
- Jose Canseco 10 1/4" A's gold plate, 2,500.......$125
- Jose Canseco mini A's plate $20
- Rod Carew 7" Angels figurine, 3,053.........$75-$150
- Steve Carlton 9" Phillies figurine, 500 .....$100-$200
- Gary Carter 7" Mets figurine, 5,008 ....$60-$125
- Gary Carter 10 1/4" Mets plate, 2,000.................$50
- Gary Carter 10 1/4" Mets gold plate, 1,000.......$125
- Gary Carter mini Mets plate $20
- Will Clark 10" Giants figurine, 1,990.......$125-$200
- Will Clark 7" Giants figurine, 1,990....................$75
- Will Clark 5" Giants figurine..........................$35-$50
- Will Clark 10 1/4" Giants plate, 10,000 65
- Will Clark 10 1/4" Giants gold plate, 2,500 ......$125
- Will Clark mini Giants plate $20
- Roger Clemens 7" Red Sox figurine, 975..........$150
- Roger Clemens 5 1/2" Red Sox figurine, 2,950...$50
- Roberto Clemente 7" Pirates figurine, 5,000 ..$75-$125
- Roberto Clemente 10 1/4" Pirates plate, 10,000.......$75
- Roberto Clemente mini Pirates plate $20
- Ty Cobb 7" Tigers figurine, 5,000..............$75-$125
- Ty Cobb 10 1/4" Tigers plate, 10,000..................$75

- Ty Cobb mini Tigers plate $20
- Eric Davis 7" Reds figurine, 1,990 ....$50-$150
- Eric Davis 5" Reds figurine, 2,950 ....$25
- Andre Dawson 7" Cubs figurine, 2,500......$60-$125
- Andre Dawson 10 1/4" Cubs plate, 10,000..........$50
- Andre Dawson 10 1/4" Cubs gold plate, 1,000 ......$125
- Andre Dawson mini Cubs plate $20
- Lenny Dykstra 7" Phillies figurine, 1,990............$125
- Lenny Dykstra 5" Phillies figurine, 2,950 ....$40
- Lenny Dykstra 10 1/4" Phillies plate, 10,000 ....$50
- Lenny Dykstra 10 1/4" Phillies gold plate, 1,000...$125
- Lenny Dykstra mini Phillies plate........................$20
- Bob Feller 7" Indians figurine, 2,500 ....$75-$125
- Bob Feller 10 1/4" Indians plate, 10,000 ....$50
- Bob Feller 10 1/4" Indians gold plate, 2,500 .....$125
- Bob Feller mini Indians plate...............................$20
- Jimmie Foxx 7" Red Sox figurine, 1,008 ....$125
- Steve Garvey 7" Dodgers figurine, 2,599....... $50-$150
- Steve Garvey 5" Dodgers figurine ....$30-$50
- Lou Gehrig 7" Yankees figurine, 5,000....$100-$125
- Lou Gehrig 10 1/4" Yankees plate, 10,000 .....$100-$125
- Lou Gehrig mini Yankees plate $20
- Kirk Gibson 7" Dodgers figurine, 2,500....$50-$125
- Kirk Gibson 10 1/4" Dodgers plate, 10,000 ....$75
- Kirk Gibson 10 1/4" Dodgers gold plate, 2,500.....$125
- Kirk Gibson mini Dodgers plate $20
- Tom Glavine 8" Braves figurine, 975.................$100
- Dwight Gooden 10" Mets figurine, 1,990............$100
- Dwight Gooden 7" Mets figurine, 5,016...$50-$125
- Dwight Gooden 5" Mets figurine, 2,950 ....$35
- Dwight Gooden 10 1/4" Mets gold plate, 3,500.....$125
- Dwight Gooden mini Mets plate.........................$125
- Mike Greenwell 7" Red Sox figurine, 2,500 .....$125
- Mike Greenwell 5" Red Sox figurine, 2,950 ....$30
- Ken Griffey Jr. 7" Mariners figurine, 1,990 ....$100-$150
- Ken Griffey Jr. 5" Mariners figurine, 2,950 ....$50
- Team Griffey 10 1/4" gold plate, Ken Sr. and Ken Jr.,
  1,991..$125
- Team Griffey mini plate, Ken Sr. and Ken Jr. $25

- Tony Gwynn 7" Padres figurine, 2,500 ......$75-$125
- Tony Gwynn 5" Padres figurine $50
- Rickey Henderson 8" A's figurine, 939....$150-$200
- Rickey Henderson 8 1/4" A's figurine, 94 AP $250
- Rickey Henderson 10 1/4" A's gold plate, 1,990 ...$125
- Rickey Henderson mini A's plate $20
- Keith Hernandez 7" Mets figurine, 2,500 ....$50
- Keith Hernandez 10 1/4" Mets plate, 2,000...........$50
- Keith Hernandez 10 1/4" Mets gold plate, 1,000 ...$175
- Keith Hernandez mini Mets plate $20
- Orel Hershiser 7" Dodgers figurine, 5,055 .....$50-$125
- Orel Hershiser 5" Dodgers figurine ....$25-$50
- Orel Hershiser 10 1/4" Dodgers plate, 10,000........$65
- Orel Hershiser 10 1/4 Dodgers gold plate, 2,500....$125
- Orel Hershiser mini Dodgers plate........................$20
- Bo Jackson 10" Royals figurine, 1,990.....$100-$200
- Bo Jackson 7" Royals figurine, 2,950.........$50-$150
- Bo Jackson 7" Royals figurine, 295 AP.............$295
- Bo Jackson 5" Royals figurine ....$25-$50
- Reggie Jackson 10" Yankees figurine, 1,987 ....$250
- Reggie Jackson 8" A's figurine, 975 ....$150
- Reggie Jackson 7" 500 Home Run Club figurine...$125
- Reggie Jackson 7" Yankees figurine, 2,500 ......$125
- Reggie Jackson 7" Angels figurine, 2,500 ....$75
- Reggie Jackson 5" Yankees figurine $50
- Gregg Jefferies 7" Mets figurine, 5,009............$125
- Gregg Jefferies 10 1/4" Mets gold plate, 3,500 ......$125
- Gregg Jefferies mini Mets plate $20
- Howard Johnson 7" Mets figurine, 5,020 ....$60-$125
- Howard Johnson 5" Mets figurine ....$25-$50
- Dave Justice 8" Braves figurine, 975.................$125
- Al Kaline 7" Tigers figurine, 2,500 ....$60-$125
- Al Kaline 10 1/4" Tigers plate, 10,000................$50
- Al Kaline 10 1/4" Tigers gold plate, 1,000........$125
- Al Kaline mini Tigers plate..................................$20
- Harmon Killebrew 7" Twins figurine, 5,573 .....$150
- Mark Langston 7" Angels figurine, 1,990 ......$50-$150
- Mickey Mantle 15" Yankees doll, 1,956 .....$100-$150
- Mickey Mantle 15" Yankees doll, 195 AP......$200-$300
- Mickey Mantle 10" Yankees figurine, 1,968.....$200
- Mickey Mantle 8" Yankees figurine, 975..........$400
- Mickey Mantle 8" Yankees figurine, 7,500.......$125
- Mickey Mantle 7" Yankees AP figurine, 106....$500
- Mickey Mantle 7" Yankees figurine, 5,536.......$100
- Mickey Mantle 7" Yankees figurine, 2,500.......$125
- Mickey Mantle 7" switch hitter, 2,401 ....$300
- Mickey Mantle 6" Yankees figurine, 2,950.......$200
- Mickey Mantle 5" Yankees figurine....................$50
- Mickey Mantle 5" Club figurine.........................$75
- Mickey Mantle mini Yankees plate, "Switch Hitter"
  ....$20
- Mickey Mantle 12" Yankees collectoval, "The Life
  of a Legend," 1,968...$195
- Mickey Mantle 10 1/4" Yankees gold plate, "Mickey
  7," 1,500 ....$200
- Mickey Mantle 8 1/2" Yankees plate, "The Golden
  Years," 5,000...$175
- Mickey Mantle mini Yankees plate, "The Golden
  Years"...$20
- Mickey Mantle/Don Mattingly 7 1/2" figurine, "Yan-
  kee Tradition," 900..$300
- Mickey Mantle/Don Mattingly 7 1/2" figurine, "Yan-
  kee Tradition," 90 AP $500
- Mickey Mantle/Don Mattingly 10 1/4" plate, "Yan-

- kee Tradition," 10,000...$65
- Mickey Mantle/Don Mattingly mini plate, "Yankee
  Tradition" $20
- Eddie Mathews 7" Braves figurine, 5,512.... $100-$150
- Don Mattingly 15" Yankees doll, 1,991 ...$125-$150
- Don Mattingly 15" Yankees doll, 200 AP.... $250-$300
- Don Mattingly 10" Yankees figurine, 1,990 ...$125-$200
- Don Mattingly 8" Yankees figurine, 975 ....$150
- Don Mattingly 7" Yankee figurine, Flanklin glove,
  500...$150-$400
- Don Mattingly 7" Yankee figurine, Franklin glove,
  2,500..$250
- Don Mattingly 6" Yankee figurine, 2,950 ....$90
- Don Mattingly 5" Yankees figurine, hitting $50
- Don Mattingly 5" Yankees figurine, fielding, 2,950 ..$50
- Don Mattingly 10 1/4" Yankees plate, "Player of the
  Year," 5,000 ....$60
- Don Mattingly 10 1/4" Yankees gold plate, "Player of
  the Year," 2,500 ....$125
- Don Mattingly mini Yankees plate, "Player of the
  Year" $20
- Don Mattingly 10 1/4" Yankees gold plate, "Yankee
  Pride"...$150
- Don Mattingly mini Yankees plate, "Yankee Pride"..$20
- Don Mattingly 10 1/4 Yankees gold plate, #23,
  1,991 ....$125
- Don Mattingly mini Yankees plate, #23............$20
- Willie Mays 7" Giants figurine, 5,660.....................
  ....$75-$150
- Willie Mays 7" Giants figurine, "Famous Catch,"
  5,000...$75-$150
- Willie Mays 5" Giants figurine ....$35-$50
- Willie Mays 8 1/2" Giants plate, "The Golden
  Years," 5,000...$125
- Willie Mays mini Giants plate, "The Golden Years"
  ....$20
- Willie Mays 10 1/4" Giants gold plate, "Famous
  Catch," 2,500...$150
- Willie Mays mini Giants plate, "Famous Catch" $20
- Willie McCovey 7" Giants figurine, 5,521... $150-$175
- Mark McGwire 10" A's figurine, 1,990 .... $150-$300
- Mark McGwire 7" A's figurine, 2,500 ....$75-$125
- Mark McGwire 5" A's figurine ....$35-$50
- Mark McGwire 10 1/4" A's gold plate, 2,500........$125
- Mark McGwire mini A's plate.............................$20
- Kevin McReynolds 7" Mets figurine, 5,022........$50
- Kevin Mitchell 7" Giants figurine, 1,990 ...$75-$150
- Kevin Mitchell 5" Giants figurine ....$30-$50
- Paul Molitor 7" Brewers figurine, 2,500 ..$65-$125
- Paul Molitor 10 1/4" Brewers plate, 10,000 ....$50
- Paul Molitor 10 1/4" Brewers gold plate, 1,000.....$125
- Paul Molitor mini Brewers plate........................$20
- Joe Morgan 7" Reds figurine, 1,900 ....$100-$200
- Joe Morgan 8" Reds figurine, 199 AP $395
- Joe Morgan 5" Reds figurine ....$35-$50
- Joe Morgan 10 1/4" Reds gold plate, 1,990.......$150
- Joe Morgan mini Reds plate $20
- Thurman Munson 10" Yankees figurine, 995 ....$150
- Thurman Munson 7" Yankees figurine, 5,000..$75-$125
- Thurman Munson 5" Yankees figurine.........$35-$50
- Thurman Munson 10 1/4" Yankees plate, 10,000....$50
- Thurman Munson mini Yankees plate $20
- Stan Musial 10 1/4" Cardinals gold plate, 1,963....$150
- Stan Musial mini Cardinals plate $20

179

- Mel Ott 7" Giants figurine, 1,008 .... $100
- Mike Piazza 7" Dodgers figurine, 975 .... $100
- Kirby Puckett 7" Twins figurine, 1,990 ...... $75-$150
- Kirby Puckett 5" Twins figurine .... $35-$50
- Cal Ripken Jr. 7" Orioles figurine, 1,990 ...... $125-$150
- Cal Ripken Jr. 5" Orioles figurine $50
- Brooks Robinson 7" Orioles figurine, 2,848... $75-$150
- Brooks Robinson 5" Orioles figurine .... $35-$50
- Brooks Robinson 10 1/4" Orioles gold plate, 1,000 ...$50
- Brooks Robinson mini Orioles plate $20
- Frank Robinson 7" Orioles figurine, 5,586 ..... $75-$150
- Jackie Robinson 7" Dodgers figurine, 5,042 ..... $75-$150
- Jackie Robinson 5" Dodgers figurine .... $30-$50
- Jackie Robinson 10 1/4" Dodgers gold plate, 1,956 .$150
- Jackie Robinson mini Dodgers plate $20
- Babe Ruth 7" Yankees figurine, 5,000 .... $125
- Babe Ruth 7" Yankees figurine, 714 .... $50-$100
- Babe Ruth 4" Club figurine $40
- Babe Ruth 10 1/4" Yankees plate, 10,000 .... $200
- Babe Ruth mini Yankees plate........................... $20
- Nolan Ryan 15" Rangers doll, 1,992 .... $125
- Nolan Ryan 15" Rangers doll, 199 AP $300
- Nolan Ryan 9" Rangers figurine, "Kings of K," 500
  .... $195
- Nolan Ryan 9" Rangers figurine, "5,000 Ks," 1,990
  .... $150-$300
- Nolan Ryan 7" Rangers figurine, "5,000 Ks," 500
  AP $195
- Nolan Ryan 5" Rangers figurine, 2,950 .... $55
- Nolan Ryan 5" Rangers figurine $50
- Nolan Ryan 10 1/4" Rangers gold plate, "5,000 Ks,"
  5,000 .... $150
- Nolan Ryan mini Rangers plate, "5,000 Ks" $20
- Nolan Ryan 10 1/4" Rangers gold plate, "300 Wins,"
  1,990 .... $150
- Nolan Ryan mini Rangers plate, "300 Wins" $20
- Ryne Sandberg 7" Cubs figurine, 975 .... $175
- Ryne Sandberg 6" Cubs figurine, 3,033 .... $50
- Mike Schmidt 8" Phillies figurine, 975 .... $225
- Mike Schmidt 8" Phillies figurine, 7,500 .... $125
- Mike Schmidt 7" Phillies figurine, 5,548 .... $100
- Tom Seaver 10" Mets figurine, 1,986.................. $75
- Tom Seaver 8" Mets figurine, 2,000.................... $75
- Tom Seaver 5" Mets figurine .... $35-$50
- Tom Seaver 9" Mets figurine, "Kings of K," 500.....$195
- Tom Seaver 10 1/4" Mets gold plate, 3,311 ...... $150
- Tom Seaver mini Mets plate $20
- Duke Snider 7" Dodgers figurine, 2,500.............. $65
- Duke Snider 5" Dodgers figurine................... $35-$50
- Duke Snider 10 1/4" Dodgers gold plate, "Boys of
  Summer," 1,500 .... $125
- Duke Snider 10 1/4" Dodgers plate, "Boys of Sum-
  mer," 5,000.. $50
- Duke Snider mini Dodgers plate, "Boys of Summer"
  .... $20
- Duke Snider 8 1/2" Dodgers plate, 5,000, "The Gold-
  en Years"... $125
- Duke Snider mini Dodgers plate, "The Golden
  Years".. $20
- Darryl Strawberry 7" Mets figurine, 5,018 ..... $60-$125
- Darryl Strawberry 5" Mets figurine, 2,950 .... $25
- Darryl Strawberry 10 1/4" Mets gold plate, 3,500
  .... $125
- Bobby Thomson 7" Giants figurine, 1,951 .... $75

- Alan Trammell 7" Tigers figurine, 2,500 .... $50-$125
- Alan Trammell 5" Tigers figurine, 2,950 .... $40
- Alan Trammell 10 1/4" Tigers plate, 10,000 .... $50
- Alan Trammell 10 1/4" Tigers gold plate, 1,000.... $125
- Alan Trammell mini Tigers plate....................... $50
- Andy Van Slyke 7" Pirates figurine, 2,500 ..... $60-$125
- Robin Ventura 8" White Sox figurine, 975 .... $85
- Frank Viola 7" Twins figurine, 2,500 .... $50-$125
- Frank Viola 10 1/4" Twins gold plate, 2,500 ..$100-$125
- Frank Viola mini Twins plate $20
- Honus Wagner 7" Pirates figurine, 5,000 .... $75-$125
- Honus Wagner 10 1/4" Pirates plate, 10,000 .... $75
- Honus Wagner mini Pirates plate $20
- Ted Williams 10" Red Sox figurine, 1,960 .. $150-$250
- Ted Williams 7" Red Sox figurine, 5,521 .... $100-$125
- Ted Williams 5" Red Sox figurine $50
- Ted Williams 10 1/4" Red Sox gold plate, 1,960... $150
- Ted Williams mini Red Sox plate $20
- Dave Winfield 7" Yankees figurine, 2,500 .... $75-$125
- Carl Yastrzemski 10 1/4" Red Sox plate, 1,500 ..$50
- Carl Yastrzemski 10 1/4" Red Sox gold plate, 1,500
  .... $125
- Carl Yastrzemski mini Red Sox plate $20
- Cy Young 7" Indians figurine, 5,000 .... $75
- Cy Young 10 1/4" Indians plate, 10,000.............. $75
- Cy Young mini Indians plate $20

Theme-related figurines/plates

- Mickey Mantle/Willie Mays/Duke Snider 12" collec-
  toval, "The Golden Years," 1,000 .... $200
- Wade Boggs/Ted Williams/Carl Yastrzemski 12"
  collectoval, "Fenway Tradition," 1,000 .... $200
- Steve Carlton/Nolan Ryan/Tom Seaver 12" collec-
  toval, "Kings of K," 1,990 .... $195
- Mickey Mantle/Willie Mays/Duke Snider 10 1/4"
  gold plate, "Greatest Centerfielders," 3,500 ..... $150
- Mickey Mantle/Willie Mays/Duke Snider mini plate,
  "Greatest Centerfielders" $20
- Duke Snider/Mickey Mantle/Willie Mays 10 1/4"
  plate, 3,500 .... $75
- Duke Snider/Mickey Mantle/Willie Mays 10 1/4"
  gold plate, 1,500 .... $150
- Duke Snider/Mickey Mantle/Willie Mays mini plate$20
- Frank Robinson/Ted Williams/Mickey Mantle/Carl
  Yastrzemski 10 1/4" gold plate, "Living Triple
  Crown," 1,000 .... $150
- Frank Robinson/Ted Williams/Mickey Mantle/Carl
  Yastrzemski 10 1/4" plate, "Living Triple Crown,"
  10,000 .... $65
- Frank Robinson/Ted Williams/Mickey Mantle/Carl
  Yastrzemski mini plate, "Living Triple Crow*n" ... $20
- Steve Carlton/Nolan Ryan/Tom Seaver 9" figurines,
  set of three, "Kings of K," 995 .... $500
- "Dem Bums" 10 1/4" plate, Brooklyn Dodgers,
  10,000... $50
- "Dem Bums" mini plate, Brooklyn Dodgers $20
- "Wait Till Next Year" 10 1/4" plate, Brooklyn Dodg-
  ers, 5,000 .... $75
- "Wait Till Next Year" mini plate, Brooklyn Dodgers
  .... $20
- Yankee Stadium 10 1/2" plate, 5,000 .... $75
- Yankee Stadium mini plate................................. $20

180

Hackett American plates

Hank Aaron signed .... $275-$350
Steve Carlton signed .... $250-$350
Gary Carter signed.................................$175
Roger Clemens signed................................$600
Whitey Ford signed $300
Steve Garvey signed.................................$225
Dwight Gooden, unsigned...........................$100
Reggie Jackson, Paluso............................$900
Reggie Jackson, Paluso............................$400
Reggie Jackson, Alexander $700
Wally Joyner signed.................................$295

Harmon Killebrew signed............................$325
Sandy Koufax signed ....$275-$500
Eddie Mathews signed......................$225-$300
Willie Mays signed............................$275-$395
Pete Rose...$45
Babe Ruth unsigned $100
Nolan Ryan signed..................................$800
Tom Seaver signed..................................$325
Tom Seaver 300.......................................$250
Don Sutton signed...................................$325

Bradford Exchange/Delphi collector plates

Legends of Baseball

1. Babe Ruth: The Called Shot $25
2. Lou Gehrig: The Luckiest Man $25
3. Ty Cobb: The Georgia Peach $28
4. Cy Young: The Perfect Game $28
5. Rogers Hornsby: The .424 Season $28
6. Honus Wagner: The Flying Dutchman $30
7. Jimmie Foxx: The Beast $30
8. Walter Johnson: The Shutout $30
9. Tris Speaker: The Gray Eagle $30
10. Christy Mathewson: 1905 World Series.$32
11. Mel Ott: Master Melvin $32
12. Lefty Grove: His Greatest Season $32
13. Shoeless Joe Jackson: Where Triples Die$32
14. Pie Traynor: Pittsburgh Champ.............$34
15. Mickey Cochrane: Black Mike $34
16. Grover Alexander $34

Take Me Out to the Ball Game

1. Wrigley Field, the Friendly Confines.......$30
2. Yankee Stadium, the House That Ruth Built...$30
3. Fenway Park, Home of the Green Monster $33
4. Briggs Stadium, Home of the Tigers........$33
5. Comiskey Park, Home of the White Sox ..$33
6. Cleveland Stadium, Home of the Indians $35
7. Memorial Stadium, Home of the Orioles .$35
8. County Stadium, Home of the Champs ...$35
9. Ebbetts Field, Home of the Dodgers $35
10. Shibe Park $37
11. Forbes Field $37

Great Moments in Baseball

1. Joe DiMaggio: The Steak $30
2. Stan Musial: 5-Homer Double-Header.....$30
3. Bobby Thomson: The Shot Heard 'Round the World $33
4. Bill Mazeroski: Winning Home Run $33
5. Don Larsen: Perfect World Series Game .$33
6. Jackie Robinson: Saved Pennant $35
7. Satchel Paige: Greatest Games $35

8. Billy Martin: The Rescue Catch...............$35
9. Dizzy Dean: World Series Shutout $35
10. Carl Hubbell: The 1934 All-State $35
11. Ralph Kiner: The Home Run...................$37
12. Enos Slaughter: The Mad Dash $37

Superstars of Baseball

1. Willie Mays $30
2. Carl Yastrzemski $30
3. Frank Robinson...$33
4. Bob Gibson $33
5. Harmon Killebrew $33
6. Don Drysdale..$35

Immortals of the Diamond

1. The Sultan of Swat, Babe Ruth $40
2. The Pride of the Yankees, Lou Gehrig.....$40
3. The Georgia Peach, Ty Cobb $40

Baseball's Diamond Moments

1. Ted Williams: Last Time at Bat..............$40

Babe Ruth Centennial

1. The 60th Homer $30

Longton Crown Tankards

Legends of Baseball Signature Series
Babe Ruth: The Called Shot........................$30
Lou Gehrig: The Luckiest Man $30
Cy Young: The Perfect Game $33
Ty Cobb: The Georgia Peach $33

The Ashton Drake Galleries

Babe Ruth: The 60th Home Run.................$80
Lou Gehrig: The Luckiest Man $80

Sports, Accessories & Memorabilia

"A Magic Night in Camden Yards,"
honors Cal Ripken Jr.'s record $45

Bobbing Head Dolls

Although bobbing head dolls didn't necessarily garner much respect when they first came over from Japan in 1960, today people are shaking their heads over how much those $2.95 dolls have appreciated in value since then.

Over the years the supply has decreased; the bobbers were not built to last, a factor which contributes to their values. It's rare when a now-scarce bobbing head doll does not have a small crack or paint chip in it.

It's even been reported in Sports Collectors Digest that some of the papier-mache dolls sold at major league stadiums in the early 1970s were used as bowling pins by stadium vendors. Others were smashed by baseball bats.

The dolls were originally sold at major league ball parks and through mail orders.

But they can be found today, if a collector is patient and persistent. Thorough perusal of a hobby publication such as Sports Collectors Digest may turn up a doll or two, especially in auction or classified ads. Card shows, garage sales, flea markets and antique shops are also good places to find these dolls.

Options to pursue in collecting bobbers would be by base color, by team, or by head type, which is either a mascot or boy's head.

The heads, attached by the neck with a spring to the body, bob, or nod, up and down at the slightest vibration. They were originally produced by Lego (a Swiss firm) and imported exclusively by Sports Specialties of Los Angeles. Many gold-based dolls still have stickers on the base which read "Sports Specialties 10203 Santa Monica Blvd. Los Angeles Calif. 67." The 67 represented a postal code.

Generally, eight categories, based on the doll's base color, are used when listing bobbing head dolls. They are: 1) Square colored bases, 1960-61; 2) Square white bases, 1961-62; 3) Caricatures, 1961-62; 4) White round miniatures, 1961-62; 5) Round green bases, 1962-64; 6) Green round bases, black players, 1962-64; 7) Round gold bases, 1965-72; and 8) Others.

In the following charts, the type of base is listed first, followed by the head types, which are represented by M, meaning team mascot head, or B, meaning boy's head. Team or city names are represented by embossed hand-painted letters, as E, or D, for paper decals. Scarcity is represented by ER, which means Extremely Rare; R, for Rare; S, for Scarce; D, for Difficult; and C, for Common. The last column represents a high/low value range for dolls in Near Mint condition.

I. Square colored bases 1960-61

These dolls were the first dolls ever made. Every franchise from 1960-61 is represented, including the expansion teams of the Minnesota Twins, New York Mets, Houston Colts and Los Angeles Angels. The Twins dolls apparently were produced in great abundance. Four teams from the minor league's Pacific Coast League were also created.

1. Baltimore Orioles (Lego on base)	green diamond (large)	M	D/E	ER	$175-$200
2. Boston Red Sox	green square	B	D/E	ER	$200-$300
3. Chicago Cubs	light blue sq.	B	D/E	ER	$175-$225
4. Cincinnati Reds	red square	B	D/E	ER	$225-$300
5. Detroit Tigers	green square	M	D/E	ER	$200-$250
6. Los Angeles Angels	blue square	B	D/E	R	$75-$100
7. Los Angeles Dodgers	blue square	B	D/E	R	$225-$275
8. Minnesota Twins	blue square	B	D	C	$45-$70
9. New York Mets	blue square	B	D/E	ER	$175-$225
10. New York Yankees	orange sq.	B	D/E	ER	$75-$150
11. Pittsburgh Pirates	orange sq.	B	D/E	R	$125-$175
12. San Francisco Giants	orange sq.	B	D/E	ER	$100-$175
13. Houston Colts	light blue sq.	B	E	ER	$150-$200
14. Washington Senators	blue square	B	E	ER	$300-$400

Minor League subset, Pacific Coast League teams, same design, 1960-61.

15. Hawaii	xxxx	B	D	ER	$325-$400
16. Portland Beavers	orange square	B	D	ER	$150-$175
17. Tacoma Giants	orange square	B	D	ER	$150-$225
18. Seattle	xxxx	B	D	ER	$150-$250

II. Square white bases 1961-62.

This series, the most difficult to complete, features 22 dolls, including the Anaheim (California) Angels and Houston Colts. The dolls in this series are perhaps the most beautiful and most desirable of all dolls. They are colorfully hand-painted, with embossed team logos on the uniform's chest.

Nine teams are represented with figural head mascots: Chicago Cubs, Cub head; Detroit Tigers, Tiger head; Cincinnati Reds, ball head; Cleveland Indians, "Wahoo" Indian head; Milwaukee Braves, Braves Indian head; Pittsburgh Pirates, Pirate head; Houston Colts, boy head with 10 gallon hat; Baltimore Orioles, Oriole bird head; and St. Louis Cardinals, Cardinal bird head.

This series is most difficult to find, especially the figurals and bobbers for the Chicago White Sox, New York Mets, Minnesota Twins, San Francisco Giants and defunct teams of the Milwaukee Braves, Los Angeles Angels, Washington Senators, Houston Colts and Kansas City A's. The Colt 45's in a blue uniform is super rare. Scarcity is represented by ER, which means Extremely Rare, or R, which means Rare.

1. Anaheim Angels	Boy's head	Decals	ER	$150-$200
2. Baltimore Orioles	Mascot	Embossed	ER	$250-$400
3. Boston Red Sox	Mascot	Embossed	ER	$175-$250
4. Chicago Cubs	Mascot	Embossed	ER	$250-$350
5. Chicago White Sox	Boy's head	Embossed	R	$175-$225
6. Cincinnati Reds	Mascot	Embossed	ER	$500-$600
7. Cleveland Indians	Mascot	Embossed	ER	$300-$400
8. Detroit Tigers	Mascot	Embossed	ER	175-$250
9. Houston Colts	Boy's head	Embossed	R	$100-$200
10. Houston Colts (blue uniform)	Boy's head	Embossed	ER	$1,000-$1,200
11. Kansas City A's	Boy's head	Decals	ER	$175-$275

12. Los Angeles Angels	Boy's head	Decals	R	$90-$165
13. Los Angeles Dodgers	Boy's head	Decals	R	$65-$150
14. Milwaukee Braves	Mascot	Embossed	ER	$200-$300
15. Minnesota Twins	Boy's head	Decals	ER	$225-$350
16. New York Mets	Boy's head	Decals	ER	$175-$300
17. New York Yankees	Boy's head	Embossed	R	$175-$225
18. Philadelphia Phillies	Boy's head	Embossed	R	$125-$185
19. Pittsburgh Pirates	Mascot	Embossed	ER	$1,000-$1,200
20. St. Louis Cardinals	Mascot	Embossed	ER	$250-$325
21. San Francisco Giants	Boy's head	Embossed/Decals	ER	$250-$375
22. Washington Senators	Boy's head	Embossed	R	$175-$250

III. Caricatures 1961-62
Clemente, Mantle, Maris, Mays

Four dolls, fairly accurate and pretty realistic in likeness, were made of individual players - Roberto Clemente, Mickey Mantle, Roger Maris and Willie Mays. Both round and square white bases were made, with the player's facsimile autograph on the front of the base. All dolls are extremely rare and very much sought after.

A) Clemente is the rarest of all the caricatures. He wasn't the most popular player of that time, but his doll is the most expensive of all dolls to locate. Only a few surface every year. No box was made with this doll, and there was no miniature made for Clemente. This 7" doll commands a hefty price of $1,200-$1,800; perhaps as few as 40 exist in any condition.

B) Mantle is not the rarest doll but certainly the most popular. It has an embossed "N.Y." or "Yankee" decal on the chest. The doll was originally issued with a box, which is worth $50-$150. The Mantle is worth $550-$800 and can often be found at most major card shows. A miniature Mantle was also made and is very difficult to find. An embossed "N.Y." or "Yankee" decal is on the chest. The mini Mantle is worth $800-$1,100.

C) Maris is rarer than Mantle, due to far less distribution than Mantle. It also includes an original box, worth $50-$150, with color pictures of the doll/player on it. An embossed "N.Y." or "Yankee" decal is on the chest. Maris is worth $475-$650. A miniature Maris was also made and is very difficult to locate. It's worth between $800-$1,000.

D) Mays is the most common of the caricatures but is found in two variations, made with either a bat or ball. A "dark variation" (the skin tone is darker) of the two types is far more difficult to find. Its value is $300-$450. The "light variation" (with a lighter skin tone) has Oriental-like eyes. This is the most common of the types and is worth between $225-$275.

IV. White round miniatures 1961-62

White rounds were intended to sit on car dashes. These dolls are extremely fragile, especially near the neck. The are about 4 1/2" tall.

There are 10 National League and 10 American League dolls. None appear to be more rarer than the others. They were boxed individually or were packaged by a league, 10 to a large box.

A few variations exist; dolls hold either a bat or ball. Reportedly some mavericks with green bases also exist. Some team decals come in script and block.

Scarcity is represented by R, which represents Rare, or ER, which means Extremely Rare.

1. Baltimore Orioles	Mascot	Decals	ER	$350-$475
2. Boston Red Sox	Boy's head	Decals	R	$225-$325
3. Chicago Cubs	Mascot	Decals	ER	$425-$450
4. Chicago White Sox	Boy's head	Decals	R	$225-$275
5. Cincinnati Reds	Mascot	Decals	ER	$350-$375
6. Cleveland Indians	Mascot	Decals	ER	$300-$500
7. Detroit Tigers	Mascot	Decals	ER	$275-$400
8. Houston Colts	Boy's head	Decals	ER	$225-$250
9. Kansas City A's	Boy's head	Decals	R	$200-$250
10. Los Angeles Angels	Boy's head	Decals	R	$125-$175
11. Los Angeles Dodgers	Boy's head	Decals	R	$150-$175
12. Milwaukee Braves	Mascot	Decals	ER	$350-$425
13. Minnesota Twins	Boy's head	Decals	R	$225-$250
14. Minneapolis Twins (Var.)	Boy's head	Decals	ER	$325-$450
15. New York Mets	Boy's head	Decals	ER	$175-$300
16. New York Yankees	Boy's head	Decals	ER	$175-$300
17. Philadelphia Phillies	Boy's head	Decals	R	$150-$275
18. Pittsburgh Pirates	Mascot	Decals	ER	$275-$375
19. St. Louis Cardinals	Mascot	Decals	ER	$275-$350
20. San Francisco Giants	Boy's head	Decals	R	$175-$300
21. Washington Senators	Boy's head	Decals	R	$275-$350

V. Round green bases 1962-64

The green round series continued with the same teams as the white base series but reduced the number of variations of curls. One major change featured the Houston Colts doll, which was made with a pistol, not a bat, in its hand. This doll is one of the more popular green base bobbers. Most dolls were made with decals, not embossed team logos. Scarcer issues are for the Pirates, Cubs and Orioles. Scarcity is represented by R, which means Rare, ER, which represents Extremely Rare, S, which represents Scarce, or D, which represents Difficult.

1. Baltimore Orioles	Mascot	Decals/Embossed	ER	$165-$225
2. Boston Red Sox	Boy's head	Decals	R	$75-$150
3. Chicago Cubs	Mascot	Decals	ER	$350-$400
4. Chicago White Sox	Boy's head	Decals	S	$75-$100
5. Cincinnati Reds	Mascot	Decals/Embossed	ER	$150-$225

6. Cleveland Indians	Mascot	Decals	ER	$225-$275
7. Detroit Tigers	Mascot	Embossed	ER	$150-$175
8. Houston Colts	Boy's head	Embossed	ER	$150-$225
9. Kansas City A's	Boy's head	Decals	ER	$350-$450
10. Los Angeles Angels	Boy's head	Decals	D	$100-$150
11. Los Angeles Dodgers	Boy's head	Decals	D	$75-$100
12. Milwaukee Braves	Mascot	Decals	ER	$150-$250
13. Minnesota Twins	Boy's head	Decals	D	$100-$125
14. New York Mets	Boy's head	Decals	S	$100-$150
15. New York Yankees	Boy's head	Decals/Embossed	R	$125-$150
16. Philadelphia Phillies	Boy's head	Decals/Embossed	R	$75-$100
17. Pittsburgh Pirates	Mascot	Decals	ER	$125-$175
18. St. Louis Cardinals	Mascot	Decals	ER	$175-$200
19. San Francisco Giants	Boy's head	Decals	S	$60-$95
20. Washington Senators	Boy's head	Decals	R	$125-$200

VI. Green round base, black players 1962-64

This series, an offshoot of the green series, is by far the most difficult and rarest series to complete. There are no mascots in the series, but the Houston Colts is different; it has a cowboy hat. Each black, boyish face is not simply a white face painted black; these bobbers have distinctive features, including larger eyes, thicker, redder lips and curly hair. All dolls are extremely rare.

1. Baltimore Orioles ....$600-$625
2. Boston Red Sox ....$1,500-$2,000
3. Chicago Cubs ....$650-$750
4. Chicago White Sox................................$600-$650
5. Cincinnati Reds ....$700-$900
6. Cleveland Indians...................................$800-$900
7. Detroit Tigers ....$600-$700
8. Houston Colts....................................$1,000-$1,500
9. Kansas City A's...................................$1,000-$1,500
10. Los Angeles Angels........................$1,000-$1,200
11. Los Angeles Dodgers ....$450-$550
12. Milwaukee Braves..........................$1,000-$1,750
13. Minnesota Twins ....$450-$500
14. New York Mets ....$750-$1,000
15. New York Yankees ....$1,000-$1,300
16. Philadelphia Phillies..............................$700-$900
17. Pittsburgh Pirates...................................$600-$800
18. St. Louis Cardinals ....$450-$525
19. San Francisco Giants ....$800-$1,000

VII. Round gold bases 1965-72

This set is the easiest and most reasonable to obtain. Most dolls are abundant and common. The series, which contains the largest number of dolls, is the last series of Japanese-made dolls. It includes teams that moved and expansion teams. The rarest, most expensive, doll in the series is the Seattle Pilot, made for a team which existed only one year. The Kansas City A's is also popular and scarce, because it is one of few to have a uniform entirely in its team colors - green jersey and gold pants. The new Oakland A's issue in a white uniform is also quite rare. But an A's doll with a yellow uniform also exists; it is exceedingly common. Two Astros dolls - a plain white uniform with blue trim and hat, or the famous "shooting star" insignia with orange hat - exist. The Padres, Cubs and Kansas City A's are tricky, but popular, as are the figurals. This series marked the end of the Japanese era of bobbers; companies in Hong Kong, Korea and Taiwan attempted to revive with plastic, but were not well distributed. From 1983 on the present Taiwan-made dolls brought back the nationwide ballpark/mail order concept. Scarcity is represented by ER, which means Extremely Rare; R, which means Rare; S, which means Scarce; D, which represents Difficult; or C, for Common.

1. Atlanta Braves	Mascot	Decals	D	$75-$125
2. Baltimore Orioles	Mascot	Decals	S	$100-$130
3. Boston Red Sox	Boy's head	Decals	D	$75-$125
4. California Angels	Boy's head	Decals	D	$75-$95
5. Chicago Cubs	Mascot	Decals	D	$100-$150
6. Chicago White Sox	Boy's head	Decals	C	$75-$95

7. Cincinnati Reds	Mascot	Decals	R	$75-$150
8. Cleveland Indians	Mascot	Decals	R	$100-$175
9. Detroit Tigers	Mascot	Decals	R	$100-$150
10. Houston Astros	Boy's head	Decals	S	$50-$100
11. Kansas City Royals	Boy's head	Decals	S	$50-$85
12. Los Angeles Angels	Boy's head	Decals	C	$50-$75
13. Los Angeles Dodgers	Boy's head	Decals	C	$60-$90
14. Milwaukee Brewers	Boy's head	Decals	C	$50-$75
15. Minnesota Twins	Boy's head	Decals	S	$100-$150
16. Montreal Expos	Boy's head	Decals	C	$75-$85
17. New York Mets	Boy's head	Decals	S	$60-$80
18. New York Yankees	Boy's head	Decals	S	$100-$135
19. Oakland A's (gold)	Boy's head	Decals	C	$50-$90
20. Oakland A's (white)	Boy's head	Decals	ER	$155-$185
21. Philadelphia Phillies	Boy's head	Decals	C	$75-$90
22. Pittsburgh Pirates	Mascot	Decals	R	$75-$125
23. St. Louis Cardinals	Mascot	Decals	R	$100-$150
24. San Diego Padres	Boy's head	Decals	S	$50-$100
25. San Francisco Giants	Boy's head	Decals	S	$75-$90
26. Seattle Pilots	Boy's head	Decals	R	$325-$400
27. Texas Rangers	Boy's head	Decals	D	$100-$140
28. Washington Senators	Boy's head	Decals	R	$100-$200

VIII.   Other bobbing heads

A) Little League baseball boy, early 1960s. This features a boy sitting on half a baseball. The ball is a bank. It's rare, and worth $100-$150.

B) Weirdos Los Angeles Dodgers, early 1960s. The dolls on these white bases feature silly expressions. The dolls are holding various items, and wearing uniforms with fractions as numbers. They go for $150 and up.

C) Pitcher/Catcher/Umpire set, early 1960s. They are extremely rare and feature blinking eyes, freckles, and feet bases. The players sell for about $100 each; the umpire is worth $150-$200.

D) Umpires, early 1960s. Several variations exist, including a square base with a scowling umpire holding a mask and broom in each hand. Another umpire has a boyish grin and is wearing a curved hat. The last is a Little League miniature on a green round base. These dolls are highly desirable, worth at least $100.

E) Green square bases, rounded corners, 1962. These are similar to the white bases, but it's doubtful there is a complete set. Dolls for the Tigers, Red Sox, Twins and Senators are known to exist, but all dolls are rare and demand prices between whites and greens.

F) Cleveland Indians, miniature boy head, late 1960s, Japanese. These 4 1/2-inch tall dolls are rare, worth between $50-$70, and were evidently given away at ballparks with a purchase.

G) Mr. and Mrs. Met gold round base, 1969. These beautiful, extremely rare dolls commemorate the Mets participation in the World Series. Mr. and Mrs. (more expensive) were made. The doll features a ball head logo/mascot, with legs crossed, leaning on a bat. It's valued at $250-$325. One (of two varieties) is a bank with a coin slot on the back.

H) Gold square bases, early 1970s. All dolls feature boy heads. The Houston Astros "shooting star" (worth $500) and the Kansas City A's green jersey/gold pants ($450) are extremely rare, but the most popular.

I) Series of plastic dolls, mid-1970s, with boxes. These dolls were never too popular, hence are worth $5-$10.

J) Plastic Henry Aaron caricature, with box, 1975. This doll, worth up to $35, is very common, due to overproduction.

Members of Cincinnati's Big Red Machine are portrayed on S.A.M. bobbers.

K) Modern heavy ceramics, by Twins Enterprises, 1983-84. The 1983 series came with a ball; the 1984 set had bats. All dolls were boxed. The dolls, made in Taiwan, have round green bases which are thicker and heavier than the 1960s Japaneses dolls. Eight dolls are mascots. The dolls are in the $10-$15 range.

L) Modern heavy ceramic, Twins Enterprises, 1988-89. These dolls, also made in Taiwan, have new designs for the eight mascots and are larger than the 1983-84 versions. They sell for between $5-$10.

M) Modern porcelain, Sports, Accessories & Memorabilia Inc., 1993-present. Each doll is hand painted and resembles the player whose name is painted on the base of the eight-inch statue. Issue prices were $40 each, with 3,000 made for each player. Values are high/low for Near Mint condition.

1. Ernie Banks, #4	$60	21. Willie Mays	$45
2. Ernie Banks, #14	$50-$70	22. Joe Morgan	$45-50
3. Johnny Bench	$40-$45	23. Stan Musial	$45
4. Yogi Berra	$50-$70	24. Satchel Paige	$45-$50
5. Rod Carew	$45	25. Jim Palmer	$45
6. Steve Carlton	$45	26. Tony Perez	$40-$45
7. Gary Carter	$40	27. Kirby Puckett	$45
8. Roger Clemens	$50	28. Cal Ripken Jr.	$55-$70
9. Roberto Clemente	$55	29. Brooks Robinson	$45
10. Ty Cobb	$50-$70	30. Pete Rose	$40-$45
11. Rollie Fingers	$40-$50	31. Babe Ruth	$75
12. Whitey Ford	$50-$70	32. Nolan Ryan, NY	$60-$70
13. Lou Gehrig	$45	33. Nolan Ryan, Cal.	$60-$70
14. Bob Gibson	$45	34. Nolan Ryan, Hou.	$60-$70
15. Ken Griffey Jr.	$55-$65	35. Nolan Ryan, Tex.	$60-$70
16. Martinez Jackson	$40	36. Tom Seaver	$65-$70
17. Reggie Jackson	$50	37. Duke Snider	$45
18. Michael Jordan	$60-$90	38. Willie Stargell	$55
19. Mickey Mantle	$65-$90	39. Ted Williams	$55-$65
20. Roger Maris	$50-$70	40. Carl Yastrzemski	$55

Yearbooks

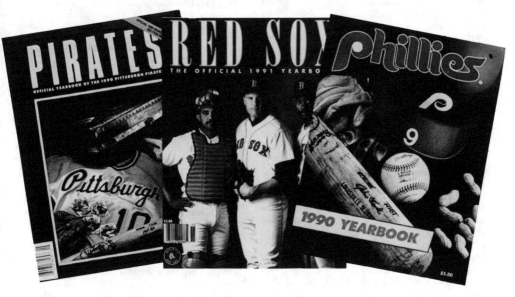

It wasn't until the 1940s and 1950s that what we now consider as yearbooks were produced by teams on a regular basis. During the 1950s many teams didn't do the actual publishing, but instead had the Jay Publishing Co. of New York put out a series of what were called "Big League Books," which served as the official yearbooks for the clubs. Jay Publishing stopped issuing them in 1965.

The main problem in creating a yearbook checklist is that there is not a general consensus as to whether a certain publication should be considered a yearbook or something else; many teams have labeled their publications with a variety of other names - magazines, roster books, photo albums and sketchbooks.

Two collectors, Ralph Deptolla and Dennis Sell, contributed a yearbook checklist which appeared in the Aug. 3, 1984, issue of Sports Collectors Digest. The two agree that in order to be classified as a yearbook, a publication must at the very least have photographs of every player on the 25-man roster, plus biographies and player statistics. If, however, a publication has photos, stats and biographies, but is labeled as a media guide, scorecard or program, then it's obviously something other than a yearbook.

Most yearbooks from the 1960s offer collectors an affordable alternative for under $100. Those from the 1950s bring the top dollars, depending on scarcity and age, while those which are autographed are even more valuable. Yearbooks should be stored in plastic holders and kept out of sunlight. Note: if yearbooks exist for 1994 and 1995, they are generally worth cover price.

Angels Yearbooks

Los Angeles Angels

1961	$150
1962 Angels baby with cake	$85-$100
1963	$35-$50
1964 Angels in action	$25-$35
1965 Angels in action	$25-$35

California Angels

1966 Anaheim Stadium	$50-$65
1967 "All About the Angels," with logo	$12-$15
1968	None issued
1969	None issued
1970	None issued
1971	None issued
1972	None issued
1973	None issued
1974	None issued
1975	None issued
1976	None issued
1977	None issued
1978	None issued
1979	None issued
1980	None issued
1981	None issued
1982	None issued
1983 Lynn, Carew, Jackson, others	$8-$12
1984 Anaheim Stadium	$5-$10
1985 25th Anniversary, Angel greats	$7-$10
1986	None issued
1987	None issued
1988	None issued
1989	None issued
1990	None issued
1991	None issued
1992 Abbott, Langston, Harvey, Finley	$12
1993 Nolan Ryan	$12
1994 and 1995	cover

Astros Yearbooks

Houston Colt 45s

1962 Baseball, pistol, Texas	$150
1963	$125
1964	$125

Houston Astros

1965 "Inside the Astrodome"	$100
1966 Astrodome	$75
1967	None issued
1968	$45
1969	None issued
1970	None issued
1971	None issued
1972	$25
1973	None issued
1974	None issued
1975	None issued
1976	None issued
1977 Photo album	$20

1978 Photo album	$20
1979 Photo album	$20
1980	None issued
1981	None issued
1982 Nolan Ryan	$12-$15
1983	None issued
1984	None issued
1985	None issued
1986	None issued
1987	None issued
1988	None issued
1989	None issued
1990	None issued
1991	None issued
1992 Luis Gonzalez	$12
1993 photo album	$12
1994 and 1995	cover

Athletics Yearbooks

Philadelphia Athletics

1949 Connie Mack	$60-$125
1950 Connie Mack Golden Jubiliee	$60-$125
1951 Team mascot (elephant)	$60-$125
1952 Team mascot (elephant)	$60-$125
1953 Elephant pitching baseball	$20
1954 Play at first base	$75

Kansas City Athletics

1955 A's batter ripping through map	$100-$150
1956 Elephant mascot	$100-$150
1957 Kansas City Municipal Stadium	$100-$150
1958 Play at first	$125
1959 Kansas City Municipal Stadium	$125
1960 Baseball wearing Athletics hat	$125
1961 Pitcher and baseball	$125
1962 A's players in action	$125
1963	$25-$40
1964 Player making a catch	$25-$40
1965 A's donkey, Finley flag	$25-$45
1966	$65
1967 Athletics pitcher	$40

Oakland Athletics

1968 Oakland Coliseum	$45-$75
1969 Connie Mack	$25-$35
1970 Monday, Odom, Jackson, others	$25
1971 Sal Bando, Bert Campaneris	$15-$25
1972 Dick Williams, Vida Blue	$15-$22
1973 Rudi, Fingers, Williams, Hunter	$20
1974 "One More in 74," two trophies	$15-$20
1975 "Keep it Alive in 75"	$20
1976 Bicentennial celebration	$15
1977 A's logo, arch of baseballs	$7-$9
1978	None issued
1979 "The Swingin 'A's," with logo	$20
1980	None issued
1981	None issued
1982 Billy Ball baseball	$5-$10
1983 A's baseball card collage	$15
1984	None issued
1985	None issued

1986	None issued
1987	None issued
1988	None issued
1989	None issued
1990	None issued
1991	None issued
1992	None issued
1993	None issued
1994 and 1995	cover

Blue Jays Yearbooks

1977 "The First Year," fans	$15-$20
1978	None issued
1979	$9
1980	$15
1981 Ernie Whitt, Jim Clancy	$15
1982 Martinez, Moseby, Whitt	$15
1983 Blue Jays baseball	$15
1984 Exhibition Stadium	$15
1985 Logo and year	$15
1986 American League baseball, bat	$15
1987 Barfield, Clancy, Whitt	$15
1988 Blue Jay player batting	$15
1989	$15
1990 George Bell	$15
1991 Player drawing	$15
1992 Roberto Alomar	$15
1993 Trophy	$15
1994 and 1995	cover

Braves Yearbooks

Boston Braves

1946	$300
1947 Billy Southworth	$150-$165
1948	None issued
1949	None issued
1950 Smiling Brave	$150
1951 Baseball diamond and ball	$125
1952 Braves players talking	$125

Milwaukee Braves

1953 Runner sliding into home	$150-$175
1954 "To the People of Milwaukee"	$75-$100
1955 Fans and stadium	$50-$60
1956 Cartoon of Braves fans	$100-$125
1957 Braves logo in crystal ball	$100-$125
1958 Brave raising World Series pennant	$100-$125
1959 Brave in hot-air balloon	$65-$70
1960 Brave with two baseball bats	$60
1961 Braves player, other N.L. players	$40-$65
1962 Braves logo	$45-$60
1963 Braves player, other N.L. players	$40
1964 Aaron, Mathews, Torre, Spahn	$40-$60
1965 Bobby Bragan, Felipe Alou	$40

Atlanta Braves

1966 Aaron, Mathews, others	$25-$50
1967 Play at home plate	$10-$30
1968 Play at second base	$10-$25
1969 Braves infielder	$15-$25

1970 Braves in action	$20
1971 Hank Aaron, Babe Ruth	$7-$9
1972 Five Braves	$5-$9
1973 Braves pitcher	$20
1974 Hank Aaron, Babe Ruth	$20
1975 Four Braves	$15
1976 Niekro, Cepeda, Aaron, others	$15
1977 Former Braves, Hank Aaron	$10
1978 Spahn, Niekro, Burdette	$10
1979 Garber stops Rose's streak	$12-$15
1980 Bob Horner, Bobby Cox	$15
1981 Dale Murphy, Bob Horner, others	$15
1982 Spahn, Horner, Aaron, others	$12-$15
1983 Phil Niekro in an Uncle Sam outfit	$10
1984 Horner, Murphy, Aaron	$10
1985 Aaron, Murphy, 20th Anniversary	$10
1986 Dale Murphy, Chuck Tanner	$12
1987 Dale Murphy	$12
1988 "Braves Illustrated"	$10
1989	None issued
1990 25 years in Atlanta	$12
1991	None issued
1992 N.L. Champions	$12
1993	None issued
1994 and 1995	cover

Brewers Yearbooks

Seattle Pilots

1969 Pilot logos, 10 pictures	$150

Milwaukee Brewers

1970 Brewers hitter	$50-$75
1971	None issued
1972	None issued
1973	None issued
1974	None issued
1975	None issued
1976	None issued
1977	None issued
1978	None issued
1979 Larry Hisle	$5-$9
1980 Gorman Thomas	$5-$9
1981 Molitor, Fingers, Yount, others	$5-$9
1982 Crowd celebrating	$12
1983 Robin Yount and fans	$10
1984 County Stadium	$5-$9
1985 George Bamberger and fans	$5-$9
1986 Brewers locker room	$5-$9
1987 Brewers baseball cards	$5-$9
1988 Paul Molitor hologram	$10
1989 Brewer greats, Hank Aaron	$12
1990 Brewers logo, Milwaukee skyline	$10
1991 Paul Molitor	$12
1992 Molitor, Yount, Gantner	$12
1993	None issued
1994 and 1995	cover

Cardinals Yearbooks

1951 Cardinal in bottom right	$250
1952 Cardinal and soldier	$125
1953 Stan Musial	$125-$175

1954 Red Schoendienst $100
1955 Cardinal pitcher gets the sign $75
1956 Cardinal pitcher gets the sign $75
1957 Cardinal circles the bases .... $40-$50
1958 Cardinal circles the bases $50
1959 Stan Musial $55
1960 Cardinal catches a ball............................... $40
1961 Simmons, Sadecki, others $40
1962 Stan Musial and his milestones .... $40-$60
1963 Musial slides into second .... $35-$50
1964 Groat, Boyer, Javier, White................... $35-$50
1965 Bob Gibson... $35
1966 New Busch Stadium photo $65
1967 World Champs................................... $50-$75
1968 Busch Stadium.. $45
1969 Brock, Flood, Gibson, others..................... $30
1970 Five Cardinal drawings .... $12-$15
1971 Brock, Torre, Gibson, others .... $12-$15
1972 Cardinals fielder $25
1973 Cardinals batter................................. $15-$20
1974 Simmons, Torre $15
1975 Brock, Gibson, others $20
1976 Centennial yearbook................................... $20
1977 Brock, Ty Cobb .... $12-$15
1978 .... None issued
1979 St. Louis city skyline $12
1980 Simmons, Hernandez................................. $10
1981.. None issued
1982.. None issued
1983 .... None issued
1984 .... None issued
1985 .... None issued
1986 .... None issued
1987.. None issued
1988 Wraparound team photo $12
1989 Coleman, Worrell .... $7-$12
1990 Herzog, Busch Stadium.............................. $10
1991 Lee Smith $12
1992 Moore, Slaughter, Musial, Guerrero, Lankford,
Jose $10
1993 Ozzie Smith $12
1994 and 1995 .... cover

Cubs Yearbooks

1934 Wraparound batting scene .... $200-$275
1939 Players' records $200
1941 Players' history/record book .... $175-$250
1942 Roster/record book .... $150-$200
1948 Logo and blue "1948" .... $100-$150
1949 Logo and blue "1949" .... $35-$50
1950 Hat and red "1950".............................. $35-$50
1951 Ball in center of red glove $60
1952 Logo, year in red and blue.................... $50-$70
1953 Cubs logo... $50
1954 Name and year... $50
1955 Name and year... $50
1956.. $75-$100
1957 Head with Cubs hat $125
1958.. None issued
1959 .... None issued
1960.. None issued
1961.. None issued

1962.. None issued
1963 .... None issued
1964 .... None issued
1965 .... None issued
1966 .... None issued
1967 .... None issued
1968 .... None issued
1969 .... None issued
1970 .... None issued
1971 .... None issued
1972 .... None issued
1973 .... None issued
1974 .... None issued
1975 .... None issued
1976 .... None issued
1977 .... None issued
1978 .... None issued
1979 .... None issued
1980 .... None issued
1981 .... None issued
1982 .... None issued
1983 .... None issued
1984 .... None issued
1985 Wrigley photo.................................... $5-$8
1986 70th Anniversary, Ryne Sandberg............ $5-$7
1987 Billy Williams, Ryne Sandberg................ $7-$8
1988 Andre Dawson.................................... $7-$9
1989 .... $12
1990 Photo of players' bats $12
1991 Ryne Sandberg $12
1992 Scoreboard, celebration $12
1993 Mark Grace... $12
1994 and 1995 .... cover

Dodgers Yearbooks

Brooklyn Dodgers

1947 League Champs $100
1948 .... None issued
1949 League Champs $250
1950 .... $175-$200
1951.. $125
1952 "The Bum" holding a sign........................... $125
1953 "The Bum" holding a bat............................ $125
1954 "The Bum" with saw, hammer.................. $125
1955 "The Bum" reaching for a star $300
1956 "The Bum" holding #6.................... $50-$125
1957 "The Bum" holding pennants .... $125-$150

Los Angeles Dodgers

1958 Autographed team baseball .... $150-$175
1959 Play at second base............................. $75-$135
1960 Dodger stadium drawing $50
1961 .... $50
1962 .... $15-$20
1963 Maury Wills.. $50
1964 1963 World Champions banner.................. $30
1965 Dodger Stadium...................................... $35
1966 Walter Alston .... $20-$25
1967 Dodger juggling crowns .... $10-$20
1968 Drysdale, Koufax, others................... $10-$20
1969 Baseball's centennial logo.................. $10-$20

1970 Dodgers and Mets mascots.....................$10-$20
1971 10th Anniversary of stadium.................$10-$20
1972 Dodger Stadium.......................................$10-$20
1973 Maury Wills, Walter Alston ....$15-$25
1974 Jimmy Wynn ....$10-$20
1975 Steve Garvey/N.L. Champions..............$12-$18
1976 Davey Lopes..$12-$18
1977 20th Anniversary, players............................$10
1978 Lasorda, Garvey, Cey, others.................$12-$15
1979 Tom Lasorda..$10-$12
1980 Dodger baseball cards $10
1981 Dusty Baker, Steve Garvey ....$10-$12
1982 World Series trophy...................................$8-$12
1983 25th Anniversary in Los Angeles.................$10
1984 "A Winning Tradition," Lasorda..............$7-$10
1985 Russell, Valenzuela, Garvey ....$9-$10
1986 Guerrero, Hershiser, Marshall.................$7-$10
1987 24 previous Los Angeles yearbooks.........$7-$10
1988 "Blueprint for Success".............................$8-$9
1989 World Series trophy..................................$6-$10
1990 Dodger greats painting ....$6-$10
1991 Dodgers Field of Dreams ....$5-$7
1992 Dodger greats ....$5-$7
1993 Hershiser, Lasorda, collage $6
1994 and 1995 ....cover

Expos Yearbooks

1969 Larry Jaster...$35-50
1970 Expos equipment and fan ....$25-$35
1971 Fan with Expos pennant ....$25-$35
1972 Four different covers, each.....................$25-$35
1973...None issued
1974...None issued
1975...None issued
1976...None issued
1977...None issued
1978...None issued
1979...None issued
1980...None issued
1981...None issued
1982 Expos celebration, All-Star logo $10
1983 Dawson, Carter, Oliver, others...............$7-$12
1984 Raines, Rose, Dawson, others ....$8-$12
1985 Wallach, Raines, Dawson, others.................$10
1986 Baseball in hand $8
1987...None issued
1988...None issued
1989...None issued
1990...None issued
1991...None issued
1992 Gary Carter $10
1993...None issued
1994 and 1995 ....cover

Giants Yearbooks

New York Giants

1947 First Year..$150-$165
1948...None issued
1949...None issued
1950...None issued
1951...$125

1952 Durocher and Giant $85
1953 Polo Grounds photo..$85
1954 Giant cutting a "1951" book..........................$85
1955 Giant holding other mascots.........................$125
1956 Giants cap ....$75-$85
1957 Photo of play at second ....$85-$100

San Francisco Giants

1958 Giant with a load of books $250
1959 Photo of a play at third ....$75-$100
1960 Al Dark, play at first.....................................$50
1961 Giants hat..$50
1962 N.L. Champs...$50
1963 Trolley car with Giants pennant.............$30-$40
1964 Child looking at Candlestick........................$30
1965 Painting of a play at second.........................$30
1966 Willie Mays with S.F. baseball ....$30-$50
1967 Willie Mays, Juan Marichal $40
1968 Willie Mays $25
1969 Mays, Bonds, McCovey $30
1970 Photos of Mays, McCovey ....$20-$25
1971 Willie McCovey ....$15-$20
1972 Willie Mays sliding into third ....$10-$15
1973 Marichal, Bonds, Speier ....$10-$15
1974 "Young Giants '74"......................................$10
1975 Gary Matthews, Mike Caldwell $12
1976...$15
1977..None issued
1978..None issued
1979..None issued
1980 Giant batter..$9
1981 Frank Robinson $10
1982 Silver Anniversary yearbook...................$8-$10
1983 Frank Robinson ....$7-$9
1984 Giants All-Star memorabilia ....$7-$9
1985 Horizontal "A History of..." ....$5-$7
1986..None issued
1987..None issued
1988..None issued
1989..None issued
1990..None issued
1991..None issued
1992 Will Clark...$12
1993..None issued
1994 and 1995 ....cover

Indians Yearbooks

1948 World Champs....................................$100-$125
1949 Logo wearing crown...............................$40-$85
1950 Fans entering stadium.............................$40-$75
1951 50th Anniversary with logo...................$60-$75
1952 Chain with Indians logo $60
1953 Umpire yelling "Play ball"....................$65-$95
1954 Lemon, Wynn, Doby, Rosen......................$100
1955 Indian wearing crown.........................$75-$100
1956 Indian mascot $75
1957 Indian mascot ....$75-$125
1958 Herb Score...$250
1959 Indians logo..$125-$175
1960 Jim Perry, Indians pitcher...........................$100
1961 ....$100
1962 ....$75

1963 .... $100
1964 Indian sliding into home $75
1965 Past and present uniforms $65
1966 Sam McDowell .... $50-$65
1967 Picture set .... $50-$65
1968 Baseball and year .... $25-$40
1969 Runner sliding into base $20
1970 Sam McDowell $25
1971 Indians in action $15
1972 Indians in action .... $7-$9
1973 Jim Perry, others $15
1974 .... None issued
1975 .... None issued
1976 .... None issued
1977 .... None issued
1978 .... None issued
1979 .... None issued
1980 .... None issued
1981 .... None issued
1982 .... None issued
1983 .... None issued
1984 Franco, Sutcliffe, others .... $5-$6
1985 .... None issued
1986 .... None issued
1987 .... None issued
1988 .... None issued
1989 Autographed team baseball $10
1990 90th Anniversary in Cleveland $10
1991 Score, Alomar, Chambliss $10
1992 Alomar, Hargrove $12
1993 .... None issued
1994 and 1995 .... cover

Mariners Yearbooks

1977 .... $50
1978 .... None issued
1979 .... None issued
1980 .... None issued
1981 .... None issued
1982 .... None issued
1983 .... None issued
1984 .... None issued
1985 Davis, Beattie, Langston $10
1986 .... None issued
1987 .... None issued
1988 .... None issued
1989 .... None issued
1990 .... None issued
1991 .... None issued
1992 .... None issued
1993 .... None issued
1994 and 1995 .... cover

Mets Yearbooks

1962 First year .... $300-$350
1963 .... $125-$150
1964 Cartoon .... $75-$100
1965 .... $50-$60
1966 .... $50
1967 Cartoon .... $50-$75
1968 Gil Hodges $45
1969 .... $100-$125

1970 Film strips, World Series celebration $35
1971 Play at the plate .... $35-$50
1972 Harrelson, McGraw, Seaver $15
1973 All-Star gallery with Mays, Seaver .... $15-$35
1974 N.L. Champions pennant $15
1975 Tom Seaver .... $15-$25
1976 Mr. Met .... $15-$20
1977 Jerry Koosman .... $10-$15
1978 .... $6-$10
1979 Mets logo .... $10-$15
1980 Mazzilli with fan, others $30
1981 Joe Torre, All-Time Mets $15
1982 George Foster, George Bamberger .... $12-$15
1983 Foster, M. Wilson, Seaver $20
1984 Orosco, Hernandez, Stawberry .... $15-$20
1985 Hernandez, Gooden, D. Johnson $15
1986 25th Anniversary logo $20
1987 World Champions logo .... $10-$15
1988 Strawberry, Gooden, Johnson, others $15
1989 Strawberry, Gooden, Carter, others $15
1990 Mets starting pitchers $15
1991 Shea Stadium $10
1992 Bonilla, Saberhagen, Murray, Torborg $15
1993 30 years at Shea $15
1994 and 1995 .... cover

Orioles Yearbooks

St. Louis Browns

1944 .... $275
1945 .... $250
1946 .... $250
1947 .... $225
1948 .... $200
1949 .... $200
1950 Browns sketchbook $200
1951 Browns logo $200
1952 .... $300
1953 .... $150

Baltimore Orioles

1954 Orioles mascot in spotlight $250
1955 Oriole mascot batting $150
1956 Oriole mascot on deck $125
1957 Oriole mascot pitching $125
1958 Oriole mascot riding a rocket $125
1959 Oriole mascot with report .... $100-$125
1960 Oriole mascot sitting on eggs $100
1961 Oriole mascot hitting opponent $75
1962 Jim Gentile $75
1963 .... $75
1964 Orioles catcher $75
1965 B. Robinson, Bauer, Bunker $75
1966 Robinsons, Blefary, Powell $50
1967 Frank Robinson and fans $50
1968 Brooks and Frank Robinson $25
1969 Dave McNally $25
1970 Boog Powell .... $20-$35
1971 B. Robinson, Palmer, others .... $15-$25
1972 Palmer, McNally, Cuellar $15
1973 Orioles player .... $12-$15
1974 Orioles jukebox .... $10-$12

1975 ....$12-$15
1976 .... None issued
1977 .... None issued
1978 .... None issued
1979 .... None issued
1980 Orioles mascot.....................................$10-$12
1981 Orioles players......................................$8-$10
1982 Frank Robinson, Earl Weaver $15
1983 Brooks Robinson ....$9-$10
1984 30th Anniversary in Baltimore ....$10-$12
1985 .... None issued
1986 Robinsons, Ripken, Murray.........................$10
1987 .... None issued
1988 .... None issued
1989 .... None issued
1990 .... None issued
1991 .... None issued
1992 .... None issued
1993 Camden Yards $10
1994 and 1995 ....cover

Padres Yearbooks

1969 Jack Murphy Stadium.................................$75
1970 .... None issued
1971 .... None issued
1972 .... None issued
1973 .... None issued
1974 .... None issued
1975 .... None issued
1976 .... None issued
1977 .... None issued
1978 .... None issued
1979 Dave Winfield ....$5-$6
1980 Dave Winfield ....$6-$7
1981 .... None issued
1982 ....$7-$12
1983 Dick Williams, Steve Garvey ....$7-$12
1984 Templeton, Williams, Garvey $12
1985 Padres hat, N.L. Championship ring $12
1986 Padres memorabilia $10
1987 .... None issued
1988 .... None issued
1989 .... None issued
1990 .... None issued
1991 .... None issued
1992 Fernandez, Gwynn, Santiago.......................$10
1993 25th Anniversary $10
1994 and 1995 ....cover

Phillies Yearbooks

1949 Batting scene ....$175-$250
1950 Phillie and sheet music $150
1951 Six player drawings $400
1952 Color stadium photo ....$100-$125
1953 Phillie batter ....$35-$75
1954 Smiling Phillie (head only).........................$100
1955 Phillie pitcher ....$75-$100
1956 Robin Roberts, Richie Ashburn..................$150
1957 Ball wearing a Phillies hat...................$50-$100
1958 Hat on pinstriped background ....$75-$80
1959 Five balls, one with a logo...................$50-$75
1960 "New Faces of 1960," eleven photos $75

1961 First edition..$150
1961 Second edition $150
1962 Four balls and logo ....$60-$75
1963 Bat, ball and logo...$75
1964 First or second edition $75
1964 Third edition, Bunning, others $75
1965 Richie Allen, Jim Bunning $45
1966 Stadium photo...$45
1967 Child eating a hot dog $45
1968 Phillie ballplayers ....$35-$45
1969 Connie Mack Stadium ....$35-$45
1970 Veterans Stadium in tree bark ....$20-$40
1971 Veterans Stadium drawing $45
1972 Stadium, fans and players............................$30
1973 12 drawings, with Carlton $45
1974 12 drawings, with Carlton, Bowa................$20
1975 Schmidt, Carlton....................................$20-$30
1976 Drawings with Schmidt, Carlton ....$12-$15
1977 Larry Bowa..$12-$15
1978 Schmidt, Carlton, photos ....$7-$9
1979 Schmidt, Rose, Carlton............................$7-$9
1980 Schmidt, Rose, Carlton.................................$30
1981 World Series ring photo $30
1982 Schmidt, Rose, Carlton................................$10
1983 Centennial celebration...........................$9-$12
1984 Schmidt, Carlton, 20 others....................$6-$7
1985 Schmidt, Carlton, Samuel, Hayes.............$7-$10
1986 Mike Schmidt at bat ....$10-$12
1987 Schmidt, Samuel, others..............................$10
1988 Veterans Stadium photo $10
1989 Jordan, V. Hayes, Schmidt $10
1990 Photo of John Kruk's equipment...................$10
1991 Veteran's Stadium $10
1992 Kruk, Dykstra, Daulton, others $10
1993 Kruk, Dykstra, Daulton, others $10
1994 and 1995 ....cover

Pirates Yearbooks

1951 Forbes Field photo....................................$250
1952 Pirate with sword and pistol $125
1953 "Buc youngster" in sailboat........................$100
1954 Honus Wagner statue.........................$100-$175
1955 Pirate batter - "It's a hit!" $100
1956 Pirate swinging at "1956" ball....................$100
1957 Pirate winding up...............................$85-$100
1958 Pirate head between two bats $65
1959 Pirate with "Pa Pitt" $50
1960 Pirate in sailboat $50
1961 Pirate on a treasure chest $35
1962 Ball wearing bandanna and cap.............$35-$50
1963 Pirate batter...$35-$50
1964 Pirate sliding into third $15
1965 Manager Harry Walker and coaches $25
1966 Wraparound Forbes Field photo.................$25
1967 Clemente, Mazeroski, others......................$25
1968 Clemente, Stargell, others $25
1969 Wraparound Forbes Field photo..................$25
1970 Three Rivers Stadium...................................$75
1971 Three Rivers Stadium...................................$75
1972 Clemente, Stargell, others $20
1973 Clemente, Stargell, others $20
1974 Stargell, Parker, others $12

1975 Historical photos..$5-$6
1976 Yosemite Sam cartoon...............................$5-$6
1977 Pirate baseball cards ....$6-$7
1978...$5-$6
1979 Dave Parker..$20
1980 "The Family of Stars".................................$5-$6
1981 Lacy, Rhoden, Madlock, others....................$10
1982 Stargell, Madlock, others..............................$10
1983 Chuck Tanner...$6-$7
1984 Madlock, Pena, Ray, others..........................$5-$6
1985 Painting of Maz's '60 homer.....................$5-$9
1986 Leland, Pena, Ray, M. Brown ....$7-$12
1987 Centennial yearbook...................................$7-$12
1988 Bonds, Bonilla, Van Slyke, others ....$7-$12
1989 Photo of official N.L. balls......................$7-$12
1990 Van Slyke bat, Leyland uniform $10
1991 Pirates greats..$10
1992 Lockerroom/uniforms....................................$10
1993 Jay Bell..$10
1994 and 1995 ....cover

Rangers Yearbooks

1972.. None issued
1973.. None issued
1974.. None issued
1975.. None issued
1976 Rangers cowgirl on horse......................$15-$25
1977 Autographed Rangers ball ....$7-$15
1978...$12
1979 Jenkins, Oliver, others................................$5-$9
1980 Arlington Stadium $15
1981 Rangers hitter ....$5-$9
1982 Rangers baseball......................................$10-$12
1983 .... None issued
1984 George Wright..$10-$12
1985 Pete O'Brien equipment $10
1986 .... None issued
1987 .... None issued
1988 Ruben Sierra..$10
1989 .... None issued
1990 Rangers helmet rack ....$6-$8
1991 20 Years in Texas...$10
1992 Nolan Ryan..$12
1993 Arlington Stadium tribute.............................$10
1994 and 1995 ....cover

Nationals/Senators Yearbooks

1947 ....$250-$400
1948 .... None issued
1949 ....$150-$350
1950 ....$125-$300
1951 .... None issued
1952 Nationals' batter $100
1953 Capitol building and baseball.........................$25
1954 Bob Porterfield, Mickey Vernon..................$75
1955 National with four bats $75
1956 Clark C. Griffith memorial.........................$100
1957 Senators pitcher ....$75-$100
1958 Roy Sievers...$100
1959 ....$50
1960 Harmon Killebrew...$65

1961 "A Team is Born".............................$100-$150
1962 Washington Stadium $75
1963 Red cover with dedication.....................$30-$45
1964 "Off the Floor in '64"....................................$15

Nationals/Senators Yearbooks

1965 Senator signing autograph $25
1966 Senators in action $20
1967 Capitol and Washington Monument.......$25-$30
1968 Pitcher delivering ....$15-$20
1969 Ted Williams..$20-$30
1970... None issued
1971... None issued

Becomes Texas Rangers

Reds Yearbooks

1948 Ewell Blackwell, Ray Lamanno.................$150
1949 Bucky Walters, Harry Gumbert..................$200
1950.. None issued
1951 75th Anniversary of N.L. ....$100-$125
1952 Crosley Field ....$100-$125
1953 Reds mascot leaning on bat...........................$75
1954 Reds mascot swinging bat..............................$75
1955 Reds mascot rising on bat...............................$75
1956 Reds mascot swinging bat..............................$75
1957 Reds mascot in space ship.....................$60-$75
1958 Reds mascot in orbit...............................$40-$50
1959 Vander Meer, Lombardi, others $50
1960 Reds mascot, Goodman, Rixey $30
1961 Reds mascot running after ball.....................$40
1962 Reds mascot raising pennant.........................$40
1963 Reds mascot yelling "Charge" $65
1964 Reds mascot in action...........................$30-$40
1965 Reds mascot making catch....................$30-$40
1966 Reds mascot reaching for ball $30
1967 Reds mascot, Crosley Field $30
1968 Autographed team baseball ....$15-$25
1969 Perez, Rose, Bench, others ....$15-$25
1970 Johnny Bench $25
1971 Rose, Bench, Anderson, others $15
1972 Bench, Perez, other film strips $15
1973 Morgan, Bench, others $10
1974 Pete Rose sliding into home $20
1975 Joe Morgan..$30
1976 Morgan, Rose, Perez $10
1977 Morgan, Bench, Foster, others $12
1978 Pete Rose $10
1979 Bench, Perez, Griffey, Foster $10
1980 Reds equipment..$8
1981 Riverfront Stadium and baseball $8
1982 Binoculars on stadium seat..............................$8
1983 Red player signing autographs $8
1984 Bats and baseball equipment $8
1985 Pete Rose, Ty Cobb.................................$8-$10
1986 .... None issued
1987 Rose, Parker, E. Davis, others $12
1988 All-Star Game logo $10
1989 Baseball with Reds logo $10
1990 Red player with fans.......................................$10

1991 World Series trophy..$10
1992 Equipment collage..$10
1993 Barry Larkin's jersey....................................$10
1994 and 1995 ....cover

Red Sox Yearbooks

1951 Fenway Park...$250
1952 Red Sox sliding into home $150
1953..None issued
1954.. None issued
1955 Red Sox fielder.................................$115-$125
1956 Red Sox owners..$75
1957 Fenway Park..................................$75-$125
1958 Red Sox signing autograph.........................$65
1959 Red Sox pitcher $65
1960 Gary Geiger $65
1961 Red Sox batter $65
1962 Carl Yastrzemski $65
1963 ....$50
1964 ....$50
1965 Dick Radatz ....$40-$45
1966 Fenway Park ....$35-$45
1967 Scott, T. Conigliaro, Yastrzemski ....$50-$75
1968 Yastrzemski, Lonborg, D. Williams..............$40
1969 Fenway Park $40
1970 Lyle, Petrocelli, Yastrzemski $40
1971 Scott, Yastrzemski, Petrocelli ....$12-$15
1972 Carl Yastrzemski and fans.......................$7-$12
1973 Carlton Fisk and fans...............................$25
1974 Carlton Fisk, with Thurman Munson $10
1975 Foxx, Williams, Yastrzemski, Fisk $10
1976 Fred Lynn $10
1977 Carl Yastrzemski ....$10-$15
1978 Jim Rice, Carl Yastrzemski ....$12-$15
1979 Jim Rice...$10
1980 Fred Lynn $8
1981 Rice, Yastrzemski, Eckersley $10
1982 Yastrzemski, Evans, Rice, Lansford $10
1983 Carl Yastrzemski $10
1984 Jim Rice...$7
1985 Tony Armas $6
1986 Wade Boggs $8
1987 Roger Clemens and Fenway Park ....$7-$9
1988 Wade Boggs, Roger Clemens....................$7-$9
1989 Dwight Evans $10
1990 Mike Greenwell, Ellis Burks........................$10
1991 Pena, Clemens, Burks....................................$10
1992 Clemens, Reardon, Viola..............................$12
1993 Roger Clemens $10
1994 and 1995 ....cover

Royals Yearbooks

1969 Pitcher inside large "R" $25
1970 Piniella, Otis, others $10
1971 Piniella, Otis, others $10
1972 Catcher's mitt with face $10
1973 Mayberry, Splittorff, others.........................$10
1974 Otis, Mayberry, Splittorff.............................$10
1975 Killebrew, McRae, Mayberry......................$15
1976...None issued
1977...None issued
1978.. None issued

1979 .... None issued
1980 .... None issued
1981 .... None issued
1982 .... None issued
1983 Bronze Royals statue ....$7-$10
1984 Royals jacket and equipment....................$7-$10
1985 Division championship celebration.......$10-$12
1986 Hand wearing World Series ring ....$5-$10
1987 Royals championship pennants ....$5-$8
1988 Fireworks over Royals Stadium $10
1989 Royals player locker $10
1990 Royals in action $10
1991 Scoreboard replay $10
1992 Newspaper format $10
1993 Memorabilia collage......................................$10
1994 and 1995 ....cover

Tigers Yearbooks

1955 ....$300
1956.. None issued
1957 Tiger sliding into home ....$150-$175
1958 Tiger Hall of Famers, with Cobb................$150
1959 Tiger batting and logo $150
1960 Tiger Stadium..$100
1961 Tiger head and five baseballs ....$50-$100
1962 Tiger head and nine players..................$75-$100
1963 Tiger head...$100
1964 Tiger head...$65
1965 Bill Freehan $65
1966 Willie Horton...$65
1967 Denny McLain $45
1968 Al Kaline ....$40-$60
1969 World Series trophy...$45
1970 Tiger hat, bats, baseballs $10
1971 Billy Martin, Kaline, Horton $20
1972 Mickey Lolich $10
1973 Tiger infielder in action $10
1974 Tiger sliding into home $10
1975 Ron LeFlore...$12-$15
1976 75th Anniversary $15
1977 Fidrych, Staub, LeFlore.........................$10-$12
1978..$8-$12
1979 Alan Trammell, Lou Whitaker ....$8-$12
1980 Trammell, Whitaker, Morris, others.........$8-$15
1981 Trammell, Whitaker, Morris, others........ $7-$15
1982 Clubhouse photo with Gibson $12
1983 Hank Greenberg, Charlie Gehringer $8
1984 Morris, Whitaker, Trammell, others.......$10-$12
1985 World Championship trophy $8
1986 Sparky Anderson $10
1987 Tiger on top of baseball....................................$8
1988 Tiger face, "Eye of the Tiger" $8
1989 "Intend-a-Pennant"...$10
1990 Roaring into the '90s Tiger............................$8
1991 Whitaker, Trammell, Fielder, others $12
1992 Anderson, Stengel $10
1993.. None issued
1994 and 1995 ....cover

Twins Yearbooks

1961 Twins batters ....$125-$175
1962 Metropolitan Stadium...................................$100
1963 Harmon Killebrew ....$75-$100

1964 Gloved hand and baseball.............................$50
1965 Autographed Twins ball ....$40-$60
1966 Tony Oliva, A.L. Champions $45
1967 Killebrew, Kaat, Oliva............................$25-$35
1968 Jim Kaat, Harmon Killebrew..................$15-$25
1969 Killebrew, Carew, Oliva, others...................$20
1970 Rod Carew $20
1971 Carew, Killebrew, Oliva, others...................$20
1972 Tony Oliva, Harmon Killebrew....................$15
1973 Frank Quilici..$15
1974 Rod Carew...$20-$25
1975 Rod Carew..$15
1976 Rod Carew..$25
1977 Past Twins yearbooks.................................$10
1978 Rod Carew..$12
1979 Twins batting helmet $10
1980 Twins baseball cards $10
1981 20th Anniversary, Rod Carew ....$8-$12
1982 Metrodome $8
1983.. None issued
1984.. None issued
1985 Yearbook/scorecard..................................$6-$10
1986 25th Anniversary celebration ....$7-$10
1987 Twins uniforms...$10
1988 World Champions celebration..................$8-$10
1989 Viola, Puckett, Gaetti, Reardon....................$10
1990 Carew, Puckett, Oliva..................................$10
1991 Uniform collage..$5-$7
1992 World Series trophy.....................................$10
1993.. None issued
1994 and 1995 .... cover

White Sox Yearbooks

1951...$250
1952...$150
1953 Comiskey Park $125
1954 White Sox batter......................................$100
1955 White Sox batter..$75
1956 White Sox sliding into home $75
1957 White Sox fielder....................................$70-$75
1958 White Sox batter.....................................$60-$65
1959 White Sox mascot with hat..........................$125
1960 White Sox fielding.................................$50-$65
1961 White Sox pitching.....................................$50
1962 White Sox batting.......................................$35
1963 White Sox fielding..................................$15-$25
1964 Fireworks over Comiskey Park ....$30-$40
1965 White Sox uniform #80.........................$25-$35
1966 White Sox batter swinging $35
1967 White Sox in action....................................$20
1968 White Sox batter at plate $20
1969 Tommy John..$20
1970 White Sox in action $40
1971...................................... None issued
1972...................................... None issued
1973...................................... None issued
1974...................................... None issued
1975...................................... None issued
1976...................................... None issued
1977...................................... None issued
1978...................................... None issued
1979...................................... None issued

1980 .... None issued
1981 .... None issued
1982 LaRussa, Luzinski, Fisk $10
1983 All-Star Game with Fisk, others....................$10
1984 Hoyt, LaRussa, Kittle, Luzinski $10
1985 .... None issued
1986 Walker, Guillen, J. Davis, Baines $12
1987 .... None issued
1988 White Sox memorabilia...............................$10
1989 .... None issued
1990 Comiskey Park ....$5-$6
1991 Comiskey Park $5
1992 Good Guys Wear Black.................................$7
1993 Cooperstown Collection $5
1994 and 1995 .... cover

Yankees Yearbooks

1950 Big League Books $300
1951 Big League Books ....$175-$250
1952 Big League Books ....$150-$200
1953 Big League Books $150
1954 Yankee with World Series bats $150
1955 Three Yankees...$250
1956 Yankee sliding into home...........................$250
1957 Yankee batting...$250
1958 Yankee fielding $150
1959 Big League Books ....$125-$150
1960 Artwork, batter ....$100-$125
1961 Artwork, pitcher $150
1962 Yankee Stadium $75
1963 Yankee holding bats $65
1964 ....$65
1965 ....$65
1966 Two autographed balls $50
1967 Mickey Mantle $50
1968 Mantle, Stottlemyre, others $25
1969 Mantle, Stottlemyre, others $50
1970 Murcer, Stottlemyre, others.........................$75
1971 Murcer, White, others..................................$10
1972 Murcer, White, Stottlemyre..........................$20
1973 Ruth, DiMaggio, Mantle, Gehrig $20
1974 Bobby Murcer, Thurman Munson.................$20
1975 25th Annual with past yearbooks $15
1976 Yankees Stadium...$25
1977 Chris Chambliss $12
1978 World Series trophy......................................$15
1979 World Series celebration ....$10-$15
1980 Yankee Stadium $8
1981 Yankees Big Apple.......................................$15
1982 Winfield, Guidry, Gossage, others $8
1983 Billy Martin $7
1984 Yankee greats $15
1985 Maris, Mantle, Ruth, Gehrig $8
1986 Yankees MVPs..$6
1987 Gehrig, Mattingly, Mantle...........................$10
1988 Mattingly, Clark, Randolph...................$10-$15
1989 Yankees memorabilia...................................$10
1990 Don Mattingly $12
1991 Pitcher vs. batter...$10
1992 Don Mattingly $12
1993 Team photo...$10
1994 and 1995 .... cover

Media guides

Media guides, as we know them today, debuted in the late 1940s. They are presented to the radio, television and newspaper beat reporters who cover major league teams throughout the season. They are designed to provide the reporters with almost every imaginable kind of biographical and statistical tidbits to liven up a broadcast or story, from who's on first, to what his favorite hobby is. Farm teams are also covered and, coupled with the chronologies of team histories, have contributed to the guides' increases in page size from the 1950s to the 1990s.

In 1948, the public relations director for the Cleveland Indians issued a 55-page guide, considered the first true modern press guide for print, radio and television. The Cincinnati Reds, however, had issued a 32-page publication in 1934, to be used by members of the radio and print media. Prior to this, teams issued roster sheets, generally one sheet folded in half or into thirds and booklets. They contained the names of players in training camp, along with a schedule of exhibition games. Few, if any, photos were used.

The guides are not found on newsstands or bookstores; they are generally available only from the reporters, who sell or give them to memorabilia dealers, or from the teams, which in recent years have given them to season ticket holders or have sold them at the stadiums, by mail or during year-end promotional sales.

The press guide provides far more extensive coverage of the team but, although it does contain profile shots of the players and key people in the organization, lacks the colorful photographs that would appear in a team yearbook.

Angels Media Guides

Los Angeles Angels

1961 Player emerging from baseball $75
1962 Baby with Angels logo $75
1963 Angels logo, Rigney, Haney $75
1964 Angels in action $75
1965 Dean Chance/Cy Young Award $40

California Angels

1966 Anaheim Stadium $75
1967 League logos and Anaheim $40
1968 Anaheim Stadium and logo $30
1969 New-look A.L. West $30
1970 Press box and player .... $12-$15
1971 Four Angels in California .... $12-$15
1972 Del Rice .... $10-$12
1973 Nolan Ryan $20
1974 Anaheim Stadium $10
1975 Dick Williams $10
1976 Angels baseball cards $10
1977 Frank Tanana $12
1978 Tanana, Ryan, Rudi $15
1979 Anaheim Stadium .... $10-$12
1980 Don Baylor $7
1981 Angels equipment $6
1982 Angels logo $7
1983 Angels in action, R. Jackson $8
1984 Angels celebrating, R. Jackson $7
1985 .... $6
1986 DeCinces, Schofield, Downing $6
1987 Donnie Moore $6
1988 Wally Joyner, Brian Downing $10
1989 All-Star Game logo $10
1990 Angels stars, Joyner, Finley $10
1991 Pitcher in action $10
1992 Bryan Harvey $10
1993 Old Angels uniforms $10
1994 .... $7
1995 .... $5

Astros Media Guides

Houston Colt 45's

1962 45's logo $150
1963 45's logo $100
1964 Player art $100

Houston Astros

1965 New logo $75
1966 Catcher's mask $75
1967 Astroturf $50
1968 Astrodome art $40
1969 Baseball anniversary $30
1970 Team roster $20
1971 Locker room scene $20
1972 Ball, bat as pool cue $20
1973 Zodiac signs $15
1974 Big orange $10
1975 Equipment .... $8-$10
1976 Bicentennial logo .... $8-$10
1977 Player art .... $6-$7
1978 Art .... $6-$7
1979 Art .... $6-$7
1980 .... $6
1981 .... $6
1982 .... $5-$6
1983 .... $5-$6
1984 .... $5-$6
1985 .... $4-$6
1986 .... $10
1987 .... $10
1988 .... $10
1989 .... $10
1990 .... $10
1991 Helmet, bat, ball $10
1992 Craig Biggio, Pete Harnisch $10
1993 Luis Gonzalez, Jeff Bagwell $10
1994 .... $7
1995 .... $5

Athletics Media Guides

Philadelphia Athletics

1928 Roster sheet $125
1929 Roster sheet $125
1930 Roster sheet (elephant) .... $75-$100
1931 Roster sheet (elephant) .... $75-$100

1932 Roster booklet (elephant) $125
1933 Roster booklet (elephant) $100
1934 Roster booklet (elephant) $100
1935 Roster booklet (elephant) $100
1936 Team mascot (elephant) .... $55-$75
1937 Team mascot (elephant) .... $50-$75
1938 Team mascot (elephant) .... $50-$75
1939 "A's" and elephant .... $50-$75
1940 Pennant and elephant .... $45-$75
1941 "A's" and baseball .... $45-$75
1942 .... $40-$45
1943 Team mascot with flag .... $40-$60
1944 Team mascot with flag .... $40-$60
1945 .... $40-$60
1946 Connie Mack .... $45-$60
1947 .... $35-$60
1948 Baseball and elephant .... $35-$60
1949 .... $60-$100
1950 Connie Mack .... $60-$100
1951 .... $60-$100
1952 Team mascot (elephant) .... $60-$100
1953 .... $60-$100
1954 Eddie Joost................................ $60-$100

Kansas City Athletics

1955 K.C. Municipal Stadium....................$75
1956 Elephant logo....................................$75
1957 Elephant logo....................................$75
1958 Elephant logo....................................$75
1959 "A's" baseball...................................$75
1960 Baseball and A's hat...........................$75
1961 K.C. Municipal Stadium....................$75
1962 ....$75
1963 Player sliding, baseball......................$75
1964 1964 and A's logo $75
1965 1965 and A's logo $30
1966 1966 and A's logo $30
1967 1967 and A's logo $30

Oakland Athletics

1968 Oakland Stadium, ball, logo $25
1969 Bando, Campaneris, Hunter $20
1970 Player at bat $20
1971 A's logo and 1971 ....$15
1972 A's logo and 1972 ....$15
1973 A's logo and 1973 ....$15
1974 A's logo and 1974 ....$15
1975 A's logo and 1975 ....$15
1976 A's logo and 1976 .... $8-$10
1977 A's logo and 1977 .... $7-$10
1978 A's logo and 1978 .... $7-$10

1979 A's logo and 1979 ....$6-$10
1980 A's logo and 1980 ....$6
1981 Billy Ball baseball.........................$6-$7
1982 Running spikes....................................$6
1983 A's jukebox $6
1984 Oakland sportswriters $6
1985 Athletics memorabilia $6
1986...$10
1987 All-time Athletics team......................$10
1988 Batter hitting $10
1989 Canseco, Eckersley, Weiss.................$10
1990 World Series trophy $10
1991 Team memorabilia $10
1992 25th anniversary, A's greats............. $10
1993 Dennis Eckersley................................$10
1994...$7
1995...$5

Blue Jays Media Guides

1977 Toronto Exhibition Stadium..............$45
1978 Blue Jays pitcher $15
1979 Blue Jays in action $15
1980 Alfredo Griffin $10
1981 Blue Jays equipment $10
1982 Blue Jays in action, Bobby Cox $10
1983 Blue Jays equipment and hat..............$10
1984 Blue Jays in action $10
1985 Blue Jays logo $10
1986 Blue Jays 10th anniversary $10
1987 Bell, Barfield, Fernandez $10
1988 George Bell $10
1989 Blue Jays stars, McGriff.....................$12
1990 Blue Jays, McGriff, Gruber...............$12
1991 Dave Stieb $10
1992 Roberto Alomar................................$12
1993 World Series trophy $10
1994 ....$7
1995...$5

Braves Media Guides

Boston Braves

1927 Roster sheet $125
1928 Roster sheet $100
1929 Roster sheet $100
1930 Roster sheet $100
1931 Roster booklet, Indian head $100
1932 Roster booklet, Indian head $100
1933 Roster booklet, Indian head $100
1934 Roster booklet, Indian head $100

1935 Roster booklet, Indian head..............$100
1936 Roster booklet.....................................$75
1937 Roster booklet.....................................$75
1938 Roster booklet, "Bees" Baseball........$75
1939 Roster booklet.....................................$75
1940 Roster booklet, Casey Stengel............$75
1941 Roster booklet, Casey Stengel............$60
1942 Roster booklet, Indian head........ $45-$60
1943 Roster booklet, Indian head........ $40-$60
1944 Booklet, Bat, flag, airplane......... $40-$60
1945 Roster booklet, Indian Head....... $40-$60
1946 Booklet, Billy Southworth.......... $40-$60
1947 Booklet, Billy Southworth........ $60-$100
1948 Roster booklet, Bob Elliott....... $60-$100
1949 Booklet, Billy Southworth........ $50-$100
1950 Roster booklet, Braves Logo .... $50-$100
1951 Roster booklet........................... $50-$100
1952 Booklet, baseball, Indian head.. $50-$100

Milwaukee Braves

1953 State of Florida $125
1954 ....$125
1955 ....$125
1956 ....$125
1957 ....$100
1958 ....$100
1959 ....$100
1960 Pennant and Indian head.....................$75
1961 Pennant and Indian head.....................$75
1962 Pennant and Indian head.....................$75
1963 Pennant and Indian head.....................$75
1964 Aaron, Alou, Mathews, Spahn $75
1965 Felipe Alou, Bobby Bragan................$75

Atlanta Braves

1966 Player hitting $40
1967 Felipe Alou $40
1968 Hands gripping bat $30
1969 Players in action $30
1970 Hank Aaron $20
1971 Foot sliding into base..........................$20
1972 Players in action .... $12-$15
1973 Players in action .... $12-$15
1974 Players in action $10
1975 "Knit" baseballs...................................$10
1976 Dave Bristol.................................. $8-$10
1977 Braves hat .... $8-$10
1978 Atlanta-Fulton Co. Stadium................$10
1979 Phil Niekro, All-Stars .... $10-$12
1980 Baseball and stadium............................$8
1981 Bob Horner, Dale Murphy............. $6-$8

1982 Joe Torre $6
1983 Bedrosian, Murphy, Niekro, Torre..$6-$7
1984 Braves logo $6
1985 Dale Murphy, Bruce Sutter ....$6-$7
1986 Bobby Cox, Chuck Tanner..................$6
1987 Braves uniform..............................$5-$6
1988...$8
1989 Gant, Glavine, Perry, Smith, Thomas $10
1990 25th anniversary logo.........................$10
1991 Ron Gant, Dave Justice......................$10
1992 Greg Olson, John Smoltz $10
1993 N.L. Champions $10
1994...$7
1995...$5

Brewers Media Guides
Seattle Pilots

1969 Pilots logo ....$100-$125
1970 Pilots logo $100

Milwaukee Brewers

1971 Newspaper clipping.....................$30-$40
1972 State of Wisconsin $10
1973 Del Crandall, George Scott $12
1974 Team mascot $10
1975 Team mascot ....$8-$10
1976 Baseball glove ....$8-$10
1977 Robin Yount.......................................$15
1978 Larry Hisle $10
1979 George Bamberger $10
1980 Cooper, Lezcano, Thomas $6
1981 Cooper, Oglivie, Yount...................$6-$8
1982 Rollie Fingers................................$7-$8
1983 Kuenn, Vuckovich, Yount ....$6-$8
1984 County Stadium...................................$6
1985 Brewers uniform #85 ....$6
1986 Brewers pitcher in action $6
1987 Ted Higuera...$6
1988 Player running $6
1989 20th anniversary logo.........................$10
1990 Player running $10
1991 Team logo $10
1992 Phil Garner $10
1993 Pat Listach...$10
1994...$7
1995...$8

Cardinals Media Guides

1926 Roster sheet......................................$200
1927 Roster sheet.......................................$125

1928 Roster sheet $125
1929 Roster sheet $100
1930 Logo and 1930, sheet........................$115
1931 Roster sheet $115
1932 Logo and 1932, booklet....................$125
1933 Logo and 1933, booklet....................$125
1934 Logo and 1934, booklet....................$115
1935 Logo and 1935, booklet....................$100
1936 Logo and 1936, booklet......................$75
1937 Logo and 1937, booklet.............. $50-$75
1938 Roster booklet.......................... $50-$75
1939 Name and year, booklet.............. $50-$75
1940 Logo and 1940, booklet.............. $45-$75
1941 Logo and 1941, booklet.............. $45-$60
1942 Logo, Statue of Liberty.............. $45-$65
1943 Flag and logo, booklet .... $40-$70
1944 Victory V and logo, booklet .... $40-$70
1945 Logo and 1945, booklet.............. $40-$60
1946 Roster booklet............................ $35-$70
1947 Team logo, booklet..................... $35-$60
1948 Logo and baseball, booklet......... $35-$60
1949 Logo and baseball, booklet......... $30-$60
1950 Baseball and players $150
1951 25th anniversary of World Champs..$125
1952 Team logo $125
1953 "It's the Cardinals" $125
1954 Team logo $125
1955 Team logo $125
1956 Team logo $100
1957 Team logo $100
1958 Team mascot......................................$75
1959 Stan Musial $100
1960 Team mascot......................................$75
1961 Broglio, McDaniel, Sadecki, Simmons $75
1962 Stan Musial $75
1963 Player in action $60
1964 Boyer, Groat, Javier, White................$60
1965 Team logo $60
1966 Busch Stadium, team logo $60
1967 Busch Stadium $60
1968 World Series trophy............................$45
1969 Bob Gibson $45
1970 Joe Torre $20
1971 Bob Gibson, Joe Torre........................$25
1972 Red Schoendienst, Joe Torre $20
1973 Brock, Gibson, Simmons, Torre........$20
1974 Cardinals uniform and hat .... $10-$15
1975 Lou Brock and team logo .... $10-$15
1976 Busch Stadium.......................... $10-$15
1977 Lou Brock, Vern Rapp .... $6-$7

1978 Cardinals equipment ....$6-$7
1979 St. Louis Arch $6
1980 Keith Hernandez ....$6-$8
1981 Whitey Herzog ....$6-$8
1982 Whitey Herzog $7
1983 World Series celebration.....................$7
1984 Player running ....$5-$6
1985 Busch Stadium, St. Louis Arch.........$10
1986 Coleman, Herzog, McGee..................$10
1987 Whitey Herzog, former managers......$10
1988 N.L. Champions celebrate..................$10
1989 Action photos, Whitey Herzog...........$10
1990 Team logo $8
1991 Joe Torre $10
1992 Todd Ziele $10
1993 Team logo $10
1994..$7
1995..$5

Cubs Media Guides

1927 The year, booklet..............................$175
1928 The year, booklet..............................$150
1929 The year, booklet..............................$150
1930 The year, booklet..............................$100
1931 Rogers Hornsby, booklet....................$100
1932 Rogers Hornsby, booklet....................$125
1933 Team mascot, booklet $100
1934 Team mascot, booklet $100
1935 Team mascot, booklet $115
1936 Team mascot, booklet $75
1937 Team mascot throwing, booklet........$75
1938 Team mascot hitting, booklet............$85
1939 Mascot with pennant, booklet $65
1940 Roster booklet $65
1941 Jimmy Wilson, booklet $65
1942 Roster booklet $65
1943 Roster booklet $65
1944 Roster booklet $65
1945 Roster booklet $75
1946 Charlie Grimm, booklet $65
1947 Team mascot, booklet $65
1948 Roster booklet $100
1949 Roster booklet $100
1950 Roster booklet $100
1951 Roster booklet $100
1952..$100
1953..$100
1954..$75
1955..$75
1956..$75

1957 ....$75
1958 Team logo...$75
1959 Team logo...$75
1960 Team logo...$50
1961 Team logo...$50
1962 Team logo...$50
1963 Team logo...$50
1964 Team logo...$50
1965 Team logo...$50
1966 Team logo...$30
1967 Team logo...$30
1968 Team logo...$30
1969 Team logo...$30
1970 Team logo................................. $15-$20
1971 Team logo................................. $15-$20
1972 Team logo...$15
1973 Team logo................................. $10-$15
1974 Team logo...$10
1975 Team logo................................... $8-$10
1976 Team logo................................... $8-$10
1977 Team logo................................... $7-$10
1978 Team logo................................... $7-$10
1979 Team logo................................... $6-$10
1980 Team logo..................................... $6-$7
1981 Team logo..................................... $6-$7
1982 Team logo..................................... $5-$7
1983 Wrigley Field, celebration .... $5-$7
1984 Autographed baseballs..........................$6
1985 Frey, Green, Sandberg, Sutcliffe $10
1986 Cubs second baseman (Sandberg) $12
1987 Billy Williams $10
1988 Andre Dawson.....................................$10
1989 Wrigley Field.......................................$10
1990 Wrigley Field.......................................$10
1991 Ryne Sandberg......................................$12
1992 Wrigley Field..$10
1993 Wrigley Field..$10
1994 ....$7
1995 ....$5

Dodgers Media Guides
Brooklyn Dodgers

1927 Roster sheet $125
1928 Name and 1928, booklet...................$150
1929 Name and 1929, booklet...................$100
1930 Name and 1930, booklet...................$100
1931 Name and 1931, booklet...................$100
1932 Name and 1932, booklet...................$100
1933 Logo and 1933, booklet....................$100
1934 Logo and 1934, booklet...................$100

1935 Logo and 1935, booklet $100
1936 Logo and 1936, booklet ....$55-$75
1937 Logo and 1937, booklet ....$55-$75
1938 Logo and 1938, booklet ....$50-$75
1939 100th anniversary logo...............$50-$75
1940 50th anniversary in Brooklyn......$45-$75
1941 Team airplane......................................$85
1942 "V" logo......................................$45-$65
1943 Roster booklet ....$40-$65
1944 Roster booklet ....$40-$65
1945 Roster booklet ....$40-$65
1946 Roster booklet ....$35-$65
1947 Roster booklet ....$35-$70
1948 Roster booklet ....$35-$65
1949 Roster booklet $150
1950 "The Bum" $125
1951 "The Bum" $125
1952..$125
1953 "The Bum" $125
1954..$125
1955 Walter Alston $125
1956 Walter Alston $100
1957 Walter Alston $100

Los Angeles Dodgers

1958 Walter Alston $75
1959 L.A. Coliseum.....................................$75
1960 Dodger Stadium drawing $30
1961 Dodger Stadium $30
1962 Cartoon and airplane $50
1963 T. Davis, Drysdale, Koufax, Wills.....$50
1964 Players celebrating $40
1965 Championship pennants $40
1966 Mascot climbing mountains...............$40
1967 Mascot juggling crowns.....................$40
1968 Walter Alston $30
1969 100th anniversary...............................$30
1970 W. Davis, Osteen, Singer, Sizemore ..$30
1971 Dodgers in action $20
1972 Dodgers in action $20
1973 Dodgers in action $10
1974 Dodgers in action $10
1975 Steve Garvey.......................................$12
1976 Buckner, Cey, Garvey, Lopes, Sutton $14
1977 Tom Lasorda ....$9-$12
1978 Baker, Cey, Garvey, Smith ....$9-$14
1979 Dodger Stadium $6
1980 Team logo $6
1981 1980 highlights.......................................$7
1982 World Series trophy, Howe, Yeager $8

1983 Sax, Guerrero, Valenzuela....................$8
1984 Fireworks over Dodger Stadium .... $5-$6
1985 Bill Russell .... $6-$7
1986 Player swinging bat .... $4-$6
1987 Dodger Stadium.................................$10
1988 Baseballs...$10
1989 World Series trophy...........................$10
1990 100th anniversary pins and pins $10
1991 Name and 1991.................................$10
1992 Team stadium $10
1993 Eric Karros.......................................$10
1994 ....$7
1995 ....$5

Expos Media Guides

1969 Team logo.......................................$75
1970 Jarry Park.......................................$40
1971 Baseball $20
1972 Action photos, Jarry Park $20
1973 Montreal photos.......................... $10-$12
1974 Gene Mauch.....................................$10
1975 Players in action .... $8-$10
1976 Players in action .... $8-$10
1977 Cash, McEnaney, Perez, D. Williams ..$6
1978 Gary Carter, Andre Dawson $10
1979 Team logo..$6
1980 Locker with uniform............................$6
1981 Pennant $6
1982 Players in action $6
1983 Hands holding a bat $6
1984 Team hats..$6
1985 Olympic Stadium with dome...............$6
1986 Baseball and team logo.......................$6
1987 Olympic Stadium with dome.............$10
1988 20th anniversary bat $10
1989 Hands giving hi-five $10
1990 Team logo...$10
1991 Team logo...$10
1992 Dennis Martinez $10
1993 25th anniversary $10
1994 ....$7
1995 ....$5

Giants Media Guides

New York Giants

1927 Name and 1927, booklet...................$150
1928 Name and 1928, booklet...................$100
1929 Name and 1929, booklet...................$100
1930 Name and 1930, booklet...................$100

1931 Name and 1931, booklet $100
1932 Name and 1932, booklet $100
1933 Name and 1933, booklet $125
1934 Name and 1934, booklet ....$60-$100
1935 Name and 1935, booklet ....$60-$100
1936 Name and 1936 ....$55-$85
1937 Name and 1937 ....$55-$85
1938 Name and 1938 ....$50-$75
1939 New York World's Fair ....$50-$75
1940 Name and 1940 ....$45-$75
1941 Name and 1941 ....$45-$60
1942 Name and 1942 ....$45-$60
1943 Name and 1943 ....$40-$60
1944 Name and 1944 ....$40-$60
1945 Name and 1945 ....$40-$60
1946 Name and 1946 ....$150
1947 Baseball with 1947..........................$150
1948 Baseball with 1948..........................$150
1949 Baseball with 1949..........................$150
1950 Polo Grounds...................................$125
1951 Team logo $125
1952 Leo Durocher, a "Giant" $125
1953 Polo Grounds...................................$125
1954 Team logo $125
1955 The "Giant" $125
1956 Team hat..$125
1957 Team hat..$125

San Francisco Giants

1958 Candlestick Park drawing $150
1959 Players in action $100
1960 Team logo $80
1961 Giants in action $80
1962 Players in action $70
1963 Candlestick Park $70
1964 Candlestick Park $70
1965 Candlestick Park $70
1966 Baseball and team logo $65
1967 Team logo $45
1968 Team logo $45
1969 Team logo $45
1970 Willie Mays, Willie McCovey $25
1971 Year of the Fox $20
1972 "Best in the West".............................$20
1973 Candlestick Park $15
1974 Matthews, Bryant, Bonds..................$15
1975 Team logo $15
1976 Team logo ....$8-$10
1977 Joe Altobelli, John Montefusco ....$7-$10
1978 Players in action $6

1979 Blue, Clark, Giants management..........$6
1980 On deck circle with team logo..............$6
1981 Golden Gate Bridge.............................$6
1982 25th anniversary in city.......................$6
1983 Team logo..$6
1984 Team logo..$6
1985 Team logo..$6
1986 Team logo..$6
1987 Team logo..$6
1988 Team logo...$10
1989 Team logo...$10
1990 Team logo...$10
1991 Team logo...$10
1992 Team uniform.....................................$10
1993 Team logo...$10
1994 ....$7
1995 ....$5

Indians Media Guides

1927 Roster sheet.....................................$125
1928 Roster sheet.....................................$100
1929 Roster sheet.....................................$100
1930 Roster sheet.....................................$100
1931 Roster sheet.....................................$100
1932 Roster booklet...................................$100
1933 Roster booklet...................................$100
1934 Roster booklet...................................$100
1935 Roster booklet...................................$100
1936 Chief and 1936, booklet............. $55-$75
1937 Chief and 1937, booklet............. $50-$75
1938 Chief and 1938, booklet............. $50-$75
1939 Chief and 1939, booklet............. $50-$75
1940 Chief and 1940, booklet............. $50-$75
1941 Chief and 1941, booklet............. $50-$60
1942 Lou Boudreau, booklet............... $55-$60
1943 Lou Boudreau, booklet............... $50-$60
1944 Mascot and year, booklet............ $40-$60
1945 Mascot and year, booklet............ $40-$60
1946 Lou Boudreau, booklet............... $45-$60
1947 Team mascot, booklet................. $35-$60
1948 Team mascot with media........ $100-$150
1949 Team mascot.....................................$100
1950 Team mascot at bat............................$100
1951 Team mascot.....................................$100
1952 Garcia, Wynn, Lemon, Feller...........$100
1953 Press box and media..........................$100
1954 Al Rosen...$100
1955 ....$100
1956 ....$100
1957 Kirby Farrell......................................$75

1958 Bobby Bragan, Frank Lane...............$75
1959 Rocky Colavito...................................$75
1960 Tito Francona.....................................$75
1961 Jim Perry...$75
1962 Team mascot......................................$75
1963 Team uniform #20..............................$75
1964 Team mascot......................................$75
1965 Team mascot......................................$35
1966 Baseball with feather..........................$35
1967 Cleveland Stadium.............................$30
1968 Autographed baseball.........................$30
1969 100th anniversary, mascot..................$30
1970 Team mascot......................................$20
1971 Team hat, feather...............................$20
1972 Players in action................................$20
1973 Team logo..$10
1974 Team logo..$10
1975 Frank Robinson..............................$8-$10
1976 Baseball with feather....................$8-$10
1977 Player hitting.................................$6-$7
1978 Baseball, logo, glove......................$6-$7
1979 Team logo.......................................$6-$7
1980 Fireworks over stadium...................$6-$7
1981 Team logo.......................................$6-$7
1982 Cleveland Stadium.........................$5-$7
1983 Team logo.......................................$5-$7
1984 Team memorabilia..........................$5-$6
1985 Bert Blyleven, Andre Thornton...........$7
1986 Past team uniforms.......................$4-$6
1987 Joe Carter..$7
1988 Indians uniform #88...........................$6
1989 Candiotti, Farrell, Jones, Swindell.....$10
1990 90 Years of Cleveland baseball..........$10
1991 Jacoby, Jones, Alomar.......................$10
1992 60 years at Cleveland Stadium...........$10
1993 Memorabilia collage..........................$10
1994..$7
1995..$5

Mariners Media Guides

1977 Kingdome...$30
1978 Baseball with team logo.....................$10
1979 Kingdome...$10
1980 Mariners equipment.............................$6
1981 Maury Wills...$7
1982 Team logo..$6
1983 Gaylord Perry, team equipment...........$8
1984 Team logo..$6
1985 Beattie, Davis, Henderson, Langston...$7
1986 Team memorabilia................................$6

1987 Team logo.................$6
1988 Team bat $10
1989 Kingdome, baseball, logo $10
1990 A.L. baseballs, team logo $10
1991 Highlights $10
1992 Team logo..................$10
1993 Team logo/Kingdome.................$10
1994 ....$7
1995 ....$5

Marlins Media Guides

1993 Logo, player...............$20
1994 ....$10
1995 ....$15

Mets Media Guides

1962 First year..................$500
1963 ....$150
1964 Shea Stadium..............$100
1965 Mr. Met.....................$100
1966 Mass media................$100
1967 Donald Grant, George Weiss...........$100
1968 Gil Hodges, crowd shot $100
1969 Gil Hodges.................$100
1970 World Series ticket, action photos......$75
1971 Scoreboard.................$50
1972 Tom Seaver..................$50
1973 Yogi Berra and pennant...............$50
1974 N.L. Champs flag $50
1975 Mets general managers $20
1976 Joe Frazier $20
1977 Mets uniform #77..............$20
1978 Team logo, hat, glove $20
1979 Willie Mays $15
1980 Team logo...................$15
1981 New York City, baseball $15
1982 George Bamberger locker.................$15
1983 Tom Seaver, others...............$15
1984 Davey Johnson...............$15
1985 Tom Seaver, Mets stars $15
1986 R. Craig, Gooden, Shea Stadium.......$15
1987 World Series ring.............$15
1988 Shea 25th anniversary...............$15
1989 Frank Cashen, Howard Johnson $15
1990 Howard Johnson $15
1991 Bud Harrelson................$15
1992 Bonilla, Murray, Saberhagen, Torborg $15
1993 Team uniform #93..............$15
1994 ....$7
1995 ....$7

Orioles Media Guides
St. Louis Browns

1927 Name and 1927, booklet $150
1928 Name and 1928, booklet $125
1929 Roster booklet $125
1930 Roster booklet $125
1931 Sportsman's Park, booklet $125
1932 Sportsman's Park, booklet ....$70-$100
1933 Sportsman's Park, booklet ....$70-$100
1934 Roster booklet ....$65-$100
1935 Roster booklet ....$65-$100
1936 Rogers Hornsby, booklet............$75-$80
1937 Team logo, booklet ....$60-$75
1938 Roster booklet ....$60-$75
1939 Roster booklet ....$60-$75
1940 Fred Haney, booklet, ...$55-$75
1941 Statue and 1941, booklet............$55-$60
1942 Roster booklet ....$55-$60
1943 Team logo, booklet ....$50-$60
1944 Roster booklet ....$70-$150
1945 ....$150
1946 Team logo, booklet $150
1947 Baseball, logo...............$150
1948 Meet the Brownies $150
1949..................................$150
1950 Team logo $150
1951 Team logo $150
1952 Team mascot $150
1953 Team mascot $150

Baltimore Orioles

1954 Team mascot $125
1955 Team mascot $100
1956 Team mascot $100
1957 Team mascot $100
1958 Team mascot $100
1959 Team mascot $100
1960 Team mascot $75
1961 Team mascot $75
1962 Team mascot $75
1963 Team mascot $75
1964 Team mascot $75
1965 Hank Bauer $40
1966 Team mascot $40
1967 Dave McNally, Brooks Robinson $50
1968 Memorial Stadium.................$40
1969 View from press box $30
1970 Orioles dugout.................$25
1971 World Series celebration...............$20
1972 Team mascot with pennants...............$15
1973 Player face drawing...............$10

1974 Orioles award winners $10
1975 Players in action $10
1976 Team logo...$10
1977 Palmer, L. May, Belanger...................$15
1978 Earl Weaver................................ $10-$12
1979 25th anniversary hats $10
1980 Players celebrating.................................$6
1981 Orioles locker room...............................$6
1982 Team logo and mascot...........................$6
1983 Frank and Brooks Robinson $8
1984 World Series celebration $6
1985 Bumbry, Palmer, Singleton $7
1986 Eddie Murray, Cal Ripken.....................$8
1987 Cal Ripken Sr. $6
1988 Team logo..$10
1989 New team uniforms $10
1990 1989 highlights $10
1991 Team stadium drawing $10
1992 Team stadium $10
1993 Team stadium $10
1994 ....$7
1995 ....$20

Padres Media Guides

1969 Preston Gomez, stadium.....................$75
1970 Jack Murphy Stadium..........................$15
1971 Jack Murphy Stadium..........................$15
1972 Padres vs. Dodgers, July 3, 1971........$15
1973 Nate Colbert...$15
1974 Player hitting $10
1975 Players in action $8
1976 Randy Jones...$8
1977 Randy Jones, Butch Metzger................$7
1978 Batter, pitcher in action $6
1979 Roger Craig, Padres stars $6
1980 Jerry Coleman, Dave Winfield.............$8
1981 Frank Howard, stadium $7
1982 Dick Williams...$6
1983 Padres memorabilia $6
1984 Team logo, Ray Kroc memorabilia $10
1985 N.L. Champions trophy $10
1986 Team logo..$10
1987 Larry Bowa..$10
1988 Tony Gwynn, Benito Santiago $10
1989 Team logo, stadium $10
1990 Players in action $10
1991 Padres uniform, ball, glove.................$10
1992 All-Star Game.......................................$10
1993 Gary Sheffield, Fred McGriff.............$10
1994 ....$7
1995 ....$5

Phillies Media Guides

1927 Roster sheet..$125
1928 Roster sheet..$100
1929 Roster sheet..$100
1930 Team logo, sheet ....$75-$100
1931 Roster sheet................................$70-$100
1932 Team logo, booklet ....$65-$125
1933 Phillies golden anniversary ....$60-$100
1934 Team logo, booklet ....$60-$100
1935 Team logo, booklet ....$55-$100
1936 Team logo, booklet ....$55-$75
1937 Team logo, booklet ....$50-$75
1938 Roster booklet ....$50-$75
1939 Roster booklet ....$50-$75
1940 Roster booklet ....$45-$75
1941 Player hitting, booklet ....$45-$60
1942 Soldier with crossed bats............$45-$60
1943 Roster booklet ....$40-$60
1944 Roster booklet ....$40-$60
1945 Roster booklet ....$40-$60
1946 Logo, Shibe Park, booklet..........$35-$60
1947 Logo, Shibe Park, booklet..........$35-$60
1948 Logo, Shibe Park, booklet..........$35-$60
1949 Roster booklet ....$30-$70
1950...$150
1951...$30-$50
1952 Shibe Park ....$25-$50
1953 Player hitting ....$25-$50
1954 Robin Roberts ....$35-$50
1955 "Get Set To Go In '55" ....$20-$50
1956 Crowd photo..................................$20-$40
1957 Crowd photo..................................$20-$40
1958 Crowd photo..................................$20-$40
1959 Team logo ....$20-$40
1960 Team logo ....$20-$40
1961 Team logo ....$15-$40
1962...$15-$20
1963...$15-$20
1964 Team hat...$150
1965 Team hat...$100
1966 Team hat...$100
1967 Team hat...$75
1968 Team hat...$75
1969 Team hat...$50
1970 Phillies "P".......................................$50
1971 Frank Luchessi $35
1972 Team logo $35
1973 Steve Carlton/Cy Young Award $25
1974 Players in action $20
1975 Players in action $20

1976 Players in action $15
1977 Division champs pennant $15
1978 Fireworks over stadium $15
1979 Team logo..$15
1980 Team logo, baseball...........................$10
1981 World Series trophy...........................$10
1982 Basket of baseballs $10
1983 100th anniversary logo $10
1984 N.L. Championship trophy $10
1985 Hands holding bat.............................$10
1986 Home plate with team logo................$10
1987 Mike Schmidt, trophies $15
1988 Steve Bedrosian, Mike Schmidt $15
1989 Nick Leyva, Lee Thomas $15
1990 Ashburn, Carlton, Roberts, Schmidt...$15
1991 Catcher's mask, baseball $15
1992 Memorabilia collage..........................$15
1993 Phillies league leaders $15
1994 ....$7
1995 ....$5

Pirates Media Guides

1927 Roster sheet $175
1928 Roster sheet $100
1929 Roster sheet $125
1930 Pirate and 1930, sheet......................$100
1931 Pirate and 1931, sheet......................$100
1932 Pirate and 1932, booklet $125
1933 Pirate and 1933, booklet .... $60-$100
1934 Pirate and 1934, booklet .... $60-$100
1935 Pirate and 1935, booklet .... $55-$100
1936 Pirate and 1936..........................$55-$75
1937 Pirate and 1937..........................$50-$75
1938 Pirate and 1938..........................$50-$75
1939 100th anniversary, Pirate...........$50-$75
1940 Pirate and 1940..........................$45-$75
1941 Pirate and 1941..........................$45-$60
1942 Pirate, Remember Pearl Harbor.. $45-$60
1943 Pirate, Buy War Bonds, Stamps . $40-$60
1944 Pirate and 1944..........................$40-$60
1945 Pirate and 1945..........................$40-$60
1946 Pirate, Buy Victory Bonds..........$35-$60
1947 Billy Herman ....$40-$60
1948 William Meyer............................$40-$60
1949 40th anniversary ....$30-$60
1950 Baseballs.....................................$30-$50
1951 Logo and 1951.................................$125
1952 Baseball and 1952.............................$125
1953 Fred Haney $125
1954 Honus Wagner statue........................$125

1955 Baseball diamond and 1955 ....$125
1956 Pirate cartoon $125
1957 Pirate cartoon $100
1958 Danny Murtaugh $100
1959 Pirate cartoon $100
1960 Pirate cartoon $75
1961 Pirate cartoon $75
1962 Pitcher $75
1963 Baseballs $75
1964 Logo and 1964 ....$60
1965 Harry Walker.......................................$60
1966 Pirate cartoon $60
1967 Pirate cartoon $45
1968 Larry Shepard and coaches $45
1969 100th anniversary, Forbes $30
1970 Three River Stadium model $30
1971 Danny Murtaugh $25
1972 World Series celebration....................$25
1973 Clemente memorial $35
1974 Three Rivers Stadium.........................$10
1975 Championship Stars, logo $10
1976 Rennie Stennett $10
1977 Players in action $6
1978 Three Pirates $6
1979 Team uniform.....................................$10
1980 Willie Stargell $9
1981 Team logo $6
1982 Team hat $6
1983 Team logo $6
1984 Bill Madlock $6
1985 Tony Pena $6
1986 Three Rivers Stadium.........................$10
1987 100th anniversary logo......................$10
1988 Pirates memorabilia...........................$10
1989 Bonilla, LaValliere, Van Slyke $10
1990 Bonds, Bonilla, Drabek, Van Slyke ...$10
1991 N.L. Champions, logo $10
1992 Doug Drabek, Don Slaught $10
1993 Jim Leyland..$10
1994...$7
1995...$5

Rangers Media Guides

1972 Team logo $30
1973 Burke, Herzog, Short $20
1974 Billy Martin..$15
1975 Hargrove, Jenkins, Martin...................$15
1976 Toby Harrah, old-timers.......................$6
1977 Team equipment, hat............................$6
1978 Billy Hunter..$6

1979 Baseball and 1979...............................$6
1980 Rangers catcher $6
1981 Fireworks over scoreboard $6
1982 Baseball with logo $6
1983 Baseball glove $6
1984 Buddy Bell, others $6
1985 Team hat $6
1986 Arlington Stadium $6
1987 Bobby Valentine................................$10
1988 Team logo and baseball.....................$10
1989 Rangers uniforms...............................$10
1990 Home plate with team logo................$10
1991 Nolan Ryan.......................................$15
1992 Julio Franco $10
1993 Arlington Stadium $10
1994 ....$7
1995 ....$5

Reds Media Guides

1927 Roster sheet $125
1928 Roster sheet $100
1929 Roster sheet $100
1930 Team logo, sheet.......................$65-$100
1931 Team logo, sheet.......................$60-$100
1932 Team logo, booklet....................$60-$100
1933 Roster booklet..........................$60-$100
1934 Cincinnati Reds, booklet ....$55-$100
1935 Team logo, booklet....................$55-$100
1936 Team logo, booklet....................$55-$75
1937 Team logo, booklet....................$50-$75
1938 Bill McKechnie, booklet ....$50-$75
1939 1869 Reds ....$50-$85
1940 Team logo..................................$45-$85
1941 Baseball, champions pennant $125
1942 Team logo, eagle $125
1943 Team logo, eagle $125
1944 Team logo, hitter $125
1945 Baseball, eagle $125
1946 Catcher and batter...........................$125
1947 Baseball and eagle $125
1948 Team logo, batter.............................$125
1949 City, team logo $125
1950 Cartoon sportswriter $100
1951 75th anniversary logo $100
1952 Team logo, eagle $100
1953 ....$100
1954 ....$100
1955 Team mascot....................................$100
1956 Birdie Tebbetts $100
1957 Schedule $100

1958 Team mascot batting $100
1959 Mayo Smith......................................$100
1960 Fred Hutchinson...............................$75
1961 Fred Hutchinson, Bill DeWitt $75
1962 Team mascot $75
1963 Team mascot $75
1964 Team mascot $75
1965 Team mascot $75
1966 Team mascot $75
1967...$75
1968...$40
1969 100th anniversary logo $40
1970 N.L. hats..$30
1971...$30
1972 Baseball field....................................$20
1973 Sparky Anderson...............................$20
1974 Jack Billingham, Don Gullett.............$15
1975 Johnny Bench....................................$15
1976 Joe Morgan, MVP Trophy $20
1977 Johnny Bench....................................$20
1978 George Foster....................................$15
1979 John McNamara $15
1980 Riverfront Stadium.............................$8
1981 Players in action.................................$8
1982 Team uniform.....................................$8
1983 Russ Nixon...$8
1984 Team logo $8
1985 Riverfront Stadium.............................$8
1986 Pete Rose...$10
1987 N.L. logos..$8
1988 All-Star Game logo $8
1989 Autographed bats $8
1990 Lou Piniella.......................................$10
1991 World Series trophy $10
1992 Equipment $10
1993 Reds locker..$10
1994...$7
1995...$5

Red Sox Media Guides

1927 Roster sheet $125
1928 Roster sheet $100
1929 Roster sheet $100
1930 Roster sheet $100
1931 Roster sheet $100
1932 Roster sheet $100
1933 Roster sheet $100
1934 Roster booklet $150
1935 Roster booklet $100
1936 Roster booklet $75

1937 Roster booklet......................................$75
1938 Roster booklet......................................$75
1939 Jimmie Foxx, booklet .... $65-$70
1940 Team logo, booklet...................... $45-$65
1941 Fenway Park, booklet .... $45-$60
1942 Baseball bats and 1942, booklet . $45-$60
1943 Tufts College batting cage .... $40-$60
1944 Roster booklet............................. $40-$60
1945 Name and 1945, booklet............. $40-$60
1946 Player in action .... $35-$70
1947 World Series pennant, booklet ... $35-$60
1948 Joe McCarthy, booklet............... $45-$60
1949 Roster booklet............................. $30-$60
1950 Team mascot................................ $30-$50
1951 Old-timer, current player $125
1952 Fenway Park $125
1953 Team logo..$125
1954 Team logo..$125
1955 Team logo..$125
1956 Name and 1956.................................$125
1957 Player in action $125
1958 Red Sox media..................................$100
1959 Player in mirror................................$100
1960 Player on horse $100
1961 Baseball glove, ball $100
1962 Carl Yastrzemski, others $125
1963 Johnny Pesky $75
1964 Team logo...$75
1965 Team logo...$75
1966 Showerhead, team logo $40
1967 Team logo...$40
1968 A.L. Championship pennant...............$40
1969 100th anniversary $40
1970 Fenway Park......................................$20
1971 Red Sox stars $20
1972 Cheering fan $10
1973 Player in action $10
1974 Darrell Johnson..................................$10
1975 Fenway Park......................................$10
1976 A.L. Championship pennant...............$10
1977 Don Zimmer $10
1978 Carl Yastrzemski, Jim Rice $15
1979 Jim Rice $12
1980 Carl Yastrzemski $12
1981 Ralph Houk...$6
1982 Ralph Houk and players $6
1983 Dwight Evans, Bob Stanley................$6
1984 Wade Boggs, Jim Rice $8
1985 Tony Armas $6
1986 Boggs, Boyd, Buckner, Gedman $8

1987 Roger Clemens, John McNamara $6
1988 Dwight Evans, Roger Clemens $8
1989 Joe Morgan..$10
1990 Fenway Park......................................$10
1991 Ellis Burks, Tony Pena.....................$10
1992 Roger Clemens, Butch Hobson..........$10
1993 Red Sox baseball $10
1994...$7
1995...$5

Rockies Media Guides

1993 Silhouette $20
1994...$10
1995...$15

Royals Media Guides

1969 Team logo $60
1970 Player hitting.....................................$20
1971 Team bat rack....................................$20
1972 Royals Stadium $15
1973 Players in action $15
1974 Royals Stadium $15
1975 Player hitting.....................................$15
1976 Whitey Herzog $10
1977 Players in action $6
1978 Players hitting, pitching $6
1979 1976-1978 A.L. West Champions........$6
1980 Team logo, scoreboard........................$6
1981 Players in action, logo $6
1982 Team logo, pitcher $6
1983 Statue of hitter...................................$6
1984 George Brett and fans $8
1985 Scoreboard (A.L. West Champions)....$6
1986 World Series trophy $6
1987 Players in action $6
1988 Fireworks over scoreboard................$10
1989 Team equipment................................$10
1990 Players in action $10
1991 George Brett......................................$12
1992 Equipment $10
1993 25th anniversary $10
1994...$7
1995...$7

Senators Media Guides

1928 Roster sheet $125
1929 Roster sheet $100
1930 Roster sheet $100
1931 Roster sheet $100

1932 Roster booklet....................................$100
1933 Roster booklet....................................$100
1933 Capitol and 1933, booklet......... $80-$115
1934 Capitol and 1934, booklet......... $80-$100
1935 Capitol and 1935, booklet......... $75-$100
1936 Capitol and 1936...............................$75
1937 Capitol and 1937...............................$75
1938 Capitol and 1938.......................$70-$75
1939 Capitol and 1939.......................$70-$75
1940 Capitol and 1940.......................$70-$75
1941 Capitol and 1941....................$60-$65
1942 Capitol and 1942....................$60-$65
1943 Capitol and 1943.......................$60-$65
1944 Capitol and 1944...............................$60
1945 Capitol and 1945...............................$60
1946 Capitol and 1946...............................$60
1947 Capitol and 1947..................$55-$60
1948 Capitol and 1948..................$55-$60
1949 Capitol and 1949.......................$55-$60
1950 Capitol and 1950...............................$50
1951 Capitol and 1951...............................$50
1952 Capitol and 1952...............................$50
1953 Capitol, bat, baseball ....$45-$50
1954 Capitol, bat, baseball ....$45-$50
1955 Capitol, bat, baseball ....$45-$50
1956 Sportswriter $40
1957 Team mascot pitching.......................$40
1958 Golden anniversary of BBWAA $40
1959 Mascot blowing out candles .... $35-$40
1960 Home run celebration $75

Becomes Minnesota Twins

1961 Doherty, Quesada, Vernon $75
1962 Stadium and team logo $75
1963 Stadium and team logo $75
1964 Stadium and team logo $60
1965 Stadium and team logo $35
1966 Stadium and team logo $25
1967 Pitcher and baseball $25
1968 Batter and baseball $25
1969 Frank Howard.....................................$25
1970 Bob Short, Ted Williams....................$25
1971 Stadium and team logo $25

Becomes Texas Rangers

Tigers Media Guides

1927 Roster sheet $125
1928 Roster sheet $100
1929 Roster sheet $100
1930 Roster sheet $100

1931 Roster booklet $100
1932 Roster booklet $100
1933 Tiger head and 1933, booklet....$60-$100
1934 Tiger head and 1934, booklet....$55-$110
1935 Tiger head and 1935, booklet....$55-$115
1936 Tiger head and 1936....................$55-$75
1937...$50-$75
1938 Tiger head and 1938....................$50-$75
1939 Tiger head and 1939....................$50-$75
1940...$45-$85
1941 Briggs Stadium............................$45-$60
1942 Flag over Briggs Stadium ....$45-$60
1943 Tiger head and 1943....................$40-$60
1944 Tiger head and 1944....................$40-$60
1945 Tiger head and 1945....................$40-$70
1946 Tiger head and 1946....................$35-$60
1947 Tiger head and 1947....................$35-$60
1948 Tiger head and 1948........................$150
1949 Tiger head and 1949........................$150
1950 Tiger head and 1950........................$150
1951 Tiger head and 1951........................$150
1952 Tiger head and 1952........................$150
1953 Tiger head and 1953........................$150
1954 Tiger head and 1954........................$100
1955 Tiger head and 1955........................$100
1956 Ray Boone, Al Kaline $100
1957 Frank Lary.......................................$100
1958 Jim Bunning $100
1959 Tiger head and 1959........................$100
1960 Tiger head and 1960..........................$75
1961 Tiger Stadium....................................$75
1962 Players and team logo $75
1963 Team logo $75
1964 Team logo $50
1965 Team logo $40
1966 Team mascot and 1966 ....$40
1967 Team mascot and 1967 ....$40
1968 Team mascot and 1968 ....$40
1969 Team mascot $30
1970 Team mascot fielding.........................$20
1971 Team mascot throwing......................$15
1972 Team mascot fielding.........................$10
1973 Team mascot fielding.........................$10
1974 Team mascot sliding $10
1975 Team mascot in field..........................$10
1976 Team mascot pitching........................$10
1977 Team mascot catching........................$10
1978 Team mascot hitting...........................$10
1979 Team logo and 1979..........................$10

1980 Team mascot in action...........................$6
1981 Tiger jumping $6
1982 Team logo..$6
1983 Greenberg and Gehringer uniforms......$6
1984 Team mascot boxing.............................$6
1985 World Series trophy, logo.....................$6
1986 Team mascot in stadium $6
1987 Baseball and Tiger................................$6
1988 ....$6
1989 "The Press Guide" and logo $10
1990 Uniform "D".......................................$10
1991 "And Once Again" $10
1992 Alan Trammell, Lou Whitaker $10
1993 Tiger greats...$10
1994 ....$7
1995 ....$5

Twins Media Guides

1961 Metropolitan Stadium drawing.........$150
1962 Metropolitan Stadium..........................$75
1963 Player hitting $75
1964 Baseball and 1964...............................$75
1965 All-Star Game hosts $40
1966 Player fielding $40
1967 Twins uniform $30
1968 Pitcher throwing $30
1969 Metropolitan Stadium.........................$25
1970 Rod Carew, Twins stars......................$25
1971 Jim Perry...$25
1972 Minnesota media $25
1973 Rod Carew $25
1974 Baseballs..$10
1975 Rod Carew, Ty Cobb..........................$15
1976 Rod Carew, Harmon Killebrew, others . $15
1977 Old press guide covers........................$10
1978 Rod Carew $10
1979 Metropolitan Stadium...........................$6
1980 Twins baseball cards.............................$6
1981 Twins bats, hats, uniforms....................$6
1982 Metrodome $6
1983 Kent Hrbek $7
1984 Twins uniforms......................................$6
1985 All-Star Game logo................................$6
1986 25th anniversary logo $6
1987 Gary Gaetti, Kirby Puckett $8
1988 World Series trophy............................$10
1989 Kirby Puckett, Frank Viola.................$10
1990 Carew, Oliva, Puckett.........................$10

1991 Drawings of Carew, Killebrew $10
1992 Celebration, World Series trophy.......$10
1993 Kirby Puckett $10
1994..$7
1995..$6

White Sox Media Guides

1927 Roster sheet.....................................$125
1928 Roster sheet.....................................$100
1929 Roster sheet.....................................$100
1930 Roster sheet.....................................$100
1931 Roster sheet.....................................$100
1932 Roster sheet.....................................$100
1933 Name and 1933, sheet ....$60-$100
1934 Name and 1934, booklet ....$55-$100
1935 Name and 1935, booklet ....$55-$100
1936 Name and 1936, booklet ....$55-$75
1937 Name and 1937, booklet ....$50-$75
1938 Name and 1938, booklet ....$50-$75
1939 Name and 1939, booklet ....$50-$75
1940 Name and 1940, booklet ....$45-$75
1941 Ted Lyons, booklet ....$50-$60
1942 Jimmy Dykes, booklet................$45-$60
1943 Buy More War Bonds, booklet ...$40-$60
1944 Back the attack, booklet ....$40-$60
1945 Roster booklet ....$40-$60
1946 Name and 1946, booklet ....$35-$60
1947 Ted Lyons, booklet $100
1948 Team mascot and 1948, booklet $100
1949 Team logo and 1949, booklet...........$100
1950 Luke Appling $100
1951 Paul Richards $100
1952 Carrasquel, Fox, Minoso, Rogovin .. $100
1953 Player in action.................................$100
1954 Team mascot $100
1955 Team mascot $100
1956 Team mascot $100
1957 Team mascot $90
1958 Team mascot $90
1959 Team mascot $90
1960 Team mascot $75
1961 Name and 1961 ....$75
1962 Player in action....................................$75
1963 Player in action....................................$75
1964 Player in action....................................$75
1965 Pitcher throwing...................................$40
1966 Batter hitting $30
1967 Player in action....................................$25
1968 Hitter up to bat $25

1969 Batter hitting $25
1970 Fielder in action $10
1971 Chuck Tanner $10
1972 Player in action $10
1973 Allen, Tanner, Wood $10
1974 Team logo $10
1975 A.L. 75th anniversary $6
1976 Team logo $6
1977 Team logo $6
1978 Team logo, hitter $6
1979 Don Kessinger $6
1980 Fans in crowd $6
1981 Pitcher in action $6
1982 Team logo $6
1983 Sportswriter equipment $6
1984 Scoreboard, A.L. West Champs $6
1985 Comiskey Park.....................................$6
1986 Aparicio, Appling, Guillen $7
1987 New White Sox uniform #87...............$6
1988 Player in action $6
1989 Former White Sox stars $6
1990 Comiskey Park 80 years $10
1991 Catcher's mask, uniform, bat.............$10
1992 Team logo..$10
1993 Team logo $10
1994 ....$7
1995 ....$6

Yankees Media Guides

1927 Roster sheet .... $150-$175
1928 Roster sheet $150
1929 Roster sheet $150
1930 Roster sheet $150
1931 Roster sheet $150
1932 Roster booklet...................................$200
1933 Roster booklet...................................$100
1934 Roster booklet...................................$100
1935 Roster booklet...................................$100
1936 Joe McCarthy, booklet............. $70-$100
1937 Joe McCarthy, booklet............. $65-$100
1938 Joe McCarthy, booklet............. $65-$100
1939 Joe McCarthy, booklet............. $65-$100
1940 Joe McCarthy, booklet............... $60-$75
1941 Joe McCarthy, booklet............... $60-$65
1942 Joe McCarthy............................. $60-$65
1943 .... $45-$65
1944 .... $45-$60
1945 Victory "V" and 1945................. $40-$60
1946 Team logo and 1946 .... $40-$60
1947 Team logo and 1947 .... $35-$65

1948 Team logo and 1948.................. $35-$60
1949 Team logo and 1949.................. $30-$65
1950 Team logo and 1950.....................$150
1951 Team logo and 1950.....................$150
1952 Team logo and 1952.....................$150
1953 Team logo and 1953.....................$150
1954 Team logo and 1954.....................$150
1955 Team logo and 1955.....................$150
1956 Team logo and 1956.....................$150
1957 Team logo and 1957.....................$150
1958 Team logo and 1958.....................$150
1959 Team logo and 1959.....................$150
1960 Yankee Stadium $100
1961 Team logo and 1961.....................$100
1962 Team logo and 1962.....................$100
1963 Team logo and 1963.....................$100
1964 Yogi Berra and logo $75
1965 Team logo $40
1966 Yankee Stadium and logo $40
1967 Team logo and hitter $40
1968 Yankee Stadium $40
1969 Yankee glove and hat $40
1970 Mel Stottlemyre................................$25
1971 Logo and players in action $20
1972 Bobby Murcer, Roy White...............$20
1973 Yankee Stadium $20
1974 Whitey Ford, Mickey Mantle...............$25
1975 Bobby Bonds, Catfish Hunter $20
1976 Yankee Stadium $20
1977 Chris Chambliss, Thurman Munson ..$25
1978 Reggie Jackson, Babe Ruth...............$25
1979 Goose Gossage, Thurman Munson $20
1980 Dick Howser, Gene Michael.............$15
1981 Team logo $20
1982 Team logo $5
1983 Billy Martin with umpire $8
1984 Righetti, Yankee no-hitters $6
1985 Don Mattingly $7
1986 Guidry, Henderson, Mattingly, Niekro $7
1987 Lou Piniella and team $15
1988 Team logo $15
1989 Dallas Green.....................................$15
1990 Baseball bat and ball $15
1991 Maas, Mattingly, Meulens, Sax $15
1992 A tradition of great moments $15
1993 Collage $4
1994...$7
1995...$5

Programs

World Series programs

1903
Pittsburgh $15,000-$30,000
Boston $15,000-$30,000

1905
Philadelphia $7,000-$16,000
New York Giants $7,000-$10,000

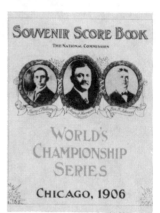

1906
Chicago Cubs $7,000-$10,000
Chicago White Sox $7,000-$7,500

1907
Detroit $10,000-$14,000
Chicago Cubs $7,000-$10,000

1908
Detroit $8,000-$12,000
Chicago Cubs $8,000-$12,500

1909
Detroit $8,000-$10,000
Pittsburgh $6,000-$10,000

1910
Chicago Cubs $5,000-$7,500
Philadelphia $5,000-$10,000

1911
Philadelphia $5,000-$6,000
New York Giants $3,000-$4,000

1912
New York Giants $2,000-$4,000
Boston Red Sox $1,500-$3,000

1913
New York Giants $2,000-$3,500
Philadelphia $2,000-$4,500

1914
Boston Braves $3,000-$5,000
Philadelphia $2,000-$3,500

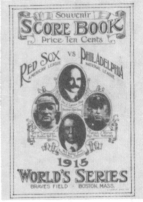

1915
Philadelphia $2,500-$3,500
Boston Red Sox $2,000-$3,500

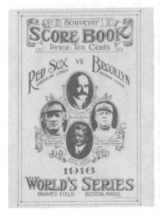

1916
Brooklyn $2,000-$5,000
Boston Red Sox $2,000-$4,000

1917
New York Giants $1,500-$3,500
Chicago $3,500-$5,000

1918
Boston Red Sox $5,000-$10,000
Chicago Cubs $3,000-$5,000

1919
Cincinnati $2,500-$4,000
Chicago $5,000-$9,000

1920
Brooklyn $2,000-$5,000
Cleveland $3,000-$7,000

1921
New York Yankees $1,500-$3,000
New York Giants $1,500-$3,000

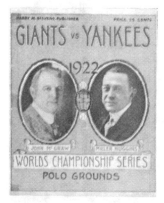

1922
New York Yankees $1,500-$2,500
New York Giants $1,500-$2,500

1923
New York Yankees $1,500-$4,000
New York Giants $1,500-$3,000

1924
New York Giants $1,500-$3,000
Washington $1,000-$2,000

1925
Pittsburgh $3,000-$5,000
Washington $500-$1,000

1926
St. Louis $1,000-$2,000
New York Yankees $700-$1,500

1927
Pittsburgh $2,000-$5,000
New York Yankees $2,000-$3,000

1928
St. Louis $1,000-$1,500
New York Yankees $1,500-$2,750

1929
Chicago Cubs $500-$1,000
Philadelphia $1,000-$1,500

1930
St. Louis $400-$750
Philadelphia $500-$1,000

1931
St. Louis $350-$750
Philadelphia $450-$750

1932
Chicago Cubs $700-$1,000
New York Yankees $750-$1,250

1933
New York Giants $700-$1,000
Washington $550-$700

1934
St. Louis $350-$600
Detroit $450-$600

1935
Chicago Cubs $350-$500
Detroit $500-$700

1936
New York Giants $200-$400
New York Yankees $375-$400

1937
New York Giants $275-$350
New York Yankees $250-$375

1938
Chicago Cubs $250-$350
New York Yankees $300-$400

1939
Cincinnati Reds $275-$350
New York Yankees $300-$350

1940
Cincinnati $300-$350
Detroit $250-$325

1941
Brooklyn $200-$400
New York Yankees $250-$300

1942
St. Louis $125-$250
New York Yankees $125-$250

1943
St. Louis $200-$250
New York Yankees $200-$250

1944
St. Louis Cardinals $175-$250
St. Louis Browns $200-$350

1945
Chicago Cubs $150-$200
Detroit $225-$350

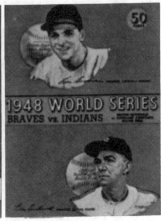

1946
St. Louis $175-$200
Boston $175-$225

1947
Brooklyn $250-$300
New York Yankees $175-$250

1948
Boston $150-$175
Cleveland $100-$175

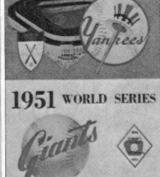

1949
Brooklyn $200-$250
New York Yankees $175-$200

1950
Philadelphia $125-$200
New York Yankees $150-$225

1951
New York Giants $150-$225
New York Yankees $150-$225

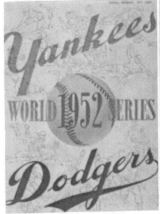

1952
Brooklyn $200-$275
New York Yankees $150-$200

1953
Brooklyn $225-$325
New York Yankees $150-$200

1954
New York Giants $200-$250
Cleveland $125-$200

1955
Brooklyn $250-$300
New York Yankees $150-$225

1956
Brooklyn $175-$300
New York Yankees $125-$200

1957
Milwaukee $100-$175
New York Yankees $100-$125

1958
Milwaukee $100-$175
New York Yankees $100-$175

1959
Los Angeles $75-$125
Chicago $150-$200

1960
Pittsburgh $100-$125
New York Yankees $75-$100

1961
Cincinnati $100-$125
New York Yankees $100-$150

1962
San Francisco Giants $150-$225
New York Yankees $75-$100

1963
Los Angeles $60-$75
New York Yankees $60-$75

1964
St. Louis $100-$125
New York Yankees $60-$75

1965
Los Angeles $30-$40
Minnesota $75-$100

1966
Los Angeles $40-$50
Baltimore $85-$125

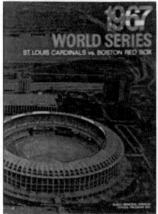

1967
St. Louis $100-$125
Boston $100-$125

1968
St. Louis $100-$125
Detroit $125-$225

1969
New York Mets $125-$150
Baltimore $50-$75

1970
Cincinnati $50-$75
Baltimore $25-$55

1971
Pittsburgh $75-$100
Baltimore $40-$50

1972
Cincinnati $50-$75
Oakland $60-$75

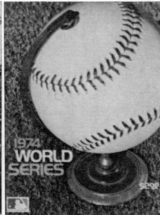

1973
New York Mets $20-$60
Oakland $60-$75

1974
Los Angeles $15-$35
Oakland $15-$35

1975
Cincinnati $25-$50
Boston $25-$50

1976
Cincinnati $15-$30
New York Yankees $20-$40

1977
Los Angeles $10-$25
New York Yankees $10-$40

1978
Los Angeles $10-$20
New York Yankees $15-$35

1979
Pittsburgh $10-$15
Baltimore $10-$15

1980
Philadelphia $10-$15
Kansas City $15-$30

1981
Los Angeles $10-$18
New York Yankees $10-$20

World Series Programs

1982
St. Louis $15-$25
Milwaukee $15-$25

1983
Philadelphia $15-$25
Baltimore $15-$25

1984
San Diego $10-$15
Detroit $10-$15

1985
Kansas City $10-$15
St. Louis $10-$15

1986
New York Mets $10-$15
Boston $10-$15

1987
St. Louis $10-$15
Minnesota $10-$15

1988
Oakland $10-$15

Los Angeles $10-$15

1989
San Francisco $10-$15
Oakland $10-$15

1990
Cincinnati $10-$15
Oakland $10-$15

1991
Atlanta $10-$12
Minnesota $10-$12

1992
Toronto $10-$12
Atlanta $10-$12

1993
Toronto $10
Philadelphia $10

1995
Atlanta $10-$15
Cleveland $10-$15

The Pittsburgh Pirates played the Cincinnati Reds in the 1974 National League Championship Series.

World Series programs

World Series programs have been published every year since 1903, except for in 1904 and 1994, when none were printed. A different program, each full of statistics, pictures, biographies and having special covers, was offered for both teams in the series until 1974. Since that time the programs have been a joint effort of the teams and have been distributed by Major League Promotion Corp. Robert D. Opie, a publisher from San Jose, Calif., reprinted classic programs in 1981 in his The Great World Series Program Collection. The programs' print runs are limited to 1,000 each. This information, and edition number, along with the indication that the program is a reprint, is contained within one of the last pages of the program. These programs generally can be purchased for between $10 to $20. The price range for original World Series programs in Excellent condition is from $10 to $15 for issues from the 1980s and 1990s, to $15,000-$30,000 for a 1903 Pittsburgh program or a 1903 Boston program. Programs for the teams which win the series generally are more valuable than those for the losers. World Series programs generally command higher prices compared to those from All-Star games, regular season games, record-breaking games and playoff games. The best programs are not torn or faded, unscored, and have the original inserts.

American League
Championship programs

1969 Baltimore...$60-$65
1969 Minnesota.................................$60-$125
1970 Baltimore................................$30-$50
1970 Minnesota..........................$100-$150
1971 Baltimore................................$30-$50
1971 Oakland ....$25-$50
1972 Detroit.................................$85-$115
1972 Oakland ....$25-$50
1973 Baltimore................................$30-$40
1973 Oakland ....$20-$50
1974 Baltimore................................$15-$40
1974 Oakland ....$300-$350
1975 Boston ....$40-$50
1975 Oakland ....$40-$50
1976 New York ....$10-$15
1976 Kansas City ....$7-$15
1977 New York ....$12-$15
1977 Kansas City ....$10-$20
1978 New York ....$7-$15
1978 Kansas City ....$10-$20
1979 Baltimore................................$60-$85
1979 California................................$7-$15
1980 New York ....$7-$10
1980 Kansas City ....$7-$12
1981 N.Y. at Oakland.....................$10-$20
1981 Oakland at N.Y.....................$10-$15
1981 K.C. at Oakland.....................$10-$20
1981 Oakland at K.C.....................$40-$60
1981 Milwaukee at N.Y. ....$10-$15
1981 N.Y. at Milwaukee ....$40-$50
1982 Milwaukee................................$60-$85
1982 California................................$7-$10
1983 Baltimore................................$7-$15
1983 Chicago................................$10-$20
1984 Detroit.................................$7-$15
1984 Kansas City ....$15-$20
1985 Toronto ....$25-$35
1985 Kansas City ....$25-$35
1986 Boston ....$7-$15
1986 California................................$20-$35
1987 Detroit.................................$6-$15
1987 Minnesota.................................$10-$20
1988 Boston ....$6-$10
1988 Oakland ....$75-$125
1989 Toronto ....$20-$30
1989 Oakland ....$20-$30
1990 Boston ....$20-$30
1990 Oakland ....$20-$30
1991 Toronto ....$20-$30
1991 Minnesota.................................$20-$30
1992 Toronto ....$20-$30
1992 Oakland ....$20-$30
1993 Toronto ....$10-$20
1993 Chicago................................$10-$20
1995 Cleveland................................$10-$20
1995 Seattle ....$10-$20

National League
Championship programs

1969 New York.................................$100-$350
1969 Atlanta.................................$40-$65
1970 Pittsburgh $300
1970 Cincinnati................................$50-$75
1971 Pittsburgh ....$30-$40
1971 San Francisco................................$1,000
1972 Pittsburgh ....$25-$40
1972 Cincinnati................................$20-$30
1973 New York.................................$50-$75
1973 Cincinnati................................$100-$175
1974 Pittsburgh ....$200-$250
1974 Los Angeles ....$150-$325
1975 Pittsburgh ....$7-$15
1975 Cincinnati................................$7-$15
1976 Philadelphia................................$7-$15
1976 Cincinnati................................$50-$75
1977 Philadelphia................................$7-$15
1977 Los Angeles ....$50-$75
1978 Philadelphia................................$7-$12
1978 Los Angeles ....$7-$15
1979 Pittsburgh ....$7-$12
1979 Cincinnati................................$12-$15
1980 Philadelphia................................$10-$15
1980 Houston ....$40-$50
1981 Houston at L.A.....................$10-$15
1981 Philadelphia at Montreal ....$15-$25
1981 Montreal at Philadelphia..............$20-$25
1981 L.A. at Montreal.....................$30-$40
1981 Montreal at L.A.....................$7-$30
1982 St. Louis ....$15-$25
1982 Atlanta.................................$7-$10
1983 Philadelphia................................$5-$15
1983 Los Angeles ....$60-$85
1984 Chicago ....$15-$20
1984 San Diego ....$20-$25
1985 St. Louis ....$25-$45
1985 Los Angeles ....$50-$60
1986 Houston ....$10-$20
1986 New York................................$15-$30
1987 St. Louis ....$6-$10
1987 San Francisco ....$15-$30
1988 New York................................$6-$10
1988 Los Angeles ....$6-$10
1989 Chicago ....$10-$15
1989 San Francisco ....$10-$15
1990 Pittsburgh ....$15-$20
1990 Cincinnati................................$15-$20
1991 Pittsburgh ....$10-$20
1991 Atlanta.................................$40-$50
1992 Pittsburgh ....$10-$20
1992 Atlanta.................................$40-$50
1993 Philadelphia................................$10-$20
1993 Atlanta.................................$10-$20
1995 Atlanta ....$10-$20
1995 Cincinnati................................$10-$20

All-Star Game programs

1933 Chicago ....$1,300-$2,500	1956 Washington ....$150-$200	1975 Milwaukee ....$40-$65
1934 New York N.L......$1,500-$3,000	1957 St. Louis.....................$150-$250	1976 Philadelphia ....$15-$25
1935 Cleveland ....$450-$600	1958 Baltimore...................$200-$250	1977 New York A.L. ....$7-$20
1936 Boston ....$3,500-$5,500	1959 Pittsburgh..................$200-$250	1978 San Diego.....................$30-$50
1937 Washington ....$500-$850	1959 Los Angeles ....$75-$100	1979 Seattle ....$10-$25
1938 Cincinnati...............$700-$1,000	1960 Kansas City ....$125-$175	1980 Los Angeles ....$20-$40
1939 New York A.L.........$800-$1,000	1960 New York A.L. ....$75-$100	1981 Cleveland ....$7-$20
1940 St. Louis ....$800-$900	1961 San Francisco.............$350-$500	1982 Montreal.......................$25-$40
1941 Detroit ....$600-$850	1961 Boston ....$300-$600	1983 Chicago A.L...................$10-$15
1942 New York N.L.....$4,000-$4,500	1962 Washington ....$150-$250	1984 San Francisco...................$5-$15
1943 Philadelphia...............$450-$700	1962 Chicago N.L...............$150-$200	1985 Minnesota........................$5-$15
1944 Pittsburgh ....$1,000-$1,250	1963 Cleveland ....$75-$125	1986 Houston...........................$5-$15
1945 ....no game	1964 New York N.L. ....$200-$325	1987 Oakland.........................$10-$15
1946 Boston ....$850-$1,100	1965 Minnesota....................$75-$125	1988 Cincinnati......................$10-$15
1947 Chicago N.L. ....$400-$550	1966 St. Louis ....$150-$250	1989 California.......................$10-$15
1948 St. Louis ....$300-$550	1967 California ....$100-$200	1990 Chicago ....$10-$15
1949 Brooklyn.................$900-$1,000	1968 Houston ....$75-$150	1991 Toronto ....$10-$15
1950 Chicago A.L. ....$250-$500	1969 Washington ....$50-$85	1992 San Diego......................$10-$15
1951 Detroit ....$150-$300	1970 Cincinnati ....$75-$150	1993 Baltimore ....$12-$15
1952 Philadelphia...............$150-$250	1971 Detroit ....$100-$200	1994 Pittsbyrgh...........................$10
1953 Cincinnati..................$175-$300	1972 Atlanta ....$20-$40	1995 Texas...................................$10
1954 Cleveland ....$175-$250	1973 Kansas City ....$150-$200	
1955 Milwaukee..................$125-$175	1974 Pittsburgh ....$20-$40	

Regular programs

Many of those who have attended a major league game have purchased a souvenir program to keep score in. Others have purchased them as reading or historical material, or perhaps to have it autographed by a player during pregame warm-ups or after the game, which increases its value. Although unscored ones are preferred, a scored program, if done neatly, does have an intrinsic value; it provides a history of what happened for that particular game, and can trigger fond memories for fans who were there. Programs from games when a record was broken or a significant event happened command premium prices.

Program design and attractiveness add to the value of a program, especially the front cover. Condition is an important factor in determining a program's value. Most collectors want them to be in nice condition, hence it will have a higher value than one which is torn, stained or missing pages. Values given in this guide are for programs in Excellent condition, those which show little wear and tear. Other factors in determining a program's value include scarcity and rarity (teams have been issuing them since the 1850s, primarily as vehicles for advertising revenue).

In general, here are the price ranges for regular season programs, with exceptions in parentheses:

Year	Price	Exceptions
pre-1900	$500-$750	(only Braves, Cardinals, Dodgers, Giants, Indians, Orioles, Phillies, Pirates, Reds, Senators and Tigers have pre-1900s programs)
1900-1910	$200-$500	
1910-1919	$75-$200	(certain Cubs, Indians, Reds, Senators and Tigers programs can be up to $250)
1920-1929	$35-$75	(certain Indians, Phillies, Pirates, Reds, Senators, Tigers and Yankees programs can be up to $100; 1920 Dodgers and Indians programs can be up to $135 each; Giants programs from 1921-24 are $80-$85)
1930-1939	$20-$35	(certain Indians, Phillies, Pirates, Tigers and Braves programs can be up to $40; certain Reds, Yankees and Dodgers programs have reached $50; Cubs programs from 1930-40 are $35-$50; A's programs from 1930-31 can be up to $75)
1940-1949	$15-$25	(certain Dodgers programs are up to $30; certain Yankees programs have reached $35)
1950-1959	$10-$25	(Baltimore programs from 1954-56 are $55-$75; 1953 Milwaukee Braves programs are $75; 1958 San Francisco Giants programs are $35; 1969 Seattle Pilots programs are $55)
1960-1969	$5-$25	(Houston Colt 45's programs can be up to $35; 1962 New York Mets programs are $60; 1961 Los Angeles Angels programs are $40; 1961 Minnesota Twins programs are $35; 1969 Montreal Expos programs are $30)
1970-1979	$5-$7.50	(1970 Milwaukee Brewer programs are $25; 1972 Texas Rangers programs are $20; 1977 Seattle Mariners programs are $15; 1977 Toronto Blue Jays programs are $12)

Periodicals

The Sporting News

The first issue of The Sporting News, an eight-page newspaper, was published by Alfred Henry Spink of St. Louis in 1886. Although other professional and collegiate sports are covered, baseball has always been TSN's primary attraction, with each weekly issue devoting coverage to every major league team. Often called the Bible of Baseball, The Sporting News has included box scores of all major league games, and has offered several attractive baseball-related photographic and artistic covers throughout the years. In the late 1960s, TSN began using color on its covers.

During the 1970s, most front covers were devoted to baseball players, with collegiate and professional football and basketball following. This continued throughout the decade, until the 1980s, when the paper began featuring more than one sport on its covers.

Those who collect TSNs, which should have their pages intact and be in at least in Very Good condition, often seek those which feature one player, members of one team, or superstars. Some people collect issues from an entire memorable season, or try to collect as many issues as possible, for the publication's historical information.

Pete Rose, Steve Carlton, Reggie Jackson and Carl Yastrzemski are among the leaders of those who have appeared on the cover the most times. Rose, Yastrzemski, Willie Mays, Hank Aaron and Roberto Clemente remain among the most popular players pictured.

Many times collectors have the covers autographed and framed. TSN did not start putting mailing labels on the front cover until the Nov. 28, 1981, issue. However, the labels are positioned so as to not detract from the cover photo.

TSN has also devoted space to the sports memorabilia hobby, with occasional ads for sports books, publications, baseball cards and memorabilia, and baseball card shows.

Common issues from the 1910s in Very Good condition sell for about $50 each; all issues thereafter until the 1960s fall in a range from $10-$30. Issues from the 1970s-1990s generally sell for $15 or less.

Issues during the regular season (April-October), as do commemorative, Opening Day, All-Star and World Series and superstar issues, generally have higher prices than those from the off-season (November-March) and have more investment potential.

These superstars are among the leaders in number of times appearing on selected TSN covers in the 1940s-1990s (Prices are given for some of the higher-priced issues):

Hank Aaron — 10/10/56 ($50), 09/24/58, 06/03/59, 07/20/63, 10/12/63, 11/23/63, 04/25/64, 07/03/65, 05/23/70, 07/29/72, 04/20/74, 08/02/82

Joe DiMaggio — 11/29/34, 10/29/36, 03/25/37, 04/29/37 ($100, with Doerr, Mungo, Gehrig), 09/30/37, 11/25/37, 12/28/39, 07/18/40, 10/24/40, 11/13/41 ($100), 02/25/43, 04/01/43, 06/17/43, 05/04/44, 01/31/46, 01/15/47, 12/03/47, 02/16/49, 04/13/49 ($200, with Ted Williams), 04/20/49, 07/06/49, 09/07/49, 01/04/50, 12/19/51 ($100), 12/26/51, 03/12/52, 02/02/55, 07/04/56 ($100, with Ted Williams, Musial), 03/22/61

Mickey Mantle — 01/03/51 ($100), 04/04/51, 04/25/51 ($300), 10/22/52, 11/12/52, 04/29/53 ($100), 06/17/53, 07/01/53, 09/14/55, 06/13/56, 10/10/56, 11/14/56, 11/28/56, 01/02/57, 01/23/57, 01/08/58, 03/29/61, 06/28/61 ($100, with Maris), 07/12/61, 09/06/61, 09/27/61 ($100, with Maris, Ruth), 03/07/62, 07/21/62, 09/22/62, 03/16/63, 04/06/68

Roger Maris — 05/01/57, 05/25/60, 07/13/60, 08/31/60, 11/16/60, 06/28/61 ($100, with Mantle), 07/12/61, 09/06/61, 09/27/61 ($100, with Mantle, Ruth), 10/11/61, 11/22/61, 01/03/62, 02/28/62, 04/29/67, 10/12/68

Willie Mays - 08/15/51, 02/24/54, 07/07/54, 07/21/54, 09/15/54, 10/13/54 ($100, with Antonelli, Avila, Lemon), 01/05/55, 02/26/58, 09/24/58, 01/28/59, 01/20/60, 03/07/62, 07/21/62, 03/16/63, 05/02/64, 07/11/64, 10/30/65, 05/21/66, 03/01/69, 01/17/70, 07/25/70, 07/17/71, 10/06/73, 07/19/75, 10/08/84

Stan Musial — 02/05/42, 10/15/42, 11/04/43, 12/09/43, 07/13/44, 11/08/45, 09/25/46, 11/27/46, 01/01/47, 02/12/47, 03/05/47, 08/20/47, 06/02/48, 12/08/48, 08/03/49, 02/28/51, 03/14/51, 10/10/51 ($200, with Feller, Fain, Roe), 11/14/51, 01/02/52, 05/12/54, 06/23/54, 07/13/55, 03/28/56, 07/04/56 ($100, with DiMaggio, Williams), 07/11/56 ($100), 02/06/57, 06/19/57, 07/10/57, 10/09/57, 05/14/58, 09/24/58, 11/05/58, 12/09/59, 09/28/60, 03/07/62, 11/24/62, 10/12/63, 10/07/67, 07/19/75, 06/20/81

Jackie Robinson — 09/11/46, 09/17/47 ($75), 11/23/49, 02/01/50, 04/19/50, 05/30/51, 12/10/52, 12/19/56, 01/16/57

Pete Rose — 10/26/63 ($30), 08/21/65, 04/20/68, 07/18/70, 07/28/73, 10/23/76, 5/20/78, 04/21/79, 07/21/79, 10/20/79, 12/29/79, 10/04/80, 06/20/81, 04/10/82, 07/25/83, 04/02/84, 09/16/85, 01/06/86, 05/26/86, 05/18/87, 04/24/89, 09/04/89, 03/12/90

Babe Ruth — 10/06/32 ($350, with Gehrig), 12/24/36, 06/23/38, 07/14/38, 10/13/38, 07/02/42, 08/13/42, 10/08/42, 10/28/43, 06/12/46, 04/23/47 ($300), 05/07/47, 03/24/48, 06/23/48 ($300), 08/25/48 ($500, death), 07/12/50, 07/26/50, 03/12/52, 09/26/56, 09/27/61, 04/20/74, 07/19/75, 07/09/84

Ted Williams — 04/13/39, 08/22/40, 06/19/41, 11/20/41, 01/01/42, 01/29/42, 12/31/42, 06/17/43, 01/31/46, 03/14/46, 05/23/46, 07/17/46, 09/18/46, 09/25/46, 11/20/46, 03/05/47, 12/31/47, 06/30/48, 04/13/49 ($200), 10/05/49, 11/30/49, 12/07/49, 12/28/49, 11/14/51, 08/05/53, 04/21/54, 07/04/56, 08/15/56, 02/20/57, 04/10/57, 05/15/57, 05/22/57, 07/10/57, 10/09/57, 01/01/58, 01/08/58, 08/27/58, 07/08/59, 12/09/59, 06/29/60, 08/17/60, 03/07/62, 01/22/66, 03/15/69, 07/19/75

The following is a list of covers with baseball players, or the main baseball story or photo contained within the issue. It wasn't until 1964 that cover photos and illustrations were standard on the front cover; prior to then, the front pages were designed like a regular newspaper.

1932

01/02/32 Bud Tinning	$30
01/14/32 Les Mallon	$30
01/21/32 Oscar Roettger	$30
01/28/32 Joyner White	$30
02/04/32 Horace Ford	$30
02/11/32 Lee Mangum	$30
02/18/32 Cubs prepare for Catalina Island	$30
02/25/32 Marv Olson, Bill Terry	$35
03/03/32 Sam Gibson, Waite Hoyt	$35
03/10/32 Edward Madjeski	$30
03/17/32 Leonard Koenecke	$30
03/24/32 William Brenzel	$30
03/31/32 Smead Jolley	$32
04/07/32 Burleigh Grimes	$35
04/14/32 Monte Weaver	$30
04/21/32 Harold Anderson	$30
04/28/32 Samuel Byrd	$30
05/05/32 William Rogell	$30
05/12/32 Walter Betts	$30
05/19/32 Ernie Lombardi	$35
05/26/32 Bill Dickey	$50
06/02/32 Fritz Knothe, Pie Traynor	$35
06/09/32 Jimmie Foxx, Bill Terry	$65
06/16/32 Mel Ott	$65
06/23/32 Dizzy Dean	$75

06/30/32 Lefty Gomez..$50

07/07/32 William Clark..$30

07/14/32 Larry French..$30

07/21/32 Oscar Melillo...$30

07/28/32 Lloyd Brown $30

08/04/32 Earl Grace...$30

08/11/32 John Jones $30

08/18/32 Ernie Orsatti $30

08/25/32 Baxter Jordan $30

09/01/32 Pepper Martin, Red Ruffing...................$45

09/08/32 Tony Freitas $30

09/15/32 Billy Herman, Joe Medwick $35

09/22/32 Evar Swanson..$30

09/29/32 Yankees vs. Cubs $150

10/06/32 Lou Gehrig, Babe Ruth $350

10/13/32 Joe Cronin, Hal Smith $32

10/20/32 Howard Maple..$30

10/27/32 John Hogan..$30

11/03/32 Del Bissonette $30

11/10/32 Fred Lindstrom..$32

11/17/32 George Susce...$30

11/24/32 George Grantham $30

12/01/32 Harry Taylor..$30

12/08/32 Babe Herman...$32

12/15/32 Travis Jackson $32

12/22/32 Hal Rhyne..$30

12/29/32 Sam West $30

1933

01/05/33 Henry Johnson...$30

01/12/33 Gus Mancuso...$30

01/19/33 Paul Andrews $30

01/26/33 Woody English...$30

02/02/33 Ossie Bluege..$30

02/09/33 Joe Moore, Honus Wagner......................$35

02/16/33 Harry Rice $30

02/23/33 Carl Reynolds..$30

03/02/33 Bud Parmelee $30

03/09/33 Bob Boken...$30

03/16/33 Beryl Richmond $30

03/23/33 Hal Schumacher, Luke Appling.............$35

03/30/33 Don Brennan $30

04/06/33 Frank Reiber..$30

04/13/33 Bill Werber..$30

04/20/33 Schoolboy Rowe $35

04/27/33 Clinton Brown $30

05/04/33 Carl Hubbell, Luke Appling...................$45

05/11/33 Pete Fox, Schoolboy Rowe $35

05/18/33 Russell Van Atta $30

05/25/33 Wally Berger $32

06/01/33 Jake Miller...$30

06/08/33 Bobby Coombs $30

06/15/33 Harley Boss $30

06/22/33 Bill McAfee...$30

06/29/33 John Jackson $30

07/06/33 First All-Star issue..................................$300

07/13/33 Chuck Fullis $30

07/20/33 Dib Williams $30

07/27/33 Rogers Hornsby, Sam Leslie..................$45

08/03/33 Dizzy Dean..$50

08/10/33 Carl Hubbell, Monte Pearson.................$40

08/17/33 D. Chapman (Nationals), Mel Ott.........$40

08/24/33 Dolph Camilli..$32

08/31/33 Dizzy and Paul Dean $50

09/07/33 Gus Mancuso...$30

09/14/33 Travis Jackson $32

09/21/33 Joey Kuhel..$30

09/28/33 Al Lopez..$32

10/05/33 World Series, Nationals/Giants............$125

10/12/33 Giants team photo $85

10/19/33 Babe Phelps $30

10/26/33 Fritz Ostermueller $30

11/02/33 Tony Piet $30

11/09/33 Red Rolfe $35

11/16/33 John Pomorski $30

11/23/33 Spud Davis $30

11/30/33 George Steinback $30

12/07/33 Reggie Grabowski....................................$30

12/14/33 Raymond Prim $30

12/21/33 John Stone $30

12/28/33 Joseph Glenn $30

1934

01/04/34 Lou Chiozza $28

01/11/34 Pete Fox...$28

01/18/34 Benny Tate $28

01/25/34 Glenn Spencer $28

02/01/34 Forrest Twogood $28

02/08/34 Edward Baecht $28

02/15/34 Henry Johnson...$28

02/22/34 Cy Blanton $28

03/01/34 Dick Ward $28

03/08/34 John Krider...$28

03/15/34 Giants' catchers $28

03/22/34 Otho Nitcholas, Lee Stine $28

03/29/34 Al Lopez..$30

04/05/34 Bill and George Dickey...........................$40

04/12/34 Augie Galan $28

04/19/34 Jack Rothrock $28

04/26/34 Johnny Pasek...$28

05/03/34 Al Spohrer $28

05/10/34 Daniel MacFayden $28

05/17/34 Carl Reynolds..$28

05/24/34 Joe Cascarella $28

05/31/34 Curt Davis $28

06/07/34 Linus Frey $28

06/14/34 Al Benton $28

06/21/34 William Urbanski.....................................$28

06/28/34 Billy Knickerbocker $28

07/05/34 Second All-Star issue $250

07/12/34 Johnny Broaca $28

07/19/34 Fred Ostermueller.....................................$28

07/26/34 Hal Lee $28
08/02/34 James Weaver................................$28
08/09/34 Alex Kampouris $28
08/16/34 Bill Myers.....................................$28
08/23/34 Zeke Bonura.................................$28
08/30/34 Buzz Boyle....................................$28
09/06/34 Jo Jo White...................................$28
09/13/34 Leslie Tietje..................................$28
09/20/34 Johnny McCarthy $28
09/27/34 Beryl Richmond...........................$28
10/04/34 World Series, Tigers/Cardinals $25
10/11/34 Cards win World Series $75
10/18/34 George Hockette..........................$28
10/25/34 Pat Malone $28
11/01/34 Oscar Melillo...............................$28
11/08/34 Lynford Lary $28
11/15/34 George Watkins............................$28
11/22/34 Dick Bartell, Johnny Vergez $28
11/29/34 Joe DiMaggio, Al Todd..........................$50
12/06/34 George Stumpf $28
12/13/34 Bill Dietrich.................................$28
12/20/34 Dutch Leonard.............................$28
12/27/34 Marvin Duke $28

1935

01/03/35 Wally Moses.................................$28
01/10/35 Steve Sundra................................$28
01/17/35 Roy Hansen $28
01/24/35 Hal Finney $28
01/31/35 Walter Millies...............................$28
02/07/35 Francis Parker...............................$28
02/14/35 Larry Bettencourt $28
02/21/35 Edward Durham............................$28
02/28/35 Eugene Schott...............................$28
03/07/35 Leon Chagnon...............................$28
03/14/35 Cliff Bolton..................................$28
03/21/35 Todd Moore..................................$28
03/28/35 Luke Sewell..................................$28
04/04/35 Clyde Hatter.................................$28
04/11/35 Babe Dahlgren..............................$28
04/18/35 Leslie Tietje..................................$28
04/25/35 Tony Lazzeri $35
05/02/35 Joseph Stripp $28
05/09/35 Johnny Whitehead.........................$28
05/16/35 Dolph Camilli...............................$30
05/23/35 Whitey Whitehead.........................$28
05/30/35 Bucky Harris, Bobo Newsom $30
06/06/35 Whitey Wilshere............................$28
06/13/35 Pep Young....................................$28
06/20/35 Leon Chagnon $28
06/27/35 Tommy Bridges............................$28
07/04/35 Cleveland All-Star issue......................$50
07/11/35 Slick Castleman.............................$28
07/18/35 William Myers $28
07/25/35 Pete Fox.......................................$28
08/01/35 Roy Henshaw $28

08/08/35 Lewis Riggs..................................$28
08/15/35 Jose Gomez $28
08/22/35 Joe Vosmik...................................$28
08/29/35 Joseph Bowman $28
09/05/35 Roxie Lawson...............................$28
09/12/35 Bud Hafey $28
09/19/35 Ivy Andrews.................................$28
09/26/35 Paul Derringer $28
10/03/35 World Series, Tigers/Cubs $95
10/10/35 Tigers win World Series................$75
10/17/35 Hal Lee...$28
10/24/35 William McGee.............................$28
10/31/35 Henry Coppola..............................$28
11/07/35 Eugene Lillard...............................$28
11/14/35 Dennis Galehouse..........................$28
11/21/35 Frank Pytlok $28
11/28/35 Whitey Whitehead.........................$28
12/05/35 Donald McNair..............................$28
12/12/35 Leroy Parmelee $28
12/19/35 Marcellus Monte Pearson.................$28
12/26/35 Monte Pearson..............................$28

1936

01/02/36 George McQuinn.........................$28
01/09/36 Frank Gabler................................$28
01/16/36 Jack Knott....................................$28
01/23/36 Roy Johnson $28
01/30/36 Babe Phelps..................................$28
02/06/36 Elburt Fletcher..............................$28
02/13/36 James DeShong $28
02/20/36 Orville Jorgens $28
02/27/36 Roy Hughes..................................$28
03/05/36 Samuel Leslie $28
03/12/36 Rudy York....................................$28
03/19/36 Alfred Todd..................................$28
03/26/36 James Oglesby...............................$28
04/02/36 Hank Greenberg $50
04/09/36 Lee John Norris $28
04/16/36 Albert Butcher..............................$28
04/23/36 Charlie Grimm $28
04/30/36 Bill and George Dickey..................$45
05/07/36 Bill Terry......................................$40
05/14/36 Dusty Rhodes................................$28
05/21/36 50th Anniversary issue...................$75
05/28/36 Frankie Frisch...............................$40
06/04/36 Steve O'Neill................................$28
06/11/36 Stuart Martin $28
06/18/36 Gabby Hartnett..............................$35
06/25/36 Monte Pearson..............................$28
07/02/36 All-Star Game issue $50
07/09/36 Augie Galan, Lou Gehrig......................$85
07/16/36 Jimmie Foxx, Lefty Grove...............$75
07/23/36 Dizzy Dean...................................$45
07/30/36 Jimmie Foxx.................................$50
08/06/36 Tom Yawkey.................................$28
08/13/36 Italo Chelini.................................$28

08/20/36 Rip Radcliff $28
08/27/36 Women baseball fans $28
09/03/36 Jimmie Foxx, Joe McCarthy $50
09/10/36 Bob Feller...$100
09/17/36 Branch Rickey $35
09/24/36 John McCarthy $28
10/01/36 Yankees (Gehrig) vs. Giants $200
10/08/36 Lou Gehrig, Yankees win Series...........$50
10/15/36 James Mosolf $28
10/22/36 Earl Averill, other Indians.....................$35
10/29/36 Joe DiMaggio, family.............................$25
11/05/36 Six comeback players.............................$28
11/12/36 Burleigh Grimes $32
11/19/36 American League officials $28
11/26/36 Lou Gehrig, Lefty Gomez $100
12/03/36 George Caster...$28
12/10/36 Winter meetings $28
12/17/36 Cookie Lavagetto $30
12/24/36 Cronin, D. Dean, Ruth............................$30
12/31/36 Hubbell, McCarthy, Rickey, Vander Meer
....$100

1937

01/07/37 Cuyler, Frisch, Goslin, others $40
01/14/37 M. Cochrane, P. Dean, other injured players
....$35
01/21/37 Ival Goodman..$26
01/28/37 Paul Dean, Branch Rickey $30
02/04/37 Vince DiMaggio, other minor leaguers..$28
02/11/37 P. Dean, Goslin, P. Waner.....................$40
02/18/37 Gabby Hartnett $28
02/25/37 St. Louis Browns $28
03/04/37 Giants in Havana $28
03/11/37 Bob Feller...$75
03/18/37 A's, White Sox in spring training $26
03/25/37 DiMaggio, Greenberg, others................$75
04/01/37 Jeff Heath $26
04/08/37 Pepper Martin...$28
04/15/37 Roxie Lawson...$26
04/22/37 Hefty ballplayers $36
04/29/37 DiMaggio, Doerr, Gehrig, Mungo $100
05/06/37 Mickey Cochrane, Hank Greenberg.......$50
05/13/37 Lamar Newsome $26
05/20/37 Gerry Walker...$26
05/27/37 Cubs trainer $26
06/03/37 Lloyd Waner..$35
06/10/37 Branch Rickey $28
06/17/37 Dick Bartell $26
06/24/37 Jimmy Dykes...$26
07/01/37 Griffith Stadium, All-Star issue $100
07/08/37 Paul Dean, Carl Hubbell $40
07/15/37 Gabby Hartnett, Charlie Root $28
07/22/37 Bucky Jordan...$26
07/29/37 Del Baker $26
08/05/37 Heinie Manush $28
08/12/37 John Wilson...$26

08/19/37 Gabby Hartnett, Mel Ott $40
08/26/37 Jim Turner $26
09/02/37 Rudy York $26
09/09/37 Joe Medwick $30
09/16/37 Kid fans $26
09/23/37 Lou Gehrig $100
09/30/37 Body parts of the stars - DiMaggio's eyes,
Gehrig's legs, etc. $75
10/07/37 Yankees vs. Giants $50
10/14/37 Yankees win World Series $100
10/21/37 Major League trainers $26
10/28/37 Ossie Vitt..$26
11/04/37 Pirate bosses $26
11/11/37 Charlie Gehringer....................................$35
11/18/37 Dodger bosses $26
11/25/37 Joe DiMaggio, Tony Lazzeri.................$60
12/02/37 Indian bosses $26
12/09/37 Milwaukee winter meetings $26
12/16/37 More winter meetings $26
12/23/37 Joe Medwick MVP celebration..............$30
12/30/37 J.T. Allen, Keller, Barrow $75

1938

01/06/38 Florida players at home $26
01/13/38 Like father, like son...............................$26
01/20/38 Grover Alexander HOF election $35
01/27/38 Cecil Travis $26
02/03/38 St. Petersburg players at home $26
02/10/38 August Mancuso......................................$26
02/17/38 Joe Gordon, other rookies......................$35
02/24/38 Harry Danning...$26
03/03/38 Lefty Gomez..$32
03/10/38 Cubs at Catalina Island...........................$26
03/17/38 Indians in New Orleans $26
03/24/38 St. Louis Browns players $26
03/31/38 Spalding factory making balls................$26
04/07/38 Vince DiMaggio, other Bees..................$28
04/14/38 Clay Bryant $26
04/21/38 First pitch presidents, Taft to FDR........$32
04/28/38 Bobby Doerr..$30
05/05/38 Bobo Newsom $26
05/12/38 Bob Feller in action $65
05/19/38 Three umpires..$26
05/26/38 Bill Dickey $35
06/02/38 Tot Pressnell..$26
06/09/38 Casey Stengel managing Bees $45
06/16/38 Sam Chapman, Dick Siebert $26
06/23/38 Babe Ruth, Dodger coach $125
06/30/38 All-Star issue...$150
07/07/38 Crosley Field $26
07/14/38 John Gee, Babe Ruth...............................$25
07/21/38 Fastest ballplayers $26
07/28/38 Ballplayers' wives...................................$28
08/04/38 Hank Greenberg $45
08/11/38 Ernie Lombardi $30
08/18/38 Major League musicians $26

08/25/38 Joe Glenn...$26
09/01/38 Lynn Myers..$26
09/08/38 Vance Page...$26
09/15/38 Miguel Gonzalez....................................$26
09/22/38 Red Ruffing...$35
09/29/38 Hank Greenberg $40
10/06/38 Yankee team picture...........................$100
10/13/38 Faces in World Series crowd, with Ruth$75
10/20/38 Major league scouts.............................$26
10/27/38 Off-season hunting, with Jimmie Foxx..$35
11/03/38 Jimmie Foxx, Ernie Lombardi $35
11/10/38 Mack's 1913 $100,000 infield $28
11/17/38 PCL presidents $26
11/24/38 Gehrig, Goslin, Simmons, vets $75
12/01/38 New Orleans winter meetings $26
12/08/38 MLB President Bramham $26
12/15/38 New Orleans winter meetings $26
12/22/38 New York winter meetings $26
12/29/38 Giles, McCarthy, VanderMeer..............$50

1939

01/05/39 Dizzy Dean, Paul Waner.......................$35
01/12/39 Baseball historians $24
01/19/39 Triumvirate to rule Yankees..................$24
01/26/39 New owners of Yankees........................$24
02/02/39 Dizzy Trout $24
02/09/39 Off-season player homes.......................$24
02/16/39 Tris Speaker $30
02/23/39 Rogers Hornsby, AA managers..............$28
03/02/39 Hot Springs, Ariz., Giants camp $24
03/09/39 Cubs at Catalina Island........................$24
03/16/39 Camilli, Lavagetto, Lazzeri...................$30
03/23/39 "Identify these Yankees".......................$24
03/30/39 Marty Marion $26
04/06/39 Browns photos......................................$24
04/13/39 ROY favorites, with Ted Williams $25
04/20/39 Bill McKechnie, Reds coaches $24
04/27/39 Zeke Bonura...$24
05/04/39 Barney McCosky...................................$24
05/11/39 Babe Dahlgren......................................$24
05/18/39 Traded Tigers, Browns..........................$24
05/25/39 Lon Warneke and father........................$24
06/01/39 Cardinals manager................................$24
06/08/39 Bill Cissell $24
06/15/39 Doubleday Field $24
06/22/39 Greenberg, Ruffing, Terry, others..........$40
06/29/39 St. Louis Browns firemen $24
07/06/39 All-Star issue $50
07/13/39 Players with complicated names $24
07/20/39 Johnny Mize...$30
07/27/39 Donald McNair.....................................$24
08/03/39 Paul Derringer, Bucky Walters $24
08/10/39 Tony Cuccinello....................................$24
08/17/39 Jimmie Dykes.......................................$24
08/24/39 Branch Rickey......................................$26
08/31/39 Boudreau, Mack, Vitt............................$28

09/07/39 Gabby Hartnett.....................................$26
09/14/39 Bob Feller...$60
09/21/39 AA pitchers $24
09/28/39 White Sox coaches $24
10/05/39 World Series, Yankees/Reds...............$100
10/12/39 World Series fans..................................$50
10/19/39 Yankee minor leaguers..........................$24
10/26/39 Leo Durocher, the Waners $50
11/02/39 Minor league managers $24
11/09/39 Hank Greenberg $26
11/16/39 Bullpen buddies....................................$24
11/23/39 Connie Mack alumni $26
11/30/39 Cincinnati winter meetings $24
12/07/39 Larry MacPhail.....................................$24
12/14/39 Winter meetings $24
12/21/39 Lefty Grove $28
12/28/39 DiMaggio, Durocher, MacPhail............$25

1940

01/04/40 Redbirds on the rise..............................$24
01/11/40 Yankee talent scouts.............................$24
01/18/40 Judge Landis...$24
01/25/40 Reds to stay in pink..............................$24
02/01/40 Judge Landis' minor league plan $24
02/08/40 Bucky Walters.......................................$24
02/15/40 Anaheim photos $24
02/22/40 Winter Haven, Giants camp $24
02/29/40 Nationals training in Orlando................$24
03/07/40 Dodgers in Belleair, Fla. $24
03/14/40 Reds in Tampa......................................$24
03/21/40 Indians in Ft. Myers, Fla. $24
03/28/40 Minor league managers $24
04/04/40 Hank Greenberg, others $30
04/11/40 Mickey Harris, Mickey Witek...............$24
04/18/40 Gabby Hartnett......................................$26
04/25/40 Managers' wives $24
05/02/40 Goose Goslin, others $26
05/09/40 Pee Wee Reese $28
05/16/40 Hal Newhouser......................................$28
05/23/40 Clyde Shown $24
05/30/40 Athletics infield $24
06/06/40 Vince DiMaggio, Paul Waner, others $26
06/13/40 Ballplayers' fathers $24
06/20/40 Ducky Medwick.....................................$28
06/27/40 Rollie Hemsley $24
07/04/40 All-Star issue $150
07/11/40 Fans make All-Star selections $26
07/18/40 DiMaggio, Greenberg, Mize $85
07/25/40 Billy Southworth $24
08/01/40 Female fans' clothing $24
08/08/40 Frankie Frisch.......................................$28
08/15/40 Barney McCosky....................................$24
08/22/40 Ted Williams $80
08/29/40 Learning from their dads $24
09/05/40 Gerald Priddy, Phil Rizzuto $30
09/12/40 Lou Novikoff, Lou Stringer $24

09/19/40 Texas League standouts $24

09/26/40 Jimmie Foxx......................................$40

10/03/40 Schoolboy Rowe, World Series $45

10/10/40 Reds win World Series.........................$65

10/17/40 Jimmy Wilson $24

10/24/40 Joe DiMaggio, Bob Feller.....................$75

10/31/40 Dodgers of yesteryear $24

11/07/40 Hank Greenberg $40

11/14/40 Frank McCormick $24

11/21/40 Ray Schalk...$24

11/28/40 Atlanta winter meetings $24

12/05/40 Charlie Grimm....................................$24

12/12/40 Winter meetings $24

12/19/40 Bob Feller..$50

12/26/40 Debs Garms..$24

1941

01/02/41 Bob Feller, Phil Rizzuto, others $80

01/09/41 Bill Klem $24

01/16/41 Leading relief pitchers.........................$24

01/23/41 William C. Tuttle $24

01/30/41 Ted Lyons..$24

02/06/41 Cardinal newcomers............................$24

02/13/41 Bobo Newsom......................................$24

02/20/41 Bobo Newsom, Al Simmons, others $25

02/27/41 Dodgers in Cuba.................................$24

03/06/41 Giants in Miami..................................$24

03/13/41 Reds in Tampa....................................$24

03/20/41 Browns, Bees in San Antonio $24

03/27/41 Front-office families............................$24

04/03/41 Minor league managers $24

04/10/41 Ty Cobb, Frankie Frisch, others...........$35

04/17/41 FDR throws out the first pitch..............$30

04/24/41 Bramham, Frick, Harridge, Landis $24

05/01/41 Bob Feller..$45

05/08/41 Larry MacPhail, others.........................$24

05/15/41 Baseball husbands and wives $24

05/22/41 Connie Mack $30

05/29/41 Branch Rickey....................................$28

06/05/41 Jimmy Dykes......................................$24

06/12/41 Brooklyn Dodgers issue $65

06/19/41 Ted Williams......................................$75

06/26/41 Appling, Boudreau, Reese, Rizzuto, others

....$45

07/03/41 Briggs Stadium, All-Star issue.............$85

07/10/41 Jeff Heath..$24

07/17/41 Sportsman's Park scoreboard.................$24

07/24/41 Foxx, Gehrig, Mize, others $80

07/31/41 300 game winners: Grove, Johnson,

Mathewson, Young, others.......................$50

08/07/41 Relief pitchers $24

08/14/41 Honus Lobert......................................$24

08/21/41 "All-Star Noisomatics" $24

08/28/41 Joe Gordon, Phil Rizzuto $30

09/04/41 Lon Warneke......................................$24

09/11/41 Hal Chase $24

09/18/41 Hal Chase $24

09/25/41 Joe McCarthy......................................$28

10/02/41 World Series issue...............................$75

10/09/41 World Champion Yankees $75

10/16/41 Baker, Roffe, Traynor, others $28

10/23/41 John Wyatt...$24

10/30/41 Minor league managers $24

11/06/41 Dolph Camilli.....................................$24

11/13/41 Joe DiMaggio......................................$100

11/20/41 Cobb, Hornsby, Jackson, T. Williams,

others $75

11/27/41 Jacksonville winter meetings $24

12/04/41 Lou Boudreau......................................$35

12/11/41 Winter meetings $24

12/18/41 Hank Greenberg $40

12/25/41 Rogers Hornsby....................................$35

1942

01/01/42 Ted Williams, others $100

01/08/42 Mel Ott...$40

01/15/42 Frisch, Gehringer, Hornsby, others $40

01/22/42 FDR to Landis: Keep Playing $30

01/29/42 Ted Williams......................................$75

02/05/42 Musial, others as minor leaguers...........$35

02/12/42 Jimmie Foxx, others............................$40

02/19/42 Mickey Cochrane, Bill Dickey, others...$35

02/26/42 Bill McKechnie $24

03/05/42 Yankee pitchers $24

03/12/42 Bruce Campbell...................................$24

03/19/42 Lou Boudreau, Burt Shotton $28

03/26/42 Mrs. McGraw, Mel Ott.........................$35

04/02/42 Ty Cobb...$45

04/09/42 Nine major league coaches...................$24

04/16/42 FDR: "Play Ball"................................$28

04/23/42 Vern Stephens $24

04/30/42 Player-managers: Boudreau, Cronin, Ott,

others $35

05/07/42 Bob Feller, Hank Greenberg, others $40

05/14/42 Navy photos $24

05/21/42 Four players wearing #3......................$24

05/28/42 Bobby Doerr.......................................$26

06/04/42 Three Phillies with glasses $24

06/11/42 Joe Gordon $26

06/18/42 Edgar Smith.......................................$24

06/25/42 Paul Waner...$26

07/02/42 All-Star issue: Gehrig, Foxx, Ruth........$50

07/09/42 Don Gutteridge...................................$24

07/16/42 Players at new positions $24

07/23/42 Chet Laabs...$24

07/30/42 Rollie Hemsley....................................$24

08/06/42 Lou Boudrea, others $30

08/13/42 Hitting pitchers: Ruth, others $60

08/20/42 Headhunting cartoon............................$24

08/27/42 Lou Novikoff caricature.........................$24

09/03/42 Reese, Rizzuto, others $30

09/10/42 Close plays $24

09/17/42 James Sewell $24
09/24/42 Joe Jackson...$50
10/01/42 World Series issue, Joe McCarthy $100
10/08/42 Famous "Babes:" Ruth, others $65
10/15/42 Stan Musial...$40
10/22/42 Ossie Bluege...$24
10/29/42 Mort Cooper $24
11/05/42 Branch Rickey $26
11/12/42 Bobo Newsom $24
11/19/42 Sam Breadon $24
11/26/42 Nick Altrock...$24
12/03/42 Judge Landis..$26
12/10/42 Al Schacht $24
12/17/42 Lefty Grove $28
12/24/42 Major leaguers' war efforts.....................$24
12/31/42 Southworth, Veeck, Williams, others ..$100

1943

01/07/43 Steve O'Neill...$22
01/14/43 Map of Northeastern U.S. $22
01/21/43 Sylvester Goedde $22
01/28/43 Bob Feller in Navy uniform $40
02/04/43 Ty Cobb as WWI captain $30
02/11/43 Cubs uniform changes.............................$22
02/18/43 Joe Cronin $22
02/25/43 Joe DiMaggio joins the Army $75
03/04/43 Griffith, Harris, Hornsby.......................$30
03/11/43 Bear Mountain (Dodgers training site) ..$22
03/18/43 Babe Dahlgren..$22
03/25/43 Paul, Lloyd Waner $22
04/01/43 Joe DiMaggio $60
04/08/43 Carl Hubbell $35
04/15/43 Franklin D. Roosevelt $30
04/22/43 Soldier reading sports page $22
04/29/43 Case, Johnson, Spence $22
05/06/43 Etten, Gordon, Johnson, Stirnweiss $25
05/13/43 "Front-Row Hits for Home Fronters" $22
05/20/43 Garbs, Simmons, Weatherly $24
05/27/43 Five new Cardinals................................$22
06/03/43 Jesse S. Flores $22
06/10/43 Dutch Leonard with rookies..................$22
06/17/43 Army (DiMaggio, Slaughter) vs. Navy
(Mize, Williams) $75
06/24/43 Dixie, Harry, G. Walker.........................$22
07/01/43 American flag...$22
07/08/43 Shibe Park: All-Star issue $24
07/15/43 Durocher, Newsom, Rickey $22
07/22/43 Dodger Bum, Giant $25
07/29/43 Gus Mancuso..$22
08/05/43 Mike Naymick...$22
08/12/43 Ford Frick $22
08/19/43 Nick Etten...$22
08/26/43 Dodger Bum playing with kids $24
09/02/43 Howie Schultz, Dodgers........................$22
09/09/43 Beauregard, W. Johnson $22
09/16/43 Cardinals team photo.............................$75

09/23/43 World Series issue, Mort Cooper $45
09/30/43 Joe McCarthy, Billy Southworth............$25
10/07/43 Red Barber $35
10/14/43 Joe McCarthy, World Series $95
10/21/43 "Break up the Yanks!" $75
10/28/43 Judge Landis, Babe Ruth.......................$65
11/04/43 Stan Musial..$50
12/02/43 Winter meetings $22
12/09/43 Frisch, Musial, Walker................................$35
12/16/43 Herb Pennock $22
12/30/43 Chandler, Griffith, McCarthy, others $60

1944

01/06/44 Carl Hubbell $35
01/13/44 Wrigley Field, Los Angeles $22
01/20/44 Branch Rickey, other owners $25
01/27/44 Babe Dahlgren, Bobo Newsom............$22
02/03/44 Baseball team owners...........................$22
02/10/44 "Little Lamzeetivee" $22
02/17/44 Clark Griffith...$25
02/24/44 Ty Cobb...$45
03/02/44 1944 A.L. schedule $22
03/09/44 1994 N.L. schedule $22
03/16/44 Durocher, C. Mack, McCarthy..............$30
03/23/44 Ralph Siewart, Joe Wood.......................$22
03/30/44 Giants jogging $22
04/06/44 Spring training photos $22
04/13/44 Full page soldier cartoon $22
04/20/44 Stadium photo $22
04/27/44 Servicemen at a game...............................$22
05/04/44 Joe DiMaggio in an Army helmet..........$60
05/11/44 Scorecard vendor......................................$22
05/18/44 Nick Etten...$22
05/25/44 No-hit Hall of Fame $25
06/01/44 Thomas Edison and night ball...............$30
06/08/44 George Sisler...$22
06/15/44 Dixie Walker $22
06/22/44 Cy Young $40
06/29/44 Browns mascot $22
07/06/44 Pirates mascot, All-Star issue.................$75
07/13/44 Stan Musial, Dixie Walker.......................$50
07/20/44 Dodger Bum $22
07/27/44 Team mascots playing cards $22
08/03/44 Connie Mack $25
08/10/44 Browns mascot $22
08/17/44 Mel Ott...$35
08/24/44 Browns mascot $22
08/31/44 Hal Newhouser, Dizzy Trout $30
09/07/44 Browns mascot $22
09/14/44 A.L. pennant race $22
09/21/44 Newhouser, O'Neill, Trout $28
09/28/44 Cardinals end season $22
10/05/44 Browns mascot $65
10/12/44 Browns mascot getting shot $50
10/19/44 Marty Marion, Vern Stephens.................$35
11/02/44 Doc Blanchard...$26

11/09/44 Dodger Bum $24
11/23/44 Marty Marion $24
11/30/44 Judge Landis dies $35
12/14/44 Baseball winter meetings $22
12/28/44 Marty Marion, Luke Sewell, others $50

1945

01/04/45 Dodger Bum "This IS Next Year!" $25
01/11/45 Hall of Fame balloting process $20
01/18/45 Willard Mullin cartoon............................$20
01/25/45 American Legion cartoon.....................$20
02/01/45 Larry MacPhail..................................$20
02/08/45 Abbott and Costello, Durocher, McCarthy, Ott..$35
02/15/45 Commissioner search committee $20
02/22/45 Search for a new commissioner $20
03/01/45 Dodger Bum $22
03/08/45 Lou Novikoff.................................$20
03/15/45 1945 A.L. schedule $20
03/22/45 1945 N.L. schedule $20
03/29/45 Larry MacPhail.............................$20
04/05/45 Leo Durocher $25
04/12/45 Browns mascot $20
04/19/45 Presidents at baseball games $20
04/26/45 Yankee and Brown mascots.................$20
05/03/45 Happy Chandler, Judge Landis $22
05/10/45 New York Giants............................$20
05/17/45 Phillie rhubarb $20
05/24/45 Giants mascot $22
05/31/45 Mort Cooper $20
06/07/45 Dave Ferriss $20
06/14/45 Howard Schultz $20
06/21/45 Indian with tomahawk.....................$20
06/28/45 Dodger Bum $22
07/05/45 Hank Greenberg $35
07/12/45 Fans discuss the All-Star Game $50
07/19/45 Al Benton $20
07/26/45 Charlie Grimm $20
08/02/45 Larry MacPhail.............................$20
08/09/45 Major League managers.......................$20
08/16/45 Al Rosen $25
08/23/45 Joe McCarthy $24
08/30/45 Bob Feller $35
09/06/45 Leo Durocher $25
09/13/45 Browns, Indians, Senators, Tigers, Yankees mascots $20
09/20/45 Dick Fowler...................................$20
09/27/45 Happy Chandler $22
10/04/45 Briggs Stadium, D. Eisenhower $85
10/11/45 Tiger licking Cub's bones, World Series $70
10/25/45 Clarence "Ace" Parker $20
11/01/45 Bill Veeck....................................$25
11/08/45 Breadon, Musial, Slaughter, others $35
11/15/45 Happy Chandler $22
11/29/45 Happy Chandler, Muddy Ruel $20

12/06/45 Player returning from war $25
12/13/45 Two baseball owners............................$20
12/27/45 Hal Newhouser, Player of the Year.......$30

1946

01/03/46 Hall of Fame elections $22
01/10/46 Sam Breadon..................................$20
01/17/46 Larry MacPhail...............................$22
01/24/46 Happy Chandler $22
01/31/46 Joe DiMaggio, Ted Williams $50
02/07/46 Mel Ott $25
02/14/46 Grapefruit League $20
02/21/46 Hank Greenberg $30
02/28/46 Mexican League $20
03/07/46 Bob Feller....................................$30
03/14/46 Ted Williams.................................$50
03/21/46 Leo Durocher $25
03/28/46 Cardinal outfielders $20
04/04/46 Johnny Mize $25
04/11/46 Mickey Owen $20
04/18/46 Peacetime baseball begins.....................$50
04/25/46 Spud Chandler................................$25
05/02/46 Tommy Henrich $25
05/09/46 Joe Cronin, Joe McCarthy......................$25
05/16/46 1946 Red Sox sluggers.......................$25
05/23/46 Ted Williams.................................$30
06/05/46 Bill Dickey, Ted Lyons $28
06/12/46 Babe Ruth....................................$50
06/19/46 Red Sox tear apart the league.................$20
06/26/46 Joe Garagiola................................$25
07/03/46 Veeck buys the Cleveland Indians $20
07/10/46 Bill Veeck, All-Star issue.....................$50
07/17/46 Ted Williams $40
07/24/46 Larry MacPhail...............................$20
07/31/46 Hal Newhouser................................$25
08/07/46 Dizzy Dean...................................$25
08/14/46 Mickey Owen, Mexican League $20
08/21/46 Mickey Owen $20
08/28/46 Feller's 98 mph pitch $30
09/04/46 Larry MacPhail...............................$20
09/11/46 Jackie Robinson $50
09/18/46 Mickey Vernon, Ted Williams...............$30
09/25/46 Stan Musial, Ted Williams....................$60
10/02/46 Eddie Collins $20
10/09/46 Frankie Frisch, World Series.................$60
10/16/46 DiMaggio, Gordon, MacPhail.................$50
10/23/46 Harry "The Cat" Brecheen, World Series $50
10/30/46 TSN 60-year chronology....................$250
11/06/46 Bob Feller....................................$25
11/13/46 Bucky Harris $20
11/20/46 Ted Williams MVP $50
11/27/46 Stan Musial MVP.............................$50
12/04/46 Leo Durocher $40
12/18/46 Walter Johnson...............................$40
12/25/46 Billy Evans $20

1947

01/01/47 Dyer, Musial, Yawkey $60
01/08/47 Little stars..$20
01/15/47 Joe DiMaggio $40
01/22/47 Branch Rickey $30
01/29/47 Bob Feller..$30
02/05/47 Pepper Martin $25
02/12/47 Sam Breadon, Stan Musial $25
02/19/47 Hank Greenberg $25
02/26/47 Hornsby, McKechnie, Speaker $25
03/05/47 Stan Musial, Ted Williams.....................$40
03/12/47 Leo Durocher, Happy Chandler $40
03/19/47 Leo Durocher, Larry MacPhail $40
03/26/47 Chandler, Durocher, MacPhail...............$40
04/02/47 Hank Greenberg $30
04/09/47 Yogi Berra, Joe Medwick $25
04/16/47 Leo Durocher $60
04/23/47 Babe Ruth...$300
04/30/47 Pete Reiser...$20
05/07/47 Babe Ruth Day $50
05/14/47 Hank Greenberg $25
05/21/47 Johnny Mize $25
05/28/47 Hal Chase $20
06/04/47 Dugout jockeys.......................................$20
06/11/47 George McQuinn.....................................$20
06/18/47 Bobby Thomson $22
06/25/47 Warren Spahn...$35
07/02/47 Ewell Blackwell $20
07/09/47 Phil Wrigley, All-Star issue $60
07/16/47 Larry Doby $60
07/23/47 Bobo Newsom...$25
07/30/47 Hall of Fame inductees...........................$25
08/06/47 Burt Shotton $20
08/13/47 Harry "The Hat" Walker $20
08/20/47 Stan Musial...$35
08/27/47 Connie Mack $25
09/03/47 Dan Bankhead $25
09/10/47 Frank McCormick $20
09/17/47 Jackie Robinson $75
09/24/47 Dixie and Harry Walker $20
10/01/47 Bucky Harris, Burt Shotton....................$75
10/08/47 Joe McCarthy, Tom Yawkey $60
10/15/47 George Weiss $50
10/22/47 Joe Kuhel $20
10/29/47 Larry MacPhail.......................................$20
11/05/47 Red Ruffing $20
11/12/47 Muddy Ruel, Zack Taylor $20
11/19/47 Snuffy Stirnweiss $20
11/26/47 Bob Elliott $20
12/03/47 Joe DiMaggio $50
12/10/47 Sam Breadon $25
12/17/47 Leo Durocher $25
12/24/47 Hugh Casey $20
12/31/47 Harris, Rickey, T. Williams $75

1948

01/07/48 Phil Masi $35
01/14/48 Stars' salaries $20
01/21/48 Sam Breadon $20
01/28/48 Bob Feller, Bill Veeck...........................$30
02/04/48 Joe McCarthy $20
02/11/48 Herb Pennock $20
02/18/48 Eddie Miller $20
02/25/48 Spring training..$20
03/03/48 Herb Pennock, Pie Traynor $25
03/10/48 Joe McCarthy $22
03/17/48 Pat Seerey $20
03/24/48 Babe Ruth...$30
03/31/48 Pesky, McCarthy, Stephens....................$22
04/07/48 Hank Greenberg $30
04/14/48 Joe McCarthy $22
04/21/48 1948 predictions $50
04/28/48 Dixie Walker $20
05/05/48 Schoolboy Rowe $20
05/12/48 Bill Meyer $20
05/19/48 Blackwell, Branca, Feller, Newhouser...$30
05/26/48 Ken Kellner $20
06/02/48 Stan Musial...$35
06/09/48 50 Home Run Club...................................$30
06/16/48 Yankee Stadium's 25th anniversary.......$25
06/23/48 Babe Ruth...$300
06/30/48 Ted Williams $40
07/07/48 Bob Lemon $20
07/14/48 Roy Campanella $40
07/21/48 Vic Raschi $25
07/28/48 Leo Durocher $22
08/04/48 Joe Tinker...$20
08/11/48 Tinker, Evers, Chance $22
08/18/48 Lou Boudreau..$24
08/25/48 Babe Ruth...$500
09/01/48 Carl Erskine..$100
09/08/48 Phil Rizzuto..$22
09/15/48 Richie Ashburn.......................................$22
09/22/48 Satchel Paige $25
09/29/48 Billy Southworth, George Stallings $20
10/06/48 1914 Miracle Braves, World Series $50
10/13/48 TSN All-Star team, World Series..........$50
10/20/48 Casey Stengel, George Weiss $20
10/27/48 Casey Stengel $25
11/03/48 Happy Chandler $20
11/10/48 Lefty Gomez...$20
11/17/48 Steve O'Neill..$20
11/24/48 Red Rolfe $20
12/01/48 Lou Boudreau..$25
12/08/48 Stan Musial...$35
12/15/48 Baseball winter meetings $20
12/22/48 Baseball winter meetings $20
12/29/48 Boudreau, Meyer, Veeck........................$40

1949

01/05/49 Pete Reiser...$30
01/12/49 20 game winners $18
01/19/49 Earl Torgeson $18
01/26/49 Dick Manville..$18
02/02/49 Bill Veeck...$20
02/09/49 Murray Dickson $18
02/16/49 Joe DiMaggio, Bob Feller $30
02/23/49 Spring training......................................$18
03/02/49 Honus Wagner......................................$20
03/09/49 Casey Stengel, 1949 Yankees $20
03/16/49 Fred Sanford $18
03/23/49 George Earnshaw $18
03/30/49 Joe McCarthy $18
04/06/49 Gene Woodling $18
04/13/49 Joe DiMaggio, Ted Williams $200
04/20/49 Joe DiMaggio $50
04/27/49 Lou Boudreau..$20
05/04/49 Chuck Connors......................................$18
05/11/49 Charlie Gehringer..................................$20
05/18/49 Bobby Shantz $18
05/25/49 Sam Breadon...$18
06/01/49 Sam Breadon...$18
06/08/49 Sam Breadon...$18
06/15/49 Mexican Leaguers reinstated.................$18
06/22/49 Frankie Frisch.......................................$18
06/29/49 Ray Boone $18
07/06/49 Joe DiMaggio $50
07/13/49 Ebbets Field, All-Star issue..................$50
07/20/49 Billy Southworth $20
07/27/49 Casey Stengel $25
08/03/49 Stan Musial...$30
08/10/49 Joe Page...$25
08/17/49 Luke Appling $20
08/24/49 Yogi Berra...$25
08/31/49 Connie Mack Day $18
09/07/49 Joe DiMaggio $50
09/14/49 Bill Klem..$18
09/21/49 Enos Slaughter $22
09/28/49 Billy Southworth $18
10/05/49 Enos Slaughter, Ted Williams...............$50
10/12/49 Casey Stengel, World Series $45
10/19/49 Branch Rickey, World Series.................$50
10/26/49 Casey Stengel $30
11/02/49 Phil Rizzuto..$20
11/09/49 Leo Durocher $18
11/16/49 Yogi Berra, Joe Garagiola.....................$25
11/23/49 Jackie Robinson $40
11/30/49 Ted Williams...$40
12/07/49 Vern Stephens, Ted Williams $25
12/14/49 Bobby Thomson $18
12/21/49 TSN All-Star team.................................$20
12/28/49 Carpenter, Stengel, Williams $60

1950

01/04/50 Joe DiMaggio $35
01/11/50 Branch Rickey.......................................$18
01/18/50 Bob Dillinger...$18
01/25/50 Virgil Trucks $18
02/01/50 Jackie Robinson $25
02/08/50 Gerry Priddy...$18
02/15/50 Ty Cobb..$30
02/22/50 Spiraling salaries $18
03/01/50 Hank Greenberg $22
03/08/50 Del Crandall $20
03/15/50 Branch Rickey.......................................$20
03/22/50 Connie Mack $20
03/29/50 Sam Jethroe $20
04/05/50 Connie Mack $20
04/12/50 Jackie Jensen, Billy Martin $25
04/19/50 Branch Rickey, Jackie Robinson...........$35
04/26/50 Luke Easter...$20
05/03/50 Jack Banta $20
05/10/50 Yogi Berra...$25
05/17/50 Edward Barrow $18
05/24/50 Ty Cobb..$25
05/31/50 Robin Roberts, Curt Simmons $20
06/07/50 Phil Rizzuto..$20
06/14/50 Bob Feller...$25
06/21/50 Boston 29, Browns 4 ....$18
06/28/50 Joe McCarthy $20
07/05/50 George Kell...$20
07/12/50 Babe Ruth, All-Star game $50
07/19/50 Luke Easter...$25
07/26/50 Ty Cobb, Babe Ruth..............................$30
08/02/50 Casey Stengel $25
08/09/50 Eddie Collins, Larry Lajoie...................$18
08/16/50 Sam Jethroe $18
08/23/50 Vern Bickford..$25
08/30/50 Preacher Roe $20
09/06/50 Hank Bauer...$18
09/13/50 Gil Hodges $20
09/20/50 Lou Boudreau..$20
09/27/50 Sal Maglie $20
10/04/50 Branch Rickey, World Series.................$50
10/11/50 Whitey Ford, World Series $50
10/18/50 Jerry Coleman, World Series $40
10/25/50 Connie Mack $18
11/01/50 Walter O'Malley, Branch Rickey $25
11/08/50 Jim Konstanty, Phil Rizzuto..................$20
11/15/50 Grover Cleveland Alexander..................$30
11/22/50 Honus Wagner..$22
11/29/50 Al Lopez...$18
12/06/50 Baseball winter meetings $18
12/13/50 Marty Marion $18
12/20/50 Happy Chandler $18
12/27/50 Happy Chandler $18

1951

01/03/51 Rizzuto, Rolfe, Weiss.............................$40
01/10/51 Yogi Berra, Phil Rizzuto.......................$25
01/17/51 Phil Rizzuto...$20
01/24/51 Tom Henrich.......................................$18
01/31/51 Mickey Mantle....................................$100
02/07/51 Jimmie Foxx, Mel Ott.........................$25
02/14/51 National League's 75th........................$25
02/21/51 Happy Chandler..................................$18
02/28/51 Stan Musial..$25
03/07/51 Red Ruffin..$18
03/14/51 Stan Musial..$25
03/21/51 Happy Chandler..................................$18
03/28/51 Fred Clarke...$18
04/04/51 Mickey Mantle....................................$50
04/11/51 Bobby Avila..$25
04/18/51 Play Ball...$40
04/25/51 Mickey Mantle....................................$300
05/02/51 Grover Alexander................................$25
05/09/51 Leo Durocher......................................$18
05/16/51 Gil McDougald.....................................$18
05/23/51 Leo Durocher......................................$20
05/30/51 Furillo, Hodges, Robinson, Snider........$35
06/06/51 Branch Rickey.....................................$18
06/13/51 Ed Lopat...$18
06/20/51 Minnie Minoso.....................................$18
06/27/51 Walter O'Malley, Buzzie Bavasi...........$20
07/04/51 1926 Cardinals....................................$18
07/11/51 Cobb, Cochrane, Gehringer.................$50
07/18/51 Roy Campanella...................................$25
07/25/51 Allie Reynolds.....................................$18
08/01/51 Dizzy and Paul Dean...........................$20
08/08/51 1951 Dodgers......................................$25
08/15/51 Willie Mays...$50
08/22/51 Charlie Gehringer...............................$30
08/29/51 Bob Feller...$30
09/05/51 Casey Stengel.....................................$30
09/12/51 Johnny Sain..$18
09/19/51 Bobby Thomson...................................$25
09/26/51 Bill Klem..$18
10/03/51 Home Run Baker, World Series............$50
10/10/51 Fain, Feller, Musial, Roe....................$200
10/17/51 Warren Giles, World Series.................$45
10/24/51 Gabe Paul...$18
10/31/51 Lou Boudreau......................................$20
11/07/51 Alvin Dark..$18
11/14/51 Stan Musial, Ted Williams...................$45
11/21/51 Yogi Berra..$25
11/28/51 Gil Hodges..$20
12/05/51 Bill Bevins...$18
12/12/51 Minnie Minoso.....................................$25
12/19/51 Joe DiMaggio......................................$100
12/26/51 Joe DiMaggio......................................$40

1952

01/02/52 Durocher, Musial, Weiss......................$75
01/09/52 Leo Durocher, Eddie Stanky................$18
01/16/52 Tommy Holmes....................................$16
01/23/52 Walter Briggs......................................$16
01/30/52 Gus Zernial..$16
02/06/52 Negro ballplayers................................$30
02/13/52 Ralph Branca, Bobby Thomson............$30
02/20/52 Johnny Mize..$20
02/27/52 Paul Waner...$16
03/05/52 Casey Stengel.....................................$18
03/12/52 Dickey, DiMaggio, Ruth.......................$30
03/19/52 Ty Cobb..$25
03/26/52 Ty Cobb..$25
04/02/52 Clem Labine..$16
04/09/52 Monte Irvin..$18
04/16/52 Play Ball...$40
04/23/52 Wilmer Mizell......................................$16
04/30/52 Walter O'Malley..................................$20
05/07/52 Walter O'Malley..................................$20
05/14/52 Ty Cobb..$22
05/21/52 Jackie Jensen......................................$15
05/28/52 Dale Mitchell.......................................$15
06/04/52 Davey Williams....................................$15
06/11/52 Ty Cobb, Rogers Hornsby.....................$25
06/18/52 Rogers Hornsby, Bill Veeck.................$18
06/25/52 Jimmy Piersall.....................................$15
07/02/52 Carl Erskine..$15
07/09/52 Leo Durocher, Casey Stengel...............$35
07/16/52 Solly Hemus..$20
07/23/52 Clark Griffith......................................$16
07/30/52 Clark Griffith......................................$16
08/06/52 Clark Griffith......................................$16
08/13/52 Jackie Jensen......................................$16
08/20/52 Bill Veeck...$18
08/27/52 Bill Loes...$16
09/03/52 Robin Roberts......................................$16
09/10/52 Early Wynn...$18
09/17/52 Hank Sauer...$16
09/24/52 Joe Black, Clint Courtney....................$16
10/01/52 1941 Dodgers, World Series.................$40
10/08/52 1952 Yankees, 1952 Dodgers...............$40
10/15/52 Johnny Mize, World Series...................$40
10/22/52 Mickey Mantle....................................$40
10/29/52 Phil Rizzuto...$18
11/05/52 Frank Lane, Bill Veeck........................$16
11/12/52 Mickey Mantle....................................$50
11/19/52 Duke Snider..$25
11/26/52 TSN All-Star team...............................$20
12/03/52 Del Webb..$16
12/10/52 Jackie Robinson..................................$25
12/17/52 Ferris Fain...$16
12/24/52 Johnny Allen.......................................$16
12/31/52 Roberts, Stanky, Weiss........................$30

1953

01/07/53 1952 Baseball thrills section $30
01/14/53 Johnny Mize $18
01/21/53 Eddie Stanky $16
01/28/53 Johnny Mize $18
02/04/53 Dizzy Dean, Al Simmons.....................$20
02/11/53 Ed Yost..$16
02/18/53 Eddie Robinson $16
02/25/53 August A. Busch Jr. $16
03/04/53 Russ Meyer...$16
03/11/53 Mickey Grasso $16
03/18/53 Browns move to Baltimore, Braves move to Milwaukee...$16
03/25/53 Braves and Browns shift $16
04/01/53 Garcia, Lemon, Wynn $20
04/08/53 Casey Stengel $18
04/15/53 Play Ball $30
04/22/53 Milwaukee opener $16
04/29/53 Mickey Mantle $100
05/06/53 Clint Courtney, Billy Martin $16
05/13/53 Bobo Holloman $16
05/20/53 Cobb, Mize, Slaughter..........................$20
05/27/53 Dave Philley $16
06/03/53 Roy Campanella $25
06/10/53 Hoyt Wilhelm......................................$16
06/17/53 Mickey Mantle $45
06/24/53 1953 Yankees winning streak $16
07/01/53 Mickey Mantle, Ed Mathews $45
07/08/53 Doby, Easter, Rosen $20
07/15/53 Charlie Dressen, Casey Stengel $30
07/22/53 Carl Furillo, Monte Irvin.....................$20
07/29/53 Robin Roberts......................................$18
08/05/53 Ted Williams.......................................$30
08/12/53 Mickey Vernon.....................................$18
08/19/53 Allie Reynolds......................................$18
08/26/53 1953 Dodger sluggers $20
09/02/53 Vic Raschi, Preacher Roe.....................$18
09/09/53 Red Schoendienst $18
09/16/53 Ed Mathews...$25
09/23/53 Yankees, Dodgers clinch.......................$20
09/30/53 1949-53 Yankees, World Series issue....$45
10/07/53 Junior Gilliam, Harvey Kuenn $20
10/14/53 Bill Veeck, World Series.......................$40
10/21/53 Rogers Hornsby....................................$18
10/28/53 Rogers Hornsby....................................$18
11/04/53 Jimmy Piersall.....................................$18
11/11/53 Nap Lajoie..$18
11/18/53 Jimmie Dykes......................................$18
11/25/53 Eddie Joost $18
12/02/53 Atlanta Crackers...................................$16
12/09/53 Walter Alston $18
12/16/53 Bob Feller...$20
12/23/53 Ed Barrow $16
12/30/53 Perini, Rosen, Stengel $35

1954

01/06/54 1953 Baseball thrills.............................$20
01/13/54 Bobo Newsom......................................$16
01/20/54 Danny O'Connell $16
01/27/54 Dickey, Maranville, Terry.....................$20
02/03/54 Spring training.....................................$16
02/10/54 Bobby Thomson $18
02/17/54 Paul Krichell.......................................$16
02/24/54 Willie Mays...$30
03/03/54 Enos Slaughter $16
03/10/54 Johnny Antonelli $16
03/17/54 Walter Alston $18
03/24/54 J.A. Robert Quinn $16
03/31/54 Don Newcombe....................................$18
04/07/54 1954 Dodgers $16
04/14/54 Baseball returns to Baltimore...............$35
04/21/54 Ted Williams.......................................$30
04/28/54 Hal Jeffcoat $16
05/05/54 Bucky Harris $16
05/12/54 Stan Musial...$75
05/19/54 Johnny Temple $16
05/26/54 Gene Baker, Ernie Banks $22
06/02/54 Art Houtteman.....................................$16
06/09/54 Ed Lopat $16
06/16/54 Roy Campanella $25
06/23/54 Hornsby, Musial, Wagner $25
06/30/54 Frank Thomas.......................................$16
07/07/54 Willie Mays, Duke Snider.....................$45
07/14/54 Dusty Rhodes, All-Star issue $30
07/21/54 Willie Mays...$35
07/28/54 Eddie Stanky $16
08/04/54 Bob Feller..$25
08/11/54 Branch Rickey......................................$16
08/18/54 Bob Lemon..$16
08/25/54 Don Mueller $16
09/01/54 Jack Harshman.....................................$16
09/08/54 Smokey Burgess....................................$16
09/15/54 Johnny Antonelli, Willie Mays $50
09/22/54 Casey Stengel $18
09/29/54 Leo Durocher, Al Lopez, World Series .$45
10/06/54 Bob Grim, Wally Moon, World Series ..$25
10/13/54 Antonelli, Avila, Lemon, Mays...........$100
10/20/54 Pinky Higgins $16
10/27/54 Connie Mack $16
11/03/54 Joe McCarthy $16
11/10/54 Joe McCarthy $16
11/17/54 A's move to Kansas City.......................$16
11/24/54 Joe Garagiola......................................$16
12/01/54 Bob Turley...$16
12/08/54 Bob Feller...$15
12/15/54 TSN All-Star team................................$20
12/22/54 Ted Kluszweski $18
12/29/54 Stan Lopata...$16

1955

01/05/55 Durocher, Mays, Stoneham....................$60
01/12/55 Nellie Fox...$16
01/19/55 Ken Boyer $18
01/26/55 Joe Nuxhall..$16
02/02/55 DiMaggio, Hartnett, Lyons, Vance........$25
02/09/55 Home Run Baker, Ray Schalk $16
02/16/55 Home Run Baker.......................................$16
02/23/55 Sad Sam Jones..$16
03/02/55 Roy Campanella $20
03/09/55 Jim Busby...$16
03/16/55 Gil Hodges $18
03/23/55 Herb Score..$16
03/30/55 Mike Higgins..$16
04/06/55 Warren Spahn...$20
04/13/55 Ken Boyer, Herb Score $35
04/20/55 Ralph Kiner $18
04/27/55 25 game winners $16
05/04/55 1955 Yankees...$20
05/11/55 Don Mueller $16
05/18/55 Harvey Kuenn $16
05/25/55 Duke Snider..$20
06/01/55 Harry Chiti $16
06/08/55 Al Kaline $25
06/15/55 Yogi Berra, Roy Campanella $25
06/22/55 Don Newcombe...$25
06/29/55 Jim Konstanty...$16
07/06/55 Dick Donovan $16
07/13/55 Stan Musial, All-Star issue.....................$30
07/20/55 Ernie Banks $25
07/27/55 Preacher Roe $20
08/03/55 Sherm Lollar...$50
08/10/55 Spitball debate...$16
08/17/55 Jimmy Piersall...$16
08/24/55 Del Ennis..$16
08/31/55 Hank Bauer...$18
09/07/55 Al Smith $16
09/14/55 Mickey Mantle $30
09/21/55 Don Mossi, Ray Narleski $18
09/28/55 Previous Yankees/Dodgers World
Series $60
10/05/55 Herb Score, Bill Virdon $25
10/12/55 Johnny Podres, World Series $200
10/19/55 Ford, Kaline, Roberts, Snider................$35
10/26/55 Roy Campanella $20
11/02/55 Clark Griffith..$16
11/09/55 Bobby Bragan..$16
11/16/55 Cy Young $18
11/23/55 Double play combos...................................$16
11/30/55 Bucky Walters $16
12/07/55 TSN All-Star team.....................................$18
12/14/55 Roy Campanella $20
12/21/55 Earl Torgeson $16
12/28/55 Bob Feller $20

1956

01/04/56 Alston, O'Malley, Snider $60
01/11/56 Gil Coan $14
01/18/56 Randy Jackson...$14
01/25/56 Pepper Martin...$14
02/01/56 Joe Cronin, Hank Greenberg....................$15
02/08/56 Joe Cronin, Hank Greenberg....................$18
02/15/56 Connie Mack $16
02/22/56 Calvin Griffith..$14
02/29/56 Robin Roberts...$16
03/07/56 Hank Greenberg $18
03/14/56 Vern Law $14
03/21/56 Greatest players from 1946-55...............$25
03/28/56 Stan Musial...$25
04/04/56 Earl Averill...$14
04/11/56 Marty Marion $14
04/18/56 Yankees vs. Dodgers................................$35
04/25/56 Minnie Minoso $14
05/02/56 Top relievers...$14
05/09/56 Bob Friend..$14
05/16/56 Bill Sarni $14
05/23/56 Vic Wertz $14
05/30/56 Dale Long $14
06/06/56 Murray Dickson $14
06/13/56 Mickey Mantle $75
06/20/56 Gabe Paul $14
06/27/56 Alvin Dark...$14
07/04/56 DiMaggio, Musial, Williams...............$100
07/11/56 Stan Musial..$100
07/18/56 Gabe Paul, All-Star issue $20
07/25/56 Tigers sold for $5.5 million....................$20
08/01/56 Bill Skowron $20
08/08/56 Fred Haney $14
08/15/56 Ted Williams $25
08/22/56 Braves pitchers $20
08/29/56 Joe Adcock..$20
09/05/56 Luis Aparicio, Frank Robinson..............$25
09/12/56 The home run $20
09/19/56 Birdie Tebbets $25
09/26/56 Babe Ruth...$45
10/03/56 Casey Stengel, World Series issue $60
10/10/56 Aaron, Mantle, Newcombe, Pierce $50
10/17/56 Don Larsen $400
10/24/56 Luis Aparicio, Frank Robinson..............$20
10/31/56 No-hit pitchers...$14
11/07/56 Al Lopez...$14
11/14/56 Mickey Mantle $30
11/21/56 Frank Lary $30
11/28/56 Mickey Mantle $30
12/05/56 Baseball's 5 greatest feats $15
12/12/56 Bob Scheffing..$14
12/19/56 Jackie Robinson $14
12/26/56 Harvey Kuenn $14

1957

01/02/57 Mantle, Paul, Tebbetts.............................$75
01/09/57 Bob Feller...$18
01/16/57 Jackie Robinson $20
01/23/57 Mickey Mantle, George Weiss...............$30
01/30/57 Duke Snider...$18
02/06/57 Stan Musial..$20
02/13/57 Sam Crawford, Joe McCarthy...............$15
02/20/57 Ted Williams $25
02/27/57 Yankees/A's trade $14
03/06/57 Phil Rizzuto..$15
03/13/57 Gil Hodges $15
03/20/57 Frank Sullivan $14
03/27/57 Marv Throneberry $14
04/03/57 Ty Cobb...$16
04/10/57 Ted Williams $20
04/17/57 Tony Kubek, Andre Rodgers $30
04/24/57 Roy Campanella $20
05/01/57 Roger Maris...$25
05/08/57 Tom Yawkey..$14
05/15/57 Ted Williams $25
05/22/57 Ted Williams $20
05/29/57 Whitey Ford $18
06/05/57 Dodgers, Giants to move.......................$25
06/12/57 Walter O'Malley $14
06/19/57 Stan Musial..$20
06/26/57 Baseball brawls, beanballs $14
07/03/57 Danny McDevitt.....................................$14
07/10/57 Stan Musial, Ted Williams....................$30
07/17/57 Ford Frick..$15
07/24/57 Yankees success system $14
07/31/57 Giants to move to San Francisco...........$14
08/07/57 Polo Grounds history.............................$15
08/14/57 Polo Grounds history.............................$20
08/21/57 Roy Sievers $14
08/28/57 Giants shift $14
09/04/57 Nellie Fox..$14
09/11/57 Frank Malzone $14
09/18/57 Walt Moryn $14
09/25/57 Al Kaline $20
10/02/57 Warren Spahn, World Series issue.........$35
10/09/57 Stan Musial, Ted Williams....................$35
10/16/57 Dodgers to move to Los Angeles $30
10/23/57 Lew Burdette..$14
10/30/57 L.A. franchise battle $15
11/06/57 Yogi Berra...$18
11/13/57 Yogi Berra...$18
11/20/57 Frank Lane $14
11/27/57 Frank Lane $20
12/04/57 Baseball winter meetings $14
12/11/57 MVP balloting..$14
12/18/57 Al Lopez..$14
12/25/57 L.A. Dodgers $15

1958

01/01/58 Hutchinson, Lane, Williams..................$35
01/08/58 Mickey Mantle, Ted Williams $15
01/15/58 Ed Mathews...$18
01/22/58 Frank Lane, George Weiss.....................$14
01/29/58 L.A. Dodgers $14
02/05/58 Roy Campanella $20
02/12/58 Stars' salaries then and now $14
02/19/58 Billy Martin...$15
02/26/58 Willie Mays $20
03/05/58 Gil Hodges, Duke Snider $18
03/12/58 Deron Johnson.......................................$14
03/19/58 Leadoff hitters.......................................$14
03/26/58 1958 Braves...$15
04/02/58 1958 Giants $15
04/09/58 1958 batting race $15
04/16/58 California here we come $30
04/23/58 Eisenhower at season opener $14
04/30/58 L.A. Dodgers $16
05/07/58 Chinese home runs $14
05/14/58 Stan Musial..$60
05/21/58 Branch Rickey.......................................$14
05/28/58 1958 Yankee pitchers............................$14
06/04/58 San Francisco Giants.............................$14
06/11/58 Ryne Duren $14
06/18/58 Yankees/Kansas City trades..................$14
06/25/58 Walter O'Malley $14
07/02/58 Gabe Paul $14
07/09/58 All-Time All-Stars $25
07/16/58 Casey Stengel..$15
07/23/58 Jackie Jensen $14
07/30/58 Phil Wrigley $14
08/06/58 Bob Turley $14
08/13/58 Philly Whiz Kids $14
08/20/58 Yankees old-timers................................$15
08/27/58 Ted Williams $25
09/03/58 Ernie Banks $18
09/10/58 Banks, Jensen, Spahn, Turley $16
09/17/58 Pete Runnels..$14
09/24/58 Aaron, Ashburn, Mays, Musial.............$35
10/01/58 George Weiss, World Series issue $30
10/08/58 Top Rookies in 1958 ....$16
10/15/58 Player/managers, World Series $25
10/22/58 Mighty Mites...$14
10/29/58 Casey Stengel..$15
11/05/58 Stan Musial..$20
11/12/58 Max Carey...$14
11/19/58 Lee MacPhail $14
11/26/58 Houston bids for franchise $14
12/03/58 Baseball winter meetings $14
12/10/58 Will Harridge...$14
12/17/58 Joe Cronin, Will Harridge $14
12/24/58 New York Yankees' homes $14
12/31/58 Brown, Stengel, Turley $25

1959

01/07/59 Will Harridge $14
01/14/59 Marty Marion $14
01/21/59 Bill Norman...$14
01/28/59 Willie Mays...$20
02/04/59 Soaring player salaries $14
02/11/59 Zack Wheat $14
02/18/59 Spring training.......................................$14
02/25/59 Bill Veeck...$15
03/04/59 Durocher, Frisch, McGraw, Stallings $15
03/11/59 Solly Hemus $14
03/18/59 Frank Lary $14
03/25/59 Ty Cobb...$18
04/01/59 Don Mossi, Ray Narleski $14
04/08/59 Play Ball $25
04/15/59 Hall of Fame historian Lee Allen...........$14
04/22/59 Clint Courtney $14
04/29/59 Woodie Held $14
05/06/59 Paul Richards $14
05/13/59 1959 Yankees woes................................$14
05/20/59 Ernie Banks $18
05/27/59 1925 Yankees $14
06/03/59 Hank Aaron $20
06/10/59 Rocky Colavito, Ed Mathews $16
06/07/59 Hoyt Wilhelm.......................................$14
06/24/59 Roy Face...$14
07/01/59 Harmon Killebrew................................$15
07/08/59 Carl Hubbell, Ted Williams $25
07/15/59 Billy Jurges..$14
07/22/59 Senators sluggers..................................$14
07/29/59 Orioles staff...$14
08/05/59 Don Drysdale $15
08/12/59 Willie McCovey $20
08/19/59 Eppa Rixey $14
08/26/59 Al Lopez..$14
09/02/59 Ty Cobb...$18
09/09/59 1959 White Sox, Bill Veeck..................$20
09/16/59 Tony Cuccinello, Al Lopez $14
09/23/59 1959 Yankees fall.................................$15
09/30/59 Bill Veeck, World Series issue..............$30
10/07/59 Early Wynn $15
10/14/59 1959 World Series summary $25
10/21/59 Larry Sherry $14
10/28/59 Wally Moon $14
11/04/59 Chuck Dressen $14
11/11/59 TSN's 1959 All-Stars $18
11/18/59 Nellie Fox...$15
11/25/59 Bob Allison $14
12/02/59 Baseball winter meetings $14
12/09/59 Stan Musial, Ted Williams....................$15
12/16/59 Billy Jurges...$15
12/23/59 Hall of Fame first basemen $18
12/30/59 Alston, Bavasi, Wynn $30

1960

01/06/60 Walter Alston $14
01/13/60 Joe Cronin $12
01/20/60 Willie Mays...$25
01/27/60 Clark Griffith.......................................$12
02/03/60 Johnny Temple $12
02/10/60 Rice, Rixey, Roush...............................$12
02/17/60 Ernie Banks $18
02/24/60 Walter O'Malley $12
03/02/60 Pete Reiser..$12
03/09/60 1960 White Sox $12
03/16/60 Walter Alston $12
03/23/60 Chuck Dressen $12
03/30/60 1960 Yankees analysis $15
04/06/60 Eddie Lopat $12
04/13/60 Play Ball $25
04/20/60 Johnson, Mathewson, Spahn, Wynn, Young
....$20
04/27/60 Rocky Colavito, Harvey Kuenn $14
05/04/60 Bill DeWitt $12
05/11/60 Ken Boyer $12
05/18/60 Lou Boudreau $12
05/25/60 Roger Maris...$25
06/01/60 Bill Veeck..$12
06/08/60 Frank Howard.......................................$12
06/15/60 Bill Mazeroski $13
06/22/60 Comiskey dynasty $12
06/29/60 Ted Williams $40
07/06/60 Roberto Clemente.................................$25
07/13/60 Roger Maris, All-Star issue $25
07/20/60 New franchises for 1962 ....$15
07/27/60 Del Crandall $12
08/03/60 Cookie Lavagetto $12
08/10/60 Jim Piersall, Casey Stengel $12
08/17/60 Ted Williams $100
08/24/60 Dick Groat $12
08/31/60 Dick Groat, Roger Maris.......................$20
09/07/60 Roy Sievers $12
09/14/60 1890s stars $12
09/21/60 Hemus, Lavagetto, Murtaugh, Richards $12
09/28/60 Stan Musial..$25
10/05/60 1927 Yankees, World Series issue $30
10/12/60 Mike Fornieles, Lindy McDaniel...........$15
10/19/60 Bobby Richardson, World Series...........$25
10/26/60 Casey Stengel $15
11/02/60 American League expansion $12
11/09/60 George Weiss $12
11/16/60 Roger Maris...$25
11/23/60 Roy Harney $12
11/30/60 Baseball winter meetings $12
12/07/60 Ralph Houk $12
12/14/60 Los Angeles Angels $12
12/21/60 John Galbreath $12
12/28/60 Billy Bruton...$12

1961

01/04/61 Mazeroski, Murtaugh, Weiss $30
01/11/61 Ted Kluszewski $13
01/18/61 Dazzy Vance, Johnny Vander Meer.......$12
01/25/61 Max Carey, Billy Hamilton...................$12
02/01/61 Walter Alston $12
02/08/61 Lindy McDaniel $12
02/15/61 Stars swan songs $14
02/22/61 Max Carey $12
03/01/61 Ralph Houk $12
03/08/61 Leo Durocher $13
03/15/61 Yankees, Tigers outfielders...................$15
03/22/61 Joe DiMaggio $18
03/29/61 Mickey Mantle $30
04/05/61 1961 managers $12
04/12/61 Presidents/Opening Day.......................$40
04/19/61 Willie Davis, Carl Yastrzemski.............$30
04/26/61 Whitey Ford $16
05/03/61 Babe Herman $14
05/10/61 Wally Moon $25
05/17/61 Jim Gentile $14
05/24/61 Alvin Dark...$14
05/31/61 Charles Finley $14
06/07/61 Pitching coach Jim Turner $14
06/14/61 Johnny Temple $14
06/21/61 Sandy Koufax...$20
06/28/61 Mickey Mantle, Roger Maris $100
07/05/61 300 game winners $20
07/12/61 Cash, Cepeda, Ford, Jay, Koufax, Mantle,
Maris, F. Robinson $60
07/19/61 George Weiss $20
07/26/61 Ty Cobb...$50
08/02/61 Red Sox immortals.................................$40
08/09/61 Ford Frick $25
08/16/61 Elston Howard.......................................$15
08/23/61 Whitey Ford $25
08/30/61 Top 1961 rookies....................................$30
09/06/61 Mickey Mantle, Roger Maris $75
09/13/61 Arroyo, Ford, Spahn..............................$40
09/20/61 Ralph Houk $40
09/27/61 Mantle, Maris, Ruth $100
10/04/61 1939 Yankees vs. Reds, World Series .. $50
10/11/61 Casey Stengel, New York Mets $200
10/18/61 Hail to the champs.................................$45
10/25/61 Yogi Berra...$15
11/01/61 Top 1961 rookies....................................$15
11/08/61 Ron Santo $12
11/15/61 Johnny Temple $12
11/22/61 Roger Maris...$60
11/29/61 Baseball winter meetings $12
12/06/61 Walter O'Malley $12
12/13/61 Ty Cobb...$14
12/20/61 Best No. 2 hitters...................................$14
12/27/61 George Sisler...$12

1962

01/03/62 Houk, Maris, Spahn, Topping...............$40
01/10/62 Al Kaline $18
01/17/62 Rogers Hornsby......................................$14
01/24/62 Hall of Fame candidates.......................$15
01/31/62 Pie Traynor..$12
02/07/62 Elston Howard.......................................$13
02/14/62 Gil Hodges $13
02/21/62 Sophomore jinx $12
02/28/62 Roger Maris...$18
03/07/62 Mantle, Mays, Musial, Spahn,
Williams $50
03/14/62 Hall of Famers who stayed with one team
....$25
03/21/62 Braves infielders....................................$12
03/28/62 Ray Schalk $12
04/04/62 Minnie Minoso $12
04/11/62 Play Ball $20
04/18/62 1962 Giants $12
04/25/62 Ford Frick $12
05/02/62 Felipe and Matty Alou $12
05/09/62 Casey Stengel $12
05/16/62 Ralph Terry $12
05/23/62 Sandy Koufax...$15
06/02/62 Luis Aparicio, Dick Howser $12
06/09/62 1962 Giants pitchers.............................$12
06/16/62 Bob Purkey..$12
06/23/62 Carl Sawatski $12
06/30/62 Don Drysdale $14
07/07/62 All-Star goats $18
07/14/62 Maury Wills $12
07/21/62 Davis, Mantle, Mays, Wagner...............$25
07/28/62 Chicago Cubs immortals $20
08/04/62 Bob Gibson..$20
08/11/62 1962 Reds $12
08/18/62 Yogi Berra...$20
08/25/62 Juan Marichal $20
09/01/62 Tom Tresh $12
09/08/62 New York Mets $20
09/15/62 Ron Fairly, Frank Howard $12
09/22/62 Donovan, Mantle, Marichal, Wills $20
09/29/62 George Weiss $12
10/06/62 Walter O'Malley, World Series issue $20
10/13/62 Ralph Houk $20
10/20/62 1962 baseball thrills $20
10/27/62 Ken Hubbs, Tom Tresh $20
11/03/62 Birdie Tebbetts $12
11/10/62 Brooks and Frank Robinson..................$30
11/17/62 Don Drysdale $14
11/24/62 Stan Musial..$18
12/01/62 George Sisler Jr. $12
12/08/62 Tom Tresh $12
12/15/62 Jack Sanford $12
12/22/62 Walter O'Malley $12
12/29/62 Don Drysdale, Maury Wills $25

1963

01/05/63 1962 World Series Game 7 .... $12-$15
01/12/63 1963's top rookie prospects .... $10-$14
01/19/63 Jim Piersall $12
01/26/63 Dean Chance .... $10-$12
02/02/63 Sam Mele .... $10-$12
02/09/63 Chicago White Sox $12
02/16/63 Sandy Koufax.................................. $15-$16
02/23/63 Johnny Pesky.................................. $10-$12
03/02/63 Dan Topping.................................... $10-$12
03/09/63 Johnny Sain $12
03/16/63 Mickey Mantle, Willie Mays $35
03/23/63 1963 Yankees .... $12-$15
03/30/63 Ralph Terry $12
04/06/63 Don Hoak $12
04/13/63 Play Ball .... $15-$18
04/20/63 Duke Snider...................................... $14-$15
04/27/63 Ernie Broglio...................................... $12-$14
05/04/63 Tony Kubek, Bobby Richardson...........$14
05/11/63 Luis Aparicio, Al Smith .... $12-$13
05/18/63 Cubs pitchers $12
05/25/63 Sandy Koufax................................... $15-$16
06/01/63 Ron Fairly...$12
06/08/63 Jim Piersall, Casey Stengel .... $12-$15
06/15/63 Gil Hodges .... $13-$15
06/22/63 Billy O'Dell...$12
06/29/63 Juan Marichal .... $12-$14
07/06/63 New York Yankees .... $12-$14
07/13/63 Casey Stengel, All-Star issue .... $18-$20
07/20/63 Aaron, Ford, Koufax, Wagner.................$20
07/27/63 Hal Woodenshick $12
08/03/63 Rich Rollins...$12
08/10/63 Frank Malzone, Carl Yastrzemski
.... $15-$16
08/17/63 Dick Ellsworth $12
08/24/63 1963 Dodgers $12
08/31/63 Warren Spahn...................................... $14-$15
09/07/63 Dick Groat $12
09/14/63 Jimmy Hall $12
09/21/63 1963's top rookies .... $14-$15
09/28/63 20 game winners .... $12-$15
10/05/63 Yankees vs. Dodgers/prior World
Series .... $20-$25
10/12/63 Aaron, Ford, Kaline, Koufax.......... $20-$30
10/19/63 Dodgers sweep the Yankees........... $20-$25
10/26/63 Pete Rose...$30
11/02/63 Dick Stuart $12
11/09/63 Yogi Berra .... $14-$15
11/16/63 Carl Yastrzemski............................. $15-$16
11/23/63 Hank Aaron .... $12-$18
11/30/63 Elston Howard.......................................$12
12/07/63 Rocky Colavito.................................. $12-$15
12/14/63 Sandy Koufax...$25
12/21/63 Leon Wagner $12
12/28/63 Jim Bouton $12

1964

01/04/64 1963 Los Angeles Dodgers $20
01/11/64 Albie Pearson .... $10-$12
01/18/64 Sandy Koufax................................. $18-$20
01/25/64 Walter Alston .... $10-$12
02/01/64 Jim "Mudcat" Grant .... $10-$12
02/08/64 Lum Harris .... $12-$15
02/15/64 Chuck Hinton .... $10-$12
02/22/64 Eddie Mathews .... $12-$15
02/29/64 Casey Stengel .... $12-$15
03/07/64 Burleigh Grimes .... $10-$12
03/14/64 Al Kaline .... $15-$20
03/21/64 Willie McCovey .... $14-$15
03/28/64 Branch Rickey .... $10-$12
04/04/64 Jim Gilliam...................................... $10-$12
04/11/64 Don Drysdale, Sandy Koufax $20
04/18/64 Play Ball .... $15-$18
04/25/64 Aaron, Mathews, Spahn $20
05/02/64 Cepeda, Mays, McCovey .... $20-$25
05/09/64 Frank Howard.................................. $10-$12
05/16/64 Tony Oliva $12
05/23/64 Richie Allen $12
05/30/64 Ron Hansen .... $10-$12
06/06/64 Dave Wickersham .... $10-$12
06/13/64 Ron Santo .... $10-$15
06/20/64 Wally Bunker .... $10-$12
06/27/64 Whitey Ford $15
07/04/64 Billy Williams $12
07/11/64 Willie Mays $25
07/25/64 Gene Mauch .... $10-$12
08/01/64 Boog Powell .... $10-$15
08/08/64 Ron Hunt .... $10-$12
08/15/64 Bill Freehan .... $10-$12
08/22/64 Johnny Callison .... $10-$15
08/29/64 Bob Allison, Harmon Killebrew $15
09/05/64 Roberto Clemente........................... $20-$30
09/12/64 Elston Howard................................. $12-$15
09/19/64 Brooks Robinson............................. $15-$20
09/26/64 Ken Boyer .... $12-$15
10/03/64 Dean Chance .... $10-$12
10/10/64 Allen, Bunker, Oliva, World Series $20
10/17/64 Yankees vs. Cardinals, World Series
.... $15-$20
10/24/64 Bing Devine, World Series $20
10/31/64 Johnny Keane .... $10-$15
12/05/64 Mel Stottlemyre, Harry Walker.............$10

1965

01/02/65 Ken Boyer, Bob Gibson .... $16-$20
02/06/65 Baseball to select new commissioner
.... $10-$12
02/27/65 Spring training.................................. $10-$15
03/20/65 Rocky Colavito................................. $10-$15
03/27/65 Juan Marichal $15
04/03/65 Bo Belinsky, Dick Stuart.................. $10-$12
04/10/65 Houston Astrodome .... $10-$12

04/17/65 Play Ball $15

04/24/65 President Johnson visits the
Astrodome $12

05/01/65 John Romano..................................$10-$12

05/08/65 Eddie Mathews...............................$12-$15

05/15/65 Tony Conigliaro ....$10-$20

05/22/65 Frank Robinson $15

05/29/65 White Sox pitchers ....$10-$15

06/05/65 Bob Gibson...$15

06/12/65 Felix Mantilla................................$10-$12

06/19/65 Wes Parker ....$10-$12

06/26/65 Vic Davalillo ....$10-$12

07/03/65 Hank Aaron ....$12-$18

07/10/65 Eddie Fisher ....$10-$20

07/17/65 Don Drysdale, Sandy Koufax ....$20-$30

07/24/65 Willie Horton ....$10-$15

07/31/65 Deron Johnson...............................$10-$12

08/07/65 Sonny Siebert ....$10-$12

08/14/65 Richie Allen $12

08/21/65 Pete Rose....................................$25-$40

08/28/65 Curt Blefary................................$10-$12

09/04/65 Vern Law....................................$10-$12

09/11/65 Sam McDowell..............................$10-$12

09/18/65 Jim Bunning ....$10-$15

09/25/65 Sandy Koufax......................................$25

10/02/65 Willie McCovey ....$12-$20

10/09/65 Jim "Mudcat" Grant, World Series $15

10/16/65 Lou Johnson ....$10-$15

10/23/65 Maury Wills, World Series ....$12-$15

10/30/65 Grant, Koufax, Mays, Oliva.......... $20-$25

11/06/65 Cal Griffth....................................$10

1966

01/08/66 Sandy Koufax.................................$20-$25

01/22/66 Ted Williams.................................$10-$15

03/05/66 Hank Aquirre..................................$10-$12

03/19/66 Dick Stuart ....$10-$12

03/26/66 Willie Davis ....$10-$12

04/02/66 Camilo Pascual...............................$10-$12

04/09/66 Brooks and Frank Robinson...........$20-$25

04/16/66 Atlanta and Anaheim stadiums $15

04/30/66 Milwaukee Braves move to Atlanta
....$10-$12

05/07/66 Larry Brown, Fred Whitfield ....$10-$12

05/14/66 Don Sutton ....$10-$15

05/21/66 Willie Mays....................................$20-$25

05/28/66 Luis Tiant ....$10-$15

06/04/66 Rick Reichardt................................$10-$12

06/11/66 Joe Morgan......................................$12-$15

06/18/66 Sandy Koufax, Juan Marichal ....$18-$25

06/25/66 Sonny Siebert ....$10-$12

07/02/66 Richie Allen ....$10-$12

07/09/66 Jim Northrup ....$10-$15

07/16/66 August A. Busch Jr. ....$12-$15

07/23/66 Gaylord Perry ....$12-$15

07/30/66 Jack Aker...$10-$15

08/06/66 Woodie Fryman.............................$10-$12

08/13/66 Boog Powell ....$10-$15

08/20/66 Orlando Cepeda.............................$10-$15

08/27/66 Baltimore Orioles ....$12-$15

09/03/66 Phil Regan ....$10-$12

09/10/66 Jim Kaat ....$10-$12

09/17/66 Willie Stargell ....$14-$15

09/24/66 Felipe and Matty Alou ....$10-$15

10/01/66 Jim Nash..$10-$12

10/08/66 Hank Bauer, World Series.............. $15-$20

10/15/66 Jim Lefebvre...................................$10-$20

10/22/66 Luis Aparicio..................................$12-$20

1967

02/25/67 Baseball cartoons ....$10-$15

03/18/67 Hoyt Wilhelm....................................$8-$15

03/25/67 Andy Etchebarren............................$8-$12

04/01/67 Chance, Grant, Kaat ....$9-$15

04/08/67 Frank Robinson $15

04/15/67 Play Ball ....$12-$15

04/22/67 Jim Fregosi ....$8-$12

04/29/67 Roger Maris......................................$25-$30

05/06/67 Whitey Ford ....$12-$20

05/13/67 Steve Hargan ....$8-$12

05/20/67 Rick Reichardt...................................$8-$12

05/27/67 Walter Alston ....$8-$12

06/03/67 Gary Nolan..$8-$12

06/10/67 Rod Carew.....................................$10-$20

06/17/67 Juan Marichal ....$9-$15

06/24/67 Al Dark, Eddie Stanky ....$8-$12

07/01/67 Jim Lonborg ....$8-$15

07/08/67 Bob Veale ....$8-$12

07/15/67 Jim McGlothlin, All-Star issue ......$12-$15

07/22/67 Tim McCarver....................................$10-$15

07/29/67 Tommy John, Gary Peters.................$8-$12

08/05/67 Dick Williams ....$8-$12

08/12/67 Joe Torre..$9-$12

08/19/67 Paul Blair ....$8-$12

08/26/67 Mike McCormick ....$8-$12

09/02/67 Gil Hodges, Frank Howard ....$9-$15

09/09/67 Rusty Staub ....$8-$15

09/23/67 Carl Yastrzemski ....$15-$30

09/30/67 Earl Wilson..$8-$12

10/07/67 Stan Musial, Red Schoendienst...... $12-$20

10/14/67 Carl Yastrzemski ....$25-$30

10/21/67 Jim Lonborg, World Series ....$15-$20

10/28/67 Bob Gibson, World Series.............. $20-$25

1968

03/02/68 Carl Yastrzeniski ....$15-$30

03/09/68 Dick Hughes ....$8-$10

03/16/68 Mark Belanger..................................$8-$12

03/23/68 Jim Bunning ....$8-$15

03/30/68 Don Wert..$8-$12

04/06/68 Mickey Mantle and family ....$25-$35

04/13/68 Lou Brock..$12-$20

04/20/68 Pete Rose ....$25-$35

04/27/68 Jim Fregosi, Bobby Knoop .... $8-$12
05/04/68 Harmon Killebrew.......................... $12-$20
05/11/68 Jerry Koosman .... $8-$15
05/18/68 Mickey Lolich .... $8-$15
05/25/68 Orlando Cepeda................................ $9-$15
06/01/68 Frank Howard.................................... $8-$12
06/08/68 Don Drysdale .... $9-$15
06/15/68 Woody Fryman.................................. $8-$15
06/22/68 Jim Hardin .... $8-$12
06/29/68 Tony Horton .... $8-$10
07/06/68 Denny McLain .... $8-$15
07/13/68 Willie McCovey, All-Star issue ..... $12-$15
07/20/68 Willie Horton .... $9-$15
07/27/68 Matty Alou .... $8-$12
08/03/68 Luis Tiant .... $8-$12
08/10/68 Glenn Beckert.................................... $8-$12
08/17/68 Reggie Jackson, Rick Monday .... $25-$35
08/24/68 Dal Maxvill .... $8-$12
08/31/68 Ted Uhlaender .... $8-$12
09/07/68 Phil Regan .... $8-$12
09/21/68 Bill Freehan.. $8-$15
09/28/68 Mike Shannon .... $8-$15
10/05/68 Denny McLain, Lefty Grove, World
Series $15
10/12/68 Roger Maris and family, World Series
.... $25-$35
10/19/68 Bob Gibson, World Series.............. $10-$20

1969

01/04/69 Denny McLain $12
03/01/69 Willie Mays.................................... $15-$20
03/15/69 Ted Williams.................................... $15
03/22/69 Denny McLain $12
03/29/69 Tony Conigliaro $12
04/05/69 100 Years of Baseball $15
04/12/69 Brock, Flood, Pinson $15
04/19/69 Don Buford.. $10
04/26/69 Tug McGraw $10
05/03/69 Mel Stottlemyre................................ $10
05/10/69 Bill Sudakis $10
05/17/69 Dave McNally $10
05/24/69 Richie Hebner.................................... $10
05/31/69 Bobby Murcer $10
06/07/69 Don Kessinger.................................... $10
06/14/69 Blue Moon Odom................................ $10
06/21/69 Lee May $10
06/28/69 Ray Culp.. $10
07/05/69 Ken Holtzman $10
07/12/69 Rod Carew.. $15
07/19/69 Powell, B. Robinson, F. Robinson $20
07/26/69 Reggie Jackson.................................... $30
08/02/69 Matty Alou $10
08/09/69 Willie McCovey $15
08/16/69 Rico Petrocelli.................................... $10
08/23/69 Phil Niekro $12
08/30/69 Steve Carlton.................................. $12-$15

09/06/69 Ron Santo $12
09/13/69 Mike Cuellar...................................... $10
09/27/69 Bobby Tolan...................................... $10
10/04/69 Billy Martin $15
10/11/69 Tom Seaver $20
10/18/69 Boog Powell $15
10/25/69 Harmon Killebrew.............................. $15
11/01/69 David (Mets)/Goliath (Orioles).............. $20

1970

01/17/70 Willie Mays.. $15
02/28/70 Roberto Clemente................................ $20
04/11/70 T. Conigliaro, R. Smith, Yastrzemski
.... $25
04/18/70 Johnny Bench $20
04/25/70 Bert Campaneris.................................. $7
05/02/70 Rusty Staub $8
05/09/70 Brant Alyea $7
05/16/70 Tony Perez $10
05/23/70 Hank Aaron $15
05/30/70 Dave Johnson $7
06/06/70 Richie Allen $8
06/13/70 Vada Pinson $8
06/20/70 Jim Merritt.. $7
06/27/70 Danny Walton $8
07/04/70 Rico Carty $8
07/11/70 Felipe Alou $7
07/18/70 Pete Rose $20
07/25/70 Willie Mays $15
08/01/70 Billy Grabarkewitz $7
08/08/70 Al Kaline .... $15-$20
08/15/70 Ray Fosse $7
08/22/70 Roy White $7
08/29/70 Dave Giusti... $7
09/05/70 Bud Harrelson $7
09/12/70 Bernie Carbo $7
09/26/70 Joe Pepitone $7
10/03/70 Gaylord Perry/Jim Perry $10
10/10/70 Danny Murtaugh $7
10/17/70 Cuellar, McNally, Palmer $12
10/24/70 Johnny Bench...................................... $15
10/31/70 World Series wrap-up $10

1971

02/27/71 Bamberger, Etchebarren, Palmer $10
04/10/71 Johnny Bench, Boog Powell $10
04/17/71 Reggie Jackson.................................... $15
04/24/71 Tony Conigliaro $10
05/01/71 Manny Sanguillen $5
05/08/71 Steve Carlton....................................... $10
05/22/71 Willie Stargell $8
06/05/71 Vida Blue $5
06/12/71 Jerry Grote... $5
06/19/71 Sonny Siebert $5
06/26/71 Dick Dietz $5
07/03/71 Fergie Jenkins...................................... $8
07/10/71 Bobby Murcer $8

07/17/71 Willie Mays...$12
07/24/71 Joe Torre...$5
07/31/71 Frank Robinson $8
08/07/71 Tony Oliva $7
08/14/71 Amos Otis $5
08/21/71 Dock Ellis $5
09/04/71 Bill Melton $5
09/25/71 Mickey Lolich $8
10/02/71 Wilbur Wood $5
10/09/71 Al Downing...$5
10/16/71 Brooks Robinson....................................$12
10/23/71 Joe Torre...$5
10/30/71 Roberto Clemente...................................$15

1972

03/04/72 Cuellar, Dobson, McNally, Palmer..........$8
04/08/72 Roberto Clemente...................................$15
04/29/72 Play Ball $7
05/13/72 Don Sutton $7
05/27/72 Milt Wilcox $5
06/03/72 Dave Kingman $5
06/10/72 Mickey Lolich $7
06/17/72 Gary Nolan $5
06/24/72 D. Baylor, T. Crowley, Grich.................$7
07/01/72 Danny Frisella, Tug McGraw $6
07/08/72 Lou Piniella $6
07/15/72 Manny Sanguillen $5
07/22/72 Joe Rudi...$5
07/29/72 Hank Aaron .... $10-$15
08/12/72 Sparky Lyle $5
08/19/72 Cesar Cedeno $5
09/02/72 Steve Carlton $10
09/23/72 Carlton Fisk...$8
09/30/72 Al Oliver $5
10/14/72 Luis Tiant $6
10/21/72 Billy Williams $7
10/28/72 Johnny Bench $12
11/04/72 Dick Williams $5

1973

01/06/73 Charlie Finley..$5
03/03/73 Rollie Fingers .... $6-$10
04/14/73 Steve Carlton $10
04/28/73 Chris Speier $5
05/05/73 Nolan Ryan..$15
05/12/73 Fred Patek, Cookie Rojas......................$5
05/19/73 Joe Morgan $7
06/02/73 Wilbur Wood $5
06/09/73 Joe Ferguson..$5
06/16/73 Joe Coleman $5
06/23/73 Ron Santo $6
06/30/73 Ron Blomberg $5
07/07/73 Bobby Bonds $5
07/14/73 John Mayberry $5
07/21/73 Bob Watson $5
07/28/73 Bench, Morgan, Rose $15
08/04/73 Bert Byleven..$5

08/11/73 Bobby Bonds...$5
08/18/73 Thurman Munson $15
08/25/73 Del Unser $5
09/01/73 Orlando Cepeda......................................$5
09/08/73 Darrell Evans...$5
09/29/73 Lou Brock..$8
10/06/73 Willie Mays............................... $10-$15
10/13/73 Jim Palmer...$8
10/20/73 Blue, Holtzman, Hunter $10
10/27/73 Jon Matlack $5
11/03/73 Mike Andrews $5

1974

03/02/74 Dick Green $4
04/06/74 Play Ball..$6
04/20/74 Hank Aaron, Babe Ruth .... $15-$25
04/27/74 Ted Simmons $4
05/04/74 Roy White $4
05/11/74 Jim Wynn $4
05/18/74 Jeff Burroughs $4
05/25/74 Ken Singleton $4
06/01/74 John Hiller...$4
06/08/74 Mike Schmidt................................ $15-$20
06/15/74 Gaylord Perry $5
06/22/74 Tommy John...$5
06/29/74 Rod Carew................................... $7-$15
07/06/74 Ralph Garr $4
07/13/74 Carlton Fisk...$6
07/20/74 Dick Williams $4
07/27/74 Mike Marshall $4
08/03/74 Steve Busby..$4
08/10/74 Greg Gross $4
08/17/74 Reggie Jackson $12
08/24/74 Jorge Orta $4
09/14/74 Richie Zisk $4
09/28/74 Reggie Smith $4
10/19/74 Bill Virdon $4
10/26/74 Steve Garvey $7
11/02/74 Brock, Burroughs, Hunter, M.
Marshall..$7

1975

01/04/75 Lou Brock...$6
03/08/75 Bobby Bonds, Jim Hunter .... $7-$12
04/12/75 Opening Day $5
04/26/75 Dave Concepcion $5
05/03/75 Frank Robinson $6
05/10/75 Greg Luzinski...$5
05/17/75 Nolan Ryan.................................. $12-$20
05/24/75 Ken Reitz..$4
05/31/75 Jim Palmer..$6
06/07/75 Madlock, Monday, Morales $6
06/14/75 Ron LeFlore $5
06/21/75 Andy Messersmith $4
06/28/75 Hal McRae $4
07/05/75 Joe Morgan..$6
07/12/75 Fred Lynn..$6

07/19/75 Mays, Musial, Ruth, Williams, Feller,
Hubbell, Kaline, Marichal $10
07/26/75 Robin Yount $15
08/02/75 Dave Parker.....................$5
08/09/75 Claudell Washington $4
08/16/75 Al Hrabosky $4
08/23/75 Jim Kaat $4
08/30/75 Larry Bowa, Dave Cash $4
09/06/75 Randy Jones $4
09/20/75 John Mayberry $4
10/04/75 Fingers, Lindblad, Todd.....................$6
10/11/75 Sparky Anderson.....................$5
10/18/75 Fred Lynn $6

1976

03/06/76 Fred Lynn $6
04/10/76 Fergie Jenkins.....................$5
04/17/76 Don Gullett.....................$4
04/24/76 Frank Tanana.....................$4
05/01/76 Larry Bowa.....................$4
05/08/76 Dave Kingman $4
05/15/76 Toby Harrah $4
05/22/76 Willie Horton $8
05/29/76 Ron Cey.....................$5
06/05/76 George Brett ....$12-$15
06/12/76 Chris Chambliss $4
06/19/76 Randy Jones $4
06/26/76 Ron LeFlore $5
07/03/76 George Foster $4
07/10/76 John Montefusco $4
07/17/76 Johnny Bench $8
07/24/76 Jim Slaton.....................$4
07/31/76 Al Oliver.....................$4
08/07/76 Dennis Leonard $4
08/14/76 Mark Fidrych.....................$5
08/21/76 Dave Cash $4
08/28/76 Rico Carty $4
09/18/76 Rick Rhoden.....................$4
09/25/76 Mickey Rivers.....................$4
10/16/76 Rawly Eastwick.....................$4
10/23/76 Cincinnati's "Big Red Machine:" Anderson,
Bench, Concepcion, Foster, Geronimo, Griffey,
Morgan, Perez, Rose $15

1977

03/05/77 Baylor, Grich, Rudi $5
03/26/77 Wayne Garland.....................$4
04/02/77 Mike Schmidt $10
04/09/77 Don Gullett, Reggie Jackson.....................$10
04/16/77 Bert Campaneris.....................$4
04/23/77 Rick Monday $4
04/30/77 Rollie Fingers.....................$4
05/07/77 Amos Otis $4
05/14/77 Joe Rudi $4
05/21/77 Ted Simmons $4
05/28/77 Ron Cey.....................$4
06/04/77 Mitchell Page $4

06/11/77 Dave Parker.....................$4
06/18/77 Richie Zisk $4
06/25/77 Bruce Sutter.....................$4
07/09/77 Butch Wynegar.....................$4
07/16/77 Jeff Burroughs.....................$4
07/23/77 Frank Tanana $4
07/30/77 Steve Carlton.....................$7
08/06/77 Joe Morgan.....................$6
08/13/77 Jim Rice.....................$6
08/20/77 Cromartie, Dawson, Valentine.....................$6
08/27/77 Billy Hunter, Bump Wills $4
09/03/77 Tommy John.....................$4
09/24/77 Graig Nettles $5
10/01/77 Greg Luzinski.....................$5
10/08/77 Al Cowens $4
10/15/77 Rod Carew $7
10/22/77 Baker, Cey, Garvey, Smith $8

1978

03/04/78 Rod Carew, George Foster.....................$7
04/08/78 Salute To 1978 Season $4
04/15/78 Lyman Bostock $4
04/22/78 Garry Templeton $4
04/29/78 Steve Kemp, Jason Thompson $4
05/06/78 Don Money.....................$4
05/13/78 Ross Grimsley $4
05/20/78 Pete Rose $9
05/27/78 Jim Rice.....................$6
06/03/78 Barr, Blue, Knepper, Montefusco $5
06/10/78 Gary Alexander $4
06/17/78 Ron Guidry.....................$6
06/24/78 Vic Davalillo, Manny Mota $4
07/01/78 Paul Splittorff $4
07/08/78 Flanagan, Martinez, McGregor,
Palmer.....................$7
07/15/78 Carew, Foster, Garvey, Guidry,
Seaver, Rice.....................$8
07/22/78 Larry Bowa.....................$4
07/29/78 Jim Sundberg.....................$4
08/05/78 Terry Puhl.....................$4
08/12/78 Paul Molitor $8
08/19/78 Jack Clark.....................$4
08/26/78 Davey Lopes.....................$4
09/16/78 Carlton Fisk $6
09/23/78 Dave Parker.....................$4
09/30/78 Rich Gossage.....................$5
10/21/78 Steve Garvey $5
10/28/78 Ron Guidry.....................$6

1979

01/06/79 Ron Guidry.....................$6
03/03/79 Spring Training issue $5
04/07/79 Guidry, Madlock, Perry, Rice $6
04/21/79 Pete Rose $7
04/28/79 Rod Carew.....................$6
05/05/79 Reggie Jackson.....................$8
05/12/79 Vida Blue $4

05/19/79 Al Oliver......$4
05/26/79 J.R. Richard......$4
06/02/79 Mike Marshall......$4
06/09/79 Gary Carter......$7
06/16/79 Fred Lynn......$6
06/23/79 Brock, Hendrick, Hernandez,
Simmons, Templeton......$7
06/30/79 Tommy John......$4
07/07/79 Roy Smalley......$4
07/21/79 Brett, Lynn, Parker, Rose......$8
07/28/79 Joe Niekro......$4
08/04/79 Don Baylor......$4
08/11/79 Willie Stargell......$6
08/18/79 Mike Flanagan......$4
08/25/79 Dave Kingman, Mike Schmidt......$8
09/15/79 Carl Yastrzemski......$7
09/22/79 Lou Brock......$6
09/27/79 Tom Seaver......$8
10/06/79 Darrell Porter......$4
10/20/79 Bench, Dent, Fingers, Jackson, Rose......$8
12/29/79 Pete Rose......$8

1980

01/12/80 Willie Stargell......$5
03/08/80 Keith Hernandez......$5
04/12/80 Mike Flanagan, Dave Winfield......$6
04/19/80 Nolan Ryan......$12
04/26/80 George Brett......$10
05/10/80 Kent Tekulve......$4
05/17/80 George Foster......$4
05/24/80 Gorman Thomas......$4
05/31/80 Ken Reitz, Champ Summers......$4
06/07/80 Dave Kingman......$4
06/14/80 Carlton Fisk......$6
06/21/80 Steve Carlton......$7
06/28/80 Reggie Smith......$4
07/05/80 Billy Martin......$6
07/12/80 Steve Garvey......$6
07/26/80 Jim Palmer, Earl Weaver......$6
08/02/80 Reggie Jackson......$8
08/09/80 Willie Wilson......$4
08/16/80 Lee Mazzilli......$4
08/23/80 Jim Bibby, Steve Stone......$4
08/30/80 Andre Dawson, Ron LeFlore......$5
09/20/80 George Brett......$8
09/27/80 Jose Cruz......$8
10/04/80 Pete Rose......$8
10/25/80 Dan Quisenberry, Mike Schmidt......$8
11/01/80 Willie Aikens......$4

1981

01/10/81 George Brett......$8
03/07/81 Rick Langford, Billy Martin......$5
03/28/81 Fred Lynn, Don Sutton......$5
04/11/81 Cooper, Oglivie, Simmons, Thomas, Yount
......$8
04/18/81 Ty Cobb, Nap Lajoie......$4

04/25/81 Bruce Sutter......$5
05/09/81 Tony Armas, Matt Keough......$4
05/16/81 Fisk, LeFlore, Luzinski......$6
05/23/81 Tim Raines, Fernando Valenzuela......$5
05/30/81 Ray Grebey, Bowie Kuhn, Marvin Miller$4
06/06/81 Gary Matthews......$4
06/13/81 Ken Singleton......$4
06/20/81 Stan Musial, Pete Rose......$8
06/27/81 On Strike......$4
07/25/81 Chuck Tanner......$4
08/07/81 R. Foster, B. Gibson, Mize......$4
08/14/81 Baseball's Back......$4
08/22/81 Goose Gossage......$4
08/29/81 Bench, Concepcion, Seaver......$6
10/31/81 Dave Winfield......$6

1982

03/06/82 Steve Garvey......$5
03/27/82 Ozzie Smith, Garry Templeton......$4
04/10/82 Perry, Rose, Stargell, Yastrzemski......$8
04/17/82 Collins, Foster, Griffey......$4
04/24/82 Al Oliver......$4
05/03/82 Rafael Ramirez......$4
05/10/82 Eddie Murray......$6
05/17/82 Keith Hernandez......$5
05/31/82 LaMarr Hoyt, Keith Moreland......$4
06/14/82 Rickey Henderson......$7
06/28/82 Carl Yastrzemski......$6
07/05/82 Gene Mauch......$4
07/12/82 Gary Carter, Andre Dawson......$6
07/26/82 Earl Weaver......$4
08/02/82 Aaron, Chandler, T. Jackson, F.
Robinson......$6
08/09/82 Cecil Cooper, Robin Yount......$7
08/23/82 Reggie Jackson, Steve Sax......$7
09/06/82 Rickey Henderson......$4
09/20/82 Dale Murphy......$4
10/11/82 Don Sutton, Robin Yount......$7
10/18/82 Cecil Cooper, Bruce Sutter......$4
10/25/82 Lonnie Smith, Robin Yount......$7

1983

01/03/83 Whitey Herzog......$4
03/07/83 Billy Martin......$4
03/21/83 Steve Garvey......$4
04/04/83 Porter, L. Smith, O. Smith, Sutter
......$4
04/11/83 Carl Yastrzemski......$6
04/18/83 Steve Kemp......$4
05/02/83 Reggie Jackson......$7
05/09/83 Nolan Ryan......$10
05/16/83 George Brett......$7
05/23/83 Greg Brock, Mike Marshall......$4
06/06/83 Steve Carlton......$6
06/13/83 Dave Stieb......$4
06/20/83 Rod Carew......$6
06/27/83 Darrell Evans......$4

Periodicals

07/04/83 TSN's All-Time All-Stars $6
07/11/83 Fernando Valenzuela..................................$4
07/25/83 Pete Rose $7
08/01/83 Alston, Kell. Marichal, B. Robinson........$6
08/08/83 Brett, MacPhail, Martin, McClelland
....$5
08/22/83 Ray Knight $4
09/12/83 Floyd Bannister $4
09/26/83 Cecil Cooper, Andre Dawson $5
10/10/83 Alexander, Fisk, Larsen, Mazeroski
....$5
10/24/83 Cal Ripken Jr., Lenn Sakata..................$10

1984

01/02/84 Bowie Kuhn $4
03/05/84 Cal Ripken Jr..$10
04/02/84 Pete Rose $7
04/09/84 Goose Gossage $4
04/23/84 Wade Boggs $6
04/30/84 Bill Madlock...$4
05/07/84 Phil Niekro, Jose Rijo $5
05/14/84 Dave Kingman $5
05/21/84 Darryl Strawberry......................................$8
05/28/84 Lemon, Parrish, Trammell, Whitaker
....$8
06/11/84 Mike Schmidt $8
06/18/84 Leon Durham $4
06/25/84 Eddie Murray $6
07/02/84 Rickey Henderson $6
07/09/84 Cronin, Foxx, Gehrig, Hubbell,
Simmons, Ruth $6
07/23/84 Tony Gwynn...$8
08/06/84 Aparicio, Drysdale, Killebrew, Reese
....$10
08/20/84 Ryne Sandberg $10
09/17/84 Kirk Gibson, Willie Hernandez...............$7
09/24/84 Kirby Puckett $10
10/08/84 Willie Mays...$7
10/15/84 Steve Garvey, Alan Trammell................ $7
10/22/84 Gibson, Trammell, Whitaker...................$7
12/31/84 Peter Ueberroth $4

1985

02/11/85 Berra, Henderson, Steinbrenner, Armstrong,
Montefusco, Torborg...$4
03/04/85 Ryne Sandberg $8
03/25/85 Bruce Sutter..$4
04/08/85 Rickey Henderson, Don Mattingly $8
04/15/85 Anderson, Gibson, Hernandez, Morris,
Trammell $7
04/22/85 LaMarr Hoyt...$4
04/29/85 Dale Murphy $4
05/13/85 Armas, Boggs, Easler, Evans, Rice..........$4
05/20/85 Billy Martin...$4
05/27/85 Terry Whitfield..$4
06/10/85 Brett, Quisenberry, Schuerholz,
Wilson $4

06/17/85 Joaquin Andujar, Mario Soto $4
06/24/85 Jack Clark, David Green baseball cards...$4
06/31/85 Dale Murphy, Eddie Murray $5
07/08/85 Vince Coleman $4
07/15/85 Bill Caudill, Gary Lavelle $4
07/29/85 Gooden, Brock, Slaughter, Vaughan, Wil-
helm $7
08/12/85 Tom Seaver $5
08/19/85 Peter Ueberroth $4
09/09/85 Pittsburgh Pirates franchise.....................$4
09/16/85 Pete Rose..$7
09/30/85 Mets-Yankees battle for Big Apple..........$6
10/07/85 Pedro Guerrero $5
10/14/85 Cardinals celebrate pennant $4
11/04/85 George Brett, Bret Saberhagen $6
12/09/85 Kirk Gibson..$5

1986

01/06/86 Pete Rose, Whitey Herzog $6
02/10/86 Ken "Hawk" Harrelson $4
02/17/86 Candlestick Park..$4
03/03/86 Brett, J. Clark, R. Henderson $6
03/17/86 Reggie Jackson...$4
03/24/86 Dave Parker, Darryl Strawberry...............$4
04/07/86 Ozzie Smith $6
04/21/86 Canseco, W. Clark, Galarraga,
Incaviglia, Carew..$7
04/28/86 Hoyt, D. Williams, Guidry $4
05/12/86 Boone, R. Jackson, Sutton........................$6
05/19/86 P. Niekro, Martin, Schmidt $4
05/26/86 Carlton, Rose, Ryan, Puckett $6
06/02/86 Robin Yount, Hubie Brooks.....................$6
06/09/96 Gooden, K. Hernandez, Leonard.............$7
06/16/86 Don Sutton $4
06/23/86 Hal Lanier, Bobby Valentine $4
06/30/86 George Steinbrenner....................................$6
07/07/86 Mike Krukow..$4
07/14/86 Wade Boggs, Bo Jackson..........................$7
07/21/86 Darling, Fernandez, Orosco $4
07/28/86 Bankhead, Clark, McDowell, Snyder, Witt,
Clemens $6
08/04/86 Glenn Davis, Mike Scott $6
08/18/86 Jose Canseco, Tim Raines.........................$6
08/25/86 Earl Weaver, Tom Lasorda $4
09/01/86 Don Mattingly, Rickey Henderson $8
09/08/86 Jack Morris $4
09/15/86 Rob Deer $5
09/29/86 G. Carter, Clemens, Ashburn $8
10/13/86 G. Davis, DeCinces, K. Hernandez, Rice $6
10/27/86 Len Dykstra, Mike Schmidt $5
11/03/86 Marty Barrett, Gary Carter......................$4
11/24/86 Lance Parrish..$5
12/15/86 Roger Clemens $5

1987

03/02/87 Dwight Gooden ....$3-$4
03/30/87 Mike Schmidt....................................$4-$5

250

04/06/87 Reggie Jackson .... $4-$5
04/13/87 Ron Guidry .... $3-$4
05/11/87 Andre Dawson $4
05/18/87 Pete Rose .... $4-$5
05/25/87 Bret Saberhagen $4
06/01/87 Rickey Henderson, Charles Hudson $4
06/08/87 Jack Clark $3
06/15/87 Eric Davis $3
07/06/87 Harold Baines, Jody Davis $3
07/13/87 Jack Morris, Alan Trammell .... $3-$4
07/27/87 Bert Blyleven, Jeff Reardon .... $3-$4
08/03/87 Whitey Herzog $3
08/10/87 Coleman, Durham, Guidry, R. Henderson,
Pettis, Strawberry $4
08/24/87 Cal Ripken Sr. $3
08/31/87 G. Bell, J. Clark, E. Davis, Dawson,
Mattingly, McGwire $4
09/07/87 Will Clark $4
10/05/87 George Bell, Alan Trammell .... $3-$4
10/19/87 Boston Red Sox, New York Mets $3
10/26/87 Greg Gagne, Willie McGee $3
11/02/87 Kent Hrbek, Kirby Puckett .... $4-$5
12/14/87 George Bell $3

1988

02/01/88 Yankees, Mets hats $3
03/07/88 Kirk Gibson, Tommy Lasorda $3
04/11/88 Kent Hrbek, Wayne Garland $3
04/25/88 Eddie Murray, Frank Robinson .... $3-$4
05/02/88 Billy Martin, Dave Winfield .... $4-$5
05/09/88 Roger Clemens .... $4-$5
05/16/88 Canseco, Parker, McGwire .... $4-$5
05/30/88 Wrigley Field $3
06/06/88 Gooden, D. Robinson, Ryan .... $6-$7
06/20/88 Greg Maddux, Mark Grace .... $4-$5
07/04/88 Andres Galarraga, Billy Martin $4
07/11/88 Baseball cards, Andy Van Slyke .... $3-$4
07/25/88 Brett, Sabo, Steinbach .... $3-$4
08/01/88 Frank Viola $3
08/08/88 Darryl Strawberry $3
08/15/88 Joe Morgan .... $3-$4
08/22/88 Alan Trammell .... $3-$4
09/05/88 Kirby Puckett, Dennis Rasmussen ..... $4-$5
10/17/88 Boggs, Canseco, Gibson, Strawberry $4
10/24/88 Kirk Gibson, Orel Hershiser $4
10/31/88 Orel Hershiser $4

1989

01/23/89 Johnny Bench, Carl Yastrzemski .... $4-$5
03/06/89 Molitor, Murray, Valentine, Van Slyke .. $4-$5
04/03/89 J. Clark, Hurst, McKeon $3
04/10/89 Ken Griffey Jr., Ken Griffey Sr. .... $7-$8
04/24/89 Ellis Burks, Pete Rose .... $4-$5
05/01/89 Gregg Jefferies $4
05/08/89 Kevin Mitchell $3
05/15/89 Brady Anderson, Cal Ripken Jr. .... $4-$5
05/22/89 Tommy John, Jose DeLeon $3

06/05/89 Ernie Whitt, Fred McGriff $4
06/12/89 Blyleven, D. Sanders, Schmidt $4
07/03/89 John Franco, Don Zimmer $3
07/24/89 Orel Hershiser, Howard Johnson $4
07/31/89 J. Franco, Palmeiro, Sierra $4
08/07/89 Lonnie Smith $3
08/14/89 Will Clark, Kevin Mitchell $4
08/21/89 Nolan Ryan .... $5-$6
08/28/89 Jose Oquendo, Mike Scott $3
09/04/89 Pete Rose .... $4-$5
09/18/89 Wade Boggs, Tony Gwynn .... $4-$5
10/16/89 McGriff, McGwire, Mitchell, Sandberg .. $5
10/23/89 Terry Kennedy, Terry Steinbach $3
10/30/89 San Francisco earthquake $4
11/06/89 Oakland A's $3
12/11/89 Kevin Mitchell $3

1990

01/08/90 J. Carter, M. Davis, Langston, Parker
.... $3-$4
01/29/90 Mike Schmidt .... $4-$5
03/05/90 Baseball lockout $3
03/12/90 Dwight Gooden, Pete Rose .... $3-$4
04/09/90 Jack McKeon, Darryl Strawberry $3
04/30/90 G. Davis, Hrbek, Puckett .... $3-$4
05/07/90 E. Davis, Larkin, O'Neill, Piniella, Sabo . $4
05/21/90 Jose Canseco, Will Clark $4
06/04/90 Cecil Fielder $4
06/11/90 Schooler, Viola, M. Williams $4
06/18/90 Len Dykstra $4
06/25/90 Nolan Ryan .... $4-$5
07/02/90 Barry Bonds, Charlie Fox $4
07/09/90 Dwight Gooden, Bret Saberhagen $3
07/23/90 Bert Blyleven, Don Drysdale $4
07/30/90 M. Davis, Heaton, Parker, Wells $3
08/06/90 Gant, Strawberry, Tapani $3
08/13/90 Nolan Ryan, George Steinbrenner $4
08/20/90 Comiskey Park, Hurst, Mattingly $4
08/27/90 Bob Welch $3
09/03/90 Jeff Ballard, Ramon Martinez $3
09/10/90 Jose Canseco, Barry Larkin $4
09/24/90 Rickey Henderson $3
10/01/90 Baines, Canseco, Lansford, McGee,
McGwire, Welch, Weiss $3
10/15/90 Chris Sabo, Andy Van Slyke $3
10/22/90 Dennis Eckersley .... $3-$4
10/29/90 Rob Dibble, Lou Piniella $3
12/17/90 Joe Carter, Fred McGriff .... $3-$4
12/31/90 Glove of money $3

1991

01/07/91 Nolan Ryan $4
03/04/91 Dave Parker $3
03/11/91 Jim Palmer $4
04/01/91 Umpire Bruce Froemming $3
04/22/91 G. Bell, J. Clark, R. Henderson,
Sanderson $3

05/13/91 Rickey Henderson, Nolan Ryan .... $4-$5
05/20/91 Rob Dibble .... $2-$3
05/27/91 Dave Justice $3
06/17/91 Andre Dawson..................................... $3-$4
07/01/91 Gambling in baseball........................... $2-$3
07/08/91 Hundley, Lankford, Van Poppel $2
07/29/91 Peter Ueberroth .... $2-$3
08/05/91 Tiger Stadium...................................... $2-$3
08/12/91 Lineups, Dennis Martinez .... $2-$3
08/19/91 Wounded baseball .... $2-$3
08/26/91 Pedro Guerrero .... $2-$3
09/09/91 Bobby Cox .... $2-$3
09/16/91 Bobby Bonilla $3
09/23/91 Terry Pendleton $3
10/14/91 John Smoltz $3
10/21/91 Kirby Puckett .... $3-$4
11/04/91 Jack Morris... $3
11/11/91 Bobby Bonilla $3
12/16/91 Bobby Bonilla $3
12/23/91 Steve Palermo, Whitey Herzog .... $2-$3

1992

03/02/92 Tom Glavine... $3
03/09/92 Kirby Puckett .... $3-$4
03/16/92 George Brett .... $3-$4
03/30/92 Cal Ripken Jr.. $3-$4
04/06/92 Joe Carter, Rob Dibble .... $2-$3
04/13/92 Jose Canseco $3
04/20/92 Camden Yards .... $2-$3
04/27/92 Butch Hobson $2
05/04/92 Barry Bonds $3
05/11/92 Tony Gwynn... $3
05/18/92 Craig Biggio .... $2-$3
05/25/92 Lenny Harris.. $2
06/01/92 Todd Hundley... $2
06/08/92 Jeff Reardon $2
06/15/92 Gary Sheffield $3
06/22/92 David Cone... $2-$3
06/29/92 Leo Durocher, Willie Randolph............... $3
07/06/92 Norm Charlton, Rob Dibble.................... $2
07/20/92 Carlton Fisk .... $2-$3
07/27/92 Robin Yount $3
08/03/92 El Beisbol $2
08/31/92 John Smoltz $3
09/14/92 Joe Carter $3
09/21/92 Fay Vincent $2
09/28/92 Jay Bell, Darrin Fletcher $2
10/05/92 Tom Glavine, Frank Thomas .... $3-$4
10/12/92 Dennis Eckersley...................................... $3
10/19/92 Steve Avery .... $2-$3
10/26/92 Ed Sprague $2
11/02/92 Joe Carter, Otis Nixon......................... $2-$3
11/23/92 Mark McGwire $3

1993

02/01/93 George Brett $4
02/22/93 How We'd Fix Baseball $2

03/01/93 Joe Siddall $2
04/05/93 Dave Winfield $3
04/19/93 Roger Clemens $3
05/17/93 Carlton Fisk $3
05/31/93 Gregg Jefferies .... $2-$3
06/14/93 Barry Bonds $4
07/05/93 Barry Bonds $4
07/19/93 Jim Abbott.. $2-$3
07/26/93 Jack McDowell...$3
08/02/93 Dave Justice $3
08/09/93 Wade Boggs, Chad Kreuter....................$3
08/16/93 Nolan Ryan, Robin Ventura $5
08/30/93 Don Mattingly .... $3-$4
09/20/93 Frank Thomas...$5
10/11/93 John Kruk $3
10/25/93 Len Dykstra $3
11/01/93 Jays Celebrate...$3

1994

01/04/94 Ted Turner.. $2-$3
02/28/94 Denis Boucher $2
03/14/94 Don Baylor $3
04/04/94 Ken Griffey Jr. $5
04/18/94 Deion Sanders $4
05/02/94 Curtis Pride... $2-$3
05/30/94 Bob Tewksbury $2
06/05/94 Carlos Delgado...$2
07/04/94 Albert Belle .... $3-$4
07/11/94 Greg Maddux $4
07/25/94 Ozzie Guillen, Kenny Lofton....................$3
08/01/94 Barry Larkin $4
08/08/94 Richard Ravitch, Kenny Rogers, Donald
Fehr...$2
08/15/94 Hickory Crawdads fans $2
08/22/94 Baseball strike photo................................$2
09/26/94 Baseball strike squabbles $2
10/31/94 Joe Carter $3
11/14/94 Ted Williams...$4

1995

02/27/95 Who's on First?
04/10/95 Cal Ripken Jr.
05/01/95 Tom Glavine
05/08/95 Frank Thomas
06/05/95 Sandy Koufax, Nolan Ryan
06/19/95 Baseball fans
07/03/95 Eddie Murray
07/10/95 Lee Smith
08/07/95 Clemens, Gant, R. Jackson, Mays
08/28/95 Benito Santiago, Eric Young
09/11/95 Lou Gehrig, Cal Ripken
10/09/95 Greg Maddux
10/30/95 Mark Lemke, Kenny Lofton
11/06/95 Atlanta Braves celebrate
12/18/95 Cal Ripken Jr.

Sporting News Baseball Guides

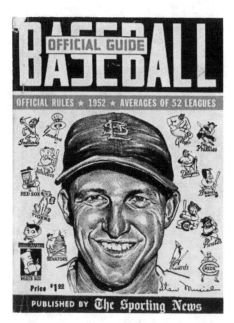

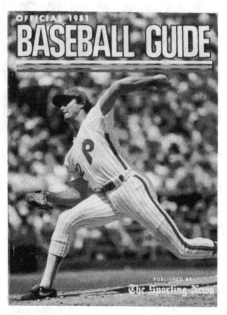

Offer complete team recaps for the previous major league season, plus statistics and lists of the award winners. From 1943-62 the guide was known as The Sporting News Baseball Guide & Record Book. It's been called The Sporting News Official Baseball Guide from 1963 to present.

1942 Baseball art	$165-$175
1943 Patriotic art	$60-$95
1944 B. Newsom/B. Dahlgren	$35-$40
1945 Marty Marion	$35-$45
1946 Hal Newhouser	$35-$45
1947 Harry Brecheen	$35-$45
1948 Ewell Blackwell	$50-$60
1949 Lou Boudreau	$50-$60
1950 P. Rizzuto/P.W. Reese	$40-$60
1951 Red Schoendienst	$40-$60
1952 Stan Musial	$35-$60
1953 Robin Roberts	$40-$60
1954 Casey Stengel	$40-$60
1955 Baseball action	$40-$60
1956 J. Coleman/B. Martin	$35-$60
1957 Mickey Mantle	$40-$60
1958 Ted Williams	$40-$60
1959 Baseballs	$40-$60
1960 Mullin "Bum" cartoon	$35-$60
1961 Trophy	$25-$35
1962 R. Maris/B. Ruth	$35-$50
1963 Mullin cartoon	$25-$50
1964 Stan Musial	$35-$50
1965 B. Robinson/K. Boyer	$35-$50

1966 W. Mays/S. Koufax	$40-$50
1967 F. Robinson/Koufax/Clemente	$40-$50
1968 Yastrzemski/Cepeda/Lonborg	$20-$35
1969 Rose/Gibson/McLain	$20-$35
1970 McCovey/Killebrew	$25-$35
1971 Bench/Gibson/Killebrew	$15-$25
1972 Jenkins/Blue/Torre	$10-$20
1973 Carlton/Bench/G. Perry	$10-$15
1974 Palmer/Jackson/Bonds	$12-$17
1975 Brock/Hunter	$15-$20
1976 Morgan/Seaver/Palmer	$15-$20
1977 Munson/Palmer	$10-$12
1978 Carew/Ryan/Carlton	$14-$15
1979 Guidry/Rice/Parker	$10-$15
1980 K. Hernandez/Baylor	$6-$10
1981 Steve Carlton	$8-$12
1982 Tom Seaver	$10-$15
1983 Robin Yount	$8-$12
1984 Cal Ripken Jr.	$10-$15
1985 Ryne Sandberg	$10-$15
1986 Willie McGee	$5-$7
1987 Roger Clemens	$10-$15
1988 Andre Dawson	$8-$10
1989 Jose Canseco	$8-$10
1990 Bret Saberhagen	$7-$10
1991 Bob Welch	$7-$10
1992 Will Clark	$7-$10
1993 Kirby Puckett	$5-$7
1994 Jack McDowell	$5-$7
1995 Ken Griffey Jr.	$7

Sporting News Baseball Register

Lists statistics for active major league players from the year before, for every player who appeared in at least one game. Minor league statistics and career accomplishments are also included.

1940 Ty Cobb	$75-$100
1941 Paul Derringer	$35-$45
1942 Joe DiMaggio	$40-$45
1943 Uncle Sam art	$30-$45
1944 Rube Waddell art	$30-$45
1945 Billy Southworth	$25-$45
1946 Baseball art	$35-$40
1947 Walter Johnson	$40-$45
1948 Baseball art	$35-$45
1949 Baseball art	$35-$45
1950 Joe DiMaggio	$35-$40
1951 Baseball art	$40-$75
1952 Baseball art	$25-$40
1953 Baseball art	$25-$40
1954 Baseball art	$22-$40
1955 Baseball art	$18-$40
1956 Baseball art	$18-$40
1957 Baseball art	$25-$40
1958 Baseball art	$15-$50
1959 Baseball art	$27-$40
1960 Baseball art	$20-$35
1961 Baseball art	$25-$35
1962 Baseball art	$25-$35
1963 Baseball art	$25-$35
1964 Yankee Stadium	$25-$35
1965 Ken Boyer	$25-$35
1966 Sandy Koufax	$25-$35
1967 Frank & Brooks Robinson	$25-$35
1968 Boston Red Sox	$20-$30
1969 Willie Horton	$20-$30
1970 Tom Seaver	$20-$25

1971 Willie Mays..................................$20-$25
1972 Joe Torre ....$17-$25
1973 Wilbur Wood ....$15-$25
1974 Pete Rose...................................$20-$25
1975 Catfish Hunter............................$15-$20
1976 Jim Palmer ....$15-$20
1977 Joe Morgan.................................$15-$20
1978 Rod Carew ....$15-$20
1979 Ron Guidry.................................$15-$20
1980 Carl Yastrzemski.........................$12-$15
1981 George Brett................................$12-$15
1982 Fernando Valenzuela ....$12-$15
1983 Bruce Sutter ....$10-$15
1984 John Denny ....$10-$15
1985 Willie Hernandez ....$10-$15
1986 Don Mattingly $10
1987 Mike Schmidt.......................................$10
1988 George Bell $10
1989 Frank Viola $10
1990 Kevin Mitchell $10
1991 Barry Bonds $10
1992 Frank Thomas $10
1993 Gary Sheffield.....................................$5-$8
1994 Lenny Dykstra...................................$5-$7
1995 Bret Saberhagen..............................$5-$7
1996 Greg Maddux ....cover

American League Red Books

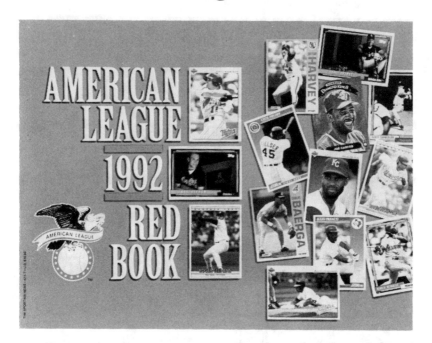

1943 Blue "V," (First Red Book)............. $25-$75
1944 Blue baseball with red seams .... $25-$50
1945 Blue baseball with red seams .... $25-$50
1946 Blue baseball with title .... $25-$45
1947 Baseball in right corner .... $25-$40
1948 Title and 1948................................ $25-$40
1949 Title and 1949................................ $25-$40
1950 Title and 1950 (1st glossy cover) .... $20-$35
1951 A.L. Golden Anniversary .... $20-$35
1952 "Play Ball!", Ted Williams .... $20-$35
1953 Shantz, Fox, Wynn, others .... $20-$35
1954 Vernon, Kuenn, Stengel, Rose .... $20-$35
1955 All-Star Team photo .... $20-$35
1956 Lemon, Stengel, managers .... $20-$30
1957 Team logos .... $17-$30
1958 50th Anniversary of BBWAA .... $17-$30
1959 Tiger sliding into home .... $17-$30
1960 Cobb, DiMaggio, Fox, Ruth, Gehrig, others.
.... $20-$35
1961 Four players with arms linked .... $17-$30
1962 Mantle, Maris, A.L. HR Leaders..... $20-$35
1963 Team pennants............................... $17-$25
1964 Killebrew, Yastrzemski, others .... $15-$25
1965 D. Chance, Powell, Oliva, others .... $12-$22
1966 McDowell, T. Conigliaro, others..... $14-$24
1967 Frank Robinson "Triple Crown" ..... $14-$24
1968 Yastrzemski "MVP/Triple Crown". $14-$24

1969 Cobb, Ruth, HOF plaques .... $14-$24
1970 Harmon Killebrew............................ $10-$20
1971 Boog Powell.................................... $10-$20
1972 Team, Major League logos .... $10-$20
1973 Team hats with Oakland in center.... $10-$20
1974 Team, Major League logos .... $10-$20
1975 Team logos..................................... $10-$15
1976 Carlton Fisk Series homer................ $10-$15
1977 Team logos, with Seattle and Toronto. $10-$15
1978 Carew, Nettles, Murray, others .... $10-$15
1979 Guidry, Rice, Carew, others............. $10-$15
1980 Orioles and Eddie Murray................. $7-$12
1981 Boddicker, Charboneau, Brett........... $7-$12
1982 1981 Playoffs team pictures.............. $7-$12
1983 Vuckovich, Yount, Ripken................. $7-$12
1984 L. Hoyt, Ripken, Quisenberry, Kittle $7-$12
1985 Stars and Detroit Tigers Series celebration...
.... $7-$8
1986 Newspaper headlines (Boggs, Seaver, others)$7
1987 Mattingly, Canseco, Clemens, others........ $7
1988 Twins World Series celebration $7
1989 1988 A.L. media guide covers $7
1990 1980s Red Book covers............................ $7
1991 League trophies, awards........................... $7
1992 Baseball cards $7
1993 George Brett, Robin Yount $7

National League Green Books

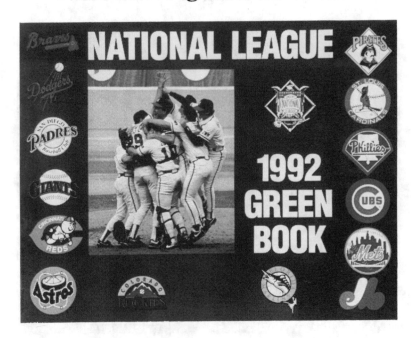

1935 Jan. 30, 1935 (First Green Book) .... $30-$60
1936 60th Birthday edition, Feb. 2, 1936 ...... $30-$50
1937 Title and Feb. 5, 1937 .... $30-$50
1938 Title and 1938 .... $30-$50
1939 Centennial edition 1839-1939 .... $30-$45
1940 Title and 1940 .... $25-$40
1941 Title and 1941 .... $25-$35
1942 Baseball diamond .... $25-$60
1943 Title and 1943 .... $25-$60
1944 Title and 1944 .... $25-$60
1945 Title and 1945 .... $25-$50
1946 BBWAA logo .... $25-$50
1947 Title and 1947 in diamond shape .... $25-$40
1948 Runner thrown out at first base .... $25-$35
1949 Team logos, pennants .... $25-$35
1950 Team logos, pennants .... $20-$30
1951 75th Anniversary, ball in glove .... $30-$30
1952 National League cities .... $20-$30
1953 National League cities .... $20-$30
1954 All-Star Team, 1st glossy cover .... $20-$30
1955 Eight stars (Mays, Musial, Spahn) ...... $20-$30
1956 Dodgers celebration photos .... $20-$30
1957 National League .... $17-$25
1958 N.L. salutes the BBWAA .... $17-$25
1959 Spahn/Musial clippings .... $17-$25
1960 Snider, McCovey, Musial, others .... $17-$25
1961 Spahn, Howard, F. Robinson, etc. .... $14-$20
1962 Map of U.S., team logos .... $14-$20
1963 1958-62 League Champs' parks .... $14-$20
1964 Stan Musial .... $14-$20

1965 List of past N.L. Champions .... $12-$20
1966 Stadiums of 1960s, seven .... $12-$20
1967 1962-66 Attendance figures .... $12-$20
1968 1967 Highlights/news clippings .... $12-$15
1969 1869 Cincinnati Red Stockings .... $12-$15
1970 Hodges, Rose, McCovey, Mets .... $12-$15
1971 Baseball with team names .... $12-$15
1972 12 bats with team names .... $12-$15
1973 Roberto Clemente memorial .... $12-$15
1974 Hank Aaron/Babe Ruth bust .... $12-$15
1975 Aaron, Brock, Schmidt, others .... $12-$15
1976 Reds World Series celebration .... $12-$15
1977 Team logos .... $12-$15
1978 12 league stars .... $12-$15
1979 League helmets, four bats .... $10-$12
1980 Baseball $7
1981 Schmidt, McGraw, All-Stars, Astros $7
1982 Valenzuela, Ryan, Schmidt, Rose $7
1983 Sax, D. Murphy, Carlton, others $7
1984 Team pennants $7
1985 Garvey, Sandberg, Gooden, Sutcliffe $7
1986 Rose, Gooden, Ryan, McGee $7
1987 Worrell, Scott, Mets, Schmidt, Raines $7
1988 .... $7
1989 Los Angeles celebration $7
1990 1980s MVPs and Cy Youngs $7
1991 Reds celebration, others $7
1992 Braves celebration $7
1993 U.S. map with team logos $7

Sports Ilustrated

Although the sport ranks second in terms of appearances on the cover, baseball is featured on the granddaddy Sports Illustrated issue of them all.

The premiere issue, of what was billed as the nation's first sports weekly, is dated Aug. 16, 1954, with a cover price of just a quarter. That issue, which now among collectors has a value of $275-$350, features the Milwaukee Braves' Eddie Mathews swinging at a pitch in Milwaukee's County Stadium. Catcher Wes Westrum and umpire Augie Donatelli are also included.

The issue's value is also driven up by the three pages of 1954 Topps baseball cards, featuring Willie Mays, Ted Williams and Jackie Robinson, printed on paper stock.

New York Yankees stars, including Mickey Mantle, are featured on 1954 Topps black-and-white and colored cards included in the magazine's second issue, dated Aug. 23, 1954. This magazine, which shows a horde of golf bags on the greens at the Masters, is as rare and as valuable as the first issue.

During Sports Illustrated's first 36 years of publication (through 1990), the magazine's cover has featured more than 360 baseball-related pictures. From 1954-1990, football tops the list, with 446 out of approximately 1,900 covers.

Leading the way for baseball players, with 10 appearances, is Reggie Jackson, who also has the distinction of holding the cover record for most different baseball uniforms worn - four, for the A's, Angels, Yankees and Orioles. Dick Groat (Phillies, Pirates and Cardinals) and Billy Martin (Rangers, Yankees, Twins) also each had three appearances. Martin is also one of only three athletes (the others are Gordie Howe and Willie Mays) to have appeared on a cover in four decades of the magazine's existence - the '50s, '60s, '70s and '80s.

The Minnesota Twins are among four teams to have been featured on three consecutive weeks. The team's streak occurred during the team's 1987 World Championship season. The Oct. 19 issue featured Greg Gagne, who was followed by Dan Gladden (Oct. 26) and a team celebration shot on Nov. 2. The team's success in 1991 led to another streak of three, beginning with the Oct. 21 issue with Kirby Puckett, followed by the Oct. 28 issue with Dan Gladden, and the Nov. 4 issue featuring Twins players celebrating a World Series championship.

The same baseball photo was used on two issue covers twice. A photo of Denny McLain was used on the July 29, 1968, issue as he was pursuing 30 wins, and again on Feb. 23, 1970, when he was in trouble for gambling.

George Brett and Mike Schmidt appeared on the April 3, 1981, baseball preview cover and again on Aug. 10, with the billing "HERE WE GO AGAIN," signfying the end of the baseball strike.

In addition to trying to collect an entire run of **SIs**, some topics to pursue include those which feature favorite players, teams, themes (World Series, All-Stars, Previews) or those named as the magazine's Sportsman of the Year. Baseball players named include:

Johnny Podres, 01/02/56; Stan Musial, 12/23/57; Sandy Koufax, 12/20/65; Carl Yastrzemski, 12/25/67; Tom Seaver, 12/22/69; Pete Rose, 12/22-29/75; Willie Stargell, 12/24-31/79; and Orel Hershiser, 12/19/88.

Father/son combinations can also be pursued. During the years they have included Ken Sr. and Ken Griffey Jr., the Ripken clan, Barry and Bobby Bonds, and Bump and Maury Wills.

First cover issues are also especially sought after by those who seek to have them autographed. These issues generally command a higher price than subsequent issues with the same player.

Generally, collectors who seek back issues want them to be in reasonable condition - unripped, uncreased - with the cover attached entirely. But the corners on many issues are often not sharp, especially from the earlier issues.

Old Sports Illustrateds can often be purchased at libraries, flea markets, through hobby publications and mail order houses, and card shops and shows. * means first cover, SOY means Sportsman of the Year.

1954

08/16/54 Eddie Mathews, Braves *............ $275-$350

1955

04/11/55 Mays*, Day, Durocher, Giants.... $100-$125
04/18/55 Al Rosen, Indians .... $75-$125
05/30/55 Herb Score, Indians * .... $15-$20
06/27/55 Duke Snider, Dodgers * $75
07/11/55 Yogi Berra, Yankees * .... $40-$50
08/01/55 Ted Williams, Red Sox * .... $75-$100
08/25/55 Don Newcombe, Dodgers * $20
09/26/55 Walter Alston, Dodgers * .... $20-$25

1956

01/02/56 Johnny Podres, Dodgers (SOY) $40
03/05/56 Stan Musial, Cardinals * .... $35-$50
04/09/56 Spring Baseball Preview $25
04/23/56 Billy Martin, Yankees * .... $20-$25
05/14/56 Al Kaline, Harvey Kuenn, Tigers * $30-$50
06/18/56 Mickey Mantle, Yankees * .... $50-$100
06/25/56 Warren Spahn, Braves *.................. $30-$50
07/09/56 Mays, Mantle, All-Stars $50
07/16/56 Kluszewski, Post, Bell, Indians....... $40-$50
07/30/56 Joe Adcock, Braves .... $15-$20
08/20/56 Second Anniversary issue .... $10-$20
09/10/56 Whitey Ford, Yankees *.................. $45-$50
10/01/56 World Series, Mickey Mantle .... $65-$75

1957

03/04/57 Mickey Mantle, Yankees .... $65-$100
04/15/57 Spring Baseball Preview $35
04/22/57 Wally Moon, Cardinals .... $12-$15
05/13/57 Billy Pierce, White Sox $15
06/03/57 Clem Labine, Dodgers .... $12-$15
07/08/57 Stan Musial, Ted Williams...................... $65
07/22/57 Hank Bauer, Yankees............................. $20
09/09/57 Roy McMillan, Reds .... $15-$20
09/30/57 Whitey Ford, Yankees, World Series...... $20
12/23/57 Stan Musial, Cardinals (SOY)................ $25

1958

03/03/58 Yankees, Spring Training............... $10-$15
03/17/58 Sal Maglie, Big League Secrets ...... $12-$15
03/31/58 Roy Sievers, Big League Secrets $20
04/14/58 Spring Baseball Preview .... $20-$25
04/21/58 Del Crandall, Big League Secrets ... $15-$25
05/19/58 Richie Ashburn, Big League Secrets $25
06/02/58 Eddie Mathews, Braves.................. $25-$40
06/23/58 Jackie Jensen, Red Sox .... $15-$20
07/07/58 Musial/Mantle/Mays .... $25-$35
07/28/58 Frank Thomas, Pirates..................... $10-$15
09/29/58 World Series.. $15

1959

03/02/59 Fred Haney, Casey Stengel $10
04/13/59 Willie Mays, Giants .... $30-$40
05/04/59 Bob Turley, Yankees....................... $12-$15
06/15/59 L.A. Coliseum baseball crowd.......... $7-$15
08/10/59 Nellie Fox/Luis Aparicio, White Sox......$55
09/28/59 Chicago White Sox $35

1960

03/07/60 Spring Training .... $10-$15
04/11/60 Baseball Preview issue............................ $25
06/06/60 Red Schoendienst, Braves............... $10-$20
07/04/60 Comiskey Park .... $8-$12
07/18/60 Candlestick Park................................ $8-$12
08/08/60 Dick Groat, Pirates $20
10/10/60 Vernon Law, Pirates....................... $10-$15

1961

03/06/61 Spring Training .... $10-$15
04/10/61 Baseball Preview issue, Musial .... $15-$20
05/15/61 Cookie Lavagetto, Twins .... $7-$15
06/26/61 Ernie Broglio, Willie Mays .... $10-$15
07/31/61 Baseball umpire.................................. $7-$10
10/02/61 Roger Maris, Yankees * .... $30-$50
10/09/61 Joey Jay, Reds .... $10-$20

1962

03/05/62 Casey Stengel, Mets .... $15-$20
04/09/62 Frank Lary, Detroit................................ $25
04/30/62 Luis Aparicio, White Sox................ $15-$20
06/04/62 Willie Mays, Giants $30
07/02/62 Mickey Mantle, Yankees .... $50-$100
07/30/62 Ken Boyer, Cardinals .... $15-$25
08/20/62 Don Drysdale, Dodgers .... $25-$35
10/01/62 World Series .... $10-$20

1963

03/04/63 Sandy Koufax, Dodgers * .... $25-$35
04/08/63 Baseball Preview issue, Killebrew $25
04/29/63 Art Mahaffey, Phillies $15
06/24/63 Roy Face, Pirates.................................... $20
07/22/63 Dick Groat, Cardinals..................... $10-$20
09/02/63 Ron Fairly, Dodgers .... $7-$15
09/30/63 Whitey Ford, Yankees..................... $20-$30

1964

03/02/64 Casey Stengel, Yogi Berra .... $15-$25
04/13/64 Sandy Koufax, Dodgers .... $30-$35
05/11/64 Al Kaline, Tigers .... $20-$35
05/25/64 Frank Howard, Dodgers .... $10-$15
07/06/64 Alvin Dark, Giants .... $8-$15
08/10/64 Johnny Callison, Phillies........................ $25
08/31/64 Brooks Robinson, Orioles $30

1965

03/01/65 Jim Bunning, Bo Belinsky, Phillies $10-$15
04/19/65 Baseball Preview $20
05/17/65 Bill Veeck, White Sox...................... $5-$6
06/21/65 Mickey Mantle, Yankees $50
07/12/65 Maury Wills, Dodgers .... $5-$8
08/09/65 Juan Marichal, Giants *.......................... $25
08/23/65 Tony Oliva, Twins .... $10-$15
10/04/65 World Series/Zoilo Versailles, Twins $12
12/20/65 Sandy Koufax, Dodgers (SOY)............... $35

1966

02/28/66 Leo Durocher, Eddie Stanky, White Sox. $9
04/18/66 Dick Groat, Phillies......................... $15-$20
05/23/66 Sam McDowell, Indians.................. $10-$15
06/06/66 Joe Morgan, Sonny Jackson, Astros $15
07/11/66 Andy Etchebarren, Orioles............... $7-$12
09/05/66 Harry Walker, Pirates......................... $5-$6
09/26/66 Gaylord Perry, Giants * .... $12-$15
10/10/66 Brooks and Frank Robinson, Orioles $35

1967

03/13/67 Jim Nash, A's.. $6
04/17/67 Maury Wills, Pirates............................... $20
05/08/67 Mickey Mantle, Ken Berry $35

Sports Illustrated

DECEMBER 20, 1965   35 CENTS

Sportsman of the Year: SANDY KOUFAX

05/15/67 Sandy Koufax, Don Drysdale, Dodgers ..$10
06/05/67 Al Kaline, Tigers..................................... $35
07/03/67 Roberto Clemente, Pirates *............ $35-$50
07/31/67 Spitball $5
08/21/67 Carl Yastrzemski, Red Sox * .... $25-$35
09/04/67 Tim McCarver, Cardinals.................. $8-$12
10/16/67 Lou Brock, Cardinals * .... $20-$25
12/25/67 Carl Yastrzemski, Red Sox (SOY).........$35

1968

03/11/68 Johnny Bench, Reds, Baseball rookies ...$20
04/15/68 Lou Brock, Cardinals $20
05/06/68 Ron Swoboda, Mets .... $8-$12
05/27/68 Pete Rose, Reds * $30
06/17/68 Don Drysdale, Dodgers .... $10-$12
07/08/68 Ted Williams, Red Sox $15
07/29/68 Denny McLain, Tigers .... $10-$15
08/19/68 Curt Flood, Cardinals .... $8-$10
09/02/68 Ken Harrelson, Red Sox.................... $8-$12
09/23/68 Denny McLain, Tigers, 30 Wins..... $25-$30
10/07/68 St. Louis Cardinals $25

1969

03/17/69 Ted Williams, Senators .... $12-$15
04/14/69 Bill Freehan, Tigers................................$20
05/19/69 Walt Alston and Dodgers .... $5-$7
06/30/69 Ron Santo, Cubs......................................$20
07/07/69 Reggie Jackson, A's * $30
07/21/69 Billy Martin, Twins............................ $5-$6
08/18/69 Hank Aaron, Braves * .... $15-$20
09/08/69 Pete Rose, Ernie Banks $35
10/05/69 Frank Robinson, Orioles .... $12-$15
10/19/69 Brooks Robinson, Orioles vs. Mets........$25
12/22/69 Tom Seaver, Mets * (SOY)....................$35

1970

02/23/70 Denny McLain, Tigers .... $10-$15
03/23/70 Dick Allen, Cardinals...................... $10-$15
04/13/70 Jerry Koosman, Mets $20
05/25/70 Hank Aaron, Braves, 3,000 Hits $20
06/22/70 Tony Conigliaro, Red Sox.............. $10-$12
07/13/70 Johnny Bench, Reds .... $15-$20
07/27/70 Willie Mays, 3,000 Hits .... $15-$20
09/07/70 Bud Harrelson, Mets .... $8-$12
09/28/70 Danny Murtaugh, Pirates .... $8-$12
10/19/70 Reds vs. Orioles .... $10-$12

1971

03/22/71 Wes Parker, Dodgers................................$6
04/12/71 Boog Powell, Orioles .... $12-$15
05/03/71 Dave Duncan, Jim Fregosi $5
05/31/71 Vida Blue, A's..................................... $8-$12
06/21/71 Jerry Grote, Mets....................................$6
07/05/71 Alex Johnson, Angels.......................... $5-$6
08/02/71 Willie Stargell, Pirates * .... $10-$15
08/30/71 Ferguson Jenkins, Cubs *................. $9-$12
09/27/71 Maury Wills, Dodgers............................$5
10/18/71 Frank Robinson, Orioles .... $8-$12

1972

03/13/72 Johnny Bench, Reds $15
03/27/72 Vida Blue, A's..$5
04/10/72 Joe Torre, Cardinals .... $10-$12
05/01/72 Willie Davis, Dodgers..............................$5
05/22/72 Willie Mays, Mets.................................$25
06/12/72 Dick Allen, White Sox .... $8-$12
07/03/72 Steve Blass, Pirates .... $5-$7
08/21/72 Sparky Lyle, Yankees .... $5-$7
09/25/72 Carlton Fisk, Red Sox $20
10/23/72 Catfish Hunter, A's .... $10-$15

1973

03/12/73 Bill Melton, White Sox .... $6-$8
04/09/73 Steve Carlton, Phillies..................... $12-$15
04/30/73 Chris Speier, Giants $5
06/04/73 Wilbur Wood, White Sox.................. $8-$10
07/02/73 Bobby Murcer/Ron Blomberg, Yankees.$10
07/30/73 Carlton Fisk, Red Sox $15
08/20/73 Claude Osteen/Bill Russell, Dodgers........$6
09/24/73 Danny Murtaugh, Pirates .... $6-$8
10/22/73 Bert Campaneris, A's........................... $8-$9

1974

03/18/74 Babe Ruth, Yankees .... $7-$10
04/08/74 Pete Rose, Reds.............................. $15-$20
04/15/74 Hank Aaron, Braves, 715th Homer.........$30
05/27/74 Jim Wynn, Dodgers...............................$5
06/17/74 Reggie Jackson, A's .... $10-$12
07/01/74 Rod Carew, Twins *........................ $10-$15
07/22/74 Lou Brock, Cardinals .... $8-$12
08/12/74 Mike Marshall, Dodgers...........................$4
10/07/74 Catfish Hunter, A's $10
10/21/74 Dodgers vs. A's......................................$7

1975

03/03/75 Reds, Spring Training issue .... $6-$9
04/07/75 Steve Garvey, Dodgers *........................$12
06/02/75 Billy Martin, Rangers..............................$6

Sports Illustrated

VIDA BLUE
PLUMBING EXECUTIVE

06/16/75 Nolan Ryan, Angels * .... $30-$35
07/07/75 Fred Lynn, Red Sox $6
07/21/75 Jim Palmer, Tom Seaver .... $15-$18
08/11/75 Baseball Boom $4
10/06/75 Reggie Jackson, A's.......................... $8-$10
10/20/75 Luis Tiant, Johnny Bench .... $10-$15
11/03/75 Johnny Bench, Reds........................ $10-$12
12/22/75 Pete Rose, Reds (SOY) $15

1976

03/15/76 Bill Veeck, White Sox........................ $4-$6
04/12/76 Joe Morgan, Reds...................................$15
05/03/76 Mike Schmidt, Phillies .... $15-$18
05/31/76 Carlton Fisk, Red Sox .... $8-$12
06/21/76 George Brett, Royals .... $15-$18
06/28/76 Bowie Kuhn $4
07/12/76 Randy Jones, Padres................................$5
08/30/76 Reggie Jackson, Orioles .... $10-$12
10/11/76 George Foster, Cincinnati .... $6-$10
11/01/76 Johnny Bench, Reds $15

1977

03/14/77 Tommy Lasorda, Dodgers................... $5-$7
03/28/77 Bump Wills, Rangers $4
04/11/77 Joe Rudi, Angels $10
05/02/77 Reggie Jackson, Yankees .... $10-$12
05/30/77 Dave Parker, Pirates .... $5-$10
06/27/77 Tom Seaver, Reds .... $10-$12
07/18/77 Rod Carew, Ted Williams............... $10-$15
08/15/77 Sadaharu Oh $10
08/29/77 Greg Luzinski, Phillies.............................$5
10/24/77 Thurman Munson, Yankees/Dodgers........$9

1978

03/20/78 Clint Hurdle, Royals...................................$6

04/10/78 George Foster, Rod Carew .... $10-$12
04/24/78 Mark Fidrych, Tigers $6
07/31/78 Billy Martin, Yankees .... $6-$8
08/07/78 Pete Rose, Reds $15
10/23/78 Yankees Best Dodgers $8

1979

03/05/79 Spring Training issue, Reds $5
03/19/79 Harry Chappas, White Sox........................$4
04/09/79 Jim Rice, Dave Parker....................... $8-$10
04/30/79 George Bamberger, Brewers....................$4
05/28/79 Pete Rose, Phillies........................... $10-$12
06/18/79 Earl Weaver, Orioles $7
07/23/79 Nolan Ryan, Angels $25
08/27/79 Yastrzemski/Rose & Golden Oldies ... $6-$9
10/22/79 Pirates vs. Orioles.............................. $7-$9
12/24/70 Willie Stargell/Terry Bradshaw (SOY)...$10

1980

03/24/80 Kirk Gibson, Tigers.......................... $8-$10
04/07/80 Keith Hernandez, Cardinals .... $6-$8
06/09/80 Darrell Porter, Royals.......................... $5-$6
07/21/80 Steve Carlton, Phillies............................$10
08/04/80 Reggie Jackson, Yankees .... $8-$10
08/18/80 J.R. Richard, Astros .... $4-$5
08/25/80 Orioles vs. Yankees...............................$4
10/06/80 Gary Carter, Expos * .... $5-$9
10/27/80 Mike Schmidt, Phillies * .... $15-$20

1981

01/05/81 Dave Winfield, Yankees * $10
03/02/81 J.R. Richard, Astros $4
03/16/81 Rollie Fingers, Brewers...........................$7
04/13/81 Mike Schmidt, George Brett $15
04/27/81 Oakland A's Aces $5
05/18/81 Fernando Valenzuela, Dodgers .... $4-$7
06/08/81 Greg Luzinski, White Sox........................$4
06/22/81 Baseball Strike $4
07/27/81 Tom Seaver, Reds .... $7-$9
08/10/81 George Brett, Mike Schmidt .... $12-$15
08/17/81 Gary Carter, Expos .... $5-$10
10/26/81 Graig Nettles, Yankees............................$5
11/02/81 Yankees vs. Dodgers .... $4-$6

1982

03/15/82 Reggie Jackson, Angels .... $6-$10
04/12/82 Steve Garvey, Dodgers................... $10-$15
05/17/82 Gaylord Perry, Mariners.......................$6
07/05/82 Kent Hrbek, Twins $4
07/19/82 Pete Rose, Carl Yastrzemski.............. $7-$9
08/09/82 Dale Murphy, Braves * .... $8-$12
09/06/82 Rickey Henderson, A's * $8
10/11/82 Robin Yount, Brewers *.................. $15-$17
10/25/82 Robin Yount, Brewers.............................$15

1983

03/14/83 Tony Perez, Pete Rose, Joe Morgan........$12
04/04/83 Gary Carter, Expos .... $8-$10
04/18/83 Tom Seaver, Mets .... $7-$10
04/25/83 Steve Garvey, Padres .... $6-$8
06/13/83 Rod Carew, Angels .... $8-$12
07/04/83 Dale Murphy, Braves .... $8-$9
07/18/83 Andre Dawson, Dave Stieb......................$4

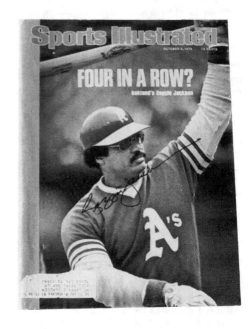

10/03/83 Steve Carlton, Phillies....................... $8-$12
10/24/83 Rick Dempsey, Orioles .... $5-$7

1984

03/12/84 George Brett, Royals...................... $10-$15
04/02/84 Yogi Berra, Yankees .... $7-$10
04/16/84 Rich Gossage/Graig Nettles, Padres ... $5-$7
04/23/84 Darryl Strawberry, Mets *................ $8-$10
05/28/84 Alan Trammell, Tigers * .... $12-$15
06/11/84 Leon Durham, Cubs $4
06/27/84 Pete Rose, Reds......................................$8
09/24/84 Rick Sutcliffe, Dwight Gooden........... $5-$6
10/22/84 Alan Trammell, Tigers .... $12-$15

1985

03/04/85 Mike Schmidt, Phillies .... $7-$9
03/18/85 Fred Lynn, Orioles $5
03/25/85 Mays/Mantle/Ueberroth .... $7-$10
04/15/85 Dwight Gooden, Mets .... $7-$8
05/06/85 Billy Martin, Yankees .... $5-$7
07/08/85 Fernando Valenzuela, Dodgers $4
08/19/85 Pete Rose, Reds......................................$6
09/02/85 Dwight Gooden, Mets $8
09/23/85 Ozzie Smith, Cardinals *................. $8-$12
10/28/85 Ozzie Smith, Cardinals.................... $8-$10
11/04/85 Royals Win World Series................. $8-$12
12/09/85 Kirk Gibson, Tigers........................... $7-$8

1986

04/14/86 Wade Boggs, Red Sox *................. $10-$15
05/12/86 Roger Clemens, Red Sox * .... $10-$15
07/14/86 Bo Jackson, Chicks .... $8-$12
07/28/86 Rickey Henderson, Yankees .... $8-$9
08/04/86 Oil Can Boyd, Red Sox............................$4
08/25/86 Ron Darling, Mets................................$5

10/06/86 Darryl Strawberry, Mets............................$7
10/20/86 Doug DeCinces, Bobby Grich............. $4-$8
10/27/86 Jim Rice, Gary Carter...............................$8
11/03/86 Ray Knight, Mets $7

1987

03/09/87 The Ripkens, Orioles....................... $10-$12
04/06/87 Cory Snyder, Joe Carter $5
04/20/87 Baseball Salaries $5
04/27/87 Rob Deer, Brewers .... $4-$5
05/11/87 Reggie Jackson, A's.................................$7
05/25/87 Eric Davis, Reds.......................................$5
07/06/87 One Day In Baseball .... $3-$4
07/13/87 Darryl Strawberry, Don Mattingly...... $8-$9
07/20/87 Andre Dawson, Cubs .... $6-$7
08/17/87 Alan Trammell, Tigers .... $6-$7
09/28/87 Ozzie Smith, Cardinals..........................$7
10/05/87 Lloyd Moseby, Blue Jays......................$5
10/19/87 Greg Gagne, Twins .... $3-$5
10/26/87 Dan Gladden, Twins........................... $3-$5
11/02/87 Twins Baseball .... $7-$9
12/14/87 Bo Jackson, Royals .... $7-$9

1988

03/07/88 Kirk Gibson, Dodgers $5
03/14/88 Umpire Pam Postema...............................$4
04/04/88 Will Clark, Mark McGwire....................$10
05/02/88 Billy Ripken, Orioles $5
05/09/88 Pete Rose, Reds .... $7-$8
07/11/88 Darryl Strawberry, Mets............................$5
07/18/88 Casey at Bat...$4
09/26/88 Dwight Evans, Red Sox .... $4-$6
10/17/88 Jose Canseco, A's............................. $8-$10
10/31/88 Orel Hershiser, Dodgers .... $7-$8
12/19/88 Orel Hershiser, Dodgers (SOY) .... $6-$8

1989

03/06/89 Wade Boggs, Red Sox......................... $6-$7
04/03/89 Pete Rose, Reds, Baseball Preview $5
05/01/89 Nolan Ryan, Rangers .... $12-$15
05/08/89 Jon Peters $4
06/12/89 Bo Jackson, Royals.................................$6
07/10/89 Rick Reuschel, Giants .... $4-$5
07/24/89 Gregg Jefferies, Mets $5
10/16/89 Rickey Henderson, A's .... $6-$8
10/30/89 Baseball, Earthquake............................$5

1990

03/12/90 Tony LaRussa, A's...................................$4
04/16/90 Ted Williams .... $5-$7
05/07/90 Ken Griffey Jr., Mariners * .... $12-$15
05/28/90 Will Clark, Gaints .... $5-$6
06/04/90 Lenny Dykstra, Phillies............................$5
07/23/90 Minor League Baseball $4
08/20/90 Jose Canseco, A's............................ $6-$10
10/01/90 Bobby Bonilla, Pirates* $5
10/22/90 Dennis Eckersley, A's..............................$5
10/29/90 Chris Sabo, Reds .... $5-$7

1991

03/04/91 Darryl Strawberry, Dodgers.....................$4
04/15/91 Nolan Ryan, Rangers .... $8-$10
05/13/91 Roger Clemens, Red Sox $6

05/27/91 Mickey Mantle, Roger Maris .... $6-$10
07/01/91 Orel Hershiser, Dodgers..................... $4-$5
07/29/91 Cal Ripken Jr., Orioles $10
09/30/91 Ramon Martinez, Dodgers .... $3-$5
10/21/91 Kirby Puckett, Twins * $10
10/28/91 Dan Gladden, Twins...............................$6
11/04/91 Minnesota Twins Celebrate................. $5-$8

1992

03/16/92 Ryne Sandberg, Cubs .... $7-$10
04/06/92 Kirby Puckett, Twins .... $5-$7
04/27/92 Deion Sanders, Braves .... $5-$6
05/04/92 Barry Bonds, Pirtes * $10
05/18/92 Baseball '92................................... $3-$4
06/01/92 Mark McGwire, A's.................................$4
07/06/92 Umpire Steve Palermo .... $3-$5
08/24/92 Deion Sanders, Braves .... $4-$5
10/05/92 George Brett, Royals .... $6-$8
10/19/92 Dave Winfield, Walt Weiss.....................$6
10/26/92 John Smoltz, Roberto Alomar $7
11/02/92 World Series, Toronto Blue Jays $6
Fall 1992 Sports Illustrated Classic Willie Mays.....$5

1993

03-01-93 George Steinbrenner .... $3-$4
03-22-93 Dwight Gooden, Mets........................ $3-$5
04-05-93 David Cone, Royals..................................$6
05-03-93 Joe DiMaggio..$10
05-24-93 Barry Bonds, Giants.......................... $4-$6
07-05-93 Mike Piazza, Dodgers .... $6-$10
07-12-93 Laurie Crews, Patti Olin .... $3-$4
07-19-93 Bob Gibson, Denny McLain $8
09-27-93 Ron Gant, Braves................................ $3-$5
11-01-93 Joe Carter, Blue Jays........................... $3-$5

1994

03-14-94 Michael Jordan......................................$20
04-04-94 Ken Griffey Jr. .... $8-$10
04-18-94 Mickey Mantle......................................$10
05-23-94 Baseball brawls......................................$4
06-06-94 Ken Griffey Jr. $10
07-18-94 Ben McDonald, Mike Mussina.................$6
08-08-94 Ken Griffey Jr., Frank Thomas..............$15
08-22-94 Baseball strike..$5

1995

02-27-95 Doc Gooden, Darryl Strawberry
05-01-95 Cal Ripken Jr.
05-15-95 Bobby Cox, Dennis Erickson, Gary Moeller
06-15-95 Matt Williams
07-10-95 Hideo Nomo
08-07-95 Cal Ripken Jr.
08-14-95 Greg Maddux
08-21-95 Mickey Mantle
09-11-95 Cal Ripken Jr.
10-02-95 Mo Vaughn
10-16-95 Ken Griffey Jr.
10-30-95 Bo Jackson
11-06-96 Atlanta Braves celebrate
12-18-95 Cal Ripken Jr.

Dell Sports Publishing
Baseball Annual

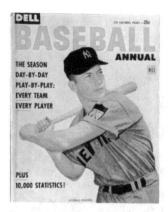  

This magazine was issued from 1952-1968, skipping 1969, and then again from 1970-1978. It had several title modifications - Dell Baseball Annual (1953-1957); Dell Sports Baseball (1958-1959 and 1970-1978); Dell Sports Magazine Baseball (1960-1963); and Dell Sports' March issue (1964-1968).

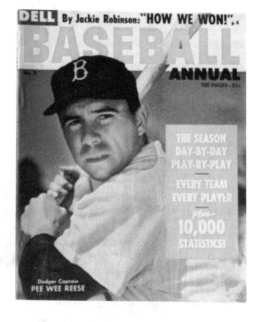

1952 Allie Reynolds	$30-$40
1953 Mickey Mantle	$45-$50
1954 Billy Martin	$35-$40
1955 Willie Mays	$30-$40
1956 Pee Wee Reese	$30-$35
1957 Mickey Mantle	$25-$35
1958 Lew Burdette	$25-$30
1959 Bob Turley	$20-$30
1960 Gil Hodges, Nellie Fox	$20-$25
1961 Richardson, Mazeroski, Ford	$20
1962 Roger Maris	$25
1963 Tom Tresh	$15-$25
1964 Sandy Koufax	$20-$25
1965 Ken Boyer, Brooks Robinson	$20-$25
1966 Sandy Koufax	$20-$25
1967 Frank Robinson	$15-$25
1968 Carl Yastrzemski	$15-$25
1970 Tom Seaver, Jerry Koosman	$15-$20
1971 Brooks Robinson	$10-$15
1972 Roberto Clemente, Vida Blue	$10-$15
1973 Richie Allen	$10-$15
1974 Hank Aaron	$10-$15
1975 Lou Brock	$8-$12
1976 Fred Lynn	$8-$10
1977	$10
1978 Reggie Jackson	$10-$15

Dell Sports Publishing
Baseball Stars

This magazine was issued from 1949-1968, known as Dell Sports Baseball Stars. In 1958-1963, and from 1964-1968, it was the May issue of Dell Sports.

1949 Stan Musial .... $45-$50
1950 Ted Williams, Joe DiMaggio $45-$50
1951 Phil Rizzuto .... $30-$35
1952 Bobby Thomson $30
1953 Robin Roberts .... $20-$30
1954 Ted Williams .... $30-$40
1955 Stan Musial .... $30-$35
1956 Mickey Mantle $35

1957 Don Larsen .... $25-$30
1958 Ted Williams .... $30-$35
1959 Warren Spahn .... $15-$25
1960 Kuenn/Aaron/Wynn .... $15-$25
1961 Vern Law $20
1962 Cepeda/Gentile/Colavito ...... $20-$25
1963 Maury Wills $20
1964 Sandy Koufax, Mickey Mantle $25
1965 Dean Chance $20
1966 Sandy Koufax $25
1967 Sandy Koufax $25
1968 Lou Brock .... $15-$20

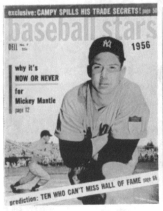
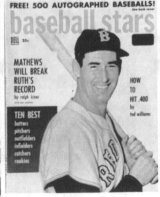

Dell Sports Publishing

Who's Who in the Big Leagues

This magazine was issued from 1953, and 1955-1958. From 1964-1968 it was issued in the June or July issues of Dell Sports.

1953 Stan Musial	$35-$45
1955 Yogi Berra	$40
1956 Roy Campanella	$25-$30
1957 Herb Score	$20-$25
1958 Willie Mays	$45
1959 Mickey Mantle	$45-$50
1960 Rocky Colavito	$20-$25
1961 Chuck Estrada	$20-$25
1962 Whitey Ford	$20-$25
1963 Harmon Killebrew	$20-$25
1964 Dick Stuart	$15-$20
1965 Willie Mays	$20-$25
1966 Tony Oliva	$15-$20
1967 Boog Powell	$15-$20
1968 Harmon Killebrew	$15-$20

Stan Musial, Willie Mays and Yogi Berra were some of the baseball superstars featured on Dell Publishing's magazine covers from the 1950s.

Who's Who In Baseball
by Baseball Magazine

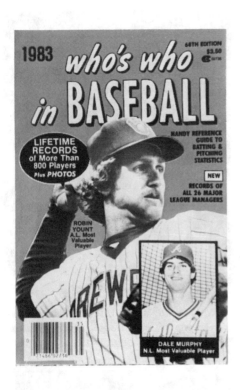

1912 Generic cover	$1,000-$1,250
1913-15	not issued
1916 Ty Cobb, A's outfielder	$500-$1,000
1917 Tris Speaker	$400-$800
1918 George Sisler	$300-$700
1919 Grover Alexander	$400-$800
1920 Babe Ruth	$350-$700
1921 Babe Ruth	$700
1922 Rogers Hornsby	$250-$500
1923 George Sisler	$300
1924 Walter Johnson	$150-$400
1925 Dizzy Vance	$250
1926 Max Carey	$100-$200
1927 Frankie Frisch	$150-$300
1928 Hack Wilson	$125-$250
1929 Bob O'Farrell	$100-$175
1930 Burleigh Grimes	$50-$125
1931 Lefty Grove	$50-$125
1932 Al Simmons	$50-$100
1933 Chuck Klein	$50-$100
1934 Bill Terry	$50-$100
1935 Dizzy Dean	$50-$100
1936 Hank Greenberg	$50-$100

1937 Lou Gehrig	$75-$150
1938 Joe Medwick	$40-$75
1939 Jimmie Foxx	$40-$75
1940 Bucky Walters	$30-$55
1941 Bob Feller	$30-$60
1942 Joe DiMaggio	$35-$80
1943 Ted Williams	$50-$80
1944 Stan Musial	$25-$45
1945 Hal Newhouser, Dizzy Trout	$25-$30
1946 Hal Newhouser	$25-$40
1947 Eddie Dyer	$25-$40
1948 Ralph Kiner, Johnny Mize	$25-$40
1949 Lou Boudreau	$25-$40
1950 Mel Parnell	$20-$30
1951 Jim Konstanty	$20-$30
1952 Stan Musial	$20-$30
1953 Hank Sauer, Bobby Shantz	$20-$30
1954 Al Rosen	$20-$25
1955 Al Dark	$20-$25
1956 Duke Snider	$20-$25
1957 Mickey Mantle	$60-$80
1958 Warren Spahn	$25-$35
1959 Bob Turley	$20-$30
1960 Don Drysdale	$25-$30
1961 Roger Maris	$20-$25
1962 Whitey Ford	$20-$25
1963 Don Drysdale	$25-$30
1964 Sandy Koufax	$20-$25
1965 Juan Marichal, Ken Boyer	$15-$20
1966 Willie Mays, Sandy Koufax	$18-$25
1967 F. Robinson, Koufax, Clemente	$20-$25
1968 Carl Yastrzemski	$18-$25
1969 Rose, Gibson, Yaz, McLain	$14-$18
1970 Seaver, Killebrew, McCovey	$12-$16
1971 Johnny Bench, Bob Gibson	$10-$15
1972 Vida Blue, Joe Torre	$10-$12
1973 Steve Carlton, Dick Allen	$10-$15
1974 Ryan, Rose, Jackson	$12-$18
1975 Lou Brock, Steve Garvey	$10-$15
1976 Joe Morgan, Fred Lynn	$9-$12
1977 Joe Morgan, Thurman Munson	$10
1978 Rod Carew, George Foster	$10
1979 Guidry, Parker, Rice	$9
1980 Willie Stargell, Keith Hernandez	$8
1981 Mike Schmidt, George Brett	$8
1982 Fernando Valenzuela, Rollie Fingers	$8
1983 Dale Murphy, Robin Yount	$8-$10
1984 Darryl Strawberry, Cal Ripken	$10
1985 Ryne Sandberg	$8
1986 Gooden, Mattingly, McGee	$8
1987 Mike Schmidt, Roger Clemens	$8
1989 Kirk Gibson, Jose Canseco	$6-$8
1990 Kevin Mitchell, Robin Yount	$8
1991 Sandberg, Ryan, Fielder	$6-$8

1992 to present @ $5-$7 each

Sport Magazine

Sport Magazine celebrated its 40th anniversary in 1986 by publishing a special collector's issue which featured stories on the "40 Who Changed Sports," including Ted Williams and Jackie Robinson.

The issue, from December 1986, is worth about $5, had 40 previous covers on its cover. Fourteen of those covers were devoted to baseball, featuring among others Joe DiMaggio, Hank Aaron, Babe Ruth, Ted Williams, Steve Carlton, Pete Rose, Carl Yastrzemski, Whitey Ford, Mickey Mantle and Willie Mays.

The magazine has been published monthly by Macfadden since September of 1946 (featuring Joe DiMaggio and his son), except for one month, January 1952, when no issue was published. Magazines typically have five or six features and lots of color photographs.

Sept. 46 Joe DiMaggio	$400-$450
April 47 Leo Durocher	$25-$30
June 47 Bob Feller	$40-$45
July 47 Eddie Dyer, Joe Cronin	$20-$25
Aug. 47 Ted Williams	$45-$60
Sept. 47 The DiMaggios	$75
April 48 Ted Williams	$40-$50
May 48 Babe Ruth	$30-$50
July 48 Ewell Blackwell	$20-$25
Aug. 48 Stan Musial	$35-$50
Sept. 48 Joe DiMaggio, Ted Williams	$75-$100
Oct. 48 Lou Gehrig	$50-$65
Feb. 49 Lou Boudreau	$20-$25
April 49 Bob Feller	$25-$35
May 49 Enos Slaughter	$30-$35
June 49 Hal Newhouser	$20-$25
July 49 Lou Boudreau, Joe Gordon	$20-$25
Aug. 49 Jackie Robinson	$25-$50
Sept. 49 Joe DiMaggio	$75-$100
Oct. 49 Christy Mathewson	$20-$25
Feb. 50 Tommy Henrich	$15-$20
April 50 Casey Stengel	$20-$25
May 50 Ralph Kiner	$15-$25
June 50 Bob Lemon	$15-$25
July 50 Stan Musial	$30-$45
Aug. 50 Art Houtteman	$15-$20
Sept. 50 Don Newcombe	$15-$25
Oct. 50 World Series	$20-$25
Nov. 50 Harry Agganis	$15-$22
April 51 Baseball	$15-$25
May 51 Baseball Jubilee	$25-$35
July 51 Ewell Blackwell	$15-$20
Aug. 51 Yogi Berra	$25-$30
Sept. 51 Ted Williams	$45-$75
Oct. 51 Jackie Robinson	$30-$45
March 52 Gil McDougald	$15-$18
April 52 Chico Carrasquel	$10-$15
May 52 Alvin Dark	$15-$20
June 52 Ralph Kiner	$20-$30

July 52 Stan Musial	$25-$40
Aug. 52 Allie Reynolds	$15-$20
Sept. 52 Mike Garcia	$15-$20
Oct. 52 J. Robinson, Pee Wee Reese	$50-$100
Nov. 52 Jackie Robinson	$15-$20
April 53 Mickey Mantle	$75-$100
May 53 Bob Lemon	$15-$25
June 53 Hank Sauer	$10-$20
July 53 Ferris Fain	$10-$15
Aug. 53 Warren Spahn	$15-$20
Sept. 53 Robin Roberts	$15-$20
Oct. 53 Roy Campanella	$25-$50
Nov. 53 Phil Rizzuto	$25-$30
Feb. 54 Eddie Mathews	$15-$20
March 54 Casey Stengel	$20-$30
April 54 Don Newcombe	$15-$20

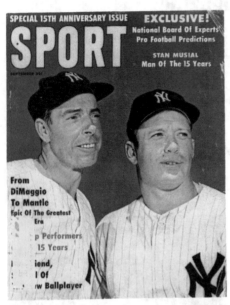

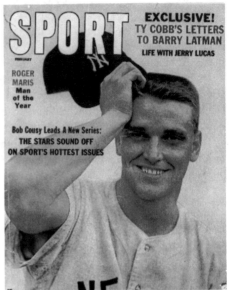

May 54 Ted Kluszewski	$15-$25	June 58 Willie Mays	$15-$25
July 54 Stan Musial	$35-$40	July 58 Herb Score	$10-$15
Aug. 54 Minnie Minoso	$15-$20	Aug. 58 Billy Martin	$12-$15
Sept. 54 Duke Snider	$35-$50	Sept. 58 Eddie Mathews	$15-$20
Oct. 54 Al Rosen	$14-$18	Oct. 58 Bob Turley	$10-$12
Feb. 55 Alvin Dark	$10-$14	Feb. 59 Lew Burdette, R. Johnson	$7-$8
April 55 Bob Turley	$12-$14	March 59 Al Kaline	$15-$25
May 55 Bobby Thomson	$10-$12	April 59 Rocky Colavito	$15-$20
June 55 Johnny Antonelli	$10-$12	May 59 Hank Bauer, Gil Hodges	$10-$12
July 55 Ned Garver	$10-$12	June 59 Mickey Mantle, Ted Williams	$35-$50
Aug. 55 Paul Richards	$8-$12	July 59 Don Newcombe, Jimmy Piersall	$8-$9
Sept. 55 Duke Snider	$30-$45	Aug. 59 Mickey Mantle	$30-$50
Oct. 55 Yogi Berra	$15-$20	Sept. 59 Ted Williams, Stan Musial	$25-$35
March 56 Walt Alston	$10-$14	Oct. 59 Warren Spahn	$12-$15
April 56 Larry Doby	$10-$12	March 60 Jackie Robinson, Willie Mays	$10-$15
May 56 Bob Lemon	$10-$14	April 60 Duke Snider	$10-$20
June 56 Willie Mays	$20-$25	May 60 Willie McCovey, Harmon Killebrew	
July 56 Ted Williams	$25-$35		$20-$25
Aug. 56 Vinegar Bend Mizell	$8-$10	June 60 Don Drysdale	$10-$12
Oct. 56 Mickey Mantle	$40-$60	July 60 Frank Howard, Luis Aparicio	$8-$10
March 57 Mickey Mantle	$50-$60	Aug. 60 Mickey Mantle	$45-$50
April 57 Eddie Mathews	$15-$20	Sept. 60 Rocky Colavito	$12-$20
May 57 Roy Campanella	$12-$14	Oct. 60 Babe Ruth	$5-$10
June 57 Early Wynn	$10-$14	Nov. 60 Roger Maris	$15-$25
July 57 Al Kaline	$15-$20	Feb. 61 Danny Murtaugh	$8-$10
Aug. 57 Joe Adcock	$8-$15	April 61 Frank Howard	$6-$8
Sept. 57 Duke Snider	$15-$25	May 61 Dick Groat	$6-$10
Oct. 57 Billy Pierce	$7-$12	June 61 Willie Mays	$10-$15
Jan. 58 Baseball Stars	$10-$15	July 61 Rocky Colavito	$10-$15
March 58 Lew Burdette	$10-$12	Aug. 61 Warren Spahn	$8-$10
April 58 Nellie Fox	$20-$25	Sept. 61 Joe DiMaggio, Mickey Mantle	$40-$50
May 58 Yogi Berra	$10-$15	Feb. 62 Roger Maris	$15-$25

April 62 Norm Cash, Vada Pinson .... $8-$10
May 62 Baseball Sluggers .... $10-$12
June 62 Hank Aaron.................................... $12-$15
July 62 Mickey Mantle .... $25-$50
Aug. 62 Rocky Colavito, Harvey Kuenn .... $10-$18
Sept. 62 Ken Boyer, Stan Musial................ $10-$15
Oct. 62 Willie Mays................................... $10-$15
Nov. 62 Tommy Davis, Jim Taylor .... $8-$10
Feb. 63 Maury Wills .... $7-$8
May 63 Mickey Mantle, Yogi Berra........... $35-$50
June 63 Maury Wills .... $7-$8
July 63 Rocky Colavito, Al Kaline .... $15-$30
Aug. 63 Willie Mays.................................. $10-$15
Sept. 63 Sandy Koufax .... $12-$15
Oct. 63 Mickey Mantle .... $25-$50
Nov. 63 Whitey Ford .... $10-$15
Dec. 63 Sport Annual.................................. $7-$10
Feb. 64 Sandy Koufax................................ $10-$15
May 64 Warren Spahn .... $8-$10
June 64 Dick Stuart...................................... $6-$9
July 64 Carl Yastrzemski .... $6-$15
Aug. 64 Joe DiMaggio, Willie Mays .... $15-$20
Sept. 64 Mickey Mantle.............................. $30-$50
Oct. 64 Willie Mays................................... $12-$15
Nov. 64 Harmon Killebrew........................ $10-$15
Feb. 65 Fred Hutchinson............................... $6-$8
April 65 Dean Chance.................................... $6-$8
May 65 Sandy Koufax .... $10-$15
June 65 Willie Mays .... $10-$15
July 65 Johnny Callison .... $5-$15
Aug. 65 Mickey Mantle .... $30-$50
Sept. 65 Lou Gehrig................................... $15-$25
Oct. 65 Sandy Koufax, Maury Wills .... $9-$10
Feb. 66 Sandy Koufax................................ $10-$15
April 66 Willie Mays, Paul Hornung............ $9-$15
May 66 Maury Wills .... $6-$7
July 66 Mickey Mantle .... $20-$50
Aug. 66 Frank Robinson .... $5-$6
Sept. 66 Willie Mays.................................... $7-$15
Oct. 66 Sandy Koufax................................... $7-$10
Feb. 67 Frank Robinson................................. $4-$6
May 67 Mickey Mantle.............................. $15-$20
June 67 Willie Mays .... $8-$15
July 67 Dick Allen, Jim Ryan .... $5-$8
Aug. 67 Roberto Clemente .... $20-$25
Sept. 67 Pete Rose....................................... $15-$20
Oct. 67 Orlando Cepeda, Johnny Unitas......... $6-$8
Feb. 68 Carl Yastrzemski.............................. $7-$10
May 68 Willie Mays .... $10-$15
June 68 Carl Yastrzemski .... $7-$10
July 68 Hank Aaron .... $7-$15
Aug. 68 Pete Rose.. $7-$12
Sept. 68 Don Drysdale .... $7-$8
April 69 Mickey Mantle.............................. $20-$35
May 69 Hall of Famers .... $6-$10

June 69 Ted Williams .... $8-$15
July 69 Tony Conigliaro .... $6-$10
Sept. 69 Cubs Stars .... $10-$20
May 70 Tom Seaver .... $9-$10
June 70 Harmon Killebrew .... $9-$10
Aug. 70 Hank Aaron..................................... $7-$15
Sept. 70 Johnny Bench .... $10-$12
May 71 Ted Williams .... $10-$12
June 71 Boog Powell .... $5-$8
July 71 Carl Yastrzemski.............................. $6-$10
Sept. 71 Willie Mays .... $8-$15
Oct. 71 Vida Blue .... $4-$5
June 72 Brooks Robinson .... $8-$10
Aug. 72 Tom Seaver .... $10-$12
Sept. 72 Frank Robinson............................... $7-$8
Aug. 73 Bobby Murcer .... $5-$8
Sept. 73 Gaylord Perry................................... $6-$7
Oct. 73 Pennant Time .... $6-$7
May 74 Hank Aaron .... $10-$15
June 74 Pete Rose .... $8-$10
Oct. 74 Reggie Jackson............................... $10-$12
May 75 Frank Robinson .... $5-$6
July 75 Bobby Bonds..................................... $5-$8
Aug. 75 Billy Martin...................................... $5-$9
April 76 Steve Garvey .... $6-$9
May 76 Tom Seaver....................................... $7-$10
Aug. 76 Pete Rose, Joe Morgan.................... $8-$15
July 77 Mark Fidrych..................................... $4-$6
Oct. 77 Rod Carew .... $5-$7
April 78 Sparky Lyle, Goose Gossage............ $6-$7
May 78 Craig Nettles...................................... $5-$7
July 78 Jim Rice... $5-$7
Aug. 78 Tom Seaver .... $7-$10
Oct. 78 Carl Yastrzemski................................ $7-$10
April 79 Pete Rose .... $6-$10
May 79 Ron Guidry .... $5-$6
June 79 Dave Parker .... $5-$6
July 79 Craig Nettles...................................... $5-$6
Aug. 79 Rod Carew .... $6-$7
Oct. 79 Reggie Jackson................................... $9-$10
April 80 Willie Stargell.................................... $5-$7
May 80 Lou Piniella .... $5-$8
July 80 Gorman Thomas................................. $5-$6
Sept. 80 Tommy John .... $5-$6
April 81 Tug McGraw .... $6-$8
May 81 Billy Martin .... $5-$6
June 81 Don Sutton .... $5-$6
July 81 Rich Gossage, Bruce Sutter................ $5-$6
April 82 Fernando Valenzuela........................ $5-$6
May 82 Reggie Jackson .... $7-$8
June 82 Tom Seaver.. $6-$7
July 82 Billy Martin .... $5-$6
March 83 Top 100 Salaries............................. $4-$6
April 83 Steve Garvey .... $5-$6
May 83 Steve Carlton .... $6-$8

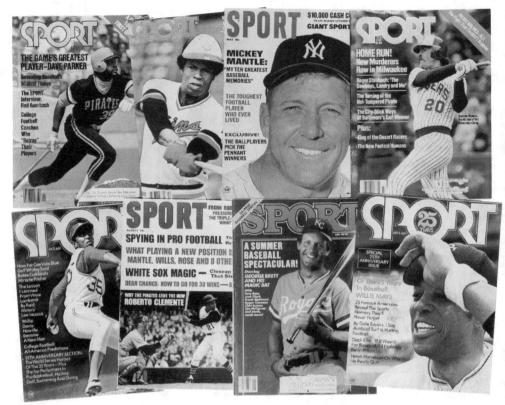

June 83 Schmidt, Dawson, Carter, Yount....... $6-$7
July 83 Reggie Jackson.................................... $7-$9
March 84 Top 100 Salaries............................. $4-$6
April 84 Cal Ripken Jr. .... $8-$10
June 84 Dale Murphy...................................... $4-$6
July 84 Baseball Managers .... $4-$6
March 85 Gary Carter .... $5-$6
April 85 Dwight Gooden .... $6-$7
May 85 Gary Matthews, Keith Hernandez ..... $4-$6
June 85 George Brett .... $6-$10
July 85 Kirk Gibson .... $5-$6
March 86 Dwight Gooden .... $4-$8
April 86 Bret Saberhagen............................... $4-$5
May 86 George Brett .... $5-$10
June 86 Top 100 Salaries .... $4-$6
July 86 P. Rose, R. Jackson, G. Carter .... $5-$6
March 87 Clemens, E. Davis, Schmidt........... $5-$8
April 87 Darryl Strawberry .... $3-$5
June 87 Top 100 Salaries .... $4-$6
July 87 Dave Parker .... $4-$5
Dec. 87 Andre Dawson, Tim Raines .... $4-$5
March 88 Jefferies, J. McDowell.................... $4-$5
April 88 Will Clark, Keith Hernandez.......... $5-$10
June 88 Top 100 Salaries .... $4-$8
March 89 Orel Hershiser................................. $4-$6

April 89 Baseball Preview .... $4-$5
June 89 Top 100 Salaries .... $3-$5
July 89 Jose Canseco .... $4-$5
Oct. 89 Dwight Gooden .... $5-$7
March 90 Bo Jackson....................................... $4-$5
April 90 Joyner, Canseco, Hershiser .... $4-$5
May 90 Sax, H. Johnson, Burks...................... $4-$6
July 90 Will Clark.. $5-$6
March 91 Ken Griffey Jr., Rickey Henderson $5-$7
April 91 R. Kelly, Reardon, H. Johnson......... $4-$6
June 91 Darryl Strawberry............................... $4-$6
July 91 Lenny Dykstra..................................... $3-$4
Oct. 91 Bo Jackson .... $4-$6
April 92 Frank Thomas, Bo Jackson .... $6-$10
May 92 Cal Ripken Jr. .... $5-$10
Jan. 93 Top 40 dominant names .... $4-$6
March 93 Steinbrenner, Sheffield, Clemens,
Winfield .... $4-$7
April 93 Bonds, Bonilla, Clemens, Canseco .. $4-$8
Jan. 94 Frank Thomas, others .... $4-$6
April 94 Joe Carter, Gonzalez, Justice............ $3-$5
Jan. 95 Griffey Jr., Frank Thomas, others ...... $4-$6
April 95 Bonds, Michael Jordan, Ripken, Thomas
.... $3-$5

Inside Sports

Oct. 79 Lemon wearing Yankees hat.......... $20-$30
April 80 Nolan Ryan.................................... $30-$40
May 80 Mark Fidrych, Johnny Bench, Magic
Johnson .... $10-$15
July 80 Ken Reitz... $5-$7
Aug. 80 Willie Randolph, Steve Garvey, Roberto
Duran.. $6-$7
April 81 George Brett $7
May 81 Outlaw Pitchers................................... $4-$7
June 81 Jim Palmer, Jan Stephenson .... $5-$7
Aug. 81 Salary Survey (Pete Rose)................. $6-$7
April 82 Steve Garvey .... $5-$7
May 82 Pete Rose .... $6-$7
March 84 Darryl Strawberry........................... $6-$7
April 84 Cal Ripken Jr., Carlton Fisk, Eddie Murray,
Ozzie Smith... $10
May 84 Fernando Valenzuela .... $5-$7
June 84 Mike Schmidt .... $5-$7
July 84 Steve Garvey, Rich Goosage.............. $5-$7
Aug. 84 Dave Winfield, George Steinbrenner.........
.... $5-$7
April 85 Kirk Gibson, Ryne Sandberg, Steve Garvey,
Dan Quisenberry .... $5-$7
May 85 Rick Sutcliffe, Gary Carter................ $4-$6
June 85 Rickey Henderson, six Dodgers .... $5-$7
July 85 Tom Seaver, Nolan Ryan, Jerry Koosman
.... $7-$9
March 86 Baseball's Best Player (Rickey Henderson
#1)... $8
April 86 1986 Baseball Preview .... $4-$6
May 86 Baseball Ratings and Inside Stuff...... $6-$8
March 87 Baseball's Best by Position .... $6-$8
April 87 1987 Baseball Preview .... $3-$6
May 87 Baseball Ratings and Inside Stuff...... $3-$6
March 88 Baseball's Best Players.................... $4-$6
April 88 1988 Baseball Preview .... $3-$6
June 88 Baseball Ratings, Inside Stuff .... $3-$6
March 89 Total Average .... $3-$6
April 89 Baseball Preview .... $3-$6
Feb. 90 Henderson, Clark, Bo Jackson, G. Carter ...
.... $4
April 90 Bo Jackson, Hershiser, McGriff, H.
Johnson, Clark, Grace, Boggs............................. $5
June 90 All-Time greats (Nolan Ryan)................ $6
Feb. 91 Clemens, Canseco, Stewart, Rijo, Gooden,
Fielder $4
April 91 Top salaries Canseco Strawberry, Clemens
.... $4
June 91 Bo Jackson... $4
Feb. 92 Larkin, Bonds, Clark, Sandberg, Canseco,
Puckett.. $5
March 92 Lee Smith, Joe Carter, Avery, Henderson
.... $4
April 93 David Cone, Greg Maddux.................... $5
May 94 Glavine, Bonds, Thomas, Gywnn, Canseco
.... $4
June 94 Barry Bonds, other sports stars............... $4
July 95 Jack McDowell, other sports stars........... $3

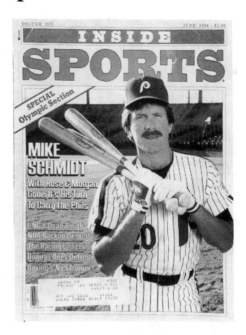

The Mike Schmidt magazine (above) is worth $7; the Fernando Valenzuela magazine (below) is also worth $7.

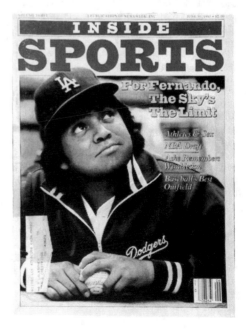

Other Magazines

Collecting general circulation news magazines with athletes on the cover, in addition to those related specifically to sports, has become very popular in recent years. Values are determined by who is pictured on the cover and the magazine's condition. Magazines in Excellent condition from the 1960s and 1970s can still be found for less than $20 in antique stores and public libraries.

Time Magazine

03/30/25 George Sisler $150
06/27/27 N.M. Butler, J.J. McGraw $100
04//11/27 Connie Mack $100
06/09/28 Rogers Hornsby $100
07/29/29 Jimmie Foxx $100
10/14/29 Bill Wrigley $75-$100
08/25/30 Wilbert Robinson $75-$100
03/08/32 Gabby Street $75
07/09/32 Col. Jacob Ruppert $50-$75
07/09/34 Lefty Gomez $50-$70
04/15/35 Jerome Herman Dean $75
10/07/35 Mickey Cochrane $20-$50
07/13/36 Joe DiMaggio $200
10/05/36 Gehrig/Hubbell $75-$85
12/21/36 Bob Feller $65-$75
08/01/38 Happy Chandler $25-$50
07/02/45 Mel Ott $100
04/21/47 Leo Durocher $40-$50
09/22/47 Jackie Robinson $75-$125
10/04/48 Joe DiMaggio $75-$125
09/05/49 Stan Musial $50-$75
04/10/50 Ted Williams $75-$125
10/01/51 Bert Lahr $40
04/28/52 Eddie Stanky $30-$40
06/13/53 Mickey Mantle $100
07/26/54 Willie Mays $45
06/13/55 "Damn Yankees" $25
07/11/55 Augie Busch $25
08/08/55 Roy Campanella $50-$65
10/03/55 Casey Stengel $30-$35
05/28/56 Robin Roberts $25-$30
07/08/57 Birdie Tebbetts $20
04/28/58 Walter O'Malley $15-$20
08/24/59 Rocky Colavito $20-$35
09/11/64 Hank Bauer $20
06/10/66 Juan Marichal $15-$20
09/13/68 Denny McLain $15-$20
09/05/69 New York Mets $20-$40
05/24/71 Vida Blue $15
07/10/72 Johnny Bench $20
08/23/73 Vida Blue $10
06/03/74 Reggie Jackson $20
08/18/75 Charley Finley $10-$15
04/26/76 Babe Ruth $10-$20
07/18/77 Rod Carew $20
07/23/79 Earl Weaver $10-$15
05/11/81 Billy Martin $10-$15
07/26/82 Yastrzemski/Rose $15

01/07/85 Peter Ueberroth $8-$15
08/19/85 Pete Rose $10-$20
04/07/86 Dwight Gooden $10-$20
07/10/89 Pete Rose $8-$10

Newsweek Magazine

04/15/33 Play at home $30-$50
04/29/33 Carl Hubbell $30-$100
09/09/33 Connie Mack $35-$75
09/30/33 Clark Griffith $30-$75
12/23/33 Judge Landis $25-$75
02/17/34 Babe Ruth $35-$100
03/17/34 Mel Ott $25-$50
10/06/34 Mickey Cochrane $25-$60
04/20/35 Judge Kenesaw Mountain Landis $25-$50
10/03/36 Carl Hubbell $25-$50
10/11/37 Carl Hubbell $20-$45
04/18/38 Rudy York $15-$30
10/10/38 Yankees/Cubs $25-$30
06/19/39 Abner Doubleday and Cooperstown $30-$75
09/16/46 Ted Williams $30-$50
06/02/47 Bob Feller $20-$40
10/06/47 Dodgers system $12-$30
04/26/48 Southworth, McCarthy $15-$25
08/08/49 Branch Rickey $15-$25
04/17/50 Mel Parnell $10-$15
03/24/52 Dodgers training $10-$15
10/04/54 Feller, Lemon $15-$25
10/03/55 Baseball, tv $8-$15

01/25/56 Mickey Mantle $65-$75
07/01/57 Stan Musial $20-$35
08/03/59 Casey Stengel $15-$25
08/14/60 Home runs $10-$15
04/26/65 The Astrodome $8-$10
10/11/65 Sandy Koufax $15-$20
10/02/67 Carl Yastrzemski $15-$20
08/13/75 Aaron, Ruth $18-$25
06/16/75 Nolan Ryan $20-$25
07/28/76 Vida Blue $7-$8
08/06/90 George Steinbrenner $5-$6

Life Magazines

04/25/38 Brooklyn Dodger $50-$75
05/01/39 Joe DiMaggio $100-$150
04/01/40 New York Giants $20-$50
09/01/41 Ted Williams $75-$125
04/01/46 St. Louis Cardinals $15-$30
08/01/49 Joe DiMaggio $75-$100
05/08/50 Jackie Robinson $50-$60
06/08/53 Roy Campanella $30-$45
09/14/53 Casey Stengel $20-$30
06/25/56 Mickey Mantle $75-$100
04/28/58 Willie Mays $25-$35
07/21/58 Roy Campanella $20-$30
08/18/61 Mantle, Maris $75
09/28/62 Don Drysdale $10-$20
08/02/63 Sandy Koufax $30-$45
07/30/65 Mickey Mantle $50-$75
09/08/67 Carl Yastrzemski $20-$25
09/26/69 Jerry Koosman $15-$20

Street & Smith's Baseball Yearbook

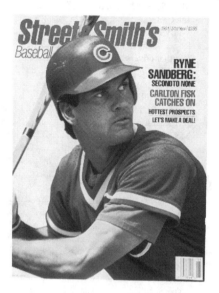

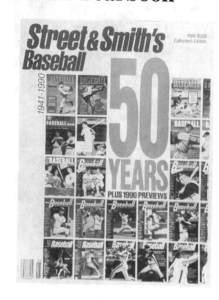

1941	Bob Feller	$100-$200
1942	Howie Pollet	$75-$125
1943	New York Giants	$85-$120
1944	Joe McCarthy	$85-$100
1945	N.Y. Giants Spring Training	$95-$110
1946	Dick Fowler	$85-$100
1947	Leo Durocher	$75-$85
1948	Joe DiMaggio	$100-$150
1949	Lou Boudreau	$85-$100
1950	J. DiMaggio/T. Williams	$100-$125
1951	J. DiMaggio/R.Kiner	$100-$125
1952	Stan Musial	$85-$110
1953	Mickey Mantle	$100-$125
1954	Eddie Matthews	$85-$110
1955	Yogi Berra	$85-$100
1956	M. Mantle/D.Snider	$75-$125
1957	Mantle, D. Larsen, Y. Berra	$75-$125
1958	B. Buhl/L. Burdette	$50-$75
1959	Mantle/Spahn/Burdette	$50-$65
1960	L. Aparicio/N. Fox	$50-$60
1961	Dick Groat	$45-$55
1962	Roger Maris	$60-$70
1963	Tom Tresh	$35-$40
	Stan Musial	$40-$50
	Don Drysdale	$40-$50
1964	Mickey Mantle	$50-$60
	Warren Spahn	$40-$50
	Sandy Koufax	$45-$50
1965	Brooks Robinson	$40-$45
	Ken Boyer	$35-$40
	Dean Chance	$30-$40
1966	Ron Swoboda	$30-$35
	Rocky Colavito	$30-$45

	Sandy Koufax	$35-$40
1967	Andy Etchebarren	$25-$35
	Harmon Killebrew	$30-$35
	Juan Marichal	$25-$35
1968	Jim Lonborg	$25-$35
	Orlando Cepeda	$30-$35
	Jim McGlothlin	$25-$35
1969	B. Gibson/D. McLain	$30-$35
1970	Tom Seaver	$35-$45
	Harmon Killebrew	$25-$30
	Bill Singer	$20-$30
1971	Boog Powell	$20-$25
	Johnny Bench	$30-$35
	Gaylord Perry	$25-$30
1972	Roberto Clemente	$40-$45
	Joe Torre	$20-$25
	Vida Blue	$20-$25
1973	Steve Carlton	$20-$25
	Johnny Bench	$20-$25
	Reggie Jackson	$25-$35
1974	Hank Aaron	$20-$25
	Pete Rose	$20-$25
	Nolan Ryan	$35-$45
1975	Lou Brock	$15-$18
	Catfish Hunter	$15-$18
	Mike Marshall	$15
1976	Fred Lynn	$15
	Joe Morgan	$17-$20
	Davey Lopes	$15
1977	Thurman Munson	$17-$20
	Mark Fidrych	$15
	Randy Jones	$15

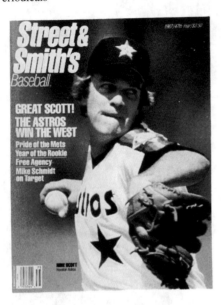

1987	G. Carter/J. Orosco	$10-$12
	Jesse Barfield	$8
	Mike Scott	$8
	Joe Carter	$8
	Wally Joyner	$8
	Roger Clemens	$10-$12
	all other covers	@$8-$12
1988	Don Mattingly	$12-$15
	Dale Murphy	$12
	Ozzie Smith	$12
	George Bell	$8
	Jeff Reardon	$8
	McGwire/Santiago	$10
	all other covers	@$8-$12
1989	Jose Canseco	$10
	Mike Greenwell	$8
	Orel Hershiser	$10
	M. Grace/C. Sabo	$9
	Kevin McReynolds	$8
	Galarraga/McGriff	$9-$10
	all other covers	@$7.50-$10
1990	Anniversary Issue	$7-$8
1991	Lou Piniella	$6
	Doug Drabek	$6
	Ryne Sandberg	$7
	Dave Justice	$6
	Nolan Ryan	$10
	Ramon Martinez	$6
	Kelly Gruber	$6
	Ken Griffey Jr.	$10
1992	Roberto Alomar	$7
	Roger Clemens	$8
	Bobby Bonilla	$7
	Terry Pendelton	$6
	Lee Smith, Jeff Bagwell, Ruben Sierra, Kirby Puckett	$7
	Frank Thomas, Cecil Fielder, Barry Larkin, Ryne Sanberg	$8
	Jim Abbott, Will Clark, Brett Butler, Jose Canseco	$7
1993	Roger Clemens	$7
	Jim Abbott	$5
	Tom Glavine	$7
	Barry Larkin	$7
	Ryne Sandberg	$7
	Dennis Eckersley	$7
	Darryl Strawberry	$5
	Roberto Alomar	$7
1994	Aaron Sele	$5
	Lenny Dykstra	$5
	Carlos Baerga	$6
	Paul Molitor	$7
	Dave Justice	$7
	Barry Bonds	$8
	Mike Piazza	$10
1995	Jimmy Key	
	Bret Saberhagen	
	Frank Thomas	

1978	Reggie Jackson	$20-$25
	Rod Carew	$17-$18
	Steve Garvey	$15-$18
1979	Ron Guidry	$15
	J.R. Richard	$15
	Burt Hooten	$15
1980	Mike Flanagan	$12
	Joe Niekro	$10
	Brian Downing	$10
1981	Mike Schmidt	$15-$20
	George Brett	$15-$20
	all other covers	@$12-$15
1982	Nolan Ryan	$30-$45
	R. Gossage/P. Rose	$15-$20
	R. Fingers/T. Seaver	$17-$20
	Valenzuela/Martin	$15
	all other covers	@$12.50-$15
1983	Steve Carlton	$12-$15
	Doug DeCinces	$10
	Robin Yount	$15-$17
	Dale Murphy	$12-$15
	all other covers	@$12-$15
1984	Carlton Fisk	$12-$15
	Pedro Guerrero	$10
	McGregor/Dempsey	$10
	all other covers	@$10
1985	Dwight Gooden	$12
	Detroit Tigers	$10
	Steve Garvey	$12
	all other covers	@$10
1986	Nolan Ryan	$20-$25
	D. Gooden/D. Mattingly	$12
	Kansas City Royals	$10
	Orel Hershiser	$14
	all other covers	@$10

Baseball Digest

Baseball Digest, the oldest surviving baseball monthly in the United States, marked its 50th anniversary in 1992. The first issue, August 1942, was a dream of Editor Herbert F. Simons, who, at the time, was a member of the Baseball Writers Association of America since 1928. The reality, a national baseball magazine, carried a cover price of 15 cents on the newsstands.

The publication, which has survived trucking and paper mill plant strikes, rising printing and publishing-related costs and a bankrupt printing plant, has covered stories on virtually every Hall of Famer, including several first-person stories. Many of the magazine's writers are also enshrined in the Baseball Hall of Fame in Cooperstown, N.Y. Some of their stories have been reprinted in Baseball Digest's 50th Anniversary issue, published in 1992.

Aug. 42	Elmer Valo	$75-$125
Oct. 42	Pete Reiser	$50
Dec. 42	Joe DiMaggio	$75
May 43	Catching a popup	$25
July 43	Play at 2nd Base	$25-$30
Aug. 43	Inside Homer	$15-$25
Sept. 43	Stan Musial	$40-$50
Oct. 43	Spud Chandler	$20-$25
Nov. 43	Johnny Lindell	$25-$30
Feb. 44	Bill Johnson	$15-$20
March 44	Joe Sewell, Bill Nicholson	$15-$20
April 44	Dixie Walker	$20-$25
May 44	Lou Boudreau	$20-$30
July 44	Vern Stephens	$15-$20
Aug. 44	Bucky Walters	$15-$20
Sept. 44	Charlie Grimm, G. Barr	$15-$20
Oct. 44	Walker Cooper	$20-$25
Nov. 44	Marty Marion	$15-$20
Feb. 45	Hal Newhouser	$10-$15
March 45	Grover Hartley	$12-$15
April 45	Dixie Walker	$10-$15
May 45	Bill Voiselle	$10-$15
July 45	Hank Borowy	$12-$15
Aug. 45	Tommy Holmes	$15-$25
Sept. 45	Stan Hack	$12-$15
Oct. 45	Hank Greenberg	$20-$25
Nov. 45	Al Lopez	$12-$15
Feb. 46	Charlie Keller	$12-$15
March 46	Phil Cavarretta	$12-$15
April 46	Bobby Doerr	$15-$20
May 46	Bob Feller	$20-$30
July 46	Joe DiMaggio, Ted Williams	$35-$50
Aug. 46	Joe Cronin	$15-$20
Sept. 46	Hank Wyse	$12-$20
Oct. 46	Boo Ferriss	$12-$20
Nov. 46	Johnny Pesky, Red Schoendienst	$12-$18
Feb. 47	Bucky Harris	$12-$15
March 47	J. Rigney, P. Knudsen	$8-$12
April 47	Johnny Van Cuyk	$8-$12
May 47	Billy Herman, Hank Greenberg	$10-$15
July 47	Lou Boudreau, Joe Gordon	$12-$15
Aug. 47	Buddy Kerr	$10-$12
Sept. 47	Ewell Blackwell	$10-$12
Oct. 47	Joe DiMaggio	$35-$50
Nov. 47	Dodgers/Phillies	$10-$12
Jan. 48	Joe Page	$12-$15
Feb. 48	Leo Durocher, Branch Rickey	$8-$15
March 48	Meyer, Ennis, Hubbard	$10-$12
April 48	Joe McCarthy	$12-$15
May 48	Art Houtteman	$10-$12
June 48	Willard Marshall	$5-$12
July 48	Ralph Kiner	$15-$17
Aug. 48	Lou Boudreau	$15-$17
Sept. 48	Stan Musial	$20-$25
Oct. 48	Hank Sauer	$10-$12
Nov. 48	Gene Bearden	$12-$15
Jan. 49	Jim Hegan	$10-$12
Feb. 49	Red Rolfe	$10-$12
March 49	Ted Williams	$25-$35
April 49	Joe DiMaggio	$30-$35
May 49	Play at the plate	$12-$15
June 49	Robin Roberts	$18-$20
July 49	Johnny Groth	$9-$10
Aug. 49	Frankie Frisch	$15-$18
Sept. 49	Vic Raschi	$10-$15
Oct. 49	Mel Parnell, Birdie Tebbetts	$10-$12
Nov. 49	Spider Jorgensen	$9-$10
Dec. 49	Tommy Henrich, Allie Reynolds	$12-$16
Jan. 50	Roy Smalley, Richie Ashburn	$10-$12
Feb. 50	Dave Koslo	$8-$10
March 50	1950 Baseball rules	$9-$11
April 50	1950 Rosters, Bob Feller	$10-$15
May 50	Stanky, Dark, J. Kramer	$8-$10
June 50	Joe DiMaggio	$20-$30
July 50	Phil Rizzuto	$12-$15
Aug. 50	Dick Sisler	$8-$10
Sept. 50	Larry Jansen, Art Houtteman	$8-$10
Oct. 50	Hoot Evers	$8-$10
Nov. 50	Jim Konstanty	$8-$10
Jan. 51	Yogi Berra, Whitey Ford	$12-$15
Feb. 51	Gil Hodges	$12-$15
March 51	Eddie Yost	$7-$8
April 51	Joe DiMaggio	$15-$25

May 51	George Earnshaw, Fogg	$7-$9
June 51	Ted Williams	$20-$25
July 51	Irv Noren	$7-$10
Aug. 51	Nellie Fox, Paul Richards	$15-$20
Sept. 51	Stan Musial	$15-$20
Oct. 51	Gil McDougald	$8-$10
Nov. 51	Charlie Dressen	$7-$8
Jan. 52	Eddie Lopat, Phil Rizzuto	$12-$15
Feb. 52	Eddie Stanky	$7-$8
March 52	Sid Gordon	$7-$10
April 52	Mike Garcia	$7-$10
May 52	George Staley	$7-$10
June 52	Pee Wee Reese	$15-$25
July 52	Ted Kluszewski	$10-$20
Aug. 52	Bobby Shantz	$7-$8
Sept. 52	Roy Campanella, Sal Maglie	$8-$10
Oct. 52	Carl Erskine	$8-$10
Nov. 52	Duke Snider	$12-$15
Jan. 53	Robin Roberts	$12-$15
Feb. 53	Eddie Mathews	$10-$15
March 53	Billy Martin	$10-$15
April 53	Mickey Mantle, Stan Musial	$20-$25
May 53	Carl Furillo	$10-$15
June 53	Bob Lemon	$8-$12
July 53	Logan, Kellner, Dorish	$7-$10
Aug. 53	Robin Roberts	$12-$15
Sept. 53	O'Connell, Strickland, Trucks	$7-$10
Oct. 53	Casey Stengel	$10-$15
Jan. 54	Billy Martin	$10-$15
March 54	Jimmy Piersall	$8-$10
April 54	Whitey Ford	$12-$15
May 54	Harvey Kuenn	$8-$10
June 54	Eddie Mathews, Morgan	$10-$12
July 54	Bob Turley	$7-$10
Aug. 54	Bob Keegan	$6-$7
Sept. 54	Willie Mays	$12-$15
Oct. 54	World Series issue	$6-$7
N,D. 54	Dusty Rhodes	$6-$7
J,F. 55	Ralph Kiner, Bill Sarni	$9-$10
Mar 55	1955 Rookies	$9-$10
April 55	Alvin Dark	$7-$8
May 55	Bob Lemon, Don Mueller	$7-$8
June 55	Bobby Avila	$6-$7
July 55	Bill Skowron	$7-$8
Aug. 55	Roy McMillian, Al Smith	$6-$7
Sept. 55	Don Newcombe	$7-$8
Oct. 55	Walter Alston, Tommy Byrne	$7-$8
Nov. 55	Johnny Podres	$8-$10
Feb. 56	Al Kaline	$15-$20
March 56	Rookie Report	$8-$9
April 56	Luis Aparicio	$10-$12
May 56	Pinky Higgins	$6-$7
June 56	Clem Labine	$7-$8
July 56	Mickey Mantle	$20-$30
Aug. 56	Dale Long	$7-$8
Sept. 56	Yogi Berra	$10-$15

Oct. 56	World Series	$10-$12
N,D. 56	Don Larsen	$15-$20
J,F. 57	Robin Roberts	$10-$12
March 57	Scouting Reports	$12-$15
April 57	Farrell, Scheffing, Tighe	$8-$10
May 57	Don Blasingame	$6-$7
June 57	Breaking up the D.P./Martin	$6-$7
July 57	Don Hoak	$6-$7
Aug. 57	Stan Musial	$10-$15
Sept. 57	Bobby Shantz	$6-$7
O,N. 57	Babe Ruth (World Series)	$10-$12
D.57,J.58	Lew Burdette	$7-$8
Feb. 58	Von McDaniel	$6-$7
March 58	Scouting Reports	$10-$15
April 58	Willie Mays, Duke Snider	$15-$20
May 58	Ted Williams	$15-$20
June 58	Stan Musial	$25-$30
July 58	Warren Spahn	$10-$12
Aug. 58	Bob Turley	$9-$10
Sept. 58	Pete Runnels	$7-$10
O,N. 58	World Series Thrills	$8-$10
D.58,J.59	Turley, Jensen, Roberts	$9-$10
Feb. 59	Baseball's Darling Daughters	$6-$7
March 59	Scouting Reports	$10-$15
April 59	Ernie Banks	$15-$20
May 59	Juan Pizarro	$6-$7
June 59	Antonelli, Pascual, Landis	$6-$7
July 59	Vada Pinson	$7-$10
Aug. 59	Hoyt Wilhelm	$8-$10
Sept. 59	Rocky Colavito, Elroy Face	$10-$15
O,N. 59	World Series, H. Wilson	$8-$10
D.59,J.60	John Roseboro, Larry Sherry	$6-$12
Feb. 60	Harvey Kuenn	$8-$12
March 60	Scouting Reports	$8-$10
April 60	Willie McCovey	$8-$9
May 60	Early Wynn	$8-$12
June 60	Bunning, Francona, McDaniel	$6-$8
July 60	Vern Law	$6-$8
Aug. 60	Dick Stuart	$7-$8
Sept. 60	Ron Hansen	$5-$6
O,N. 60	Dick Groat	$8-$10
D.60,J.61	Bill Virdon	$5-$6
Feb. 61	Ralph Houk	$6-$7
March 61	Scouting Reports	$7-$8
April 61	Tony Kubek	$7-$8
May 61	Glen Hobbie	$5-$6
June 61	Earl Battey	$4-$6
July 61	Wally Moon	$4-$6
Aug. 61	Norm Cash	$6-$8
Sept. 61	Whitey Ford	$8-$10
O,N. 61	Koufax, Robinson, M&M Boys	$12-$15
D.61,J.62	Elston Howard, Ralph Terry	$6-$7
Feb. 62	Joey Jay	$5-$6
March 62	Scouting Reports	$8-$10
April 62	Orlando Cepeda	$8-$10
May 62	Jim Landis	$8-$10

June 62	Mickey Mantle	$25-$30
July 62	Dick Donovan	$5-$6
Aug. 62	20 Dramatic Home Runs	$7-$8
Sept. 62	Rich Rollins	$5-$6
O,N. 62	Frank Howard, Tom Tresh	$6-$8
D.62,J.63	Ralph Terry	$6-$7
Feb. 63	Ty Cobb, Maury Wills	$8-$10
March 63	Scouting Reports	$8-$10
April 63	1963 Rosters	$7-$10
May 63	Dean, Drysdale, Grove	$8-$10
June 63	Al Kaline	$15-$20
July 63	Jim O'Toole	$5-$6
Aug. 63	Jim Bouton	$5-$6
Sept. 63	Denny LeMaster	$5-$6
O,N. 63	Al Downing	$5-$6
D.63,J.64	Don Drysdale, Sandy Koufax	$7-$8
Feb. 64	Roger Maris	$15-$20
March 64	Scouting Reports	$8-$10
April 64	Sandy Koufax	$10-$12
May 64	Harmon Killebrew	$8-$10
June 64	Tommy Davis, Carl Yastrzemski	$8-$10
July 64	Jim Maloney	$5-$6
Aug. 64	Dave Nicholson	$5
Sept. 64	Dennis Bennett, Willie Smith	$4-$6
O,N. 64	Miracle Braves	$7-$9
D.64,J.65	Dick Groat	$10-$15
Feb. 65	Winter Trades, Pete Rose	$7-$8
March 65	Scouting Reports	$10-$12
April 65	Which Tag is Phony?	$5-$6
May 65	Bill Freehan	$5-$8
June 65	Tony Conigliaro	$6-$8
July 65	Yankees' Six Mistakes	$6-$8
Aug. 65	Don Drysdale	$7-$8
Sept. 65	Joe Morgan, Pete Ward	$6-$7
O,N. 65	Biggest W.S. Mysteries	$5-$6
D.65,J.66	Sandy Koufax	$9-$10
Feb. 66	Willie Mays	$9-$10
March 66	Scouting Reports	$8-$10
April 66	1966 Rosters	$7-$10
May 66	Sam McDowell	$5-$6
June 66	Should Rules Be Changed?	$4-$6
July 66	Juan Marichal	$10-$15
Aug. 66	Gene Alley, Bill Mazeroski	$6-$7
Sept. 66	George Scott	$5-$6
O,N. 66	World Series Special	$5-$7
D.66,J.67	Palmer, Drabowsky, Bunker	$6-$7
Feb. 67	Allison, Drysdale, Mathews	$6-$8
March 67	Scouting Reports	$8-$10
April 67	1967 Rosters	$7-$10
May 67	Roger Maris	$12-$15
June 67	Juan Marichal, Gaylord Perry	$8-$10
July 67	Denny McLain, Jimmy Wynn	$4-$6
Aug. 67	Joel Horlen	$4-$6
Sept. 67	Tim McCarver	$5-$10
O,N. 67	World Series Special	$5-$6
D. 67,J.68	Bob Gibson	$7-$10

Feb. 68	Billy Williams	$6-$7
March 68	Scouting Reports	$8-$10
April 68	1968 Rosters	$7-$10
May 68	Carew, Johnstone, R. Nye	$6-$7
June 68	Nelson Briles, Cookie Rojas	$4-$6
July 68	Jerry Koosman	$7-$10
Aug. 68	Andy Kosco	$4-$6
Sept. 68	Matty Alou, Ken Harrelson	$5-$6
O,N. 68	Bob Gibson, Denny McLain	$6-$8
D.68,J.69	World Series	$5-$8
Feb. 69	Mickey Mantle	$20-$30
March 69	Scouting Reports	$7-$10
April 69	1969 Rosters	$7-$10
May 69	Al Lopez	$5-$6
June 69	Ernie Banks	$10-$12
July 69	Tony Conigliaro	$8-$10
Aug. 69	Frank Robinson	$6-$8
Sept. 69	Baseball Flirts With Tragedy	$4-$6
Oct. 69	World Series Special	$5-$7
Nov. 69	Super Stars of the '70s	$7-$8
Dec. 69	Tom Seaver	$9-$12
Jan. 70	Harmon Killebrew	$9-$12
Feb. 70	Joe Pepitone	$5-$8
March 70	Gene Alley	$5-$8
April 70	Tony Perez	$5-$10
May 70	Roberto Clemente	$10-$20
June 70	Mel Stottlemyre	$5-$10
July 70	Ken Holtzman	$6-$8
Aug. 70	Sal Bando	$6-$8
Sept. 70	Jim Hickman	$6-$8
Oct. 70	Jim Palmer	$8-$10
Nov. 70	Johnny Bench	$10-$15
Dec. 70	Billy Williams	$10-$15
Jan. 71	Brooks Robinson	$10-$15
Feb. 71	Sal Bando, Juan Marichal	$6-$8
March 71	Carl Yastrzemski	$8-$12
April 71	Bob Gibson	$6-$8
May 71	Willie Mays	$10-$15
June 71	Tony Oliva	$6-$8
July 71	Hank Aaron	$7-$10
Aug. 71	Vida Blue	$6-$8
Sept. 71	Joe Pepitone	$6-$8
Oct. 71	World Series	$5-$7
Nov. 71	Bobby Murcer	$6-$8
Dec. 71	Joe Torre	$4-$5
Jan. 72	Steve Blass	$3-$5
Feb. 72	Earl Williams	$3-$5
March 72	Frank Robinson	$6-$7
April 72	Bill Melton	$4-$5
May 72	1972 Rosters	$5-$6
June 72	Reggie Jackson	$10-$12
July 72	Richie Allen	$5-$7
Aug. 72	Bud Harrelson	$3-$5
Sept.72	Roberto Clemente	$7-$8
Oct. 72	Gary Nolan	$3-$5
Nov. 72	Carlton Fisk	$7-$8

Periodicals

Date	Subject	Price
Dec. 72	Richie Allen	$7-$5
Jan. 73	Pete Rose	$7-$8
Feb. 73	Cesar Cedeno	$4-$5
March 73	Harmon Killebrew	$5-$6
April 73	Don Kessinger	$3-$5
May 73	Nolan Ryan	$10-$12
June 73	Tom Seaver	$7-$10
July 73	Pete Rose	$7-$8
Aug. 73	R. Allen, C. May, B. Melton	$4-$5
Sept. 73	Ken Holtzman	$3-$5
Oct. 73	Bill Russell	$3-$5
Nov. 73	Jose Cardenal	$3-$5
Dec. 73	Willie Stargell	$5-$6
Jan. 74	Berra, Campaneris (Series)	$5-$6
Feb. 74	Willie Mays	$6-$8
March 74	Bobby Grich	$3-$5
April 74	Hank Aaron	$7-$8
May 74	Ted Sizemore	$3-$5
June 74	Felix Milan	$3-$5
July 74	Brooks Robinson	$5-$8
Aug. 74	Tony Perez	$4-$5
Sept. 74	Tommy John	$4-$5
Oct. 74	Dick Allen	$4-$5
Nov. 74	Bando, Campaneris, Jackson	$6-$7
Dec. 74	Lou Brock	$4-$5
Jan. 75	Rollie Fingers	$4-$5
Feb. 75	Steve Garvey	$4-$5
March 75	Jeff Burroughs	$3-$5
April 75	Catfish Hunter	$4-$5
May 75	Mike Schmidt	$7-$10
June 75	Rod Carew	$4-$5
July 75	Nolan Ryan	$8-$12
Aug. 75	Rick Monday	$3-$5
Sept. 75	Johnny Bench	$5-$6
Oct. 75	Vida Blue	$3-$5
Nov. 75	Fred Lynn	$3-$5
Dec. 75	Joe Morgan	$4-$6
Jan. 76	Pete Rose	$6-$8
Feb. 76	Jim Palmer	$4-$6
March 76	George Brett	$6-$8
April 76	Carlton Fisk	$5-$6
May 76	Frank Tanana	$3-$5
June 76	Rick Manning	$3-$5
July 76	Bill Madlock	$3-$5
Aug. 76	Randy Jones	$3-$5
Sept. 76	Larry Bowa	$3-$5
Oct. 76	Mickey Rivers	$3-$5
Nov. 76	Mark Fidrych	$5-$6
Dec. 76	Joe Morgan	$5-$6
Jan. 77	World Series highlights	$4-$6
Feb. 77	Thurman Munson	$5-$8
March 77	Amos Otis	$3-$5
April 77	Mark Fidrych	$3-$5
May 77	John Montefusco	$3-$6
June 77	Steve Carlton	$4-$5
July 77	Dave Parker	$5-$6
Aug. 77	Ivan DeJesus, Manny Trillo	$3-$5
Sept. 77	Carl Yastrzemski	$7-$8
Oct. 77	Steve Garvey	$4-$5
Nov. 77	Bump Wills	$3-$5
Dec. 77	George Foster	$3-$5
Jan. 78	Reggie Jackson	$7-$8
Feb. 78	Willie McCovey	$4-$6
March 78	Rod Carew	$5-$6
April 78	Tom Seaver	$5-$6
May 78	Cesar Cedeno	$4-$5
June 78	Garry Templeton	$4-$6
July 78	Dave Kingman	$4-$6
Aug. 78	Jim Rice	$5-$6
Sept. 78	Ron Guidry	$5-$6
Oct. 78	Rich Gale, Clint Hurdle	$4-$6
Nov. 78	Reggie Smith	$4-$6
Dec. 78	Dave Parker	$4-$5
Jan. 79	World Series highlights	$4-$6
Feb. 79	Dave Winfield	$5-$6
March 79	Greg Luzinski	$4-$6
April 79	Rich Gossage	$4-$6
May 79	Jack Clark	$4-$6
June 79	Steve Garvey	$4-$6
July 79	Al Oliver	$4-$6
Aug. 79	Bill Buckner	$4-$6
Sept. 79	Tommy John	$3-$5
Oct. 79	Mike Schmidt	$5-$6
Nov. 79	Omar Moreno	$3-$5
Dec. 79	George Brett	$6-$7
Jan. 80	Mike Flanagan	$3-$5
Feb. 80	Paul Molitor	$4-$5
March 80	Gary Carter	$4-$5
April 80	Willie Stargell	$4-$5
May 80	Don Baylor	$3-$5
June 80	J.R. Richard, Nolan Ryan	$5-$7
July 80	Baumgarten, Burns, Trout	$3-$5
Aug. 80	Ken Landreaux	$3-$5
Sept. 80	Steve Carlton	$4-$5
Oct. 80	Reggie Jackson	$5-$6
Nov. 80	Joe Charboneau	$3-$5
Dec. 80	George Brett	$4-$5
Jan. 81	Tug McGraw	$4-$5
Feb. 81	Eddie Murray	$4-$5
March 81	Rickey Henderson	$4-$5
April 81	Mike Schmidt	$5-$6
May 81	Gary Carter	$4-$5
June 81	Cecil Cooper	$3-$5
July 81	Carlton Fisk	$4-$5
Aug. 81	Fernando Valenzuela	$4-$5
Sept. 81	Danny Darwin	$3-$5
Oct. 81	Ron Davis	$3-$5
Nov. 81	Pete Rose	$6-$8
Dec. 81	Tim Raines	$4-$5
Jan. 82	Steve Garvey	$4-$5

Feb. 82	Carney Lansford	$3-$5
March 82	Rollie Fingers	$4-$5
April 82	Dave Winfield	$4-$5
May 82	Nolan Ryan	$6-$8
June 82	Jerry Reuss	$4-$5
July 82	Salome Barojas	$3-$5
Aug. 82	Dale Murphy	$4-$5
Sept. 82	Rickey Henderson	$5-$6
Oct. 82	Robin Yount	$6-$8
Nov. 82	Kent Hrbek	$4-$5
Dec. 82	Ozzie and Lonnie Smith	$4-$5
Jan. 83	Darrell Porter	$3-$5
Feb. 83	Mario Soto	$3-$5
March 83	Doug DeCinces	$3-$5
April 83	Willie McGee	$4-$5
May 83	Pete Vuckovich	$3-$5
June 83	Cal Ripken Jr.	$8-$10
July 83	Tony Pena	$4-$5
Aug. 83	Dave Stieb	$4-$5
Sept. 83	Chris Chambliss	$3-$5
Oct. 83	Ron Kittle	$3-$5
Nov. 83	Steve Carlton	$4-$5
Dec. 83	Carlton Fisk	$4-$5
Jan. 84	Rick Dempsey	$3-$5
Feb. 84	Wade Boggs	$6-$8
March 84	Dale Murphy	$4-$5
April 84	Mike Boddicker	$3-$5
May 84	Andre Dawson	$4-$5
June 84	Lance Parrish	$3-$5
July 84	Bill Madlock	$3-$5
Aug. 84	Leon Durham	$3-$5
Sept. 84	Gwynn, C. Martinez, McReynolds	$4-$5
Oct. 84	Ryne Sandberg	$5-$8
Nov. 84	Keith Hernandez	$3-$5
Dec. 84	Mark Langston	$4-$5
Jan. 85	Alan Trammell	$3-$5
Feb. 85	Don Mattingly	$5-$8
March 85	Frank Viola	$3-$5
April 85	Jack Morris	$3-$5
May 85	Tony Gwynn	$4-$5
June 85	Dwight Gooden	$4-$5
July 85	Bruce Sutter	$3-$5
Aug. 85	Pete Rose	$4-$5
Sept. 85	Lonnie Smith	$4-$5
Oct. 85	Ron Guidry	$3-$5
Nov. 85	Pedro Guerrero	$3-$5
Dec. 85	Dwight Gooden	$4-$5
Jan. 86	Willie McGee	$3-$5
Feb. 86	Bret Saberhagen	$3-$5
March 86	Tom Browning	$3-$5
April 86	Harold Baines	$3-$5
May 86	Darryl Strawberry	$4-$5
June 86	Eddie Murray	$5-$6
July 86	Bert Blyleven	$3-$5

Aug. 86	Roger Clemens	$5-$8
Sept. 86	Gary Carter	$4-$5
Oct. 86	Jose Canseco, Wally Joyner	$4-$5
Nov. 86	Bill Doran	$3-$5
Dec. 86	Roger Clemens, Ted Higuera	$6-$8
Jan. 87	Wade Boggs, Don Mattingly	$6-$8
Feb. 87	Sid Fernandez	$3-$5
March 87	Mike Scott	$3-$5
April 87	Chris Brown	$3-$5
May 87	Pete O'Brien	$3-$5
June 87	Eric Davis, Jody Davis	$3-$5
July 87	Mike Witt	$3-$5
Aug. 87	Rickey Henderson	$4-$5
Sept. 87	Jack Clark, Ozzie Smith	$4-$5
Oct. 87	Mark McGwire	$4-$5
Nov. 87	George Bell	$3-$5
Dec. 87	Kevin Seitzer	$3-$5
Jan. 88	Andre Dawson	$4-$5
Feb. 88	Frank Viola	$3-$5
March 88	Jimmy Key	$3-$5
April 88	Kevin McReynolds, Mike Pagliarulo	$3-$5
May 88	Eric Davis	$3-$5
June 88	K.C. Royals pitchers	$3-$5
July 88	Andy Van Slyke	$3-$5
Aug. 88	Dave Winfield	$6-$8
Sept. 88	Greg Maddux	$4-$5
Oct. 88	Kirby Puckett	$4-$5
Nov. 88	Jose Canseco	$4-$5
Dec. 88	Danny Jackson	$3-$5
Jan. 89	Jose Canseco	$4-$5
Feb. 89	Orel Hershiser	$3-$5
March 89	Gregg Jefferies	$3-$5
April 89	Kirk Gibson	$3-$5
May 89	Cory Snyder	$3-$5
June 89	Fred McGriff	$4-$5
July 89	Will Clark	$4-$5
Aug. 89	Nolan Ryan	$6-$8
Sept. 89	Bo Jackson	$4-$5
Oct. 89	Dave Stewart	$3-$5
Nov. 89	Howard Johnson	$3-$5
Dec. 89	Dwight Smith, Jerome Walton	$3-$5
Jan. 90	Abbott, Clark, Ryan	$6-$8
Feb. 90	Ruben Sierra	$3-$5
March 90	Ken Griffey Jr.	$6-$8
April 90	Canseco, McGwire, Steinbach	$4-$5
May 90	Gibson, Strawberry, Winfield	$4-$5
June 90	Mark Grace	$3-$5
July 90	Bob Geren, Lou Whitaker	$3-$5
Aug. 90	Bobby Bonilla, Frank Viola	$3-$5
Sept. 90	Ozzie Guillen	$3-$5
Oct. 90	Rickey Henderson	$3-$5
Nov. 90	Cecil Fielder	$4-$5
Dec. 90	Sandy Alomar, Dave Justice	$3-$5
Jan. 91	Bob Welch	$3-$4

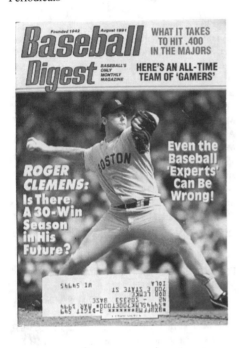

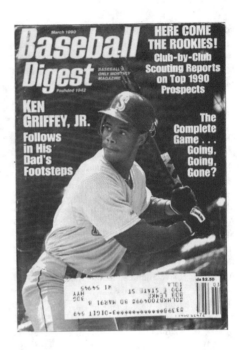

Feb. 91	Chris Sabo	$3-$4
March 91	Ray Lankford	$3-$4
April 91	Charlton, Dibble, Myers	$3-$4
May 91	Darryl Strawberry	$3-$4
June 91	Tim Raines	$3-$4
July 91	Kevin Mitchell	$3-$4
Aug. 91	Roger Clemens	$4-$5
Sept. 91	Robin Yount	$4-$5
Oct. 91	Cal Ripken Jr.	$6-$8
Nov. 91	Roberto Alomar, Rafael Palmeiro	$4-$5
Dec. 91	Chuck Knoblauch	$3-$4
Jan. 92	Steve Avery	$3-$4
Feb. 92	Kirby Puckett	$4-$5
March 92	Felix Jose	$3-$4
April 92	Frank Thomas	$5-$6
May 92	Wade Boggs	$4-$5
June 92	Gladden, Mack, Olson	$3-$4
July 92	Howard Johnson	$3-$4
Aug. 92	Mark McGwire	$3-$4
Sept. 92	Juan Guzman	$3-$4
Oct. 92	Kirby Puckett	$4-$5
Nov. 92	Dennis Eckersley, Tom Glavine	$4-$5
Dec. 92	Pat Listach	$3-$4
Jan. 93	Roberto Alomar	$4-$5
Feb. 93	Gary Sheffield	$4-$5
March 93	Tim Wakefield	$2-$4
April 93	Jose Canseco	$3-$4
May 93	Mike Mussia, Curt Schilling	$2-$4
June 93	Robin Ventura	$2-$4
July 93	Carlos Baerga, Juan Gonzalez	$3-$4
Aug. 93	Barry Bonds	$4-$5
Sept. 93	Joe Carter	$3-$4
Oct. 93	John Kruk	$2-$4
Nov. 93	Frank Thomas	$5-$6
Dec. 93	Mike Piazza, Tim Salmon	$6-$8
Jan. 94	Paul Molitor	$4-$5
Feb. 94	Randy Johnson	$3-$4
March 94	Greg Maddux	$4-$5
April 94	Carlos Baerga	$3-$4
May 94	Lenny Dykstra	$2-$4
June 94	Rafael Palmeiro, Chris Sabo	$2-$4
July 94	Lance Johnson	$2-$3
Aug. 94	Matt Williams	$3-$4
Sept. 94	unknown	cover
Oct. 94	Cal Ripken Jr., Ozzie Smith	$6-$8
Nov. 94	Jimmy Key	$2-$4
Dec. 94	Bob Hamelin	$2-$3
Jan. 95	Jeff Bagwell	
Feb. 95	Tony Gwynn	
March 95	Raul Mondesi	
April 95	Kenny Lofton	
May 95	Don Mattingly	
June 95	Fred McGriff	
July 95	Cal Ripken Jr.	
Aug. 95	Eddie Murray	
Sept. 95	John Valentin	
Oct. 95	Barry Larkin	
Nov. 95	Mickey Mantle	
Dec. 95	Hideo Nomo	

Baseball Magazine

April 1912 Player $90
May 1912 Opening Day $90
Dec. 1912 Football player $90
March 1913 Frank Chase $90
April 1915 Walter Johnson $150
May 1916 Joe Jackson................................ $150
Sept. 1916 Brown paper (no cover) $20
Oct. 1916 Brown paper (no cover).............. $40
Nov. 1916 Brown paper (no cover)............. $40
Jan. 1917 John McGraw $35
Feb. 1917 St. Louis players $50
March 1917 Tris Speaker $95
Nov. 1917 Baseball fans.............................. $65
March 1920 Pat Moran $75
Sept. 1920 Cleveland player $90
Oct. 1922 Play at third................................ $35
March 1923 Batter and catcher $45
Nov. 1924 Batter $45
May 1925 Pitcher $35
Nov. 1925 Pitcher, World Series................ $50
Feb. 1926 Fielder.. $35
April 1926 Play at the plate $45
May 1926 Pitcher $35
Aug. 1926 Eddie Collins, George Sisler $35
Sept. 1926 Catcher $45
Feb. 1927 Batter $40
April 1927 Play at first............................... $35
July 1927 Robert O'Farrell $35
Aug. 1927 Catcher...................................... $35
Oct. 1927 Joe McCarthy $30
May 1928 Pitcher $35
June 1928 First baseman $45
July 1928 Batter and catcher $35
Aug. 1928 Batter $45
Sept. 1928 Play at third $35
Jan. 1929 Play at plate $40
Feb. 1929 Sliding into base $40
March 1929 Catcher $40
April 1929 Base runner $40
May 1929 Pitcher $40
June 1929 Batter... $35
July 1929 Play at second $40
Aug. 1929 Mickey Cochrane $40
Sept. 1929 Batter $40
Jan. 1930 Pitcher illustration $30
Feb. 1930 Pitcher illustration $30
March 1930 Lefty Grove $30
April 1930 Batter illustration $40
May 1930 Al Simmons $40
June 1930 Batter illustration $40
July 1930 Grover Alexander $30
Aug. 1930 Pitcher illustration $25
Sept. 1930 Play at the plate $40
Oct. 1930 Pitcher illustration $40
Nov. 1930 World Series crowd $25
Jan. 1931 Pitcher illustration $35
March 1931 Fielder illustration $30
April 1931 Play at second $35
May 1931 1930-31 Champions banner $35
June 1931 Batter illustration $35
July 1931 Catcher and batter $25
Aug. 1931 Rabbit Maranville $30
Sept. 1931 Play at second $30

Oct. 1931 Wes Ferrell $35
Nov. 1931 World Series number $25
Dec. 1931 Fielder....................................... $30
Jan. 1932 Unknown $35
Feb. 1932 Chuck Klein $45
March 1932 Play at the plate $75
April 1932 Pepper Martin............................ $35
May 1932 "Play ball".................................. $35
June 1932 Max Carey $35
July 1932 Fielder illustration $30
Aug. 1932 Catcher illustration $35
Sept. 1932 George Earnshaw $35
Oct. 1932 Earl Averill................................. $50
Nov. 1932 World Series number $35
Dec. 1932 Joe McCarthy, President Roosevelt.......... $75
Feb. 1933 Jimmie Foxx $45
March 1933 John Heydler $35
April 1933 Dale Alexander.......................... $35
May 1933 25th Anniversary issue $45
June 1933 Bill Terry $45
July 1933 Red Faber $35
Aug. 1933 Play at second........................... $35
Feb. 1934 William Harridge $40
May 1934 Play at the plate $35
June 1934 Bob O'Farrell.............................. $35
July 1934 Jimmy Dykes.............................. $35
Sept. 1934 Mel Harder $30
Jan. 1935 Ford Frick $35
July 1935 Charles Dressen $30
Sept. 1935 Mel Ott..................................... $45
Oct. 1935 Hank Greenberg $45
Jan. 1936 Buddy Myers $30
Feb. 1936 Gabby Hartnett........................... $40
March 1936 Steve O'Neill $35
May 1936 "Play ball".................................. $35
June 1936 Roger Cramer $35
July 1936 Joe Medwick $75
Aug. 1936 Bill Dickey $35
Sept. 1936 Lon Warneke............................. $35
Oct. 1936 World Series bleacher fans.......... $35
Nov. 1936 Joe McCarthy, Bill Terry $30
Dec. 1936 Luke Appling $35
Jan. 1937 Play at first................................. $40
Feb. 1937 Hal Trotsky $35
March 1937 Leo Durocher $40
April 1937 Johnny Allen.............................. $35
May 1937 "Play ball".................................. $35
June 1937 Burleigh Grimes $35
July 1937 Wally Moses $35
Aug. 1937 Dick Bartell $35
Oct. 1937 Play at the plate $35
Dec. 1937 Charlie Gehringer $40
Jan. 1938 Joe Medwick $35
Feb. 1938 Gee Walker $30
March 1938 Play at the plate $30
April 1938 Catcher's mask $30
June 1938 Gus Mancuso $30
July 1938 Frank Crosetti $30
Aug. 1938 Gabby Hartnett, umpire.............. $75
Sept. 1938 Red Rolfe $30
Oct. 1938 World Series issue....................... $75
Nov. 1938 Gabby Hartnett, Joe McCarthy $30
Dec. 1938 Dizzy Dean $30

Jan. 1939 Ernie Lombardi	$35
Feb. 1939 Bob Feller	$35
March 1939 Play at the plate	$35
April 1939 Bobby Doerr	$35
May 1939 Dick Bartell, Hank Leiber, Gus Mancuso.	$30
June 1939 Abner Doubleday	$75
July 1939 Baseball action photos	$75
Sept. 1939 Dodgers on the mound	$35
Oct. 1939 Red Rolfe	$50
Nov. 1939 Bucky Walters, Joe DiMaggio	$50
Dec. 1939 Ted Williams	$50
Jan. 1940 Terry Moore	$25
Feb. 1940 Baseball close-up	$25
March 1940 Pete Coscarart, Charlie Dressen, Leo Durocher	$25
April 1940 Joe Gordon	$25
May 1940 Umpire Bill Klem	$25
June 1940 Bob Feller, Rollie Hemsley, Ossie Vitt	$35
July 1940 Ernie Lombardi, Johnny Mize	$35
Aug. 1940 Flash Gordon	$25
Sept. 1940 Harry Danning	$25
Oct. 1940 Joe DiMaggio	$50
Nov. 1940 Reds' team photo	$30
Dec. 1940 Tigers/Reds World Series	$30
Jan. 1941 Jimmy Wilson	$25
Feb. 1941 Connie Mack	$25
March 1941 Babe Young	$25
April 1941 Joe McCarthy	$25
May 1941 Bucky Walters	$25
June 1941 Jake Early, Ban Johnson	$25
July 1941 Johnny Hopp, Babe Young	$25
Aug. 1941 Ted Williams	$45
Sept. 1941 Dolf Camilli, Enos Slaughter	$25
Oct. 1941 Umpire Bill Summers	$30
Nov. 1941 Yankees team	$30
Dec. 1941 Billy Herman	$30
Jan. 1942 Lou Boudreau	$50
Feb. 1942 Mel Ott, team executives	$40
March 1942 Play at the plate	$35
April 1942 Ebbets Field	$35
May 1942 Hank Greenberg	$45
June 1942 Enos Slaughter	$35
July 1942 Play at the plate	$35
Aug. 1942 Paul Waner	$35
Sept. 1942 Joe Gordon, Elmer Valo	$35
Oct. 1942 Play at the plate	$35
Nov. 1942 Joe McCarthy, Billy Southworth	$35
Dec. 1942 Cal Griffith	$35
Jan. 1943 Pee Wee Reese	$35
Feb. 1943 Johnny Pesky, Phil Rizzuto	$35
March 1943 Jimmy Brown	$30
April 1943 Play at the plate	$30
May 1943 Play at the plate	$25
June 1943 Play at the plate	$30
July 1943 Arguing with an umpire	$30
Aug. 1943 Play at first	$30
Sept. 1943 Arky Vaughn	$30
Oct. 1943 Bill Johnson	$50
Nov. 1943 Joe McCarthy, Billy Southworth	$30
Dec. 1943 Frank Crosetti	$25
Jan. 1944 Play at the plate	$25
Feb. 1944 Play at third	$20
March 1944 Yankee bat boy	$20
April 1944 Pirate player	$25
May 1944 Senators pitchers	$25
June 1944 "Buy Bonds"	$25
July 1944 Jimmie Foxx	$35
Aug. 1944 Play at third	$20
Sept. 1944 Play at the plate	$25
Oct. 1944 The Cooper brothers	$25
Nov. 1944 Detroit Tiger players	$25
Dec. 1944 Cardinals team photo	$25
Jan. 1945 Play at the plate	$25
Feb. 1945 Ford Frick, William Harriot	$25
March 1945 Play at the plate	$25
April 1945 "Play ball"	$25
May 1945 Joe Cronin, Tom Yawkey	$15
June 1945 "Buy Bonds"	$25
July 1945 Happy Chandler	$25
Aug. 1945 Rundown play	$25
Sept. 1945 Milwaukee Braves players	$25
Oct. 1945 Chicago Cubs players	$25
Nov. 1945 Chief Bender, Connie Mack	$25
Dec. 1945 Charlie Grimm, Steve O'Neill	$25
Jan. 1946 Play at the plate	$25
Feb. 1946 Play at the plate	$25
March 1946 Play at the plate	$25
April 1946 Leo Durocher, Joe McCarthy, Mel Ott	$35
May 1946 Lou Boudreau, Bob Feller	$35
June 1946 President Truman	$25
July 1946 Pee Wee Reese, Pete Reiser	$35
Aug. 1946 Rudy York	$25
Sept. 1946 Play at third	$25
Oct. 1946 Bobby Doerr, Ted Williams	$45
Nov. 1946 Bob Feller, Hal Newhouser	$40
Dec. 1946 Cardinal team photo	$25
Jan. 1947 Johnny Pesky	$25
Feb. 1947 George Case	$25
March 1947 Happy Chandler	$25
April 1947 Play at the plate	$25
May 1947 Eddie Stanky	$45
June 1947 Ted Williams	$45
July 1947 Pete Reiser, Andy Seminick	$35
Aug. 1947 Luke Appling	$25
Sept. 1947 Ewell Blackwell	$25
Oct. 1947 Cincinnati Reds	$25
Nov. 1947 Ralph Kiner, Johnny Mize	$30
Dec. 1947 Jackie Robinson	$45
Jan. 1948 Play at third	$25
Feb. 1948 Joe Cronin, Joe McCarthy	$35
March 1948 Yogi Berra, Jack Conway	$30
April 1948 Play at the plate	$25
May 1948 Tommy Holmes, Danny Litwhiler, Connie Ryan	$25
June 1948 President Truman	$20
July 1948 Clyde Kluttz, Johnny Mize	$25
Aug. 1948 Steve O'Neill, Dizzy Trout	$25
Sept. 1948 Stan Musial	$35
Oct. 1948 Lou Boudreau, Mike Guerra	$50
Nov. 1948 Connie Mack	$20
Dec. 1948 Lou Boudreau	$25
Jan. 1949 Joe DiMaggio, Bobby Doerr, Ted Williams	$60
Feb. 1949 Gil Coan, Joe Dobson	$25
March 1949 Pat Mullin	$25
April 1949 Bob Swift, Birdie Tebbets	$25
June 1949 Griffith Stadium	$25
July 1949 Ralph Branca	$25
Aug. 1949 Del Rice	$25
Sept. 1949 Casey Stengel	$25
Oct. 1949 Richie Ashburn, Clyde McCullough, Andy Seminick	$35
Nov. 1949 Connie Mack	$30

Dec. 1949 Ford Frick, William Harridge, Casey Stengel $20
Jan. 1950 Red Sox pitchers $20
Feb. 1950 Roy Sievers $20
March 1950 Tommy Henrich, Johnny Mize, Casey Stengel $20
April 1950 Sherm Lollar, Birdie Tebbets $20
May 1950 Stan Musial $25
June 1950 Earl Torgeson $20
July 1950 Connie Mack $25
Aug. 1950 Eddie Sawyer $20
Sept. 1950 Johnny Lipon $20
Oct. 1950 Richie Ashburn $35
Dec. 1950 Yankee Stadium $35
Jan. 1951 Play at second $20
Feb. 1951 Billy Goodman $20
March 1951 Braves vs. Cubs $20
April 1951 Joe Garagiola $15
May 1951 Vern Bickford, Johnny Sain, Warren Spahn $20
June 1951 Casey Stengel $20
July 1951 Eddie Sawyer, Casey Stengel $15
Sept. 1951 Gil Hodges $35
Oct. 1951 World Series issue $25
Nov. 1951 Bob Feller $25
Dec. 1951 Cy Young $25
Jan. 1952 Out at the plate $20
March 1952 Ned Garver $20
April 1952 Rogers Hornsby, Eddie Stanky $40
May 1952 Richie Ashburn, Del Ennis, Tommy Brown $35
June 1952 Willie Mays $35
July/Aug. 1952 All-Star Game issue $20
Sept. 1952 Babe Ruth anniversary issue $35

Oct. 1952 Pennant issue $45
Nov./Dec. 1952 World Series issue $20
April 1953 Pee Wee Reese, Hank Sauer, Bobby Shantz $35
May 1953 Solly Hemus, Johnny Mize $20
June 1953 Joe DiMaggio, Hoot Evers, Allie Reynolds $40
July 1953 Billy Bruton, Mickey Mantle $45
Aug. 1953 Luke Applng, Ray Boone, Dick Gernert ... $15
Sept. 1953 Karl Drews, Mickey Vernon, Del Wilber $20
Oct. 1953 Gus Bell, Gil Hodges $35
Nov. 1953 Pee Wee Reese, Phil Rizzuto, Robin Roberts, Red Schoendienst $35
Aug. 1954 Mickey Mantle $20
Sept. 1954 Casey Stengel $10
Oct. 1954 World Series issue $10
March 1955 Connie Mack $15
May 1955 illustration $10
June 1955 illustration $10
July 1955 All-Star Game issue $15
May 1956 "Play Ball" $25
June 1956 Ted Williams $30
July 1956 Mickey Mantle $40
Aug. 1956 Bob Friend $20
Oct. 1956 Casey Stengel $20
May 1957 Don Larsen $20
Sept. 1957 Bob Feller $20
Nov. 1964 Johnny Callison $30
Dec. 1964 Brooks Robinson $30
Jan. 1965 Cardinals team photo $20
Feb. 1965 Cleveland's Municipal Stadium $20
March 1965 Frank Howard $30
April 1965 Wally Bunker $20

Famous Sluggers of...
Famous Slugger Yearbook

Illustrated artwork was used for the years which do not appear in this list.

Values range from $60 (1927) to $6 (1978).

1933 Jimmie Foxx, Chuck Klein
1934 Lou Gehrig, Paul Waner
1935 Arky Vaughn, Buddy Myer
1936 Lou Gehrig, Mel Ott
1937 Charlie Gehringer, Joe Medwick
1939 Jimmie Foxx, Ernie Lombardi
1940 Joe DiMaggio
1941 Joe DiMaggio, others
1942 Joe DiMaggio, Ted Williams
1943 Ted Williams, Ernie Lombardi
1944 Stan Musial
1945 Dixie Walker, Lou Boudreau
1947 Stan Musial, Mickey Vernon
1948 Lefty O'Doul
1949 Ted Williams, Stan Musial
1950 Jackie Robinson, Ted Williams
1951 Ralph Kiner

1956 Al Kaline, Richie Ashburn
1957 Mickey Mantle, Hank Aaron, Ted Kluszewski
1958 Ted Williams
1959 Stan Musial
1960 Rocky Colavito, others
1961 Ernie Banks
1962 Roger Maris
1963 Tommy Davis, Pete Runnels
1964 Tommy Davis, Carl Yastrzemski
1965 Roberto Clemente, Tony Oliva
1966 Roberto Clemente, Tony Oliva
1967 Frank Robinson, Matty Alou
1968 Roberto Clemente, Carl Yastremski
1969 Pete Rose, Carl Yastrzemski
1970 Pete Rose, Rod Carew
1971 Johnny Bench, Alex Johnson
1972 Willie Stargell, others
1973 Dick Allen
1974 Hank Aaron
1975 Johnny Bench

Comic Books

A-1 Comics

Magazine Enterprises
1944-1955
89) Home Run, Stan Musial $125

All-Pro Sports

All-Pro Sports
(black and white)
1) Unauthorized bio - Bo Jackson, baseball $2.50

The All-Star Story of the Dodgers

Stadium Communications
April 1979
1F) Roy Campanella, Sandy Koufax, Jackie Robinson
....$2

All-Time Sports Comics

Hillman Periodicals
Oct.-Nov. 1949
5) Baseball $75
7) Baseball $75

The Amazing Willie Mays

Famous Funnies Publications
September 1954
1) Willie Mays (c) $400

Babe

"The Amazon of the Ozarks"
Prize/Headline Feature
June-July 1948
2) Baseball (c) $30

Babe Ruth Sports Comics

Harvey Publications
April 1949-February 1951
2) Baseball (c) $175
3) Joe DiMaggio (c) $150
4) Bob Feller (c) $125
8) Yogi Berra (c) $115
9) Stan Musial (c) $125

Baseball Classics

Personality
1) Willie Mays..$2.75
1a) Willie Mays with trading cards $5
2) Lou Gehrig $2.75
2a) Lou Gehrig with trading cards $5

Baseball Comics

Will Eisner Productions
Spring 1949
1) Rube Rooky...$425

Baseball Comics

Personality
1) Frank Thomas $2.75
1a) Frank Thomas with cards $5
2) Rickey Henderson $2.75
2a) Rickey Henderson with cards............................$5
3) Nolan Ryan $2.75
3a) Nolan Ryan with cards $5
4) Cal Ripken Jr..$2.75
4a) Cal Ripken Jr. with cards $5

Baseball Greats

Dark Horse
1) Jimmy Piersall story $2.95

Baseball Heroes

Fawcett Publications
1952
Babe Ruth Hall of Fame Biographies.................$450

Baseball Legends

Revolutionary
1) Babe Ruth...$2.50
2) Ty Cobb..$2.50
3) Ted Williams...$2.50
4) Mickey Mantle..$2.50
5) Joe DiMaggio...$2.50
6) Jackie Robinson..$2.50
7) Sandy Koufax...$2.50
8) Willie Mays..$2.50
9) Honus Wagner...$2.50
10) Roberto Clemente $2.50
11) Yogi Berra..$2.50
13) Hank Aaron..$3
14) Carl Yastrzemski...$3
15) Satchel Paige $3
16) Johnny Bench...$3
17) Shoeless Joe Jackson.......................................$3
18) Lou Gehrig $3

Baseball Sluggers

Personality Comics
1) Ken Griffey Jr. $2.75
1a) limited edition $5
2) Dave Justice $2.75
2a) limited edition $5
3) Frank Thomas $2.75
3a) limited edition $5
4) Don Mattingly $2.75
4a) limited edition $5

Baseball Superstars

Revolutionary $3 each
Hank Aaron; Jim Abbott; Alomar brothers; Steve
Avery, Tom Glavine; Johnny Bench; Yogi Berra;
George Brett; Jose Canseco; Roger Clemens; Joe
DiMaggio; Dennis Eckersley; Carlton Fisk; Lou Geh-
rig; Ken Griffey Jr.; Rickey Henderson; Bo Jackson;
Mickey Mantle; Billy Martin; Willie Mays; Mark
McGwire; Kirby Puckett; Cal Ripken Jr.; Pete Rose;
Nolan Ryan; Babe Ruth; Ryne Sandberg; Darryl
Strawberry; Frank Thomas; Honus Wagner; Ted Will-
iams; Dave Winfield; Carl Yastrzemski; Annual #1
Nolan Ryan.

Baseball Thrills

Ziff-Davis Publishing Co.
1951-1952
10) Bob Feller...$200
2) Yogi Berra..$150
3) Joe DiMaggio...$150

Baseball Thrills 3-D

3-D Zone
May 1990
1) Ty Cobb, Ted Williams..................................cover

Best Pitchers

Personality
1) Nolan Ryan ....cover
1a) Nolan Ryan with cards ....cover
2) Dwight Gooden ....cover
2a) Dwight Gooden with cards...........................cover
3) Roger Clemens ....cover
3a) Roger Clemens with cards............................cover

Bill Stern's Sports Book

Ziff-Davis Publishing Co.
1951-1952
1) Ewell Blackwell $90

Blue Bolt

Funnies Inc./Novelty Press/Premium Group of Comics
1940-1949
8-1 Baseball cover..$22
9-1 Baseball cover..$22
10-1 Baseball cover..$24

Blue Devil

DC Comics
1984-1986
26) Special baseball issue..................................$1.50

Brooks Robinson

Magnum
May 1992
1) photo...$1.75

Calling All Boys

Parents' Magazine Institute
1946-1948
7) Baseball...$14
12) Baseball...$40

Comics Revue

St. John Publishing Co.
1947-48
3) Iron Vic baseball cover $27.50

Daredevil Comics

Lev Gleason Publications
July 1941-Sept. 1956
25) baseball cover..$175

DC Superstars

National Periodical Publications/DC Comics
1976-1978
10) Superhero Baseball Special.........................$4.25

Don Newcombe

Fawcett Publications
1950
1) Baseball Star $200

Famous Funnies

Eastern Color
1933-1955
22) Baseball cover $300
58) Baseball cover $140

Jack Armstrong

Parents' Institute
1947-1949
7) Baffling Mystery on the Diamond $50

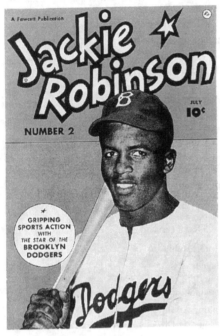

Jackie Robinson

Fawcett Publications
1950-1952
No # Famous Plays of Jackie Robinson.............$450
2) Famous Plays of Jackie Robinson...................$300
3) Famous Plays of Jackie Robinson...................$250
4) Famous Plays of Jackie Robinson...................$250
5) Famous Plays of Jackie Robinson...................$250
6) Famous Plays of Jackie Robinson...................$250

King Comics

David McKay Publications
Starring Popeye
1936-1952
39) Baseball..$200
61) Phantom Baseball...$125
156) Baseball $35

Krazy Komics

Timely
1942-1948
24) Baseball...$40

Larry Doby, Baseball Hero

Fawcett Publications
1950
1) baseball..$400

Li'l Abner

Harvey Publications
1947-1955
83) Baseball...$60

Mel Allen Sports Comics

Visual Editions
1949-1950
2) Lou Gehrig $70

Mickey Mantle Comics

Magnum
1) Rise to Big Leagues $3

Negro Heroes

Parents' Magazine Institute
1947-1948
2) Jackie Robinson $375

Phil Rizzuto

Fawcett Publications
1951
The Sensational Story of the American League's
MVP $350

Power Pack

1984-1991
13) Baseball issue $2

The Pride of the Yankees

Magazine Enterprises
No # The Life of Lou Gehrig $425

Ralph Kiner, Home Run King

Fawcett Publications
1950
No # Life Story of the Famous Pittsburgh Slugger.....
$300

Real Heroes Comics

Parents' Magazine Institute
1941-1946
6) Lou Gehrig $85
14) Pete Gray...$30

Real Life Comics

Nedor/Better/Standard Publications
1941-1952
24) Babe Ruth..$65
41) Jimmie Foxx...$35

Roy Campanella, Baseball Hero

Fawcett Publications
1950
No # Life Story of the Battling Dodgers Catcher$325

Sport Comics

Street & Smith Publications
1940-1941
1) Lou Gehrig $275
3) Phil Rizzuto...$125

Sports Action

Marvel Comics
1950-1952
3) Hack Wilson...$100
7) Jim Konstanty $90
8) Ralph Kiner $90

Sports Classics

Personality Comics
1) Babe Ruth...$2.50
1a) with trading cards $5
2) Mickey Mantle $2.50
2a) with trading cards $5
3) Ty Cobb..$2.50
3a) with trading cards $5
4) Ted Williams..$2.50
4a) with trading cards $5
5 Jackie Robinson...$2.50
5a) with trading cards $5

Sports Personalities

Personality Comics
1992
2) Nolan Ryan $2.50
2a) limited edition $5
3) Rickey Henderson $2.50
3a) limited edition $5
8) George Brett..$2.50
8a) limited edition $5
12) Ken Griffey Jr. $2.50
12a) with trading cards $5
14) Pete Rose..$2.50
14a) with trading cards $5

Sports Stars

Parents' Magazine Institute
1946
2) Baseball Greats $125

Sport Thrills

Star Publications
1950-1951
11) Ted Williams, Ty Cobb....................................$90
12) Joe DiMaggio, Phil Rizzuto $65
14) baseball cover...$65
15) baseball cover...$65

Supersnipe Comics

Street & Smith's Publications
1942-1949
2-4 Baseball $175
3-3 Baseball $150
3-11 Baseball Pitcher..$150
4-8 Baseball Star $115

Target Comics

Funnies Inc./Novelty Publishing/Star Publications
1940-1949
9-5 Baseball..$30

Thrilling True Story of the Baseball Giants

Thrilling True Story of the Baseball Yankees
Fawcett Publications
1952
No # Famous Giants of the Past...........................$375
No # Baseball Yankees..$350

True Comics

True Comics/Parents' Magazine Press
1941-1950
3) Baseball Hall of Fame......................................$100
6) Baseball World Series $95
15) Bob Feller...$45
37) Baseball $25
44) El Senor Goofy, baseball $25
49) Baseball $20
71) The Story of Joe DiMaggio............................$25
77) Lou Boudreau...$25
78) Stan Musial $25
84) includes baseball $115

True Sport Picture Stories

Street & Smith Publications
1942-1949
1-5 Joe DiMaggio..$160
1-7 Mel Ott $85
2-3 Carl Hubbell $70
2-7 Stan Musial $75
2-10 Connie Mack $70
3-2 The Philadelphia Athletics $60
3-3 Leo Durocher $60
3-12 Red Sox vs. Senators....................................$60
4-1 Spring Training in full spring...........................$55
4-2 How to Pitch 'Em Where They Can't Hit 'Em$55

Vic Verity Magazine

Vic Verity Publications
1945
5) Championship Baseball Game $35

WOW Comics

Fawcett Publications
1940-1948
69) Tom Mix Baseball...$50

Yogi Berra

Fawcett Publications
1957
1) Yogi Berra...$350

Young All-Stars

DC Comics
June 1987
7) Baseball Game ....cover

Books

The outlook for baseball books as collectibles is very good; prices of quality used baseball books are relatively low. However, prices have been rising, and, as more and more collectors discover this over-looked area of the memorabilia hobby, prices will escalate accordingly. For lovers of baseball literature and for investors, there is no better time than now to buy quality baseball books.

Four main factors determine the value of a used baseball book: scarcity, desirability, condition, and edition. Generally, scarcity adds to the value of a baseball book, but not significantly unless the book is considered desirable in the first place. In other words, hundreds of fairly hard-to-find baseball books are not particularly valuable because there is no demand for them. However, desirable books that are scarce always command premium prices.

Many older baseball books, especially those published in the 19th century, are the exceptions to this rule. These older books, such as Henry Chadwick's The Game of Baseball (1868) and Jacob Morse's Sphere and Ash (1888), are not very entertaining to the average contemporary reader, but they are extremely rare and historically important. Thus, each easily sells for thousands of dollars.

Desirability is ultimately in the eye of the reader/buyer, but the author, the subject, the degree of originality, and the overall quality or "readability" of the book are the main factors that determine a book's standing with collectors. Baseball card collectors should have little trouble understanding that condition greatly affects the value of baseball books. Torn or missing pages, coffee cup rings on the cover, general wear and tear on the spine - such defects definitely reduce any book's value.

Two particularly important aspects of condition to be aware of are: 1) "ex libre" books, i.e. discards from libraries, are considered damaged goods and are shunned by collecting purists; and 2) a lack of a dust jacket (if issued) significantly reduces the value of a book, sometimes up to 50 percent or more. Closely related to condition is the matter of a book's edition. To be worth top dollar a book should be a first printing of a first edition.

Two other influences on value are worth noting. First, although an autograph normally lessons the value of a premier baseball card, it enhances a baseball book, whether the book is signed by the author or the subject(s), or both. Second, a biography is not necessarily valuable because the subject is a superstar.

For example, Mickey Mantle is a magic name in the baseball card market, but there is no scarce (or particularly outstanding) Mantle biography. Thus a much hard-to-find biography of a lesser player, such as Rocky Colavito (Don't Knock the Rock), is considered more valuable than any Mantle biography.

Of course, there is no guarantee that any baseball book will appreciate dramatically, so the average collector would be well advised to collect books he enjoys for his own sake.

Because there are so many baseball books, with a few hundred new ones published annually, most collectors should consider specializing. Four common approaches to specialization are collecting by quality, team, genre (e.g., record books, fiction, picture books, general histories), or topic. Some of the most popular topics for baseball book collectors are ballparks, the Negro Leagues, biographies and the minors.

Finally, there is a wide variety of sources for used baseball books. The top sources, ranging from the least to the most productive, are: garage sales, card shows, library sales, antiquarian book sales, hobby periodicals (such as Sports Collectors Digest), used book stores, and used baseball book dealers who issue mail-order catalogs. Remaindered books at cut-rate prices can also be found in new-book book stores, but these offerings will always be recently published books that either didn't sell well or were over-printed.

Listed below are some of the best baseball books ever published, books which would form the foundation of any worthy collections. While not truly rare, first editions of many of these titles are becoming quite scarce. Because there is no comprehensive used baseball book price guide, it is difficult to state exact values for these books with any certainty; however, collectors can expect to see these books priced in the following ranges: up to $50; $50-$75; and more than $75.

Babe, The Legend Comes to Life, Robert Creamer, 1974, ($50) - Considered by many as the best sports biography ever written, Babe increases our affection and respect for baseball's foremost hero.

Ball Four, Jim Bouton, 1970, ($50) - Although rather tame by today's standards, Bouton's tell-all shocker of 1970 is still the funniest baseball book in captivity.

The Ballparks, Bill Shannon, 1965, (more than $75) - This photo-history, the first book on its subject, is tough to find and high on many collectors' want-lists.

Baseball: The Early Years (1960) and *Baseball: The Golden Age (1971),* Harold Seymour, ($50-$75) - This as-yet-uncompleted triology ranks as baseball literature's most highly regarded general history.

The Baseball Encyclopedia, first edition, ($50) - Now in its eighth edition, the original edition of the most famous baseball record book comes in a neat boxed slip cover.

Baseball I Gave You All The Best Years Of My Life, edited by Richard Grossinger and Kevin Kerrane, ($50) - A mind-bending anthology of eclectic poetry and prose, *Baseball I Gave You* is hard to find but worth the trouble.

The Boys Of Summer, Roger Kahn, 1971, ($50) - The book that immortalized that Brooklyn Dodgers of the early 1950s, *The Boys of Summer* is the quintessential classic baseball book.

Bush League, Robert Obojski, ($50-$75) - Conceived as a companion to *The Baseball Encyclopedia, Bush League* was published in 1975 but it is still the best reference book on the minors.

The Celebrant, Eric Rolfe Greenberg, (more than $75) - A novel about Christy Mathewson and his biggest fan, *The Celebrant* is a scarce book with a big following.

The Cincinnati Game, Lonnie Wheeler, 1988, ($50) - This is the most innovative team history ever, but only 3,000 copies of the hardback were published.

The Chrysanthemum and the Bat, Robert Whiting, ($50-$75) - The first major treatment of Japanese baseball, this is also a book about the clash of two cultures.

Eight Men Out, Eliot Asinof, ($50-$75) - This is the best book about baseball's most infamous scandal, the fixed 1919 World Series.

A *False Spring,* Pat Jordan, ($50) - This beautifully-written coming-of-age autobiography about failure in the minor leagues reads like a novel.

The Fireside Book of Baseball, Vol I, II, & III, edited by Charles Einstein, ($50, $50 and more than $75) - These are the first great (and still unsurpassed) anthologies of baseball literature. Vol. III is especially tough to locate.

The Glory of Their Times, Lawrence Ritter, 1966, ($85) - This collection of first-person accounts by players from the '20s is a favorite with collectors.

The Great American Baseball Card Flipping, Trading and Bubble Gum Book, Brendan C. Boyd and Fred C. Harris, (A) - Recently reprinted, this most nostalgic of all baseball books was the first to demonstrate the enormous appeal of baseball cards.

The Long Season, 1960, and *Pennant Race,* Jim Brosnan, ($50-$75 each) - Great inside looks at major league baseball, Brosnan's diaries remain the only books to be entirely written by an active major league player.

Only the Ball Was White, Robert Peterson, (more than $75) - This pioneering history of Negro League baseball is a must for anyone interested in its popular topic.

Putnam Sports Series, various authors, (more than $75) - Written by the leading sportswriters of the '50s, these team histories have stood the test of time and fetch increasingly higher prices.

Shoeless Joe, W. P. Kinsella, (more than $75) - The novel that "Field of Dreams" was based on, Shoeless Joe is highly sought-after by collectors of American fiction as well as collectors of great baseball books.

Ty Cobb, Charles C. Alexander, (A) - This great biography of baseball's fiercest immortal was underestimated and underprinted by its original publisher.

The Ultimate Baseball Book, edited by Dan Okrent, ($50) - Great photos and superb writing by an all-star lineup highlight this coffee-table spectacular.

Veeck As In Wreck, Bill Veeck and Ed Linn, ($50-$75) - Baseball's maverick promoter tells how it's done in a consistently entertaining and seldom-offered-for-sale book.

— Mike Shannon

Mike Shannon is the editor and publisher of Spitball: the Literary Baseball Magazine, 6224 Collegevue Place, Cincinnati, Ohio, 45224. Spitball magazine annually awards the Casey Award to the best baseball book of the year. Previous winners include:

1983: *The Celebrant,* Eric Rolfe Greenberg

1984: *Bums: An Oral History of the Brooklyn Dodgers,* Peter Golenbock

1985: *Good Enough to Dream,* Roger Kahn

1986: *The Bill James Historical Baseball Abstract,* Bill James

1987: *Diamonds are Forever,* Peter Gordon/Paul Weinman

1988: *Blackball Stars,* John Holway

1989: *The Pitch that Killed,* Mike Sowell

1990: *Baseball: The People's Game,* Harold Seymour

1991: *To Everything a Season: Shibe Park and Urban Philadelphia,* Bruce Kuklick

1992: *The Negro Baseball Leagues: A Photographic History,* Phil Dixon and Patrick J. Hannigan

1993: *Diamonds: The Evolution of the Ballpark,* Michael Gershman

1994: *Lords of the Realm,* John Helyar

1995: *Walter Johnson, Baseball's Big Train,* Henry Thomas

The following prices are taken from catalogs from Wayne Greene and R. Plapinger, two leading used books dealers. Greene can be contacted at 945 West End Avenue #5D, New York, N.Y. 10025; Plapinger can be reached at P.O. Box 1062, Ashland, Ore. 97520. HC means hard cover. Books are all first editions.

Classics

Babe: The Legend Comes to Life, by Robert W. Creamer, Simon & Schuster (1974), HC, $50.
Ball Four, by Jim Bouton with Leonard Schecter, World (1970), HC, $50, signed $65.
How Life Imitates the World Series, by Tom Boswell, Doubleday (1982), HC, $25.
I Had a Hammer, by Hank Aaron with Lonnie Wheeler, Harper/Collins (1991), HC, signed, $40-$60, unsigned, $15.
Late Innings, by Roger Angell, Simon & Schuster (1982), HC, $15-$50.
Once More Around the Park, by Roger Angell, Ballantine (1991), HC, $20.
Season Ticket, by Roger Angell, Houghton Mifflin, (1988), HC, $20.
The Heart of the Order, by Tom Boswell, Doubleday (1989), HC, $15.
The Image of Their Greatness, by Lawrence Ritter and Donald Honig, HC, $35.
The Summer Game, by Roger Angell, Viking (1972), HC, $25-$50.
The Ultimate Baseball Book, by Daniel Okrent and Harry Levine, $19.95, HC, $50-$90.
Ty Cobb, by Charles C. Alexander, Oxford (1984), HC, $65.
Why Time Begins on Opening Day, by Tom Boswell, Doubleday (1984), HC, $20-$35.

Biographies/Autobiographies

The Hank Aaron Story, by Milton Shapiro, Messner (1961), HC, $15.
Aaron R.F., by Henry Aaron and Furman Bisher, World (1968), HC, $65.
Hank Aaron - Quiet Superstar, by Al Hirshberg, Putnam (1974), HC, $30.
Hank Aaron 715, by Pat Reshen, Arco (1974), HC, $30.
The Man Who Made Milwaukee Famous, by Don Money (Hank Aaron), Agape (1976), HC, $45.
Crash, by Tom Whitaker and Dick Allen, Ticknor & Fields (1989), HC, $15-$25.
You Can't Beat the Hours, by Mel Allen and Ed Fitzgerald, Harper (1964), HC, $75.
The Bob Allison Story, by Hal Butler, Messner (1967), HC, $50.
My Life in Baseball, by Felipe Alou with Herm Weiskopf, Word (1967), HC, signed, $45.
Alston and the Dodgers, Walter Alston with Si Burick, Doubleday (1966), HC, $22.50.
A Year at a Time, by Walt Alston and Jack Tobin, Word (1976), HC, $17.50.
Bless You Boys, Sparky Anderson with Dan Ewald (1984 season recap), Contemporary (1984), HC, $15.
Sparky!, by Sparky Anderson with Dan Ewald, Prentice Hall (1990), HC, signed, $40.
Mr. Cub, by Ernie Banks and Jim Enright, Follet (1971), HC, $40.
Don Baylor, by Don Baylor and Claire Smith, St. Martin's (1989), HC, $20.
Bo - Pitching and Wooing, by Maury Allen (Bo Belinsky), Dial (1973), HC, signed, $45.
Hardball, by George Bell with Bob Elliot, Key Porter (1990), HC, $35.
From Behind the Plate, by Johnny Bench with George Kalinsky, Rutledge (1972), HC, $30.
Johnny Bench - King of the Catchers, by Lou Sabin, Putnam (1977), HC, $7.50.
Catch You Later, by Johnny Bench with William Brashler, Harper & Row (1979), HC, $30, signed, $75.
Moe Berg - Athlete, Scholar, Spy, by Lewis Kaufman, et. al., Little, Brown (1974), HC, $65.
The Catcher Was A Spy, by Nicholas Dawidoff (Moe Berg), Pantheon (1994), HC, $17.
Yogi Berra - The Muscle Man, by Ben Epstein, Barnes (1951), HC, $150.
Yogi Berra, by Joe Trimble, Barnes (1952), HC, $40.
The Yogi Berra Story, by Gene Roswell, Messner (1958), HC, $40.
Yogi, Yogi Berra with Ed Fitzgerald, Doubleday (1961), HC, $30-$45, signed $75.
The Story of Yogi Berra, by Gene Schoor, Doubleday (1976), HC, $40.
Yogi, It Ain't Over, Yogi Berra with Tom Horton, McGraw Hill (1989), HC, $12.50.
Ewell Blackwell, by Lou Smith, Barnes (1951), HC, $65.
Vida, His Own Story, by Vida Blue and Bill Libby, Prentice Hall (1972), HC, $12.50.

Vida Blue - Coming Up Again, by Don Kowet, Putnam (1974), HC, $12.50.

Player-Manager, Lou Boudreau with Ed Fitzgerald, Little, Brown (1949), HC, $40.

I'm Glad You Didn't Take It Personally, by Jim Bouton with Leonard Schecter, Morrow (1971), HC, signed, $20.

I Managed Good, But Boy Did They Play Bad, Jim Bouton with Neil Offen, Playboy (1973), HC, signed, $20.

Ball Four Plus Five: An Update (1970-80), by Jim Bouton, Stein & Day (1981), HC, $20.

Ken Boyer, by Jack Zanger, Nelson (1965), HC, $60.

You Can't Hit The Ball With The Bat On Your Shoulder, by Bobby Bragan and Jeff Guinn, Summit (1992), HC, $25.

The George Brett Story, by John Garrity, Coward McCann & Geoghegan (1981), HC, $45.

Stealing is My Game, by Lou Brock with Franz Schulze, Prentice Hall (1976), HC, $45-$65.

The Jim Bunning Story, by Jim Bunning and Ralph Bernstein, Lippincott (1965), HC, $40.

Roy Campanella, by Dick Young, Grosset & Dunlap (1952), HC, $30.

It's Good to Be Alive, by Roy Campanella, Little, Brown (1959), HC, $45.

Roy Campanella - Man of Courage, by Gene Schoor, Putnam (1959), HC, $60.

Carew, by Rod Carew and Ira Berkow, Simon & Schuster (1979), HC, $35, signed, $60.

A Dream Season, by Gary Carter and John Hough Jr. (recaps 1986 season), HBJ (1987), HC, $10.

The Gamer, by Gary Carter, Word (1993), HC, signed, $40.

My Ups & Downs in Baseball, by Orlando Cepeda, Putnam (1968), HC, $15-$50.

Orlando Cepeda, by Bob Stevens and Richard Keller, Woodford (1987), HC, signed, $25.

Rocket Man, by Roger Clemens with Peter Gammons, S. Greene (1987), HC, $30.

Clemente, by Kal Wagenheim (Roberto Clemente), Praeger (1973), HC, $45.

The Life of Roberto Clemente, by Paul Robert Walker, HBJ (1988), HC, $15.

Ty Cobb - Idol of Baseball Fandom, by Sverre Braathen, Avondale (1928), HC, inscribed, $800.

The Tiger Wore Spikes, by John McCallum (Ty Cobb), Barnes (1956), HC, $45.

My Life in Baseball - The True Record, by Ty Cobb with Al Stump, Doubleday (1961), HC, $45-$125.

Ty Cobb - The Greatest, by Robert Rubin, Putnam (1978), HC, $75.

Ty Cobb, by Charles Alexander, Oxford (1984), HCThe Hank Aaron Story, by Milton Shapiro, Messner (1961), HC, $15.

Don't Knock the Rock, by Gordon Cobbledick (Rocky Colavito), World (1966), HC, $150.

"Commy," The Life Story of the Grand Old Roman of Baseball, by G.W. Axelson (Charles A. Comiskey), The Reilly & Lee Co. (1919), HC, $150-$250.

Seeing It Through, by Tony Conigliaro with Jack Zanger, Macmillan (1970), HC, $15.

Jocko, by Jocko Conlon and Robert Creamer, Lippincott (1967), HC, $25.

Inside Pitch - by Roger Craig and Vern Plagenhoef (pitching coach recaps 1984 Detroit Tigers season), Eerdman's (1984), HC, $12.50.

Slugging It Out In Japan, by Warren Cromartie and Robert Whiting, Kodansha Intl. (1991), HC, $20.

When in Doubt, Fire the Manager, by Alvin Dark and John Underwood, Dutton (1980), HC, $30.

The Tommy Davis Story, by Patrick Russell, Doubleday (1969), HC, $75.

America's Dizzy Dean, by Curt Smith, Bethany Press (1978), HC, $17.50-$25.

Joe DiMaggio, Yankee Clipper, by Tom Meany, Barnes (1951), HC, $65.

Where Have You Gone Joe DiMaggio?, by Maury Allen, Dutton (1975), HC, $25.

The DiMaggio Albums, by Richard Whittingham (two volumes), Putnam (1982), HC, $25.

Joe DiMaggio, by George DeGregorio, Scarborough (1983), HC, $45.

Joe DiMaggio: Baseball's Yankee Clipper, by Jack B. Moore, Praeger (1987), HC, $55.

Pride Against Prejudice, by Joseph Thomas Moore (Larry Doby), Praeger (1988), HC, $12.50.

One Last Round for the Shuffler, by Tom Clark ("Shufflin'" Phil Douglas), Truck Books (1979), HC, $35.

The Don Drysdale Story, by Milton Shapiro, Messner (1964), HC, $75.

Once a Bum, Always a Dodger, by Don Drysdale with Bob Verdi, St. Martin's (1990), HC, $12.50.

The Comeback, by Ryne Duren and Robert Drury, Lorenz (1978), HC, $45.

The Leo Durocher Story, by Gene Schoor, Messner (1955), HC, $10.

Nice Guys Finish Last, by Leo Durocher and Ed Linn, Simon & Schuster (1975), HC, $35.

Nails, Lenny Dykstra with Marty Noble, Doubleday (1987), HC, $25.

Dock Ellis in the Country of Baseball, by Dock Ellis and Donald Hall, Coward McCann (1976), HC, $20-$25.

Umpiring From The Inside, by Billy Evans, self-published (1947); $150.

Strikeout Story, by Bob Feller, Barnes (1947), HC, $40.

Bob Feller, by Gene Schoor, Doubleday (1962), HC, $45.

No Big Deal, by Mark Fidrych with Tom Clark, Lippincott (1977), HC, $20.

Yankee Stranger, by Ed Figueroa and Dorothy Harshman, Exposition Press (1982), HC, $20.

Slick, by Whitey Ford and Phil Pepe, Morrow (1987), HC, signed, $45.

The George Foster Story, by Malka Drucker with George Foster, Holiday House (1979), HC, $25.

Double X: Jimmie Foxx Baseball's Forgotten Slugger, by Bob Gorman, Holy Name Society (1990), HC, $15.

Behind the Mask, by Bill Freehan, World (1970), HC, $30.

Frank Frisch - The Fordham Flash, by Frank Frisch and J. Roy Stockton, Doubleday (1962), HC, $65.

Garvey, by Steve Garvey with Skip Rozin, Times (1986), HC, $12.50, signed, $30.

Lou Gehrig - Pride of the Yankees, by Paul Gallico, Grosset & Dunlap (1942), HC, $35.

Lou Gehrig - Boy of the Sand Lots, by Guernsey Van Riper, Bobbs-Merrill (1949), HC, $25.

Iron Horse, by Ray Robinson (Lou Gehrig), Norton (1990), HC, $17.50.

Take Time for Paradise, by A. Bartlett Giamatti, Summit (1989), HC, $15.

From Ghetto to Glory, by Bob Gibson with Phil Pepe, Prentice Hall (1968), HC, signed, $65.

A Stranger to the Game, by Bob Gibson with Lonnie Wheeler, Viking (1994), HC, signed, $50.

Josh Gibson, by William Brashler, Harper & Row (1978), HC, $125.

Rookie, by Richard Woodley (Dwight Gooden), Doubleday (1985), HC, $27.50.

Dwight Gooden - Strikeout King, by Nathan Aaseng, Lerner (1988), HC, $10.

One Armed Wonder, by William C. Kashatus (Pete Gray), McFarland (1995), HC, $14.

The Story of My Life, by Hank Greenberg with Ira Berkow, Times Books (1989), HC, $22.50-$30.

Calvin: Baseball's Last Dinosaur, by Jon Kerr (Calvin Griffith), William C. Brown (1990) HC, $40.

Jolly Cholly's Story, by Charlie Grimm and Ed Prell, Regnery (1968), HC, $25.

Guidry, by Ron Guidry and Peter Golenbock, Prentice Hall (1980), HC, $15.

Tony!, by Tony Gwynn and Jim Geschke, Contempory (1986), HC, $25.

Hawk, by Ken Harrelson and Al Hirshberg, Viking (1969), HC, $25.

Off Base, by Rickey Henderson with John Shea, Harper/Collins (1992), HC, $10.

If At First, by Keith Hernandez and Mike Bryan, McGraw Hill (1986), HC, $15, signed, $35.

Out of the Blue, by Orel Hershiser and Jerry Jenkins, Wolgemuth & Hyatt (1989), HC, $15.

White Rat, by Whitey Herzog with Kevin Horrigan, Harper & Row (1987), HC, $10.

The High Hard One, by Kirby Higbe and Martin Quigley, Viking (1967), HC, $85.

Gil Hodges: The Quiet Man, by Marino Amoruso, Erickson (1991), HC, $25.

My War With Baseball, by Rogers Hornsby with Bill Surface, McKay (1953), HC, $85.

The Willie Horton Story, by Hal Butler, Messner (1970), HC, $25.

The Jock's Itch, by Tom House, Contemporary (1989), HC, $15.

Frank Howard: The Gentle Giant, by Al Hirshberg, Putnam (1973), HC, $40.

Between the Lines, by Steve Howe with Jim Greenfield, Masters (1989), HC, $12.50.

Catfish, Million Dollar Pitcher, by Bill Libby (Jim Hunter), Coward McCann (1976), HC, $12.50.

Catfish Hunter, by Irwin Stambler, Putnam (1976), HC, $20.

Catfish, by Jim "Catfish" Hunter and Armen Keteyian, McGraw Hill (1988), HC, $10.

Bo Knows Bo, by Bo Jackson with Dick Schaap, Doubleday (1990), HC, $15.

Reggie Jackson, the $3 Million Man, by Maury Allen, Harvey (1978), HC, $15.

The Reggie Jackson Story, by Bill Libby, Lothrop (1979), HC, $20.

Reggie, by Reggie Jackson with Mike Lupica, Villard (1984), HC, $15.

Mr. October, by Maury Allen (Reggie Jackson), Times (1981), HC, $20.

Say It Ain't So Joe - The Story of Shoeless Joe Jackson, by Donald Gropman, Little, Brown (1979), HC, $50-$60.

Shoeless Joe and Ragtime Baseball, by Harvey Frommer (Shoeless Joe Jackson), Taylor (1992), HC, $15.

Like Nobody Else, by Ferguson Jenkins and George Vass, Regnery (1973), signed, $60.

The Tommy John Story, by Tommy and Sally John with Joe Muser, Revell (1978), HC, signed, $40.

Ban Johnson, by Gene Murdock, Greenwood (1982), HC, $60.

Walter Johnson, by Roger Treat, Messner (1948), HC, $150.

Walter Johnson - Baseball's Big Train, by Henry Thomas, Phenom (1995), HC, $25.

Temporary Insanity, by Jay Johnstone with Rick Talley, Contemporary (1985), HC, signed, $20.

Over the Edge, by Jay Johnstone with Rick Talley, Contemporary (1987), HC, signed, $25.

Cleon, by Cleon Jones with Ed Hershey, Coward McCann (1970), HC, $25.

The Al Kaline Story, by Al Hirshberg, Messner (1964), HC, signed, $60.

Al Kaline and the Detroit Tigers, by Hal Butler, Regnery (1973), HC, $55.

The Harmon Killebrew Story, by Hal Butler, Messner (1966), HC, $15.

Harmon Killebrew, Baseball's Superstar, Deseret (1971), HC, $125.

Ralph Kiner, The Heir Apparent, by Tom Meany, Barnes (1951), HC, $45.

Kiner's Korner, by Ralph Kiner and Joe Gergen, Arbor (1987), HC, $25.

Jim Konstanty, by Frank Yeutter, Barnes (1951), HC, $17.50.

Sandy Koufax - Strikeout King, Arnold Hano, Putnam (1964), HC, $40.

Koufax, by Sandy Koufax with Ed Linn, Viking (1966), HC, signed, $100.

Hardball, by Bowie Kuhn, Times (1987), HC, $50.

Judge Landis and 25 Years of Baseball, by J.G. Taylor Spink, Crowell (1947), HC, $22.50.

The Artful Dodger, by Tommy Lasorda with David Fisher, Arbor House (1985), HC, $20.

The Wrong Stuff, by Bill Lee with Dick Lally, Viking (1984), HC, $12.50.

Breakout, by Ron LeFlore with Jim Hawkins, Harper & Row (1978), HC, $15.

Prophet of the Sandlots, by Mark Winegardner (scout Tony Luccadello), Atlantic Monthly (1990), HC, $25.

Fred Lynn, Young Star, by Bill Libby, Putnam (1977), HC, signed, $40.

Fred Lynn, The Hero from Boston, by Ed Dolan and Richard Lyttle, Icarus (1982), HC, $25.

Connie Mack, by Fred Lieb, Putnam (1945), HC, $35.

My 66 Years in the Big Leagues, by Connie Mack, Winston (1950), HC, $50.

My Nine Innings, by Lee MacPhail, Meckler (1989), HC, $25.

The Sal Maglie Story, by Milton Shapiro, Messner (1966), HC, $27.50-$45.

The Mickey Mantle Story, by Mickey Mantle and Ben Epstein, Holt (1953), $150.

Mickey Mantle of the Yankees, by Gene Schoor, Putnam (1958), HC, $10.

Mickey Mantle - Yankee Slugger, by Milton Shapiro, Messner (1962), HC, $12.50.

Mickey Mantle - Mr. Yankee, by Al Silverman, Putnam (1963), HC, $50.

The Quality of Courage, by Mickey Mantle, Doubleday (1964), HC, $45.

The Mick, by Mickey Mantle with Herb Gluck, Doubleday (1985), HC, $25.

A Pitcher's Story, by Juan Marichal with Charles Einstein, Doubleday (1967), HC, $50.

Roger Maris: A Man For All Seasons, by Maury Allen, Donald Fine & Co. (1986), HC, $20-$30.

Roger Maris: A Title To Fame, by Harvey Rosenfeld, Praire House (1991), HC, $15.

The Return of Billy the Kid, by Norman Lewis Smith (Billy Martin), Coward McCann (1977), HC, $17.50.

Billy Martin, by Gene Schoor, Doubleday (1980), HC, $17.50.

Billyball, Billy Martin with Phil Pepe, Doubleday (1987), HC, $12.50.

The Last Yankee, by David Falkner (Billy Martin), Simon & Schuster (1992), HC, $15.

Wild, High and Tight, by Peter Golenbock (Billy Martin), St. Martin's (1994), HC, $15.

The Eddie Mathews Story, by Al Hirshberg, Messner (1961), HC, signed, $75.

Eddie Mathews and the National Pastime, by Eddie Mathews and Bob Buege, Douglas American (1994), HC, signed, $45.

Pitching in a Pinch, by Christy Mathewson, Putnam (1912), HC, $350.

Christy Mathewson, by Gene Schoor with Henry Gilfond, Messner (1953), HC, $25.

They Call Me Sarge, by Fred Mitchell with Gary Matthews, Bonus (1985), HC, $15.

The Willie Mays Story, by Ken Smith, Greenberg (1954), HC, $100.

Born to Play Ball, Willie Mays and Charles Einstein, Putnam (1955), HC, $45.

Willie Mays Story, by Milton Shapiro, Messner (1960), HC, $45.

The Willie Mays Album, by Howard Liss, Hawthorn (1966), HC, $75.

My Life In and Out of Baseball, by Willie Mays and Charles Einstein, Dutton (1966), HC, $15

Willie Mays - Baseball Superstar, by Sam and Beryl Epstein, Garrard (1975), HC, $12.50.

Willie's Time, by Charles Einstein (Willie Mays), Lippincott (1979), HC, $30.

Say Hey, Willie Mays with Lou Sahadi, Simon & Schuster (1988), HC, $10, signed, $85.

Oh, Baby, I Love It, by Tim McCarver with Ray Robinson, Villard (1987), HC, $12.50.

John McGraw, by Charles C. Alexander, Viking (1988), HC, $35.

Screwball, by Tug McGraw and Joe Durso, Houghton-Mifflin (1974), HC, signed, $40.

Nobody's Perfect, by Denny McLain with Dave Diles, Dial (1975), HC, $20.

Strikeout, by Denny McLain with Mike Nahrstedt, Sporting News (1988), HC, $15, signed, $40.

Joe Morgan: A Life In Baseball, by Joe Morgan with David Falkner, Norton (1933), HC, signed, $60.

Thurman Munson - Pressure Player, by Bill Libby, Putnam (1978), HC, $30.

Thurman Munson, by Thurman Munson with Martin Appel, Coward McCann (1978), HC, $35.

Ask Dale Murphy, by Dale Murphy with Curtis Patton, Algonquin (1987), HC, $12.50.

Stan Musial - The Man, by Tom Meany, Barnes (1951), HC, $40.

The Stan Musial Story, by Gene Schoor and Henry Gilfond, Messner (1955), HC, $35.

Stan Musial - The Man, by Irv Goodman, Nelson (1961), HC, $30.

Stan Musial, by Ray Robinson, Putnam (1963), HC, $9.

Stan Musial - The Man's Own Story, by Stan Musial and Bob Broeg, Doubleday (1964), HC, $60.

The Man, Stan Musial, Then and Now, Stan Musial and Bob Broeg, Bethany (1977), HC, $45.

Knuckler - The Phil Niekro Story, Wilfred Binette, Hallux Bros. (1970), HC, $25, signed, $60.

Knuckleballs, by Phil Niekro and Tom Bird, Freundlich (1986), HC, $20.

Sadahura Oh, by Sadahura Oh and David Falkner, Times (1984), HC, $30.

Pitchin' Man, by Satchel Paige and Hal Lebovitz, Cleveland News (1948), HC, $35.

Maybe I'll Pitch Forever, by Satchel Paige and David Lipman, Doubleday (1962), HC, $75.

Andy Pafko - The Solid Man, by John Hoffman, Barnes (1951), HC, $65.

Behind the Mask, by Dave Pallone and Alan Steinberg, Viking (1990), HC, $12.50.

Joe, You Coulda Made Us Proud, by Joe Pepitone and Barry Stainback, Playboy (1975), HC, $25.

Me and the Spitter, by Gaylord Perry and Bob Sudyk, Sunday Review Press (1974), HC, $50.

The Truth Hurts, by Jimmy Piersall, Contemporary (1984), HC, $12.50.

Sweet Lou, by Lou Piniella and Maury Allen, Putnam (1986), HC, $20.

Snap Me Perfect, by Darrell Porter and William Deerfield, Nelson (1984), HC, $10.

Kirby Puckett - Fan Favorite, by Ann Bauleke (biography for younger readers), Lerner (1993), HC, $15.

I Love This Game, by Kirby Puckett with Mike Bryan, Harper/Collins (1993), HC, $12.50.

Ted "Double Duty" Radcliffe, by Kyle McNary, McNary (1994), HC, signed, $30.

Phil Regan, by Phil Regan and James Hefley, Zondervan (1968), HC, signed, $65.

The Bobby Richardson Story, by Bobby Richardson, Revell (1965), HC, signed, $50.

Branch Rickey, by Arthur Mann, Houghton-Mifflin (1957), HC, inscribed, $40.

Branch Rickey, by Murray Polner, Atheneum (1982), HC, $45.

Phil Rizzuto, by Joe Trimble, Barnes (1951), HC, $30.

Phil Rizzuto: A Yankee Tradition, by Dan Hirshberg, Sagamore (1993), HC, signed, $60.

O Holy Cow! The Selected Verse of Phil Rizzuto, by Hart Seely and Tom Peyer, Ecco (1993), $10.

The Brooks Robinson Story, by Jack Zanger, Messner (1967), HC, $15.

Putting It All Together, by Brooks Robinson and Fred Bauer, Hawthorn (1971), HC, $30.

Third Base Is My Home, by Brooks Robinson and Jack Tobin, Word (1974), HC, $30.

Extra Innings, by Frank Robinson and Berry Stainback, McGraw-Hill (1988), HC, $17.50.

My Life in Baseball, by Frank Robinson and Al Silverman, Doubleday (1975), HC, $12.50.

My Own Story, by Jackie Robinson and Wendell Smith, Greenberg (1948), HC, $100.

The Jackie Robinson Story, by Arthur Mann, FJ Low (1950), HC, $55.

Wait Till Next Year, by Jackie Robinson and Carl Rowan, Random House (1960), HC, $40.

Jackie Robinson of the Brooklyn Dodgers, by Milton Shapiro, Messner (1965), HC, $20.

Jackie Robinson - Baseball's Gallant Fighter, by Sam and Beryl Epstein, Garrard (1974), HC, $45.

Jackie Robinson - A Life Remembered, by Maury Allen, Watts (1987), HC, $25.

I Never Had It Made, by Jackie Robinson and Alfred Duckett, Putnam (1972), HC, $35.

The Pete Rose Story, by Pete Rose, World (1970), HC, $27.50.

Pete Rose, They Call Him Charlie Hustle, by Bill Libby, Putnam (1972), HC, $20.

Charlie Hustle, by Pete Rose with Bob Hertzel, Prentice Hall (1975), HC, $15.

Pete Rose, Mr. .300, by Keith Brandt, Putnam (1977), HC, $12.50.

Pete Rose, My Life in Baseball, by Pete Rose, Doubleday (1979), HC, $75.

Pete Rose: My Story, by Pete Rose with Roger Kahn, Macmillan (1989), HC, $7.50.

Hustle: The Myth, Life and Lies of Pete Rose, by Michael Y. Sokolove, Simon & Schuster (1990), HC, $17.50.

Super Scout - Thirty Five Years of Major League Scouting, by Jim Russo and Bob Hammel, Bonus (1992), HC, $15.

Babe Ruth, by Tom Meany, Barnes (1947), HC, $30.

The Babe Ruth Story, by Babe Ruth and Bob Considine, Dutton (1948), HC, $50.

Babe Ruth - Baseball Boy, by Guernsey Van Riper, Bobbs-Merrill (1954), HC, $25.

Babe Ruth, His Story in Baseball, by Lee Allen, Putnam (1966), HC, $17.50.

Babe Ruth's America, by Robert Smith, Crowell (1974), HC, $40.

Babe Ruth: His Life and Legend, by Karl Wagenheim, Praeger (1974), HC, $45.

The Life That Ruth Built, by Marshall Smelser (Babe Ruth), Quadrangle (1975), HC, $75.

Babe Ruth - Sultan of Swat, by Lois P. Nicholson, Goodwood (1994), HC, $20.

Nolan Ryan - Fireballer, by Bill Libby, Putnam (1975), HC, $35.

Throwing Heat, by Nolan Ryan and Harvey Frommer, Doubleday (1988), HC, $15.

Miracle Man: Nolan Ryan, by Nolan Ryan with Jerry Jenkins, Word (1992), HC, $10.

Second to None, by Ryne Sandberg, Bonus (1995), HC, signed, $50.

Ron Santo: For Love of Ivy, by Ron Santo with Randy Minkoff, Bonus (1993), HC, signed, $50.

Sax!, by Steve Sax and Steve Delsohn, Contemporary (1986), HC, signed, $20.

Clowning Through Baseball, by Al Schact, Barnes (1941), HC, $30.

Tom Seaver of the Mets, by George Sullivan, Putnam (1971), HC, $20.

Inside Corner - Talks with Tom Seaver, by Joel Cohen, Atheneum (1974), HC, $30.

Tom Seaver - Portrait of a Pitcher, by Malka Drucker with Tom Seaver, Holiday (1978), HC, $20.

Seaver, by Gene Schoor (Tom Seaver), Contemporary (1986), HC, $15.

The Blooper Man, by Elson Smith (Rip Sewell), J. Pohl (1981), HC, $25.

The Ted Simmons Story, by Jim Brosnan, Putnam (1977), HC, $30.

Country Hardball, by Enos Slaughter and Kevin Reid, Tudor (1981), HC, $45.

Wizard, by Ozzie Smith with Rob Rains, Contemporary (1982), HC, $25.

The Duke Snider Story, by Irwin Winehouse, Messner (1964), HC, $20.

The Duke of Flatbush, by Duke Snider with Bill Gilbert, Zebra (1988), HC, $20, signed, $50.

A.G. Spalding and the Rise of Baseball, by Peter Levine, Oxford (1985), HC, $30.

Willie Stargell, by Bill Libby, Putnam (1973), HC, $10.

Willie Stargell - An Autobiography, by Willie Stargell and Tom Bird, Harper & Row (1984), HC, $25.

Rusty Staub of the Expos, by John Robertson, Prentice Hall (1971), HC, $45.

Casey Stengel - Baseball's Greatest Manager, by Gene Schoor, Messner (1953), HC, $12.50.

Casey Stengel, by Frank Graham Jr., John Day (1958), HC, $15-$25.

Casey at the Bat, by Casey Stengel and Harry T. Paxton, Random House (1962), HC, $25.

Casey, by Joseph Durso (Casey Stengel), Prentice Hall (1967), HC, $25, signed, $35.

Casey Stengel, by Norman MacLean, Drake (1976), HC, $40.

Stengel: His Life and Times, by Robert W. Creamer, Simon & Schuster (1984), HC, $30.

Tomorrow, I'll Be Perfect, by Dave Stieb and Kevin Boland, Doubleday (1986), HC, signed, $45.

Darryl, by Darryl Strawberry and Art Rust Jr., Bantam (1992), HC, $12.50.

Triumph Born of Tragedy, by Andre Thornton and Al Janssen, Harvest House (1983), HC, $25.

El Tiante, by Luis Tiant and Joe Fitzgerald, Doubleday (1976), HC, $25.

Fernando!, by Mike Littwin (Fernando Valenzuela), Bantam (1981), HC, $10.

Veeck As In Wreck, by Bill Veeck with Ed Linn, Putnam (1962), HC, signed, $200.

The Hustler's Handbook, by Bill Veeck with Ed Linn, Putnam (1965), HC, $65.

The Kid from Cuba, James Terzian (Zoilo Versailles), Doubleday (1967), HC, $30.

The Ginger Kid, by Irving Stein (Buck Weaver), Brown and Benchmark (1992), HC, $12.50.

It's What You Learn After You Know It All That Counts, by Earl Weaver and Barry Stainback, Doubleday (1982), HC, $20.

Five O'Clock Comes Early, by Bob Welch and George Vecsey, Morrow (1982), HC, $35.

Billy, the Classic Hitter, by Billy Williams and Irv Haag, Rand McNally (1974), HC, $50.

Ted Williams, by Arthur Sampson, Barnes (1950), HC, $45.

My Turn at Bat, by Ted Williams with John Underwood, Simon & Schuster (1969) HC, $45.

Ted Williams: Seasons of the Kid, by Richard Cramer, Prentice Hall (1991), HC, $45.

The Last .400 Hitter, by John B. Holway (Ted Williams), William C. Brown (1991), HC, $20.

Ted Williams - A Baseball Life, by Michael Seidel, Contemporary (1991), HC, $20.

It Pays to Steal, by Maury Wills and Steve Gardner, Prentice Hall (1963), HC, $10.

How to Steal a Pennant, by Maury Wills and Don Freeman, Putnam (1976), HC, $12.50.

On the Run, by Maury Wills and Mike Celizic, Carroll & Graf (1991), HC, $15, signed, $30.

Hack, by Robert Boone and Gerald Grunska (Hack Wilson), Highland Press (1978), HC, $75.

Dave Winfield - 23 Million Dollar Man, by Gene Schoor, Stein & Day (1982), HC, $30.

Winfield - A Player's Life, by Dave Winfield with Tom Parker, Norton (1988), HC, $10, signed, $35.

Dave Winfield - 3,000 and Counting, by the St. Paul Pioneer Press, Andrews & McMeel (1993), HC, $15.

Philip K. Wrigley, by Paul Angle, Rand McNally (1975), HC, $65.

Yaz, by Carl Yastrzemski with Al Hirshberg, Viking (1968), HC, $30.

Batting, by Carl Yastrzemski with Al Hirshberg, Viking (1972), HC, $25.

Historical

After the Miracle, by Maury Allen (1969 Mets, 20 years later), Watts (1989), HC, $20.

The Armchair Book of Baseball, by John Thorn, Scribner's (1985), HC, $15.

Backstage at the Mets, by Lindsey Nelson and Al Hirshberg, Viking (1966), HC, $30.

Ballplayers Are Human Too, by Ralph Houk and Charles Dexter, Putnam (1962), HC, $27.50.

Baseball Between the Lines, by Donald Honig, Coward McCann (1976), HC, $35.

Baseball is a Funny Game, by Joe Garagiola with Martin Quigley, Lippincott (1960), HC, $30.

Baseball Rookies Who Made Good, by M.G. Bonner (Mantle, Williams, Ruth, etc.), Knopf (1954), $35.

Baseball's 100, by Maury Allen (his picks as the best), Galahad (1982), HC, $17.50.

Baseball Through a Knothole, by Bill Borst (history of baseball in St. Louis), Krank (1980), HC, $15.

Baseball When the Grass Was Real, by Donald Honig, Coward McCann (1975), HC, $35.

Bats, by Davey Johnson and Peter Golenbock (New York Mets' 1985 season), Putnam (1986), HC, $45.

Beating the Bushes, by Frank Dolson (life in the minors), Icarus (1982), HC, $30.

The Best Seat in Baseball, But You Have to Stand, by Lee Gutkind (1974 season from an umpiring crew's viewpoint), Dial (1975), HC, $30-$40.

Beyond the Sixth Game, by Peter Gammons (Boston Red Sox from the sixth game of the 1975 World Series on), Houghton-Mifflin (1985), HC, $25.

Black Diamonds, by John Holway, Meckler (1989), HC, $20.

Bleachers - A Summer in Wrigley Field, by Lonnie Wheeler, Contemporary (1988), HC, $30.

The Boston Red Sox, by Fred Lieb, Putnam (1947), HC, $45.

The Boston Red Sox, by Tom Meany, Barnes (1956), HC, $35.

The Boys of Summer, by Roger Kahn, Harper & Row (1972), HC, $50.

The Boys Who Would Be Cubs, by Joseph Bosco (a year with the Class A Peoria Cubs), Morrow (1990), HC, $12.50-$20.

The Broadcasters, by Red Barber, Dial (1970), HC, $50.

The Bronx Zoo, by Sparky Lyle and Peter Golenbock, Crown (1979), HC, $10, signed, $40.

Bums, by Peter Golenbock (Brooklyn Dodgers baseball), Putnam (1984), HC, $30.

Bush League, by Robert Obojski (history of the minors), Macmillan (1975), HC, $50.

Can't Anybody Here Play This Game?, by Jimmy Breslin (New York Mets' first year), Viking (1963), HC, $40.

Catch - A Major League Life, by Ernie Whitt and Greg Cable (Blue Jays' 1988 season as seen by team's catcher), McGraw Hill - Ryerson, HC, $27.50.

Champagne and Baloney, by Tom Clark (recaps Oakland's prominence in the 1970s), Harper & Row (1976), $17.50.

Charlie O & the Angry A's, by Bill Libby, Doubleday (1975), $20.

The Chicago Cubs, by Warren Brown, Putnam (1946), HC, $50-$75.

The Chicago White Sox, by Warren Brown, Putnam (1952), HC, $75-$90.

The Chrysanthemum and the Bat, by Robert Whiting (baseball in Japan), Dodd, Mead (1977), HC, $50.

The Cincinnati Reds, by Lee Allen, Putnam (1948), HC, $135.

The Cincinnati Reds, by Ritter Collett, Jordan-Powers (1976), HC, $125.

Colorado Rockies - The Inaugural Season, by Rich Clarkson and Bob Baron, Fulcrum (1993), HC, $45.

The Crooked Pitch, by Martin Quigley, Algonquin (1984), HC, $35.

The Cubs of 69, by Rick Talley (recaps the bittersweet 1969 season), Contemporary (1989), HC, $20.

The Curse of the Bambino, by Dan Shaughnessy, Dutton (1990), HC, $25.

The Curse of Rocky Colavito, by Terry Pluto, Simon & Schuster, HC, $20.

A Day In The Bleachers, by Arnold Hano (Game 1 of the 1954 World Series), Crowell (1955), HC, $35-$125.

The Detroit Tigers, by Fred Lieb, Putnam (1946), HC, $65.

Diamonds in the Rough, by Ken Rappoport (minor league baseball), Tempo (1979), HC, $10.

Diamonds in the Rough, by David Hanneman (memoirs of scout Tony Luccadello), Diamond (1989), HC, $12.50.

Diamonds in the Rough, by Joel Zoss and John Bowman (history of baseball), Macmillan (1989), HC, $30.

Diary of a Yankee Hater, by Bob Marshall, Watts (1981), HC, $7.50.

The Dizziest Season, by G.H. Fleming (1934 Gashouse Gang), Morrow (1984), HC, $40-$50.

The Dodgers, by Frank Graham, Putnam (1945), HC, $65-$100.

Down to the Wire, by Jeff Miller (1967 American League pennant race), Taylor (1992), HC, $12.50.

Eight Men Out, by Eliot Asinof (1919 Black Sox scandal), Holt Rinehart & Winston (1963), HC, $50-$75.

A False Spring, by Pat Jordan, Dodd & Mead (1975), HC, $50.

The Fireside Book of Baseball (baseball anthologies), by Charles Einstein, Simon & Schuster (1956), HC, $50-$100.

First to Last, by Larry Fox (New York Mets' 1969 season), Harper (1970), HC, $35.

Five O'Clock Lightning, by Tommy Henrich and Bill Gilbert, Birch Lane (1992), HC, $45.

Five Seasons, by Roger Angell, Simon & Schuster (1977), HC, $15.

The Gashouse Gang, by J. Roy Stockton, Barnes (1945), HC, $25-$45.

The Girls of Summer, by Lois Browne (history of the All American Girls Professional Baseball League), Harper/Collins (1992), HC, $17.50.

The Glory of Their Times, by Lawrence Ritter, Macmillan (1966), HC, $85.

The Go-Go Chicago White Sox, by Dave Condon, Coward McCann (1960), HC, $45-$75.

Good Enough to Dream, by Roger Kahn (onwer of the Utica Blue Sox), Doubleday (1985), HC, $12.50, signed, $20.

The Great Chase: The Dodgers-Giants Pennant Race of 1951, by Harvey Rosenfeld, MacFarland (1992), HC, $27.50.

The Greatest Game Ever Played, by Jerry Izenberg, Holt (1987), HC, $25.

Green Diamonds, by Jay Acton with Nick Bakalar (minor league baseball), Zebra (1993), HC, $15.

Hardball - A Season in the Projects, by Daniel Coyle, Putnam (1993), HC, $12.50.

The High Hard One, by Kirby Higbe with Martin Quigley, Viking (1967), HC, $100.

Home Games, by Bobbie Bouton and Nancy Marshall (wives' series of letters to their husbands), St. Martin's (1983), HC, $15.

The Home Run Heard Round The World, by Ray Robinson (1951 Giants vs. Dodgers), Harper/Collins (1991), HC, $15.

The Hot Stove League, by Lee Allen (history and anecdotes), Barnes (1955), HC, $150-$175.

I Don't Care If I Never Come Back, by Art Hill, Simon & Schuster (1980), HC, $20.

The Imperfect Diamond, by Lee Lowenfish and Tony Lupien, Stein & Day (1980), HC, $20.

Inside the Yankees, by Ed Linn (1977 New York Yankees), Ballantine (1978), HC, $7.50.

Invisible Men, by Donn Rogosin (Negro Leagues), Atheneum (1983), HC, $60.

It's Anybody's Ball Game, by Joe Garagiola, Contemporary (1988), HC, $12.50.

Joe DiMaggio - The Golden Year 1941, by Al Silverman, Prentice Hall (1969), HC, $60.

Joy In Mudville, by George Vecsey (1969 Mets), McCall (1970), HC, $15.

July 2, 1903, by Mike Sowell (Ed Delahanty's death), Macmillan (1992), HC, $15.

Kings of the Hill, by Nolan Ryan with Mickey Herskowitz (Ryan summarizes pitchers), Harper/Collins, HC, $12.50.

Kiss It Goodbye, by Shelby Whitfield (the last season of the Washington Senators), Abelard-Schuman (1973), HC, $25.

Lady in the Lockerroom, by Susan Fornoff (female sports reporter), Sagamore (1993), HC, $12.50.

Lightning In A Bottle, by Herbert F. Crehan with James W. Ryan (1967 Boston Red Sox), Branden (1992), $17.50.

The Long Season, by Jim Brosnan (diary of the 1959 season), Harper & Row (1960), HC, $60, signed, $85.

Louisville Slugger, by Jan Arrow (history of bat making), Pantheon (1984), HC, $30.

Love Letters to the Mets, by Bill Adler, Simon & Schuster (1965), $50.

Major League Memories Series, by Bruce Chadwick and David Spindel, team summaries and artifacts for the Los Angeles Dodgers (1993), $15; Boston Red Sox (1992), $12.50; Cincinnati Reds (1994), $8.

The Man in the Crowd - Confessions of a Sports Addict, by Stanley Cohen, Random House (1981), HC, $15.

The Man in the Dugout, by Donald Honig, Follett (1977), HC, $20.

The Man Who Stole First Base, by Eric Nadel and Craig R. Wright (135 off-beat stories), Taylor (1989), $12.50.

Men At Work, by George F. Will, Macmillan (1990), HC, $10.

The Men in Blue, by Larry Gerlach, Viking (1980), HC, $35.

The Men of Autumn, by Dom Forker (1949-53 New York Yankees), Taylor (1989), HC, $20.

Men of the Reds Machine, by Ritter Collett (1970s Cincinnati Reds), Landfall (1976), HC, $35.

The Mets Will Win the Pennant, by William Cox, Putnam (1964), HC, $40.

The Milwaukee Braves, a Baseball Eulogy, by Bob Buege, Douglas (1988), HC, $25.

The Minors, by Neil J. Sullivan (historical overview of the minor leagues), St. Martin's (1990), HC $17.50

Miracle at Coogan's Bluff, by Thomas Kiernan (1951 Giants), Crowell (1975), HC, $35.

Misfits!, J. Thomas Hetrick (1899 Cleveland Spiders), McFarland (1991) HC, $25.

My Baseball Diary, by James Farrell (novelist's viewpoint on the game he followed all his life), Barnes (1957), HC, $40-$50.

My Baseball Scrapbook, by Bob Broeg (St. Louis Cardinal beat writer), River City (1983), HC, $45.

My Favorie Summer 1956, by Mickey Mantle and Phil Pepe, Doubleday (1991), HC, $15.

The Neighborhood of Baseball, by Barry Gifford (Chicago Cubs from the 1950s-80s), Dutton (1981), HC, $20.

The New Baseball Reader, by Charles Einstein (baseball anthologies), Viking (1991), HC, $20.

New York City Baseball, by Harvey Frommer (1947-57 baseball in New York), Macmillan (1980), HC, $35.

Nine Innings, by Daniel Okrent (1982 Brewer/Orioles game), Ticknor & Fields (1985), HC, $15.

1947: When All Hell Broke Loose in Baseball, by Red Barber, Doubleday (1982), HC, $45.

No Cheering in the Press Box, by Jerome Holtzman, Holt, Rinehart & Winston (1974), HC, $30.

No Joy in Mudville, by Ralph Andreano, Schenkman (1965), HC, $25.

October 1964, by David Halberstam (recaps pennant race and World Series), Villard (1994), HC, $15.

One Strike Away, by Dan Shaughnessy (1986 Red Sox season), Beaufort (1987), HC, $25.

Only the Ball Was White, by Robert Peterson (Negro Leagues), Prentice Hall, HC, $100.

The Only Ticket Off The Island, by Gare Joyce (a season in the Dominican Republic's Winter League), Lester & Orpen Dennys (1990), HC, $40.

Our Game, by Charles C. Alexander (history of the game), Holt (1991), HC, $17.50.

Out of My League, by George Plimpton, Harper (1961), HC, $25.

Pen Men, by Bob Cairns (life in the bullpen), St. Martin's (1992), HC, $10.

The Perfect Game, by Tom Seaver and Dick Schaap (1969 Mets), Dutton (1970), HC, $12.50.

The Philadelphia Phillies, by Fred Lieb and Stan Baumgartner, Putnam (1953), HC, $225.

The Philadelphia Phillies - The Team that Wouldn't Die, by Hal Bodley (1981), HC, $45.

Pine Tarred and Feathered, by Jim Kaplan (Sports Illustrated writer), Algonquin (1985), HC, $17.50.

Pinstripe Pandemonium, by Geoffrey Stokes (Yankees' 1983 season), Harper & Row (1984), HC, $10.

The Pirates - We Are Family, Lou Sahadi, Times (1980), HC, $25.

Pitchers Do Get Lonely, by Ira Berkow, Atheneum (1988), HC, $15.

The Pitch That Killed, by Mike Sowell, Macmillan (1989), HC, $20.

The Pittsburgh Pirates, by Fred Lieb, Putnam (1948), HC, $100-$135.

Play Ball, by John Feinstein (baseball's troubled times), Villard (1993), HC, $12.50.

Playing Around, by Donald Hall, et. al. (1973 spring training with the Pittsburgh Pirates), Little, Brown (1974), HC, $30.

The Psychologist At Bat, by David F. Tracy (team psychologist for the St. Louis Browns), Sterling (1951), HC, $50.

Roger Maris at Bat, by Roger Maris and Jim Ogle, Duell (1961 season), Sloan and Pearce (1962), HC, $60.

The Rookies, by Ed Walton, Stein & Day (1982), HC, $12.50.

Safe at Home, by Sharon Hargrove (baseball wife tells her story), by Texas A&M (1989), HC, $17.50.

The St. Louis Cardinals, by Fred Lieb, Putnam (1944), HC, $30.

A Season in the Sun, by Roger Kahn, Harper & Row (1977), HC, signed $50.

Season of Dreams, by Tom Kelly and Ted Robinson (Minnesota Twins' 1991 season), Voyager Press (1992), HC, $17.50.

The Seattle Pilots Story, by Carson Van Lindt, Marabou (1993), HC, $10.

The Short Season, by David Falkner (spring training atmosphere), Times (1986), HC, $45.

Some Are Called Clowns, Bill Heward and Dimitri Gat (season with pitcher/manager of the 1973 Indianapolis Clowns), Crowell (1974), HC, $50-$60.

Streak: Joe DiMaggio and the Summer of 1941, by Michael Seidel, McGraw Hill (1988), HC, $12.50-$20.

The Suitors of Spring, by Pat Jordan, Dodd Mead (1973), HC, $10.

Superstars and Screwballs, by Richard Goldstein (baseball in Brooklyn), Dutton (1991), HC, $15.

Sweet Seasons, by Dom Forker (1955-64 New York Yankees), Taylor (1990), HC, $20.

Ted Williams - The Golden Year 1957, by Edwin Pope, Prentice Hall (1970), HC, signed, $275.

The Twenty-Four Inch Home Run, by Michael Bryson (baseball oddities and anecdotes), Contemporary (1990), HC, $15.

Ball Four has had several editions published, including a Japanese version.

The 26th Man, by Steve Fireovid and Mark Winegardner (story of a veteran minor leaguer), Macmillan (1991), HC, $20.

They Kept Me Loyal to the Yankees, by Victor Debs (tribute to former Yankees), Rutledge (1993), HC, $25.

Tomahawked, by Bill Zack (1992 Braves season), Simon & Schuster (1993), HC, $15.

Total Baseball, by John Thorn and Pete Palmer, Warner (1989), HC, $25.

Two Spectacular Seasons, by William B. Mead (1930 and 1968 seasons recapped), Macmillan (1990), HC, $12.50.

Up From the Minor Leagues, by Donald Honig, Cowles (1970), HC, $40.

View from the Dugout, Ed Richter (1963 Philadelphia Phillies season), Chilton (1964), HC, $27.50.

Voices from the Great Black Baseball Leaguers, by John Holway, Dodd Mead (1975), HC, $125.

Voices of the Game, by Curt Smith (chronicles baseball broadcasting), Diamond (1987), HC, $30.

Wait Til Next Year, by Chris Jennison (New York City baseball from the 1940s and '50s), Norton (1974), signed by Duke Snider, $40.

Want To Be A Baseball Champion, by Ethan Allen (demonstrates baseball offensive strategies), General Mills (1946), HC, $45.

We Won Today, by Kathleen Parker (diary of a 1976 Mets fan), Doubleday (1977), HC, $25-$35.

When the Cheering Stops, by Lee Heiman, Dave Weiner and Bill Gutman (profiles 21 players from the 1950s and 1960s), Macmillan (1990), HC, $15.

The Whiz Kids, by Harry Paxton (1950 Phillies), McKay (1950), HC, $110.

Winning, by Earl Weaver and John Sammis (instructional), Morrow (1972), HC, $20.

Wild and Outside, by Stefan Fatsis (1994 season of the independent Northern League of Professional Baseball), Walker (1995), HC, $25.

The Wit and Wisdom of Yogi Berra, by Phil Pepe, Hawthorn (1974), HC, $17.50.

The World Champion Pittsburgh Pirates, by Dick Groat and Bill Surface (1961 Pirates season), Coward McCann (1961), HC, $65.

Yankee Batboy, by Joe Carrieri and Zander Hollander, Barnes (1945), HC, $30.

The Year of the Tiger, by Jerry Green, Coward McCann (1969), HC, $40.

The Year the Mets Lost Last Place, by Paul Zimmerman and Dick Schaap, World (1969), HC, $20.

The Year They Called off the World Series, by Benton Stark (details the 1904 season), Avery (1991), HC, $15.

You Gotta Have Wa, by Robert Whiting (baseball in Japan), Macmillan (1989), HC, $15-$20.

Bookmarks

1993 DiamondMarks bookmarks

While they look like baseball cards and were sold in foil packs like baseball cards, DiamondMarks were licensed as bookmarks. Issued by Barry Colla Productions, the 2 1/2" by 5" cards feature Colla's trademark, high-quality player photos on front and back. The UV-coated fronts feature black borders with the player's name in white above the photos and a color team logo beneath. Backs, also bordered in black, feature color player photos in an open book design. There is a portrait photo on the left and a head-and-shoulders reproduction of the front photo at right. A bookmark with a team logo is incorporated in the design. The 120-card set is unnumbered and worth $20 in Mint condition. Individual cards are worth .25 to .75, unless noted.

Atlanta Braves - Steve Avery, Ron Gant, Tom Glavine, David Justice ($1), Terry Pendleton, Deion Sanders ($1), John Smoltz

Chicago Cubs - Mark Grace, Randy Myers, Ryne Sandberg ($2), Jose Vizcaino

Cincinnati Reds - Bobby Kelly, Barry Larkin, Kevin Mitchell, Jose Rijo, Reggie Sanders

Colorado Rockies - Dante Bichette, Daryl Boston, Andres Galarraga, Charlie Hayes

Florida Marlins - Orestes Destrade, Dave Magadan, Benito Santiago, Walt Weiss

Houston Astros - Jeff Bagwell ($1), Craig Biggio, Ken Caminiti, Luis Gonzalez

Los Angeles Dodgers - Brett Butler, Eric Davis, Orel Hershiser, Eric Karros, Ramon Martinez, Mike Piazza ($3), Darryl Strawberry

Montreal Expos - Moises Alou, Delino DeShields, Marquis Grissom, Dennis Martinez, Larry Walker

New York Mets - Bobby Bonilla, Dwight Gooden, Howard Johnson, Eddie Murray

Philadelphia Phillies - Darren Daulton, Lenny Dykstra, Dave Hollins, John Kruk

Pittsburgh Pirates - Jay Bell, Al Martin, Orlando Merced, Andy Van Slyke

St. Louis Cardinals - Gregg Jefferies, Tom Pagnozzi, Ozzie Smith, Todd Zeile

San Diego Padres - Derek Bell, Tony Gwynn, Fred McGriff, Gary Sheffield

San Francisco Giants - Barry Bonds ($1.50), John Burkett, Will Clark ($1.25), Matt Williams

Baltimore Orioles - Brady Anderson, Mike Mussina, Cal Ripken Jr. ($2)

Boston Red Sox - Roger Clemens, Andre Dawson, Mike Greenwell, Mo Vaughn

California Angels - Chad Curtis, Gary DiSarcina, Tim Salmon ($1.50), J.T. Snow

Chicago White Sox - Bo Jackson, Frank Thomas ($3), Robin Ventura

Cleveland Indians - Sandy Alomar Jr., Carlos Baerga, Albert Belle, Kenny Lofton

Detroit Tigers - Cecil Fielder, Tony Phillips, Mickey Tettleton, Alan Trammell

Kansas City Royals - George Brett ($1), Wally Joyner, Mike McFarlane, Brian McRae

Milwaukee Brewers - Darryl Hamilton, Pat Listach, B.J. Surhoff, Robin Yount

Minnesota Twins - Kent Hrbek, Chuck Knoblauch, Kirby Puckett, Dave Winfield

New York Yankees - Wade Boggs, Don Mattingly, Danny Tartabull

Oakland A's - Dennis Eckersley, Rickey Henderson, Mark McGwire, Ruben Sierra, Terry Steinbach

Seattle Mariners - Ken Griffey Jr. ($3), Edgar Martinez, Pete O'Brien, David Valle

Texas Rangers - Jose Canseco ($1), Juan Gonzalez ($1.50), Ivan Rodriguez, Nolan Ryan ($3)

Toronto Blue Jays - Roberto Alomar, Pat Borders, Joe Carter, Juan Guzman, Paul Molitor, Dave Stewart

1993 DiamondMarks inserts

Randomly inserted into packs of DiamondMarks cards at the rate of one per 48-pack carton was a series of eight cards featuring the baseball artwork of Terry Smith. The inserts are the same size as the regular cards and have the same basic black-bordered design, but both sides are UV-coated. Beneath the fantasy design player artwork on the front is the player's name. On the back the open book design is used, with a small player profile on the left and a Barry Cola photo portrait on the right, plus a team logo.

The complete set of eight cards is worth $75 in Mint condition. Individual cards are worth $11 each, unless noted. The players featured are: Roberto Alomar, Barry Bonds ($15), Ken Griffey Jr. ($18.50), David Justice, John Olerud, Nolan Ryan ($22), Frank Thomas ($15) and Robin Yount.

1993 DiamondMarks promos

In the same format as the regular-issue Diamond-Mark cards, these promos were produced to preview the concept for dealers and collectors. The promo cards feature different photos than those used on the regular cards. The cards are unnumbered. A complete set of eight cards is worth $75 in Mint condition. The players featured are: Roberto Alomar ($11), Will Clark ($15), Dennis Eckersley ($11), Ken Griffey Jr. ($25), Juan Gonzalez ($15), Kirby Puckett ($15), Ryne Sandberg ($18.50) and Frank Thomas ($25).

10

Commemoratives

Gateway Stamp Co.

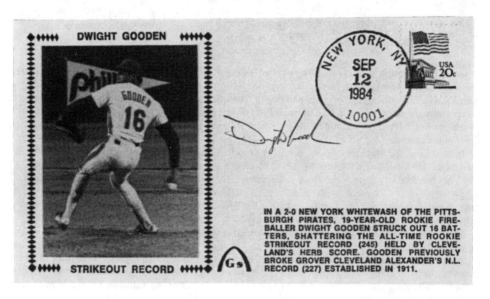

DWIGHT GOODEN

GOODEN 16

STRIKEOUT RECORD

NEW YORK, NY
SEP 12 1984
10001

USA 20c

IN A 2-0 NEW YORK WHITEWASH OF THE PITTS-
BURGH PIRATES, 19-YEAR-OLD ROOKIE FIRE-
BALLER DWIGHT GOODEN STRUCK OUT 16 BAT-
TERS, SHATTERING THE ALL-TIME ROOKIE
STRIKEOUT RECORD (245) HELD BY CLEVE-
LAND'S HERB SCORE. GOODEN PREVIOUSLY
BROKE GROVER CLEVELAND ALEXANDER'S N.L.
RECORD (227) ESTABLISHED IN 1911.

Gateway Stamp Co. Inc., of Florissant, Mo., has been producing full-color "silk" commemorative cachets since 1977, when the company produced a set of three cachets commemorating the 50th anniversary of the flight of Charles Lindbergh. Since that time the company has planned more than 540 sports-related cachets, primarily baseball issues. The limited-edition envelopes are postmarked on the historic dates by the United States Postal Service, which only dates items submitted before midnight. Gateway has employees who track a player's progress toward a milestone accomplishment; they also follow the player, with a determined number of stamped cachets to be postmarked, until the even has occurred. When the event has happened, the employee has the Post Office in that city hand-cancel the envelopes. Whenever possible, Gateway also incorporates philatelic cancellations on the envelopes.

The cachets feature gold borders, biographical information and full-color silk cachets, which are actual event photos, publicity photos, or artists' renditions. A primary attraction of the cachets is that Gateway has designed the envelopes to be autographed, and obtains the signatures of the players represented on them. Values of the covers are determined by condition (cleanliness, crispness of corners, centering, positioning of copy, clarity of postmarks) and autographs - quality and player represented.

Z Silk Cachets

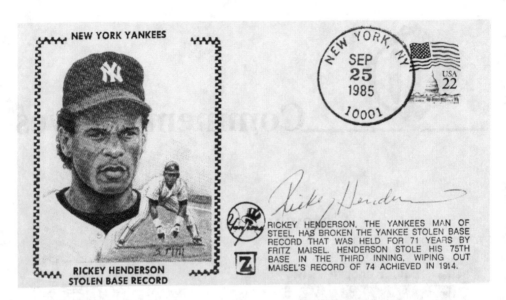

When Don Mattingly tied Dale Long's record of eight homers in eight consecutive games, Historic Limited Editions was there to capture the event on a silk-cacheted philatelic cover. The process begins with a staff artist who does an original painting of a ballplayer or event. The painting is then reproduced on specially-manufactured silk-like cloth in full color. These silk cachets are then applied by hand to envelopes which have been stamped and postmarked by the post office in the corresponding city where the event occurred.

In the case of the Mattingly record, company president John Zaso, with a few minutes to spare before a midnight deadline, flew to Arlington, Texas, to secure a postmark with the date of the event - July 18, 1987. Six hundred envelopes were created. Generally, 200 to 600 covers are produced per event, depending on the player and/or event involved and potential demand by collectors. Mattingly has been one of the more popular players. Several events, including the World Series, playoffs, All-Star games and Hall of Fame inductions, are commemorated annually. Year-end award winners are also recognized.

The covers are suitable for autographing, although the company does offer a limited number already signed by the players. Investment potential varies, but some command far more than the original issue price. For example, the cachet honoring Reggie Jackson's 500th home run had an issue price of $4 but is now up to $150 autographed. Historic Limited Editions is located in New Canaan, Conn.

In the following checklist, based on Mint condition, an a after the value means the item is autographed. The prices are the current retail prices on the market

Subject	Company	Description	Value
Hank Aaron	Colorano	FDI of Ruth stamp, 7/6/83	$7
Hank Aaron	Colorano	World Stamp Expo, 11/30/89	$5
Hank Aaron	Colorano	20th anniversary of home run 715, 4/8/94	$7
Hank Aaron	Galasso	715th home run anniversary, 4/8/84	$10
Hank Aaron	Gateway	Hall of Fame Induction, 8/1/82	$40a
Hank Aaron	Little Sun	20th anniversary of 715th home run, 4/8/94	$10
Hank Aaron	Little Sun	40th anniverary of 1st home run, 4/23/94	$10
Hank Aaron	Z Silk	Braves uniform retirement	$5
Jim Abbott	Colorano	no hitter, 9/4/93	$7
Jim Abbott	Z Silk	no-hitter set of 2, 9/4/93	$14
Cal Abrams	Z Silk	Hall of Fame induction, 6/12/88	$7
All-Star logo, 1979	Gateway	1979 in Seattle, 7/17/79	$10
All-Star logo, 1983	Gateway	1983 in Chicago (AL), 7/6/83	$15a

All-Star logo, 1989	Gateway	1989 in Anaheim, 7/11/89	$5
All-Star logo, 1990	Z Silk	1990 in Chicago (NL), 7/10/90	$5
All-Star logo, 1992	Z Silk	1992 in San Diego, 7/14/92	$5
100 autographed by Padres representative Gary Sheffield			$25
All-Star logo, 1995	Z Silk	1995, lists lineups	$5
Sandy Alomar Jr.	Z-Silk	1991 All-Star Game	$5
Walter Alston	Gateway	Hall of Fame induction, 7/31/83	$60a
Walter Alston	Z Silk	Hall of Fame induction, 7/31/83	$10
Walter Altson	Z Silk	Brooklyn Dodgers series, 11/28/89	$5
American League strike	Z Silk	AL logo, 8/14/94	$5
Sandy Amoros	Z Silk	anniversary of 1955 World Series catch, 10/4/88	$5
Anaheim Stadium	Gateway	25th anniversary, 4/19/91	$5
100 autographed by Rick Reichardt, who hit first home run there			$15
Anaheim Stadium	Z Silk	Ballpark series, 7/1/90	$5
100 autographed by Jimmy Piersall, Marcelino Lopez, Jay Johnstone and Clyde Wright			$30
Sparky Anderson	Gateway	100 wins both leagues, 9/23/84	$17a
Luis Aparicio	Gateway	Hall of Fame induction, 8/12/84	$25a
Luke Appling	Gateway	50th anniversary of Hall of Fame, 6/12/89	$5
100 autographed by Chico Carrasquel and Don Kolloway			$25
Arlington Stadium	Gateway	last game played	$5
Arlington Stadium	Z Silk	The Ball Park, 1st game, 4/1/94	$5
Arlington Stadium	Z Silk	Ballpark series, 4/21/90	$5
100 autographed by Nolan Ryan, $50, or Juan Gonzalez			$25
Luis Arroyo	Z Silk	salute to the 1961 Yankees, 7/14/90	$5
Richie Ashburn	Z Silk	1995 Hall of Fame induction, Mets or Phillies uniform	$5
Richie Ashburn	Z Silk	Phillies uniform retirement	$5
Astrodome	Gateway	25th anniversary, 4/12/90	$5
150 autographed by Dick Allen, who hit the first home run there			$20
Astrodome	Z Silk	Ballpark series, 9/30/90	$5
Atlanta-Fulton County Stadium	Gateway	25th anniversary, 4/12/90	$5
Carlos Baerga	Gateway	home run record, 4/8/93	$20a
Jeff Bagwell	Z Silk	1994 MVP	$5
Jeff Bagwell	Z Silk	1994 Gold Glove	$5
Baltimore Memorial Stadium	Gateway	last game, 10/6/91	$5
200 autographed by Jim Gentile			$15
Baltimore Memorial Stadium	Z Silk	Ballpark series, 4/15/89	sold out
200 signed by Earl Weaver and Jim Palmer			$30
Baltimore Orioles	Gateway, losing streak ends, 4/29/88, signed by Frank Robinson		$25
Baltimore Orioles	Z Silk	Opening Day 1983, team logo	$5
Dan Bankhead	Z Silk	Brooklyn's first black pitcher, 5/30/92	$5
Ernie Banks	Gateway	50th anniversary All-Star Game, 7/6/83	$60a
Ernie Banks	Z Silk	Cubs uniform retirement	$5
Red Barber	Z Silk	first Dodgers broadcast anniversary, 4/18/88	$5
Red Barber	Z Silk	first TV game anniversary, 8/26/88	$5
Bret Barberie	Gateway	Florida Marlins' first hit	$20a
Jesse Barfield	Z Silk	traded to the Yankees, 4/30/89	$4.50
Len Barker	Gateway	perfect game, 5/15/81	$35
Al Barlick	Gateway	Hall of Fame induction, 7/23/89	$20a
Al Barlick	Z Silk	Hall of Fame election, 1/15/89	$5
Al Barlick	Z Silk	Hall of Fame induction, 7/23/89	$5
200 autographed by Barlick			$20
Rex Barney	Z Silk	Brooklyn Dodger Hall of Fame, 6/11/89	$5
Marty Barrett	Z Silk	1986 AL playoffs, 10/15/86	$5
Hank Bauer	Z Silk	Yankee Old-Timers' Day 1991	$5
Steve Bedrosian	Z Silk	1987 Cy Young Award, 11/9/87	$5
Hank Behrman	Z Silk	Brooklyn anniversary of 1947 World Series, 5/30/92	$5
Cool Papa Bell	Gateway	Black Heritage 50th, 9/16/83	$95
Johnny Bench	Gateway	Hall of Fame induction, 7/23/89	$40a
Johnny Bench	Z Silk	Hall of Fame induction, 1/9/89	$6

Commemoratives

Moe Berg	Little Sun	50th anniversary of war effort	$7.50
Yogi Berra	Z Silk	salute to the 1961 Yankees, 3/30/93	$5
Yogi Berra	Z Silk	uniform retired	$5
Joe Black	Z Silk	Brooklyn anniversary of 1952 season	$5
Johnny Blanchard	Z Silk	salute to the 1961 Yankees, 7/14/90	$5
200 autographed by Blanchard			$15
Bert Blyleven	Gateway	3,000 strikeouts, set of 2, 8/1/86	limited availability
Wade Boggs	Z Silk	1987 batting title, 10/4/87	$6
Wade Boggs	Z Silk	200 hits six straight seasons, 9/20/88	$6
Wade Boggs	Z Silk	1993 All-Star Game	$5
Wade Boggs	Z Silk	1995 All-Star Game	$5
Barry Bonds	Z Silk	1992 NL MVP, 11/18/92	$5
Barry Bonds	Z Silk	1993 NL MVP	$5
Barry Bonds	Z Silk	1993 Gold Glove	$5
Bobby Bonilla	Z Silk	1992 Mets' home opener, 4/5/92	$5
Bob Boone	Gateway	all-time catching record, 9/16/87	$20a
Boston Braves Field	Z Silk	Ballpark series, 9/21/90	$5
100 autographed by Warren Spahn and Johnny Sain			$30
Ken Boswell	Z Silk	salute to the 1969 Mets, 11/17/92	$4.50
Lou Boudreau	Gateway	50th anniversary Hall of Fame, 6/12/89	$17a
Clete Boyer	Z Silk	salute to the 1961 Yankees, 7/14/89	$5
100 autographed by Boyer			$15
Ralph Branca	Z Silk	famous pitch to Bobby Thomson	$5
George Brett	Colorano	3,000 hits, 9/30/92	$10
George Brett	Galasso	pine tar game, 1983	$10
George Brett	Z Silk	pine tar game, set of 2, 1983	$30
George Brett	Z Silk	1985 AL playoffs, 10/16/85	$10
George Brett	Z Silk	1991 Opening Day, 4/8/91	$8
George Brett	Z Silk	3,000 hits, 10/3/92	$10
Lou Brock	Gateway	3,000 hits set of 2, 8/14/79	$20a
Lou Brock	Gateway	Hall of Fame induction, 7/28/85	$20a
Lou Brock	Z Silk	Hall of Fame election, 1/8/85	$8
Lou Brock	Z Silk	Hall of Fame induction, 7/28/85	$8
Brooklyn Dodgers	Z Silk	clinch flag in 1941, pictures Whit Wyatt, Freddy Fitzsimmons	
and Dixie Walker			$5
Brooklyn Dodgers	Z Silk	1938 photo of Stainback, Hassett, Cuyler and Ruth	$5
Brooklyn Dodgers	Z Silk	1941 pennant parade	$5
Brooklyn Dodgers	Z Silk	1941 World Series, Mickey Owen and Tommy Henrich	$5
Brooklyn Dodgers	Z Silk	1955 World Series, group celebration	$5
Brooklyn Dodgers	Z Silk	1956 pennant, Don Bessent pictured	$5
Tommy Brown	Z Silk	Brooklyn anniversary 50th season, 5/29/92	$5
Tom Browning	Gateway	perfect game, 9/16/88	$17a
Tom Browning	Z Silk	perfect game, 9/16/88	$10
Busch Stadium	Gateway	25th anniversary, 5/12,91	$5
Busch Stadium	Z Silk	Ballpark series, 9/30/90	$5
Francisco Cabrera	Z Silk	1992 NL playoffs	$5
Camden Yards	Gateway	inaugural game, 4/6/92	$5
Camden Yards	Z Silk	Ballpark series, inaugural game, 4/6/92	$10
Dolph Camilli	Z Silk	Brooklyn series, 8/23/89	$5
Roy Campanella	Gateway	50th anniversary of Hall of Fame, 6/12/89	$650a
Roy Campanella	Z Silk	anniversary of 1955 MVP Award	$5
Roy Campanella	Z Silk	last game at Ebbets Field	$5
Roy Campanella	Z Silk	paralyzed	$5
Roy Campanella	Z Silk	anniversary of 1949 All-Star Game, 7/12/88	$7
Roy Campanella	Z Silk	uniform retired	$5
Canada	Gateway	FDI 150th anniversary of baseball in Canada, 9/14/88	$5
Candlestick Park	Gateway	30th anniversary, 4/12/90	$5
200 autographed by Felipe, Matty and Jesus Alou			$40
Candlestick Park	Z Silk	Ballpark series, 4/12/88	$5
Jose Canseco	Gateway	40 home runs/40 stolen bases, 9/23/88	$75a
Jose Canseco	Z Silk	1988 AL playoffs, 10/9/88	$8
Rod Carew	Colorano	Hall of Fame induction, 7/21/91	$6

Rod Carew	Gateway	3,000 hits, set of 2, 8/4/84	$30a
Rod Carew	Gateway	Hall of Fame induction	$40a
Rod Carew	Z Silk	Hall of Fame induction, 7/21/91	$6
Steve Carlton	Galasso	3,508 strikeouts passes Walter Johnson, 5/20/83	$10
Steve Carlton	Gateway	1979 All-Star Game, 7/17/79	$30a
Steve Carlton	Gateway	3,000 strikeouts, set of 2, 4/29/81	limited availability
Steve Carlton	Gateway	all-time strikeout record, 6/7/83	$40a
Steve Carlton	Gateway	300 wins, 9/23/83	limited availability
Steve Carlton	Gateway	4,000 strikeouts, 8/5/86	$30a
Steve Carlton	Gateway	left-handed strikeout record, 7/6/90	$100a
Steve Carlton	Z Silk	1983 NL playoffs, 10/8/83	$12
Steve Carlton	Z Silk	1994 Hall of Fame induction	$5
Steve Carlton	Z Silk	uniform retired	$5
Gary Carter	Z Silk	traded to the Mets, 12/10/84	$5
Gary Carter	Z Silk	Opening Day 1985	$5
Happy Chandler	Gateway	Hall of Fame induction, 8/1/82	$75a
Ed Charles	Z Silk	salute to the 1969 Mets, 11/17/92	$5
Gino Cimoli	Z Silk	Brooklyn anniversary of 1957 season	$5
Cincinnati Reds	Gateway	14-run first inning, with 10 autographs	$150a
Will Clark	Gateway	1988 All-Star logo, 7/12/88	$25a
Will Clark	Gateway	1989 All-Star logo, 7/11/89	$25a
Will Clark	Gateway	1991 All-Star Game	$5
Will Clark	Z Silk	1989 NL playoffs MVP, 10/9/89	$5
Roger Clemens	Galasso	20 strikeouts in a game, 4/29/86	$50a
Roger Clemens	Gateway	20 strikeouts in a game, 4/29/86	$250a
Roger Clemens	Z Silk	1986 Cy Young Award, 11/12/86	$10
Roger Clemens	Z Silk	1987 Cy Young Award, 11/11/87	$10
Roger Clemens	Z Silk	1991 Cy Young Award	$7
Roberto Clemente	Gateway	FDI of Clemente stamp, 8/17/84	$5
Roberto Clemente	Z Silk	uniform retired	$5
Roberto Clemente	Z Silk	statue dedication, 7/8/94	$5
Cleveland Stadium	Colorano	last game played	$6
Cleveland Stadium	Gateway	last game played, 4/3/93	$5
autographed by Mel Harder			$15a
Jim Coates	Z Silk	salute to 1961 Yankees, 7/14/90	$5
100 autographed by Coates			$15
Vince Coleman	Gateway	rookie stolen base record, 8/15/85	$19a
Vince Coleman	Z Silk	1985 NL Rookie of the Year, 11/27/85	$10
Colorado Rockies	Z Silk	inaugural game	$6
Comiskey Park	Gateway	last game played, 9/30/90	$6
Comiskey Park	Gateway	first game played, 4/18/91	$5
Comiskey Park	Z Silk	Ballpark series, 9/30/90	$5
100 autographed by Minnie Minoso			$20
David Cone	Z Silk	1994 Cy Young Award	$5
Jocko Conlon	Gateway	50th anniverary Hall of Fame, 6/12/89	$5
Marty Cordova	Z Silk	1995 Rookie of the Year	$5
Joe Cowley	Gateway	no hitter, 9/16/86	$75a
Billy Cox	Z Silk	Brooklyn series, 6/17/89	$5
Roger Craig	Z Silk	Brooklyn series, anniversary of 1955 series	$5
100 autographed by Craig			$15
Crosley Field	Z Silk	Ballpark series, 4/8/91	$5
Cubs vs. Tigers	Z Silk	1995 Hall of Fame exhibition game	$5
Tony Cuccinello	Z Silk	1933 All-Star	$5
Ray Dandridge	Gateway	Hall of Fame induction, 7/26/87	$25a
Ray Dandridge	Z Silk	Hall of Fame election, 1/15/87	$6
Ray Dandridge	Z Silk	Hall of Fame induction, 7/26/87	$6
Alvin Davis	Z Silk	1984 Rookie of the Year	$5
Eric Davis	Gateway	three grand slams in a month, 5/30/87	$20a
Mark Davis	Z Silk	1989 Cy Young Award, 11/13/89	$5
Andre Dawson	Z Silk	1987 MVP, 11/2/87	$6
Andre Dawson	Z Silk	300th stolen base, 9/22/90	$5
Leon Day	Z Silk	1995 Hall of Fame induction	$5

Jim Deshaies	Gateway	strikeout record, 9/23/86	$15a
Rob Dibble	Z Silk	1990 NL playoff co-MVP	$7
Bill Dickey	Gateway	50th anniversary of All-Star Game, 1983	$95a
Bill Dickey	Z Silk	uniform retired	$5
Jack Dilauro	Z Silk	salute to the 1969 Mets	$5
Joe DiMaggio	Gateway	40th anniversary of 56-game hitting streak, 7/16/81	limited availability
Joe DiMaggio	Gateway	50th anniversary of 56-game hitting streak, 7/16/91	limited availability
Joe DiMaggio	Z Silk	50th anniversary of 56-game hitting streak, set of 2	$20
Joe DiMaggio	Z Silk	Pride of the Yankees 1991	$10
Joe DiMaggio	Z Silk	Yankee Memorial Park 7/24/86	$10
Joe DiMaggio	Z Silk	uniform retired	$5
DiMaggio/T. Williams	Z Silk	50th anniversary 1941 season, 7/17/91	$10
DiMaggio/T. Williams	Z Silk	co-captains 1991 All-Star Game	$10
Art Ditmar	Z Silk	salute to 1961 Yankees	$4.50
Larry Doby	Little Sun	Indians retire uniform number, 6/3/94	$10
Dodger Stadium	Gateway	25th anniversary, 4/13/87	$10
Dodger Stadium	Z Silk	Ballpark series, 4/6/92	$5
100 autographed by "Sweet" Lou Johnson			$15
100 autographed by Eric Karros			$20
Bobby Doerr	Gateway	Hall of Fame induction, 8/3/86	$17a
Bobby Doerr	Z Silk	Hall of Fame election, 1/8/86	$6
Bobby Doerr	Z Silk	Hall of Fame induction, 8/3/86	$6
Doubleday Field	Z Silk	Ballpark series, 7/22/91	$5
Al Downing	Z Silk	salute to 1961 Yankees	$5
Chuck Dressen	Z Silk	Brooklyn series, 11/6/91	$5
Don Drysdale	Gateway	Hall of Fame induction, 8/12/84	$50a
Don Drysdale	Z Silk	Brooklyn series, anniversary 1956 opener	$15
Leo Durocher	Z Silk	Brooklyn series, anniversary 1941 World Series	$5
Leo Durocher	Z Silk	7th National Convention, 7/24/86	$6
Leo Durocher	Z Silk	1994 Hall of Fame (New York Giants)	$5
Leo Durocher	Z Silk	1994 Hall of Fame (Brooklyn)	$5
Leo Durocher	Z Silk	suspended	$5
Earthquake	Gateway	1989 World Series interruption, 10/17/89	$5
100 autographed by Giants Manager Roger Craig			$15
Ebbets Field	Gateway	80th anniversary of opening, 4/4/93	$5
Ebbets Field	Z Silk	Ballpark series, 4/9/90	$5
100 autographed by Tony Cuccinello and "Frenchy" Bordagaray			$30
Ebbets Field	Z Silk	demolition	$5
Dennis Eckersley	Z Silk	1990 playoff MVP, 10/10/90	$5
Dennis Eckersley	Z Silk	1992 MVP Award	$5
Dennis Eckersley	Z Silk	1992 Cy Young Award	$5
Bruce Edwards	Z Silk	Brooklyn anniversary 1946 season	$5
Dock Ellis	Little Sun	25th anniversary of no hitter, 6/12/95	$15
Carl Erskine	Z Silk	anniversary of 2nd no hitter, 5/12/88	$5
Carl Erskine	Z Silk	anniversary of 1st no hitter, 6/19/88	$5
Darrell Evans	Gateway	oldest player to hit 40 home runs, 10/2/85	$50a
Darrell Evans	Gateway	400th home run, 9/22/88	$17a
Bob Feller	Gateway	50th anniversary of first game, 8/23/86	$17a
Bob Feller	Z Silk	50th anniversary of no hitter, 4/16/90	$5
Fenway Park	Gateway	75th anniversary, 4/20/87	limited availability
Fenway Park	Z Silk	Ballpark series	$5
100 autographed by Rico Petrocelli			$15
200 autographed by Dom DiMaggio, Bobby Doerr and Boo Ferriss			$30
Rick Ferrell	Gateway	Hall of Fame induction, 8/12/84	$25a
Cecil Fielder	Colorano	50 home run season, 10/3/90	$7
Cecil Fielder	Gateway	over the roof home run at Tiger Stadium	$40a
Cecil Fielder	Gateway	50 home run season, 10/3/90	$25a
Cecil Fielder	Z Silk	11th member of 50 home run club	$7
Rollie Fingers	Colorano	Hall of Fame induction, 8/2/92	$5
Rollie Fingers	Gateway	all-time saves record, 4/13/85	$20a

Rollie Fingers	Gateway	Hall of Fame induction, 8/2/92	$20a
Rollie Fingers	Z Silk	Hall of Fame induction, 8/2/92	$5
Carlton Fisk	Gateway	1,807 games caught, 8/19/88	limited availability
Carlton Fisk	Z Silk	1991 All-Star Game, 7/9/91	$6
500 Home Run Club	Gateway	signed by all 12 living members	$750a
Florida Marlins	Z Silk	inaugural game	$6
Florida Marlins	Z Silk	Opening Day 1993	$5
Florida Marlins	Z Silk	expansion draft day	$5
Florida Marlins/	Z Silk	Ballpark series	$5
Joe Robbie Stadium			
Whitey Ford	Gateway	Hall of Fame induction, 6/12/79	$80a
Whitey Ford	Z Silk	salute to 1961 Yankees	$5
Bob Forsch	Gateway	1st no hitter, 4/16/78	limited avialability
Bob Forsch	Gateway	2nd no hitter, 9/26/83	$20a
Carl Furillo	Z Silk	Brooklyn anniversary of 1955 World Series	$5
Eddie Gaedel	Gateway	40th anniversary of pinch hit appearance, 8/19/91,	
autographed by pitcher Bob Cain			$15a
Gary Gaetti	Z Silk	1987 AL playoffs, 10/12/87	$5
Augie Galan	Z Silk	Brooklyn anniversary of 1942 season	$5
Andres Galarraga	Gateway	First Colorado Rockies hit	$25a
Billy Gardner	Gateway	salute to 1961 Yankees, 8/26/94	$5
Steve Garvey	Galasso	1,117 consecutive games, 4/15/83	$10
Steve Garvey	Gateway	1,000 consecutive games, 6/7/82	$20a
Steve Garvey	Gateway	1,118 consecutive games, 6/16/83	$20a
Steve Garvey	Gateway	Padres retire uniform, 4/16/88	$20a
Steve Garvey	Z Silk	1984 NL playoffs	$10
Lou Gehrig	Colorano	FDI of Gehrig stamp, 6/10/89	$5
Lou Gehrig	Gateway	FDI of Gehrig stamp, 6/10/89	$8
250 autographed by Babe Dahlgren, who took over for Gehrig			$15a
Lou Gehrig	Gateway	50th anniversary of retirement, 7/4/89	limited availability
500 autographed by Yankee first baseman Don Mattingly			$60
Lou Gehrig	Z Silk	Yankee Memorial Park, 7/13/85	$5
Lou Gehrig	Z Silk	uniform retired	$5
Charlie Gehringer	Gateway	50th anniversary of All-Star Game, 4/16/83	$175a
Gary Gentry	Z Silk	salute to 1969 Mets, 5/20/89	$5
Bob Gibson	Gateway	Hall of Fame induction, 8/12/81	$25a
Kirk Gibson	Gateway	1988 World Series MVP, 10/15/88	$25a
Kirk Gibson	Z Silk	1984 AL playoffs, 10/5/84	$10
Kirk Gibson	Z Silk	1988 MVP Award, 11/15/88	$6
Jim Gilliam	Z Silk	Brooklyn series, 11/5/91	$5
Al Gionfriddo	Z Silk	anniversary of 1947 World Series catch	$5
100 autographed by Gionfriddo			$15
Lefty Gomez	Gateway	50th anniversary of All-Star Game, 4/16/83	$60a
Doc Gooden	Gateway	rookie strikeout record, 9/26/84	$30a
Doc Gooden	Gateway	youngest 20-game winner, 8/25/85	$30a
Doc Gooden	Z Silk	1984 Rookie of the Year, 11/20/84	$10
Doc Gooden	Z Silk	K Day, Shea Stadium, 4/15/85	$6
Doc Gooden	Z Silk	youngest 20-game winner, 8/25/85	$6
Doc Gooden	Z Silk	1985 Cy Young Award, 11/13/85	$10
Doc Gooden	Z Silk	1988 All-Star Game, 7/12/88	$10
Goose Gossage	Gateway	300th career save, 8/6/88	$17a
Pete Gray	Little Sun	50th anniversary of debut, 4/14/94	$10
Tommy Greene	Colorano	no hitter, 5/23/91	$5
Griffith Stadium	Z Silk	Ballpark series, 9/21/90	$5
100 autographed by Mickey Vernon and Eddie Yost			$25
100 autographed by Bennie Daniels and Gene Woodling			$25
Ken Griffey Jr.	Colorano	1992 All-Star Game	$7
Ken Griffey Jr. and Sr.	Gateway	Junior's major league debut, set of two	$50a
Ken Griffey Jr. and Sr.	Gateway	father/son on same team	$50a
Ken Griffey Jr.	Z Silk	1992 Gold Glove Award	$7
Ken Griffey Jr.	Z Silk	1994 All-Star Game	$7
Jerry Grote	Z Silk	salute to 1969 Mets, 5/20/89	$5

Commemoratives

Name	Maker	Description	Price
Ron Guidry	Gateway	1979 All-Star Game, 7/17/79	$5
Ozzie Guillen	Z Silk	1985 Rookie of the Year, 11/25/83	$6
Tony Gwynn	Z Silk	1991 home opener, 4/9/91	$6
Tony Gwynn	Z Silk	1994 All-Star Game	$5
Harvey Haddix	Gateway	30th anniversary of perfect game, 5/26/94	$30a
Bob Hale	Z Silk	salute to 1961 Yankees, 6/9/95	$5
Bob Hamelin	Z Silk	1994 Rookie of the Year	$5
Bud Harrelson	Z Silk	salute to 1969 Mets, 5/20/89	$5
autographed 100 by Harrelson			$15
Ernie Harwell	Gateway	Hall of Fame induction	$17a
Joe Hattan	Z Silk	Brooklyn anniversary of 1950 season, 6/11/89	$5
Buddy Hassett	Z Silk	Brooklyn Dodger Hall of Famer	$5
Andy Hawkins	Gateway	no hitter, 7/1/90	$15a
Andy Hawkins	Z Silk	traded to Yankees, 9/30/89	$5
Ed Head	Z Silk	Brooklyn anniversary of no hitter, 3/17/92	$5
Rickey Henderson	Colorano	all-time stolen base king	$7
Rickey Henderson	Gateway	stolen base record, 8/27/82	$40a
Rickey Henderson	Gateway	all-time stolen bases, 5/1/91	$50a
Rickey Henderson	Z Silk	lead-off home run record, 4/28/89	$6
Rickey Henderson	Z Silk	1989 AL playoffs, 10/8/89	$6
Rickey Henderson	Z Silk	breaks Cobb's stolen base record, set of 2, 5/26/90 and 5/29/90	$25
Rickey Henderson	Z Silk	1990 AL playoffs, 10/10/90	$6
Rickey Henderson	Z Silk	breaks Brock's stolen base record, set of 2, 4/28/91 and 5/1/91	$25
Rickey Henderson	Z Silk	1991 All-Star Game	$6
Babe Herman	Z Silk	13-year career	$5
Billy Herman	Gateway	50th anniversary of Hall of Fame, 6/12/89	$30a
Billy Herman	Z Silk	Brooklyn anniversary of 1941 season, 8/12/89	$5
Gene Hermanski	Z Silk	Brooklyn Dodgers Hall of Fame induction, 6/12/88	$5
Keith Hernandez	Z Silk	2,000th hit, 9/15/87	$5
Willie Hernandez	Z Silk	1984 Cy Young Award, 10/30/84	$5
Willie Hernandez	Z Silk	1984 MVP Award, 11/6/84	$5
Orel Hershiser	Gateway	59 scoreless innings, 9/28/88	$75a
Orel Hershiser	Z Silk	1988 Cy Young Award, 11/10/88	$6
Orel Hershiser	Z Silk	1988 NL playoffs	$6
Kirby Higbe	Z Silk	Brooklyn anniversary of 1941 season, 9/7/89	$5
Gil Hodges	Z Silk	four home runs	$5
Gil Hodges	Z Silk	Brooklyn anniversary of 1955 World Series 10/1/88	$5
Gil Hodges	Z Silk	salute to 1969 Mets, 11/18/92	$5
William Holbert	Z Silk	1995 Hall of Fame induction	$5
Bob Horner	Gateway	four home runs in a game, 7/6/86	$18a
Charlie Hough	Gateway	Florida Marlins' first pitch	$20a
Ralph Houk	Z Silk	salute to 1961 Yankees, 7/14/90	$5
100 autographed by Houk			$15
Elston Howard	Z Silk	salute to 1961 Yankees, 7/14/90	$5
Carl Hubbell	Gateway	50th anniversary of All-Star feat, 7/10/84	$95a
Catfish Hunter	Gateway	Hall of Fame induction, 7/26/87	$20a
Catfish Hunter	Z Silk	Hall of Fame election, 1/15/87	$6
Catfish Hunter	Z Silk	Hall of Fame induction, 7/26/87	$8
Monte Irvin	Gateway	50th anniversary of Hall of Fame, 6/12/89	$17a
Bo Jackson	Galasso	professional debut, 6/30/86	$50a
Bo Jackson	Gateway	1989 All-Star Game	$75a
Bo Jackson	Z Silk	1993 AL playoffs	$5
Reggie Jackson	Colorano	Hall of Fame induction, as a Yankee	$6
Reggie Jackson	Colorano	Hall of Fame induction, as an Angel	$6
Reggie Jackson	Gateway	1977 World Series, three home runs, 10/18/77	$300a
Reggie Jackson	Gateway	1979 All-Star appearance	$50a
Reggie Jackson	Gateway	400th home run, 8/11/80	$50a
Reggie Jackson	Gateway	500th home run, 9/17/84	$150a
Reggie Jackson	Gateway	500th home run, numbered version	$200a
Reggie Jackson	Z Silk	Yankees Old-Timers Day 1991	$5

Reggie Jackson	Z Silk	Hall of Fame induction, as Yankee, as Yankee with father,	
as an Athletic, as an Angel or as an Oriole			$5 each
Travis Jackson	Gateway	Hall of Fame induction, 8/1/82	$60a
Jacobs Field, Cleveland	Colorano	inaugural game, 4/4/94	$7.50
Jacobs Field, Cleveland	Gateway	inaugural game, 4/4/94	$5
Jacobs Field, Cleveland	Z Silk	Ballpark series	$5
Johnny James	Z Silk	salute to 1961 Yankees	$5
Fergie Jenkins	Colorano	1991 Hall of Fame induction, 7/21/91	$5
Fergie Jenkins	Gateway	3,000 strikeouts, set of 2, 5/25/83	$20a
Fergie Jenkins	Gateway	Canadian Hall of Fame induction, 11/19/87	$5
Fergie Jenkins	Z Silk	1991 Hall of Fame induction, 7/21/91	$5
Howard Johnson	Z Silk	1991 All-Star Game	$5
Judy Johnson	Gateway	Black Heritage 50th anniversary, 9/16/83	$75a
Randy Johnson	Z Silk	1995 Cy Young Award	$5
Walter Johnson	Gateway	all-time strikeout leader	$25a
Cleon Jones	Z Silk	salute to 1969 Mets, 5/20/89	$5
100 autographed by Jones			$15
Johnny Jorgensen	Z Silk	career highlights, 4/30/95	$5
Wally Joyner	Gateway	rookie All-Star, 7/15/86	$20a
Wally Joyner	Z Silk	Angels vs. Yankees, 4/27/91	$5
Jim Kaat	Gateway	25 years, 4/5/83	$15a
Al Kaline	Gateway	Hall of Fame induction, 8/30/80	limited availability
Eric Karros	Z Silk	1992 Rookie of the Year	$5
George Kell	Gateway	Hall of Fame induction, 7/31/83	$25a
George Kell	Z Silk	Hall of Fame induction, 7/31/83	$10
Harmon Killebrew	Gateway	Hall of Fame induction, 8/12/84	$25a
Ralph Kiner	Gateway	50th anniversary of Hall of Fame, 6/12/89	$17a
Clyde King	Z Silk	Brooklyn anniversary of first game, 6/21/88	$5
100 autographed by King			$15
Clyde King	Z Silk	Brooklyn Dodger Hall of Fame induction, 6/11/89	$5
Dave Kingman	Gateway	400th home run, 8/10/85	$30a
Chuck Knoblauch	Z Silk	1991 Rookie of the Year	$5
Jerry Koosman	Z Silk	salute to 1969 Mets, 5/20/89	$5
100 signed by Koosman			$15
Sandy Koufax	Gateway	50th anniversary of Hall of Fame, 6/12/89	$40a
Sandy Koufax	Little Sun	vs. Bob Hendley, no hitter vs. one hitter	$15
Sandy Koufax	Z Silk	uniform retired	$5
Ed Kranepool	Z Silk	salute to 1969 Mets, 5/20/89	$5
100 signed by Kranepool			$15
Tony Kubek	Z Silk	salute to 1961 Yankees	$5
Los Angeles Coliseum	Z Silk	Ballpark series, 9/30/90	$5
100 autographed by Don Drysdale and Wally Moon			$60
Clem Labine	Z Silk	Brooklyn anniversary of first game, 8/28/88	$5
Rick Langford	Gateway	21 complete games, 9/6/80	$150a
Rick Langford	Gaterway	22 complete games, 9/12/80	$35a
Barry Larkin	Z Silk	1995 MVP	$5
Don Larsen	Gateway	30th anniversary of World Series perfect game, 10/8/86	$20a
Don Larsen	Z Silk	30th anniversary of World Series perfect game	$6
Tommy Lasorda	Z Silk	Brooklyn anniversary of first game, 8/5/88	$5
100 autographed by Lasorda			$25
Tommy Lasorda	Z Silk	500th meeting between SF/LA teams, 4/12/85	$5
100 autographed by Lasorda			$25
Cookie Lavagetto	Z Silk	ends Bivins' no-hit bid	$5
Cookie Lavagetto	Z Silk	Brooklyn Dodgers Hall of Fame, 6/12/88	$5
Cookie Lavagetto	Z Silk	Brooklyn anniversary of 1947 World Series	$5
Tony Lazzeri	Gateway	Hall of Fame induction, 7/21/91	$5
100 autographed by Frank Crosetti			$17a
Bob Lemon	Gateway	50th anniversary of Hall of Fame, 6/12/89	$17a
Buck Leonard	Gateway	Black Heritage 50th anniversary, 9/16/83	$30a
Jeff Leonard	Z Silk	1987 NL playoffs, 10/14/87	$5
Pat Listach	Z Silk	1992 Rookie of the Year	$5
Billy Loes	Z Silk	Brooklyn anniversary of 1953 World Series, 10/3/89	$5

Commemoratives

Ernie Lombardi	Z Silk	Hall of Fame election, 1/8/86	$5
Ernie Lombardi	Z Silk	Hall of Fame induction, 8/3/86	$5
Al Lopez	Gateway	50th anniversary of the Hall of Fame, 6/12/89	$80a
Hector Lopez	Z Silk	salute to 1961 Yankees, 7/14/89	$5
100 signed by Lopez			$15
Fred Lynn	Gateway	1979 All-Star Game, 7/17/79	$20a
Duke Maas	Z Silk	salute to 1961 Yankees	$5
Larry MacPhail	Z Silk	Brooklyn anniversary of 1941 World Series	$5
Greg Maddux	Z Silk	1992 Cy Young Award	$5
Greg Maddux	Z Silk	1993 Cy Young Award	$5
Greg Maddux	Z Silk	1994 Cy Young Award	$5
Greg Maddux	Z Silk	1995 Cy Young Award	$5
Sal Maglie	Z Silk	Brooklyn anniversary of no hitter, 11/18/85	$5
Willie McGee	Gateway	NL switch-hitting record, 10/6/85	$18a
Willie McGee	Z Silk	1985 MVP Award, 11/18/85	$6
Mantle/Maris	Gateway	anniversary of 1961 season, autographed by Mantle	$125
Mickey Mantle	Gateway	40th anniversary of Hall of Fame, 6/12/79	$175a
Mickey Mantle	Z Silk	Heroes of Baseball, 7/5/80	$7
Mickey Mantle	Z Silk	reinstated in baseball, 2/14/85	$7
Mickey Mantle	Z Silk	throws first pitch, 4/16/85	$7
Mickey Mantle	Z Silk	salute to 1961 Yankees, 7/14/90	$5
Mickey Mantle	Z Silk	Old-Timers Day 1991, 7/27/91	$5
Mickey Mantle	Z Silk	uniform retired	$5
Mickey Mantle	Z Silk	memorial, Texas postmark	$5
Mickey Mantle	Z Silk	memorial, different postmark	$5
Mickey Mantle	Z Silk	funeral	$5
Mickey Mantle	Z Silk	honored	$5
Mickey Mantle	Z Silk	laid to rest	$5
Juan Marichal	Gateway	Hall of Fame induction, 7/31/83	$20a
Juan Marichal	Z Silk	Hall of Fame induction, 7/31/83	$10
Roger Maris	Colorano	30th anniversary of 61 home runs, 10/1/91	$6
Roger Maris	Z Silk	Pride of the Yankees, 4/15/85	$5
Roger Maris	Z Silk	Yankee Memorial Park, 7/16/88	$5
Roger Maris	Z Silk	salute to 1961 Yankees, 7/14/89	$5
Billy Martin	Colorano	memorial, 12/19/89	$6
Billy Martin	Gateway	remembrance, 12/29/89	$5
Billy Martin	Z Silk	Yankees honor Billy Martin, 8/10/86	$5
Billy Martin	Z Silk	Billy is back V, 10/10/87	$5
Billy Martin	Z Silk	memorial, 12/29/89	$5
JC Martin	Z Silk	salute to 1969 Mets, 11/19/92	$7
Dennis Martinez	Colorano	perfect game, 7/28/91	$20a
Eddie Mathews	Gateway	50th anniverary of Hall of Fame, 6/12/89	$5
Eddie Mathews	Z Silk	uniform retired	$10
Mattingly/Gwynn	Galasso	1984 batting leaders	$10
Don Mattingly	Galasso	most doubles in a season, 10/4/86	$35a
Don Mattingly	Gateway	batting record, 10/5/86	$35a
Don Mattingly	Gateway	consecutive home runs, 7/18/87	$150a
Don Mattingly	Gateway	grand slams, 9/29/87	$5
Don Mattingly	Z Silk	1989 All-Star Game	$5
Don Mattingly	Z Silk	1992 Gold Glove Award, 11/5/92	$5
Don Mattingly	Z Silk	1993 Gold Glove Award	$5
Don Mattingly	Z Silk	season finale, 1993	$5
Don Mattingly	Z Silk	Opening Day, 1994	$5
Don Mattingly	Z Silk	1994 Gold Glove Award	$10
Willie Mays	Galasso	Giants retire uniform, 8/20/83	$10
Willie Mays	Galasso	30th anniversary of World Series catch	$10
Mays/McCovey	Galasso	Giant Runners, 3/23/83	$150a
Willie Mays	Gateway	Hall of Fame induction, 8/2/79	$7
Willie Mays	Z Silk	reinstated into baseball, 2/14/85	$5
Willie Mays	Z Silk	uniform retired	$5
Mike McCormick	Z Silk	career highlights, 4/28/95	$10
Willie McCovey	Galasso	25th anniversary of pro debut, 7/30/84	

Willie McCovey	Gateway	500th home run, set of 2, 6/3/78	$125a
Willie McCovey	Gateway	Hall of Fame induction, 8/3/86	$25a
Willie McCovey	Z Silk	Hall of Fame election, 1/8/86	$8
Willie McCovey	Z Silk	Hall of Fame induction, 8/3/86	$8
Danny McDevitt	Z Silk	salute to 1961 Yankees	$4.50
Jack McDowell	Z Silk	1993 Cy Young Award	$5
Tug McGraw	Z Silk	salute to 1969 Mets, 5/20/89	$5
Mark McGwire	Gateway	rookie home run record, 8/14/87	$40a
Mark McGwire	Gateway	five home runs in two games, 6/28/87	$50a
Metrodome	Z Silk	Ballpark series	$5
Ducky Medwick	Z Silk	first appearance against Cardinals as a Dodger	$5
Ed Miksis	Z Silk	Brooklyn Dodger Hall of Fame, 6/12/88	$5
Mile High Stadium/ Denver	Gateway	first Colorado game	$5
Minnie Minoso	Gateway	five decades of baseball, 10/4/80	$300a
Kevin Mitchell	Z Silk	1989 MVP Award, 11/22/89	$5
Johnny Mize	Gateway	Hall of Fame induction, 8/2/81	$25a
Paul Molitor	Gateway	39-game hitting streak, 8/25/87	$30a
Paul Molitor	Z Silk	stolen base feat, 7/26/87	$5
Paul Molitor	Z Silk	39-game hitting streak, 7/26/87	$5
Raul Mondesi	Z Silk	1994 Rookie of the Year	$5
Wally Moon	Little Sun	25th anniversary of moon landing	$15a
Joe Morgan	Gateway	Hall of Fame induction, 8/6/90	$15a
Joe Morgan	Z Silk	Hall of Fame induction, 8/5/90	$25a
Jack Morris	Gateway	no hitter, 4/7/84	$22a
Randy Myers	Z Silk	1990 NL playoff co-MVP	$7
Municipal Stadium/ Kansas City	Z Silk	Ballpark series	$5
Dale Murphy	Gateway	1983 All-Star Game	limited availability
Eddie Murray	Gateway	1,500 RBI, 5/23/92	$40a
Stan Musial	Gateway	hit record broken, 8/10/81	$40a
Charlie Neal	Z Silk	Brooklyn anniversary of 1956 season, 5/29/92	$5
Craig Nettles	Z Silk	Yankee Old-Timers Day, 19991	$5
Hal Newhouser	Gateway	Hall of Fame induction, 8/2/92	$20a
Hal Newhouser	Z Silk	Hall of Fame induction, 8/2/92	$5
100 autographed by Newhouser			$20
Don Newcombe	Z Silk	anniversary of 1956 MVP and Cy Young awards	$5
New York Mets	Z Silk	Opening Day 1993, with starting lineup	$5
New York Yankees	Z Silk	Opening Day 1993, with starting lineup	$5
Phil Niekro	Gateway	3,000 strikeouts, set of 2, 7/4/84	$20a
Phil Niekro	Gateway	300 wins, 6/10/85	$20a
Phil Niekro/Steve Carlton	Gateway	300-game winner teammates, 4/9/87, signed by both	$50
Phil Niekro/Don Sutton	Gateway	300-game winners, 8/28/86, signed by both	$60a
Phil Niekro/Joe Niekro	Gateway	winningest brother combination, signed by both	$25a
Juan Nieves	Gateway	no hitter, 4/15/87	$20a
Hideo Nomo	Z Silk	1995 All-Star Game	$5
Hideo Nomo	Z Silk	1995 Rookie of the Year	$5
Oakland A's	Z Silk	1992 home opener, with starting lineup listed	$5
Oakland/Alameda/ County Stadium	Gateway	25th anniversary, 4/17/93	$5
Lefty O'Doul	Z Silk	shown on horseback leading a parade	$5
Luis Olmo	Z Silk	Brooklyn anniversary of 1945 season, 5/17/92	$5
Greg Olson	Z Silk	1989 Rookie of the Year, 11/7/89	$5
Olympic baseball team	Gateway	1984 team reunited, 21 autographs	$200
Olympic baseball team	Gateway	1988 team reunited, 22 autographs	$200
Walter O'Malley	Z Silk	Brooklyn anniversary Ebbets finale	$5
Paul O'Neill	Z Silk	Opening Day 1994	$5
Mickey Owen	Z Silk	Brooklyn Dodger Hall of Fame, 6/12/88	$5
Andy Pafko	Z Silk	Brooklyn anniversary, trade to Dodgers, 6/14/88	$5
Satchell Paige	Gateway	40th anniversary Hall of Fame, 6/12/79	$400a
Erv Palica	Z Silk	Brooklyn anniversary of great game, 3/17/92	$5
Dave Palmer	Gateway	5-inning perfect game, 4/22/84	$15a

Jim Palmer	Gateway	Hall of Fame induction, 8/5/90	$5
Jim Palmer	Z Silk	1983 AL playoffs, 10/8/83	$6
Jim Palmer	Z Silk	Hall of Fame induction, 8/5/90	$6
Jim Palmer/Joe Morgan	Z Silk	Hall of Fame induction	$6
Chan Ho Park	Gateway	major league debut, 4/8/94	$30a
Dave Parker	Gateway	1979 All-Star Game, 7/17/79	$20a
Gaylord Perry	Colorano	1991 Hall of Fame induction (Rangers)	$5
Gaylord Perry	Gateway	300 wins, set of 2, 5/6/82	$20a
Gaylord Perry	Gateway	Hall of Fame induction, as a Giant or an Indian	$20a
Gaylord Perry/Jim Perry	Gateway	winningnest brother combination, autographed by both	$40a
Gaylord Perry	Z Silk	1991 Hall of Fame induction (Royals)	$5
Phil Phifer	Z Silk	bat boy at Carl Erskine's no hitter	$4
Mike Piazza	Z Silk	1993 Rookie of the Year	$5
Joe Pignatano	Z Silk	salute to 1969 Mets, 5/20/89	$5
Pittsburgh Pirates	Z Silk	1994 home opener, logo and lineups	$5
Bud Podbielan	Z Silk	career highlights, 4/29/95	$5
Johnny Podres	Z Silk	Brooklyn anniversary, 10/4/88	$5
Polo Grounds	Z Silk	Ballpark series, 10/4/88	limited availability
Kirby Puckett	Gateway	10 consecutive hits, 8/30/87	$40a
Jeff Reardon	Gateway	40 saves both leagues, 9/30/88	$17a
Jack Reed	Z Silk	salute to 1961 Yankees	$4.50
Pee Wee Reese	Gateway	Hall of Fame induction, 8/12/84	$5
Pee Wee Reese	Z Silk	joins military	$5
Pee Wee Reese	Z Silk	uniform retired	$5
Pete Reiser	Z Silk	Brooklyn anniversary of 1941 season, 5/25/89	$5
Hal Reniff	Z Silk	salute to 1961 Yankees, 6/9/95	$5
Jim Rice	Gateway	1983 All-Star Game	$20a
Bobby Richardson	Z Silk	salute to 1961 Yankees, 7/14/90	$5
100 autographed by Richardson			$15
Dave Righetti	Gateway	no hitter, 7/4/83	$20a
Jose Rijo	Z Silk	1990 World Series MVP, 10/20/90	
Cal Ripken Jr.	Gateway	consecutive innings played, 9/14/87	limited availability
Cal Ripken Jr.	Gateway	2,131 consecutive games played	limted availability
Cal Ripken Jr.	Z Silk	1990 Hall of Fame Game in Cooperstown	$10
Cal Ripken Jr.	Z Silk	1991 All-Star Game	$7
Cal Ripken Jr.	Z Silk	1992 All-Star Game, 7/14/92	$10
Cal Ripken Jr.	Z Silk	1993 All-Star Game	$7
Cal Ripken Jr.	Z Silk	1993 Silver Slugger Award	$7
Cal Ripken Jr.	Z Silk	1994 All-Star Game	$7
Cal Ripken Jr.	Z Silk	2,000th hit	$25a
Cal Ripken Jr.	Z Silk	ties Gehrig's record	$7
Cal Ripken Jr.	Z Silk	breaks Gehrig's record	$7
Cal Ripken Jr.	Z Silk	1995 All-Star Game	$5
Ripken Jr./Pendleton	Z Silk	AL/NL MVP Awards	$10
Phil Rizzuto	Z Silk	Pride of the Yankees	$5
Phil Rizzuto	Z Silk	Hall of Fame induction, 7/31/94	$5
Phil Rizzuto	Z Silk	Phil Rizzuto Day, 8/9/94	$5
Phil Rizzuto	Z Silk	DiMaggio honors Rizzuto, 8/9/94	$5
Phil Rizzuto	Z Silk	uniform retired	$5
Robin Roberts	Gateway	50th annivesary of the Hall of Fame, 6/12/89	$17a
Robin Roberts	Z Silk	uniform retired	$5
Brooks Robinson	Gateway	Hall of Fame induction, 7/31/83	$20a
Brooks Robinson	Z Silk	Hall of Fame induction, 7/31/83	$10
Frank Robinson	Gateway	Hall of Fame induction, 8/1/82	$25a
Frank Robinson	Z Silk	uniform retired (Orioles)	$5
Jackie Robinson	Gateway	40th anniversary of first game played	$5
100 autographed by Johnny Sain, first pitcher Robinson faced			$15
100 autographed by Dick Littlefield, only player to be traded for Robinson			$25
Jackie Robinson	Gateway	First Day Issue of stamp, 8/2/82	$5
Jackie Robinson	Little Sun	50th anniversary of first pro contract	$10
Jackie Robinson	Z Silk	Brooklyn anniversary of signing with Dodgers	limited availability
100 autographed by Al Campanis and Clyde Sukeforth			$25

Jackie Robinson	Z Silk	Brooklyn anniversary of first game played	$5
Jackie Robinson	Z Silk	retires	$5
Jackie Robinson	Z Silk	anniversary of 1949 MVP award	$5
Jackie Robinson	Z Silk	uniform retired	$5
Preacher Roe	Z Silk	Brooklyn anniversary of 1949 season, 10/2/89	$5
Ed Roebuck	Z Silk	Brooklyn series, 4/18/89	$5
Pete Rose	Galasso	4,000 hits, 4/13/84	$10
Pete Rose	Gateway	all-time NL hit record, set of 2, 6/10/81	$35a
Pete Rose	Gateway	3,000 hits, set of 2, 5/5/78	$50a
Pete Rose	Gateway	44-game hitting streak, game 37, 7/24/78	$35
Pete Rose	Gateway	44-game hitting streak, game 38, 7/25/78	$35
Pete Rose	Gateway	44-game hitting streak, game 44, 7/31/78	$50
Pete Rose	Gateway	44-game hitting streak, night it ended, 8/1/78	$75
Pete Rose	Gateway	4,000 hits, 4/13/84	$75a
Pete Rose	Gateway	3,309 games played, 6/29/84	$60a
Pete Rose	Gateway	managerial debut, 8/17/84	limited availability
Pete Rose	Gateway	4,192 hits, all-time record, set of 4, 9/1/94	$75a
Pete Rose	Gateway	banishment, 8/24/89	$30
Pete Rose	Z Silk	banishment, 8/24/89	$10
John Roseboro	Z Silk	Brooklyn anniversary of 1957 season, 5/17/92	$5
Ed Roush	Gateway	70th anniversary of batting title, 9/30/87	$5a
Royals Stadium	Z Silk	Ballpark series, 7/1/91	$5
100 autographed by John Mayberry, who hit the first home run there			$15
Babe Ruth	Gateway	FDI of Ruth stamp, 7/6/83	$10
100 autographed by Silas Johnson, the last to strike Ruth out			$25
Babe Ruth	Z Silk	Yankee Memorial Park, 7/13/85	$5
Babe Ruth	Z Silk	100th birthday, set of 3	$15
Nolan Ryan	Galasso	3,509 strikeouts, 4/27/83	$20
Nolan Ryan	Gateway	3,000 strikeouts, set of 2, 7/4/80	$50a
Nolan Ryan	Gateway	5th no hitter, 9/26/81	$300a
Nolan Ryan	Gateway	3,509 strikeouts, 4/27/83	$50a
Nolan Ryan	Gateway	4,000 strikeouts, 7/11/85	$50a
Nolan Ryan	Gateway	5,000 strikeouts, 8/22/89	$150a
Nolan Ryan	Gateway	6th no hitter, 6/11/90	$50a
Nolan Ryan	Gateway	300 wins, 7/31/90	$50a
Nolan Ryan	Gateway	7th no hitter, 5/1/91	limited availability
Nolan Ryan	Gateway	27th season, 4/9/93	$50a
Nolan Ryan	Z Silk	3,000 strikeouts, 7/4/80	$10
Nolan Ryan	Z Silk	salute to 1969 Mets, 5/20/89	$6
Nolan Ryan	Z Silk	1991 Opening Day, 4/8/91	$6
Nolan Ryan	Z Silk	22 seasons with 100 strikeouts, 7/2/91	$10
Nolan Ryan	Z Silk	1993 Opening Day	$6
Nolan Ryan	Z Silk	retires, 10/3/93	$6
Nolan Ryan	Z Silk	set of 4 for each team he's played on, 10/3/93	$30
Nolan Ryan	Z Silk	special pictorial postmark, Alvin, Texas	$6
Nolan Ryan	Z Silk	retires, set of 7 honoring his no hitters	$35
Bret Saberhagen	Colorano	no hitter, 8/26/91	$8
Bret Saberhagen	Z Silk	youngest 20-game winner, 9/30/85	$300a
Bret Saberhagen	Z Silk	1985 Cy Young Award, 11/11/85	$6
Bret Saberhagen	Z Silk	1989 Cy Young Award, 11/15/89	$6
Bret Saberhagen	Z Silk	no hitter, 8/26/91	$40a
Chris Sabo	Z Silk	1988 Rookie of the Year, 11/1/88	$5
St. Louis Browns	Gateway	40th anniversary of last game in St. Louis	$5
St. Louis Cardinals	Z Silk	100th anniversary	$5
Tim Salmon	Z Silk	Rookie of the Year	$5
San Diego Padres	Gateway	three home runs to start the game, autographed by	
Marvell Wynne, Tony Gwynn and John Kruk, 4/13/87			$75
San Diego Padres	Gateway	20th anniversary, autographed by Randy Jones	$17
Benito Santiago	Gateway	rookie hit streak, 10/2/87	$20a
Benito Santiago	Z Silk	1987 Rookie of the Year, 11/4/88	$5
Mike Schmidt	Gateway	400th home run, 5/15/85	$50a
Mike Schmidt	Gateway	500th home run, 4/18/87	$50a

Commemoratives

Mike Schmidt	Z Silk	Phillies retire uniform, 5/26/90	$10
Mike Schmidt	Z Silk	536th home run, ties Mantle, 6/17/88	$10
Mike Schmidt	Z Silk	uniform retired	$5
Mike Schmidt	Z Silk	Hall of Fame election, 1/9/95	$5
Mike Schmidt	Z Silk	Hall of Fame induction #1 cachet, 7/30/95	$5
Mike Schmidt	Z Silk	Hall of Fame induction #2 cachet, 7/30/95	$5
Red Schoendienst	Gateway	Hall of Fame induction, 7/23/89	$20a
Red Schoendienst	Z Silk	Hall of Fame election, 1/15/89	$5
Red Schoendienst	Z Silk	Hall of Fame induction, 7/23/89	$5
Mike Scott	Gateway	no hitter, 9/25/86	$17a
Mike Scott	Z Silk	1986 Cy Young Award, 10/15/86	$5
Mike Scott	Z Silk	1986 NL playoffs	$8
Seals Stadium	Z Silk	Ballpark series, 4/15/88	$8
Tom Seaver	Colorano	Hall of Fame induction, 8/2/92	$5
Tom Seaver	Galasso	returns to Mets, 4/5/83	$10
Tom Seaver	Gateway	3,000 strikeouts, set of 2, 4/18/81	$30a
Tom Seaver	Gateway	uniform retirement, 7/24/84	$30a
Tom Seaver	Gateway	Opening Day record, 4/9/85	$30a
Tom Seaver	Gateway	300 wins, 8/4/85	$30a
Tom Seaver	Gateway	Hall of Fame induction, 8/2/92	$40a
Tom Seaver	Gateway	no hitter	limited availability
Tom Seaver	Z Silk	15 opening day, 4/9/85	$5
Tom Seaver	Z Silk	returns to Mets, 6/6/87	$5
Tom Seaver	Z Silk	retires, 6/22/87	$5
Tom Seaver	Z Silk	Mets retire uniform, 7/24/88	$5
Tom Seaver	Z Silk	salute to 1969 Mets, 5/20/89	$5
Tom Seaver	Z Silk	Hall of Fame induction, 8/2/92	$5
Tom Seaver	Z Silk	returns to Mets postmark (4/5/83) and Hall of Fame induction postmark (8/2/92)	$16a
Tom Seaver postmark (8/2/92)	Z Silk	300 wins postmark (8/4/84 and Hall of Fame induction	$20a
Tom Seaver	Z Silk	uniform #41 retired	$5
Joe Sewell	Gateway	50th anniversary of Hall of Fame, 6/12/89	$5
Art Shamsky	Z Silk	salute to 1969 Mets, 11/19/92	$5
Shea Stadium	Gateway	25th anniversary, 4/17/89	limited availability
Shea Stadium	Z Silk	salute to 1969 Mets, 5/20/89	$5
Shea Stadium	Z Silk	Ballpark series, 4/3/89	$5
100 autographed by Bud Harrelson, Ed Kranepool and Cleon Jones			$30
Sheffield/McGriff	Gateway	back-to-back homer runs in consecutive innings, 8/6/92, autographed by both	$40
Rollie Sheldon	Z Silk	salute to 1961 Yankees	$5
Shibe Park	Z Silk	Ballpark series	$5
Connie Mack Stadium			$20
100 autographed by Richie Ashburn			$5
George Shuba	Z Silk	Brooklyn Dodger Hall of Fame, 6/12/88	$5
Moose Skowron	Z Silk	Yankee Old Timers Day 1991	$5
Moose Skowron	Z Silk	salute to 1961 Yankees, 7/14/90	$15
100 autographed by Skowron			$25a
Enos Slaughter	Gateway	Hall of Fame induction, 7/28/85	$6
Enos Slaughter	Z Silk	Hall of Fame election, 1/8/85	$6
Enos Slaughter	Z Silk	Hall of Fame induction, 7/28/85	$5
Enos Slaughter	Z Silk	Yankee Old Timers Day 1991	$22a
Lee Smith	Gateway	300th save, 8/25/91	$22a
Lee Smith	Gateway	all-time save record, 4/13/93	$25a
Ozzie Smith	Gateway	10th straight All-Star Game, 7/14/92	$10
Ozzie Smith	Z Silk	1985 NL playoffs, 10/16/85	$25a
Duke Snider	Gateway	Hall of Fame induction, 8/3/80	$5
Duke Snider	Z Silk	uniform retired	$5
Duke Snider	Z Silk	belts four World Series home runs	$5
Casey Stengel	Z Silk	classic photo	$50a
Warren Spahn	Gateway	300 wins, 5/6/82	limited availability
Sportsman's Park	Z Silk	Ballpark series, 10/15/90	

Bill Stanford	Z Silk	salute to 1961 Yankees	$4.50
Eddie Stanky	Z Silk	Brooklyn anniversary of 1941 season	$5
Willie Stargell	Gateway	Hall of Fame induction, 7/31/88	$20a
Willie Stargell	Z Silk	Hall of Fame election, 1/12/88	$6
Willie Stargell	Z Silk	Hall of Fame induction, 7/31/88	$6
Rusty Staub	Gateway	100 pinch hits, 9/21/83	$20a
Rusty Staub	Gateway	last game, set of 2, 7/13/86	$30a
Casey Stengel	Little Sun	60th anniversary, 2/23/94	$10
Dave Stewart	Gateway	no hitter, 6/29/90	$25a
Dave Stewart	Z Silk	1988 World Series MVP	$5
Terry Steinbach	Gateway	1988 All-Star Game	$15a
Darryl Strawberry	Z Silk	1985 All-Star Game	$5
Darryl Strawberry	Z Silk	1986 All-Star Game	$5
Darryl Strawberry	Z Silk	1988 All-Star Game	$5
Darryl Strawberry	Z Silk	1991 opener, first Dodger game	$5
Rick Sutcliffe	Z Silk	1984 Cy Young Award, 10/23/84	$10
Don Sutton	Gateway	3,000 strikeouts, set of 2, 6/24/83	$20a
Don Sutton	Gateway	300 wins, 6/18/86	$20a
Danny Tartabull	Z Silk	season finale 1993	$5
Ralph Terry	Gateway	50th annivesary of All-Star Game	$100
Ralph Terry	Z Silk	salute to 1961 Yankees, 11/18/92	$100
Texas Trio	Gateway	home run record, signed by Juan Gonzalez, Rafael Palmero and	
Dean Palmer			limited availability
Frank Thomas	Z Silk	1993 All-Star Game	$5
Frank Thomas	Z Silk	1993 MVP	$5
Frank Thomas	Z Silk	1994 MVP	$5
Leroy Thomas	Z Silk	salute to 1961 Yankees	$5
Bobby Thomson	Gateway	40th anniversary of 1951 playoffs	$17a
Jim Thorpe	Gateway	FDI of Thorpe stamp, 5/24/84	$5
Three Rivers Stadium	Gateway	25th anniversary	$5
Three Rivers Stadium	Z Silk	Ballpark series	$5
Tiger Stadium	Gateway	80th anniversary	$5
Tiger Stadium	Gateway	Ballpark series	$5
Tigers vs. Cubs	Z Silk	1995 Hall of Fame exhibition game	$5
Earl Torgeson	Z Silk	salute to 1961 Yankees	$4.50
Toronto Skydome	Z Silk	Ballpark series	$5
Tom Tresh	Z Silk	salute to 1961 Yankees, 7/14/90	$5
Triple Crown	Gateway	autographed by Ted Williams, Mickey Mantle, Frank Robinson,	
Carl Yastrzemski			$400a
Bob Turley	Z Silk	salute to 1961 Yankees, 7/14/90	$5
100 autographed by Turley			$15
Fernando Valenzuela	Gateway	ERA record, 4/28/85	$35a
Fernando Valenzuela	Z Silk	1986 All-Star Game	$6
Chris Van Cuyk	Z Silk	Brooklyn Dodgers' 15-run inning	$5
Johnny Vandermeer	Gateway	back-to-back no hitters, set of 2	limited availability
Johnny Vandermeer	Z Silk	back-to-back no hitters	limited availabilty
Andy Van Slyke	Gateway	1988 All-Star Game	$25a
Arky Vaughn	Z Silk	Hall of Fame election, 3/6/85	$5
Arky Vaughn	Z Silk	Hall of Fame induction, 7/8/85	$5
Arky Vaughn	Gateway	Hall of Fame induction, 7/8/85	$5
Mo Vaughn	Z Silk	1995 MVP	$5
Veterans Park	Z Silk	Ballpark series	7/1/91 $5
100 autographed by Jim Bunning, who won the first game there			$20
Frank Viola	Z Silk	1988 Cy Young Award	$5
Dixie Walker	Z Silk	Brooklyn anniversary of first game, 8/7/89	$5
Rube Walker	Z Silk	Brooklyn anniversary of 1951 season, 5/17/92	$5
Jerome Walton	Z Silk	1989 Rookie of the Year	$5
Washington Park	Z Silk	Ballpark seriers	$5
Al Weis	Z Silk	salute to 1969 Mets, 11/18/92	$5
Walt Weiss	Z Silk	1989 Rookie of the Year	$5
Mark Whiten	Gateway	four home runs in a game, 9/8/93	$20a
Hoyt Wilhelm	Gateway	Hall of Fame induction, 7/28/85	$20a

Hoyt Wilhelm	Z Silk	Hall of Fame election, 1/8/85	$5
Hoyt Wilhelm	Z Silk	Hall of Fame induction, 7/28/85	$5
Billy Williams	Gateway	Hall of Fame induction, 7/26/86	$5
Billy Williams	Z Silk	Hall of Fame election, 1/15/87	$6
Billy Williams	Z Silk	Hall of Fame induction, 7/26/87	$6
Dick Williams	Z Silk	Brooklyn Dodgers series, 11/7/91	$5
100 autographed by Williams			$15
Ted Williams	Gateway	50th anniversary of .400 season, 9/28/91	$20
Ted Williams	Z Silk	co-captain 1991 All-Star Game	$10
Ted Williams	Z Silk	set of four cachets	$25
Ted Williams	Z Silk	uniform retired	$5
Ted Williams	Z Silk	50th anniversary of 1941 season	$5
Willie, Mickey and the Duke	Gateway	autographed by Mays, Mantle and Snider, 1/14/89	$300
Maury Wills	Gateway	25th anniversary of 104 stolen bases, 10/3/87	$17a
Dave Winfield	Colorano	400th home run, 8/14/91	$7
Dave Winfield	Colorano	3,000th hit, 9/16/93	$7
Winfield/Mattingly	Galasso	1984 batting race	$10
Dave Winfield	Gateway	1979 All-Star Game	$30a
Dave Winfield	Gateway	400th home run, 8/14/91	$30a
Dave Winfield	Gateway	3,000th hit, 9/16/93	$35a
Mike Witt	Gateway	perfect game, 9/30/84	$17a
Todd Worrell	Gateway	rookie saves record, 8/10/86	$17a
Todd Worrell	Z Silk	1986 Rookie of the Year	$5
Wrigley Field	Gateway	first night game, set of 2, 8/8/88	$10
Wrigley Field	Z Silk	Ballpark series, 4/23/90	limited availability
100 autographed by Phil Cavarretta and Andy Pafko			$20
100 autographed by Glenn Beckert			$20
Wrigley Field, Los Angeles	Z Silk	Ballpark series, 10/1/90	$5
Whit Wyatt	Z Silk	Brooklyn anniversary of 1941 season, 9/24/89	$5
100 autographed by Wyatt			$15
Early Wynn	Gateway	300 wins, 5/6/82	$50a
Yankee Stadium	Gateway	70th anniversary photo	$5
Yankee Stadium	Gateway	70th anniversary art	$5
Yankee Stadium	Z Silk	Ballpark series	$5
Carl Yastrzemski	Gateway	3,000 hits, 9/12/79	$100a
Carl Yastrzemski	Gateway	Hall of Fame induction, 7/23/89	limited availability
Carl Yastrzemski	Z Silk	Hall of Fame election, 1/15/89	$10
Carl Yastrzemski	Z Silk	uniform retired	$5
Eric Young	Gateway	first rookie home run	$20a
Robin Yount	Colorano	3,000 hits, 9/9/92	$10
Robin Yount	Colorano	retirement announcement, 2/11/94	$7
Robin Yount	Gateway	3,000 hits, 9/9/92	$40a
Robin Yount	Z Silk	1989 MVP, 11/20/89	$7
Robin Yount	Z Silk	3,000 hits	$10

Gateway World Series cachets

A is autographed, U is unautographed

1978

Game 1: Oct. 10, 1978, Los Angeles, Calif. Stadium artwork. A by Reggie Jackson ($75), Steve Garvey ($60), Ed Figueroa ($40).

Game 2: Oct. 11, 1978, Los Angeles, Calif. Ron Cey and Davey Lopes. A by Cey, Lopes or Don Sutton ($45), Garvey ($60), Sutton and Catfish Hunter ($75), Garvey and Hunter ($80).

Game 3: Oct. 13, 1978, Bronx, N.Y. Graig Nettles. A by Ron Guidry ($50), Nettles ($45).

Game 4: Oct. 14, 1978, Bronx, N.Y. Tommy Lasorda, Cey and Garvey. A by Lasorda ($50), Reggie Jackson ($75), Reggie Smith ($45), Garvey ($60).

Game 5: Oct. 15, 1978, Bronx, N.Y. Thurman Munson. U ($35).

Game 5: Reggie Jackson. sold out.

Game 6: Oct. 17, 1978, Los Angeles, Calif. World Series trophy. A by Hunter ($50), Yogi Berra ($60).

1979

Game 1: Oct. 10, 1979, Baltimore, Md. Stadium artwork. A by Mark Belanger ($20), Eddie Murray ($25), Frank Robinson ($25), WillieStargell ($25), John Lowenstein ($20).
Game 1: Mike Flanagan. U ($20).
Game 2: Oct. 11, 1979, Baltimore, Md. Jim Palmer. A by Palmer ($25).
Game 2: Kent Tekulve. U ($10).
Game 3: Oct. 12, 1979, Pittsburgh, Pa. Kiko Garcia. U ($10).
Game 4: Oct. 13, 1979, Pittsburgh, Pa. Earl Weaver. A by Weaver ($20), U ($10).
Game 5: Oct. 14, 1979, Pittsburgh, Pa. Dave Parker and Rick Dempsey. A by Parker ($25), Dempsey or Bill Madlock ($20), Mike Flanagan or Tim Foli ($15).
Game 6: Oct. 16, 1979, Baltimore, Md. Kent Tekulve. U ($10).
Game 6: Oct. 16, 1979, Baltimore, Md. Jim Palmer. A by Palmer ($25), U ($10).
Game 7: Oct. 17, 1979, Baltimore, Md. Willie Stargell and Bill Robinson. A by Stargell ($25), Robinson ($20), U ($10).

1980

Game 1: Oct. 14, 1980, Philadelphia, Pa. Stadium artwork. A by Bob Boone, Bake McBride or Frank White ($20).
Game 2: Oct. 15, 1980, Philadelphia, Pa. Steve Carlton. A by Carlton ($35), U ($15).
Game 3: Oct. 17, 1980, Kansas City, Kan. George Brett. A by Brett ($50), Amos Otis ($20), U ($15).
Game 4: Oct. 18, 1980, Kansas City, Kan. Willie Mays Aikens. U ($10), A by Larry Christenson ($20).
Game 5: Oct. 19 1980, Kansas City, Kan. Bob Boone and Darrell Porter. A by Manny Trillio, Del Unser or Tug McGraw ($20).
Game 6: Oct. 21, 1980, Philadelphia, Pa. Mike Schmidt. A by Schmidt ($50), U ($15).

1981

Game 1: Oct. 20, 1981, Bronx, N.Y. Stadium artwork. A by Ron Guidry, Bob Lemon or Dave Righetti ($15), U ($10).
Game 2: Oct. 21, 1981, Bronx, N.Y. Goose Gossage. A by Gossage ($15).
Game 3: Oct. 23, 1981, Los Angeles, Calif. Fernando Valenzuela. U ($10).
Game 3: Oct. 23, 1981, Los Angeles, Calif. Ron Cey. A by Cey and Tommy Lasorda ($30), U ($10).
Game 4: Oct. 24, 1981, Los Angeles, Calif. Steve Garvey. A by Garvey ($20).
Game 5: Oct. 25, 1981, Los Angeles, Calif. Jerry Reuss. A by Reuss ($15), U ($10).
Game 6: Oct. 28, 1981, Bronx, N.Y. Steve Yeager and Steve Howe. A by Yeager, Cey or Dusty Baker ($15), U ($10).

1982

Game 1: Oct. 12, 1982, St. Louis, Mo. Stadium artwork. A by Tommy Herr ($15), U ($10).
Game 2: Oct. 13, 1982, St. Louis, Mo. Darrell Porter. A by Porter ($15), U ($10).
Game 2: Oct. 13, 1982, St. Louis, Mo. Ted Simmons. A by Simmons ($15), U ($10).
Game 3: Oct. 15, 1982, Milwaukee, Wis. Joaquin Andujar. A by Willie McGee ($15), U ($10).
Game 4: Oct. 16, 1982, Milwaukee, Wis. Cecil Cooper. A by Cooper ($15), Ozzie Smith ($25), U ($10).
Game 5: Oct. 17, 1982, Milwaukee, Wis. Robin Yount. A by Yount ($35), or U ($20).
Game 6: Oct. 19, 1982, St. Louis, Mo. Keith Hernandez. A by Hernandez ($15), U ($10).
Game 6: Oct. 19, 1982, St. Louis, Mo. Darrell Porter. A by Porter ($15), U ($10).
Game 7: Oct. 20, 1982, St. Louis, Mo. Bruce Sutter. A by Sutter, McGee or Lonnie Smith ($15), U ($10).

1983

Game 1: Oct. 11, 1983, Baltimore, Md. Stadium artwork. A by Joe Morgan ($25), Al Holland ($15).
Game 2: Oct. 12, 1983, Baltimore, Md. Mike Boddicker. A by Boddicker ($15), U ($7.50).
Game 3: Oct. 14, 1983, Philadelphia, Pa. Rick Dempsey.. A by Dempsey ($15), U ($7.50).
Game 3: Oct. 14, 1983, Philadelphia, Pa. Joe Morgan. A by Morgan ($25).
Game 4: Oct. 15, 1983, Philadelphia, Pa. John Denny. A by Denny ($15), U ($7.50).
Game 5: Oct. 16, 1983, Philadelphia, Pa. Rick Dempsey. A by Dempsey ($15), U ($7.50).
Game 5: Oct. 16, 1983, Philadelphia, Pa., Eddie Murray. A by Murray ($25), U ($7.50).

1984

Game 1: Oct. 9, 1984, San Diego, Calif. Stadium artwork. U ($7.50).
Game 2: Oct. 10, 1984, San Diego, Calif. Kurt Bevacqua and Terry Kennedy. A by Kennedy ($15), U ($7.50).
Game 3: Oct. 12, 1984, Detroit, Mich. Willie Hernandez. A by Hernandez ($15), U ($7.50).
Game 4: Oct. 13, 1984, Detroit, Mich. Alan Trammell. A by Trammell ($15), U ($7.50).
Game 5: Oct. 14, 1984, Detroit, Mich. Kirk Gibson. A by Gibson ($25), U ($7.50).

1985

Game 1: Oct. 19, 1985, Kansas City, Mo. Stadium artwork. A by Ozzie Smith ($25), U ($7.50).
Game 2: Oct. 20, 1985, Kansas City, Mo. Terry Pendleton. A by Pendleton ($15), U ($7.50).
Game 3: Oct. 22, 1985, St. Louis, Mo. Frank White photo. A by White ($15), U ($7.50).
Game 4: Oct. 23, 1985, St. Louis, Mo. John Tudor. A by Tudor ($15), U ($7.50).
Game 5: Oct. 24, 1985, St. Louis, Mo. Willie Wilson. U ($7.50).
Game 6: Oct. 26, 1985, Kansas City, Mo. Charlie Leibrandt. A by Leibrandt ($15), U ($7.50).
Game 7: Oct. 27, 1985, Kansas City, Mo. Bret Saberhagen and George Brett. A by Saberhagen ($25), by Saberhagen and Brett ($75).

1986

Game 1: Oct. 18, 1986, New York, NY. Stadium artwork. A by Davey Johnson or Bill Buckner ($15), U ($7.50).
Game 2: Oct. 19, 1986, New York, N.Y. Dwight Gooden. A by Gooden ($25), U ($10).
Game 2: Oct. 19, 1986, New York, N.Y. Roger Clemens. A by Clemens ($35), U ($10).
Game 3: Oct. 21, 1986, Boston, Mass. Lenny Dykstra. A by Dykstra ($20), U ($7.50).
Game 4: Oct. 22, 1986, Boston, Mass. Gary Carter. A by Carter ($20), U ($10).
Game 5: Oct. 23, 1986, Boston, Mass. Bruce Hurst. A by Hurst ($15), U ($7.50).
Game 6: Oct. 25, 1986, New York, N.Y. Keith Hernandez. A by Hernandez ($15), U ($7.50).
Game 6: Oct. 25, 1986, New York, N.Y. Wade Boggs. A by Boggs ($25), U ($10).
Game 7: Oct. 27, 1986, New York, N.Y. Ray Knight. A by Knight ($15), U ($7.50).

1987

Game 1: Oct. 17, 1987, Minneapolis, Minn. Stadium artwork. A by Kirby Puckett ($30), Tom Brunansky ($15), U ($7.50).
Game 2: Oct. 18, 1987, Minneapolis, Minn. Bert Blyleven. A by Blyleven ($15), U ($7.50).
Game 3: Oct. 20, 1987, St. Louis, Mo. Vince Coleman. A by Coleman ($15), U ($7.50).
Game 4: Oct. 21, 1987, St. Louis, Mo. Tom Lawless. A by Lawless ($15).
Game 5: Oct. 22, 1987, St. Louis, Mo. Ozzie Smith. A by Smith ($25), U ($10).
Game 6: Oct. 24, 1987, Minneapolis, Minn. Kent Hrbek. A by Hrbek ($15).
Game 7: Oct. 25, 1987, Minneapolis, Minn. Frank Viola. A by Viola ($15), U ($7.50).

1988

Game 1: Oct. 15, 1988, Los Angeles, Calif. Stadium artwork. A by Jose Canseco ($25), U ($7.50).
Game 2: Oct. 16, 1988, Los Angeles, Calif. Orel Hershiser. A by Hershiser ($20), U ($7.50).
Game 3: Oct. 18, 1988, Oakland, Calif. Mark McGwire. A by McGwire ($20).
Game 4: Oct. 19, 1988, Oakland, Calif. Mike Scioscia. A by Scioscia ($15), U ($7.50).
Game 5: Oct. 20, 1988, Oakland, Calif. Mickey Hatcher. A by Hatcher ($15), U $7.50.

1989

Game 1: Oct. 14, 1989, Oakland, Calif. Stadium artwork. A by Matt Williams ($20), U ($7.50).
Game 2: Oct. 15, 1989, Oakland, Calif. Rickey Henderson. A by Henderson ($25), U ($7.50).
Earthquake: Oct. 17, 1989, San Francisco, Calif. Earthquake artwork. A by Roger Craig ($15), U ($7.50).
Game 3: Oct. 27, 1989, San Francisco, Calif. Dave Stewart. A by Stewart ($20), U ($7.50).
Game 4: Oct. 28, 1989, San Francisco, Calif. Mike Moore. A by Moore ($15), U ($7.50).

1990

Game 1: Oct. 16, 1990, Cincinnati, Ohio. Stadium artwork. A by Lou Piniella or Eric Davis ($15), U ($7.50).
Game 2: Oct. 17, 1990, Cincinnati, Ohio. Billy Hatcher and Carney Lansford. A by Hatcher ($15), U ($7.50).
Game 3: Oct. 19, 1990, Oakland, Calif. Chris Sabo. A by Sabo ($15).
Game 3: Oct. 19, 1990, Oakland, Calif. Rob Dibble. A by Dibble and Norm Charlton ($25), U ($10).
Game 4: Oct. 20, 1990, Oakland, Calif. Jose Rijo. A by Rijo ($15).

1991

Game 1: Oct. 19, 1991, Minneapolis, Minn. Stadium artwork. A by Tom Glavine ($15).
Game 2: Oct. 20, 1991, Minneapolis, Minn. Ron Gant. A by Gant ($15), U ($7.50).
Game 3: Oct. 22, 1991, Atlanta, Ga. Steve Avery. A by Avery ($15), U ($7.50).
Game 4: Oct. 23, 1991, Atlanta, Ga. Lonnie Smith and Brian Harper. U ($7.50).
Game 5: Oct. 24, 1991, Atlanta, Ga. Mark Lemke. A by Lemke ($15), U ($7.50).
Game 6: Oct. 26, 1991, Minneapolis, Minn. Kirby Puckett. U ($7.50).
Game 7: Oct. 27, 1991, Minneapolis, Minn. Jack Morris. U ($7.50).

Colorano World Series cachets

1991 - sold as an unautographed set of 7 cachets ($30), pictured are Dan Gladden/Greg Olson, Chuck Knoblauch, Lonnie Smith, Brian Harper/Mark Lemke, Kirby Puckett and Jack Morris.

1992 - sold as an unautographed set of 6 cachets ($30), pictured are Roberto Alomar, Lonnie Smith, Dave Winfield, Juan Guzman, action play at first and Blue Jays' celebration.

1993 - sold as an unautographed set of 6 cachets ($30), pictured are Lenny Dykstra/Mariano Duncan, Jim Eisenreich, Paul Molitor, Duane Ward, Mitch Williams and Lenny Dykstra.

Historic Limited Editions
Z Silk World Series cachets

1983 Orioles/Phillies - sold as unautographed set of 5 ($35), pictured are Garry Maddox, Mike Boddicker, Jim Palmer, Rich Dauer and Rick Dempsey.

1984 Tigers/Padres - sold as an unautographed set of 5 ($30), pictured are Jack Morris, Kurt Bevacqua, Marty Castillo, Alan Trammell and Kirk Gibson.

1985 Royals/Cardinals - sold as an unautographed set of 7 ($30), pictured are Cesar Cedeno, Terry Pendleton, Bret Saberhagen, Tito Landrum, Danny Jackson, Dane Iorg amd George Brett.

1986 Mets/Red Sox - sold as an unautographed set of 7 ($30), pictured are Bruce Hurst, Wade Boggs, Lenny Dykstra, Gary Carter, Bruce Hurst, Mooike Wilson and Jesse Orosco.

1987 Twins/Cardinals - sold as an unautographed set of 7 ($30), pictured are Dan Gladden, Tim Laudner, Vince Coleman, Tom Lawless, Curt Ford, Kent Hrbek and Greg Gagne.

1988 Dodgers/A's - sold as an unautographed set of 5 ($25), pictured are Kirk Gibson, Orel Hershiser, Bob Welch, Jay Howell and Orel Hershiser.

1989 A's/Giants - sold as an unautographed set of 4 ($20), pictured are Walt Weiss, Terry Steinbach, Dave Stewart and Rickey Henderson.

1990 A's/Reds - sold as an unautographed set of 4 ($20), pictured are Eric Davis, Barry Larkin, Chris Sabo and Jose Rijo.

1991 Braves/Twins - sold as an unautographed set of 7 ($30), pictured are Greg Gagne, Scott Leius, Dave Justice, Mark Lemke, Terry Pendleton, Kirby Puckett and Jack Morris.

1992 Braves/Blue Jays - sold as an unautographed set of 6 ($25), pictured are Damon Berryhill, Ed Sprague, Roberto Alomar, group of Blue Jays, Lonnie Smith and Pat Borders.

1993 Blue Jays/Phillies - sold as an unautographed set of 6 ($25), pictured are Lenny Dykstra/Milt Thompson, Darren Daulton/Roberto Alomar, Paul Molitor, Duane Ward, Mitch Williams and Lenny Dykstra.

Bull's Eye cachets

These cachets feature the artwork of Scott Forst and include a certificate of authenticity with each one that has been autographed. Each cachet has either a full color photo or an art silk. All issue numbers are included; each cachet is numbered.

1) All-Star Game, 25th Anniversary of the 1969 Classic (300), art silk of Hank Aaron, Willie McCovery and Ron Santo $7.50

2) 1994 All-Star Game, Three Rivers Stadium, Pittsburgh, Pa. (450), art silk of stadium and all-star montage, 7/12/94, includes team rosters $6

3) 1995 All-Star Game, The Ballpark, Arlington, Texas (375), art silk of stadium and all-star montage, 7/11/95, includes team rosters $6

4) Grover Cleveland Alexander, 373rd and final victory (325), photo silk, has him in a Cardinal uniform $7.50

5) Arlington Stadium, last game played, special pictorial cancellation (250), photo silk $7.50

6) The Ballpark at Arlington, inaugural game, special pictorial cancellation (300), photo silk $7.50

7) Brett Butler, 2,000th career hit (200), photo silk...$20a

8) Roberto Clemente, a tribute, 60th birthday special pictorial cancellation (300), photo silk, with flag or Puerto Rico stamp ($7.50); with 1984 Clemente stamp $9.50; autographed by Luis Clemente (100), Roberto's son ....($16)

9) Cleveland Stadium, last game played (300), Mel Harder throws out the first pitch..................$17a

10) Coors Stadium, inaugural game (325), art silk $7.50

11) Chili Davis, 1,000th RBI (110), photo silk, 7/23/94..$25a

12) Forbes Field, 85th anniversary, special pictorial cancellation (325), photo silk, ($6); 100 autographed by Hal Smith and Bill Virdon ....($25)

13) Jimmie Foxx, 500th home run (325), photo silk...$7.50

14) Harvey Haddix, 35th anniversary of 12-inning perfect game, special pictorial cancellation (300), photo silk $7.50

15) Jacobs Field, inaugural game, special pictorial cancellation (300), photo silk....................$7.50

16) Ramon Martinez, 1995 no hitter (225), photo silk..$18a

17) Don Mattingly, 2,000 hits (100), photo silk $12

18) Bill Mazeroski, anniversary of his 1960 World Series home run (300), photo silk $17a

19) Willie McCovey, anniversary of his 500th home run (300), photo silk $25a

20) Denny McLain, anniversary of his 30-win season (100), photo silk $25a

21) Kent Merker, ho hitter (125), photo silk $12

22) Raul Mondesi, opening day 1994, special pictorial cancellation (200), photo silk $25

23) Chan Ho Park, first Korean to play in the Majors, on Dodgers' Opening Day (200), photo silk, autographed in Korean ($20); autographed in Korean and English...$25

24) Mike Piazza, 1993 season finale, 1993 N.L. Rookie of the Year (300), photo silk $40a

25) Cal Ripken Jr., 2,000th consecutive game (325), photo silk $7.50

26) Frank Robinson, anniversary of his 500th home run (325), photo silk, 9/13/94 ....$25a

27) Nolan Ryan, final game at Arlington (100), photo silk, autographed...................................sold out

28) Tim Salmon, 1993 season finale, 1993 A.L. Rookie of the Year (350), photo silk $30a

29) Willie Stargell, anniversary of the home run he hit out of Dodger Stadium (300), photo silk, autographed by Stargell ($20); autographed by Stargell and pitcher Alan Foster............................$27

30) Ted Williams, anniversary of his 500th home run (300), photo silk $7.50

Bull's Eye World Series editions

These feature full color art silk montage of stadiums and artwork by Scott Forst.

1) 1919 World Series, 75th anniversary of the Black Sox scandal (325), montage of the eight players involved..$7.50

2) 1944 World Series, 50th anniversary of the Cardinals vs. Browns (325), 100 autographed by Max Lanier or Harry Brecheen ($15 each); 75 autographed by Don Gutteridge ($15); unautographed (sold out)

3) 1945 World Series, 50th anniversary of the Tigers vs. Cubs (450), 100 autographed by Hal Newhouser and Phil Cavarretta ($27), or Virgil Trucks or Claude Passeau ($15 each), 150 unautographed ..$7.50

4) 1949 World Series, 45th anniversary of the Yankees vs. Dodgers (325), 100 autographed by Preacher Roe ($15) or 225 unautographed..$7.50

5) 1954 World Series, 40th anniversary of the Giants vs. Indians (325), 100 autographed by Dusty Rhodes or Alvin Dark ($15 each), or 125 unautographed $7.50

6) 1958 World Series, 35th anniversary of the Yankees vs. Braves (350), full color silk of Hank Bauer hitting a home run; 100 autographed by Bauer and Bob Turley ($25); 100 autographed by Eddie Mathews and Lew Burdette ($30); 100 autographed by Whitey Ford ($25); 50 unautographed $10

7) 1959 World Series, 35th anniversary of the Dodgers vs. White Sox (325), 100 autographed by Series MVP Larry Sherry or Charlie Neal ($15 each), or by Chuck Essegian and Norm Larker ($22), or unautographed $7.50

8) 1963 World Series, 30th anniversary of the Dodgers vs. Yankees (350), photo silk of the Dodgers celebrating, 100 autographed by Tommy Davis and Willie Davis, or Frank Howard and Moose Skowron, or Johnny Podres and John Roseboro ($25), or unautographed $10

9) 1964 World Series, 30th anniversary, Yankees vs. Cardinals (325), 100 autographed by Curt Flood ($25), 100 autographed by Joe Pepitone ($15), or 125 unautographed $7.50

10) 1968 World Series, 25th anniversary, Cardinals vs. Tigers (350), photo silk of the Tigers celebrating, 100 autographed by Mickey Lolich and Denny McLain ($25), 100 autographed by Al Kaline ($25), 50 unautographed $10

11) 1974 World Series, 20th anniversary, Dodgers vs. A's (325), 100 autographed by Series MVP Rollie Fingers ($20), or Joe Rudi ($15), 50 autographed by Davey Lopes ($15), 75 unautographed......$7.50

Wild Horse cachets

Individually hand-painted sports cachets since 1988, numbered and signed by Wild Horse artist Warren Reed.

1) Grover C Alexander, "Reflections of the Past," 6/10/89, 90 at $35, 10 artist proofs at $50
2) Sandy Alomar Jr., 4/8/91, 100 at $35
3) Richie Ashburn, Hall of Fame induction, 7/30/95, 85 at $35, 10 artist proofs at $50
4) Johnny Bench/Pete Rose, 7/21/91, 175 at $40
5) Black Sox scandal, Landis/Jackson/Felsch, 9/30/90, 90 at $35, 9 artist proofs at $50
6) Cardinals "Yesterday's Images," Gibson/Musial/Brock, 7/21/91, 15 artist proofs at $60
7) Steve Carlton, Hall of Fame induction, 7/31/94, 95 at $40
8) Roberto Clemente/Willie Stargell, "Yesterday's Images," 7/8/94, 96 at $40
9) Mickey Cochrane/Connie Mack/Lefty Grove, "Reflections of the Past," 6/10/89, 90 at $35
10) Dizzy Dean, "Reflections of the Past," 6/10/89, 90 at $35
11) Don Drysdale, "A Tribute," 8/2/82, artist proofs only at $75
12) Leo Durocher, Hall of Fame induction, 7/31/94, 102 at $35
13) Rollie Fingers, Hall of Fame induction, 8/2/92, 100 at $50
14) Josh Gibson, "Reflections of the Past," 6/10/89, 90 at $35
15) Hank Greenberg, "Reflections of the Past," 6/10/89, 90 at $35
16) Charlie Grimm, "Reflections of the Past," 7/10/90, 90 at $35
17) Gil Hodges, 8/2/82, 115 at $35
18) Rogers Hornsby, "Reflections of the Past," 6/10/89, 85 at $35, 10 artist proofs at $50
19) Shoeless Joe Jackson, "Reflections of the Past," 6/10/89, 85 at $35, 10 artist proofs at $50
20) Mickey Mantle Memorial, 8/13/95, 140 at $35
21) Christy Mathewson, "Reflections of the Past," 6/10/89, 90 at $35, 10 artist proofs at $50
22) Mel Ott, "Reflections of the Past," 6/10/89, 90 at $35, 10 artist proofs at $50
23) Satchel Paige, "Reflections of the Past," 6/10/89, 85 at $35, 10 artist proofs at $50
24) Phil Rizzuto, Hall of Fame induction, 7/31/94, 100 at $35, 20 at $50
25) Benito Santiago, San Diego Padres, 4/9/91, 123 at $35
26) Mike Schmidt, Hall of Fame induction, 7/30/95, 110 at $35, 10 artist proofs at $50
27) Darryl Strawberry, Los Angeles Dodgers, 4/12/91, 100 at $35
28) Triple Crown, Mantle/Yastrzemski/F. Robinson, 135 at $60
29) 1992 World Series, Blue Jays/Braves, set of 5, 95 at $150

Commemoratives

1976 A&P Kansas City Royals

Identical in format to the Brewers' set issued around Milwaukee, these 5 7/8" by 9" photos picture players without their caps in posed portraits. The cards were given away four per week with the purchase of selected grocery item specials. Cards have a players' association logo in the upper-left corner, and a black facsimile autograph on front. Backs are blank. The complete set is worth $15 in Near Mint condition; individual cards are worth .50, unless noted. The players in the set are: Doug Bird, George Brett ($10), Steve Busby, Al Cowens, Al Fitzmorris, Dennis Leonard, Buck Martinez, John Mayberry, Hal McRae ($2.50), Amos Otis, Fred Patek, Tom Poquette, Mel Rojas, Tony Solaita, Paul Splittorff and Jim Wohlford.

1976 A&P Milwaukee Brewers

The Hank Aaron and Robin Yount cards from this regional issue support the set price. The set was issued by the A&P grocery chain. The oversized - 5 7/8" by 9" - cards, actually printed on semi-gloss paper, were given out at the stores in 1976. The complete set is woth $24 in Near Mint condition; individual cards are worth .50, unless noted. The players in the set are: Hank Aaron ($12), Pete Broberg, Jim Colburn, Mike Hegan, Tim Johnson, Von Joshua, Sixto Lezcano, Don Money, Charlie Moore, Darrell Porter, George Scott ($1), Bill Sharp, Jim Slaton, Bill Travers, Robin Yount ($10) and County Stadium.

1969 Atlantic-Richfield Boston Red Sox

One of many larger-format (8" by 10") baseball premiums sponsored as gas station giveaways in the late 1960s and early 1970s was this set of Boston Red Sox player pictures by artist John Wheeldon. The set is sponsored by the Atlantic-Richfield Oil Co. Done in pastel colors, the pictures feature a large por-

trait and smaller action picture against a bright background. A facsimile autograph is penciled in beneath the pictures, and the player's name is printed in the white bottom border. The backs are printed in black-and-white and include biographical and career data, full major and minor league stats, a self-portrait and biography of the artist and the logos of the team, players' association and sponsor. The pictures are unnumbered. A complete set of 12 in Near Mint condition is worth $75; individual pictures are $6, unless noted. The players in the set are: Mike Andrews, Tony Conigliaro ($9), Ray Culp, Russ Gibson, Dalton Jones, Jim Lonborg ($7.50), Sparky Lyle ($7.50), Syd O'Brien, George Scott ($7.50), Reggie Smith ($7.50), Rico Petrocelli ($7.50) and Carl Yastrzemski ($24).

1969 Citgo New York Mets

One of several regional issues in the Mets World Series Championship season of 1969, this unnumbered set of player portraits was sponsored by Citgo, whose gas stations distributed the pictures with fuel purchases. Fronts feature large portraits and smaller action pictures of the player, done in pastels, set against a bright pastel background. The paintings are the work of noted celebrity artist John Wheeldon. Beneath the pictures is a facsimile autograph. The player's name is printed in the bottom border. Backs are printed in black-and-white and include a biography and career details, full major and minor league stats and a self portrait and biography of the artist. Logos of the Mets, the players' association and the sponsor complete the back design. The complete set of eight is worth $60 in Near Mint condition; individual cards are worth $6, unless noted. The players in the set are: Tommie Agee ($7.50), Ken Boswell, Gary Gentry, Jerry Grote, Cleon Jones, Jerry Koosman ($7.50), Ed Kranepool and Tom Seaver ($22).

1947 Cleveland Indians picture pack

The first of many annual issues of player photo packs, the 1947 version offered "autographed" photos of all 25 players on the team's roster as of July 1. All players were presented in studio quality portraits in a 5" by 7" format, lithographed on heavy paper with a facsimile autograph. A thin white border surrounds the photo. Backs are blank. The photos were sold in sets for 50 cents. The complete set of 25 is worth $125 in Near Mint condition; common players are worth $4, unless noted. The players in the set are: Don Black ($6), Lou Boudreau ($9), Eddie Bockman, Jack Conway, Hank Edwards, "Red" Embree, Bob Feller ($45), Les Fleming, Allen Gettel, Joe Gordon, Steve Gromek, Mel Harder ($6), Jim Hegan, Ken Keltner ($6), Ed Klieman, Bob Lemon ($12), Al Lopez ($12), George Metkovich, Dale Mitchell ($6), Hal Peck, Eddie Robinson, Hank Ruszkowski, Pat Seerey, Bryan Stephens and Les Willis ($6).

1984 Farmer Jack Detroit Tigers

Though there is no indication on the pictures themselves, this issue was a promotion by the Farmer Jack grocery store chain. Printed on semi-gloss paper, the color photos are bordered in white and measure 6" by 9." A facsimile autograph is printed on the front of each unnumbered card. The complete set of 16 is worth $15 in Mint condition; individual cards are worth .50, unless noted. The players in the set are: Dave Bergman, Darrell Evans ($1), Barbaro Garbey, Kirk Gibson ($1), John Grubb, Willie Hernandez, Larry Herndon, Howard Johnson ($1.50), Chet Lemon (.75), Jack Morris (.90), Lance Parrish ($1), Dan Petry, Dave Rozema, Alan Trammell ($4), Lou Whitaker ($2.50) and Milt Wilcox.

1973 Jewel Food baseball photos

Jewel Foods, a Midwestern grocery chain, issued three team sets of large-format baseball player photos in 1973. The 5 7/8" by 9" blank-back photos are full color and feature a facsimile autograph. Photos, each unnumbered, were sold in groups of four per week or a nickel or dime per picture. There are 25 Milwaukee Brewers in the issue ($45 in Near Mint condition), and 16 each for the Chicago Cubs ($45 in Near Mint condition) and Chicago White Sox ($30 in Near Mint condition). Individual photos are $2, unless noted. The 16 Cubs featured are: Jack Aker, Glenn Beckert ($3), Jose Cardenal, Carmen Fanzone, Burt Hooten, Fergie Jenkins ($7.50), Don Kessinger ($3), Jim Hickman, Randy Hundley ($3), Bob Locker, Rick Monday, Milt Pappas, Rick Reuschel, Ken Rudolph, Ron Santo ($7.50) and Billy Williams ($9). The 16 White Sox featured are: Dick Allen ($5), Mike Andrews, Stan Bahnsen, Eddie Fisher, Terry Forster, Ken Henderson, Ed Hermann, John Jeter, Pat Kelly, Eddie Leon, Carlos May, Bill Melton, Tony Muser, Jorge Orta, Rick Reichardt and Wilbur Wood. The 25 Milwaukee Brewers are: Jerry Bell, John Briggs, Ollie Brown, Billy Champion, Jim Colburn, Bob Coluccio, John Felske, Pedro Garcia, Rob Gardner, Bob Heise, Tim Johnson, Joe Lahoud, Frank Linzy, Skip Lockwood, Dave May, Bob Mitchell, Don Money ($3), Bill Parsons, Darrell Porter, Eduardo Rodriguez, Ellie Rodriguez, George Scott ($4), Chris Short, Jim Slaton and Pete Vukovich.

1984 Jewel Food Chicago Cubs

Similar in format to previous issues by the Midwestern food company, this 16-piece set of 1984 National League East pennant winers is printed on 6" by 9" paper. Fronts feature a

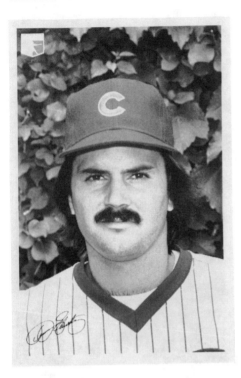

Gary Matthews, Keith Moreland, Ryne Sandberg ($8), Scott Sanderson ($1.50), Lee Smith ($3), Tom Stoddard, Rick Sutcliffe ($2), Steve Trout and Gary Woods.

1958-60 Los Angeles Dodgers premium pictures

Apparently issued over a period of years from 1958 through at least 1960, these black-and-white, 8 1/2" by 11" premium pictures were sold as a set through Dodgers souvenir outlets, although the makeup of the set changed with the comings and goings of players. The blank-backed pictures feature on the front a pencil portrait of the player, with his name printed toward the bottom. The signature of sports artist Nicholas Volpe also appears on the front. The cards are unnumbered. A complete set of 15 is worth $250 in Near Mint condition; individual pictures are worth $10, unless noted. The players in the set are: Walter Alston ($12), Roy Campanella ($25), Don Drysdale ($20), Carl Erskine, Carl Furillo ($12.50), Jim Gilliam ($12.50), Gil Hodges ($15), Clem Labine, Wally Moon, Don Newcombe, Johnny Podres, Pee Wee Reese ($20), Rip Repulski, Vin Scully/Jerry Doggett and Duke Snider ($25).

1963 Los Angeles Dodgers pin-ups

TOM DAVIS

chest-to-cap color player photo with a black facsimile autograph. A logo and copyright notice by the players' association is at the upper left. A complete set of 16 photos is $23 in Mint condition; indvidual photos are .75, unless noted. The players in the set are: Larry Bowa, Ron Cey (.90), Jody Davis, Bob Dernier, Leon Durham, Dennis Eckersley ($3), Richie Hebner,

Borrowing on the concept of the 1938 Goudey Heads-up cards, this set was sold, probably at the stadium souvenir stands, in a white envelope labeled "Los Angeles Dodgers Pin-Ups." The cards feature large full-color head-and-cap photos set atop cartoon ballplayers' bodies. Cards are printed on 7 1/4" by 8 1/2" semi-gloss cardboard with blank backs. The player's name appears in black on the front, along with the instructions "Push out character carefully. Take scissors and trim white around player's head." Each figure was die-cut to allow its easy removal from the background. A complete set of 10 is worth $150 in Near Mint condition; commons are worth $10-$12, unless noted. The players in the set are: Tommy Davis, Willie Davis, Don Drysdale ($20), Ron Fairly, Frank Howard ($15), Sandy Koufax ($45), Joe Moeller, Stan Perranoski, John Roseboro and Maury Wills ($15).

1969 New York News New York Mets Portfolio of Stars

To commemorate the New York Mets' miracle season of 1969, one of the city's daily newspapers, The News, issued a portfolio of player portraits done by its editorial cartoonist. The 9" by 12" pencil drawings are printed on heavy textured paper and were sold as a set in a folder labeled "The 1969 Mets/A Portfolio of Stars." The black-and-white drawings are on a white background. A facsimile player autograph is in the lower left corner, while the artist's signature, Stark, the paper's logo and a union label are in the lower right. The photos are unnumbered. A complete set of 20 pictures in Near Mint condition is worth $300; individual pictures are worth $8, unless noted. The players in the set are: Tommie Agee, Ken Boswell, Don Cardwell, Donn Clendenon ($10), Wayne Garrett, Gary Gentry, Jerry Grote, Bud Harrelson ($10), Gil Hodges ($12), Cleon Jones, Jerry Koosman, Ed Kranepool, Jim McAndrew, Tug McGraw ($10), Nolan Ryan ($150), Tom Seaver ($45), Art Shamsky, Ron Swoboda, Ron Taylor and Al Weis.

1969 Oakland A's picture pack

These blank-backed, black-and-white player portraits were sold in a picture pack. Photos measure approximately 4 5/8" by 7" and are unnumbered. A complete set of 12 is worth $35 in Near Mint condition; common players are $2, unless noted. The players in the set are: Sal Bando, Bert Campaneris ($3), Danny Cater, Chuck Dobson, Dick Green, Mike Hershberger, Jim Hunter ($8), Reggie Jackson ($18), Lew Krausse, Rick Monday ($3), Jim Nash and John Odom ($3).

1950 Pittsburgh Pirates photo pack

The player photos in this picture pack, which was sold at Forbes Field, measure 6 1/2" by 9" and are printed in black-and-white on heavy, blank-backed paper. A facsimile auto-graph is printed on the front of each picture, although all were written in the same hand. Several of the photos from this set were the basis for the color paintings found on 1951 Bowman cards. The cards are unnumbered. A complete set of 26 is worth $175 in Near Mint condition; common players are worth $8, unless noted. The players in the set are: Ted Beard, Gus Bell ($12), Pete Castiglione, Cliff Chambers, Dale Coogan, Murry Dickson, Bob Dillinger, Froilan Fernandez, Johnny Hopp, Ralph Kiner ($18), Vernon Law ($12), Vic Lombardi, Bill MacDonald, Clyde McCullough, Bill Meyer, Ray Mueller, Danny Murtaugh, Jack Phillips, Mel Queen, Stan Rojek, Henry Schenz, George Strickland, Earl Turner, Jim Walsh, Bill Werle and Wally Westlake.

1966 Pure Oil Atlanta Braves pictures

In the team's first year in Atlanta a set of Braves premium pictures done by noted portrait artist Nicholas Volpe was sponsored by Pure Oil. The 8 1/2" by 11" pictures were given away with gas purchases. Fronts feature a larger pastel portrait and smaller full-figure action picture of the player set against a black background. A facsimile autograph was penciled in at the bottom, along with the artist's signature. The player's name was printed in black in the white bottom border. A complete set of 12 pictures is worth $125 in Near Mint condition; individual pictures are $7.50, unless noted. The players in the set are: Hank Aaron ($40), Felipe Alou ($12), Frank Bolling, Bobby Bragan, Rico Carty ($9), Tony Cloninger, Mack Jones, Denny LeMaster, Eddie Mathews ($22), Denis Menke, Lee Thomas and Joe Torre ($12).

1969 San Diego Padres premium pictures

Unlike most of the contemporary large-format (8 1/2" by 11") premium pictures, this issue carries no advertising and appears to have been a team issue during the Padres' inaugural year. Fronts feature large portraits and smaller action pictures of the player against a dark background with a facsimile auto-graph at the bottom and the player's name printed in the white bottom border. The signature of the artist appears in the lower left corner. The artwork was done by Nicholas Volpe, who produced many similar items for teams in all sports in the 1960s, '70s and '80s. The backs have a large team logo in the center and a sketch of the artist at the bottom. There is evidence to suggest that the picture of Cito Gaston is scarcer than the other seven. A complete set of eight pictures is worth $60 in Near Mint condition; individual pictures are $7.50, unless noted. The players in the set are: Ollie Brown, Tommy Dean, Al Ferrara, Clarence Gaston ($15), Preston Gomez, Johnny Podres ($9), Al Santorini and Ed Spiezio.

1969 Seattle Pilots premium pictures

This set of 8 1/2" by 11" premium pictures is based on the artwork of John Wheeldon, who also did contemporary issues for the Mets, Twins and Red Sox. The pastels feature large portraits and small action pictures with a large facsimile autograph at the bottom. In the white bottom border the player's name is printed in black. The backs are black-and-white and feature biographical data, a comprehensive career summary amd complete minor and major league stats. There is a self-portrait and biographical sketch of the artist on the back, too. At the bottom are the logos of the players' association and the player's team. The unnumbered premiums were given away at selected Pilots home games during the team's lone season in Seattle. They were later sold for 25 cents each in the concession stands. A complete set of eight pictures is worth $75 in Near Mint condition; individual pictures are $8, unless noted. The players in

the set are: Wayne Comer, Tommy Harper ($10), Mike Heagan, Jerry McNertney, Don Mincher, Ray Oyler, Marty Pattin and Diego Segui.

1953-57 Spic and Span Milwaukee Braves 7x10 photos

This regional set was issued by Spic and Span Dry Cleaners of Milwaukee over a four-year period and consists of 13 large (7" by 10") photos of Braves players. Of all the various Spic and Span sets, this one seems to be the easiest to find. The fronts feature a player photo with a facsimile autograph below. The Spic and Span logo also appears on the front, while the back is blank. A photo of Milwaukee County Stadium also exists but is not generally considered to be part of the set. A complete set of 13 player pictures is worth $225 in Near Mint condition; individual players are worth $10, unless noted. The players in the set are: Joe Adcock ($15), Bill Bruton, Bob Buhl, Lew Burdette ($15), Del Crandall ($15), Jack Dittmer, John Logan ($15), Ed Mathews ($50), Chet Nichols, Dan O'Connell, Andy Pafko ($15), Warren Spahn ($50) and Bob Thomson ($15).

1987 Sun Foods Milwaukee Brewers

Though they are nowhere identified on the cards, Sun Foods was the sponsor of this team set, issuing four cards per week. Measuring 6" by 9", the cards were licensed only by the players' association and therefore do not feature team uniform logos. Bareheaded players are photographed against a blue

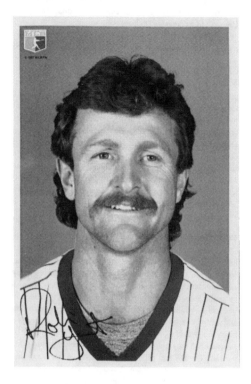

tures were given away at Super Value grocery stores. The premiums feature large portraits and smaller action pictures painted in pastels, against a pastel background. A facsimile autograph is printed below the pictures and the player's name is printed in the bottom border. At 7 3/4" by 9 3/8" the Twins portraits are somewhat smaller than similar contemporary issues. Backs are printed in black-and-white and include a self-portrait and biography of the artist. Player information includes biographical bits, a lengthy career summary and complete major and minor league stats. A team and sponsor logo are also included on the unnumbered card backs. A complete set of 12 pictures is worth $80 in Near Mint condition; individual pictures are worth $6, unless noted. The players in the set are: Brent Alyea, Leo Cardenas, Rod Carew ($17.50), Jim Kaat ($9), Harmon Killebrew ($15), George Mitterwald, Tony Oliva ($9), Ron Perranoski, Jim Perry, Rich Reese, Luis Tiant ($7.50) and Cesar Tovar.

1962 Union Oil Los Angeles Dodgers premium pictures

One of the many premiums issued by Union Oil during the Dodgers' early years in Los Angeles, this set of player pictures is the most popular with collectors. The 8 1/2" by 11" pictures feature a large color pastel portrait of the player on the front, along with a smaller action picture. The player's name is printed in the white border below. The artist's signature and a 1962 copyright are printed below the portrait. Backs are printed in black-and-white and include a career summary and complete minor and major league stats, a profile of sports artist Nicholas Volpe and an ad at the bottom for Union Oil and its Union 76 brand of gasoline. The portraits are unnumbered. A complete set of 24 pictures in Near Mint condition is worth $125; individual pictures are $6, unless noted. The players in the set are: Larry Burright, Doug Camilli, Andy Carey, Tom Davis ($7.50), Willie Davis ($7.50), Don Drysdale ($12), Ron Fairly, Jim Gilliam ($7.50), Tom Harkness, Frank Howard ($8), Sandy Koufax ($15), Joe Moeller, Wally Moon, Ron Perranoski, Johnny Podres ($7.50), Ed Roebuck, John Roseboro, Larry Sherry, Norm Sherry, Duke Snider ($15), Daryl Spencer, Lee Walls, Stan Williams and Maury Wills ($7.50).

1964 Union Oil Los Angeles Dodgers premium pictures

Paired pastel portraits, one in uniform and one without, from sports artist Nicholas Volpe are featured on these large format (8 1/2" by 11") premium pictures sponsored by Union Oil. The player's name is printed in the bottom border while the artist's signature and copyright date are printed beneath the portraits. Backs are in black-and-white and feature personal data about the

background, with a black facsimile autograph at the bottom. An MLBPA logo appears in the upper left. Backs are blank. The photos are unnumbered. A complete set of 16 pictures is worth $15 in Mint condition; individual photos are .50, unless noted. The players in the set are: Glenn Braggs, Greg Brock, Mark Clear, Cecil Cooper ($1), Rob Deer, Jim Gantner, Ted Higuera, Paul Molitor ($3), Juan Nieves, Dan Plesac, Billy Jo Robidoux, Bill Schroeder, B.J. Surhoff (.75), Dale Sveum, Bill Wegman (.75) and Robin Yount ($5).

1970 Super Value Minnesota Twins

One of many Minnesota Twins regional issues from the team's first decade, this set of player portraits was painted by noted celebrity artist John Wheeldon. Individual player pic-

player and artist, complete minor and major league stats and Union Oil/Union 76 logos. The pictures are unnumbered. A complete set of 18 in Near Mint condition is worth $90; individual pictures are $6, unless noted. The players in the set are: Tommy Davis ($7.50), Willie Davis ($7.50), Don Drysdale ($18), Ron Fairly, Jim Gilliam ($7.50), Frank Howard ($8), Sandy Koufax ($22), Bob Miller, Joe Moeller, Wally Moon, Phil Ortega, Wes Parker, Ron Perranoski, John Podres ($7), John Roseboro, Dick Tracewski, Lee Walls and Maury Wills ($7.50).

1969 Union Oil Los Angeles Dodgers premium pictures

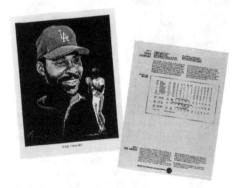

Because of the odd number known, it is likely additional pictures will be added to this checklist in the future. The premiums are similar in format to earlier and later sets sponsored by Union Oil and created by sports artist Nicholas Volpe. Fronts have a pastel player portrait and an action drawing against a black background. Backs are in black-and-white and have a player biography, stats and career summary, along with a word about the artist and an ad for Union Oil/Union 76. The pictures are unnumbered. A complete set of 13 is worth $75 in Near Mint condition; individual pictures are $6, unless noted. The players in the set are: Walt Alston ($9), Jim Brewer, Willie Davis ($7.50), Don Drysdale ($17.50), Ron Fairly, Tom

Haller, Jim Lefebvre, Claude Osteen, Wes Parker, Paul Popovich, Bill Singer, Bill Sudakis and Don Sutton ($10).1982 Union Oil Los Angeles Dodgers premium pictures

A whole new generation of Los Angeles Dodgers was portrayed in the pastel renderings by sports artist Nicholas Volpe on these large format (8 1/2" by 11") premiums sponsored by Union Oil Co. Fronts feature large portraits and smaller action pictures. Backs, in black-and-white, have player data, complete minor and major league stats, a profile of the artist and a Union Oil/Union 76 ad. The pictures are unnumbered. A complete set of 26 is worth $12 in Mint condition; individual pictures are .25 to .50, unless noted. The players in the set are: Dusty Baker, Mark Belanger, Ron Cey, Terry Forster, Steve Garvey ($2), Pedro Guerrero, Burt Hooton, Steve Howe, Ken Landreaux, Tom Lasorda, Mike Marshall, Rick Monday, Jose Morales, Tom Niedenfeur, Jorge Orta, Jerry Reuss, Ron Roenicke, Bill Russell, Steve Sax, Mike Scioscia, Vin Scully, Dave Stewart ($1), Derrell Thomas, Fernando Valenzuela ($1), Bob Welch and Steve Yeager.

1963 Western Oil Minnesota Twins

Issued by Mileage and DS gas stations, these 8 1/2" by 11" heavy paper portraits are the work of sports artist Nicholas Volpe. Each front has a pastel portrait and action rendering against a black background. The player's name appears as a facsimile autograph in white on the painting and is printed in black in the white bottom border. Backs have biographical data and a career summary of the player at the top. At center is a black box with complete major and minor league stats. At lower center is a biography of the artist and, on most pictures, his portrait. The DS and Mileage logos of the Western Oil and Fuel Co. appear at the bottom. A complete set of 24 pictures is worth $75 in Near Mint condition; individual pictures are $5, unless noted. The players in the set are: Bernie Allen, Bob Allison ($8), George Banks, Earl Battey ($6), Bill Dailey, John Goryl, Lenny Green, Jim Kaat ($8), Jimmie Hall, Harmon Killebrew ($15), Sam Mele, Don Mincher, Ray Moore, Camilo Pascual ($6), Jim Perry, Bill Pleis, Vic Power ($6), Garry Roggenburk, Jim Roland, Rich Rollins, Lee Stange, Dick Stigman, Zoilo Versalles ($6) and Jerry Zimmerman.

1964 Western Oil Minnesota Twins

Identical in format to the previous year's issue, the 1964 set of Twins pictures features the use of a second portrait of the player in civilian dress rather than an action picture. The 1964 issue also uses a background of pastel colors, rather than all black, and, on the backs, an oval/arrow logo for Western brand gas, along with the Mileage and DS logos. A complete set of 15 pictures in Near Mint condition is worth $60; individual pictures are $5, unless noted. The players in the set are: Bernie Allen, Bob Allison ($6), Earl Battey ($6), Bill Dailey, Jimmie Hall, Jim Kaat ($7.50), Harmon Killebrew ($15), Don Mincher, Tony Oliva ($15), Camilo Pascual ($6), Bill Pleis, Jim Roland, Rich Rollins, Dick Stigman and Zoilo Versalles ($6).

Perez-Steele postcards

Perez-Steele
Hall of Fame art postcards

In its first postcard set issued in 1980, Perez-Steele Galleries of Fort Washington, Pa., produced the first of four limited-edition sets. The first set is devoted to members of the Hall of Fame and is updated every two years to add the new inductees. 10,000 numbered sets are produced each time. The postcards are generally collected autographed; the prices below are for autographed postcards. "I" means it's impossible that the player could have signed the postcard. Generally, unsigned postcards range from $5-$35, with the following exceptions: Jackie Robinson, Roberto Clemente, Sandy Koufax and Willie Mays are $40 each; Satchell Paige is $45; Earl Averill, Joe DiMaggio and Ted Williams are $50 each; Stan Musial is $55; Lou Gehrig is $60; Ty Cobb is $75; Babe Ruth is $100; and Mickey Mantle is $150. The first value is for an unsigned card; the second is for an autographed one.

First Series (Brown, 1980)

Pee Wee Reese

1 Ty Cobb. . . . .$75 un, I
2 Walter Johnson . . . .$30 un, I
3 Christy Mathewson . . . .$10 un, I
4 Babe Ruth . . . .$100 un, I
5 Honus Wagner. . . . .$10 un, I
6 Morgan Bulkeley. . . . .$5 un, I
7 Ban Johnson . . . .$5 un, I
8 Nap Lajoie. . . . .$5 un, I
9 Connie Mack. . . . .$5 un, I
10 John McGraw . . . .$5 un, I
11 Tris Speaker. . . . .$10 un, I
12 George Wright. . . . .$5 un, I
13 Cy Young . . . .$10 un, I
14 Grover Alexander . . . .$5 un, I
15 Alexander Cartwright . . . .$5 un, I
16 Henry Chadwick . . . .$5 un, I
17 Cap Anson. . . . .$5 un, I
18 Eddie Collins. . . . .$5 un, I
19 Candy Cummings . . . .$5 un, I
20 Charles Comiskey . . . .$5 un, I
21 Buck Ewing. . . . .$5 un, I

22 Lou Gehrig . . . .$60 un, I

23 Willie Keeler . . . .$5 un, I

24 Hoss Radbourne . . . .$5 un, I

25 George Sisler . . . .$10 un, I

26 A.G. Spalding . . . .$5 un, I

27 Rogers Hornsby . . . .$10 un, I

28 Kenesaw Landis . . . . $5un, I

29 Roger Bresnahan . . . .$5 un, I

30 Dan Brouthers . . . .$5 un, I

Second Series (Green, 1980)

31 Fred Clarke . . . .$5 un, I

32 Jimmy Collins . . . .$5 un, I

33 Ed Delahanty . . . .$5 un, I

34 Hugh Duffy . . . .$5 un, I

35 Hughie Jennings . . . .$5 un, I

36 King Kelly . . . .$5 un, I

37 Jim O'Rourke . . . .$5 un, I

38 Wilbert Robinson . . . .$5 un, I

39 Jesse Burkett . . . .$5 un, I

40 Frank Chance . . . .$5 un, I

41 Jack Chesbro . . . .$5 un, I

42 Johnny Evers . . . .$5 un, I

43 Clark Griffith . . . .$10 un, I

44 Thomas McCarthy . . . .$5 un, I

45 Joe McGinnity . . . .$5 un, I

46 Eddie Plank . . . .$5 un, I

47 Joe Tinker . . . .$5 un, I

48 Rube Waddell . . . .$5 un, I

49 Ed Walsh . . . .$5 un, I

50 Mickey Cochrane . . . .$10 un, I

51 Frankie Frisch . . . .$15 un, I

52 Lefty Grove . . . .$20 un, I

53 Carl Hubbell . . . .$25 un, $60-$80

54 Herb Pennock . . . .$10 un, I

55 Pie Traynor . . . .$5 un, I

56 Mordecai Brown . . . .$5 un, I

57 Charlie Gehringer . . . . $20 un, $60

58 Kid Nichols . . . .$5 un, I

59 Jimmy Foxx . . . .$15 un, I

60 Mel Ott . . . .$10 un, I

Third Series (Blue, 1980)

61 Harry Heilmann . . . .$5 un, I

62 Paul Waner . . . .$5 un, I

63 Edward Barrow . . . .$5 un, I

64 Chief Bender . . . .$5 un, I

65 Tom Connolly . . . .$5 un, I

66 Dizzy Dean . . . .$35 un, I

67 Bill Klem . . . .$5 un, I

68 Al Simmons . . . .$10 un, I

69 Bobby Wallace . . . .$5 un, I

70 Harry Wright . . . . $5 un, I

71 Bill Dickey . . . . $20 un, $75-$80

72 Rabbit Maranville . . . . $5 un, I

73 Bill Terry . . . . $20 un, $65-$80

74 Frank Baker . . . . $5 un, I

75 Joe DiMaggio . . . . $50 un, $250-$300

76 Gabby Hartnett . . . . $5 un, I

77 Ted Lyons . . . . $10 un, $200-$250

78 Ray Schalk . . . . $5 un, I

79 Dazzy Vance . . . . $5 un, I

80 Joe Cronin . . . . $15 un, $750

81 Hank Greenberg . . . . $20 un, $300

82 Sam Crawford . . . . $5 un, I

83 Joe McCarthy . . . . $10 un, I

84 Zack Wheat . . . . $10 un, I

85 Max Carey . . . . $ 5un, I

86 Billy Hamilton . . . . $5 un, I

87 Bob Feller . . . . $15 un, $25-$35

88 Bill McKechnie . . . . $5 un, I

89 Jackie Robinson . . . . $40 un, I

90 Edd Roush . . . . $10 un, $65-$80

Fourth Series (1981, Red)

91 John Clarkson . . . . $5 un, I

92 Elmer Flick . . . . $5 un, I

93 Sam Rice . . . . $5 un, I

94 Eppa Rixey . . . . $5 un, I

95 Luke Appling . . . . $10 un, $40

96 Red Faber . . . . $5 un, I

97 Burleigh Grimes . . . . $10 un, $200

98 Miller Huggins . . . . $10 un, I

99 Tim Keefe . . . . $5 un, I

100 Heinie Manush . . . . $5 un, I

101 John Ward . . . . $5 un, I

102 Pud Galvin . . . . $5 un, I

103 Casey Stengel . . . . $25 un, I

104 Ted Williams . . . . $50 un, $225-$325

105 Branch Rickey . . . . $5 un, I

106 Red Ruffing . . . . $10 un, $400

107 Lloyd Waner . . . . $10 un, $3,500

108 Kiki Cuyler . . . . $5 un, I

109 Goose Goslin . . . . $10 un, I

110 Joe Medwick . . . . $10 un, I

111 Roy Campanella . . . . $20 un, $175

112 Stan Coveleski . . . . $10 un, $400

113 Waite Hoyt . . . . $10 un, $450-$550

114 Stan Musial . . . .$55 un, $80

115 Lou Boudreau . . . .$10 un, $20

116 Earle Combs . . . . $10 un, I

117 Ford Frick . . . . $5 un, I

118 Jesse Haines . . . . $10 un, I

119 David Bancroft . . . . $5 un, I
120 Jake Beckley . . . . $5 un, I

Fifth Series (1981, Yellow)

121 Chick Hafey. . . . . $10 un, I
122 Harry Hooper. . . . . $5 un, I
123 Joe Kelley . . . . $5 un, I
124 Rube Marquard . . . . $5 un, I
125 Satchel Paige . . . . $45 un, $3,500
126 George Weiss . . . . $5 un, I
127 Yogi Berra. . . . . $15 un, $25
128 Josh Gibson . . . . $5 un, I
129 Lefty Gomez . . . . $20 un, $55-$65
130 William Harridge. . . . . $5 un, I
131 Sandy Koufax . . . . $40 un, $70
132 Buck Leonard . . . . $15 un, $30
133 Early Wynn . . . . $10 un, $20
134 Ross Youngs . . . . $5 un, I
135 Roberto Clemente . . . . $40 un, I
136 Billy Evans . . . . $5 un, I
137 Monte Irvin . . . . $10 un, $20
138 George Kelly . . . . $10 un, $300
139 Warren Spahn . . . . $10 un, $20-$30
140 Mickey Welch. . . . . $5 un, I
141 Cool Papa Bell. . . . . $20 un, $65-$80
142 Jim Bottomley . . . . $5 un, I
143 Jocko Conlan. . . . . $10 un, $45-$60
144 Whitey Ford. . . . . $15 un, $25
145 Mickey Mantle . . . . . $150 un, $300-$350
146 Sam Thompson . . . . $5 un, I
147 Earl Averill . . . . $50 un, $550
148 Bucky Harris . . . . $10 un, I
149 Billy Herman. . . . . $10 un, $25
150 Judy Johnson . . . . $20 un, $80

Sixth Series (1981, Orange)

151 Ralph Kiner. . . . . $10 un, $15-$25
152 Oscar Charleston . . . . $5 un, I
153 Roger Connor . . . . $5 un, I
154 Cal Hubbard . . . . $5 un, I
155 Bob Lemon . . . . $10 un, $20
156 Freddie Lindstrom. . . . . $5 un, I
157 Robin Roberts . . . . $10 un, $20
158 Ernie Banks. . . . . $15 un, $30-$35
159 Martin DiHigo. . . . . $5 un, I
160 John Lloyd. . . . . $5 un, I
161 Al Lopez . . . . $15 un, $75
162 Amos Rusie. . . . . $5 un, I
163 Joe Sewell . . . . $10 un, $45-$60
164 Addie Joss . . . . $5 un, I
165 Larry MacPhail . . . . $5 un, I

Brooks Robinson

166 Eddie Mathews. . . . . $10 un, $20
167 Warren Giles . . . . $20 un, I
168 Willie Mays . . . . $40 un, $60
169 Hack Wilson. . . . . $10 un, I
170 Al Kaline . . . . $15 un, $20
171 Chuck Klein. . . . . $10 un, I
172 Duke Snider . . . . $10 un, $25
173 Tom Yawkey . . . . $5 un, I
174 Rube Foster . . . . $5 un, I
175 Bob Gibson . . . . $10 un, $20
176 Johnny Mize. . . . . $15 un, $25
A. Abner Doubleday. . . . . $5 un, I
B. Stephen C. Clark . . . . $5 un, I
C. Paul S. Kerr . . . . $5 un, I
D. Edward W. Stack . . . . $5 un, $15

Seventh Series (1983, Brown)

177 Hank Aaron . . . . $15 un, $25
178 Happy Chandler . . . . $15 un, $35
179 Travis Jackson . . . . $10 un, $75
180 Frank Robinson . . . . $10 un, $25
181 Walter Alston. . . . . $20 un, $800
182 George Kell . . . . $10 un, $12
183 Juan Marichal. . . . . $10 un, $20
184 Brooks Robinson . . . . $10 un, $20

Eighth Series (1985, Green)

185 Luis Aparicio. . . . . $10 un, $20
186 Don Drysdale. . . . . $10 un, $30
187 Rick Ferrell . . . . $10 un, $30
188 Harmon Killebrew. . . . . $15 un, $25
189 Pee Wee Reese . . . . $15 un, $30
190 Lou Brock . . . . $10 un, $20
191 Enos Slaughter. . . . . $10 un, $20
192 Arky Vaughan. . . . .$5 un, I
193 Hoyt Wilhelm . . . . $10 un, $15

Ninth Series (1987, Blue)

194 Bobby Doerr . . . . $10 un, $15
195 Ernie Lombardi . . . .$5 un, I
196 Willie McCovey . . . . $5 un, $20
197 Ray Dandridge. . . . . $5 un, $20
198 Catfish Hunter. . . . . $10 un, $20
199 Billy Williams. . . . .$5 un, $10-$15
E. Perez-Steele Galleries

Tenth Series (1989, Red)

200 Willie Stargell . . . . $5 un, $15
201 Al Barlick. . . . .$5 un, $15
202 Johnny Bench. . . . . $5 un, $20-$25
203 Red Schoendienst. . . . . . . $5 un, $15-$20
204 Carl Yastrzemski . . . . $5 un, $30
F. George Bush/Edward D. Stack

Eleventh Series (1991)

205 Joe Morgan. . . . . $5 un, $15
206 Jim Palmer . . . . $5 un, $15-$20
207 Rod Carew . . . .$5 un, $25
208 Ferguson Jenkins . . . . $5 un, $10-$15
209 Tony Lazzeri . . . . $5 un, I
210 Gaylord Perry. . . . .$5 un, $15
211 Bill Veeck . . . . $5 un, I

Post 1991 releases

Steve Carlton. . . . . $5 un, $30
Phil Rizzuto. . . . . $15 un, $35

Perez-Steele Great Moments Checklist

In 1985, Perez-Steele Galleries offered 5,000 numbered sets of Great Moments postcards, with periodical updates. These cards are generally purchased for the autograph, or to be autographed; the prices listed are for signed postcards. "I" means it's impossible that the player could have signed the card. Generally, unsigned cards sell for about $5-$15 each, except for higher priced cards for players such as Babe Ruth, Lou Gehrig, Ted Williams, Mickey Mantle, Stan Musial and Charlie Gehringer.

First Series (1985)

1 Babe Ruth . . . .$20 un, I
2 Al Kaline. $25
3 Jackie Robinson. I
4 Lou Gehrig . . . .$30 un, I
5 Whitey Ford. . . . .$20-$30
6 Christy Mathewson. I
7 Roy Campanella . . . . $12 un, $200
8 Walter Johnson I
9 Hank Aaron. $30-$35
10 Cy Young I
11 Stan Musial $75
12 Ty Cobb. . . . .$20 un, I

Second Series (1987)

13 Ted Williams. . . . . $100-$135
14 Warren Spahn $20
15 The Waner Brothers I
16 Sandy Koufax . . . .$35-$60
17 Robin Roberts . . . .$12-$15
18 Dizzy Dean I
19 Mickey Mantle . . . . $150-$250
20 Satchel Paige. I

CATFISH HUNTER

21 Ernie Banks . . . . $25-$35
22 Willie McCovey $25
23 Johnny Mize $20
24 Honus Wagner I

Third Series (1988)

25 Willie Keeler I
26 Pee Wee Reese $35
27 Monte Irvin . . . . $12-$15
28 Eddie Mathews . . . . $10-$20
29 Enos Slaughter $20
30 Rube Marquard I
31 Charlie Gehringer . . . . $30-$40
32 Roberto Clemente I
33 Duke Snider $25
34 Ray Dandridge $20
35 Carl Hubbell . . . . $35-$50
36 Bobby Doerr . . . . $10-$15

Fourth Series (1988)

37 Bill Dickey . . . . $55-$60
38 Willie Stargell . . . . $10-$15
39 Brooks Robinson . . . . $10-$15
40 Tinker-Evers-Chance I
41 Billy Herman $20
42 Grover Alexander I
43 Luis Aparicio . . . . $10-$20
44 Lefty Gomez . . . . $40-$50
45 Eddie Collins I
46 Judy Johnson I
47 Harry Heilmann I
48 Harmon Killebrew $25

Fifth Series (1990)

49 Johnny Bench $30
50 Max Carey I
51 Cool Papa Bell $80
52 Rube Waddell I
53 Yogi Berra . . . . $15-$25
54 Herb Pennock I
55 Red Schoendienst . . . . $10-$20
56 Juan Marichal . . . . $10-$20
57 Frankie Frisch I
58 Buck Leonard . . . . $15-$25
59 George Kell . . . . $10-$15
60 Chuck Klein I

Sixth Series (1990)

61 King Kelly I
62 Jim Hunter . . . . $10-$15
63 Lou Boudreau . . . . $10-$20
64 Al Lopez . . . . $60-$70
65 Willie Mays $30
66 Lou Brock $20
67 Bob Lemon . . . . $10-$20

68 Joe Sewell, Improbable $50
69 Billy Williams . . . . $10-$15
70 Rick Ferrell . . . . $15-$20
71 Arky Vaughan I
72 Carl Yastrzemski . . . . $15-$30

Seventh Series (1991)

73 Tom Seaver $35
74 Rollie Fingers $20
75 Ralph Kiner $20
76 Frank Baker I
77 Rod Carew $25
78 Goose Goslin I
79 Gaylord Perry $15
80 Hack Wilson I
81 Hal Newhouser $15
82 Early Wynn $20
83 Bob Feller $20
84 Branch Rickey I

Eighth Series (1992)

85 Jim Palmer $25
86 Al Barlick $15
87 Willie, Mickey & Duke $150
88 Hank Greenberg I
89 Joe Morgan $20
90 Chief Bender I
91 Reese, Robinson I
92 Jim Bottomley I
93 Ferguson Jenkins $15
94 Frank Robinson $25
95 Hoyt Wilhelm $15
96 Cap Anson I

Perez-Steele Celebration checklist

This 45-card set was issued in 1989 to commemorate the 50th anniversary of the Baseball Hall of Fame and the Galleries' 10th anniversary. There were 10,000 sets made. The set will not be updated; a complete set has 44 Hall of Famers and one checklist. Cards are 3 1/2-by-5 1/4 inches in size. The prices below are for signed cards. "I" means it is impossible that the player could have signed the card. Unsigned cards are generally about $8-$10 each, but are generally more for players such as Mickey Mantle, Stan Musial and Ted Williams.

1 Hank Aaron . . . . $22-$25
2 Luis Aparicio. $20
3 Ernie Banks . . . . $20-$35
4 Cool Papa Bell. . . . . $35-$50
5 Johnny Bench . . . . $15-$30
6 Yogi Berra. . . . . $15-$20
7 Lou Boudreau . . . . $10-$15
8 Roy Campanella $200
9 Happy Chandler. $25
10 Jocko Conlan. . . . . $150-$500
11 Ray Dandridge. . . . . $15-$20
12 Bill Dickey . . . . $45-$50
13 Bobby Doerr . . . . $10-$15
14 Rick Ferrell . . . . $15-$20
15 Charlie Gehringer . . . . $25-$40
16 Lefty Gomez I
17 Billy Herman. . . . . $10-$15
18 Catfish Hunter. . . . . $10-$15
19 Monte Irvin . . . . $10-$15
20 Judy Johnson. I
21 Al Kaline. $20
22 George Kell. . . . . $10-$15
23 Harmon Killebrew. . . . . $10-$20
24 Ralph Kiner. . . . . $10-$20
25 Bob Lemon . . . . $10-$20
26 Buck Leonard . . . . $15-$25
27 Al Lopez . . . . $45-$70
28 Mickey Mantle . . . . $125-$250
29 Juan Marichal . . . . $10-$15
30 Eddie Mathews . . . . $10-$15
31 Willie McCovey . . . . $10-$20
32 Johnny Mize . . . . $15-$20
33 Stan Musial . . . . $30-$50
34 Pee Wee Reese . . . . $15-$35
35 Brooks Robinson. . . . . $10-$15
36 Joe Sewell . . . . $25-$40
37 Enos Slaughter. . . . . $10-$20

Collectors usually pursue Perez-Steele Celebration cards to have the players autogragh them.

38 Duke Snider . . . . $10-$25
39 Warren Spahn. . . . . $10-$20
40 Willie Stargell . . . . $10-$15
41 Bill Terry I
42 Billy Williams . . . . $10-$15
43 Ted Williams . . . . $80-$175
44 Carl Yastrzemski . . . . $15-$25

Perez-Steele Master Works checklist

This 50-card set was produced in two 25-card series beginning in 1990 and features 10 players on five different postcard styles. The players are Charlie Gehringer, Mickey Mantle, Willie Mays, Duke Snider, Warren Spahn, Yogi Berra, Johnny Mize, Willie Stargell, Ted Williams and Carl Yastrzemski. Four designs are modeled after the the 1888 Goodwin Champions baseball card set, the 1908 Rose cards, the Ramly 1909 set, and the 1911 gold-bordered T205 set. The last design was created by the artist, Dick Perez. There were 10,000 sets produced. Prices are for individual cards.

Charlie Gehringer
($6 unsigned, $50 signed)
1 Ramly
2 Goodwin
3 Rose
4 Gold Border
5 Perez-Steele

Mickey Mantle
($20 unsigned, $150 signed)
6 Ramly
7 Goodwin
8 Rose
9 Gold Border
10 Perez-Steele

Willie Mays
($7 unsigned, $35 signed)
11 Ramly
12 Goodwin
13 Rose
14 Gold Border
15 Perez-Steele

Duke Snider
($6 unsigned, $20 signed)
16 Ramly
17 Goodwin
18 Rose
19 Gold Border
20 Perez-Steele

Warren Spahn
($6 unsigned, $20 signed)
21 Ramly
22 Goodwin
23 Rose
24 Gold Border
25 Perez-Steele

Yogi Berra
($7 unsigned, $25 signed)
26 Ramly
27 Goodwin
28 Rose
29 Gold Border
30 Perez-Steele

Johnny Mize
($6 unsigned, $35 signed)
31 Ramly
32 Goodwin
33 Rose
34 Gold Border
35 Perez-Steele

Willie Stargell
($6 unsigned, $20 signed)
36 Ramly
37 Goodwin
38 Rose
39 Gold Border
40 Perez-Steele

Ted Williams
($20 unsigned, $125 signed)
41 Ramly
42 Goodwin
43 Rose
44 Gold Border
45 Perez-Steele

Carl Yastrzemski
($10 unsigned, $30 signed)
46 Ramly
47 Goodwin
48 Rose
49 Gold Border
50 Perez-Steele

Postcards

1955-60 Bill and Bob
Milwaukee Braves postcards

Nolan Ryan

One of the most popular and scarce of the 1950s color postcard series is the run of Milwaukee Braves postcards known as "Bill and Bob's." While some of the 20 cards do carry a photo credit acknowledging the pair, and a few add a Bradenton, Fla. (spring training home of the Braves), address, little else is known about the issuer. The cards themselves appear to have been purchased by the players to honor photo and autograph requests. Several of the cards carry facsimile autographs pre-printed on the front. The cards feature crisp full-color photos on their borderless fronts. Postcard backs have a variety of printing including card numbers, photo credits, a Kodachrome logo and a player name. Some cards are found with some of those elements, some with none. There is some question whether the Frank Torre card is actually a Bill and Bob product because it is 1 1/16" narrower than the standard 3 1/2" by 5 1/2" format of the other cards, features the player with a Pepsi bottle in his hand and is rubber-stamped on the back with a Pepsi bottler's address. The Torre card is usually collected along with the rest of the set, which is worth $1,450 in Near Mint condition.

The players in the set are: Hank Aaron ($475), Joe Adcock ($70, fielding), Adcock ($60, bat on shoulder), Adcock ($60, kneeling), Billy Bruton ($70, kneeling), Bruton ($90, throwing), Bob Buhl ($35), Lou Burdette ($35), Gene Conley ($35), Wes Covington ($60, with one bat), Covington ($60, with seven bats), Del Crandall ($35, with one bat), Crandall ($35, with two bats), Chuck Dressen ($55), Charlie Grimm ($90), Fred Haney ($55), Bob Keely ($70), Eddie Mathews ($175), Warren Spahn ($150), and Frank Torre ($90).

1994 Capital Cards
1969 New York Mets postcards

Capital Cards produced a 32-card postcard set of members of the 1969 World Champion New York Mets from Ron Lewis paintings, limited to 25,000 sets. Capital Cards also produced 5,000 uncut sheets that are individually numbered and carried a suggested retail price of $99.95. The boxed postcard set retailed for $39.95. The cards could also be purchased with autographs. A complete set of 32 is worth $20 in Mint condition; individual cards are worth .50, unless noted.

The players in the set are: 1. Logo card, 2. Gil Hodges ($2.50), 3. Rube Walker, 4. Yogi Berra ($3), 5. Joe Pignatano, 6. Ed Yost, 7. Tommie Agee, 8. Ken Boswell, 9. Don Cardwell, 10. Ed Charles, 11. Donn Clendenon, 12. Jack DiLauro, 13. Duffy Dyer, 14. Wayne Garrett, 15. Rod Gaspar, 16. Gary Gentry, 17. Jerry Grote, 18. Bud Harrelson (.75), 19. Cleon Jones (.75), 20. Cal Koonce, 21. Jerry Koosman (.90), 22. Ed Kranepool (.75), 23. J.C. Martin, 24. Jim McAndrew, 25. Tug McGraw (.75), 26. Bob Pfeil, 27. Nolan Ryan ($6), 28. Tom Seaver ($3), 29. Art Shamsky, 30. Ron Swoboda (.75), 31. Ron Taylor and 32. Al Weis.

1932 Charles Denby Cigars
Chicago Cubs postcards

Actually a series of postcards, this Chicago Cubs set issued by the Charles Denby Co. in 1932 is the last known tobacco issue produced before World War II. The cards are a standard postcard size (5 1/4" by 3 3/8") and feature a glossy black-and-white player photo with a facsimile autograph. In typical postcard style, the back of the card is divided in half, with a printed player profile on the left and room for the mailing address on the right. The back also includes an advertisement for Charles Denby cigars, the mild five-cent cigar "for men who like to inhale." Only five different subjects have been reported to date, but there is speculation that more probably exist. A complete set of five is worth $500 in Near Mint condition. The players are: Elwood English ($80), Charles J. Grimm ($110), William Herman ($175), William F. Jurges ($80) and Lonnie Warneke ($80).

338

1907 Dietsche
Chicago Cubs postcards

1907-09 Dietsche
Detroit Tigers postcards

Three apparent annual issues (1907-09) of the home team by Detroit postcard publisher A.C. Dietsche, these 3 1/2" by 5 1/2" black-and-white postcards have most of the photographic background on the front blacked out. On the back, along with the postcard legalities, are a short player biography and a dated copyright line. The postcards were reportedly sold in sets for 25 cents. A complete set of 35 postcards sells for $5,500 in Near Mint condition; individual cards are worth $75, or $90 for those issued from 1908-09, unless noted.

The players in the set are: 1907 - 1a. Ty Cobb, batting ($750), 1b. Cobb, fielding ($1,100), 2. William Coughlin, 3. Sam Crawford ($125), 4. Bill Donovan, 5. Jerome Downs, 6. Hughie Jennings ($125), 7. David Jones, 8. Ed Killian, 9. George Mullin, 10. Charles O'Leary, 11. Fred Payne, 12. Claude Rossman, 13. Germany Schaefer, 14. Schaefer and O'Leary ($90), 15. Charles Schmidt and 16. Ed Siever - 1908-09 - 1. Henry Beckendorf, 2. Donie Bush, 3. Ty Cobb ($900), 4. James Delahanty, 5. Bill Donovan, 6. Hughie Jennings ($125), 7. Tom Jones, 8. Matthew McIntyre, 9. George Moriarty, 10. Germany Schaefer, 11. Oscar Stanage, 12. Ed Summers, 13. Ira Thomas, 14. Edgar Willett, 15. George Winter, 16. Ralph Works and 17. Detroit Tigers team ($100).

1953-55 Dormand postcards

This series of early Cubs postcards was published by the same Detroit printer who issued Tigers postcards series from 1907-09. The Dietsche Cubs postcards are scarcer than the Tigers issues. The 3 1/2" by 5 1/2" black-and-white cards have most of the photographic background blacked out on the front. The player's name may or may not appear on the front. Postcard-style backs include a short career summary and a dated copyright line. A complete set of 15 postcards is worth $1,200 in Near Mint condition. Individual cards are worth $100, unless noted. The players are: Mordecai Brown ($125), Frank Chance ($150), John Evers ($150), Arthur Hoffman, John Kling, Carl Lundgren, Pat Moran, Orvie Overall, John Pfeister, Ed Ruelbach, Frank Schulte, Jimmy Sheckard, James Slagle, Harry Steinfeldt and Joseph Tinker ($150).

This mid-1950s issue features only selected players from the New York Yankees, Brooklyn Dodgers, Chicago White Sox and Philadelphia A's. Apparently produced on order by the players by Louis Dormand, a Long Island, N.Y., photographer, the cards were used to honor fan requests for photos and autographs. All of the cards have a facsimile autograph printed on the front. Otherwise, the fronts of these standard-size 3 1/2" by 5 1/2" postcards feature only sharp color photos with no border. Backs, printed in blue or green, feature a few biographical or career details, one or two lines identifying the producer and usually a product and series number. Most have a Kodachrome logo. Some cards do not have all of these elements and several are found blank-backed. The Gil Hodges card is considerably scarcer than the others in the set, with those of Jim Konstanty, Elston Howard and Casey Stengel also seldom seen. There are also oversized versions for Phil Rizzuto and Mickey Mantle. A variation of Johnny Sain's card shows his Arkansas Chevrolet dealership in a photo above the player's picture. The complete set of cards, without the oversized cards included, is worth $2,500 in Near Mint condition. Individual cards are worth $25, unless noted.

The players are: Hank Bauer ($30), Yogi Berra ($60), Don Bollweg, Roy Campanella ($150), Chico Carrasquel, Jerry Coleman, Joe Collins ($30, patch on sleeve), Collins ($25, no patch), Frank Crosetti ($40), Carl Erskine ($50), Whitey Ford ($50), Carl Furillo ($60), Tom Gorman, Gil Hodges ($400), Ralph Houk, Elston Howard ($125), Jim Konstanty ($125), Ed Lopat, Mickey Mantle ($200, bat on shoulder), Mantle ($100, batting), Mantle ($250, 6" by 9"), Billy Martin ($45), Jim McDonald, Gil McDougald ($30, large autograph), McDougald ($45, small autograph), Bob Miller, Willie Miranda, Johnny Mize ($75), Irv Noren, Billy Pierce ($35), Pee Wee Reese ($60), Allie Reynolds ($45), Phil Rizzuto ($45, autograph parallel), Rizzuto ($45, autograph angles), Rizzuto ($150, 9" by 12"), Ed Robinson ($40), Johnny Sain ($35, beginning windup), Sain ($30, leg kick), Sain ($75, auto dealership), Ray Scarborough, Bobby Shantz ($35), Charlie Silvera, Bill Skowron ($45), Enos Slaughter ($75), Casey Stengel ($150), and Gene Woodling ($30).

1962 Ford
Detroit Tigers postcards

Because baseball card collectors have to compete with auto memorabilia hobbyists for these scarce cards, they are among the most valuable postcard issues of the early 1960s. In standard 3 1/2" by 5 1/2" postcard format, the full-color cards feature photos taken on a golf course with the players posed in front of various new Fords. White backs have a name, position and team, with a box for a stamp. Probably given out in conjunction with autograph appearances at car dealerships (they are frequently found autographed), the set lacks some of the team's biggest stars (Al Kaline, Norm Cash) but includes coaches and even team trainer Jack Homel. Probably because of lack of demand, the coaches' and trainer's cards are the scarcest to find today. A complete set of 16 postcards is worth $950 in Near Mint condition; individual postcards are worth $60, unless noted. The players in the set are: Hank Aguirre, Steve Boros ($80), Dick Brown, Phil Cavaretta ($90), Rocky Colavito ($125), Jim Bunning ($95), Terry Fox, Purn Goldy, Jack Homel ($90), Ron Kline, Don Mossi, George Myatt ($80), Ron Nischwitz, Larry Osborne, Mike Roarke ($90) and Phil Regan.

1991 Ron Lewis
Negro Leagues postcards

The 1991 Negro League Living Legends postcard set features paintings by artist Ron Lewis. Cards measure 3 1/2" by 5 1/2" and are stamped with a number within the 10,000 sets produced. In between the player's image and his name at the bottom of the card is ample space for an autograph. The 30-card set was created as a fund raiser for the Negro League Baseball Players Association. It is worth $25 in Mint condition; individual cards are .50, unless noted. The players

Willie Mays

in the set are: 1. George Giles, 2. Bill Cash, 3. Bob Harvey, 4. Lyman Bostock Sr. (.75), 5. Ray Dandridge ($2), 6. Leon Day ($1.50), 7. Verdell "Lefty" Mathis, 8. Jimmie Crutchfield (.75), 9. Clyde McNeal, 10. Bill Wright, 11. Mahlon Duckett, 12. William "Bobby" Robinson, 13. Max Manning, 14. Armando Vazquez, 15. Jehosie Heard (.75), 16. Quincy Trouppe (.75), 17. Wilmer Fields, 18. Lonnie Blair, 19. Garnett Blair, 20. Monte Irvin ($2), 21. Willie Mays ($6), 22. Buck Leonard ($4), 23. Frank Evans, 24. Josh Gibson Jr. ($4), 25. Ted "Double Duty" Radcliffe ($1), 26. Josh Johnson, 27. Gene Benson, 28. Lester Lockett, 29. Cowan "Bubba" Hyde and 30. Rufus Lewis.

1994 Ron Lewis
Negro League postcards

BUCK O'NEIL

A second series of postcards honoring players of the Negro Leagues was produced by artist Ron Lewis in September 1994. In this set, more emphasis was placed on multi-player cards. Many of the cards also feature detailed backgrounds of street scenes with vintage vehicles, old-time stadiums, etc. Cards measure 3 1/2" by 5 1/2" and have a wide front border with the player(s) name printed at the bottom and space above for autographing. Postcard backs are printed in black and include a few career stats, a card number and the card's position among the limited edition of 10,000. A complete set of 32 cards is worth $25 in Mint condition; individual cards are worth $1, unless noted.

The players in the set are: 1. Willie Ways, Ernie Banks, Hank Aaron ($4), 2. Bill Wright, Lester Lockett, Lyman Bostock Sr., 3. Josh Gibson, Josh Gibson Jr., Buck Leonard ($2.50), 4. Max Manning, Monte Irvin, Leon Day ($1.50), 5. Armando Vazquez, Minnie Minoso, Martin DiHigo ($1.50), 6. Ted "Double Duty" Radcliffe ($1.50), 7. Bill Owens, Turkey Stearnes, Bobby Robinson, 8. Wilmer Fields, Edsall Walker,

Josh Johnson, 9. Artie Wilson, Lionel Hampton ($1.50), 10. Earl Taborn, 11. Barney "Bonnie" Serrell, 12. Rodolfo "Rudy" Fernandez, 13. Willie Pope, 14. Ray Noble, 15. Jim "Fireball" Cohen, 16. Henry Kimbro, 17. Charlie Biot, 18. Al Wilmore, 19. Sam Jethroe ($1.50), 20. Tommy Sampson, 21. Charlie Rivera, 22. Claro Duany, 23. Russell Awkard, 24. Art "Superman" Pennington, 25. Wilmer Harris, 26. Napolean "Nap" Gulley, 27. Emilio Navarro, 28. Andy Porter, 29. Willie Grace, 30. Red Moore, 31. Buck O'Neill ($2) and 32. Stanley Glenn.

1980 Minnesota Twins postcards

One of the scarcest in a long line of Twins team issues, this postcard set features the photos of Barry Fritz, whose initials appear on the back. Card fronts feature borderless color photos, with or without a black facsimile autograph overprinted (cards without autographs are worth twice the values quoted here). Backs of the 3 1/2" by 5 1/2" cards have a ghost-image team logo at left, above which is the player name and a few biographical details. The cards are unnumbered. A complete set of 33 is worth $60 in Near Mint condition; common players are worth $2.25, unless noted.

The players in the set are: Glenn Adams, Sal Butera, John Castino, Doug Corbett, Mike Cubbage, Dave Edwards, Roger Erickson, Terry Felton, Danny Goodwin, John Goryl, Darrell Jackson, Ron Jackson, Harmon Killebrew ($12), Jerry Koosman ($4), Karl Kuehl, Ken Landreaux, Pete Mackanin, Mike Marshall, Gene Mauch, Jose Morales, Willie Norwood, Camilo Pascual, Hosken Powell, Bobby Randall, Pete Redfern, Bombo Rivera, Roy Smalley, Rick Sofield, John Verhoeven, Rob Wilfong, Butch Wynegar, Geoff Zahn and Jerry Zimmerman.

1981 Minnesota Twins postcards

The photography of Barry Fritz is again featured on the Twins' 1981 color postcard issue. Players are posed on front of the borderless, 3 1/2" by 5 1/2" cards. A black facsimile autograph appears on the front, as well. A few biographical details appear on the back. The cards are unnumbered. A complete set of 34 is worth $15 in Mint condition; individual players are worth .50. The players in the set are: Glenn Adams, Fernando Arroyo, Chuck Baker, Sal Butera, John Castino, Don Cooper, Doug Corbett, Dave Engle, Roger Erickson, Billy Gardner, Danny Goodwin, Johnny Goryl, Mickey Hatcher, Darrell Jackson, Ron Jackson, Greg Johnston, Jerry Koosman, Karl Kuehl, Pete Mackanin, Jack O'Connor, Johnny Podres, Hosken Powell, Pete Redfern, Roy Smalley, Ray Smith, Rick Sofield, Rick Stelmaszek, John Verhoeven, Gary Ward, Rob Wilfong, Al Williams, Butch Wynegar and Metropolitan Stadium.

1985 New York Mets postcards - Wally Backman, Billy Beane, Bruce Berenyi, John Bettendorf, Jeff Bittiger, Terry Blocker, Gary Carter, Kevin Chapman, John Christensen, Ron Darling, Len Dykstra, Sid Fernandez, George Foster, Brent Gaff, Ron Gardenhire, Wes Gardner, John Gibbons, Dwight Gooden, Tom Gorman, Danny Heep, Keith Hernandez, Vern Hoscheit, Clint Hurdle, Davey Johnson, Howard Johnson, Ray Knight, Ed Lynch, Roger McDowell, Kevin Mitchell, Jesse Orosco, Bill Robinson, Ronn Reynolds, Rafael Santana, Calvin Schiraldi, Doug Sisk, Mel Stottlemyre, Darryl Strawberry, Laschelle Tarver, Bobby Valentine and Mookie Wilson.

1987 New York Mets postcards - Rick Anderson, Wally Backman, Jose Bautista, Terry Blocker, Bob Buchanan, Tom Burns, Mark Carreon, Gary Carter, Charlie Corbell, Reggie Dobie, Len Dykstra, Kevin Elster, Sid Fernandez, John Gibbons, Brian Givens, Dwight Gooden, Bud Harrelson, Keith Hernandez, Vern Hoscheit, Clint Hurdle, Davey Johnson, Howard Johnson, Arthur Jones, Ralph Kiner, Marcus Lawton, Terry Leach, Barry Lyons, Dave Magadan, Lee Mazzilli, Tim McCarthy, Roger McDowell, Kevin McReynolds, Keith Miller, John Mitchell, Bob Murphy, Randy Myers, Bob Ojeda, Greg Olson, Jesse Orosco, Al Pedrique, Sam Perlozzo, Bill Robinson, Zoilo Sanchez, Rafael Santana, Doug Sisk, Arthur Smith, Mel Stottlemyre, Darryl Strawberry, Gary Thorne, Tim Teufel, Gene Walter, Dave West, Mookie Wilson and team photo.

1951-59 Photo-Film Fotos
Pittsburgh Pirates postcards

This series of black-and-white postcards was issued over a period which seems to have spanned virtually the entire decade of the 1950s. In standard 3 1/2" by 5 1/2" size, the cards have minor variations in size and styles of type used for the player typography on the backs. Some cards are seen with pre-printed autographs on the front. Most of the cards have printing on the back which includes versions of "Genuine Photo-Film Fotos, Inc., New York, N.Y., U.S.A." and "Souvenir of Forbes Field Home of the Pittsburgh Pirates." The checklist here, arranged alphabetically, indicates by the use of "a, b, c" and "d" suffixes for different known poses for that particular player. Future additions to the checklist are likely, so no complete set price is given. Individual players are worth $15, unless noted.

The players in the set include: Gair Allie, Toby Atwell, Tony Bartirome, Ron Blackburn, Don Carlsen, Pete Castiglione (a), Castiglione (b), Cliff Chambers, Dick Cole, Dale Coogan, Bobby Del Greco, Roy Face (a, $20), Face (b, $20), Face (c, $20), Hank Foiles, Gene Freese, Bob Friend (a, $17), Friend (b, $17), Friend (c $17), Dick Groat ($20), Fred Haney, Ralph Kiner ($50), Ron Kline (a), Kline (b), Clem

Koshorek, Vern Law (a, $17), Law (b, $17), Law (c, $17), Law (d, $17), Dale Long (a), Long (b), Jerry Lynch (a), Lynch (b), Bill MacDonald, Bill Mazeroski (a, $30), Mazeroski (b, $30), Danny Murtaugh, Johnny O'Brien, Bob Oldis, Laurin Pepper, Hardy Peterson, Jack Phillips, Buddy Pritchard, Bob Purkey, Dino Restelli, Bob Smith, Red Swanson, Frank J. Thomas (a, $17), Thomas (b, $17), Thomas (c, $17), Bill Virdon, Lee Walls (a), Walls (b), Junior Walsh, Pete Ward, Fred Waters, Bill Werle and Wally Westlake.

1983 San Francisco Giants postcards - Jim Barr, Dave Bergman, Fred Breining, Bob Brenly, Mark Calvert, Mike Chris, Jack Clark, Chili Davis, Darrell Evans, Atlee Hammaker, Mike Krukow, Duane Kuiper, Bill Laskey, Gary Lavelle, Johnnie LeMaster, Jeff Leonard, Renie Martin, Milt May, Andy McGaffigan, Greg Minton, Tom O'Malley, Joe Pettini, Frank Robinson, Champ Summers, Max Venable, Joel Youngblood, coaches (Don Buford) and coaches (Tom McCraw, Danny Ozark, Herm Starrette, John Van Ornum).

1987 San Franciso Giants postcards - Mike Aldrete, Randy Bockus, Bob Brenly, Chris Brown, Will Clark, Keith Comstock, Roger Craig, Chili Davis, Mark Davis, Kelly Downs, Bill Fahey, Scott Garrelts, Jim Gott, Atlee Hammaker, Mike Krukow, Mike LaCoss, Jeffrey Leonard, Bob Lillis, Gordy MacKenzie, Candy Maldonado, Willie Mays, Willie McCovey, Bob Melvin, Eddie Milner, Jose Morales, Jon Perlman, Jeff Robinson, Norm Sherry, Chris Speier, Harry Spilman, Robby Thompson, Jose Uribe, Mark Wasinger, Joel Youngblood and Don Zimmer.

1985 Seattle Mariners postcards - Salome Barojas, Jim Beattie, Karl Best, Barry Bonnell, Phil Bradley, Ivan Calderon, Al Chambers, Chuck Cottier, Al Cowens, Dave Henderson, Deron Johnson, Jim Mahoney, Marty Martinez, Mike Morgan, John Moses, Edwin Nunez, Jack Perconte, Ken Phelps, Jim Presley, Domingo Ramos, Phil Regan, Harold Reynolds, Phil Roof, Donnie Scott, Gorman Thomas, Ed Vande Berg and Matt Young.

1978 team postcard sets

Atlanta Braves - Brian Asselstine, Bob Beall, Tommy Boggs, Barry Bonnell, Cloyd Boyer, Tom Burgess, Jeff Burroughs, Rick Camp, Dave Campbell, Chris Cannizzaro, Darrel Chaney, Bobby Cox, Adrian Devine, Jamie Easterly, Gene Garber, Cito Gaston, Preston Hanna, Bob Horner, Glenn Hubbard, Max Leon, Mickey Mahler, Gary Matthews, Larry McWilliams, Phil Niekro, Tom Paciorek, Biff Pocoroba, Pat Rockett, Dick Ruthven, Buddy Jay Solomon and Ted Turner.

Baltimore Orioles - Mark Belanger, Nelson Briles, Al Bumbry, Terry Crowley, Rich Dauer, Doug DeCinces, Rick Dempsey, Mike Flanagan, Jim Frey, Kiko Garcia, Larry Harlow, Ellie Hendricks, Pat Kelly, Joe Kerrigan, Carlos Lopez, Dennis Martinez, Tippy Martinez, Lee May, Scott McGregor, Ray Miller, Andres Mora, Eddie Murray, Jim Palmer, Cal Ripken, Brooks Robinson, Frank Robinson, Gary Roenicke, Ken Singleton, Dave Skaggs, Billy Smith, Don Stanhouse, Earl Stephenson, Tim Stoddard and Earl Weaver.

Detroit Tigers - Tiger Stadium, Fernando Arroyo, Steve Baker, Jack Billingham, Gates Brown, Tim Corcoran, Jim Crawford, Steve Dillard, Mark Fidrych, Steve Foucault, Fred Gladding, Fred Hatfield, Jim Hegan, John Hiller, Ralph Houk, Steve Kemp, Ron LeFlore, Phil Mankowski, Milt May, Jack Morris, Lance Parrish, Aurelio Rodriguez, Dave Rozema, Jim Slaton, Charlie Spikes, Mickey Stanley, Rusty Staub, Bob Sykes, Bruce Taylor, Jason Thompson, Dick Tracewski, Alan Trammell, Mark Wagner, Lou Whitaker, Milt Wilcox and John Wockenfuss.

Houston Astros - Jesus Alou, Joaquin Andujar, Floyd Bannister, Dave Bergman, Enos Cabell, Cesar Cedeno, Jose Cruz, Tom Dixon, Ken Forsch, Julio Gonzalez, Wilbur Howard, Art Howe, Deacon Jones, Rafael Landestoy, Mark Lemongello, Bob Lillis, Bo McLaughlin, Joe Niekro, Tony Pacheco, Gene Pentz, Terry Puhl, Luis Pujols, J.R. Richard, Joe Sambito, Jimmy Sexton, Bill Virdon, Dennis Walling, Bob Watson, Rick Williams and Mel Wright.

Minnesota Twins - Glenn Adams, Glenn Borgmann, Rod Carew, Rich Chiles, Mike Cubbage, Roger Erickson, Dan Ford, Dave Goltz, Dave Johnson, Tom Johnson, Craig Kusick, Jose Morales, Willie Norwood, Hosken Powell, Bob Randall, Pete Redfern, Bombo Rivera, Gary Serum, Roy Smalley, Greg Thayer, Paul Thormodsgard, Rob Wilfong, Larry Wolfe, Butch Wynegar and Geoff Zahn.

San Francisco Giants - Joe Altobelli, Rob Andrews, Jim Barr, Vida Blue, Jack Clark, John Curtis, Darrell Evans, Ed Halicki, Vic Harris, Tom Heintzelman, Larry Herndon, Marc Hill, Mike Ivie, Skip James, Bob Knepper, Gary Lavelle, Johnnie LeMaster, Bill Madlock, Willie McCovey, Lynn McGlothen, Randy Moffitt, John Montefusco, Mike Sadek, Terry Whitfield and Charlie Williams.

St. Louis Cardinals - Ken Boyer, Lou Brock, John Denny, Jim Dwyer, Pete Falcone, Bob Forsch, Maurice Mozzali, Jerry Mumphrey, Claude Osteen, Mike Phillips, Vern Rapp, Eric Rasmussen, Ken Reitz, Dave Ricketts, Sonny Ruberto, Buddy Schultz, Tony Scott, Ted Simmons, Gary Sutherland, Steve Swisher, Garry Templeton, Mike Tyson, John Urrea and Pete Vuckovich.

Toronto Blue Jays - Alan Ashby, Doug Ault, Bob Bailor, Rick Bosetti, Rico Carty, Rick Cerone, Jim Clancy, Victor Cruz, Bobby Doerr, Sam Ewing, Jerry Garvin, Luis Gomez, Don Leppert, John Mayberry, Dave McKay, Bob Miller, Balor Moore, Jackie Moore, Tom Murphy, Tom Underwood, Willie Upshaw, Otto Velez, Harry Warner, Mike Willis and Al Woods.

Pins

Press Pins

Press pins, which have been issued since 1911, are distributed to members of the media by the host teams for World Series and All-Star games. The lapel pins provide the reporters legitimate access to cover the game.

Enamel pins have replaced the fairly ornate pins, with ribbons and medals, of the early years. Many are quite simple in their designs, which is a factor in the value of the pin; generally, the better-looking, better-conditioned pins are more valuable. Also, pins for the teams which lost usually cost less than those of the winners. But rarity and the reputation of the team are the main factors. Each team, except the 1918 Chicago Cubs, has issued a pin.

Phantom pins are those which are created by teams which might end up in post-season play, but don't, by failing to make the World Series; teams must decide to produce pins before the season is over. Several major league teams already have unused, undated pins available for future use.

All-Star pins first appeared in 1938, skipping 1939, 1940, 1942, 1944 and 1945, and then running consecutively since 1946. There are usually fewer All-Star pins available for collectors, because not as many have been made; fewer reporters cover this game compared to the number who cover the World Series.

Hall of Fame pins were first produced in 1982 by L.B. Balfour Co. to honor Hall of Fame inductees. Those players have their names featured on the pins, which are given to the media and dignitaries who attend the induction ceremonies.

The following pin listings show the year, the manufacturer, type of fastener, color and value.

In general, here's a price range for World Series pins for each decade:

1910s	$2,500-$18,000	1960s	$50-$300
1920s	$375-$4,000	1970s	$50-$375
1930s	$225-$5,000	1980s	$25-$175
1940s	$250-$2,400	1990s	$50-$150
1950s	$125-$500		

This 1928 pin, with its original card, is worth up to $2,400.

World Series

1911 **Philadelphia Athletics:** Allen A. Kerr; brooch; blue...$13,850-$18,000
1912 **New York Giants:** Whitehead & Hoag; brooch; blue ....$6,500-$12,500
1912 **Boston Red Sox:** Unknown; threaded post; red..$3,500-$5,000
1913 **New York Giants:** Whitehead & Hoag; threaded post; blue ....$5,000-$10,000
1913 **Philadelphia Athletics:** J.E. Caldwell; brooch; blue/green ....$6,000-$6,500
1914 **Boston Braves:** Bent & Bush; threaded post; blue..$5,000-$5,500
1914 **Philadelphia Athletics:** J.E. Caldwell; brooch; blue/white/green ....$6,500-$11,000
1915 **Philadelphia Phillies:** J.E. Caldwell; brooch; red..$6,000-$11,000
1915 **Boston Red Sox:** Bent & Bush; threaded post; gold...$4,000-$5,500
1916 **Brooklyn Dodgers:** Dieges & Clust; threaded post; blue/white..........................$4,000-$4,400
1916 **Boston Red Sox:** Bent & Bush; threaded post; red/blue..$4,000-$5,000
1917 **New York Giants:** Unknown; brooch; gold..$4,500-$7,000
1917 **Chicago White Sox, with banner:** Greenduck; threaded post; blue ....$4,000-$9,500
1918 **Boston Red Sox:** Bent & Bush; threaded post; gold...$3,000-$5,500
1919 **Cincinnati Reds:** Gustave Fox; threaded post; gold...$2,500-$4,750
1919 **Chicago White Sox, with banner:** Greenduck; threaded post; gold...................$5,000-$12,000
1920 **Brooklyn Dodgers:** Unknown; threaded post; red...$2,500-$3,000
1920 **Cleveland Indians enamel:** Unknown; threaded post; green/white.....................$1,500-$3,000
1920 **Cleveland Indians celluloid button:** Unknown; safety brooch; black/white ....$2,500-$3,500
1921 **New York Yankees/Giants:** Whitehead & Hoag; brooches; blue/white..............$2,000-$2,500
1922 **New York Yankees/Giants:** Whitehead & Hoag; brooches; blue/white..............$3,000-$4,000

This collection of World Series pins is from New York Yankees

1923 New York Yankees: Dieges & Clust; threaded post; red/white/blue .... $2,300-$3,800
1924 New York Giants: Dieges & Clust; threaded post; blue.. $845-$1,500
1924 Washington Senators: Dieges & Clust; threaded post; red/white/blue................ $1,000-$1,500
1925 Pittsburgh Pirates: Whitehead & Hoag; threaded post; black/white................... $1,500-$2,500
1925 Washington Senators: Dieges & Clust; threaded post; blue................................ $1,375-$2,000
1926 St. Louis Cardinals: Unknown; threaded post; red .... $1,300-$2,400
1926 New York Yankees: Dieges & Clust; threaded post; red/white/blue .... $1,200-$1,500
1927 Pittsburgh Pirates: Whitehead & Hoag; threaded post; black/white................... $1,100-$2,000
1927 New York Yankees: Dieges & Clust; threaded post; red/white/blue .... $2,000-$2,300
1928 St. Louis Cardinals: St. Louis Button; threaded post; red/white/blue .... $875-$1,200
1928 New York Yankees: Dieges & Clust; threaded post; red/white/blue .... $1,850-$2,400
1929 Chicago Cubs: Hipp & Coburn; threaded post; red/white/blue............................. $1,500-$2,350
1929 Philadelphia Athletics: Unknown; threaded post; blue/white...................................... $375-$800
1930 St. Louis Cardinals: St. Louis Button; threaded post; red/white/blue .... $500-$1,000
1930 Philadelphia Athletics: Unknown; threaded post; blue/white............................... $3,000-$5,000
1931 St. Louis Cardinals: St.Louis Button; threaded post; red/white/blue .... $650-$900
1931 Philadelphia Athletics: Unknown; threaded post; blue/white................................ $1,300-$1,500
1932 Chicago Cubs: Dieges & Clust; threaded post; black/white................................. $1,900-$2,200
1932 New York Yankees: Dieges & Clust; threaded post; gold .... $1,000-$1,200
1933 New York Giants: Dieges & Clust; threaded post; red/green/blue .... $235-$700
1933 Washington Senators: Dieges & Clust; threaded post; gold .... $700-$950
1934 St. Louis Cardinals: St. Louis Button; threaded post; red/white .... $650-$800
1934 Detroit Tigers: Dieges & Clust; threaded post; black/white .... $600-$750

World Series Pins

1912 Red Sox
$3,500-$5,000

1930 Cardinals
$500-$1,000

1936 Yankees
$550-$800

1935 Chicago Cubs: S.D. Childs; brooch; red/white/blue .... $2,200-$3,000
1935 Detroit Tigers: Unknown; threaded post; black .... $600-$800
1936 New York Giants: Dieges & Clust; threaded post; black/white/orange .... $275-$400
1936 New York Yankees: Dieges & Clust; threaded post; red/white/blue .... $550-$800
1937 New York Giants: Dieges & Clust; threaded post; black/orange .... $225-$350
1937 New York Yankees: Dieges & Clust; threaded post; red/white/blue .... $450-$600
1938 Chicago Cubs: Lambert Bros.; brooch; red/white/blue .... $1,400-$2,250
1938 New York Yankees: Dieges & Clust; threaded post; red/white/blue .... $475-$750
1939 Cincinnati Reds: Bastian Bros.; threaded post, brooch; red/white/blue .... $275-$425
1939 New York Yankees: Dieges & Clust; threaded post; red/white/blue .... $400-$750
1940 Cincinnati Reds: Bastian Bros.; threaded post, brooch; red/white/blue .... $425-$475
1940 Detroit Tigers: Unknown; threaded post; gold .... $475-$650
1941 Brooklyn Dodgers: Dieges & Clust; threaded post; red/white/blue .... $450-$725
1941 New York Yankees: Dieges & Clust; threaded post; red/white/blue .... $275-$475
1942 St. Louis Cardinals: St. Louis Button; safety brooch; red/white/black .... $2,000-$2,400
1942 New York Yankees: Dieges & Clust; threaded post, brooch; silver .... $275-$400
1943 St. Louis: St. Louis Button; safety brooch; red/black/white .... $1,000-$2,000
1943 New York Yankees: Dieges & Clust; threaded post, brooch; silver .... $300-$500
1944 St. Louis Cardinals: St. Louis Button; threaded post; copper .... $450-$575
1944 St. Louis Browns: St. Louis Button; threaded post; copper .... $500-$575
1945 Chicago Cubs: Unknown; threaded post; red/white/blue .... $400-$550
1945 Detroit Tigers: Unknown; threaded post; red/blue .... $425-$575
1946 St. Louis Cardinals: St. Louis Button; threaded post; red/white/silver .... $350-$500
1946 Boston Red Sox: Balfour; threaded post; red/white .... $300-$575
1947 Brooklyn Dodgers: Dieges & Clust; threaded post, brooch; blue .... $400-$800
1947 New York Yankees: Dieges & Clust; threaded post; red/white/blue .... $500-$600
1948 Boston Braves: Balfour; threaded post; red/white/copper .... $400-$475
1948 Cleveland Indians: Balfour; threaded post; red/white/black .... $250-$400
1949 Brooklyn Dodgers: Dieges & Clust; threaded post, brooch; blue .... $350-$400
1949 New York Yankees: Dieges & Clust; threaded post, brooch red/white/blue .. $300-$400
1950 Philadelphia Phillies: Martin; needle post; red/silver .... $250-$350
1950 New York Yankees: Dieges and Clust; threaded post, brooch red/white/blue.... $250-$375

World Series Pins

1937 Giants
$225-$350

1941 Yankees
$275-$475

1945 Cubs
$400-$550

1951 New York Giants: Dieges & Clust; threaded post; black/white .... $150-$175
1951 New York Yankees: Dieges & Clust; threaded post, brooch; red/white/blue .... $125-$175
1952 Brooklyn Dodgers: Dieges & Clust; threaded post, brooch; red/blue .... $300-$400
1952 New York Yankees: Balfour; threaded post, brooch; red/white/blue........................ $200-$300
1953 Brooklyn Dodgers: Dieges & Clust; threaded post, brooch; white/blue .... $275-$350
1953 New York Yankees: Balfour; threaded post and brooch; red/white/blue.................... $250-$325
1954 New York Giants: Dieges and Clust; threaded post; black/white .... $150-$200
1954 Cleveland Indians: Balfour; threaded post; red/white/blue/black............................. $250-$300
1955 Brooklyn Dodgers: Dieges & Clust; threaded post, brooch; silver/white/blue .... $400-$500
1955 New York Yankees: Balfour; threaded post, brooch; red/white/blue........................ $125-$275
1956 Brooklyn Dodgers: Dieges & Clust; clasps; silver/white/blue................................ $500-$750
1956 New York Yankees: Balfour; threaded post, brooch; red/white/blue........................ $200-$300
1957 Milwaukee Braves: Balfour; threaded post; copper/red.................................... $150-$200
1957 New York Yankees: Balfour; threaded post, brooch; red/white/blue........................ $150-$200
1958 Milwaukee Braves: Balfour; threaded post; black/white .... $200-$275
1958 New York Yankees: Balfour; threaded post, brooch white/blue .... $175-$200
1959 Los Angeles Dodgers: Balfour; threaded post, charm, brooch; white/blue .... $125-$250
1959 Chicago White Sox: Balfour; threaded post, brooch; blue/green .... $175-$275
1960 Pittsburgh Pirates: Josten; threaded post; black/white .... $175-$250
1960 New York Yankees: Balfour; threaded post, brooch white/blue .... $100-$150
1961 Cincinnati Reds: Balfour; threaded post, charm; red/white/blue .... $100-$175
1961 New York Yankees: Balfour; threaded post, brooch; red/white/blue........................ $125-$225
1962 San Francisco Giants: Balfour; threaded post; white .... $200-$275
1962 New York Yankees: Balfour; threaded post, brooch; red/white/blue........................ $100-$150
1963 Los Angeles Dodgers: Balfour; threaded post; blue .... $125-$150
1963 New York Yankees: Balfour; needle post, brooch; red/white/blue .... $100-$175
1964 St. Louis Cardinals: Josten; threaded post, brooch; red............................. $125-$200
1964 New York Yankees: Balfour; needle post; red/white/blue .... $175-$200
1965 Los Angeles Dodgers: Balfour; needle post, charm; blue .... $50-$150
1965 Minnesota Twins: Balfour; needle post; red/white/blue .... $50-$125
1966 Los Angeles Dodgers: Balfour; needle post, charm; blue .... $50-$150
1966 Baltimore Orioles: Balfour; needle post, clasp, charm, brooch; black/white/orange . $175-$200
1967 St. Louis Cardinals: Balfour; needle post, charms; red/white/black........................... $75-$100
1967 Boston Red Sox: Balfour; needle post, charm; red/white/blue .... $150-$200
1968 St. Louis Cardinals: Balfour; needle post, charms; red/white/black......................... $75-$125
1968 Detroit Tigers: Balfour; needle post, charms; blue .... $125-$200
1969 New York Mets: Balfour; needle post, charm; blue/orange .... $200-$300

World Series Pins

1947 Yankees
$775

1948 Indians $450

1952 Yankees $300

1969 Baltimore Orioles: Balfour; needle post, charms, clasp, brooch; black/white/orange $150-$200
1970 Cincinnati Reds: G.B. Miller; needle post, charms; red/white/black .... $125-$150
1970 Baltimore Orioles: Jenkins; needle post, clasp, charm, brooch; black/white/orange.. $100-$150
1971 Pittsburgh Pirates: Balfour; needle post; black .... $75-$150
1971 Baltimore Orioles: Balfour; needle post, clasp, brooch; black/white/orange .... $100-$150
1972 Cincinnati Reds: Balfour; needle post, charm; red/white .... $100-$150
1972 Oakland A's: Balfour; needle post, charm; green/white .... $125-$250
1973 New York Mets: Balfour; needle post, charm; orange/blue .... $125-$150
1973 Oakland A's: Josten; needle post, charms; green/white .... $200-$275
1974 Los Angeles Dodgers: Balfour; needle post, charms; blue .... $125-$150
1974 Oakland A's: Josten; needle post; green/white .... $300-$375
1975 Cincinnati Reds: Balfour; needle post, charms; red .... $100-$200
1975 Boston Red Sox: Balfour; needle post, charms; red/white .... $125-$200
1976 Cincinnati Reds: Balfour; needle post, charms; red .... $125-$175
1976 New York Yankees: Balfour; needle post; red/white/blue .... $125-$175
1977 Los Angeles Dodgers: Balfour; needle post, charms; red/white/blue.......................... $125-$150
1977 New York Yankees: Balfour; needle post, charms; blue.. $75-$125
1978 Los Angeles Dodgers: Balfour; needle post, charms; blue/white................................ $75-$100
1978 New York Yankees: Balfour; needle post, charms; red/white/blue .... $50-$125
1979 Pittsburgh Pirates: Balfour; needle post; gold.. $50-$125
1979 Baltimore Orioles: Balfour; needle post, clasp, charm, brooch; white/black/orange ... $50-$100
1980 Philadelphia Phillies: Balfour; needle post; gold.. $50-$75
1980 Kansas City Royals: Green Co.; needle post, charms; blue/white .... $50-$175
1981 Los Angeles Dodgers: Balfour; needle post, charms; red/white/blue.......................... $50-$100
1981 New York Yankees: Balfour; needle post; blue .... $75-$100
1982 St. Louis Cardinals: Balfour; needle post, charms; red .... $50-$75
1982 Milwaukee Brewers: Balfour; needle post, charms; blue .... $50-$100
1983 Philadelphia Phillies: Balfour; needle post, charms; red/white/green .... $40-$75
1983 Baltimore Orioles: Balfour; needle post, charm, brooch; orange/white/black.............. $65-$100
1984 San Diego Padres: Balfour; needle post, charms; brown/white .... $25-$75
1984 Detroit Tigers: Balfour; needle post, charms; blue .... $45-$75
1985 Kansas City Royals: Green Co.; needle post, charms; blue/white .... $75-$100
1985 St. Louis Cardinals: Balfour; needle post, charms; red/black.................................. $75-$100
1986 New York Mets: Balfour; needle post, charms; blue/orange..................................... $100-$135
1986 Boston Red Sox: Balfour; needle post, charms; red/white/blue .... $75-$125

World Series Pins

1955 Yankees
$125-$275

1956 Yankees
$200-$300

1960 Yankees
$100-$150

1987 St. Louis Cardinals: Balfour; needle post, charms; red/white/gold .... $100-$125
1987 Minnesota Twins: Josten; needle post, charms; gold .... $75-$125
1988 Oakland A's: .... $60-$75
1988 Los Angeles Dodgers: .... $50-$75
1989 San Francisco Giants: .... $75-$100
1989 Oakland A's: .... $75-$100
1990 Cincinnati Reds: .... $125-$150
1990 Oakland A's: .... $75-$100
1991 Atlanta Braves: .... $60-$100
1991 Minnesota Twins: .... $60-$100
1992 Atlanta Braves: .... $100-$125
1992 Toronto Blue Jays: .... $125-$150
1993 Philadelphia Phillies: .... $50-$100
1993 Toronto Blue Jays: .... $125-$150
1995 Atlanta Braves .... $100-$150
1995 Cleveland Indians .... $100-$150

1963 Yankees
$100-$175

1965 Giants
Phantom $125-$150

1976 Reds
$125-$175

1985 Royals
$75-$100

1986 Red Sox
$75-$125

1985 Cardinals
$75-$100

1983 Orioles
$65-$100

Phantoms

1938 Pittsburgh Pirates: Whitehead & Hoag; threaded post; red/white/black .... $500-$1,000
1944 Detroit Tigers: Unknown; threaded post; red/white/blue .... $375-$500
1945 St. Louis Cardinals: St. Louis Button; threaded post; red/white .... $475-$600
1946 Brooklyn Dodgers: Dieges & Clust; threaded post, brooch .... $125-$275
1948 Boston Red Sox: Balfour; threaded post; red/white/blue .... $1,200-$1,800
1948 New York Yankees: Dieges & Clust, threaded post; red/white/blue .... $1,600-$1,800
1949 St. Louis Cardinals: Unknown; threaded post; red/white/black .... $450-$725
1949 Boston Red Sox: Balfour; threaded post; red/white/blue .... $950-$1,400
1950 Brooklyn Dodgers: Balfour; threaded post; red/white/blue .... $1,600-$2,400
1951 Cleveland Indians: Balfour; threaded post; red/white/black .... $1,200-$1,750

World Series Pins

1951 Brooklyn Dodgers: Dieges & Clust; threaded post, brooch; red/white/blue .... $125-$400
1952 New York Giants: Dieges & Clust; threaded post, brooch; white/black .... $275-$350
1955 Chicago White Sox: Unknown; threaded post; red/white/blue .... $800-$1,400
1955 Cleveland Indians: Balfour; threaded post; red/white/blue/black .... $600-$800
1956 Milwaukee Braves: Balfour; threaded post; red/copper .... $100-$150
1959 San Francisco Giants: Balfour; threaded post; white/black .... $550-$800
1959 Milwaukee Braves: Balfour; threaded post, charm; red/copper .... $400-$500
1960 Chicago White Sox: Balfour; threaded post; red/white .... $1,200-$1,600
1960 Baltimore Orioles: Balfour; threaded post; red/green/black .... $800-$1,250
1963 St. Louis Cardinals: Josten; threaded post; red .... $75-$150
1964 Philadelphia Phillies: Martin; needle post; red/blue .... $15-$30
1964 Chicago White Sox: Balfour; needle post; red/white/blue .... $800-$1,100
1964 Baltimore Orioles: Balfour; needle post; orange/white/black .... $625-$850
1964 Cincinnati Reds: Balfour; needle post, brooch; red/white/black .... $200-$250
1965 San Francisco Giants: Balfour; threaded post; white/black .... $125-$150
1966 Pittsburgh Pirates: Balfour; needle post; black .... $375-$450
1966 San Francisco Giants: Balfour; threaded post; white/black .... $950-$1,200
1967 Minnesota Twins: Balfour; needle post; red/white/blue .... $50-$60
1967 Chicago White Sox: Balfour; needle post; red/white/blue .... $75-$100
1969 San Francisco Giants: Balfour; needle post; white/black .... $100-$150
1969 Atlanta Braves: Josten; needle post and charm; blue .... $45-$75
1969 Minnesota Twins: Balfour; needle post; red/white/blue .... $75-$150
1970 California Angels: Balfour; needle post; red/white/blue .... $450-$500
1970 Chicago Cubs: Balfour; needle post; blue/white .... $450-$500
1971 San Francisco Giants: Balfour; needle post; black .... $125-$150
1971 Oakland A's (smaller pin): Unknown; needle post; green/white .... $100-$150
1971 Oakland A's (larger pin): Balfour; needle post, charm; green/white .... $650-$750
1972 Chicago White Sox: Balfour; needle post; red/white/blue .... $875-$1,000
1972 Pittsburgh Pirates: Balfour; needle post; no color .... $600-$750
1974 Texas Rangers: Balfour; needle post; red/white/blue/gold .... $400-$550
1975 Oakland A's: Josten; needle post; green/white .... $300-$450
1976 Philadelphia Phillies: Balfour; needle post; no color .... $35-$75
1977 Boston Red Sox: Balfour; needle post, charm; red/blue .... $50-$75
1978 San Francisco Giants: Balfour; needle post; black/orange .... $30-$50
1978 Cincinnati Reds: Balfour; needle post, charm; red .... $75-$100
1978 Milwaukee Brewers: .... $50-$75
1979 Montreal Expos: Balfour; needle post; no color .... $50-$75
1979 California Angels: Balfour; needle post; red/white/blue .... $200-$250
1979 Houston Astros: Balfour; needle post; white/blue .... $850-$900
1980 Houston Astros: Balfour; needle post, charm; blue/orange .... $150-$200
1981 Oakland A's: Balfour; needle post, charm; green .... $55-$85
1981 Chicago Cubs: Balfour; needle post; red/white/blue .... $175-$200
1981 Philadelphia Phillies: Balfour; needle post; red/white .... $45-$75
1982 Los Angeles Dodgers: Balfour; needle post, charm; red/white/blue .... $125-$150
1983 Milwaukee Brewers: Balfour; needle post; white/black .... $200-$250
1983 Chicago White Sox: Balfour; needle post; red/blue .... $40-$50
1983 Pittsburgh Pirates: Balfour; needle post; black .... $200-$275
1984 Chicago Cubs: Balfour; needle post, charm; red/black .... $125-$200
1985 Toronto Blue Jays: Balfour; needle post, charm; red/white/blue .... $200-$250
1986 California Angels: Gem Peddler; needle post, charm; no color .... $175-$200
1986 Houston Astros: Balfour; needle post, charm; red/blue .... $75-$150
1987 Detroit Tigers: Balfour; needle post; blue/white/gold .... $125-$175
1987 New York Yankees: Balfour; threaded post; blue/white/gold .... $175-$200
1987 New York Mets: Balfour; needle post; orange/black/white/gold .... $200-$225

1987 San Francisco Giants: Balfour; needle post; black/white/gold.............................$75-$100
1987 Boston Red Sox:...$150-$175
1988 Boston Red Sox:...$75-$100
1990 Pittsburgh Pirates:..$300-$350
1990 Boston Red Sox:...$60-$75

All-Star Pins

1938 Cincinnati: Bastian Brothers; safety pin; red/white/blue.....................$7,000-$8,000
1941 Detroit: Dodge; threaded post; blue..$2,200-$2,500
1943 Philadelphia: Unknown; threaded post; silver..$1,200-$1,500
1946 Boston: Balfour; threaded post; red...$575-$1,000
1947 Chicago: Unknown; threaded post; red/white/blue.......................................$1,100-$1,850
1948 St. Louis: St. Louis Button; threaded post; brown/white ....$650-$2,250
1949 Brooklyn: Balfour; threaded post, brooch; blue..$325-$400
1950 Chicago: Balfour; threaded post, brooch; red/white ....$150-$325
1951 Detroit: Unknown; threaded post, brooch; red/white/blue............................$250-$375
1952 Philadelphia: Martin; needle post; red/white/blue......................................$175-$400
1953 Cincinnati: Robbins; threaded post; red/white/black....................................$225-$375
1954 Cleveland: Balfour; threaded post; red/white/black.....................................$250-$375
1955 Milwaukee: Balfour; brooch; gold..$175-$350
1956 Washington: Balfour; threaded post, clasp; red/white/blue............................$225-$350
1957 St. Louis: Balfour; threaded post, brooch; black/red....................................$300-$350
1958 Baltimore: Balfour; threaded post, charm; black/white/orange........................$400-$650
1959 Los Angeles: Balfour; threaded post, brooch; blue/white ....$100-$150
1959 Pittsburgh: Balfour; threaded post; red/white/black.....................................$225-$400
1960 Kansas City: Balfour; threaded post; red...$200-$325
1960 New York Yankees: Balfour; threaded post; red/white/blue.............................$200-$400
1961 Boston: Balfour; needle post; red/white/blue ....$400-$500
1961 San Francisco: Balfour; threaded post; white..$475-$600
1962 Chicago: Balfour; needle post; red/white/blue...$250-$350
1962 Washington: Balfour; threaded post, clasp; white/blue..................................$200-$250
1963 Cleveland: Balfour; threaded post; red/white/blue/black...............................$75-$150
1964 New York (Shea Stadium): Balfour; needle post, charm; blue/orange ....$200-$250
1965 Minnesota: Balfour; needle post; red/white/blue...$100-$175
1966 St. Louis: Balfour; needle post; red..$35-$80
1967 California: Balfour; needle post, charm; blue/white..$50-$150
1968 Houston: Balfour; needle post, charm; blue/white..$100-$125
1969 Washington: Balfour; needle post, clasp; blue ....$75-$150
1970 Cincinnati: Balfour; needle post, charm; red/white/black ....$75-$100
1971 Detroit: Balfour; needle post, charms; red/white/blue ....$100-$175
1972 Atlanta: Balfour; needle post, charm; red/blue..$75-$125
1973 Kansas City: Balfour; needle post, charm; blue ....$75-$150
1974 Pittsburgh: Balfour; needle post; gold...$175-$275
1975 Milwaukee: Unknown; brooch; gold...$50-$100
1976 Philadelphia: Balfour; needle post; gold ....$50-$75
1977 New York Yankees: Balfour; (pin)...$100-$125
1977 New York: Balfour; (charm); gold...$30-$50
1978 San Diego: Balfour; needle post, charm, brooch; brown/blue ....$40-$80
1979 Seattle: Balfour; needle post, charm, brooch; blue/white ....$30-$60
1980 Los Angeles: Balfour; needle post, charm; gold ....$30-$60
1981 Cleveland: Balfour; needle post, charm; red/white/blue.................................$25-$50
1982 Montreal: Balfour; needle post, straight pin; gold..$60-$75

1983 Chicago: Balfour; needle post, charms; red/blue .... $25-$50
1984 San Francisco: Balfour; needle post, charm; orange/black/white .... $20-$35
1985 Minnesota: Peter David; needle post, charms; red/white/blue..................................... $20-$25
1986 Houston: Balfour; needle post, charms; red/white/blue/silver....................................... $65-$125
1987 Oakland: Josten; needle post; copper .... $75-$90
1988 Cincinnati: Josten; needle post; red/white/blue/silver.. $75-$100
1989 California: .... $55-$75
1990 Chicago: .... $125-$150
1991 Toronto: .... $100-$125
1992 San Diego: .... $20-$100
1993 Baltimore: .... $100-$150
1994 Pittsburgh: $125
1995 Texas: .... $50-$100

Hall of Fame

1982: Balfour; charms and standard needle post: Hank Aaron, Happy Chandler, Travis Jackson, Frank Robinson .... $400-$700
1983: Balfour; charms and standard needle post: Walter Alston, George Kell, Juan Marichal, Brooks Robinson: .... $400-$525
1984: Balfour; charms and standard needle post: Luis Aparicio, Don Drysdale, Harmon Killebrew, Rick Ferrell, Pee Wee Reese .... $225-$375
1985: Balfour; charms and standard needle post: Lou Brock, Enos Slaughter, Arky Vaughan, Hoyt Wilhelm... $250-$350
1986: Balfour; charms and standard needle post: Bobby Doerr, Ernie Lombardi, Willie McCovey...... $225-$350
1987: Balfour; charms and standard needle post: Ray Dandridge, Jim Hunter, Billy Williams$500-$650
1988: Balfour; charms and standard needle post: Willie Stargell... $500-$650
1989: Al Barlick, Johnny Bench, Red Schoendienst, Carl Yastrzemski .... $500-$650
1990: Joe Morgan, Jim Palmer .... $450-$650
1990: (1936 inductees) Ty Cobb, Walter Johnson, Christy Mathewson, Babe Ruth, Honus Wagner$750
1991: Rod Carew, Fergie Jenkins, Gaylord Perry, Tony Lazzeri, Bill Veeck........................ $375-$575
1991: (1937 inductees) Morgan Bulkeley, Ban Johnson, Nap Lajoie, Connie Mack, John McGraw, Tris Speaker, George Wright, Cy Young $700
1992: Rollie Fingers, Bill McGowan, Hal Newhouser, Tom Seaver $400
1992: (1938 inductees) Grover Cleveland Alexander, Alexander Cartwright, Henry Chadwick ...$375
1992: (1955 inductees) Frank Baker, Joe DiMaggio, Gabby Hartnett, Ted Lyons, Ray Schalk, Dazzy Vance..$495
1993: Reggie Jackson..$450
1993: (1939 inductees) Charles Comiskey, Buck Ewing, Cap Anson, Candy Cummings, Eddie Collins $400
1993: (1939 inductees) Charles Radbourne, George Sisler, Al Spalding, Lou Gehrig, Wee Willie Keeler..$500
1994: Steve Carlton, Leo Durocher, Phil Rizzuto .... $425-$450
1994: (1942 inductee) Rogers Hornsby $375
1994: (1966 inductees) Casey Stengel, Ted Williams $375
1995: Richie Ashburn, Leon Day, William Hulbert, Mike Schmidt, Vic Willis....................$375
1995: (1944 inductee) Kenesaw Mountain Landis $375
1995: (1969 inductees) Roy Campanella, Stan Coveleski, Waite Hoyt, Stan Musial $375

1985 Fun Food Buttons

Fun Foods of Little Silver, N.J. issued a set of 133 full-color metal pins in 1985. The buttons, which are 1-1/4" in diameter and have a "safety pin" back, have bright borders which correspond to the player's team colors. The button backs are numbered and contain the player's 1984 batting or earned run average. The buttons were available as complete sets through hobby dealers and were also distributed in packs (three buttons per pack) through retail stores.

		MT	NM	EX
	Complete set:	18.00	13.50	7.25
	Common player:	.10	.08	.04
1	Dave Winfield	.40	.30	.15
2	Lance Parrish	.15	.11	.06
3	Gary Carter	.25	.20	.10
4	Pete Rose	.80	.60	.30
5	Jim Rice	.10	.08	.04
6	George Brett	.75	.60	.30
7	Fernando Valenzuela	.15	.11	.06
8	Darryl Strawberry	.20	.15	.08
9	Steve Garvey	.20	.15	.08
10	Rollie Fingers	.20	.15	.08
11	Mike Schmidt	1.25	.90	.50
12	Kent Tekulve	.10	.08	.04
13	Ryne Sandberg	.75	.60	.30
14	Bruce Sutter	.10	.08	.04
15	Tom Seaver	.30	.25	.12
16	Reggie Jackson	.70	.50	.30
17	Rickey Henderson	.50	.40	.20
18	Mark Langston	.10	.08	.04
19	Jack Clark	.10	.08	.04
20	Willie Randolph	.10	.08	.04
21	Kirk Gibson	.15	.11	.06
22	Andre Dawson	.20	.15	.08
23	Dave Concepcion	.10	.08	.04
24	Tony Armas	.10	.08	.04
25	Dan Quisenberry	.10	.08	.04
26	Pedro Guerrero	.10	.08	.04
27	Dwight Gooden	.15	.11	.06
28	Tony Gwynn	.40	.30	.15
29	Robin Yount	.50	.40	.20
30	Steve Carlton	1.00	.70	.40
31	Bill Madlock	.10	.08	.04
32	Rick Sutcliffe	.10	.08	.04
33	Willie McGee	.10	.08	.04
34	Greg Luzinski	.15	.11	.06
35	Rod Carew	.40	.30	.15
36	Dave Kingman	.15	.11	.06
37	Alvin Davis	.10	.08	.04
38	Chili Davis	.25	.20	.10
39	Don Baylor	.15	.11	.06
40	Alan Trammell	.20	.15	.08
41	Tim Raines	.20	.15	.08
42	Cesar Cedeno	.10	.08	.04
43	Wade Boggs	.75	.60	.30
44	Frank White	.10	.08	.04
45	Steve Sax	.10	.08	.04
46	George Foster	.10	.08	.04
47	Terry Kennedy	.10	.08	.04
48	Cecil Cooper	.10	.08	.04
49	John Denny	.10	.08	.04
50	John Candelaria	.10	.08	.04
51	Jody Davis	.10	.08	.04
52	George Hendrick	.10	.08	.04
53	Ron Kittle	.10	.08	.04
54	Fred Lynn	.15	.11	.06
55	Carney Lansford	.10	.08	.04
56	Gorman Thomas	.10	.08	.04
57	Manny Trillo	.10	.08	.04
58	Steve Kemp	.10	.08	.04
59	Jack Morris	.12	.09	.05
60	Dan Petry	.10	.08	.04
61	Mario Soto	.10	.08	.04
62	Dwight Evans	.10	.08	.04
63	Hal McRae	.10	.08	.04
64	Mike Marshall	.10	.08	.04
65	Mookie Wilson	.10	.08	.04
66	Graig Nettles	.10	.08	.04
67	Ben Oglivie	.10	.08	.04
68	Juan Samuel	.10	.08	.04
69	Johnny Ray	.10	.08	.04
70	Gary Matthews	.10	.08	.04
71	Ozzie Smith	.20	.15	.08
72	Carlton Fisk	.40	.30	.15
73	Doug DeCinces	.10	.08	.04
74	Joe Morgan	.60	.45	.25
75	Dave Stieb	.10	.08	.04
76	Buddy Bell	.10	.08	.04
77	Don Mattingly	.90	.70	.35
78	Lou Whitaker	.15	.11	.06
79	Willie Hernandez	.10	.08	.04
80	Dave Parker	.20	.15	.08
81	Bob Stanley	.10	.08	.04
82	Willie Wilson	.10	.08	.04
83	Orel Hershiser	.15	.11	.06
84	Rusty Staub	.15	.11	.06
85	Goose Gossage	.15	.11	.06
86	Don Sutton	.25	.20	.10
87	Al Holland	.10	.08	.04
88	Tony Pena	.10	.08	.04
89	Ron Cey	.10	.08	.04
90	Joaquin Andujar	.10	.08	.04
91	LaMarr Hoyt	.10	.08	.04
92	Tommy John	.15	.11	.06
93	Dwayne Murphy	.10	.08	.04
94	Willie Upshaw	.10	.08	.04
95	Gary Ward	.10	.08	.04
96	Ron Guidry	.15	.11	.06
97	Chet Lemon	.10	.08	.04
98	Aurelio Lopez	.10	.08	.04
99	Tony Perez	.20	.15	.08
100	Bill Buckner	.10	.08	.04
101	Mike Hargrove	.10	.08	.04
102	Scott McGregor	.10	.08	.04
103	Dale Murphy	.40	.30	.15
104	Keith Hernandez	.10	.08	.04
105	Paul Molitor	.45	.35	.20
106	Bert Blyleven	.10	.08	.04
107	Leon Durham	.10	.08	.04
108	Lee Smith	.12	.09	.05
109	Nolan Ryan	2.00	1.50	.80
110	Harold Baines	.10	.08	.04
111	Kent Hrbek	.12	.09	.05
112	Ron Davis	.10	.08	.04
113	George Bell	.12	.09	.05
114	Charlie Hough	.10	.08	.04
115	Phil Niekro	.15	.11	.06
116	Dave Righetti	.10	.08	.04
117	Darrell Evans	.10	.08	.04
118	Cal Ripken, Jr.	2.00	1.50	.80
119	Eddie Murray	.60	.45	.25
120	Storm Davis	.10	.08	.04
121	Mike Boddicker	.10	.08	.04
122	Bob Horner	.10	.08	.04
123	Chris Chambliss	.10	.08	.04
124	Ted Simmons	.10	.08	.04
125	Andre Thornton	.10	.08	.04
126	Larry Bowa	.10	.08	.04
127	Bob Dernier	.10	.08	.04
128	Joe Niekro	.10	.08	.04
129	Jose Cruz	.10	.08	.04
130	Tom Brunansky	.10	.08	.04
131	Gary Gaetti	.10	.08	.04
132	Lloyd Moseby	.10	.08	.04
133	Frank Tanana	.10	.08	.04

1969 Kelly's Potato Chips Pins

Consisting of 20 pins, each measuring approximately 1-3/16" in diameter, this set was issued by Kelly's Potato Chips in 1969 and has a heavy emphasis on St. Louis Cardinals. The pin has a black and white player photo in the center surrounded by either a red border (for A.L. players) or a blue border (for N.L. players) that displays the player's team and name at the top and bottom. "Kelly's" appears to the left while the word "Zip!" is printed to the right. The pins are unnumbered.

		NM	EX	VG
Complete set:		150.00	75.00	45.00
Common player:		1.50	.70	.45
(1)	Luis Aparicio	7.00	3.50	2.00
(2)	Ernie Banks	15.00	7.50	4.50
(3)	Glenn Beckert	1.50	.70	.45
(4)	Lou Brock	10.00	5.00	3.00
(5)	Curt Flood	2.00	1.00	.60
(6)	Bob Gibson	10.00	5.00	3.00
(7)	Joel Horlen	1.50	.70	.45
(8)	Al Kaline	10.00	5.00	3.00
(9)	Don Kessinger	1.50	.70	.45
(10)	Mickey Lolich	2.50	1.25	.70
(11)	Juan Marichal	8.00	4.00	2.50
(12)	Willie Mays	22.00	11.00	6.50
(13)	Tim McCarver	2.50	1.25	.70
(14)	Denny McLain	2.50	1.25	.70
(15)	Pete Rose	20.00	10.00	6.00
(16)	Ron Santo	2.50	1.25	.70
(17)	Joe Torre	1.50	.70	.45
(18)	Pete Ward	1.50	.70	.45
(19)	Billy Williams	7.00	3.50	2.00
(20)	Carl Yastrzemski	15.00	7.50	4.50

1969 Major League Baseball Players Ass'n Pins

Issued by the Major League Baseball Players Association in 1969, this unnumbered set consists of 60 pins - 30 players from the N.L. and 30 from the A.L. Each pin measures approximately 7/8" in diameter and features a black-and-white player photo. A.L. players are surrounded by a red border, while N.L. players are framed in blue. The player's name and team appear at the top and bottom. Also along the bottom is a line reading "1969 MLBPA MFG. R.R. Winona, MINN."

		NM	EX	VG
Complete set:		350.00	175.00	105.00
Common player:		1.50	.70	.45
(1)	Hank Aaron	30.00	15.00	9.00
(2)	Richie Allen	6.00	3.00	1.75
(3)	Felipe Alou	3.00	1.50	.90
(4)	Max Alvis	1.50	.70	.45
(5)	Luis Aparicio	8.00	4.00	2.50
(6)	Ernie Banks	16.00	8.00	4.75
(7)	Johnny Bench	16.00	8.00	4.75
(8)	Lou Brock	8.00	4.00	2.50
(9)	George Brunet	1.50	.70	.45
(10)	Johnny Callison	2.00	1.00	.60
(11)	Rod Carew	14.00	7.00	4.25
(12)	Orlando Cepeda	6.00	3.00	1.75
(13)	Dean Chance	1.50	.70	.45
(14)	Roberto Clemente	30.00	15.00	9.00
(15)	Willie Davis	2.00	1.00	.60
(16)	Don Drysdale	14.00	7.00	4.25
(17)	Ron Fairly	2.00	1.00	.60
(18)	Curt Flood	5.00	2.50	1.50
(19)	Bill Freehan	2.00	1.00	.60
(20)	Jim Fregosi	2.00	1.00	.60
(21)	Bob Gibson	14.00	7.00	4.25
(22)	Ken Harrelson	1.50	.70	.45
(23)	Bud Harrelson	1.50	.70	.45
(24)	Jim Ray Hart	1.50	.70	.45
(25)	Tommy Helms	1.50	.70	.45
(26)	Joe Horlen	1.50	.70	.45
(27)	Willie Horton	2.00	1.00	.60
(28)	Frank Howard	5.00	2.50	1.50
(29)	Tony Horton	2.00	1.00	.60
(30)	Al Kaline	16.00	8.00	4.75
(31)	Don Kessinger	2.00	1.00	.60
(32)	Harmon Killebrew	16.00	8.00	4.75
(33)	Jerry Koosman	2.00	1.00	.60
(34)	Mickey Lolich	4.00	2.00	1.25
(35)	Jim Lonborg	2.00	1.00	.60
(36)	Jim Maloney	1.50	.70	.45
(37)	Juan Marichal	14.00	7.00	4.25
(38)	Willie Mays	30.00	15.00	9.00
(39)	Tim McCarver	4.00	2.00	1.25
(40)	Willie McCovey	14.00	7.00	4.25
(41)	Sam McDowell	2.00	1.00	.60
(42)	Denny McLain	4.00	2.00	1.25
(43)	Rick Monday	2.00	1.00	.60
(44)	Tony Oliva	4.00	2.00	1.25
(45)	Joe Pepitone	2.00	1.00	.60
(46)	Boog Powell	5.00	2.50	1.50
(47)	Rick Reichardt	1.50	.70	.45
(48)	Pete Richert	1.50	.70	.45
(49)	Brooks Robinson	16.00	8.00	4.75
(50)	Frank Robinson	16.00	8.00	4.75
(51)	Pete Rose	30.00	15.00	9.00
(52)	Ron Santo	4.00	2.00	1.25
(53)	Mel Stottlemyre	2.00	1.00	.60
(54)	Ron Swoboda	1.50	.70	.45
(55)	Luis Tiant	2.00	1.00	.60
(56)	Joe Torre	3.00	1.50	.90
(57)	Pete Ward	1.50	.70	.45
(58)	Billy Williams	10.00	5.00	3.00
(59)	Jim Wynn	2.00	1.00	.60
(60)	Carl Yastrzemski	30.00	15.00	9.00

1956 PM15 Yellow Basepath Pins

These pins were issued circa 1956; the sponsor of this 32-pin set is not indicated. The set, which has been assigned the American Card Catalog designation PM15, is commonly called "Yellow Basepaths" because of the design of the pin, which features a black-and-white player photo set inside a green infield with yellow basepaths. The unnumbered pins measure 7/8" in diameter. The names of Kluszewski and Mathews are misspelled.

		NM	EX	VG
Complete set (32):		2200.	1100.	660.00
Common player:		25.00	12.50	7.50
(1)	Hank Aaron	175.00	87.00	52.00
(2)	Joe Adcock	25.00	12.50	7.50
(3)	Luis Aparicio	60.00	30.00	18.00
(4)	Richie Ashburn	75.00	37.00	22.00
(5)	Gene Baker	25.00	12.50	7.50
(6)	Ernie Banks	90.00	45.00	27.00
(7)	Yogi Berra	90.00	45.00	27.00

(8)	Bill Bruton	25.00	12.50	7.50
(9)	Larry Doby	35.00	17.50	10.50
(10)	Bob Friend	25.00	12.50	7.50
(11)	Nellie Fox	40.00	20.00	12.00
(12)	Jim Greengrass	25.00	12.50	7.50
(13)	Steve Gromek	25.00	12.50	7.50
(14)	Johnny Groth	25.00	12.50	7.50
(15)	Gil Hodges	75.00	37.00	22.00
(16)	Al Kaline	90.00	45.00	27.00
(17)	Ted Kluzewski (Kluszewski)	50.00	25.00	15.00
(18)	Johnny Logan	25.00	12.50	7.50
(19)	Dale Long	25.00	12.50	7.50
(20)	Mickey Mantle	450.00	225.00	135.00
(21)	Ed Mathews	60.00	30.00	18.00
(22)	Minnie Minoso	40.00	20.00	12.00
(23)	Stan Musial	175.00	87.00	52.00
(24)	Don Newcombe	40.00	20.00	12.00
(25)	Bob Porterfield	25.00	12.50	7.50
(26)	Pee Wee Reese	75.00	37.00	22.00
(27)	Robin Roberts	50.00	25.00	15.00
(28)	Red Schoendienst	40.00	20.00	12.00
(29)	Duke Snider	90.00	45.00	27.00
(30)	Vern Stephens	25.00	12.50	7.50
(31)	Gene Woodling	25.00	12.50	7.50
(32)	Gus Zernial	25.00	12.50	7.50

1938 PM8
Our National Game Pins

This unnumbered 30-pin set issued in the 1930s carries the American Card Catalog designation of PM8 and is known as "Our National Game." The pins, which measure 7/8" in diameter, have a "tab" rather than a pin back. The black-and-white player photo is tinted blue, and the player's name and team are printed in a band near the bottom.

		NM	EX	VG
Complete set (30):		800.00	400.00	240.00
Common player:		12.00	6.00	3.50
(1)	Wally Berger	12.00	6.00	3.50
(2)	Lou Chiozza	12.00	6.00	3.50

(3)	Joe Cronin	30.00	15.00	9.00
(4)	Frank Crosetti	16.00	8.00	4.75
(5)	Jerome (Dizzy) Dean	50.00	25.00	15.00
(6)	Frank DeMaree (Demaree)	12.00	6.00	3.50
(7)	Joe DiMaggio	150.00	75.00	45.00
(8)	Bob Feller	40.00	20.00	12.00
(9)	Jimmy Foxx (Jimmie)	40.00	20.00	12.00
(10)	Lou Gehrig	150.00	75.00	45.00
(11)	Charles Gehringer	30.00	15.00	9.00
(12)	Lefty Gomez	30.00	15.00	9.00
(13)	Hank Greenberg	30.00	15.00	9.00
(14)	Irving (Bump) Hadley	12.00	6.00	3.50
(15)	Leo Hartnett	30.00	15.00	9.00
(16)	Carl Hubbell	30.00	15.00	9.00
(17)	John (Buddy) Lewis	12.00	6.00	3.50
(18)	Gus Mancuso	12.00	6.00	3.50
(19)	Joe McCarthy	30.00	15.00	9.00
(20)	Joe Medwick	30.00	15.00	9.00
(21)	Joe Moore	12.00	6.00	3.50
(22)	Mel Ott	30.00	15.00	9.00
(23)	Jake Powell	12.00	6.00	3.50
(24)	Jimmy Ripple	12.00	6.00	3.50
(25)	Red Ruffing	30.00	15.00	9.00
(26)	Hal Schumacher	12.00	6.00	3.50
(27)	George Selkirk	12.00	6.00	3.50
(28)	"Al" Simmons	30.00	15.00	9.00
(29)	Bill Terry	30.00	15.00	9.00
(30)	Harold Trosky	12.00	6.00	3.50

1932 PR2
Orbit Gum Pins Numbered

Issued circa 1932, this skip-numbered set of small (13/16" in diameter) pins was produced by Orbit Gum and carries the Amerian Card Catalog designation of PR2. A player lithograph is set against a green background with the player's name and team printed on a strip of yellow below. The pin number is at the very bottom.

		NM	EX	VG
Complete set:		1200.	500.00	300.00
Common player:		15.00	7.50	4.50
1	Ivy Andrews	15.00	7.50	4.50
2	Carl Reynolds	15.00	7.50	4.50
3	Riggs Stephenson	18.00	9.00	5.50
4	Lon Warneke	15.00	7.50	4.50
5	Frank Grube	15.00	7.50	4.50
6	Kiki Cuyler	30.00	15.00	9.00
7	Marty McManus	15.00	7.50	4.50
8	Lefty Clark	15.00	7.50	4.50
9	George Blaeholder	15.00	7.50	4.50
10	Willie Kamm	15.00	7.50	4.50
11	Jimmy Dykes	18.00	9.00	5.50
12	Earl Averill	30.00	15.00	9.00
13	Pat Malone	15.00	7.50	4.50
14	Dizzy Dean	95.00	47.00	28.00
15	Dick Bartell	15.00	7.50	4.50
16	Guy Bush	15.00	7.50	4.50
17	Bud Tinning	15.00	7.50	4.50

		NM	EX	VG
18	Jimmy Foxx	50.00	25.00	15.00
19	Mule Haas	15.00	7.50	4.50
20	Lew Fonseca	15.00	7.50	4.50
21	Pepper Martin	25.00	12.50	7.50
22	Phil Collins	15.00	7.50	4.50
23	Bill Cissell	15.00	7.50	4.50
24	Bump Hadley	15.00	7.50	4.50
25	Smead Jolley	15.00	7.50	4.50
26	Burleigh Grimes	30.00	15.00	9.00
27	Dale Alexander	15.00	7.50	4.50
28	Mickey Cochrane	35.00	17.50	10.50
29	Mel Harder	15.00	7.50	4.50
30	Mark Koenig	15.00	7.50	4.50
31a	Lefty O'Doul (Dodgers)	45.00	22.00	13.50
31b	Lefty O'Doul (Giants)	25.00	12.50	7.50
32a	Woody English (with bat)	15.00	7.50	4.50
32b	Woody English (without bat)	45.00	22.00	13.50
33a	Billy Jurges (with bat)	15.00	7.50	4.50
33b	Billy Jurges (without bat)	45.00	22.00	13.50
34	Bruce Campbell	15.00	7.50	4.50
35	Joe Vosmik	15.00	7.50	4.50
36	Dick Porter	15.00	7.50	4.50
37	Charlie Grimm	18.00	9.00	5.50
38	George Earnshaw	15.00	7.50	4.50
39	Al Simmons	30.00	15.00	9.00
40	Red Lucas	15.00	7.50	4.50
51	Wally Berger	15.00	7.50	4.50
52	Jim Levey	15.00	7.50	4.50
58	Ernie Lombardi	30.00	15.00	9.00
64	Jack Burns	15.00	7.50	4.50
67	Billy Herman	30.00	15.00	9.00
72	Bill Hallahan	15.00	7.50	4.50
92	Don Brennan	15.00	7.50	4.50
96	Sam Byrd	15.00	7.50	4.50
99	Ben Chapman	15.00	7.50	4.50
103	John Allen	15.00	7.50	4.50
107	Tony Lazzeri	30.00	15.00	9.00
111	Earl Combs (Earle)	30.00	15.00	9.00
116	Joe Sewell	30.00	15.00	9.00
120	Vernon Gomez	35.00	17.50	10.50

1932 PR3
Orbit Gum Pins Unnumbered

This set, issued by Orbit Gum circa 1932, has the American Card Catalog designation PR3. The pins are identical to the PR2 set, except they are unnumbered.

		NM	EX	VG
Complete set (60):		2160.	1080.	648.00
Common player:		27.00	13.50	8.00
(1)	Dale Alexander	27.00	13.50	8.00
(2)	Ivy Andrews	27.00	13.50	8.00
(3)	Earl Averill	55.00	27.00	16.50
(4)	Dick Bartell	27.00	13.50	8.00
(5)	Wally Berger	27.00	13.50	8.00
(6)	George Blaeholder	27.00	13.50	8.00
(7)	Jack Burns	27.00	13.50	8.00
(8)	Guy Bush	27.00	13.50	8.00

		NM	EX	VG
(9)	Bruce Campbell	27.00	13.50	8.00
(10)	Bill Cissell	27.00	13.50	8.00
(11)	Lefty Clark	27.00	13.50	8.00
(12)	Mickey Cochrane	65.00	32.00	19.50
(13)	Phil Collins	27.00	13.50	8.00
(14)	Kiki Cuyler	55.00	27.00	16.50
(15)	Dizzy Dean	135.00	67.00	40.00
(16)	Jimmy Dykes	27.00	13.50	8.00
(17)	George Earnshaw	27.00	13.50	8.00
(18)	Woody English	27.00	13.50	8.00
(19)	Lew Fonseca	27.00	13.50	8.00
(20)	Jimmy Foxx	80.00	40.00	24.00
(21)	Burleigh Grimes	55.00	27.00	16.50
(22)	Charlie Grimm	27.00	13.50	8.00
(23)	Lefty Grove	80.00	40.00	24.00
(24)	Frank Grube	27.00	13.50	8.00
(25)	Mule Haas	27.00	13.50	8.00
(26)	Bump Hadley	27.00	13.50	8.00
(27)	Chick Hafey	55.00	27.00	16.50
(28)	Jesse Haines	55.00	27.00	16.50
(29)	Bill Hallahan	27.00	13.50	8.00
(30)	Mel Harder	27.00	13.50	8.00
(31)	Gabby Hartnett	55.00	27.00	16.50
(32)	Babe Herman	35.00	17.50	10.50
(33)	Billy Herman	55.00	27.00	16.50
(34)	Rogers Hornsby	90.00	45.00	27.00
(35)	Roy Johnson	27.00	13.50	8.00
(36)	Smead Jolley	27.00	13.50	8.00
(37)	Billy Jurges	27.00	13.50	8.00
(38)	Willie Kamm	27.00	13.50	8.00
(39)	Mark Koenig	27.00	13.50	8.00
(40)	Jim Levey	27.00	13.50	8.00
(41)	Ernie Lombardi	55.00	27.00	16.50
(42)	Red Lucas	27.00	13.50	8.00
(43)	Ted Lyons	55.00	27.00	16.50
(44)	Connie Mack	70.00	35.00	21.00
(45)	Pat Malone	27.00	13.50	8.00
(46)	Pepper Martin	35.00	17.50	10.50
(47)	Marty McManus	27.00	13.50	8.00
(48)	Lefty O'Doul	35.00	17.50	10.50
(49)	Dick Porter	27.00	13.50	8.00
(50)	Carl Reynolds	27.00	13.50	8.00
(51)	Charlie Root	27.00	13.50	8.00
(52)	Bob Seeds	27.00	13.50	8.00
(53)	Al Simmons	55.00	27.00	16.50
(54)	Riggs Stephenson	27.00	13.50	8.00
(55)	Bud Tinning	27.00	13.50	8.00
(56)	Joe Vosmik	27.00	13.50	8.00
(57)	Rube Walberg	27.00	13.50	8.00
(58)	Paul Waner	55.00	27.00	16.50
(59)	Lon Warneke	27.00	13.50	8.00
(60)	Pinky Whitney	27.00	13.50	8.00

1930 PR4
Cracker Jack Pins

Although no manufacturer is indicated on the pins themselves, this 25-player set was apparently issued by Cracker Jack in the early 1930s. Each pin measures 13/16" in diameter and features a line drawing of a player portrait. The unnumbered pins are printed in blue and gray with a background of yellow. The player's name appears below.

		NM	EX	VG
Complete set (25):		800.00	400.00	240.00
Common player:		17.00	8.50	5.00
(1)	Charles Berry	17.00	8.50	5.00
(2)	Bill Cissell	17.00	8.50	5.00
(3)	KiKi Cuyler	30.00	15.00	9.00
(4)	Dizzy Dean	45.00	22.00	13.50
(5)	Wesley Ferrell	17.00	8.50	5.00
(6)	Frank Frisch	30.00	15.00	9.00
(7)	Lou Gehrig	115.00	57.00	34.00
(8)	Vernon Gomez	30.00	15.00	9.00
(9)	Goose Goslin	30.00	15.00	9.00

(10)	George Grantham	17.00	8.50	5.00
(11)	Charley Grimm	17.00	8.50	5.00
(12)	Lefty Grove	35.00	17.50	10.50
(13)	Gabby Hartnett	30.00	15.00	9.00
(14)	Travis Jackson	30.00	15.00	9.00
(15)	Tony Lazzeri	30.00	15.00	9.00
(16)	Ted Lyons	30.00	15.00	9.00
(17)	Rabbit Maranville	30.00	15.00	9.00
(18)	Carl Reynolds	17.00	8.50	5.00
(19)	Charles Ruffing	30.00	15.00	9.00
(20)	Al Simmons	30.00	15.00	9.00
(21)	Gus Suhr	17.00	8.50	5.00
(22)	Bill Terry	30.00	15.00	9.00
(23)	Dazzy Vance	30.00	15.00	9.00
(24)	Paul Waner	30.00	15.00	9.00
(25)	Lon Warneke	17.00	8.50	5.00

1933 PX3
Double Header Pins

Issued by Gum Inc. circa 1933, this unnumbered set consists of 43 metal discs approximately 1-1/4" in diameter. The front of the pin lists the player's name and team beneath his picture. The numbers "1" or "2" also appear inside a small circle at the bottom of the disc, and the wrapper advised collectors to "put 1 and 2 together and make a double header." The set is designated as PX3 in the American Card Catalog.

		NM	EX	VG
Complete set (43):		900.00	450.00	270.00
Common player:		25.00	12.50	7.50
(1)	Sparky Adams	25.00	12.50	7.50
(2)	Dale Alexander	25.00	12.50	7.50
(3)	Earl Averill	45.00	22.00	13.50
(4)	Dick Bartell	25.00	12.50	7.50
(5)	Walter Berger	25.00	12.50	7.50
(6)	Jim Bottomley	45.00	22.00	13.50
(7)	Lefty Brandt	25.00	12.50	7.50
(8)	Owen Carroll	25.00	12.50	7.50

(9)	Lefty Clark	25.00	12.50	7.50
(10)	Mickey Cochrane	50.00	25.00	15.00
(11)	Joe Cronin	45.00	22.00	13.50
(12)	Jimmy Dykes	25.00	12.50	7.50
(13)	George Earnshaw	25.00	12.50	7.50
(14)	Wes Ferrell	25.00	12.50	7.50
(15)	Neal Finn	25.00	12.50	7.50
(16)	Lew Fonseca	25.00	12.50	7.50
(17)	Jimmy Foxx	90.00	45.00	27.00
(18)	Frankie Frisch	50.00	25.00	15.00
(19)	Chick Fullis	25.00	12.50	7.50
(20)	Charley Gehringer	45.00	22.00	13.50
(21)	Goose Goslin	45.00	22.00	13.50
(22)	Johnny Hodapp	25.00	12.50	7.50
(23)	Frank Hogan	25.00	12.50	7.50
(24)	Si Johnson	25.00	12.50	7.50
(25)	Joe Judge	25.00	12.50	7.50
(26)	Chuck Klein	45.00	22.00	13.50
(27)	Al Lopez	45.00	22.00	13.50
(28)	Ray Lucas	25.00	12.50	7.50
(29)	Red Lucas	25.00	12.50	7.50
(30)	Ted Lyons	45.00	22.00	13.50
(31)	Firpo Marberry	25.00	12.50	7.50
(32)	Oscar Melillo	25.00	12.50	7.50
(33)	Lefty O'Doul	30.00	15.00	9.00
(34)	George Pipgras	25.00	12.50	7.50
(35)	Flint Rhem	25.00	12.50	7.50
(36)	Sam Rice	45.00	22.00	13.50
(37)	Muddy Ruel	25.00	12.50	7.50
(38)	Harry Seibold	25.00	12.50	7.50
(39)	Al Simmons	45.00	22.00	13.50
(40)	Joe Vosmik	25.00	12.50	7.50
(41)	Gerald Walker	25.00	12.50	7.50
(42)	Pinky Whitney	25.00	12.50	7.50
(43)	Hack Wilson	45.00	22.00	13.50

1909 PX7
Domino Discs

Domino Discs, distributed by Sweet Caporal Cigarettes from 1909 to 1912, are among the more obscure 20th-century tobacco issues. Although the disc set contains many of the same players - some even pictured in the same poses - as the Sweet Caporal P2 pin set, the discs have always lagged behind the pins in collector appeal. The Domino Discs, so called because each disc has a large, white domino printed on the back, measure approximately 1-1/8" in diameter and are made of thin card cardboard surrounded by a metal rim. The fronts of the discs contain a player portrait set against a background of either red, green or blue. The words "Sweet Caporal Cigarettes" appear on the front along with the player's last name and team. There are 135 different major leaguers featured in the set, each pictured in two different poses for a total of 270 different subjects. Also known to exist as part of the set is a "game disc" which pictures a "generic" player and contains the words "Home Team" against a red background on one side and "Visiting Team" with a green background on the reverse. Because each of the 135 players in the set can theoretically be found with three different background colors and with varying numbers of dots on the dominoes, there is almost an impossible number of variations available. Collectors, however, generally collect the discs without regard to background color or domino arrangement. The Domino Disc set was assigned the designation PX7 in the American Card Catalog.

		NM	EX	VG
Complete set:		5500.	2700.	1650.
Common player:		25.00	12.50	7.50
(1)	Red Ames	25.00	12.50	7.50
(2)	Jimmy Archer	25.00	12.50	7.50
(3)	Jimmy Austin	25.00	12.50	7.50
(4)	Home Run Baker	60.00	30.00	18.00
(5)	Neal Ball	25.00	12.50	7.50
(6)	Cy Barger	25.00	12.50	7.50
(7)	Jack Barry	25.00	12.50	7.50
(8)	Johnny Bates	25.00	12.50	7.50
(9)	Beals Becker	25.00	12.50	7.50
(10)	George Bell	25.00	12.50	7.50
(11)	Chief Bender	60.00	30.00	18.00
(12)	Bill Bergen	25.00	12.50	7.50
(13)	Bob Bescher	25.00	12.50	7.50
(14)	Joe Birmingham	25.00	12.50	7.50
(15)	Roger Bresnahan	60.00	30.00	18.00
(16)	Al Bridwell	25.00	12.50	7.50
(17)	Mordecai Brown	60.00	30.00	18.00
(18)	Bobby Byrne	25.00	12.50	7.50
(19)	Nixey Callahan	25.00	12.50	7.50
(20)	Howie Camnitz	25.00	12.50	7.50
(21)	Bill Carrigan	25.00	12.50	7.50
(22)	Frank Chance	60.00	30.00	18.00
(23)	Hal Chase	40.00	20.00	12.00
(24)	Ed Cicotte	40.00	20.00	12.00
(25)	Fred Clarke	60.00	30.00	18.00
(26a)	Ty Cobb ("D" on cap)	600.00	300.00	180.00
(26b)	Ty Cobb (no "D" on cap)	600.00	300.00	180.00
(27)	Eddie Collins	60.00	30.00	18.00
(28)	Doc Crandall	25.00	12.50	7.50
(29)	Birdie Cree	25.00	12.50	7.50
(30)	Bill Dahlen	25.00	12.50	7.50
(31)	Jim Delahanty	25.00	12.50	7.50
(32)	Art Devlin	25.00	12.50	7.50
(33)	Josh Devore	25.00	12.50	7.50
(34)	Red Dooin	25.00	12.50	7.50
(35)	Mickey Doolan	25.00	12.50	7.50
(36)	Patsy Dougherty	25.00	12.50	7.50
(37)	Tom Downey	25.00	12.50	7.50
(38)	Larry Doyle	25.00	12.50	7.50
(39)	Louis Drucke	25.00	12.50	7.50
(40)	Clyde Engle	25.00	12.50	7.50
(41)	Tex Erwin	25.00	12.50	7.50
(42)	Steve Evans	25.00	12.50	7.50
(43)	Johnny Evers	60.00	30.00	18.00
(44)	Cecil Ferguson	25.00	12.50	7.50
(45)	Russ Ford	25.00	12.50	7.50
(46)	Art Fromme	25.00	12.50	7.50
(47)	Harry Gaspar	25.00	12.50	7.50
(48)	George Gibson	25.00	12.50	7.50
(49)	Eddie Grant	35.00	17.50	10.50
(50)	Clark Griffith	60.00	30.00	18.00
(51)	Bob Groom	25.00	12.50	7.50
(52)	Bob Harmon	25.00	12.50	7.50
(53)	Topsy Hartsel	25.00	12.50	7.50
(54)	Arnold Hauser	25.00	12.50	7.50
(55)	Dick Hoblitzell	25.00	12.50	7.50
(56)	Danny Hoffman	25.00	12.50	7.50
(57)	Miller Huggins	60.00	30.00	18.00
(58)	John Hummel	25.00	12.50	7.50
(59)	Hugh Jennings	60.00	30.00	18.00
(60)	Walter Johnson	300.00	150.00	90.00
(61)	Ed Karger	25.00	12.50	7.50
(62a)	Jack Knight (Yankees)	25.00	12.50	7.50
(62b)	Jack Knight (Senators)	25.00	12.50	7.50
(63)	Ed Konetchy	25.00	12.50	7.50
(64)	Harry Krause	25.00	12.50	7.50
(65)	Frank LaPorte	25.00	12.50	7.50
(66)	Nap Lajoie	150.00	75.00	45.00
(67)	Tommy Leach	25.00	12.50	7.50
(68)	Sam Leever	25.00	12.50	7.50
(69)	Lefty Leifield	25.00	12.50	7.50
(70)	Paddy Livingston	25.00	12.50	7.50
(71)	Hans Lobert	25.00	12.50	7.50
(72)	Harry Lord	25.00	12.50	7.50
(73)	Nick Maddox	25.00	12.50	7.50
(74)	Sherry Magee	25.00	12.50	7.50
(75)	Rube Marquard	60.00	30.00	18.00
(76)	Christy Mathewson	300.00	150.00	90.00
(77)	Al Mattern	25.00	12.50	7.50
(78)	George McBride	25.00	12.50	7.50
(79)	John McGraw	60.00	30.00	18.00
(80)	Harry McIntire	25.00	12.50	7.50
(81)	Matty McIntyre	25.00	12.50	7.50
(82)	Larry McLean	25.00	12.50	7.50
(83)	Fred Merkle	25.00	12.50	7.50
(84)	Chief Meyers	25.00	12.50	7.50
(85)	Clyde Milan	25.00	12.50	7.50
(86)	Dots Miller	25.00	12.50	7.50
(87)	Mike Mitchell	25.00	12.50	7.50
(88a)	Pat Moran (Cubs)	25.00	12.50	7.50
(88b)	Pat Moran (Phillies)	25.00	12.50	7.50
(89)	George Mullen (Mullin)	25.00	12.50	7.50
(90)	Danny Murphy	25.00	12.50	7.50
(91)	Red Murray	25.00	12.50	7.50
(92)	Tom Needham	25.00	12.50	7.50
(93)	Rebel Oakes	25.00	12.50	7.50
(94)	Rube Oldring	25.00	12.50	7.50
(95)	Fred Parent	25.00	12.50	7.50
(96)	Dode Paskert	25.00	12.50	7.50
(97)	Barney Pelty	25.00	12.50	7.50
(98)	Eddie Phelps	25.00	12.50	7.50
(99)	Deacon Phillippe	25.00	12.50	7.50
(100)	Jack Quinn	25.00	12.50	7.50
(101)	Ed Reulbach	25.00	12.50	7.50
(102)	Lew Richie	25.00	12.50	7.50
(103)	Jack Rowan	25.00	12.50	7.50
(104)	Nap Rucker	25.00	12.50	7.50
(105a)	Doc Scanlon (Scanlan) (Superbas)	25.00	12.50	7.50
(105b)	Doc Scanlon (Scanlan) (Phillies)	25.00	12.50	7.50
(106)	Germany Schaefer	25.00	12.50	7.50
(107)	Boss Schmidt	25.00	12.50	7.50
(108)	Wildfire Schulte	25.00	12.50	7.50
(109)	Jimmy Sheckard	25.00	12.50	7.50
(110)	Hap Smith	25.00	12.50	7.50
(111)	Tris Speaker	100.00	50.00	30.00
(112)	Harry Stovall	25.00	12.50	7.50
(113a)	Gabby Street (Senators)	25.00	12.50	7.50
(113b)	Gabby Street (Yankees)	25.00	12.50	7.50
(114)	George Suggs	25.00	12.50	7.50
(115)	Ira Thomas	25.00	12.50	7.50
(116)	Joe Tinker	60.00	30.00	18.00
(117)	John Titus	25.00	12.50	7.50
(118)	Terry Turner	25.00	12.50	7.50
(119)	Heinie Wagner	25.00	12.50	7.50
(120)	Bobby Wallace	60.00	30.00	18.00
(121)	Ed Walsh	60.00	30.00	18.00
(122)	Jack Warhop	25.00	12.50	7.50
(123)	Zach Wheat	60.00	30.00	18.00
(124)	Doc White	25.00	12.50	7.50
(125a)	Art Wilson (dark cap, Pirates)	25.00	12.50	7.50
(125b)	Art Wilson (dark cap, Giants)	25.00	12.50	7.50
(126a)	Owen Wilson (white cap, Giants)	25.00	12.50	7.50
(126b)	Owen Wilson (white cap, Pirates)	25.00	12.50	7.50
(127)	Hooks Wiltse	25.00	12.50	7.50
(128)	Harry Wolter	25.00	12.50	7.50
(129)	Cy Young	250.00	125.00	75.00

1910 P2 Sweet Caporal Pins

Expanding its premiums to include more than just trading cards, the American Tobacco Co. issued a series of baseball pins between 1910 and 1912. The sepia-colored pins, each measuring 7/8" in diameter, were distributed under the Sweet Caporal brand name. The set includes 152 different major league players, but because of numerous "large letter" variations, collectors generally consider the set complete at 204 different pins. Fifty of the players are pictured on a second pin that usually displays the same photo but has the player's name and team designation printed in larger letters. Two players (Roger Bresnahan and Bobby Wallace) have three pins each. It is now generally accepted that there are 153 pins with "small letters" and another 51 "large letter" variations in a complete set. Research among advanced collectors has shown that 19 of the pins, including six of the "large letter" variations, are considered more difficult to find. The back of each pin has either a black or a red paper insert advertising Sweet Caporal Cigarettes. The red backings, issued only with the "large letter" pins, are generally less common. The Sweet Caporal pins are closely related to the popular T205 Gold Border tobacco cards, also issued by the American Tobacco Co. about the same time. All but nine of the players featured in the pin set were also pictured on T205 cards, and in nearly all cases the photos are identical. The Sweet Caporal pins are designated as P2 in the American Card Catalog. The complete set price includes all variations.

		NM	EX	VG
Complete set:		5500.	2750.	1650.
Common player:		20.00	10.00	6.00
(1)	Ed Abbaticchio	20.00	10.00	6.00
(2)	Red Ames	20.00	10.00	6.00
(3a)	Jimmy Archer (small letters)	20.00	10.00	6.00
(3b)	Jimmy Archer (large letters)	25.00	12.50	7.50
(4a)	Jimmy Austin (small letters)	20.00	10.00	6.00
(4b)	Jimmy Austin (large letters)	25.00	12.50	7.50
(5)	Home Run Baker	40.00	20.00	12.00
(6)	Neal Ball	20.00	10.00	6.00
(7)	Cy Barger	20.00	10.00	6.00
(8)	Jack Barry	20.00	10.00	6.00
(9)	Johnny Bates	20.00	10.00	6.00
(10)	Beals Becker	20.00	10.00	6.00
(11)	Fred Beebe	20.00	10.00	6.00
(12a)	George Bell (small letters)	20.00	10.00	6.00
(12b)	George Bell (large letters)	25.00	12.50	7.50
(13a)	Chief Bender (small letters)	40.00	20.00	12.00
(13b)	Chief Bender (large letters)	65.00	32.00	19.50
(14)	Bill Bergen	20.00	10.00	6.00
(15)	Bob Bescher	20.00	10.00	6.00
(16)	Joe Birmingham	20.00	10.00	6.00
(17)	Kitty Bransfield	45.00	22.00	13.50
(18a)	Roger Bresnahan (mouth closed, small letters)	40.00	20.00	12.00
(18b)	Roger Bresnahan (mouth closed, large letters)	120.00	60.00	36.00
(19)	Roger Bresnahan (mouth open)	40.00	20.00	12.00
(20)	Al Bridwell	20.00	10.00	6.00
(21a)	Mordecai Brown (small letters)	40.00	20.00	12.00
(21b)	Mordecai Brown (large letters)	65.00	32.00	19.50
(22)	Bobby Byrne	20.00	10.00	6.00
(23)	Nixey Callahan	20.00	10.00	6.00
(24a)	Howie Camnitz (small letters)	20.00	10.00	6.00
(24b)	Howie Camnitz (large letters)	25.00	12.50	7.50
(25a)	Bill Carrigan (small letters)	20.00	10.00	6.00
(25b)	Bill Carrigan (large letters)	25.00	12.50	7.50
(26a)	Frank Chance (small letters)	45.00	22.00	13.50
(26b)	Frank Chance (large letters)	65.00	32.00	19.50
(27)	Hal Chase (different photo, small letters)	20.00	10.00	6.00
(28)	Hal Chase (different photo, large letters)	30.00	15.00	9.00
(29)	Ed Cicotte	35.00	17.50	10.50
(30a)	Fred Clarke (small letters)	40.00	20.00	12.00
(30b)	Fred Clarke (large letters)	65.00	32.00	19.50
(31a)	Ty Cobb (small letters)	300.00	150.00	90.00
(31b)	Ty Cobb (large letters)	400.00	200.00	120.00
(32a)	Eddie Collins (small letters)	40.00	20.00	12.00
(32b)	Eddie Collins (large letters)	90.00	45.00	27.00
(33)	Doc Crandall	20.00	10.00	6.00
(34)	Birdie Cree	45.00	22.00	13.50
(35)	Bill Dahlen	20.00	10.00	6.00
(36)	Jim Delahanty	20.00	10.00	6.00
(37)	Art Devlin	20.00	10.00	6.00
(38)	Josh Devore	20.00	10.00	6.00
(39)	Wild Bill Donovan	45.00	22.00	13.50
(40a)	Red Dooin (small letters)	20.00	10.00	6.00
(40b)	Red Dooin (large letters)	25.00	12.50	7.50
(41a)	Mickey Doolan (small letters)	20.00	10.00	6.00
(41b)	Mickey Doolan (large letters)	25.00	12.50	7.50
(42)	Patsy Dougherty	20.00	10.00	6.00
(43a)	Tom Downey (small letters)	20.00	10.00	6.00
(43b)	Tom Downey (large letters)	25.00	12.50	7.50
(44a)	Larry Doyle (small letters)	20.00	10.00	6.00
(44b)	Larry Doyle (large letters)	25.00	12.50	7.50
(45)	Louis Drucke	20.00	10.00	6.00
(46a)	Hugh Duffy (small letters)	40.00	20.00	12.00
(46b)	Hugh Duffy (large letters)	65.00	32.00	19.50
(47)	Jimmy Dygert	20.00	10.00	6.00

(48a)	Kid Elberfeld (small letters)	20.00	10.00	6.00
(48b)	Kid Elberfeld (large letters)	25.00	12.50	7.50
(49a)	Clyde Engle (small letters)	20.00	10.00	6.00
(49b)	Clyde Engle (large letters)	25.00	12.50	7.50
(50)	Tex Erwin	20.00	10.00	6.00
(51)	Steve Evans	20.00	10.00	6.00
(52)	Johnny Evers	40.00	20.00	12.00
(53)	Cecil Ferguson	20.00	10.00	6.00
(54)	John Flynn	20.00	10.00	6.00
(55a)	Russ Ford (small letters)	20.00	10.00	6.00
(55b)	Russ Ford (large letters)	25.00	12.50	7.50
(56)	Art Fromme	20.00	10.00	6.00
(57)	Harry Gaspar	20.00	10.00	6.00
(58a)	George Gibson (small letters)	20.00	10.00	6.00
(58b)	George Gibson (large letters)	25.00	12.50	7.50
(59)	Eddie Grant	45.00	22.00	13.50
(60)	Dolly Gray	20.00	10.00	6.00
(61a)	Clark Griffith (small letters)	40.00	20.00	12.00
(61b)	Clark Griffith (large letters)	65.00	32.00	19.50
(62)	Bob Groom	20.00	10.00	6.00
(63)	Bob Harmon	20.00	10.00	6.00
(64)	Topsy Hartsel	20.00	10.00	6.00
(65)	Arnold Hauser	45.00	22.00	13.50
(66)	Ira Hemphill	20.00	10.00	6.00
(67a)	Buck Herzog (small letters)	20.00	10.00	6.00
(67b)	Buck Herzog (large letters)	25.00	12.50	7.50
(68)	Dick Hoblitzell	20.00	10.00	6.00
(69)	Danny Hoffman	20.00	10.00	6.00
(70)	Harry Hooper	20.00	10.00	6.00
(71a)	Miller Huggins (small letters)	40.00	20.00	12.00
(71b)	Miller Huggins (large letters)	65.00	32.00	19.50
(72)	John Hummel	20.00	10.00	6.00
(73)	Hugh Jennings (different photo, small letters)	40.00	20.00	12.00
(74)	Hugh Jennings (different photo, large letters)	65.00	32.00	19.50
(75a)	Walter Johnson (small letters)	120.00	60.00	36.00
(75b)	Walter Johnson (large letters)	165.00	82.00	49.00
(76)	Tom Jones	45.00	22.00	13.50
(77)	Ed Karger	20.00	10.00	6.00
(78)	Ed Killian	45.00	22.00	13.50
(79a)	Jack Knight (small letters)	20.00	10.00	6.00
(79b)	Jack Knight (large letters)	25.00	12.50	7.50
(80)	Ed Konetchy	20.00	10.00	6.00
(81)	Harry Krause	20.00	10.00	6.00
(82)	Rube Kroh	20.00	10.00	6.00
(83)	Nap Lajoie	80.00	40.00	24.00
(84a)	Frank LaPorte (small letters)	20.00	10.00	6.00
(84b)	Frank LaPorte (large letters)	25.00	12.50	7.50
(85)	Arlie Latham	20.00	10.00	6.00
(86a)	Tommy Leach (small letters)	20.00	10.00	6.00
(86b)	Tommy Leach (large letters)	25.00	12.50	7.50
(87)	Sam Leever	20.00	10.00	6.00
(88)	Lefty Leifield	20.00	10.00	6.00
(89)	Hans Lobert	20.00	10.00	6.00
(90a)	Harry Lord (small letters)	20.00	10.00	6.00
(90b)	Harry Lord (large letters)	25.00	12.50	7.50
(91)	Paddy Livingston	20.00	10.00	6.00
(92)	Nick Maddox	20.00	10.00	6.00
(93)	Sherry Magee	20.00	10.00	6.00
(94)	Rube Marquard	40.00	20.00	12.00
(95a)	Christy Mathewson (small letters)	120.00	60.00	36.00
(95b)	Christy Mathewson (large letters)	145.00	72.00	43.00
(96a)	Al Mattern (small letters)	20.00	10.00	6.00
(96b)	Al Mattern (large letters)	25.00	12.50	7.50
(97)	George McBride	20.00	10.00	6.00
(98a)	John McGraw (small letters)	50.00	25.00	15.00
(98b)	John McGraw (large letters)	80.00	40.00	24.00
(99a)	Larry McLean (small letters)	20.00	10.00	6.00
(99b)	Larry McLean (large letters)	25.00	12.50	7.50
(100)	Harry McIntyre (Cubs)	20.00	10.00	6.00
(101a)	Matty McIntyre (White Sox, small letters)	20.00	10.00	6.00
(101b)	Matty McIntyre (White Sox, large letters)	25.00	12.50	7.50
(102)	Fred Merkle	20.00	10.00	6.00
(103)	Chief Meyers	20.00	10.00	6.00
(104)	Clyde Milan	20.00	10.00	6.00
(105)	Dots Miller	20.00	10.00	6.00
(106)	Mike Mitchell	20.00	10.00	6.00
(107)	Pat Moran	20.00	10.00	6.00
(108a)	George Mullen (Mullin) (small letters)	20.00	10.00	6.00
(108b)	George Mullen (Mullin) (large letters)	25.00	12.50	7.50
(109)	Danny Murphy	20.00	10.00	6.00
(110a)	Red Murray (small letters)	25.00	12.50	7.50
(110b)	Red Murray (large letters)	20.00	10.00	6.00
(111)	Tom Needham	45.00	22.00	13.50
(112a)	Rebel Oakes (small letters)	20.00	10.00	6.00
(112b)	Rebel Oakes (large letters)	25.00	12.50	7.50
(113)	Rube Oldring	20.00	10.00	6.00
(114)	Charley O'Leary	20.00	10.00	6.00
(115)	Orval Overall	45.00	22.00	13.50
(116)	Fred Parent	20.00	10.00	6.00
(117a)	Dode Paskert (small letters)	20.00	10.00	6.00
(117b)	Dode Paskert (large letters)	25.00	12.50	7.50
(118)	Barney Pelty	20.00	10.00	6.00
(119)	Jake Pfeister	20.00	10.00	6.00
(120)	Eddie Phelps	20.00	10.00	6.00
(121)	Deacon Phillippe	20.00	10.00	6.00
(122)	Jack Quinn	20.00	10.00	6.00
(123)	Ed Reulbach	20.00	10.00	6.00
(124)	Lew Richie	20.00	10.00	6.00
(125)	Jack Rowan	20.00	10.00	6.00
(126a)	Nap Rucker (small letters)	20.00	10.00	6.00
(126b)	Nap Rucker (large letters)	25.00	12.50	7.50
(127)	Doc Scanlon (Scanlan)	45.00	22.00	13.50
(128)	Germany Schaefer	20.00	10.00	6.00
(129)	Jimmy Scheckard (Sheckard)	20.00	10.00	6.00
(130a)	Boss Schmidt (small letters)	20.00	10.00	6.00
(130b)	Boss Schmidt (large letters)	25.00	12.50	7.50
(131)	Wildfire Schulte	20.00	10.00	6.00
(132)	Hap Smith	20.00	10.00	6.00
(133a)	Tris Speaker (small letters)	65.00	32.00	19.50
(133b)	Tris Speaker (large letters)	90.00	45.00	27.00
(134)	Oscar Stanage	20.00	10.00	6.00
(135)	Harry Steinfeldt	20.00	10.00	6.00
(136)	George Stone	20.00	10.00	6.00
(137a)	George Stoval (Stovall) (small letters)	20.00	10.00	6.00
(137b)	George Stoval (Stovall) (large letters)	25.00	12.50	7.50
(138a)	Gabby Street (small letters)	20.00	10.00	6.00
(138b)	Gabby Street (large letters)	25.00	12.50	7.50
(139)	George Suggs	20.00	10.00	6.00
(140a)	Ira Thomas (small letters)	20.00	10.00	6.00
(140b)	Ira Thomas (large letters)	25.00	12.50	7.50
(141a)	Joe Tinker (small letters)	40.00	20.00	12.00
(141b)	Joe Tinker (large letters)	65.00	32.00	19.50
(142a)	John Titus (small letters)	20.00	10.00	6.00
(142b)	John Titus (large letters)	25.00	12.50	7.50
(143)	Terry Turner	25.00	12.50	7.50
(144)	Heinie Wagner	20.00	10.00	6.00
(145a)	Bobby Wallace (with cap, small letters)	40.00	20.00	12.00
(145b)	Bobby Wallace (with cap, large letters)	65.00	32.00	19.50
(146)	Bobby Wallace (without cap)	40.00	20.00	12.00
(147)	Ed Walsh	40.00	20.00	12.00
(148)	Jack Warhop	45.00	22.00	13.50
(149a)	Zach Wheat (small letters)	40.00	20.00	12.00
(149b)	Zach Wheat (large letters)	65.00	32.00	19.50
(150)	Doc White	20.00	10.00	6.00
(151)	Art Wilson (Giants)	45.00	22.00	13.50
(152)	Owen Wilson (Pirates)	20.00	10.00	6.00
(153)	Hooks Wiltse	20.00	10.00	6.00
(154)	Harry Wolter	20.00	10.00	6.00
(155a)	Cy Young (small letters)	70.00	35.00	21.00
(155b)	Cy Young (large letters)	100.00	50.00	30.00

1956 Topps Pins

One of Topps first specialty issues, the 60-pin set of ballplayers issued in 1956 contains a high percentage of big-name stars which, combined with the scarcity of the pins, makes collecting a complete set extremely challenging. Compounding the situation is the fact that some pins are seen far less often than others, though the reason is unknown. Chuck Stobbs, Hector Lopez and Chuck Diering are unaccountably scarce. Measuring 1-1/8" in diameter, the pins utilize the same portraits found on 1956 Topps baseball cards. The photos are set against a solid color background.

		NM	EX	VG
Complete set (60):		2750.	1350.	825.00
Common player:		18.00	9.00	5.50
(1)	Hank Aaron	120.00	60.00	35.00
(2)	Sandy Amoros	18.00	9.00	5.50
(3)	Luis Arroyo	18.00	9.00	5.50
(4)	Ernie Banks	60.00	30.00	18.00
(5)	Yogi Berra	80.00	40.00	24.00
(6)	Joe Black	18.00	9.00	5.50
(7)	Ray Boone	18.00	9.00	5.50
(8)	Ken Boyer	20.00	10.00	6.00
(9)	Joe Collins	18.00	9.00	5.50
(10)	Gene Conley	18.00	9.00	5.50
(11)	Chuck Diering	225.00	112.00	67.00
(12)	Dick Donovan	18.00	9.00	5.50
(13)	Jim Finigan	18.00	9.00	5.50
(14)	Art Fowler	18.00	9.00	5.50
(15)	Ruben Gomez	18.00	9.00	5.50
(16)	Dick Groat	20.00	10.00	6.00
(17)	Harvey Haddix	18.00	9.00	5.50
(18)	Jack Harshman	18.00	9.00	5.50
(19)	Grady Hatton	18.00	9.00	5.50
(20)	Jim Hegan	18.00	9.00	5.50
(21)	Gil Hodges	40.00	20.00	12.00
(22)	Bobby Hofman	18.00	9.00	5.50
(23)	Frank House	18.00	9.00	5.50
(24)	Jackie Jensen	20.00	10.00	6.00
(25)	Al Kaline	65.00	32.00	19.50
(26)	Bob Kennedy	18.00	9.00	5.50
(27)	Ted Kluszewski	25.00	12.50	7.50
(28)	Dale Long	18.00	9.00	5.50
(29)	Hector Lopez	200.00	100.00	60.00
(30)	Ed Mathews	45.00	22.00	13.50
(31)	Willie Mays	120.00	60.00	35.00
(32)	Roy McMillan	18.00	9.00	5.50
(33)	Willie Miranda	18.00	9.00	5.50
(34)	Wally Moon	18.00	9.00	5.50
(35)	Don Mossi	18.00	9.00	5.50
(36)	Ron Negray	18.00	9.00	5.50
(37)	Johnny O'Brien	18.00	9.00	5.50
(38)	Carlos Paula	18.00	9.00	5.50
(39)	Vic Power	18.00	9.00	5.50
(40)	Jim Rivera	18.00	9.00	5.50
(41)	Phil Rizzuto	40.00	20.00	12.00
(42)	Jackie Robinson	100.00	50.00	30.00
(43)	Al Rosen	24.00	12.00	7.25
(44)	Hank Sauer	18.00	9.00	5.50
(45)	Roy Sievers	18.00	9.00	5.50
(46)	Bill Skowron	20.00	10.00	6.00
(47)	Al Smith	18.00	9.00	5.50
(48)	Hal Smith	18.00	9.00	5.50
(49)	Mayo Smith	18.00	9.00	5.50
(50)	Duke Snider	75.00	37.00	22.00
(51)	Warren Spahn	60.00	30.00	18.00
(52)	Karl Spooner	18.00	9.00	5.50
(53)	Chuck Stobbs	175.00	87.00	52.00
(54)	Frank Sullivan	18.00	9.00	5.50
(55)	Bill Tremel	18.00	9.00	5.50
(56)	Gus Triandos	18.00	9.00	5.50
(57)	Bob Turley	20.00	10.00	6.00
(58)	Herman Wehmeier	18.00	9.00	5.50
(59)	Ted Williams	125.00	62.50	37.50
(60)	Gus Zernial	18.00	9.00	5.50

1983 MLBPA pins

This pin set of 36, commonly mistaken for the 1969 Major League Baseball Player's Association version which is patterned after, has 18 unnumbered pins for each league; American Leaguers have red borders, National Leaguers have blue borders. Each pin is 7/8" in diameter and contains a black-and-white player mug shot.

Hank Aaron, blue .... $6-$9
Bob Allison, red $2
Yogi Berra, red.. $4.50
Roy Campanella, blue .... $6-$9
Norm Cash, red .... $2-$4.50
Orlando Cepeda, blue................................ $4.50
Roberto Clemente, blue .... $7-$10
Joe DiMaggio, red................................ $15-$20
Bobby Doerr, red .... $3-$6
Don Drysdale, blue .... $6-$7.5
Bob Feller, red .... $4.50-$9
Whitey Ford, red...................................... $4.50
Nelson Fox, red.............................. $4.50-$7.50
Frank Howard, red .... $2-$4.50
Jim Hunter, red................................. $4.50-$6
Al Kaline, red................................. $4.50-$7.50
Sandy Koufax, blue....................... $4.50-$7.50
Mickey Mantle, red .... $15-$22
Juan Marichal, blue............................ $4.50-$6
Eddie Mathews, blue.......................... $4.50-$6
Willie Mays, blue...................................... $6-$9
Willie McCovey, blue................................ $4.50
Stan Musial, blue .... $4.50-$7.50
Tony Oliva, red .... $3-$4.50
Satchel Paige, red.......................... $4.50-$15
Phil Rizzuto, red....................................... $4.50
Robin Roberts, blue .... $4.50-$6
Brooks Robinson, red................................ $4.50
Jackie Robinson, blue .... $9-$11
Ron Santo, blue.. $4.50
Bill Skowron, red .... $3-$4.50
Duke Snider, blue.......................... $4.50-$7.50
Warren Spahn, blue.................................. $4.50
Billy Williams, blue................................ $4.50-$6
Ted Williams, red................................. $9-$15
Maury Wills, blue .... $3-$6

PM10 Stadium Photo issues

These pins were issued in various sizes and were sold at ball parks around the country; the most popular pin size is 1 3/4". All of the pins have black-and-white photos on various color backgrounds, as noted after the players' names.

1. Hank Aaron, blue $275
2. Sandy Amoros, blue $50
3. Harry Anderson, black $75
4. Johnny Antonelli, white/N.Y. $45
    Johnny Antonelli, black, white/S.F. $25
5. Richie Ashburn, gray............................ $135
6. Dick Bartell, photo in circle $15
7. Gus Bell, white $85
8. Yogi Berra, blue $50
    Yogi Berra, white $75
    Yogi Berra, gray more expensive............ $95
9. Joe Black, white/profile........................... $95
    Joe Black, white/portrait $50
    Joe Black, black/white.......................... $25
10. Don Bollweg, gray $20
11. Lou Boudreau, white............................ $15
    Lou Boudreau, cap is red/blue............. $250
12. Eric Bressoud, gray $20
13. Billy Bruton, white.............................. $25
14. Dolph Camilli, white........................... $15
15. Roy Campanella, white $75
    Roy Campanella, blue $95
    Roy Campanella, ivory........................... $75
16. Chico Carrasquel, White Sox $125
17. Phil Cavaretta, stars in border $150
18. Orlando Cepeda, dirty white $45
    Orlando Cepeda, railing $50
19. Roberto Clemente, We remember........ $30
20. Gerry Coleman, gray $15
21. Tony Conigliaro, gray $50
    Tony Conigliaro, gray/teeth showing.... $50
22. Morton Cooper, white/black $15
23. Billy Cox, white $15
    Billy Cox, ivory.................................... $45
24. Al Dark, white.................................... $15
25. Jim Davenport, gray $95
    Jim Davenport, ivory............................ $95
26. Jerome (Dizzy) Dean, black $50
27. Bill Dickey, Yankees.......................... $145
28. Dom DiMaggio, black.......................... $50
    Dom DiMaggio, ivory $15
29. Joe DiMaggio, green $275
    Joe DiMaggio, black $275
    Joe DiMaggio, white $275
    Joe DiMaggio, light blue...................... $65
    Joe DiMaggio, white circle $300
    Joe DiMaggio, autograph $275
30. Larry Doby, white $15
    Larry Doby, black $65

    Larry Doby, Congratulations $85
31. Luke Easter, Indians............................ $65
32. Del Ennis, dirty gray $95
    Del Ennis, brown $95
33. Carl Erskine, white.............................. $35
34. Bob Feller, white................................. $15
    Bob Feller, autograph.......................... $175
35. Whitey Ford, white $70
36. Nelson Fox, foxes $250
37. Carl Furillo, black/white, facing right..$125
    Carl Furillo, black/white, facing left...... $95
    Carl Furillo, ivory $125
    Carl Furillo, blue................................ $145
38. Len Gabrielson, SF $75
39. Ned Garver, white............................. $125
40. Lou Gehrig, photo in circle................. $300
41. Junior Gilliam, small print $95
    Junior Gilliam, large print.................... $95
42. Lefty Gomez, Yankees........................ $125
43. Ruben Gomez, black/white, photo
    in circle $15
44. Billy Goodman, white........................... $65
45. Granny Hamner, gray.......................... $125
46. Jim Hart, ear missing $125
47. Gabby Hartnett, black $50
48. Grady Hatton, Reds.............................. $75
49. Jim Hegan, name in red $250
50. Tom Henrich, light gray....................... $50
    Tom Henrich, white $20
51. Mike Higgins, black............................. $15
52. Gil Hodges, white/eyes left.................. $75
    Gil Hodges, white/eyes front $125
    Gil Hodges, black/white....................... $75
    Gil Hodges, orange $75
53. Elston Howard, white............................ $25
54. Carl Hubbell, photo in circle............... $125
    Carl Hubbell, white circle $25
55. Monte Irvin, black............................... $40
    Monte Irvin, white circle $125
    Monte Irvin, white $125
56. Forrest "Spook" Jacobs, black/white $20
57. Jackie Jensen, black $25
    Jackie Jensen, natural........................... $50
    Jackie Jensen, white $95
58. Walter Johnson, Senators.................... $250
59. Willie Jones, gray................................ $85
60. Harmon Killebrew, natural $175
61. Ralph Kiner, white circle $175
62. Ted Kluszewski, white.......................... $75
63. Jim Konstanty, gray $145
64. Ed Kranepool, white $20
65. Hal Lanier, black circle $125
66. Big Bill Lee, black/gray $15
67. Bob Lemon, white................................ $15
    Bob Lemon, white circle..................... $145
68. Jim Lemon, white circle...................... $125

69. Whitey Lockman, black/white $15
70. Stan Lopata, gray $125
71. Sal Maglie, black/white $45
72. Frank Malzone, ivory $45
    Frank Malzone, natural $15
73. Mickey Mantle, blue/ear missing $250
    Mickey Mantle, ivory, baseball style .. $175
    Mickey Mantle, blue, name at wrist ... $135
    Mickey Mantle, white/name at elbow ... $125
    Mickey Mantle, white/both hands
      visible $40
    Mickey Mantle, white/eyes closed $300
    Mickey Mantle, with Teresa Brewer $50
74. Juan Marichal, black $135
75. Marty Marion, white circle $135
76. Roger Maris, yellow $25
    Roger Maris, pink $50
    Roger Maris, orange $25
    Roger Maris, white $125
77. Willie Mays, gray/S.F. $175
    Willie Mays, white/N.Y. $45
    Willie Mays, gray/N.Y. $195
    Willie Mays, natural/S.F. $145
    Willie Mays, S.F./stands $275
    Willie Mays, white circle $175
    Willie Mays, turquoise $250
78. Willie McCovey, gray $50
79. Gil McDougald, dirty gray $15
80. Clift Melton, photo in circle $15
81. Bill Meyer, white circle $125
82. Orestes Minoso, white circle $145
83. Bill Monbouquette, gray $15
84. Don Mueller, white $15
85. Bobby Murcer, white $15
86. Danny Murtaugh, white circle $150
87. Stan Musial, yellow $45
    Stan Musial, white $250
    Stan Musial, white/ear noticeable $225
88. Don Newcombe, ivory $25
    Don Newcombe, blue $75
    Don Newcombe, white/mouth open $30
89. Dan O'Connell, photo in a white border . $15
90. Andy Pafko, black $145
91. Joe Page, ivory $35
92. Leroy Paige, ivory $175
93. Mel Parnell, white $15
94. Joe Pepitone, white $20
95. Gaylord Perry, white $50
96. Johnny Pesky, white $65
97. Rico Petrocelli, gray $50
98. Jimmy Piersall, ivory $30
99. Johnny Podres, white $45
100. Johnny Pramesa, dirty gray $75
101. Dick Radatz, gray $30
102. Vic Raschi, white $45
103. Pee Wee Reese, white $75
     Pee Wee Reese, gray/B on cap $45

     Pee Wee Reese, gray/ear missing $125
     Pee Wee Reese, light gray $75
104. Pete Reiser, photo in circle $15
105. Bill Rigney, black/white $15
106. Phil Rizzuto, ivory $50
107. Robin Roberts, black/white $20
     Robin Roberts, brown $125
108. Jackie Robinson, yellow $50
     Jackie Robinson, red $250
     Jackie Robinson, ROY $125
     Jackie Robinson, blue $125
     Jackie Robinson, gray/white $275
     Jackie Robinson, white $275
     Jackie Robinson, white/ear missing ... $300
     Jackie Robinson, natural $125
109. Preacher Roe, white $125
110. Saul Rogovin, photo in circle $15
111. Stan Rojek, white circle $125
112. Al Rosen, white $15
113. Charles Herbert Ruffing, gray $25
114. Babe Ruth, black $400
115. Chuck Schilling, white $65
     Chuck Schilling, white $65
116. George Scott, white $15
117. Andy Seminick, gray $125
118. Bobby Shantz, white $20
     Bobby Shantz, gray $125
119. Frank Shea, black/white $15
120. Curt Simmons, brown $125
121. Enos Slaughter, black $85
122. Roy Smalley, white circle $125
123. Duke Snider, dirty gray $45
     Duke Snider, blue $175
     Duke Snider, black $95
124. Dick Stuart, gray $50
125. Hank Thompson, white circle $45
126. Bobby Thomson, ivory $40
127. Gus Triandos, light gray $70
128. Robert Lee Trice, natural $75
129. Eddie Waitkus, gray $125
130. Dixie Walker, white circle $45
131. Bill Werle, white circle $145
132. Sam White, white $15
133. Ted Williams, black/white, name on
     bottom $75
     Ted Williams, black/white, name on
     top $175
     Ted Williams, black $175
     Ted Williams, white $175
     Ted Williams, white $175
     Ted Williams, natural, name at bottom .. $75
134. Gene Woodling, natural $145
135. Whitlow Wyatt, photo in circle $15
136. Carl Yastrzemski, gray $150
     Carl Yastrzemski, white $150
137. Gus Zernial, gray $125

Crane Potato Chips team pins

Crane Potato Chips issued 7/8" team pins during the 1960s. Generally, the pins can be purchased for about $10 each, with the Yankees, Mets and Dodgers selling for $15 each. In 1961 the company issued two versions - dated (red, black and white) and undated (red, white and blue) for all 18 major league teams. In 1963 the company issued dated, red, black and yellow pins for all 20 teams. Variations exist for the Braves (red stripe, $10, or no stripe, $12) and Red Sox (black background, $10, or yellow background, $12). The 1964 dated pins are gold, red and light blue and range from $5-$15 each. The 1965 pins, which are also dated, are silver, red and dark blue. The 1967 pins, which are not dated, have red, white and light blue borders. Pins from 1968 are red, yellow and black and are dated. The undated pins from 1969 are dark blue, white and orange, while those from 1984, which are dated, have two styles - a base path for National League teams and a baseball style for American League teams.

Guy's Potato Chips

This company issued pins from 1964-66. Generally, pins sell for about $10 each. The 1964 pins, which are undated, are red, white and light blue. Variations exist for the Braves (red stripe or no stripe) and Red Sox (white background or blue background). The 1965 pins are dated and are red, yellow and light blue. Once again, variations exist for the Braves (red stripe or no stripe) and Red Sox (blue background or yellow background). The 1966 pins are also dated and are yellow, brown and green.

Win Craft Major League Baseball stamp pins

Carlos Baerga, Jeff Bagwell, Dante Bichette, Wade Boggs, Barry Bonds, Will Clark, Roger Clemens, Lenny Dykstra, Cecil Fielder, Tom Glavine, Juan Gonzalez, Mark Grace, Ken Griffey Jr., Tony Gwynn, Dave Justice, John Kruk, Greg Maddux, Mike Mussina, John Olerud, Hideo Nomo (2), Mike Piazza, Kirby Puckett, Cal Ripken Jr., Ivan Rodriguez, Tim Salmon, Deion Sanders, Dave Winfield - $5 each

Ticket Stubs, Schedules

Ticket stubs do not command high prices unless they are from World Series, All-Star or playoff games, or from a game in which a significant achievement or record occurred. Generally, the stubs are in either Poor or Fair condition, because they have been bent and are worn, or Very Good to Excellent because they have been preserved. Full, unused tickets are worth more money than stubs, and are generally for seats which went unsold for a playoff or World Series game, or one in which a baseball milestone occurred. Shortly after Nolan Ryan won his 300th game in 1990, unused tickets were being offered for $60; an unused ticket and program were priced at $75. Special commemorative certificates, printed by the respective teams, also add to the value and make for an attractive display.

Other tickets which would command premium prices would be those for games such as when Reggie Jackson hit his three homers in the sixth game of the 1977 World Series, and the 1956 World Series game when Don Larsen pitched a perfect game against the Brooklyn Dodgers. One ticket stub from that game sold for $532 in a 1992 auction. It was autographed, framed and matted and included a photo of the final pitch and a copy of the box score.

Other examples from auction results have shown prices realized from games from the 1922 and 1923 World Series (at the Polo Grounds and Yankee Stadium) were between $177-$296, while a 1920 Cleveland Indians full ticket from Game 4 sold for $967. A full ticket from Stan Musial's last game, Sept. 29, 1963, at St. Louis, sold for $242, while a full ticket from Catfish Hunter's perfect game on May 8, 1968, at Oakland, sold for $370. A 1978 All-Star Game full ticket from San Diego sold for $77. But in general, ticket stubs shouldn't set you back more than $30.

Alan Rosen, in his book Mr. Mint's Insider's Guide to Investing in Baseball Cards and Collectibles, advises collectors to not buy old tickets unless they have seat numbers, which are generally printed in a different ink color in a separate press run. Those without, generally from the 1940s and 1950s, and sold in large blocks, are usually worthless because they aren't artist's proofs.

Tickets

Note: The first ticket price is for a full ticket, the second is a stub. A means All-Star, P means playoff game, WS means World Series.

Boston Braves tickets: 1936 A ($400/$200); 1914 WS ($1,600/$800); 1948 WS ($200/$100-$145).

Brooklyn Dodgers tickets: 1949 A ($170/$85); 1916 WS ($1,200/$600-$750); 1920 WS ($800/$400); 1941-47-49 WS ($200-$250/$75-$200); 1952-53-56 WS ($125-$150/$75-$150); 1955 WS ($250/$95-$125).

Colorado Rockies tickets: None.

Florida Marlins tickets: None.

Houston Colt 45s tickets: None.

Kansas City A's tickets: 1960 A ($70/$35).

Milwaukee Braves tickets: 1955 A ($150/$75-$150); 1957-58 WS ($150-$200/$40-$75).

New York Giants tickets: 1934 A ($400/$200); 1942 A ($200/$100); 1905 WS ($2,500/$1,200); 1911-12-13 WS ($1,600/$600-$800); 1917 WS (1,200/$600); 1921-22-23-24 WS ($800/$400); 1933-36-37 WS ($400/$125-$200); 1951 WS ($150/$75-$125).

Philadelphia A's tickets: 1943 A ($200/$100); 1905 WS ($2,500/$1,200); 1910-11-13-14 WS ($1,600/$800); 1915 WS ($1,200/$600); 1930-31 WS ($400/$175-$275).

St. Louis Browns tickets; 1948 A ($200/$100); 1944 WS ($200/$75-$125).

Seatle Pilots tickets: None.

Washington Senators tickets: 1937 A ($400/$200); 1956 A ($150/$75); 1962 A ($75/$35-$75); 1969 A ($75/$35); 1924-25 WS ($800/$400); 1933 WS ($400/$75-$200).

Atlanta Braves tickets: 1972 A ($55/$15); 1969 P ($30/$15); 1982 P ($15/$5); 1991-92 P ($10/$5); 1991-92 WS ($20/$10).

Cincinnati Reds tickets: 1938 A ($400/$200); 1953 A ($150/$75-$175); 1970 A ($40/$20-$65); 1988 A ($30/$15-$50); 1970-72-73-75-76-79 P ($35-$75/$20-$55); 1990 P ($18/$10); 1993-95 P ($100/$30-$60); 1919 WS ($2,000/$1,000); 1939 WS ($400/$200); 1940 WS ($200/$100-$125); 1961 WS ($70/$35-$75); 1970-75-76 WS ($40-$145/$15-$60); 1990 WS ($125/$45).

Houston Astros tickets: 1868 A ($70/$35-$100); 1986 A ($30/$15); 1981-86 P ($28/$15).

Los Angeles Dodgers tickets: 1959 A ($150/$100-$175); 1980 A ($30/$15-$25); 1974-77-78 P ($45/$20); 1981-83-85-88 P ($45/$25); 1959 WS ($150/$75); 1963-65-66 WS ($65-$125/$40-$50); 1974-77-78 WS ($75$125/$35-$60); 1981-88 WS ($30-$75/$15-$40).

San Diego Padres tickets: 1978 A ($40/$20); 1992 A ($20/$10); 1984 P ($28/$15); 1984 WS ($75/$65).

San Francisco Giants tickets: 1961 A ($70/$35); 1984 A ($30/$15); 1971 P ($38/$15); 1987-89 P ($28/$15); 1962 WS ($300/$65-$125); 1989 WS ($30/$15).

Chicago Cubs tickets: 1947 A ($175-$200/$125); 1962 A ($150-$200/$35); 1990 A ($125/$60); 1984 P ($35/$15); 1989 P ($30/$15); 1906-07-08 WS ($2,000/$1,000); 1910 WS ($1,600/$800); 1918 WS ($1,200/$600); 1929 WS ($600/$250-$300); 1932-35-38 WS ($400/$150-$200); 1945 WS ($200/$100).

Montreal Expos tickets: 1982 A ($175/$100); 1981 P ($28/$15).

New York Mets tickets: 1964 A ($70/$35); 1969 P ($65/$50); 1973 P ($125/$35); 1986-88 P ($28/$15); 1969 WS ($350/$95); 1973 WS ($225/$40-$75); 1986 WS ($250/$75-$100).

Philadelphia Phillies tickets: 1952 A ($150/$75); 1976 A ($40/$20); 1976-77-78 P ($38/$20-$35); 1980-83 P ($60/$25); 1993 P ($40/$20); 1915 WS ($1,200/$600); 1950 WS ($250/$100-$145); 1980-83 WS ($30/$15); 1993 WS ($100/$40).

Pittsburgh Pirates tickets: 1944 A ($200/$100); 1959 A ($150/$75); 1974 A ($100-$125/$30-$45); 1970-71-72-74-75-79 ($75/$20-$45), 1990-91-92 P ($18/$10); 1903 WS ($6,000/$3,000); 1909 WS ($2,000/$1,000); 1925 WS ($800/$400); 1927 WS ($600/$300); 1960 WS ($70/$40-$100); 1971-79 WS ($75-$100/$20-$45).

St. Louis Cardinals tickets: 1940 A ($200/$100); 1957 A ($85-$150/$45); 1966 A ($70/$35); 1982-85-87 P ($28/$15); 1926-28 WS ($600/$300-$375); 1930-31-34 WS ($400/$175-$200); 1942-43-44-46 WS ($200/$100); 1964-67-68 WS ($70/$45-$75); 1982-85-87 WS ($75-$100/$35-$45).

Baltimore Orioles tickets: 1958 A ($200/$100); 1993 A ($150/$40); 1969 P ($50-$75/$25-$50); 1970-71 P ($30-$65/$15-$45); 1973-74 P ($20-$50/$30-$40); 1979 P ($20/$7); 1983 P ($15/$5); 1966 WS ($100/$40); 1969-70 WS ($70/$35-$45); 1971 WS ($50/$20-$45); 1979 WS ($100/$40); 1983 WS ($50/$30).

Boston Red Sox tickets: 1946 A ($200/$100); 1961 A ($75/$35); 1975 P ($45/$20); 1986-88 P ($90/$15-$25); 1990 P ($20/$10); 1903 WS ($6,000/$3,000); 1915-16-18 WS ($1,200/$600); 1946 WS ($50/$70); 1967 WS ($70-$100/$40-$85); 1975 WS ($40/$20); 1986 WS ($30/$15).

Cleveland Indians tickets: 1935 A ($400/$200); 1954 A ($150/$75-$125); 1963 A ($70/$35); 1981 A ($30/$15); 1920 WS ($800/$200-$350); 1948 WS ($200/$75-$150); 1954 WS ($150/$55-$95).

Detroit Tigers tickets: 1941 A ($200/$100); 1951 A ($150/$75); 1971 A ($40/$20); 1972 P ($38/$18); 1984-87 P ($30-$50/$30); 1908-09 WS ($2,000/$1,000); 1934-35 WS ($400/$150-$200); 1940-45 WS ($200/$100-$125); 1968 WS ($70/$45); 1984 WS ($30-$50/$30).

Milwaukee Brewers tickets: 1975 A ($45/$20); 1982 P ($28/$15-$20); 1982 WS ($75-$100/$35).

New York Yankees tickets: 1939 A ($275-$400/$200); 1960 A ($70/$35); 1977 A ($40/$20); 1976-77-78 P ($38/$15-$20); 1980-81 P ($28/$15-$20); 1921-22-23 WS ($800/$400); 1926-27-28 WS ($600/$225-$300); 1932-36-37-38-39 WS ($400/$125-$200); 1941-42-43-47-49 WS ($200/$85-$150); 1950-51-52-53-55-56-57-58 WS ($125-$150/$75-$125); 1960-61-62-63-64 WS ($200/$35-$75); 1976-77-78 WS ($40/$25); 1981 WS ($30/$15).

Toronto Blue Jays tickets: 1991 A ($175-$65); 1985-89 P ($28-$35/$15); 1991-92 P ($20-$65/$10); 1993 P ($45/$20); 1992-93 WS ($100-$200/$15-$50).

California Angels tickets: 1967 A ($150/$85); 1989 A ($30-$60/$15-$45); 1979-82 P ($30/$15-$30); 1986 ($25/$10).

Chicago White Sox tickets: 1933 A ($400/$200-$250); 1950 A ($150/$75); 1983 A ($30-$75/$15); 1986 P ($15/$5); 1993 P ($60/$15); 1906 WS ($2,000/$1,000); 1917 WS ($1,200/$600); 1919 WS ($3,000/$1,500); 1959 WS ($150/$75-$95).

Kansas City Royals tickets: 1973 A ($40/$20); 1976-77-78 P ($38/$18); 1980-81-84-85 P ($28/$15); 1980-85 WS ($100-$125/$40-$45).

Minnesota Twins tickets: 1965 A ($70-$125/$35); 1985 A ($30/$15-$20); 1969 P ($65/$30); 1970-87 P ($35-$65/$15-$25); 1991 P ($20-$45/$10-$20); 1965 WS ($100-$150/$35-$50); 1987 WS ($75-$100/$35-$60); 1991 WS $100/$35-$50).

Oakland A's tickets: 1987 A ($30/$15); 1971-72-73-74-75 P ($38/$20-$30); 1988-89 P ($50-$65/$15-$20); 1990-92 P ($18/$10); 1972-73-74-75 WS ($75-$125/$40-$65); 1988-89 WS ($100-$125/$15-$45); 1990 WS ($20/$10).

Seattle Mariners tickets: 1979 A ($40/$20).

Texas Rangers tickets: 1995 A ($125/$50-$75).

Full ticket sheets

1965 Minnesota Twins: WS 1, 2, 6, 7 ....$265
1982 St. Louis Cardinals: WS 1, 2, 6, 7 ....$525
1982 Chicago White Sox (yellow): ALCS 1,2; WS 3, 4, 5..$25
1982 Chicago White Sox (tan): ALCS 1, 2; WS 3, 4, 5...$25
1982 Chicago White Sox (green): ALCS 1, 2; WS 3, 4, 5...$25
1982 Chicago White Sox (orange): ALCS 1, 2; WS 3, 4, 5...$25
1982 Chicago White Sox (purple): ALCS 1, 2; WS 3, 4, 5..$25
1984 Minnesota Twins: ALCS 1, 2; WS A, B, C, D..$40
1987 St. Louis Cardinals: NLCS 1, 2, 6, 7; WS 3, 4, 5...$595
1989 San Francisco Giants: WS 3, 4, 5...$295
1992 Minnesota Twins: ALCS 3, 4, 5; WS 3, 4, 5..$50

1960-64 Chicago White Sox ticket stubs

From 1960-64, tickets to Chicago White Sox home games at Comiskey Park were issued bearing player photographs. Along with the photos on the backs of the 1 5/16" by 2 5/8" ticket stubs are career information and facsimile autographs. Photos were generally re-used from year to year and color variations, depending on the type of ticket, are known. Players from each year are listed here alphabetically. The complete set of tickets is $450 in Near Mint condition; common players are worth $6, unless noted.

The players each year are: 1960 - Luis Aparicio ($15), Earl Battey, Frank Baumann, Dick Donovan, Nelson Fox ($12), Gene Freese, Ted Kluszewski ($12), Jim Landis, Barry Latman, Sherm Lollar, Al Lopez ($9), Turk Lown, Orestes Minoso ($10), Bill Pierce, Jim Rivera, Bob Shaw, Roy Sievers, Al Smith, Gerry Staley and Early Wynn ($9).

The players for 1961 are: Aparicio ($15), Baumann, Camilo Carreon, Sam Esposito, Fox ($12), Billy Goodman, Landis, Lollar, Lopez ($9), Cal McLish, J.C. Martin, Minoso ($10), Pierce, Juan Pizarro, Bob Roselli, Herb Score ($7.50), Shaw, Sievers, Smith, Staley and Wynn ($9).

The players for 1962 are: Aparicio ($15), Baumann, Buzhardt, Carreon, Joe Cunningham, Bob Farley, Eddie Fisher, Fox ($12), Landis, Lollar, Lopez ($9), Turk Lown, Martin, McLish, Gary Peters, Pizarro, Floyd Robinson, Roselli, Score ($7.50), Al Smith, Charles Smith and Wynn ($9).

The players for 1863 are: Baumann, Buzhardt, Carreon, Cunningham, Dave DeBusschere ($8), Fisher, Fox ($12), Ron Hansen, Ray Herbert, Mike Hershberger, Grover Jones, Mike Joyce, Frank Kreutzer, Landis, Lopez ($9), Martin, Maxwell, Dave Nicholson, Pizarro, Robinson, Charlie Smith, Pete Ward, Al Weis, Hoyt Wilhelm ($9) and Dom Zanni.

The players for 1964 are: Fritz Ackley, Baumann, Don Buford, Buzhardt, Carreon, Cunningham, DeBusschere ($8), Fisher, Jim Golden, Hansen, Herbert, Hershberger, Horlen, Landis, Lopez ($9), Martin, Nicholson, Peters, Pizarro, Robinson, Gene Stephens, Ward and Wilhelm ($9).

Schedules

If you search through the scrapbooks, wallets and shoe boxes of memorabilia long enough, inevitably you'll find an annual schedule or two for a favorite team of yesteryear.

Schedules, or skeds for short, offer collectors an inexpensive alternative to the big-ticket items which anchor any fan's collection. The limits are endless.

Although the most common form is a pocket schedule, skeds come in all shapes, sizes and for all sports. Collegiate sports such as baseball, football and hockey often utilize sked-cards, which are usually a single piece of paper or tagboard stock with artwork on one side and a game schedule on the back. Professional sports teams generally use folded skeds, similar to sked-cards, but with multiple panels separated by folds. These types of schedules are commonly provided by the major league teams' ticket offices. Other schedule varieties include matchbook covers, schedule cups, ticket brochures, decals, magnets, rulers, napkins, place mats, stickers, key chains, plastic coin purses and poster skeds.

The easiest way to begin or add to a schedule collection is to contact professional teams for ticket information. You'll usually get a response, especially if you send a self-addressed stamped envelope, which means the team isn't paying postage and already has a pre-addressed envelope to send back. When mailing to Canada, remember that any SASEs sent to the Montreal Expos or Toronto Blue Jays require Canadian postage.

Because schedules are primarily advertising pieces through which the sponsors can reach a wide, varying target audience, the sponsors themselves can be a source for schedules. Other possible sources can be found by determining who advertises in the team's yearbook and programs. Radio and television sponsors, and stations which carry the broadcasts, also often produce skeds, as may those who advertise on the television and radio broadcasts.

Off-the-wall skeds can be found in a variety of locations, such as restaurants, which often offer matchbook schedules, liquor stores, sporting goods stores, museums, banks and credit unions, motels and hotels, and ticket offices. When traveling, remember to check gas stations, convenience stores, and kiosks which are located along interstate rest stops.

Another way to obtain schedules is by trading, searching for prospective partners in classified ads in hobby publications such as Sports Collectors Digest and sked newsletters.

If the conventional shoe box or scrapbook is not used for displaying schedules, many pocket schedules will fit into eight- or nine-pocket baseball card plastic sheets which are held together in an album. These sheets protect the skeds from getting dinged and folded. Oversized schedules may fit into 5-by-7 inch, dollar bill-sized, or postcard-sized plastic sheets.

Condition is not a critical factor in determining a schedule's value, but it is important. It's more valuable if it isn't damaged, ripped or torn, or marked on. Schedules for defunct teams carry a slight premium value compared to other schedules of the same year, as do localized, scarcer schedules and those featuring team or player photos.

Schedules and their general values: 1901-1909 ($150); 1910-19 ($100); 1920-29 ($75); 1930-39 ($35); 1940-49 ($30); 1950-59 ($25); 1960-69 ($15); 1970-79 ($10); 1980-85 ($2); 1986-on ($1).

Medallions

1955 Armour Coins

In 1955, Armour inserted a plastic "coin" in its packages of hot dogs. A raised profile of a ballplayer is on the front of each coin along with the player's name, position, birthplace and date, batting and throwing preference, and 1954 hitting or pitching record. The coins, which measure 1-1/2" in diameter and are unnumbered, came in a variety of colors, including the more common ones in aqua, dark blue, light green, orange, red and yellow. Scarcer colors are black, pale blue, lime green, very dark green, gold, pale orange, pink, silver, and tan. Scarce colors are double the value of the coins listed in the checklist that follows. Twenty-four different players are included in the set. Variations exist for Harvey Kuenn (letters in his name are condensed or spaced) and Mickey Mantle (name is spelled Mantle or incorrectly as Mantel). The complete set price includes the two variations.

		NM	EX	VG
Complete set:		1200.	600.00	350.00
Common player:		17.50	8.75	5.25
(1)	John "Johnny" Antonelli	22.00	11.00	6.50
(2)	Larry "Yogi" Berra	88.00	44.00	26.00
(3)	Delmar "Del" Crandall	22.00	11.00	6.50
(4)	Lawrence "Larry" Doby	27.00	13.50	8.00
(5)	James "Jim" Finigan	17.50	8.75	5.25
(6)	Edward "Whitey" Ford	88.00	44.00	26.00
(7)	James "Junior" Gilliam	30.00	15.00	9.00
(8)	Harvey "Kitten" Haddix	17.50	8.75	5.25
(9)	Ranson "Randy" Jackson (name actually Ransom)	30.00	15.00	9.00
(10)	Jack "Jackie" Jensen	27.00	13.50	8.00
(11)	Theodore "Ted" Kluszewski	35.00	17.50	10.50
(12a)	Harvey E. Kuenn (spaced letters in name)	37.00	18.50	11.00
(12b)	Harvey E. Kuenn (condensed letters in name)	60.00	30.00	18.00
(13a)	Charles "Mickey" Mantel (incorrect spelling)	215.00	107.00	64.00
(13b)	Charles "Mickey" Mantle (correct spelling)	550.00	275.00	165.00
(14)	Donald "Don" Mueller	30.00	15.00	9.00
(15)	Harold "Pee Wee" Reese	60.00	30.00	18.00
(16)	Allie P. Reynolds	27.00	13.50	8.00
(17)	Albert "Flip" Rosen	27.00	13.50	8.00
(18)	Curtis "Curt" Simmons	17.50	8.75	5.25
(19)	Edwin "Duke" Snider	88.00	44.00	26.00
(20)	Warren Spahn	60.00	30.00	18.00
(21)	Frank Thomas	50.00	25.00	15.00
(22)	Virgil "Fire" Trucks	17.50	8.75	5.25
(23)	Robert "Bob" Turley	27.00	13.50	8.00
(24)	James "Mickey" Vernon	17.50	8.75	5.25

1959 Armour Coins

After a three-year layoff, Armour again inserted plastic baseball "coins" into its hot dog packages. The coins retained their 1-1/2" size but did not include as much detailed information as in 1955. Missing from the coins' backs is information such as birthplace and date, team, and batting and throwing preference. The fronts contain the player's name and, unlike 1955, only the team nickname is given. The set consists of 20 coins which come in a myriad of colors. Common colors are navy blue, royal blue, dark green, orange, red, and pale yellow. Scarce colors are pale blue, cream, grey-green, pale green, dark or light pink, pale red, tan, and translucent coins of any color with or without multi-colored flecks in the plastic mix. Scarce colors are double the value listed for coins in the checklist. In 1959, Armour had a write-in offer of 10 coins for $1. The same 10 players were part of the write-in offer, accounting for why half of the coins in the set are much more plentiful than the other.

	NM	EX	VG
Complete set:	550.00	275.00	165.00
Common player:	15.00	7.50	4.50
(1) Hank Aaron	67.00	33.00	20.00
(2) John Antonelli	22.00	11.00	6.50
(3) Richie Ashburn	34.00	17.00	10.00
(4) Ernie Banks	60.00	30.00	18.00
(5) Don Blasingame	15.00	7.50	4.50
(6) Bob Cerv	15.00	7.50	4.50
(7) Del Crandall	22.00	11.00	6.50
(8) Whitey Ford	50.00	25.00	15.00
(9) Nellie Fox	22.00	11.00	6.50
(10) Jackie Jensen	40.00	20.00	12.00
(11) Harvey Kuenn	22.00	11.00	6.50
(12) Frank Malzone	15.00	7.50	4.50
(13) Johnny Podres	22.00	11.00	6.50
(14) Frank Robinson	36.00	18.00	11.00
(15) Roy Sievers	15.00	7.50	4.50
(16) Bob Skinner	15.00	7.50	4.50
(17) Frank Thomas	20.00	10.00	6.00
(18) Gus Triandos	15.00	7.50	4.50
(19) Bob Turley	27.00	13.50	8.00
(20) Mickey Vernon	22.00	11.00	6.50

1960 Armour Coins

The 1960 Armour coin issue is identical in number and style to the 1959 set. The unnumbered coins, which measure 1-1/2" in diameter, once again came in a variety of colors. Common colors for 1960 are dark blue, light blue, dark green, light green, red-orange, dark red, and light yellow. Scarce colors are aqua, grey-blue, cream, tan, and dark yellow. Scarce colors are double the value of the coins in the checklist. The Bud Daley coin is very scarce, although it is not exactly known why. Theories for the scarcity center on broken printing molds, contract disputes, and that the coin was only inserted in a test product that quickly proved to be unsuccessful. As in 1959, a mail-in offer for 10 free coins was made available by Armour.

	NM	EX	VG
Complete set:	1450.	725.00	425.00
Common player:	9.00	4.50	2.75
(1a) Hank Aaron (Braves)	55.00	27.00	16.50
(1b) Hank Aaron (Milwaukee Braves)	90.00	45.00	27.00
(2) Bob Allison	15.00	7.50	4.50
(3) Ernie Banks	22.00	11.00	6.50
(4) Ken Boyer	12.00	6.00	3.50
(5) Rocky Colavito	18.50	9.25	5.50
(6) Gene Conley	12.00	6.00	3.50
(7) Del Crandall	12.00	6.00	3.50
(8) Bud Daley	900.00	450.00	270.00
(9a) Don Drysdale (L.A condensed)	25.00	12.50	7.50
(9b) Don Drysdale			
(space between L. and A.)	32.00	16.00	9.50
(10) Whitey Ford	25.00	12.50	7.50
(11) Nellie Fox	18.50	9.25	5.50
(12) Al Kaline	37.00	18.50	11.00
(13a) Frank Malzone (Red Sox)	9.00	4.50	2.75
(13b) Frank Malzone (Boston Red Sox)	30.00	15.00	9.00
(14) Mickey Mantle	125.00	62.00	37.00
(15) Ed Mathews	33.00	16.50	10.00
(16) Willie Mays	55.00	27.00	16.50
(17) Vada Pinson	12.00	6.00	3.50
(18) Dick Stuart	12.00	6.00	3.50
(19) Gus Triandos	9.00	4.50	2.75
(20) Early Wynn	25.00	12.50	7.50

1969 Citgo Coins

This 20-player set of small (about 1" in diameter) metal coins was issued by Citgo in 1969 to commemorate professional baseball's 100th anniversary. The brass-coated coins, susceptible to oxidation, display the player in a crude portrait with his name across the top. The backs honor the 100th anniversary of pro ball. The coins are unnumbered but are generally checklisted according to numbers that appear on a display card which was available from Citgo by mail.

	NM	EX	VG
Complete set:	95.00	47.00	28.00
Common player:	1.50	.70	.45
1 Denny McLain	3.00	1.50	.90
2 Dave McNally	1.50	.70	.45
3 Jim Lonborg	1.50	.70	.45
4 Harmon Killebrew	7.50	3.75	2.25
5 Mel Stottlemyre	1.50	.70	.45
6 Willie Horton	1.50	.70	.45
7 Jim Fregosi	2.25	1.25	.70
8 Rico Petrocelli	1.50	.70	.45
9 Stan Bahnsen	1.50	.70	.45
10 Frank Howard	3.00	1.50	.90
11 Joe Torre	2.25	1.25	.70
12 Jerry Koosman	1.50	.70	.45
13 Ron Santo	3.00	1.50	.90
14 Pete Rose	22.00	11.00	6.50
15 Rusty Staub	3.00	1.50	.90
16 Henry Aaron	25.00	12.50	7.50
17 Richie Allen	4.50	2.25	1.25
18 Ron Swoboda	1.50	.70	.45
19 Willie McCovey	7.50	3.75	2.25
20 Jim Bunning	3.00	1.50	.90

1965 Old London Coins

These 1-1/2" diameter metal coins were included in Old London snack food packages. The 40 coins in this set feature two players from each of the major leagues' 20 teams, except St. Louis (3) and the New York Mets (1). Coin fronts have color photos and player names, while the silver-colored coin backs give brief biographies of each player. An Old London logo is also displayed on each coin back. Space Magic Ltd. produced the coins. This is the same company which produced similar sets for Topps in 1964 and 1971.

Medallions

		NM	EX	VG
	Complete set (40):	625.00	300.00	185.00
	Common player:	4.50	2.25	1.25
(1)	Henry Aaron	65.00	32.00	19.50
(2)	Richie Allen	7.25	3.75	2.25
(3)	Bob Allison	5.75	3.00	1.75
(4)	Ernie Banks	30.00	15.00	9.00
(5)	Ken Boyer	7.25	3.75	2.25
(6)	Jim Bunning	10.00	5.00	3.00
(7)	Orlando Cepeda	7.50	3.75	2.25
(8)	Dean Chance	4.50	2.25	1.25
(9)	Rocky Colavito	10.00	5.00	3.00
(10)	Vic Davalillo	4.50	2.25	1.25
(11)	Tommy Davis	6.50	3.25	2.00
(12)	Ron Fairly	5.00	2.50	1.50
(13)	Dick Farrell	4.50	2.25	1.25
(14)	Jim Fregosi	5.00	2.50	1.50
(15)	Bob Friend	5.00	2.50	1.50
(16)	Dick Groat	6.50	3.25	2.00
(17)	Ron Hunt	4.50	2.25	1.25
(18)	Chuck Hinton	4.50	2.25	1.25
(19)	Ken Johnson	4.50	2.25	1.25
(20)	Al Kaline	30.00	15.00	9.00
(21)	Harmon Killebrew	25.00	12.50	7.50
(22)	Don Lock	4.50	2.25	1.25
(23)	Mickey Mantle	160.00	80.00	48.00
(24)	Roger Maris	35.00	17.50	10.50
(25)	Willie Mays	65.00	32.00	19.50
(26)	Bill Mazeroski	10.00	5.00	3.00
(27)	Gary Peters	4.50	2.25	1.25
(28)	Vada Pinson	7.25	3.75	2.25
(29)	Boog Powell	7.25	3.75	2.25
(30)	Dick Radatz	4.50	2.25	1.25
(31)	Brooks Robinson	30.00	15.00	9.00
(32)	Frank Robinson	30.00	15.00	9.00
(33)	Tracy Stallard	4.50	2.25	1.25
(34)	Joe Torre	6.50	3.25	2.00
(35)	Leon Wagner	4.50	2.25	1.25
(36)	Pete Ward	4.50	2.25	1.25
(37)	Dave Wickersham	4.50	2.25	1.25
(38)	Billy Williams	20.00	10.00	6.00
(39)	John Wyatt	4.50	2.25	1.25
(40)	Carl Yastrzemski	55.00	27.00	16.50

1962 Salada-Junket Dessert Coins

These 1-3/8" diameter plastic coins were issued in packages of Salada Tea and Junket Pudding mix. There are 221 different players available, with variations bringing the total of different coins to 261. Each coin has a paper color photo inserted in the front which contains the player's name and position plus the coin number. The plastic rims come in six different colors, coded by team. Production began with 180 coins, but the addition of the New York Mets and Houston Colt .45's to the National League allowed the company to expand the set's size. Twenty expansion players were added along with 21 other players. Several players' coins were dropped after the initial 180 run, causing some scarcities.

		NM	EX	VG
	Complete set (no variations):	2725.	1350.	800.00
	Complete set (with variations):	7900.	3950.	2350.
	Common player (1-180):	3.25	1.75	1.00
	Common player (181-221):	8.75	4.50	2.75
1	Jim Gentile	5.00	2.50	1.50
2	Bill Pierce	114.00	57.00	34.00

3	Chico Fernandez	3.25	1.75	1.00
4	Tom Brewer	27.00	13.50	8.00
5	Woody Held	3.25	1.75	1.00
6	Ray Herbert	33.00	16.50	10.00
7a	Ken Aspromonte (Angels)	12.00	6.00	3.50
7b	Ken Aspromonte (Indians)	5.50	2.75	1.75
8	Whitey Ford	27.00	13.50	8.00
9	Jim Lemon	3.25	1.75	1.00
10	Billy Klaus	3.25	1.75	1.00
11	Steve Barber	38.00	19.00	11.50
12	Nellie Fox	16.50	8.25	5.00
13	Jim Bunning	9.75	5.00	3.00
14	Frank Malzone	5.50	2.75	1.75
15	Tito Francona	3.25	1.75	1.00
16	Bobby Del Greco	3.25	1.75	1.00
17a	Steve Bilko (red shirt buttons)	7.75	4.00	2.25
17b	Steve Bilko (white shirt buttons)	6.00	3.00	1.75
18	Tony Kubek	60.00	30.00	18.00
19	Earl Battey	3.25	1.75	1.00
20	Chuck Cottier	3.25	1.75	1.00
21	Willie Tasby	3.25	1.75	1.00
22	Bob Allison	4.25	2.25	1.25
23	Roger Maris	34.00	17.00	10.00
24a	Earl Averill (red shirt buttons)	7.75	4.00	2.25
24b	Earl Averill (white shirt buttons)	4.25	2.25	1.25
25	Jerry Lumpe	3.25	1.75	1.00
26	Jim Grant	29.00	14.50	8.75
27	Carl Yastrzemski	70.00	35.00	21.00
28	Rocky Colavito	13.00	6.50	4.00
29	Al Smith	3.25	1.75	1.00
30	Jim Busby	38.00	19.00	11.50
31	Dick Howser	3.25	1.75	1.00
32	Jim Perry	3.25	1.75	1.00
33	Yogi Berra	35.00	17.50	10.50
34a	Ken Hamlin (red shirt buttons)	7.75	4.00	2.25
34b	Ken Hamlin (white shirt buttons)	4.25	2.25	1.25
35	Dale Long	3.25	1.75	1.00
36	Harmon Killebrew	24.00	12.00	7.25
37	Dick Brown	3.25	1.75	1.00
38	Gary Geiger	3.25	1.75	1.00
39a	Minnie Minoso (White Sox)	27.00	13.50	8.00
39b	Minnie Minoso (Cardinals)	17.50	8.75	5.25
40	Brooks Robinson	39.00	19.50	11.50
41	Mickey Mantle	125.00	62.00	37.00
42	Bennie Daniels	3.25	1.75	1.00
43	Billy Martin	12.00	6.00	3.50
44	Vic Power	5.50	2.75	1.75
45	Joe Pignatano	3.25	1.75	1.00
46a	Ryne Duren (red shirt buttons)	7.75	4.00	2.25
46b	Ryne Duren (white shirt buttons)	5.50	2.75	1.75
47a	Pete Runnels (2B)	12.00	6.00	3.50
47b	Pete Runnels (1B)	6.50	3.25	2.00
48a	Dick Williams (name on right)	1090.	545.00	327.00
48b	Dick Williams (name on left)	4.25	2.25	1.25
49	Jim Landis	3.25	1.75	1.00
50	Steve Boros	3.25	1.75	1.00
51a	Zoilo Versalles (red shirt buttons)	7.75	4.00	2.25
51b	Zoilo Versalles (white shirt buttons)	5.50	2.75	1.75
52a	Johnny Temple (Indians)	19.00	9.50	5.75
52b	Johnny Temple (Orioles)	5.50	2.75	1.75
53a	Jackie Brandt (Oriole)	8.75	4.50	2.75
53b	Jackie Brandt (Orioles)	926.00	463.00	278.00
54	Joe McClain	3.25	1.75	1.00
55	Sherm Lollar	5.50	2.75	1.75
56	Gene Stephens	3.25	1.75	1.00
57a	Leon Wagner (red shirt buttons)	7.75	4.00	2.25
57b	Leon Wagner (white shirt buttons)	5.50	2.75	1.75
58	Frank Lary	3.25	1.75	1.00
59	Bill Skowron	7.75	4.00	2.25
60	Vic Wertz	6.50	3.25	2.00
61	Willie Kirkland	3.25	1.75	1.00
62	Leo Posada	3.25	1.75	1.00
63a	Albie Pearson (red shirt buttons)	7.75	4.00	2.25
63b	Albie Pearson (white shirt buttons)	4.25	2.25	1.25
64	Bobby Richardson	13.00	6.50	4.00
65a	Marv Breeding (SS)	16.50	8.25	5.00
65b	Marv Breeding (2B)	5.50	2.75	1.75
66	Roy Sievers	87.00	43.00	26.00
67	Al Kaline	35.00	17.50	10.50
68a	Don Buddin (Red Sox)	17.50	8.75	5.25
68b	Don Buddin (Colts)	5.00	2.50	1.50
69a	Lenny Green (red shirt buttons)	7.75	4.00	2.25
69B	Lenny Green (white shirt buttons)	5.50	2.75	1.75
70	Gene Green	35.00	17.50	10.50
71	Luis Aparicio	16.50	8.25	5.00
72	Norm Cash	7.75	4.00	2.25
73	Jackie Jensen	44.00	22.00	13.00
74	Bubba Phillips	3.25	1.75	1.00
75	Jim Archer	3.25	1.75	1.00
76a	Ken Hunt (red shirt buttons)	7.75	4.00	2.25

76b	Ken Hunt (white shirt buttons)	4.25	2.25	1.25
77	Ralph Terry	4.25	2.25	1.25
78	Camilo Pascual	3.25	1.75	1.00
79	Marty Keough	38.00	19.00	11.50
80	Cletis Boyer	5.00	2.50	1.50
81	Jim Pagliaroni	3.25	1.75	1.00
82a	Gene Leek (red shirt buttons)	7.75	4.00	2.25
82b	Gene Leek (white shirt buttons)	4.25	2.25	1.25
83	Jake Wood	3.25	1.75	1.00
84	Coot Veal	35.00	17.50	10.50
85	Norm Siebern	5.50	2.75	1.75
86a	Andy Carey (White Sox)	44.00	22.00	13.00
86b	Andy Carey (Phillies)	8.75	4.50	2.75
87a	Bill Tuttle (red shirt buttons)	8.25	4.25	2.50
87b	Bill Tuttle (white shirt buttons)	5.50	2.75	1.75
88a	Jimmy Piersall (Indians)	16.50	8.25	5.00
88b	Jimmy Piersall (Senators)	8.75	4.50	2.75
89	Ron Hansen	41.00	20.00	12.50
90a	Chuck Stobbs (red shirt buttons)	7.75	4.00	2.25
90b	Chuck Stobbs (white shirt buttons)	4.25	2.25	1.25
91a	Ken McBride (red shirt buttons)	7.75	4.00	2.25
91b	Ken McBride (white shirt buttons)	4.25	2.25	1.25
92	Bill Bruton	3.25	1.75	1.00
93	Gus Triandos	3.25	1.75	1.00
94	John Romano	3.25	1.75	1.00
95	Elston Howard	7.75	4.00	2.25
96	Gene Woodling	4.25	2.25	1.25
97a	Early Wynn (pitching pose)	65.00	32.00	19.50
97b	Early Wynn (portrait)	29.00	14.50	8.75
98	Milt Pappas	4.25	2.25	1.25
99	Bill Monbouquette	3.25	1.75	1.00
100	Wayne Causey	3.25	1.75	1.00
101	Don Elston	3.25	1.75	1.00
102a	Charlie Neal (Dodgers)	13.50	6.75	4.00
102b	Charlie Neal (Mets)	4.25	2.25	1.25
103	Don Blasingame	3.25	1.75	1.00
104	Frank Thomas	41.00	20.00	12.50
105	Wes Covington	4.25	2.25	1.25
106	Chuck Hiller	3.25	1.75	1.00
107	Don Hoak	4.25	2.25	1.25
108a	Bob Lillis (Cardinals)	33.00	16.50	10.00
108b	Bob Lillis (Colts)	4.25	2.25	1.25
109	Sandy Koufax	44.00	22.00	13.00
110	Gordy Coleman	3.25	1.75	1.00
111	Ed Matthews (Mathews)	22.00	11.00	6.50
112	Art Mahaffey	4.25	2.25	1.25
113a	Ed Bailey			
	(red period above "i" in Giants)	12.00	6.00	3.50
113b	Ed Bailey (white period)	4.25	2.25	1.25
114	Smoky Burgess	5.50	2.75	1.75
115	Bill White	4.25	2.25	1.25
116	Ed Bouchee	27.00	13.50	8.00
117	Bob Buhl	3.25	1.75	1.00
118	Vada Pinson	4.25	2.25	1.25
119	Carl Sawatski	3.25	1.75	1.00
120	Dick Stuart	4.25	2.25	1.25
121	Harvey Kuenn	63.00	31.00	19.00
122	Pancho Herrera	3.25	1.75	1.00
123a	Don Zimmer (Cubs)	11.00	5.50	3.25
123b	Don Zimmer (Mets)	5.50	2.75	1.75
124	Wally Moon	4.25	2.25	1.25
125	Joe Adcock	5.50	2.75	1.75
126	Joey Jay	3.25	1.75	1.00
127a	Maury Wills (blue "3" on shirt)	18.50	9.25	5.50
127b	Maury Wills (red "3" on shirt)	7.75	4.00	2.25
128	George Altman	3.25	1.75	1.00
129a	John Buzhardt (Phillies)	18.50	9.25	5.50
129b	John Buzhardt (White Sox)	5.50	2.75	1.75
130	Felipe Alou	4.25	2.25	1.25
131	Bill Mazeroski	9.75	5.00	3.00
132	Ernie Broglio	3.25	1.75	1.00
133	John Roseboro	4.25	2.25	1.25
134	Mike McCormick	3.25	1.75	1.00
135a	Chuck Smith (Phillies)	19.50	9.75	5.75
135b	Chuck Smith (White Sox)	6.50	3.25	2.00
136	Ron Santo	5.50	2.75	1.75
137	Gene Freese	3.25	1.75	1.00
138	Dick Groat	5.50	2.75	1.75
139	Curt Flood	4.25	2.25	1.25
140	Frank Bolling	3.25	1.75	1.00
141	Clay Dalrymple	3.25	1.75	1.00
142	Willie McCovey	38.00	19.00	11.50
143	Bob Skinner	3.25	1.75	1.00
144	Lindy McDaniel	3.25	1.75	1.00
145	Glen Hobbie	3.25	1.75	1.00
146a	Gil Hodges (Dodgers)	38.00	19.00	11.50
146b	Gil Hodges (Mets)	24.00	12.00	7.25
147	Eddie Kasko	3.25	1.75	1.00
148	Gino Cimoli	44.00	22.00	13.00
149	Willie Mays	76.00	38.00	23.00
150	Roberto Clemente	76.00	38.00	23.00
151	Red Schoendienst	6.50	3.25	2.00
152	Joe Torre	4.25	2.25	1.25
153	Bob Purkey	3.25	1.75	1.00
154a	Tommy Davis (3B)	11.00	5.50	3.25
154b	Tommy Davis (OF)	5.50	2.75	1.75
155a	Andre Rogers (incorrect spelling)	11.00	5.50	3.25
155b	Andre Rodgers (correct spelling)	4.25	2.25	1.25
156	Tony Taylor	3.25	1.75	1.00
157	Bob Friend	3.25	1.75	1.00
158a	Gus Bell (Redlegs)	8.75	4.50	2.75
158b	Gus Bell (Mets)	4.25	2.25	1.25
159	Roy McMillan	3.25	1.75	1.00
160	Carl Warwick	3.25	1.75	1.00
161	Willie Davis	4.25	2.25	1.25
162	Sam Jones	63.00	31.00	19.00
163	Ruben Amaro	3.25	1.75	1.00
164	Sam Taylor	3.25	1.75	1.00
165	Frank Robinson	28.00	14.00	8.50
166	Lou Burdette	5.50	2.75	1.75
167	Ken Boyer	5.50	2.75	1.75
168	Bill Virdon	4.25	2.25	1.25
169	Jim Davenport	3.25	1.75	1.00
170	Don Demeter	3.25	1.75	1.00
171	Richie Ashburn	49.00	24.00	14.50
172	John Podres	4.25	2.25	1.25
173a	Joe Cunningham (Cardinals)	54.00	27.00	16.00
173b	Joe Cunningham (White Sox)	18.50	9.25	5.50
174	ElRoy Face	5.50	2.75	1.75
175	Orlando Cepeda	7.75	4.00	2.25
176a	Bobby Gene Smith (Phillies)	22.00	11.00	6.50
176b	Bobby Gene Smith (Mets)	6.50	3.25	2.00
177a	Ernie Banks (OF)	60.00	30.00	18.00
177b	Ernie Banks (SS)	27.00	13.50	8.00
178a	Daryl Spencer (3B)	16.50	8.25	5.00
178b	Daryl Spencer (1B)	4.25	2.25	1.25
179	Bob Schmidt	33.00	16.50	10.00
180	Hank Aaron	76.00	38.00	23.00
181	Hobie Landrith	8.75	4.50	2.75
182a	Ed Broussard	436.00	218.00	131.00
182b	Ed Bressoud	38.00	19.00	11.50
183	Felix Mantilla	8.75	4.50	2.75
184	Dick Farrell	8.75	4.50	2.75
185	Bob Miller	8.75	4.50	2.75
186	Don Taussig	8.75	4.50	2.75
187	Pumpsie Green	12.00	6.00	3.50
188	Bobby Shantz	12.00	6.00	3.50
189	Roger Craig	13.00	6.50	4.00
190	Hal Smith	8.75	4.50	2.75
191	John Edwards	8.75	4.50	2.75
192	John DeMerit	8.75	4.50	2.75
193	Joe Amalfitano	8.75	4.50	2.75
194	Norm Larker	8.75	4.50	2.75
195	Al Heist	8.75	4.50	2.75
196	Al Spangler	8.75	4.50	2.75
197	Alex Grammas	8.75	4.50	2.75
198	Gerry Lynch	8.75	4.50	2.75
199	Jim McKnight	8.75	4.50	2.75
200	Jose Pagen (Pagan)	8.75	4.50	2.75
201	Junior Gilliam	21.00	10.50	6.25
202	Art Ditmar	8.75	4.50	2.75
203	Pete Daley	8.75	4.50	2.75
204	Johnny Callison	28.00	14.00	8.50
205	Stu Miller	8.75	4.50	2.75
206	Russ Snyder	8.75	4.50	2.75
207	Billy Williams	33.00	16.50	10.00
208	Walter Bond	8.75	4.50	2.75
209	Joe Koppe	8.75	4.50	2.75
210	Don Schwall	33.00	16.50	10.00
211	Billy Gardner	18.50	9.25	5.50
212	Chuck Estrada	8.75	4.50	2.75
213	Gary Bell	8.75	4.50	2.75
214	Floyd Robinson	8.75	4.50	2.75
215	Duke Snider	54.00	27.00	16.00
216	Lee Maye	8.75	4.50	2.75
217	Howie Bedell	8.75	4.50	2.75
218	Bob Will	8.75	4.50	2.75
219	Dallas Green	12.00	6.00	3.50
220	Carroll Hardy	19.50	9.75	5.75
221	Danny O'Connell	12.00	6.00	3.50

1963 Salada-Junket Dessert Coins

A much smaller set of baseball coins was issued by Salada/Junket in 1963. The 63 coins issued were called "All-Star Baseball Coins" and included most of the top players of the day. Unlike 1962, the coins were made of metal and measured a slightly larger 1-1/2" diameter. American League players have blue rims on their coins, while National Leaguers are rimmed in red. Coin fronts contain no printing on the full-color player photos, while backs list coin number, player name, team and position, along with brief statistics and the sponsors' logos.

		NM	EX	VG
Complete set (63):		1100.	550.00	325.00
Common player:		5.00	2.50	1.50
1	Don Drysdale	20.00	10.00	6.00
2	Dick Farrell	5.00	2.50	1.50
3	Bob Gibson	20.00	10.00	6.00
4	Sandy Koufax	35.00	17.50	10.50
5	Juan Marichal	18.00	9.00	5.50
6	Bob Purkey	5.00	2.50	1.50
7	Bob Shaw	5.00	2.50	1.50
8	Warren Spahn	18.00	9.00	5.50
9	Johnny Podres	5.00	2.50	1.50
10	Art Mahaffey	5.00	2.50	1.50
11	Del Crandall	6.50	3.25	2.00
12	John Roseboro	6.50	3.25	2.00
13	Orlando Cepeda	8.00	4.00	2.50
14	Bill Mazeroski	11.00	5.50	3.25
15	Ken Boyer	8.00	4.00	2.50
16	Dick Groat	7.00	3.50	2.00
17	Ernie Banks	30.00	15.00	9.00
18	Frank Bolling	5.00	2.50	1.50
19	Jim Davenport	5.00	2.50	1.50
20	Maury Wills	7.00	3.50	2.00
21	Tommy Davis	6.50	3.25	2.00
22	Willie Mays	70.00	35.00	21.00
23	Roberto Clemente	70.00	35.00	21.00
24	Henry Aaron	70.00	35.00	21.00
25	Felipe Alou	6.50	3.25	2.00
26	Johnny Callison	6.50	3.25	2.00
27	Richie Ashburn	19.00	9.50	5.75
28	Eddie Mathews	20.00	10.00	6.00
29	Frank Robinson	22.50	11.00	6.75
30	Billy Williams	19.00	9.50	5.75
31	George Altman	5.00	2.50	1.50
32	Hank Aguirre	5.00	2.50	1.50
33	Jim Bunning	9.00	4.50	2.75
34	Dick Donovan	5.00	2.50	1.50
35	Bill Monbouquette	5.00	2.50	1.50
36	Camilo Pascual	6.50	3.25	2.00
37	David Stenhouse	5.00	2.50	1.50
38	Ralph Terry	6.50	3.25	2.00
39	Hoyt Wilhelm	18.00	9.00	5.50
40	Jim Kaat	11.00	5.50	3.25
41	Ken McBride	5.00	2.50	1.50
42	Ray Herbert	5.00	2.50	1.50
43	Milt Pappas	6.50	3.25	2.00
44	Earl Battey	5.00	2.50	1.50
45	Elston Howard	8.00	4.00	2.50
46	John Romano	5.00	2.50	1.50
47	Jim Gentile	5.00	2.50	1.50
48	Billy Moran	5.00	2.50	1.50
49	Rich Rollins	5.00	2.50	1.50
50	Luis Aparicio	19.00	9.50	5.75
51	Norm Siebern	5.00	2.50	1.50
52	Bobby Richardson	15.00	7.50	4.50
53	Brooks Robinson	30.00	15.00	9.00
54	Tom Tresh	11.00	5.50	3.25
55	Leon Wagner	5.00	2.50	1.50
56	Mickey Mantle	110.00	55.00	33.00
57	Roger Maris	40.00	20.00	12.00
58	Rocky Colavito	11.00	5.50	3.25
59	Lee Thomas	5.00	2.50	1.50
60	Jim Landis	5.00	2.50	1.50
61	Pete Runnels	6.50	3.25	2.00
62	Yogi Berra	25.00	12.50	7.50
63	Al Kaline	25.00	12.50	7.50

1964 Topps Coins

The 164 metal coins in this set were issued by Topps as inserts in the company's baseball card wax packs. The series is divided into two principal types, 120 "regular" coins and 44 All-Star coins. The 1 1/2" diameter coins feature a full-color background for the player photos in the "regular" series, while the players in the All-Star series are featured against plain red or blue backgrounds. There are two variations of the Mantle, Causey and Hinton coins among the All-Star subset.

		NM	EX	VG
Complete set (164):		700.00	350.00	210.00
Common player:		2.50	1.25	.70
1	Don Zimmer	2.50	1.25	.70
2	Jim Wynn	2.50	1.25	.70
3	Johnny Orsino	2.50	1.25	.70
4	Jim Bouton	3.00	1.50	.90
5	Dick Groat	3.00	1.50	.90
6	Leon Wagner	2.50	1.25	.70
7	Frank Malzone	2.50	1.25	.70
8	Steve Barber	2.50	1.25	.70
9	Johnny Romano	2.50	1.25	.70
10	Tom Tresh	3.00	1.50	.90
11	Felipe Alou	3.00	1.50	.90
12	Dick Stuart	2.50	1.25	.70
13	Claude Osteen	2.50	1.25	.70
14	Juan Pizarro	2.50	1.25	.70
15	Donn Clendenon	2.50	1.25	.70
16	Jimmie Hall	2.50	1.25	.70
17	Larry Jackson	2.50	1.25	.70
18	Brooks Robinson	12.50	6.25	3.75
19	Bob Allison	2.50	1.25	.70
20	Ed Roebuck	2.50	1.25	.70
21	Pete Ward	2.50	1.25	.70
22	Willie McCovey	8.00	4.00	2.50
23	Elston Howard	3.00	1.50	.90
24	Diego Segui	2.50	1.25	.70
25	Ken Boyer	3.00	1.50	.90
26	Carl Yastrzemski	15.00	7.50	4.50
27	Bill Mazeroski	4.00	2.00	1.25
28	Jerry Lumpe	2.50	1.25	.70
29	Woody Held	2.50	1.25	.70
30	Dick Radatz	2.50	1.25	.70
31	Luis Aparicio	7.00	3.50	2.00
32	Dave Nicholson	2.50	1.25	.70
33	Ed Mathews	12.00	6.00	3.50
34	Don Drysdale	16.00	8.00	4.75
35	Ray Culp	2.50	1.25	.70
36	Juan Marichal	7.00	3.50	2.00
37	Frank Robinson	11.00	5.50	3.25
38	Chuck Hinton	2.50	1.25	.70
39	Floyd Robinson	2.50	1.25	.70

40	Tommy Harper	2.50	1.25	.70	130	Leon Wagner (All-Star)	2.50	1.25	.70
41	Ron Hansen	2.50	1.25	.70	131a	Mickey Mantle			
42	Ernie Banks	15.00	7.50	4.50		(All-Star, lefthanded)	60.00	30.00	18.00
43	Jesse Gonder	2.50	1.25	.70	131b	Mickey Mantle			
44	Billy Williams	8.00	4.00	2.50		(All-Star, righthanded)	50.00	25.00	15.00
45	Vada Pinson	3.00	1.50	.90	132	Albie Pearson (All-Star)	2.50	1.25	.70
46	Rocky Colavito	5.00	2.50	1.50	133	Harmon Killebrew (All-Star)	12.00	6.00	3.50
47	Bill Monbouquette	2.50	1.25	.70	134	Carl Yastrzemski (All-Star)	15.00	7.50	4.50
48	Max Alvis	2.50	1.25	.70	135	Elston Howard (All-Star)	3.00	1.50	.90
49	Norm Siebern	2.50	1.25	.70	136	Earl Battey (All-Star)	2.50	1.25	.70
50	John Callison	2.50	1.25	.70	137	Camilo Pascual (All-Star)	2.50	1.25	.70
51	Rich Rollins	2.50	1.25	.70	138	Jim Bouton (All-Star)	3.00	1.50	.90
52	Ken McBride	2.50	1.25	.70	139	Whitey Ford (All-Star)	10.00	5.00	3.00
53	Don Lock	2.50	1.25	.70	140	Gary Peters (All-Star)	2.50	1.25	.70
54	Ron Fairly	2.50	1.25	.70	141	Bill White (All-Star)	2.50	1.25	.70
55	Roberto Clemente	25.00	12.50	7.50	142	Orlando Cepeda (All-Star)	3.00	1.50	.90
56	Dick Ellsworth	2.50	1.25	.70	143	Bill Mazeroski (All-Star)	4.00	2.00	1.25
57	Tommy Davis	2.50	1.25	.70	144	Tony Taylor (All-Star)	2.50	1.25	.70
58	Tony Gonzalez	2.50	1.25	.70	145	Ken Boyer (All-Star)	3.00	1.50	.90
59	Bob Gibson	12.00	6.00	3.50	146	Ron Santo (All-Star)	2.50	1.25	.70
60	Jim Maloney	2.50	1.25	.70	147	Dick Groat (All-Star)	2.50	1.25	.70
61	Frank Howard	3.00	1.50	.90	148	Roy McMillan (All-Star)	2.50	1.25	.70
62	Jim Pagliaroni	2.50	1.25	.70	149	Hank Aaron (All-Star)	22.00	11.00	6.50
63	Orlando Cepeda	4.00	2.00	1.25	150	Roberto Clemente (All-Star)	25.00	12.50	7.50
64	Ron Perranoski	2.50	1.25	.70	151	Willie Mays (All-Star)	22.00	11.00	6.50
65	Curt Flood	2.50	1.25	.70	152	Vada Pinson (All-Star)	3.00	1.50	.90
66	Al McBean	2.50	1.25	.70	153	Tommy Davis (All-Star)	2.50	1.25	.70
67	Dean Chance	2.50	1.25	.70	154	Frank Robinson (All-Star)	12.50	6.25	3.75
68	Ron Santo	2.50	1.25	.70	155	Joe Torre (All-Star)	2.50	1.25	.70
69	Jack Baldschun	2.50	1.25	.70	156	Tim McCarver (All-Star)	2.50	1.25	.70
70	Milt Pappas	2.50	1.25	.70	157	Juan Marichal (All-Star)	8.00	4.00	2.50
71	Gary Peters	2.50	1.25	.70	158	Jim Maloney (All-Star)	2.50	1.25	.70
72	Bobby Richardson	3.00	1.50	.90	159	Sandy Koufax (All-Star)	18.00	9.00	5.50
73	Lee Thomas	2.50	1.25	.70	160	Warren Spahn (All-Star)	12.00	6.00	3.50
74	Hank Aguirre	2.50	1.25	.70	161a	Wayne Causey			
75	Carl Willey	2.50	1.25	.70		(All-Star, N.L. on back)	15.00	7.50	4.50
76	Camilo Pascual	2.50	1.25	.70	161b	Wayne Causey			
77	Bob Friend	2.50	1.25	.70		(All-Star, A.L. on back)	2.50	1.25	.70
78	Bill White	2.50	1.25	.70	162a	Chuck Hinton			
79	Norm Cash	3.00	1.50	.90		(All-Star, N.L. on back)	15.00	7.50	4.50
80	Willie Mays	25.00	12.50	7.50	162b	Chuck Hinton			
81	Duke Carmel	2.50	1.25	.70		(All-Star, A.L. on back)	2.50	1.25	.70
82	Pete Rose	22.00	11.00	6.50	163	Bob Aspromonte (All-Star)	2.50	1.25	.70
83	Hank Aaron	25.00	12.50	7.50	164	Ron Hunt (All-Star)	2.50	1.25	.70
84	Bob Aspromonte	2.50	1.25	.70					
85	Jim O'Toole	2.50	1.25	.70					
86	Vic Davalillo	2.50	1.25	.70					
87	Bill Freehan	2.50	1.25	.70					
88	Warren Spahn	10.00	5.00	3.00					
89	Ron Hunt	2.50	1.25	.70					
90	Denis Menke	2.50	1.25	.70					
91	Turk Farrell	2.50	1.25	.70					
92	Jim Hickman	2.50	1.25	.70					
93	Jim Bunning	4.50	2.25	1.25					
94	Bob Hendley	2.50	1.25	.70					
95	Ernie Broglio	2.50	1.25	.70					
96	Rusty Staub	3.00	1.50	.90					
97	Lou Brock	8.00	4.00	2.50					
98	Jim Fregosi	2.50	1.25	.70					
99	Jim Grant	2.50	1.25	.70					
100	Al Kaline	15.00	7.50	4.50					
101	Earl Battey	2.50	1.25	.70					
102	Wayne Causey	2.50	1.25	.70					
103	Chuck Schilling	2.50	1.25	.70					
104	Boog Powell	3.50	1.75	1.00					
105	Dave Wickersham	2.50	1.25	.70					
106	Sandy Koufax	18.00	9.00	5.50					
107	John Bateman	2.50	1.25	.70					
108	Ed Brinkman	2.50	1.25	.70					
109	Al Downing	2.50	1.25	.70					
110	Joe Azcue	2.50	1.25	.70					
111	Albie Pearson	2.50	1.25	.70					
112	Harmon Killebrew	12.00	6.00	3.50					
113	Tony Taylor	2.50	1.25	.70					
114	Alvin Jackson	2.50	1.25	.70					
115	Billy O'Dell	2.50	1.25	.70					
116	Don Demeter	2.50	1.25	.70					
117	Ed Charles	2.50	1.25	.70					
118	Joe Torre	3.00	1.50	.90					
119	Don Nottebart	2.50	1.25	.70					
120	Mickey Mantle	50.00	25.00	15.00					
121	Joe Pepitone (All-Star)	2.50	1.25	.70					
122	Dick Stuart (All-Star)	3.00	1.50	.90					
123	Bobby Richardson (All-Star)	2.50	1.25	.70					
124	Jerry Lumpe (All-Star)	2.50	1.25	.70					
125	Brooks Robinson (All-Star)	12.00	6.00	3.50					
126	Frank Malzone (All-Star)	2.50	1.25	.70					
127	Luis Aparicio (All-Star)	8.00	4.00	2.50					
128	Jim Fregosi (All-Star)	2.50	1.25	.70					
129	Al Kaline (All-Star)	15.00	7.50	4.50					

1971 Topps Coins

Measuring 1-1/2" in diameter, the latest edition of the Topps coins was a 153-piece set. The coins feature a color photograph surrounded by a colored band on the front. The band carries the player's name, team, position and several stars. Backs have a short biography, the coin number and encouragement to collect the entire set. Back colors differ, with #s 1-51 having a brass back, #s 52-102 chrome backs, and the rest have blue backs. Most of the stars of the period are included in the set.

		NM	EX	VG
Complete set (153):		300.00	150.00	90.00
Common player:		.90	.45	.25
1	Cito Gaston	1.50	.70	.45
2	Dave Johnson	.90	.45	.25
3	Jim Bunning	2.00	1.00	.60
4	Jim Spencer	.90	.45	.25
5	Felix Millan	.90	.45	.25
6	Gerry Moses	.90	.45	.25
7	Fergie Jenkins	5.00	2.50	1.50

8	Felipe Alou	1.50	.70	.45
9	Jim McGlothlin	.90	.45	.25
10	Dick McAuliffe	.90	.45	.25
11	Joe Torre	1.25	.60	.40
12	Jim Perry	.90	.45	.25
13	Bobby Bonds	1.50	.70	.45
14	Danny Cater	.90	.45	.25
15	Bill Mazeroski	3.00	1.50	.90
16	Luis Aparicio	5.00	2.50	1.50
17	Doug Rader	.90	.45	.25
18	Vada Pinson	1.50	.70	.45
19	John Bateman	.90	.45	.25
20	Lew Krausse	.90	.45	.25
21	Billy Grabarkewitz	.90	.45	.25
22	Frank Howard	1.50	.70	.45
23	Jerry Koosman	1.25	.60	.40
24	Rod Carew	8.00	4.00	2.50
25	Al Ferrara	.90	.45	.25
26	Dave McNally	.90	.45	.25
27	Jim Hickman	.90	.45	.25
28	Sandy Alomar	.90	.45	.25
29	Lee May	.90	.45	.25
30	Rico Petrocelli	1.25	.60	.40
31	Don Money	.90	.45	.25
32	Jim Rooker	.90	.45	.25
33	Dick Dietz	.90	.45	.25
34	Roy White	.90	.45	.25
35	Carl Morton	.90	.45	.25
36	Walt Williams	.90	.45	.25
37	Phil Niekro	3.25	1.75	1.00
38	Bill Freehan	1.25	.60	.40
39	Julian Javier	.90	.45	.25
40	Rick Monday	.90	.45	.25
41	Don Wilson	.90	.45	.25
42	Ray Fosse	.90	.45	.25
43	Art Shamsky	.90	.45	.25
44	Ted Savage	.90	.45	.25
45	Claude Osteen	.90	.45	.25
46	Ed Brinkman	.90	.45	.25
47	Matty Alou	.90	.45	.25
48	Bob Oliver	.90	.45	.25
49	Danny Coombs	.90	.45	.25
50	Frank Robinson	7.00	3.50	2.00
51	Randy Hundley	.90	.45	.25
52	Cesar Tovar	.90	.45	.25
53	Wayne Simpson	.90	.45	.25
54	Bobby Murcer	.90	.45	.25
55	Tony Taylor	.90	.45	.25
56	Tommy John	1.50	.70	.45
57	Willie McCovey	7.00	3.50	2.00
58	Carl Yastrzemski	10.00	5.00	3.00
59	Bob Bailey	.90	.45	.25
60	Clyde Wright	.90	.45	.25
61	Orlando Cepeda	2.00	1.00	.60
62	Al Kaline	7.00	3.50	2.00
63	Bob Gibson	7.00	3.50	2.00
64	Bert Campaneris	.90	.45	.25
65	Ted Sizemore	.90	.45	.25
66	Duke Sims	.90	.45	.25
67	Bud Harrelson	.90	.45	.25
68	Jerry McNertney	.90	.45	.25
69	Jim Wynn	.90	.45	.25
70	Dick Bosman	.90	.45	.25
71	Roberto Clemente	15.00	7.50	4.50
72	Rich Reese	.90	.45	.25
73	Gaylord Perry	5.00	2.50	1.50
74	Boog Powell	1.50	.70	.45
75	Billy Williams	5.00	2.50	1.50
76	Bill Melton	.90	.45	.25
77	Nate Colbert	.90	.45	.25
78	Reggie Smith	.90	.45	.25
79	Deron Johnson	.90	.45	.25
80	Catfish Hunter	5.00	2.50	1.50
81	Bob Tolan	.90	.45	.25
82	Jim Northrup	.90	.45	.25
83	Ron Fairly	.90	.45	.25
84	Alex Johnson	.90	.45	.25
85	Pat Jarvis	.90	.45	.25
86	Sam McDowell	.90	.45	.25
87	Lou Brock	6.00	3.00	1.75
88	Danny Walton	.90	.45	.25
89	Denis Menke	.90	.45	.25
90	Jim Palmer	7.00	3.50	2.00
91	Tommie Agee	.90	.45	.25
92	Duane Josephson	.90	.45	.25
93	Willie Davis	.90	.45	.25
94	Mel Stottlemyre	.90	.45	.25
95	Ron Santo	1.25	.60	.40
96	Amos Otis	.90	.45	.25
97	Ken Henderson	.90	.45	.25
98	George Scott	.90	.45	.25
99	Dock Ellis	.90	.45	.25
100	Harmon Killebrew	7.00	3.50	2.00

101	Pete Rose	25.00	12.50	7.50
102	Rick Reichardt	.90	.45	.25
103	Cleon Jones	.90	.45	.25
104	Ron Perranoski	.90	.45	.25
105	Tony Perez	1.50	.70	.45
106	Mickey Lolich	1.25	.60	.40
107	Tim McCarver	1.25	.60	.40
108	Reggie Jackson	12.00	6.00	3.50
109	Chris Cannizzaro	.90	.45	.25
110	Steve Hargan	.90	.45	.25
111	Rusty Staub	1.50	.70	.45
112	Andy Messersmith	.90	.45	.25
113	Rico Carty	.90	.45	.25
114	Brooks Robinson	7.00	3.50	2.00
115	Steve Carlton	7.00	3.50	2.00
116	Mike Hegan	.90	.45	.25
117	Joe Morgan	5.00	2.50	1.50
118	Thurman Munson	5.00	2.50	1.50
119	Don Kessinger	.90	.45	.25
120	Joe Horlen	.90	.45	.25
121	Wes Parker	.90	.45	.25
122	Sonny Siebert	.90	.45	.25
123	Willie Stargell	5.00	2.50	1.50
124	Ellie Rodriguez	.90	.45	.25
125	Juan Marichal	5.00	2.50	1.50
126	Mike Epstein	.90	.45	.25
127	Tom Seaver	7.00	3.50	2.00
128	Tony Oliva	1.50	.70	.45
129	Jim Merritt	.90	.45	.25
130	Willie Horton	.90	.45	.25
131	Rick Wise	.90	.45	.25
132	Sal Bando	.90	.45	.25
133	Ollie Brown	.90	.45	.25
134	Ken Harrelson	.90	.45	.25
135	Mack Jones	.90	.45	.25
136	Jim Fregosi	.90	.45	.25
137	Hank Aaron	15.00	7.50	4.50
138	Fritz Peterson	.90	.45	.25
139	Joe Hague	.90	.45	.25
140	Tommy Harper	.90	.45	.25
141	Larry Dierker	.90	.45	.25
142	Tony Conigliaro	2.00	1.00	.60
143	Glenn Beckert	.90	.45	.25
144	Carlos May	.90	.45	.25
145	Don Sutton	2.50	1.25	.70
146	Paul Casanova	.90	.45	.25
147	Bob Moose	.90	.45	.25
148	Leo Cardenas	.90	.45	.25
149	Johnny Bench	8.00	4.00	2.50
150	Mike Cuellar	.90	.45	.25
151	Donn Clendenon	.90	.45	.25
152	Lou Piniella	.90	.45	.25
153	Willie Mays	15.00	7.50	4.50

1987 Topps Coins

For the first time since 1971, Topps issued a set of baseball "coins." Similar in design to the 1964 edition, the metal discs measure 1-1/2" in diameter. The aluminum coins were sold on a limited basis in retail outlets. Three coins and three sticks of gum were found in a pack. The coin fronts feature a full-color photo along with the player's name, team and position in a white band at the bottom. Gold-colored rims are found for American League players; National League players have silver-colored rims. Backs are silvered and carry the coin number, player's name and personal and statistical information.

		MT	NM	EX
	Complete set:	12.50	9.50	5.00
	Common player:	.15	.11	.06
1	Harold Baines	.15	.11	.06
2	Jesse Barfield	.15	.11	.06
3	George Bell	.15	.11	.06
4	Wade Boggs	.70	.50	.30
5	George Brett	.75	.60	.30
6	Jose Canseco	.70	.50	.30
7	Joe Carter	.25	.20	.10
8	Roger Clemens	.40	.30	.15
9	Alvin Davis	.15	.11	.06
10	Rob Deer	.15	.11	.06
11	Kirk Gibson	.20	.15	.08
12	Rickey Henderson	.60	.45	.25
13	Kent Hrbek	.20	.15	.08
14	Pete Incaviglia	.15	.11	.06
15	Reggie Jackson	.50	.40	.20
16	Wally Joyner	.25	.20	.10
17	Don Mattingly	.75	.60	.30
18	Jack Morris	.15	.11	.06
19	Eddie Murray	.45	.35	.20
20	Kirby Puckett	.45	.35	.20
21	Jim Rice	.15	.11	.06
22	Dave Righetti	.15	.11	.06
23	Cal Ripken, Jr.	3.00	2.25	1.25
24	Cory Snyder	.15	.11	.06
25	Danny Tartabull	.20	.15	.08
26	Dave Winfield	.45	.35	.20
27	Hubie Brooks	.15	.11	.06
28	Gary Carter	.25	.20	.10
29	Vince Coleman	.20	.15	.08
30	Eric Davis	.20	.15	.08
31	Glenn Davis	.15	.11	.06
32	Steve Garvey	.25	.20	.10
33	Dwight Gooden	.20	.15	.08
34	Tony Gwynn	.35	.25	.14
35	Von Hayes	.15	.11	.06
36	Keith Hernandez	.15	.11	.06
37	Dale Murphy	.25	.20	.10
38	Dave Parker	.25	.20	.10
39	Tony Pena	.15	.11	.06
40	Nolan Ryan	2.00	1.50	.80
41	Ryne Sandberg	1.00	.70	.40
42	Steve Sax	.15	.11	.06
43	Mike Schmidt	.75	.60	.30
44	Mike Scott	.15	.11	.06
45	Ozzie Smith	.35	.25	.14
46	Darryl Strawberry	.20	.15	.08
47	Fernando Valenzuela	.20	.15	.08
48	Todd Worrell	.15	.11	.06

		MT	NM	EX
4	Wade Boggs	1.00	.70	.40
5	Harold Baines	.15	.11	.06
6	Ivan Calderon	.15	.11	.06
7	Jose Canseco	1.00	.70	.40
8	Joe Carter	.30	.25	.12
9	Jack Clark	.15	.11	.06
10	Alvin Davis	.15	.11	.06
11	Dwight Evans	.15	.11	.06
12	Tony Fernandez	.15	.11	.06
13	Gary Gaetti	.15	.11	.06
14	Mike Greenwell	.30	.25	.12
15	Charlie Hough	.15	.11	.06
16	Wally Joyner	.30	.25	.12
17	Jimmy Key	.15	.11	.06
18	Mark Langston	.15	.11	.06
19	Don Mattingly	1.50	1.25	.60
20	Paul Molitor	.40	.30	.15
21	Jack Morris	.15	.11	.06
22	Eddie Murray	.60	.45	.25
23	Kirby Puckett	.60	.45	.25
24	Cal Ripken, Jr.	3.00	2.25	1.25
25	Bret Saberhagen	.15	.11	.06
26	Ruben Sierra	.25	.20	.10
27	Cory Snyder	.15	.11	.06
28	Terry Steinbach	.15	.11	.06
29	Danny Tartabull	.25	.20	.10
30	Alan Trammell	.25	.20	.10
31	Devon White	.25	.20	.10
32	Robin Yount	.70	.50	.30
33	Andre Dawson	.25	.20	.10
34	Steve Bedrosian	.15	.11	.06
35	Benny Santiago	.20	.15	.08
36	Tony Gwynn	.40	.30	.15
37	Bobby Bonilla	.25	.20	.10
38	Will Clark	.45	.35	.20
39	Eric Davis	.20	.15	.08
40	Mike Dunne	.15	.11	.06
41	John Franco	.15	.11	.06
42	Dwight Gooden	.25	.20	.10
43	Pedro Guerrero	.15	.11	.06
44	Dion James	.15	.11	.06
45	John Kruk	.25	.20	.10
46	Jeffrey Leonard	.15	.11	.06
47	Carmelo Martinez	.15	.11	.06
48	Dale Murphy	.25	.20	.10
49	Tim Raines	.25	.20	.10
50	Nolan Ryan	2.25	1.75	.90
51	Juan Samuel	.15	.11	.06
52	Ryne Sandberg	1.25	.90	.50
53	Mike Schmidt	1.25	.90	.50
54	Mike Scott	.15	.11	.06
55	Ozzie Smith	.40	.30	.15
56	Darryl Strawberry	.30	.25	.12
57	Rick Sutcliffe	.15	.11	.06
58	Fernando Valenzuela	.15	.11	.06
59	Tim Wallach	.15	.11	.06
60	Todd Worrell	.15	.11	.06

1988 Topps Coins

This edition of 60 lightweight metal coins is similar in design to Topps' 1964 set. The 1988 coins are 1-1/2" in diameter and feature full-color player portraits under crimped edges in silver, gold and pink. Curved under the photo is a red and white player name banner pinned by two gold stars. Coin backs list the coin number, player name, personal information and career summary in black letters on a silver background.

		MT	NM	EX
	Complete set:	12.00	9.00	4.75
	Common player:	.15	.11	.06
1	George Bell	.15	.11	.06
2	Roger Clemens	.60	.45	.25
3	Mark McGwire	.60	.45	.25

1989 Topps Coins

Similar in format to previous Topps coins, this 60-piece set features 1-1/2" diameter coins with rolled colored edges. A shooting star device printed over the player photo gives his name, team and position. Backs have a few biographical details and a summary of the player's previous season performance printed in black on silver. The coins were sold three per pack, with each pack including an offer card for an album to house the pieces.

Medallions

		MT	NM	EX
Complete set (60):		9.00	6.75	3.50
Common player:		.10	.08	.04
1	Kirk Gibson	.10	.08	.04
2	Orel Hershiser	.15	.11	.06
3	Chris Sabo	.10	.08	.04
4	Tony Gwynn	.35	.25	.14
5	Brett Butler	.10	.08	.04
6	Bobby Bonilla	.12	.09	.05
7	Jack Clark	.10	.08	.04
8	Will Clark	.40	.30	.15
9	Eric Davis	.12	.09	.05
10	Glenn Davis	.10	.08	.04
11	Andre Dawson	.15	.11	.06
12	John Franco	.10	.08	.04
13	Andres Galarraga	.15	.11	.06
14	Dwight Gooden	.12	.09	.05
15	Mark Grace	.15	.11	.06
16	Pedro Guerrero	.10	.08	.04
17	Ricky Jordan	.10	.08	.04
18	Mike Marshall	.10	.08	.04
19	Dale Murphy	.12	.09	.05
20	Eddie Murray	.35	.25	.14
21	Gerald Perry	.10	.08	.04
22	Tim Raines	.15	.11	.06
23	Juan Samuel	.10	.08	.04
24	Benito Santiago	.12	.09	.05
25	Ozzie Smith	.20	.15	.08
26	Darryl Strawberry	.12	.09	.05
27	Andy Van Slyke	.10	.08	.04
28	Gerald Young	.10	.08	.04
29	Jose Canseco	.60	.45	.25
30	Frank Viola	.10	.08	.04
31	Walt Weiss	.10	.08	.04
32	Wade Boggs	.35	.25	.14
33	Harold Baines	.10	.08	.04
34	George Brett	.75	.60	.30
35	Jay Buhner	.15	.11	.06
36	Joe Carter	.15	.11	.06
37	Roger Clemens	.25	.20	.10
38	Alvin Davis	.10	.08	.04
39	Tony Fernandez	.10	.08	.04
40	Carlton Fisk	.15	.11	.06
41	Mike Greenwell	.12	.09	.05
42	Kent Hrbek	.12	.09	.05
43	Don Mattingly	.80	.60	.30
44	Fred McGriff	.35	.25	.14
45	Mark McGwire	.20	.15	.08
46	Paul Molitor	.20	.15	.08
47	Rafael Palmeiro	.15	.11	.06
48	Kirby Puckett	.50	.40	.20
49	Johnny Ray	.10	.08	.04
50	Cal Ripken, Jr.	1.00	.70	.40
51	Ruben Sierra	.15	.11	.06
52	Pete Stanicek	.10	.08	.04
53	Dave Stewart	.12	.09	.05
54	Greg Swindell	.10	.08	.04
55	Danny Tartabull	.10	.08	.04
56	Alan Trammell	.12	.09	.05
57	Lou Whitaker	.10	.08	.04
58	Dave Winfield	.25	.20	.10
59	Mike Witt	.10	.08	.04
60	Robin Yount	.25	.20	.10

1990 Topps Coins

Sixty of the game's top stars and promising rookies are featured in this fourth annual coin set. Fronts of the 1-1/2" diameter coins feature a player photo with a symbolic infield in front of and behind the photo. The player's name and team appear below. Most coins feature natural aluminum coloring on the rolled edges and on the back. Special coins of major award winners have different colors in the background and edges. Backs feature a coin number, minimal biographical data and a previous season career summary. Coins were sold three per pack which included an offer card for a coin holder and Topps magazine subscription offer.

		MT	NM	EX
Complete set (60):		9.00	6.75	3.50
Common player:		.10	.08	.04
1	Robin Yount	.30	.25	.12
2	Bret Saberhagen	.10	.08	.04
3	Gregg Olson	.10	.08	.04
4	Kirby Puckett	.45	.35	.20
5	George Bell	.10	.08	.04
6	Wade Boggs	.35	.25	.14
7	Jerry Browne	.10	.08	.04
8	Ellis Burks	.10	.08	.04
9	Ivan Calderon	.10	.08	.04
10	Tom Candiotti	.10	.08	.04
11	Alvin Davis	.10	.08	.04
12	Chili Davis	.12	.09	.05
13	Chuck Finley	.10	.08	.04
14	Gary Gaetti	.10	.08	.04
15	Tom Gordon	.10	.08	.04
16	Ken Griffey, Jr.	.60	.45	.25
17	Rickey Henderson	.20	.15	.08
18	Kent Hrbek	.15	.11	.06
19	Bo Jackson	.25	.20	.10
20	Carlos Martinez	.10	.08	.04
21	Don Mattingly	.35	.25	.14
22	Fred McGriff	.25	.20	.10
23	Paul Molitor	.20	.15	.08
24	Cal Ripken, Jr.	.60	.45	.25
25	Nolan Ryan	.60	.45	.25
26	Steve Sax	.10	.08	.04
27	Gary Sheffield	.15	.11	.06
28	Ruben Sierra	.15	.11	.06
29	Dave Stewart	.10	.08	.04
30	Mickey Tettleton	.10	.08	.04
31	Alan Trammell	.10	.08	.04
32	Lou Whitaker	.10	.08	.04
33	Kevin Mitchell	.10	.08	.04
34	Mark Davis	.10	.08	.04
35	Jerome Walton	.10	.08	.04
36	Tony Gwynn	.25	.20	.10
37	Roberto Alomar	.20	.15	.08
38	Tim Belcher	.10	.08	.04
39	Craig Biggio	.10	.08	.04
40	Barry Bonds	.40	.30	.15
41	Bobby Bonilla	.15	.11	.06
42	Joe Carter	.15	.11	.06
43	Will Clark	.25	.20	.10
44	Eric Davis	.12	.09	.05
45	Glenn Davis	.10	.08	.04
46	Sid Fernandez	.10	.08	.04
47	Pedro Guerrero	.10	.08	.04
48	Von Hayes	.10	.08	.04
49	Tom Herr	.10	.08	.04
50	Howard Johnson	.10	.08	.04
51	Barry Larkin	.20	.15	.08
52	Joe Magrane	.10	.08	.04
53	Dale Murphy	.12	.09	.05
54	Tim Raines	.15	.11	.06
55	Willie Randolph	.10	.08	.04
56	Ryne Sandberg	.50	.40	.20
57	Dwight Smith	.10	.08	.04
58	Lonnie Smith	.10	.08	.04
59	Robby Thompson	.10	.08	.04
60	Tim Wallach	.10	.08	.04

Chicagoland Processing Enviromint Corp.

Nolan Ryan liked one particular medallion commemorating his 300th win so much that he gave one to each of his Texas Rangers teammates. The medallion, created by Chicagoland Processing Enviromint Corp., remains one of the company's most popular.

The company's silver medallions, dating back to 1985, are officially licensed by Major League Baseball. The one-troy ounce medallions are made from silver extracted from recycled film; the company annually keeps an estimated 12 million pounds of scrap out of landfills.

Chicagoland does not produce coins from any non-precious metal material. Limited-edition medallions are created only to commemorate events or special occasions, thus limiting the variety of coins produced and making them more valuable.

Regarding mintage, the company follows the same format for all events. Mintage on Division Champions is 5,000, Conference Champions or American League/National League Champions is 10,000 and the Super Bowl and World Series Champions is 25,000. Individual player mintages is limited to 15,000 each. Each medallion is individually numbered.

After a medallion has been sold out, the company destroys the dies to ensure there is never a second mintage; the company vows it has never duplicated a second edition and never will.

In addition to baseball, Chicagoland has minted medallions licensed by the National Hockey League, the National Football League, the National Basketball Association, the National Collegiate Athletic Association, Paramount Pictures, Warner Bros., Winterland Productions, Carolco Licensing, Curtis Licensing, Determined Productions, MCA Records and Apple Records. Non-sport events commemorated by the company have included Batman's 50th anniversary, Star Trek's 25th anniversary, and the history of the Beatles.

The company is located in Mt. Prospect, Ill. The initial release price for the company's medallions has usually been $29.95. S/O means the medallion is sold out.

Major League Baseball medallions

1995 releases, team-related, each is a regular and 24k, unless noted.
1995 World Series Event medallion
1995 World Series Champion Atlanta Braves , 3-piece proof set, and 1-ounce
pure gold
1995 American League Champion Cleveland Indians , 1-ounce pure gold
1995 National League Champion Atlanta Braves , 3-piece proof set, 1-ounce pure gold each includes a regular, 24k, and fine bronze, unless noted.
1995 American League Central Division Champion Cleveland Indians
1995 American League Eastern Division Champion Boston Red Sox , 3-piece set
1995 American League Western Division Champion Seattle Mariners
1995 National League Central Division Champion Cincinnati Reds , 3-piece set
1995 National League Eastern Division Champion Atlanta Braves , 3-piece set
1995 National League Western Division Champion Los Angeles Dodgers , 3-piece set

1995 National League Wild Card Colorado Rockies
1995 American League Wild Card New York Yankees
Cleveland Indians/Eddie Murray 2-piece set regular, 24k
Tampa Bay Devil Rays - New Franchise regular, 24k
Arizona Diamond Backs - New Franchise regular, 24k
Tampa Bay/Arizona 2-piece silver set, 2-piece 24k set
Colorado Rockies - Coors Field Opening Day regular, 1-ounce gold
Texas Rangers - Arlington Stadium Opening Game regular, 1-ounce gold, 24k
Old Arlington Stadium regular, 24k
Old/New Arlington Stadium 2-piece set
Cleveland Indians New Stadium Opening Game regular, 1-ounce gold, 24k
Cleveland Indians Old/New stadiums 2-piece silver set, 24k
Milwaukee Brewers 25th Anniversary regular, 24k
Colorado Rockies Record-Breaking Attendance regular
Cleveland Indians Final Game at Municipal Stadium regular, 24k
Baltimore Memorial Stadium regular
Miami Marlins Franchise
Miami Marlins Inuaugural Season
Colorado Rockies Franchise
Colorado Rockies Inaugural Season
Marlins/Rockies Inaugural Season 2-piece set

Medallions

Pittsburgh Pirates 1994 All-Star Game regular, 24k
Texas Rangers 1995 All-Star Game regular, 24k
Texas Rangers 1995 All-Star Game/Ballpark in Arlington
   2-piece regular, 2-piece 24k
1955 Brooklyn Doders Cooperstown Collection
New York Giants Cooperstown Collection
1995 releases, players: each includes regular, 24k, bronze and
   3-piece proof set, unless noted
Roberto Alomar - Baltimore Orioles
Carlos Baerga - Cleveland Indians 1995 All-Star
Albert Belle - Cleveland Indians 1995 All-Star
Dante Bichette - Colorado Rockies 1995 All-Star regular, 24k
   bronze, 3-piece proof set
Wade Boggs - New York Yankees 1995 All-Star
Barry Bonds - San Francisco Giants 1995 All-Star
Jay Buhner - Seattle Mariners 1995 All-Star
Jose Canseco - Boston Red Sox 1995 All-Star
Steve Carlton - Philadelphia Phillies regular
Joe Carter - Toronto Blue Jays 1995 All-Star
Vinnie Castilla - Colorado Rockies 1995 All-Star
Will Clark - Texas Rangers 1995 All-Star
Roger Clemens - Boston Red Sox 1995 All-Star
Roberto Clemente - Pittsburgh Pirates 1994 All-Star regular, 24k
Roberto Clemente - Pittsburgh Pirates Career Commemorative
   regular, 24k
Roberto Clemete - 2-piece silver card and coin set
Darren Daulton - Philadelphia Phillies 1995 All-Star
Lenny Dykstra - Philadelphia Phillies 1995 All-Star
Dennis Eckersley - Oakland A's 1995 All-Star
Cecil Fielder - Detroit Tigers regular, 24k, 3-piece proof set
Andres Galarraga - Colorado Rockies 1995 All-Star
Tom Glavine - Atlanta Braves 1995 All-Star
Juan Gonzalez - Texas Rangers 1995 All-Star
Mark Grace - Chicago Cubs 1995 All-Star
Ken Griffey Jr. - Seattle Mariners 1995 All-Star
Tony Gwynn - San Diego Padres 1995 All-Star
Rickey Henderson - Oakland A's 1995 All-Star
Reggie Jackson - Hall of Fame regular, 1-ounce gold
Randy Johnson - Seattle Mariners 1995 All-Star
Randy Johnson - Seattle Mariners 1995 Cy Young Award
Chipper Jones - Atlanta Braves 1995 All-Star
Dave Justice - Atlanta Braves 1995 All-Star
Eric Karros - Los Angeles Dodgers 1995 All-Star
Chuck Knoblauch - Minnesota Twins 1995 All-Star
Kenny Lofton - Cleveland Indians 1995 All-Star
Los Angeles Dodgers rookies (Eric Karros, Mike Piazza,
   Raul Mondesi)
Greg Maddux - Atlanta Braves 1995 Cy Young Award

Mickey Mantle - New York Yankees legend bronze, gold,
   3-piece proof set, card and coin set
Dennis Martinez - Cleveland Indians 1995 All-Star
Edgar Martinez - Seattle Mariners 1995 All-Star
Tino Martinez - Seattle Mariners 1995 All-Star
Don Mattingly - New York Yankees 1995 All-Star
Fred McGriff - Atlanta Braves 1995 All-Star
Mark McGwire - Oakland A's 1995 All-Star
Jack McDowell - New York Yankees 1995 All-Star
Kevin Mitchell - Cincinnati Reds
Paul Molitor - Toronto Blue Jays regular, 24k, bronze
Eddie Murray - Cleveland Indians 3,000th career hit regular,
   24k, 1-ounce gold, 3-piece proof set
Hideo Nomo - Los Angeles Dodgers regular, 24k, bronze
Hideo Nomo - Los Angeles Dodgers 1995 Rookie of the Year
John Olerud - Toronto Blue Jays 1995 All-Star
Terry Pendleton - Florida Marlins 1995 All-Star
Mike Piazza - Los Angeles Dodgers 1995 All-Star
Kirby Puckett - Minnesota Twins 1995 All-Star
Manny Ramirez - Cleveland Indians 1995 All-Star
Cal Ripken Jr. - Baltimore Orioles consecutive games streak ,
   card and coin set, 24k card and coin set
Ivan Rodriguez - Texas Rangers 1995 All-Star
Nolan Ryan - Texas Rangers retirement regular, bronze, card
   and coin set
Bret Saberhagen - Colorado Rockies 1995 All-Star
Tim Salmon - California Angels 1995 All-Star
Mike Schmidt - Philadelphia Phillies 1995 Hall of Fame Induc-
   tion regular, 24k, bronze, 1-ounce gold
Ozzie Smith - St. Louis Cardinals 1995 All-Star
Frank Thomas - Chicago White Sox 1995 All-Star regular,
   24k, bronze
Mo Vaughn - Boston Red Sox 1995 All-Star
Matt Williams - San Francisco Giants 1995 All-Star
Dave Winfield - Cleveland Indians 1995 All-Star

Collector cards

Cal Ripken Jr. - Baltimore Orioles consecutive games played
   streak silver, 24k
Atlanta Braves - 1995 World Series Champions silver, 24k
Mickey Mantle - New York Yankees legend silver, 24k,
   bronze
Coors Field - Inaugural season regular, 24k
Roberto Clemente - career commemorative regular, 24k
Nolan Ryan - strikeouts 24k, bronze
Nolan Ryan - career commemorative silver

	Mintage		Issue	Value
* Cleveland Indians, 3-piece proof set	250	S/O	1995	$125
* Cleveland Indians, 3-piece AL Central	95	S/O	1995	$125
* Seattle Mariners, AL West 3-piece set	95	S/O	1995	$125
* Colorado Rockies, NL Wildcard 3-piece set	95	S/O	1995	$125
* Colorado Rockies/Coors Field Opening, 24k	405	S/O	1995	$50
* New York Yankees, AL Wildcard 3-piece set	95	S/O	1995	$125
* Colorado Rockies record-breaking attendance	5,000		1993	$30
* 1993 Rockies/Andres Galarraga 2-piece set	1,000		1993	$30
* Indians final game at Municipal Stadium	10,000		1993	$30
* Indians final game at Municipal Stadium, pure gold	61	S/O	1993	$850
* Arlington Stadium Old and New	1,000	S/O	1993	$75
* Kansas City Royals 25th Anniversary	286	S/O	1993	$30
* Montreal Expos 25th Anniversary	48	S/O	1993	$30
* San Diego Padres 25th Anniversary	82	S/O	1993	$30
* Toronto Blue Jays Back-to-Back 2-piece set (note: issue price was $82.95)	400	S/O	1993	$175
* 1993 three-piece World Series Champs set (note: issue price was $125)	500	S/O	1993	$255
* 1993 seven-piece World Series Champs set (note: issue price was $250)	500	S/O	1993	N/A

* 1993 Toronto Blue Jays World Series Champs	9,972		1993	$30
* 1993 Toronto Blue Jays World Series Champs, gold	13	S/O	1993	$850
(note: issue price was $850)				
* 1993 Philadelphia Phillies N.L. Champs	2,790	S/O	1993	$30
* 1993 Toronto Blue Jays A.L. Champs	3,155	S/O	1993	$30
* 1993 Division Winners				
Toronto Blue Jays	2,867	S/O	1993	$30
Atlanta Braves	1,090	S/O	1993	$30
Chicago White Sox	1,278	S/O	1993	$30
Philadelphia Phillies	896	S/O	1993	$30
* Miami Marlins inaugural	10,000		1993	$30
* Colorado Rockies inaugural	10,000		1993	$30
* Inaugural 2-piece set	1,000		1993	$82.50
(note: issue price was $82.50)				
* 1992 three-piece World Series Champs set	500	S/O	1992	$290
(note: issue price was $125)				
* 1992 seven-piece World Series Champs set	500	S/O	1992	$440
(note: issue price was $250)				
* 1992 Toronto Blue Jays World Series Champions	25,000	S/O	1992	$60
* 1992 Toronto Blue Jays World Series Champions, gold	67	S/O	1992	$850
(note: issue price was $850)				
* 1992 Toronto Blue Jays A.L. Champions	10,000	S/O	1992	$55
* 1992 Atlanta Braves N.L. Champions	3,332	S/O	1992	$30
* 1992 Atlanta Braves N.L. Champions, gold	unknown		1992	$850
(note: issue price was $850)				
* 1992 Division Winners				
Toronto Blue Jays	5,000	S/O	1992	$58
Atlanta Braves	1,452	S/O	1992	$30
Oakland A's	515	S/O	1992	$30
Pittsburgh Pirates	557	S/O	1992	$30
* St. Louis Cardinals 100th Anniversary	5,000		1992	$30
* Baltimore Memorial Stadium	48,000		1992	$30
* Oakland A's 25th Anniversary	96	S/O	1991	$30
* 1991 Minnesota Twins World Series Champions	13,101	S/O	1991	$30
* 1991 Minnesota Twins A.L. Champions	1,315	S/O	1991	$30
* 1991 Atlanta Braves N.L. Champions	2,600	S/O	1991	$50
* 1991 Division Winners				
Minnesota Twins	N/A	S/O	1991	$30
Atlanta Braves	2,744	S/O	1991	$35
Toronto Blue Jays	4,500	S/O	1991	$75
Pittsburgh Pirates	1,300	S/O	1991	$40
* Miami Marlins franchise	10,000		1991	$30
* Colorado Rockies franchise	10,000		1991	$30
* New York Giants Cooperstown Collection	10,000		1991	$35
* 1990 Cincinnati World Series Champions	9,005	S/O	1990	$30
* 1990 Cincinnati N.L. Champions	2,050	S/O	1990	$30
* 1990 Oakland A's A.L. Champions	750	S/O	1990	$30
* 1990 Division Winners				
Cincinnati Reds	1,050	S/O	1990	$55
Oakland A's	150	S/O	1990	$75
Boston Red Sox	450	S/O	1990	$50
Pittsburgh Pirates	450	S/O	1990	$50
* Comiskey Park Commemorative Old & New	43,931		1990	$30
* Wrigley Field 75th Anniversary	10,000		1990	$30
* Dodgers 100th Anniversary	5,000		1990	$30
* 1955 Brooklyn Dodgers Cooperstown Collection	10,000		1990	$35
* Chicago Cubs 1989 Division Championship	10,000		1989	$30
* 1989 Oakland A's World Series Champions	6,550	S/O	1989	$35

Medallions

* 1989 Oakland A's A.L. Champions	6,550	S/O	1989	$32.50
* 1989 San Francisco Giants N.L. Champions	8,100	S/O	1989	$35
* 1989 Division Winners				
San Francisco Giants	600	S/O	1989	$35
Oakland A's	900	S/O	1989	$35
Chicago Cubs	6,200	S/O	1989	$35
Toronto Blue Jays	2,300	S/O	1989	$75
* Wrigley Field First Night Game	39,012	S/O	1988	$42.50
* 1988 L.A. Dodgers World Series Champions	2,225	S/O	1988	$30
* 1988 Los Angeles Dodgers N.L. Champions	4,050	S/O	1988	$32.50
* 1988 Oakland A's A.L. Champions	4,250	S/O	1988	$32.50
* 1988 Division Winners				
Oakland A's	800	S/O	1988	$35
Boston Red Sox	500	S/O	1988	$45
New York Mets	1,100	S/O	1988	$35
Los Angeles Dodgers	800	S/O	1988	$35
* 1987 Minnesota Twins World Series Champions	25,000	S/O	1987	$45
* 1987 Minnesota Twins A.L. Champions	5,000		1987	$35
* 1987 St. Louis Cardinals N.L. Champions	N/A	S/O	1987	$35
* 1987 Division Winners				
Minnesota Twins	3,000	S/O	1987	$35
San Francisco Giants	1,000	S/O	1987	$35
Detroit Tigers	1,800	S/O	1987	$35
St. Louis Cardinals	1,500	S/O	1987	$35
* 1986 N.Y. Mets World Series Champions	25,000		1987	$30
* Comiskey Park 75th Anniversary	680	S/O	1985	$125
* Team Commemorative - All teams (logos/names)	1,000 each			$30
* Pittsburgh Pirates All-Star 1994	5,000		1994	$30
* 1993 All-Star Team, 10-piece set	51	S/O	1993	$450
(note: issue price was $450)				
* Baltimore Orioles All-Star 1993	766	S/O	1993	$30
* San Diego Padres All-Star 1992	1,063	S/O	1992	$30
* Toronto Blue Jays All-Star 1991	5,000	S/O	1991	$60
* Chicago Cubs All-Star 1990	7,700	S/O	1990	$30
* California Angels All-Star 1989	2,000	S/O	1989	$45
* All-Star 1991 for Commissioner's Office	500	S/O	1991	N/A
* All-Star 1990	10,000		1990	$30
* All-Star 1990 for Commissioner's Office	400	S/O	1990	N/A
* All-Star 1989	2,000	S/O	1989	$45
* All-Star 1989 for Commissioner's Office	350	S/O	1989	N/A
* All-Star 1988	2,000	S/O	1988	$45
* All-Star 1988 for Commissioner's Office	300	S/O	1988	N/A
* All-Star 1987 for Commissioner's Office	300	S/O	1987	N/A

Players

* Roberto Alomar - Toronto Blue Jays	130	S/O	1993	$30
Roberto Alomar - Toronto Blue Jays 24k	125	S/O	1993	$50
Roberto Alomar - Toronto Blue Jays bronze	50	S/O	1993	$15
Roberto Alomar - 1995 All-Star	25	S/O	1995	$30
Roberto Alomar - 1995 All-Star 24k	5	S/O	1995	$50
Roberto Alomar - 1995 All-Star bronze	20	S/O	1995	$15
Roberto Alomar - 1995 All-Star 3-piece set	12	S/O	1995	$125
* Albert Belle - Cleveland Indians	140	S/O	1993	$30
Albert Belle - Cleveland Indians 24k	85	S/O	1993	$50
Albert Belle - Cleveland Indians bronze	30	S/O	1993	$15
* Johnny Bench - 1989 Hall of Fame	10,635	S/O	1989	$30
* Blue Jay Bashers - Alomar, Carter & White	1,813	S/O	1992	$30
Blue Jay Bashers - Olerud, Alomar & Molitor	925	S/O	1993	$30

* Wade Boggs - 1987 A.L. Batting Champ	1,249	S/O	1988	$50
Wade Boggs - New York Yankees	13,751		1993	$30
* Barry Bonds - 1993 N.L. MVP	390	S/O	1993	$30
Barry Bonds - 1993 N.L. MVP 24k	15	S/O	1993	$50
Barry Bonds - 1993 N.L. MVP bronze	500	S/O	1993	$15
Barry Bonds/San Francisco Giants generic, 2-piece set	500		1993	$30
* George Brett - 3 Decades of Batting Titles	2,033	S/O	1991	$30
George Brett - 3,000th career hit	6,035	S/O	1992	$30
George Brett/Robin Yount 3,000th hit, 2-piece set	1,000	S/O	1992	$95
(note: issue price was $82.95)				
* Jose Canseco - 40/40 Oakland A's	5,893	S/O	1990	$40
Jose Canseco - 40/40 Texas Rangers	9,000		1992	$30
* Steve Carlton - 4-Time Cy Young Winner	15,000		1990	$30
* Joe Carter - Toronto Blue Jays	90	S/O	1993	$30
Joe Carter - Toronto Blue Jays 24k	125	S/O		$50
Joe Carter - Toronto Blue Jays bronze	30	S/O		$15
* Will Clark- San Francisco Giants	2,389		1990	$50
* Roger Clemens - 1986-87 Cy Young Winner	740	S/O	1990	$60
* Roberto Clemente - 1973 Hall of Fame	1,560	S/O	1988	$55
* Ty Cobb - New York Giants	1,093	S/O	1988	$65
* Darren Daulton - Philadelphia Phillies	70	S/O	1993	$30
Darren Daulton - Philadelphia Phillies 24k	20	S/O		$50
Darren Daulton - Philadelphia Phillies bronze	30	S/O		$15
* Mark Davis - 1989 Cy Young Winner	270	S/O	1989	$65
* Andre Dawson - 1987 N. L. MVP	10,900	S/O	1990	$35
Andre Dawson - Boston Red Sox	4,100		1993	$30
* Lenny Dykstra - Philadelphia Phillies	50	S/O	1993	$30
Lenny Dykstra - Philadelphia Phillies 24 k	15	S/O	1993	$50
Lenny Dykstra - Philadelphia Phillies bronze	30	S/O	1993	$15
* Dennis Eckersley - 40 Saves/3 straight years	400	S/O	1992	$50
Dennis Eckersley - 1992 Cy Young Winner	105	S/O	1992	$30
* Cecil Fielder - A.L. Home Run/RBI Leader	15,000		1991	$30
* Rollie Fingers - Oakland A's	115	S/O	N/A	$30
* Carlton Fisk - Most Career Hits by a Catcher	15,000		1990	$30
* Andres Galarraga - 1993 N.L. Batting Champion	483	S/O	1993	$30
Andres Galarraga - 1993 N.L. Batting Champion bronze	20	S/O	1993	$15
* Steve Garvey - 1,207 Consecutive Games Played	450	S/O	1989	$30
* Lou Gehrig - 2,130 Consecutive Games Played	1,352	S/O	1987	$55
* Kirk Gibson - 1988 N.L. MVP	600	S/O	1988	$45
* Tom Glavine - Atlanta Braves	580	S/O	1992	$30
* Juan Gonzalez - Texas Rangers	189	S/O	1993	$30
Juan Gonzalez - Texas Rangers 24k	125	S/O	1993	$50
Juan Gonzalez - Texas Rangers bronze	495	S/O	1993	$15
* Dwight Gooden - 1985 Cy Young Winner	625	S/O	1989	$30
* Mark Grace - Chicago Cubs	95	S/O	1993	$30
Mark Grace - Chicago Cubs 24k	36	S/O	1993	$50
Mark Grace - Chicago Cubs bronze	30	S/O	1993	$15
* Ken Griffey Jr. & Sr. - Mariners/Reds	3,300	S/O	1990	$95
Ken Griffey Jr. & Sr. - Mariners	3,700	S/O	1990	$65
Ken Griffey Jr. - Seattle Mariners	805	S/O	1993	$30
Ken Griffey Jr. - Seattle Mariners 24k	125	S/O	1993	$50
Ken Griffey Jr. - Seattle Mariners bronze	499	S/O	1993	$15
Ken Griffey Jr. - All-Star 3-piece	95	S/O	1995	$125
* Tony Gwynn - 1987, '88, '89 Batting Champion	1,075	S/O	1990	$50
* Rickey Henderson - All-Time Stolen Bases	7,109	S/O	1990	$45
Rickey Henderson - Toronto Blue Jays	7,891		1993	$30
* Orel Hershiser - 1988 Cy Young Winner	725	S/O	1989	$45
* Bo Jackson - L.A. Raiders/K.C. Royals	4,400	S/O	1990	$45

Bo Jackson - White Sox/White Sox error	N/A		1990	$75
Bo Jackson - L.A. Raiders/White Sox	N/A		1991	$35
Bo Jackson - Chicago White Sox	15,000		1992	$30
* Reggie Jackson - 1993 Hall of Fame	15,000		1993	$30
Reggie Jackson - 1993 Hall of Fame, gold	44		1993	$850
(note: issue price was $850).				
Reggie Jackson - Hall of Fame, 2-piece set	100	S/O	1993	$125
(note: issue price was $82.95)				
* Randy Johnson - Seattle Mariners	125	S/O	1993	$30
Randy Johnson - Seattle Mariners 24k	20	S/O	1993	$50
Randy Johnson - Seattle Mariners bronze	30	S/O	1993	$15
* Ferguson Jenkins - 1991 Hall of Fame	1,300		1991	$30
* Howard Johnson - N.L. Home Run/RBI Leader	680		1991	$30
* Michael Jordan - Birmingham Barons	8,014	S/O	1994	$30
* Dave Justice - 1990 Rookie of the Year	1,434	S/O	1991	$30
* Harmon Killebrew - 1984 Hall of Fame	801		1991	$30
* Chuck Knoblauch - Minnesota Twins	345	S/O	1993	$30
* Greg Maddux - 1992 N.L. Cy Young Winner	309	S/O	1992	$45
Greg Maddux - Atlanta Braves	14,691		1993	$30
Greg Maddux - 1993 N.L. Cy Young Winner	14,600		1993	$30
Greg Maddux - 1993 N.L. Division, 2-piece set	500		1993	$82.95
(note: issue price was $82.95)				
* Mickey Mantle - New York Yankees legend	9,000	S/O	1995	$30
* Don Mattingly - Most Grand Slams, season	2,805		1988	$30
* Jack McDowell - 1993 A.L. Cy Young Winner	190	S/O	1993	$30
Jack McDowell - 1993 A.L. Cy Young Winner 24k	125	S/O	1993	$50
Jack McDowell - 1993 A.L. Cy Young Winner bronze	30	S/O	1993	$30
Jack McDowell/Frank Thomas, 2-piece set	1,000	S/O	1993	$85
* Mark McGwire - 30 Homers 1st Four Seasons	450	S/O	1991	$30
* Kevin Mitchell - 1989 N.L. MVP	1,200	S/O	1990	$45
Kevin Mitchell - Seattle Mariners	108	S/O	19199392	$55
Kevin Mitchell - Cincinnati Reds	13,692		1993	$30
* Paul Molitor - 39-Game Hitting Streak	11,001	S/O	1990	$35
Paul Molitor - Toronto Blue Jays	3,999		1992	$30
* Joe Morgan - 1990 Hall of Fame	1,225		1990	$30
* Hideo Nomo - 1995 All-Star	1,900	S/O	1995	$30
Hideo Nomo - 1995 All-Star 24k	405	S/O	1995	$50
Hideo Nomo - 1995 All-Star bronze	1,900	S/O	1995	$15
Hideo Nomo - 1995 All-Star 3-piece set	95	S/O	1995	$125
* John Olerud - 1993 A.L. Batting Champion	495	S/O	1993	$30
John Olerud - 1993 A.L. Batting Champion 24k	125	S/O	1993	$50
* Greg Olson - 1989 A.L. Rookie of the Year	630	S/O	1990	$35
* Terry Pendleton - 1991 N.L. Batting Champion	900	S/O	1991	$45
Terry Pendleton - 1991 N.L. MVP	14,100		1991	$30
* Mike Piazza - 1993 Rookie of the Year	170	S/O	1993	$30
Mike Piazza - 1993 Rookie of the Year 24k	65	S/O	1993	$50
Mike Piazza - 1993 Rookie of the Year bronze	500	S/O	1993	$15
Mike Piazza/Tim Salmon 2-piece set	70	S/O	1993	$82.50
* Kirby Puckett - 1989 A.L. Batting Champion	2,200	S/O	1990	$50
Kirby Puckett - Minnesota Twins	50	S/O	1993	$30
Kirby Puckett - Minnesota Twins 24k	20	S/O	1993	$50
Kirby Puckett - Minnesota Twins bronze	30	S/O	1993	$15
* Cal Ripken - 1991 A.L. MVP	15,000		1992	$30
Cal Ripken Jr. - Baltimore Orioles	560	S/O	1993	$30
Cal Ripken Jr. - Baltimore Orioles 24k	125	S/O	1993	$50
Cal Ripken Jr. - Baltimore Orioles bronze	200	S/O	1993	$15
Cal Ripken Jr. - 1995 All-Star 24k	405	S/O	1995	$50
Cal Ripken Jr. - 1995 All-Star 3-piece set	95	S/O	1995	$125

* Brooks Robinson - 1983 Hall of Fame	1,475	S/O	1991	$30
* A's Rookies (McGwire, Weiss, Canseco)	15,000		1990	$30
* Pete Rose - All-Time Hit Leader	25,000	S/O	1985	$65
* Babe Ruth - New York Yankees	2,382	S/O	1987	$49.95
* Nolan Ryan - 300th Victory	15,000	S/O	1990	$95
Nolan Ryan - 300th Victory 24k	285	S/O	N/A	$50
Nolan Ryan - 5,000th Strikeout	15,000	S/O	1989	$85
Nolan Ryan - 5,000th Strikeout 24k	365	S/O	N/A	$50
Nolan Ryan - 7th No-Hitter	15,000	S/O	1991	$45
Nolan Ryan - 7th No-Hitter	250	S/O	N/A	$50
Nolan Ryan - Retirement, matched 2-piece set	500	S/O	1993	$145
(note: issue price was $125)				
Nolan Ryan - Retirement, gold	95	S/O	1993	$850
(note: issue price was $850)				
Nolan Ryan - Retirement 24k	1,000	S/O	1993	$50
* Bret Saberhagen - 1988 A.L. Cy Young Winner	352	S/O	1990	$65
Bret Saberhagen - New York Mets	14,700		N/A	$30
Bret Saberhagen - 1995 National League	14	S/O	1995	$30
Bret Saberhagen - 1995 National League 24k	10	S/O	1995	$50
Bret Saberhagen - 1995 National League bronze	15	S/O	1995	$15
* Chris Sabo - 1988 N.L. Rookie of the Year	1,315	S/O	1989	$30
* Tim Salmon - 1993 Rookie of the Year	134	S/O	1993	$30
Tim Salmon - 1993 Rookie of the Year 24k	110	S/O	1993	$50
Tim Salmon - 1993 Rookie of the Year bronze	65	S/O	1993	$15
* Ryne Sandberg - All-Time Errorless Streak	6,057	S/O	1990	$30
* Deion Sanders - Atlanta Braves	545	S/O	1992	$30
* Mike Schmidt - Player of the Decade	10,000	S/O	1990	$45
Mike Schmidt - 1995 Hall of Fame, 3-piece set	95	S/O	1995	$125
* Tom Seaver - 300th Win	377	S/O	1987	$750
Tom Seaver - 1992 Hall of Fame	15,000		1992	$30
* Ozzie Smith - St. Louis Cardinals	340	S/O	1993	$30
Ozzie Smith - St. Louis Cardinals 24k	109	S/O	1993	$50
Ozzie Smith - St. Louis Cardinals bronze	1,200		1993	$15
* Darryl Strawberry - New York Mets	1,200	S/O	1990	$45
Darryl Strawberry - Los Angeles Dodgers	13,800		1991	$30
* Frank Thomas - 1993 A.L. MVP	867	S/O	1993	$30
Frank Thomas - 1993 A.L. MVP 24k	125	S/O	1993	$50
Frank Thomas - 1993 A.L. MVP bronze	255	S/O	1993	$15
Frank Thomas - 1994 A.L. MVP	235	S/O	1994	$30
Frank Thomas - 1993 A.L. MVP 24k	110	S/O	1994	$50
Frank Thomas - 1993 A.L. MVP bronze	325	S/O	1994	$15
Frank Thomas - 1995 All-Star 3-piece	95	S/O	1995	$125
* Frank Viola - 1988 N.L. Cy Young Winner	300	S/O	1988	$30
* Jerome Walton - 1989 N.L. Rookie of the Year	900	S/O	1990	$55
* Billy Williams - 1987 Hall of Fame	690	S/O	1991	$30
* Matt Williams - San Francisco Giants	90	S/O	1993	$30
Matt Williams - San Francisco Giants 24k	20	S/O	1993	$50
Matt Williams - San Francisco Giants	30	S/O	1993	$15
* Dave Winfield - Toronto Blue Jays	389	S/O	1992	$60
Dave Winfield - Minnesota Twins	14,611		1993	$30
* Robin Yount - 1989 A.L. MVP	2,387	S/O	1990	$35
Robin Yount - 3,000th career hit	12,114	S/O	1992	$30

Stamps

There have been six general issue baseball postage stamps issued by the United States. They are listed with prices according to the 1996 Brookman stamp price guide, using Fine-Very Fine grading conditions.

1) 1939 3-cent Baseball Centennial, violet - a sheet for $110; block of 4 for $11; unused stamp, $2.30; used stamp, 20 cents.

2) 1969 6-cent Professional Baseball Centenary, multicolored - a sheet for $50; block of 4 for $4.95; an unused stamp, $1.10; a used stamp, 15 cents.

3) 1982 20-cent Jackie Robinson, multicolored - a sheet for $95; block, $9.50; unused, $1.95; used, 15 cents.

4) 1983 20-cent Babe Ruth, blue - sheet, $100; block, $10.50; unused, $2.75; used, 15 cents.

5) 1984 20-cent Roberto Clemente, multicolored - sheet, $130; block, $12.75; unused, $3; used, 15 cents.

6) 1988 25-cent Lou Gehrig, multicolored - sheet, $38.50; block, $4; unused, 85 cents; used, 15 cents.

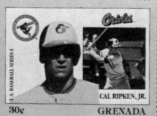

Two post offices in the Caribbean, Grenada and St. Vincent, have issued multi-player sheets of stamps. (Values for these stamps are from Scott's 1996 Standard Postage Stamp Catalogue, Volume 1A). In 1988, Grenada, licensed by Major League Baseball, issued nine sheets portraying 79 past and present baseball stars. Sheets of nine stamps (each stamp is 30 cents in East Caribbean currency) can be purchased from stamp dealers for $2 each; the whole set can be purchased for $17.50-$20. Three players from each team were depicted, except the Yankees. Individual stamps generally sell for 20 cents each.

The groups of nine are: A) Johnny Bench, Dave Stieb, Reggie Jackson, Harold Baines, Wade Boggs, Pete O'Brien, Stan Musial, Wally Joyner and Grover Cleveland Alexander.

B) Jose Cruz, American League logo, Al Kaline, Chuck Klein, Don Mattingly, Mike Witt, Mark Langston, Hubie Brooks and Harmon Killebrew.

C) Jackie Robinson, Dwight Gooden, Brooks Robinson, Nolan Ryan, Mike Schmidt, Gary Gaetti, Nellie Fox, Tony Gwynn and Dizzy Dean.

D) Luis Aparicio, Paul Molitor, Lou Gehrig, Jeffrey Leonard, Eric Davis, Pete Incaviglia, Steve Rogers, Ozzie Smith and Randy Jones.

E) Gary Carter, Hank Aaron, Gaylord Perry, Ty Cobb, Andre Dawson, Charlie Hough, Kirby Puckett, Robin Yount and Don Drysdale.

F) Mickey Mantle, Roger Clemens, Rod Carew, Ryne Sandberg, Mike Scott, Tim Raines, Willie Mays, Bret Saberhagen and Honus Wagner.

G) George Brett, Joe Carter, Frank Robinson, Mel Ott, Benito Santiago, Teddy Higuera, Lloyd Moseby, Bobby Bonilla and Warren Spahn.

H) Ernie Banks, National League logo, Julio Franco, Jack Morris, Fernando Valenzuela, Lefty Grove, Ted Williams, Darryl Strawberry and Dale Murphy.

I) Roberto Clemente, Cal Ripken Jr., Bob Feller, George Bell, Mark McGwire, Alvin Davis, Pete Rose, Dan Quisenberry and Babe Ruth.

On Dec. 7, 1988, St. Vincent issued a $2 stamp honoring Hall of Famer Babe Ruth. This stamp is worth $1.50. On May 3, 1989, St. Vincent issued another sheet of two $2 stamps - one features team logos for the 1988 World Series participants - the Oakland A's and Los Angeles Dodgers; the other shows the Dodgers celebrating. Individual stamps are worth $1.50; the sheet is worth $3.

On July 23, 1989, St. Vincent issued a set of 12 $2 stamps featuring Hall of Famers Bob Feller, Ernie Banks, Al Kaline, Stan Musial, Ty Cobb, Jackie Robinson, Ted Williams, Willie Mays, Lou Gehrig, Red Schoendienst, Carl Yastrzemski and Johnny Bench. Individual stamps are worth $1.50 each; the complete set is worth $18. Major League Baseball and the Major League Baseball Players Association gave approval for the stamps. A $5 1989 All-Star Game stamp, listing the starting lineups for the game in California, was also issued; it's worth $3.75.

Three other sheets of nine 60-cent stamps were also issued at the same time. Two sheets feature rookies, mainly from 1989. The first sheet shows Tom McCarthy, Jerome Walton, Dante Bichette, Gaylord Perry, Ramon Martinez, Carl Yastrzemski, John Smoltz, Ken Hill and Randy Johnson. The second has Bob Milacki, Babe Ruth, Jim Abbott, Gary Sheffield, Gregg Jefferies, Kevin Brown, Cris Carpenter, Johnny Bench and Ken Griffey Jr. The third sheet has nine award winners - Chris Sabo, Walt Weiss and Willie Mays (Rookie of the Year winners); Kirk Gibson, Ted Williams and Jose Canseco (MVP winners); and Gaylord Perry, Orel Hershiser and Frank Viola (Cy Young Award winners). In each case, sheets of nine are worth $4; individual stamps are worth 45 cents.

In September, 1989, St. Vincent issued two sheets of nine 60-cent stamps featuring members of the World Champion Los Angeles Dodgers. The sheets are worth $4 each; individual stamps are worth 45 cents. One sheet has Jay Howell, Alejandro Pena; Mike Davis, Kirk Gibson; Fernando Valenzuela, John Shelby; Jeff Hamilton, Franklin Stubbs; Dodger Stadium; Ray Searage, John Tudor; Mike Sharperson, Mickey Hatcher; coaches Amalfitano, Cresse, Ferguson, Hines, Mota, Perranoski and Russell; and John Wetteland, Ramon Martinez. The second sheet has Tim Belcher, Tim Crews; Orel Hershiser, Mike Morgan; Mike Scioscia, Rick Dempsey; Dave Anderson, Alfredo Griffin; team emblem; Kal Daniels, Mike Marshall; Eddie Murray, Willie Randolph; Tommy Lasorda, Jose Gonzalez; and Lenny Harris, Chris Gwynn and Billy Beane.

On Nov. 30, 1989, St. Vincent issued nine more sheets of nine 30-cent stamps. The sheets are $2 each; individual stamps are 22 cents each. The sheets feature 1) Early Wynn, Cecil Cooper, Joe DiMaggio, Kevin Mitchell, Tom Browning, Bobby Witt, Tim Wallach, Bob Gibson and Steve Garvey; 2) Rick Sutcliffe, Bart Giamatti, Cory Snyder, Rollie Fingers, Willie Hernandez, Sandy Koufax, Carl Yastrzemski, Ron Darling and Gerald Perry; 3) Mike Marshall, Tom Seaver, Bob Milacki, Dave Smith, Robin Roberts, Kent Hrbek, Bill Veeck, Carmelo Martinez and Rogers Hornsby; 4) Barry Bonds, Jim Palmer, Lou Boudreau, Ernie Whitt, Jose Canseco, Ken Griffey Jr., Johnny Vander Meer, Kevin Seitzer and Dave Drabecky; 5) Glenn Davis, Nolan Ryan, Hank Greenberg, Richie Allen, Dave Righetti, Jim Abbott, Harold Reynolds, Dennis Martinez and Rod Carew; 6) Joe Morgan, Tony Fernandez, Ozzie Guillen, Mike Greenwell, Bobby Valentine, Doug DeCinces, Mickey Cochrane, Willie McGee and Von Hayes; 7) Frank White, Brook Jacoby, Boog Powell, Will Clark, Ray Kroc, Fred McGriff, Willie Stargell, John Smoltz and B.J. Surhoff; 8) Keith Hernandez, Eddie Mathews, Tom Paciorek, Alan Trammell, Greg Maddux, Ruben Sierra, Tony Oliva, Chris Bosio and Orel Hershiser; 9) Casey Stengel, Jim Rice, Reggie Jackson, Jerome Walton, Bob Knepper, Andres Galarraga, Christy Mathewson, Willie Wilson and Ralph Kiner. Two misspellings occurred; Fingers is spelled Finger, while Cochrane is Cochpane.

Nolan Ryan is featured on a sheet of nine $2 stamps issued Nov. 30, 1989. Individual stamps are worth $1.50; the sheet is worth $13.50. Ryan's achievements recognized on the stamps include: a) 383 league leading strikeouts in 1973, b) no hitter on May 15, 1973, c) no hitter on July 15, 1973, d) no hitter on Sept. 28, 1974, e) no hitter on June 1, 1975, f) no hitter on Sept. 26, 1981, g) won 100+ games in both leagues, h) struck out 200+ batters in 13 seasons, and i) 5,000 career strikeouts. Boston Red Sox outfielder Mike Greenwell was also featured on a 30-cent stamp; individual stamps are worth 22 cents.

On Aug. 5, 1992, St. Vincent issued a boxed set of 64x89mm $4 stamps featuring 12 Hall of Famers; a complete set is worth $36. The stamps were printed on thin cards; to affix the stamps, one had to remove the backing, which contained the player's statistics. The players in the set are Ty Cobb, Dizzy Dean, Bob Feller, Whitey Ford, Lou Gehrig, Rogers Hornsby, Mel Ott, Satchel Paige, Babe Ruth, Casey Stengel, Honus Wagner and Cy Young. Two $5 stamps, honoring players from New York - the Mets' Howard Johnson and the Yankees' Don Mattingly - were issued Nov. 9, 1992. These stamps are worth $3.75 each. On Dec. 21, 1992, three $2 stamps were issued honoring Hall of Famers Roberto Clemente, Hank Aaron and Tom Seaver. These stamps are worth $1.50 each. A $2 stamp for Hall of Famer Reggie Jackson was issued Oct. 4, 1993. The stamp is also worth $1.50.

Blankets, pennants leathers, silks

1937 BF104 Blankets

A throwback to the 1914 B18 blankets, little is known about these 3-1/2"-square felts. They were designated as BF104 in the American Card Catalog. The issue date attributed here is approximate; it can be more accurately pinpointed when additions to the checklist are forthcoming. The issuer and manner of distribution remain a mystery.

		NM	EX	VG
	Common player:	75.00	37.50	22.00
(1)	Moe Berg	400.00	200.00	120.00
(2)	Thornton Lee	75.00	37.50	22.00
(3)	Rudy York	75.00	37.50	22.00

1916 BF2 Felt Pennants

Issued circa 1916, this unnumbered set consists of 97 felt pennants with a small black-and-white player photo glued to each. The triangular pennants measure approximately 8-1/4" long, while the photos are 1-3/4" by 1-1/4" and appear to be identical to photos used for The Sporting News issues of the same period. The pennants list the player's name and team. The pennants were reportedly given away as premiums with the purchase of Ferguson's Bakery products.

		NM	EX	VG
	Complete set:	9500.	4500.	2500.
	Common player:	55.00	27.00	16.50
(1)	Grover Alexander	155.00	77.00	46.00
(2)	Jimmy Archer	55.00	27.00	16.50
(3)	Home Run Baker	95.00	47.00	28.00
(4)	Dave Bancroft	95.00	47.00	28.00
(5)	Jack Barry	55.00	27.00	16.50
(6)	Chief Bender	95.00	47.00	28.00
(7)	Joe Benz	55.00	27.00	16.50
(8)	Mordecai Brown	95.00	47.00	28.00

(9)	George J. Burns	55.00	27.00	16.50
(10)	Donie Bush	55.00	27.00	16.50
(11)	Hick Cady	55.00	27.00	16.50
(12)	Max Carey	95.00	47.00	28.00
(13)	Ray Chapman	90.00	45.00	27.00
(14)	Ty Cobb	675.00	337.00	202.00
(15)	Eddie Collins	95.00	47.00	28.00
(16)	Shano Collins	55.00	27.00	16.50
(17)	Commy Comiskey	95.00	47.00	28.00
(18)	Harry Coveleskie (Coveleski)	55.00	27.00	16.50
(19)	Gavvy Cravath	55.00	27.00	16.50
(20)	Sam Crawford	95.00	47.00	28.00
(21)	Jake Daubert	55.00	27.00	16.50
(22)	Josh Devore	55.00	27.00	16.50
(23)	Red Dooin	55.00	27.00	16.50
(24)	Larry Doyle	55.00	27.00	16.50
(25)	Jean Dubuc	55.00	27.00	16.50
(26)	Johnny Evers	95.00	47.00	28.00
(27)	Red Faber	95.00	47.00	28.00
(28)	Eddie Foster	55.00	27.00	16.50
(29)	Del Gainer (Gainor)	55.00	27.00	16.50
(30)	Chick Gandil	90.00	45.00	27.00
(31)	Joe Gedeon	55.00	27.00	16.50
(32)	Hank Gowdy	55.00	27.00	16.50
(33)	Earl Hamilton	55.00	27.00	16.50
(34)	Claude Hendrix	55.00	27.00	16.50
(35)	Buck Herzog	55.00	27.00	16.50
(36)	Harry Hooper	95.00	47.00	28.00
(37)	Miller Huggins	95.00	47.00	28.00
(38)	Shoeless Joe Jackson	1100.	550.00	330.00
(39)	Seattle Bill James	55.00	27.00	16.50
(40)	Hugh Jennings	95.00	47.00	28.00
(41)	Walter Johnson	350.00	175.00	105.00
(42)	Fielder Jones	55.00	27.00	16.50
(43)	Joe Judge	55.00	27.00	16.50
(44)	Benny Kauff	55.00	27.00	16.50

(45)	Bill Killefer	55.00	27.00	16.50
(46)	Nap Lajoie	100.00	50.00	30.00
(47)	Jack Lapp	55.00	27.00	16.50
(48)	Doc Lavan	55.00	27.00	16.50
(49)	Jimmy Lavender	55.00	27.00	16.50
(50)	Dutch Leonard	55.00	27.00	16.50
(51)	Duffy Lewis	55.00	27.00	16.50
(52)	Hans Lobert	55.00	27.00	16.50
(53)	Fred Luderus	55.00	27.00	16.50
(54)	Connie Mack	95.00	47.00	28.00
(55)	Sherry Magee	55.00	27.00	16.50
(56)	Al Mamaux	55.00	27.00	16.50
(57)	Rabbit Maranville	95.00	47.00	28.00
(58)	Rube Marquard	95.00	47.00	28.00
(59)	George McBride	55.00	27.00	16.50
(60)	John McGraw	95.00	47.00	28.00
(61)	Stuffy McInnes (McInnis)	55.00	27.00	16.50
(62)	Fred Merkle	55.00	27.00	16.50
(63)	Chief Meyers	55.00	27.00	16.50
(64)	Clyde Milan	55.00	27.00	16.50
(65)	Otto Miller	55.00	27.00	16.50
(66)	Pat Moran	55.00	27.00	16.50
(67)	Ray Morgan	55.00	27.00	16.50
(68)	Guy Morton	55.00	27.00	16.50
(69)	Eddie Murphy	55.00	27.00	16.50
(70)	Rube Oldring	55.00	27.00	16.50
(71)	Dode Paskert	55.00	27.00	16.50
(72)	Wally Pipp	65.00	32.00	19.50
(73)	Pants Rowland	55.00	27.00	16.50
(74)	Nap Rucker	55.00	27.00	16.50
(75)	Dick Rudolph	55.00	27.00	16.50
(76)	Reb Russell	55.00	27.00	16.50
(77)	Vic Saier	55.00	27.00	16.50
(78)	Slim Sallee	55.00	27.00	16.50
(79)	Ray Schalk	95.00	47.00	28.00
(80)	Wally Schang	55.00	27.00	16.50
(81)	Wildfire Schulte	55.00	27.00	16.50
(82)	Jim Scott	55.00	27.00	16.50
(83)	George Sisler	95.00	47.00	28.00
(84)	George Stallings	55.00	27.00	16.50
(85)	Oscar Stanage	55.00	27.00	16.50
(86)	Jeff Tesreau	55.00	27.00	16.50
(87)	Joe Tinker	95.00	47.00	28.00
(88)	Lefty Tyler	55.00	27.00	16.50
(89)	Hippo Vaughn	55.00	27.00	16.50
(90)	Bobby Veach	55.00	27.00	16.50
(91)	Honus Wagner	400.00	200.00	120.00
(92)	Ed Walsh	95.00	47.00	28.00
(93)	Buck Weaver	90.00	45.00	27.00
(94)	Ivy Wingo	55.00	27.00	16.50
(95)	Joe Wood	55.00	27.00	16.50
(96)	Ralph Young	55.00	27.00	16.50
(97)	Heinie Zimmerman	55.00	27.00	16.50

1936-37 BF3 Felt Pennants

The checklist for this obscure set of felt pennants issued circa 1936-1937 is not complete, and new examples are still being reported. The pennants do not carry any manufacturer's name and their method of distribution is not certain, although it is believed they were issued as a premium with candy or gum. The pennants vary in size slightly but generally measure approximately 2-1/2" by 4-1/2" and were issued in various styles and colors, including red, yellow, white, blue, green, purple, black and brown. Most of the printing is white,

although some pennants have been found with red or black printing, and the same pennant is often found in more than one color combination. The pennants feature both individual players and teams, including some minor league clubs. Advanced collectors have categorized the BF3 pennants into the following 11 design types, depending on what elements are included on the pennant: Type I: Player's name and figure. Type II: Player's name, team nickname and figure. Type III: Player's name and team nickname. Type IV: Team nickname and figure. Type V: Team nickname with emblem. Type VI: Team nickname only. Type VII: Player's name and team nickname on two-tailed pennant displayed inside the BF3 pennant. Type VIII: Player's name, year, and team nickname on ball. Type IX: Player's name, year on ball and team nickname. Type X: Team nickname and year. Type XI: Minor league and team.

		NM	EX	VG
Complete set:		7500.	3500.	2200.
Common pennant:		25.00	12.50	7.50
Type I				
(1)	Luke Appling (batting)	42.00	21.00	12.50
(2)	Wally Berger (fielding)	25.00	12.50	7.50
(3)	Zeke Bonura			
	(fielding ground ball)	25.00	12.50	7.50
(4)	Dolph Camilli (fielding)	25.00	12.50	7.50
(5)	Ben Chapman (batting)	25.00	12.50	7.50
(6)	Mickey Cochrane (catching)	42.00	21.00	12.50
(7)	Rip Collins (batting)	25.00	12.50	7.50
(8)	Joe Cronin (batting)	42.00	21.00	12.50
(9)	Kiki Cuyler (running)	42.00	21.00	12.50
(10)	Dizzy Dean (pitching)	60.00	30.00	18.00
(11)	Frank Demaree (batting)	25.00	12.50	7.50
(12)	Paul Derringer (pitching)	25.00	12.50	7.50
(13)	Bill Dickey (catching)	60.00	30.00	18.00
(14)	Jimmy Dykes (fielding)	25.00	12.50	7.50
(15)	Bob Feller (pitching)	60.00	30.00	18.00
(16)	Wes Ferrell (batting)	25.00	12.50	7.50
(17)	Wes Ferrell (running)	25.00	12.50	7.50
(18)	Jimmy Foxx (batting)	60.00	30.00	18.00
(19)	Larry French (batting)	25.00	12.50	7.50
(20)	Franky Frisch (running)	42.00	21.00	12.50
(21)	Lou Gehrig			
	(fielding at 1st base)	250.00	125.00	75.00
(22)	Lou Gehrig (throwing)	250.00	125.00	75.00
(23)	Charles Gehringer (running)	42.00	21.00	12.50
(24)	Lefty Gomez (pitching)	42.00	21.00	12.50
(25)	Goose Goslin (batting)	42.00	21.00	12.50
(26)	Hank Greenberg (fielding)	42.00	21.00	12.50
(27)	Charlie Grimm (running)	30.00	15.00	9.00
(28)	Lefty Grove (pitching)	42.00	21.00	12.50
(29)	Gabby Hartnett (catching)	42.00	21.00	12.50
(30)	Rollie Hemsley (catching)	25.00	12.50	7.50
(31)	Billy Herman			
	(fielding at 1st base)	42.00	21.00	12.50
(32)	Frank Higgins (fielding)	25.00	12.50	7.50
(33)	Rogers Hornsby (batting)	42.00	21.00	12.50
(34)	Carl Hubbell (pitching)	42.00	21.00	12.50
(35)	Chuck Klein (throwing)	42.00	21.00	12.50
(36)	Tony Lazzeri (batting)	42.00	21.00	12.50
(37)	Hank Leiber			
	(fielding ground ball)	25.00	12.50	7.50
(38)	Ernie Lombardi (catching)	42.00	21.00	12.50
(39)	Al Lopez (throwing)	42.00	21.00	12.50
(40)	Gus Mancuso (running)	25.00	12.50	7.50
(41)	Heinie Manush (batting)	42.00	21.00	12.50
(42)	Pepper Martin (batting)	30.00	15.00	9.00
(43)	Joe McCarthy (kneeling)	42.00	21.00	12.50
(44)	Wally Moses (running)	25.00	12.50	7.50
(45)	Van Mungo (standing)	25.00	12.50	7.50
(46)	Mel Ott (throwing)	60.00	30.00	18.00
(47)	Schoolboy Rowe (pitching)	30.00	15.00	9.00
(48)	Babe Ruth (batting)	425.00	212.00	127.00
(49)	George Selkirk (batting)	25.00	12.50	7.50
(50)	Luke Sewell (sliding)	25.00	12.50	7.50
(51)	Joe Stripp (batting)	25.00	12.50	7.50
(52)	Hal Trosky (fielding)	25.00	12.50	7.50
(53)	Floyd Vaughan			
	(running, script signature)	42.00	21.00	12.50
(54)	Floyd Vaughan			
	(running, not script signature)	42.00	21.00	12.50
(55)	Joe Vosmik (running)	25.00	12.50	7.50
(56)	Paul Waner (batting)	42.00	21.00	12.50
(57)	Lon Warneke (pitching)	25.00	12.50	7.50
(58)	Jimmy Wilson			
	(fielding ground ball)	25.00	12.50	7.50
Type II				
(1)	Luke Appling (batting)	42.00	21.00	12.50
(2)	Luke Appling			
	(batting, name in script)	42.00	21.00	12.50

(3)	Zeke Bonura (batting)	25.00	12.50	7.50
(4)	Dolph Camilli (batting)	25.00	12.50	7.50
(5)	Joe Cronin (throwing)	42.00	21.00	12.50
(6)	Dizzy Dean (batting)	70.00	35.00	21.00
(7)	Frank Demaree (batting)	25.00	12.50	7.50
(8)	Bob Feller (pifthing)	70.00	35.00	21.00
(9)	Wes Ferrell (throwing)	25.00	12.50	7.50
(10)	Larry French (batting)	25.00	12.50	7.50
(11)	Frank Frisch (fielding)	42.00	21.00	12.50
(12)	Lou Gehrig (batting)	150.00	75.00	45.00
(13)	Lou Gehrig (fielding)	150.00	75.00	45.00
(14)	Hank Greenberg (throwing)	42.00	21.00	12.50
(15)	Charlie Grimm (fielding)	30.00	15.00	9.00
(16)	Charlie Grimm (throwing)	30.00	15.00	9.00
(17)	Lefty Grove (batting)	42.00	21.00	12.50
(18)	Lefty Grove (pitching)	42.00	21.00	12.50
(19)	Gabby Hartnett (batting)	42.00	21.00	12.50
(20)	Billy Herman (batting)	42.00	21.00	12.50
(21)	Tony Lazzeri (running)	42.00	21.00	12.50
(22)	Tony Lazzeri (throwing)	42.00	21.00	12.50
(23)	Hank Leiber (batting)	25.00	12.50	7.50
(24)	Ernie Lombardi (batting)	42.00	21.00	12.50
(25)	Pepper Martin (batting)	33.00	16.50	10.00
(26)	Ducky Medwick (batting)	42.00	21.00	12.50
(27)	Joe Stripp (batting)	25.00	12.50	7.50
(28)	Bill Terry (fielding)	42.00	21.00	12.50
(29)	Floyd Vaughan (batting)	42.00	21.00	12.50
(30)	Joe Vosmik (throwing)	25.00	12.50	7.50
(31)	Paul Waner (batting)	42.00	21.00	12.50
(32)	Lon Warneke (batting)	25.00	12.50	7.50
(33)	Lon Warneke (pitching)	25.00	12.50	7.50

Type III

(1)	Wally Berger	25.00	12.50	7.50
(2)	Zeke Bonura	25.00	12.50	7.50
(3)	Dolph Camilli	25.00	12.50	7.50
(4)	Ben Chapman	25.00	12.50	7.50
(5)	Kiki Cuyler	42.00	21.00	12.50
(6)	Dizzy Dean	70.00	35.00	21.00
(7)	Frank Demaree	25.00	12.50	7.50
(8)	Bill Dickey	60.00	30.00	18.00
(9)	Joe DiMaggio (name in script)	250.00	125.00	75.00
(10)	Bob Feller (name in script)	60.00	30.00	18.00
(11)	Wes Ferrell	25.00	12.50	7.50
(12)	Jimmie Foxx	45.00	22.00	13.50
(13)	Larry French	25.00	12.50	7.50
(14)	Frank Frisch	42.00	21.00	12.50
(15)	Lou Gehrig (name in script)	250.00	125.00	75.00
(16)	Charles Gehringer	42.00	21.00	12.50
(17)	Lefty Gomez	50.00	25.00	15.00
(18)	Hank Greenberg	60.00	30.00	18.00
(19)	Lefty Grove	42.00	21.00	12.50
(20)	Gabby Hartnett	25.00	12.50	7.50
(21)	Billy Herman (name in script)	42.00	21.00	12.50
(22)	Roger Hornsby (Rogers)	50.00	25.00	15.00
(23)	Carl Hubbell	42.00	21.00	12.50
(24)	Chuck Klein	42.00	21.00	12.50
(25)	Tony Lazzeri	42.00	21.00	12.50
(26)	Ernie Lombardi	40.00	20.00	12.00
(27)	Al Lopez	42.00	21.00	12.50
(28)	Johnny Marcum	25.00	12.50	7.50
(29)	Pepper Martin	30.00	15.00	9.00
(30)	Ducky Medwick	42.00	21.00	12.50
(31)	Van Mungo	25.00	12.50	7.50
(32)	Billy Myers	30.00	12.50	7.50
(33)	Mel Ott	40.00	20.00	12.00
(34)	Schoolboy Rowe	25.00	15.00	9.00
(35)	George Selkirk	25.00	12.50	7.50
(36)	Luke Sewell	25.00	12.50	7.50
(37)	Bill Terry	42.00	21.00	12.50
(38)	Pie Traynor	42.00	21.00	12.50
(39)	Hal Trosky	25.00	12.50	7.50
(40)	Floyd Vaughan	42.00	21.00	12.50
(41)	Lon Warneke	25.00	12.50	7.50
(42)	Earl Whitehill	25.00	12.50	7.50
(41)	Earl Whitehill			

Type IV

(1)	Athletics (fielder)	25.00	12.50	7.50
(2)	Browns (catcher)	25.00	12.50	7.50
(3)	Cubs (batter)	25.00	12.50	7.50
(4)	Dodgers (batter)	25.00	12.50	7.50
(5)	Dodgers (fielder)	25.00	12.50	7.50
(6)	Giants (standing by base)	25.00	12.50	7.50
(7)	Giants (two players)	25.00	12.50	7.50
(8)	Phillies (pitcher)	25.00	12.50	7.50
(9)	Reds (batter)	25.00	12.50	7.50
(10)	Reds (pitcher)	25.00	12.50	7.50
(11)	White Sox (batter)	25.00	12.50	7.50
(12)	White Sox (catcher)	25.00	12.50	7.50
(13)	White Sox (pitcher)	25.00	12.50	7.50
(14)	Yankees (batter)	42.00	21.00	12.50
(15)	Yankees (fielding ball, from waist up)	42.00	21.00	12.50

Type V

(1)	Athletics (bat)	25.00	12.50	7.50
(2)	Athletics (elephant)	25.00	12.50	7.50
(3)	Bees (bee)	25.00	12.50	7.50
(4)	Browns (bat)	25.00	12.50	7.50
(5)	Cardinals (bat)	25.00	12.50	7.50
(6)	Cardinals (cardinal)	25.00	12.50	7.50
(7)	Cardinals (four birds flying)	25.00	12.50	7.50
(8)	Cubs (cub)	25.00	12.50	7.50
(9)	Cubs (cub's head)	25.00	12.50	7.50
(10)	Dodgers (ball, bat and glove)	25.00	12.50	7.50
(11)	Dodgers (ball)	25.00	12.50	7.50
(12)	Giants (crossed bats and ball)	25.00	12.50	7.50
(13)	Indians (Indian)	25.00	12.50	7.50
(14)	Indians (Indian's head)	25.00	12.50	7.50
(15)	Indians (Indian's head with hat)	25.00	12.50	7.50
(16)	Phillies (Liberty Bell)	25.00	12.50	7.50
(17)	Pirates (skull and crossbones)	25.00	12.50	7.50
(18)	Red Sox (ball and bat)	25.00	12.50	7.50
(19)	Red Sox (bat)	25.00	12.50	7.50
(20)	Reds (ball)	25.00	12.50	7.50
(21)	Senators (bat)	25.00	12.50	7.50
(22)	Senators (Capitol building)	25.00	12.50	7.50
(23)	Tigers (cap)	25.00	12.50	7.50
(24)	Tigers (tiger)	25.00	12.50	7.50

Type VI

(1)	Cardinals	25.00	12.50	7.50
(2)	Cubs	25.00	12.50	7.50
(3)	Dodgers	25.00	12.50	7.50
(4)	Giants	25.00	12.50	7.50
(5)	Indians	25.00	12.50	7.50
(6)	Phillies (Phillies on spine)	25.00	12.50	7.50
(7)	Pirates (Pirates on spine)	25.00	12.50	7.50
(8)	Pirates (no Pirates on spine)	25.00	12.50	7.50
(9)	Yankees	42.00	21.00	12.50

Type VII

(1)	Luke Appling	40.00	20.00	12.00
(2)	Dolph Camilli	25.00	12.50	7.50
(3)	Joe DiMaggio	250.00	125.00	75.00
(4)	Lou Gehrig	250.00	125.00	75.00
(5)	Earl Grace	25.00	12.50	7.50
(6)	Rollie Hemsley	25.00	12.50	7.50
(7)	Carl Hubbell	45.00	22.00	13.50
(8)	Bob Johnson	25.00	12.50	7.50
(9)	Al Lopez	40.00	20.00	12.00
(10)	Joe Medwick	40.00	20.00	12.00
(11)	Frank Pytlak	25.00	12.50	7.50
(12)	Arky Vaughn	40.00	20.00	12.00
(13)	Paul Waner	40.00	20.00	12.00

Type VIII

(1)	Larry French	25.00	12.50	7.50

Type IX

(1)	Zeke Bonura	25.00	12.50	7.50
(2)	Stan Bordagaray	25.00	12.50	7.50
(3)	Clint Brown	25.00	12.50	7.50
(4)	Clay Bryant	25.00	12.50	7.50
(5)	Guy Bush	25.00	12.50	7.50
(6)	Sugar Cain	25.00	12.50	7.50
(7)	Tex Carleton	25.00	12.50	7.50
(8)	Phil Cavaretta (Cavarretta)	25.00	12.50	7.50
(9)	Irving Cherry	25.00	12.50	7.50
(10)	Ripper Collins	25.00	12.50	7.50
(11)	Tony Cuccinello	25.00	12.50	7.50
(12)	Curt Davis	25.00	12.50	7.50
(13)	Dizzy Dean	50.00	25.00	15.00
(14)	Paul Dean	33.00	16.50	10.00
(15)	Frank Demaree	25.00	12.50	7.50
(16)	Bill Dietrich	25.00	12.50	7.50
(17)	Vince DiMaggio	33.00	16.50	10.00
(18)	Wes Flowers	25.00	12.50	7.50
(19)	Vic Frasier	25.00	12.50	7.50
(20)	Larry French	25.00	12.50	7.50
(21)	Linus Frey	25.00	12.50	7.50
(22)	Augie Galan	25.00	12.50	7.50
(23)	Charlie Grimm	30.00	15.00	9.00
(24)	Geo. Haas	25.00	12.50	7.50
(25)	Stan Hack	25.00	12.50	7.50
(26)	Gabby Hartnett	42.00	21.00	12.50
(27)	Billy Herman	42.00	21.00	12.50
(28)	Walt Highbee (Kirby Higbe)	25.00	12.50	7.50
(29)	Roy Johnson	25.00	12.50	7.50
(30)	Baxter Jordan	25.00	12.50	7.50

		NM	EX	VG
(31)	Billy Jurges	25.00	12.50	7.50
(32)	Vernon Kennedy	25.00	12.50	7.50
(33)	Mike Kreevich	25.00	12.50	7.50
(34)	Bill Lee	25.00	12.50	7.50
(35)	Alf Lopez	42.00	21.00	12.50
(36)	Andy Lotshaw	25.00	12.50	7.50
(37)	Ted Lyons	42.00	21.00	12.50
(38)	Dan MacFayden	25.00	12.50	7.50
(39)	Henry Majeski	25.00	12.50	7.50
(40)	Pepper Martin	30.00	15.00	9.00
(41)	Stuart Martin	25.00	12.50	7.50
(42)	Joe Marty	25.00	12.50	7.50
(43)	Bill McKechnie	25.00	12.50	7.50
(44)	Joe Medwick	42.00	21.00	12.50
(45)	Steve Mesner	25.00	12.50	7.50
(46)	Hank Meyer	25.00	12.50	7.50
(47)	Johnny Mize	42.00	21.00	12.50
(48)	Gene Moore	25.00	12.50	7.50
(49)	Terry Moore	30.00	15.00	9.00
(50)	Brusie Ogrodowski	25.00	12.50	7.50
(51)	Tony Piet	25.00	12.50	7.50
(52)	Ray Radcliff	25.00	12.50	7.50
(53)	Bob Reis	25.00	12.50	7.50
(54)	Les Rock	25.00	12.50	7.50
(55)	Chas. Root	25.00	12.50	7.50
(56)	Larry Rosenthal	25.00	12.50	7.50
(57)	Luke Sewell	30.00	15.00	9.00
(58)	Merv Shea	25.00	12.50	7.50
(59)	Tuck Stainback	25.00	12.50	7.50
(60)	Hank Steinbacher	25.00	12.50	7.50
(61)	Monty Stratton	30.00	15.00	9.00
(62)	Ken Sylvestri	25.00	12.50	7.50
(63)	Billie Urbanski	25.00	12.50	7.50
(64)	Fred Walker	25.00	12.50	7.50
(65)	Lon Warnecke	25.00	12.50	7.50
(66)	Johnnie Whitehead	25.00	12.50	7.50
Type X				
(1)	Yankees (1936 Champions)	42.00	21.00	12.50
Type XI				
(2)	Bears (International League)	25.00	12.50	7.50
(3)	Blues (American Association)	25.00	12.50	7.50
(4)	Brewers (American Association)	25.00	12.50	7.50
(5)	Chicks (Southern Association)	25.00	12.50	7.50
(6)	Colonels (American Association)	25.00	12.50	7.50
(7)	Giants (International League)	25.00	12.50	7.50
(8)	Maple Leafs (International League)	25.00	12.50	7.50
(9)	Millers (American Association)	25.00	12.50	7.50
(10)	Mud Hens (American Association)	25.00	12.50	7.50
(11)	Orioles (International League)	25.00	12.50	7.50
(12)	Red Birds (American Association)	25.00	12.50	7.50
(13)	Saints (American Association)	25.00	12.50	7.50
(14)	Smokies (Southern Association)	25.00	12.50	7.50
(15)	Travelers (Southern Association)	25.00	12.50	7.50

1914 B18 Blankets

These 5-1/4"-square flannels were issued in 1914 wrapped around several popular brands of tobacco. The flannels, whose American Card Catalog designation is B18, picked up the nickname blankets because many of them were sewn together to form bed covers or throws. Different color combinations on the flannels exist for all 10 teams included in the set. The complete set price in the checklist that follows does not include higher-priced variations.

		NM	EX	VG
Complete set:		4800.	2400.	1440.
Common player:		25.00	12.50	7.50
(1a)	Babe Adams (purple pennants)	48.00	24.00	14.50
(1b)	Babe Adams (red pennants)	58.00	29.00	17.50
(2a)	Sam Agnew (purple basepaths)	50.00	25.00	15.00
(2b)	Sam Agnew (red basepaths)	58.00	29.00	17.50
(3a)	Eddie Ainsmith (green pennants)	25.00	12.50	7.50
(3b)	Eddie Ainsmith (brown pennants)	25.00	12.50	7.50
(4a)	Jimmy Austin (purple basepaths)	50.00	25.00	15.00
(4b)	Jimmy Austin (red basepaths)	58.00	29.00	17.50
(5a)	Del Baker (white infield)	25.00	12.50	7.50
(5b)	Del Baker (brown infield)	95.00	47.00	28.00
(5c)	Del Baker (red infield)	285.00	142.00	85.00
(6a)	Johnny Bassler (purple pennants)	48.00	24.00	14.50
(6b)	Johnny Bassler (yellow pennants)	95.00	47.00	28.00
(7a)	Paddy Bauman (Baumann) (white infield)	25.00	12.50	7.50
(7b)	Paddy Bauman (Baumann) (brown infield)	95.00	47.00	28.00
(7c)	Paddy Bauman (Baumann) (red infield)	285.00	142.00	85.00
(8a)	Luke Boone (blue infield)	25.00	12.50	7.50
(8b)	Luke Boone (green infield)	25.00	12.50	7.50
(9a)	George Burns (brown basepaths)	25.00	12.50	7.50
(9b)	George Burns (green basepaths)	25.00	12.50	7.50
(10a)	Tioga George Burns (white infield)	25.00	12.50	7.50
(10b)	Tioga George Burns (brown infield)	95.00	47.00	28.00
(10c)	Tioga George Burns (red infield)	95.00	47.00	28.00
(11a)	Max Carey (purple pennants)	95.00	47.00	28.00
(11b)	Max Carey (red pennants)	105.00	52.00	31.00
(12a)	Marty Cavanaugh (Kavanagh) (white infield)	25.00	12.50	7.50
(12b)	Marty Cavanaugh (Kavanagh) (brown infield)	135.00	67.00	40.00
(12c)	Marty Cavanaugh (Kavanagh) (red infield)	285.00	142.00	85.00
(12d)	Marty Kavanaugh (Kavanagh)	25.00	12.50	7.50
(13a)	Frank Chance (green infield)	55.00	27.00	16.50
(13b)	Frank Chance (brown pennants, blue infield)	55.00	27.00	16.50
(13c)	Frank Chance (yellow pennants, blue infield)	285.00	142.00	85.00
(14a)	Ray Chapman (purple pennants)	55.00	27.00	16.50
(14b)	Ray Chapman (yellow pennants)	95.00	47.00	28.00
(15a)	Ty Cobb (white infield)	395.00	197.00	118.00
(15b)	Ty Cobb (brown infield)	575.00	287.00	172.00
(15c)	Ty Cobb (red infield)	3500.	1750.	1050.
(16a)	King Cole (blue infield)	25.00	12.50	7.50
(16b)	King Cole (green infield)	25.00	12.50	7.50
(17a)	Joe Connolly (white infield)	25.00	12.50	7.50
(17b)	Joe Connolly (brown infield)	95.00	47.00	28.00
(18a)	Harry Coveleski (white infield)	25.00	12.50	7.50
(18b)	Harry Coveleski (brown infield)	95.00	47.00	28.00
(18c)	Harry Coveleski (red infield)	95.00	47.00	28.00
(19a)	George Cutshaw (blue infield)	25.00	12.50	7.50
(19b)	George Cutshaw (green infield)	25.00	12.50	7.50
(20a)	Jake Daubert (blue infield)	30.00	15.00	9.00
(20b)	Jake Daubert (green infield)	30.00	15.00	9.00
(21a)	Ray Demmitt (white infield)	25.00	12.50	7.50
(21b)	Ray Demmitt (brown infield)	95.00	47.00	28.00
(21c)	Ray Demmitt (red infield)	95.00	47.00	28.00
(22a)	Bill Doak (purple pennants)	48.00	24.00	14.50
(22b)	Bill Doak (yellow pennants)	95.00	47.00	28.00
(23a)	Cozy Dolan (purple pennants)	48.00	24.00	14.50
(23b)	Cozy Dolan (yellow pennants)	95.00	47.00	28.00
(24a)	Larry Doyle (brown basepaths)	30.00	15.00	9.00
(24b)	Larry Doyle (green basepaths)	30.00	15.00	9.00
(25a)	Art Fletcher (brown basepaths)	25.00	12.50	7.50
(25b)	Art Fletcher (green basepaths)	25.00	12.50	7.50
(26a)	Eddie Foster (brown pennants)	25.00	12.50	7.50
(26b)	Eddie Foster (green pennants)	25.00	12.50	7.50
(27a)	Del Gainor (white infield)	25.00	12.50	7.50
(27b)	Del Gainor (brown infield)	95.00	47.00	28.00

ID	Description			
(28a)	Chick Gandil (brown pennants)	42.00	21.00	12.50
(28b)	Chick Gandil (green pennants)	42.00	21.00	12.50
(29a)	George Gibson (purple pennants)	48.00	24.00	14.50
(29b)	George Gibson (red pennants)	55.00	27.00	16.50
(30a)	Hank Gowdy (white infield)	25.00	12.50	7.50
(30b)	Hank Gowdy (brown infield)	95.00	47.00	28.00
(30c)	Hank Gowdy (red infield)	285.00	142.00	85.00
(31a)	Jack Graney (purple pennants)	48.00	24.00	14.50
(31b)	Jack Graney (yellow pennants)	95.00	47.00	28.00
(32a)	Eddie Grant (brown basepaths)	30.00	15.00	9.00
(32b)	Eddie Grant (green basepaths)	25.00	12.50	7.50
(33a)	Tommy Griffith (white infield, green pennants)	25.00	12.50	7.50
(33b)	Tommy Griffith (white infield, red pennants)	285.00	142.00	85.00
(33c)	Tommy Griffith (brown infield)	95.00	47.00	28.00
(33d)	Tommy Griffith (red infield)	285.00	142.00	85.00
(34a)	Earl Hamilton (purple basepaths)	50.00	25.00	15.00
(34b)	Earl Hamilton (red basepaths)	55.00	27.00	16.50
(35a)	Roy Hartzell (blue infield)	25.00	12.50	7.50
(35b)	Roy Hartzell (green infield)	25.00	12.50	7.50
(36a)	Miller Huggins (purple pennants)	90.00	45.00	27.00
(36b)	Miller Huggins (yellow (pennants)	155.00	77.00	46.00
(37a)	John Hummel (blue infield)	25.00	12.50	7.50
(37b)	John Hummel (green infield)	25.00	12.50	7.50
(38a)	Ham Hyatt (purple pennants)	48.00	24.00	14.50
(38b)	Ham Hyatt (red pennants)	55.00	27.00	16.50
(39a)	Shoeless Joe Jackson (purple pennants)	1000.	500.00	300.00
(39b)	Shoeless Joe Jackson (yellow pennants)	1350.	675.00	405.00
(40a)	Bill James (white infield)	25.00	12.50	7.50
(40b)	Bill James (brown infield)	95.00	47.00	28.00
(40c)	Bill James (red infield)	95.00	47.00	28.00
(41a)	Walter Johnson (brown pennants)	285.00	142.00	85.00
(41b)	Walter Johnson (green pennants)	285.00	142.00	85.00
(42a)	Ray Keating (blue infield)	25.00	12.50	7.50
(42b)	Ray Keating (green infield)	25.00	12.50	7.50
(43a)	Joe Kelley (Kelly) (purple pennants)	48.00	24.00	14.50
(43b)	Joe Kelley (Kelly) (red pennants)	55.00	27.00	16.50
(44a)	Ed Konetchy (purple pennants)	48.00	24.00	14.50
(44b)	Ed Konetchy (red pennants)	55.00	27.00	16.50
(45a)	Nemo Leibold (purple pennants)	48.00	24.00	14.50
(45b)	Nemo Leibold (yellow pennants)	95.00	47.00	28.00
(46a)	Fritz Maisel (blue infield)	25.00	12.50	7.50
(46b)	Fritz Maisel (green infield)	25.00	12.50	7.50
(47a)	Les Mann (white infield)	25.00	12.50	7.50
(47b)	Les Mann (brown infield)	95.00	47.00	28.00
(47c)	Les Mann (red infield)	95.00	47.00	28.00
(48a)	Rabbit Maranville (white infield)	55.00	27.00	16.50
(48b)	Rabbit Maranville (brown infield)	155.00	77.00	46.00
(48c)	Rabbit Maranville (red infield)	360.00	180.00	108.00
(49a)	Bill McAllister (McAllester) (purple basepaths)	50.00	25.00	15.00
(49b)	Bill McAllister (McAllester) (red basepaths)	55.00	27.00	16.50
(50a)	George McBride (brown pennants)	25.00	12.50	7.50
(50b)	George McBride (green pennants)	25.00	12.50	7.50
(51a)	Chief Meyers (brown basepaths)	25.00	12.50	7.50
(51b)	Chief Meyers (green basepaths)	25.00	12.50	7.50
(52a)	Clyde Milan (brown pennants)	25.00	12.50	7.50
(52b)	Clyde Milan (green pennants)	25.00	12.50	7.50
(53a)	Dots Miller (purple pennants)	48.00	24.00	14.50
(53b)	Dots Miller (yellow pennants)	95.00	47.00	28.00
(54a)	Otto Miller (blue infield)	25.00	12.50	7.50
(54b)	Otto Miller (green infield)	25.00	12.50	7.50
(55a)	Willie Mitchell (purple pennants)	48.00	24.00	14.50
(55b)	Willie Mitchell (yellow pennants)	95.00	47.00	28.00
(56a)	Danny Moeller (brown pennants)	25.00	12.50	7.50
(56b)	Danny Moeller (green pennants)	25.00	12.50	7.50
(57a)	Ray Morgan (brown pennants)	25.00	12.50	7.50
(57b)	Ray Morgan (green pennants)	25.00	12.50	7.50
(58a)	George Moriarty (white infield)	25.00	12.50	7.50
(58b)	George Moriarty (brown infield)	95.00	47.00	28.00
(58c)	George Moriarty (red infield)	285.00	142.00	85.00
(59a)	Mike Mowrey (purple pennants)	48.00	24.00	14.50
(59b)	Mike Mowrey (red pennants)	55.00	27.00	16.50
(60a)	Red Murray (brown basepaths)	25.00	12.50	7.50
(60b)	Red Murray (green basepaths)	25.00	12.50	7.50
(61a)	Ivy Olson (purple pennants)	48.00	24.00	14.50
(61b)	Ivy Olson (yellow pennants)	95.00	47.00	28.00
(62a)	Steve O'Neill (purple pennants)	48.00	24.00	14.50
(62b)	Steve O'Neill (red pennants)	95.00	47.00	28.00
(62c)	Steve O'Neill (yellow pennants)	95.00	47.00	28.00
(63a)	Marty O'Toole (purple pennants)	48.00	24.00	14.50
(63b)	Marty O'Toole (red pennants)	55.00	27.00	16.50
(64a)	Roger Peckinpaugh (blue infield)	30.00	15.00	9.00
(64b)	Roger Peckinpaugh (green infield)	30.00	15.00	9.00
(65a)	Hub Perdue (white infield)	25.00	12.50	7.50
(65b)	Hub Perdue (brown infield)	95.00	47.00	28.00
(65c)	Hub Purdue (red infield)	285.00	142.00	85.00
(66a)	Del Pratt (purple basepaths)	50.00	25.00	15.00
(66b)	Del Pratt (red basepaths)	55.00	27.00	16.50
(67a)	Hank Robinson (purple pennants)	50.00	25.00	15.00
(67b)	Hank Robinson (yellow pennants)	95.00	47.00	28.00
(68a)	Nap Rucker (blue infield)	25.00	12.50	7.50
(68b)	Nap Rucker (green infield)	25.00	12.50	7.50
(69a)	Slim Sallee (purple pennants)	48.00	24.00	14.50
(69b)	Slim Sallee (yellow pennants)	95.00	47.00	28.00
(70a)	Howard Shanks (brown pennants)	25.00	12.50	7.50
(70b)	Howard Shanks (green pennants)	25.00	12.50	7.50
(70c)	Howard Shanks (white infield)	21.00	10.50	6.25
(71a)	Burt Shotton (purple basepaths)	50.00	25.00	15.00
(71b)	Burt Shotton (red basepaths)	55.00	27.00	16.50
(72a)	Red Smith (blue infield)	25.00	12.50	7.50
(72b)	Red Smith (green infield)	25.00	12.50	7.50
(73a)	Fred Snodgrass (brown basepaths)	25.00	12.50	7.50
(73b)	Fred Snodgrass (green basepaths)	25.00	12.50	7.50
(74a)	Bill Steele (purple pennants)	48.00	24.00	14.50
74b	Bill Steele (yellow pennants)	95.00	47.00	28.00
(75a)	Casey Stengel (blue infield)	155.00	77.00	46.00
(75b)	Casey Stengel (green infield)	175.00	87.00	52.00
(76a)	Jeff Sweeney (blue infield)	25.00	12.50	7.50
(76b)	Jeff Sweeney (green infield)	25.00	12.50	7.50
(77a)	Jeff Tesreau (brown basepaths)	25.00	12.50	7.50
(77b)	Jeff Tesreau (green basepaths)	25.00	12.50	7.50
(78a)	Terry Turner (purple pennants)	48.00	24.00	14.50
(78b)	Terry Turner (yellow pennants)	95.00	47.00	28.00
(79a)	Lefty Tyler (white infield)	25.00	12.50	7.50
(79b)	Lefty Tyler (brown infield)	95.00	47.00	28.00
(79c)	Lefty Tyler (red infield)	285.00	142.00	85.00
(80a)	Jim Viox (purple pennants)	48.00	24.00	14.50
(80b)	Jim Viox (red pennants)	55.00	27.00	16.50
(81a)	Bull Wagner (blue infield)	25.00	12.50	7.50
(81b)	Bull Wagner (green infield)	25.00	12.50	7.50
(82a)	Bobby Wallace (purple basepaths)	95.00	47.00	28.00
(82b)	Bobby Wallace (red basepaths)	95.00	47.00	28.00
(83a)	Dee Walsh (purple basepaths)	50.00	25.00	15.00
(83b)	Dee Walsh (red basepaths)	55.00	27.00	16.50
(84a)	Jimmy Walsh (blue infield)	25.00	12.50	7.50
(84b)	Jimmy Walsh (green infield)	25.00	12.50	7.50
(85a)	Bert Whaling (white infield)	25.00	12.50	7.50
(85b)	Bert Whaling (brown infield)	95.00	47.00	28.00
(85c)	Bert Whaling (red infield)	285.00	142.00	85.00
(86a)	Zach Wheat (blue infield)	95.00	47.00	28.00
(86b)	Zach Wheat (green infield)	95.00	47.00	28.00
(87a)	Possum Whitted (purple pennants)	48.00	24.00	14.50
(87b)	Possum Whitted (yellow pennants)	95.00	47.00	28.00
(88a)	Gus Williams (purple basepaths)	50.00	25.00	15.00
(88b)	Gus Williams (red basepaths)	55.00	27.00	16.50
(89a)	Owen Wilson (purple pennants)	48.00	24.00	14.50
(89b)	Owen Wilson (yellow pennants)	95.00	47.00	28.00
(90a)	Hooks Wiltse (brown basepaths)	25.00	12.50	7.50
(90b)	Hooks Wiltse (green basepaths)	25.00	12.50	7.50

1913 Cravats Felt Pennants

Little is known about this felt pennant issue, including the complete checklist. The name "Cravats" in the baseball above the player picture may represent the issuer, or describe the issue; the word "cravat" is an arcane term for a triangular piece of cloth. The pennants measure 4-1/8" across the top and are 9" long. Background colors are dark, with all printing in white. At center is a line art represntation of the player, with his name horizontally beneath and his team nickname vertically at bottom. At top is a bat and ball logo with the "Cravats" name. Most specimens are seen with a metal ring reinforcing the hole punched at top center. The known checklist points to 1913 as the most probably year of issue.

		NM	EX	VG
Common Player:		75.00	37.00	22.00
(1)	Eddie Ainsmith	75.00	37.00	22.00
(2)	Hugh Bedient	75.00	37.00	22.00
(3)	Ray Caldwell	75.00	37.00	22.00
(4)	Jack Coombs	75.00	37.00	22.00
(5)	C.S. Dooin	75.00	37.00	22.00
(6)	Lawrence Doyle	75.00	37.00	22.00
(7)	Ed Konethy (Konetchy)	75.00	37.00	22.00
(8)	James Lavender	75.00	37.00	22.00
(9)	John J. McGraw	200.00	100.00	60.00
(10)	Stuffy McInnes (McInnis)	75.00	37.00	22.00
(11)	Christy Mathewson	400.00	200.00	120.00
(12)	J.T. (Chief) Meyer (Meyers)	75.00	37.00	22.00
(13)	Nap Rucker	75.00	37.00	22.00
(14)	Tris Speaker	250.00	125.00	75.00
(15)	Ed Sweeney	75.00	37.00	22.00
(16)	Jeff Tesreau	75.00	37.00	22.00
(17)	Ira Thomas	75.00	37.00	22.00
(18)	Joe Tinker	225.00	110.00	65.00
(19)	Ed Walsh	200.00	100.00	60.00

1912 L1 Leathers

One of the more unusual baseball collectibles of the tobacco era, the L1 "Leathers" were issued by Helmar Tobacco Co. in 1912 as a premium with its "Turkish Trophies" brand of cigarettes. The set featured 25 of the top baseball players and shared a checklist with the closely-related

S81 "Silks," which were another part of the same promotion. The "Leathers," advertised as being 10" by 12", featured drawings of baseball players on horsehide-shaped pieces of leather. The drawings were based on the pictures used for the popular T3 Turkey Red series issued a year earlier. Twenty of the 25 players in the "Leathers" set are from the T3 set. Five pitchers (Rube Marquard, Rube Benton, Marty O'Toole, Grover Alexander and Russ Ford) not pictured in T3 were added to the "Leathers" set, and the Frank Baker error was corrected. According to the promotion, each "Leather" was available in exchange for 50 Helmar coupons. In addition to the 25 baseball stars, the "Leathers" set also included more than 100 other subjects, including female athletes and bathing beauties, famous generals, Indian chiefs, actresses, national flags, college mascots and others.

		NM	EX	VG
Complete set:		68500.	34000.	20000.
Common player:		1700.	850.00	500.00
86	Rube Marquard	3400.	1700.	1020.
87	Marty O'Toole	1700.	850.00	500.00
88	Rube Benton	1700.	850.00	500.00
89	Grover Alexander	4500.	2250.	1350.
90	Russ Ford	1700.	850.00	500.00
91	John McGraw	3400.	1700.	1020.
92	Nap Rucker	1700.	850.00	500.00
93	Mike Mitchell	1700.	850.00	500.00
94	Chief Bender	3400.	1700.	1020.
95	Home Run Baker	3400.	1700.	1020.
96	Nap Lajoie	4500.	2250.	1350.
97	Joe Tinker	3400.	1700.	1020.
98	Sherry Magee	1700.	850.00	500.00
99	Howie Camnitz	1700.	850.00	500.00
100	Eddie Collins	3400.	1700.	1020.
101	Red Dooin	1700.	850.00	500.00
102	Ty Cobb	11000.	5500.	3300.
103	Hugh Jennings	3400.	1700.	1020.
104	Roger Bresnahan	3400.	1700.	1020.
105	Jake Stahl	1700.	850.00	500.00
106	Tris Speaker	4000.	2000.	1200.
107	Ed Walsh	3400.	1700.	1020.
108	Christy Mathewson	5500.	2750.	1650.
109	Johnny Evers	3400.	1700.	1020.
110	Walter Johnson	5500.	2750.	1650.

1909 S74 Silks - White

Designated as S74 in the "American Card Catalog," these small, delicate fabric collectibles are popular with advanced collectors. The silks were issued as premiums with several different brands of cigarettes: Turkey Red, Old Mill, Helmar, and, rarely, Red Sun. The satin-like silks can be found in two different styles, either "white" or "colored." The white silks measure 1 7/8" by 3" and were originally issued with a brown paper backing that carried an advertisement for one of the cigarette brands. The backing also advised that the silks were "useful in making pillow covers and other fancy articles for home decoration." Many undoubtedly were used for such purposes, making silks with the paper backing still intact more difficult to find. White silks must, however, have the backing intact to command top value. Although similar, the S74 "colored" silks, as their name indicates, were issued in a variety of colors. They are also slightly larger, measuring 1-

7/8" by 3-1/2", and were issued without a paper backing. The colored silks, therefore, contained the cigarette brand name on the lower front of the fabric (No colored silks advertising the Helmar brand are known to exist.). There are 121 different players reported: six have been found in two poses, resulting in 127 different subjects. Ninety-two subjects are known in the "white" silk, while 120 have been found in the "colored." The silks feature the same players pictured in the popular T205 Gold Border tobacco card set.

		NM	EX	VG
Complete set (92):		23500.	11500.	7000.
Common player:		150.00	75.00	45.00
(1)	Home Run Baker	300.00	150.00	90.00
(2)	Cy Barger	150.00	75.00	45.00
(3)	Jack Barry	150.00	75.00	45.00
(4)	Johnny Bates	150.00	75.00	45.00
(5)	Fred Beck	150.00	75.00	45.00
(6)	Beals Becker	150.00	75.00	45.00
(7)	George Bell	150.00	75.00	45.00
(8)	Chief Bender	300.00	150.00	90.00
(9)	Roger Bresnahan	300.00	150.00	90.00
(10)	Al Bridwell	150.00	75.00	45.00
(11)	Mordecai Brown	300.00	150.00	90.00
(12)	Bobby Byrne	150.00	75.00	45.00
(13)	Howie Camnitz	150.00	75.00	45.00
(14)	Bill Carrigan	150.00	75.00	45.00
(15)	Frank Chance	325.00	162.00	97.00
(16)	Hal Chase	200.00	100.00	60.00
(17)	Fred Clarke	300.00	150.00	90.00
(18)	Ty Cobb	1750.	875.00	525.00
(19)	Eddie Collins	300.00	150.00	90.00
(20)	Doc Crandall	150.00	75.00	45.00
(21)	Lou Criger	150.00	75.00	45.00
(22)	Jim Delahanty	150.00	75.00	45.00
(23)	Art Devlin	150.00	75.00	45.00
(24)	Red Dooin	150.00	75.00	45.00
(25)	Mickey Doolan	150.00	75.00	45.00
(26)	Larry Doyle	150.00	75.00	45.00
(27)	Jimmy Dygert	150.00	75.00	45.00
(28)	Kid Elberfield (Elberfeld)	150.00	75.00	45.00
(29)	Steve Evans	150.00	75.00	45.00
(30)	Johnny Evers	300.00	150.00	90.00
(31)	Bob Ewing	150.00	75.00	45.00
(32)	Art Fletcher	150.00	75.00	45.00
(33)	John Flynn	150.00	75.00	45.00
(34)	Bill Foxen	150.00	75.00	45.00
(35)	George Gibson	150.00	75.00	45.00
(36)	Peaches Graham (Cubs)	150.00	75.00	45.00
(37)	Peaches Graham (Rustlers)	150.00	75.00	45.00
(38)	Clark Griffith	300.00	150.00	90.00
(39)	Topsy Hartsel	150.00	75.00	45.00
(40)	Arnold Hauser	150.00	75.00	45.00
(41)	Charlie Hemphill	150.00	75.00	45.00
(42)	Tom Jones	150.00	75.00	45.00
(43)	Jack Knight	150.00	75.00	45.00
(44)	Ed Konetchy	150.00	75.00	45.00
(45)	Harry Krause	150.00	75.00	45.00
(46)	Tommy Leach	150.00	75.00	45.00
(47)	Rube Marquard	300.00	150.00	90.00
(48)	Christy Mathewson	650.00	325.00	195.00
(49)	Al Mattern	150.00	75.00	45.00
(50)	Amby McConnell	150.00	75.00	45.00
(51)	John McGraw	300.00	150.00	90.00
(52)	Harry McIntire (McIntyre)	150.00	75.00	45.00
(53)	Fred Merkle	150.00	75.00	45.00
(54)	Chief Meyers	150.00	75.00	45.00
(55)	Dots Miller	150.00	75.00	45.00
(56)	Danny Murphy	150.00	75.00	45.00
(57)	Red Murray	150.00	75.00	45.00
(58)	Tom Needham	150.00	75.00	45.00
(59)	Rebel Oakes	150.00	75.00	45.00
(60)	Rube Oldring	150.00	75.00	45.00
(61)	Orval Overall	150.00	75.00	45.00
(62)	Fred Parent	150.00	75.00	45.00
(63)	Fred Payne	150.00	75.00	45.00
(64)	Barney Pelty	150.00	75.00	45.00
(65)	Deacon Phillippe	150.00	75.00	45.00
(66)	Jack Quinn	150.00	75.00	45.00
(67)	Bugs Raymond	150.00	75.00	45.00
(68)	Ed Reulbach	150.00	75.00	45.00
(69)	Doc Scanlon (Scanlan)	150.00	75.00	45.00
(70)	Germany Schaefer	150.00	75.00	45.00
(71)	Admiral Schlei	150.00	75.00	45.00
(72)	Wildfire Schulte	150.00	75.00	45.00
(73)	Dave Shean	150.00	75.00	45.00
(74)	Jimmy Sheckard	150.00	75.00	45.00
(75)	Hap Smith (Superbas)	150.00	75.00	45.00
(76)	Harry Smith (Rustlers)	500.00	250.00	150.00
(77)	Fred Snodgrass	150.00	75.00	45.00
(78)	Tris Speaker	400.00	200.00	120.00
(79)	Harry Steinfeldt (Cubs)	150.00	75.00	45.00
(80)	Harry Steinfeldt (Rustlers)	150.00	75.00	45.00
(81)	George Stone	150.00	75.00	45.00
(82)	Gabby Street	150.00	75.00	45.00
(83)	Ed Summers	150.00	75.00	45.00
(84)	Lee Tannehill	150.00	75.00	45.00
(85)	Joe Tinker	300.00	150.00	90.00
(86)	John Titus	150.00	75.00	45.00
(87)	Terry Turner	150.00	75.00	45.00
(88)	Bobby Wallace	300.00	150.00	90.00
(89)	Doc White	150.00	75.00	45.00
(90)	Ed Willett	150.00	75.00	45.00
(91)	Art Wilson	150.00	75.00	45.00
(92)	Harry Wolter	150.00	75.00	45.00

1910 S74 Silks - Colored

		NM	EX	VG
Complete set (120):		21500.	10750.	6450.
Common player:		125.00	62.00	37.00
(1)	Red Ames	125.00	62.00	37.00
(2)	Jimmy Archer	125.00	62.00	37.00
(3)	Home Run Baker	250.00	125.00	75.00
(4)	Cy Barger	125.00	62.00	37.00
(5)	Jack Barry	125.00	62.00	37.00
(6)	Johnny Bates	125.00	62.00	37.00
(7)	Beals Becker	125.00	62.00	37.00
(8)	George Bell	125.00	62.00	37.00
(9)	Chief Bender	250.00	125.00	75.00
(10)	Bill Bergen	125.00	62.00	37.00
(11)	Bob Bescher	125.00	62.00	37.00
(12)	Roger Bresnahan (mouth closed)	300.00	150.00	90.00
(13)	Roger Bresnahan (mouth open)	300.00	150.00	90.00
(14)	Al Bridwell	125.00	62.00	37.00
(15)	Mordecai Brown	250.00	125.00	75.00
(16)	Bobby Byrne	125.00	62.00	37.00
(17)	Howie Camnitz	125.00	62.00	37.00
(18)	Bill Carrigan	125.00	62.00	37.00
(19)	Frank Chance	300.00	150.00	90.00
(20)	Hal Chase	200.00	100.00	60.00
(21)	Ed Cicotte	215.00	107.00	64.00
(22)	Fred Clarke	250.00	125.00	75.00
(23)	Ty Cobb	1750.	875.00	525.00
(24)	Eddie Collins	250.00	125.00	75.00
(25)	Doc Crandall	125.00	62.00	37.00
(26)	Bill Dahlen	125.00	62.00	37.00
(27)	Jake Daubert	125.00	62.00	37.00
(28)	Jim Delahanty	125.00	62.00	37.00
(29)	Art Devlin	125.00	62.00	37.00
(30)	Josh Devore	125.00	62.00	37.00
(31)	Red Dooin	125.00	62.00	37.00
(32)	Mickey Doolan	125.00	62.00	37.00
(33)	Tom Downey	125.00	62.00	37.00

(34)	Larry Doyle	125.00	62.00	37.00
(35)	Hugh Duffy	250.00	125.00	75.00
(36)	Jimmy Dygert	125.00	62.00	37.00
(37)	Kid Elberfield (Elberfeld)	125.00	62.00	37.00
(38)	Steve Evans	125.00	62.00	37.00
(39)	Johnny Evers	250.00	125.00	75.00
(40)	Bob Ewing	125.00	62.00	37.00
(41)	Art Fletcher	125.00	62.00	37.00
(42)	John Flynn	125.00	62.00	37.00
(43)	Russ Ford	125.00	62.00	37.00
(44)	Bill Foxen	125.00	62.00	37.00
(45)	Art Fromme	125.00	62.00	37.00
(46)	George Gibson	125.00	62.00	37.00
(47)	Peaches Graham	125.00	62.00	37.00
(48)	Eddie Grant	125.00	62.00	37.00
(49)	Clark Griffith	250.00	125.00	75.00
(50)	Topsy Hartsel	125.00	62.00	37.00
(51)	Arnold Hauser	125.00	62.00	37.00
(52)	Charlie Hemphill	125.00	62.00	37.00
(53)	Dick Hoblitzell	125.00	62.00	37.00
(54)	Miller Huggins	250.00	125.00	75.00
(55)	John Hummel	125.00	62.00	37.00
(56)	Walter Johnson	625.00	312.00	187.00
(57)	Davy Jones	125.00	62.00	37.00
(58)	Johnny Kling	125.00	62.00	37.00
(59)	Jack Knight	125.00	62.00	37.00
(60)	Ed Konetchy	125.00	62.00	37.00
(61)	Harry Krause	125.00	62.00	37.00
(62)	Tommy Leach	125.00	62.00	37.00
(63)	Lefty Leifield	125.00	62.00	37.00
(64)	Hans Lobert	125.00	62.00	37.00
(65)	Rube Marquard	250.00	125.00	75.00
(66)	Christy Mathewson	625.00	312.00	187.00
(67)	Al Mattern	125.00	62.00	37.00
(68)	Amby McConnell	125.00	62.00	37.00
(69)	John McGraw	300.00	150.00	90.00
(70)	Harry McIntire (McIntyre)	125.00	62.00	37.00
(71)	Fred Merkle	125.00	62.00	37.00
(72)	Chief Meyers	125.00	62.00	37.00
(73)	Dots Miller	125.00	62.00	37.00
(74)	Mike Mitchell	125.00	62.00	37.00
(75)	Pat Moran	125.00	62.00	37.00
(76)	George Moriarty	125.00	62.00	37.00
(77)	George Mullin	125.00	62.00	37.00
(78)	Danny Murphy	125.00	62.00	37.00
(79)	Red Murray	125.00	62.00	37.00
(80)	Tom Needham	125.00	62.00	37.00
(81)	Rebel Oakes	125.00	62.00	37.00
(82)	Rube Oldring	125.00	62.00	37.00
(83)	Orval Overall	125.00	62.00	37.00
(84)	Fred Parent	125.00	62.00	37.00
(85)	Dode Paskert	125.00	62.00	37.00
(86)	Billy Payne	125.00	62.00	37.00
(87)	Barney Pelty	125.00	62.00	37.00
(88)	Deacon Phillippe	125.00	62.00	37.00
(89)	Jack Quinn	125.00	62.00	37.00
(90)	Bugs Raymond	125.00	62.00	37.00
(91)	Ed Reulbach	125.00	62.00	37.00
(92)	Jack Rowan	125.00	62.00	37.00
(93)	Nap Rucker	125.00	62.00	37.00
(94)	Doc Scanlon (Scanlan)	125.00	62.00	37.00
(95)	Germany Schaefer	125.00	62.00	37.00
(96)	Admiral Schlei	125.00	62.00	37.00
(97)	Wildfire Schulte	125.00	62.00	37.00
(98)	Dave Shean	125.00	62.00	37.00
(99)	Jimmy Sheckard	125.00	62.00	37.00
(100)	Happy Smith	125.00	62.00	37.00
(101)	Fred Snodgrass	125.00	62.00	37.00
(102)	Tris Speaker	425.00	212.00	127.00
(103)	Jake Stahl	125.00	62.00	37.00
(104)	Harry Steinfeldt	125.00	62.00	37.00
(105)	George Stone	125.00	62.00	37.00
(106)	Gabby Street	125.00	62.00	37.00
(107)	Ed Summers	125.00	62.00	37.00
(108)	Lee Tannehill	125.00	62.00	37.00
(109)	Joe Tinker	250.00	125.00	75.00
(110)	John Titus	125.00	62.00	37.00
(111)	Terry Turner	125.00	62.00	37.00
(112)	Bobby Wallace	250.00	125.00	75.00
(113)	Zack Wheat	250.00	125.00	75.00
(114)	Doc White (White Sox)	125.00	62.00	37.00
(115)	Kirby White (Pirates)	125.00	62.00	37.00
(116)	Ed Willett	125.00	62.00	37.00
(117)	Owen Wilson	125.00	62.00	37.00
(118)	Hooks Wiltse	125.00	62.00	37.00
(119)	Harry Wolter	125.00	62.00	37.00
(120)	Cy Young	600.00	300.00	180.00

1912 S81 Silks

The 1912 S81 "Silks," so-called because they featured pictures of baseball players on a satin-like fabric rather than paper or cardboard, are closely related to the better-known T3 Turkey Red cabinet cards of the same era. The silks, which featured 25 of the day's top baseball players among its other various subjects, were available as a premium with Helmar "Turkish Trophies" cigarettes. According to an advertising sheet, one silk could be obtained for 25 Helmar coupons. The silks measure 7" by 9" and, with a few exceptions, used the same pictures featured on the popular Turkey Red cards. Five players (Rube Marquard, Rube Benton, Marty O'Toole, Grover Alexander and Russ Ford) appear in the "Silks" set that were not included in the T3 set. In addition, an error involving the Frank Baker card was corrected for the "Silks" set. (In the T3 set, Baker's card actually pictured Jack Barry.) Several years ago a pair of New England collectors found a small stack of Christy Mathewson "Silks," making his, by far, the most common. Otherwise, the "Silks" are generally so rare that it is difficult to determine the relative scarcity of the others. Baseball enthusiasts are usually only attached to the 25 baseball players in the "Silks" premium set, but it is interesting to note that the promotion also offered dozens of other subjects, including "beautiful women in bathing and athletic costumes, charming dancers in gorgeous attire, natiional flags and generals on horseback."

		NM	EX	VG
Complete set (25):		47500.	23000.	14000.
Common player:		1000.	500.00	300.00
90	Russ Ford	1175.	587.00	352.00
91	John McGraw	3500.	1750.	1050.
92	Nap Rucker	1000.	500.00	300.00
93	Mike Mitchell	1000.	500.00	300.00
94	Chief Bender	2500.	1250.	750.00
95	Home Run Baker	2500.	1250.	750.00
96	Nap Lajoie	3500.	1750.	1050.
97	Joe Tinker	2500.	1250.	750.00
98	Sherry Magee	1000.	500.00	300.00
99	Howie Camnitz	1000.	500.00	300.00
100	Eddie Collins	2500.	1250.	750.00
101	Red Dooin	1000.	500.00	300.00
102	Ty Cobb	8500.	4250.	2550.
103	Hugh Jennings	2500.	1250.	750.00
104	Roger Bresnahan	2500.	1250.	750.00
105	Jake Stahl	1150.	575.00	345.00
106	Tris Speaker	3750.	1875.	1125.
107	Ed Walsh	2500.	1250.	750.00
108	Christy Mathewson	3000.	1500.	900.00
109	Johnny Evers	2500.	1250.	750.00
110	Walter Johnson	4500.	2250.	1350.
111	Rube Marquard	2500.	1250.	750.00
112	Marty O'Toole	1000.	500.00	300.00
113	Rube Benton	1000.	500.00	300.00
114	Grover Alexander	2750.	1375.	825.00

Pennants

Since almost every kid who had a felt pennant tacked it up on his bedroom wall, it's unusual to find a vintage pennant in well-preserved, investment grade condition. Most, measuring 12x30, have pin holes in them and can be purchased for less than $50. Today's versions, often available at stadiums and arenas, are made in large quantities, so look for 1950s and before models, and concentrate on pennants for popular teams, championship teams, teams which no longer exist, or those which commemorate a specific event. Some of the best places to find several pennants would be at larger card shows or through sports memorabilia auctions. Sometimes a pennant or two will turn up in an antique shop, too. Although it probably isn't going to offer big returns as an investment piece, a pennant can still add a nice decorative touch to any memorabilia display.

Pennants

- 1920s Cleveland Indians, red with white letters
....$135
- 1930s Boston Braves, batting scene, red $125
- 1934-35 Detroit Tigers pennant winners, black-and-white on orange $375
- 1935 Detroit Tigers World Champs scroll pennant, orange on black $350
- Early-1940s Boston Red Sox, large baseball over the stadium, gray and red $100
- Early-1940s Brooklyn Dodgers, batter and catcher, white on red $285
- Early-1940s Brooklyn Dodgers, "Brooklyn Dodgers: Our Champs," white on purple $395
- Mid-1940s Boston Red Sox, batter hitting pitched ball, white on red $135
- Late-1940s Brooklyn Dodgers, shows catcher and batter from backside, white on blue $175
- Late-1940s New York Yankees, player sliding into tag, white on blue $95
- Late-1940s Philadelphia Phillies signature pennant with names and numbers, Fightin' Phillies, white and red...$195
- Late-1940s St. Louis Cardinals, two birds on a bat, red, yellow and white on red $65
- Late-1940s St. Louis Browns, player making a catch, orange on blue $175
- 1940s Boston Red Sox, runner sliding into base, white on red $145
- 1940s Brooklyn Dodgers, player sliding into tag, blue on white $150
- 1940s Chicago Cubs, large C in Chicago, white on blue..$110
- 1940s Chicago Cubs, player sliding into a tag, black on orange $95
- 1940s Chicago White Sox, infield play in progress, white on dark blue $125
- 1940s Cincinnati Reds, Cincinnati in Gothic letters, white and red $150
- 1940s Cleveland Indians, Indian with full headdress, white on red $80
- 1940s Detroit Tigers, black tiger head on orange$85
- 1940s New York Giants, batter, catcher and umpire, white and blue $125
- 1948 Cleveland Indians American League Champs/World Series, multi-color on dark red.................$195
- Early-1950s Brooklyn Dodgers, red, white and blue $295
- Early-1950s Philadelphia A's, white on blue $85
- Mid-1950s Chicago Cubs Wrigley Field, Cub playing with a ball, white on blue $75
- Mid-1950s Baltimore Orioles, bird on a baseball, white and pink on red $100
- Mid-1950s New York Yankees, Uncle Sam, multi-color on blue $125
- Late-1950s Baltimore Orioles, bird pitching over Memorial Stadium...$95

- Late-1950s San Francisco Giants, mascot on the bridge, white, gray and pink and green $85
- 1950s Chicago Cubs, two cubs standing, white and peach on blue..$55
- 1950s Chicago White Sox, winged foot, white and yellow on blue $75
- 1950s Detroit Tigers, Tiger head inside Tiger Stadium..$60
- 1950s New York Giants, orange and white on black $60
- 1950s New York Yankees, Yankee logo, red and blue on white $95
- 1950s Philadelphia Phillies, "Go Phillies Go" with batting scene $60
- 1950s Philadelphia Phillies, elephant with a ball in its trunk, white and blue $125
- 1950s-60s Pittsburgh Pirates, black with Pirate head with a sword in his mouth $90
- 1950 Philadelphia Phillies, "Fightin' Phillies," with tag scene and players' names and numbers around it, white on red $165
- 1950 New York Yankees American League Champs, player sliding into a tag $125
- 1950 New York Yankees American League Champions, "Bronx Bombers" batter, white on blue $375
- 1954 New York Giants World Series $125
- 1955 Brooklyn Dodgers National League Champs, scroll, Bum, multi-color on blue $475
- 1957 Milwaukee Braves World Champions, names of players, white and purple.....................................$250
- 1958 Milwaukee Braves National League Champs, Indian dancing, player names, white and red $110
- 1958 Milwaukee Braves 1958 National League Champs scroll pennant $100
- 1959 Chicago White Sox American League Champs, white on blue $125
- Early-1960s Chicago Cubs, Wrigley Field, multi-color on blue $55
- Early-1960s Houston Colt 45s, blue and orange on white $65
- Early-1960s New York Mets, skyline, team logo, blue and white on dark blue $85
- Mid-1960s San Francisco Giants, SF in block, Giants logo, bat, black on orange $65
- Late-1960s Baltimore Orioles, bird on top of an O, bat and glove, black on orange................................$65
- Late-1960s New York Mets, shows Shea, Mr. Met and Liberty on blue $45
- Late-1960s Washington Senators, white on red..$60
- 1960s Atlanta Braves, multi-color on navy $35
- 1960s Pittsburgh Pirates, multi-color on black ...$40
- 1960s St. Louis Cardinals, multi-color on red $40
- 1960s San Francisco Giants, play at the plate, black on orange $85

- 1960s Washington Senators, pitcher and capital, red, white and blue $75
- 1960 Pittsburgh Pirates 1960 National League Champions, pirate holding a sword.....................$135
- 1960 St. Louis Browns, shows batter, white on brown...$55
- 1961 Cincinnati Reds picture pennant $135
- 1961 Cincinnati Reds National League Champions, players' names, red and blue on white $110
- 1961 New York Yankees picture pennant $250
- 1962 Dodger Stadium grand opening, blue and red vertical pennant $75
- 1963 New York Mets black-and-white picture pennant $155
- 1964 Philadelphia Phillies picture pennant.........$85
- 1965 Houston Colt .45s/Houston Astrodome, double-sided pennant...$150
- 1965 World Series Los Angeles Dodgers vs. Minnesota Twins, multi-color on blue felt............$85
- 1966 Baltimore Orioles team picture pennant $100
- 1966 Chicago White Sox team picture pennant, red and blue on white $110
- 1966 New York Mets team picture pennant $135
- 1966 World Series Los Angeles Dodgers vs. Baltimore Orioles, bird over Dodger Stadium $65
- 1966-67 California Angels, Anaheim Stadium...$55
- 1967 Boston Red Sox vs. St. Louis Cardinals World Series at Fenway Park, black and red on white ...$125
- 1967 St. Louis Cardinals National League Champions...$40
- 1968 Chicago White Sox picture pennant $85
- 1968 Detroit Tigers American League Champions, black and orange on white.....................................$85
- 1968 St. Louis Cardinals National League Champions/ World Series, white and pink on red $65
- 1969 Baltimore Orioles World Series picture pennant $110
- 1969 Boston Red Sox picture pennant...............$55
- 1969 Cincinnati Reds picture pennant $95
- 1969 Houston Astros...$20
- 1969 Kansas City Royals $40
- 1969 Montreal Expos...$35
- 1969 Mickey Mantle Day at Yankee Stadium....$55
- 1969 New York Mets World Champions, orange on blue $95
- 1969 Seattle Pilots, MLB logo, Seattle in script, multi-colored on red $185
- 1969-71 Washington Senators, red and blue on white $75
- Early-1970s Chicago White Sox, batter on sock in red circle $45
- Early-1970s Cleveland Indians, Chief Wahoo with bat and ball $45
- Early-1970s Minnesota Twins, TC in dot over I in Minnesota, white on blue $35
- 1970s Baltimore Orioles $10
- 1970s Houston Astros $10
- 1970s Milwaukee Brewers.................................$10

- 1970s St. Louis Cardinals $10
- 1970s San Diego Padres, crossed bats with padre, white on brown..$55
- 1970s San Francisco Giants $10
- 1970 Baltimore Orioles team picture, orange and black on white $75
- 1970 Baltimore Orioles picture pennant $125
- 1970 Milwaukee Brewers, barrel man swinging a bat, gold on blue $55
- 1971 Pittsburgh Pirates color team photo pennant $95
- 1971 Pittsburgh Pirates National League Champs scroll, black and gold on white..............................$60
- 1972 All-Star Game in Atlanta, red and blue on white $55
- 1973 Boston Red Sox Fenway Park, white and green on red $75
- 1973 Chicago White Sox American League Western Division Champions $10
- 1973 New York Mets World Champs signature pennant $45
- 1973 New York Mets "You Gotta Believe, Mets #1 Again," 1973 Champions, blue on white $75
- 1973 New York Mets Eastern Division Champs scroll pennant, white and orange on blue $65
- 1973 Oakland A's American League Champs scroll pennant $45
- 1974 Cincinnati Reds picture pennant $95
- 1974 Hank Aaron Home Run King, dated April 8, 1974 ....$45
- 1974 Los Angeles Dodgers World Series signature pennant $50
- 1975 Boston Red Sox World Series signature pennant $55
- 1975 Boston Red Sox World Champions phantom $25
- 1975 Boston Red Sox American League Champions scroll pennant $50
- 1975 Cincinnati Reds picture pennant $65
- 1975 Cincinnati Reds World Champs signature pennant $65
- 1976 Cincinnati Reds World Champs trophy $45
- 1977 New York Yankees picture pennant $55
- 1977 All-Star Game at Yankee Stadium.............$30
- 1977 Los Angeles Dodgers National League Champs scroll pennant, blue on white $50
- 1978 "Do it Pete! Do it Pete!" for Rose's hitting streak, 7/25/78 at Shea Stadium....................................$55
- 1979 Baltimore Orioles American League Champions signature pennant...$45
- 1979 California Angels American League West Champions scroll pennant $65
- 1979 Philadelphia Phillies picture pennant, black-and-white $75
- 1979 Pittsburgh Pirates World Champions scroll pennant $45
- 1980 Kansas City World Series scroll pennant, blue and gold on white $45
- 1980 New York Yankees $10

• 1980 New York Yankees American League Eastern Division Champs, blue and red on white $35
• 1980 Philadelphia Phillies World Champions scroll pennant, "We're #1"...$45
• 1981 All-Star Game in Cleveland, Chief Wahoo on a star $45
• 1981 New York Yankees American League Champions scroll pennant $45
• 1982 Milwaukee Brewers American League Eastern Division Champs, blue and gold on white $40
• 1983 50th All-Star Game at Comiskey Park.......$10
• 1983 Carl Yastrzemski retirement day pennant..$55
• 1983 Baltimore Orioles World Champions, scroll pennant, black and orange on white $45
• 1983 Philadelphia Phillies National League Champs, maroon, blue and red on white $40
• 1984 Chicago Cubs World Series $20
• 1984 Detroit Tigers World Champions scroll pennant, blue and orange on black......................................$55
• 1984 Kansas City Royals American League Western Division Champions, scroll $35
• 1984 San Diego Padres National League Western Division Champions......................................$10
• 1985 Kansas City Royals American League Western Division Champions, scroll $35
• 1985 Los Angeles Dodgers National League Western Division Champions...$10
• 1986 Boston Red Sox American League Eastern Division Champions...$10
• 1986 Boston Red Sox World Series....................$10
• 1986 New York Mets World Champs signature pennant $35
• 1986 New York Yankees color team picture $35
• 1987 Minnesota Twins World Series..................$10
• 1988 All-Star Game in Cincinnati $10
• 1989 Chicago Cubs National League Eastern Division Champions..$10
• 1993 Florida Marlins' Opening Day...................$20
• 1994 All-Star Game in Pittsburgh......................$10

1950 American Nut & Chocolate Pennants

Although there is nothing on these small (1 7/8" by 4") felt pennants to identify the issuer, surviving ads show that the American Nut & Chocolate Co. of Boston sold them as a set of 22 for 50 cents. The pennants of American League players are printed in blue on white, while National Leaguers are printed in red on white. The pennants feature crude line-art drawings of players on the left, along with a facsimile autograph. The pennants carry an American Card Catalog designation of F510. The complete set of 22 pennants is worth $350 in Near Mint condition; individual pennants are worth $15, unless noted. The players in the set are: Ewell Blackwell, Harry

Brecheen, Phil Cavarretta, Bobby Doerr ($17.50), Bob Elliott, Boo Ferriss, Joe Gordon, Tommy Holmes, Charles Keller, Ken Keltner, Whitey Kurowski, Ralph Kiner ($20), Johnny Pesky, Pee Wee Reese ($35), Phil Rizzuto ($30), Johnny Sain ($17.50), Enos Slaughter ($17.50), Warren Spahn ($25), Vern Stephens, Earl Torgeson, Dizzy Trout and Ted Williams ($65).

1992 Win Craft player pennants

1. Jim Abbott..$3
2. Wade Boggs...$4
3. George Brett...$5
4. Jose Canseco $4
5. Will Clark...$4
6. Andre Dawson $3
7. Dwight Gooden $3
8. Mark Grace $3
9. Ken Griffey Jr. $5
10. Rickey Henderson $4
11. Orel Hershiser $3
12. Kent Hrbek $3
13. Bo Jackson $3
14. Chuck Knoblauch...$3
15. Don Mattingly $4
16. Mark McGwire...$4
17. Kevin Mitchell $3
18. Paul Molitor $4
19. Kirby Puckett $5
20. Kirby Puckett $5
21. Cal Ripken MVP...$5
22. Nolan Ryan $6
23. Ryne Sandberg $4
24. Ozzie Smith..$3
25. Darryl Strawberry $3
26. Frank Thomas $5
27. Alan Trammell..$3
28. Andy Van Slyke..$3
29. Robin Yount..$4

Auctions

How to buy through the mail

Sports Collectors Digest, as do all Krause Publications hobby publications, screens its advertisers to weed out dishonesty, but these guidelines are helpful when buying collectibles through the mail:

1) Read the entire ad carefully before you order.

2) Condition and authenticity of the merchandise should be guaranteed.

3) For quicker service, send a money order or certified check instead of a personal check.

4) Pack and unpack the items carefully; damaged or broken items can't always be blamed on the post office. If damaged product should arrive, take the entire contents to the post office and file a claim.

How to buy at auctions and through auction houses

1) Learn the bidding process; rules for buying vary from state to state.

2) Listen to the auctioneer for a while to determine nuances and his acknowledgments of bids; a scratch of your nose might mean you just bid.

3) Bidding may be done by voice or by hand raising.

4) Many auction houses do not take responsibility for the correctness of description, authenticity, genuineness or condition of the item. So, go early and look at the items in person. Check out the condition, size and whether the item has been repaired or restored.

5) Items are often sold "as is" and the house, in issuing catalogs, does not take responsibility or issue warranties regarding the description or physical condition, size, quality, rarity, importance or historical relevance, or errors.

6) The highest bid accepted is usually the buyer's, but disputes may result. If so, bidding is often reopened, but only between the two, with the highest bidder becoming the owner. Then it's his responsibility and risk for relocating the item. Sometimes the house will send the purchased property to a public warehouse for the account, risk and expense of the purchaser.

7) At unrestricted sales, or those without a reserve, the consignors of the items being sold are not supposed to bid. If they do bid back their own items, they still pay the full sales commission.

8) Most auctioneers reserve the right to refuse a bid if it does not match the item's value or is a nominal advance over the previous bid. He's looking to make the most on a bid. If the auctioneer decides an opening bid is below the reserve value for the article offered, he may reject the same and withdraw the article from the sale. A buyer's premium, often 10 percent, is generally added on to the successful bid, and is payable by the purchaser as part of the total purchase price.

9) Get there early to browse, pick up a bidder's number, and get a good seat.

10) Local auctions will probably accept personal checks, but traveler's checks are wise for out-of-town auctions.

11) When dealing as a consignor, read the contract in its entirety before signing it and understand what you've just signed.

Telephone auctions

Convey the lot you wish to bid on and your absolute top bid. Normal bidding progresses with bids being raised by the regular 10 percent. When someone tops your current bid, the auctioneer automatically increases your bid by the mandatory 10 percent. This process continues until your absolute top bid is reached.

Often the times are designated and the bidding ends promptly, with no exceptions.

Pre-registration by potential bidders is usually required a few days in advance. A bidding number is obtained at that time and is later given when the auction occurs. Then the lots and absolute top bids for each are given and the process continues.

Bidders are generally discouraged from calling immediately after the auction to check on results. Winners are contacted within the next day; those wishing results may generally do so after the auction's deadline by sending an SASE for a prices realized list.

Absentee bids are encouraged, too, but require top limits on the bids for each lot. Lots are purchased for the absentee bidders at the lowest possible price under their top limit. For example: If you write in with an absentee top limit bid of $500 and the highest bid received by other phone bidders is $300, you win the lot for $330 - ($300 plus 10 percent) plus the 10 percent buyer's fee.

Centerfield Collectibles Inc.
Spring Training Auction
March 14-15, 1996

• Satchel Paige autographed baseball, Lee MacPhail American League ball $1,287
• 1955 Cleveland Indians Phantom World Series press pin $605
• Cal Ripken Jr. game-used bat, brown Louisville Slugger, cracked and repaired, 1980-83 .... $1,947
• 1982 Hall of Fame Induction press pin, for class which included Hank Aaron, Happy Chandler, Travis Jackson and Frank Robinson $303
• 1983 Hall of Fame Induction press pin, for class which included George Kell, Walter Alston, Juan Marichal and Brooks Robinson $292
• 1984 Hall of Fame Induction press pin, for class which included Don Drysdale, Luis Aparicio, Harmon Killebrew, Rick Ferrell, and Pee Wee Reese $152
• 1985 Hall of Fame Induction press pin, for class which included Lou Brock, Enos Slaughter, Arky Vaughn and Hoyt Wilhelm $150
• 1986 Hall of Fame Induction press pin, for class which included Bobby Doerr, Ernie Lombardi and Willie McCovey $125
• 1987 Hall of Fame Induction press pin, for class which included Ray Dandridge, Catfish Hunter and Billy Williams $225
• 1989 Hall of Fame Induction press pin, for class which included Johnny Bench, Carl Yastrzemski, Al Barlick and Red Schoendienst $225
• 1990 Hall of Fame Induction press pin, for class which included Joe Morgan and Jim Palmer $225
• 1995 Hall of Fame Induction press pin, for class which included Richie Ashburn, Leon Day, Mike Schmidt, William Hulbert and Vic Willis $480
• Michael Jordan game-used Birmingham Barons cap, fitted, name and number stitched inside $714
• Reggie Jackson game-used Oakland A's cap, 1970s, name and number under the sweatband $433
• 1995 American League All-Stars autographed baseball, signed by 24 players $242
• 1995 National League All-Stars autographed baseball, signed by 30 players $443
• Phil Niekro 1983 game-used Atlanta Braves road blue jersey, autographed, with tags $576
• St. Louis Cardinals blue and red warm-up jacket, early 1970s.................................... $366
• Don Denkinger game-used American League umpire's cap, 1976, autographed.... $76

• Gaylord Perry game-used San Francisco Giants cap, 1960s-early 1970s $98
• 1994 Birmingham Barons collector's edition yearbook/scorecard, pictures Michael Jordan $40
• Joe DiMaggio autographed "Joltin' Joe DiMaggio" sheet music, from 1941 .... $87
• Babe Ruth baseball scorer, circa 1920s, 2x4, works, resembles an umpire's clicker $117
• Robin Yount 3,000th hit game full ticket and program $55
• Jacobs Field's first game ever full ticket and program, April 4, 1994, Indians vs. Mariners $83
• Lot of four small pieces of Astroturf from Veteran's Stadium in Philadelphia.............. $29
• "I Was There Mickey Mantle Day" pennant, 12x30, from June 8, 1969 .... $184
• Joe DiMaggio alarm clock, 3" face, works, 1970s... $237
• Willie Mays/Hank Aaron lot of 50 promotional matchbooks, from 1975, Mays as a Met, Aaron as a Brewer, notes "1,415 Home Runs".. $63
• Pete Rose lot of 50 promotional matchbooks, Rose as a Red, notes his 4,256 hits $69
• Leather strap key chain/scorer, from 1920s, works, face depicts baseball diamond and outfield $96
• Home Run Cigarettes pack, original, unopened, from 1930s-40s, depicts batter and catcher on each side $176
• Baseball pencil case from the pre-war era, metal, 2x 8 1/2, features full color player on the front.. $200
• 1961 All-Star Game full ticket, from Boston's Fenway Park $200
• Brooklyn Dodgers felt pennant, 1930s, red with white printing, shows a batter........... $333
• 1964 Philadelphia Phillies Phantom World Series press pin $40
• 1967 Minnesota Twins Phantom World Series press pin $41
• San Diego Padres lineup card from June 16, 1987, signed by Manager Larry Bowa, includes Tony Gwynn, Benito Santiago and Kevin Mitchell... $25
• St. Louis Cardinals 1950s popcorn holder/ megaphone $50
• Philadelphia Phillies home dugout card from Aug. 7, 1978, vs. St. Louis, includes Larry Bowa, Mike Schmidt, Bob Boone, Ted Simmons and Keith Hernandez $31
• Philadelphia Phillies home dugout card from June 6, 1978, vs. San Francisco, includes Mike Schmidt, Bob Boone, Darrell Evans, Will Clark and Willie McCovey.................................... $43
• 1965 Philadelphia Phillies Phantom World Series program $110

Centerfield Collectibles Inc.
Off Season Auction
Feb. 16, 1996

• Triple Crown autographed print, framed and matted, pictures Frank Robinson, Ted Williams, Mickey Mantle and Carl Yastrzemski, 26x31 ....$536

• Ted Williams Cooperstown Bat Collection "Famous Players Series" bat, autographed.....$999

• Ted Williams autographed player model H&B bat $1,128

• 3,000 Hit Club baseball, signed by all 12 living members, including Hank Aaron, George Brett, Lou Brock, Rod Carew, Al Kaline, Willie Mays, Eddie Murray, Stan Musial, Pete Rose, Dave Winfield, Carl Yastrzemski and Robin Yount................$660

• Joe DiMaggio autographed New York Yankees fitted cap $268

• Willie, Mickey and the Duke autographed print, framed and matted, signed by all three $509

• Mike Schmidt Cooperstown Bat Collection "Famous Players Series" bat, autographed.....$333

• Kirby Puckett game-used Louisville Slugger bat, uncracked, #34 on both ends, Minnesota Twins stamped below his name $295

• 1986 All-Star Game program from Houston, autographed by 15 Hall of Famers, includes Hank Aaron, Joe DiMaggio, Willie Mays, Stan Musial, Duke Snider and Ted Williams $389

• Frank Thomas game-used Chicago White Sox cap, autographed $102

• Hank Aaron 1970s Atlanta Braves replica blue jersey and cap, both signed................$167

• Frank Thomas game-worn Reebok preseason turf shoes, size 14, from 1995 ....$113

• Cal Ripken Jr. 2,131th game commemorative ticket, by Nike, one of 10,000 printed, given to fans who attended the game $222

• Twelve official 1994 World Series baseballs, by Rawlings, each is sealed................$125

• Wade Boggs game-used Louisville Slugger bat, uncracked, with lots of pine tar, signed, 1986-89................$515

• Dave Righetti 1987 game-used New York Yankees road jersey, with tags................$532

• Pete Rose 1984 game-used Montreal Expos road jersey, blue, with tags................$576

• Frank Thomas game-used Reebok batting gloves, each autographed, 1995 season.....$248

• Mickey Mantle autographed New York Yankees fitted cap $213

• Sandy Koufax Los Angeles Dodgers road gray replica jersey, signed................$139

• Ernie Banks Chicago Cubs home white replica wool jersey, unsigned................$119

• Jose Canseco game-used Oakland A's pants, signed, 1993 season $101

• Mike Jorgensen game-used New York Mets blue batting practice jersey, early 1980s......$92

• Jay Tibbs game-used Baltimore Orioles black batting practice jersey, 1988................$57

• Tony Solaita game-used Kansas City Royals road jersey and pants, 1975-76 ....$208

• Tom Acker game-used baseball sleeves sweatshirt, Wilson, tan with blue sleeves, Acker in marker on the collar $57

• Frank Linzy, game-used baseball sleeves shirt, from 1970 Cardinals season, Rawlings, number in collar................$25

• Hank Aaron autographed fitted Milwaukee Braves cap, 755 added $50

• Frank Robinson autographed fitted Baltimore Orioles cap $44

• Stan Musial autographed fitted St. Louis Cardinals cap, HOF 1969 added $61

• Dick Such game-used Texas Rangers cap, 1983-85 ....$24

• Steve Comer game-used Texas Rangers cap, 1978-82 ....$21

• Rob Andrews game-used San Francisco Giants cap, 1977-79 ....$15

• Danny Darwin game-used Texas Rangers cap, 1978-84................$21

• Cracker Jack Old-Timers Baseball Classic cap, 1983, adjustable $18

• Phil Rizzuto autographed New York Yankees adjustable cap $39

• Joe DiMaggio autographed reproduction of 1936 World Series program $238

• Joe DiMaggio autographed reproduction of 1938 World Series program $122

• Joe, Vince and Dom DiMaggio autographed 3x5 index card................$167

• Joe DiMaggio autographed "Joltin Joe DiMaggio" 1941 sheet music, two pages, has DiMaggio picture on the front $545

• Joe DiMaggio autographed "Mrs. Robinson" 1968 sheet music, six pages................$110

• Joe DiMaggio autographed Life Magazine issue, May 1, 1939 ....$212

• Joe DiMaggio autographed Life Magazine issue, Aug. 1, 1949................$200

• Joe DiMaggio autographed The National Police Gazette magazine, from August 1949, has DiMaggio, Ted Williams and Stan Musial on the cover................$133

• Joe DiMaggio autographed May 1938 Baseball Magazine issue $158

• 1970s Babe Ruth framed Coca-Cola print, 19x25 .... $36

• 1970s Willie Mays framed Coca-Cola print, 19x25, autographed $67

• 1970s Casey Stengel framed Coca-Cola print, 19x25, autographed........................... $25

• 1951 Chicago White Sox Bowman 20-card reprint set, laminated on a 19x23 plaque..... $36

• 1951 Chicago Cubs Bowman 19-card reprint set, laminated on a 19x23 plaque $40

• 1953 Detroit Tigers Topps Archives 16-card reprint set, laminated on a 19x23 plaque..... $66

• 1986 New York Mets 1987 Topps cards, 28 laminated on a 19x25 plaque with an aerial view of Shea Stadium in the center...................... $50

• 1969 Jim Beam commemorative bottle for baseball's 100 Year Centennial Anniversary, 11" tall, four colors $74

• 1970s Ted Williams pocket watch, shows Williams in his Red Sox uniform, works .. $131

• Roberto Clemente professional baseball stamp collector's pin, 1x1 1/2" with hand-painted enamel colors and brash finish, depicts the Postal Series stamp made of him $18

• Joe DiMaggio's Restaurant and Cocktail Lounge matchbook, orange and blue with a picture of him and a facsimile autograph, without matches.. $18

• Carl Yastrzemski autographed 22x33 advertising display poster for Hillshire Farms and Kahn's Meats, dry mounted $75

• Roberto Clemente Hartland statue $81

• Nolan Ryan Hartland statue $74

• Frank Thomas game-used autographed black belt, from 1995 season $70

• Unopened case of Cal Ripken Jr. commemorative Wheaties boxes, 16 total, with Oriole logo.. $142

• Joe DiMaggio autographed 1989 National Baseball Hall of Fame Engagement Calendar, special 50th anniversary special, cover also pictures Lou Gehrig and Jimmie Foxx........ $43

• "Little Johnny Strikeout" record, two albums, with book-type sleeve telling Joe DiMaggio's story... $67

• Lot of three All-Star Baseball Games by Cadaco/Cadaco Ellis, 1960, 1962 and 1989 editions, with all pieces $80

• Lot of two baseball board games, includes 1955 Tudor Tru-Action Electric Baseball and 1969 Ideal All-Pro Baseball, games are complete $25

• 1969 Minnesota Twins pocket schedule ... $21

• 1973 Pittsburgh Pirates pocket schedule, features Roberto Clemente on the front $26

• 1984 All-Star Game press pin, for game in San Francisco $58

• President Gerald R. Ford autographed American League baseball $98

• Ted Williams autographed American League baseball $118

• Mickey Mantle autographed American League baseball... $131

• Harvey Kuenn autographed American League baseball... $307

• Fred McGriff game-used Worth bat, black, cracked, 1995 .... $177

• Eddie Murray game-used Louisville Slugger bat, brown, 1980-83 .... $5354

• Carlos Baerga game-used Louisville Slugger bat, black, 1986-89 .... $156

Alan "Mr. Mint" Rosen March 4, 1996, telephone auction

More than 100 bobbing head doll lots were offered during Alan "Mr. Mint" Rosen's March 4, 1996, telephone auction, his largest auction to date. The bobbers, purchased from Steve Townsend, were among the more than 450 items for sale by the Montvale, N.J., memorabilia dealer.

A Roberto Clemente bobber lead the way, selling for $1,460. Mickey Mantle's round-based bobber sold for $525; his square-based one sold for $495. A Roger Maris mini sold for $500. Willie Mays' light-faced doll and dark-faced version brought in $265 and $365.

The top 10 team-related bobbers were all black dolls from 1962-66: Washington Senators, $1,150; Cleveland Indians, $960; Philadelphia Phillies, $675; St. Louis Cardinals, $665; Los Angeles Angels, $650; Baltimore Orioles, $590; Los Angeles Dodgers, $590; Detroit Tigers, $500; Chicago Cubs, $495; and Chicago White Sox, $400.

The next six were 1961-62 Pittsburgh Pirates mascot, square white base, $550; 1961-62 Cincinnati Reds mascot, square base, $440; 1961-62 Cleveland Indians mascot, square white base, $400; 1961-62 Cleveland Indians mascot, green round mini, $400; 1967-72 Houston Astros gold base, with shooting star, $405; and 1961-62 Baltimore Orioles white round mini, $365.

Other items included: a complete set of 23 1960 Armour coins sold for $1,010, while a complete set of 26 1955 coins sold for $660 and a complete set of 20 1959 coins brought in $365. A 1956 Mickey Mantle Big League Star statue, in its original package, sold for $935, while a 1968 Topps Mickey Mantle plak sold for $665. Mantle's 1952 Star-Cal decal sold for $810.

Baseballs signed by the 1941 World Champion New York Yankees, the 1948 Yankees and 1956 Champion Yankees brought in $1,145, $590, and $880 respectively. A George Sisler autographed baseball sold for $1,200, while a 1934 American League All-Stars ball reached $8,750.

A Honus Wagner cancelled check, issued Jan. 6, 1920, for $43.97, sold for $1,800. Carl Yastrzemski's 1970 American League baseball contract with the Boston Red Sox, payable to Yaz for $125,000, sold for $360. Reggie Jackson's New York Yankees signed paycheck for $148,596, on a Yankee team check dated 1/2/79, sold for $240.

World Series press pins from 1916 (Brooklyn Dodgers), and 1927 (New York Yankees) sold for $2,865 and $1,950. A program from the 1920 Brooklyn Dodgers/Cleveland Indians World Series sold for $1,870, while All-Star Game programs from 1935 (Cleveland), 1939 (Yankee Stadium), 1942 (New York Giants), 1951 (Detroit Tigers) and 1961 (San Francisco) brought $545, $800, $1,725, $275 and $365.

A 1946 phantom World Series program for the Brooklyn Dodgers and Boston Red Sox sold for $400, while a 1949 St. Louis Cardinals phantom World Series ticket sold for $100.

World Series Black Bats and prices realized included 1937 New York Giants ($600), 1939 Cincinnati Reds ($550), 1941 New York Yankees ($305), 1947 Brooklyn Dodgers ($570), 1947 Yankees ($200), 1948 Cleveland Indians ($535), 1949 Yankees ($440), 1950 Yankees (350), 1952 Yankees ($425), 1957 Milwaukee Braves ($405) and 1957 Yankees ($405).

A complete set of 18 Hartland statues, in Excellent-Mint condition, sold for $3,600, while an early 1950s Mickey Mantle Fan Club pin and membership card sold for $1,750. A Roger Maris stadium pin (3 1/2") and 10x10 full-color proof sheet of 16 stadium pin paper proofs sold for $250.

Several other pins which were sold, and prices realized, included: 1938 Knot Hole Gang pin, "On To Nicollet Park," $70; 1947 Jackie Robinson "Rookie of the Year" pin, with ball and ribbon, $260; 1930s Dizzy Dean pin with figural ball and ribbon, $110; and a Babe Ruth memorial pin with black ribbon and ball, $275. A 1910 Sweet Caporal P2 set of 204 pins, in Near Mint condition, sold for $4,360. It included all known variations.

A circa 1917 figural four-wheel celluloid scorer, in the shape of a glove with an advertisement for Thistle shoes, sold for $120. A 1915 five-wheel scorer promoting "Lazarus Pennant Winners" sold for $125.

A 1930s Curtiss Baby Ruth Candy Bar promotional megaphone sold for $85, while Elroy Face's 1960 World Series game-used glove sold for $500.

Results from Rosen's 195-lot Dec. 4., 1995, telephone auction include:

- 1912 L1 Leather Tris Speaker, $2,000; Frank Baker $1,000
- 1955 Armour coin set with Mickey Mantle variation $665
- 1883 A.J. Reach Baseball Guide, first issue $1,300
- 1933 Who's Who in Baseball, #1 issue, Mint condition $550
- 1941 complete Brooklyn Dodgers World Series ticket, for Game 5 at Ebbets Field $265
- 1949 New York Yankees World Series Black Bat $710
- 1950 New York Yankees World Series Black Bat $365
- 1971 Pittsburgh Pirates World Series Black Bat $220
- 1973 New York Mets World Series Black Bat $200
- Mickey Mantle bobbing head doll, with original box $935
- Roberto Clemente bobbing head doll, Mint condition $1,200
- 1960s Aurora statues, complete set of 6, includes Willie Mays, Johnny Unitas, Dempsey vs. Firpo, Jim Brown, Jerry West and Babe Rith, with original boxes..................................$1,100
- Ty Cobb autographed souvenir photo album, four pages with two photos and signature inside $730
- Dizzy Dean autographed baseball, with original box $1,075
- 1948 Boston Braves National League Champions autographed baseball, includes 21 signatures $365
- 1950 Brooklyn Dodgers autographed baseball, includes 25 signatures................$810

• 1977 New York Yankees autographed baseball, includes 27 signatures from this World Championship team $770

• Jackie Robinson autographed 7x9 color magazine photo $400

• A dozen Mickey Mantle autographed baseballs, official American League balls $1,420

• A dozen Nolan Ryan autographed baseballs, official American League balls $400

• 48 copies of Hank Aaron's autobiography, "I Had A Hammer," each is autographed...... $660

• 500 Home Run Club lithograph, #1 of 1,000, signed by all 11 living members of the club $2,925

• 500 Home Run Club autographed bat, #11 of 300, Rawlings, signed by all 11 living members $2,475

• 500 Home Run Club autographed ball, includes all 11 members............................ $730

• Warren Spahn game-used Milwaukee Braves cap, with name tag inside $590

• Mickey Mantle autographed New York Yankees old-timers jersey, circa 1979......$1,815

• Don Mattingly 1989 New York Yankees game-used road jersey, includes tags $1,500

North Shore Sports
Feb. 27, 1996,
telephone auction

Mr. Memorabilia
March 15, 1996,
telephone auction

Historic baseballs and memorabilia from baseball's most prolific switch-hitter, Mickey Mantle, were the highlights in North Shore Sports' Feb. 27, 1996, telephone auction, conducted by the Northbrook, Ill., auction house.

Mickey Mantle's 1954 New York Yankee home flannel sold for $77,000, as did a 1937 Lou Gehrig Yankee road flannel. Mantle's 1960 team-issued wool jacket also sold for $20,020.

Mantle's first home run baseball, signed and dated, sold for $41,250. Mantle inscribed it "My first H.R. in the majors, May 1, 1951, 4:50 pm, Chicago," and "6th Inning off of Randy Gumpert." The ball used for his 500th home run, also signed and dated, brought in $24,200, while his 346th/1,000th RBI and 404th home run balls went for $12,375 and $6,600.

A few unique items which sold at the auction included a letter from President Richard Nixon congratulating Harmon Killebrew for his 500th homer ($2,420). A jersey worn by voodoo worshipper Pedro Cerrano in the movie "Major League" sold for $1,060, while the uniform worn by Richard Pryor in the movie "Bingo Long" had a winning bid of $1,210.

Other top sellers included Ernie Banks' 500th Home Run Trophy, for $12,100; his Hall of Fame plaque, for $13,090; and Joe DiMaggio's 1941 MVP ring, made for a friend, for $4,235.

Michael Jordan's game-used Birmingham Barons jersey sold for $6,655, while his practice jersey sold for $1,952. Sandy Koufax's signed 1966 Los Angeles Dodgers home flannel was another hot item, selling for $15,400.

Nolan Ryan items and their winning bids included a 1980s Houston Astros home rainbow jersey ($6,435), a 1987 Astros warm-up jacket ($3,190), a 1991 home Texas Rangers jersey ($2,310), a 1993 Rangers road jersey ($3,995), and a 1989 Rangers batting practice jersey ($2,970).

Mr. Memorabilia's March 15, 1996, telephone auction from Sykesville, Md., featured several items from Baltimore's professional teams, with Cal Ripken items setting the pace.

The lineup card from Ripken's first full game, dated Aug. 21, 1981, sold for $2,500. The card has Ripken batting eighth, playing shortstop, and is signed by manager Earl Weaver. Possibly the earliest known official lineup card from Ripken's record-setting 2,131 consecutive game streak, dated June 6, 1982, the sixth game in the streak, sold for $4,540.

The home run ball hit by Pittsburgh Pirates slugger Willie Stargell to win Game 7 of the 1979 World Series sold for $3,000. The ball was obtained from a member of the grounds crew, who caught the ball at his station in the bullpen.

Sheet music for "I Can't Get to First Base With You," written by Mrs. Lou Gehrig and Fred Fisher, sold for $2,000. The 1935 music shows Lou Gehrig (and a genuine autograph) on the front, with a photo of Mrs. Gehrig in the lower right corner.

Christie's East auction
Oct. 5, 1995

Mickey Mantle's 1951 New York Yankees rookie jersey brought one of the top prices ever paid for a post-war uniform at Christie's East's Oct. 5, 1995, auction in the city where he made his mark on baseball.

The jersey, which Mantle wore in Game 1 of the World Series against the cross-town New York Giants, sold for $74,000, including the buyer's fees. In that game, Mantle tore up his knee after tripping on a sprinkler in the outfield, and was unable to participate in the rest of the Series.

The 500-lot auction brought in $780,000 for the New York auction house. The baseball Babe Ruth hit for a home run in the third-inning of the first All-Star Game in 1933, at Chicago's Comiskey Park, sold for $44,850, making it the second highest realization. The ball, which was signed by Ruth and several other American League All-Stars, had a pre-sale estimate of $8,000-$10,000.

Ruth's parlor player grand piano, purchased by the Babe in 1929, sold for less than the $20,000-$30,000 estimate, but did bring in $17,250. Included with the piano were more than 100 player rolls of music.

Several other Ruth items were sold during the auction. A 1940s Babe Ruth bronze electric clock sold for $3,350. The clock, which features a bust of Ruth between two baseballs, had a pre-sale estimate of $1,500-$2,000.

An 11x14 studio-type signed photo of Ruth taken in the late 1920s sold for $8,050, against a pre-sale estimate of $1,000-$1,500. A ball signed by Ruth and Lou Gehrig during the 1930s sold for $2,700, while a Ty Cobb ball brought $1,840.

Cobb's monogrammed robe from the 1930s failed to meet its $15,000-$20,000 reserve and went unsold, as did a 1934 Gehrig home Yankees flannel jersey. The bidding reached $90,000, but fell short of the pre-sale estimate of $120,000-$150,000. Roberto Clemente's 1971 Pittsburgh Pirates jersey, perhaps the only one in existence that he signed, also fell short of its $40,000-$50,000 reserve.

A pair of ticket stubs from the 1903 World Series, pitting Pittsburgh against Boston, sold for $11,500. The lot included a small scrapbook of newspaper articles, too, about baseball's first-ever World Series

A 14k gold pin with 20 diamonds, given to members of the 1905 World Champion New York Giants, sold for $14,375, while the glove Ray Knight used in the 1986 World Series sold for $1,265. Knight, who played for the New York Mets, was the MVP of the Series.

A nine-page letter written by Ty Cobb on May 5, 1955, sold for $5,520. The letter contains Cobb's thoughts on baseball in general and includes his player evaluations of Phil Rizzuto, Joe DiMaggio and Ted Williams.

An H&B bat, used and cracked by Williams while he was a member of the Minneapolis Millers in 1938, sold for $4,830. Lou Gehig's 1930s Yankees cap sold for $16,100.

Cal Ripken Jr. memorabilia was also popular. The only remaining set of press plates used to produce the front page of the Baltimore Sun for Sept. 7, 1995, sold for $2,185. The plate featured special coverage of Ripken's consecutive games played record and included four aluminum color printing plates, with the image plate featuring Ripken's signature.

Ripken's 1985 home Baltimore Orioles jersey, autographed on the front tail, went unsold after failing to meet its $4,000-$6,000 reserve. A game-used cap, however, sold for $863, while a game-used batting helmet sold for $2,300.

Hall's Nostalgia fall 1995 auction results

• Ty Cobb autographed baseball, signed and dated June 19, 1917 .... $4,000

• Babe Ruth's pencil autograph on the blank side of an old Russell Dry Docks Inc. business card $750

• Three 1960 Mickey Mantle Armour coins, blue, green and orange $200

• 1947 Detroit Tigers autographed baseball, with 27 signatures $200

• Joe DiMaggio New York Yankees autographed replica cap, with acrylic display case $180

• Ted Williams Day commemorative folder, signed $100

• Hardcover copy of the 1933 Who's Who in the Major Leagues, by Speed Johnson $220

• A collection of 124 baseball stadium postcards from the 1940s through 1980s $270

• Autographed "500 Home Run Club" lithograph, by Ron Lewis $1,700

• 11 single-signed baseballs, one for each member of the 500 Home Run Club $450

• 1912 Boston Red Sox World Series program $1,300

• Mickey Mantle bobbing head doll $400

• 1949 New York Yankees autographed baseball, includes Joe DiMaggio $500

• First issue of Sports Illustrated, with baseball card pullout and special folder $325

• Bunker Hills Breweries 1917 baseball calendar, pictures the 1915-16 Boston Red Sox World Champions, including Babe Ruth, calendar missing, but advertising picture intact $280

Robert Edward Auctions June 10, 1995

• Christy Mathewson's 1903 Major League player's contract, for the National League's New York Giants for the 1903 season, dated Sept. 15, 1902, and signed by Mathewson, club President John T. Brush, and Manager John McGraw, a witness... $12,894.56

• Lou Gehrig game-used New York Yankees cap, Spalding, circa 1930, shows moderate wear, "L. Gehrig" is stitched inside........... $13,202.56

• Henry Chadwick autographed baseball diamond and letter, 4x6, circa 1840s, field diagram which identifies positions and includes a letter signed by Chadwick which relates to the controversy regarding the origins of the game........... $7,035.84

• Cap Anson single-signed baseball, circa 1900, signed "AC Anson"................ $16,390.96

• Babe Ruth Reach Home Run Special baseball with box, box features Ruth on the cover, ball has facsimile Ruth signature $1,538.88

• Earliest U.S. Patent baseball, an original sample sent to the U.S. Patent Office for the very first patent ever to be awarded for a baseball, includes tag with patent number, is actually one a half of a ball so it shows the inside $18,219.04

• Autographed banquet program honoring the 1907 World Champion Chicago Cubs, held Oct. 17, 1907, at the Congress Hotel in Chicago, inside autograph page features 21 signatures, including Joe Tinker, Johnny Evers, Frank Chance and Cap Anson $5,040

• Mickey Mantle high school graduation matted photo, original photo with postcard backing $900.48

• Shibe Park cornerstone trowel, from the ceremonies for laying the cornerstone for the new ballpark in 1908, engravings identify the trowel's use $3,272.64

• 1888 Cap Anson game-used bat plus related 1907 Sporting Life newspaper article, which indicates who the owner of the bat was and that Anson did give it to him.................. $20,598.72

• 1927 Pie Traynor 310-page scrapbook, presented to him by the boys at the Gusky Orphanage, it includes 100s of newspaper articles and pictures $369.60

• Sheet music collection of 38, spanning from 1910 to 1950, includes "Pride of the Yankees," "I Love Mickey," and "Take Me Out To The Ball Game".. $616

• Negro American League baseball, official Wilson, with original box and wrapping $3,862.88

• Buck Weaver autographed Soldier Boy tobacco pack, "for smoke or chew," unopened $845.60

• Pre-1900 baseball glove, first baseman's or catcher's mitt, leather and cloth, like a pot holder.. $446.88

• Original wire photo of Babe Ruth signing boxes of baseballs, dated June 23, 1927, with caption attached to the back $636.16

• Bob Feller's game-used baseball shoes, black leather, both autographed $2,996

• Limited-edition Mickey Mantle/Roger Maris autographed Louisville Slugger, commemorates their home runs in 1961, only 115 were made $3,597.44

• 500 Home Run Club autographed bat, Adirondack, signed by the 11 members who were living in 1988 .... $1,631.84

• Babe Ruth personal check, dated April 12, 1935, made out for $13.20 to National Exhibition Co. (corporate name of the New York Giants) $1,713.60

• "Batterin' Babe" sheet music, from 1919, pictures Babe Ruth with the Boston Red Sox $308

• Hillerich & Bradsby metal sign, 1940s, red, white and black metal, the centerpiece for a wooden easel store display.................. $900.48

• Ted Williams Creamy Root Beer counter display sign, 1950s, cardboard advertising sign with easel stand $677.60

• Yogi Berra/Mickey Mantle Yoo Hoo advertising display, 24x30, "The Drink of Champions," autographed by Berra, framed $1,568

• Ted Williams' 517th home run bat, Louisville Slugger used to hit #517 on Sept. 2, 1960, against Washington................. $8,161.44

• Christy Mathewson Bucknell University freshman yearbook, published in 1900, has several pictures of the multi-sport athlete $819.84

• Reggie candy bar store display, counter standup display includes a pad of mail-in promotions for Reggie Jackson autographed baseballs... $271.04

• Reggie Jackson commemorative candy bar wrapper, famed and autographed proof, dated Feb. 22, 1978, given to members of the press to unveil the new candy bar $1,018.08

• Honus Wagner cigar band, perfect condition, has a full-color stone litho portrait of Wagner $2,240

• 500 Home Run autographed baseball, signed by the 11 living members on an American League baseball $957.60

• Early 1960s Yoo Hoo 11x14 cardboard counter display, pictures eight New York Yankees, including Yogi Berra, Whitey Ford and Mickey Mantle................................... $1,197.28

• Major League Indoor Base Ball Game, Philadelphia Game Co., 1912, complete with all pieces, cover pictures 16 stars of the era $3,279.36

• Joe Tinker cigar box, circa 1910, two sides picture Tinker...................................... $677.60

• 1930s Diamond Dust punchboard, from the 1930s, features 15 players (11 Hall of Famers), including Babe Ruth and Lou Gehrig, chances were sold for 5 cents each with the chance to win prizes.. $222.80

• 1949 "Pride of the Yankees" movie poster one-sheet, 27x41, Gary Cooper stars in this film chronicling the life of Lou Gehrig $2,458.40

• "Safe at Home" movie poster, 60x40, features images of Roger Maris and Mickey Mantle, from 1962 ....$1,400

Leland's 1995 auction results

• Baseball autographed by President John F. Kennedy while he was in Cuba in 1963 ...$27,500

• 1927 World Champion New York Yankees autographed baseball $26,400

• 1928 World Champion New York Yankees autographed baseball $19,800

• Babe Ruth 1922-31 game-used Hillerich & Bradsby bat, cracked at handle............. $13,200

• Babe Ruth two-inch brass locker tag, with his name and number on one side and "Locker 3, Yankee Stadium, The Bronx, New York" on the other.. $2,475

• Babe Ruth's custom-made set of Vic Ghezzi Grand Slam Model golf clubs, from 1930s, with bag $2,750

• Mickey Mantle 1965-68 game-used Hillerich & Bradsby bat... $7,700

• Roger Maris autographed baseball $990

• 1923 New York Yankees World Champions 14k gold watch fob................................. $2,750

• 1937 New York Yankees World Championship pocket watch $2,475

• 1952 New York Yankees World Championship Wittnauer pocket watch . $1,100

• New York Yankees' owner George Weiss' 1953 14k World Championship ring $9,350

• Hank Bauer's 1958 New York Yankees World Championship 14k gold ring....... $8,250

• Carl Yastrzemski's complete Boston Red Sox home uniform, from when he got his 3,000th hit... $3,575

• Ted Williams' blue satin 1969-71 Washington Senators jacket $1,650

• Keith Hernandez's 1978 Rawlings Gold Glove Award $4,400

• Babe Ruth 1931 autographed baseball, includes message inscribed to a sick child $3,630

• Walter Johnson 1930 autographed baseball, with personal message............................ $3,219

• 1925 New York Yankees autographed baseball, with Babe Ruth and 12 others......$1,065

• 1953 World Champion New York Yankees autographed baseball $1,099

• Cast iron Detroit Tigers doorstop, from turn of the century, has a standing tiger holding a bat $1,150

• Willie Mays bobbing head doll, with the box.. $424

• Goose Gossage game-used Mizuno glove, from 1991, autographed $358

• Robin Yount game-used Louisville Slugger, autographed $330

• Dale Murphy 1984 Atlanta Braves road uniform, with spikes................................$1,089

• Harmon Killebrew's 1970 All-Star Game bat... $879

• Boston Braves figural stadium seat $725

• Briggs Stadium figural stadium seat.$1,320

• Polo Grounds figural stadium seat ...$1,597

• Ron Kline's 1950s Pittsburgh Pirates equipment trunk, 25x20x100, with team logo and his number... $484

• Paul Blair's 1974 Rawlings Gold Glove Award... $3,896

• Babe Ruth/Lou Gehrig autographed baseball $3,300

• 1943 World Champion New York Yankees autographed baseball, with 28 signatures$3,344

• 1951 World Champion New York Yankees autographed baseball, with 25 signatures ..$600

• 1961 World Champion New York Yankees autographed baseball, with 24 signatures ..$600

• 1963 Pittsburgh Pirates autographed baseball $484

• 1969 World Champion New York Mets autographed baseball................................$1,180

• 1926 New York Yankees World Series press pin $733

• 1959 Los Angeles Dodgers World Series press pin $211

• 1963 Los Angeles Dodgers World Series press pin $178

• 1973 Oakland A's World Series press pin $121

• 1982 Hall of Fame press pin, for Frank Robinson and Hank Aaron......................... $248

• 1994 Hall of Fame press pin, for Leo Durocher, Steve Carlton and Phil Rizzuto...................... $220

• 1993 Los Angeles Dodgers batting helmet, signed by the team $363

• Andres Galarraga's 1991 game-used Montreal Expos batting helmet................. $231

• Carlos Baerga's 1990 game-used Cleveland Indians jersey $1,464

• Roberto Clemente game-used Louisville Slugger bat, 1960s, cracked handle repaired with nails...$1,320

• 1930s Louisville Slugger reproduction store display bat rack, used to hold 36 bats $1,121

• Mickey Mantle bobbing head doll, with box $440

• George Brett game-used bat, with pine tar, cracked $605

• Hank Aaron game-used Adirondack bat, 1970s...$1,331

• Jose Rijo's 1990 Cincinnati Reds World Series warm-up jacket, signed by the Series MVP... $405

• Lenny Dykstra six-finger Regent autographed glove, with name and "Nails" stitched in red $330

• Dwight Gooden game-used spikes, 1991, autographed $110

• Babe Ruth autographed baseball $1,320

• 1950 Brooklyn Dodgers autographed baseball $702

• 1963 World Champion New York Yankees autographed ball $369

• 1965 World Champion Minnesota Twins autographed ball

• 1975 World Champion Cincinnati Reds autographed ball $495

• 1980 World Champion Philadelphia Phillies autographed ball $242

• Ball signed by all 11 living members of the 500 Home Run Club $545

• Roger Maris bobbing head doll, with box $468

• Unscored scorecard for a game between the Negro League's Indianapolis Clowns and Memphis Red Sox $275

• 1930s autograph album, with 700 signatures from 1932-34, includes Babe Ruth, Lou Gehrig, Jimmie Foxx, Honus Wagner, Rogers Hornsby $4,442

• Collection of 118 3x5 index cards signed by Hall of Famers, includes Ty Cobb, Roberto Clemente, Honus Wagner, Pie Traynor $2,420

• One-page contract signed by Thurman Munson to appear in a golf tournament $333

• Herb Pennock's 1925-26 New York Yankees contact, signed by the Hall of Famer and team officials $880

• Full ticket from Pete Rose's Sept. 11, 1985, game when he had his record 4,192nd hit, signed $315

• Babe Ruth autographed baseball $3,548

• Lou Gehrig/Babe Ruth autographed baseball $3,545

• Ball used in Nolan Ryan's fifth no hitter, signed and dated $3,328

• Baseball scuffed by Tommy John, confiscated by home plate umpire Dallas Parks in 1979, signed $420

• Pete Rose's 385th home run baseball, signed and dated $394

• 1976 Cincinnati Reds autographed baseball, World Champions $586

• 1978 New York Yankees autographed baseball, World Champions $1,271

• Harmon Killebrew's 1971 All-Star Game used bat $2,200

• Ken Griffey Jr.'s 1993 game-used Seattle Mariners jersey and undershirt, autographed $1,980

• Gary Carter's game-used Montreal Expos batting helmet, autographed $495

• Robin Yount's 1980 Milwaukee Brewers game-used batting helmet $605

• 1992 Atlanta Braves batting helmet, signed by the team $1,100

• Dave Winfield autographed game-used Cooper glove, 1993 .... $605

• Hank Aaron's 1970s Atlanta Braves undershirt, with name and number on it $220

• Don Mattingly's 1992 New York Yankees game-used cap $394

• Jeff Bagwell's 1994 game-used Houston Astros cap $275

• Ozzie Smith's 1992 game-used St. Louis Cardinals cap $212

• Nap Lajoie autographed baseball $3,001

• Ty Cobb autographed baseball $2,160

• Ted Turner's 1991 salesman's sample National League Champions ring, "Worst to First" $3,163

• 1927 World Series program, Pittsburgh vs. New York Yankees, scored $1,540

• Ticket stub from Roger Maris' record-setting 61st home run game, Oct. 1, 1961, Yankee Stadium $1,065

• 1953 Brooklyn Dodgers autographed baseball, National League Champions, 20 signatures $1,029

• Wire service photo of Joe DiMaggio and Marilyn Monroe taken just before their Jan. 14, 1954, wedding $355

• 1948 Babe Ruth watch $275

• 1926 St. Louis Cardinals World Series program $646

• 1962 Wrigley Field All-Star Game press pin $220

• 1993 Toronto Blue Jays World Series press pin $121

• 1994 Pittsburgh Pirates All-Star Game press pin $165

• Al Kaline's 1970s game-used spikes, autographed $492

• Johnny Bench's game-used turf shoe $275

• Gary Carter game-used 1974 Montreal Expos jersey $880

• Bo Jackson's game-used 1990 Kansas City Royals home jersey $551

• Tony Gwynn game-used San Diego Padres cap, autographed $200

• Slat back seat from Yankee Stadium, seat #3 .... $847

• Double seat from Pittsburgh's Forbes Field, seat #s 1, 2 .... $968

• Figural end seat from Cincinnati's Crosley Field $2,200

Leland's Nov. 19-20, 1994, Grand Slam auction

The boyhood home where Mickey Mantle honed his skills was perhaps the most unusual item to be offered in an auction over the last few years.

The home, which sits just off Route 66, in Commerce, Okla., sold for $60,500 in Leland's Grand Slam auction Nov. 19-20, 1994. The buyer intended to dismantle the home, which carried a pre-sale estimate of $30,000-$40,000, and relocate it in a tourist area as a Mickey Mantle museum.

Mantle, who moved there in 1935 when he was 4 years old, wrote about the one-story house quite extensively in his 1985 autobiography "The Mick." He lived there until 1944.

The old tin barn which was in the backyard was also included in the deal. Mantle used the barn to pitch against; its dents and marks are evidence of its use.

A Lou Gehrig Day plaque, created by Dieges for Gehrig's moving July 4, 1939, oratory, sold for $16,500. The brass plaque, 5x10, reads "American Sportsman - To Lou Gehrig" and has a tribute below, with the names of his teammates listed, too.

A Shoeless Joe Jackson game-used Louisville Slugger bat, "Black Betsy," sold for $12,100. The 35.5" bat, which has a facsimile signature, shows exceptional wear from Jackson's use as a member of the Chicago White Sox.

Other items in the auction, and prices realized:

• Two magazine photos and two 1976 Topps cards, all signed in blue ball-point by Thurman Munson.. $1,430

• Paul Blair's 1978 World Champion New York Yankees World Series ring, 14k gold with blue stone and diamonds, plus NY logo and inscriptions "Blair 1978 Pride/Tradition 2" and "Greatest Comeback in History" $6,050

• Billy Martin signed 1977 World Series telegram from Frank Sinatra, from Western Union, dated Oct. 11, 1977, it reads "Dear Billy don't believe Tommy Lasorda. We love you. Love Frank Sinatra, Jilly Rizzo," signed by Billy Martin..$1,650

• Yankee Stadium seat, antique-style slat back seat, from the 1923 opening, all original, with #13 on the top slat $1,430

• "Reggie" candy bar collection, includes sealed carton of 36 candy bars, advertising display and box display..............................$605

• Don Mattingly's New York Yankees suitcase, with the NY logo with #23 in the middle $385

• 1951 Yankees-Dodgers phantom World Series program, complete, for a series that was never played...$825

• Leo Durocher's 1940s Brooklyn Dodgers coat, full length, blue with huge chenille B on it $2,530

• Jackie Robinson's 1954 All-Star Game presentational tray, silver plate engraved "All-Star Game 1954 Jackie Robinson American League 11 National League 9," some scratches $1,430

• 1942 Detriot Black Sox letter from President Louis Taylor to Detroit Tigers General Manager J.A. Zeller, on Black Sox green and blue letterhead, it reads "What we are primarily interested in, Mr. Zeller, is to give the patrons of the City of Detroit the same caliber of baseball as you give them each season. We want to put Negro baseball on the same plane as our white brethren have it now" $495

• Wrigley Field folding chair, repainted, from the 1930s, wood and cast iron $275

• Los Angeles Dodgers stadium banner, 70x110, blue and white, flew at Cincinnati's Crosley Field in the late 1960s.................. $495

• Tris Speaker 1933 Kansas City Baseball Club stock certificate, signed three times by Speaker $1,045

• Joe Jackson 32" Louisville Slugger decal bat, with art nouveau pattern $4,400

• Margo Adams pendant from Wade Boggs, heart-shaped 18k necklace pendant he gave to her in 1984, with Boggs' #26 in the middle.... $990

• Ted Williams Boston Red Sox game-used undershirt, wool McAulife with dark blue sleeves and Williams' name embroidered in the collar $2,475

• Roger Maris 61st home run ticket stub, from Oct. 1, 1961, when Maris hit #61 off Boston's Tracy Stallard $1,045

• Roger Maris 61st home run program, from the same game, scored in pencil, with "Maris Hits 61st Home Run" written on it $1,045

• Forbes Field turnstile, 40", from 1909, fire engine red with solid brass top and glass-encased counter and window for ticker tape........ $6,050

• 1971 World Champion Pittsburgh Pirates banner, 36x38, flew above the streets in the city, it reads "Welcome Pittsburgh Pirates 1971 World Champs"... $715

• Roberto Clemente 1972 Pittsburgh Pirates knit home white uniform, with pants and all tags, possibly worn in the playoffs.................$9,350

• Willie Stargell "Black Man's Shaver," a Remington Electric which pictures Stargell on the box, still works......................................$83

• 1993 Ken Griffey Jr. Louisville Slugger bat, black, he smashed it across his knee after striking out $880

• George Brett game-used spikes, royal blue Nikes, both signed in silver........................$605

• Kirby Puckett game-used glove, from 1991, this jet-black Wilson model has Puckett's name stitched in red on the thumb....................$1,650

• Gary Carter game-used shin guards, black Rawlings, each is signed............................$550

• Frank Thomas game-used Mizuno first baseman's glove, from 1991, has #35 and Thomas on it, signed...............................$2,090

• Prototype 1969 Montreal Expos Wilson flannel, created for a press conference, Gene Mauch model, button-down style $605

• Christy Mathewson Tuxedo Tobacco cardboard advertising sign, 24x32 framed, portrait shot of Mathewson, who endorses the product $7,150

• 1950s diecut Al Kaline Cooper Tire cardboard sign, 17x20, black-and-white photo of Kaline throwing $550

• Cy Young store-model glove, 1930s Hutch, with facsimile signature $660

• Babe Ruth wristwatch, 1949 Exacta Time, shows Ruth in the center with bats over his shoulder, has a metal band $880

• 1930s Babe Ruth-brand underwear, button-down white cotton, has "Babe Ruth" tag in the collar $220

• Babe Ruth 2" locker tag, brass circle incised, "Babe Ruth 3" on the front, "Locker 3, Yankee Stadium, The Bronx, New York" on the back, intended to be a key chain for locker keys $1,980

• Babe Ruth's 1916-17 Boston Red Sox player contract, pays him $3,500 per season as a pitcher, signed by the team president, Joseph Lannin, on Jan 6., 1916 ....$29,700

• The world's largest baseball bat, 10 feet, to scale, 1930s ash "Genuine W.G. Smith Model" used as an advertising piece.....................$1,760

• Stan Musial's last game program, from Sept. 29,1963, at Busch Stadium in St. Louis, unscored $990

• 19th century baseball, hard, dark brown leather, inner twine shows its age.............. $385

• 1973 Rollie Fingers Fireman of the Year Award, white fire helmet with "Rollie Fingers Oakland A's" on the sides, "Fireman of Year 1973 #34" on the front, signed.................. $660

• 1955 All-Star Game belt buckle, 14k with large diamond in the center flanked by two crossed figural bats, it reads "All Star 1955 Award" and was inscribed to Eddie Brannick, the New York Giants travelling secretary....... $660

• Lou Gehrig "Rawhide" movie sheet, 27x41 one-sheet, this 1941 horse opera starred Gehrig in his only movie appearance $605

• 1949 "Pride of the Yankees" movie sheet, 27x41 one-sheet, stars Gary Cooper as Lou Gehrig, with an inset image of Babe Ruth $1,650

• "Safe at Home" movie sheet, 27x41 one-sheet, features Mickey Mantle and Roger Maris in back-to-back batting stances $825

• "The Babe Ruth Story" movie sheet, 27x41 one-sheet, from the 1948 rendition of Ruth's life, big red block letters used for the title..... $1,210

• Heydler baseball in box, "Official National League Cushioned Cork Center" ball, with Spalding 1918 logos and "John A. Heydler" facsimile signature.................................. $1,320

• 1910 World Champion Philadelphia A's cello mirror, an Owens Drug Co. ad which says "World's Champions 1910" and has 17 ovals around it with player mug shots $1,100

• 1893 Zimmer's Baseball Game, 21x21x1.5, by McLoughlin Brothers of New York $14,300

• Christ Mathewson Big 6 game, 17x22, image of Mathewson runs the length of this roulette game $1,045

• 1930s Babe Ruth's Baseball Game, by Milton Bradley, features rendition of Ruth at bat on the cover $715

• Max Carey's 1933 All-Star Game cap, used in the first-ever mid-summer classic, dark blue wool with "NL" stitched in white on the front, "M. Carey" is stitched inside the band. $11,000

• 1951 American League Golden Anniversary patch, worn on Boston Red Sox jerseys, says "American League 1901-1951 Golden Anniversary" $440

• King & His Court jersey, worn by Eddie Feigner, the famed fast-pitch softball player, All-American style blue with red and white stripes and stars.. $880

• "Pride of the Yankees" Academy Award, 13", "Presented to Daniel Mandell In Recognition Of The Film Editing Of The 'Pride Of The Yankees' 1942," the film which chronicles the life of Lou Gehrig..........$16,830

• Ernie Banks 1971 Chicago Cubs road jersey, flannel with tags, name written in black marker on the collar..$13,200

• Wrigley Field turnstile, original blue, side-turning style $1,320

• Darryl Strawberry's 1986 New York Mets jacket, signed, name on the back, with #18 and 25th Anniversary patch $330

• Darryl Strawberry's 1986 World Series trophy, golden flags circle the base, which has enamels for the Mets and Red Sox on it and Strawberry's name engraved on it $4,675

• Waddell & Davis paddle baseball game, 4x6, compliments of Camden Tea Co., pictures Rube Waddell and Harry Davis, with five holes in it $605

• Circa 1910 Washington Senators pennant, 26" blue felt, depicts a player and says "Washington...American League B.B.C." $1,210

• 1950s Philadelphia Phillies usherette uniform, complete, includes satiny pink vest and cap, with "Phillies" monogrammed on them, plus three gray skirts..$468

• 1954 Cleveland Indians World Series cufflinks and tie-bar, given to team personnel instead of rings, 14k figural Indians in red enamels with matching rubies, engraved "American League Champions 1954 All-Time Record 111 Games Won" $3,300

• Nolan Ryan's second no-hitter ticket stub, from July 15, 1973, pitted Ryan's California Angels in Detroit against the Tigers $1,210

• Don Larsen's perfect game World Series program, from Game 5 of the 1956 World Series, scored $495

• Catfish Hunter's perfect game ticket, unused, from the May 8, 1968, game in Oakland, signed $220

• Jim Abbott no-hitter baseball, came from the Yankees and is autographed "Jim Abbott 9/4/93 Game Ball"..$1,540

• Nolan Ryan baseball from his 7th no-hitter, signed and dated.....................................$4,125

• New York Yankees souvenir batting helmet, signed by more than 70 greats from the 1970s and 1980s, includes Billy Martin, Reggie Jackson, Thurman Munson, Yogi Berra, Catfish Hunter $2,090

• New York Mets pitcher Anthony Young's equipment from his record-breaking 19-game losing streak in 1993, includes a black Wilson glove, Pony spikes, Mets pullover warm-up, uncracked Adirondack bat and a baseball signed "Anthony Young 19" $715

• Complete run of 14 National League team-signed baseballs from 1993, includes 383 signatures, with managers on the sweet spots $825

• Willie Mays San Francisco Giants equipment bag and pants, orange and black canvas bag, has "24 San Francisco Giants" on one end and "Willie Mays" on the other, includes 1968 Spalding pants with tags............................ $825

• Willie Mays game-used glove, MacGregor, with "Mays" written in marker on the thumb $4,950

• Sadaharu Oh Japanese-manufactured game-used bat, with pine tar, cracked but restored, also includes three autographed baseballs $1,650

• "At Home With Jackie Robinson" Bond Bread poster, 11x15, a companion to the 1947 card set, this unused color cardboard window poster shows Robinson as a Brooklyn Dodger rookie, plus his wife and child $1,100

Mr. Mint's 24th Dec. 6, 1993, telephone auction

New York Yankee memorabilia was the center of attention during Alan "Mr. Mint" Rosen's 24th major telephone auction Dec. 6, 1993, in

Montvale, N.J. But there were plenty of unusual items for non-Yankee fans, too.

Honus Wagner's personal shaving kit sold for $970, against a minimum bid of $500. The gold-plated Gillette safety razor box is engraved with the letters "J.H.W." Inside the purple velvet-lined box is a razor-blade holder and a very ornate initialed two-piece razor. It came from the Wagner estate and included a letter of authenticity from Leslie Wagner Blair, the granddaughter of Honus Wagner.

Leland's Nov. 20-21, 1993, Doubleheader auction

Boston Red Sox first baseman Bill Buckner has kept his sense of humor regarding the 1986 World Series, when he made a costly error in Game 6 to allow the winning run to score for the New York Mets.

The 10k-gold diamond-studded ring Buckner was awarded after the Mets ultimately went on to win the World Series was up for bids in Leland's Nov. 20-21, 1993, Doubleheader auction. The ring sold for $33,000, against a presale estimate of $6,500-$7,500 made by the New York City auction house.

In a letter which accompanied the ring, Buckner wrote: "Hope you enjoy my 1986 World Series ring (Losers reward). The nightmare of 1986 is over! I'm off the hook. Your pal, Bill Buckner."

The ring has a diamond-studded "B" on a maroon stone, framed by the words "American League Champions." "Buckner 6" (his uniform number) and a Red Sox logo are on one side, while an image of Fenway Park and the date, 1986, are on the other.

Leland's Feb. 20, 1993, Souvenirs auction

The contract which sent Babe Ruth from the Boston Red Sox to the New York Yankees was one of several big-ticket items sold during Leland's Feb. 20, 1993, Souvenirs auction.

The New York city auction house had a phone bidder who paid $99,000 for the 1919 contract, which detailed the conditions and sale of Ruth from the Red Sox to the Yankees, including a stipulation that if Ruth demanded a raise over his $10,000 salary, the Red Sox would help the Yankees pay the increase. The six-page typed document, dated Dec. 26, 1919, was notarized by Yankees' owner Jacob Ruppert and Red Sox President Harry Frazee.

A 43-pound bronze commemorative slab identical to one given to Mickey Mantle on his day at Yankee Stadium in 1969 sold for $33,000. The 24x18-inch slab, which lists Mantle's accomplishments, is one of only three known to exist; one is at Mantle's New York restaurant, while another is in Yankee Stadium's Yankee Park.

Pete Rose's 1978 Silver Wraith Rolls Royce, with "PETE" Ohio license plates, sold for $44,000, while his 1975 World Series Most Valuable Player ring sold for $12,000. His 3,000th hit baseball, as noted by Rose on the ball, sold for $13,750.

Leland's Aug. 4, 1992, Hall of Fame auction

What would you pay for the ball Mookie Wilson hit through Bill Buckner's legs to give the New York Mets a victory over the Boston Red Sox in Game 6 of the 1986 World Series?

One ex "Major Leaguer" was willing to pay the highest price ever paid for one baseball, according to Joshua Evans, the owner of Leland's, the New York city auction house which put the ball up for bids in its Hall of Fame auction Aug. 4, 1992.

Evans had estimated the ball would sell for between $8,000-$10,000. But a telephone bidder, actor Charlie Sheen, he of "Eight Men Out"

and "Major League" movie fame, paid $93,500 for the ball.

An autographed Mets warm-up jacket Seaver wore between 1967-69 sold for $11,000, but contained an item inside its pocket which Evans deemed priceless; he gave the item - a toothpick - a presale estimate of "?".

The toothpick, which eventually sold for $440, included a letter of authenticity from Seaver, which stated, in part, "This is a toothpick left in my Mets warm-up jacket worn by me in the late 60's (sic). I had given this to my good friend Arthur Richman. It is 100% authentic, original and unrestored."

Richard Wolffers auction Sept. 8, 1993

The first patented baseball and patented bat, contributed by the U.S. Patent Office, were among the items which were sold during a Richard Wolffers auction Sept. 8, 1993.

The 14-inch model bat, which sold for $41,250, included a handwritten tag dated Oct. 30, 1886, and was issued to George W. Hill. The bat was slit at the top of the barrel, allowing it to be packed with rubber or leather. The designer claimed this would send the ball further when it was hit.

The baseball, which had patent number 79719 handwritten on its tag, sold for $14,300. The ball, which was cut in half to show its construction and stuffing, was issued to inventor Henry A. Alden and was dated July 7, 1868.

A baseball signed by Joe DiMaggio and his wife Norma Jean (Marilyn Monroe) sold for $9,350.

Sotheby's auction Feb. 29, 1992

• Madonna baseball uniform: Pink jumper worn by singer Madonna in the baseball movie "League of Their Own;" Rockford Peaches emblem; GPBL patch; #5......................$7,150.
• A piece of Joe DiMaggio's wedding cake: Nov. 19, 1939; DiMaggio weds actress Dorothy Arnold in San Francisco; guests were given cake wrapped in cellophane to take home; two bisque columns and a rose; includes wedding and reception invitations and a picture of the newlyweds cutting the cake ....$1,210.

Prices realized for uniforms

* Ernie Banks' 1970 Chicago Cubs jersey, $13,200, Leland's, Nov. 20-21, 1993
* Roberto Clemente's 1967 Pittsburgh Pirates road jersey, $13,200, Leland's, Nov. 20-21, 1993
* Ty Cobb's 1921-22 Detroit Tigers jersey, $82,500, Sotheby's, Feb. 29, 1992
* Joe DiMaggio's 1939 New York Yankees jersey, $132,000, Richard Wolffers, Sept. 8, 1993
* Joe DiMaggio's 1941 New York Yankees uniform, $99,000, Sotheby's, Feb. 29, 1992
* Lou Gehrig's 1927 New York Yankees home pinstripe jersey, $363,000, Richard Wolffers, Sept. 9, 1992
* Lou Gehrig's 1937-39 New York Yankees gray flannel road jersey, $198,000, Richard Wolffers, Sept. 8, 1993
* Lou Gehrig's red-white-blue pinstriped jersey, used when he and several other American players toured Japan in 1931, $110,000, Leland's, Feb. 20, 1993
* Sandy Koufax's 1966 Los Angeles Dodgers jersey, $24,200, Richard Wolffers, June 2, 1993
* Mickey Mantle's 1960 New York Yankees home jersey, $111,100, Leland's, Jan. 2, 1992
* Mickey Mantle's 1967 New York Yankees road jersey, $71,500, Leland's, July 24, 1991
* Roger Maris' 1961 New York Yankees flannel pinstripe, $132,000, Sotheby's, Feb. 29, 1992
* Roger Maris' 1960 New York Yankees home jersey, $66,000, Leland's, Jan. 2, 1992
* Eddie Mathews' 1965 Milwaukee Braves home jersey, autographed, $24,200, Richard Wolffers, June 2, 1993
* Willie Mays' 1954 New York Giants flannel road jersey, $31,900, Richard Wolffers, Feb. 18, 1993
* Willie Mays' 1965 San Francisco Giants road jersey and pants, $13,200, Richard Wolffers, June 2, 1993
* John McGraw's 1913-14 New York Giants flannel road jersey and pants, $15,950, Richard Wolffers, Sept. 8, 1993
* Stan Musial's 1962 St. Louis Cardinals jersey, signed, $25,300, Richard Wolffers, Feb. 18, 1993
* Stan Musial's 1956 St. Louis Cardinals jersey, $14,300, Richard Wolffers, Sept. 8, 1993
* Jackie Robinson's 1950 Brooklyn Dodgers home flannel jersey, $55,000, Richard Wolffers, Feb. 18, 1993
* Pete Rose's 1981 Philadelphia Phillies road jersey, $3,025, Leland's, Nov. 20-21, 1993
* Babe Ruth's 1938 Brooklyn Dodgers road flannel, $176,000, Richard Wolffers, Sept. 9, 1992
* Babe Ruth's 1929-30 New York Yankees gray flannel road jersey, $132,000, Leland's, Nov. 20-21, 1993
* Babe Ruth's 1926 New York Yankees World Series home jersey, $82,500, Leland's, Jan. 15, 1992
* Tom Seaver's 1969 New York Mets home jersey, $55,000, Leland's, Aug. 2, 1992
* Warren Spahn's 1962 Milwaukee Braves home jersey, signed, $16,500, Richard Wolffers, June 2, 1993
* Casey Stengel's 1924 Boston Braves jersey, $7,700, Richard Wolffers, Sept. 8, 1993
* Honus Wagner's flannel Pittsburgh Pirates jersey, $115,500, Richard Wolffers, Sept. 8, 1993
* Ted Williams' 1941 Boston Red Sox road jersey, from the season he hit .406, $71,500, Leland's, Nov. 20-21, 1993
* Ted Williams' 1955 Boston Red Sox jersey, signed, $93,500, Richard Wolffers, Sept. 8, 1993
* Carl Yastrzemski's 1975 Boston Red Sox road jersey, $3,025, Leland's Nov. 20-21, 1993

Miscellaneous

Advertising/promotional

• Dizzy Dean Falstaff Beer advertising fan, 1940s, features color photo of Dean.. $85
• Don Drysdale Spalding Glove 11x18 advertising poster........ $95
• Steve Garvey autographed Sports Illustrated poster, 24x36 .... $30
• 1937 Lou Gehrig Camels color cartoon ad from April 17, 1937, issue of Time magazine.. $45
• Lou Gehrig 36x24 poster issued by the U.S. Post Office promoting his stamp... $50
• Mickey Mantle Holiday Inn postcard, color photo shows Mantle in a dugout lounge of the motel $35
• 1956 Eddie Mathews Greyhound Bus promotional, 8x10 with Milwaukee Braves schedule.. $75
• 1960s Willie Mays Alaga Syrup advertising poster, 10x20, has Mays endorsing the product, says "Say Hey! Love that real ribbon cane flavor"... $95
• Cal Ripken Jr./Lou Gehrig special Nike commemorative piece for Ripken's record-breaking 2,131st game, dated Sept. 6, 1995, only available at the game..................................... $80
• Pete Rose Norelco T-shirt advertising "Norelco Hustles Harder For You" $95
• 1985 Pete Rose video counter display, 14 1/2x10, heavy cardboard.. $125
• 1990 Nolan Ryan popsicle stick for Good Humor promotion $45
• 1990 Nolan Ryan Mother's Cookies shelf advertisement $135
• Mike Schmidt "Drink Your Milk" ad display $50
• Duke Snider Cooper Tires advertising sign, 1960-61 cardboard sign with a black-and-white batting pose of Snider, 21x21.. $400
• Ted Williams movie 3D store display standup, early 1950s $1,500
• Ted Williams 1950s Moxie advertising piece, small cardboard die-cut card, slipped into each six-pack carton of Moxie, it has Williams' endorsement, shows him kneeling with a bat.......................... $250
• 1958 Ted Williams Louisville Slugger advertising card, 5x6, black-and-white photo on the front, player model gloves on the back $250
• 1960s large cellophane bag, pictures Ted Williams, details for the Sears/Williams insulated underwear which came in it............... $10
• 1994 cardboard standup advertising sign, says "Coming Right After Labor Day," promotes Ken Burns' "Baseball" documentary, 12x18... $20
• 1993 Budweiser large inflatable glove advertising the World Series.. $100

• 1951 Iron City Beer Pittsburgh Pirates advertising schedule, 21x13... $150
• Louisville Slugger bats "Over the Fence Records" promotional poster, features stars who use Hillerich & Bradsby bats, such as Gehrig, Hornsby, DiMaggio and Williams, 1950s, 11x17, black-and-white $100
• Louisville Slugger poster for the 1949 All-Star Game, features Williams, Jackie Robinson and Musial, 1950s, 11x17, black-and-white $110
• Louisville Slugger bat poster, "It's Performance That Makes Them Famous," features Mantle, Jackie Robinson and others, 1950s, 11x17, black-and-white $95
• Louisville Slugger bat poster, "Star Performance," features Musial, DiMaggio, Williams and Mize, 1950s, 11x17, black-and-white $85
• Louisville Slugger bat poster, "Gunning for new home run records," features Mantle, Snider, Berra and others, 1950s, 11x17, black-and-white $110
• Louisville Slugger bat poster, "Their Big Sticks Keep Blasting Out The Hits," includes Williams, Jackie Robinson, Kiner and others, 1950s, 11x17, black-and-white............................. $85
• Louisville Slugger bat poster, features facsimile signatures of several players who use the bats, 1950s, 11x17, black-and-white $50
• 1920s Martin's Liniment unused bottle with box, pictures pitcher Mike Martin on both, used to rub down pitchers' arms, paperwork includes several player endorsements $200
• 1993 McDonald's glasses, feature Nolan Ryan or Roberto Clemente.. $35-$45 each
• Circa 1910 Piedmont Cigarettes advertising hand-held cardboard fan, shaped like a baseball with a ball with a smiling face on it $200
• Rawlings glove poster, features Mantle with his gloves, 1950s, 8 1/2x11, black-and-white... $85
• Rawlings glove poster, features Mantle and Bauer, "Rawlings Gloves are a favorite with the Yankees," 1950s, 8 1/2x11, black-and-white $50
• Rawlings glove poster, features Musial, "Look At The Record, Rawlings Makes the Gloves Preferred By Most Major Leaguers," 1950s, 8 1/2x11, black-and-white................... $35
• Seagram's 16x20 mirrors, 1970s, feature Gehrig, Mays, Banks, Hodges, Young, Cobb, Ruth, or Clemente............$100-$150 each
• Spalding advertising poster for the "Babe Ruth Story," 1950s, 11x17, black-and-white... $95
• 1983 United States Postal Service poster advertising the new Babe Ruth stamp $15

1960 MacGregor cards

The MacGregor Sporting Goods Co. was one of the pioneers in celebrity marketing, creating an advisory staff in 1960 to promote its products. The 25-card set features black-and-white photography of several stars and lesser lights, and even a couple of managers. The cards are 3 3/4" by 5" with a thin white border and the words "MacGregor Baseball Advisory Staff of Champions" on the bottom panel. The cards are unnumbered and are blank-backed, and include a facsimile autograph in white on the front photo. A complete set of 25 cards is worth $825 in Near Mint condition. Individual cards are worth $15, unless noted. The players featured are: Hank Aaron ($185), Richie Ashburn ($45), Gus Bell, Lou Berberet, Jerry Casale, Del Crandall, Art Ditmar, Gene Freese, James Gilliam ($22), Ted Kluszewski ($35), Jim Landis, Al Lopez ($22), Willie Mays ($185), Bill Mazeroski ($35), Mike McCormick, Gil McDougald ($22), Russ Nixon, Bill Rigney, Robin Roberts ($35), Frank Robinson ($65), John Roseboro ($18.50), Red Schoendienst ($30), Bill Skowron ($22), Daryl Spencer and Johnny Temple.

1965 MacGregor cards

The 1965 MacGregor set is similar to earlier issues, with only a slight change in dimension to 3 1/2" by 5" and reduced in size to only 10 players. The cards are blank-backed and unnumbered and have a glossy finish. The complete set of 10 cards is worth $275 in Near Mint condition. Individual cards are worth $8, unless noted. The players in the set are: Roberto Clemente ($125), Al Downing, Johnny Edwards, Ron Hansen, Deron Johnson, Willie Mays ($125), Tony Oliva ($15), Claude Osteen, Bobby Richardson ($12) and Zoilo Versalles.

1955 Rawlings Stan Musial

Though missing from Topps and Bowman card sets from 1954-57, Cardinals superstar Stan Musial wasn't entirely unavailable on baseball cards. In about 1955 he appeared on a series of six cards found on boxes of Rawlings baseball gloves carrying Musial's endorsement. The cards feature black-and-white photos of Musial set against a blue background. Because the cards were part of a display box, they are blank-backed. Depending on the position on the box, the cards measure 2" by 3" (#1a and 2a) or 2 1/2" by 3 3/4" (#1-4). Cards are numbered in a yellow star at upper left. A complete set of 6 is worth $1,200 in Near Mint condition; individual cards are worth $200. The set of cards are: 1. Musial portrait, 1a. Musial portrait with bat, 2. Musial kneeling, 2a. Musial portrait, 3. Musial swinging, 4. Musial batting pose.

A *Rawlings* TRADING CARD

1964 Rawlings glove box

Measuring about 2 3/8" by 4" when properly cut off the glove boxes on which they were printed, these full-color cards show stars of the day posing with their Rawlings glove prominently displayed. The blank-backed unnumbered cards are checklisted alphabetically. The quality of the cutting should be considered in grading these cards. In actuality, the cards were not meant to be cut from the boxes, but rather to show which premium photo was packed inside the glove box. A complete set of 8 is worth $450; individual cards are worth $25, unless noted. The players in the set are: Ken Boyer ($35), Willie Davis, Dick Groat, Mickey Mantle ($200), Brooks Robinson ($60), Warren Spahn ($50), Tom Tresh and Billy Williams.

1964 Rawlings premium photos

One premium photo was inserted into each baseball glove box sold by Rawlings in 1964. The 8" by 9 1/2" full-color photos were advertised on the outside of the boxes in miniature form. Each photo pictures a player posed with his Rawlings leather prominently displayed. A black facsimile autograph is printed on the front. A complete set of 8 is worth $400; individual cards are worth $15, unless noted. The players in the set are: Ken Boyer ($25), Willie Davis, Dick Groat, Mickey Mantle ($200), Brooks Robinson ($85), Warren Spahn ($75), Tom Tresh and Billy Williams ($45).

1969 Rawlings Reggie Jackson

How this card was distributed is not certain today. If there are any other cards in the series they are not known. This black-and-white card of Reggie Jackson measures 3" by 5" and features a closeup portrait on the front, with a white strip at the bottom which holds a facsimile autograph. The back has Jackson's minor league stats, career highlights and a Rawlings ad. The card is worth $90 in Near Mint condition.

Baseballs

• Official National League Baseball, which Luis Tiant signed and gave to Bill Madlock, it says "To Dog, Best of Luck, From Your Friend, Luis Tiant, 9-30-81" $40
• Cal Ripken Jr. autographed special official American League baseball, has orange stitching, #8 on side panel, 2,130 and 2,131 on other side $85
• Baseball signed by 11 living members of the 500 Home Run Club (Aaron, Banks, Jackson, Killebrew, Mantle, Mathews, Mays, McCovey, Frank Robinson, Schmidt, Williams)...$750
• Baseball signed by eight members of the 300 Wins Club (Carlton, Niekro, Perry, Ryan, Seaver, Spahn, Sutton, Wynn) $275
• Baseball signed by four players with 100 or more stolen bases in a season (Brock, Coleman, Henderson, Wills)$100
• Baseball signed by nine pitchers with 3,000 or more strikeouts (Blyleven, Carlton, Gibson, Jenkins, Niekro, Perry, Ryan, Seaver, Sutton)....................................... $350
• Baseball signed by the "Magnificent Seven" outfielders (Aaron, DiMaggio, Mantle, Mays, Snider, Frank Robinson, Williams) $4,500
• 1988 Team USA Olympic baseball, signed by 20 players $60
• April 22, 1993, ball used during Chris Bosio's no hitter, inscribed, includes autographed unused game ticket... $225
• Baseball used in Game 3 of the 1921 World Series, Yankees vs. New York Giants, Oct. 7, 1921, noted as being the final out in the Giants' 13-5 win $2,700
• Baseball used in Game 2 of the 1923 World Series, Yankees vs. New York Giants, Oct. 11, 1923........................ $5,500
• Official baseballs for 1986 and 1989 World Series games, unused and unsigned..$40 each
• Official baseballs for the 1982, 1984, 1987 and 1989 All-Star games, unused and unsigned ....$30-$40 each
• 1950s Wilson official baseballs, sealed and unopened $75
• 1975 MacGregor Hank Aaron 715th home run baseball with facsimile autograph... $45
• Special Don Larsen baseball, commemorates his no-hit game in the 1957 World Series, in original wrap $100

Fotoball USA Inc., San Diego, Calif., has issued during the 1990s synthetic baseballs with retired and current baseball players' likenesses, and baseballs featuring team rosters and logos. They include: Roberto Alomar, Moises Alou, Brady Anderson, Steve Avery, Carlos Baerga, Jeff Bagwell, Ernie Banks, Jay Bell, Albert Belle, Johnny Bench, Andy Benes, Jason Bere, Craig Biggio, Dante Bichette, Wade Boggs, Barry Bonds, Bobby Bonilla, Jay Buhner, Ellis Burks, Brett Butler, Ken Caminiti, Jose Canseco, Chuck Carr, Joe Carter, Will Clark, Roberto Clemente, Roger Clemens, David Cone, Darren Daulton, Lenny Dykstra, Cecil Fielder, Travis Fryman, Andres Galarraga, Tom Glavine, Juan Gonzalez, Mark Grace, Ken Griffey Jr., Marquis Grissom, Tony Gwynn, Rickey Henderson, Gregg Jefferies, Randy Johnson, Wally Joyner, Dave Justice, Eric Karros, Jeff King, Chuck Knoblauch, John Kruk, Mark Langston, Barry Larkin, Kenny Lofton, Greg Maddux, Kirt Manwaring, Don Mattingly, Jack McDowell, Fred McGriff, Mark McGwire, Brian McRae, Orlando Merced, Paul Molitor, Raul Mondesi, Hal Morris, Eddie Murray, Mike Mussina, David Nied, Hideo Nomo, Rafael Palmeiro, Mike Piazza, Phil Plantier, Kirby Puckett, Jose Rijo, Cal Ripken Jr., Brooks Robinson, Ivan Rodriguez, Alex Rodriguez, Bret Saberhagen, Tim Salmon, Gary Sheffield, Ruben Sierra, Ozzie Smith, Lee Smith, Sammy Sosa, Frank Thomas, Andy Van Slyke, Greg Vaughn, Mo Vaughn, Robin Ventura, Larry Walker, Matt Williams, Ted Williams, Dave Winfield and Carl Yastrzemski.

Bats

• A Famous Slugger plastic bat rack and miniature player bats; circa late 1950s, offered by Famous Slugger Yearbooks ....$75-$100
• Hank Aaron 715 Home Runs Magnavox bat in original box $375
• Jose Canseco's used aluminum softball bat, from Rock 'n Jock competition, signed $225
• Kansas City Athletics Dick Green "Green Bat Day" bat, 1960s.. $85
• Mickey Mantle/Willie Mays 1968 Transogram "Zippee" bat and ball set with cardboard picture container $150
• 1969 Louisville Slugger plastic bats bank, includes Mantle, Clemente and Rose, with original box.......................... $85

Beer cans/pop cans

More than 50 commemorative baseball-related beer cans have been produced featuring major league players, minor league teams and six major league teams (Pirates, Twins, Cubs, White Sox, Reds and Orioles). Many have team/player photos, drawings, schedules or stats incorporated into the design and were sold for a limited time in a limited area. Beer can trade shows are the best places to find older cans no longer sold in stores. Most collectors prefer cans which have been opened from the bottom.

Anheuser-Busch, St. Louis, Mo., issued a Red Schoendienst commemorative bank can in 1977, honoring the dedication of Schoendienst Field, Feb. 20, 1977, in Germantown, Ill.

C. Schmidt & Sons Inc., Philadelphia, Pa., issued four Casey's Lager Beer cans in 1980 featuring Duke Snider, Richie Ashburn, Whitey Ford and Monte Irvin.

National Brewing Co., Baltimore, Md., issued a National Bohemian Beer can with a 1970 Baltimore Orioles schedule and a can in 1992 commemorating Baltimore's Memorial Stadium from 1954-91. Adolph Coors Co., Golden, Colo., issued a can in 1992 commemorating the Baltimore Orioles' 1991 season.

G. Heileman Brewing Co., La Crosse, Wis., has done several cans. Old Style 16-ounce brands in 1990 featured Comiskey Park, Ron Santo, Billy Williams, Fergie Jenkins and the 1990 Divisional Championship. A 1991 Old Style Light can featured Billy Williams, while 1992 Special Export 16-ounce green cans honor the 1961-91 Minnesota Twins and 1992 Special Export Light 16-ounce blue cans honor the 1961-91 Minnesota Twins.

Hudepohl Brewing Co., Cincinnati, Ohio, issued cans in 1976 and 1977 commemorating the 1975 and 1976 World Champion Cincinnati Reds. There are two varieties in 1976 - with either a cream or grey box score background.

Pittsburgh Brewing Co., Pittsburgh, Pa., issued Iron City Beer & Draft cans, focusing on the Pittsburgh Pirates. The 1973 cans featured Three Rivers Stadium. Ten 1974 cans featured the Pirates' team record from 1887-1973; participation in the World Series; 1974 home schedule; 1974 TV schedule; 1974 roster of pitchers, catchers; 1974 roster of infielders, outfielders; 1960 World Series; 1971 World Series; World Championships from 1950-73; and a letter from the brewery's president. Two 1980 cans featured the 1979 World Champions and a salute to the 1979 champs. A 1988 can featured "Hardball 88," while a 1990 can honored the Pittsburgh Tradition. Two 1991 cans were issued featuring the Eastern Division Championship and ticket stubs.

1977-78 Royal Crown Cola pop cans

They don't fit into plastic sheets, they rust and they may leak, and all they do is collect dust. But if you have the room to display or store them, Royal Crown cans featuring baseball players on them pose a fairly inexpensive challenge to collectors.

The cans, issued in 1977-78, feature more than a dozen Hall of Famers, even though the team insignias are blacked out on the players' caps. The cans, produced prior to the introduction of today's one-piece aluminum pop cans, are constructed in three parts - a top, center and bottom which are crimped and soldered together. Rust may appear at the seams if the cans are in storage for a while; if the can still has soda inside it, you can expect it to spring a leak, due to the acidity of the cola. Cans are more valuable when they appear to be full, so they should be opened from the bottom.

There were 70 cans produced in 1977; in 1978 100 cans were made. Many of the players appeared in both sets, some with the same black-and-white pictures, some with different ones. The photos were set in a plain, white circle; 1978 cans have a red border around the circle. No insignias appeared on the players' caps, indicating RC didn't pay the teams for the rights to reproduce their logos.

Both years used the same basic blue color scheme, with red and white trim. Cans from 1977 had player biographical data in a square, while those produced in

1978 had a career-highlights summary inside a baseball. At the bottom of the ball was the can number, designated as "No. x of 100."

The biggest problem with buying RC cans is not the cost, but rather finding the cans. Many dealers do not take them to card shows because they are too bulky and take up valuable table space. Nor are the cans generally advertised for sale in hobby papers because it usually costs more to mail them than they are worth. The first price listed below is for a can; the second value is for the can flats, the 5x8 3/8" square tin strips used to make the cans.

1977 Royal Crown pop cans

Sal Bando, $3/$6
Mark Belanger, $1-$3.50/$6
Johnny Bench, $10/$30
Vida Blue, $3-$5/$6
Bobby Bonds, $2-$3/$6
Bob Boone, $1-$3/$6
Larry Bowa, $1/$6
Steve Braun, $3/$6
George Brett, $10/$25
Lou Brock, $10-$15/$20
Bert Campaneris, $2/$6
Bill Campbell, $1-$3/$6
Jose Cardenal, $1/$6
Rod Carew, $5-$10/$25
Dave Cash, $1-$3/$6
Cesar Cedeno, $1-$3/$6
Ron Cey, $2/$6
Chris Chambliss, $2-$4/$6
Dave Concepcion, $2/$7
Mark Fidrych, $2/$6
Rollie Fingers, $8-$10/$15
George Foster, $2-$3/$6
Wayne Garland, $3/$6
Ralph Garr, $1-$3/$6
Steve Garvey, $3.50-$5/$7
Bobby Grich, $1-$3/$6
Ken Griffey, $2- $3.50/$6
Don Gullett, $1-$3/$6
Mike Hargrove, $3/$6
Catfish Hunter, $5/$15
Randy Jones, $1/$6
Dave Kingman, $4/$8
Dave LaRoche, $1/$6
Ron LeFlore, $2/$6
Greg Luzinski, $2/$6
Fred Lynn, $2-$3.50/$6
Bill Madlock, $1/$6
Jon Matlack, $1-$4/$8
Gary Matthews, $1-$3/$6
Bake McBride, $1/$6
Hal McRae, $2-$3/$6
Andy Messersmith, $1-$3/$6
Rick Monday, $1/$6

John Montefusco, $1-$3/$6
Joe Morgan, $10/$20
Thurman Munson, $5-$10/$10
Al Oliver, $2-$3.50/$6
Amos Otis, $1/$6
Jim Palmer, $5-$10/$25
Dave Parker, $2-$3/$6
Fred Patek, $1/$6
Gaylord Perry, $10/$20
Marty Perez, $1/$6
Tony Perez, $2-$4/$8
J.R. Richard, $1/$6
Pete Rose, $10/$35
Joe Rudi, $2-$3/$6
Mike Schmidt, $10/$35
Tom Seaver, $10-$12/$35
Bill Singer, $1/$6
Rusty Staub, $1-$4/$6
Don Sutton, $2/$7
Gene Tenace, $2/$6
Luis Tiant, $2/$7
Ellis Valentine, $1-$3/$6
Claudell Washington, $1-$3/$6
Butch Wynegar, $1/$6
Carl Yastzremski, $10-$15/$30
Robin Yount, $10-$15/$20
Richie Zisk, $1.50-$2/$6

1978 Royal Crown pop cans

1. Don Sutton, $2-$3.50/$6
2. Bill Singer, $1/$5
3. Pete Rose, $10-$15/$30
4. Gene Tenace, $1-$3/$5
5. Dave Kingman, $2-$3.50/$5
6. Dave Cash, 1-$3/$5
7. Joe Morgan, $10/$15
8. Mark Belanger, $1-$3.50/$5
9. Steve Braun, $1/$5
10. Butch Wynegar, $3/$5
11. Ken Griffey, $2-$3.50/$5
12. Ron LeFlore, $1-$3/$5
13. George Foster, $2-$3/$5
14. Tony Perez, $4/$7

15. Thurman Munson, $5-$10/$10
16. Bill Campbell, $1-$3/$5
17. Andy Messersmith, $1-$3/$5
18. Mike Schmidt, $10-$15/$30
19. Ron Cey, $3/$5
20. Chris Chambliss, $3/$5
21. Ralph Garr, $1-$3/$5
22. Dave LaRoche, $1-$3/$5
23. George Brett, $10/$20
24. Bob Boone, $3/$5
25. Jeff Burroughs, $1-$3/$5
26. Bake McBride, $3/$5
27. Gary Matthews, $3/$5
28. Don Gullett, $1/$5
29. Rick Monday, $1-$3/$5
30. Al Oliver, $3.50/$5
31. Ellis Valentine, $3/$5
32. Mike Hargrove, $3/$5
33. Hal McRae, $2/$5
34. Rollie Fingers, $7-$10/$12
35. Dave Parker, $3/$5
36. Tom Seaver, $10/$30
37. Wayne Garland, $3/$5
38. Jon Matlack, $3/$5
39. Richie Zisk, $3/$5
40. Joe Rudi, $3/$5
41. Sal Bando, $3-$5/$5
42. Greg Luzinski *, $2/$5
43. Vida Blue *, $3/$5
44. Bobby Bonds, $2-$3/$6
45. Jim Palmer, $7/$20
46. Claudell Washington, $1-$3/$5
47. Dave Concepcion, $2/$6
48. Rod Carew, $10/$20
49. J.R. Richard, $3/$5
50. Rich Gossage, $2/$6
51. Cesar Cedeno, $2/$5
52. Bert Campaneris, $2/$5
53. Marty Perez, $1/$5
54. Bill Madlock, $2/$5
55. Amos Otis, $2/$5
56. Robin Yount, $10/$15
57. Bobby Grich, $1-$3/$5

58. Catfish Hunter, $5-$10/$12
59. Butch Hobson, $3/$5
60. Larry Bowa, $2/$5
61. Randy Jones *, $1-$3/$5
62. Richie Hebner, $1/$5
63. Fred Patek, $1/$5
64. John Denny, $1/$5
65. Johnny Bench, $10/$25
66. Doyle Alexander, $3/$5
67. Dusty Baker, $2/$5
68. Bert Blyleven, $3/$5
69. Lyman Bostock, $1/$5
70. Bill Buckner, $1-$3/$5
71. Steve Carlton, $10-$12/$25
72. John Candelaria, $1/$5
73. Andre Dawson, $4/$6
74. Al Cowens, $1/$5
75. Eddie Murray, $7/$30
76. Dan Driessen, $3/$5
77. Jim Rice, $3.50/$6
78. Garry Maddox, $3/$5
79. Larry Hisle, $3/$5
80. Al Hrabosky, $3/$5
81. Reggie Jackson, $10/$25
82. Tommy John, $3/$5
83. Willie McCovey, $10/$15
84. Sparky Lyle, $3/$5
85. Tug McGraw, $3/$5
86. Paul Splittorff, $3/$5
87. Bobby Murcer, $4/$8
88. Graig Nettles, $4/$6
89. Phil Niekro, $4/$7
90. Lou Piniella, $3.50/$6
91. Rick Reuschel, $3/$5
92. Frank Tanana, $3/$5
93. Nolan Ryan, $40/$75
94. Garry Templeton, $3/$5
95. Reggie Smith,$3/$5
96. Bruce Sutter, $1-$3.$5
97. Jason Thompson, $3/$5
98. Mike Torrez, $3/$5
99. Rick Wise, $1/$5
100. Bump Wills, $3/$5

* indicates the player photo is different from that used on the 1977 can.

Books

• George Brett El Segundo High School sophomore yearbook, 1969 ....$450
• Eddie Collins "Fan Favorites" composition notebook, cover features Collins in a hitting pose $250
• Dom DiMaggio's 1934 high school senior yearbook....$175
• Lou Gehrig Risque Pocket Comic Book, 4x2 1/2, 1930s, fictional story about Gehrig and Mae West $800
• Lou Gehrig 5" advertising bat, circa 1942, advertises for an upcoming book about Gehrig $150
• Tony Gwynn's 1977 high school yearbook, includes action photos $175

• Christy Mathewson "Fan Favorites" composition notebook, cover features Mathewson in a pitching pose $450
• 1964 Baseball "Finer Points" booklets set of 12, for Little, Junior, Midget and Babe Ruth players, comic book style, 3x5, illustrates techniques needed to win, giveaway items by TCF Bank $50
• 1965 Hood Ice Cream baseball instructional booklets, lot of five contains hints for Little Leaguers, Babe Ruth players $35
• 1965 New York Mets coloring book, Mr. Met on the cover ....:... $85

Bottle caps

1967-68 Coca Cola

These bottle caps were issued in 1967-68. Some of the players had changed teams from one year to the next, so some were dropped and others were added in 1968. The caps issued in 1967 are identified by an a; those issued in 1968 have a b. The caps were issued on bottles of Coke, Tab, Sprite, Fresca and some flavors of Fanta. Although Coke caps are more common, there is no difference in price for the same player on different sodas. This was a national promotion, but only the All-Stars were issued across the country. Each major league team at the time was produced, except the St. Louis Cardinals. They were distributed in the local area of that team only, which makes completing a set of all 19 teams very difficult. The All-Stars are the most readily available, so a cap of the same player is generally more valuable from the regional set than the All-Star set. The numbering is on the inside of the cap. The system for the regional sets begins with an alphabetical designation sometimes corresponding to the team name (T for Tigers) and a number from 1-18. However, for the two cities which have two teams (New York and Los Angeles), the numbers go to 35. The All-Stars are numbered in one of two ways. The Major League All-Stars are numbered from 1-35 with no alphabetical designation; this set was produced for those areas which did not have a major league city near by. The other set is divided between National (N19-N35) and American (A19-A35) League All-Stars. This set is a continuation of the regional sets. There were also eight game caps which could be sent in to Coca Cola along with complete team sets for prizes, among which were the 1967 Dexter Press oversized cards. The bottle caps are condition-sensitive because most were bent with a bottle opener and discarded.

All common All-Stars in Near Mint are $1 each, unless noted

All common regionals in Near Mint are $1.50 each, unless noted

Major League All-Stars

1. Richie Allen, $2.50
2. Pete Rose, $25
3. Brooks Robinson, $15
4. Marcelino Lopez
5. Rusty Staub, $2
6. Ron Santo, $2.50
7. Jim Nash
8. Jim Fregosi
9. Paul Casanova
10. Willie Mays, $35
11. Willie Stargell, $7
12. Tony Oliva, $2.50
13. Joe Pepitone
14. Juan Marichal, $6
15. Jim Bunning, $2.50
16. Claude Osteen
17. Carl Yastrzemski, $20
18. Harmon Killebrew, $8.50
19. Henry Aaron, $35
20. Joe Torre, $2.50
21. Ernie Banks, $15
22. Al Kaline, $15
23. Frank Robinson, $14
24. Max Alvis
25. Elston Howard, $2.50
26. Gaylord Perry, $5
27. Bill Mazeroski, $2.50
28. Ron Swoboda
29. Vada Pinson
30. Joe Morgan, $7
31. Cleon Jones
32. Willie Horton
33. Leon Wagner
34. George Scott
35. Ed Charles

National League All-Stars

N19. Henry Aaron, $35
N20. Jim Bunning, $2.50
N21. Joe Torre, $2.50
N22. Claude Osteen
N23. Ron Santo, $2.50
N24. Joe Morgan, $7
N25. Richie Allen, $2.50
N26. Ron Swoboda
N27. Ernie Banks, $15
N28. Bill Mazeroski, $2.50
N29. Willie Stargell, $7
N30. Pete Rose, $25
N31. Gaylord Perry, $5
N32. Rusty Staub, $2
N33. Vada Pinson
N34. Juan Marichal, $6
N35. Cleon Jones

American League All-Stars

A19. Al Kaline, $15
A20. Frank Howard, $2.50
A21. Brooks Robinson, $15
A22. George Scott
A23. Willie Horton
A24. Jim Fregosi
A25. Ed Charles
A26. Harmon Killebrew, $8.50
A27. Tony Oliva, $2.50
A28. Joe Pepitone
A29. Elston Howard, $2.50
A30. Jim Nash
A31. Marcelino Lopez
A32. Frank Robinson, $14
A33. Leon Wagner
A34. Max Alvis
A35. Paul Casanova

Atlanta Braves

B1a. Gary Geiger
B1b. Cecil Upshaw
B2a. Ty Cline
B2b. Tito Francona
B3. Henry Aaron, $45
B4a. Gene Oliver
B4b. Pat Jarvis
B5. Tony Cloninger
B6a. Denis Menke
B6b. Phil Niekro, $7.50
B7a. Denny LeMaster
B7b. Felix Milan
B8. Woody Woodward
B9. Joe Torre, $3
B10. Ken Johnson
B11a. Bob Bruce
B11b. Marty Martinez
B12. Felipe Alou
B13. Clete Boyer
B14a. Wade Blasingame
B14b. Sonny Jackson
B15a. Don Schwall
B15b. Deron Johnson
B16a. Dick Kelley
B16b. Claude Raymond
B17. Rico Carty
B18. Mack Jones

Baltimore Orioles

O1. Dave McNally
O2a. Luis Aparicio, $5
O2b. Jim Hardin
O3. Paul Blair
O4. Frank Robinson, $18
O5a. Jim Palmer, $14
O5b. Bruce Howard
O6a. Russ Snyder
O6b. John O'Donoghue
O7a. Stu Miller
O7b. Dave May
O8. Dave Johnson
O9. Andy Etchebarren
O10. Brooks Robinson, $20
O11. John Powell, $3
O12a. Sam Bowens
O12b. Pete Richert
O13. Curt Blefary
O14a. Ed Fisher
O14b. Mark Belanger
O15. Wally Bunker
O16a. Moe Drabowsky
O16b. Don Buford
O17. Larry Haney
O18. Tom Phoebus

Boston Red Sox

R1. Lee Stange
R2a. Carl Yastrzemski, $25
R2b. Gary Waslewski
R3a. Don Demeter
R3b. Gary Bell
R4a. Jose Santiago
R4b. John Wyatt
R5. Darrell Brandon
R6. Joe Foy
R7a. Don McMahon
R7b. Ray Culp
R8. Dalton Jones
R9a. Mike Ryan
R9b. Gene Oliver
R10a. Bob Tillman
R10b. Jose Santiago
R11. Rico Petrocelli
R12. George Scott
R13a. George Smith
R13b. Mike Andrews
R14a. Dennis Bennett
R14b. Dick Ellsworth
R15a. Hank Fischer
R15b. Norm Sieburn
R16. Jim Lonborg
R17a. Jose Tartabull
R17b. Jerry Adair
R18a. George Thomas
R18b. Elston Howard, $3.50

California Angels

L19. Len Gabrielson
L20. Jackie Hernandez
L21. Paul Schaal
L22. Lou Burdette
L23. Jimmie Hall
L24. Fred Newman
L25. Don Mincher
L26. Bob Rodgers
L27. Jack Sanford
L28. Bobby Knoop
L29. Jose Cardenal
L30. Jim Fregosi
L31. George Brunet
L32. Marcelino Lopez
L33. Minnie Rojas
L34. Jay Johnstone
L35. Ed Kirkpatrick

Chicago Cubs

C1. Ferguson Jenkins, $12
C2. Ernie Banks, $20
C3. Glenn Beckert
C4. Bob Hendley
C5. John Boccabella
C6. Ron Campbell
C7. Ray Culp
C8. Adolfo Phillips
C9. Don Bryant
C10. Randy Hundley
C11. Ron Santo, $3
C12. Lee Thomas
C13. Billy Williams, $8.50
C14. Ken Holtzman
C15. Cal Koonce
C16. Curt Simmons
C17. George Alman
C18. Byron Browne

Chicago White Sox

L1. Gary Peters

L2. Jerry Adair
L3. Al Weiss
L4. Pete Ward
L5. Hoyt Wilhelm, $6
L6. Don Buford
L7. John Buzhardt
L8. Wayne Causey
L9. Gerald McNertney
L10. Ron Hansen
L11. Tom McCraw
L12. Jim O'Toole
L13. Bill Skowron
L14. Joel Horlen
L15. Tommy John, $4
L16. Bob Locker
L17. Ken Berry
L18. Tommie Agee

Cincinnati Reds

F1. Floyd Robinson
F2. Leo Cardenas
F3. Gordy Coleman
F4. Tommy Harper
F5. Tommy Helms
F6. Deron Johnson
F7. Jim Maloney
F8. Tony Perez, $10
F9. Don Pavletich
F10. John Edwards
F11. Vada Pinson
F12. Chico Ruiz
F13. Pete Rose, $32
F14. Billy McCool
F15. Joe Nuxhall
F16. Milt Pappas
F17. Art Shamsky
F18. Dick Simpson

Cleveland Indians

I1. Luis Tiant, $5
I2. Max Alvis
I3. Larry Brown
I4a. Rocky Colavito, $4
I4b. Tommy Harper
I5a. John O'Donoghue
I5b. Vern Fuller
I6a. Pedro Gonzalez
I6b. Jose Cardenal
I7a. Gary Bell
I7b. Dave Nelson
I8. Sonny Siebert
I9. Joe Azcue
I10. Lee Maye
I11. Chico Salmon
I12. Leon Wagner
I13a. Fred Whitfield
I13b. Eddie Fischer
I14. Jack Kralick
I14b. Stan Williams
I15. Sam McDowell
I16a. Dick Radatz
I16b. Steve Hargan
I17. Vic Davalillo
I18a. Chuck Hinton
I18b. Duke Sims

Detroit Tigers

T1a. Larry Sherry
T1b. Ray Oliver
T2. Norm Cash, $5
T3a. Jerry Lumpe
T3b. Mike Marshall, $5
T4a. Dave Wickersham

T4b. Mickey Stanley
T5. Joe Sparma
T6. Dick McAuliffe
T7a. Fred Gladding
T7b. Gates Brown
T8. Jim Northrup
T9. Bill Freehan
T10. Earl Wilson
T11. Dick Tracewski
T12. Don Wert
T13a. Jake Wood
T13b. Dennis Ribant
T14. Mickey Lolich, $5
T15a. Johnny Podres
T15b. Denny McLain, $6.50
T16a. Bill Monbouquette
T16b. Ed Mathews, $12
T17. Al Kaline, $20
T18. Willie Horton

Houston Astros

H1. Dave Guisti
H2. Bob Aspromonte
H3. Ron Davis
H4a. Claude Raymond
H4b. Julio Gotay
H5a. Barry Latman
H5b. Fred Gladding
H6a. Chuck Harrison
H6b. Lee Thomas
H7a. Bill Heath
H7b. Wade Blasingame
H8a. Sonny Jackson
H8b. Denis Menke
H9. John Bateman
H10. Ron Brand
H11a. Aaron Pointer
H11b. Doug Rader
H12. Joe Morgan, $9
H13. Rusty Staub, $3
H14. Mike Cuellar
H15. Larry Dierker
H16a. Dick Farrell
H16b. Denny LeMaster
H17a. Jim Landis
H17b. Jim Wynn
H18a. Ed Mathews, $12
H18b. Don Wilson

Kansas City Athletics

K1. Jim Nash
K2. Bert Campaneris
K3. Ed Charles
K4. Wes Stock
K5. John Odom
K6. Ozzie Chavarria
K7. Jack Aker
K8. Dick Green
K9. Phil Roof
K10. Rene Lachemann
K11. Mike Hershberger
K12. Joe Nossek
K13. Roger Repoz
K14. Chuck Dobson
K15. Jim Hunter, $12
K16. Lew Krausse
K17. Danny Kater
K18. Jim Gosger

Los Angeles Dodgers

L1. Phil Regan
L2. Bob Bailey

L3. Ron Fairly
L4a. Joe Moeller
L4b. Jim Brewer
L5. Don Sutton, $8.50
L6a. Ron Hunt
L6b. Tom Haller
L7a. Jim Brewer
L7b. Rocky Colavito, $4
L8a. Lou Johnson
L8b. Jim Grant
L9a. John Roseboro
L9b. Jim Campanis
L10. Jeff Torborg
L11a. John Kennedy
L11b. Zoilo Versalles
L12. Jim Lefebvre
L13. Wes Parker
L14a. Bob Miller
L14b. Bill Singer
L15. Claude Osteen
L16a. Ron Perranoski
L16b. Len Gabrielson
L17. Willie Davis
L18. Al Ferrara

Minnesota Twins

M1a. Ron Kline
M1b. Rich Reese
M2. Bob Allison
M3a. Earl Battey
M3b. Ron Perranoski
M4a. Jim Merritt
M4b. John Roseboro
M5. Jim Perry
M6. Harmon Killebrew, $10
M7. Dave Boswell
M8. Rich Rollins
M9. Jerry Zimmerman
M10. Al Worthington
M11. Cesar Tovar
M12a. Sandy Valdespino
M12b. Jim Merritt
M13a. Zoilo Versalles
M13b. Bob Miller
M14. Dean Chance
M15a. Jim Grant
M15b. Ted Uhlaender
M16. Jim Kaat, $4
M17. Tony Oliva, $3
M18a. Andy Kosco
M18b. Rod Carew, $50

New York Mets

V19. Chuck Hiller
V20. Johnny Lewis
V21. Ed Kranepool
V22. Al Luplow
V23. Don Cardwell
V24. Cleon Jones
V25a. Bob Shaw
N7. Tom Seaver, $50
V26. John Stephenson
V27. Ron Swoboda
V28. Ken Boyer
V29. Ed Bressoud
V30. Tommy Davis
V31. Roy McMillan
V32. Jack Fisher
V33. Tug McGraw
V34. Jerry Grote
V35. Jack Hamilton

425

New York Yankees

V1. Mel Stottlemyre, $3.50
V2. Ruben Amaro
V3. Jake Gibbs
V4. Dooley Womack
V5. Fred Talbot
V6. Horace Clark
V7. Jim Bouton, $3.50
V8. Mickey Mantle, $75
V9. Elston Howard, $3.50
V10. Hal Reniff
V11. Charley Smith
V12. Bobby Murcer, $3.50
V13. Joe Pepitone
V14. Al Downing
V15. Steve Hamilton
V16. Fritz Peterson
V17. Tom Tresh
V18. Roy White

Philadelphia Phillies

P1. Richie Allen, $3
P2. Bob Wine
P3. Johnny Briggs
P4. John Callison
P5. Doug Clemons

P6. Dick Groat
P7. Dick Ellsworth
P8. Phil Linz
P9. Clay Dalrymple
P10. Bob Uecker, $8.50
P11. Cookie Rojas
P12. Tony Taylor
P13. Bill White
P14. Larry Jackson
P15. Chris Short
P16. Jim Bunning, $3
P17. Tony Gonzalez
P18. Don Lock

Pittsburgh Pirates

E1. Al McBean
E2. Gene Alley
E3. Donn Clendenon
E4. Bob Veale
E5. Pete Mikkelsen
E6. Bill Mazeroski, $3
E7. Steve Blass
E8. Manny Mota
E9. Jim Pagliaroni
E10. Jesse Gonder
E11. Jose Pagan

E12. Willie Stargell, $9
E13. Maury Wills, $4
E14. Roy Face
E15. Woodie Fryman
E16. Vernon Law
E17. Matty Alou
E18. Roberto Clemente, $50

San Francisco Giants

G1. Bob Bolin
G2. Ollie Brown
G3. Jim Davenport
G4a. Tito Fuentes
G4b. Bob Barton
G5a. Norm Sieburn
G5b. Jack Hiatt
G6. Jim Hart
G7. Juan Marichal, $7.50
G8. Hal Lanier
G9a. Tom Haller
G9b. Ron Hunt
G10a. Bob Barton
G10b. Ron Herbal
G11. Willie McCovey, $10
G12. Mike McCormick
G13. Frank Linzy

G14. Ray Sadecki
G15. Gaylord Perry, $6
G16. Lindy McDaniel
G17. Willie Mays, $45
G18. Jesus Alou

Washington Senators

S1. Bob Humphreys
S2. Bernie Allen
S3. Ed Brinkman
S4. Pete Richert
S5. Camilio Pascual
S6. Frank Howard, $3
S7. Casey Cox
S8. Jim King
S9. Paul Casanova
S10. Dick Lines
S11. Dick Nen
S12. Ken McMullen
S13. Bob Saverine
S14. Jim Hannan
S15. Darold Knowles
S16. Phil Ortega
S17. Ken Harrelson
S18. Fred Valentine

Baseball game caps - "Match the Stars" or "Tops & Tips"

19. SS Fields Ball, Throws to 2nd Baseman to Force Runner
20. 2nd Baseman Relays to 1st Baseman
21. 1st Baseman Completes Double Play
22. Pitcher Fields Bunt, Throws to 2nd Baseman to Force Runner at Second
23. 2nd Baseman Relays to 1st Baseman

24. 1st Baseman Completes Double Play
25. Centerfielder Makes Catch, Then Throws Quickly to Catcher
26. Catcher Takes Throw, Tags Out Runner Trying to Score After Catch

---

Buttons/Pins/Badges

1970s-80s Sports Photo Association, 3"

$20 - Reggie Jackson, Yankees; $18 - Johnny Bench, Reds; Mike Schmidt, Phillies; Robin Yount, Brewers; $14 - Billy Martin, A's; Jim Palmer, Orioles; $13 - Lee Mazzilli, Mets; Lee Mazzilli, Yankees; Rusty Staub, Mets; $12 - Rod Carew, Angels; Rick Cerone, Yankees; Catfish Hunter, Yankees; Tommy John, Yankees; Dave Kingman, Mets; Eddie Murray, Orioles; $10 - Gary Carter, Expos; Larry Christiansen, Phillies; Steve Garvey, batting; Steve Garvey, kneeling; Richie Hebner, Phillies; Tug McGraw, Phillies; Tom Seaver, Reds; Ken Singleton, Orioles; $9 - Bob Boone, Phillies; Larry Bowa, Phillies; Rick Sutcliffe, Cubs; $8 - Rich Gossage, Yankees; Ross Grimsley, Expos; Jerry Mumphrey, Yankees; Ron Reed, Phillies; Ellis Valentine, Expos; Fernando Valenzuela

1970s-80s Hall of Famers, 3"

$20 - Duke Snider, Dodgers; Ted Williams, Red Sox; $18 - Hank Greenberg, Tigers; $15 - Bob Gibson, Cardinals; Monte Irvin, N.Y. Giants; George Kell, Red Sox

1970s-80s standup buttons, 3 1/2"

$20 - Hank Aaron, Braves; Hank Aaron, 715-4/8/74; Lou Brock, Stolen Base King; Reggie Jackson, A's;

Willie Mays, Mets; Pete Rose, Reds; $15 - Richie Allen, White Sox; Luis Aparicio, Red Sox; Vida Blue, A's; Juan Marichal, Giants; Joe Morgan, Reds; Willie Stargell, Pirates; Don Sutton, Dodgers; Maury Wills, Dodgers; $12 - Carlton Fisk, Red Sox; $10 - Stan Bahnsen, White Sox; Glenn Beckert, Cubs; Dwight Evans, Red Sox; Ken Holtzman, Red Sox; Dave Kingman, Giants; Mickey Lolich, Tigers; Bill Madlock, Cubs; Joe Rudi, A's; Luis Tiant, Red Sox

Miscellaneous team pins

• Baltimore Orioles, ball, bats and Oriole, red, white and blue, 3/4" $10
• Boston Red Sox, Red Sox logo $10
• California Angels, halo over ball with wings, logo, 3/4" $10
• Cleveland Indians, Indian logo, 3/4" $10
• Kansas City Royals, 1985 World Champions, 3" $5
• Los Angeles Dodgers, ball and logo, red, white and blue, 3/4" $10
• Milwaukee Braves, Indian running, tomahawk and drums, 2" 1954 .... $45
• Minnesota Twins, 1965 American League Champions $65
• Minnesota Twins, 1987 World Champions $5
• Oakland Athletics, elephant logo, 3/4" $10
• Philadelphia Phillies, ball, stars and logo, 3/4" $10
• Philadelphia Phillies, Fightin Phillies, player leaning on bat logo $10
• Pittsburgh Pirates, Pirate logo, 3/4" $10
• St. Louis Cardinals, small pennant with team logo $60
• San Diego Padres, Padre swinging a bat, 1 1/2" $15
• San Francisco Giants, "I Am A Giant Fan," 3/4" $12

Ace Novelty player pins

In 1990, Ace Novelty Inc., Bellevue, Wash., issued MVP Major League Players collectors lapel pins which feature current players and include a 1990 Score baseball card. American League players are: Jim Abbott, Harold Baines, George Bell, Bert Blyleven, Wade Boggs, George Brett, Jose Canseco, Roger Clemens, Alvin Davis, Brian Downing, Dennis Eckersley, Tony Fernandez, Carlton Fisk, Julio Franco, Gary Gaetti, Dan Gladden, Tom Gordon, Mike Greenwell, Ken Griffey Jr., Ozzie Guillen, Rickey Henderson, Teddy Higuera, Kent Hrbek, Bo Jackson, Brook Jacoby, Doug Jones, Wally Joyner, Chet Lemon, Jeffrey Leonard, Don Mattingly, Fred McGriff, Mark McGwire, Paul Molitor, Jack Morris, Gregg Olson, Kirby Puckett, Harold Reynolds, Dave Righetti, Bill Ripken, Cal Ripken Jr., Nolan Ryan, Bret Saberhagen, Steve Sax, Ruben Sierra, Lee Smith, Cory Sndyer, Dave Stewart, Dave Stieb, B.J. Surhoff, Greg Swindell, Mickey Tettleton, Bobby Thigpen, Alan Trammell, Greg Walker, Lou Whitaker, Dave Winfield and Robin Yount.

National Leaguers are: Barry Bonds, Bobby Bonilla, Tom Brunansky, Brett Butler, Jack Clark, Will Clark, Eric Davis, Glenn Davis, Andre Dawson, Billy Doran, Doug Drabek, Shawon Dunston, Lenny Dykstra, Sid Fernandez, Andres Galarraga, Kirk Gibson, Tom Glavine, Doc Gooden, Mark Grace, Ken Griffey Sr., Pedro Guerrero, Tony Gwynn, Billy Hatcher, Von Hayes, Tom Herr, Orel Hershiser, Danny Jackson, Howard Johnson, Dennis Martinez, Roger McDowell, Kevin Mitchell, Dale Murphy, Tim Raines, Dennis Rasmussen, Chris Sabo, Ryne Sandberg, Benito Santiago, Mike Scioscia, Mike Scott, Lonnie Smith, Ozzie Smith, John Smoltz, Darryl Strawberry, Fernando Valenzuela, Andy Van Slyke, Frank Viola, Tim Wallach, Jerome Walton, Matt Williams, Mitch Williams and Todd Worrell.

Starshots Sports Collectibles

In 1991, Starshots Sports Collectibles, Palm Desert, Calif., issued a series of sports celebrity badges which each fold into a display easel. There were 54 baseball players represented, 27 from each league. The complete set is worth $200. American Leaguers are Jim Abbott ($8), Sandy Alomar Jr. ($4), Wade Boggs ($12), George Brett ($15), Jose Canseco ($12), Roger Clemens ($18), Cecil Fielder ($12), Carlton Fisk ($15), Ken Griffey Jr. ($33), Kelly Gruber ($4), Rickey Henderson ($15), Wally Joyner ($6), Don Mattingly ($18), Mark McGwire ($12), Paul Molitor ($15), Dave Parker ($6), Kirby Puckett ($22), Billy Ripken ($4), Cal Ripken Jr. ($30), Nolan Ryan ($25), Bret Saberhagen ($8), Steve Sax ($4), Ruben Sierra ($8), Dave Stieb ($4), Alan Trammell ($10), Bob Welch ($4) and Dave Winfield ($10).

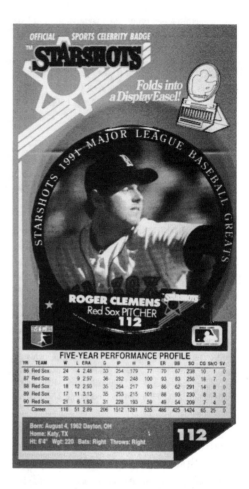

YR	TEAM	W	L	ERA	G	IP	H	R	ER	BB	SO	CG	ShO	SV
86	Red Sox	24	4	2.48	33	254	.179	77	70	67	238	10	1	0
87	Red Sox	20	9	2.97	36	282	248	100	93	83	256	18	7	0
88	Red Sox	18	12	2.93	35	264	217	93	86	62	291	14	8	0
89	Red Sox	17	11	3.13	35	253	215	101	88	93	230	8	3	0
90	Red Sox	21	6	1.93	31	228	193	59	49	54	209	7	4	0
Career		116	51	2.89	206	1512	1281	535	486	425	1424	65	25	0

Born: August 4, 1962 Dayton, OH
Home: Katy, TX
Ht: 6'4" Wgt: 220 Bats: Right Throws: Right

National Leaguers are Barry Bonds ($20), Bobby Bonilla ($6), Will Clark ($15), Eric Davis ($4), Glenn Davis ($4), Andre Dawson ($10), Delino DeShields ($4), Doug Drabek ($4), Shawon Dunston ($4), Lenny Dykstra ($8), Ron Gant ($10), Dwight Gooden ($6), Tony Gwynn ($15), Orel Hershiser ($8), Dave Justice ($8), Barry Larkin ($8), Kevin McReynolds ($4), Kevin Mitchell ($6), Eddie Murray ($10), Chris Sabo ($6), Ryne Sandberg ($12), Benito Santiago ($4), Mike Scioscia ($4), Ozzie Smith ($12), Darryl Strawberry ($6), Tim Wallach ($4) and Matt Williams ($12).

1995 Pinnacle Team Pinnacle Pin Trade Cards

In one of the hobby's first major attempts to cross-promote pin and baseball card collecting, 1995 Series II Pinnacle packs offered a special insert set of cards which could be redeemed for a collector's pin of the same player. Seeded at the rate of one per every 48 regular baseball card packs and one per every 36 jumbo packs, the pin redemption cards were valid until Nov. 15, 1995. Players featured on the cards/pins are: Greg Maddux, Mike Mussina, Mike Piazza, Carlos Delgado, Jeff Bagwell, Frank Thomas, Craig Biggio, Roberto Alomar, Ozzie Smith, Cal Ripken Jr., Matt Williams, Travis Fryman, Barry Bonds, Ken Griffey Jr., Dave Justice, Albert Belle, Tony Gwynn and Kirby Puckett.

Coins

In the 1990s, Bandai America, Cerritos, Calif., issued sport stars collectors coins of major league baseball players, minted in brass (including Mike Scioscia, Alan Trammell, Jim Abbott, Dale Murphy, Andy Van Slyke, Nolan Ryan, Darryl Strawberry).

Computer mouse pads

In 1995, Chris Martin Enterprises produced a line of computer mouse pads featuring 14 Major League Baseball players. Each full-color pad, which measures 7 1/2x7 1/4, has a large action shot with a photo inset, along with the player's name at the bottom of the pad. The team logo is in the upper left corner, while the Pro Pads logo is in the upper right. MLB and MLBPA logos are at the bottom. The players featured include: Albert Belle, Barry Bonds, Juan Gonzalez, Ken Griffey Jr., Tony Gwynn, Ryan Klesko, Barry Larkin, Greg Maddux, Mark McGwire, Hideo Nomo, Mike Piazza, Kirby Puckett, Cal Ripken Jr., and Frank Thomas.

Credit cards

1981 Perma-Graphics
Super Star credit cards

Issued in 1981 by Perma-Graphics of Maryland Heights, Mo., this innovative 32-card set was printed on high-impact, permanently-laminated vinyl to give the appearance of a real credit card. The front of the wallet-sized cards includes career statistics and highlights, along with an "autograph panel" for obtaining the player's signature.

The prices below are for cards in Mint condition.

Complete set (32)	$40
1. Johnny Bench	$3
2. Mike Schmidt	$4
3. George Brett	$4
4. Carl Yastrzemski	$2.50
5. Pete Rose	$4
6. Bob Horner	$1
7. Reggie Jackson	$2.50
8. Keith Hernandez	$1
9. George Foster	$1
10. Garry Templeton	$1
11. Tom Seaver	$2.50
12. Steve Garvey	$1.25
13. Dave Parker	$1
14. Willie Stargell	$2
15. Cecil Cooper	$1
16. Steve Carlton	$2.50
17. Ted Simmons	$1
18. Dave Kingman	$1.25
19. Rickey Henderson	$3
20. Fred Lynn	$1
21. Dave Winfield	$3
22. Rod Carew	$2.50
23. Jim Rice	$1
24. Bruce Sutter	$1
25. Cesar Cedeno	$1
26. Nolan Ryan	$8
27. Dusty Baker	$1
28. Jim Palmer	$3
29. Gorman Thomas	$1
30. Ben Oglivie	$1
31. Willie Wilson	$1
32. Gary Carter	$1.25

1981 Perma-Graphics
All-Star credit cards

Using the same "credit card" style of its previous issue, Perma-Graphics issued an 18-card set in the fall of 1981 featuring the starting players from the 1981 All-Star Game. The front of the card contains a full-color photo, plus the player's name, position and team. The back includes personal data, career records, highlights and an autograph panel. The prices below are for cards in Mint condition.

Complete set (18)	$35
1. Gary Carter	$1.25
2. Dave Concepcion	$1
3. Andre Dawson	$1.25
4. George Foster	$1
5. Davey Lopes	$1
6. Dave Parker	$1.25
7. Pete Rose	$4
8. Mike Schmidt	$4
9. Fernando Valenzuela	$1.25
10. George Brett	$5
11. Rod Carew	$2.50
12. Bucky Dent	$1
13. Carlton Fisk	$1.25
14. Reggie Jackson	$2.50
15. Jack Morris	$1
16. Willie Randolph	$1
17. Ken Singleton	$1
18. Dave Winfield	$3

1982 Perma-Graphics
All-Star credit cards

Perma-Graphics issued its second "All-Star Credit Card" set in the fall of 1982. Consisting of 18 cards, the set pictured starters from both leagues in the 1982 All-Star Game. It was also available in a limited-edition gold version, which is generally two to three times the value of the regular edition. The prices below are for cards in Mint condition.

Complete set (18) $25
1. Dennis Eckersley.................................$1.50
2. Cecil Cooper.......................................$1
3. Carlton Fisk..$1.50
4. Robin Yount..$3
5. Bobby Grich.......................................$1
6. Rickey Henderson $3
7. Reggie Jackson...................................$2
8. Fred Lynn $1
9. George Brett.......................................$4
10. Gary Carter.......................................$1.25
11. Dave Concepcion $1
12. Andre Dawson....................................$1.25
13. Tim Raines $1
14. Dale Murphy $1.25
15. Steve Rogers......................................$1
16. Pete Rose $3
17. Mike Schmidt $3
18. Manny Trillo $1

1982 Perma-Graphics
Super Star credit cards

Perma-Graphics reduced its "Superstar Credit Card Set" to 24 players in 1982, maintaining the same basic credit card appearance. The player photos on the front of the cards are surrounded by a wood-tone border and the backs include the usual personal data, career statistics, highlights and autograph panel. The set was also issued in a limited-edition gold version. These special gold cards are generally worth two to three times the value of a regular-edition card. The prices below are for cards in Mint condition.

Complete set (24) $35
1. Johnny Bench $2
2. Tom Seaver $2
3. Mike Schmidt $3
4. Gary Carter...$1.25
5. Willie Stargell $2
6. Tim Raines $1
7. Bill Madlock..$1
8. Keith Hernandez...................................$1
9. Pete Rose $3
10. Steve Carlton $2
11. Steve Garvey $1.25
12. Fernando Valenzuela...........................$1.25
13. Carl Yastrzemski.................................$2
14. Dave Winfield $2
15. Carney Lansford..................................$1
16. Rollie Fingers $1.50
17. Tony Armas $1
18. Cecil Cooper.......................................$1
19. George Brett $3
20. Reggie Jackson....................................$2
21. Rod Carew $2
22. Eddie Murray......................................$1.50
23. Rickey Henderson $2
24. Kirk Gibson $1

1983 Perma-Graphics
All-Star credit cards

The final issue from Perma-Graphics, this 18-card set was produced in the fall of 1983 and features the 18 starting players from the 1983 All-Star Game. Similar to other Perma-Graphics sets, the cards were printed on wallet-size vinyl to give the appearance of a real credit card. The set was also available in a limited-edition gold version, which carries a value two to three times a regular set or card. The prices below are for cards in Mint condition.

Complete set (18)......................................$25
1. George Brett...$2
2. Rod Carew $1.50
3. Fred Lynn $1
4. Jim Rice $1
5. Ted Simmons $1
6. Dave Stieb $1
7. Manny Trillo $1
8. Dave Winfield.......................................$2
9. Robin Yount...$2
10. Gary Carter...$1.25
11. Andre Dawson $1.25
12. Dale Murphy $1.50
13. Al Oliver $1
14. Tim Raines $1
15. Steve Sax $1
16. Mike Schmidt.......................................$2
17. Ozzie Smith...$1.50
18. Mario Soto $1

1983 Perma-Graphics
Super Star credit cards

Similar in design to its previous sets, Perma-Graphics increased the number of cards in its 1983 "Superstar" set to 36, including 18 players from each league. The fronts of the vinyl cards have a full-color photo with the player's name, team, league and position below. The backs contain career records, highlights and an autograph panel. The cards were also issued in a special gold edition, which are valued at two to three times a regular-edition card. The prices below are for card in Mint condition.

Complete set (36)......................................$30
1. Bill Buckner...$1
2. Steve Carlton..$3
3. Gary Carter..$1.25
4. Andre Dawson $1.25
5. Pedro Guerrero......................................$1
6. George Hendrick $1
7. Keith Hernandez $1
8. Bill Madlock $1
9. Dale Murphy $1.50
10. Al Oliver $1
11. Dave Parker...$1.25
12. Darrell Porter $1

13. Pete Rose $3
14. Mike Schmidt $4
15. Lonnie Smith $1
16. Ozzie Smith $2
17. Bruce Sutter $1
18. Fernando Valenzuela $1.25
19. George Brett $4
20. Rod Carew $2
21. Cecil Cooper $1
22. Doug DeCinces $1
23. Rollie Fingers $1.50
24. Damaso Garcia $1
25. Toby Harrah $1
26. Rickey Henderson $3
27. Reggie Jackson $3
28. Hal McRae $1
29. Eddie Murray $2
30. Lance Parrish $1
31. Jim Rice $1
32. Gorman Thomas $1
33. Willie Wilson $1
34. Dave Winfield $3
35. Carl Yastrzemski $2.50
36. Robin Yount $3

Equitable Life sports prints

The 1960s Equitable Life Assurance Sports Hall of Fame Portraits print set of at least 95 athletes includes 21 different baseball players. Since there were two artists, Robert Riger (1964-67) and George Loh (1961-69), who created the black-and-white prints, it is believed that at least two series were released. The prints were advertised in magazines. Equitable Life offered a 26-print set through the mail, and included a 4x7, 32-page booklet featuring all the subjects and short bios. The set, recently priced at $100, includes Babe Ruth, Carl Hubbell, Lefty Grove, Bob Feller and Allie Reynolds. Later players featured were: Ernie Banks, Roy Campanella, Johnny Evers, Lou Gehrig, Tommy Henrich, Al Kaline, Jerry Koosman, Mickey Mantle, Eddie Mathews, Willie Mays, Stan Musial, Pee Wee Reese, Robin Roberts, Brooks Robinson, Red Ruffing and Warren Spahn.

Folders

In 1988, the Sheaffer Eaton Co., Pittsfield, Mass., produced 9 1/2x11 3/4 two-pocket portfolios of 130 1988 Topps baseball cards; five players from each major league team were selected. Each folder showed the front and back of the player's card and opened to offer two pockets for storage. They were originally offered individually at several retail outlets for between 99 cents to $1.49 each or all-star assortments of 50 pieces each. Dealers had to buy team boxes containing 10 folders of each of the five players. A complete set of 1988 Topps/Sports Shots Portfolios sells for $150. All players listed are $1 each, unless noted: Harold Baines, Jesse Barfield, Marty Barrett, Steve Bedrosian, Buddy Bell, George Bell, Mike Boddicker, Wade Boggs

($2.50), Barry Bonds ($2.50), Bobby Bonilla ($1.50), Phil Bradley, George Brett ($3), Hubie Brooks, DeWayne Buice, Brett Butler, Ivan Calderon, Jose Canseco ($2.50), Gary Carter ($1.25), Joe Carter ($1.50), Jack Clark, Will Clark ($2), Roger Clemens ($2), Vince Coleman ($1.25), Ron Darling, Alvin Davis, Chili Davis, Eric Davis, Glenn Davis, Jody Davis, Andre Dawson ($1.50), Bo Diaz, Bill Doran, Brian Downing, Mike Dunne, Dwight Evans, Brian Fisher, Carlton Fisk ($1.25), John Franco, Gary Gaetti, Greg Gagne, Andres Galarraga ($1.50), Kirk Gibson, Dwight Gooden ($1.25), Rich Gossage, Pedro Guerrero, Tony Gwynn, Billy Hatcher, Von Hayes, Keith Hernandez, Rickey Henderson ($2), Orel Hershiser ($1.25), Teddy Higuera, Charlie Hough, Kent Hrbek ($1.50), Pete Incaviglia, Bo Jackson ($1.50), Brook Jacoby, Dion James, Wally Joyner, Terry Kennedy, Jimmy Key, John Kruk ($1.25), Mark Langston, Barry Larkin ($1.50), Jeffrey Leonard, Don Mattingly ($3), Lance McCullers, Mark McGwire ($1.50), Kevin Mitchell ($1.25),

Paul Molitor ($1.50), Jack Morris, Lloyd Moseby, Dale Murphy ($1.50), Dwayne Murphy, Eddie Murray ($2), Matt Nokes, Pete O'Brien, Lance Parrish, Larry Parrish, Tony Pena, Gerald Perry, Dan Plesac, Luis Polonia, Jim Presley, Kirby Puckett ($3), Dan Quisenberry, Tim Raines ($1.25), Willie Randolph, Rick Reuschel, Harold Reynolds, Jim Rice, Dave Righetti, Cal Ripken Jr. ($4), Nolan Ryan ($4), Bret Saberhagen, Juan Samuel, Ryne Sandberg ($3), Benito Santiago ($1.25), Steve Sax, Mike Schmidt ($2.50), Mike Scott, Larry Sheets, Ruben Sierra, Lee Smith, Ozzie Smith ($1.50), Zane Smith, Cory Snyder, Dave Stewart ($1.25), Dave Stieb, Darryl Strawberry ($1.25), B.J. Surhoff, Rick Sutcliffe, Pat Tabler, Bobby Thigpen, Alan Trammell ($1.50), Fernando Valenzuela, Andy Van Slyke, Frank Viola, Ozzie Virgil, Greg Walker, Tim Wallach, Mitch Webster, Bob Welch, Lou Whitaker, Devon White, Willie Wilson, Dave Winfield ($1.50), Mike Witt, Todd Worrell and Robin Yount ($2.50).

In its second year, the number of baseball card folders produced by Sheaffer Eaton dropped from 130 to 39. The format remains the same, but the designs copy the style of Topps' 1989 cards. The 1989 folders are considerably scarcer than the 1988s. A complete set sells for $45. Individual folders are $1, unless noted. The players in the set are: Wade Boggs ($1.50), George Brett ($3), Ellis Burks, Jose Canseco ($1.50), Will Clark ($1.50), Roger Clemens ($1.50), David Cone, Eric Davis, Andre Dawson, Dennis Eckersley, Dwight Evans, Andres Galarraga ($1.25), Kirk Gibson, Doc Gooden ($1.25), Mike Greenwell, Tony Gwynn ($1.50), Dave Henderson, Rickey Henderson ($1.50), Keith Hernandez, Orel Hershiser, Jay Howell, Danny Jackson, Greg Jefferies ($1.25), Mike Marshall, Don Mattingly ($2.50), Mark McGwire ($1.50), Kevin McReynolds, Paul Molitor ($1.50), Kirby Puckett ($2), Dave Righetti, Mike Scioscia, Mike Scott, Ozzie Smith ($1.50), Terry Steinbach, Dave Stewart, Darryl Strawberry ($1.25), Alan Trammell, Frank Viola and Dave Winfield ($1.50).

Food/drink

Cereal boxes

1983 Fernando Valenzuela Corn Flakes box $50
1987 Minnesota Twins Wheaties box $35
1990 Cincinnati Reds Wheaties box $30
1991 Johnny Bench Wheaties box $50
1991 Rod Carew Wheaties box $125
1991 Joe Morgan Wheaties box $50
1991 Jim Palmer Wheaties box $50
1991 Minnesota Twins Wheaties box $30
1991 Minnesota Twins Frosted Flakes box $30
1992 Lou Gehrig 60 Years of Sports Heritage (Wheaties) $10
1992 Willie Mays 60 Years of Sports Heritage (Wheaties) $10
1992 Babe Ruth 60 Years of Sports Heritage (Wheaties) $10
1993 Nolan Ryan Corn Flakes box $25
1993 Reggie Jackson Mini-Wheats box $20
1993 Ken Griffey Jr. Frosted Flakes box $25
1993 Nolan Ryan Corn Flakes box $25
1994 Roberto Clemente Corn Flakes box $30
1995 Cal Ripken Wheaties box, without Orioles logo, $30, with logo $15
1995 Atlanta Braves World Series champs Wheaties box $25
1995 Cleveland Indians American League champs Wheaties box $25

Other Wheaties boxes have pictured on the cover: Hank Aaron ($75), Sparky Anderson ($15), Johnny Bench ($15), Yogi Berra ($75), Lou Boudreau ($50), Roy Campanella ($75), Ron Cey ($25), Joe DiMaggio ($100), Bob Feller ($75), Jimmie Foxx ($100), Lou Gehrig ($150), Hank Greenberg ($100), Lefty Grove ($85), Carl Hubbell ($65), Ralph Kiner ($60), Ernie Lombardi ($75), Willie Mays ($80), Stan Musial ($85), Hal Newhouser ($75), Mel Ott ($100), Pee Wee Reese ($60), Phil Rizzuto ($60), Brooks Robinson ($50), Jackie Robinson ($125), Pete Rose ($20), Al Rosen ($50), Babe Ruth ($150), Eddie Stanky ($60) and Ted Williams ($100).

1971 Milk Duds

These cards were issued on the backs of five-cent packages of Milk Duds candy. Most collectors prefer to collect complete boxes, rather than cut-out cards, which measure approximately 1 13/16" by 2 5/8" when trimmed tightly. Values quoted here are for complete boxes. The set includes 37 National League and 32 American League players. Card numbers appear on the box flap, with each number from 1 through 24 being shared by three different players. A suffix (a, b and c) has been added for the collector's convenience. Harmon Killebrew, Brooks Robinson and Pete Rose were double-printed. A complete set of 72 cards is worth $1,400 in Near Mint condition. Individual cards are worth $7, unless noted.

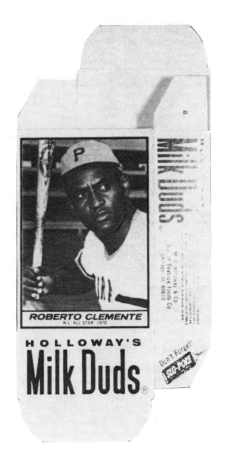

1a Frank Howard, $9
1b Fritz Peterson
1c Pete Rose, $65
2a Johnny Bench, $30
2b Rico Carty
2c Pete Rose, $65
3a Ken Holtzman
3b Willie Mays, $50
3c Cesar Tovar

4a Willie Davis, $8.50
4b Harmon Killebrew, $17.50
4c Felix Milan
5a Billy Grabarkewitz
5b Andy Messersmith
5c Thurman Munson, $17.50
6a Luis Aparicio, $17.50
6b Lou Brock, $17.50
6c Bill Melton

7a Ray Culp
7b Willie McCovey, $22.50
7c Luke Walker
8a Roberto Clemente, $45
8b Jim Merritt
8c Claude Osteen
9a Stan Bahnsen
9b Sam McDowell, $8
9c Billy Williams, $17.50
10a Jim Hickman
10b Dave McNally
10c Tony Perez, $12.50
11a Hank Aaron, $50
11b Glenn Beckert
11c Ray Fosse
12a Alex Johnson
12b Gaylord Perry, $17.50
12c Wayne Simpson
13a Dave Johnson
13b George Scott
13c Tom Seaver, $30
14a Bill Freehan, $8.50
14b Bud Harrelson
14c Manny Sanguillen
15a Bob Gibson, $20
15b Rusty Staub, $9
15c Roy White
16a Jim Fregosi
16b Catfish Hunter, $17.50

16c Mel Stottlemyre
17a Tommy Harper
17b Frank Robinson, $24
17c Reggie Smith
18a Orlando Cepeda, $9
18b Rico Petrocelli
18c Brooks Robinson, $24
19a Tony Oliva, $9
19b Milt Pappas
19c Bobby Tolan
20a Ernie Banks, $25
20b Don Kessinger
20c Joe Torre, $8
21a Fergie Jenkins, $17.50
21b Jim Palmer, $18.50
21c Ron Santo, $12
22a Randy Hundley
22b Denis Menke
22c Boog Powell, $9
23a Dick Dietz
23b Tommy John, $9
23c Brooks Robinson, $24
24a Danny Cater
24b Harmon Killebrew, $17.50
24c Jim Perry

Miscellaneous food/drink

- Ballpark in Arlington Coca-Cola bottle, 1994, unopened, 8-ounce $3
- Jim Beam Baseball 100th Anniversary whiskey decanter, 1969 .... $100
- 1955 Biggie's Restaurant paper napkin, features Stan Musial batting illustration, red, green and white design $12.50
- Camden Yards, Baltimore Orioles' park Coca-Cola bottle, July 13, 1993, unopened, 8-ounce $9
- 1979 Canada Dry pop cans, featuring Steve Carlton, Pete Rose or Mike Schmidt .... $35 each
- 1975 Grafs Cola can commemorating the 1975 All-Star Game in Milwaukee $35
- Houston Astrodome 30th Anniversary Coca-Cola bottle, 1965-95, unopened, 8-ounce $3
- Mickey Mantle's Restaurant soup bowl $65
- Mickey Mantle's Restaurant sauce bowl $30
- Reggie candy bar wrapper from 1978 .... $25
- Cal Ripken Jr. commemorative Coca-Cola six-pack of bottles $20
- 1970s Pete Rose Restaurant glass ashtray, red and white with block lettering, 4" diameter with corners $30
- 1984 Alan Trammell unopened Coca-Cola can, World Champions $30
- Washington Senators Beer, full bottles, with labels $50
- Ted Williams Root Beer wooden crate, refinished $145
- Yoo Hoo chocolate can, 6", featuring 1961 New York Yankees caps of Mantle, Berra, Ford, Richardson, Skowron $100

1952 Coca-Cola Playing Tips

While it was more widely distributed than the three test cards, the 10-card set of playing tip cards is still scarce today. Apparently only issued in the metropolitan New York region, the cards include only players from the Yankees, Giants and Dodgers. Fronts feature paintings of players in action, though the artwork bears little actual resemblance to the players named. The phrase "Coke is a natural" is in the background on pennants, panels, etc. The player's name, team and position are included in the picture. In the portion of the card meant to be inserted into the soda bottle carton, the home schedule of the player's team for 1952 is presented. Printed on back are tips for playing the position of the pictured player. Cards are irregularly shaped, measuring about 3 1/2" at their widest point, and 7 1/2" in length. The unnumbered cards are checklisted here in alphabetical order. A complete set of 10 cards is worth $3,500 in Near Mint condition. The players in the set are: Hank Bauer ($350), Carl Furillo ($450), Gil Hodges ($600), Ed Lopat ($250), Gil McDougald ($300), Don Mueller ($200), Pee Wee Reese ($600), Bobby Thomson, 3B ($300), Bobby Thomson, hitting ($300) and Wes Westrum ($200).

1952 Coca-Cola Playing Tips Test Cards

Apparently a regional issue to test the concept of baseball playing tips cards inserted into cartons of soda bottles, these test cards have a number of differences to the version which was more widely issued. The test cards are printed in black, red and yellow on the front, which features a drawing of the player with a bottle of Coke, along with his name in script and his team. Backs are printed in red on gray cardboard. The playing tips on back do not necessarily conform to the position of the player on the front. Mays' card has a biography instead of a playing tip. The cards are irregularly shaped, measuring about 3 1/2" at their widest point, and about 7 1/2" in length. The complete set of three cards is worth $4,500 in Near Mint condition. The players in the set are Willie Mays ($3,500) and two Phil Rizzuto cards ($500 each).

1963 Pepsi-Cola Colt .45's

This 16-card set was distributed regionally in Texas in bottled six-packs of Pepsi. The cards were issued on panels 2 3/8" by 9 1/8", which were fit in between the bottles in each carton. Values quoted here are for complete panels. A standard 2 3/8" by 3 3/4" card was printed on each panel, which also included promos for Pepsi and the Colt .45's, as well as a team schedule. Card fronts were black-and-white posed action photos with blue and red trim. Player name and position and Pepsi logo are also included. Card backs offer player statistics and career highlights. The John Bateman card, which was apparently never distributed publicly, is among the rarest collectible baseball cards of the 1960s. The complete set, excluding the Bateman card, is worth $210 in Near Mint condition. Individual players in the set are worth $8, unless noted. The players in the set are: Bob Aspromonte, John Bateman ($500), Bob Bruce, Jim Campbell, Dick Farrell, Ernie Fazio, Carroll Hardy, J.C. Hartman, Ken Johnson, Bob Lillis, Don McMahon, Pete Runnels ($15), Al Spangler, Rusty Staub ($30), Johnny Temple and Carl Warwick ($60).

1977 Pepsi-Cola Baseball Stars

An Ohio regional promotion (the checklist is extra heavy with Indians and Reds players), large numbers of these cards found their way into hobby dealers' hands with the result that they are fairly common even today. Designed to be inserted into cartons of soda, the cards have a 3 3/8" diameter central disc attached with perforations to a baseball glove design. A tab beneath the glove contains the checklist (the card discs themselves are unnumbered) and a coupon on the back for ordering a player T-shirt, the offer for which is made on the back of the player. The players' association logo appears on the front, but the producer, Mike Schecter Associates, did not seek licensing by Major League Baseball, with the result that uniform logos have been removed from the black-and-white player photos. Prices are shown for complete glove/disc/tab cards. Values for unattached player discs would be no more than one-half of those shown. A complete set of 72 cards is worth $80 in Near Mint condition. Individual cards are worth .50 to .70 cents, unless noted. The players featured are: Robin Yount ($6), Rod Carew ($3), Butch Wynegar, Manny Sanguillen, Mike

Hargrove, Larvell Blanks, Jim Kern, Pat Dobson, Rico Carty, John Grubb, Buddy Bell, Rick Manning, Dennis Eckersley ($1.75), Wayne Garland, Dave LaRoche, Rick Waits, Ray Fosse, Frank Duffy, Duane Kuiper, Jim Palmer ($3), Fred Lynn ($1.50), Carlton Fisk ($1.50), Carl Yastrzemski ($4), Nolan Ryan ($10), Bobby Grich ($1), Ralph Garr, Richie Zisk, Ron LeFlore, Rusty Staub ($1), Mark Fidrych, Willie Horton, George Brett ($6), Amos Otis, Reggie Jackson ($6), Don Gullett, Thurman Munson ($1.75), Al Hrabosky, Mike Tyson, Gene Tenace, George Hendrick, Chris Speier, John Montefusco, Pete Rose ($6), Johnny Bench ($6), Dan Driessen, Joe Morgan ($3), Dave Concepcion, George Foster, Cesar Geronimo, Ken Griffey Sr., Gary Nolan, Santo Alcala, Jack Billingham, Pedro Borbon, Rawly Eastwick, Fred Norman, Pat Zachary, Jeff Burroughs, Manny Trillo, Bob Watson, Steve Garvey ($1), Don Sutton, John Candelaria, Willie Stargell ($3), Jerry Reuss, Dave Cash, Tom Seaver ($3), Jon Matlack, Dave Kingman, Mike Schmidt ($6), Jay Johnstone and Greg Luzinski.

1978 Pepsi-Cola Superstars

This 40-card complete set is worth $30 in Near Mint condition. Individual cards are worth .25 to .35 cents, unless noted. The players in the set are: Sparky Anderson (.50), Rick Auerbach, Doug Bair, Buddy Bell, Johnny Bench ($2), Bill Bonham, Pedro Borbon, Larry Bowa, George Brett ($3), Jeff Burroughs, Rod Carew ($1), Dave Collins, Dave Concepcion, Dan Driessen, George Foster, Steve Garvey (.40), Cesar Geronimo, Ken Griffey Sr., Ken Henderson, Tom Hume, Reggie Jackson ($2), Junior Kennedy, Dave Kingman, Ray Knight, Mike Lum, Bill Madlock, Joe Morgan ($1), Paul Moskau, Fred Norman, Jim Palmer ($1), Pete Rose ($2), Nolan Ryan ($3.50), Manny Sarmiento, Tom Seaver ($1.50), Ted Simmons, Dave Tomlin, Don Werner, Carl Yastrzemski ($2) and Richie Zisk.

1960 Post Cereal

These cards were issued on the backs of Grape Nuts cereal and measure an oversized 7" by 8 3/4". The nine cards in the set include five baseball players, two football players (Johnny Unitas, $400, and Frank Gifford, $400) and two basketball players (Bob Pettit, $400, and Bob Cousy, $450). The full-color photos were placed on a color background and bordered by a wood frame design. The cards covered the entire back of the cereal box and were blank-backed. Card fronts also include the player's name and team and a facsimile autograph. A panel on the side of the box contains player biographical information. A scarce set, the cards are very difficult to obtain in Mint condition. A Mint condition set of nine is worth $4,500. The baseball players in the set are Don Drysdale ($400), Al Kaline ($450), Harmon Killebrew ($300), Eddie Mathews ($300) and Mickey Mantle ($1,500).

Franklin Mint

In the 1970s and 1980s the Franklin Mint has issued several sterling-silver medals featuring baseball players on them, including Babe Ruth, Lou Gehrig, Connie Mack, Roberto Clemente, Hank Aaron and Jackie Robinson. Among numismatists, most of these medallions do not command much more than issue price, which is usually less than $20.

Game-used lineup cards

• 1971 Minnesota Twins lineup card, includes Carew, Oliva, Killebrew, Blyleven, undated.. $35
• 1973 Oakland A's lineup card, signed by Dick Williams, from Aug. 28, 1973, game $75
• Boston Red Sox lineup card for 1975 American League Championship Series Game 3 .... $375

Hall of Fame items

Since 1936, the National Baseball Hall of Fame and Museum, in Cooperstown, N.Y., has offered several plaque postcards honoring those enshrined.

The companies producing the postcards have been the Albertype Co., of Brooklyn, N.Y., (1936-52, black-and-white); Artvue Post Card Co., of New York, (1953-63, black-and-white); and since 1964, in brown-and-yellow, by Curteichcolor - 3D Natural Color Reproduction and "Mike Roberts Color Productions" of Oakland, Calif. These are generally collected to be autographed, and generally cost about $25, depending on who's pictured. A complete Artvue set of 50, unsigned, is worth about $500.

1981-84 Hall of Fame metallic plaque-cards

Between 1981-84, the National Baseball Hall of Fame and Museum issued a set of metallic baseball cards reproducing the plaques of the baseball greats inducted to that time. The plaques are pictured on 2 1/2" by 3 1/2" blank-backed gold anodized aluminum. Every detail of the plaque is fully and faithfully reproduced. The set was sold in series through the Hall of Fame's gift shop. The complete set of 187 unnumbered cards is worth $2,000 in Mint condition.

The players in the set are: $125 - Babe Ruth; $100 - Joe DiMaggio, Lou Gehrig, Mickey Mantle, Ted Williams; $75 - Hank Aaron, Roberto Clemente, Ty Cobb, Willie Mays, Jackie Robinson; $60 - Ernie Banks, Yogi Berra, Roy Campanella, Al Kaline, Christy Mathewson, Satchel Paige, Duke Snider, Cy Young; $50 - Dizzy Dean, Whitey Ford, Jimmie Foxx, Josh Gibson, Hank Greenberg, Walter Johnson, Brooks Robinson, Frank Robinson, Warren Spahn, Casey Stengel, Honus Wagner; $45 - Bill Dickey, Don Drysdale, Rube Foster, Charles Gehringer, Rogers Hornsby, Harmon Killebrew, Buck Leonard, Pee Wee

Reese; $40 - Grover Alexander, Cap Anson, Cool Papa Bell, Frank Chance, John Evers, Lefty Gomez, Nap Lajoie, Eddie Mathews, Johnny Mize, Juan Marichal, Tris Speaker, Joe Tinker; $35 - Chief Bender, Oscar Charleston, Mickey Cochrane, Eddie Collins, Joe Cronin, Martin Dihigo, Bob Feller, Bob Gibson, Rabbit Maranville, Stan Musial, Mel Ott, Robin Roberts; $30 - Luis Aparicio, Jim Bottomley, Roger Bresnahan, Mordecai Brown, Jake Chesbro, Charles Comiskey, Frank Frisch, Goose Goslin, Lefty Grove, Carl Hubbell, Monte Irvin, Judy Johnson, Al Lopez, Heinie Manush; $25 - Home Run Baker, Jocko Conlan, Sam Crawford, Ford Frick, Warren Giles, Clark Griffith, Gabby Hartnett, William Harridge, Harry Heilmann, Schoolboy Hoyt, Miller Huggins, Travis Jackson, Hugh Jennings, Willie Keeler, George Kell, Highpockets Kelly, King Kelly, Ralph Kiner, Chuck Klein, Kenesaw Landis, Bob Lemon, Fred Lindstrom, Ted Lyons, Connie Mack, Rube Marquard, Joe McCarthy, John McGraw, Joe Medwick, Eddie Plank, Sam Rice, Branch Rickey, Wilbert Robinson, Al Simmons, George Sisler, Bill Terry, Pie Traynor, Dazzy Vance, Hack Wilson, Early Wynn; $20 - Walter Alston, Luke Appling, Jacob Beckley, Lou Boudreau, Happy Chandler, Fred Clarke, Stan Coveleski, Kiki Cuyler, Ed Delahanty, Rick Ferrell, Burleigh Grimes, Chick Hafey, Pop Haines, Bucky Harris, Bill Herman, Harry Hooper, Addie Joss, Joe Kelley, Pop Lloyd, Iron Man McGinnity, Bill McKechnie, Edd Roush, Red Ruffing, Ray Schalk, Joe Sewell, Rube Waddell, Ed Walsh, Lloyd Waner, Paul Waner, Zack Wheat; $15 - Earl Averill, David Bancroft, Ed Barrow, Dan Brouthers, Morgan Bulkeley, Jesse Burkett, Max Carey, Alexander Cartwright, Henry Chadwick, John Clarkson, James Collins, Earle Combs, Thomas Connolly, Roger Connor, Candy Cummings, Hugh Duffy, Bill Evans, Buck Ewing, Urban Faber, Elmer Flick, Pud Galvin, William Hamilton, Cal Hubbard, Ban Johnson, Timothy Keefe, Bill Klem, Larry McPhail, Thomas McCarthy, Kid Nichols, James O'Rourke, Herb Pennock, Hoss Radbourne, Eppa Rixey, Amos Rusie, Al Spalding, Sam Thompson, Roderick Wallace, John Ward, George Weiss, Mickey Welch, George Wright, Harry Wright, Ross Youngs.

Twenty players enshrined in Cooperstown have also been depicted on 6 3/4-inch statuettes, produced by Sports Hall of Fame, Long Island, N.Y., in 1963. The statuettes were issued in two 10-player series, with the second series statues being more scarce. Jimmie Foxx is considered the scarcest, and usually brings the highest price. The other players are Ty Cobb, Mickey Cochrane, Joe Cronin ($500), Bill Dickey ($95), Joe DiMaggio (slightly yellow, EX, no box, $35), Bob Feller ($95), Lou Gehrig ($150-$200), Hank Greenberg, Rogers Hornsby ($60), Walter Johnson ($95), Christy Mathewson ($50), John McGraw (EX+,

no box, $300), Jackie Robinson (Nr. Mt., no box, $160), Babe Ruth (bent, otherwise Mint in box, $45), George Sisler ($200), Tris Speaker ($200), Pie Traynor ($50), Honus Wagner ($60) and Paul Waner (Mint, rewrapped box, $300). The given prices are advertised or auction prices realized; the statues are in Mint condition with box, unless noted.

Highland Mint

1993 Highland Mint

The Highland Mint produced replicas of several Topps rookie cards and other prominent cards in bronze and silver. Limited to 1,000 in silver and 5,000 in bronze, the company produced cards of many current stars along with a replica of Brooks Robinson's 1957 rookie card. The cards carried a suggested retail price of $235 for the silver and $50 for the bronze. Cards measure 2 1/2" by 3 1/2" and are 1/10" thick. Each Mint-Card has a serial number engraved on the edge and is sold in a heavy lucite holder, packaged with a certificate of authenticity in a plastic book-style folder. The number produced is listed after the player's name.

Complete set, silver (17)	$4,000
Complete set, bronze (17)	$850
Roberto Alomar, 1988 Topps silver, 214	$235
Roberto Alomar, 1988 Topps bronze, 928	$50
Barry Bonds, 1986 Topps silver, 596	$235
Barry Bonds, 1986 Topps bronze, 2,677	$50
George Brett, 1975 Topps silver, 999	$260
George Brett, 1975 Topps bronze, 3,560	$50
Will Clark, 1986 Topps silver, 150	$275
Will Clark, 1986 Topps bronze, 1,044	$50
Roger Clemens, 1985 Topps silver, 432	$235
Roger Clemens, 1985 Topps bronze, 1,789	$50
Juan Gonzalez, 1990 Topps silver, 365	$235
Juan Gonzalez, 1990 Topps bronze, 1,899	$50
Ken Griffey Jr., 1992 Topps gold, 500	$500
Ken Griffey Jr., 1992 Topps silver, 1,000	$265
Ken Griffey Jr., 1992 Topps bronze, 5,000	$65
Don Mattingly, 1984 Topps silver, 414	$235
Don Mattingly, 1984 Topps bronze, 1,550	$50
Kirby Puckett, 1985 Topps silver, 359	$235
Kirby Puckett, 1985 Topps bronze, 1,723	$50
Cal Ripken Jr., 1992 Topps silver, 1,000	$235
Cal Ripken Jr., 1992 Topps bronze, 4,065	$50
Brooks Robinson, 1957 Topps silver, 796	$235
Brooks Robinson, 1957 Topps bronze, 2,043	$50
Nolan Ryan, 1992 Topps silver, 999	$750
Nolan Ryan, 1992 Topps bronze, 5,000	$145
Ryne Sandberg, 1992 Topps silver, 430	$235
Ryne Sandberg, 1992 Topps silver, 1,932	$50
Ozzie Smith, 1979 Topps silver, 211	$235
Ozzie Smith, 1979 Topps bronze, 1,088	$50
Frank Thomas, 1992 Topps gold, 500	$500
Frank Thomas, 1992 Topps silver, 1,000	$235
Frank Thomas, 1992 Topps bronze, 5,000	$50
Dave Winfield, 1974 Topps silver, 266	$235
Dave Winfield, 1974 Topps bronze, 1,216	$50
Robin Yount, 1975 Topps silver, 349	$235
Robin Yount, 1975 Topps bronze, 1,564	$50

1994 Highland Mint

In 1994 the Highland Mint continued its production of Mint-Cards, but reduced its print runs to 750 for silver and 2,500 for bronze. Suggested retail prices remained the same as the previous year. In mid-year, the company announced it would cease production of Topps replica cards. Instead, the Mint-Cards would reproduce the designs of Pinnacle brand cards.

Complete set, gold (2):	$1,500
Complete set, silver (12):	$2,750
Complete set, bronze (12):	$550
Jeff Bagwell, 1992 Pinnacle silver, 750	$235
Jeff Bagwell, 1992 Pinnacle bronze, 2,500	$50
Ernie Banks, 1954 Topps silver, 437	$235
Ernie Banks, 1954 Topps bronze, 920	$50
Johnny Bench, 1969 Topps silver, 500	$235
Johnny Bench, 1969 Topps bronze, 1,384	$50
Dave Justice, 1990 Topps silver, 265	$235
Dave Justice, 1990 Topps bronze, 1,396	$50
Greg Maddux, 1992 Pinnacle silver, 750	$235
Greg Maddux, 1992 Pinnacle bronze, 2,500	$50
Paul Molitor, 1979 Topps silver, 260	$235
Paul Molitor, 1979 Topps bronze, 369	$50
Mike Piazza, 1992 Topps gold, 374	$500
Mike Piazza, 1992 Topps silver, 750	$235
Mike Piazza, 1992 Topps bronze, 2,500	$50
Nolan Ryan, 1992 Pinnacle Then & Now gold, 500	$500
Nolan Ryan, 1992 Pinnacle Then & Now silver, 1,000	$235
Nolan Ryan, 1992 Pinnacle Then & Now bronze, 5,000	$50
Tim Salmon, 1993 Topps silver, 264	$235
Tim Salmon, 1993 Topps bronze, 768	$50
Deion Sanders, 1989 Topps silver, 187	$235
Deion Sanders, 1989 Topps bronze, 668	$50
Mike Schmidt, 1974 Topps silver, 500	$235
Mike Schmidt, 1974 Topps bronze, 1,641	$50
Carl Yastrzemski, 1960 Topps silver, 500	$235
Carl Yastrzemski, 1960 Topps bronze, 1,072	$50

1995 Highland Mint

The first releases for the Highland Mint in 1995 featured basketball star Michael Jordan, as depicted as a baseball player on Upper Deck cards.

Michael Jordan, Upper Deck Rare Air gold, 500	$650
Michael Jordan, Upper Deck Rare Air silver, 1,000	$235
Michael Jordan, Upper Deck Rare Air bronze, 5,000	$50

Jewelry/trophies

• George Brett Silver Gillette special award trophy for being the leading vote-getter for the 1981 All-Star Game, signed $3,250
• Cito Gaston's San Diego Padres Baseball Writers Association MVP Award $895
• Josten's National League Player of the Week presentation watch with box $295
• 100th anniversary of baseball commemorative watch, the face depicts a red, white and blue 100th anniversary baseball player logo, with baseball bats as hour hands, plus a black leather band and gold encasement $125
• 1948 Babe Ruth wristwatch, works $595
• 1955 Elroy Face Dapper Dan Award for outstanding contribution to baseball, sterling silver award $1,650

• 1956 Mickey Mantle New York Yankees World Series Championship ring, salesman's sample $7,000
• 1956 New York Yankees World Champs ladies watch, 14k with diamonds $895
• 1960 Mickey Mantle/Roger Maris All-Star kid's watch, with new band $145
• 1960 New York Yankees 14k World Series ring, vs. the Pittsburgh Pirates $4,950
• 1964 St. Louis Cardinals 14k World Series ring, white gold championship ring, vs. the New York Yankees $2,995
• 1967 Sporting News/Rawlings Gold Glove Award, presented to California Angels shortstop Jim Fregosi, shows his model glove, flanked by two gold baseballs, on a base with his picture $3,995
• 1968 Harmon Killebrew watch, Swiss-made, face features Killebrew photo with a facsimile autograph against a green baseball diamond background, includes a black imitation leather band $295
• 1969 Nolan Ryan New York Mets 10k World Series ring, salesman's sample $2,850
• 1970 Baltimore Orioles World Series championship ring, Frank Robinson salesman's sample $1,795
• 1971 Pittsburgh Pirates 10k World Series ring, vs. the Baltimore Orioles, salesman's sample $3,500
• 1974 Oakland A's 10k World Series ring, Charles Finley salesman's sample, vs. the Los Angeles Dodgers $2,750
• 1974 Rawlings Mitsui Japanese Central Gold Glove Award, just like an American version, presented to Clete Boyer $3,495
• 1975 Cincinnati Reds 10k World Series ring, Joe Morgan salesman's sample white gold championship ring, vs. the Boston Red Sox $3,150
• 1977 All-Star Game 10k yellow-gold ring, for the game in New York, belonged to a Yankee executive $2,250
• 1978 Los Angeles Dodgers 14k World Series ring, vs. the New York Yankees, salesman's sample $3,500
• 1978 New York Yankees 10k World Series ring, Reggie Jackson salesman's sample $3,500
• 1979 George Brett June 1979 Player of the Month Award $1,750
• 1980 Philadelphia Phillies World Series ring, Pete Rose salesman's sample, vs. the Kansas City Royals $2,100
• 1981 Los Angeles Dodgers World Series trophy, presented to Danny Goodman $3,850
• 1981 Manny Mota presentation award/plaque, "Los Angeles Dodgers 1981 World Champions" and "145 Pinch Hits Major League Record" $695
• 1982 Bob Boone Eraser Mate 1982 Best Defense Catcher Award, with a large lucite baseball diamond with an engraved colored plaque $995
• 1984 All-Star Game ring, for the game in San Francisco, with original presentation box $1,250
• 1985 Kansas City Royals 10k World Series Champions pendant with diamonds $2,000
• 1985 Kansas City Royals 10k World Series ring, George Brett salesman's sample $3,695
• 1985 Kansas City Royals World Series trophy, sample, autographed by Bret Saberhagen $1,750
• 1986 Boston Red Sox World Series ring, with presentation box, vs. the New York Mets $2,850
• 1987 Minnesota Twins World Series ring, Frank Viola, vs. the St. Louis Cardinals $2,100
• 1988 Los Angeles Dodgers World Championship 10k pendant, vs. the Oakland A's $1,500
• 1989 San Francisco Giants National League Champions ring, 14k gold plated, Will Clark salesman's sample $2,250
• 1990 Oakland A's World Series ring, vs. the Cincinnati Reds, salesman's sample $3,500
• 1990 Cincinnati Reds World Series ring, vs. the Oakland A's, salesman's sample $4,500
• 1991 Atlanta Braves 10k World Series ring, yellow-gold salesman's sample, vs. the Minnesota Twins $3,500
• 1992 Roberto Alomar World Series MVP trophy, has his name engraved on the front, includes two press pins attached to the base of the award $6,000
• 1993 All-Star Game ring, in Baltimore, made for a non-player $395
• 1993 Philadelphia Phillies National League Champs 10k gold ring, Lenny Dykstra salesman's sample $2,395
• 1995 All-Star Game ring, in Texas, made for a front office executive $995

435

Leaf products

1994 Leaf Slide Show

A new level of high-tech insert card production values was reached with the creation of Leaf's "Slide Show" cards. The cards feature a printed acetate center sandwiched between cardboard front and back. The see-through acetate portion of the card is bordered in white to give it the appearance of a slide. The player's name, location and date of the photo are printed on the front of the "slide," with a card number on the back. The pseudo-slide is bordered in black (Series I) or white (Series II), with a blue "Slide Show" logo at the bottom and a silver-foil Leaf logo. Backs of the inserts have a few sentences about the featured player from Frank Thomas, Leaf's official spokesman in 1994. The first five cards were released in Series I baseball card packs; cards 6-10 were in Series II packs. The odds of finding a Slide Show insert are one per every 54 packs. A complete set (10) is worth $60 in Mint condition. The players are 1. Frank Thomas, $20; 2. Mike Piazza, $8; 3. Darren Daulton, $2; 4. Ryne Sandberg, $5; 5. Roberto Alomar, $4; 6. Barry Bonds, $6; 7. Juan Gonzalez, $4; 8. Tim Salmon, $2.50; 9. Ken Griffey Jr., $20; 10. Dave Justice, $3.

1995 Leaf Slide Show

The hold-to-light technology which Leaf debuted with its 1994 Slide Show inserts continues in 1995 with a cross-series concept. The same eight players are featured on these cards in both Series I and Series II. Each has three clear photos at the center, between the spokes of a silver-foil wheel. When both the player's cards are placed side-by-side, the six-piece see-through photo device is complete. Silver-foil and black borders surround the photo wheel on each side of the card. The Slide Show inserts are found on an average of just over one per box among all types of pack configurations. Cards were issued with a removable plastic protector on the front. A complete set (16) is worth $80 in Mint condition. The same checklist and values are used for both series: 1. Raul Mondesi, $6; 2. Frank Thomas, $15; 3. Fred McGriff, $5; 4. Cal Ripken Jr., $16; 5. Jeff Bagwell, $7.50; 6. Will Clark, $5; 7. Matt Williams, $5; 8. Ken Griffey Jr., $15.

Linnett Superstars

This frequently encountered set of 36 cards has enjoyed little collector interest since its issue in 1976. Officially known as "Pee-Wee Superstars," the cards measure 4" by 5 5/8." Player portraits by artist Charles Linnett are rendered in black-and-white pencil and set against a pale yellow background. Players are shown without caps or uniforms (most appear to be wearing white T-shirts). According to the logos at the top the set was fully licensed by the players' association and Major League Baseball, and team logos do appear in the lower-left corner. A facsimile autograph in red or purple appears on each card. Front borders are bright

purple, red, green, dark brown or white. Card backs feature either a photo of an antique auto or a drawing of a historic sailing ship. Each of the 12 different back designs appears on one card from each team set. The Linnetts were sold in panels of six perforated cards. An offer on the back of each card set makes 8x10 premium portraits of each player available for 95 cents. The premium pictures have about the same value as the cards. Only the World Champion Cincinnati Reds, American League Champion Boston Red Sox and National League runner-up Los Angeles Dodgers are represented in the set.

A complete panel set of six (all 36 cards) is worth $15, while a complete set of 36 individual cards is worth $12. Common players are .50, unless noted.

Panel 1 ($6.50) features Don Gullett, Johnny Bench ($2), Tony Perez (.90), Mike Lum, Ken Griffey (.60) and George Foster (.60). Panel 2 ($8) features Joe Morgan ($1.50), Pete Rose ($3), Dave Concepcion (.60), Cesar Geronimo, Dan Driessen and Pedro Borbon. Panel 3 ($7) features Carl Yastrzemski ($2), Fred Lynn (.90), Dwight Evans (.60), Ferguson Jenkins ($1), Rico Petrocelli and Denny Doyle.

Panel 4 ($5) features Luis Tiant (.60), Carlton Fisk ($1), Rick Burleson, Bill Lee, Rick Wise and Jim Rice (.75). Panel 5 ($5) features Davey Lopes (.60), Steve Garvey ($1), Bill Russell (.60), Ron Cey (.60), Steve Yeager and Doug Rau. Panel 6 ($4.75) features Don Sutton ($1), Joe Ferguson, Mike Marshall, Bill Buckner (.60), Rick Rhoden and Ted Sizemore.

Magnets

1989 Phoenix Magnetables

The first of what was intended to be a long line of sports-themed "magnetables" (magnetic collectibles), this 156-piece set of baseball players never caught on and the line ended. Measuring 2" x 3" with rounded corners, these items feature color player photos attached to a magnetic backing. Fronts include the player and the team name in orange strips, and in the lower-left corner the word "Phoenix" and a copyright line for Major League Baseball and the players' association. The unnumbered pieces are checklisted here alphabetically. A complete set in Mint condition is $60; individual magnets are worth 50 cents to 90 cents, unless noted.

1. Alan Anderson	40. Dwight Evans	79. Wally Joyner	118. Kevin Reimer
2. Roberto Alomar, $2	41. Felix Fermin	80. Carney Lansford	119. Bill Ripken
3. Sandy Alomar Jr.	42. Tony Fernandez	81. Barry Larkin	120. Cal Ripken Jr., $2.50
4. Harold Baines	43. Carlton Fisk	82. Tim Laudner	121. Nolan Ryan, $6
5. Marty Barrett	44. Tim Flannery	83. Vance Law	122. Chris Sabo
6. Kevin Bass	45. Julio Franco	84. Manny Lee	123. Luis Salazar
7. Dave Bergman	46. Greg Gagne	85. Chet Lemon	124. Juan Samuel
8. Mike Boddicker	47. Andres Galarraga	86. Jeffrey Leonard	125. Ryne Sandberg, $2.50
9. Wade Boggs, $2	48. Dave Gallagher	87. Jose Lind	126. Rafael Santana
10. Phil Bradley	49. Ron Gant	88. Steve Lyons	127. Mike Schmidt, $3
11. Mickey Brantley	50. Jim Gantner	89. Candy Maldonado	128. Steve Sax
12. George Brett, $2.50	51. Kirk Gibson	90. Mike Marshall	129. Dick Schofield
13. Tom Brookens	52. Paul Gibson	91. Ramon Martinez	130. Kevin Seitzer
14. Hubie Brooks	53. Dan Gladden	92. Don Mattingly, $2	131. John Shelby
15. Tom Browning	54. Dwight Gooden	93. Willie McGee	132. Ruben Sierra
16. Tom Brunansky	55. Mark Grace	94. Fred McGriff, $1.25	133. Don Slaught
17. Ellis Burks	56. Mike Greenwell	95. Mark McGwire, $1.50	134. Ozzie Smith
18. Randy Bush	57. Ken Griffey Jr., $4	96. Kevin McReynolds	135. Van Snider
19. Brett Butler	58. Pedro Guerrero	97. Bobby Meacham	136. Cory Snyder
20. Jose Canseco, $2	59. Ozzie Guillen	98. Luis Medina	137. Darryl Strawberry, $1.25
21. Gary Carter	60. Tony Gwynn	99. Kevin Mitchell	138. B.J. Surhoff
22. Joe Carter, $1.25	61. Jeff Hamilton	100. Paul Molitor	139. Pat Tabler
23. Jack Clark	62. Lenny Harris	101. Lloyd Moseby	140. Danny Tartabull
24. Will Clark, $2	63. Billy Hatcher	102. Darryl Motley	141. Wayne Tolleson
25. Roger Clemens, $1.50	64. Mickey Hatcher	103. Rance Mulliniks	142. Jim Traber
26. Vince Coleman	65. Dave Henderson	104. Dale Murphy	143. Alan Trammell
27. David Cone	66. Rickey Henderson, $1.75	105. Matt Nokes	144. Andy Van Slyke
28. Kal Daniels	67. Keith Hernandez	106. Jose Oquendo	145. Frank Viola
29. Eric Davis	68. Orel Hershiser	107. Joe Orsulak	146. Greg Walker
30. Chili Davis	69. Jack Howell	108. Rafael Palmeiro	147. Walt Weiss
31. Glenn Davis	70. Kent Hrbek	109. Tony Pena	148. Lou Whitaker
32. Jody Davis	71. Bo Jackson	110. Terry Pendleton	149. Devon White
33. Andre Dawson	72. Brook Jacoby	111. Gerald Perry	150. Frank White
34. Jose DeJesus	73. Chris James	112. Tom Prince	151. Mookie Wilson
35. Rick Dempsey	74. Dion James	113. Kirby Puckett	152. Willie Wilson
36. Bob Dernier	75. Gregg Jefferies	114. Tim Raines	153. Dave Winfield, $1
37. Brian Downing	76. Steve Jeltz	115. Rafael Ramirez	154. Craig Worthington
38. Cameron Drew	77. Doug Jennings	116. Johnny Ray	155. Gerald Young
39. Kevin Elster	78. Tommy John	117. Jody Reed	156. Robin Yount, $2

Chris Martin Enterprises 1994 Pro Mags

Borderless color player action photos are featured on this set of blank-backed, round-cornered 2 1/8" by 3 3/8" magnets produced by former NFL player Chris Martin (sets were also made of football and basketball player magnets). The flexible, UV-coated magnets have a color team logo in an upper corner and a "Pro Mags" logo in the other. At the bottom is the player's name, magnet number, the logos of the MLBPA and MLB licensors and a Chris Martin Enterprises copyright line. Magnets were sold in blister packs of five, with a 2 1/8" by 3/4" team logo magnet and a checklist card of Joe Carter, for about $5. Autographed magnets of Carter were randomly inserted into packs. The complete set of 140 magnets is worth $100. Individual magnets are worth $1-$1.50, unless noted.

1. Terry Pendleton
2. Ryan Klesko
3. Fred McGriff
4. Dave Justice
5. Greg Maddux
6. Brady Anderson
7. Ben McDonald
8. Cal Ripken Jr., $3
9. Mike Mussina
10. Jeffrey Hammonds
11. Roger Clemens
12. Andre Dawson
13. Mike Greenwell
14. Mo Vaughn
15. Otis Nixon
16. Chad Curtis
17. Mark Langston
18. Tim Salmon
19. Chuck Finley
20. Eduardo Perez
21. Steve Buechele

22. Mark Grace
23. Sammy Sosa
24. Derrick May
25. Shawon Dunston
26. Jack McDowell
27. Tim Raines
28. Frank Thomas, $3
29. Robin Ventura
30. Julio Franco
31. John Smiley
32. Barry Larkin
33. Jose Rijo
34. Reggie Sanders
35. Kevin Mitchell
36. Sandy Alomar Jr.
37. Carlos Baerga
38. Albert Belle
39. Manny Ramirez
40. Eddie Murray
41. Dante Bichette
42. Ellis Burks

43. Andres Galarraga
44. Greg W. Harris
45. David Nied
46. Cecil Fielder
47. Kirk Gibson
48. Mickey Tettleton
49. Lou Whitaker
50. Travis Fryman
51. Jeff Conine
52. Charlie Hough
53. Benito Santiago
54. Gary Sheffield
55. Dave Magadan
56. Jeff Bagwell
57. Luis Gonzalez
58. Andujar Cedeno
59. Craig Biggio
60. Doug Drabek
61. Tom Gordon
62. Brian McRae
63. David Cone
64. Wally Joyner
65. Jeff Montgomery
66. Eric Karros
67. Tom Candiotti
68. Delino DeShields
69. Orel Hershiser
70. Mike Piazza
71. Darryl Hamilton
72. Kevin Seitzer
73. B.J. Surhoff
74. John Jaha
75. Greg Vaughn
76. Kent Hrbek
77. Kirby Puckett
78. Kevin Tapani
79. Dave Winfield
80. Chuck Knoblauch
81. Moises Alou
82. Wil Cordero
83. Marquis Grissom
84. Pedro J. Martinez
85. Larry Walker
86. Jim Abbott
87. Wade Boggs
88. Don Mattingly
89. Luis Polonia
90. Danny Tartabull
91. Bobby Bonilla
92. Todd Hundley
93. Dwight Gooden
94. Jeromy Burnitz

95. Bret Saberhagen
96. Dennis Eckersley
97. Mark McGwire
98. Ruben Sierra
99. Terry Steinbach
100. Rickey Henderson
101. Darren Daulton
102. Lenny Dykstra
103. Dave Hollins
104. John Kruk
105. Curt Schilling
106. Carlos Garcia
107. Jay Bell
108. Don Slaught
109. Andy Van Slyke
110. Orlando Merced
111. Ray Lankford
112. Mark Whiten
113. Todd Ziele
114. Ozzie Smith
115. Gregg Jefferies
116. Derek Bell
117. Andy Benes
118. Phil Plantier
119. Tony Gwynn
120. Bip Roberts
121. Barry Bonds, $2
122. John Burkett
123. Robby Thompson
124. Darren Lewis
125. Willie McGee
126. Jay Buhner
127. Ken Griffey Jr., $3
128. Randy Johnson
129. Eric Anthony
130. Edgar Martinez
131. Kevin Brown
132. Jose Canseco, $2
133. Juan Gonzalez
134. Will Clark
135. Ivan Rodriguez
136. Roberto Alomar
137. Joe Carter
137a. Joe Carter autographed, $15
138. Juan Guzman
139. Paul Molitor
140. John Olerud

Marbles

In 1968 Creative Creations Inc. produced a series of Official Major League Baseball Player Marbles which were sold in packages of 20 for a suggested retail price of $1.49. Twenty Hall of Famers are in the set. Each marble was two pieces of clear, hard plastic with a round 3/4" disc inserted into it. The front featured the player's face against a pastel background. His team's logo was airbrushed from his cap. The back had a facsimile autograph and the word JAPAN. The 20 marbles were packaged in a 12"-square colorful cardboard store hanger display which featured larger photos of the players in the pack, plus facsimile autographs of many of the 120 players. Although the blister-packed display piece encourages buyers to "Collect All 24 Series," apparently only 120 marbles were released, not 240 as promised. Original packages of 20 marbles, even without major superstars, can sell for between $35-$50, while common players range from $3-$5. Superstars such as Pete Rose have been sold for as much as $150.

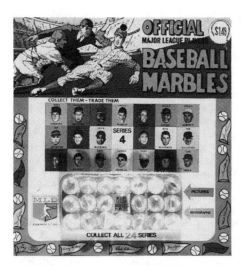

1968 Baseball Player Marbles

Hank Aaron
Tommie Aaron,$5
Tommie Agee
Richie Allen
Gene Alley
Bob Allison, $5
Felipe Alou
Jesus Alou
Matty Alou, $5
Max Alvis
Mike Andrews, $5
Luis Aparicio, $18
Bob Aspromonte, $5
Stan Bahnsen
Bob Bailey, $5

Ernie Banks
Glenn Beckert, $5
Gary Bell, $5
Johnny Bench
Ken Berry, $5
Paul Blair
Bob Bolin
Dave Boswell, $5
Nelson Briles, $5
Lou Brock
Wally Bunker
Johnny Callison
Norm Cash
Orlando Cepeda
Dean Chance
Roberto Clemente
Donn Clendenon
Tony Cloninger, $5
Tommy Davis

Al Downing
Curt Flood
Bill Freehan
Jim Fregosi
Bob Gibson, $25
Jim "Mudcat" Grant
Jerry Grote
Jimmie Hall
Tom Haller
Ron Hansen, $5
Steve Hargan, $5
Ken Harrelson
Jim Hart, $5
Jim Holt
Joe Horlen, $5
Willie Horton
Frank Howard, $12
Dick Hughes, $5
Randy Hundley, $5
Ron Hunt
Jim "Catfish" Hunter
Pat Jarvis
Julian Javier, $5
Tommy John, $9
Deron Johnson
Mack Jones, $5
Jim Kaat
Al Kaline
Don Kessinger, $5
Harmon Killebrew
Jerry Koosman, $6
Jim Lefebvre, $5
Mickey Lolich
Jim Lonborg, $5
Juan Marichal
Roger Maris, $27
Eddie Mathews
Jerry May, $5
Willie Mays
Dick McAuliffe
Tim McCarver
Willie McCovey
Sam McDowell, $5

Denny McLain, $6
Dave McNally
Dennis Menke
Jim Merritt
Bob Miller
Rick Monday, $5
Joe Morgan
Gary Nolan
Jim Northrup
Rich Nye, $5
Tony Oliva, $10
Milt Pappas, $5
Camilo Pascual
Joe Pepitone
Tony Perez
Jim Perry, $5
Gary Peters, $5
Fritz Peterson, $5
Rico Petrocelli, $5
Vada Pinson
Boog Powell
Pete Reichardt, $5
Brooks Robinson, $30
Frank Robinson
Pete Rose
Chico Salmon, $5
Ron Santo
George Scott
Tom Seaver
Dick Selma
Mike Shannon
Joe Sparma, $5
Willie Stargell
Mel Stottlemyre, $5
Luis Tiant
Cesar Tovar, $5
Tom Tresh, $5
Pete Ward
Billy Williams, $12
Maury Wills
Earl Wilson, $5
Dooley Womack

In 1991, Spectra Star, a Pacoima, Calif.-based marketer of toys and sporting goods, produced a series of 20 SuperStar marbles featuring baseball players inside. The full-color, one-inch diameter "Rad Rollers" were offered in four sets of five players, based on the division in which the players compete. American League East players are Robin Yount, Cecil Fielder, Cory Sndyer, Fred McGriff and Cal Ripken Jr.; American League West players are Ken Griffey Jr., Jose Canseco, Nolan Ryan, Kirby Puckett and Jim Abbott. National League East players are Tim Raines, Darryl Strawberry, Barry Bonds, Len Dykstra and Ryne Sandberg; National League West players are Ron Gant, Chris Sabo, Craig Biggio, Fernando Valenzuela and Benito Santiago. The packages of five originally sold for $4-$5.

1969-70 Chemtoy Superballs, featuring a photo of a Major League Baseball players on the inside. Superballs are $4-$6.50 each, unless noted.

Atlanta Braves - Hank Aaron ($40,) Ken Aspromonte, Orlando Cepeda ($8), Pat Jarvis, Felix Millan, Milt Pappas, Bob Tillman

Baltimore Orioles - Mark Belanger, Paul Blair, Don Buford, Mike Cuellar ($8), Andy Etchebarren, Dave Johnson ($8), Jim Palmer ($20), Tom Phoebus, Boog Powell ($9), Ed Watt

Boston Red Sox - Mike Andrews, Tony Conigliaro ($35), Russ Gibson, Dalton Jones, Jim Lonborg ($8), Rico Petrocelli, Jose Santiago, Tom Satriano, George Scott, Sonny Siebert, Reggie Smith, Lee Stange

California Angels - Sandy Alomar ($9), Lloyd Allen, Joe Azcue, Ed Fisher, Jim Fregosi, Jim Hicks, Jay Johnstone, Lefty Phillips, Roger Repoz, Rick Reichardt, Greg Washburn

Chicago Cubs - John Callison, Leo Durocher, Jim Hickman, Ken Holtzman, Randy Hundley, Ron Santo

Chicago White Sox - Ken Berry, Ron Hansen, Joe Horlen, Tommy John ($10), Carlos May, Bill Melton, Billy Wynne

Cincinnati Reds - Jack Fisher, Tony Perez ($35), Bobby Tolan, Bobby Woodward

Cleveland Indians - Jose Cardenal, Dean Chance, Alvin Dark, Dick Ellsworth, Ray Fosse ($8), Vern

Fuller, Richie Scheinblum ($8), Duke Sims, Russ Snyder, Ted Uhlaender, Zoilo Versalles ($8)

Detroit Tigers - Norm Cash, Willie Horton, Denny McLain ($8), Jim Northrup, Joe Sparma, Mickey Stanley

Houston Astros - Jesus Alou, Larry Dierker, Denis Menke, Norm Miller, Joe Morgan ($10), Joe Pepitone, Doug Rader, Hector Torres, Don Wilson

Kansas City Royals - Jerry Adair, Tom Burgmeier, Jim Campanis, Mike Hedlund, Pat Kelly, Lou Piniella ($8)

Los Angeles Dodgers - Jim Brewer, Willie Crawford, Len Gabrielson, Billy Grabarkewitz, Andy Kosco, Claude Osteen, Ted Sizemore, Jeff Torborg

Minnesota Twins - Bobby Allison, Leo Cardenas, Joe Coleman, Jim Kaat ($9), Harmon Killebrew ($40), George Mitterwald, Rich Reese, Cesar Tovar ($8)

Montreal Expos - Ron Brand, Kevin Collins, Angel Hermosa, Coco Laboy, Gary Sutherland, Bobby Wine

New York Mets - Ken Boswell, Gary Gentry, Jerry Grote, Bud Harrelson, Cleon Jones, Jerry Koosman, Ron Swoboda

New York Yankees - Jake Gibbs, Ralph Houk, Gene Michael, Fritz Peterson, Mel Stottlemyre ($7), Tom Tresh ($10)

Oakland A's - Sal Bando, Bert Campaneris ($10), Don Mincher, Ramon Webster

Philadelphia Phillies - John Boozer, John Briggs, Woodie Fryman, Ron Stone, Bill Wilson

Pittsburgh Pirates - Richie Hebner

San Diego Padres - Jack Baldschun, Chris Cannizzaro, Dick Kelley, Clay Kirby, Roberto Pena, Gary Ross, Tommie Sisk

San Francisco Giants - Bobby Bonds ($8), Jim Davenport, Dick Dietz, Tito Fuentes, Jim Ray Hart, Ron Hunt, Hal Lanier, Willie Mays ($45), Mike McCormick, Willie McCovey ($20), Gaylord Perry ($10)

Seattle Pilots - Gene Brabender ($10), Wayne Comer ($10), Tom Harper ($10), Mike Hegan ($10), George Lauzerique ($10), Jim Pagliaroni ($10), Rich Rollins ($10)

Washington Senators - Ed Brinkman, Casey Cox, Mike Epstein, Chuck Hinton, Frank Howard ($20), Ed Stroud, Ted Williams ($40), Del Unser

Matches

Collecting matchcovers has been an organized hobby since the 1939 New York World's Fair. Today, there are at least 24 clubs, with at least 4,000 members. Amongst the gamut of subjects, ranging from beer, to politics to transportation, sports covers remain the most popular, with an estimated thousands of people having sports covers in their collections. The easiest types to find are those from motels, banks and restaurants, with 50 out of every 100 coming from restaurants. Sports VIPs - players such as Mickey Mantle, Joe DiMaggio and Lefty O'Doul who have lent their names and likenesses for advertising purposes - remain quite popular among those who collect the restaurants/hotel covers.

In the late 1870s, approximately 100 small companies joined to form the Diamond Match Co. in Barberton,

Ohio. The company's first baseball set, which appeared in 1934, is the largest. The set, called the silver border (because of the silver line framing the player's photo) or U-1 (Sports Collectors Bible designation) set, has 200 different players featured, each with four different background colors - red, green, blue and orange. Thus, there are 800 covers to be collected.

Hall of Famers in the set include Jim Bottomley, Kiki Cuyler, Dizzy Dean, Leo Durocher, Rick Ferrell, Frankie Frisch, Charlie Gehringer, Chick Hafey, Jesse Haines, Gabby Hartnett, Billy Herman, Waite Hoyt, Carl Hubbell, Chuck Klein, Bill Klem, Ernie Lombardi, Al Lopez, Ted Lyons, Rabbit Maranville, Bill McKechnie, Joe Medwick, Met Ott, Casey Stengel, Dazzy Vance, Lloyd Waner, Paul Waner and Hack Wilson. Prices for the non-Hall of Famers range from $5-$20, while HOFers are about $75 each in Mint condition, with matches that haven't been struck.

The second set, U-2, was produced in 1935 and is the most difficult to assemble. Each of the 24 covers has a black border entirely around the picture on the front and history on the back. There are eight each of three colors - red, green and blue. Eleven Hall of Famers are represented.

The third set, U-3, was produced in 1935 and 1936 with green, red and blue colors. Two smaller sets were also produced through 1938. Those designated as U-4 and U-5 consist of a combined 23 players, each having three different colors (green, blue and red), making the set complete at 69. However, the set is available in two styles - with brown ink or black ink. The final set, U-6, has 14 covers in it.

Milk cartons

1961-62 Cloverleaf Dairy Minnesota Twins

Although produced in both 1961 and 1962, these unnumbered cards picturing members of the Minnesota Twins are generally collected as one 31-card set. Measuring approximately 3 3/4" by 7 3/4", the cards were actually side panels from Cloverleaf Milk cartons. Complete cartons are valued at about twice the prices listed. The front of the card includes a player photo with name, position, personal data and yearly statistics appearing below. Printing on the cartons is in shades of green. A complete set of 31 cards is $800 in Near Mint condition. Individual cards are worth $30 unless noted. The players are: Bernie Allen, George Banks, Earl Battey, Joe Bonikowski, Billy Gardner, Paul Giel, John Goryl, Lenny Green, Jim Kaat ($45), Jack Kralick, Don Lee, Jim Lemon, Georges Maranda, Billy Martin ($65), Orlando Martinez, Don Mincher, Ray Moore, Hal Naragon, Camilo Pascual ($35), Vic Power ($35), Pedro Ramos, Rich Rollins, Theodore Sadowski, Albert Stange, Dick Stigman, Chuck Stobbs, Bill Tuttle, Jose Valdivielso, Zoilo Versalles ($35), Gerald Zimmerman and Manager/Coaches.

1963 French Bauer Milk Caps

This regional set of cardboard milk bottle caps was issued in the Cincinnati area in 1963 and features 30 members of the Cincinnati Reds. The unnumbered, blank-backed cards are approximately 1 1/4" in diameter and feature rather crude drawings of the players with their names in script alongside the artwork and the words "Visit Beautiful Crosley Field/See The Reds in Action" along the outside. An album was issued to house the set. A complete set of 30 is worth $550 in Near Mint condition; individual caps are worth $5, unless noted. The album is worth $100. The players are: Don Blasingame, Leo Cardenas, Gordon Coleman, William O. DeWitt, John Edwards, Jesse Gonder, Tommy Harper, Bill Henry, Fred Hutchinson ($8), Joey Jay, Eddie Kasko, Marty Keough, Jim Maloney ($8), Joe Nuxhall ($8), Reggie Otero, Jim O'Toole, Jim Owens, Vada Pinson ($18), Bob Purkey, Frank Robinson ($60), Richard Rohde, Pete Rose ($225), Ray Shore, Dick Sisler, Bob Skinner, John Tsitorius, Jim Turner, Ken Walters, Al Worthington, and Dom Zanni.

1986 Meadow Gold Statistics Backs

Beatrice Foods produced this set of 20 cards on specially-marked boxes of Meadow Gold Double Play popsicles, fudgesicles and bubble gum coolers. They came in two-card panels and have full-color player pictures with player name, team and position printed below the photo. Card backs are printed in red ink and feature player career highlights. The cards measure 2 3/8" by 3 1/2" and were distributed in the West and Midwest. It is considered one of the toughest 1986 regional sets to complete. A complete panel set is worth $40 in Mint condition; a complete singles set is worth $20 in Mint condition.

Panel 1 ($5) - George Brett ($2), Fernando Valenzuela (.40); Panel 2 ($3.50) - Dwight Gooden (.60), Dale Murphy ($1.50); Panel 3 ($7) - Don Mattingly ($1.50), Reggie Jackson ($2); Panel 4 ($6) - Dave Winfield ($1), Pete Rose ($2); Panel 5 ($4) - Wade Boggs ($1.50), Willie McGee (.50); Panel 6 ($8) - Cal Ripken ($3), Ryne Sandberg ($2); Panel 7 ($2.50) - Carlton Fisk (.80), Jim Rice (.40); Panel 8 ($5) - Steve Garvey (.60), Mike Schmidt ($2); Panel 9 ($2) - Bruce Sutter (.40), Pedro Guerrero (.30); Panel 10 ($2) - Rick Sutcliffe (.50), Rich Gossage (.50).

1986 Meadow Gold Blank Backs

This set was the second set to be distributed by Meadow Gold Dairy (Beatrice Foods) in 1986. It was issued on Double Play ice cream cartons, one card per package. Full-color player photos have team logos and insignias airbrushed away. This 16-card set is very similar to the Meadow Gold popsicle set, but the photos are different in some instances. The cards measure 2 3/8" by 3 1/2." The Willie McGee card is reportedly tougher to find than the other cards in the set. The complete set of 16 is worth $50 in Mint condition; individual cards are worth $2-$4. The players in the set are: George Brett, Wade Boggs, Carlton Fisk, Steve Garvey, Dwight Gooden, Pedro Guerrero, Reggie Jackson, Don Mattingly, Willie McGee, Dale Murphy, Cal Ripken Jr., Pete Rose, Ryne Sandberg, Mike Schmidt, Fernando Valenzuela and Dave Winfield.

1986 Meadow Gold Milk

The third set from Meadow Gold from 1986 came on milk cartons - on pint, quart and half-gallon size containers. The cards measure 2 1/2" by 3 1/2" and feature drawings instead of photographs. Different dairies distributed the cards in various colors of ink. The cards can be found printed in red, brown or black ink. The crude drawings have prevented this rare set from being higher in price. A complete set of 11 cards is worth $100 in Mint condition. The players in the set are: Wade Boggs ($10), George Brett ($12), Steve Carlton ($8), Dwight Gooden ($6), Willie McGee ($4), Dale Murphy ($8), Cal Ripken Jr. ($12), Pete Rose ($16), Ryne Sandberg ($12), Mike Schmidt ($12) and Fernando Valenzuela ($6).

1986 Schnucks Milk St. Louis Cardinals

These milk carton panels were issued by Schnucks supermarkets in the St. Louis and southwestern Illinois areas. The 3 3/4" by 7 1/2" blank-backed panels feature black-and-white photos of 24 different St. Louis players along with personal information and 1985 player statistics. A mascot and schedule card were also include in the set. The complete set of 26 is worth $30 in Mint condition; individual photos are $1, unless noted.

The players in the set are: Jack Clark, Vince Coleman ($2), Tim Conroy, Danny Cox, Ken Dayley, Bob Forsch, Mike Heath, Tom Herr, Rick Horton, Clint Hurdle, Kurt Kepshire, Jeff Lahti, Tito Landrum, Mike Lavalliere ($1.50), Tom Lawless, Willie McGee ($2.50), Jose Oquendo, Rick Ownbey, Terry Pendleton ($4), Pat Perry, Ozzie Smith ($8), John Tudor, Andy Van Slyke ($2.50), Todd Worrell, Fred Bird (mascot) and 1986 Cardinals schedule.

441

Miscellaneous items

• 1939 Baseball's 100th Anniversary mechanical bat pencil, Louisville Slugger .... $25-$30
• Late-1940s Hall of Fame kid's beanie, blue with white letters $50
• Aug. 28, 1973, recall contract between the Cincinnati Reds and Indianapolis bringing George Foster, Joel Youngblood, Will McEnaney, Rawly Eastwick and Joe Hague back to the major leagues for $100 .... $25
• 1975 American League Championship Series announcers' notes about the Boston Red Sox starting lineup $95
• 1985 Play Ball calendar, with Harmon Killebrew on the cover, Nolan Ryan, Eddie Murray, Al Kaline, Dale Murphy on the inside $45
• Actual Major League regulation-size pitching rubber from before it was set in the mound, autographed "Tom Seaver 331 Ws" and "Phil Niekro 318 wins" $75

Movie memorabilia

A variety of means are used to advertise newly-released movies, including posters, lobby cards, inserts, half-sheets, press kits, video posters and stand-ups. Original full-size movie posters generally measure 27x41 and have a five-digit National Screen Service code printed at the bottom; the first two numbers indicate the year the film was released. "Advance" posters are also sometimes made to promote coming attractions; because they are printed in smaller quantities, these posters are generally more valuable than regular posters. Most older movie posters will be folded into eighths; they were folded so they could be mailed easier.

Lobby cards generally are 11x14 and contain eight separate photos. Inserts are 14x36, and oftentimes have the same design as their larger movie poster counterparts. Half-sheets generally look the same as a full-size poster, but are 22x28. Video posters are used by stores to publicize the release of a movie on home video; generally they have the movie company's video logo on them. Stand-ups are cardboard fold-outs, usually found in a theater lobby. Press kits contain production information, cast lists, black-and-white photos and data used by movie reviewers. The price of a kit is usually determined by the number of photos it includes.

When looking for originals, look for the NSS code, and look for those without pin holes or fading or creases, which lessen the value. Posters can be found at movie memorabilia shops and sports card shops, too. Mail order businesses are also a source, as are video stores and movie theaters themselves.

For new movies, full-size poster prices begin at around $10-$15. Bull Durham posters featuring Kevin Costner by himself are around $35, while those with Costner and Susan Sarandon are about $25. Other movies posters from the 1980s which range from $20-$30 include Field of Dreams (1989), Eight Men Out (1988) and The Natural (1984). 1970s movie posters in the $35-$50 range include The Bad News Bears (1976), Bad News Bears in Breaking Training (1977), The Bad

News Bears Go To Japan (1978), Bang the Drum Slowly (1973) and Bingo Long Traveling All-Stars and Motor Kings (1976).

1940s-1950s examples include: The Stratton Story (1949) poster $325, inserts/half sheets $250; The Jackie Robinson Story (1950) poster $350, lobby card $250; The Pride Of St. Louis (1952) poster $225-$400, lobby card $50; Fear Strikes Out (1957) poster $250; The Babe Ruth Story (1948) poster $425; The Winning Team (1952) poster $325; Pride of the Yankees (1942) poster $3,000; It Happens Every Spring (1949) poster $325; Take Me Out To The Ballgame (1949) poster $330-$525, inserts/half-sheets $425; Damn Yankees (1958) poster $285, lobby cards $65; Angels in the Outfield (1951) poster $275; Safe at Home! poster $300-$450.

Miscellaneous

• Lou Gehrig "Rawhide" movie press book, 11x17 1/2", cover features Gehrig, inside includes newspaper-like accounts of his career, plus pages of available movie posters that could be placed in movie theaters to advertise the movie .... $400-$500
• "Little Big League" Castle Rock Entertainment promotional wool and leather jacket made for the movie, brand new $225
• "Major League 2" Cleveland Indians home jersey and pants, worn by David Keith $650
• "Major League 2" Cleveland Indians game jersey, practice jersey, pants, hat, undershirt, #00, worn by Omar Epps (Willie Mays Hayes) $1,650
• Mickey Mantle "The American Dream Comes to Life" video tape $20
• 1984 "The Natural" movie promotional package and videotape, includes glossy 9x12 Academy Awards promotional booklet with Robert Redford on the cover, a Roy Hobbs baseball card, a promotional baseball, a 21x33 color poster of Redford in his movie role, and a sealed copy of the video $90
• Tom Selleck's "Mr. Baseball" white-blue cotton jersey, with pants, made by Descente, #54 .... $895

Music

More than 500 records in the form of baseball recordings have been made. The first actual baseball record - "Casey at the Bat" - was released in 1907 as performed by T. Wolfe Hopper, a prominent actor of that era. This piece is one of the most prolific pieces of baseball literature, as is "Take Me Out to the Ballgame," whose lyrics are sung the third most frequently in the United States (behind "Happy Birthday" and the National Anthem). The song has been done by more than 30 different artists since it was first released in 1910. Historical broadcasts and significant events such as Carlton Fisk's dramatic home run in the 1975 World Series have also been captured on record. The best place to find records are at garage sales, flea markets and used record stores and thrift shops.

Some of the players who have been featured on records include Joe DiMaggio (Little Johnny Strikeout, without dust jacket $45, $175 with); Jackie Robinson and Pee Wee Reese (Slugger at the Bat, two records, 1949, $200); Babe Ruth (Babe Ruth, Babe Ruth, We Love You); Mickey Mantle (I Love Mickey, sung by Theresa Brewer, $85); Willie Mays (Say Hey, Willie Mays, $100); Mays, Mantle and Duke Snider (Willie, Mickey and the Duke); Tony Oliva (My Favorite Music); and Waite Hoyt (The Best of Waite Hoyt In The Rain, $50).

Players

"Move Over Babe, Here Comes Henry Aaron" 45 rpm, $15, 33 1/3 rpm $35
"Hank Aaron, A Night To Remember" 45 rpm $15
"The Ballad of Roberto Clemente" 45 rpm $20
"Tony Conigliaro, Limited Man" 45 rpm $20
"That Holler Guy" by Joe Garagiola, 45 rpm with original sleeve .... $40-$100
"Ralph Kiner Talks to the Amazin' Mets" - Gil Hodges, Tom Seaver, Tommie Agee, etc., 33 1/3 rpm $75
"Sandy Koufax Talks With Vin Scully," Union 76 record in original sleeve, 1966 .... $50
"My Favorite Hits," Mickey Mantle album .... $150-$175
"1969 Mickey Mantle, A Day To Remember" 45 rpm $40
"A Day To Remember," Mickey Mantle 33 1/3 rpm $75

"Ode to Billy Martin" 45 rpm $25
"Denny McLain's Greatest Hits," 1963, 33 1/3 rpm......... $45
"Stan the Man Musial's Hit Record," by Phillips 66, includes booklet with Musial demonstrating hitting techniques................$25-$60
"He's a Hero to Us All," Nolan Ryan, by Jerry Jeff Walker, 1990 .... $12
"Babe Ruth: The Legend Comes to Life" 33 1/3 rpm $35
"Babe Ruth's Home Run Story," 1920, 78 rpm, with Ruth's actual voice .... $350-$1,200
Ted Williams 78 rpm photo record (1946), includes original envelope $225
Carl Yastrzemski album $25

Teams/other

"The Impossible Dream: 1967 Red Sox" ....$20-$35
"Super Sox 75," Boston's 1975 season $20
"Yes We Can," highlights of the California Angels' first 19 years, from 1961-79 .... $50
"The Sound of the Dodgers," Vin Scully, Jimmy Durante and Stubby Kaye, with Willie Davis and Maury Wills on the cover $35
"Go Get 'Em Braves," 33 1/3 rpm 1961 Braves $40
"Meet the Mets" 33 1/3 rpm, with dust jacket $70
"The Amazing Mets," 1969 season recap ....$20-$30
"Get Metsmerized," 1986 Mets recap $20
"Return to Glory," Yankees' 1977 season $35
"Ain't No Stoppin' Us Now" 45 rpm, 1980 Phillies season recap $55
"The Phantastic Phillies," 1980 recap $30
"The Impossible Pirates," 1960 recap, Bill Mazeroski home run cover, 33 1/3 rpm ....$45-$250
"The Impossible Pirates," 1960 season, 33 1/3 rpm $250
St. Louis Cardinals World Champions 1964, narrated by Harry Caray, Jack Buck $45
"The Giants Win The Pennant," 1962 Giants recap......... $50
"Baseball - The First 100 Years," 33 1/3 rpm ....$20-$45
"Baseball in the Great Yankee Tradition" 45rpm $65
"Casey at the Bat," 45 rpm, $45, 33 1/3 rpm $35
"The Greatest Moments in Sports," 33 1/3 rpm, with Ruth/Gehrig cover ....$45-$65
"Yankee Stadium's 50 Years" $45
"Yankee Stadium, The Sounds of Half a Century," narrated by Mel Allen $20
"Baseball Tips from the Stars," by Willie Mays, #1 How to Bat, 1962 .... $25
"Baseball Tips from the Stars," by Spahn, Drysdale, Podres and Jay, #2 How to Pitch, 1962 .... $25
"Baseball Tips from the Stars," by Willie Mays, #3 How to Field, 1962 .... $25
Talkin' Baseball records for the Mets, Astros, Phillies, Indians, Orioles, Red Sox, Pirates, Reds, Tigers, Cubs, Dodgers, Braves, Rangers and Giants..$25 each
Sears/Ted Williams batting tips with 45 rpm on how to be a better hitter $135

Sheet music

"Oh! You Babe Ruth" sheet music $1,141
"Safe at Home" sheet music.. $60
"I Can't Miss That Ball Game," 1910 sheet music $50
"Meet the Mets" official songsheet of the team $95
"The Milwaukee Braves Song," 1953 sheet music $45
"The National Game" sheet music, by John Phillip Sousa, 1925 .... $145
"Tigers on Parade" sheet music, 1934, roaring Tiger on the front, dedicated to Mickey Cochrane and his Tigers............... $85-$95
Ty Cobb "King of Clubs" sheet music, Cobb pose on the front $1,500
"Come Play Ball With Me Deary," 1909 sheet music, features women playing baseball, wearing Chicago and Yankee uniforms $175
"Where The Shy Little Violets Grow," 1928 sheet music, features photo of Hall of Fame pitcher Waite Hoyt at the piano $30

1971 Mattel Instant Replay Records

These 2 3/8" diameter plastic records were produced in conjunction with a hand-held, battery operated record player. Paper inserts featured illustrations of players in baseball, football and basketball, as well as various racing vehicles and airplanes. The audio recounts career highlights of the depicted player. Additional records were sold in sets of four. The complete set of 11 records sells for $200. Individual prices, in Near Mint, are: Hank Aaron ($25), Ernie Banks ($20), Al Kaline ($20), Sandy Koufax ($30), Roger Maris ($40), Willie Mays ($25, plays one side only, was included with record player purchase), Willie McCovey ($20), Tony Oliva ($10), Frank Robinson ($20), Tom Seaver ($25), and Willie Stargell ($20).

1962 Auravision 33 1/3 rpm records

Similar in design and format to the 16-record set which was issued in 1964, this test issue can be differentiated by the stats on the back. On the 1962 record, Mantle is shown in a right-handed batting posed, as compared to a follow-through on the 1964 record. While Jim Gentile and Rocky Colavito are shown in the uniforms of K.C. A's on the 1964 records, they are shown as a Tiger (Colavito) and Oriole (Gentile) on the earlier version. The set of six sells for $500. Individual prices are: Rocky Colavito ($95), Whitey Ford ($75), Jim Gentile ($45), Mickey Mantle ($125), Roger Maris ($95), Willie Mays ($175).

1964 Auravision 33 1/3 rpm records

Never a candidate for the Billboard "Hot 100," this series of baseball picture records has been popular with collectors due to the high-quality photos on front and back. On the grooved front side of the 6 3/4" x 6 3/4" plastic laminated cardboard record is a color player photo with facsimile autograph, Sports Record trophy logo and 33 1/3" RPM notation. A color border surrounds the photo and is carried over to the unrecorded back side. There is another photo on back, along with a career summary and complete major and minor league stats and instructions for playing the record. In the bottom border is a copyright notice by Sports Champions Inc., and a notice that the Auravision Record is a product of Columbia Records. A hole in the center of the record could be punched out for playing. The records featured a five-minute interview with the player by sportscaster Marty Glickman. Large quantities of the records made their way into the hobby as remainders. For early-1960s baseball items they remain reasonably priced today. The Mays record is unaccountably much scarcer than the others.

There were 50,000 copies made of each player, with an estimated 1,000 complete sets in existence, due to a fire which destroyed the bulk of them. The unnumbered set of 16 sells for $400. The individuals prices are: Bob Allison ($8.50), Ernie Banks ($42), Ken Boyer ($17), Rocky Colavito ($25), Don Drysdale ($38), Whitey Ford ($42), Jim Gentile ($8.50), Al Kaline ($38), Sandy Koufax ($50), Mickey Mantle ($110), Roger Maris ($50), Willie Mays ($110), Bill Mazeroski ($25), Frank Robinson ($38), Warren Spahn ($38) and Pete Ward ($8.50).

Newspapers

Chances are, every Major League baseball team has had its name splashed across the front page of a newspaper. And sometimes, even players make the front page, too. These papers not only offer a glimpse of baseball's storied past, but they offer affordable alternatives for today's ambitious collectors.

Historical sports moments, such as Hank Aaron's 715th home run or Babe Ruth's death, which are captured in the headlines make the best collectibles, and most valuable ones, too, oftentimes ranging from $100-$500. But some papers have hit four-figures, too, including those covering the 1919 Chicago Black Sox scandal and Babe Ruth's 60th home run. Great events are often easier newspapers to find, too, compared to the average daily story of your favorite player or team.

Value is determined by several factors, including what section features the story. Was the story on the front page of the entire newspaper, or just the sports page? Are the photos game shots, or posed? Who's pictured? Is it a photo taken the day before, or is it a stock shot which has had repeated use?

Condition plays a role in the value of a newspaper, too. Because of the high acidic content in the paper, and the fact newspapers were not made to be saved, they deteriorate over time. Papers should be stored flat (unfolded) in Mylar and other acid-free materials. Vinyl holders should be avoided. A spray called Wei-T'O claims it will protect prints, books, paper and works of art from brittleness and yellowing, and extends the life of the item two to four times.

Two sources for newspapers catalogs include: Jim Lyons Historical Newspapers, Dept. 4, 970 Terra Bella Ave., Suite 3, Mountain View, Calif. 94043; or Box Seat Collectibles, P.O. 2013, Halesite, N.Y. 11743.

• Feb. 3, 1936, New York Times: "Ty Cobb Achieves Highest Niche in Modern Baseball Hall of Fame"....................... $125
• June 6, 1941, New York Times" "Gehrig, Iron Man of Baseball, Dies at the Age of 37" $125
• July 8, 1941, New York Times: "A.L. Favored to Score 6th All-Star Victory Today".. $35
• Aug. 20, 1951, New York Times: "Small Man In Big Leagues: A Veeck Stunt" $75
• Sept. 30, 1962, Los Angeles Times: "Spahn Breaks Record for Southpaws With 327th Win"..................................... $20
• Oct. 21, 1969, New York Daily News: "Mets Ticker Tape Parade".. $20
• April 23, 1970, Des Moines Register: "Seaver Fans Record 10 In Row".. $50
• May 18, 1970, Des Moines Register: "Aaron Collects 3,000th Career Hit".. $75
• Oct. 15, 1976, New York Newsday: "Next, It's The Reds" $50
• Oct. 21, 1982, St. Louis Post: "World Champs! Cardinals Wrap It Up"... $25
• Oct. 28, 1986, New York Daily News: "Title Town! Mets Rally To Win It All" $40

In 1972, Baltimore Sun newspapers included comic inserts, 22x14, featuring full-color artistic drawings of players. They included: Roberto Clemente, Reggie Jackson, and Willie Mays ($95 each); Tom Seaver and Brooks Robinson ($75 each); Frank Robinson, Jim Palmer, Bob Gibson and Johnny Bench ($65 each); Mickey Lolich and Boog Powell ($35 each); and Bobby Grich, Paul Blair, Dave McNally, Pat Dobson, Merv Rettenmund, Dave Johnson, Andy Etchebarren, Don Buford and Mark Belanger ($25 each).

Patches/decals

Penn Emblem

In 1979, Penn Emblem, a prestigious emblem manufacturer from Philadelphia, issued a line of 100 Major League Baseball player patches, for a suggested retail price of $2.50 each. Each 2 1/2"x 3 1/2" patch featured a multi-color, three dimensional embroidered portrait of a contemporary baseball favorite. The players included are: Buddy Bell, Johnny Bench, Vida Blue, Bobby Bonds, Bob Boone, Larry Bowa, George Brett, Lou Brock, Rick Burleson, Jeff Burroughs, Bert Campaneris, John Candelaria, Rod Carew, Steve Carlton, Gary Carter, Dave Cash, Cesar Cedeno, Ron Cey, Chris Chambliss, Jack Clark, Dave Concepcion, Cecil Cooper, Jose Cruz, Andre Dawson, Dan Driessen, Rawly Eastwick, Dwight Evans, Mark Fidrych, Rollie Fingers, Carlton Fisk, George Foster, Steve Garvey, Rich Gossage, Bobby Grich, Ross Grimsley, Ron Guidry, Mike Hargrove, Keith Hernandez, Larry Hisle, Bob Horner, Roy Howell, Reggie Jackson, Tommy John, Jim Kern, Chet Lemon, Davey Lopes, Greg Luzinski, Fred Lynn, Garry Maddox, Bill Madlock, Jon Matlack, John Mayberry, Lee Mazilli, Rick Monday, Don Money, Willie Montanez, John Montefusco, Joe Morgan, Thurman Munson, Bobby Murcer, Graig Nettles, Phil Niekro, Al Oliver, Amos Otis, Jim Palmer, Dave Parker, Fred Patek, Tony Perez, Lou Piniella, Biff Pocoroba, Darrell Porter, Jim Rice, Pete Rose, Joe Rudi, Rick Rueschel, Nolan Ryan, Manny Sanguillen, Mike Schmidt, George Scott, Tom Seaver, Ted Simmons, Reggie Smith, Willie Stargell, Rennie Stennett, Jim Sundberg, Bruce Sutter, Frank Tanana, Garry Templeton, Gene Tenace, Jason Thompson, Joe Torre, Ellis Valentine, Bob Watson, Frank White, Lou Whitaker, Bump Wills, Dave Winfield, Butch Wynegar, Carl Yastrzemski and Richie Zisk.

Star-Cal decals, type I

The Meyercord Co., of Chicago, issued two sets of baseball player decals in 1952. The type I Star-Cal decal set consists of 68 different major leaguers, each pictured on a large 4 1/8" by 6 1/8" decal. The player's name and facsimile autograph appear on the decal, along with the decal number listed on the checklist here. Values shown are for decals complete with outer directions envelopes. A complete set of 68 is worth $3,200 in Near Mint condition; individual players are worth $17, unless noted.

The players in the set are: 70a) Allie Reynolds, $21; 70b) Ed Lopat; 70c) Yogi Berra, $55; 70d) Vic Raschi; 70e) Jerry Coleman; 70f) Phil Rizzuto, $55; 70g) Mickey Mantle, $800; 71a) Mel Parnell; 71b) Ted Williams, $200; 71c) Ted Williams, $200; 71d) Vern Stephens; 71e) Billy Goodman; 71f) Dom DiMaggio, $21; 71g) Dick Gernert; 71h) Hoot Evers; 72a) George Kell, $29; 72b) Hal Newhouser, $29; 72c) Hoot Evers; 72d) Vic Wertz; 72e) Fred Hutchinson; 72f) Johnny Groth; 73a) Al Zarilla; 73b) Billy Pierce, $21; 73c) Eddie Robinson; 73d) Chico Carrasquel; 73e) Minnie Minoso, $23; 73f) Jim Busby; 73g) Nellie Fox, $23; 73h) Sam Mele; 74a) Larry Doby, $21; 74b) Al Rosen, $21; 74c) Bob Lemon, $29; 74d) Jim Hegan; 74e) Bob Feller, $45; 74f) Dale Mitchell; 75a) Ned Garver; 76a) Gus Zernial; 76b) Ferris Fain; 76c) Bobby Shantz, $21; 77a) Richie Ashburn, $29; 77b) Ralph Kiner, $29; 77c) Curt Simmons; 78a) Bobby Thomson, $21; 78b) Alvin Dark; 78c) Sal Maglie; 78d) Larry Jansen; 78e) Willie Mays, $315; 78f) Monte Irvin, $29; 78g) Whitey Lockman; 79a) Gil Hodges, $34; 79b) Pee Wee Reese, $45; 79c) Roy Campanella, $55); 79d) Don Newcombe, $21; 79e) Duke Snider, $85; 79f) Preacher Roe; 79g) Jackie Robinson, $175; 80a) Eddie Miksis; 80b) Dutch Leonard; 80c) Randy Jackson; 80d) Bob Rush; 80e) Hank Sauer; 80f) Phil Cavarretta; 80g) Warren Hacker; 81a) Red Schoendienst, $29; 81b) Wally Westlake; 81c) Cliff Chambers; 81d) Enos Slaughter; 81e) Stan Musial, $150; 81f) Stan Musial, $150; and 81g) Jerry Staley.

1952 Star-Cal decals, type 2

Also produced by Chicago's Meyercord Co. in 1952, these Star-Cal decals are similar to the type I variety, except the decal sheets are smaller, measuring 4 1/8" by 3 1/16". Also, each sheet features two players instead of one. A complete set is worth $1,450 in Near Mint condition; individuals are worth $14, unless noted.

The players in the set are: 84a) Vic Raschi, Allie Reynolds, $21; 84b) Yogi Berra, Ed Lopat, $55; 84c) Jerry Coleman, Phil Rizzuto, $45; 85a) Ted Williams, Ted Williams, $200; 85b) Dom DiMaggio, Mel Parnell, $17; 85c) Billy Goodman, Vern Stephens; 86a) George Kell, Hal Newhouser, $29; 86b) Hoot Evers, Vic Wertz; 86c) Johnny Groth, Fred Hutchinson; 87a) Eddie Robinson, Eddie Robinson; 87b) Chico Carrasquel, Minnie Minoso, $17; 87c) Nellie Fox, Billy Pierce, $21; 87d) Jim Busby, Al Zarilla; 88a) Jim Hegan, Bob Lemon, $23; 88b) Larry Doby, Bob Feller, $55; 88c) Dale Mitchell, Al Rosen, $17; 89a) Ned Garver, Ned Garver; 89b) Ferris Fain, Gus Zernial; 89c) Richie Ashburn, Richie Ashburn, $23; 89d) Ralph Kiner, Ralph Kiner, $29; 90a) Monte Irvin, Willie Mays, $250; 90b) Larry Jansen, Sal Maglie; 90c) Al Dark, Bobby Thomson, $17; 91a) Gil Hodges, Pee Wee Reese, $60; 91b) Roy Campanella, Jackie Robinson, $145; 91c) Preacher Roe, Duke Snider, $65; 92a) Phil Cavarretta, Dutch Leonard; 92b) Randy Jackson, Eddie Miksis; 92c) Bob Rush, Hank Sauer; 93a) Stan Musial, Stan Musial, $145; 93b) Red Schoendienst, Enos Slaughter, $23; and 93c) Cliff Chambers, Wally Westlake.

Phone cards

Several sports-related themes have been used on phone cards, which are prepaid cards offering callers an alternative from using coins. Through a phone card, the caller has purchased phone time in advance. A $10 card entitles the caller to $10 worth of long distance phone time.

The cards, similar to credit cards, have an 800-number and a personal identification number on the back; they are punched in before the telephone number is dialed. A computer voice informs the caller how much time remains on the card and calculates time as it is used. When the time is used up, the card can be thrown away or kept as a collectible.

The cards are collectibles for several reasons - they offer the same beauty and themes of stamps, the monetary value of coins and paper money, and the trading appeal of sports cards. Generally, the most desirable cards are those which feature images of popular people, places or events. The print runs are often limited, too.

Condition also plays a factor in how valuable the card is; if a card has been used it can not be considered to be in Mint condition. Cards tend to scratch easily, so it's wise to examine the surface closely.

New phone cards can be found in a growing number of places - hobby shops, bus stations, post offices, airport gift shops, or any high pedestrian traffic area. Generally, used cards are an affordable alternative for those who are starting a phone card collection.

1994 Ameritech

Frank Thomas set of 4, $40

Robin Yount set of 4, $35

1995 AmeriVox Legends of Baseball Phone Cards

Sold only as a complete set in a cardboard fold-out collector's album, these $10 phone cards feature four Hall of Famers. Player photos on the 2 1/8x3 3/8 plastic cards have had uniform logos airbrushed away. The AmeriVox logo appears at the top and there is a red facsimile autograph at the bottom. The denomination appears in the lower-right corner. Backs are printed in black-and-white and contain information for using the cards, the player's name and the serial number from within an announced production of 5,000 sets. Marked sample cards of each player also exist. Individual cards of the four - Yogi Berra, Harmon Killebrew, Brooks Robinson and Duke Snider - are $10 each; the complete set in Mint condition is $40.

1995 Classic Phone Card Promos

Issued in mid-1995 to promote its forthcoming series of licensed baseball player phone cards, these 2 1/8x3 3/8 cards are printed on plastic and feature borderless color action photos on the fronts. Backs are printed in black and carry a sales message for the issue. Each $10-denominated promo card is overprinted on front and back: "For Promotional Use Only." The cards are unnumbered. A complete set of 8 is worth $45 in Mint condition. The players in the set are: Cal Ripken Jr. ($15); Frank Thomas, Ken Griffey Jr. ($12 each); Barry Bonds, Mike Piazza ($5 each); Juan Gonzalez ($3.50); Will Clark, Ozzie Smith ($2.50 each).

1995 Classic Phone Cards

Five special cards honoring Cal Ripken, and bilingual cards of Manny Ramirez and Hideo Nomo, are featured in Classic's Major League Baseball phone card set, at the time of its issue the largest ever to feature individual players. Each of the 2 1/8x3 3/8 plastic cards was sold in an individual blister pack and carries $10 worth of long distance phone time. Fronts feature borderless color action photos and have team logos; backs are in black-and-white and have instructions for using the cards. The complete set of is worth $550 in Mint condition; common players are $10.

The players in the set are: Roberto Alomar, Kevin Appier, Jeff Bagwell, Carlos Baerga, Albert Belle, Dante Bichette, Craig Biggio, Wade Boggs, Barry Bonds, Jose Canseco, Joe Carter, Will Clark, Roger Clemens, Jeff Conine, Len Dykstra, Darren Daulton, Cecil Fielder, Travis Fryman, Andres Galarraga, Ron Gant, Juan Gonzalez, Mark Grace, Ken Griffey Jr. ($25), Tony Gwynn, Rickey Henderson, Randy Johnson, Chipper Jones ($15), Dave Justice, Jeff Kent, Barry Larkin, Kenny Lofton, Greg Maddux, Fred McGriff, Mark McGwire, Don Mattingly, Raul Mondesi, Eddie Murray, Mike Mussina, Denny Neagle, Hideo Nomo (Japanese/English, $25; regular, $20), Paul O'Neill, Mike Piazza, Carlos Perez, Kirby Puckett, Manny Ramirez (Spanish/English), Cal Ripken Jr. (five specials $25 each; autographed, $200; regular, $25; $100 redemption card, $125), Ivan Rodriguez, Tim Salmon, Deion Sanders, Reggie Sanders, Ozzie Smith, Sammy Sosa, Frank Thomas ($15), Mo Vaughn, Robin Ventura, Larry Walker and Matt Williams.

1996 Classic/Sports Cards Phone Card

This card, commemorating Cal Ripken's 2,131st game, was available exclusively by subscribing to Sports Cards magazine in the spring of 1995. The card is the standard 3 3/8x2 1/8 plastic format. The card is worth $5 in Mint condition.

1994 Diamond Connection Ken Griffey Jr. Phone Cards

In conjunction with MCI, Diamond Connection produced a five-card phone card issue of Ken Griffey Jr. The set was introduced with a promo card giveaway at the 1994 National Sports Collectors Convention in Houston. Printed in color on plastic 2 1/8x3 3/8 format, the cards picture Griffey in a variety of batting poses and portraits. Backs are in black-and-white and have details for using the cards. The issue was limited to 5,000 numbered sets, which are each worth $40 in Mint condition. Individual cards are worth $10 each. The six are: 1) promo card, 2 units; 2) 10 units, batting; 3) 10 units, batting; 4) 10 units, batting; 5) 10 units, portrait; 6) 10 units, portrait.

GTS 1969 New York Mets Phone Cards

One of the first multi-player phone card issues was this 32-card series from Global Telecommunications Solutions honoring the 25th anniversary of the "Miracle Mets'" 1969 World's Championship. Cards picture team members in color portraits by sports artist Ron Lewis. A gold-foil headline in the top white border reads "'69 Mets Collector Edition." Backs of the 2 1/8" by 3 3/8" plastic cards are printed in black-and-white and contain instructions for using the phone card. Each of the unnumbered phone cards had a nominal value of five minutes of phone time. The complete set of 32 cards is worth $225 in Mint condition. Individual cards are worth $6 to $8, unless noted. The players featured are: Tommie Agee, Yogi Berra ($15), Ken Boswell, Don Cardwell, Ed Charles, Donn Clendenon, Jack DiLauro, Duffy Dyer, Wayne Garrett, Rod Gaspar, Gary Gentry, Jerry Grote, Bud Harrelson, Gil Hodges ($12), Cleon Jones, Cal Koonce, Jerry Koosman, Ed Kranepool, J.C. Martin, Jim McAndrew, Tug McGraw, Bobby Pfeil, Joe Pignatano, Nolan Ryan ($60), Tom Seaver ($30), Art Shamsky, Ron Swoboda, Ron Taylor, Rube Walker, Al Weis, Ed Yost and the Mets logo.

1995 GTS Major League Baseball Team Logo cards

complete set (30) $180

individual cards $6

1995 MCI

Mickey Mantle/Bobby Murcer Oklahoma City charity card
.... $50

1995 Southwestern Bell

Stan Musial set (10) $175

1995 Topps Stadium Club
Phone Card inserts (Ring Leaders)

An interactive contest carrying through the "Ring Leaders" insert card set theme featured randomly inserted phone cards picturing All-Star Game players' rings. The 2 1/8x3 3/8 plastic cards could be found in regular, silver and gold editions. By using the card for a long distance call, the holder could determine if it was a further winner. Regular card winners received a set of Stadium Club Ring Leaders insert cards. Winners on a silver card received a complete set of the 13 different phone cards in all three versions. Gold card winners received the genuine All-Star ring pictured on the card. Approximately 217,000 phone cards were inserted in the program; odds of finding a regular card were about one per 40 packs; silver, one per 237 packs; and gold, one per 2,955 packs. Cards picturing the 1988 and 1989 All-Star rings were not issued. Phone cards with the number panel on back scratched off are worth 40-60% of values quoted. A complete set of regular cards is worth $30 in Mint condition; a complete silver set is worth $100; a complete gold set is worth $250. Common regular cards are worth $3; common silver cards are worth $10; common gold cards are worth $20. The cards are: 1980 Los Angeles, 1981 Cleveland, 1982 Montreal, 1983 Chicago A.L., 1984 San Francisco, 1985 Minnesota, 1986 Houston, 1987 Oakland, 1990 Chicago N.L., 1991 Toronto, 1992 San Diego, 1993 Baltimore and 1994 Pittsburgh.

1994 Upper Deck/GTS
Mickey Mantle Phone Cards

Upper Deck and Global Telecommunication Solutions combined to produce this set of phone cards paralleling the Mantle Heroes insert cards found in the regular Upper Deck baseball card packs. The phone cards were sold in two series of five cards each for $59.95 per series. Fronts of the 2 1/8x3 3/8 plastic cards feature black-and-white or color photos of Mantle, along with a career highlight. Backs are printed in black and have instructions for using the card. A card picturing the 1869 Cincinnati Red Stockings was included as a random insert in the first series of Mantle phone card sets. A complete set of 10 in Mint condition is $150, with individual cards ranging from $12.50 to $20. The cards portray: 1) portrait, 2) 1951: The Early Years, 3) 1953: Tape Measure Home Runs, 4) 1956: Triple Crown Season, 5) 1957: Second Consecutive MVP, 6) 1961: Chasing the Babe, 7) 1964: Series Home Run Record, 8) 1967: 500th Home Run, 9) 1974: Hall of Fame, 10) portrait. The Red Stockings phone card is worth $65.

1995 Upper Deck/GTS Phone Cards

In conjunction with Global Telecommunications Service, Upper Deck issued a series of 15 phone cards described as being the first licensed by Major League Baseball and the Players Association. Measuring about 2 1/8x3 3/8, with rounded corners, the cards were printed on heavy plastic and utilized the basic format and photos from the players' 1994 Upper Deck baseball cards. Issue price, with phone time, was $12 each. The complete set, in Mint condition, is worth $180. Individual cards are worth $12 each, except Cal Ripken Jr., who's at $45, and Frank Thomas and Ken Griffey Jr., each at $25. The players featured are: Roberto Alomar, Jeff Bagwell, Barry Bonds, Roger Clemens, Cecil Fielder, Griffey Jr., Tony Gwynn, Dave Justice, Don Mattingly, Fred McGriff, Kirby Puckett, Ripken Jr., Gary Sheffield, Ozzie Smith and Thomas.

Player-related souvenirs

• Hank Aaron 715 Home Run King T-shirt $65
• 1974 Hank Aaron theme spiral notebook, color photo of Aaron on the front $20
• Johnny Bench's Battle of the Superstars warm-up jacket, worn during that competition, signed "Catch Ya Later, Johnny Bench" $575
• Johnny Bench's scarlet baseball school nylon jacket, signed "Catch Ya Later, Johnny Bench" $175
• Johnny Bench/Pete Rose Lincoln-Mercury dealership 8x11 1/2 letterhead $20
• 1971 Johnny Bench/Pete Rose Lincoln-Mercury dealership bumper decals, unused $40
• 1971 Johnny Bench/Willis Reed Keds gym shoe box, with size 12 shoes included, has large cards of Bench and Reed on the top $175
• Johnny Bench's 1973 Cincinnati Reds player contract offering him $85,000 per year, refused by Bench $1,195
• Johnny Bench Stroh's Beer keychain, shaped like a ticket, dated Aug. 11, 1984, commemorates the retirement of Bench's uniform $40
• Wade Boggs' Boston Red Sox check, payable to him for $55.86, dated Feb. 28, 1983, matted and framed with an 8x10 photo $250
• Roberto Clemente 20x28 charcoal sketch for "Roberto Clemente Night," from Bill Madlock $1,750
• Ty Cobb writing tablet, 6x9 lined notepad with Cobb on the cover surrounded by baseball-related newspaper clippings $175
• Del Crandall porcelain glove ashtray $110
• 1930s Dizzy Dean Winner's Bread pin, brass bat and ball with a facsimile autograph down the bat $45
• Joe DiMaggio Fisherman's Wharf Restaurant menu, with facsimile autograph $50
• Joe DiMaggio Fisherman's Wharf Restaurant pennant, red, 1940s $200
• Joe DiMaggio Bakelite plastic pencil bat, 1940s Louisville Slugger, facsimile autograph on the barrel $80
• Joe DiMaggio matchbook, 1950, from his San Francisco restaurant, matches in tact, pictures DiMaggio in front of the locker $25
• Lou Gehrig wooden bat pencil, with mechanical lead, features image of Gehrig batting $50
• 1971 Harmon Killebrew 500 Home Runs insulated plastic mug, miniature baseballs depict his milestone home runs, shows the then six members of the 500 Home Run Club $25
• Don Larsen Oct. 6, 1956, World Series commemorative plate, has Yankee Stadium box score, signed by Larsen and Yogi Berra $400

• Official Pennsylvania governor's proclamation for Connie Mack Day, April 15, 1941 .... $500
• Roger Maris/Eddie Mathews Louisville Slugger pen and pencil bat set, 1960s $60
• Mickey Mantle's Restaurant in New York, menu and napkins $30
• 1968 Mickey Mantle's Isometric "Minute a Day Home Gym," exercise system, shows Mantle's face on the box $95
• "Say Hey! Buy USA" Willie Mays bumper sticker $45
• 1981 Willie Mays/Ronald Reagan postcard from the White House $55
• Joe Medwick 1930s wooden pencil bat, facsimile autograph on the barrel $35
• Joe Morgan Kahn's Wieners commemorative coin, still in the bubble pack $4
• 1980 contract signed by Lou Piniella with Wiffle Ball to appear on the box side.. $15
• 1980 contract signed by Jimmy Piersall with Xerox Corp. to promote its educational materials $15
• Babe Ruth knife keychain.. $75
• 1920s "Bambino" Tobacco rolling papers, original pack of papers made for Bambino Tobacco, wrapper pictures Babe Ruth swinging a bat.. $300
• 1930s Babe Ruth belt buckle $265
• Babe Ruth musical bat, 1930s, 4" wooden harmonica . $150
• 1940-50 Babe Ruth League booster pin, red, white and blue with a silhouette of Ruth $24
• 1948 slide picturing Babe Ruth and William Bendix during filming of the Babe Ruth Story, a promo item for the world premier $15.75
• 1949-50 Babe Ruth commemorative brass coin, 1 1/4" diameter.. $35
• 1990 Nolan Ryan "He's a Hero to Us All" CD $75
• Early-1980s Nolan Ryan Gillette premium blue windbreaker, with facsimile autograph.. $125
• 1977 contract signed by Ron Santo to appear at the American Airlines Golf Tournament................................. $12.75
• Willie Stargell stars, two, given to Pittsburgh Pirates players during the 1979 season.. $85
• 1978 statement signed by Don Sutton retaining his amateur status with the U.S. Golf Association $10.75
• Tony Taylor Night keychain, from Aug. 9, 1975, has two photos and facsimile autograph... $45
• Joe Tinker cigar band $125
• 1986 life-size Bob Uecker face mask, by Miller Lite...... $7
• Ted Williams Sears box of Target Load Shotgun shells, 12-gauge, 25 in box $850
• Ted Williams Jimmy Fund tag $45
• Ted Williams 1959 "Jimmy Fund" membership card and hang tab $150
• Carl Yastrzemski Boston Red Sox check, made payable to him for $1,655, dated June
• 15, 1977, matted and framed with and 8x10 photo $250

Playing cards

1985 Chicago Cubs playing cards

A regular 52-card deck plus two jokers comprise this set produced by long-time Cubs broadcaster Jack Brickhouse, whose photo and trademark phase "Hey Hey" are featured on the back of each card. Card fronts have a black-and-white photo with the player's name and a date underneath. Traditional suit and value markings of a playing card deck are included in the corners of the 2 1/2" by 3 1/2" round-cornered cards. The cards are arranged in chronological order. The complete set of 54 cards is worth $8 in Mint condition;

individual cards are worth a dime, unless noted. The two Joker cards feature Ron Cey and Jack Brickhouse and Harry Caray.

Hearts - A Jack Brickhouse, 2 1876 Champions, 3 Cap Anson, 4 Joe Tinker/Johnny Evers/Frank Chance/ Harry Steinfeldt (.25), 5 Ed Reulbach, 6 Mordecai Brown, 7 Jim Vaughn, 8 Joe McCarthy, 9 Jimmy Cooney, 10 Rogers Hornsby (.25), J Hack Wilson, Q Hack Wilson/Babe Ruth/Lou Gehrig (.25), K Babe Ruth (.50)

Clubs - A Lon Warneke, 2 Augie Galan, 3 1935 Pennant-winning Cubs, 4 Dizzy Dean (.25), 5 Gabby Hartnett, 6 Billy Herman, 7 Charlie Root, 8 Charlie Grimm, 9 Andy Pafko (.15), 10 Stan Hack, J Phil Cavarretta, Q National League Champs, K Bill Nicholson

Diamonds - A Burt Hooten, 2 Fergie Jenkins (.15), 3 Ron Santo (.15), 4 Ken Holtzman, 5 1969 Cubs, 6 Billy Williams (.15), 7 Ken Hubbs (.25), 8 Don Cardwell, 9 Lou Boudreau (.15), 10 Dale Long, J Sam Jones, Q Ernie Banks, K Hank Sauer (.50)

Spades - A Leon Durham, 2 Keith Moreland, 3 Gary Mathews, 4 Bob Dernier, 5 1984 Eastern Division Champs, 6 Ryne Sandberg (.50), 7 Jim Frey, 8 Rick Sutcliffe, 9 Jody Davis, 10 Dallas Green, J Bill Madlock, Q Rick Reuschel, K Milt Pappas

1977-78 Cubic Corp. Sports Decks playing cards

Playing cards featuring pencil drawings of stars in various sports were produced on a limited basis in the late 1970s by Cubic Corp. of San Diego. The cards were standard bridge size (2 1/4" by 3 1/2") with rounded corners and featured the artwork of Al Landsman along with a facsimile autograph within a colored frame. Each deck had the same athlete on the back and sold for $1.60. There is no indication of the manufacturer on individual cards; it is only found on the box. It is believed most of the decks were only produced in limited sample quantities. Similar cards were produced for Pepsi and are listed thereunder. Only the baseball players are checklisted here, in alphabetical order. A complete set of baseball, boxed decks, is worth $300 in Near Mint condition; a complete set of baseball, one card each, is worth $24.

1a) Johnny Bench bd	$25
1b) Johnny Bench sc	$2
2a) Catfish Hunter bd	$15
2b) Catfish Hunter sc	$1.50
3a) Randy Jones bd	$12
3b) Randy Jones sc	.50
3a) Mickey Mantle bd	$200
4b) Mickey Mantle sc	$10
5a) Butch Metzger bd	$12
5b) Butch Metzger sc	.50
6a) Stan Musial bd	$60
6b) Stan Musial sc	$4
7a) Pete Rose bd	$45
7b) Pete Rose sc	$4
8a) Tom Seaver bd	$30
8b) Tom Seaver sc	$3
9a) Frank Tanana bd	$12
9b) Frank Tanana sc	.50

1969 Globe Import playing cards

Measuring 1 5/8x2 1/4, with black-and-white photos and blank backs, these cards have rather muddy player action photos in the center of each card, with the player's name reversed out of a black strip at the bottom. A complete set of 52 cards in Near Mint condition is worth $3; individuals are worth .05-.10, unless noted.

Hearts - A Willie Mays (.50), 2 Chris Short, 3 Tony Conigliaro, 4 Bill Freehan, 5 Willie McCovey (.25), 6 Joel Horlen, 7 Ernie Banks (.40), 8 Jim Wynn, 9 Brooks Robinson (.40), 10 Orlando Cepeda (.25), J Al Kaline (.40), Q Gene Alley, K Rusty Staub (.10)

Clubs - A Richie Allen, 2 Reggie Smith, 3 Jerry Koosman, 4 Tony Oliva, 5 Bud Harrelson, 6 Rick Reichardt, 7 Billy Williams (.25), 8 Pete Rose (.40), 9 Jim Maloney, 10 Tim McCarver, J Max Alvis, Q Ron Swoboda, K Johnny Callison

Diamonds - A Bob Gibson (.25), 2 Paul Casanova, 3 Juan Marichal (.25), 4 Jim Fregosi, 5 Earl Wilson, 6 Tony Horton, 7 Harmon Killebrew (.25), 8 Tom Seaver (.35), 9 Curt Flood, 10 Frank Robinson (.40), J Bob Aspromonte, Q Lou Brock (.25), K Jim Lonborg

Spades - A Ken Harrelson, 2 Denny McLain, 3 Rick Monday, 4 Richie Allen, 5 Mel Stottlemyre, 6 Tommy John, 7 Don Mincher, 8 Chico Cardenas, 9 Willie Davis, 10 Campy Campaneris, J Ron Santo, Q Al Ferrara, K Clete Boyer

1977 Pepsi Cincinnati Reds playing cards

Similar to a multi-sport series produced by Cubic Corp., these playing card sets feature on the backs the pencil drawings of Al Landsman. Each boxed deck featured one Reds star player with a red border. Also on each card back are a facsimile autograph and a Pepsi logo. Cards are 2 1/4" by 3 1/2" with rounded corners. Decks were available by sending in 250 16-ounce Pepsi cap liners or a combination of cash and cap liners. A complete set of boxed decks is worth $24 in Near Mint condition; a complete set, with one card each, is worth $6. A common boxed deck is worth $8. The players in the set are: Johnny Bench (bd $10; sc $3); Joe Morgan (bd $8, sc $2); and Pete Rose (bd $12, sc $4).

1933 Rittenhouse Candy playing cards (E285)

Designed to resemble a set of playing cards, this set, issued circa 1933 by the Rittenhouse Candy Co. of Philadelphia, carries the ACC designation E285 and is generally considered to be the last of the E-card issues. Each card measures 1 7/16" by 2 1/4" and features a small black-and-white player photo in the center of the playing card design. The backs of the cards usually consist of just one large letter and were part of a promotion in which collectors were instructed to find enough different letters to spell "Rittenhouse Candy Co." Other backs explaining the contest and the prizes available have also been found, as have backs with numbers. Because it was designed as a deck of playing cards, the set is complete at 52 cards, featuring 46 different players (six are pictured on two cards each). Cards have been found in red, orange, green and blue. The complete set of 52 cards is worth $5,000 in Near Mint condition. Individual cards are worth $50, unless noted. The players featured are: Dick Bartell, Walter Berger, Max Bishop, James Bottomley ($100), Fred Brickell, Sugar Cain, Ed Cihocki, Phil Collins, Roger Cramer, Hughie Critz, Joe Cronin ($110), Kiki Cuyler ($100), George Davis, Spud Davis, Jimmy Dykes ($55), George Earnshaw, Jumbo Elliot, Lou Finney, Jimmy Foxx ($150), Frankie Frisch ($100, 3 of Spades), Frankie Frisch ($100, 7 of Spades), Lefty Grove ($125), Mule Haas, Chick Hafey ($100), Leo Hartnett ($100), Babe Herman ($55), William Herman ($100), Kid Higgins, Rogers Hornsby ($125), Don Hurst (Jack of Diamonds), Don Hurst (6 of Spades), Chuck Klein ($100), Leroy Mahaffey, Gus Mancuso, Rabbit McNair, Bing Miller, Lefty O'Doul ($60), Mel Ott ($110), Babe Ruth ($1,000, Ace of Spades), Babe Ruth ($1,000, King of Clubs), Al Simmons ($100), Bill Terry ($110), Pie Traynor ($100), Rube Walberg, Lloyd Waner ($100), Lloyd Warner ($100, Waner), Paul Waner ($100), Paul Warner ($100, Waner), Pinkey Whitney, Dib Williams, Hack Wilson ($100, 9 of Spades) and Hack Wilson ($100, 9 of Clubs).

1990 U.S. Playing Card All-Stars

Sold as a box set, these cards are in the standard 2 1/2" by 3 1/2" format but have rounded corners. Each card features a color player photo with the upper left and lower right corners inset to provide for the playing card designations. A team logo appears in the lower left corner. On American League players' cards (Clubs and Spades) the player's name and position appear in white in a blue box beneath the photo. On the National Leaguers' cards (Hearts and Diamonds) the box is red and the printing black. Card backs are identical, with blue borders and a multi-colored "1990 Baseball Major League" logo on a pinstriped white center panel. The U.S. Playing Card Co. logo is at the bottom. A complete set of 56 cards is worth $4 in Mint condition. Individuals worth .05-.10, unless noted.

Hearts - A Ramon Martinez, K Darryl Strawberry, Q Kevin Mitchell, J Bobby Bonilla, 10 Benito Santiago, 9 Andre Dawson (.20), 8 Matt Williams, 7 John Franco, 6 Ozzie Smith (.20), 5 Chris Sabo, 4 Ryne Sandberg (.40), 3 Jeff Brantley, 2 Mike Scioscia. (.05)

Clubs - A Bob Welch, K Rickey Henderson (.25), Q George Bell, J Wade Boggs (.30), 10 Dave Stieb, 9 Bobby Thigpen, 8 Dennis Eckersley, 7 Ellis Burks, 6 Ozzie Guillen, 5 Brook Jacoby, 4 Gregg Olson, 3 Bret Saberhagen, 2 Lance Parrish

Diamonds - A Frank Viola, K Barry Bonds (.35), Q Will Clark (.30), J Tony Gwynn (.25), 10 Shawon Dunston, 9 Lenny Dykstra, 8 Dave Smith, 7 Neal Heaton, 6 Barry Larkin, 5 Tim Wallach, 4 Roberto Alomar (.25), 3 Dennis Martinez, 2 Greg Olson

Spades - A Roger Clemens, K Cecil Fielder (.20), Q Dave Parker (.20), J Ken Griffey Jr. (.50), 10 Alan Trammell, 9 Chuck Finley/Cal Ripken Jr., 8 Kirby Puckett (.20), 7 Doug Jones, 6 5 Kelly Gruber, 4 Steve Sax, 3 Randy Johnson, 2 Sandy Alomar

Wild Cards/Jokers - Jack Armstrong Joker, Julio Franco Joker, Rob Dibble/Randy Myers Wild Card, Mark McGwire/Jose Canseco Wild Card (.25)

1991 U.S. Playing Card All-Stars

In a standard 2 1/2" by 3 1/2" format, with rounded corners, this 56-card set was produced by the country's leading maker of playing cards and sold as a boxed set. Fronts have a color player photo with the top-left and bottom-right corners inset to include playing card designations. A team logo appears in the upper right corner. On American Leaguers' cards (Hearts and Diamonds), the players' name and position appear in white in a green stripe beneath the photo. National League players (Clubs and Spades) have a yellow stripe with black printing. Backs are red bordered with a colorful "1991 Baseball Major League All-Stars" logo on a pinstriped white center panel. The U.S. Playing Card Co. logo is at the bottom. A complete set of 56 cards in Mint condition is worth $4; individuals are worth .05-.10, unless noted.

Hearts - A Jack Morris, K Dave Henderson, Q Roberto Alomar (.20), J Rickey Henderson (.20), 10 Roger Clemens, 9 Ruben Sierra, 8 Paul Molitor (.15), 7 Rick Aguilera, 6 Julio Franco, 5 Mark Langston, 4 Joe Carter, 3 Jack McDowell, 2 Ozzie Guillen

Clubs - A Tony Gwynn (.15), K Ivan Calderon, Q Chris Sabo, J Andre Dawson (.15), 10 Lee Smith, 9 Craig Biggio, 8 Juan Samuel, 7 Frank Viola, 6 Barry Larkin, 5 Mike Morgan, 4 Howard Johnson, 3 John Smiley, 2 Paul O'Neill

Diamonds - A Ken Griffey Jr. (.50), K Cal Ripken Jr. (.50), Q Cecil Fielder (.20), J Sandy Alomar, 10 Dennis Eckersley, 9 Harold Baines, 8 Jimmy Key, 7 Bryan Harvey, 6 Rafael Palmeiro, 5 Jeff Reardon, 4 Kirby Puckett (.20), 3 Scott Sanderson, 2 Carlton Fisk (.15)

Spades - A Tom Glavine, K Ozzie Smith (.20), Q Ryne Sandberg (.40), J Benito Santiago, 10 Rob Dibble, 9 Terry Pendleton, 8 Brett Butler, 7 Dennis Martinez, 6 George Bell, 5 Tom Browning, 4 John Kruk, 3 Pete Harnisch, 2 Eddie Murray (.15)

Wild Cards/Jokers - Bobby Bonilla Joker, Danny Tartabull Joker, Wade Boggs Wild Card (.25), Will Clark Wild Card (.25)

1992 U.S. Playing Card Aces

This 56-card boxed set features 13 top players in each of four major statistical categories, ranked by performance. Hearts feature RBI leaders, Clubs depict home run hitters, batting average leaders are featured on Diamonds and Spades have pitchers with the lowest ERAs. Card fronts feature full-bleed color photos, with the playing card suit and rank overprinted in the upper-left and lower-right corners. A team logo is in the lower-left, along with a black box containing the player's name and position in gold. Backs have a red, white and gold "Major League Baseball 1992 Aces" against a black background. The 2 1/2" by 3 1/2" cards have rounded corners. A complete set of 56 cards in Mint condition is worth $4; individuals are worth .05-.15, unless noted.

Hearts - A Cecil Fielder (.20), K Jose Canseco (.25), Q Howard Johnson, J Cal Ripken Jr. (.20), 10 Barry Bonds (.25), 9 Ruben Sierra, 8 Cal Ripken Jr. (.40), 7 Frank Thomas (.50), 6 Joe Carter, 5 Fred McGriff, 4 Ron Gant, 3 Andre Dawson, 2 Juan Gonzalez (.30)

Clubs - A Jose Canseco (.25), K Cecil Fielder (.20), Q Howard Johnson, J Cal Ripken Jr. (.40), 10 Matt Williams, 9 Cal Ripken Jr., 8 Ron Gant, 7 Frank Thomas (.50), 6 Andre Dawson, 5 Fred McGriff, 4 Danny Tartabull, 3 Mickey Tettleton, 2 Chili Davis

Diamonds - A Julio Franco, K Wade Boggs (.25), Q Willie Randolph, J Ken Griffey Jr. (.40), 10 Paul Molitor (.15), 9 Cal Ripken Jr. (.40), 8 Rafael Palmeiro (.40), 7 Terry Pendleton, 6 Kirby Puckett (.20), 5 Hal Morris, 4 Frank Thomas (.50), 3 Tony Gwynn (.15), 2 Danny Tartabull

Spades - A Dennis Martinez, K Jose Rijo, Q Tom Glavine, J Tim Belcher, 10 Roger Clemens, 9 Tom Candiotti, 8 Pete Harnisch, 7 Jose DeLeon, 6 Mike Morgan, 5 Bill Wegman, 4 Jim Abbott, 3 Nolan Ryan (.50), 2 Mike Moore

Roger Clemens Joker, Tom Glavine Joker, Home Run Rummy Game Instructions, Header Card

1992 U.S. Playing Card All-Stars

Players from the 1992 All-Star Game are featured in this set of 56 playing cards. In playing card format of 2 1/2" by 3 1/2" with rounded corners, the cards have a photo on the front with a team logo in the upper right corner. Traditional playing card suits and values are in the upper left and lower right corners. Player names are in a yellow (American League) or red (National League) box beneath the photo. Backs have a large product logo on a white background with a dark blue-green border. Appropriate licenser and manufacturer logos appear at the bottom. The set was sold in a box featuring miniature representations of some of the cards. A complete set of 56 cards in Mint condition is worth $5; individuals are worth .10, unless noted.

Clubs - A Roberto Alomar (.25), K Wade Boggs (.45), Q Mark McGwire, J Sandy Alomar Jr., 10 Edgar Martinez, 9 Carlos Baerga (.25), 8 Paul Molitor (.20), 7 Ruben Sierra (.15), 6 Chuck Knoblauch (.15), 5 Robin Ventura (.20), 4 Charles Nagy, 3 Juan Guzman, 2 Joe Carter (.20)

Spades - A Ken Griffey Jr. (.75), K Kirby Puckett (.45), Q Cal Ripken Jr. (.50), J Jose Canseco (.45), 10 Roger Clemens (.25), 9 Kevin Brown, 8 Rick Aguilera, 7 Jack McDowell, 6 Jeff Montgomery, 5 Travis Fryman, 4 Brady Anderson, 3 Roberto Kelly, 2 Ivan Rodriguez (.15)

Hearts - A Andy Van Slyke, K Fred McGriff (.20), Q Ozzie Smith (.20), J Ryne Sandberg (.50), 10 John Kruk (.15), 9 Mike Sharperson, 8 Gary Sheffield (.15), 7 Will Clark (.25), 6 Tony Fernandez, 5 David Cone, 4 Tom Pagnozzi, 3 Larry Walker, 2 Greg Maddux (.15)

Diamonds - A Tony Gwynn (.25), K Barry Bonds (.45), Q Terry Pendleton (.15), J Benito Santiago, 10 Tom Glavine, 9 Lee Smith, 8 John Smoltz, 7 Norm Charlton, 6 Bip Roberts, 5 Craig Biggio, 4 Doug Jones, 3 Ron Gant (.15), 2 Bob Tewksbury

Dennis Eckersley Wild Card, Mike Mussina/Mark Langston Joker, Darren Daulton/Dennis Martinez Joker, advertising card

1992 U.S. Playing Card team sets

Besides several All-Star sets, the U.S. Playing Card Co. in 1992 issued playing card sets for several teams. All were issued as a 56-card boxed set in a similar format. Cards are 2 1/2" by 3 1/2" with rounded corners. Fronts feature player photos with inserts at the upper left and lower right corners to allow playing card suit designations and ratings. The player's name and position appears in a colored strip beneath the photo. Backs feature a large color team logo set against a gray background with either dark blue or red pinstriping and heavy vertical side bars.

Each team set is worth $4.50 in Mint condition, with individual cards worth between .05 and .20, unless noted.

Atlanta Braves

Hearts - A Otis Nixon, K Ron Gant, Q Juan Berenguer, J Dave Justice (.25), 10 Tom Glavine, 9 Jeff Treadway, 8 Lonnie Smith, 7 Kent Mercker, 6, Brian Hunter, 5 Armando Reynoso, 4 Sid Bream, 3 Mike Stanton, 2 Deion Sanders

Clubs - A Terry Pendleton, K Charlie Leibrandt, Q Jeff Blauser, J Pete Smith, 10 Otis Nixon, 9 Ron Gant, 8 Juan Berenguer, 7 Dave Justice (.25), 6 Rico Rossy, 5 Marvin Freeman, 4 Kent Mercker, 3 Armando Reynoso, 2 Mark Lemke

Diamonds - A Steve Avery, K Greg Olson, Q Rafael Belliard, J Brian Hunter, 10 Terry Pendleton, 9 Charlie Leibrandt, 8 John Smoltz, 7 Rico Rossy, 6 Jim Clancy, 5 Jeff Blauser, 4 Mike Heath, 3 Pete Smith, 2 Marvin Freeman

Spades - A Tom Glavine, K Jeff Treadway, Q Lonnie Smith, J John Smoltz, 10 Steve Avery, 9 Greg Olson, 8 Rafael Belliard, 7 Sid Bream, 6 Mike Stanton, 5 Mike Heath, 4 Mark Lemke, 3 Deion Sanders, 2 Jim Clancy

National League logo Joker, National League logo Joker, 1992 Atlanta Braves home schedule, Atlanta Braves history

Boston Red Sox

Hearts - A Roger Clemens (.25), K Greg Harris, Q Jeff Gray, J Jack Clark, 10 Wade Boggs (.30), 9 Carlos Quintana, 8 Tony Fossas, 7 Phil Plantier, 6 Jeff Reardon, 5 Danny Darwin, 4 Dennis Lamp, 3 John Marzano, 2 Matt Young

Clubs - A Mike Greenwell, K Jody Reed, Q John Marzano, J Luis Rivera, 10 Roger Clemens (.25), 9 Jack Clark, 8 Jeff Gray, 7 Dan Petry, 6 Tony Pena, 5 Greg Harris, 4 Dana Kiecker, 3 Dan Petry, 2 Danny Darwin

Diamonds - A Joe Hesketh, K Ellis Burks, Q Mo Vaughn (.25), J Tom Brunansky, 10 Mike Greenwell, 9 Jody Reed, 8 Kevin Morton, 7 Tom Bolton, 6 Luis Rivera, 5 Matt Young, 4 Tony Fossas, 3 Dana Kiecker, 2 Steve Lyons

Spades - A Wade Boggs (.30), K Carlos Quintana, Q Phil Plantier, J Tony Pena, 10 Jeff Reardon, 9 Ellis Burks, 8 Joe Hesketh, 7 Dennis Lamp, 6 Tom Brunansky, 5 Steve Lyons, 4 Kevin Morton, 3 Mo Vaughn (.25), 2 Tom Bolton

American League logo Joker, American League logo Joker, 1992 Boston Red Sox home schedule, Boston Red Sox team history

Chicago Cubs

Hearts - A Andre Dawson, K Chuck McElroy, Q Chico Walker, J Jerome Walton, 10 Danny Jackson, 9 Ryne Sandberg (.35), 8 Mark Grace, 7 Paul

Assenmacher, 6 Chico Walker, 5 Bob Scanlan, 4 Doug Dascenzo, 3 Rick Wilkins, 2 Dwight Smith

Clubs - A George Bell, K Shawon Dunston, Q Doug Dascenzo, J Hector Villanueva, 10 Dave Smith, 9 Andre Dawson, 8 Chuck McElroy, 7 Luis Salazar, 6 Shawn Boskie, 5 Danny Jackson, 4 Heathcliff Slocumb, 3 Jose Vizcaino, 2 Gary Scott

Diamonds - A Greg Maddux, K Paul Assenmacher, Q Les Lancaster, J Frank Castillo, 10 Frank Castillo, 9 George Bell, 8 Jerome Walton, 7 Mike Harkey, 6 Jose Vizcaino, 5 Ced Landrum, 4 Gary Scott, 3 Ced Landrum, 2 Shawn Boskie

Spades - A Ryne Sandberg (.35), K Mark Grace, Q Luis Salazar, J Bob Scanlan, 10 Dwight Smith, 9 Greg Maddux, 8 Heathcliff Slocumb, 7 Shawon Dunston, 6 Hector Villanueva, 5 Les Lancaster, 4 Dave Smith, 3 Mike Harkey, 2 Frank Castillo

National League logo Joker, National League logo Joker, 1992 Chicago Cubs home schedule, Chicago Cubs team history

Detroit Tigers

Hearts - A Cecil Fielder (.25), K Mickey Tettleton, Q Walt Terrell, J Lloyd Moseby, 10 John Cerutti, 9 Frank Tanana, 8 Alan Trammell, 7 Paul Gibson, 6 Jerry Don Gleaton, 5 Dan Galeker, 4 Steve Searcy, 3 Dave Bergman, 2 Andy Allanson

Clubs - A Tony Phillips, K Pete Incaviglia, Q Skeeter Barnes, J Rob Deer, 10 Cecil Fielder (.25), 9 Mickey Tettleton, 8 Skeeter Barnes, 7 Scott Aldred, 6 Travis Fryman, 5 Pete Incaviglia, 4 David Haas, 3 Walt Terrell, 2 Dan Galeker

Diamonds - A Bill Gullickson, K Lou Whitaker, Q Travis Fryman, J Milt Cuyler, 10 Tony Phillips, 9 Dave Bergman, 8 Mike Henneman, 7 John Shelby, 6 Scott Livingstone, 5 Lloyd Moseby, 4 David Haas, 3 Steve Searcy, 2 John Cerutti

Spades - A Frank Tanana, K Mike Henneman, Q Jerry Don Gleaton, J Alan Trammell, 10 Bill Gullickson, 9 Lou Whitaker, 8 Paul Gibson, 7 Andy Allanson, 6 Milt Cuyler, 5 Rob Deer, 4 John Shelby, 3 Scott Livingstone, 2 Scott Aldred

American League logo Joker, American League logo Joker, 1992 Detroit Tigers home schedule, Detroit Tigers team history

Minnesota Twins

Hearts - A Kirby Puckett (.25), K Jack Morris, Q Rick Aguilera, J Scott Leius, 10 Scott Erickson, 9 Kevin Tapani, 8 Chuck Knoblauch, 7 Greg Gagne, 6 Mike Pagliarulo, 5 Pedro Munoz, 4 Steve Bedrosian, 3 Paul Abbott, 2 Junior Ortiz

Clubs - A Shane Mack, K Kent Hrbek, Q Dan Gladden, J Carl Willis, 10 Kirby Puckett, 9 Jack Morris, 8 Rick Aguilera, 7 Scott Leius, 6 Terry Leach, 5 Mike Pagliarulo, 4 Junior Ortiz, 3 Al Newman, 2 Allan Anderson

Diamonds - A Brian Harper, K Chili Davis, Q Randy Bush, J Gene Larkin, 10 Shane Mack, 9 Kent Hrbek, 8 Dan Gladden, 7 Carl Willis, 6 Mark Guthrie, 5 Terry Leach, 4 David West, 3 Allan Henderson, 2 Al Newman

Spades - A Scott Erickson, K Kevin Tapani, Q Chuck Knoblauch, J Greg Gagne, 10 Brian Harper, 9 Chili Davis, 8 Randy Bush, 7 Gene Larkin, 6 Pedro Munoz, 5 Mark Guthrie, 4 Steve Bedrosian, 3 David West, 2 Paul Abbott

American League logo Joker, American League logo Joker, 1992 Minnesota Twins home schedule, Minnesota Twins team history

1993 U.S. Playing Card Aces

Major League superstars with the top 1992 statistical performances in four major categories are featured in this set of playing cards. Spades feature the 13 lowest ERAs; Hearts depict the baker's dozen stolen base leaders; the 13 players with the highest home run totals and batting average are featured on Clubs and Diamonds, respectively. The 2 1/2" by 3 1/2" cards have rounded corners and traditional playing cards suits and values in the upper left and lower right corners. Borderless color player photos are featured on the front, with color team logos in the lower left. Player names and positions are printed in a black box at the bottom. Backs have a red background with a large product logo and smaller licenser and manufacturer logos at the bottom. The box in which the cards were sold is enhanced with gold foil and features miniature representations of some of the cards. A complete set of 56 cards is $5 in Mint condition; individual cards are worth .05-.10, unless noted.

Clubs - A Juan Gonzalez, K Mark McGwire (.20), Q Cecil Fielder (.25), J Fred McGriff (.25), 10 Barry Bonds (.45), 9 Albert Belle (.30), 8 Joe Carter (.20), 7 Gary Sheffield, 6 Mickey Tettleton (.15), 5 Rob Deer, 4 Ken Griffey Jr. ($1.50), 3 Darren Daulton, 2 Dave Hollins

Spades - A Bill Swift, K Greg Maddux (.15), Q Curt Schilling, J Roger Clemens (.20), 10 Kevin Appier, 9 Dennis Martinez, 8 Mike Mussina, 7 Mike Morgan, 6 Jose Rijo, 5 Juan Guzman, 4 Greg Swindell, 3 Sid Fernandez, 2 Tom Glavine

Hearts - A Marquis Grissom, K Kenny Lofton (.20), Q Pat Listach, J Brady Anderson, 10 Luis Polonia, 9 Roberto Alomar (.20), 8 Rickey Henderson (.15), 7 Delino DeShields, 6 Tim Raines, 5 Steve Finley, 4 Bip Roberts, 3 Ozzie Smith (.20), 2 Chad Curtis

Diamonds - A Edgar Martinez, K Gary Sheffield, Q Kirby Puckett (.45), J Andy Van Slyke, 10 John Kruk (.15), 9 Bip Roberts, 8 Frank Thomas ($1.50), 7 Paul Molitor (.20), 6 Tony Gwynn (.20), 5 Shane Mack, 4 Carlos Baerga (.20), 3 Terry Pendleton, 2 Roberto Alomar (.20)

Cal Ripken Jr. Wild Card, National League logo Joker, American League logo Joker, advertising card

1993 U.S. Playing Card 1992 Rookies

Top rookies of the 1992 season are featured in full-color on the fronts of these playing cards. Player name and position are printed in white in a green stripe beneath the photo. A team logo is in the upper right corner. Backs are printed in dark green with gold pinstripes and a large gold, red and purple logo. The complete set of 56 cards is worth $4 in Mint condition; individual cards are worth .05-.10, unless noted.

Clubs - A Kenny Lofton (.50), K Cal Eldred, Q Bob Zupcic, J Alan Mills, 10 Reggie Sanders (.25), 9 Ruben Amaro Jr., 8 Scott Servais, 7 Jeff Frye, 6 Arthur Rhodes, 5 Eric Young, 4 John Patterson, 3 Mark Wohlers (.20), 2 Eric Fox

Spades - A Eric Karros (.25), K Chad Curtis (.15), Q Rusty Meacham, J Moises Alou (.20), 10 Royce Clayton (.15), 9 Ed Taubensee, 8 David Haas, 7 Jeff Kent, 6 David Nied, 5 Derek Bell (.15), 4 Pedro Astacio, 3 Wil Cordero, 2 Butch Henry

Hearts - A Pat Listach, K Gary DiSarcina, Q Scott Livingstone, J Donovan Osborne, 10 Derrick May, 9 Robert Wickham, 8 Rey Sanchez, 7 Monty Fariss, 6 Jeff Branson, 5 John Vander Wal, 4 Dan Walters, 3 Greg Colbrunn, 2 Pat Mahomes

Diamonds - A Dave Fleming, K Tim Wakefield (.25), Q Andy Stankiewicz, J Scott Cooper (.15), 10 Frank Seminara, 9 Roberto Hernandez, 8 Lenny Webster, 7 John Doherty, 6 Brian Jordan, 5 Brian Williams, 4 Kevin Koslofski, 3 Anthony Young, 2 Reggie Jefferson

National League Rookie of the Year Eric Karros Joker, American League Rookie of the Year Pat Listach Joker, rookie qualification rules, checklist

1994 U.S. Playing Card 1993 Rookies

The top rookies from the 1993 season are featured on this deck of playing cards; several players appear on more than one card in the deck. Fronts have color player photos in the center, with traditional playing card suits and values in the upper left and lower right borders. A team logo is in the upper right. The player's name and position appear in white in a purple strip in the lower left. Backs are purple with a large product logo at the top center and licenser/licenses logos at the bottom. Cards measure 2 1/2" by 3 1/2" with rounded corners and were sold in a specially-decorated cardboard box. The complete set of 56 cards is worth $4 in Mint condition; individual cards are worth .05-.10, unless noted.

Clubs - A Mike Piazza (.25), K Tim Salmon (.20), Q Troy Neel, J Al Martin, 10 J.T. Snow (.15), 9 Jeromy Burnitz, 8 Bret Boone, 7 Jeff Conine (.15), 6 Carlos Garcia, 5 Craig Paquette, 4 Ryan Thompson, 3 Wil Cordero, 2 Vinny Castilla

Spades - A Greg McMichael, K Jason Bere, Q Armando Reynoso, J Pedro J. Martinez, 10 Rene Arocha, 9 Kirk Rueter, 8 Aaron Sele (.15), 7 Steve Cooke, 6 Angel Miranda, 5 Tim Pugh, 4 Trevor Hoffman, 3 Steve Reed, 2 Paul Quantrill

Hearts - A Kevin Stocker, K Mike Piazza (.25), Q Jeff Conine, J Troy Neel, 10 David Hulse, 9 Brent Gates, 8 Rich Amaral, 7 Mike Lansing, 6 Tim Salmon (.20), 5 Al Martin, 4 Erik Pappas, 3 Carlos Garcia, 2 Alex Arias

Diamonds - A Chuck Carr., K David Hulse, Q Mike Lansing, J Rich Amaral, 10 Carlos Garcia, 9 Lou Frazier, 8 Wayne Kirby, 7 Al Martin, 6 Wil Cordero, 5 Brent Gates, 4 Phil Hiatt, 3 Joe Kmak, 2 Jeff McNeeley

Rookie of the Year Tim Salmon Joker, Rookie of the Year Mike Piazza Joker, checklist, rookie qualification rules

1994 U.S. Playing Card Aces

Statistical leaders from the 1993 season were featured on this deck of playing cards. Pitchers with the lowest ERAs are shown on the Spades; stolen base leaders are featured on the Hearts; home run hitters are depicted on the Clubs; and Diamonds host the batting average leaders. Cards are 2 1/2" by 3 1/2" with rounded corners. Fronts have full-bleed photos with the suit and value of the playing card in the upper left and lower right corners. The player's name, position and team logo are at the lower left. Backs are printed in dark blue with vertical silver stripes at each side and a red, white and blue "Baseball Aces" logo at the top. Licensing logos appear at the bottom. The complete set of 56 cards is worth $4 in Mint condition; individual cards are worth .05-.10, unless noted.

Clubs - A Barry Bonds (.25), K Juan Gonzalez (.25), Q Ken Griffey Jr. (.50), J Frank Thomas (.50), 10 Dave Justice (.15), 9 Albert Belle (.15), 8 Matt Williams, 7 Fred McGriff, 6 Rafael Palmeiro, 5 Ron Gant, 4 Mike Piazza (.20), 3 Bobby Bonilla, 2 Phil Plantier

Spades - A Greg Maddux, K Jose Rijo, Q Kevin Appier, J Mark Portugal, 10 Bill Swift, 9 Steve Avery, 8 Wilson Alvarez, 7 Pete Harnisch, 6 Tom Glavine, 5 John Burkett, 4 Jack McDowell, 3 Jimmy Key, 2 Tom Candiotti

Hearts - A Kenny Lofton (.15), K Chuck Carr, Q Roberto Alomar (.15), J Luis Polonia, 10 Marquis Grissom, 9 Rickey Henderson, 8 Chad Curtis, 7 Otis Nixon, 6 Gregg Jefferies, 5 Darren Lewis, 4 Delino DeShields, 3 Eric Young, 2 Brett Butler

Diamonds - A Andres Galarraga, K John Olerud, Q Gregg Jefferies, J Barry Bonds (.25), 10 Paul Molitor (.15), 9 Roberto Alomar (.15), 8 Kenny Lofton (.15), 7 Mark Grace, 6 Carlos Baerga (.15), 5 Jeff Bagwell (.15), 4 Mike Piazza (.20), 3 Frank Thomas (.50), 2 John Kruk

National League logo Joker, American League logo Joker, checklist, advertising card

1994 U.S. Playing Card team sets

Atlanta Braves

The most popular Braves are pictured on up to three of the cards in this deck. In 2 1/2" by 3 1/2" round-cornered format, the large color photos on the card fronts have their upper left and lower right corners clipped to display traditional playing card suits and values. The player name and position are printed in black in a gold strip below the photo. Backs have the Braves logo on a dark blue background with red stripes on the left and right edges. Brand and licenser logos are at the bottom. The cards were sold in a colorful box. The complete set of 56 is worth $4 in Mint condition. Individual cards are worth .05-.15, unless noted.

Clubs - A Ron Gant, K Fred McGriff (.20), Q John Smoltz, J Greg McMichael, 10 Rafael Belliard, 9 Dave Gallagher, 8 Dave Justice (.25), 7 Deion Sanders (.25), 6 Steve Avery, 5 Pedro Borbon, 4 Mark Wohlers, 3 Terry Pendleton, 2 Chipper Jones (.25)

Spades - A Jeff Blauser, K Tom Glavine, Q Mark Wohlers, J Kent Mercker, 10 Ramon Caraballo, 9 Deion Sanders (.25), 8 Greg Maddux (.20), 7 Javier Lopez (.25), 6 Steve Bedrosian, 5 Charlie O'Brien, 4 Mike Potts, 3 Ryan Klesko (.50), 2 Mike Stanton

Hearts - A Dave Justice (.25), K Deion Sanders (.25), Q Steve Avery, J Mike Stanton, 10 Terry Pendleton, 9 Ryan Klesko (.50), 8 Jeff Blauser, 7 Milt Hill, 6 Tom Glavine, 5 Bill Pecota, 4 Rafael Belliard, 3 Javier Lopez (.25), 2 Mark Lopez

Diamonds - A Greg Maddux (.20), K Terry Pendleton, Q Mark Lemke, J Bill Pecota, 10 Steve Bedrosian, 9 Mike Kelly, 8 Ron Gant, 7 Fred McGriff (.20), 6 John Smoltz, 5 Tony Tarasco, 4 Greg McMichael, 3 Kent Merker, 2 Ron Gant

Atlanta Braves logo Joker, National League logo Joker, checklist, 1994 Atlanta Braves home schedule

1994 U.S. Playing Card Baltimore Orioles

The 1994 Baltimore Orioles are featured in this deck of playing cards. Color photos of the players have clipped corners to display traditional playing card suits and values in the upper left and lower right corners. Beneath the photo is an orange strip with the player's name and position in white. Backs have a large Orioles logo on a pinstriped background. Company and licenser logos are at the bottom. Cards measure 2 1/2" by 3 1/2" with rounded corners. The set was sold in a colorful cardboard box. The complete set of 56 cards is worth $5 in Mint condition. Individual players are worth .05-.15, unless noted.

Clubs - A Chris Hoiles, K Rafael Palmeiro (.35), Q Jeffrey Hammonds (.50), J Jack Voigt, 10 Brad Pennington, 9 Cal Ripken Jr. ($1), 8 Ben McDonald, 7 David Segui, 6 Damon Buford, 5 Arthur Rhodes, 4 Jeff Tackett, 3 Paul Carey, 2 Mike Cook

Spades - A Mark McLemore, K Harold Baines, Q Jamie Moyer, J Alan Mills, 10 Sherman Obando, 9 Mike Mussina, 8 Brady Anderson, 7 Mike Devereaux, 6 Tim Hulett, 5 Leo Gomez, 4 Jim Poole, 3 Kevin McGehee, 2 Manny Alexander

Hearts - A Cal Ripken Jr. ($1), K Ben McDonald, Q David Segui, J Damon Buford, 10 Arthur Rhodes, 9 Jeff Tackett, 8 Mark McLemore, 7 Harold Baines, 6 Jamie Moyer, 5 Alan Mills, 4 Sid Fernandez, 3 John O'Donoghue, 2 Harold Baines

Diamonds - A Mike Mussina, K Brady Anderson, Q Mike Devereaux, J Tim Hulett, 10 Leo Gomez, 9 Jim Poole, 8 Chris Hoiles, 7 Rafael Palmeiro (.25), 6 Chris Sabo, 5 Jack Voight, 4 Jeffrey Hammonds (.50), 3 Brad Pennington, 2 Mike Oquist

Baltimore Orioles logo Joker, American League logo Joker, checklist, 1994 Baltimore Orioles home schedule

1994 U.S. Playing Card Philadelphia Phillies

Veterans and rookies on the roster of the 1994 Phillies are featured in this deck of playing cards; the most popular players appear on up to three cards each. In standard 2 1/2" by 3 1/2" round-corner format, the large color photos have their top left and bottom right corners clipped to display traditional playing card suits and values. The player's name and position are printed in black on a red strip beneath the photo. A complete set of 56 cards is worth $4 in Mint condition. Individual cards are worth .05-.15, unless noted.

Clubs - A Pete Incaviglia, K John Kruk (.25), Q Ben Rivera, J Mariano Duncan, 10 Roger Mason, 9 Terry Mulholland, 8 Darren Daulton, 7 Curt Schilling, 6 Terry Mulholland, 5 Kevin Stocker, 4 Mickey Morandini, 3 Milt Thompson, 2 Lenny Dykstra (.25)

Spades - A Dave Hollins, K Jim Eisenrich, Q Tyler Green, J Kim Batiste, 10 Ricky Jordan, 9 Brad Brink, 8 Tony Longmire (.25), 7 Tommy Greene, 6 Wes Chamberlain, 5 Lenny Dykstra (.25), 4 David West, 3 Todd Pratt, 2 Danny Jackson

Hearts - A Lenny Dykstra (.25), K Darren Daulton, Q Curt Schilling, J Milt Thompson, 10 Mike Williams, 9 Kevin Stocker, 8 Kevin Foster, 7 Dave Hollins, 6 Ricky Jordan, 5 Ben Rivera, 4 Pete Incaviglia, 3 Kim Batiste, 2 Tony Longmire (.25)

Diamonds - A Terry Mulholland, K Tommy Greene, Q Mickey Morandini, J Jim Eisenrich, 10 Wes Chamberlain, 9 Todd Pratt, 8 David West, 7 John Kruk (.25), 6 Jim Eisenrich, 5 Danny Jackson, 4 Mariano Duncan, 3 Roger Mason, 2 Brad Brink

Philadelphia Phillies logo Joker, National League logo Joker, checklist, 1994 Philadelphia Phillies home schedule

1995 U.S. Playing Card Aces

Baseball's 1994 statistical leaders in home runs (Clubs), ERA (Spades), stolen bases (Hearts) and batting average (Diamonds) are featured in this deck of playing cards. Measuring a standard 2 1/2" by 3 1/2" with rounded corners, the cards have borderless action photos on the front with traditional playing card suits and denominations in the upper left and lower right corners. The player's color team logo, name and position appear in the lower left corner. Backs are silver with black side stripes and a red-and-black Aces logo in the center. Sets were sold in a colorful cardboard box. The complete set of 56 cards is worth $4 in Mint condition; individual cards are worth .05-.10, unless noted.

Clubs - A Matt Williams, K Ken Griffey Jr. ($1), Q Jeff Bagwell, J Frank Thomas ($1), 10 Barry Bonds (.25), 9 Albert Belle, 8 Fred McGriff, 7 Jose Canseco (.25), 6 Andres Galarraga, 5 Kevin Mitchell, 4 Cecil Fielder, 3 Dante Bichette, 2 Joe Carter

Spades - A Greg Maddux, K Steve Ontiveros, Q Bret Saberhagen, J Doug Drabek, 10 Roger Clemens, 9 David Cone, 8 Jeff Fassero, 7 Shane Reynolds, 6 Mike Mussina, 5 Jose Rijo, 4 Bobby Jones, 3 Randy Johnson, 2 Steve Trachsel

Hearts - A Kenny Lofton, K Vince Coleman, Q Otis Nixon, J Craig Biggio, 10 Deion Sanders, 9 Marquis Grissom, 8 Chuck Knoblauch, 7 Chuck Carr, 6 Brady Anderson, 5 Darren Lewis, 4 Barry Bonds (.25), 3 Alex Cole, 2 Brian McRae

Diamonds - A Tony Gwynn, K Jeff Bagwell, Q Paul O'Neill, J Albert Belle, 10 Frank Thomas ($1), 9 Kenny Lofton, 8 Wade Boggs (.25), 7 Paul Molitor, 6 Moises Alou, 5 Hal Morris, 4 Will Clark (.25), 3 Kevin Mitchell, 2 Gregg Jefferies

American League logo Joker, National League logo Joker, checklist, MicroMini Team card order form

1927 W560

Although assigned a "W" number, this set is not a "strip card" issue in the same sense as the rest of the "W" baseball card sets, although W560 cards are frequently found in uncut sheets of three or four across or down. Uncut sheets of 16 cards, in four rows of four cards each, are also known to exist. Cards in the W560 set measure 1 3/4" by 2 3/4" and are designed like a deck of playing cards, with the pictures on the various suits - either hearts, clubs, spades, diamonds or jokers. The set includes movie stars, aviators and other athletes, in addition to baseball players. Because they are designed as a deck of playing cards, the cards are printed in either red or black. A complete set of 49 baseball cards in Near Mint condition is worth $2,750. Individual cards are worth $28, unless noted.

1. Vic Aldridge
2. Lester Bell
3. Larry Benton
4. Max Bishop
5. Del Bissonette
6. Jim Bottomley, $50
7. Guy Bush
8. W. Clark
9. Andy Cohen
10. Mickey Cochrane, $50
11. Hugh Critz
12. Kiki Cuyler, $50
13. Taylor Douthit
14. Fred Fitzsimmons
15. Jim Foxx, $315
16. Lou Gehrig, $450
17. Goose Goslin, $50
18. Sam Gray
19. Lefty Grove, $75
20. Jesse Haines, $50
21. Babe Herman, $35
22. Rogers Hornsby, $125
23. Waite Hoyt, $50
24. Henry Johnson
25. Walter Johnson
26. Willie Kamm
27. Remy Kremer
28. Fred Lindstrom, $50
29. Fred Maguire
30. Fred Marberry
31. Jonnny Mostil
32. Buddy Myer
33. Herb Pennock, $50
34. George Pipgras
35. Flint Rhem
36. Babe Ruth, $700
37. Luke Sewell
38. Willie Sherdel
39. Al Simmons, $50
40. Thomas Thevenow
41. Fresco Thompson
42. George Uhle
43. Dazzy Vance, $50
44. Rube Walberg
45. Lloyd Waner, $50
46. Paul Waner, $50
47. Fred "Cy" Williams, $35
48. Jim Wilson
49. Glenn Wright

Posters/art

• "American Royalty," George Brett - 1990 Costacos Brothers $8
• "Bash & Dash," Jose Canseco - 1990 Costacos Brothers $5
• "Battle of the Bay," 1989 Giants/A's World Series - by Chevron Classic $8
• "Boston Greats" - 24x18, by Robert Stephen Simon $25
• "Boys of Summer" (Duke Snider, Gil Hodges, Jackie Robinson, Pee Wee Reese and Roy Campanella) - 18x24, by Robert Stephen Simon $25
• "Chill Out," Bo Jackson - 1990s Pepsi $5
• Dizzy Dean - 1991 Busch $5
• Catfish Hunter - 1976 Redman Tobacco $10
• Reggie Jackson - 1991 Busch $5
• "The King of Swing," Tony Gwynn - 1990 Costacos Brothers $5
• "Long Ball Hitters" - 1991 Post Cereal (Sandberg, Bonds, Fielder and five others) $5
• Mickey Mantle - 1989 Wiz $12
• "Mickey at Night" - 18x24, by Robert Stephen Simon $25
• M&M Boys, Mantle and Maris - 24x18, by Robert Stephen Simon $25
• Stan Musial - 1986 Busch $5
• Brooks Robinson - 1983 Crown $8
• Ted Williams - 1988 Busch $5
• "Texas Heat," Nolan Ryan - 1990 Costacos Brothers $8
• "Willie, Mickey and the Duke" - 18x24, by Robert Stephen Simon $25
• 1978 World Series program covers, 1903-77 - 1978 Squirt $6
• "Yankee Greats" - 28x22, by Gayle Gibson $30
Artwork/lithographs
• Hank Aaron and Sadaharu Oh - lithograph, by Michael Elins, signed by all $155
• Roberto Alomar - 18x24 lithograph, by Angelo Marino, signed by both $90
• Johnny Bench, the Catcher - 38x19, serigraph, limited edition, by Leroy Neiman, signed by both $2,500

• Roger Clemens - lithograph, by Michael Gardner, signed by both.. $130
• Roberto Clemente - 18x24 lithograph, by Angelo Marino $75
• Joe DiMaggio - 24x18, open edition, autographed, by Angelo Marino $700
• Joe DiMaggio - 16x20, oil, by Frank Stapleton $500
• Joe DiMaggio - 18x24 lithograph, by Angelo Marino, signed by both... $595
• Whitey Ford - 18x24 lithograph, by Angelo Marino, signed by both... $100
• Ken Griffey Jr. - 16x20 lithograph, by J. Charles, signed by both.. $75
• Tony Gwynn - 18x24 lithograph, by Angelo Marino, signed by both.. $95
• Sandy Koufax - 28x22, limited edition, autographed, by Leroy Beachy... $350
• Mickey Mantle, Hall of Fame Performance - 20x16, by James Amore... $200
• Mickey Mantle - 20x16, limited edition, by James Amore $225
• Mickey Mantle, the Last World Series - 12x16, limited edition, by James Amore.. $200
• Mickey Mantle - 24x21, pencil, autographed, by Glen Banse $3,600
• Mickey Mantle - 3D, 12x14 of his 1952 Topps card, autographed, by Jeff Frankel..................................... $3,000
• Mickey Mantle - 24x18, open edition, autographed, by Angelo Marino $700
• Mickey Mantle - 37 1/2x24, limited edition, autographed, by Burt Silverman $800
• Willie Mays - 16x20 lithograph, by Ron Lewis, signed by both.. $125
• 1969 Mets - 28x22, limited edition, by Joseph Catalano $200
• Cal Ripken Jr. - 18x24 lithograph, by Angelo Marino ... $75
• Pete Rose - 26x22, limited edition, autographed, by Lewis Watkins $250
• A Tradition of Excellence (Brooks Robinson and Cal Ripken Jr.) - 30x41, limited edition, autographed by both, by Tony Capparellio $700
• Nolan Ryan - 24x18, open edition, autographed, by Angelo Marino.. $600
• Nolan Ryan - 18x24 lithograph, by Angelo Marino....... $90
• Ryan Express - 20x17, open edition, by Kenneth Gatewood $35
• Mike Schmidt - 28x22, limited edition, autographed, by Frank Stapleton.. $375
• Warren Spahn and Johnny Sain - 17x22 lithograph, by Ron Lewis, signed by all $80
• Frank Thomas - 25x36 lithograph, by Frank Stapleton $275
• We Wanna Play (Ken Griffey Jr. and Frank Thomas) - 21x16, open edition, by Kenneth Gatewood........................... $35
• Ted Williams - 18x24 lithograph, by Angelo Marino $75
• Ted Williams, the End of an Era - 22x26, limited edition, autographed, by Lewis Watkins..................................... $950
• Ted Williams, 1941 - 30x22, limited edition, autographed, by Lewis Watkins... $950
• Yankee Greats - Lou Gehrig, Mickey Mantle, Babe Ruth and Joe DiMaggio, 28x22, limited edition by Joseph Catalano $200
• Carl Yastrzemski, Triple Crown - 22x28, limited edition, autographed, by Walt Peterson $200
Costacos Brothers Sports, Seattle, Wash., has issued several fantasy posters picturing modern baseball players.

Norman Rockwell's 37x24 oil on canvas painting of "Gee, Thanks Brooks," shows Brooks Robinson signing for a youngster at the stadium, was commissioned in 1971 as an advertisement for the Rawlings sporting goods company, sold for $222,500 in an auction.

Two preliminary versions of the painting, a 37 3/4" by 28 1/4" charcoal on paper, and a 19 1/2" by 14 1/2" oil on paper, sold for $37,375 and $18,400.

Norman Rockwell's 40 1/4x38 1/2 charcoal on paper painting of "The Rookie," shows Ted Williams casting a wary eye at a young rookie, appeared on a Saturday Evening Post cover March 2, 1957, sold for $85,000 in an auction.

Sports Illustrated posters

During the late 1960s and early 1970s, Sports Illustrated produced several posters featuring hockey, basketball, football and baseball players. The posters, made available through ads in the magazine beginning in 1969, originally sold for $1.50 each. Today, some have reached $200, including Mickey Mantle, Roberto Clemente and Willie Mays. The year listed behind a player's name is the year the poster was released. The year of release of some posters is not known, so those posters are indicated by 1968-70.

Sports Illustrated posters

Hank Aaron, 1968 ....$35-$45
Tommie Agee, 1968-70 ....$8-$15
Richie Allen, 1968 ....$10-$15
Gene Alley, 1968 ....$8-$15
Felipe Alou, 1968..$8-$15
Max Alvis, 1968...$8-$15
Mike Andrews, 1969..$8-$12
Bob Aspromonte, 1968-70.....................................$10-$15
Ernie Banks, 1968...$20-$30
Glenn Beckert, 1968-70 ....$8-$20
Gary Bell, 1968 (Indians).....................................$10-$15
Gary Bell, 1968 (Pilots)...$10-$20
Bobby Bonds, 1970..$10-$18
Clete Boyer, 1968 ....$8-$12
Lou Brock, 1968 ....$18-$25
Johnny Callison, 1968..$10-$15
Bert Campaneris, 1968..$10-$15
Leo Cardenas, 1968..$10-$15
Rod Carew, 1970..$25-$45
Paul Casanova, 1968...$10-$15
Orlando Cepeda, 1968..$10-$18
Roberto Clemente, 1968 ....$125-$200
Tony Conigliaro, 1968 ....$12-$20
Mike Cuellar, 1970 ....$8-$15
Tommy Davis, 1968..$10-$20
Willie Davis, 1968 ....$10-$15
Don Drysdale, 1968 ....$18-$30
Mike Epstein, 1970 ....$8-$15
Al Ferrara, 1968 ....$8-$12
Curt Flood, 1968 ....$10-$15
Bill Freehan, 1968..$10-$15
Jim Fregosi, 1968...$8-$15
Bob Gibson, 1968 ....$18-$25
Bud Harrelson, 1968..$8-$15
Ken Holtzman, 1970 ....$8-$15
Joe Horlen, 1968 ....$8-$15
Tony Horton, 1968..$8-$12
Frank Howard, 1968 ....$12-$20
Reggie Jackson, 1969..$90-$120
Ferguson Jenkins, 1968-70 ....$25-$50
Tommy John, 1968 ....$10-$18
Cleon Jones, 1970..$8-$15
Al Kaline, 1968 ....$18-$25
Harmon Killebrew, 1968..$25-$35
Jerry Koosman, 1968 ....$10-$18
Let's Go Mets, 1969..$25-$45
Mickey Lolich, 1970 ....$10-$18
Jim Lonborg, 1968 ....$8-$15
Jim Maloney, 1968...$8-$15
Mickey Mantle, 1968 ....$150-$225
Juan Marichal, 1968..$20-$35
Willie Mays, 1968..$125-$200
Bill Mazeroski, 1968...$12-$18
Tim McCarver, 1968..$10-$15
Mike McCormick, 1968..$8-$15
Willie McCovey, 1968..$75-$150
Sam McDowell, 1970 ....$8-$15
Denny McLain, 1968 ....$12-$18
Don Mincher, 1968 (Angels)....................................$8-$15
Don Mincher, 1968 (Pilots).......................................$8-$20
Rick Monday, 1968..$10-$15
Bobby Murcer, 1968-70..$10-$18
Phil Niekro, 1970 ....$12-$20
John Odom, 1968-70..$10-$15
Tony Oliva, 1968..$12-$18
Wes Parker, 1970 ....$8-$12
Tony Perez, 1970 ....$12-$20
Rico Petrocelli, 1968...$8-$15

Boog Powell, 1968-70...$10-$18
Rick Reichart, 1968...$8-$15
Brooks Robinson, 1968 ....$50-$100
Frank Robinson, 1968 ....$30-$50
Pete Rose, 1968 ....$25-$50
Ron Santo, 1968 ....$10-$15
Tom Seaver, 1968 ....$50-$85
Chris Short, 1968...$8-$15
Bill Singer, 1970 ....$8-$15
Reggie Smith, 1968..$8-$15
Rusty Staub, 1968..$10-$18
Mel Stottlemyre, 1968..$10-$15
Ron Swoboda, 1968...$8-$15
Cesar Tovar, 1968 ....$10-$15
Roy White, 1968-70..$8-$12
Walt Williams, 1970 ....$8-$12
Earl Wilson, 1968...$8-$15
Jimmy Wynn, 1968 ....$8-$15
Carl Yastrzemski, 1968 ....$25-$40

During the 1990s, Starline Inc., East Elmhurst, N.Y., has issued indvidual and team collage posters, paper bookcovers featuring player photos, door posters, posters featuring team collages, jigsaw puzzles and greeting cards.

TV Sports Mailbag/Photo File, Elmsford, N.Y., has also issued glossy photographs and lithographs of current and retired players, and several 8x10 card sets, featuring Nolan Ryan, baseball's 300-game winners and Hall of Fame inductees.

Programs

• All American Girls League World Series scorecard, Fort Wayne vs. Rockford Peaches $250
• George Brett or Robin Yount 3,000th hit programs ......$22 each
• Tom Glavine autographed 1995 World Series program, MVP $55
• Chipper Jones autographed 1995 World Series program $50
• Mickey Mantle 1965 "Mickey Mantle Day" program, signed $200
• Nolan Ryan 7th no-hitter program, May 13, 1991.........$85
• Nolan Ryan 300th win program, signed by Tom Seaver, Steve Carlton, Warren Spahn, Early Wynn and Phil Niekro...........$125
• Nolan Ryan 300th win program, signed $85
• Pete Rose's 4,192nd hit game program, with box score enclosed, $20, signed $40

7-Eleven cups

1972-73 7-Eleven cups

In 1972-73, 7-Eleven convenience stores gave away, with the purchase of a soda or 14-ounce Slurpee crushed-ice drink, cups which feature portraits of Major League baseball players.

The 5 5/16" tall plastic cups are 3 1/4" in diameter at the top and 2 1/8" inches at the bottom. The player's full-color sketched picture is on one side of the cup above his name and the team name; on the opposite side in between his team's logo and the 7-Eleven logo is a brief biography.

The 1972 60-cup set includes 18 Hall of Famers. Twenty-one of the players were carried over to the 1973 set; all but seven (Dick Allen, Lou Brock, Cesar Cedeno, Ralph Garr, Willie Mays, Vada Pinson and

Tom Seaver) were the same portraits. The 1973 cups differed little from the 1972 cups; the major change in format was that in 1972 the player's name and team name are flush left above his biography, while in 1973 they were centered.

The 80-cup 1973 series includes 20 old-time Hall of Famers, whose cups were the same format and styles as the current players' cups, except the portraits were done in gold rather than in color.

7-Eleven later produced full-color cups using reproduced photos. These, and the earlier cups, have not survived in quantity or quality, in part because too much dishwashing took its toll on them. Also, the cups are very susceptible to cracking, so don't put too much pressure on them.

1972 7-Eleven cups

Hank Aaron	$25-$30
Tommie Agee	$6
Rich Allen	$7-$8
Sal Bando	$6
Johnny Bench	$25
Steve Blass	$6
Vida Blue	$7-$8
Lou Brock	$20
Norm Cash	$6
Cesar Cedeno	$6
Orlando Cepeda	$10
Roberto Clemente	$35-$50
Nate Colbert	$7
Willie Davis	$7
Ray Fosse	$6-$7
Ralph Garr	$6
Bob Gibson	$20
Bud Harrelson	$7-$8
Frank Howard	$9
Ron Hunt	$6-$7
Reggie Jackson	$40
Ferguson Jenkins	$15
Alex Johnson	$7
Deron Johnson	$8
Al Kaline	$15
Harmon Killebrew	$15-$20
Mickey Lolich	$7-$12
Jim Lonborg	$7
Juan Marichal	$15-$25
Willie Mays	$35

Willie McCovey	$15-$25
Denny McLain	$7
Dave McNally	$6-$7
Bill Melton	$7
Andy Messersmith	$6
Bobby Murcer	$7-$12
Tony Oliva	$7-$10
Amos Otis	$6
Jim Palmer	$15-$20
Joe Pepitone	$7-$8
Jim Perry	$6
Lou Piniella	$7-$10
Vada Pinson	$10
Dave Roberts	$6
Brooks Robinson	$25-$30
Frank Robinson	$15-$20
Pete Rose	$25
George Scott	$6
Tom Seaver	$25
Sonny Siebert	$8
Reggie Smith	$8
Willie Stargell	$12-$25
Bill Stoneman	$7
Mel Stottlemyre	$7-$9
Joe Torre	$8
Maury Wills	$7
Don Wilson	$6
Rick Wise	$7-$8
Wilbur Wood	$7
Carl Yastrzemski	$25

1973 7-Eleven cups

Hank Aaron	$15
Dick Allen	$7-$8
Dusty Baker	$4-$6
Johnny Bench	$15
Yogi Berra	$10-$12
Larry Biittner	$6
Steve Blass	$4-$6
Lou Boudreau *	$6
Lou Brock	$5
Roy Campanella *	$10-$15-$35
Bert Campaneris	$4-$6
Rod Carew	$9
Steve Carlton	$9
Cesar Cedeno	$4
Ty Cobb *	$15-$35
Nate Colbert	$4-$6
Willie Davis	$4
Bill Dickey *	$10
Bob Feller *	$10-$35
Carlton Fisk	$6-$8
Bill Freehan	$4-$7
Ralph Garr	$4-$6
Lou Gehrig *	$15, $65
Charlie Gehringer *	$8-$10-$35
Bob Gibson	$10
Hank Greenberg *	$10-$15-$35
Bobby Grich	$4-$8
Lefty Grove *	$6-$35
Toby Harrah	$6
Richie Hebner	$4
Ken Henderson	$4-$8
Carl Hubbell *	$6-$35
Jim "Catfish" Hunter	$7-$13
Reggie Jackson	$15-$20
Walter Johnson *	$10-$15
Don Kessinger	$4-$8
Leron Lee	$4-$6
Mickey Lolich	$4-$8

459

Sparky Lyle $4
Greg Luzinski $5
Mike Marshall .... $4-$6
Mickey Mantle * .... $20-$25-$95
Carlos May .... $4-$6
Lee May .... $4-$6
John Mayberry .... $4-$6
Willie Mays * $20
John McGraw * .... $6-$10-$35
Joe Medwick * .... $6-$35
Joe Morgan .... $5-$12
Thurman Munson .... $9-$25
Bobby Murcer .... $8-$12
Stan Musial * .... $12-$15-$35
Gary Nolan .... $4-$6
Tony Oliva .... $8-$9
Al Oliver .... $4-$6
Claude Osteen .... $4-$6
Jim Palmer $6
Gaylord Perry .... $5-$12
Lou Piniella $4
Vada Pinson $4
Brooks Robinson $15
Ellie Rodriguez .... $4-$6
Joe Rudi .... $4-$6
Red Ruffing * .... $6-$12
Babe Ruth * .... $15-$25-$55
Nolan Ryan .... $35-$45
Manny Sanguillen .... $4-$6
Ron Santo $9
Richie Scheinblum $4
Tom Seaver $25
Ted Simmons $6
Reggie Smith $4
Chris Speier .... $4-$6
Don Sutton .... $5-$12
Luis Tiant $4
Pie Traynor * .... $8-$12-$35
Honus Wagner * .... $10-$20-$35
Billy Williams .... $6-$10
Wilbur Wood .... $4-$7
Carl Yastrzemski .... $15-$20
* Old-time Hall of Famer

1982 cups

George Brett $35, Rod Carew $25, Rollie Fingers $25, Carlton Fisk $35, Rickey Henderson $25, Eddie Murray $25, Pete Rose $35, Nolan Ryan $85, Mike Schmidt $45, Dave Winfield $25

Sportscasters

1977-79 Sportscaster cards

This massive set of full-color cards, which includes players from dozens of different sports - some of them very obscure - contains more than 2,000 different subjects, making it one of the biggest sets of trading cards ever issued. Available by mail subscription from 1977-1979, the Sportscaster cards are large, measuring 6 1/4" by 4 3/4". Subscribers were mailed one series of 24 cards each for $1.89, plus postage, every month or so. The cards are not numbered, making it very difficult to assemble a complete set. The set has an international flavor to it, including such sports as rugby, soccer, lawn bowling, fencing, karate, bicycling, curling, skiing, bullfighting, auto racing, mountain climbing, hang

gliding, yachting, sailing, badminton, bobsledding, etc. Each card has a series of legends in the upper right corner to assist collectors in the various methods of sorting. Most popular among American collectors are the baseball, football, and basketball stars in the set, which includes the 140 baseball subjects listed here. The checklist includes many Hall of Famers and future Hall of Famers. The card backs contain detailed write-ups of the player featured. Because the set was issued in series, and many collectors dropped out of the program before the end, cards in the higher series are especially scarce. This accounts for the prices on some of the superstar cards, issued in early series, being lower than for some of the lesser-known players. A complete set of baseball cards only is worth $800 in Near Mint condition.

The players in the set are: Hank Aaron, $8; Danny Ainge, $90; Emmett Ashford, $8; Ernie Banks, $8; Johnny Bench, $5; Vida Blue, $6; Bert Blyleven, $3; Bobby Bonds, $12; Lyman Bostock, $3; George Brett, $12; Lou Brock, $4.50; Jeff Burroughs, $3; Roy Campanella, $21; John Candelaria, $3.50; Rod Carew, $7; Steve Carlton, $7; Ron Cey, $3; Roberto Clemente, $35; Steve Dembowski, $9; Joe DiMaggio, $12; Dennis Eckersley, $8; Mark Fidrych, $5; Carlton Fisk, $20; Mike Flanagan, $9; Steve Garvey, $15; Ron Guidry, $15; Gil Hodges, $15; Catfish Hunter, $5; Tommy John, $3.25; Randy Jones, $3; Dave Kingman, $5; Sandy Koufax, $9; Tommy Lasorda, $15; Ron Leflore, $3; Greg Luzinski, $3; Billy Martin, $10; Willie Mays, $9; Lee Mazzilli, $6; Willie McCovey, $15; Joe Morgan, $6; Thurman Munson, $5; Stan Musial, $10; Phil Niekro, $11; Jim Palmer, $6; Dave Parker, $5; Freddie Patek, $3; Gaylord Perry, $5; Jim Piersall, $8; Vada Pinson, $3; Rick Reuschel, $3; Jim Rice, $3; J.R. Richard, $8; Brooks Robinson, $8; Frank Robinson, $12; Jackie Robinson, $9; Pete Rose, $5; Joe Rudi, $3; Babe Ruth, $11; Tom Seaver, $9; Warren Spahn, $6; Monty Stratton, $8; Craig Swan, $7; Frank Tanana, $3; Ron Taylor, $9; Garry Templeton, $3; Gene Tenace, $3; Bobby Thomson, $3; Andre Thornton, $3; Johnny VanderMeer, $3; Ted Williams, $8; Maury Wills, $3; Hack Wilson, $10; Dave Winfield, hitting, $15; Dave Winfield, portrait, $10; and Cy Young, $5.

Theme cards are: the 1927 Yankees, $5; the 1969 Mets, $6; All-Star Game (Joe Morgan and Steve Garvey), $5; Amateur Draft (Rick Monday), $3; At-A-Glance Reference (Tom Seaver), $8; Babe Ruth Baseball (Ed Figueroa), $10; Baltimore Memorial Stadium, $9; Boston's Fenway Park, $6; Brother vs. Brother (Joe Niekro), $8; Busch Memorial Stadium, $9; Candlestick Park, $8; Cape Cod League (Jim Beattie), $6; a Century and a Half of Baseball (Johnny Bench), $5; Cy Young Award (Tom Seaver), $8; the Dean Brothers (Dizzy and Paul Dean), $12; Designated Hitter (Rusty Staub), $8; Dodger Stadium, $8; Perfect Game (Don Larsen), $8; the Double Steal (Davey Lopes), $3; Fenway Park, $8; the Firemen (Goose Gossage), $11; Forever Blowing Bubbles (Davey Lopes) $6; the Forsch Brothers (Bob and Ken Forsch), $10; Four Home Runs in a Game (Mike Schmidt), $7; 400-Homer Club (Duke Snider), $12; Great Moments (Bob

Gibson), $5; Great Moments (Ferguson Jenkins), $5; Great Moments (Mickey Lolich), $5; Great Moments (Carl Yastrzemski), $7; Hidden Ball Trick (Carl Yastrzemski), $3; Hit and Run (George Foster), $3; Hitting the Cutoff Man, $3; Hitting Pitchers (Don Drysdale), $8; Infield Fly Rule (Bobby Grich), $3;

Instruction (Rod Carew), $5; Interference (Johnny Bench), $5; Iron Mike (Pitching Machine), $8; Keeping Score, $5; Like Father, Like Son (Roy Smalley), $10; Lingo I (Gary Carter), $4; Lingo II (Earl Weaver), $3; Little Leagues to Big Leagues (Hector Torres), $7; Maris and Mantle (Mickey Mantle and Roger Maris), $20; Measurements (Memorial Stadium), $3; the Money Game (Dennis Eckersley), $15; NCAA Tournament (Aggies vs. Longhorns), $4; the Oakland A's, 1971-75, $6; the Perfect Game (Sandy Koufax), $8; the Pickoff (Luis Tiant), $3; the Presidential Ball (William Howard Taft), $5; Relief Pitching (Mike Marshall), $3; the Rules (Hank Aaron), $5; Rundown, $3; 7th Game of the World Series (Bert Campaneris), $7; Shea Stadium, $8; the 3,000 Hit Club (Roberto Clemente), $20; Training Camps (Orioles), $8; Triple Crown (Carl Yastrzemski), $12; Triple Play (Rick Burleson), $8; Triple Play (Bill Wambsganss), $3; Umpires Strike, $5; Veterans Stadium, $9; Wrigley Marathon (Mike Schmidt), $7; and Yankee Stadium, $3. Beyond sports, baseball-related themes include: Clemente Award (Andre Thornton), $12; Clowns (Al Schact and Nick Altrock), $12; Fellowship of Christian Athletes (Don Kessinger), $12; High School Record Book (David Clyde), $8; Hutchinson Award (Al Kaline), $12; and Walkie Talkie (Yogi Berra), $12.

Stadium seats

Although many of the stadium seats offered in auctions have been restored, they are commanding the same amounts of dollars as those in their natural state. Generally, it's a matter of preference on how collectors want their seats - "lived in" or restored to their original, "pristine" state - and if they are going to display them or actually use them.

Before buying a seat, research the ballpark, especially the paint color of the seat, to aid in determining authenticity. Auction houses and newsletters are also available to offer historical information and price structures.

Advertised and auction-result values for various styles of seats from five of the eight original National League ballparks debuting in the 1800s-early 1900s include: Wrigley Field (1930s, $100); Crosley Field (non-aisle, $200-$500); Ebbets Field: (blue, straight-backed, free-standing, $2,000-$5,000); Polo Grounds (figural seats, $2,500) and Braves Field (aisle seats; $5,000).

Values for various styles of seats from five of the eight original American League ballparks include: Comiskey Park (folding chairs, $280; round-back or straight-back, $250); Yankee Stadium (straight-back, $500-$800); Tiger Stadium (single seat, $150-$200);

Griffith Stadium (three-seater, $1,650-$2,000); and Fenway Park (straight-back, single-seater, $1,500-$1,800).

Team souvenirs, items

• 1954 Baltimore Orioles round metal pocket schedule.... $75
• 1960s Baltimore Orioles popcorn holder/megaphone $40
• Baltimore Orioles matchbook, 1966 and 1970 World Champions.. $25
• 1985 Baltimore Orioles glasses, set of six, includes Ripken, Davis, Murray, Boddicker, Dempsey and Lynn............. $150
• 1948 Boston Braves World Series leather wallet, features Indian head and tomahawk on the front with the date, made to hold playing cards, etc.. $185
• 1937 baseball team visors, banana-shaped, visors have team name, date and baseball logo, Boston Red Sox, New York Giants, Chicago Cubs and New York Yankees........$45 each
• 1959 Boston Red Sox crystal dish, etched with date ... $195
• 1920s Brooklyn Dodgers team letterhead, 8 1/2x11, pictures an engraving of Ebbets Field, includes return address envelope $100
• 1951 Chicago White Sox charm bracelet, gold, with small bat and ball, "White Sox" and "51" are attached $75
• 1969 Chicago Cubs bullpen white glass coffee cup, features facsimile autographs of the team's relievers $55
• Chicago White Sox Lite Beer beer tapper handle, 3x6, heavy plastic $10
• 1951 Chicago White Sox 12" metal ruler $12
• Pocket hanky with letter H on it, attached to a 1960 Chicago White Sox schedule, 3 1/2x7 .... $10
• 1952 Cincinnati Reds ice scraper, mounted on original cardboard display $30
• 1970s Cincinnati Reds Marathon Oil bumper sticker, "Team of the '70s" $10

Miscellaneous

- 1975 Cincinnati Reds World Champs drinking glass, 5 1/2" tall, with facsimile autographs $20
- 1975 Cincinnati Reds Icee plastic drinking glass, 5 1/2" tall, with Icee Bear on one side, playoff and World Series stats on the other.. $5
- Cleveland Indians Chief Wahoo rubber doll, by Rempel Co. of Akron, Ohio, without feather... $45
- 1948 Cleveland Indians 10" plate, center features Cleveland Stadium $250
- 1960s Cleveland Indians cloth iron-on patch $25
- 1977 Cleveland Indians Coca-Cola plastic place mat, features Bell, Manning and Grubb... $10
- 1950s Detroit Tigers or New York Yankees bat pencils, $12 each
- 1960s Los Angeles Dodgers keychain on original card . $45
- Milwaukee Braves souvenir fan, red and black Braves mascot, black wooden handle... $20
- 1950s Milwaukee Braves plastic ring.............................. $30
- 1950s Milwaukee Braves beaded belt $65
- 1960s Milwaukee Braves drinking glasses, lot of seven, each has a team logo and an opponent's (Mets, Cubs, Giants, Dodgers, Reds, Cards and Phillies)................................... $100
- 1961 "Play Ball With the Braves!" place mat, red, white and blue design features Milwaukee County Stadium and schedule, 10x14... $20
- 1982 Milwaukee Brewers McDonald's place mats, in original envelope, signed by Yount, Sutton, Cooper, Vuckovich, Fingers, Caldwell, Moore, Oglivie, Gantner and Simmons $225
- 1982 Milwaukee Brewers Harvey's Wallbangers ceramic coffee cup... $35
- Minnesota Twins Metropolitan Stadium bricks, original stadium bricks, available with red, blue, orange or gray paint edge $35
- 1960s Minnesota Twins charm bracelet, gold, with gold bat and ball... $25
- 1960s Minnesota Twins pen/pencil set, in original placard $40
- 1965 Minnesota Twins American League Champions souvenir patch, red, white and blue, with Twins logo in the center, 4 1/2x6 1/2, from the World Series $50
- 1965 World Series Minnesota Twins clubhouse pass, issued to Joe Garagiola $75
- 1969 Minnesota Twins all-time team ruler, red on white, features Killebrew, Carew, Oliva, Allison and Kaat........ $25
- 1969 House of Pancakes place mat featuring New York Mets players $75
- 1969 New York Mets World Champions glass mug...... $45
- 1973 New York Mets cigarette lighter, silver-toned, features 1973 World Series logo.. $150
- New York Yankees beach towel, signed by Joe DiMaggio $200
- 1940s New York Yankees fountain pen and retractable pencil, each shaped like a baseball bat, with Yankee logo $200
- 1950s New York Yankees or Boston Red Sox straw hats, with felt band including team name and baseball player, sold at stadiums .... $50 each
- New York Yankees Yankee Stadium "Special Police" badge, #160, 1950s-1960s, silver metal, worn by police $295
- 1962-63 New York Yankees/New York Mets plastic bat pen $25
- Oakland A's inflatable seat cushion, 1972-74 World Champions $45
- Philadelphia Athletics fishing hat, blue and white $65
- Philadelphia Phillies set of six sandwich bags, feature Schmidt, Luzinski, Bowa, Lonborg, McGraw and Cash .. $95
- 1980 Philadelphia Phillies World Champs metal ashtray$45
- 1980 Philadelphia Phillies World Champions ceramic baseball bank... $55

- 1952 Pittsburgh Pirates ice scraper, still in the original package.. $15
- 1960 Pittsburgh Pirates souvenir scrapbook, empty, front cover has a gold Pirate mascot head and the words "1960 World Champions".. $40
- 1960 Pittsburgh Pirates plastic baseball bank, with facsimile autographs $195
- 1971 Pittsburgh Pirates World Champions glass mug.... $35
- 1944 World Series pen/pencil set, in original box, barrels read "1944 World Series St. Louis Cardinals vs. St. Louis Browns"... $135
- 1967 St. Louis Cardinals schedule on a vinyl car litter bag $45
- 1960 San Francisco Giants Christmas card, photo of Candlestick Park on the cover... $35
- 1942 Griffith Stadium property tax stub for stadium land and surrounding parcels in Washington, D.C., all stubs are labeled "Clark & Ann Griffith c/o Washington Baseball Club" ... $50
- 1960s Washington Senators beach baseball $135
- 1960s Washington Senators popcorn holder/megaphone$45
- 1960s Washington Senators ceramic baseball glove dish with bat in pocket $65
- Mid-1960s megaphone, has all the American and National League team logos, by F.R. Woods of Cooperstown, N.Y.$75
- 1969 uniform patches, 3" diameter each, for Senators, Royals, Brewers, Red Sox, Yankees, Indians, Twins, Mets, Astros and Reds, each.. $20

Tickets/skeds

- 1910 Pittsburgh Pirates pocket mirror/schedule, has schedule on the celluloid front and a mirror on the back $400
- 1924 American League pocket schedule $50
- Chicago Cubs' first night game full ticket, Aug. 8, 1988$85
- Toronto Blue Jays inaugural season Opening Day ticket, 1977, $100, signed by Bill Singer, Opening Day pitcher$125
- Hank Aaron hits #714, opening day ticket in Cincinnati, 1974 .... $145
- George Brett 3,000th hit full ticket, $75, signed........... $150
- Rod Carew 3,000th hit full ticket, $95, signed $150
- Steve Carlton 300th win ticket stub, signed................... $75
- Reggie Jackson 500th home run full ticket, $175, signed.... $250
- Sandy Koufax's 1964 no-hitter ticket stub, June 4, 1964, with newspaper clippings $225
- Roger Maris' 60th home run ticket stub, Sept. 26, 1961$475
- Eddie Murray's 3,000th hit ticket stub $55
- Cal Ripken Jr. embossed ticket from Sept. 5, 1995, unsigned $90
- Cal Ripken Jr. embossed ticket from Sept. 6, 1995, unsigned $160
- Pete Rose 4,000 hit certificate, says "I Was There," signed $25
- Pete Rose's 4,192nd hit ticket, Sept. 11, 1985, signed . $225
- Pete Rose's 4,192nd hit full ticket, framed, signed and matted with an autographed photo from the game, Sept. 11, 1985, $325
- Nolan Ryan 6th no-hitter full ticket, framed and matted with an autographed photo from the game $225
- Nolan Ryan 7th no-hitter full ticket, May 13, 1991, unsigned, $65, signed $125
- Nolan Ryan 300th win full ticket, May 13, 1991 .... $75
- Nolan Ryan 300th win full ticket, May 13, 1991, autographed $150
- Nolan Ryan first attempt at 300 wins, July 25, 1990, ticket vs. New York Yankees $35
- Nolan Ryan's last game full ticket, Sept. 22, 1993........ $125
- Mike Schmidt's 500th home run, full ticket, April 18, 1987, signed $165
- Tom Seaver's 300th win ticket stub................................ $100
- Dave Winfield's 3,000th hit ticket stub $55
- Robin Yount 3,000th hit full ticket, $60, signed........... $125

Topps baseball-card related

1989 Topps Heads Up! Test Issue

Much rarer than the 1990 issue, this 24-card test set debuted the bizarre "shrunken head" format of a die-cut player's head and cap printed on heavy cardboard, approximately 4 1/2" by 6 1/2" in size and sold one per pack. Backs feature both a small plastic suction cup and an adhesive strip for hanging the card. The player's name and team are printed in black on the back. The complete set of 24 is worth $2,500. The players are: Ellis Burks, Ricky Jordan and Frank Viola, at $75 each; Eric Davis, at $90; Jim Abbott, Dwight Gooden, Mike Greenwell, Bo Jackson, Gregg Jefferies, and Gary Sheffield, at $100 each; Wade Boggs, Mark Grace, Mark McGwire, Dale Murphy, Ozzie Smith and Darryl Strawberry, at $150 each; Jose Canseco, Will Clark, Tony Gwynn, Don Mattingly, Kirby Puckett and Ryne Sandberg, at $200 each; Mike Schmidt, at $250; and Ken Griffey Jr., at $300.

1990 Topps Heads Up!

Following a much rarer test issue of the previous year, this 24-piece set received wider distribution, but proved unpopular with collectors. On heavy cardboard, die-cut to approximately 5" by 6", these novelties featured only a head-and-cap photo of the player. Backs have the player's name and team, along with an adhesive strip and plastic suction cup which could be used to "hang" the player on a window. The complete set of 24 is worth $7.50. Players in the set, worth 25-35 cents unless noted, are: Jim Abbott, Craig Biggio, Jose Canseco, Will Clark, Dennis Eckersely, John Franco, Dwight Gooden, Tom Gordon, Ken Griffey Jr. ($2), Tony Gwynn, Bo Jackson, Don Mattingly, Mark McGwire, Kevin Mitchell, Gregg Olson, Rafael Palmeiro, Kirby Puckett, Harold Reynolds, Bret Saberhagen, Ryne Sandberg ($1), Gary Sheffield, Dwight Smith, Jerome Walton and Craig Worthington.

1991 Topps Superstar Stand-Ups

Another of Topps' efforts to market candy containers with a baseball player theme, the 1991 Superstar Stand-Ups were a test issue. Sold in a color-printed paper envelope, the Stand-Ups were a hard plastic container filled with candy tablets. In bright see-through colors, the containers measure 2 1/16" by 2 9/16" and are vaguely shaped like a head and shoulders. A paper label attached to the front of the plastic has a player portrait with his team name in a banner above and his name in a strip at the bottom. Backs have a baseball design on the label with a Topps 40th anniversary logo at the top. The player's name, team and position are in color bars at the bottom, with the item number on the left. At center are the player's height, weight, birth date, batting and throwing preference, and the year and the number of his Topps rookie card. Both back and front labels are printed in color. The complete set of 36 is worth $75. The players are: Jim Abbott ($3), Sandy Alomar ($1.50), Wade Boggs ($6), Barry Bonds ($6), Bobby Bonilla ($1.50), George Brett ($6), Jose Canseco ($7.50), Will Clark ($6), Roger Clemens ($2.50), Eric Davis ($1.50), Andre Dawson ($1.50), Len Dykstra ($1.50), Cecil Fielder ($2.50), Carlton Fisk ($1.50), Dwight Gooden ($2), Mark Grace ($1.50), Ken Griffey Jr. ($9), Tony Gwynn ($6), Rickey Henderson ($5), Bo Jackson ($3), Dave Justice ($3), Kevin Maas ($1.50), Ramon Martinez ($1.50), Don Mattingly ($6), Ben McDonald ($1.50), Mark McGwire ($2.50), Kevin Mitchell ($1.50), Cal Ripken Jr. ($7.50), Nolan Ryan ($10), Ryne Sandberg ($6), Ozzie Smith ($2.50), Dave Stewart ($1.50), Darryl Strawberry ($2), Frank Viola ($1.50), Matt Williams ($2), and Robin Yount ($3).

1992 Topps Triple Header Photo Balls

Picture a slightly oversized ping pong ball painted like a baseball with the heads and facsimile autographs of three different players on it and you've got the idea behind this test issue. Very limited in distribution, the team balls were sold in a small box with a package of candy. The complete set is worth $75; individual balls are worth $3-$5.

Atlanta Braves - Ron Gant, Tom Glavine, Dave Justice

Baltimore Orioles - Ben McDonald, Gregg Olson, Cal Ripken Jr.

Boston Red Sox - Wade Boggs, Roger Clemens, Mike Greenwell

California Angels - Chuck Finley, Wally Joyner, Dave Winfield

Chicago Cubs - George Bell, Mark Grace, Ryne Sandberg

Chicago White Sox - Carlton Fisk, Frank Thomas, Robin Ventura

Cincinnati Reds - Eric Davis, Barry Larkin, Chris Sabo

Cleveland Indians - Sandy Alomar Jr., Alex Cole, Mark Lewis

Detroit Tigers - Cecil Fielder, Tony Phillips, Alan Trammell

Houston Astros - Jeff Bagwell, Craig Biggio, Ken Caminiti

Kansas City Royals - George Brett, Bret Saberhagen, Danny Tartabull

Los Angeles Dodgers - Ramon Martinez, Eddie Murray, Darryl Strawberry

Milwaukee Brewers - Paul Molitor, Greg Vaughn, Robin Yount

Minnesota Twins - Scott Erickson, Kent Hrbek, Kirby Puckett

Montreal Expos - Ivan Calderon, Delino DeShields, Dennis Martinez

New York Mets - Vince Coleman, Dwight Gooden, Howard Johnson

New York Yankees - Don Mattingly, Willie Randolph, Steve Sax

Oakland A's - Jose Canseco, Dave Henderson, Rickey Henderson

Philadelphia Phillies - Len Dykstra, John Kruk, Dale Murphy

Pittsburgh Pirates - Barry Bonds, Bobby Bonilla, Andy Van Slyke

San Diego Padres - Tony Gwynn, Fred McGriff, Benito Santiago

San Francisco Giants - Will Clark, Kevin Mitchell, Matt Williams

Seattle Mariners - Ken Griffey Jr., Ken Griffey Sr., Harold Reynolds

St. Louis Cardinals - Pedro Guerrero, Ozzie Smith, Todd Zeile

Texas Rangers - Julio Franco, Juan Gonzalez, Nolan Ryan

Toronto Blue Jays - Roberto Alomar, Joe Carter, Kelly Gruber

Toys

• Plastic team rings, sold in gumball machines in 1969 - Atlanta Braves, Houston Astros, New York Mets, Oakland A's, Philadelphia Phillies, Kansas City Royals, California Angels, Chicago White Sox, Minnesota Twins, San Diego Padres, Boston Red Sox, Cincinnati Reds, Pittsburgh Pirates, St. Louis Cardinals, Cleveland Indians, New York Yankees, San Francisco Giants, Baltimore Orioles and Montreal Expos all $5 each; Seattle Pilots and Washington Senators, $10 each

• Johnny Bench wiffle ball and bat, Bench's image on the box $75

• George Brett batting tee, in box, 1980s $75

• George Brett wiffle ball and bat.......................... $65

• 1978 Rod Carew K-Tel batting trainer, in original box $75

• Rocky Colavito's Own Baseball Game, Trans-O-Gram, 1960, 22x22, features Colavito on the box $225

• Jackie Jensen wiffle ball, in original box............ $45

• Mickey Mantle/Willie Mays Transogram wiffle ball holder display, with two baseballs $95

• Pete Rose softball-size Wiffle ball, with box...... $45

• 1978 Pete Rose batting trainer, in original box. $175

• 1972 ABC Wide World of Sports 250-piece puzzle, features Richie Allen on the box $55

1970 Action Cartridge

This set of boxes with baseball players' pictures on them was issued by Action Films Inc., of Mountain View, Calif., in 1970-71. The boxes, measuring 2 5/8" by 6" by 1" deep, contained 8mm film cartridges of various professional athletes demonstrating playing tips. The movie series includes 12 baseball players. (Other sports represented were football, golf, tennis, hockey and skiing.) The movie cartridges are occasionally collected today, as are the boxes, which feature attractive, color player portraits. The photos appear inside an oval and include a facsimile autograph. The values listed are for complete boxes, but without the movie cartridge. A complete set of 12 is worth $425. Individual boxes are: Tom Seaver ($65), Dave McNally ($9.50), Bill Freehan ($11.50), Willie McCovey ($40), Glenn Beckert/Don Kessinger ($9.50), Brooks Robinson ($50), Hank Aaron ($95), Reggie Jackson ($85), Pete Rose ($85), Lou Brock ($35), Willie Davis ($9.50) and Rod Carew ($45).

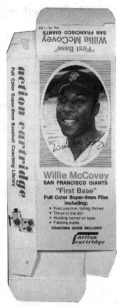

1985 Pocket Whoozit?

These sports picture game cards feature nine photos on each card, with three trivia questions on the back for each player. Among the cards with baseball-related people are: Nellie Fox, Mel Ott and Red Faber ($10); Ford Frick, Mickey Cochrane and Sam Crawford ($5); Kiki Cuyler, Rabbit Maranville and Christy Mathewson ($6); Gil Hodges, Gabby Hartnett and Lyman Bostock ($6); Shoeless Joe Jackson and Ken Hubbs ($7); Jackie Robinson, Paul Waner and Zack Wheat ($7); Kenesaw Landis and Billy Goodman ($5); Joe DiMaggio, Phil Wrigley, Ernie Shore and George Sisler ($7); Frank McCormick, Bob Meusel, Joe Medwick and Johnny Mize ($7); Max Carey, Ernie Nevers and Roger Breshnahan ($5); Pee Wee Reese and Phil Rizzuto ($4); Monty Stratton, Fred Clarke and Charlie Grimm ($4); Maury Wills, Jacob Ruppert, Frank Chance, Earle Combs, Pie Traynor and Abner Doubleday ($5).

Sports Puzzles

Sports Puzzles Inc., Palatine, Ill.: "Signa" Chip puzzles, 15 1/2" by 18, suitable for autographing, featuring major league players. Each 250-piece puzzle had two photos of the player - one large, one small - and included one piece which was designed to have the player sign. Signa Chip offered pre-signed chips through a mail-in order. The players represented in the series are: Barry Bonds, George Brett, Jose Canseco, Will Clark, Roger Clemens, Eric Davis, Andre Dawson, Kirk Gibson, Dwight Gooden, Mark Grace, Mike Greenwell, Rickey Henderson, Orel Hershiser, Bo Jackson, Gregg Jefferies, Don Mattingly, Mark McGwire, Kirby Puckett, Ryne Sandberg, Ozzie Smith, Darryl Strawberry, Alan Trammell, Frank Viola and Robin Yount.

1974 Topps Puzzles

One of the many test issues by Topps in the mid-1970s, the 12-player jigsaw puzzle set was an innovation which never caught on with collectors. The 40-piece puzzles (4 3/4" by 7 1/2") feature color photos with a decorative lozenge at the bottom naming the player, team and position. The puzzles came in individual wrappers picturing Tom Seaver. The Nolan Ryan puzzle is almost always found off-center. Well-centered Ryan puzzles will command a significant premium. The complete set of 12 puzzles is worth $975 in Near Mint condition. The players are: Hank Aaron ($150), Dick Allen ($40), Johnny Bench ($100), Bobby Bonds ($25), Bob Gibson ($75), Reggie Jackson ($125), Bobby Murcer ($25), Jim Palmer (75), Nolan Ryan ($200), Tom Seaver ($100), Willie Stargell ($75) and Carl Yastrzemski ($100).

Viewmaster's 1953 Baseball Stars

Bright, sharp Kodachrome images of Baseball Hall of Famers spring to life in this 21-player set of three reels issued by Viewmaster in 1953. All of the photos were shot in spring training in Florida, which accounts for the lack of some teams being represented in the set. Each reel, featuring seven players, was in its own blue-and-cream colored envelope and included a 3 1/2x13 8-page fold-out brochure giving biographical details, stats and a facsimile autograph of the seven players. A yellow-and-green envelope was made to hold all three reels, too. Reel 725 players are: Al Rosen, Phil Rizzuto, Jackie Jensen, Preacher Roe, Whitey Lockman, Minnie Minoso and Yogi Berra. Reel 726 players are Johnny Mize, Bob Lemon, Al Schoendienst, Ferris Fain, Monte Irvin, Bob Shantz and Sid Gordon. Reel 727 players are Bob Thomson, Grady Hatton, Vic Wertz, Mel Parnell, Gene Woodling, Sal Maglie and Roy Campanella.

Travel bags
(given to members of the press)

• 1975 All-Star Game, Milwaukee, small drawstring, gold bag $15
• 1979 All-Star Game, Seattle, white vinyl and blue trim $20
• 1982 All-Star Game, Montreal, blue vinyl portfolio $15
• 1984 World Series, tan canvas $15

Wire photos

• Circa 1915 Hank Gowdy $25
• 1920 Tris Speaker, Cleveland, fielding pose, 7x9 .... $65
• Late-1920s Babe Ruth signing a New York Yankee contract with Jacob Ruppert and Ed Barrow, 7x9 .... $95
• 1928 Lou Gehrig, World Series action, fielding play $45
• Circa 1931 Pepper Martin, with two articles attached to the back $25
• 1932 Cy Young, Cleveland, pitching pose, 7x9 .... $45
• Feb. 26, 1932, 6x8 black-and-white glossy of Dizzy Dean in action $25
• 1934 Paul "Daffy" Dean, St. Louis, pitching pose, 7x9
• Oct. 4, 1934, 7x9 black-and-white glossy of Dizzy Dean and Charlie Gehringer in action during the Cardinals/Tigers World Series $25
• 1936 Red Ruffing, New York Yankee 5x7 batting pose $45
• 1937 Frankie Frisch, St. Louis, pose, 7x9 .... $45
• 1938 Joe Cronin, Boston, fielding pose, 6x8 .... $30

• 1938 Tommy Henrich, New York, batting pose, 5x7 ..... $25
• 1938 Pie Traynor, Pittsburgh, dugout shot, 5x8 .... $25
• July 2, 1940, 5 1/2x7 1/2 black-and-white of Mr. and Mrs. Lefty Grove with their newborn daughter $15
• 1941 Joe DiMaggio, batting pose, 8x11 .... $75
• 1942 Arky Vaughn, Brooklyn, fielding pose, 6 1/2x8 1/2$45
• 1946 New York Giants team photo, 8x10 .... $50
• 1948 Joe DiMaggio scoring on a home run, 7 1/2x8 $35
• 1948 Carl Furillo, Brooklyn, choosing a bat, 7x9.......... $30
• 1948 Babe Ruth's funeral, five wire service photos showing the funeral procession $475
• Early 1950s Casey Stengel/Whitey Ford closeup shot ... $30
• 1950 Ralph Kiner, Pittsburgh, home run trot, 7x9 .... $25
• Oct. 5, 1950, 7x9 black-and-white glossy of Joe DiMaggio in action during the World Series, with Al Barlick and Bill Dickey also pictured $25
• 1954 Ted Williams batting pose, 9x7 .... $95
• 1955 World Series, shows Whitey Ford on the mound in six frames $25
• 1956 World Series, shows Roy Campanella tagging out Phil Rizzuto $20
• 1956 World Series, shows Jackie Robinson sliding into second as Billy Martin covers $20
• 1959 Nellie Fox, signs a contract for the season, 8x10 .. $35
• 1961 Roberto Clemente, in uniform with his son, 8x10 . $30
• June 20, 1960, 7x10 black-and-white glossy of the Reds' Tommy Harper sliding into Ron Hunt of the Mets $7.75
• Denny McLain, 1968 World Series Game 6, pitching pose closeup, 8x10 .... $25
• 1970s Nolan Ryan, California, pitching pose, 7x9 .... $25
• 1971 Leo Durocher, argues a call at first as the Cubs' manager, signed $25

Baseball videos

Several teams have put out season-highlights tapes over the years, and several players have done instructional tapes, too, such as Steve Garvey, Charlie Lau and Maury Wills. A Greatest Sports Legends series features among others Hank Aaron, Roberto Clemente, Lou Gehrig, Stan Musial and Ted Williams. World Series moments and the lighter side of baseball have also been captured on video.

Among the top baseball-related videos, as selected by David Craft, Sports Collectors Digest's Tale of the Tape columnist:

1) An Amazin' Era - The New York Mets 1962-1986; 2) The Boys of Summer; 3) The Chicago White Sox: A Visual History; 4) Detroit Tigers: The Movie; 5) Forever Fenway: 75 Years of Red Sox Baseball; 6) The Glory of Their Times; 7) The History of the Game; 8) New York Yankees: The Movie; 9) St. Louis Cardinals: The Movie; 10) Chicago and the Cubs: A Lifelong Love Affair; 11) Pinstripe Power: The Story of the 1961 New York Yankees; 12) Reds: The Official History of the Cincinnati Reds; 13) Centennial: 100 Years of Phillies Baseball.

Among the most memorable baseball movies, as selected by Craft: 1) Pride of St. Louis; 2) Pride of the Yankees; 3) A Love Affair: The Eleanor and Lou Gehrig Story; 4) The Babe Ruth Story; 5) The Jackie Robinson Story; 6) The Bingo Long Traveling All-Stars And Motor Kings; 7) Don't Look Back: The Story Of Leroy "Satchel" Paige; 8) One In A Million: The Ron LeFlore Story; 9) Fear Strikes Out; 10) The Stratton Story; 11) Damn Yankees; 12) Take Me Out To The Ball Game; 13) Angels In The Outfield; 14) Elmer the Great; 15) Bang The Drum Slowly; 16) The Natural; 17) Bull Durham and 18) Eight Men Out.

- 1948 All-Star Game, 16 mm film, with original box $45
- 1964 "Casey at the Mets" 8mm film with box, Casey Stengel's New York Mets $70
- 1969 New York Mets Super 8 movie film in original box .... $50-$65
- 1970 All-Star Game, 8 mm film, box has Pete Rose and Ray Fosse on it $45
- 1971 World Series Super 8 movie film, has Roberto Clemente on the box $55

Baseball games

Baseball-related games are the most popular of all sports games; more than 300 board and card games exist. The game recognized as the first professional baseball game, The New Parlor Game of Baseball, was produced in 1869. Published by M.B. Sumner, the game included team rosters and lineup cards.

The first data-enhanced game based on player statistics appeared in 1950, when APBA Game Co. of Lancaster, Pa., created a dice and card game. The company produces new player game cards annually. The first game to be endorsed by a player - the Rube Walker & Harry Davis Baseball Game - was produced in 1905 by Champion Athletics. Since that time several athletes have loaned their names to games - Hank

Aaron, Bob Feller, Lou Gehrig, Walter Johnson, Mickey Mantle, Christy Mathewson, Willie Mays, Babe Ruth and Carl Yastrzemski, to name a few.

Generally, player or team-related games are in greater demand than generic games, while board games are more valuable than card games. Game values are also determined in part by age (older is more valuable); company (McLoughlin Bros., Bliss, Singer, Selchow and Righter, Parker Bros., Cadaco-Ellis and Milton Bradley are tops); graphics/illustrations (those with higher quality of lithography and highly-detailed, colorful illustrations, especially on the box, are more valuable); box and board style (wooden boxes are more valuable, then heavy cardboard; metal games are more valuable than cardboard ones); theme; the region in which the item is being sold; rarity; implements (game parts); and completeness (missing game cards or integral parts may drop a value by 50 percent). The American Game Collectors Association has archives of game instructions and can supply copies by contacting AGCA, 49 Brooks Ave., Lewiston, Maine, 04240.

Condition is also a big factor in determining game values. Look for games which are in Very Good or Excellent condition - those which are not faded, water stained, covered with soot or mildew, and have all the parts and instructions.

The best places to find board games are at game conventions, collectibles shows, antique shops, flea markets, and through auction houses and hobby publications, such as Krause Publications' Toy Shop and Today's Collector publications. When buying sight-unseen through the mail, however, get as detailed of a description about condition beforehand, and inquire if the seller has return policy if material is not satisfactory.

Many games are repairable, but that's best left to an archivist or other professional who can clean your game using special materials such as acid-free glue and paper. Rubber cement thinner can be used to remove price stickers or tape on the outside box cover on games which are taped shut. Mildew can be cleaned with a bathroom mildew remover and a damp sponge, but test a small area first.

Games should be kept out of extremely cold or hot temperatures and places with wide temperature fluctuations. Direct sunlight, spotlights and other bright lights should be avoided, too, to prevent fading. Damp areas can cause mildew buildup, so a dehumidifier is recommended. Also, although stacking is not suggested, if you are going to stack your games, do so by cross-stacking them, alternating them vertically and horizontally, so that the weight of the games on top do not crush those underneath.

Note: Because so few exist in that condition, games from 1844-1945 are not priced in Mint condition. Prices fluctuate, too, oftentimes based on auction fever, which tends to drive prices up. Remember, value is what someone is willing to pay, not necessarily the selling price.

Baseball Board Games

Name	Company	Year	Type	Good	Ex	Mint
ABC Baseball Game	xxx	1910s	board	$430	$715	xxx
Action Baseball	Pressman	1965	board	$35	$50	$75
Alexander's Baseball Game	xxx	1930s	board	$245	$400	xxx
All Pro Baseball	Ideal	1950	board	$45	$70	$110
All-Star Baseball Game	Whitman	1935	board	$100	$165	xxx
All-Star Baseball	Cadaco-Ellis	1959-60	board	$40	$65	$90
All-Star Baseball Game	Cadaco-Ellis	1962	board	$15	$25	$40
All-Star Baseball	Cadaco	1989	board	$12	$20	$30
All-Star Electric Baseball & Football	Harett-Gilmar	1955	board	$35	$60	$90
All-Time Greats Baseball Game	Midwest Research	1971	board	$15	$25	$35
Alpha Baseball Game	Redlich Mfg. Co.	1930s	board	$110	$180	$275
APBA Baseball Master Game	APBA	1975	board	$35	$60	$90
ASG Baseball	3M	1989	board	$12	$20	$30
ASG Major League Baseball	Gerney Games	1973	board	$55	$90	$135
Atkins Real Baseball	Atkins & Co.	1915	board	$450	$750	xxx
Autograph Baseball Game	F.J.Raff	1948	board	$110	$180	$275
Auto-Play Baseball Game	Auto-Play Games Co.	1911	board	$425	$700	xxx
Aydelott's Parlor Baseball	Aydelott's Base Ball Card Co.	1910	board	$195	$325	xxx
Babe Ruth Baseball Game	xxx	1933	board	$640	$1,075	xxx
Babe Ruth National Game of Baseball	Keiter-Fry Mfg. Co.	1929	board	$550	$910	xxx
Babe Ruth's Baseball Game	Milton Bradley	1936	board	$200	$500	xxx
Babe Ruth's Official Baseball Game	Toy Town Corp.	1940s	board	$430	$715	xxx
Ballplayer's Baseball Game	Jon Weber	1955	board	$30	$50	$75
Bambino	Johnson Store Equipment Co.	1933	board	$295	$490	xxx
Bambino Baseball Game	Mansfield-Zesiger Mfg. Co.	1946	board	$145	$250	xxx
Base-Ball, Game of	McLoughlin Bros.	1886	board	$750	$1,300	xxx
Baseball	George Parker	1885	board	$700	$1,000	xxx
Baseball	George B. Doan & Co.	1920	board	$70	$100	xxx
Baseball	J. Ottman Litho Co.	1915	board	$140	$200	xxx
Baseball Game	All-Fair	1930	board	$100	$125	xxx
Baseball	All-Fair	1946	board	$30	$45	$60
Baseball	Milton Bradley	1940s	board	$35	$50	xxx
Baseball	Samuel Lowe Co.	1942	board	$15	$25	xxx
Baseball, Football & Checkers	Parker Bros.	1957	board	$35	$60	$90
Baseball & Checkers	Milton Bradley	1910s	board	$75	$150	xxx
Baseball Card All-Star Game	Captoys	1987	card	$6	$10	$15
Baseball Card Game	Ed-U-Cards	1950s	card	$20	$35	$50
Baseball Challenge	Tri-Valley Games	1980	board	$15	$25	$35
Base Ball Dominoes	Evans	1910	board	$250	$400	xxx
Baseball Game	Brinkman Engineering	1925	board	$95	$135	xxx
Baseball Game	Corey Games	1943	board	$70	$100	xxx
Baseball Game	Parker Bros.	1949	board	$10	$17	$25
Baseball Game	Parker Bros.	1950	board	$10	$15	$22
The Baseball Game	Horatio	1988	board	$12	$20	$30
Baseball Game & G-Man Target Game	Marks Bros.	1940	board	$100	$165	xxx
Baseball's Greatest Moments	Ashburn Ind.	1979	board	$5	$8	$12
Baseballitis Card Game	Baseballitis Card Co.	1909	card	$125	$205	xxx
Baseball Knapp Electro Game Set	Knapp	1929	board	$125	$175	xxx
Baseball Mania The Board Game	Baseball Mania	1993	board	$14	$21	$30
Baseball Strategy	Avalon Hill	1973	board	$10	$15	$20
Baseball Wizard Game	Morehouse Mfg.	1916	board	$265	$450	xxx
Base Hit	Games Inc.	1944	board	$55	$90	xxx
Bases Full	Hand Skill Game	1930	skill	$45	$70	xxx

Miscellaneous

Name	Company	Year	Type	Good	Ex	Mint
Batter-Rou Baseball Game	Memphis Plastic	1950s	board	$100	$165	$250
Batter Up Card Game	Ed-U-Cards	1949	card	$25	$40	$60
Batter Up	M. Hopper	1946	board	$30	$50	$75
Bee Gee Baseball Dart Target	Bee Gee	1935s	board	$70	$115	xxx
Bible Baseball	Standard Publishing Co.	1950	board	$10	$16	$25
Big League Baseball Card Game	Whitman Publishing	1933	card	$35	$60	xxx
Big League Baseball Game	J. Chein & Co.	1930s	board	$42	$60	xxx
Big League Baseball Game	A.E. Gustafson	1938	board	$85	$125	xxx
Big League Baseball	Saalfield	1959	board	$55	$90	$135
Big League Baseball Game	3M Corp.	1966	board	$55	$90	$135
Big League Baseball	3M Corp.	1971	board	$14	$21	$30
Big Six: Christy Mathewson Indoor Baseball Game	Piroxloid Products Corp.	1922	board	$775	$1,300	xxx
Big 6 Sports Games	Gardner & Co.	1950s	board	$175	$295	$450
Bob Feller's Big League Baseball	Saalfield Artcraft	1950	board	$75	$150	$250
Bobby Shantz's Baseball Game	Realistic Games	1954	board	$80	$150	$225
Boston Baseball Game	Boston Game Co.	1906	board	$495	$825	xxx
Boston Red Sox Game	Ed-U-Cards	1964	card	$55	$90	$135
Broadcast Baseball	J. Pressman & Co.	1938-40	board	$70	$100	xxx
Carl Hubbell Mechanical Baseball	Gotham	1950	board	$100	$200	$300
Carl Yastrzemski's Action Baseball	Pressman	1962	board	$90	$145	$195
Casey on the Mound	Kamm Games Inc.	1947	board	$190	$275	xxx
Challenge the Yankees	Hasbro	1960s	board	$125	$225	$325
The Champion Game of Base Ball	Schultz	1889	board	$4,100	$6,800	xxx
The Champion Base Ball Game	New York Game Co.	board	1913	$140	$200	xxx
The Champion Game of Baseball	Proctor Amusement Co.	1890s	board	$60	$100	xxx
Championship Baseball	Championship Games Inc.	1966	board	$10	$20	$30
Championship Baseball	Milton Bradley	1984	board	$18	$28	$40
Championship Base Ball Parlor Game	Grebnelle Novelty Co.	1914	board	$1,050	$1,750	xxx
Charlie Brown's All Star Baseball Game	Parker Bros.	1965	board	$35	$60	$90
Chicago Game Series Base Ball	George Doan Co.	1890s	board	$1,175	$1,950	xxx
Classic Major League Baseball Classic green		1987	game	$115	$175	$250
Classic Major League Baseball Classic yellow update		1987	board	$18	$28	$40
Classic Major League Baseball Classic red		1988	board	$7.50	$10	$15
Classic Major League Baseball Classic blue		1988	board	$10	$14	$20
Classic Major League Baseball Classic		1989	board	$18	$28	$40
Classic Major League Baseball Classic 1989 travel orange		1989	board	$10	$14	$20
Classic Major League Baseball Classic		1989	update	$7.50	$10	$15
Classic Major League Baseball Classic		1990	cards	$7.50	$10	$15
Classic Major League Baseball Classic		1990	Series II	$6	$9	$13
Classic Major League Baseball Classic		1990	Series III	$7.50	$10	$15
Classic Major League Baseball Classic		1991	board	$6	$9	$13
College Base Ball Game	Parker Bros.	1898	board	$350	$900	xxx
Computer Baseball	Epoch Playtime	1966	board	$25	$40	$65
Danny McFayden's Stove League Baseball Game	National Games Co.	1927	board	$295	$490	xxx
Dennis The Menace Baseball Game	xxx	1960	board	$20	$50	$70
The Diamond Game of Base Ball	McLoughlin Bros.	1894	board	$1,275	$2,150	xxx
Diceball	Ray-Fair Co.	1938	board	$90	$145	xxx
Diceball!	Intellijedx	1993	board	$12	$18	$25
The Dicex Baseball Game	Chester S. Howland	1925	board	$195	$325	xxx
Double Game Board	Parker Bros.	1926	board	$165	$275	xxx
Double Header Baseball	Redlich Mfg. Co.	1935	board	$145	$250	xxx
Durgin's New Baseball Game	Durgin & Palmer	1885	board	$425	$700	xxx

Name	Company	Year	Type	Good	Ex	Mint
Earl Gillespie Baseball Game	Wei-gill Inc.	1961	board	$25	$40	$65
Egerton R. Williams Baseball Game	The Hatch Co.	1886	card	$2,500	$5,000	xxx
Electric Baseball	Einson-Freeman Publishing Corp.	1935	board	$35	$60	xxx
Electric Baseball	Jim Prentice	1940s	board	$55	$80	xxx
Electric Baseball	Jim Prentice	1950s	board	$30	$45	$65
Electric Magnetic Baseball	xxx	1900	board	$175	$295	xxx
Ethan Allen's All-Star Baseball	Cadaco Ltd.	1941	board	$60	$150	xxx
Ethan Allen's All-Star Baseball Game	Cadaco-Ellis	1942	board	$60	$150	xxx
Ethan Allen's All-Star Baseball Game	Cadaco-Ellis	1946	board	$28	$42	$60
Ethan Allen's All-Star Baseball Game	Cadaco-Ellis	1955	board	$22	$35	$50
Extra Innings	J. Kavanaugh	1975	board	$15	$25	$35
Fan-I-Tis	C.W. Marsh	1913	board	$110	$180	xxx
Follow the Stars, Watts Indoor Baseball League	H. Allan Watts	1922	board	$225	$375	xxx
Fortune Telling & Baseball Game	xxx	1889	board	$85	$140	xxx
Game of Base Ball	J.H. Singer	1888	board	$325	$550	xxx
Game of Baseball	Milton Bradley	1910	board	$100	$150	xxx
Game of Baseball	Milton Bradley	1925	board	$42	$60	xxx
Game of Baseball	Canada Games Co.	1925	board	$210	$300	xxx
Game of Batter Up	Fenner Game Co.	1908	card	$100	$165	xxx
George Brett's 9th-Inning Baseball Game	Brett Ball	1981	board	$16	$25	$40
Get The Balls Baseball Game	xxx	1930	board	$20	$30	xxx
Gil Hodges Pennant Fever	Research Games	1970	board	$65	$100	$150
Golden Trivia Game	Western Pub.	1984	board	$6	$10	$15
Gonfalon Scientific Base Ball	General Specialties Corp.	1930	board	$110	$180	xxx
Goose Goslin's Scientific Baseball Game	Wheeler Toy Co.	1935	board	$250	$400	xxx
Graham McNamee Radio Scoreboard World Series Baseball Game	Radio Sports Inc.	1937	board	$250	$400	xxx
Grand Slam	Sming Game Co.	1979	board	$14	$21	$30
Graphic Baseball	North Western	1930s	board	$165	$275	xxx
The Great American Baseball Game	William Dapping	1906	board	$145	$250	xxx
The Great American Game	Frantz Toys	1925	board	$110	$180	xxx
The Great American Game of Baseball	Pittsburgh Brewing Co.	1907	board	$145	$250	xxx
The Great American Game of Baseball	Hustler Toy Co.	1923	board	$105	$175	xxx
Great American Game of Pocket Baseball	Neddy Pocket Game Co.	1910	dice	$140	$200	xxx
Great Mails Baseball Card Game	Walter Mails Baseball Game Co.	1919	board	$2,475	$4,100	xxx
Great Pennant Races	Great Pennant Races	1980	board	$14	$21	$28
Grebnelle Championship Base Ball Parlor Game	Grebnelle Novelty Co.	1914	board	$150	$250	xxx
Hank Aaron Baseball Game	Ideal	1973	board	$50	$80	$125
Hank Aaron's Eye Ball Game	xxx	1960s	board	$85	$145	$215
Hank Bauer's "Be A Manager"	Bamo Enterprises	1953	board	$75	$125	$175
Hatfield's Parlor Base-Ball Game	Hatfield Co.	1914	board	$140	$200	xxx
Hening's In-Door Game of Professional Baseball	Inventor's Co.	1889	board	$525	$875	xxx
Home Baseball Game	McLoughlin Bros.	1900	board	$900	$1,700	xxx
Home Baseball Game	McLoughlin Bros.	1910	board	$775	$1,100	xxx
Home Baseball Game	Rosebud Art. Co.	1936	board	$100	$150	xxx
Home Diamond, The Great Baseball Game	Phillips Co.	1913	board	$175	$295	xxx
Home Run King	Selrite Products Inc.	1930s	board	$275	$450	xxx
Home Run with Bases Loaded	T.V. Morrison	1935	board	$205	$350	xxx
Home Team Baseball Game	Ben Dickenson	1917	board	$140	$200	xxx
Home Team Baseball Game	Ben Dikenson/Selchow & Righter	1918	board	$140	$200	xxx

Name	Company	Year	Type	Good	Ex	Mint
Home Team Baseball Game	Selchow & Righter	1957	board	$35	$60	$90
Home Team Baseball Game	Selchow & Righter	1964	board	$14	$20	$30
Houston Astros Baseball Challenge Game	Croque Ltd.	1980	board	$15	$25	$35
In-Door Baseball	E. Bommer Foundation	1926	board	$100	$180	xxx
Inside Base Ball Game	Popular Games Co.	1913	board	$300	$500	xxx
Jackie Robinson Baseball Game	Gotham Pressed Steel Corp.	1948	board	$425	$725	xxx
Jacmar Big League Electric Baseball	Jacmar	1952	board	$100	$175	$250
JDK Baseball	JDK Baseball	1982	board	$10	$16	$25
Joe "Ducky" Medwick's Big Leaguer Baseball Game	Johnson-Breier Co.	1939	card	$125	$200	xxx
Jose Canseco's Perfect Baseball Game	Perfect Game Co.	1991	board	$8	$13	$20
Junior Baseball Game	Benjamin-Seller Mfg. Co.	1913	board	$100	$165	xxx
Kellogg's Baseball Game	Kellogg's	1936	board	$21	$30	xxx
KSP Baseball	Koch Sports Products	1983	board	$15	$25	$35
Las Vegas Baseball	Samar Enterprises	1987	board	$8	$13	$20
Lawson's Patent Base Ball Playing Cards	T.H. Lawson & Co.	1884	card	$350	$700	xxx
League Parlor Baseball	Bliss	1880s	board	$1,050	$1,750	xxx
League Parlor Baseball	R. Bliss Mfg.	1889s	board	$600	$1,000	xxx
Leslie's Base Ball Game	Perfection Novelty & Advertising Co.	1909	board	$145	$250	xxx
Lew Fonseca, The Carrom Baseball Game	Carrom Co.	1930s	board	$525	$875	xxx
LF Baseball	Len Feder	1980	board	$12	$20	$30
Line Drive	Lord & Freber Inc.	1953	board	$60	$100	$125
Little League Baseball Game	Standard Toycraft Inc.	1950s	board	$25	$45	$70
Longball	Ashburn Industries	1975	board	$30	$50	$75
Look All-Star Baseball Game	Progressive Research	1960	board	$35	$60	$90
Lou Gehrig's Official Playball	Christy Walsh	1930s	board	$525	$875	xxx
Lucky 7th Baseball Game	All-American Games Co.	1937	board	$55	$90	xxx
"Mac" Baseball Game	McDowell Mfg. Co.	1930s	board	$145	$250	xxx
Main Street Baseball	Main Street Toy Co.	1989	board	$20	$35	$55
Major League Ball	National Game Makers	1921	board	$325	$550	xxx
Major League Indoor Base Ball	Philadelphia Game Mfg. Co.	1913	board	$650	$1,000	xxx
The Major League Baseball Game	xxx	1910	card	$85	$145	xxx
Major League Baseball	Negamco	1959	board	$12	$18	$25
Major League Baseball Magnetic Dart Game	Pressman	1958	board	$55	$90	$135
Major League Indoor Baseball Game	Philadelphia Game Mfg. Co.	1912	board	$4,200	$6,000	xxx
Manage Your Own Team	Warren	1950s	board	$55	$90	$135
Mather's Parlor Base Ball Game	Mathers	1908	board	$350	$500	xxx
Mickey Mantle's Baseball Action Game	Kohner Bros.	1960s	board	$50	$125	$175
Mickey Mantle's Big League Baseball	Gardner & Co.	1962	board	$125	$250	$325
Mickey Mouse Baseball	Post Cereal	1936	board	$55	$90	xxx
Montreal Expos Super Baseball	Super Sports Games	1979	board	$7.50	$10	$15
MVP Baseball, The Sports Card Game	Ideal	1989	board	$8	$13	$20
National American Base Ball Game	Parker Bros.	1910	card	$110	$180	xxx
The National Base Ball Game	National Baseball Playing	1913	card	$700	$1,200	xxx
The National Game of Base Ball	McLoughlin	1901	board	$500	$875	xxx
The National Game	National Game Co.	1889	board	$875	$1,450	xxx
National League Ball Game	Yankee Novelty Co.	1890	board	$350	$575	xxx
NBC Baseball Game of the Week	Hasbro	1969	board	$25	$40	$65
New Baseball Game	Clark & Martin	1885	board	$165	$275	xxx
The New Parlor Game, Baseball	M.B. Sumner	1869	board	$7,000	$10,000	xxx
New York Recorder Newspaper Supplement Baseball Game	xxx	1896	board	$430	$715	xxx

Name	Company	Year	Type	Good	Ex	Mint
Official Baseball Game	Milton Bradley	1965	card	$175	$295	$450
Official Baseball Game	Milton Bradley	1953	board	$100	$165	$250
Official Baseball Game	Milton Bradley	1970	board	$55	$85	$125
Official Denny McLain Magnetik Game	Gotham	1968	board	$115	$195	$295
Official Dizzy and Daffy Dean Nok-Out Baseball Game	Nok-Out Manufacturing Co.	1930	board	$350	$575	xxx
Our National Ball Game	McGill & DeLany	1887	board	$425	$650	xxx
Our No. 7 Baseball Game Puzzle	Satisfactory Co.	1910	board	$110	$180	xxx
Ozark Ike's Complete 3 Game Set	Builtrite	1956	board	$55	$90	$135
Parlor Baseball	E.B. Pierce	1878	board	$1,750	$2,900	xxx
Parlor Base Ball	American Parlor Base Ball Co.	1903	board	$165	$250	xxx
Parlor Baseball Game, Chicago vs. Boston	xxx	1880s	board	$2,100	$3,000	xxx
Parker Bros. Baseball Game	Parker Bros.	1950	board	$45	$70	$110
Pat Moran's Own Baseball Game	Smith, Kline & French	1919	board	$325	$550	xxx
Pee-Wee (Pee Wee Reese Marble Game)	Pee Wee Enterprises	1956	board	$175	$295	$450
Peg Base Ball	Parker Bros.	1908	board	$105	$175	xxx
Pennant Chasers Baseball Game	Craig Hopkins	1946	board	$25	$45	$70
Pennant Drive	Accu-Stat Game Co.	1980	board	$8	$13	$20
Pennant Puzzle	L.W. Harding	1909	board	$250	$400	xxx
Pennant Winner	Wolverine Supply & Manufacturing Co.	1939	board	$175	$295	xxx
The Philadelphia Inquirer Baseball Game	Philadelphia Inquirer	1896	board	$145	$250	xxx
Photo-Electric Baseball	Cadaco-Ellis	1951	board	$55	$90	$135
Pinch Hitter	J&S Corp.	1938	board	$110	$180	xxx
Play Ball	National Game Co.	1920	board	$145	$250	xxx
Pocket Baseball	Toy Creations	1940	board	$15	$25	xxx
Pocket Edition Major League Baseball Game	Anderson	1943	board	$85	$140	xxx
Polar Ball Baseball	Bowline Game Co.	1940	board	$90	$145	xxx
Poosh-em-up Slugger Bagatelle	North Western Products	1946	board	$30	$75	$105
Popular Indoor Baseball Game	Egerton R. Williams	1896	board	$500	$850	xxx
Pro Baseball	xxx	1940s	board	$70	$115	xxx
Pro Baseball Card Game	Just Games	1980s	card	$6	$10	$60
Pursue the Pennant	Pursue the Pennant	1984	board	$25	$40	$60
Psychic Base Ball Game	Psychic Base Ball Corp.	1927	card	$60	$150	xxx
Psychic Base Ball Game	Parker Bros.	1935	board	$175	$295	xxx
Radio Baseball	Toy Creations	1939	board	$50	$125	xxx
Real Action Baseball Games	Real-Action Games	1966	board	$20	$35	$50
Real Baseball Card Game	National Baseball	1900	board	$110	$180	$275
Realistic Baseball	Realistic Game & Toy Co.	1925	board	$205	$350	xxx
Red Barber's Big League Baseball Game	G&R Anthony Inc.	1950s	board	$350	$575	$900
Replay Series Baseball	Bond Sports Ent.	1983	board	$6	$10	$15
Robin Roberts Sports Club Baseball Game	Dexter Wayne	1960	board	$100	$165	$250
Roger Maris' Action Baseball	Pressman Toy Co.	1962	board	$50	$125	$175
Roll-O Junior Baseball Game	Roll-O Mfg.	1922	board	$325	$550	xxx
Roulette Base Ball Game	W. Bartholomae	1929	board	$115	$195	xxx
Rube Bressler's Baseball Game	Ray B. Bressler	1936	board	$130	$215	xxx
Rube Waddell & Harry Davis Baseball Game	Inventors and Investors Corp.	1905	board	$875	$1,450	xxx
St. Louis Cardinals Baseball Card Game	Ed-U-Cards	1964	board	$35	$55	$85
Sandlot Slugger	xxx	1960s	board	$35	$60	$90
Say Hey! Willie Mays Baseball Game	Toy Development Co.	1954	board	$200	$350	$525
Scott's Baseball Card Game	Scott's Baseball Cards	1989	card	$12	$20	$30
Skor-It Bagatelle	Northwestern Products	1930s	board	$145	$250	xxx

Miscellaneous

Name	Company	Year	Type	Good	Ex	Mint
Slide Kelly! Baseball Game	B.E. Ruth Co.	1936	board	$70	$115	xxx
Slugger Baseball Game	Marks Bros.	1930	board	$110	$180	xxx
Snappet Catch Game with Harmon Killebrew	Killebrew Inc.	1960	board	$55	$90	$135
Spin Cycle Baseball	Pressman	1965	board	$25	$40	$65
Sporting News Baseball	Mundo Games	1986	board	$8	$13	$20
Sport-O-Rama	Pin-Bo	1950s	board	$35	$60	$90
A Sports Illustrated Game, Baseball	Time Inc.	1975	board	$25	$40	$65
Sports Illustrated Baseball	Sports Illustrated	1972	board	$25	$40	$65
Sports Illustrated Pennant Race	Avalon Hill-Sports Illustrated	1982	board	$7.50	$10	$15
Star Baseball Game	W.P. Ulrich	1941	card	$70	$115	xxx
Statis Pro Baseball	Avalon Hill	1979	board	$17	$28	$40
Strategy Manager Baseball	McGuffin-Ramsey	1967	board	$20	$35	$50
Strat-O-Matic Baseball	Strat-O-Matic	1961	board	$100	$165	$250
Strat-O-Matic Baseball	Strat-O-Matic	1969	board	$10	$15	$25
Strike-Like	Saxon Toy Corp.	1940s	board	$55	$90	xxx
Strike Out	All-Fair Inc.	1920s	board	$175	$295	xxx
Strike 3 by Carl Hubbell	Tone Products Corp.	1946	board	$275	$475	$725
Superstar Baseball	Sports Illustrated	1966	board	$30	$50	$75
Superstar Baseball	Sports Illustrated-Time Inc.	1974	board	$12	$18	$25
Swat Baseball	Milton Bradley	1948	board	$20	$35	$50
Tiddle Flip Baseball	Modern Craft Ind.	1949	board	$20	$35	$50
Time Travel Baseball	Time Travel	1979	board	$8	$12	$18
Tom Seaver Game Action Baseball	Pressman Toy Co.	1969	board	$50	$125	$175
Toto, The New Game	Baseball Toto Sales Co.	1925	board	$55	$90	xxx
Triple Play	National Games Inc.	1930s	board	$12	$20	xxx
Tru-Action Electric Baseball Game	Tudor	1955	board	$25	$50	$80
Ty Cobb's Own Game of Baseball	National Novelty Co.	1924	board	$350	$650	xxx
U-Bat-It	Schultz III Star Co.	1920s	board	$70	$115	xxx
Ultimate Sports Trivia	Ram Games	1992	board	$17	$25	$35
Uncle Sam's Base Ball	J.C. Bell	1890	board	$525	$875	xxx
Wachter's Parlor Base Ball	Wachter	1888	board	$145	$250	xxx
Walter Johnson Base Ball Game	Walter Johnson Baseball Game	1920s	board	$125	$250	xxx
Walter Johnson Base Ball Game	Walter Johnson Baseball Game	1930s	board	$195	$325	xxx
Waner's Baseball Game	Waner's Baseball Inc.	1939	board	$350	$575	xxx
Whirly Bird Play Catch	Game Innovation Industries	1958	board	$20	$35	$50
Whiz Baseball	Electric Game Co.	1945	board	$42	$60	xxx
Wil-Croft Baseball	Wil-Croft	1971	board	$10	$16	$25
William's Popular Indoor Baseball	Hatch Co.	1889	card	$700	$1,175	xxx
Willie Mays Push Button Baseball	Eldon Champion	1965	board	$175	$295	$450
Willie Mays "Say Hey" Baseball	Centennial Games	1958	board	$190	$295	$450
Win A Card Trading Game	Milton Bradley	1965	board	$350	$575	$900
Winko Baseball	Milton Bradley	1945	board	$45	$70	xxx
Wiry Dan's Electric Baseball Game	Harrett-Gilmore	1950	board	$15	$40	$65
World's Championship Baseball	Champion Amusement Co.	1910	board	$175	$295	xxx
World's Championship Baseball Game	Beacon Hudson Co.	1930s	board	$100	$150	xxx
World's Greatest Baseball Game	J. Woodlock	1977	board	$30	$50	$80
World Series Baseball Game	Radio Sports	1940s	board	$205	$350	xxx
World Series Big League Baseball Game	E.S. Lowe	1945	board	$115	$150	xxx
World Series Parlor Baseball	Clifton E. Hooper	1916	board	$150	$250	xxx
"You're Out" Baseball Game	Corey Games	1941	board	$85	$140	xxx
Zimmer Baseball Game	McLoughlin Bros.	1885	board	$1,300	$2,150	xxx

Sources

The following sources have been used for information or to help determine prices:

Baker, Mark Allen. Sports Collectors Digest Baseball Autograph Handbook, second edition. Krause Publications, Iola, Wis. 1991.

Bevans, Don and Ron Menchine. Baseball Team Collectibles. Wallace-Homestead Book Co., Radnor, Pa. 1994.

Cooper, Mark W. Baseball Games, Home Versions of the National Pastime 1860s-1960s. Schiffer Publishing Ltd., Atglen, Pa. 1995.

Hudgeons, Marc. The Official 1996 Blackbook Price Guide of United States Postage Stamps, Eighteenth Edition. Random House, New York, N.Y. 1995.

Korbeck, Sharon. 1997 Toys & Prices, fourth edition. Krause Publications, Iola, Wis. 1996.

Malloy, Roderick A. Malloy's Sports Collectibles Value Guide. Wallace-Homestead Book Co., Radnor, Pa. 1993.

Rosen, Allen. Mr. Mint's Insider's Guide to Investing in Baseball Cards and Collectibles. Warner Books, New York, N.Y. 1991.

Whitehall, Bruce. Games: American Boxed Games and Their Makers 1822-1992 With Values. Wallace-Homestead Book Co., Radnor, Pa. 1992.

Also, for Chapter 17 Auctions, the respective auction catalogs have been used for descriptions for items in auctions by Sotheby's, Leland's Inc., Christie's East and Richard Wolffers.

The December 1986 issue of Sport magazine and the 35th anniversary issue of Sports Illustrated, from 1990, have been used to determine cover photos.

Back issues of Sports Collectors Digest, Baseball Cards Magazine, and Baseball Card News have also been used to compile checklists, prices and provide background material.

Dealers

1) Autographs

Albersheim Autographs, 14755 Ventura Blvd., Suite 806, Sherman Oaks, Calif. 91403.
Anaconda Sports, P.O. Box 660, One Anaconda Drive, Lake Katrine, N.Y. 12449.
Ball Park Heroes, 1531 J Street, Bedford, Ind. 47421.
Brigandi Coin Co., 60 West 44th St., New York, N.Y. 10036.
Broadway Rick's Strike Zone, 1840 North Federal Highway, Boynton Beach, Fla. 33435-2833.
Left Field Collectibles, 7855 Blvd. East, Suite 261, North Bergen, N.J. 07047.
Mark Jordan Inc., 1000 Ballpark Way #306, Arlington, Texas 76011.
M.D.'s Sports Connection, 280 Albright Drive, Loveland, Ohio 45140.
MVP Autographs & Sports Memorabilia, 4839 E. Greenway, Suite 210, Scottsdale, Ariz. 85254-1654.
Quality Autographs & Memorabilia of Virginia, P.O. Box 25274, Alexandria, Va. 22313-5274.
Rich Altman Hollywood Collectibles, 3942 North 46th Ave., Hollywood, Fla. 33021.
The Score Board Inc., 1951 Old Cuthbert Road, Cherry Hill, N.J. 08034.
SLS, P.O. Box 640332, Oakland Gardens, N.Y. 11364.
The Sports Alley Inc., 15545 E. Whittier Blvd., Whittier, Calif. 90603.
Sports Collectors Store, 1040 S. LaGrange Road, LaGrange, Ill. 60525.

2) Uniforms

Ball Park Heroes, 1531 J Street, Bedford, Ind. 47421.
Broadway Rick's Strike Zone, 1840 North Federal Highway, Boynton Beach, Fla. 33435-2833.
California Sports Investments, 2785 Pacific Coast Highway, Suite #129, Torrance, Calif. 90505.
E&R Galleries, P.O. Box 15, New Rochelle, N.Y. 10804-0015.
It's Truly Unique, Box 28821, Gladstone, Mo. 64188.
The Man of Steal, 231 Market Place, Suite 212, San Ramon, Calif. 94583.
M.D.'s Sports Connection, 280 Albright Drive, Loveland, Ohio 45140.
Sebring Sports Inc., 427 Forks-of-the-River Parkway, Sevierville, Tenn. 37862.
The Sports Alley Inc., 15545 E. Whittier Blvd., Whittier, Calif. 90603.
Sports Heroes, 3 Westchester Plaza, Elmsford, N.Y. 10523.

3) Equipment

Ball Park Heroes, 1531 J Street, Bedford, Ind. 47421.
Bob McCann, 108 Village Green Drive, Gilbertsville, Pa. 19525.
Broadway Rick's Strike Zone, 1840 North Federal Highway, Boynton Beach, Fla. 33435-2833.
California Sports Investments, 2785 Pacific Coast Highway, Suite #129, Torrance, Calif. 90505.
Chris Ingstrup, 16 Windsor Drive, Freehold, N.J. 07728.
Corey Leiby, 1603 Village Road, Orwigsburg, Pa. 17961.
David Bushing, 217 Homewood Ave., Libertyville, Ill. 60048.
Dot & Lou's Collectibles, P.O. Box 7020, West Orange, N.J. 07052.
E&R Galleries, P.O. Box 15, New Rochelle, N.Y. 10804-0015.
Everything Baseball Inc., 388 Ramapo Valley Road, Oakland, N.J. 07436.
It's Truly Unique, Box 28821, Gladstone, Mo. 64188.
Left Field Collectibles, 7855 Blvd. East, Suite 261, North Bergen, N.J. 07047.
M.D.'s Sports Connection, 280 Albright Drive, Loveland, Ohio 45140.
Sebring Sports Inc., 427 Forks-of-the-River Parkway, Sevierville, Tenn. 37862.
The Sports Alley Inc., 15545 E. Whittier Blvd., Whittier, Calif. 90603.
John F. Taube, 412 N. Nassau Ave., Margate, N.J. 08402.
Zane Burns, 9116 Oden Court, Brentwood, Tenn. 37027.

4) Statues/Figurines

All-Star Celebrity Collectibles, 1207 Nilgai Place, Ventura, Calif. 93003.
B&E Collectibles, 950 Broadway, Thornwood, N.Y. 10594.
Bill Daniels, 510 Indianapolis Ave., P.O. Box 607, Lebanon, Ind. 46052.
Bob McCann, 108 Village Green Drive, Gilbertsville, Pa. 19525.
Bob Rothschild, 5 Fillmore Drive, Clarksburg, N.J. 08510.
Down-Maine Limited, 2315 Griffin Road, Unit #1, Leesburg, Fla. 34748.
E&R Galleries, P.O. Box 15, New Rochelle, N.Y. 10804-0015.
Kirk's Cards, 6841 Pearl Road, Middleburg Heights, Ohio 44130.
The Minnesota Connection, 17773 Kenwood Trail, Lakeville, Minn. 55044.
PM Sportscards, P.O. Box 31011, Bloomington, Minn. 55431.
Romito Enterprises, 232 Elmtree Road, New Kensington, Pa. 15068.
Tim Hunter, 1668 Golddust Drive, Sparks, Nev. 89436.

5) Yearbooks

Stan Martucci, 106 Rosedale Ave., SCD-B, Staten Island, N.Y. 10312.

6) Media Guides

B&E Collectibles, 950 Broadway, Thornwood, N.Y. 10594.
E&R Galleries, P.O. Box 15, New Rochelle, N.Y. 10804-0015.
Phil's Collectibles, P.O. Box 95, Briarcliff Manor, N.Y. 10510-0095.
Stan Martucci, 106 Rosedale Ave., SCD-B, Staten Island, N.Y. 10312.

7) Programs

Alan Getz, 237 E. Valley Parkway, Escondido, Calif. 92025.
B&E Collectibles, 950 Broadway, Thornwood, N.Y. 10594.
Chicago Sportscards Ltd., P.O. Box 702, Wheeling, Ill. 60090.
Ed Taylor's Baseball Dreams, 982 Monterey St., San Luis Obispo, Calif. 93401.
E&R Galleries, P.O. Box 15, New Rochelle, N.Y. 10804-0015.
Phil's Collectibles, P.O. Box 95, Briarcliff Manor, N.Y. 10510-0095.
Sports Collectors Store, 1040 S. LaGrange Road, LaGrange, Ill. 60525.
Stan Martucci, 106 Rosedale Ave., SCD-B, Staten Island, N.Y. 10312.

8) Periodicals

B&E Collectibles, 950 Broadway, Thornwood, N.Y. 10594.
Centerfield Collectibles Inc., P.O. Box 522, Ambler, Pa. 19002.
Ed Taylor's Baseball Dreams, 982 Monterey St., San Luis Obispo, Calif. 93401.
E&R Galleries, P.O. Box 15, New Rochelle, N.Y. 10804-0015.

Ken Domonkos, P.O. Box 4177, River Edge, N.J. 07661.
Phil's Collectibles, P.O. Box 95, Briarcliff Manor, N.Y. 10510-0095.
Sports Collectors Store, 1040 S. LaGrange Road, LaGrange, Ill. 60525.
Stan Martucci, 106 Rosedale Ave., SCD-B, Staten Island, N.Y. 10312.

9) Books

B&E Collectibles, 950 Broadway, Thornwood, N.Y. 10594.
Bill Rosenthal's All Sports, 16617 Music Grove Court, Rockville, Md. 20853.
Bob Rothschild, 5 Fillmore Drive, Clarksburg, N.J. 08510.
R. Plapinger Baseball Books, P.O. Box 1062, Ashland, Ore. 97520.
Phil's Collectibles, P.O. Box 95, Briarcliff Manor, N.Y. 10510-0095.
Sports Collectors Store, 1040 S. LaGrange Road, LaGrange, Ill. 60525.

10) Commemoratives

Bill Daniels, 510 Indianapolis Ave., P.O. Box 607, Lebanon, Ind. 46052.
Gateway Stamp Co. Inc., P.O. Box D, Florissant, Mo. 63031-0040.
Historic Limited Editions, P.O. Box 1236, New Canaan, Conn. 06840.

11) Perez-Steele postcards

Bill Daniels, 510 Indianapolis Ave., P.O. Box 607, Lebanon, Ind. 46052.

12) Pins

Allegheny Collectibles Ltd., P.O. Box 288, 613 Elm St., Tionesta, Pa. 16353.
Chris Ingstrup, 16 Windsor Drive, Freehold, N.J. 07728.
Lew Lipset, P.O. Box 137, Centereach, N.Y. 11720.
Novak Enterprises, 1150 Cushing Circle #334, St. Paul, Minn. 55108.
The Political Gallery, 5335 N. Tacoma Ave., Suite 24, Indianapolis, Ind. 46220.
Recollectics, P.O. Box 1011, Darien, Conn. 06820.

13) Tickets/Schedules

Alan Getz, 237 E. Valley Parkway, Escondido, Calif. 92025.
Ed Taylor's Baseball Dreams, 982 Monterey St., San Luis Obispo, Calif. 93401.
E&R Galleries, P.O. Box 15, New Rochelle, N.Y. 10804-0015.
Lew Lipset, P.O. Box 137, Centereach, N.Y. 11720.
Novak Enterprises, 1150 Cushing Circle #334, St. Paul, Minn. 55108.

14) Medallions

Chicagoland Processing Enviromint, 501 W. Algonquin Road, Mt. Prospect, Ill. 60056.

15) Stamps

16) Pennants

Bob Rothschild, 5 Fillmore Drive, Clarksburg, N.J. 08510.
Kirk's Cards, 6841 Pearl Road, Middleburg Heights, Ohio 44130.
Rick Haskins, 4431 Cinnabar Drive, Dallas, Texas 75227.
Sports Card Heaven, 3740 SW 64th Ave., Davie, Fla. 33314.

17) Auctions

Centerfield Collectibles Inc., P.O. Box 522, Ambler, Pa. 19002.
Christie's East, 219 East 67th St., New York, N.Y. 10021.
Leland's, 245 Fifth Ave., Suite 902, New York, N.Y. 10016.
Richard Wolffers Auctions Inc., 133 Kearny St., Suite 400, San Francisco, Calif. 94108.
Sotheby's, 1334 York Avenue at 72nd St., New York, N.Y. 10021.

18) Miscellaneous

Bill Rosenthal All Sports, 16617 Music Grove Court, Rockville, Md. 20853.
Bob Rothschild, 5 Fillmore Drive, Clarksburg, N.J. 08510.
Bob McCann, 108 Village Green Drive, Gilbertsville, Pa. 19525.
Bill Daniels, 510 Indianapolis Ave., P.O. Box 607, Lebanon, Ind. 46052, lithographs and artwork.

Chris Ingstrup, 16 Windsor Drive, Freehold, N.J. 07728.

Columbia City Collectibles Co., 830 S. Bluegrass Drive, Columbia City, Ind. 46725, Linnett portraits, 7-Eleven cups, marbles.

Dave Berman, 377 Golf Drive, Oceanside, N.Y. 11572.

Elaine's Fine Art & Sports Memorabilia, The Pavillion, 500 East 77th St., Suite 2918, New York, N.Y. 10162, Artwork

Everything Baseball Inc., 388 Ramapo Valley Road, Oakland, N.J. 07436.

Fred & Joan Budde's Double-Header Sports, 4109 Farmington Ave., SE, Delano, Minn. 55328.

Howard's Sports Collectibles, 128 East Main St., P.O. Box 84, Leipsic, Ohio 45856, lithographs.

Jon Grimm, 306 E. Lincoln Ave., Oshkosh, Wis. 54901.

The Minnesota Connection, 17773 Kenwood Trail, Lakeville, Minn. 55044, cereal boxes.

Phils Collectibles, P.O. Box 95, Briarcliff Manor, N.Y. 10510-0095, RC Cola cans.

Rich Altman Hollywood Collectibles, 3942 North 46th Ave., Hollywood, Fla. 33021.

The Sports Alley Inc., 15545 E. Whittier Blvd., Whittier, Calif. 90603.

TG Sports Enterprises, 99 Snelling Ave. N., St. Paul, Minn. 55104.

a) Rings/Awards

It's Truly Unique, Box 28821, Gladstone, Mo. 64188.

Out of this World Memorabilia, 1418 Brett Place, Suite 123, San Pedro, Calif. 90732.

The Ring Man, P.O. Box 18194, Philadelphia, Pa. 19116.

b) Highland Mint Topps replica rookie cards

The Highland Mint, 4100 North Riverside Drive, Melbourne, Fla. 32937.

c) Sportscaster cards

Ed Taylor's Baseball Dreams, 982 Monterey St., San Luis Obispo, Calif. 93401.

Kevin Savage Cards/Mid-America Sports, 3509 Briarfield Blvd., Maumee, Ohio 43537.

Mid-Atlantic Sports Cards Inc., 22 SCD South Morton Ave., Morton, Pa. 19070-1708.

San Diego Sports Collectibles, 10639 Roselle St., Suite A, San Diego, Calif. 92121.

d) Movie posters

Tary Enterprises Inc., 550 Kinderkamack Road, Oradell, N.J. 07649.

e) Newspapers

Box Seat Collectibles, P.O. Box 2013, Halesite, N.Y. 11743.

Jim Lyons, 970 Terra Bella Ave., Suite 3, Mountain View, Calif. 94043.

f) Games

Carousel Card Coin & Collectibles, Rt. 1 Box 88e, Henderson, Minn. 56044, gloves, records and buttons, games, tickets.

Everything Baseball Inc., 388 Ramapo Valley Road, Oakland, N.J. 07436.

Acknowledgments

Thanks to everyone at Krause Publications who somewhere along the process helped create this book. These teammates especially deserve extra credit and many thanks for their help and cooperation:

Tom Payette, who followed the roadmaps while styling this book, and Cheryl Mueller, who did the paste-up work. Lori Anderson, Bonnie Tetzlaff and Jim Cihlar, for their efforts in shepherding this through the channels.

Duke Tuomi, who supplied items from his private collection for this book's cover. I was like an ants-in-my-pants "See-and-Say" preschooler making his first trip to the zoo; I wanted to spend all night looking at Duke's collection. It was a blast, and the lasagna wasn't bad, either. Bob Lemke, who also provided material for the cover, as did Jason Stonelake, who supplied the Philadelphia Phillies jersey. Shawn "his-last-name-isn't-spelled-just-like-the-Los-Angeles-Lakers'-leader-of-Show-Time" Reilly, whose name is spelled correctly in this book, for trusting me to dodge deer on the way to and from work and safely return his S.A.M. Nolan Ryan bobbers in tact. Too bad I wasn't working on a book about Marilyn Monroe...

Rick Hines, one of the few people who has probably looked at and owns all three editions of this book. But he might have to buy this one...Thanks, Rick - this book is for collectors like you...

Kim Schierl and Ross Hubbard, for their creative talents in designing this fabulous book cover. The cover has four themes - 1: Games (I bought them all as I rummaged around the neighboring counties on a monthly road trip to look for such items and hardcover books. I excitedly purchased the electric baseball game for $25, just before the deadline for this cover shot was nearing. It's in Mint condition, and, besides my Kansas City Chiefs/Minnesota Vikings Super Bowl IV electric football game, is the centerpiece of my games collection.); 2: Duke's stuff; 3: Nolan Ryan memorabilia (besides Robin Yount, Ryan is one of my favorite players; I've built a very modest Ryan collection); and 4: Equipment (a few of the items pictured are not really game-used, such as my "I-pretend-this-belonged-to-George-Brett" Kansas City Royals cap, which I wore for about six months, the typical time I wear a particular cap until I get a knew one.).

Sharon Korbeck and Tom Michael, who graciously offered their knowledge on board games and book prices.

Sports Collectors Digest's Tom Hultman, who provided miscellaneous information for this book. He has used the previous editions to compile player memorabilia checklists which have appeared in SCD.

Dave Bushing and Joe Phillips, for use of values from their Vintage Baseball Glove Pocket Price Guide, and Dave Miedema and Mike Shannon, whose previous efforts were reused.

Finally, thanks to Steve Ellingboe, who, as publisher, believed in this project and me when we did the first edition. It paved the way for this one...And thanks to those who purchased the previous editions. Without your support, a third edition wouldn't have been possible...

— Mark K. Larson

About the Author

The author, Mark K. Larson, joined the Sports Collectors Digest editorial staff in 1988. Since that time, he's intermittently worked on Krause Publications' annual and standard baseball card price guides, plus the football, basketball and hockey card books; he's co-authored Mickey Mantle Memorabilia and the Sports Collectors Digest Minor League Baseball Card Price Guide; he's written 101 Sports Card Investments; and he's edited Team Baseballs, Getting Started in Card Collecting, and his personal favorite, a book which is highly under-appreciated, SCD's The Sports Card Explosion, which makes a great read when your favorite team is experiencing a rain delay...

Larson, a card and memorabilia collector for 25 years, doesn't have any idea how much his stuff is worth. That's not what is important to him. It's the spine-tingling moments such as when he witnessed Nolan Ryan win his 300th game and Robin Yount collect his 3,000th hit, and the memories generated by those moments, which are priceless...He plans to be in Cooperstown in 1999 when Yount and Ryan are inducted into the Baseball Hall of Fame.

About the cover

These four collages are used on this book's cover:

1) **Games**
   1979 Strat-O-Matic Baseball ($10-$15)
   1971 Big League Baseball, by 3M ($30)
   1981 Statis Pro Baseball, Game of Professional Baseball, by Sports Illustrated ($40)
   1989 All-Star Baseball, by Cadaco ($30)
   1958 Tudor Tru-Action Electric Baseball Game ($80)

2) **Equipment**
   Philadelphia Phillies replica jersey ($50-$75)
   Kansas City Royals replica cap ($10)
   1950s Eddie Kasko kid's model glove ($55)
   Jim Palmer autographed baseball ($25)
   Charlie Moore autographed baseball ($10)
   Brooks Robinson autographed baseball ($25-$30)
   George Brett Rawlings player model glove ($75)
   Dana Kiecker autographed baseball ($10)
   Tony Oliva mini Louisville Slugger bat ($15)
   Dana Kiecker autographed mini Louisville Slugger bat ($10)
   Rogers Hornsby mini Louisville Slugger bat ($200-$300)
   Willie Stargell Hall of Fame commemorative Louisville Slugger bat ($185)
   Gorman Thomas game-used Seattle Mariners jersey ($250-$400)

3) **Duke's stuff**
   Gorman Thomas game-used Seattle Mariners jersey ($250-$400)
   1950s Chicago White Sox pennant ($50-$75)
   Eddie Mathews Hartland statue ($100-$175)
   Stan Musial: "The Man's" Own Story, as told to Bob Broeg ($60)
   Yogi, It Ain't Over...Yogi Berra, with Tom Horton ($12.50)
   I Love This Game, My Life and Baseball, by Kirby Puckett ($12.50)
   Sparky, by Sparky Anderson, with Dan Ewald ($40, signed)
   Kent Tekulve Pittsburgh Pirates Tribute program ($20)
   1977 Joe Morgan RC Cola can ($10)
   1985 All-Star Game button ($5)
   1964 Ken Boyer Auravision record ($17)
   1960s Louisville Slugger coin bank ($100)
   Stan Musial Day pin ($30)
   Milwaukee Braves 50th Anniversary program ($50-$75)
   1992 Detroit Tigers yearbook ($10)
   1941 All-Star Game program, Cleveland ($850)
   1931 World Series program ($750)
   1917 World Series program ($3,500)
   1940s Cleveland Indians fan ($20)

4) **Nolan Ryan tribute**
   Nolan Ryan Corn Flakes box ($25)
   Nolan Ryan 11x14 black-and-white print ($5)
   Nolan Ryan "Feel the Heat" video ($35)
   Nolan Ryan Kenner Stadium Stars statue ($48)
   Nolan Ryan Sports, Accessories and Memorabila bobbers ($60-$70 each)
   Nolan Ryan 300th win ticket stub ($35)
   Nolan Ryan 300th win medallion by Chicagoland Processing Enviromint ($95)
   Nolan Ryan 300th win newspaper, Milwaukee Journal ($25-$35)
   Nolan Ryan commemorative baseball, by Mennon ($?)
   Nolan Ryan autographed 8x10 photo ($40)

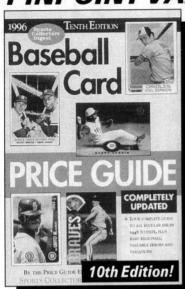